A GUIDE TO THE COLLECTIONS OF THE
MULTICULTURAL HISTORY SOCIETY OF ONTARIO

A GUIDE TO THE COLLECTIONS OF THE MULTICULTURAL HISTORY SOCIETY OF ONTARIO

Compiled by Nick G. Forte

Edited and With an Introduction by
Gabriele Scardellato

Multicultural History Society of Ontario
1992

The Multicultural History Society of Ontario is a research centre on the campus of the University of Toronto. It was created in 1976 by a group of academics, civil servants, librarians, and archivists who saw a need for a special effort to preserve materials relevant to the province's immigrant and ethnic history. The Society receives support from the Ministry of Culture and Communications of the Province of Ontario, and St. Michael's College, University of Toronto.

Canadian Cataloguing in Publication Data

Multicultural History Society of Ontario
    A guide to the collections of the Multicultural History
    Society of Ontario

Includes index
ISBN 0-919045-58-8

1. Minorities - Private collections - Canada.
2. Multiculturalism - Private collections - Canada.
3. Multicultural History Society of Ontario
I. Forte, Nick G. II. Scardellato, Gabriele Pietro, 1951 -   .
III. Title.

Z1395.E4M8 1992   026'.3058'00971   C91-095712-6

CONTENTS

PREFACE

The Multicultural History Society of Ontario (MHSO) falls into the category of institutions that serve the function of what might be called transmission belts whose task is to process raw data and make it accessible in the form of publications, conferences, and exhibits to both professional and non-professional audiences. During this last decade of the twentieth century, the MHSO will carry out its function as an informational transmission belt, specifically in the field of ethnic studies, through the completion of four major research projects. These include guides to the research holdings of the MHSO, a multicultural data base for the Province of Ontario, a national bibliography of Canada's peoples, and encyclopedic or analytical works about the peoples of Ontario and Canada.

The first project concerns the preparation of comprehensive published guides to the collections of the MHSO under the general editorship of Dr. Gabriele Scardellato. The present volume is one of these guides and lists the photographic, manuscript, and related collections of the MHSO, most of which are housed in the Archives of Ontario. Another guide will provide full listings of the MHSO's collection of microfilm and paper-copy runs of over 500 ethnic newspapers representing some 50 ethnocultural groups. The second project concerns the creation of an on-going data base that lists a wide variety of resources dealing with all aspects of Ontario's multicultural population that has been commissioned by the province's Ministry of Culture and Communications.

The third project responds to the well-known principle that no serious scholarly project can be undertaken before a researcher has a firm grasp of the existing literature on the subject. It is with this caveat in mind that the MHSO has initiated the *National Bibliography of Canada's Peoples*. Building on the 1972 bibliography complied by Andrew Gregorovich, the MHSO will issue decennial updates, the first of which will cover the years 1972 through 1979. The second update will cover the decade 1980 through 1989. Our scope is large: to list all publications, wherever they appear, that deal with individual groups or with some aspect of ethnic studies in Canada.

The fourth project consists of an analytical history of the peopling of Ontario and an *Encyclopedia of Canada's Peoples*. The all-Canadian encyclopedia is being coordinated by a resident project committee assisted by a nation-wide advisory committee. It will include easy-to-read and accessible information on every people who inhabits Canada, regardless of size or time of arrival—from the Aboriginal Peoples, the French, and the English, to the Friulians, the Macedonians, and the Goans.

Each of the four major projects of the Multicultural History Society of Ontario is interrelated. The resulting publications will underline the fact that our Society is a scholarly institution which realizes its duty not only to serve all segments of the public of Ontario and of Canada, but to function as well as a resource centre for an ever-increasing number of scholars, government officials, and cultural figures from other countries who are interested in the Canadian experience and in how we promote knowledge about the many peoples that inhabit this land. I a very pleased to add this preface to the first published result of the MHSO research projects. May this comprehensive volume serve its users well as they continue to chart the course of knowledge about the fascinatingly diverse human nature of our society.

Paul Robert Magocsi
Toronto, Ontario
July 1992

INTRODUCTION

The Multicultural History Society of Ontario was established in 1976 with a one-time grant from what was then the Province of Ontario's WINTARIO funding programme. From its beginning, those responsible for the project, in particular the founding director and president, the late Professor Robert F. Harney, sought to create a "well-catalogued archival and library collection of ethnocultural material"[1] which would be open to both the general public and scholars. The creation of this research facility was seen as "one of the first steps toward a province which recognized the variety of its historical records which help free people from ignorance of one another and dangerous dependence on stereotypes."[2] In pursuit of these aims the Society worked with a general mandate to preserve and record the province's immigrant and ethnic history. This Guide is a description of the Society's past achievements and continuing commitment to its original mandate of collection, preservation, and dessemination.

The creation of the Society occurred in an atmosphere which was receptive to the pursuit of multiculturalism as a national and provincial ideology. It followed from the work of the Royal Commission on Bilingualism and Biculturalism in the late 1960s and, in particular, the appearance of its fourth volume, *The Cultural Contribution of the Other Ethnic Groups*.[3] As an ideology, multiculturalism found both support and impetus through the coming-of-age of Canada's post-World War II immigrants. In many instances, in the iteration of this ideological statement, this cohort acted with older groups and individuals from the inter-war or earlier periods who had been long in the land even if invisible and almost certainly, unacknowledged. The ideology embedded in the federal version of Multiculturalism policy can be understood as a type of "coming-of-age" statement of these intermingled generations.

Federally, the ideology came to be enacted through a Multiculturalism policy, enunciated in 1971 by the then prime minister, Pierre Trudeau, and which is usually summarized with the paraphrase 'two nations, many cultures.' Acting in part, at least, on the recommendation of volume four of the Royal Commission, large portions of the programmes devised to implement the policy were designed to assist "Canadian scholars and learned societies to give high priority to research concerning immigration and ethnic relations and their effects on our social, economic, political, and cultural life."[4]

In Ontario, the federal initiative to recognize the country's cultural diversity led to a series of provincially-sponsored Heritage Ontario meetings. A number of the submissions made at these meetings called for the establishment of a government-funded research institution which would be devoted to the study of the province's multicultural heritage. The creation of such an institution became a perennial recommendation of the Ontario Advisory Council on Multiculturalism, which had come into being. The activity at the provincial government level converged with the interest and research of a number of academics.

These individuals were concerned to save "the records of immigrant lives and ethnic associations," in particular because this undertaking was deemed to be an important aspect of what was then the "new history from the bottom up." To quote Professor Harney who, with a number of colleagues, government officials, and members of various ethnocultural groups, was actively engaged with these concerns, the creation of a research institute would allow the compilation of a data base of a new kind. The new data base was sought not "merely for the purpose of discrediting the invented tradition then in use as 'Ontario history', but rather to open up the possibility of other readings and emplotments of the province's history before 1945 and more especially of its postwar experience."[5]

The result of this convergence of interests, of ideological reconfiguration, of direct or veiled challenges to the "established canon," or invented tradition, was the foundation of the Multicultural History Society of Ontario in 1976. The work of the MHSO, under the intellectual guidance of Robert F. Harney as its first academic director and president, and buttressed by a board of directors who had struggled with him to affect the creation of the institution, was assigned to a number of new Society employees who were hired specifically to receive and order collections or donations. In turn, these professionals were assisted by a wide range of interested and dedicated community scholars.[6] Equally, if not more important, was the activity which was begun through the recruitment of both paid and volunteer researchers.

By the end of its second year of operation, the MHSO counted over fifty paid community researchers and other staff. It was largely their enterprise which enabled the Society to amass the bulk of the collections described here.

When the Wintario funding was exhausted, the MHSO went through inevitable changes. In particular, research activity was curtailed and the staff that remained, lead by Robert Harney, entered into a struggle to convert what had been intended as a fixed-term project into a permanent institution. The transitional years, 1982–84, were anxious ones, but the Society emerged with a sound foundation on which archival collecting activity—as well as other undertakings like conferences, publishing, and exhibitions—could continue to grow, albeit with a reduced capacity. Shortly after this transition, Professor Harney began a project to publish guides to the materials which had been collected by the Society. The task initially was assigned to the Society's then Research Resources Coordinator, Mr. Ewald Schaefer.

Working with a framework far different than that eventually chosen for the present project, Schaefer produced guides in the form of pamphlets for two Multicultural History Society Collections, the Finnish and the South Asian.[7] The intent was to "offer a preliminary reconnaissance of what has been preserved..." and to "show the *lacunae* in the collections."[8] In contrast, the present *Guide* was undertaken with a very different methodology than that of the Schaefer pamphlets, and in the compilation we were also able to use a different technology, that which is now made available through personal computers.

At Professor Harney's request, I assumed responsibility for the Guide project in 1988, shortly after I had been hired as the Coordinator for the Society's Research Resources Centre (library and archives). Nick Forte, the Guide's compiler, was already at work on a part-time basis to produce further pamphlets in the MHSO Ethnic Collections Series. His sources were the finding aids, material submission report forms, and interview log forms which had been drawn up as collections were assembled by the Society's researchers. Forte began by extracting information from these records and transferring it to index cards in preparation for typing as a "camera-ready" manuscript. Methodologically, he followed the lead of the Finnish and South Asian pamphlets. In these two pamphlets, the contents of a collection are subdivided into five sections which include: (1) Resource and Research Library; (2) Archival

Holdings; (3) Oral History; (4) Photographs and; (5) Newspapers.

At my suggestion, this approach to a collection was modified so that the process by which it was originally created could be reproduced, and the role of individual or institutional donations—which were gathered by MHSO researchers and which form the bulk of every collection—could be acknowledged. At the same time, the technology for recording and storing the information for eventual publication as a Guide, also was changed.

The organization of the material presented in this Guide is determined largely by the procedures followed as the donations were submitted and processed. The donations were recorded originally on Material Submission Report (MSR) forms, which were numbered consecutively and by now have reached the 14,000 mark. These forms were designed to record: (1) the name and address of a donor, lender, or interviewee; (2) the name of the researcher responsible for the submission and; (3) the contents. The latter portion of the MSR is subdivided to allow for the description of the different types of material within the donation.

A submission might consist of all or some of "Written Material," which includes printed as well as manuscript documents, "Photographs," and "Tapes." Generally, a "tape" is a recording of an interview which seeks to document the immigrant or ethnic experience of the interviewee. Each recording is accompanied by its own "Identification Form" which provides biographical and other information about an interviewee, and a "Tape Release" form; the latter determines the access which will be allowed to researchers wishing to use a recording. In the compilation of this Guide the information from all of these forms was summarized, if necessary, and entered into a micro-computer data base software programme.

In the entries recorded below, every effort has been made to provide readers with a useful summary of donations processed by the Society to the end of 1987.[9] Each entry begins with the name of the donor and a brief indication of the geographical location—generally city and province—of the donor's residence *at the time the donation was made*. The first portion of the donation description which follows the name and address, is a brief general summary of its entire contents as recorded on the Material Submission Report with particular emphasis on any manuscript or similar materials—personal correspondence, for example, as well as passports, identity cards and so forth—which might be included. This is followed by more specific information about each component of the donation. If photographs were part of the donation, they are noted in a separate paragraph which follows the general description. The photograph description is followed, in turn, by a paragraph that describes an oral history interview if one was recorded and, finally, the end of the entry lists in bibliographic format any printed materials which might have been part of the donation. If warranted because of length, the bibliographic lists might be subdivided according to the types of printed materials (pamphlets, monographs, newsletters and so forth) in the donation.

Within any of the Guide's ethnocultural or similar subsections all donations by individuals are listed first (alphabetically by donor surname), and these entries are followed by a separate section, subdivided by a double line, for institutional donors that are listed alphabetically by institutional name. Where materials have been acquired for the MHSO's collections through means other than donations, these have been described according to the title of the project which might have produced them. A joint MHSO and Archives of Ontario ethnic press microfilming project is a good example. Titles microfilmed by the project are listed in the "institutional donor" portion of a collection though technically neither institution was a "donor" for this material. Whenever a donor could not be ascribed, as with materials housed in the Society's Research Resources Centre library and purchased specifically for that collection, then the Society itself is treated as the "institutional donor."

After the compiler began to work on the Guide as a full-time employee of the MHSO, the Archives of Ontario, as the permanent repository for the photographic, manuscript and other components of the Society's collections, produced a comprehensive inventory to the Society's photograph collection. This inventory, prepared by Linda Baier, proved extremely useful in the compilation of the Guide and *must* be considered the preferred finding aid for researchers who wish to use the photographic portions of the collections.[10] Shortly after the inventory of photographs was produced the Archives of Ontario also began to issue individual inventories of ethnocultural group records for those portions of the Society collections which are housed in the Archives and serviced there. These undertakings at the Archives of Ontario were aimed at bringing the descriptions of the MHSO papers into line with institutional standards that would enhance public access to the collections. Again, where available, these archival inventories proved useful for compiling the present Guide. However, as with the photographs, researchers should note that the Archival inventories *must* be consulted and *must* be considered the primary finding aids for anyone wishing to access what the Archives of Ontario have termed the *Multicultural*

History Society of Ontario Papers.[11] In contrast, this Guide is the first successful attempt to provide a comprehensive listing of the thousands of hours of oral history recordings housed and serviced at the MHSO, and to unite these records with their component donation parts.

Within the current Guide, as with the Society's collections in general, there is one over-riding organizational principle; namely, the subdivision of collections according to ethnocultural groups. This principle results from the methods which were followed in gathering materials for the collections. As already noted, from the beginning of the MHSO's research efforts an important and ultimately successful decision was taken to engage community researchers, both paid and volunteer, who "spoke the mother tongue of the group whose historical records were being gathered." These individuals came from "every age group, educational level, and walk of life" and "the individual community researcher and the contacts and networks of trust he or she created" formed "the core of the Society's approach both in method and ethos."[12] However, even though researchers were assigned on the basis of mother-tongue skills for a particular group, in certain instances the records which they gathered were processed according to other organizational assumptions.

For example, donations gathered by a Friulan-speaking researcher from donors from the Friuli region of northeastern Italy were processed as part of the MHSO's Italian-Canadian collection. Similarly, records gathered from Spanish speakers were organized under that rubric although none of them appears to be Spanish in the sense of being immigrants from Spain. They are, instead, immigrants from various Central and South American countries. The German collection was organized along similar lines, although it clearly contains donations from immigrants from Germany as well as from German-speaking donors outside of the national territory known as Germany which is not itself, of course, an entity that has been permanently fixed over time.

In an effort to resolve some of these contradictions and possible inconsistencies, some re-organization of the collections has been accomplished for this Guide. The so-called Spanish collection, for example, has been re-arranged as the Latin-American collection. Further steps could have been taken to subdivide this into Central- and South-American, for example, and then into national groupings—Bolivian, Colombian, Argentine, and so forth—but this did not seem to be warranted given the relatively small numbers of donations within these categories and our inability to determine whether further subdivisions are required within a national heading. Instead, those readers who might be interested in

Bolivian Canadians will find a cross-reference in the index to "(see Latin-American)." Within that subheading the country of origin of every donor has been noted, if available, in the description of the donation. The index, apart from cross-references of this type, also lists all donors alphabetically by surname. Further, it includes entries for each group-collection described in the Guide with sub-listings of the geographic locations where materials were collected or donations were made.

Readers should understand that these groupings or re-organizations are not intended as statements about cultural or ethnic or national identity nor should they be seen as fixed descriptions about what may or may not be considered an ethnocultural group. Rather, they are an effort to preserve a sense of the entire MHSO collection as it was originally compiled (something of its institutional provenance) combined with a desire to make the material more accessible to researchers.

Finally, a word about language. The researchers who were responsible for bringing the donations to the MHSO were selected to work with any given group, as noted, on the basis of their language and related skills. In some cases, to judge by the Society records which they compiled, they were skilled and meticulous and worked hard to ensure that names, for example, were recorded correctly and, if necessary, with all of their diacritical and other markings. Others were either not so skilled or not so meticulous. We have tried in the present Guide—in particular in the editorial stage of the project—to ensure that names, foreign-language terms, and similar information, is reproduced correctly. In that effort we owe a large measure of thanks to the many individuals who, as in earlier days of the Society's history, willingly provided their language and other skills—including often detailed knowledge of individual collections—in proof-reading various portions of the manuscript. We hope the end result is worthy both of Bob Harney's original dream for a "data base of a new kind" and of the thousands of personal histories which have been entrusted to the Multicultural History Society of Ontario.

Gabriele Scardellato
Head, Research and Publications
Multicultural History Society of Ontario

1. Robert F. Harney, "A History of the Multicultural History Society of Ontario," *Polyphony: The Bulletin of the Multicultural History Society of Ontario*, vol. 9, no. 1, 1987, p. 1.

2. *Loc. cit.*

3. Book IV: *The Cultural Contribution of the Other Ethnic Groups,* report of the Royal Commission on Bilingualism and Biculturalism (Ottawa: The Queen's Printer, 1969).

4. On the introduction of the federal policy of Multiculturalism see, for example, Robert F. Harney, "'So Great A Heritage as Ours': Immigration and the Survival of the Canadian Polity," in Pierre Anctil and Bruno Ramirez, eds., *If One Were to Write a History ... Selected Writings by Robert F. Harney* (Toronto: Multicultural History Society of Ontario, 1991), pp. 227-269.

5. Harney, "History," p. 1.

6. A *partial* list of these scholars is reproduced in Harney, *ibid.*, p. 7.

7. Ewald Schaefer, comp., *Finnish Canadian Collection*, MHSO Ethnic Collections Series, No. 1. (Toronto: Multicultural History Society of Ontario, 1986) and *idem.*, *The South Asian Canadian Collection*, MHSO Ethnic Collections Series, No. 2. (Toronto: Multicultural History Society of Ontario, 1986).

8. Robert F. Harney, "The Finnish Canadian Collection," introduction to Ewald Schaefer, comp., *The Finnish Canadian Collection*, MHSO Ethnic Collection Series, No. 1 (Toronto: Multicultural History Society of Ontario, 1986) n.p.

9. The closing date adopted for entries to be included in the Guide inevitably will be seen as arbitrary. However, the choice was guided by the date for the end of Mr. Schaefer's employment with the Society, the beginning of Mr. Forte's part-time work in compiling additional guide pamphlets and other considerations. Obviously, those donations that are not included here because they were not processed at the time of compilation *will* be included when supplements to the Guide are published. Supplements will be published, as required, to keep up with the continuing accession of

records collections by the Society.

10. *Inventory of the Multicultural History Society of Ontario Papers, F 1405, Photographic Records* (Toronto: Archives of Ontario, 1990) prepared by Linda Baier. The compilation of this archival quality inventory of the Multicultural History Society of Ontario's collections, and those inventories described below, was accomplished under the direction of Mr. Paul Yee, former Coordinator of the Multicultural Unit in the Archives of Ontario, and his staff.

11. Researchers and others should note that record donations were re-organized when received by the Society so that photographs, because of their particular requirements for preservation, for example, are housed and accessed separately in the Archives of Ontario from other portions of the Multicultural History Society of Ontario Papers. As stated, the inventories produced by the Archives of Ontario must be treated as the primary finding aids by researchers wishing to access the Papers. The present Guide attempts to provide only an overview of the contents of each donation and should not be used as an Archives of Ontario inventory.

12. Harney, "A History," p. 8.

ACKNOWLEDGMENTS

A special thank you is owed first to all those people, too numerous to name here individually, who gave freely of their time and skills to proof-read and correct portions of the manuscript. Secondly, the staff of the Multicultural History Society of Ontario, both past and present, led by the Society's Publications Assistant, Maryann Strevel Zugic, has been particularly helpful with what at times must have appeared to be an endless amount of editorial revision of the original data bases.

Thirdly, the Society's researchers, many of whom, although not all, are named in the *Guide* entries, were instrumental in gathering the donations and building the collections. Without them, of course, and the donors who entrusted their records to the Society, a *Guide* would not have been possible.

ALLEN, MARY
TORONTO, ONT.
Interviewed on 23, 30 July 1982; 3 hrs.; 3 tapes; English; by Roy Thompson. Spent the first few years after her arrival in Canada in Winnipeg and Toronto, discusses family life, and the Eureka Friendly Club.

AYLESTOCK, WILLIAM LLOYD
TORONTO, ONT.
Interviewed on 13 May 1982; 1 hr.; 1 tape; English; by Diana Braith-waite. Born in Glenallen, Ont., grew up in Drayton, Ont., worked as a machinist with Victory Aircraft, and studied to be a jazz percussionist.

BAILEY, ISOBEL LOUISE
TORONTO, ONT.
Interviewed on 6 Aug. 1982; .5 hr.; 1 tape; by Donna Bailey. Born in Nova Scotia in 1910, moved to Toronto, c. 1930s, discusses the Depression years.

BAILEY, PAUL E.
PICKERING, ONT.
Interviewed on 8 Aug. 1982; 2 hrs.; 2 tapes; English; by Donna Bailey. Born in Halifax, Nova Scotia, moved to Winnipeg, Manitoba, and then to Toronto. He discusses the 1949 strike by the Canadian Seamans' Union, his employment with C.N. Railway, and incidents of racial strife.

BANCROFT, GEORGE WINSTON
TORONTO, ONT.
Interviewed on 25 Aug. 1982; 2 hrs.; 2 tapes; English; by Donna Bailey. Emigrated from Guyana to Canada in 1948, worked as a factory hand, and a porter for the railway.

BELFON, CONSTANCE
TORONTO, ONT.
Interviewed on 8 Feb. 1983; 1 hr.; 1 tape; English; by Roy Thompson. Originally from Boston, Massachusetts, moved to Toronto in the 1930s, involved in the Home Service Association.

BELL, ARCHIBALD ALEXANDER
ST. CATHARINES, ONT.
Interviewed on 26 Aug. 1982; 1 hr.; 1 tape; English; by Roy Thompson. An account of his social and religious life in St. Catharines.

BELL, VIOLET E.
TORONTO, ONT.
3 photographs: Herbert Bell partici-pating in veterans' activities after military service, 1940-50. Taped interview.
Interviewed on 3 Sept. 1980; 1.5 hrs.; 2 tapes; English; by Lorraine Hubbard. Born in Toronto.

BLACKMAN, VIOLET
TORONTO, ONT.
Interviewed on 15 Jan. 1979: 2 hrs.; 2 tapes; English; by Huguette

Casimir. Recounts her childhood in Jamaica, her immigration to Canada in 1920, her work experience, and her participation in the Universal African Improvement Association (U.A.I.A.).

BLAKE, RONALD
TORONTO, ONT.
 See Home Service Association Collection.

BRAITHWAITE, DANIEL OBEDIAH
TORONTO, ONT.
 Interviewed on 23 Sept., 14 Oct. 1981; 1.5 hrs.; 2 tapes; English; by Diana Braithwaite. Originally from Nova Scotia, moved to Toronto, c. 1930s, involved in the U.A.I.A., the Negro Credit Union, and the Canadian Negro Newspaper; recounts his struggles against racism.

BRAITHWAITE, DANIEL OBEDIAH
TORONTO, ONT.
 Interviewed on 17 Aug. 1978; 1.5 hrs.; 2 tapes; by Arleigh Holder. Originally from Nova Scotia, discusses the breaking down of racial barriers, the removal of the book *Little Black Sambo* from Toronto's schools, his involvement in the U.N.I.A., and the Toronto Negro Study Group.

BRAITHWAITE, HENRY A.
TORONTO, ONT.
 Interviewed on 17 Nov., 2, 23 Dec. 1981; 2.25 hrs.; 3 tapes; English; by Diana Braithwaite. Born in Montreal, Quebec, discusses his working experience, the Depression, and military service overseas.

BRAITHWAITE, JUNE A.
TORONTO, ONT.
 Interviewed on 20 Oct. 1981; .75 hr.; 1 tape; English; by Diana Braithwaite. Grew up in Campbellville, Ont., discusses her involvement with the church, and the U.A.I.A. Comments on Black awareness, pride, and racism.

BRAITHWAITE, LEONARD A.
TORONTO, ONT.
 Interviewed on 11, 16, 20, 27 Aug., 2 Sept. 1982; 4 hrs.; 4 tapes; English; by Donna Bailey. Born in Toronto.

BRAITHWAITE, RELLA MARJORIE
TORONTO, ONT.
 Interviewed on 26 July 1981; 1 hr.; 1 tape; English; by Diana Braithwaite. Born in Lebanon, Ont., moved to Toronto in 1938, discusses early community organizations, and prominent figures like Marcus Garvey.

BRAITHWAITE, RELLA MARJORIE
TORONTO, ONT.
 12 photographs: the Braithwaite family; and family members while in the military service in Toronto, n.d. Taped interview.
 Interviewed on 15 Sept. 1978; .75 hr.; 1 tape; English; by Diana Braithwaite. Discusses her early life in Ont.
 Garvey, Marcus. "The Case of the Negro for International Racial Adjustment, Before the English People." Speech delivered at the Royal Albert Hall, London, England, 6 June 1928.
 Garvey, Marcus, ed. *The Black Man*. Vol. 3, no. 10, 1938.

BREWTON, OSCAR A.
TORONTO, ONT.
Oscar Brewton Collection. Scrap books, 1944-73. .8 meters. Taped interview.
Interviewed on 25 July 1978; .75 hr.; 1 tape; English; by Diana Braithwaite. Grew up in Florida, and attended Tuskegge Institute where he was lectured by Booker T. Washington. He became a podiatrist, discusses incidents of prejudice.

BUDD, ALBERT
TORONTO, ONT.
Interviewed on 12 March 1979; 1 hr.; 1 tape; English; by Ruth Lewis. Born in London, Ont., discusses his family life, his employment with the railway, and his involvement in several community organizations.

BUDD, RALPH
TORONTO, ONT.
Interviewed on 2 Aug. 1978; .5 hr.; 1 tape; English; by Arleigh Holder. Discusses growing up in a small town, working on the railroad, and starting his own business. Talks about the influx of West Indians, and how it has benefited Toronto's Black community.

CARTY, DONALD
TORONTO, ONT.
41 photographs: the Carty family in New Brunswick and Ont., 1914-15; family members in the Canadian Armed Service, 1914, 1945; and family recreational activities, 1935-40. Taped interview.
Interviewed on 25 May, 28 June 1982; 2 hrs.; 2 tapes; English; by Diana Braithwaite. Grew up in New Brunswick, moved to Ont. while in WWII military service.

CHATTERS, VERNA
TORONTO, ONT.
Interviewed on 11 Oct. 1980; 1 hr.; 1 tape; English; by W. O. Brooks. Born in Dresden, Ont., moved to Windsor in 1916, discusses her family history.

CHRISTIAN, CLEO ANNE
WAUBAUSHENE, ONT.
Interviewed on 13, 14 Aug. 1980; 1.5 hrs.; 2 tapes; English; by W. O. Brooks. Originally from England, she arrived in Canada in 1912, discusses her early years in Toronto, and her involvement in the War Amps Programme during WWI.

CLARKE, JOSEPH EDWARD
TORONTO, ONT.
Interviewed on 1 Aug. 1978; 3 hrs.; 3 tapes; English; by Diana Braithwaite. Born and raised in Toronto, involved in the Universal African Improvement Association, and other Black organizations.

COOK, VERDA B.
TORONTO, ONT.
Interviewed on 20 Aug. 1980; 1 hr.; 1 tape; English; by Lorraine Hubbard. Born in Toronto, describes work life, and survival during the Depression.

COOK, VERDA B.
TORONTO, ONT.
1 photograph: the Jackson family in Toronto, c. 1890-1900. Taped interview.
Interviewed on 19 Sept. 1980; 1.75 hrs.; 2 tapes; English; by Lorraine Hubbard. Born in Toronto, founding member of Eureka Friendly Club in 1905.

CUZZENS, BEULAH
WINDSOR, ONT.
 Interviewed on 3, 5 Nov. 1980; 1.5
hrs.; 2 tapes; English; by Vivian
Chavis. Grew up in London, Ont.,
became a member of the Professional
Business Women's Association, and
the Inter-Church Council.

CUZZENS, BEULAH
WINDSOR, ONT.
 Interviewed on 23 Sept. 1980; 1 hr.;
1 tape; English; by Vivian Chavis.
Born and raised in Chatham, Ont.,
discusses community life, sports, and
migration of Blacks to the U.S. in
search of work.

DARRELL, ALEXANDER
TORONTO, ONT.
 Interviewed on 20 May 1982; .75
hr.; 1 tape; English; by Donna
Bailey. Emigrated from Bermuda in
1947, involved in the Home Service
Association.

DARRELL, ALICE LOUISE
TORONTO, ONT.
 Interviewed on 17, 20 May, 4 June
1982; 3 hrs.; 4 tapes; English; by
Donna Bailey. Emigrated from Bermuda in 1947, discusses child rear-
ing, and community activities.

DAWSON, EVERETT
ST. CATHARINES, ONT.
 Interviewed on 14 Aug. 1982; 1 hr.;
1 tape; English; by Roy Thompson.
Grew up in Toronto, discusses his
involvement with the U.A.W. in St.
Catharines.

DEAN, DARRYL
TORONTO, ONT.
 "Commonwealth Caribbean: Canada
Conference." 1966. Commemorative

booklet.
 "Project School-to-School." 1968.
Poster. .5 cm (2 items).
 Blizzard, F. H. "West Indians in
Canada: A Select Annotated Bibli-
ography." The University of Guelph
Library, 1970. 40 pp.

FREEMAN, GORMAN WILLIAM
NORTH BUXTON, ONT.
 Interviewed on 25 Aug. 1982; 2
hrs.; 2 tapes; English; by Vivian
Chavis. Born in Ont.

GAIREY, HARRY
TORONTO, ONT.
 8 photographs: employees at
C.P. Railway, n.d.

———.
TORONTO, ONT.
 Interviewed on 9 July 1977; 2 hrs.; 2
tapes; English; by Kenneth Amoroso.

———.
TORONTO, ONT.
 Interviewed in June, Aug. 1978; 7.5
hrs.; 11 tapes; English; by Donna
Hill. Immigrated to Canada from
Jamaica in 1914, worked for C.P.
Railway most of his life, active in
organizations such as the U.N.I.A.,
and the African Communities League.
See *A Black Man's Toronto.*

———.
TORONTO, ONT.
 Interviewed on 23 Sept. 1980; 1 hr.;
1 tape; English; by Lorraine
Hubbard.

GRIZZLE, NORMAN W.
TORONTO, ONT.
 Interviewed on 1 Sept. 1982; 1 hr.;
1 tape; English; by Donna Bailey.
Grew up in Toronto, co-founder of

the Young Peoples' Association, and involved in the Home Service Association.

HARDING, WILFRED
DRESDEN, ONT.
Interviewed on 27 Aug. 1980; 1 hr.; 1 tape; English; by Vivian Chavis. Grew up in Chatham, Ont., discusses community life.

HAYES, E.
THORNHILL, ONT.
The Negro Directory.
May, Oct. 1966; March 1967; March, Oct. 1968; March 1970; March, Oct. 1974; March, Oct. 1975; March 1978. 4 cm.

HAYES, ESTHER P.
TORONTO, ONT.
Interviewed on 15 Jan. 1983; 2 hrs.; 2 tapes; English; by Roy Thompson. Moved from Cape Breton, Nova Scotia.

HAYES, HAROLD
TORONTO, ONT.
Interviewed on 21 Jan. 1983; 1 hr.; 1 tape; English; by Roy Thompson. Grew up in Toronto, worked with the railway, describes Caribbean influences in early Toronto.

HILL, DAN
TORONTO, ONT.
Hill, Dan. *Human Rights in Canada: A Focus on Racism.* n.d.
Contrast. Toronto, 1969-77. Incomplete. .4 meters.
The Islander. Vol. 1, no. 1. Toronto, 15 Aug. 1973 - 16 June 1977. Incomplete. 4 cm.

HUNT, ALBERT EDWARD
TORONTO, ONT.
Interviewed on 30 June 1982; 1 hr.; 1 tape; English; by Donna Bailey. Born in Toronto in 1895, worked with the railroad most of his life.

JACKMAN, REV. HAROLD
TORONTO, ONT.
Interviewed on 24 July 1978; 1 hr.; 1 tape; English; by Diana Braithwaite. Immigrated to Canada from Trinidad in 1967. Discusses the slaying of Emmanuel Jacques, the role he played in "cleaning up" Yonge Street in Toronto, and the prejudice that exists in the Canadian church. Sends a message for Black businesses.

JENKINS, FERGUSON H.
TORONTO, ONT.
Interviewed on 3 Oct. 1980; 1 hr.; 1 tape; English; by Vivian Chavis. From Windsor, Ont., discusses his life history, including his career as a professional baseball player.

JOHNSON, LEONARD
TORONTO, ONT.
Interviewed on 3 Aug. 1978; 1 hr.; 1 tape; English; by Hugette Casimir. Born and raised in Toronto, discusses his working experiences as a porter with the railway, his views on politics, and the start of his bookstore.

JOHNSTON, GWENDOLYN
TORONTO, ONT.
Interviewed on 22 Feb. 1979; 1 hr.; 1 tape; English; by Ruth Lewis. Her ancestors travelled from Maryland, U.S. via the underground railroad, discusses her involvement in literary services for Blacks (Third World Bookstore).

JOHNSTON, LEONARD
TORONTO, ONT.
Interviewed on 24, 27, 30 Nov.
1981; 2.5 hrs.; 3 tapes; English; by
Diana Braithwaite. Born in Toronto in
1918, active in the Canadian Progressive Left.

JOHNSTON, ROY W.
TORONTO, ONT.
Interviewed on 24, 29 Sept., 28 Oct.
1980; 2.5 hrs.; 3 tapes; English; by
F. Brooks. Born and raised in
Toronto, discusses his early life, his
WWII experiences, his community
involvement, and Canadian attitudes.

JONES, IAN
TORONTO, ONT.
See Harriet Tubman Collection.

LAWS, DUDLEY EZEKIEL
TORONTO, ONT.
Interviewed on 1 Dec. 1981; 1 hr.; 1
tape; English; by Diana Braithwaite.
Born in Jamaica in 1934, Arrived in
Toronto, via England in 1965,
worked as awelder, and a construc-
tion worker, involved in the Universal
African Improvement Association.

LAWSON, WILLIAM ALEXANDER
TORONTO, ONT.
Interviewed on 25 Jan. 1979; 1 hr.;
1 tape; English; by Ruth Lewis. Grew
up in Drayton, Ont., discusses his
work experiences, and his
West–Indian relations.

LEWSEY, MARJORIE
TORONTO, ONT.
Interviewed on 7 March 1979; 1 hr.;
1 tape; English; by Huguette Casimir.
Grew up in Toronto, relates her

childhood experiences to her participation in various organizations, such
as the Elks, and the U.A.I.A.

MARKHAM, REV. A. S.
TORONTO, ONT.
Interviewed on 6 Feb. 1979; 1 hr.; 1
tape; English; by Huguette Casimir.

MARSHALL, DUDLEY
TORONTO, ONT.
Interviewed on 19 July 1978; 1 hr.;
1 tape; English; by Arleigh Holder.
Emigrated from Barbados, discusses
lives of Blacks in the early 1900s, his
involvement in the Universal African
Improvement Association, and his
friendship with Marcus Garvey.

MCALEER, BERTHA E. A.
TORONTO, ONT.
12 photographs: the interior and
exterior of African Methodist Episco-
pal Churches; and parishioners in
Toronto, Hamilton, Windsor,
Chatham, and Oakville, 1890-1961.
Taped interview.
Interviewed on 23, 28 April 1982;
2.5 hrs.; 3 tapes; English; by
Lorraine Hubbard. Born in
Amherstburg, Ont., grew up in
Toronto, active member of the
U.N.I.A. Ladies' League, and the
Home Service Association.

METZGER, PAT
BARRIE, ONT.
Interviewed on 20 Aug. 1982; .75
hr.; 1 tape; English; by Roy
Thompson.

MILBURN, KEN
CHATHAM, ONT.
Interviewed on 28 Sept. 1980; 1 hr.;
1 tape; English; by W. O. Brooks.
Grew up in Chatham, Ont., discusses

his family history, and work experiences, and comments on being "coloured."

MILBURN, WANDA
CHATHAM, ONT.
Interviewed on 28 Sept. 1980; 1 hr.; 1 tape; English; by W. O. Brooks. Born in Chatham, Ont., discusses family, previous occupations, and discrimination she faced when searching for work.

NICHOLSON, HOPE K.
ST. CATHARINES, ONT.
Interviewed on 13 Aug. 1982; 1 hr.; 1 tape; English; by Roy Thompson. Grew up near St. Catharines, and worked in construction.

NICHOLSON, NORMA
ST. CATHARINES, ONT.
Interviewed on 29 Jan. 1983; 1 hr.; 1 tape; English; by Roy Thompson. Grew up in Hamilton, Ont., discusses life during the Depression, and discrimination.

OLIVER, W. P.
HALIFAX, NOVA SCOTIA
Oliver, W. P. "A Brief Summary of Nova Scotia Negro Communities." 1964. Unpublished. .5 cm.

PERRY, LLOYD
TORONTO, ONT.
Interviewed on 9, 16 Nov. 1981; 27 July 1982; 2 hrs.; 2 tapes; English; by Kim Bernhardt. Born in Halifax, Nova Scotia, moved to North Buxton, Ont., and finally to Toronto, discusses his life history.

ROBBINS, WESTON
TORONTO, ONT.
Interviewed on 25 Sept. 1980; 1.75

hrs.; 2 tapes; English; by Vivian Chavis. Grew up in Kent County, discusses his family history, and the community of North Buxton, Ont.

ROBBINS-CHAVIS, VIVIAN
NORTH BUXTON, ONT.
Interviewed on 1, 30 Aug. 1980; 1 hr.; 1 tape; English; by W. O. Brooks. Born in North Buxton, Ont., Discusses early community life.

SHADD, PHILIP
MERLIN, ONT.
Interviewed on 27 Sept. 1980; 1 hr.; 1 tape; English; by W. O. Brooks. Born and raised in Merlin, Ont., discusses family, and early community life.

SIMPSON, MELVIN E.
TORONTO, ONT.
Interviewed on 24 Nov. 1981; .5 hr.; 2 tapes; English; by Larry Hill. Born in Toronto, a musician in his youth. Later worked for the railway, and went into the brokerage business, comments on the racial discrimination he faced at some workplaces.

TAYLOR, ROSE
TORONTO, ONT.
8 photographs: the Johnson and Roberts families, n.d. Taped interview.
Interviewed on 4 June 1982; 1 hr.; 1 tape; English; by Donna Bailey. Born in Oakville, Ont., a member of Eureka Friendly Club.

TAYLOR, SHELDON
TORONTO, ONT.
Canadian Observer. 12 Dec. 1914 - 14 June 1919. 1 reel of microfilm.

TERRELL, KINGSLEY
CHATHAM, ONT.
Interviewed on 6 Aug. 1980; 1 hr.; 1 tape; English; by Wanda Milburn. Raised in Chatham, Ont., original member of the Chatham All-Stars.

THOMPSON, DAWN SOPHIE
BARRIE, ONT.
Interviewed on 13 July 1982; .75 hr.; 1 tape; English; by Roy Thompson. Born and raised in Toronto.

THOMPSON, HAZEL AMELIA
TORONTO, ONT.
Interviewed on 15 July 1982; 1 hr.; 1 tape; English; by Roy Thompson. Born and raised in Barrie, Ont.

THOMPSON, HERBERT MELVIN
BARRIE, ONT.
Interviewed on 13 Nov. 1982; 1 hr.; 1 tape; English; by Roy Thompson. Born and raised in Barrie.

THOMPSON, PERCY
BARRIE, ONT.
Interviewed on 13 July 1982; .75 hr.; 1 tape; English; by Roy Thompson. Born and raised in Barrie, Ont., discusses the Depression years, and previous employment.

THORNE, HATTIE
TORONTO, ONT.
Interviewed on 22 June, 6, 22 July 1982; 3 hrs.; 3 tapes; English; by Donna Bailey. Born in Richmond, Virginia, U.S.; grew up in Winnipeg, Manitoba, organized the first trade unions in the C.N. Railway, and was involved in the U.N.I.A.

WATKINS, HILDA VIOLA
WINDSOR, ONT.
Interviewed on 19 Oct. 1980, 12 Jan. 1981; 2 hrs.; 2 tapes; English; by Vivian Chavis. Born in North Buxton, Ont., was instrumental in the organization of the Hour-a-Day Study Club.

WELLS, NELLIE ROSINA
TORONTO, ONT.
Interviewed on 10 Sept., 28 Oct. 1980; 3 hrs.; 3 tapes; English; by Lorraine Hubbard. Born in Toronto in 1909, member of the Home Service Association.

WHITE, JOHN EDGAR
TORONTO, ONT.
Interviewed on 9 Aug. 1982; 1 hr.; 1 tape; English; by Donna Bailey. Born in Halifax, Nova Scotia in 1925, moved to Toronto in 1949, active in the Black Coalition, and founding member of the Toronto Negroes Progress Club.

WHITE, VIVIAN
TORONTO, ONT.
Portia White Collection. Contains scrapbooks and personal documents, 1901-62. .7 meters.

WILLIAMS, GERALDINE
TORONTO, ONT.
Interviewed on 15 Dec. 1981; 1 hr.; 1 tape; English; by Donna Bailey. Born in Collingwood, Ont. in 1914, worked as a domestic, a member of the U.N.I.A.

WILSON, FREDERICK
TORONTO, ONT.
Interviewed on 31 May 1980;

1.5 hrs.; 2 tapes; English; by Kim Bernhardt. Grew up in Toronto, worked as a machinist for 48 years.

BLACK RESOURCES AND INFORMA-
TION CENTRE
TORONTO, ONT.
 Collection includes brochures, pro-
grammes, and annual reports,
1976-77. 5 cm.
 Black Resources and Information
Centre. "Some Facts About B.R.I.C."
1976. 11 pp.
_____. "B.R.I.C.: Serving Canada's
Black Community." n.d. 10 pp.
_____. "Arrest and Detention: Your
Rights and Duties." n.d. 5 pp.
_____. "Black Grassroots Organiz-
ing." n.d. 8 pp.
B.R.I.C. News. May, June, July,
Nov. 1976; Feb., March, July 1977.
1 cm.

CARIBBEAN CULTURAL COMMITTEE
TORONTO, ONT.
 A collection of commemorative
booklets and minutes, 1968-76. 4 cm.
 "Caribana '73." 1973. .25 cm.

CARIBBEAN TORONTO SECRETARIAT
TORONTO, ONT.
 Miscellaneous printed items, c.
1970s. 1 cm. Photograph.
 1 photograph: two founding members
of the Caribbean Toronto Secretariat,
1976.
Exchange. Spring 1976. 7–page
newsletter.

HARRIET TUBMAN YOUTH CENTRE
TORONTO, ONT.
 Includes annual reports, a brochure,
and miscellaneous papers, 1972-77. 8
cm (2 files).

"Lost Women: Harriet Tubman, the
Moses of Her People." *Ms Magazine.*
Aug. 1973. 4 pp.

HOME SERVICE ASSOCIATION
TORONTO, ONT.
 Records, 1948-64, which include
financial statements, annual reports,
and correspondence. 5 cm (2 files).
RESTRICTED
 Black Heritage Canada Group. *Black
Heritage in Ontario.* 1972. 21 pp.
 *A Manual for Servicing the Needs of
Toronto's Black Community.* BCCP.
n.d. Pamphlet.

LIBERATION SUPPORT MOVEMENT
RICHMOND, BRITISH COLUMBIA
 Liberation Support Movement. Inter-
view with MPLA Sixth Region Com-
mander, Seta Likambuila. Richmond,
British Columbia: Liberation Support
Movement, c. 1970s. 36 pp.

MULTICULTURAL HISTORY SOCIETY
OF ONTARIO
TORONTO, ONT.
 Brown, Trevor C. "The West Indian
Immigrant in Canada." July 1973.
Unpublished.
 Burpee, Joyce. "The Black Presence
in the Canadian Mosaic: A Study of
Perception and the Practice of Dis-
crimination Against Blacks in Met-
ropolitan Toronto." Ontario Human
Rights Commission, 1975.
_____. *A Brief Pictorial History of
Blacks in Nineteenth Century Ontario.*
n.d. 30 pp.
 Campbell, Horace. *Four Essays on
Neo-Colonialism in Uganda: The Bar-
barity of Idi Amin.* Toronto:
Afro-Carib Publications, 1975.
 Chambers, Catharine. "Annotated
Bibliography: Black Women in
Canada." 29 Oct. 1986. Unpublished.

Cromwell, Liz. *Canadian Jungle Tea*. Toronto: Khoisan Artists, 1975. A book of poems. 47 pp.

Gairey, Harry. *A Black Man's Toronto, 1914-1980: The Reminiscences of Harry Gairey*. Toronto: Multicultural History Society of Ontario, 1981. 43 pp.

Gibson, Clint. *Portrait of a Black Artist*. Toronto: Gibson Art Establishment, 1984. Kichwa, Morena. *Bushman's Brew*. Toronto: Goathair Press, 1974. A book of poems. 28 pp.

Kwandela, Odimumba (J. Ashton Braithwaite). *The Righteous Blackman*. Toronto: 21st Century, 1970. A book of poems. 13 pp.

Lacovia, R. M. "Caribbean Aesthetics: A Prolegomenon." *Black Images Monographs*. Vol. 2, no. 2.

Roberts, Alfie. *Black Liberation and World Revolution: Prison Interview with Rosie Douglas*. Quebec: Mondiale Publishers, 1975.

Saul, John S. *Canada and Mozambique*. Toronto: DEC/TCLPAC, 1974. 81 pp.

Shreiber, Jan. *West Indian Immigrants in Toronto Schools*. Toronto: The Toronto Board of Education, 1970.

Anti-Apartheid Movement of Canada. "South Africa: Some Basic Facts." 1970. 7 pp.

Black Dial Directory. *Black Dial Directory, 1976-77*. Toronto: Trevor Sessing, 1977. 80 pp.

Black Education Project. "The Black Education Project, 1969-72." Toronto. 8 pp.

Contrast. Toronto, Oct. 1969 - Nov. 1989. 15 reels of microfilm.

Dawn of Tomorrow. London, Ont., 14 Jan. 1923 - April 1972. 2 reels of microfilm.

Dixie Magazine: The Times-Picayune. New Orleans, May 1984 (2 issues).

"A Minority Report." *The Toronto Star*. 3 Nov. 1985.

Nova Scotia Human Rights Commission. *Pictorial on Black History: Nova Scotia*. Halifax: Nova Scotia Human Rights Commission, c. 1970s.

Riendeau, Roger. *An Enduring Heritage: Black Contributions to Early Ontario*. Toronto: Dundurn Press Ltd., 1984. Booklet.

Papers on the Black Community. Toronto: Ministry of Culture and Recreation, 1975. .5 cm.

Spear: Canadian Magazine of Truth and Soul. Vol. 6, no. 5, 1976. 55 pp.

Anansi: For All People Week, 17- 23 April 1978. Toronto: Toronto Board of Education, Teaching Aids Department, 1978. Curriculum package.

Unity Press. Windsor, Ont., 30 July - 24 Aug. 1970. 1 reel of microfilm.

ONTARIO BLACK HISTORY SOCIETY
TORONTO, ONT.
Collection includes an annual report, 1986, and leaflets, c. 1970s. 1 cm.

"The Writings of Fred Landon." Toronto: Ontario Black History Society, 1983. Black History Bibliography Series, no. 1.

ONTARIO ETHNIC NEWSPAPER MICROFILM PROJECT
TORONTO, ONT.
Black Liberation News. July 1969 - Feb 1970. 1 reel of microfilm.

UNIVERSAL AFRICAN IMPROVEMENT ASSOCIATION
TORONTO, ONT.
Records, 1929-77, which include a constitution, minutes, annual reports, financial accounts, correspondence,

membership lists, clippings, and
newsletters; and a report from the
Ladies' Division. 1 reel of microfilm.
Photographs.

 Photographs: various members of the
U.N.I.A.; and Marcus Garvey, n.d.

AMERICAN COLLECTION

ALLEN, E. D.
BROWNSVILLE, ONT.
 Interviewed on 10 June 1985; .5 hr.;
1 tape; English; by M. Lipowski.
Arrived in Canada in 1930, worked
for the Canadian Leaf Tobacco Company, compares tobacco farming
techniques in the southern U.S. to
those in Ont.

BLANK, ABRAHAM
TORONTO, ONT.
 Personal papers, n.d. .5 cm (6
items). Taped interview.
 Interviewed on 3 Dec. 1978; 2 hrs.;
2 tapes; English; by Janice
Spellerberg. Post-WWII immigrant,
came to Canada because of the draft
status in both Israel, and the U.S.

BONANNO, TOM
SPARTA, ONT.
 Interviewed in Jan. 1979; .75 hr.; 1
tape; English; by Mary Mullins.
Arrived in Canada in 1969 as a war
resister, discusses his early life in
New York.

BURDICK, MARY P.
TORONTO, ONT.
 Interviewed on 21 Jan. 1979; 2 hrs.;
2 tapes; English; by Janice
Spellerberg. Grew up in Florida and
New Orleans, Louisianna, migrated to
Toronto with her future husband in
the 1960s.

BUSH, STEVEN
TORONTO, ONT.
 Personal papers, programmes,

reviews, and 2 posters. 2 cm (17
items). Taped interview.
 Interviewed on 15 Jan. 1979; 1.5
hrs.; 2 tapes; English; by Janice
Spellerberg. Immigrated to Canada in
the 1960s, settled in Toronto, discusses theatre, and political conditions
in the U.S.

CLARKE, FRED
WATERFORD, ONT.
 Interviewed on 23 July 1985; 1 hr.;
1 tape; English; by Anne Schooley.
Discusses tobacco farming, and ethnic
groups in the Delhi tobacco region.

DRAGON, BRYAN AND G. SMITH
SPARTA, ONT.
 Interviewed on 11 Nov. 1978; .75
hr.; 1 tape; English; by Mary
Mullins. Arrived in Canada in 1969,
discusses personal struggles related to
the U.S. draft.

EAKER, YATES
DELHI, ONT.
 Interviewed on 14 June 1985; 1 hr.;
1 tape; English; by Anne Schooley.
Born in North Carolina in 1908,
arrived in Canada in 1929, worked
cutting tobacco.

GUTHRIE, A.
SIMCOE, ONT.
 Interviewed in May 1978; 1 hr.; 1
tape; English; by David Judd. Discusses tobacco farming in the Delhi
region.

HAMILTON, WILLIAM
VANESSA, ONT.
 Interviewed on 18 July 1977; 1 hr.;
1 tape; English; by David Judd. Discusses family farm in Virginia, and
his migration to southern Ont. where
he sharecropped in tobacco. Also discusses farming in the 1930s, and
farming anecdotes in southwestern
Ont.

HENNESSEY, DANIEL R.
CANNINGTON, ONT.
 Interviewed on 16 Jan. 1979; 2 hrs.;
2 tapes; English; by Mary Mullins.
Emigrated from New Jersey in 1967
as a draft dodger, pursued a career as
an actor in Toronto.

HOLMAN, DON
TORONTO, ONT.
 Interviewed on 25 Jan. 1979; 2 hrs.;
2 tapes; English; by Janice
Spellerberg. Fled to Canada in the
late 1960s. Discusses anti-draft feelings, and activities in the U.S.

HOPPER, KEN
TORONTO, ONT.
 Interviewed on 1 Dec. 1978; 1 hr.; 1
tape; English; by Janice Spellerberg.
Left the U.S. in the 1960s as a draft
resister, pursued a career as an artist
in Toronto.

JOHNSON, ELIZABETH
DELHI, ONT.
 Interviewed on 10 April 1985; 1 hr.;
1 tape; English; by Stacia Johnson.
Born in Kentucky in 1902, migrated
to the Delhi region with her husband
in 1928. He worked cutting tobacco,
and they bought a farm in 1947.

JONES, LAURA
TORONTO, ONT.
 6 photographs: community life on
Baldwin Street in Toronto, 1969-72.
Taped interview.
 Interviewed on 20 Dec. 1978; .75
hr.; 1 tape; English; by Mary
Mullins. Quakers in resistance of the
war, immigrated to Canada in the
1960s.

LAWRENCE, KENT
COMBEMERE, ONT.
 7 photographs: interior and exterior
views of Kent Lawrence's house in
Toronto, 1978. Taped interview.
 Interviewed on 17 Oct. 1978; 2 hrs.;
2 tapes; English; by Mary Mullins.
Originally from Vermont, immigrated
to Canada in 1970 through the
T.A.D.P. (Toronto Anti-Draft Program), settled in Toronto.

MULLINS, PHILIP M.
TORONTO, ONT.
 Interviewed on 7 Jan. 1979; 2.5 hrs.;
3 tapes; English; by Janice
Spellerberg. Discusses his anti-war
activities in the U.S., his immigration
to Canada in the 1960s, and the building of a cohesive, co-operative
American community in Toronto.

ORMSBY, MICHAEL
TORONTO, ONT.
 Interviewed on 8 Nov. 1978; 1 hr.;
1 tape; English; by Janice
Spellerberg. Discusses student activities in New York, and reasons for
immigrating to Canada in the late
1960s.

PHILLIPS, E. W.
DELHI, ONT.
 Interviewed on 24 April 1985; 1 hr.;
1 tape; English; by Stacia Johnson.

Grew up in the U.S., returned to Delhi in 1946, discusses employment on tobacco farms, politics, and various immigrant groups in the Delhi region.

PHILLIPS, JOHN F.
TORONTO, ONT.
  4 photographs: people and store fronts on Baldwin Street in Toronto, n.d. Taped interview.
  Interviewed on 10 Jan. 1979; 1.5 hrs.; 2 tapes; English; by Mary Mullins. Draft resister, immigrated to Canada in the late 1960s or early 1970s, discusses the American community on Baldwin Street in Toronto.

RICHARDSON, WOODROW
DELHI, ONT.
  Interviewed on 16 May 1985; 1 hr.; 1 tape; English; by Anne Schooley. Born 1913 in Virginia, moved to Tillsonburg, Ont. in 1930 to harvest tobacco, discusses the political economy, and techniques used in tobacco farming in the Delhi region.

SPELLERBERG, JANICE
TORONTO, ONT.
  3 photographs: street vending in Toronto, 1973-75. Taped interview.
  Interviewed on 30 Jan. 1979; 1.5 hrs.; 2 tapes; English; by Mary Mullins. Born in Missouri, immigrated to Toronto with husband, who was a draft dodger, in 1969, recounts her involvement in the Kansas City Group, and the various jobs she held in Canada, Europe, and South Africa.

STARBUCK, FLETCHER
TORONTO, ONT.
  1 photograph: taken by donor, a professional photographer, 1973. Taped interview.

Interviewed on 5 Nov. 1978; 2 hrs.; 2 tapes; English; by Mary Mullins. Born in California, migrated to Canada in 1967 to avoid the draft, much transience between Toronto, Montreal, and Vancouver, lived in the Baldwin Street district of Toronto. *Arts Canada*. Nos. 192-95, 1974. 1.5 cm.

STARBUCK, MADELYN AVERITTE
TORONTO, ONT.
  3 photographs: Madelyn Averitte Starbuck and George Mullins, 1970. Taped interview.
  Interviewed on 28 Oct. 1978; 1 hr.; 1 tape; English; by Mary Mullins. Born in Florida, moved to Ont. in 1960s, settled on Baldwin Street in Toronto, where she operated a leather shop.

STEPHENS, GARY LEON
TORONTO, ONT.
  Interviewed on 14 Jan. 1979; .75 hr.; 1 tape; English; by Janice Spellerberg. Born in Oklahoma, immigrated to Toronto in the 1960s, involved in theatre production.

TETTEMER, FRANKLIN
TORONTO, ONT.
  Interviewed on 28 Jan. 1979; 1 hr.; 1 tape; English; by Phillip Mullins. Born in Pennsylvania, immigrated to Toronto in 1969 to avoid the draft, lived in communal settings throughout Ont., including one on Baldwin Street in Toronto.

WILSON, JAMES E.
BARRY'S BAY, ONT.
  1 photograph: plate printer. Taped interview.
  Interviewed on 3 Jan. 1979; 2 hrs.; 2 tapes; English; by Mary Mullins.

Originally from North Carolina, he
immigrated to Canada in the late
1960s. He settled in Toronto where
he opened a commune, and ventured
into the arts and crafts business.
Discusses his anti-draft activities, and
the importance of the Amerindian
culture in his life.

ZIMMERMAN, DAVID R.
TORONTO, ONT.
 Interviewed on 9 Jan. 1979; 1 hr.; 1
tape; English; by Mary Mullins.
Originally from New Jersey, fled to
Canada in the 1960s in resistance to
draft, lived in the Baldwin Street
community of Toronto.

AMERICAN CLUB OF TORONTO
TORONTO, ONT.
 Membership application. .25 cm.
 The Eagle. Jan. 1979. Bulletin. .5
cm.

AMERICAN WOMEN'S CLUB
TORONTO, ONT.
 Records, 1947-76, which include
minutes, correspondence, and two
scrapbooks. 1 reel of microfilm.

ARAB COLLECTION

AHMED, QUTBI M.
TORONTO, ONT.
Interviewed on 20 July 1978; 1 hr.;
1 tape; English; by Anab Whitehouse.
Discusses the Jami mosque and its
purpose, the Islamic faith, and the
problems of adjustment faced by
Muslims living in Canada.

AZIZ, NABIL N.
SUDBURY, ONT.
Interviewed on 17 April 1984; .5
hr.; 1 tape; English; by Kareem Toni.
Discusses the history of the Aziz fam-
ily.

AZZEH, FAHMI
SUDBURY, ONT.
Interviewed on 2 Aug. 1984; .5 hr.;
1 tape; English; by Kareem Toni.
Emigrated from Palestine in 1968.

BANGASH, ZAFAR U.
TORONTO, ONT.
Interviewed on 2 Dec. 1978; 1 hr.; 1
tape; English; by Anab Whitehouse.
Discusses the founding, and history of
the *Crescent* newspaper.

BARRACH, EVELYN
TORONTO, ONT.
3 photographs: unidentified, n.d.

BHATTI, ABRAR M.
TORONTO, ONT.
Interviewed on 25 July 1978; 1 hr.;
1 tape; English; by AnabWhitehouse.
Discusses the founding of the Jami
mosque, and the Muslim Society of
Toronto.

BURKET, KASSIM
LONDON, ONT.
Collection includes letters, and photographs (11 items). Taped interview.
7 photographs: donor's restaurant;
and a picnic in Springbank Park, all
taken in London, Ont.
Interviewed on 26 July 1979; 1 hr.;
1 tape; English/Arabic; by Mazen
Nasruddin. Emigrated from Lebanon
in the mid-1920s, discusses his
employment history, restaurant business, and involvement in his community.

DABOUS, MORRIS
SUDBURY, ONT.
Interviewed on 23 July 1984; .5 hr.;
1 tape; English; by Kareem Toni.
Discusses the history of the Dabous
family.

DATARDINA, MUHAMMAD–ASGHAR
AND FARHANA SUBHANI
TORONTO, ONT.
Interviewed on 23 Sept. 1978; 1.25
hrs.; 2 tapes; English; by Anab
Whitehouse. Discusses the function of
the Islamic Community Services of
Toronto.

EGAB, M. A.
SUDBURY, ONT.
Interviewed on 23 July 1984; .5 hr.;
1 tape; English; by Kareem Toni.
Discusses personal history.

FARAH, ANIS
SUDBURY, ONT.
Interviewed on 26 July 1984; .5 hr.;

1 tape; English; by Kareem Toni.
Emigrated from Palestine, via
Lebanon.

HADDAD, F.
SUDBURY, ONT.
Interviewed on 25 July 1984; .5 hr.;
1 tape; English; by Kareem Toni.
Discusses personal history.

MIRZA, MUHAMMAD YAQUB
TORONTO, ONT.
Interviewed on 23 July 1978; 1.25
hrs.; 2 tapes; English; by Anab
Whitehouse. Past president of the
Muslim Students' Association, dis-
cusses its goals and activities.

NASSAN, OMAR
LONDON, ONT.
5 photographs: the Hassan family;
and Muslim community activities in
Toronto and London, 1948-75. Taped
interview.
Interviewed on 19 Aug. 1979; 1 hr.;
1 tape; English; by Mazen Nasruddin.
Arrived in Canada in
the early 1940s, worked at General
Motors most of his life.

PETERS, JIM
TORONTO, ONT.
Announcements and flyers issued by
the Arab Palestine Association, the
Lebanese National Movement, the
Canadian Arab Friendship Associ-
ation, the Arab Community Centre of
Toronto, and the Arab Canadian Club
of Toronto, 1977-80; along with scat-
tered issues of Arab journals and
newspapers. 5.5 cm. 1 reel of micro-
film. Canadian Arab Federation. *The
Arab Dawn.* 1968-78. Incomplete (34
issues).
Canadian Arab Federation Journal.
April, June, July, Aug., Sept., Oct.

1972 (7 issues).
*The Canadian Arab Society of Lon-
don.* n.d. News bulletins (7 issues).
Jameel's Journal. Nov. 1972 - Sum-
mer 1973 (4 issues).
Middle East Digest and Newsletter.
Jan. 1962 - Sept. 1969. 1 reel of
microfilm.

SEEDE, AHMED EL
LONDON, ONT.
Interviewed on 19 July 1979; 1 hr.;
1 tape; English; by Mazen Nasruddin.
Arrived in Canada in 1927, farmed in
Saskatchewan, operated a variety
store in London, Ont., and played an
important role in building the London
Muslim Mosque.
*The Action Committee on
American-Arab Relations, 1965-66.*
Illustrated yearbook. 97 pp.
Federation of Islamic Associations.
July 1956, July 1966, and July 1967.
Yearbooks for the 5th, 15th, and 16th
annual conventions in the U.S., and
Canada. 6 cm.

TONI, KAREEM
SUDBURY, ONT.
List of Arab community members in
the Sudbury area before 1965, and the
Sudbury Arabic Club minutes,
1970-75. 3 cm.

WHITEHOUSE, WILLIAM
TORONTO, ONT.
Interviewed on 26, 27, 29 July 1979;
2.5 hrs.; 3 tapes; English; by Anab
Whitehouse. Discuss incidents of pla-
giarism at the University of Toronto.

YOUSSEF, TONI
SUDBURY, ONT.
Interviewed on 13 July 1984; .5 hr.;

1 tape; English; by Kareem Toni.
Discusses the history of the Youssef
family.

ZAZAR, SAID
TORONTO, ONT.
Interviewed on 11 Oct. 1978; 1.25
hrs.; 2 tapes; English/Arabic; by
Anab Whitehouse. Discusses the
history and functions of the Islamic
Medical Association of North
America.

====

ARAB CANADA CLUB OF TORONTO
TORONTO, ONT.
Constitution and list of objectives,
n.d., a historical sketch of the club,
and flyers, 1970-78. 4.5 cm.
Arab Canada Club of Toronto.
Building Fund Hafleh. 1969, 1970,
1974 (3 issues). 2 cm.

BRANTFORD MUSLIM ASSOCIATION
BRANTFORD, ONT.
Minutes, general correspondence,
statements of accounts, and invita-
tions, 1975-78. 2.5 cm.
The Brantford Expositor. July 1975.
Islam Canada. May 1975 (1 issue).

CAMBRIDGE MUSLIM ASSOCIATION
CAMBRIDGE, ONT.
Minutes and correspondence,
1976-78, list of Muslims in the Cambridge area, teaching aids in Arabic,
notices, and brochures. 1.5 cm. Photographs.
3 photographs: the Cambridge Muslim Association activities, 1976-77.
Al-Manar-Al-Islami. 1977, 1978 (2
issues).
Islam Canada. 1977 (2 issues).

CANADIAN ARAB FRIENDSHIP
SOCIETY OF TORONTO
TORONTO, ONT.
Records, 1972-77, which include a
constitution, correspondence, reports,
press releases, and miscellaneous
printed items. 1 reel of microfilm.

CANADIAN ARAB PROFESSIONAL
ASSOCIATION
OTTAWA, ONT.
Constitution, 1975; correspondence,
1974-77; financial report, annual
budget, 1976; and miscellaneous
printed items, 1974-77. 3.5 cm.

CANADIAN ARAB SOCIETY OF LON-
DON
LONDON, ONT.
"Proceedings of the Canadian Arab
Heritage Conference." 1976. 34 pp.
*The Arab World and Canada: Pros-
pects for Cooperation.* 1976. .5 cm.
*The Arab Heritage of Western Civili-
zation.* 1976. .5 cm.
The Arab Case for Oil and Justice.
1976. .5 cm.
Arabic for English Beginners. 1975.
62 pp.
Arabic for Beginners, Book II. 1974.
42 pp.
Conversational Arabic. 1975. 99 pp.
Lebanon Handicrafts. n.d. 24 pp.
*People's Democratic Republic of
Yemen.* 1974. 12 pp.

CANADIAN FRIENDS OF THE MIDDLE
EAST
LONDON, ONT.
General correspondence, 1972-75,
and miscellaneous Arabic grammar,
and history publications, 1972-77. 4.5
cm.

CANADIAN SOCIETY OF MUSLIMS
TORONTO, ONT.
Newsletter. March 1977, Jan. 1978
(2 issues).

ISLAMIC FRATERNAL ASSOCIATION OF
MUSLIMS OF YUGOSLAVIA
TORONTO, ONT.
Letters patent, correspondence,
receipt book, membership booklet,
and greeting cards, 1974-78. 4 cm.

ISLAMIC SCHOOL OF OTTAWA
OTTAWA, ONT.
Miscellaneous records, n.d. 1 reel of
microfilm. Photographs.
11 photographs: activities at the
Islamic School of Ottawa; and
mosques in Alberta, 1938-75.

KINGSTON ISLAMIC SOCIETY
KINGSTON, ONT.
Correspondence, receipt book, programmes, press releases, and
newsclippings, 1970-77. 3 cm. Photographs.
10 photographs: activities at schools;
and celebrations of the Kingston
Islamic Society, 1967-77.

MUSLIM ASSOCIATION OF HAMILTON
HAMILTON, ONT.
Constitution, annual report, directory, and newsletter, 1976-78. 1.5
cm. Photographs.
6 photographs: activities of the Muslim Association of Hamilton,
1976-77.

MUSLIM BENEVOLENT SOCIETY
LADIES' CLUB
OTTAWA, ONT.
Brochures and souvenir booklets. 1.5
cm. Photographs.
3 photographs: the St. Elijah's
Young Ladies' Society, 1938-39;

tombs and sepulchral monuments,
1948, Ottawa.
*Federation of Islamic Associations in
the U.S. and Canada*. 1955. Souvenir
programme from the 4th annual convention. 1 cm.

MUSLIM STUDENTS' ASSOCIATION OF
CANADA
TORONTO, ONT.
Constitution and list of objectives,
1975, flyers and an Islamic calendar,
1976-78. 2.5 cm.
*Education and Recreation of Mus-
lims*. 1978. 2nd annual conference in
Ont. .25 cm.
Islamic Horizons. 1978 (3 issues).
Islamic Teaching Centre News. 1978
(1 issue).
The News. 1978 (1 issue).

OTTAWA MUSLIM ASSOCIATION
OTTAWA, ONT.
Constitution and record of by-laws,
correspondence, annual reports, and
newsclippings, 1965-78. 1.5 cm. Pho-
tographs.
10 photographs: activities of the
Ottawa Muslim Association, 1977-78.
The Canadian Muslim. 1968-78.
Newsletter (2 issues).

OTTAWA MUSLIMS WOMEN'S AUXILI-
ARY
OTTAWA, ONT.
Constitution and minutes, 1973-77.
Publications and Islamic teaching
aids. 1 reel of microfilm.
The Canadian Muslim. 1977-78 (3
issues).
*Ottawa Muslim Association Direc-
tory, 1938-1978*. .5 cm.
Islam Canada. Sept. 1977, March
1980 (2 issues).

Muslim Students' Association.
Islam—Unique and Universal. 1972.
12 pp.

ST. MARY'S COPTIC ORTHODOX
CHURCH
OTTAWA, ONT.
Church Council minutes, 1970-78;
church newsletter, 1976-78; and
calendars and invitations. 5.5 cm.

ARMENIAN COLLECTION

ABDALYAN, ANI
TORONTO, ONT.
 Armenian Concert of Anoush Opera,
1981. 1 leaflet. Photographs.
 20 photographs: the Armenian Relief
Society summer school in Toronto,
1981; and Homemetmen Basketball
World Tournament, 1981. 1 cm.

ADAMS, A.
HAMILTON, ONT.
 Personal documents. .5 cm (3 items).
Photographs.
 17 photographs: family and friends
of Michael Adams in Hamilton,
Vancouver, Kharpert, Kingston,
Toronto, and Guelph, 1912–44; and a
picnic organized by the Armenian
Revolutionary Federation in
Hamilton.

ADOURIAN, ONNIG
HAMILTON, ONT.
 Interviewed on 14 Sept. 1979; 2.5
hrs.; 3 tapes; English; by John
Apramian. Arrived in Canada in the
early 1920s with a large group of
Armenian orphans known as the
Georgetown Boys. They were brought
to southwestern Ont. to work on
farms.

ADOURIAN, PAUL
TORONTO, ONT.
 Interviewed on 6 March 1979; 3.5
hrs.; 4 tapes; English; by John
Apramian. One of the Georgetown
Boys discusses his life history.

ALOIAN, ALICE
ST. CATHARINES, ONT.
 Personal documents, n.d. 1 cm.
Photograph. Taped interview.
 1 photograph: the Boyagian family in
St. Catharines, Ont. 1918.
 Interviewed on 18 Aug. 1977; .5 hr.;
1 tape; English; by E. Kashikjian.
Her parents operated a boarding
house in St. Catharines, Ont. Dis-
cusses the history of the Aloian, and
Boyagian families.

ALOIAN, BERJ
ST. CATHARINES, ONT.
 Interviewed in Sept. 1977; 1 hr.; 1
tape; English; by E. Kashikjian.
Active member of Tashnag Club in
St. Catharines, Ont.

ALOIAN, MR. AND MRS.
ST. CATHARINES, ONT.
 2 photographs: Armenian war
heroes, c. 1909.

ANONYMOUS
 8 photographs: early Armenian
immigrants, n.d.

ANONYMOUS
 10 photographs: unidentified family.

APRAMIAN, JOHN
HAMILTON, ONT.
 43 photographs: orphaned Armenian
children known as the Georgetown
Boys, 1920-30. See also Georgetown
Armenian Boys' Association.

Ararat Magazine. Vol. 1, no. 1, 1926 - vol. 2, no. 5, 1927. 1 reel of microfilm.

ARTINIAN, GULVART
ST. CATHARINES, ONT.
 Interviewed in Aug. 1977; 1 hr.; 1 tape; Armenian; by E. Kashikjian. The history of a post–WWI immigrant in St. Catharines, Ont.

ARTINIAN, HARRY R.
ST. CATHARINES, ONT.
 Extensive notes illustrating the history of the Armenian Canadian community, 1914-80. 78 photographs.

AVEDESIAN, REGGIE
ST. CATHARINES, ONT.
 2 sheets of "Bulgour" patent, a copy of company letterhead, interview transcripts, and clippings, n.d. .5 cm. Photographs.
 3 photographs: Armenian workers at Galt Malleable Iron Co. in Galt, Ont., 1937.

AVEDISIAN, A.
ST. CATHARINES, ONT.
 25 photographs: activities of the Armenian Revolutionary Federation, the Armenian Relief Society, and the Armenian Youth Federation in Montreal, St. Catharines, Toronto, and Galt, 1926–78; and a children's theatrical play, and dance group in St. Catharines, 1975-78.

AYVAZIAN, A.
BURLINGTON, ONT.
 1 photograph: Armenian Resistance participants, Van, c. 1908-11.

BERBERIAN, DIKRAN
TORONTO, ONT.
 Interviewed on 14 Oct. 1979; 1 hr.; 1 tape; English; by John Apramian. An Armenian orphan who came to Canada in the 1920s discusses his personal history.

BOGHOSIAN, BOGHOS
TORONTO, ONT.
 Interviewed on 15 Aug. 1977; 1 hr.; 1 tape; English; by John Apramian. One of the Georgetown Boys who arrived in the 1920s.

BOYADJIAN, ARAM
ARLINGTON, MASSACHUSETTS AND KILWORTHY, ONT.
 Interviewed on 12 Sept. 1978; 1 hr.; 1 tape; English; by John Apramian. An Armenian orphan who came to Canada in the 1920s.

BUZBUZIAN, V.
GUELPH, ONT.
 An Armenian handwritten notebook of letters, n.d., 2 photocopies of Arek village before 1915 in the Ottoman Empire. 2 cm (13 items). Photographs.
 11 photographs: family residences and businesses in Guelph, Ont.; and sculptures by Armand Buzbuzian, n.d.

CORKIGIAN, C.
HAMILTON, ONT.
 See Armenian Community Centre of Hamilton.

COURIAN, PAUL
TORONTO, ONT.
 Personal documents, n.d. 1 cm. Photographs.

99 photographs: the Courian family; and views of Algonquin Park, Ont., Greece, and Turkey, 1894–1945.

DAVIES (MOORADIAN), A. B.
HAGERSVILLE, ONT.
Armenian handwritten notebooks of plays, poems, speeches, programmes, and songs, n.d. 7.5 cm (24 items). Photographs.
12 photographs: the Mooradian family in Cairo, Egypt, Hamilton, Ont., and Arek (Keghi), 1910-50; and a theatrical production, 1916.
8 photographs: Armenian refugees in Egypt (mainly children); Armenian religious ceremonies; and Armenians with a flag during military service, c. 1918-19.

DAYIAN, JERRY
ST. CATHARINES, ONT.
Interviewed on 22 Aug. 1979; 1 hr.; 1 tape; English; by John Apramian. Arrived in Canada in the 1920s as a Georgetown orphan.

DERSTEPHANIAN, GEORGE
BRANTFORD, ONT.
17 photographs: the Der Stepanian family in Brantford and St. Catharines, 1919-50; Armenian Freedom Fighter during military service, c. 1915; and workers at Brantford Laundry Ltd. in Ont., 1936-41.

DERSTEPHANIAN, K.
BRANTFORD, ONT.
Papers from the Canadian Armenian Congress. .5 cm (3 items). Photographs. Taped interview.
4 photographs: the Stephanian family; and a theatrical play in Brantford, c. 1935. Taped interview.

Interviewed on 16 May 1978; 2 hrs.; 2 tapes; English; by H. Nahabedian and R. F. Harney.

EVARIAN, P.
HAMILTON, ONT.
9 photographs: the Evarian family, 1920-70.

GEORGIAN, GEORGE
HAMILTON, ONT.
Interviewed on 15 July 1978; 2 hrs.; 2 tapes; English; by John Apramian. Arrived in Canada as a Georgetown orphan in the 1920s.

GROOM, HARRY
HAMILTON, ONT.
Interviewed on 17 Oct. 1977; 1 hr.; 1 tape; English; by John Apramian. Immigrated to Canada in the 1930s.

HACHIGIAN, A.
HAMILTON, ONT.
30 photographs: the Melkonian and Mooradian families; groups of children at the Gibson School, and a baseball team; and paintings by Alice Melkonian Hachigian, 1917-25.

HAGOPIAN, HAIG
TORONTO, ONT.
Interviewed on 12 Sept. 1979; 3 hrs.; 3 tapes; English; by John Apramian. One of the Georgetown Armenian orphans who arrived in Canada in 1927.

HATCH, HARRY
HAMILTON, ONT.
2 photographs: the donor while in the military, 1941, 1943. Taped interview.
Interviewed on 8 Sept. 1979; 3 hrs.;

3 tapes; English; by John Apramian. One of the Georgetown Boys who arrived in 1923.

HOUROIAN, MAMPRE
DEARBORN, MICHIGAN
See Darmon Union Association.

HUMPARTZOOMIAN, MRS. NEVART
BRANTFORD, ONT.
"The Armenian Community Centre." n.d. Pamphlet. Photograph.
1 photograph: the Humpartzoomian family in Brantford, Ont., n.d.

ISHKHANIAN, PAUL
TORONTO, ONT.
Armenian General Benevolent Union. 1979. Booklet commemorating the 25th anniversary of Alex Manoogian's presidency of the A.G.B.U. 1 cm.

JACKSON, ERNEST (MISAG TOMADJIAN)
HAMILTON, ONT.
Interviewed on 29 Aug. 1978; 1.5 hrs.; 2 tapes; English; by John Apramian. Georgetown Armenian orphan who arrived in the 1920s.

KALAGIAN, MARIAM
ST. CATHARINES, ONT.
Interviewed on 15 Sept. 1977; 1 hr.; 1 tape; Armenian; by E. Kashikjian. Inter-war immigrant discusses her personal history.

KALAGIAN, MARY
ST. CATHARINES, ONT.
1 photograph: the Armenian Relief Society in St. Catharines, c. 1955. Taped interview.
Interviewed on 18 Aug. 1977; 1 hr.; 1 tape; Armenian; by E. Kashikjian. Active member of the Armenian Relief Society.

KALAGIAN, PARAVON
ST. CATHARINES, ONT.
Personal documents, n.d. 1 cm. Photographs.
9 photographs: religious ceremony at St. Gregory the Illuminator Church; and farming activities, 1930-60.

KAPRIELIAN, ANNA AND ROBERT MELKONIAN
HAMILTON, ONT.
Interviewed on 23 July 1980; 1.5 hrs.; 2 tapes; Armenian; by Isabel Kaprielian. Armenian folk music.

KAPRIELIAN, ISABEL
TORONTO, ONT.
George Mardekian's dinner menu, n.d., an announcement of a play held in the Armenian community of St. Catharines, c. 1920s, a circular of the opening of the Armenian Community Centre of Toronto, 1979, and various publications. 9 cm. Photographs.
17 photographs: boarding houses, churches, schools, and clubhouses, c. 1970-80.
7 photographs: the Kaprielian family, 1928-45; and a group at the Gibson School in Hamilton, 1940.
Niepage, Martin. *The Horrors of Aleppo.* London: T. Fisher Unwin Ltd., 1975.
Armenian Newsletter. No. 2-27. Toronto, 1977–79. .5 cm.
The Free Republic of Armenia. 1918-68. Pamphlet commemorating the 50th anniversary of the Armenian Republic founding.
The Free Republic of Armenia. 1979. Genocide pamphlet.
Our School. Toronto, n.d. Armenian Day School pamphlet. .5 cm.
Our School. Toronto, 1969. Pamphlet commemorating the pontifical visit of Khoren I.

Revolutionary Album. Aleppo: Eastern Press. 12 pamphlets. 3 cm.
Silver Jubilee Booklet of the Holy Trinity Armenian Church. Toronto, 1978. .5 cm.

KAPRIELIAN, ISABEL
TORONTO, ONT.
A collection of Armenian publications, which includes church souvenir booklets, almanacs, constitutions, periodicals, and pamphlets from the U.S., Lebanon, and France, c. 1910-1960. 17 cm. 1 reel of microfilm.
Darpinian, Rupen. *Socialism and Bolshevism*. Boston: Hairenik, 1922.
Hovaghimian, M. *Everyone's Almanac*. Constantinople: Theotig, 1921. 1 reel of microfilm.
Kasparian, Rev. Yeghishe. *American-Armenian Almanac*. Boston: Hairenik, 1935.

KAPRIELIAN, JACK AND ANNA
HAMILTON, ONT.
13 photographs: the Kaprielian family; Armenian picnics; and Armenian Red Cross members in Hamilton, and Brantford, 1921-70
20th Anniversary Album of the Armenian Red Cross. Boston: Hairenik, 1930. Some pages pertaining to Ont. chapters.
Hamakeghi Patriotic Society. *New Keghi*. 1965. Members of the organization lived in Canada and the U.S., but were originally from Keghi, Armenian Province of Erzerum, Ottoman Empire.

KAPRIELIAN, NORMAN
HAMILTON, ONT.
The collection includes family papers, Armenian publications from North America, naturalization papers,

a passport, 1924; a cookbook, n.d.; Armenian handwritten notes, and poetry by Lucy Kaprielian.
Armenian Relief Society. "H.O.M." n.d., and miscellaneous printed items. 15 cm. Photographs.
8 photographs: the Kaprielian family; school photograph taken in Hamilton, n.d.; and the Armenian cavalry, n.d.
Mandalian, James. *What Do the Armenians Want?* Armenian National Committee, U.S., 1946. 15 pp., in English.
Missakian, James. *A Searchlight on the Armenian Question, 1878-1950*. Boston: American Committee for the Independence of Armenia, Hairenik, 1950. 154 pp., in English.
Tashjian, James. *The Armenians of the U.S. and Canada*. Boston: Armenian Youth Federation, Hairenik, 1947.
Tourigian, Mihran. *The Keghi Front*. Beirut: Hrazdan, 1926. Booklet. 86 pp.
The Alphabet. n.d. Armenian Elementary Reader. 30 pp.
Hairenik Daily, 1914-60. Compilation of various *Hairenik* issues. 1 cm.
Veejag (Ascension). n.d. Religious poems in Armenian/Turkish, with English translation sheets.

KAPRIELIAN, NORMAN
HAMILTON, ONT.
Chakmakjian, Haroutioun. *Armeno-American Letter Writer*. Boston: Yeran Press, 1914. Book of letters in English/Armenian. 1 reel of microfilm. See *Polyphony: The Bulletin of the Multicultural History Society of Ontario*. Vol. 3, no. 1 (1982).
Armenian-English Conversation. Boston: E. A. Yeran, n.d. An illustrated conversation, and guide book.

Religious hymn book (Protestant, Constantinople), 1926. 1 reel of microfilm.

KAPRIELIAN, NORMAN
HAMILTON, ONT.
 Armenian poems, n.d., and a handwritten note, c. 1970s. 1 cm.
 Apramian, John. *The Georgetown Boys*. n.d. Story of approximately one hundred Armenian orphans who were brought to a farm in Georgetown, Ont. 2 cm.
 Boyajian, Durtad. *Popular Legends from Armenian History*. Boston: Hairenik, n.d. Pamphlet.
 Elementary English Reader. n.d. (Used by early settlers). 1 cm.
 20th Anniversary Commemorative Book of Armenian Trinity Church. Toronto. 1973. .5 cm., in English.
 L'Arménie Persecutée. Lausanne: Union of Christian Youth, c. 1890s. .5 cm., in French. *Hairenik*. Boston: Hairenik Press, Nov. 1923 (monthly, containing articles and poetry by Armenian writers). .5 cm.

KAPRIELIAN, PAUL
HAMILTON, ONT.
 A collection of periodicals, programmes, pamphlets, books, menus, and a certificate, c. 1920-70. 3 reels of microfilm. Photographs.
 86 photographs: the Kaprielian family, 1920-69; Armenian school children, 1938-44; and Armenian picnics, choirs, and folk dance groups, 1936-60, all taken in Hamilton.
 Darpinian, Rupen. *Mer Badasghane H. Khachaznounee* (Our Answer to H. Khachaznounee). Boston: Hairenik, 1923. 166 pp., in Armenian.
 Zartarian, R. *Meghraked* (River of

Honey). Boston: Hairenik Press, 1927. 127 pp., in Armenian.
 Kantzaran (Treasury). Constantinople, n.d. 287 pp., in Armenian.
 Patriotic Society of Keghi. Detroit, Michigan, 1937. 20th anniversary commemorative book. 1 reel of microfilm.

KASHIKJIAN, ESTHER
LONDON, ONT.
 Postcards from Soviet Armenia, a church questionnaire, and minutes, c. 1930. 1.5 cm. Photographs.
 5 photographs: social activities at St. Gregory's the Illuminator Church in St. Catharines, c. 1960s.
 11 photographs: the "Holiday Festival" in London, 1975.

KASSABIAN, N.
TORONTO, ONT.
 Recorded in 1979; 3.5 hrs.; 4 tapes; Armenian; by Isabel Kaprielian. Audio recordings of an Armenian church service, consecration, and nuptial discussion.

KELEJIAN, PERCY
ST. CATHARINES, ONT.
 Interviewed on 27 Sept. 1979; 2 hrs.; 2 tapes; English; by John Apramian. An orphan who immigrated to Canada in 1923.

KERBEKIAN, YEPREM
TORONTO, ONT.
 Interviewed on 9 July 1978; 2.5 hrs; 3 tapes; English; by John Apramian. Georgetown orphan who came to Canada in the 1920s.

KLOIAN, ARDASHES
DETROIT, MICHIGAN
 Collection of personal papers,

printed material, and a handwritten
memoir, c. 1920s. 1 reel of microfilm. Photographs. Taped interview.
 4 photographs: Armenian orphans in
Kharpet, 1920; and the Patriotic
Society of Keghi, n.d.
 Interviewed in Sept. 1980; 2.5 hrs.;
3 tapes; Armenian; by Isabel
Kaprielian. Arrived in the early
1920s, discusses transience between
Canada, and the U.S.

KREKORIAN, VARSENIG
ST. CATHARINES, ONT.
 A collection of announcements,
newsclippings, programmes, and a
brief autobiography, 1910-1930,
which refer to the Armenian Union of
Canada. 4.5 cm (18 items). Photo-
graphs. Taped interview.
 12 photographs: social gatherings,
and a funeral at St. Gregory the
Illuminator Church in St. Catharines;
and activities of the Armenian Youth
Association, 1928-52.
 Interviewed on 28 Oct. 1977; 1 hr.;
1 tape; Armenian; by E. Kashikjian.
Inter-war immigrant, active in the
Armenian community of St.
Catharines.

KRIKORIAN, EDNA
ST. CATHARINES, ONT.
 2 books in English/Armenian, and
clippings, n.d. Photographs.
 118 photographs: the Mgerdich
Krikorian family in Turkey and St.
Catharines, Ont., 1910-74; parish
activity at St. Gregory the Illuminator
Church in St. Catharines, 1930-50;
and a strike at McKinnon Industries
in St. Catharines, 1969.

MAGARIAN, KIRK
TORONTO, ONT.
 18 photographs: various meetings, a

group of Georgetown Boys in
Toronto and Detroit, Michigan,
1915-70. Taped interview.
 Interviewed on 10 Oct. 1979; 3 hrs.;
3 tapes; English; by John Apramian.
Georgetown orphan who arrived in
the mid-1920s.

MARDEROSSIAN, M.
TORONTO, ONT.
 4 photographs: the Armenian Cultural Centre in Toronto, n.d.

MAVIAN, ZORIG
SOUTHFIELD, MICHIGAN
 See Astghapert Educational Society.

MELKONIAN, A.
HAMILTON, ONT.
 1 photograph: "The Wounded Soldier," n.d. A play.

MELKONIAN, R.
STONEY CREEK, ONT.
 35 photographs: the Melkonian and
Mooradian families in Egypt and
Hamilton; student sports activities,
parades, and processions in Hamilton,
c. 1928-53; Armenian volunteers in
the Palestine military, 1915-17; andan
Arabian rebellion in Cairo, Egypt,
1919.

MINOIAN, M.
ST. CATHARINES, ONT.
 17 photographs: the Minoian family
in St. Catharines, 1905-60.

MOORADIAN, F.
BRANTFORD, ONT.
 Collection of personal papers, a
diary, and a passport, n.d. 2 cm.
Photographs. Taped interview.
 Interviewed on 16 May 1978; .5 hr.;

1 tape; English; by H. Nahabedian. Arrived in Canada in 1926, established Armenian Club in Brantford, Ont.

MOORADIAN, V.
BRANTFORD, ONT.
 3 photographs: the donor as an Armenian volunteer in French army, fighting Turks in Cilicia, c. 1919–20; and Mr. and Mrs. Mooradian in Hamilton and Detroit, Michigan in the early 1920s.

MUJEREDIAN, GILBERT
TORONTO, ONT.
 Interviewed on 8 Sept. 1979; 1 hr.; 1 tape; English; by John Apramian. Georgetown orphan who arrived in 1923.

NAHABEDIAN, REV. H.
TORONTO, ONT.
 73 photographs: Armenian gravestones in a Brantford cemetery; buildings of the Armenian Community Centre, Central School; and Hunchak Club in Brantford, Ont., n.d.

NAHABEDIAN, V.
TORONTO, ONT.
 Collection of personal papers, certificates, and a passport, n.d. 1.5 cm (6 items). Photographs.
 7 photographs: the Armenian Cultural Centre in Brantford, 1980;and members of the Armenian Union of Canada in Toronto, 1928.

PALVETZIAN, CHARLES
GALT, ONT.
 Collection of 4 pamphlets, and a membership card to the Keghi Fraternal Society,
1915-65. 2.5 cm. Photographs.
 17 photographs: the Palvetzian fam-

ily in Armenia, Corfu, Greece, and Galt, Ont.; and religious ceremonies, the "Madagh" service, in St Catharines, 1915–67.

POSTALIAN, JAMES
TORONTO, ONT.
 Interviewed on 14 July 1979; 2 hrs.; 2 tapes; English; by John Apramian. Georgetown orphan who came to Canada in 1926.

POSTIAN, N.
LONDON, ONT.
 5 photographs: believed to be the Postian family, c. 1960s.

RACIAN, MARGARET
HAMILTON, ONT.
 7 photographs: the Racian family in Greece, 1920-40.

RICE, T.
HAMILTON, ONT.
 10 photographs: employment in mills and foundries, 1939-45; and Victory Lane Parade, 1941, all taken in Hamilton.

SAHAGIAN, M. AND E. SERAGANIAN
BRANTFORD, ONT.
 17 photographs: the Sahagian family in Brantford, Niagara Falls, Turkey, and Bulgaria; the Armenian Red Cross; and a carpet factory in Brantford, 1919–36.

SARKESIAN, MRS. NEVART
DETROIT, MICHIGAN
 22 photographs: U.S. conferencesand projects of the Patriotic Society of Keghi, 1948-60; and people in, and from Keghi, 1914-60.
 Sheedanian, Armen. *Avazagabede* (The Brigand Boss). Boston: Yeran Pub., 1915. 540 pp.

Vratzian, Simon, ed. *Hairenik*. Boston: Hairenik Press, 1945. 270 pp.
Nishan Palanjian School: Past and Present. Beirut, Lebanon, 1972-73. 60 pp.
Samuel Mooradian School in Sévres, France. Venice, Italy: Meghitarist Press, 1938. 31 pp.
Simon Zavarian Armenian Community Centre. Detroit, Michigan: Armenian Revolutionary Federation, n.d. Commemorative booklet. 64 pp.

SARKESIAN, MRS. NEVART
DETROIT, MICHIGAN
Patriotic Society of Keghi. 1958. 25th anniversary booklet. 38 pp.

SARKISIAN, SARKIS
FERGUS, ONT.
Interviewed on 18 Sept. 1978; 2 hrs.; 2 tapes; English; by John Apramian. Georgetown orphan who came to Canada in 1923.

SARKISSIAN, MRS.
BRANTFORD, ONT.
Interviewed on 16 May 1978; 1 hr.; 1 tape; English; by H. Nahabedian, and R. F. Harney.

SHEHIRIAN, E.
TORONTO, ONT.
Two phonograph records—Armenian Christmas chants, and "To the Memory of D. Varoojan and Siamanto." Photograph.
1 photograph: Veejag celebration, 1970.
Shehirian, E. *We Learn Armenian*. Toronto: Armenian Recordings, 1973. Armenian language primer. 56 pp.
Armenian Young Men's Assocation of Toronto. *Newsletter*. 1931-32. 3 pp.
Everyman's Handbook, 1964. pp.

225-28, 237, 244-248 only.
Canadian Armenian Young People's Association. *Genetics*. 1930. 174 pp.
Veejag. n.d. Poems.

SHEHIRIAN, E. AND A. SRABIAN
TORONTO, ONT.
Recorded on 9, 10 June 1980; 1.5 hrs.; 2 tapes; Armenian; by Isabel Kaprielian. Armenian folk music.

SHIRINIAN, MAMPRE
TORONTO, ONT.
Interviewed on 8 Aug. 1979; 2 hrs.; 2 tapes; English; by John Apramian. Georgetown orphan who arrived in 1924.

SIMIGIAN, M.
HAMILTON, ONT.
Collection of personal documents, marriage certificates, and a report card, c. 1920s. 1.5 cm. Photographs.
30 photographs: the Simigian and Manougian families; the Armenian Choir, a Christmas concert, a beauty contest, picnics and parties; and a funeral, and other religious rites.

SNIDERMAN, S.
TORONTO, ONT.
Collection of material belonging to Levon and Peruz Babayan, which includes correspondence, clippings, pamphlets, periodicals, books, programmes, menus, Christmas cards, and a postcard; and artifacts—1 plaque, 2 medals, and 1 cloth game, n.d. 16 cm. Photographs.
35 photographs: family and friends of Levon Babayan in Armenia, Montreal, Quebec, Toronto, and Constantinople, 1900-62; and activities of the Armenian Relief Association of Canada, and the Armenian General Benevolent Union, 1962.

SOLOMONIAN, ALICE
ST. CATHARINES, ONT.
1 newspaper article from the *St. Catharines Standard* about the donor's father, Nishan Krekorian, a survivor of the Titanic tragedy, n.d. .25 cm. Photograph. Taped interview.
1 photograph: the donor's father, Nishan Krekorian, 1975.
Interviewed in Sept. 1977; 1 hr.; 1 tape; English; by E. Kashikjian. active in the Armenian community of St. Catharines.

SOUIN, M.
TORONTO, ONT.
1 photograph: young Toronto Armenians, c. 1930.

TANELIAN, EGLANTINE
HAMILTON, ONT.
Interviewed on 17 Sept. 1977; .5 hr.; 1 tape; Armenian; by John Apramian. Arrived in 1930, indentured as a domestic.

TATARIAN, M.
TORONTO, ONT.
Collection of family diaries, correspondence, Armenian Congress material, clippings, and printed items. 10 cm. Photographs.
113 photographs: Setrak B. Tatarian and his family, 1900-71; his service in the Turkish Army, 1918-19; and his employment with Standard Oil Co. in Constantinople, 1920-22, and in agriculture in Woodstock, Ont., 1924.

TEGHTSOONIAN, O.
TORONTO, ONT.
5 letters of reference, and 1 Armenian handwritten notebook, 1936. 1.5 cm. Photographs.
9 photographs: the Teghtsoonian

family and businesses (rug concession) 1930-40; executive members of the Armenian General Benevolent Union, 1943; and a picnic of the Canadian Armenian Young People's Association, c. 1928.
Achdjian, K. *The Rug.* n.d. Booklet.
Armenian General Benevolent Union Convention. 1972. Booklet.

TOPALIAN, ONNIG (JACK)
TORONTO, ONT.
Interviewed on 10 Oct. 1979; 2 hrs.; 2 tapes; English; by John Apramian. Came to Canada in 1923, as a Georgetown orphan.

TOROSIAN, HYGUS
ST. CATHARINES, ONT.
Minutes, financial statements, and books from the Osnag Educational Society, and various printed items from the Armenian General Benevolent Union, and Keghi Fraternal Society in St. Catharines, 1904-64. 2 reels of microfilm. 7 photographs.

TOROSIAN, HYGUS
ST. CATHARINES, ONT.
Collection of family documents, clippings, minutes, and by-laws of various Armenian organizations in Ont., 1909-61. 1 reel of microfilm. Photographs.
10 photographs: taken between 1909 and 1961.

TOROSIAN, HYGUS
ST. CATHARINES, ONT.
Collection includes boarding house accounts, Armenian textbooks, notebooks, minutes, and segments of handwritten autobiographies, n.d. 3 reels of microfilm. Photographs.
73 photographs: the Torosian family; religious ceremonies at St. Gregory

the Illuminator Church; and the
Armenian Red Cross, all taken on
Bradford Street in St. Catharines,
Ont.

TOURIKIAN, H.
TORONTO, ONT.
5 photographs: the Armenian Quarter
in Beirut, 1975-76. Donor's father
operated the "Lux Hotel" in Beirut.

TROPER, HAROLD
TORONTO, ONT.
1 photograph: Garabed Negararian
(from Nicomedia) in Port Hope, Ont.,
1887.

VARTERESSIAN, ONNIG
OAKVILLE, ONT.
Interviewed on 13 July 1978; 4 hrs.;
4 tapes; English; by John Apramian.
Georgetown orphan who came to
Canada in the 1920s.

VASSOYIAN, LEVON
TORONTO, ONT.
Interviewed on 7 July 1978; 1 hr.; 1
tape; English; by John Apramian.
Georgetown orphan who arrived in
the 1920s.

WOODLEY, HARRY
MONTREAL, QUEBEC
7 photographs: Marash and Zeitoun;
and Rev. Harry Woodley, 1914–18.

ARMENIAN COMMUNITY CENTRE
HAMILTON, ONT.
Minutes, 1962-70. 1 cm.

ARMENIAN COMMUNITY CENTRE
TORONTO, ONT.
Financial report of Armenian Com-
munity Building Fund, 1979; 15

newspaper clippings; and 44 printed
items, which include announcements,
invitations, and programmes issued by
the Armenian Community Centre,
n.d. Additional publications, in
Armenian .75 meters.
Armenian Dance Ensemble. n.d. 20
pp.
Armenian School Textbook. 1916. 80
pp.
Caravan '79—Armenian Pavillion. 3
booklets.
Church of St. Philip. Hamilton,
Ont., 1955. 20 pp.
Echo: Armenian Tabloid Toronto.
Feb. 1972 - Nov. 1976. Complete. .5
meters.
Hamazkine. 1979. 10th anniversary
booklet of Armenian Summer School.
54 pp.
Letters and (*Kir-ou-Kirk*). n.d. 12
pp.
*Outreach: A Publication of the Prel-
acy of the Armenian Apostolic Church
of America.* Vol. 1, no. 1, 1978. 8
pp.

ARMENIAN GENERAL BENEVOLENT
UNION
TORONTO, ONT.
Includes an annual report, an histori-
cal sketch, and patent letters of the
Armenian General Benevolent Union,
n.d. 1 cm.

ARMENIAN RELIEF SOCIETY AND
ARMENIAN ETHNIC HERITAGE PRO-
JECT
TORONTO, ONT.
Recorded on 29 July 1981; .75 hr.; 1
tape; English; by Isabel Kaprielian.
"Sounds of Armenia," segment of a
teaching aid package.

ARMENIAN RELIEF SOCIETY
TORONTO, ONT.
Collection of pamphlets published by
the Armenian Relief Society:
Armenian Khatchkar (Stone Cross).
1976. 11 pp.
Elements of Armenian Architecture.
1976. 20 pp.
The Land of the Armenians. 1976. 31
pp.
Medieval Armenian Costumes. 1976.
20 pp.
*My Origins: Discovering and
Recording Family History.* 1976. 17
pp.
Sights and Sounds of Armenia. 1976.
23 pp.

ARMENIAN RELIEF SOCIETY SUMMER
SCHOOL
TORONTO, ONT.
19 photographs: the Armenian Relief
Society Summer School, n.d. Taped
recording.
Recorded on 14 Aug. 1981; .5 hr.; 1
tape; Armenian; by Ani Abdalyan.
Songs and choir lessons.

ARMENIAN RELIEF SOCIETY SUMMER
SCHOOL
TORONTO, ONT.
Recorded on 14 Aug. 1981; .75 hr.;
1 tape; Armenian; by Ani Abdalyan.
Student recitals.

ARMENIAN REVOLUTIONARY FEDER-
ATION
TORONTO, ONT.
Collection of records, newsletters,
commemorative booklets, and
circulars from the Armenian Revolutionary Federation, the Armenian
Relief Society, the Armenian Youth
Federation, and the Armenian Cultural Federation, 1968-81. 1 reel of
microfilm. Photographs.

68 photographs: life with the
Armenian Relief Society, the
Armenian Revolutionary Federation,
and the Tashnak Club; and Armenian
community activity–schools,
churches, store fronts, employment,
and handicrafts in St. Catharines,
Hamilton, and Montreal, 1914-80.

ASTGHAPERT EDUCATIONAL SOCIETY
SOUTHFIELD, MICHIGAN
Constitution, correspondence, min-
utes, financial statements, and an
historical sketch of the village of
Astghapert, n.d. 1 reel of microfilm.

CANADIAN ARMENIAN YOUNG
PEOPLE'S ASSOCIATION
TORONTO, ONT.
Minutes of the Canadian Armenian
Young People's Association, 1929.
1.5 cm. Photograph.
1 photograph: a group in Toronto,
1934.

DARMON UNION ASSOCIATION
DEARBORN, MICHIGAN
Collection includes a constitution,
1918, minutes, financial records, and
membership lists, n.d. 1 reel of
microfilm.

GEORGETOWN ARMENIAN BOYS'
ASSOCIATION
GEORGETOWN, ONT.
Personal files on Georgetown Boys,
c. 1920-40. 5 reels of microfilm.

GIBSON SCHOOL
HAMILTON, ONT.
Gibson School register, n.d. 2.5 cm.

HAMAZKAIN ARMENIAN CULTURAL
ASSOCIATION
HAMILTON, ONT.
Collection includes a ratified consti-

tution, minutes, newsletters, and a
membership list, 1977-79. 1 reel of
microfilm.

MULTICULTURAL HISTORY SOCIETY
OF ONTARIO
TORONTO, ONT.
  Baliozian, Ara. *The Armenians,
Their History and Culture: A Short
Introduction*. Toronto: Kar Pub.
House, 1975. 211 pp.
  Hagopian, John D. *Kiss Me: I'm
Armenian*. Phoenix, Arizona:
Jurobian, 1982. Memoir. 139 pp.
  Nor Serount. Toronto: Holy Trinity
Armenian Church, 1955 - April 1974.
1 meter.

PATRIOTIC SOCIETY OF KEGHI
DETROIT, MICHIGAN
  Records, which include the Society's
by-laws and goals, dues books,
annual reports, correspondence,
posters, maps, and minutes of meetings, and annual conventions. 2 reels
of microfilm. See N. Sarkesian for
photographs.

AUSTRIAN COLLECTION

BIBERSTEINER, INGE
TORONTO, ONT.
See Austrian Society of Toronto.

DENTAY-KRAUS, GRETA
TORONTO, ONT.
Personal papers, n.d. .25 cm. Photographs. Taped interview.
3 photographs: documents, n.d.; and Greta Kraus, n.d.
Interviewed on 12 June 1979; 1 hr.; 2 tapes; English; by S. Bauer. Immigrated to Canada in 1939, discusses her career in music.

DISSAUER, HERBERT
TORONTO, ONT.
Interviewed on 5 Feb. 1979; 1.5 hrs.; 2 tapes; English/German; by K. Lundy. Arrived in Canada in 1971, an executive member of the Austrian Club in Toronto.

DZIUMA, ADOLPHINE
TORONTO, ONT.
Interviewed on 4 June 1979; .75 hr.; 1 tape; German; by S. Bauer. Arrived in Canada in 1953, moved to Toronto in 1968, an executive member of the Austrian Society of Toronto.

GSCHAIDER, ADOLF
TORONTO, ONT.
Interviewed on 24 Feb. 1979; 1.5 hrs.; 2 tapes; English; by K. Lundy. Post-WWII immigrant, a member of the Austrian Club, discusses his return visits to Austria.

HODGKINSON, MARIA
TORONTO, ONT.
Interviewed on 19 Nov. 1979; .75 hr.; 1 tape; English; by H. Martens. Post-WWII immigrant and war bride, a career woman, discusses difficulties with West Indian housemaids, labour, and racial problems.

HOHENDORF, JOHN
WINDSOR, ONT.
Interviewed on 12 Feb. 1980; .75 hr.; 1 tape; English; by T. Bozek. His father immigrated to Canada, and the family followed in 1937; discusses the history, and immigrant experiences of Transylvanian Saxons.

ISTL, FREDERIC A.
TORONTO, ONT.
Interviewed on 17 May 1979; .5 hr.; 1 tape; English; by S. Bauer. Post-WWII immigrant, co-founded the Canadian Austrian Society of Toronto in 1968.

JESSNER, IRENE
TORONTO, ONT.
Interviewed on 10 July 1980; 1 hr.; 1 tape; English; by M. Karin. Post-WWII immigrant, discusses her career in music.

JUCHART, WALTER
TORONTO, ONT.
Letters, 1977 (4 items). Photographs. Taped interview.
5 photographs: the 5th anniversary of the Chess Club (part of the Edelweiss Club) in Toronto, 1973.

Interviewed on 19 March 1979; 1.5 hrs.; 2 tapes; German; by K. Lundy. Arrived in 1957, actively involved in the Austrian Club.

LABIB, INEZ
TORONTO, ONT.
Interviewed on 19 Jan. 1979; 1 hr.; 1 tape; English; by K. Lundy. Immigrated in 1966. Discusses the family business, and the differences between Canadian and Austrian culture.

LISKA, RODOLPHE
TORONTO, ONT.
Interviewed on 24 May 1979; 1.75 hrs.; 2 tapes; English; by S. Bauer. Immigrated to Canada in 1954, discusses family business, and his involvement in the Canadian Austrian Society of Toronto.

MAUTNER, LORENZ
TORONTO, ONT.
Personal papers, 1938-47. .25 cm. Photographs. Taped interview.
2 photographs: the Mautner family; and a document, n.d.
Interviewed on 23 May 1979; 1 hr.; 1 tape; English/German; by S. Bauer. Arrived in Canada in 1940, discusses hardships encountered during WWII due to Jewish ancestry.

MINICOLA, SUSAN
TORONTO, ONT.
Interviewed on 6 Nov. 1978; 1 hr.; 1 tape; English; by K. Lundy. Post-WWII immigrant, discusses her ethnic, and Canadian identity.

MOHR, INGEBORG
TORONTO, ONT.
Interviewed in July 1980; 1 hr.; 1tape; English; by M. Karin. Arrived in Toronto in mid-1950s, discusses her career as an artist (painter).

PATZAK, GERTRUDE
TORONTO, ONT.
Interviewed on 6 June 1979; .75 hr.; 1 tape; English; by S. Bauer. Arrived in Canada in 1951, discusses work experiences, and involvement in Canadian–Austrian organizations.

PELCIS, HELEN
OTTAWA, ONT.
See Austrian Society of Ottawa.

PILLER, HAROLD
TORONTO, ONT.
Interviewed on 5 June 1979; .5 hr.; 1 tape; English; by S. Bauer. Immigrated to Canada in 1953, discusses his family, and his tool–and–die business.

PILLER MARIA
TORONTO, ONT.
See Canadian Austrian Society of Toronto.

PRAXMARER, RUDOLPH
TORONTO, ONT.
Interviewed on 3 June 1979; 1 hr.; 1 tape; English; by S. Bauer. Arrived in Canada in 1954, discusses his business establishment, and involvement in the Canadian Austrian Society of Toronto.

RASCHKE, JOHN
TORONTO, ONT.
Personal papers including his passport, and identification card; and a menu, n.d. Taped interview.
Interviewed on 14 June 1979; 1.25 hrs.; 2 tapes; English; by S. Bauer. Arrived in Canada in the 1950s with government assistance, discusses his

employment history, and involvement in Austrian ethnic organizations.

ROM, RUTHARD E.
OAKVILLE, ONT.
 Interviewed on 30 Sept. 1978; 1.5 hrs.; 2 tapes; English; by K. Lundy.
 Immigrated to Canada in 1958 from South Africa, very exuberant about his business ventures, and Canadian economic opportunities in general.

SEIPT, SHANNETTE
TORONTO, ONT.
 Interviewed on 25 Sept. 1978; 1 hr.; 1 tape; English; by K. Lundy. Born in Montreal, Quebec; discusses her Austrian heritage.

ULLMANN, KARL
TORONTO, ONT.
 Interviewed on 6 April 1979; 1.5 hrs.; 2 tapes; English/German; by K. Lundy. Immigrated to Canada in 1967 shortly after his girlfriend, discusses employment history, and involvement in Austrian Club.
 Klub Im Wandel. n.d. Journal issue celebrating the 25th anniversary of the Austrian Club. 48 pp.

⸻

AUSTRIAN SOCIETY OF OTTAWA
OTTAWA, ONT.
 Records, 1965-78, which include constitution and by-laws, minutes, correspondence, bank slips, programmes, announcements, and membership lists. 2 reels of microfilm. Photographs.
 69 photographs: recreational activities, concerts, receptions, folk danc-ing, picnics, and parades in Ottawa, 1967-77.
 Newsletter. 1965-78. 1 reel of microfilm.

CANADIAN AUSTRIAN SOCIETY OF TORONTO
TORONTO, ONT.
 The collection contains constitution, correspondence, minutes, financial records, invitations, and programmes, 1968-79. 14 cm. Photographs.
 13 photographs: famous Austrians and buildings; and Austrians kayaking, n.d.
 Newsletter. 1968-78. 5.5 cm.

WINDSOR AUSTRIAN CLUB (W. WOLF)
WINDSOR, ONT.
 The collection contains a constitution, correspondence, programmes, and clippings, 1972-80. 3.5 cm. Photographs.
 8 photographs: recreational activities; and folk dancing, 1977-78.
 "40 Years of Teutonia Club, Windsor." n.d. Booklet.
 "The Corn Ear in the Wind." n.d.
 Der Osterreicher. April, June, Dec. 1979.

CLOET, JOSEPH
DELHI, ONT.
 Material of the Cloet family, c.
1960. .5 cm.

JAENEN, CORNELIUS J.
OTTAWA, ONT.
 List of people from Ont.'s Belgian
community who did not report for
military duty, 1945, and a letter from
the donor, n.d. .5 cm.

DEMEYERE, CYRIL
TILLSONBURG, ONT.
 Interviewed on 21 July 1977; .5 hr.;
1 tape; English; by Kathleen Jones.
Discusses farming in southwestern
Ont., and his involvement with vari-
ous organizations.

DUWIJN, ALBERT FRANCOIS
DELHI, ONT.
 Belgian passport of donor, 1928. .5
cm.

GESQUIERE, GEORGES J.
LANGTON, ONT.
 Interviewed on 24 July 1977; .5 hr.;
1 tape; English; by Kathleen Jones.
Discusses his childhood in Belgium,
and his farming experiences in southwestern Ont.

LANNOO, ACHIEL
DELHI, ONT.
Interviewed on 19 July 1977; .5 hr.;
1 tape; English/Flemish; by Kathleen
Jones. Discusses his early life in Belgium, the journey to Canada, the
hardships he encountered, and his
employment in Canada.

LANNOO, ACHIEL
DELHI, ONT.
 Collection of family papers which
includes 4 Belgian passports, 1950,
1959; a marriage book, 1921; 2 Belgian identity cards, 1937, 1941; a
C.P. Railway identity card, 1948; a
tax statement, 1949; 2 copies of
"Campaign News" pertaining to a
new church building, 1955; 2 bills,
1951, 1957; 4 tobacco farm contracts,
1948-51; a postcard, 1966; and a
Church Building Fund circular, 1955.
2 cm. Photographs.
 4 photographs: Belgians farming
tobacco in Delhi, Ont., 1928-29.

VANCOMPERNALLE, DEMETRIE
DELHI, ONT.
 1 photograph: Belgians farming
tobacco in Delhi, Ont., 1942.

VAN DE MAELE, JULIA
DELHI, ONT.
 Immigration documents of Julia and
Pierre Van de Maele, 1928. .5 cm.

VANDENBUSSCHE, GERARD
DELHI, ONT.
 Interviewed on 8 April 1985; 1.75
hrs.; 2 tapes; English; by Stacia
Johnson. Discusses influx of Belgians
in 1930s, development of the Belgian
Hall up to 1948, and problems
encountered with farming.

VANDENHEEDE, CONRAD
DELHI, ONT.
Interviewed on 17 April 1985; 1.75 hrs.; 2 tapes; English; by Stacia Johnson. Born in Belgium in 1902. Describes his father's work as a butcher. He came to Ont. in 1924, where he became a tobacco share-grower, and later bought a farm in Lynnville, Ont., which he eventually sold to his eldest son in the 1950s.

VERBUYST, MARIA
DELHI, ONT.
Interviewed on 30 May 1985; 1 hr.; 1 tape; English; by Anne Schooley. Discusses her family history in Belgium, the transatlantic crossing in 1924, her work farming sugar beets in Windsor, and sharecropping. She returned to Belgium, and re-immigrated to Canada in 1939, where she grew tobacco for 31 years.

VERHAEGHE, EDMUND
DELHI, ONT.
Interviewed on 20 July 1977; .5 hr.; 1 tape; English; by Kathleen Jones. Discusses family history in Belgium, post-WWII transatlantic crossing, and farm work in Delhi region.

VERVALLE, OCTAAF
DELHI, ONT.
Interviewed on 31 July 1985; 1 hr.; 1 tape; English; by Anne Schooley. Discusses family history in Belgium, arrival in Canada in 1924, and tobacco farming in the Delhi region in the 1930s.

MULTICULTURAL HISTORY SOCIETY OF ONTARIO
TORONTO, ONT.
Magee, Joan. *The Belgians in Ontario*. Toronto: Dundurn Press, 1987. 271 pp.

R. F. PROVINCIAL CAPUCHIN FATHERS
ORANGEVILLE, ONT.
Transcription of letters, 1927-29 and 1938-39, from the archives of Belgian Capuchin Fathers in Canada. 2 cm. *20th Anniversary of St. Philip Neri Parish, 1952-72*. Booklet. 20 pp.

BRITISH COLLECTION

CROSIER, GEORGE
DELHI, ONT.
 Interviewed on 21 July 1977; .75
hr.; 1 tape; English; by David Judd.
Discusses his career as a tobacco
farmer in the Delhi region including
his relations with "New Canadians"
and other groups.

DOWRAD, RAY
TORONTO, ONT.
 Interviewed on 2 May 1979; 2 hrs.;
2 tapes; English; by Margaretha
Bolin. Discusses her origins as an
English-born daughter of Romanian
immigrants in England. Immigrated to
Canada in the late 1940s.

KENT, MR. AND MRS. GORDON G.
DELHI, ONT.
 Interviewed on 22 & 25 Jul. 1977; 2
hrs.; 2 tapes; English; by David Judd.
Discussion of life in the Delhi region
as both tobacco farmers and small
business proprietors.

LE FEVRE, ROBIN AND ELIZABETH
KINGSTON
TORONTO, ONT.
 Interviewed on 8 Aug. 1982; 1.5
hrs.; 2 tapes; English; by Roman
Bielski. Interview with couple
engaged to be married; he British by
birth and she born in Vancouver,
B.C. He arrived in Canada in late
1950s, university education in
Toronto and so forth.

POLLARD, WILFRID
DELHI, ONT.
 Interviewed on 12 July 1977; 1 hr.;
1 tape; English; by David Judd.
Discusses various phases of immigration to the Delhi area and observations about New Canadians and so
forth.

VICKERY, L.S.
DELHI, ONTARIO
 Interviewed on 13 July 1977; 1 hr.;
1 tape; English; by David Judd. Interview focusses on tobacco farming in
the Leamington and Norfolk areas of
southern Ont. and on post-war immigration to the area.

WALLIS, WALTER
SIMCOE, ONT.
 Interviewed on 26 July 1977; 1 hr.;
1 tape; English; by David Judd.
Tobacco farming and marketing
boards are the focus of this interview
inlcuding the interviewee's term as a
marketing board member.

WILSON, DORA
DELHI, ONT.
 Interviewed on 3 Aug. 1977; .75 hr.;
1 tape; English; by David Judd.
Discusses her father's tobacco
farming experiences, his role as
police chief in Delhi, Ont. in 1930s
and experiences with ethnic groups in
business.

BULGARIAN COLLECTION

BONCHEFF, GEORGE
TORONTO, ONT.
5 photographs: employment in agriculture in Toronto, 1939-54. Taped interview.
Interviewed on 8 March 1977; 1 hr.; 1 tape; English/Bulgarian; by Irene Markoff. Immigrated to Canada, c. 1920s. Discusses the voyage of his "mail-order bride" to Canada, their marriage in 1939, the jobs he had in slaughter houses, on farms, and with C.P. Railway. Eventually, they purchased their own land, and built a successful market-gardening business. Involved in Toronto's Bulgarian community.

DAMYANOFF, DAMYAN
TORONTO, ONT.
6 photographs: the donor in Toronto, 1914; the donor while working in construction in Pembroke, Washago, and Bobcaygeon, 1915-19; and the Macedonian Canadian People's League, 1953. Taped interview.
Interviewed on 14 April 1977; 1.5 hrs.; 1 tape; English/Bulgarian; by Irene Markoff. Born in Troyan, Bulgaria in 1897 where he learned the furrier trade. Immigrated to Canada in 1913. Discusses the jobs he held as a maker of tin, dockworker, waterboy for C.P. Railway, labourer in a stone quarry in Wasago, hoisting engineer in Toronto, violinist for the Balkansko Eho Ochestra, and administrator for the *Novo Vreme* newspaper in Toronto.

DIMITROFF, MILKA
TORONTO, ONT.
Interviewed on 4 June 1977; 1.5 hrs.; 2 tapes; English/Bulgarian; by Irene Markoff. Born in Kustendil, Bulgaria in 1905, married and immigrated to Canada in 1928.

DOULOFF, GEORGE
TORONTO, ONT.
Membership card of the Vambel Benevolent Society, n.d. .25 cm. Taped interview.
Interviewed on 14 May 1977; 1 hr.; 1 tape; English/Bulgarian; by Irene Markoff. Belonged to the Macedonian/Bulgarian contingent of the International Brigade in the Spanish Civil War, immigrated to Canada in 1930. Discusses prejudice, and the disappearance of Christo Botev, a cultural organization.

DULOFF, ANTON
TORONTO, ONT.
Interviewed on 28 May 1977; 1 hr.; 1 tape; English/Bulgarian; by Irene Markoff. Arrived in Canada in 1916, returned to Bulgaria in 1927, and re-immigrated to Canada in 1929, involved in the Balkanski Unak, and the Vambel Benevolent Society in Toronto.

ELIEFF, VASILKA
TORONTO, ONT.
Interviewed on 22 June 1977; .5 hr.; 1 tape; Bulgarian; by Irene Markoff. Arrived in 1924, Discusses her earlier years in Bulgaria, her transatlantic

crossing to Canada in 1924, and her husband's poolroom at Queen and Parliament Streets, a member of the Balkanski Unak, a sports organization.

EVANOFF, METHODY
TORONTO, ONT.
Interviewed on 11 July 1977; 1 hr.; 1 tape; English/Bulgarian; by Irene Markoff. Immigrated to Canada in 1930, discusses the village where he lived prior to immigrating, and his restaurant business ventures in Toronto.

EVANOFF, VLADO
TORONTO, ONT.
Interviewed on 11 April 1977; 1 hr.; 1 tape; English/Bulgarian; by Irene Markoff. Donor's father immigrated to Canada in 1911, donor and his mother arrived in 1927, discusses territorial disputes in the Balkans, his transatlantic crossing, and his work in Toronto.

GEORGEFF (GEORGEVICH), ANTON
TORONTO, ONT.
Interviewed on 13 April 1977; 1 hr.; 1 tape; Bulgarian/English; by Irene Markoff. Donor's father immigrated to Canada in 1912, donor arrived in 1930, discusses his homeland during the Balkan War, and his shoe-repair business of the early 1940s.

GRUDEFF, JOHN
TORONTO, ONT.
Interviewed on 9 Feb. 1977; 1 hr.; 1 tape; Bulgarian/English; by Irene Markoff. Immigrated to Canada in the 1910s, obtained post-secondary education in Toronto, co-founded the First Benevolent Society, and the Bulgarian Canadian Society.

KALEFF, JIM
TORONTO, ONT.
Interviewed on 16 March 1977; 1 hr.; 1 tape; Bulgarian; by Irene Markoff. Immigrated to Canada in 1930, discusses his early life in Bulgaria, his numerous jobs in Ont., and his return visit to Bulgaria in 1960.

KANTAROFF, KRIS
TORONTO, ONT.
Interviewed on 1 Feb. 1977; 1.5 hrs.; 2 tapes; Bulgarian/English; by Irene Markoff. Immigrated in the 1910s, discusses his arranged marriage to a woman in his home village, his poolroom business, and his involvement in the community theatre, and choir at Sts. Cyril and Methody Church.

KOLEFF, NICK
HAMILTON, ONT.
Interviewed on 8 July 1977; 1.75 hrs.; 2 tapes; English/Bulgarian; 1913, rented a farm in Saskatchewan, worked as a barber, a carpenter, and later opened a restaurant in Hamilton. Donor joined his father in 1929, and worked in the family restaurant.

KOLESHKOVA, VESELINA
ST. CATHARINES, ONT.
2 photographs: the Mutual Benefit Society picnic in Niagara Falls, 1937; and the Raduvensko Association in St. Catharines, 1945. Taped interview.
Interviewed on 18 June 1977; .75 hr.; 1 tape; English/Bulgarian; by Irene Markoff. Immigrated to Canada in the 1920s.

KOTCHEFF, TODOR
TORONTO, ONT.
Interviewed on 13 March 1977; 1 hr.; 1 tape; English/Bulgarian; by

Irene Markoff. Immigrated to Canada in 1925, worked in the restaurant business.

MARKOFF, JOSEPH
TORONTO, ONT.
3 photographs: Bulgarian Canadians with a visiting Bulgarian theatrical group, 1937; a wedding, 1950; and a child in traditional Bulgarian costume, 1948, all taken in Toronto. Taped interview.
Interviewed on 27 March 1977; 1 hr.; 1 tape; English/Bulgarian; by Irene Markoff. Immigrated to Canada in the 1920s, volunteered to fight with the International Brigade in Spain in the late 1930s. Discusses the jobs he held in construction, tobacco farming, restaurants, and on the railway.

MATOV, GEORGE
TORONTO, ONT.
Interviewed on 20 June 1977; 1.5 hrs.; 2 tapes; Bulgarian/English; by Irene Markoff. Immigrated to Canada in the mid-1920s, his wife-to-be immigrated in 1929, they owned a shipping agency in Toronto.

MIHAILOFF, REV. VASIL
TORONTO, ONT.
Interviewed on 7 Feb. 1977; 1 hr.; 1 tape; English; by Irene Markoff. Arrived in Toronto in 1938; a priest at Sts. Cyril and Methodius Bulgaro-Macedonian Church in Toronto, discusses Bulgarian immigrants to Canada, and divisions within the local church.

MLADENOFF, PANDO
TORONTO, ONT.
Interviewed on 23 June 1977; 2.5 hrs.; 2 tapes; English/Bulgarian; by Irene Markoff. Post-WWII immigrant, discusses his pre-migration experiences in his home village, and Bulgaria.

MOUSMANIS, YOTO
TORONTO, ONT.
Interviewed on 7 June 1977; 1 hr.; 1 tape; Bulgarian/English; by Irene Markoff. Immigrated to Canada in 1927, a restaurateur, and a prominent member of the Dambeni Benevolent Society.

NAIDENOFF, RADOICO
TORONTO, ONT.
Interviewed on 20 May 1977; 1 hr.; 1 tape; English/Bulgarian; by Irene Markoff. Immigrated to Canada in 1924, his wife-to-be immigrated in 1938, worked in the poolroom, and restaurant business.

NICOLOFF, RAINA
TORONTO, ONT.
Interviewed on 2 March 1977; .75 hr.; 1 tape; Bulgarian/English; by Irene Markoff. Immigrated to Canada in 1928, a member of the Bulgaro-Macedonian club, Christo Botev, in Toronto.

NIKOLOFF, TINKA
TORONTO, ONT.
Interviewed on 6 July 1977; 1 hr.; 1 tape; Bulgarian; by Irene Markoff. Husband was a restaurateur, both were members of club Christo Botev.

PANOFF, DANCHO
THOROLD, ONT.
Interviewed on 18 June 1977; 1 hr.; 1 tape; Bulgarian/English; by Irene Markoff. Immigrated to Canada in 1930, worked as a farmer, and a mechanic.

PETROFF, MINCHO
SOUTH THOROLD, ONT.
 Interviewed on 18 June 1977; 1 hr.;
1 tape; Bulgarian; by Irene Markoff.
Immigrated to Canada in 1930, a
member of the Raduvenian Benefit
Association in Thorold.

PEYCHOFF, SAVKA
TORONTO, ONT.
 Interviewed on 16 June 1977; .5 hr.;
1 tape; Bulgarian; by Irene Markoff.
Immigrated to Canada in 1940,
married Ampe Peychoff, and together
they opened a restaurant in the 1950s.

RALLEY, DINCHO
TORONTO, ONT.
 Charter and member's card of the
Bulgarian Canadian People's League
Christo Botev; and membership book
of Macedonian People's League of
Canada. 1.5 cm. Taped interview.
 Interviewed on 26 May 1977; 2 hrs.;
3 tapes; English/Bulgarian; by Irene
Markoff. Pre-WWI immigrant,
recounts his formative years, his par-
ticipation in left-wing
Bulgarian/Macedonian organizations
in Canada, and his involvement in the
Macedonian partisan movement.

STOEFF, ELENKA
TORONTO, ONT.
 Interviewed on 15 June 1977; 3 hrs.;
2 tapes; Bulgarian; by Irene Markoff.
Donor's husband immigrated to
Canada in 1912, donor arrived in
1924, began a poolroom business,
members of the Bugarian Benevolent
Society.

TODOROFF, JOHN
TORONTO, ONT.
 Interviewed on 16 June 1977; 1 hr.;
1 tape; Bulgarian/English; by

Irene Markoff. Immigrated to Canada
in 1914, worked as a farmer, and a
meat-packer.

TODOROFF, VILLIE
TORONTO, ONT.
 Interviewed on 15 June 1977; 1 hr.;
1 tape; Bulgarian/English; by Irene
Markoff. Post-WWII immigrant.

TSENOFF, VALKO
TORONTO, ONT.
 Interviewed on 6 July 1977; 1 hr.; 1
tape; Bulgarian/English; by
Irene Markoff. Donor's father immigrated to Canada three times 1910,
1913, and 1923. Donor joined his
father in 1923, worked as a waterboy,
and flagman for the C.P. Railway.

MULTICULTURAL HISTORY SOCIETY
OF ONTARIO
TORONTO, ONT.
 Novo Vreme. 20 March 1942 - 19
April 1957. 8 reels of microfilm.

BYELORUSSIAN COLLECTION

ZINIAK, MARIA
TORONTO, ONT.
 2 photographs: Byelorussian Evangelical Baptist Fraternity in Toronto,
n.d. Collection includes correspondence, 1951-73, a religious brochure,
and clippings. 3 cm. Photographs.
 76 photographs: activities of the
Byelorussian National Association
including exhibitions, folk dancing,
demonstrations, beauty contests,
national celebrations, and parades in
Toronto, 1948-71.
 Bielaruski Holas. Toronto.
Byelorussian monthly magazine.

BYELORUSSIAN NATIONAL ASSO-
CIATION
TORONTO, ONT.
 Political pamphlets, and flyers, c.
1950s. 1 cm.
 Byelorussian Literary Magazine.
Nos. 7, 12; 1962, 1972. .5 cm.

BYELORUSSIAN GREEK ORTHODOX
CHURCH (FATHER P. WIELIKI)
TORONTO, ONT.
 Ostrowski, W. *About the Origin of
the Name "White Russia."* 1975. 32
pp.
 _____. *The Ancient Names of
Byelorussia.* 1968. .5 cm.

BYELORUSSIAN LITERARY ASSOCI-
ATION OF CANADA AND THE U.S.
TORONTO, ONT.
 Correspondence, 1950-73. 2 cm.

MULTICULTURAL HISTORY SOCIETY
OF ONTARIO
TORONTO, ONT.
 Bielaruski Holas. Jan. 1975-Dec.
1976. 1 reel of microfilm.
 Byelorussia U.S.S.R. Moscow:
Novosty Press, 1972. Illustrated. 82
pp., in English.
 Sobornost. Eastern Churches
Review. Vol. 7, no. 2, 1985. .5 cm.

MULTICULTURAL NEWSPAPER
MICROFILM PROJECT
TORONTO, ONT.
 Bielarus. Toronto, Feb. 1964-
Jan./March 1986. 2 reels of micro-
film.

ONTARIO ETHNIC NEWSPAPER
MICROFILM PROJECT
TORONTO, ONT.
 Bielaruski Emihrant. Feb. 1948-April
1954. 1 reel of microfilm.

ST. EUFROSSINIA BYELORUSSIAN
GREEK ORTHODOX CHURCH
TORONTO, ONT.
 10 photographs: clergy and congre-
gation at St. Eufrossinia Church in
Toronto, 1949-69.

CHINESE COLLECTION

CANNON, JOHN
TORONTO, ONT.
 Collection includes brochures, flyers, and leaflets related to the Bethune Memorial House, the Chinese Catholic Centre News, and the Toronto Chinese Baptist Church, et al., c. 1970s. 2 cm.
 Anniversary of Toronto Chinese Baptist Church Eastside Mission. n.d. 1 cm.

CHAN, ANTHONY B.
TORONTO, ONT.
 "The Chinese Community in Canada: Background and Teaching Resources." n.d. 5 pp.

CHAN, DAVID
WINDSOR, ONT.
 Interviewed on 7 Sept. 1980; 1 hr.; 1 tape; English/Chinese; by Alice Hsieh. Presbyterian minister.

CHANG, FANG GEE
SUDBURY, ONT.
 Interviewed on 14 July 1978; .75 hr.; 1 tape; Chinese; by Chang Lee. Pre-WWII immigrant.

CHANG, YOY SEE
SUDBURY, ONT.
 20 photographs: the Chang and Lee families; and weddings, and festivities in Hong Kong, and Sudbury, 1944-72. Taped interview.
 Interviewed on 18 June 1978; 1 hr.; 1 tape; Chinese; by Chang Lee. Pre-WWII immigrant.

CHAN, PETER
TORONTO, ONT.
 Flyers and a Toronto Super 8 Film programme, 1977. .25 cm.

CHEUNG, MR.
THUNDER BAY, ONT.
 Interviewed on 30 April 1978; 1 hr.; 1 tape; Chinese; by A. Cheng. Pre-WWII immigrant.

CHAI, H. C.
TORONTO, ONT.
 1 flyer. .25 cm.

CHIK, WAI CHUN (CHINESE STUDENTS' ASSOCIATION)
WINDSOR, ONT.
 Interviewed on 31 Jan. 1981; .5 hr.; 1 tape; Chinese; by Alice Hsieh.

CHIU, C. M.
TORONTO, ONT.
 Immigration papers, 1977. .25 cm.

CHIU, FUN LAN
WINDSOR, ONT.
 Interviewed on 17 July 1980; 1 hr.; 1 tape; English; by Alice Hsieh. Discusses religious beliefs.

CHIU, REX
TORONTO, ONT.
 Constitution and flyers of the York University Chinese Students' Association, 1977. .25 cm.
 Chinese Student Monthly. Vols. 1-3. 1977. 40 pp.
 Woodgreen Community Centre. 1983. Newsletter. 2 pp.

CHONG, HENRY
TORONTO, ONT.
Report on the Chinese Outreach Project by the Woodgreen Community Centre, 1974. 1 cm.

CHOW, DAVID
SUDBURY, ONT.
Interviewed on 6 Sept. 1978; .5 hrs.; 1 tape; English; by Chang Lee. Post-WWII immigrant.

CHOW, HONG
SUDBURY, ONT.
Interviewed on 21 June 1978; .25 hr.; 1 tape; Chinese; by Chang Lee. Immigrated to Canada in 1953 via Hong Kong.

CHOW, TING-BONG
SUDBURY, ONT.
Interviewed on 28 Aug. 1978; .5 hr.; 1 tape; English; by Chang Lee. Post-WWII immigrant.

CHUN, MIAO
WINDSOR, ONT.
Membership forms, newsletters, and posters, n.d. (9 items).

FONG, CHEE WING
SUDBURY, ONT.
Interviewed on 26 July 1978; .5 hr.; 1 tape; Chinese; by Chang Lee. Post-WWII immigrant.

FONG, CHI-KIU
TORONTO, ONT.
Records of the Chinese Students' Association. 1 cm (11 items).
China and Ourselves. 1977. Newsletter. 11 pp.

FUNG, WINNIE
OTTAWA, ONT.
A collection of eulogies of Sun Yat-Sen, n.d., in Chinese, and flyers. 1 reel of microfilm.

HOPE, YING
TORONTO, ONT.
Newsclippings and photographs, n.d. .5 cm.
2 photographs: Freemason's lion dance team, 1931; and a group at a youth conference, 1951.

HSIEH, DICK
WINDSOR, ONT.
17 photographs: the Taiwanese University Alumni Association

KAN, CHAN PUI
SUDBURY, ONT.
Interviewed on 6 Sept. 1978; 1 hr.; 1 tape; Chinese; by Chang Lee. Post-WWII immigrant.

KAN, FONG CHE
TORONTO, ONT.
Questionnaire from *The Crossroads*. .25 cm.

KING, MILDRED QUAN
TORONTO, ONT.
4 photographs: the Chinese C.G.I.T. and War Relief, n.d.

KING, PETER LEE
TORONTO, ONT.
1 photograph: Toronto's first all-Chinese hockey team, c. 1949.

KWAN, MING YET
SUDBURY, ONT.
Interviewed on 25 July 1978; 1 hr.; 1 tape; Chinese; by Chang Lee.

LAM, MR. AND MRS. E.
SUDBURY, ONT.
Interviewed on 24 Aug. 1978; .5 hr.;

1 tape; English; by Chang Lee.
Post-WWII immigrant.

LAM, JEAN
TORONTO, ONT.
 Interviewed on 18 Aug. 1983; 1 hr.;
1 tape; English; by Dora Nipp.
Post-WWII immigrant.

LAM, J.
THUNDER BAY, ONT.
 Interviewed in Fall 1977; 1 hr.; 1
tape; Chinese; by A. Cheng.
Pre-WWII immigrant.

LEE, CHOW QUEN
SUDBURY, ONT.
 3 photographs: the Lee family; and
the Sudbury parade, 1960s. Taped
interview.
 Interviewed on 15 June 1978; 1 hr.;
1 tape; Chinese; by Chang Lee.
Post-WWII immigrant.

LEE, EDWARD
WINDSOR, ONT.
 5 photographs: the Lee family; and
Lee after returning from military service in WWII. Taped interview.
 Interviewed on 28 Dec. 1979; 2 hrs.;
2 tapes; English; by Alice Hsieh.

LEE, GUM
SUDBURY, ONT.
 Interviewed on 11 Aug. 1978; .5 hr.;
1 tape; Chinese; by Chang Lee.
Post-WWII immigrant.

LEE, JOHN
SUDBURY, ONT.
 Interviewed on 6 Sept. 1978; .25
hr.; 1 tape; Chinese/English; by
Chang Lee. Post-WWII immigrant.

LEE, LILLIAN
WINDSOR, ONT.
 Interviewed on 1 Dec. 1979; 1 hr.; 1
tape; English; by Alice Hsieh. Member of the E.C.C.C.A.

LEE, MARIA
TORONTO, ONT.
 Report on Outreach Programme,
posters about community events, and
papers of Mount Sinai Hospital, c.
1970s. "A Protocol on the Chinese
Community Hearing Screening."
Nov. 1977. 2 cm. Photographs.
 84 photographs: activities of the Chinese Summer School, taken mainly in
Toronto's Chinatown, 1977.
 Chinese Student Monthly. Toronto,
n.d. (1 issue). 8 pp.

LEE, S.
MONTREAL, QUEBEC
 Immigration certificate, 1918, and
papers from the Chinese Students'
Association 1.5 cm. Photographs.
 2 photographs: personal documents,
1918-24.
 The Woodgreen Scanner. 1976
Newsletter. 10 pp.
 Media. 1977 (1 issue). 41 pp.

LEE, SHING
THUNDER BAY, ONT.
 Interviewed in Fall 1977; 1 hr.; 1
tape; Chinese; by A. Cheng.
Pre-WWII immigrant.

LEE, SHONG
SUDBURY, ONT.
 Interviewed on 12 August 1978; .25
hrs.; 1 tape; Chinese; by Chang Lee.
Arrived in Toronto in 1965 via Hong
Kong to join husband.

LEE, WAI-KWOK
TORONTO, ONT.
Minutes of Chinese Canadians for
Mutual Advancement, 1976; speech
by K. Dock Yip on immigration and
multiculturalism; and a Chinese
Students' Association circular,
1976-77. 1 cm.

LEE, WAI-MAN
TORONTO, ONT.
Collection of posters, n.d.(21 items).
*Ontario Chinese Business Telephone
Directory*. 1977-78. 3 cm.

LEE, YEW SHONG
SUDBURY, ONT.
Interviewed on 14 Aug. 1978; .5 hr.;
1 tape; Chinese; by Chang Lee.
Immigrated to Canada in 1953.

LEE, YEW
SUDBURY, ONT.
Personal documents, 1943-50, a
scrapbook of clippings on the Chinese
community in Sudbury, and a menu
of Capital Cafe. 5 cm. Photographs.
40 photographs: the Lee family in
China, and Sudbury, 1913-67; school
children; and restaurants operated by
the Lee family.

LEUNG, LOK FUNG
TORONTO, ONT.
Records of the Chinese-Canadians
Education Association, which include
by-laws, minutes, and correspon-
dence, 1977- . 1 cm.

LEUNG, PAUL
TORONTO, ONT.
Open letter from the Chinese Com-
munity Centre, n.d., and a poster.

LI, BELINDA
TORONTO, ONT.
Collection of letters, programmes,
posters, and leaflets regarding Chinese Canadian organizations; minutes
of the South-East Spadina Steering
Committee, 1977; a membership list
of the Chinese Canadians for Mutual
Advancement, and an open letter
from the Chinese Parents' Association, 1975. 4 cm.
Harbourfront News. 1977 (1 issue).
.25 cm.
XUN. Nov. 1977 (1 issue). Student
magazine for Erindale Chinese
Students' Association. 45 pp.

LI, PETER
TORONTO, ONT.
Programmes, flyers, and posters of
the Mid-Autumn Festival, 1976. .5
cm.
Mid-Autumn Festival. 1976. Special
issue. 1 cm.

LIU, GRACE
LONDON, ONT.
Toronto Chinese Community Church.
Vol 1., Jan. 1977 - May 1977. 1.5
cm.

LOCK, TOM
TORONTO, ONT.
Clippings, and a concert programme,
n.d. 1.5 cm. Photographs.
8 photographs: the Lock family at
picnics, events for young people, and
on a basketball team in Toronto, n.d.

LOO, LIM SING
TORONTO, ONT.
Handwritten genealogical history of
Lim Sing Loo, n.d., newsclippings,
annual reports of the Chinese Benevolent Association of Canada, 1954-55;
and annual reports of the Chinese

Community Centre, 1973. 5 cm.
Lee's Association of Canada Monthly. 1960-62. 2 cm.

LOW, DAVID
THUNDER BAY, ONT.
1 immigration bond, n.d. 4 pp.
Photographs. Taped interview.
2 photographs: a parade in Fort
William, c. 1940-50.
Interviewed in Fall 1977; 1 hr.; 1
tape; Chinese; by A. Cheng. Immigrated to Canada in 1955.

LUMB, JEAN
TORONTO, ONT.
Interviewed on 18 Aug. 1983; 1 hr.;
1 tape; English; by Dora Nipp. Her
experiences as a Chinese Canadian
and Chinese-Canadian woman.

MIAO, CHUN
WINDSOR, ONT.
Written material on Buddha, n.d. 17
pp. Taped interview.
Interviewed on 7 July 1980; 1 hr.; 1
tape; Chinese; by Alice Hsieh. Discusses Buddhism.

MOK, SUM LENG
WINDSOR, ONT.
Interviewed on 28 May 1980; 1 hr.;
1 tape; Chinese; by Alice Hsieh. The
history of the Chinese Church
Alliance.

MOK, REV. SAMUEL
WINDSOR, ONT.
Recorded on 20 July 1980; 1 hr.; 1
tape; Chinese; by Alice Hsieh.
Church service.

MOK, REV. SAMUEL (CHINESE
ALLIANCE CHURCH)
WINDSOR, ONT.
Recordeded on 25 May 1980; 1 hr.;

1 tape; Chinese; by Alice Hsieh.
Church service. See Chinese Alliance
Church.

MOY, FRANK
TORONTO, ONT.
Collection includes a series of
unpublished essays on Chinese Canadians; a list of Chinese associations in
Toronto, 1974; 2 menus, and community flyers, and clippings, c.
1970s. 6 cm.
*A Needs Study of the Chinese in
Kensington*. 1975. 1 cm.
*50th Anniversary of Shing Wah Daily
News*. n.d. Booklet. 48 pp.
Mon Sheon Foundation. 1971. 6th
annual report. 43 pp.
Mon Sheon Home for the Aged.
1975. Booklet. 10 pp.
*Report on the First
Chinese-Canadian National Conference on Immigration and Citizenship*.
1976. 1 cm.
*KMI: Yearbook of the Ontario
Branch*. n.d. 16 pp.
*The 23rd Conference of the Chinese
Freemasons in Ontario*. n.d. Report.
1 cm.

NG, JULIA
SUDBURY, ONT.
Interviewed on 14 June 1978; .5 hr.;
1 tape; English; by Chang Lee.
Immigrated to Canada in 1965.

NG, SHERRY
TORONTO, ONT.
Interviewed on 29 July 1978; 1 hr.;
1 tape; English; by A. M. Nicholson.
Post-WWII immigrant.

PANG, K. L.
THUNDER BAY, ONT.
Immigration certificate, 1910. 2 pp.
Photographs. Taped interview.

6 photographs: the Pang family, n.d. Interviewed on 12 Feb. 1978; 1 hr.; 1 tape; Chinese; by A. Cheng. Immigrated to Canada in 1920.

QUAN, L.
OTTAWA, ONT.
Information on Ottawa's Chinese Community Service Centre, and flyers. .25 cm.

SANG, HO LOK
TORONTO, ONT.
Objectives and outline of the "Immigration Policy Study Committee," flyers, and election material, 1975-77. .5 cm.
Media. 1972-77. Student magazine. Incomplete. 7 cm.
Chinese Students' Association at University of Toronto. 1 cm.
China Week Special Issue. 1976. .25 cm.

SHING-YU, MR.
TORONTO, ONT.
Articles and clippings regarding the culinary business, n.d. 1 cm. Photographs.
20 photographs: culinary contest, n.d.

SING, DON YAN
THUNDER BAY, ONT.
Personal papers and immigration documents, n.d. 1.5 cm. Photographs.
6 photographs: Don Yan Sing, n.d.

STANTON, MICHAEL
TORONTO, ONT.
Canada China Programme. 1977. Newsletter. 6 pp.

TON, LAM DU
WINDSOR, ONT.
Interviewed on 2 Aug. 1980; .5 hr.; 1 tape; Chinese; by Alice Hsieh. Discusses religious beliefs.

TONG, NANCY
TORONTO, ONT.
16mm film, a description of the film, and a resume for the producer of the film, 1977. .25 cm.

TSANG, ANGIE
TORONTO, ONT.
Chinese Workers' Group newsletter, n.d. 1 pp.

TSUI, HELEN (ESSEX COUNTY CHINESE-CANADIAN ASSOCIATION)
WINDSOR, ONT.
5 newsletters from the Essex County Chinese-Canadian Association. .25 cm. Taped interview.

TSUI, HELEN
WINDSOR, ONT.
Interviewed on 6 Dec. 1979; 1 hr.; 1 tape; English; by Alice Hsieh. Post-WWII immigrant, and teacher, discusses the history of the Chinese Heritage School.

TWU, SHYR-JIANN
WINDSOR, ONT.
Interviewed on 24 Nov. 1979; 1 hr.; 1 tape; English; by Alice Hsieh. Post-WWII immigrant. See Taiwanese Universities Alumni Association.

WAH, CHUNG
SUDBURY, ONT.
Interviewed on 21 Aug. 1978; 1 hr.; 1 tape; English; by Chang Lee. Post-WWII immigrant, past president of the Sudbury Chinese Association.

WONG, CHUCK
SUDBURY, ONT.
 Interviewed on 5 Sept. 1978; 1 hr.;
1 tape; English; by Chang Lee.
Post-WWII immigrant, originally
from Hong Kong.

WONG, GEORGE
SUDBURY, ONT.
 Interviewed on 6 Sept. 1978; .5 hr.;
1 tape; English; by Chang Lee. Born
and raised in Malaysia, immigrated to
Canada after WWII.

WONG, JEW
SUDBURY, ONT.
 Interviewed on 2 July 1978; 1 hr.; 1
tape; Chinese; by Chang Lee.
Post-WWII immigrant discusses Com-
munist takeover in China.

WONG, MAN
THUNDER BAY, ONT.
 Immigration papers, 1918, and a
menu. 1.5 cm. Photographs. Taped
interview.
 3 photographs: Man Wong in Thunder Bay, 1930-50.
 Interviewed in Autumn 1977; 1 hr.;
1 tape; Chinese; by A. Cheng. Immigrated to Canada in 1918.

WONG, LIN-YING LEE
TORONTO, ONT.
 3 photographs: the Wong, Lee, and
Chan families in traditional Chinese
dress, n.d.

WU, BETTY
WINDSOR, ONT.
 *Insight: Chinese Students' Associ-
ation of University of Windsor.* 1976.
2 cm.

YANG, CHIH-SHAO
WINDSOR, ONT.
 Interviewed on 24 Nov. 1979; .5
hr.; 1 tape; English; by Alice Hiesh.
Originally from Formosa, Taiwan, he
immigrated to Canada after WWII.

YAO, DICK
TORONTO, ONT.
 Personal papers and a speech given
by Bill Wow of the Chinese Business
Association, 1977. .25 cm.

YEE, LEE
THUNDER BAY, ONT.
 Immigration and citizenship certificates, 1918, 1964; 3 bonds, n.d., and
a menu. 1 cm. Photographs. Taped
interview.
 4 photographs: Lee Yee in Sudbury,
n.d;
 Interviewed on 20 Nov. 1977; 1 hr.;
1 tape; Chinese; by A. Cheng. Immigrated to Canada in c. 1918, paid
head tax on arrival in Victoria.

YOUNG, HARRY
SUDBURY, ONT.
 Collection includes a Chinese mailing
list for Sudbury, 1965; the Head Tax
Certificate of Lum Jack, 1912; the
registration certificate of Lum Jack,
n.d; 4 festival programmes; and clippings, c. 1950s. 3 cm. Photographs.
Taped interview
 Over 60 photographs: the activities
of Sudbury's Chinese community,
parades, and processions, 1937-77.
 Interviewed on 1 Aug. 1982; 2 hrs.;
2 tapes; English; by Dora Nipp. Born
in Montreal, Quebec in 1905, moved
to North Bay, where the donor's
mother operated a laundry to support
the family. The family returned to
China, and the donor re-immigrated
to Canada in the early 1920's.

Condit, I. M. *English-Chinese Reader.* 1882. 133 pp.
Inco Triangle. 1947, 1952-53. 1 cm.
Windsor Chinese Youth Book. Jan. 1956. 100 pp.

YOUNG YING
SUDBURY, ONT.
Interviewed on 18 June 1978; 1 hr.; 1 tape; Chinese; by C. Lee. Paid a Head Tax of $500 to immigrate to Canada in 1914, and settled in North Bay. Discusses his work, and the dreadful working conditions.

YU, BISMARK H.
WINDSOR, ONT.
Collection includes a constitution, a membership booklet, minutes, annual reports, and miscellaneous items from the University of Windsor Chinese Students' Association. 3 cm. Taped interview.
Interviewed on 2 March 1980; 1 hr.; 1 tape; English; by Alice Hsieh. Post-WWII immigrant, discusses involvement in the Chinese Students' Association at the University of Windsor.

YU, OLIVER
OTTAWA, ONT.
Ga Mei De. May, July 1977. 2 cm.
Green Pastures. n.d. (1 issue). .25 cm.

YU, SHING
TORONTO, ONT.
9 photographs: Shing Yu with entries in culinary competitions, c. 1977.

CANADA AND CHINA FRIENDSHIP ASSOCIATION
WINDSOR, ONT.
Interview recorded on 14 Dec. 1980; 1 hr.; 1 tape; English; by Alice Hsieh.

CHINESE ALLIANCE CHURCH (SUNDAY SCHOOL)
WINDSOR, ONT.
Recorded on 1 June 1980; 1 hr.; 1 tape; Chinese; by Alice Hsieh. Sunday School songs.

CHINESE BAPTIST CHURCH
WINDSOR, ONT.
Interviewed on 23 Nov. 1980; 2 hrs.; 2 tapes; Chinese; by Alice Hsieh. Church services with Pastor Gaspard Kam-to Lam.
"The Chinese Baptist Church Weekly Report." 23 Nov. 1980.

CHINESE BAPTIST CHURCH
WINDSOR, ONT.
Recorded on 16 Nov. 1980; 2 hrs.; 2 tapes; Chinese; by Alice Hsieh. Church services.

CHINESE CANADIANS FOR MUTUAL ADVANCEMENT (LEO CHAN)
TORONTO, ONT.
Collection includes community programmes, bulletins, flyers, and a poster. 2 cm.
Chan, Leo. "Immigrant Settlement and Adaption Programme: Some Reactions to the New Policy." 1977. Unpublished. 9 pp.
Chinese-Canadians for Mutual Advancement. Vol. 1, nos. 5-6, 1977. .25 cm.

CHINESE IN SUDBURY (MRS. CHOW
LEE)
SUDBURY, ONT.
 Recording date unknown; 1 hr.; 1
tape; English; by Alice Hsieh.
Recorded radio programme.

CHINESE PRESBYTERIAN CHURCH
WINDSOR, ONT.
 Chinese hymnal, 1965; a citizenship
guide, 1979; St. Andrew's Presby-
terian Church reports; information
sheets; and a poster, 1980. 2 cm.
Taped recording.
 Recorded on 12 Oct. 1980; 2 hrs.; 2
tapes; English/Chinese; by Alice
Hsieh. Thanksgiving service
Newsletter. Oct. 1980. .25 cm.
 St. Andrew's Annual Report. 1980. 1
cm.

CHINESE PRESBYTERIAN CHURCH
WINDSOR, ONT.
 Recorded on 28 Sept. 1980; .5 hr.; 1
tape; English/Chinese; by Alice
Hsieh. Church service.

CHINESE PRESBYTERIAN CONGREGA-
TION
WINDSOR, ONT.
 Interviewed on 21 Sept. 1980; 1 hr.;
1 tape; English/Chinese; by Alice
Hsieh. Discusses church services.

CHINESE PRESBYTERIAN CONGREGA-
TION
WINDSOR, ONT.
 Interviewed on 7 Sept. 1980; 1 hr.;
1 tape; English/Chinese; by Alice
Hsieh. Church service.

CHINESE UNITED CHURCH
TORONTO, ONT.
 Brief history of the Church's Chinese
School, and staff directory, 1976. .25
cm.

COMMITTEE FOR A FAIR MEDIA
TORONTO, ONT.
 Open letters to editors of news-
papers. .25 cm.

THE CROSSROADS MONTHLY
TORONTO, ONT.
 Collection includes the constitution
and membership forms for the Council of Chinese Canadians in Ontario,
printed items of the Canton pavillion
at Toronto's Caravan Festival, and
correspondence, reports, and clippings from the South-East Spadina
Development, 1970-77. 11 cm. Photographs.
 138 photographs: the development of
Toronto's Chinatown, 1970-76.
 Chi-Kiu, Fong. *Crossroads: Collection of Short Stories.* Toronto: Crossroads, 1977. .5 cm.
 Ka Fa Monthly. 1977 (1 issue). 1
cm.

ESSEX COUNTY CHINESE CANADIAN
ASSOCIATION
WINDSOR, ONT.
 Invitations, announcements, flyers, a
poster, and records, 1978-80, which
include financial statements, and
annual reports. 5.5 cm.
 E.C.C.C.A. Annual Book. 1978. 28
pp.
 E.C.C.C.A. Newsletter. 1978-80. 2
cm.

FEDERATION OF CHINESE CANADIANS
IN ONTARIO
TORONTO, ONT.
 Collection includes by-laws, minutes,
letters, a constitution, a proposal of
Cecil Street Community Centre, lists
of Federation members, Chinese
student associations, and church and
Chinatown groups, c. 1977. 3 cm.

GRANGE PARK RESIDENTS' ASSOCI-
ATION
TORONTO, ONT.
  Information sheets, n.d. (2 issues).
10 pp.

MID-AUTUMN FESTIVAL ORGAN-
IZATION COMMITTEE
TORONTO, ONT.
  Programmes and flyers, 1976. 1 cm.

MON SHEONG FOUNDATION
TORONTO, ONT.
  Collection includes an annual report,
1976, and a fund-raising letter, 1977.
2 cm. Photographs.
  37 photographs: activities at the Mon
Sheong Foundation, and the Mon
Sheong Home for the Aged in
Toronto, 1970-77.
  *Annual Report of the Mon Sheong
Foundation.* 1974. 1.5 cm.

MULTICULTURAL HISTORY SOCIETY
OF ONTARIO
TORONTO, ONT.
  Chinese Express. 1977-78. .5
meters.
  Hung Chung She Po. Jan. 1954 -
Dec. 1956. 6 reels of microfilm.
  K'uai Pao Chinese Express. Jan.
1971 - Dec. 1986; 1 Oct. 1987 - 26
Jan. 1989. 81 reels of microfilm.
  Shing Wah Daily News. 1973,
1977-78.
  Shing Wah Yat Po. 29 May 1923; 30
June 1954 - 31 Dec. 1969; Jan. 1970
- Dec. 1987; 2 Jan. 1988 - 30 Dec.
1989. 107 reels of microfilm.
  Watt Way Weekly. 1977. Incomplete.
3 cm.

MULTICULTURAL NEWSPAPER
MICROFILM PROJECT
TORONTO, ONT.
  Capital Chinese News. Ottawa. May

1983 - Dec. 1987. 3 reels of micro-
film.
  Chinese Canadian Community News.
Ottawa. 20 July 1979 - Dec. 1987. 3
reels of microfilm.
  Chinese Community Newsletter.
Ottawa. 4 July - 5 Dec. 1977. 1 reel
of microfilm.
  *National Capital Chinese Community
Newsletter.* Ottawa. Feb. 1981 - April
1983. 1 reel of microfilm.

SAPERE AUDE BOOKROOM
TORONTO, ONT.
  Regulations and nomination form for
executive committee of the Toronto
Chinese Business Association, and a
notice of an annual meeting, 1977.
.25 cm.

SOUTH-EAST SPADINA STEERING
COMMITTEE
TORONTO, ONT.
  Documents of the South-East Spadina
Plan, 1975-78; and a brief history of
Children's World Chinese School,
1977. 4 cm. Photographs.
  8 photographs: Chinese Canadians
participating in a meeting regarding
South-East Spadina Part II Plan,
1977.
  The Future of South-East Spadina.
1977. .25 cm.
  The Kensington. 1977. Newsletter.
.25 cm.
  South-East Spadina News. 1976. 1
cm.

ST. STEPHEN COMMUNITY HOUSE
(MARY LING)
TORONTO, ONT.
  Collection includes reports, flyers,
leaflets, and posters by St. Stephens
Community House. 3 cm.

TAIWANESE UNIVERSITIES ALUMNI
ASSOCIATION (S. TWU)
WINDSOR, ONT.
  Collection includes a constitution,
and a movie poster, 1979. .5 cm.
Photographs. Taped interview.
3 photographs: Association's recre-
ational activities, 1977-78.

TORONTO CHINESE BAPTIST CHURCH
(YOUTH DEPARTMENT)
TORONTO, ONT.
  Image. Vol. 1, nos. 1-2, 1977. 2
cm.

UNIVERSITY OF TORONTO SETTLE-
MENT
TORONTO, ONT.
  Meeting notice and election resumes,
1977, and 1 poster. .25 cm.

WINDSOR CHINESE ALLIANCE
CHURCH (REV. MOK)
WINDSOR, ONT.
  Collection includes church pro-
grammes, leaflets, and news cards. .5
cm. Taped interview.
  A Chinese Foreigner in China. July,
1980. 6 pp.
  Alliance Men in Action. Spring,
1980. 15 pp.
  Bible. 1975. 1518 pp., in Chinese.
  The Cross. Jan. 1980. 14 pp.
1980. 15 pp.
  Hymns of Praise. 1977. 633 pp.
  How to Fire a Pastor. June 1980. 6
pp.
  The Missionary Mantle. Feb. 1980.
.25 cm.
  Sunday School's Song Book. 1980.
51 pp.
  *Every Home Crusade Prayer Bull-
etin.*

WOODGREEN CHINESE CANADIAN
ASSOCIATION (CHINESE CULTURAL
CLASSES)
TORONTO, ONT.
  Collection includes minutes, correspondence, financial statements, lists
of students, teacher's journal, and
curriculum material, 1975–77. 1 reel
of microfilm.

WOODGREEN COMMUNITY CENTRE
TORONTO, ONT.
  Activities programme, 1976; social
notices, a poster, and a constitution of
the Centre's Elderly Persons Club.
1.5 cm. *Newsletter.* 1977. 4 pp.

BELJO, ANTE
SUDBURY, ONT.
 Invitation to the Croatian Youth
Festival in Sudbury, 1977. .5 cm.
 *The Third Canadian-Croatian Folk-
lore Festival*. Toronto: Croatian
Folklore Ensemble, Croatian Folklore
Federation of Canada, 1977. 1 cm.,
in English/Croatian.

BUČAR, NIKOLA
TIMMINS, ONT.
 Interviewed on 3 Feb. 1980; 2 hrs.;
3 tapes; English; by A. Buchar.
Pre-WWII immigrant recollects work-
ing life during the Great Depression,
and political divisions among Croatian
Canadians.

BUCHAR, ANA
SCHUMACHER, ONT.
 1 photograph: Frank and Mary
Buchar, n.d.
 5 photographs: Schumacher orchestras, 1938-55. Taped interview.
 Interviewed on 10 Nov. 1979; .5
hr.; 1 tape; English; by Frank
Buchar. Pre-WWII immigrant.

BUCHAR, FRANK
SCHUMACHER, ONT.
 Interview recorded in 1953; 1 hr.; 1
tape; English; by Frank Buchar.
Donor's commentary on videotape of
Croatian picnics and festivities in
Schumacher, Ont.

BUCHAR, F. J.
SOUTH PORCUPINE, ONT.
 The collection includes minutes of

the first Croatian Peasant Party convention, 1932; minutes of the third
and sixth conventions of the Croatian
Fraternal Union of America, 1932,
1943; printed items and artifacts (2
postcards, 1 pin, and 2 ribbons of the
Peasant Party, and stationery used by
Croatian Hall). 10.5 cm. Photographs.
 2 photographs: J. Krnjević, c. 1962;
and Croat Orchestral Group in
Schumacher, c. 1952.
 17 photographs: the Croatian National Hall in Schumacher, 1940-57; the
Croatian National Home in Hamilton,
1946; and working life at a northern
Ont. mine, n.d.

CIMPRICH, MARGARET
SCHUMACHER, ONT.
 12 photographs: Croatian weddings,
funerals, and orchestras, and mining
work in Schumacher, Ont., 1920-51.
 *Milijoni Sada Žive Neće Nikad
Umrijeti*. New York: Izdanje, International Bible Students' Association,
1920. 123 pp.

DRAVOJ, JOSIP
HAMILTON, ONT.
 Financial statement of the Croatian
Peasant Party, H.S.S., 1965. .25 cm.

DUKOVAC, MARTIN AND KATE
GRIMSBY, ONT.
 5 photographs: the Dukovac family
in South Porcupine, Ont., c. 1928; a
funeral at Kirkland Lake, Ont., c.
1930; and a wedding in Timmins,
Ont., c. 1929-55. Taped interview.

Interviewed on 22 Dec. 1979; .5 hr.; 1 tape; English; by Frank Buchar. Pre-WWII immigrants.

FRANKOVICH, MARKO
TIMMINS, ONT.
5 photographs: Croatian Ladies' Association, 1954; Christmas festivities, 1950; orchestral groups and welcoming committee for J. Krnjević, c. 1950; and traditional costume worn at an annual picnic, 1953.

KOLICH, ANNIE
SCHUMACHER, ONT.
Interviewed on 23 Nov. 1979; .5 hr.; 1 tape; English; by Frank Buchar. Discussion on continuity of Croatian traditions in Canada.

KOLAKOVICH, MATO
SOUTH PORCUPINE, ONT.
Various publications, including music books used at the Croatian Hall. 6 cm. Photographs. See F. J. Buchar Collection.
5 photographs: J. Krnjević and J. Krznarich, leaders in the Croatian Peasant Party, n.d.
Pedeset-Godišnjica, 1884-94. Pittsburgh: Croatian Fraternal Union of America. 52 pp., in Croatian.

KOVACICH, JOSEPH
SAULT STE. MARIE, ONT.
Interviewed on 19 Sept. 1977; 2 hrs.; 2 tapes; Croatian/English; by Zlata Godler.

KRUŽIĆ, MARIJAN
TORONTO, ONT.
7 photographs: prominent Yugoslavians—Maryan Kružić, Steve Miošić, Stevan Serdar, and Nikola Ivanišević in Toronto, and Belgrade, 1979. Taped interview.

Interviewed on 23 Feb. 1979; 1.5 hrs; 2 tapes; Serbo-Croatian; by Vic Tomovich. Discusses Yugoslavian workers' movement in Canada, 1929-35.

KRZNARIĆ, J.
SCHUMACHER, ONT.
The Krznarić collection is an extensive assortment of materials on the activities of the Croatian Peasant Party (H.S.S.) in Canada and abroad. It includes various documents from the H.S.S., 1947-50; a Supreme Committee declaration, n.d., correspondence and financial papers concerning the *Croatian Voice* newspaper, 1968-69; and personal letters to Pere Perković from M. Zvorkin, V. Maček, and I. Krnjević, n.d. 3 reels of microfilm.
Spomenica na dvadeset godina Hrvatskih Seljačkih Organizacija u Kanadi. Winnipeg, 1952. 173 pp.

MATAN, ALEK AND ANA
SUDBURY, ONT.
Interviewed on 21 Jan. 1982; 2 hrs.; 2 tapes; Croatian; by Ljubo Krasić. Immigrated to Canada in 1926, recounts his work experience as a miner in northern Ont.

MATIJEVIĆ, ROSE
SUDBURY, ONT.
7 photographs: orchestras, the Croatian Women's Club and the Croatian Peasant Party in Sudbury, 1938-57.

MIOŠIĆ, STEVE
TORONTO, ONT.
Interviewed on 23 Feb. 1979; 1 hr.; 1 tape; Serbo-Croatian; by Vic Tomovich. Editor of Croatian, and Yugoslavian newspapers from 1935.

PANDZICH, STEVE
SAULT STE. MARIE, ONT.
 Charter of incorporation of the
Croatian Peasant Party of Ontario,
1931; donor's Yugoslavian passports,
1937; and Canadian registration card,
1940. 1.5 cm. Photographs. Taped
interview.
 7 photographs: opening of the
Croatian home in Thunder Bay, c.
1932; and harvest festival in Sault
Ste. Marie, Ont., 1967.
 Interviewed on 19 Sept. 1977; 1 hr.;
1 tape; Croatian; by Zlata Godler.
Pre-WWII immigrant, discusses community life in Sault Ste. Marie, Ont.,
and work at the Algoma Steel Co.

PRPIĆ, BOŽO
ZAGREB, YUGOSLAVIA
 Interviewed in July 1977; 1 hr.; 1
tape; Serbo-Croatian; by Vic
Tomovich. Discusses life in Canada
between 1928-43.

SALAMON, TONY
SAULT STE. MARIE, ONT.
 Minutes of the Croatian Catholic
Society, No. 73, Sault Ste. Marie,
Ont., 1936-76. Incomplete. 4 cm.
Taped interview.
 Interviewed on 19 Sept. 1977; 1 hr.;
1 tape; Croatian; by Zlata Godler.
Arrived in Canada in 1919.

SIAUS, MATE
ZAGREB, YUGOSLAVIA
 Interviewed in July 1977; 1 hr.; 1
tape; Serbo-Croatian; by Vic
Tomovich. Discusses the Yugoslavian
community in Vancouver, British
Columbia, and the labour movement
among Yugoslav-Canadians.

VUKOVICH, ANTON
SCHUMACHER, ONT. 2 photographs:
the first Croatian Party convention in
Toronto, 1932. Taped interview.
 Interviewed on 29 Oct. 1979; .5 hr.;
1 tape; English; by Frank Buchar.
WWI immigrant, relates early work
experiences in Canada, and involve-
ment in the building of the Croatian
Hall.

VUKOVICH, JOSEPH
SCHUMACHER, ONT.
 4 photographs: family in
Schumacher, 1951-53. Taped inter-
view.
 Interviewed on 8 March 1980; 1 hr.;
1 tape; English/Croatian; by Frank
Buchar. WWI immigrant, discusses
work in British Columbia and in
Schumacher, Ont.; involvement with
Croatian Hall; and life in Croatia.

———————————

CROATIAN PEASANT PARTY
SCHUMACHER, ONT.
 Minutes and records, 1935-58; and
correspondence between J. Krznarić
and J. Krnjević, n.d. 3 reels of
microfilm.

CROATIAN PEASANT SOCIETY
SUDBURY, ONT.
 By-laws, 1932; minutes, 1932-74;
and cash books, 1933-65. 3 reels of
microfilm.

CROATIAN SOCIETY
SCHUMACHER, ONT.
 Minutes and records of the Croatian
Society (Schumacher Branch), c.
1936-38; minutes and records of the
Croatian Women's Society
(Schumacher Branch); and historical
record book of the Croatian Catholic

Group, 1912-32. 1 reel of microfilm.
Hrvatski Glas (Croatian Voice Almanac). Winnipeg, Manitoba, 1935, 1937, 1939, 1965, 1971, 1974. Illustrated, in Croatian.

CROATIAN WOMEN'S CLUB
SUDBURY, ONT.
Minutes, 1936-39, 1944-50; cash book, 1947-52; and correspondence, 1939. 1 reel of microfilm. Photographs.
4 photographs: members of the Croatian Women's Club, some in traditional costume, 1938-66.

KANADSKOG JUGOSLAVENSKOG KLUBA
WINDSOR, ONT.
Minutes, 1929, 1933, 1935, 1949. 1 reel of microfilm.

LEAGUE OF CANADIAN CROATS
ST. CATHARINES, ONT.
Executive Board minutes, 1942-45, and an assortment of flyers issued by the League. 1 reel of microfilm.

MULTICULTURAL HISTORY SOCIETY
OF ONTARIO
TORONTO, ONT.
Meheš, Mirko. *I stvoti čovjek Boga.* Toronto, 1979. 49 pp., in Croatian.
Rasporich, Anthony W. *For a Better Life: A History of the Croatians in Canada.* Toronto: McCelland and Stewart Ltd., 1982. 279 pp.
Borba. Toronto, 21 May 1932 - 19 Sept. 1936. 3 reels of microfilm.
Croatia, 1956-76. Toronto: Croatian National Soccer Club, 1976. Illustrated, 1 cm.
Croatians in Sudbury Centennial. Sudbury, Ont.: Canadian-Croatian Folklore Festival, 1983. 208 pp., in English.

Novosti. Toronto, Jan. 1944 - June 1948. 3 reels of microfilm.
Slobodna Misao. Toronto, 22 Sept. 1936 - 15 Aug. 1960. 5 reels of microfilm.
The 4th Canadian-Croatian Folklore Festival. Ottawa: The Croatian Canadian Club and Croatian Folklore Federation of Canada, 1978. Illustrated. 1 cm.

CZECH COLLECTION

BAŤA, THOMÁŠ
TORONTO, ONT.
Interviewed on 8 April 1978; 1 hr.; 1 tape; English; by Rose Wilcox. An account of the months before the outbreak of WWII, and the donor's migration to Canada.

BRAUN, FRANK
HAMILTON, ONT.
Interviewed on 5 Sept. 1978; 1 hr.; 1 tape; English; by Jana Cipris. Arrived in Canada in 1949, was active in the Czech Association which assisted newly arrived Czech immigrants.

BRZOBOHATÝ, HANA
HAMILTON, ONT.
Interviewed on 8 Aug. 1978; 1 hr.; 1 tape; Czech; by Jana Cipris. Immigrated to Canada in 1972, member of Czech Association in Hamilton.

BUDAHAZY, DANIEL
HAMILTON, ONT.
Interviewed on 18 July 1978; 1.5 hrs.; 2 tapes; Czech; by Jana Cipris. Arrived in Canada in 1976.

BUDLOVSKÝ, KAREL
HAMILTON, ONT.
Interviewed on 12 June 1978; .5 hr.; 1 tape; English; by Jana Cipris. Arrived in Canada in 1968.

CECHA, B.
HAMILTON, ONT.
50 photographs: the Czech community in Batawa, Ont.; the Bata Shoe Factory; factory employee residences; sports activities of the Sokol; and Czech language school, and festivals, 1939-65.
Dvořáková, Jarmila. *Umělec na Útěku*. Toronto: Naše Hlasy, 1960. 32 pp., in Czech.
Snížek, Jan. *Kdo Uteče, Vyhraje*. Toronto: Naše Hlasy, 1956. 58 pp., in Czech.
Alois Jirásek. n.d. Pamphlet about a Czech leader. .25 cm., in Czech.
Památník Československé Kanady. Toronto: Czechoslovak National Alliance in Canada, 1942. 207 pp., in Czech.
Poupě (Rosebud). 1937-38. A children's reader, in Czech (4 issues).
Sokol Looking Forward. Toronto: Sokol Gymnastic Association, 1958. 1 cm., in English.
Telocvičné Jednoty Sokol. Batawa, Ont., 1940, 1941, 1945, 1950. 4 annual reports of the Sokol Gymnastic Association. 2 cm., in Czech.
Všesokolských Sletů v Praze, 1882-1938. An illustrated history of Sokol. .5 cm., in Czech.

ČECHOVÁ, MILADA
HAMILTON, ONT.
Interviewed on 19, 20 June 1978; 2 hrs.; 2 tapes; Czech; by Jana Cipris. Immigrated to Canada in 1939, recollections of Batawa, Ont.
Jirák, Karel B. *Antonín Dvořák, 1841-1961*. New York, 1961. 31 pp., in English.
Merbout, Cyril N. *Lidice*. Praze: Ministerstvo Informací, 1945. 29 pp.,

in Czech.
Pulcová, Marie and Vladivoj Pulec. *40 Let ČSR.* Obris Praha, n.d. History booklet about socialist Czechoslovakia. 65 pp., in Czech.
Zápisky o Zlíně. Prague: Tribuna, 1935. 27 pp., in Czech.

ČERMÁK, JOSEF
TORONTO, ONT.
Personal documents, 1940s, identity card from Ludwigsburg refugee camp, military certificates, proof of good wartime conduct, postponement of army service, and deletion from voters' list, 1948. 3.5 cm. Taped interview.
Interviewed on 29 March 1977; 1 hr.; 1 tape; English; by Rose Wilcox. Immediate post-WWII immigrant, former editor of *Naše Hlasy,* and executive member of the Czechoslovak Society of Arts and Sciences.
Čermák, Josef. *Going Home.* New York: Vantage Press, 1963. 161 pp.
_____. *Pokorné Navraty.* Stockholm: Križrice Lyriky, 1955. Booklet of poems.

CHOROŠ, JOE
SIMCOE, ONT.
Interviewed on 12 July 1977; .5 hr.; 1 tape; English; by David Judd. Immigrated to Canada where he settled first in Alberta and then in Ont. He was a tobacco farmer for 19 years.

CIPRIS, HANA
HAMILTON, ONT.
25 short stories concerning emigration. Unpublished. 3.5 cm.
RESTRICTED
Interviewed on 1 Sept. 1980; 1.75 hrs.; 2 tapes; Czech; by Jana Cipris.

Discusses Moravian, Slovak, and Czech traditional bonds.

CIPRIS, SYLVA
HAMILTON, ONT.
Immigration documents and correspondence, 1969-70. .5 cm. Taped interview.
Interviewed on 13 June 1978; 1 hr.; 1 tape; English; by Jana Cipris. Arrived in Canada in 1969.

CMUNT, JOSEPH
TORONTO, ONT.
19 photographs: citizenship, education, employment, and military documents, 1912-44. Taped interview.
Interviewed on 9 March 1977; 1 hr.; 1 tape; English; by Rose Wilcox. Arrived in the 1930s, a member of Czech Sokol in the mid-1940s.

CORN, GEORGE
TORONTO, ONT.
Personal documents (photographed) 1945-73: refugee camp indentification certificates, tags, and Alberta farm work contract; and Sokol membership cards, Czech National Association of Canada membership certificate, membership booklet of the Company of the National Revolution, and charter of the Czech National Association, 1977. 2.5 cm. Taped interview.
Interviewed on 29 March 1977; 1 hr.; 1 tape; English; by Rose Wilcox. Fled to Canada via Germany in 1949.

DOČKÁLEK, JAN
TORONTO, ONT.
Published material, scattered issues of Ont. Czech journals, 1949-76. 4.5 cm.
A Gem of the Canadian Mosaic: Pictures of the Life and the Work of

Canadians of Czechoslovak Origin.
Toronto: Masaryk Memorial Inst.,
1957.

FABŠIC, JIŘÍ
HAMILTON, ONT.
 Interviewed on 23 June 1978; 1 hr.;
1 tape; English; by Jana Cipris.
Arrived in Canada in 1949.

FLOSSMAN, MARIE
HAMILTON, ONT.
 Personal documents, including immigration, and refugee camp certificates, c. 1950-59. .5 cm. Taped
interview.
 Interviewed on 29 May 1978; 1 hr.;
1 tape; Czech; by Jana Cipris.
Arrived in Canada in 1950.

GABRIEL, MARIE
HAMILTON, ONT.
 Interviewed on 19 July 1978; .75
hr.; 1 tape; English; by Jana Cipris.
Arrived with husband in 1932, settled
in Kenora, Ont.

HANZLÍKOVÁ, MARIE
HAMILTON, ONT.
 Interviewed on 30 July 1980; 1.5
hrs.; 2 tapes; Czech/English; by Jana
Cipris. Immediate post-WWII immi-
grant, a member of the Czechoslovak
Association in Hamilton.

HAŠEK, FRANTISEK
HAMILTON, ONT.
 Interviewed on 10 Aug. 1978; 1 hr.;
1 tape; English; by Jana Cipris.
Immigrated to Canada via Germany in
1951.

HAVRLANT, LIDA
TORONTO, ONT.
 Interviewed on 16 March 1978; 1

hr.; 1 tape; English/Czech; by Rose
Wilcox. Post-WWII immigrant.

HOLÝ, KAREL
HAMILTON, ONT.
 Interviewed on 26 July 1978; 1 hr.;
1 tape; English; by Jana Cipris.
Arrived in Canada in 1951.

HRČEK, JOSEF
HAMILTON, ONT.
 1 printed item, 1977. .5 cm. 5 post-
cards from Koprivnice,
Chechoslovakia, n.d. Photographs.
Taped interview.
 Interviewed on 30 May 1978; 1 hr.;
1 tape; Czech; by Jana Cipris.
Immediate post-WWII immigrant,
Immigrated to Canada through Ger-
many.

HYNEK, ANTONÍN
HAMILTON, ONT.
 Interviewed on 7 June 1978; .75 hr.;
1 tape; Czech; by Jana Cipris.
Arrived in Canada in 1948.

JANEČEK, MIKE
MISSISSAUGA, ONT.
 Donor's biography, 1974; and
multicultural programmes, and
articles, 1963-77. 1.5 cm. Photograph.
 1 photograph: Ethnic Press Association Christmas party in Toronto,
1979.

JANÍCĚK, REV. B.
MONTREAL, QUEBEC
 Věstník. 1973-78. 1 reel of micro-
film.

KLIMEK, MIROSLAV
HAMILTON, ONT.
 Interviewed on 26 Aug. 1980; 2
hrs.; 2 tapes; Czech; by Jana Cipris.

Immediate post-WWII immigrant, discussion of Czech traditional customs.

KOTÁČKOVÁ, LUDMILA
HAMILTON, ONT.
Interviewed on 28 May 1978; 1 hr.; 1 tape; Czech; by Jana Cipris. Immigrated to Canada in 1968.

KRAUS, EVA
HAMILTON, ONT.
Interviewed on 20 July 1978; 1.25 hrs.; 2 tapes; English; by Jana Cipris. Immigrated to Canada via Germany in 1949.

KUBÁNEK, JOSEF
BURLINGTON, ONT.
11 photographs: the Kubánek family in Europe, and Midland, Ont., 1929-57. Taped interview.
Interviewed on 14 July 1978; .75 hr.; 1 tape; Czech; by Jana Cipris. Immigrated to Canada in 1956, employed in the shoe-making industry most of his life.

LANC, ANA
BURLINGTON, ONT.
4 photographs: family wearing traditional Czech costumes, 1918-55. Taped interview.
Interviewed on 1 Aug. 1978; .5 hr.; 1 tape; English; by Jana Cipris. Parents arrived in Canada in the early 1900s.
Orac, Napsal J. *Devčica Slovače.* n.d. Booklet. 79 pp., in Czech.
Kam Jdeš?-Kniha Útěchy Pro Doby Trudně. V Praze, 1898. 400 pp., in Czech.

LENK, JARMILA
HAMILTON, ONT.
Interviewed on 15 Aug. 1978; .75

hr.; 1 tape; English; by Jana Cipris. Immigrated to Canada in 1969, husband a member of the Czechoslovak Association.

MAREK, BŘETISLAW
HAMILTON, ONT.
Interviewed on 19 June 1978; 1 hr.; 1 tape; Czech; by Jana Cipris. Arrived in Canada in 1976.

MEISEL, JOHN
TORONTO, ONT.
Interviewed on 29 Sept. 1977; 1 hr.; 1 tape; English; by Rose Wilcox. Post-WWII immigrant.

MEISEL-WILCOX, ROSE M.
TORONTO, ONT.
11 photographs: the Meisel family in Czechoslovakia, and Batawa, and Toronto, Ont. 1931-51.

MRÁZ, L'UBA
TORONTO, ONT.
Interviewed on 4 Jan. 1978; 1 hr.; 1 tape; English; by Rose Wilcox. Immediate post-WWII immigrant.

OBR, HUBERT
HAMILTON, ONT.
8 photographs: the Obr family in Germany; their voyage to Canada; and various locations in Canada, 1950-51. Taped interview.
Interviewed on 4 Aug. 1978; 1.5 hrs.; 2 tapes; English; by Jana Cipris. Immigrated to Canada via Germany in 1950.

PETREK, DAGMAR
HAMILTON, ONT.
2 photographs: the Czechoslovak National Association convention in

Montreal, 1968; and dancers in traditional Czech costumes. Taped interview.
Interviewed on 8 Aug. 1978; 1 hr.; 1 tape; Czech; by Jana Cipris. Immigrated to Canada via Germany in 1949, member of the Czechoslovak Association, discusses Czech identity.

PETŘÍČEK, JAROMIR
TORONTO, ONT.
Interviewed on 11 Feb. 1978; 1 hr.; 1 tape; English; by Rose Wilcox. Immediate post-WWII immigrant.

POLÁČKOVÁ-HENLEY, KÁČA
HAMILTON, ONT.
Interviewed in 1978; 1 hr.; 1 tape; English; by Jana Cipris. Immigrated to Canada via the U.S. in the early 1970s.

PROCHÁZKA-BENEŠ, JIŘÍ
TORONTO, ONT.
Newsclippings about a restaurant in Lindsay, Ont. previously owned by donor, n.d. .25 cm. Taped interview.
Interviewed on 13 March 1977; 1 hr.; 1 tape; English; by Rose Wilcox. Post-WWII immigrant, was a restaurateur in Toronto, Ont.

REINIŠ, MILADA
WATERLOO, ONT.
Interviewed in 1978; 1 hr.; 1 tape; English/Czech; by Jana Cipris. Publisher of *Západ* magazine, and member of the Czech National Association in Kitchener.
Západ. May 1979 - June 1988. 9 cm.

RONZA, ANTONIN
BURLINGTON, ONT.
Interviewed on 18 July 1978; 1 hr.; 1 tape; English; by Jana Cipris.

Immigrated to Canada in 1939 as an employee of Bata Shoes.

RONZA, HENRIETTA
COLLINGWOOD, ONT.
2 copies of St. Catharines Folk Arts Festival map, May, June 1978. .25 cm. Taped interview.
Interviewed on 31 May 1978; 1.5 hrs.; 2 tapes; Czech; by Jana Cipris. Arrived in Canada in 1970, and operated a family restaurant.

ROUSOVÁ, IVA
HAMILTON, ONT.
Interviewed c. 1978; 1.5 hrs.; 2 tapes; Czech; by Jana Cipris. Post-WWII immigrant.

RUBEŠ, JAN L.
TORONTO, ONT.
2 photographs: the Rubes family in Czechoslovakia, 1938. Taped interview.
Interviewed on 16 Sept. 1977; .5 hr.; 1 tape; English/Czech; by Rose Wilcox. Immediate post-WWII immigrant, discusses musical, and acting career.

RUS, REV. SVATOPLUK
CHATHAM, ONT.
Interviewed on 2 Sept. 1980; 1 hr.; 1 tape; English; by Jana Cipris. Discusses history of Czech community in Chatham.

ŠACH, FATHER JOSEF V.
BURLINGTON, ONT.
Printed items, c. 1960s, including anti-communist pamphlets, and a short history of St. Adalbert Mission, n.d. 2 cm. Taped interview.
Interviewed on 19 July 1978; .75 hr.; 1 tape; English; by Jana Cipris. Post-WWII immigrant, chaplain at St.

Joseph hospital, and co-founder of Czech St. Adalbert Mission.

SEMERÁD, HANA
ST. CATHARINES, ONT.
Interviewed in Aug. 1980; 1 hr.; 1 tape; English; by Jana Cipris. Post-WWII immigrant, involved in the Czech Association in St. Catharines.

ŠEVČÍK, DAVID
KITCHENER, ONT.
Interviewed in July 1980; 1.5 hrs.; 2 tapes; English; by Jana Cipris. Post-WWII immigrant, involved in the Czech National Association in Kitchener, Ont.

SKOUTAJAN, HANNS
TORONTO, ONT.
1 newsclipping, "From Refugee to Man of the Cloth." n.d., and a sermon from St. James-Bond United Church, 1977. .5 cm. Photographs. Taped interview.
9 photographs: the Skoutajan family in Saskatchewan, 1939-41.
Interviewed on 24 Nov. 1977; 2 hrs.; 2 tapes; English; by Rose Wilcox. Immigrated to Canada in 1939 as part of the C.P. Railway, and C.N. Railway settlement scheme.

ŠOLC, LADISLAV
HAMILTON, ONT.
Interviewed in July 1980; 1 hr.; 1 tape; Czech; by Jana Cipris. Post-WWII immigrant.

STARK, KAROL
KITCHENER, ONT.
C.P. Railway menu, 1939; Sokol membership card, n.d., bulletins of the Czechoslovak Association, n.d.; and newsclippings, and programmes documenting Czech immigrant activities in Ont., c. 1950s. Photograph. Taped interview.
1 photograph: delegation from the Czechoslovak National Alliance of Canada in Ottawa, 1950.
Interviewed, c. 1978; 1 hr.; 1 tape; Czech; by Jana Cipris. Arrived in Canada in 1939, worked in Batawa, Ont., member of the Czechoslovak National Association.

URBAN, LOUIS
KITCHENER, ONT.
Interviewed on 10 Aug. 1978; 1 hr.; 1 tape; English; by Jana Cipris. Post-WWII immigrant, member of the Czech Alliance, and the Czech Association in Kitchener.

VAJDÍK, TONY
CHATHAM, ONT.
8 photographs: procession on "Czechslovak Day" in Chatham lead by the donor, Tony Vajdík, 1941; and Building Committee of St. Anthony's Church in Chatham, 1956. Taped interview.
Interviewed on 12 Aug. 1980; 2.5 hrs.; 3 tapes; Czech; by Jana Cipris. Discusses religious life at St. Anthony's Church in Chatham.

VEJVALKA, MARIE
HAMILTON, ONT.
Personal immigration papers and certificates, c. 1946-69. 1 cm. Taped interview.
Interviewed on 5 June 1978; 1 hr.; 1 tape; Czech; by Jana Cipris. Arrived in Canada in 1973.

VŠETULA, FRANK
CHATHAM, ONT.
The collection includes newsclippings of Czech events in Chatham (dances,

visits by ambassador, display of
crafts, elections, marriage announcements), 1931-54; souvenir programmes of Czech plays, concerts,
and national celebrations in Chatham,
c. 1930-41; and receipt for a loan
from employer, Dominion Sugar Co.,
1924. 1 reel of microfilm. Photographs. Taped interview.
 4 photographs: Czechoslovak Day
procession in Chatham, 1941(?).
 Interviewed on 27 Aug. 1980; 1.5
hrs.; 2 tapes; Czech; by Jana Cipris.
Father was a sugarbeet labourer in
Chatham in the 1920s.

WÁGNER, VÍT
THOROLD, ONT.
 7 photographs: life and work in a
lumbercamp at Heron Bay, 1951-53.
Taped interview.
 Interviewed on 26 Aug. 1980; 1 hr.;
1 tape; Czech; by Jana Cipris.
Immediate post-WWII immigrant,
member of the Czechoslovak Association.

WILCOX, ROSE M.
TORONTO, ONT.
 Personal documents, 1931, 1940. .5
cm. Photographs.
 19 photographs: reproductions of
travel documents, 1933-42.

ZIMMER, DAGMAR
HAMILTON, ONT.
 6 photographs: the Zimmer family,
1950-52; and pilgrimage in Chatham,
Ont., 1955. Taped interview.
 Interviewed on 25 July 1978; 1.5
hrs.; 2 tapes; English; by Jana Cipris.
Arrived in Canada in early 1950s,
member of the Sparta soccer team.
 *Vlastivéda Moravská. Musejní spolek
v Brné.* 1914. Demographic study of
Moravia. 459 pp.

ZRALÝ, VÁCLAV
KITCHENER, ONT.
Interviewed on 31 July 1978; 1.5
hrs.; 2 tapes; Czech; by Jana Cipris.
Immigrated to Canada in 1956, mem-
ber of the Czech Association.

BLUE MOUNTAIN RESORTS LTD.
COLLINGWOOD, ONT.
 Correspondence, n.d., and miscellaneous printed items (brochures,
newsclippings, price lists, advertisements). 4.5 cm. Photographs.
 22 photographs: activities and struc-
tures at Blue Mountain, 1950-70; the
Weider family, 1958-70; and paintings by Walter Trier, n.d.

CZECHOSLOVAK BAPTIST CHURCH
(REV. J. NOVÁK)
TORONTO, ONT.
 Hymn books, and church bulletins,
c. 1955-78. 9 cm.
 Slavná Naděje. 1957-58, 1975-78 (13
issues).
 Marek, Karel. *Co s Krěstanstvím?.*
Toronto: Nákladem, 1954. 143 pp.,
in Czech.

CZECHOSLOVAK NATIONAL ALLIANCE
OF CANADA
TORONTO, ONT.
 The Czechoslovak National Alliance
of Canada was formed in 1939 to
preserve a free, and democratic
Czechoslovakia. In 1960, its name
was changed to the Czechoslovak
National Association. Collection
includes membership lists, 1939-45. 1
reel of microfilm. Photograph.
 1 photograph: Karel Buzek, n.d.
 Buzek, Karel. *Památnik
Československé Kanady.* Toronto,
1942. 1 reel of microfilm.

CZECHOSLOVAK NATIONAL ASSOCI-
ATION OF CANADA
HAMILTON, ONT.
 Records, 1968-78, and correspon-
dence, 1978. 1 reel of microfilm.
Taped interview with J. Fabsic.

CZECHOSLOVAK NATIONAL ASSOCI-
ATION OF CANADA
ST. CATHARINES, ONT.
 Charter and by-laws, 1960, 1969,
1970; minutes of Headquarters Folk
Arts Council, 1971-76; correspon-
dence, mostly with the Association of
East Central Europeans, n.d.; book-
lets; and newletters. 1972. Congress
programme. 3 cm. 1 reel of micro-
film.
 Věstník. 1975-76.

CZECH SOCIAL CLUB
OTTAWA, ONT.
 Correspondence, 1976-78, and items,
1967-78. 4 cm. Photographs.
 7 photographs: recreational and
educational activities organized by the
Czech Ottawa Club, 1977-78.

KLUB NOVÝCH (CZECHOSLOVAK
NEWCOMERS' CLUB)
TORONTO, ONT.
 Charter and letters patent, 1972;
Club's information bulletin, 1966-79,
and membership items. 12 cm.
 Hlas Nových (superseded by
Kanadské Listy in 1973). June 1966 -
Dec. 1979.
 5 Let Klubu Nových. 1971. History
of Klub Novych's first five years. .5
cm.

MASARYK MEMORIAL INSTITUTE INC.
TORONTO, ONT.
 Financial records, 1979. 1 cm. Pho-
tograph.

1 photograph: the executive of
Masaryk Memorial Institute of
Toronto, 1980.

MULTICULTURAL NEWSPAPER
MICROFILM PROJECT
TORONTO, ONT.
 Čas. 1 June 1949 - Dec. 1949. 1 reel
of microfilm.
 Naše Hlasy. 8 March 1975 - Dec.
1987. 4 reels of microfilm.
 Nový Domov. 2 March 1950 - 17
Dec. 1987. 16 reels of microfilm.

SLOVAKOTOUR (A. J. BANIK)
TORONTO, ONT.
 Travel brochures, 1978, and pamphlets from Czechoslovakia, n.d. 12
cm.

ST. ADALBERT ROMAN CATHOLIC
CZECH MISSION
BURLINGTON, ONT.
 Correspondence with Apostolic
authorities in Prague, and Lomouc,
1972-78; financial statements of St.
Vojtěch Church in Hamilton, 1972;
and St. Adalbert newsletters, and
bulletins, 1972-78. 11.5 cm. Photographs.
 11 photographs: pilgrimages in
Chatham, and Midland, Ont.,
1976-77, including children in traditional Czech costumes.

ST. ANTHONY'S CHURCH
CHATHAM, ONT.
 Papers of Rev. P.L. Gáboŕík,
1940-77, comprise parish correspondence, church calendars, sermons,
bulletins, and programmes. Also
included are 4 film reels of church
events, and ceremonies. .4 meters.
Photographs.
 20 photographs: activities at St.
Anthony's Church in Chatham,

1960-70, and Our Lady of Sorrows
Church in Sarnia, n.d.
 Over 60 photographs and postcards:
the Consoler Fathers of Gethsemane,
1933-72.

ST. WENCESLAUS ROMAN CATHOLIC
CHURCH
TORONTO, ONT.
 Marriage and baptismal registers,
1951-78. 1 reel of microfilm.

UNION OF CZECH PROTESTANTS IN
CANADA
TORONTO, ONT.
 Correspondence with the United
Church of Canada, Sokol Gymnastic
Association, 1952-62, and published
works by Protestants in exile in Ger-
many, 1919-66. 9 cm. Photographs.
 9 photographs: gymnastic meets in
Toronto, Ont., and Chicago, Illinois,
1972-77.

YOUNG PEOPLE'S THEATRE (SUSAN
RUBEŠ)
TORONTO, ONT.
 Promotional material on Young
People's Theatre, 1970s. 2 cm. See J.
Rubeš.

DANISH COLLECTION

BROLUND, JENNY E.
TORONTO, ONT.
 Pedersen, Kirstine. *Mine
Erindringer*. Unpublished. 153 pp.

CLEMMENSEN, ANNA M.
TORONTO, ONT.
 Immigration documents, n.d. 1 cm.
Taped interview.
 Interviewed in March 1979; 1 hr.; 1
tape; English; by Lisbet Abbott.
Arrived in Canada in 1927.

ENGBERG, IDUN AND JACOB
PASS LAKE, ONT.
 12 photographs: schools, picnics,
folk dancing, and work in logging and
agriculture, 1931-43, all taken in the
Pass Lake community. Taped interview.
 Interviewed on 26 April 1978; 1.5
hrs.; 2 tapes; English; by Harold
Hogstad. Pre-WWI immigrants.

JENSEN, CHRISTIAN
TORONTO, ONT.
 Personal papers, 1938-67, and con-
stitution of St. Ansgar Danske
Evangeliske Lutherske Manighed,
n.d. 1 cm. Taped interview.
 Interviewed on 12 Nov. 1978; 1.5
hrs.; 2 tapes; Danish; by Lisbet
Abbott. Arrived in Canada in 1928.

JESSEN, JOHN W.
TORONTO, ONT.
 14 photographs: family and dwellings; and employment in gardening in
Sheridan, Hamilton, and

Bowmanville, 1922-77.
Taped interview.
 Interviewed on 2 March 1979; 1 hr.;
1 tape; English; by Lisbet
Abbott. Arrived in Canada in 1922.

JOHANSEN, ANNA V.
TORONTO, ONT.
 Personal documents, 1907-45. 1 cm.
Photographs. Taped interview.
 9 photographs: the Johansen and the
Nielsen families in Denmark,
Toronto, and Ottawa, 1917-74.
 Interviewed on 1 Dec. 1978; 1 hr.; 1
tape; Danish; by Lisbet Abbott.
Arrived in Canada in 1926.
 The Danish-Canadian Club. "Wel-
come Home." Booklet. 1946.

MELLERUP, CARL F.
THUNDER BAY, ONT.
 3 photographs: Carl Mellerup in St.
John Ambulance Sservice, 1945-78.
Taped interview.
 Interviewed on 25 March 1978; .5
hr.; 1 tape; English; by Harold
Hogstad. Immigrated to Canada in
1923.

MIKKELSEN, FRED A.
PASS LAKE, ONT.
 9 photographs: mostly of cabins in
Pass Lake, 1929-51; and Salem
Lutheran Church, 1951. Taped inter-
view.
 Interviewed on 25 April 1978; 1 hr.;
1 tape; English; by Harold Hogstad.
Settled in the Pass Lake area in the
1920s.

NIELSEN, ARTHUR F.
TORONTO, ONT.
1 graduation book, n.d. .25 cm.
Photographs. Taped interview.
21 photographs: war destruction and
pillage in China, 1914-24.
Interviewed on 2 April 1979; 1 hr.;
1 tape; English; by Lisbet Abbott.
Arrived in Canada in 1923.

ØSTERGAARD, LISELOTTE
RICHMOND HILL, ONT.
Clippings and list of participants in
"Queens of Light" (beauty pageant).
.25 cm. Photographs.
20 photographs: the "Lucia" pageant;
and religious ceremonies at the Danish Lutheran Church in Toronto,
1964-77.

OVERGAARD-THOMSEN, POUL
TORONTO, ONT.
1 passport, 1946. .25 cm. Photographs. Taped interview.
9 photographs: activities and clergy
at the Danish Lutheran Church in
Toronto, 1965.
Interviewed on 25 March 1979; 2
hrs.; 2 tapes; English; by Lisbet
Abbott. Immigrated to Canada in
1946.

PEDERSEN, ANE KIRSTINE
TORONTO, ONT.
Interviewed on 6 Oct. 1978; 1.5
hrs.; 2 tapes; Danish; by Lisbet
Abbott. Immigrated to Canada in
1927.

PETERSEN, KAREN
TORONTO, ONT.
Correspondence, 1923-68. 1 cm.
Photographs.
Over 150 photographs: the Petersen
family in Denmark, Saskatchewan,

and Manitoba, 1920-60; and employment in a lumber camp.

RASMUSSEN, CHRIS
HAMILTON, ONT.
7 scrapbooks, 1930s-50s. 13 cm.

SØRENSEN, LARS
TORONTO, ONT.
Danish passport, n.d., soldier's
record book, 1920, naturalization
certificate, 1933, and personal diary,
1927-31. 5 cm.

SØRENSEN, MICHAEL AND DAGMAR
TORONTO, ONT.
Immigration documents, 1975-76.
.25 cm. Photographs. Taped interview.
8 photographs: the Sørensen family
in Saskatchewan; and their farm in
Milton, Ont., 1921-27.
Interviewed on 16 Oct. 1978; 2 hrs.;
2 tapes; English; by Lisbet Abbott.
Arrived in Canada in 1926.

THEIL, HENRY
TORONTO, ONT.
Interviewed on 23 Oct. 1978; 1 hr.;
1 tape; English; by Lisbet Abbott.
Arrived in Canada in 1927.

VIBE-PETERSEN, ERIK
TORONTO, ONT.
Immigration documents, 1927-32. .5
cm. Photographs. Taped interview.
4 photographs: family in Nova
Scotia, and Saskatchewan, 1926-46.
Interviewed on 4 April 1979; 1.5
hrs.; 2 tapes; English; by Lisbet
Abbott. Arrived in Canada in 1927.

WESTERGAARD, KNUD
TORONTO, ONT.
De Danskes Vej. n.d. 21 pp.

CLUB DAN HANDBALL CLUB
TORONTO, ONT.
Records of Danish handball team,
1975-77. 1 reel of microfilm.

DANISH-CANADIAN CLUB
KINGSTON, ONT.
Records, 1968-77, which include
constitution, minutes, correspondence,
treasurer's reports, and miscellaneous
items: flyers, invitations, and tickets.
1 reel of microfilm.

DANISH-CANADIAN CLUB
ST. CATHARINES, ONT.
Club minute book, 1954-69. 1 cm.

DANISH-CANADIAN CLUB
WATERLOO, ONT.
Records, 1965-77, which include
minutes, correspondence, financial
statements, annual reports, and miscellaneous items: invitations, programmes, song sheets, photographs,
mailing lists, notices of meetings and
social activities, list of scholarship
winners, and clippings. Bulletins of
Scandinavian Canadian Club,
1965-66. 1 reel of microfilm.
Newsletters. 1965–73. Microfilm.

DANISH CANADIAN SOCIETY
(C. HASMUSSEN)
HAMILTON, ONT.
The collection contains correspondence of Axel Christensen, 1938;
constitutional guidelines, and minutes
of the Viking Club, n.d.; and miscellaneous records, constitution, correspondence, cash book, membership
lists, invitations, and clippings,
1945-77. 6 cm. Photographs.
25 photographs: religious ceremony;
associational and family life; and

military service, c. 1956-66, of
Hamilton's Danish community.
Danish Canadian Society Bulletins.
1967-72. .5 cm.
R.N.A.F. Training Centre. "Fare-
well to Canada." 1945. 72 pp.
Sunset Villa Bulletin. 1977 (1 issue).

DANISH CHURCH OF THE NIAGARA
PENINSULA
GRIMSBY, ONT.
Church records, 1970s; and Danish
prayer and hymn books, 1905. 3 cm.
Dansk Kirke I Udlandet. 1971-77.
Incomplete (22 issues).
Deres Kirke. 1977 (1 issue).
Månedens Prædike. 1977-78. Church
sermons (6 issues).

DANISH CLUB OF OTTAWA
OTTAWA, ONT.
Records, 1975-77. 1 reel of micro-
film.

DANISH GOLDEN AGE CLUB
TORONTO, ONT.
Minute book, members lists, yearly
programme, and club song book,
1974-78. 3 cm.

DANISH LADIES' AUXILIARY
TORONTO, ONT.
Minutes, 1958-77. 1 reel of micro-
film.

DANISH LUTHERAN CHURCH
GRIMSBY, ONT.
1 annual report, 1977-78. .5 cm.

DANISH LUTHERAN CHURCH
WILLOWDALE, ONT.
The collection contains minutes,
financial reports, brief history of
church, bulletins, clippings, notices,

and flyers, 1966-77. 4 cm. 1 reel of microfilm.
Church Bulletins. 1973-78. Incomplete. 2 cm.

FEDERATION OF DANISH ASSOCIATIONS IN CANADA
TORONTO, ONT.
Vokser Sammen. 1981. Conference publication. 1 cm.

LADIES' AUXILIARY OF DANISH LUTHERAN CHURCH
TORONTO, ONT.
Records, 1974-79, which include minutes, bulletins, constitution, and miscellaneous items. 1 reel of microfilm.

LARSON, CARK
TORONTO, ONT.
Dansk Kirkeblad. 1928-33. 1 reel of microfilm.

ONTARIO COUNCIL OF UNIVERSITY LIBRARIES AND ONTARIO ETHNIC NEWSPAPER MICROFILM PROJECT
TORONTO, ONT.
Viking. 16 Aug. 1928 - 13 March 1931 weekly. 1 reel of microfilm.

ROYAL DANISH GUARD ASSOCIATION
KITCHENER, ONT.
Membership list, executive list, overseas membership handbook, Association's songbook, invitation, programme, and letterhead, 1951-66. 2 cm.
Garderbladet. 1967-68 (40 issues). Incomplete.
Vagtparaden. 1967-68 (23 issues). Incomplete.

ST. ANSGAR DANISH MEN'S CLUB
LONDON, ONT.
Includes club constitution, minute book, cash book, and membership lists, 1962-64. 1 cm.
Meddelelse. 1963. 1 newsletter.

ST. ANSGAR LUTHERAN CHURCH
TORONTO, ONT.
Church records, 1938-78. 1 reel of microfilm.
Anniversary Booklet of St. Ansgar Lutheran Church. n.d. 22 pp.

ST. ANSGARD DANISH LUTHERAN CHURCH
LONDON, ONT.
Church records, 200 church sermons, personal history of Pastor Emil Nommesen, and letters regarding Nommesen's appointment, 1931-68; also, Ladies' Aid minute book, 1968-75. 12 cm. Photographs.
13 photographs: activities at St. Ansgard Church, 1953-69.

SUNSET VILLA ASSOCIATION
PUSLINCH, ONT.
Records, 1950-74, include constitution, minutes, correspondence, ledger book, dues forms, mailing list, and announcements. 1 reel of microfilm. Photographs.
10 photographs: activities of Sunset Villa Association, n.d.
Sunset Villa Bulletin. 1968, 1978. 1 cm.
Sunset Villa News. 1971- (3 issues).

DANUBE-SWABIAN COLLECTION

AMBERG, LUCY
MISSISSAUGA, ONT.
 Interviewed on 22 March 1979; .75
hr.; 1 tape; English; by H. Martens.
Immediate post-WWII immigrant,
discusses activities of
German-Catholic congregation at St.
Patrick's Church in Toronto.

BERENCZ, FERDINAND
TORONTO, ONT.
 Immigration and work papers,
1951-54. .5 cm. Photographs. Taped
interview.
 29 photographs: 1939-74, the
Berencz family; festivities; wedding
in Austria; and tobacco harvest in
Delhi, Ont.
 Interviewed on 15 Feb. 1978; 1.25
hrs.; 2 tapes; English/German; by
Bernard Dandyk. Arrived in Canada
in 1953, executive member of the
Donauschwabe Club.
 Heimatbote. Nov. 1975, Feb., April
1978 (3 issues).

KEPPLER, CASPAR
KITCHENER, ONT.
 Immigration documents, 1927. 1 cm.
Taped interview.
 Interviewed on 13 Sept., 17 Nov.
1977; 2 hrs.; 2 tapes; Ger-
man/English; by Bernard Dandyk.
Arrived in Canada in the 1920s.
 *25th Anniversary of the Canadian
Schwaben Sick Benefit Association,
1931-53*. 22-26 Feb. 1956. 16 pp.

KIEFER, OTTO
KITCHENER, ONT.
 3 family trees: C. Schweitzer, B.
Kiefer, Johann Kiefer, and K.
Schnurr, n.d.; and two letters regard-
ing Franz Schweitzer, 1870, 1872. 1
cm. Taped interview.
 Interviewed on 4 Aug. 1977; 1 hr.; 1
tape; German; by Bernard Dandyk.
Immigrated to Canada in 1955.
 Aptiner Heimatblaetter. June 1977.
.25 cm.
 *Totenbuch der Apatiner
Gemeinschaft*. 1977. .25 cm.

KNIPL, ELISABETH
TORONTO, ONT.
 Interviewed on 26 April 1979; .5
hr.; 1 tape; English; by H. Martens.
Arrived in Canada in 1953, describes
her involvement in the
German-Catholic congregation of St.
Patrick's Parish.

KRAR, JOHN AND MARY
WELLAND, ONT.
 Interviewed on 1 Aug. 1977; 4 hrs.;
4 tapes; English; by Rosa Frey.
Arrived in Canada in 1927-28.

KROEG, STEFAN
TORONTO, ONT.
 Interviewed on 1 June 1978; 1.5
hrs.; 2 tapes; English; by Bernard
Dandyk. Arrived in Canada in 1948.
 *25 Jahre, Pfarrgemeinde, St.
Michael der Deutschen Katholiken,
1949-74*. Windsor. 56 pp.
 Haus der Deutschkanadier, 10 Jahre.
Montreal, Quebec, April 1978. 76 pp.

Tag der Donauschwaben. Kitchener, Sept. 1970. 32 pp.

LICKER, MATHEW
KITCHENER, ONT.
 Personal papers, 1928-38. 1 cm.
Photographs. Taped interview.
 4 photographs: documents, 1904-34.
Interviewed on 27 July 1977; 2 hrs.;
2 tapes; English/German; by Bernard
Dandyk. Arrived in 1928, active in
the Schwaben Club.

METTLER, JOHN
KITCHENER, ONT.
 Constitution and bulletins of Canadian Schwaben Benefit Association, 1947-1960. 1 cm.
Summerfest. Alliance of Danube Schwabians of Canada. 14-15 July 1962. 40 pp.
Tag der Donauschwaben. Alliance of Danube Schwabians of Canada. 5-6 Sept. 1970. 28 pp.
25th Anniversary Booklet, 1931-56. Canadian Schawben Sick Benefit Association. Kitchener. 1 cm.
Oktoberfest Booklet. Canadian Schawben Sick Benefit Association. Kitchener, 6 Oct. 1962. .5 cm.

MITTERFELNER, KATHERINE
TORONTO, ONT.
 Interviewed on 27 June 1979; 1.5 hrs.; 2 tapes; English; by H. Martens. Interwar immigrant, personal maid to Lady Eaton, member of St. Patrick's parish.

PITZER, SISTER MARY AGNES
TORONTO, ONT.
 Interviewed on 27 Jan. 1979; 1.5 hrs.; 2 tapes; English; by H. Martens. Pre-WWII immigrant, discusses

social activities of the German-Catholic congregation at St. Patrick's Parish.

SAWER, ANTON
TORONTO, ONT.
 Interviewed on 26 April 1979; .75 hr.; 1 tape; English; by H. Martens. Arrived in Canada in 1948, served as treasurer of the Catholic Settlement (Toronto) Credit Union.

SCHMIDT, ADAM
KITCHENER, ONT.
 Interviewed on 5 Aug. 1977; 1 hr.; 1 tape; English; by B. Dandik. Interwar immigrant.

SCHMIDT, MARIE
KITCHENER, ONT.
 Immigration papers, 1929-50. 1 cm.
Photographs. Taped interview.
 11 photographs: family in Austria, Romania, and Kitchener, c. 1918-28.
Interviewed on 28 Sept. 1977; 2 hrs.; 2 tapes; English/German; by Bernard Dandyk. Post-WWII immigrant.

SIEBER, FRANK
KITCHENER, ONT.
 Interviewed on 14 Nov. 1977; 2 hrs.; 2 tapes; English/German; by Bernard Dandyk. Arrived in Canada in 1951.

STICHMANN, ELIZABETH AND MATTHEW
PORT PERRY, ONT.
 Interviewed on 28 Aug. 1977; 2 hrs.; 2 tapes; English; by Rosa Frey. Immigrated to Canada in the late 1920s.
Das Erste Jahrzehnt der Deutsch-Katholischen Gemeinde. 2-4 Sept. 1939. The first ten years of the

German-Catholic parish, "St.
Patrick's." 1 reel of microfilm.
*Fibel Fur Wolkschulen Mit Deutscher
Unterrichts-Sprache*. 1928. A reading
and writing practice book, in Ger-
man. 1 reel of microfilm.

TELIPASA, MARY
TORONTO, ONT.
 Interviewed on 28 March 1979; 1
hr.; 1 tape; English; by H. Martens.
Arrived in Canada in 1949, describes
activities at St. Patrick's Parish in
Toronto.

WEKERLE, ANTON
THORNHILL, ONT.
 Interviewed on 10 March 1979; 1.25
hrs.; 2 tapes; English; by H. Martens. Immigrated to Canada in 1947.

SCHWABEN CLUB (ADOLF FISCHER)
KITCHENER, ONT.
 Interviewed on 25 July 1977; 1 hr.;
1 tape; English/German; by Bernard
Dandyk. Discusses history of the
Schwaben Club in Kitchener.

VERBAND AND VEREINIGUNG DER
DONAU SCHWABEN
TORONTO, ONT.
 Correspondence, circulars, pro-
grammes, menus, and events lists,
1972-78. 2 cm. Taped interview with
Ferdinand Berencz.

DUTCH COLLECTION

AKKERHUIS, JOE
TORONTO, ONT.
 Personal documents and bibliographi-
cal item, 1941- . 1 cm (6 items).
Taped interview.
 Interviewed on 12 May 1979; 1 hr.;
1 tape; English; by E. Hietkamp.
Immigrated to Canada in 1952.

ASSINCK, A.
TORONTO, ONT.
 Dutch passport and 2 advertising
booklets. .25 cm (3 items). Photographs. Taped interview.
 14 photographs: employment in agriculture and lumber industry in
Dunsford, 1949; and storefronts and
dwellings in Markham, Ont.,
1953-55.
 Interviewed on 27 April 1977; 1 hr.;
1 tape; English; by Mark Boekelman.
Immigrated to Canada in 1948.

ATRILL, MRS.
TORONTO, ONT.
 Interviewed on 14 June 1977; 1 hr.;
1 tape; English; by Nancy Jones.
Dutch war bride.

BAARTS, LARRY
THUNDER BAY, ONT.
 3 personal and business scrapbooks
and 2 typescript reports, n.d. 5 cm. 1
reel of microfilm. Photographs.
Taped interview.
 54 photographs: Larry Baarts at
work in pulp and paper industry in

Temiskaming, Iroquois Falls,
1926-31; and family in Holland,

1914-27.
 Interviewed on 25 April, 25 June
1978, 22 Sept. 1979, 25 Jan. 1980; 4
hrs.; 4 tapes; English; by Henry
Kamphof. Pre-WWII immigrant.
 Community News. Dec. 1979. 8 pp.
 *Memory Diamonds: Eternal As the
Sky*. n.d. Catalogue of Baarts' jewel-
lery business.
 Ontario Innkeeper. May/June 1978.
.5 cm.

BADER, LUKE
KITCHENER, ONT.
 Interviewed on 18 July 1979; 1 hr.;
1 tape; English; by E. Murphy.
Immigrated to Canada in 1950.

BAKKER, TIM
NORTHERN ONT.
 Personal documents and letters. 2 cm
(16 items). Photographs. Taped interview.
 78 photographs: the Bakker family;
and employment in mining, farming,
and logging in Manitoba, Sioux
Lookout, and Gowganda, 1948-53.
 Interviewed on 4 Dec. 1978; 2 hrs.;
2 tapes; English; by Henry Kamphof.
Post-WWII immigrant.

BOEKELMAN, MARK
TORONTO, ONT.
 8 photographs: n.d.
 Contactblad voor Emigranten.
1973-74.
 De Emigrant. 1972. Newsletter.
 Der Nederlandse Courant.
March-July 1977.
 De Watcher. 1977.

Duca Post. 1977.
Dutch-Canadian Credit Union News.
Chatham, 1976.
Emigratie. 1962-64.
Emigratie Koelier. 1973.
Handleiding voor nieuwe inwoners
van Canada. 1954.
Hollandia News. 1977.
In Touch on Time. 1977.
Migration from the Netherlands to
Canada. n.d. Leaflet.
Speelman's Bookhouse Catalogue.
1968-69.
The Banner. 1977.
Unity and Friendship. 1976. News-
letter.

BOEKELMAN, MARK
TORONTO, ONT.
DUCA Credit Union. *Annual Report.*
1975, 1976.
Dutch Credit Union. *Insight.*
Oshawa, 1977.
First Christian Reformed Church of
Toronto. *1950+25=1975.*
Netherlands Reformed Congregations
in Ontario. *Church News.* 1973.
St. Willibrod Credit Union. *Annual*
Report. 1976.
Canada: Questions and Answers.
n.d.
Clarion. Dec. 1975- Nov. 1976.
Contact-Orgaan. Jan.-April 1970.
Credits for Immigrants. n.d.
De Emigratie in Lijnen en Cijfers.
1975.
Destination Canada. 1966.
Hoe is het...in Canada?. n.d.
Nieuwsbrief. May 1977. 8 pp.
Santa Claus: The Dutch Way. n.d.
Pamphlet and sheet music.
The Guide. Jan.-June, Aug.-Sept.
1975; March-Oct. 1976.
Werken Wonen En Leven in Canada.
1972.

BOEKELMAN, MARK
TORONTO, ONT.
Announcements of the Nederlands
Bazaar Comite', leaflets, flyer of
Toronto Amsterdam Twin Cities
Association, menu and programme of
8th Biennial Conference Canadian
Ethnic Press Federation, and 2 post-
cards, c. 1970s. 2 cm (10 items).
Schenk, M. *Juliana, Queen of the*
Netherlands. n.d.
Calvinist Contact. 21 Jan. 1975. .5
cm.
Dutch-Canadian Seniors Clubs,
Dutch News. 1977. 21 pp.
National Union of Christian Schools.
Annual Report. 1976-77. .5 cm.
_____. Directory, 1976-77.
Pioneer Christian Monthly, Dec.
1975-May 1976. Scattered issues.
Holland Club. *Windmill Whispers.*
Guelph. Newsletter. Sept. 1977. 20
pp.

BOONSTRA, FRED
DUNDAS, ONT.
Included are leaflets, newsclippings,
and typescripts. 4 cm (14 items).
50 Years of the Christian Reformed
Church in Chatham, Ont. 1976. 40
pp.
Hamilton Christian Reformed Church,
50th Anniversary Commemorative
Booklet. 1979.
_____. *Chronology.* 1979. .5 cm.

BOONSTRA, MARTIN
DRAYTON, ONT.
Personal documents and letters. 2 cm
(12 items). Photograph. Taped inter-
view.
1 photograph: graduation class from
Police Academy in Holland, 1941.
Interviewed on 5 June 1978; 2 hrs.;
2 tapes; English; by E. Hietkamp.
Post-WWII immigrant.

BOSGOED, WILLIAM AND DIANE
TURKEY POINT, ONT.
 Interviewed on 1 Aug. 1979; 2 hrs.;
2 tapes; English; by E. Murphy.
Post-WWII immigrants.

BOTMAN, REV. PETER
TORONTO, ONT.
 4 photographs: the Botman family in
Holland, n.d.
 Interviewed on 16 March 1979; 2
hrs.; 2 tapes; English; by E. Murphy.
Immigrated to Canada in 1961.

BOUW, CORNELIUS AND MARIA
SIMCOE, ONT.
 Personal papers, 1955-?. .25 cm.
Photographs. Taped interview.
 13 photographs: the Bouw family,
1937-69, religious life in various
places, 1937-55; and Dutch immi-
grants en route to Canada, 1955, in
Holland and Simcoe.
 Interiewed on 25 Feb. 1979; 1 hr.; 1
tape; English; by E. Murphy.
Post-WWII immigrant.

BOWEN, JANSJE
TORONTO, ONT.
 Interviewed on 18 July 1977; 2 hrs.;
2 tapes; English; by Nancy Jones.
Dutch war bride.

BRITNELL, CORRIE
ANGUS, ONT.
 Interviewed on 31 May 1977; 1 hr.;
1 tape; English; by Nancy Jones.
Dutch war bride.

BROUWER, J.
TORONTO, ONT.
 Promotional material, and yearbook
of Radio Nederland, c. 1975-77. 2
cm.

BROWN, MARIA J.
TORONTO, ONT.
 Interviewed on 13 June 1977; 1 hr.;
1 tape; English; by Nancy Jones.
Dutch war bride.

CHAPMAN, AGNES
TORONTO, ONT.
 Interviewed on 3 August 1977; 1 hr.;
1 tape; English; by Nancy Jones.
Dutch war bride.

COHEN, ALBERT
TORONTO, ONT.
 1 passport (photographed). .25 cm.
Taped interview.
 Interviewed on 11 May 1977; 2 hrs.;
2 tapes; English; by Mark
Boekelman. Arrived in 1956.

COPELAND, NELLIE
TORONTO, ONT.
 Interviewed on 9 August 1977; 2
hrs.; 2 tapes; English; by Nancy
Jones. Dutch war bride.

COULTER, A.
TORONTO, ONT.
 Interviewed on 25 July 1977; 1 hr.;
1 tape; English; by Nancy Jones.
Dutch war bride.
DAVENPORT, MRS.
GALT, ONT.
 Interviewed on 20 June 1977; 1 hr.;
1 tape; English; by Nancy Jones.
Dutch war bride.

DEEN, HERMAN
DRAYTON, ONT.
 Personal documents, n.d., copy of
Dutch-Canada Anthem, 1970. 2 cm.
Photographs. Taped interview.
 4 photographs: portraits and dwell-
ings of the Deen family in Holland,
and Drayton, 1946-77.
 Interviewed on 21 June 1978; 2 hrs.;

2 tapes; English; by E. Hietkamp.
Post-WWII immigrant.

DEFFETT, G.
TORONTO, ONT.
 Interviewed on 4 Aug. 1977; 1 hr.; 1
tape; English; by Nancy Jones. Dutch
war bride.

DELHEY, WILLIAM
APPLE HILL, ONT.
 Interviewed on 31 July 1977; 1 hr.;
1 tape; English; by Hask
uir. Dutch farming in Ont.

DE NIEUWE, KEES
TORONTO, ONT.
 2 schedules for the Toronto and District Soccer League, 1967; 3
newsclippings; summaries of soccer
games, 1965; and statistics of team
members' scoring record, 1965. 2 cm
(9 items). Photographs.
 8 photographs: Neerlandia Soccer
Club team members in Toronto,
1959-67.

DEN OTTER, TIENY
DRAYTON, ONT.
 18 photographs: family in Holland
and Drayton, 1931-78. Taped interview.
 Interviewed on 20 June 1978; 1 hr.;
1 tape; English; by E. Hietkamp.
Post-WWII immigrant.

DEWAR, ANN
CORNWALL, ONT.
 Interviewed on 8 July 1977; 1 hr.; 1
tape; English; Hakvitz. Arrived in
Canada in 1953.

DE WIT, JOHN
VAL CARON, ONT.
 Interviewed on 22 June 1982; 1.75

hrs.; 2 tapes; English; by G. Schinko.
Arrived in Canada in 1951.

DE YONG, JACOB
EMO, ONT.
 10 photographs: portraits and dwellings of the De Jong family in Holland, Manitoba, and Emo, 1931-51.
Taped interview.
 Interviewed on 3 Aug. 1978; 1 hr.; 1
tape; English; by Henry Kamphof.

DOBBIN, WILHELMINA
PETERBOROUGH, ONT.
 Questionnaire regarding war bride
experience, 1978. 3 pp.

DUGAN, HILDE
TORONTO, ONT.
 Interviewed on 27 July 1977; 1 hr.;
1 tape; English; by Nancy Jones.
Dutch war bride.

DYKSTRA, FRANK AND LYNN
HAGERSVILLE, ONT.
 2 photographs: family in Holland,
n.d. Taped interview.
 Interviewed on 3 March 1979; 2
hrs.; 2 tapes; English; by E. Murphy.
Arrived in Canada in 1950.

EDMUNDSON, WILLEMINA
TORONTO, ONT.
 Interviewed on 25 Aug. 1977; 1 hr.;
1 tape; English; by Nancy Jones.
Dutch war bride.

ELIENS, REV. JOSEPH
CALEDONIA, ONT.
 Interviewed on 24 July 19??; 2 hrs.;
2 tapes; English; by E. Murphy.
Immigrated to Canada in 1952.

ESSILINK, J. C.
DEVLIN, ONT.
 Personal documents, letters, and

clippings, 1950-60. 2 cm (10 items).
Photographs. Taped interview.
22 photographs: the Essilink family
in Holland, Alberta, and Devlin,
1948-77; dwelling in Emo; and
farming activity in Devlin, 1960-70.
Interviewed on 31 July 1978; 1 hr.;
1 tape; English; by Henry Kamphof.
Post-WWII immigrant.

FERDINANDS, CLAUDE
TORONTO, ONT.
Interviewed on 17 Feb. 1979; 2 hrs.;
2 tapes; English; by S. Sugunasiri.
Immigrated to Canada in 1958.
FILIATRAULT, FREDRICA
SUDBURY, ONT.
Interviewed on 26 July 1982; 2 hrs.;
2 tapes; English; by G. Schinko.
Arrived in Canada in 1947.

FINN, REV. JOSEPH
PORT DOVER, ONT.
Interviewed on 4 Aug. 1979; 2 hrs.;
2 tapes; English; by E. Murphy.
Church life among Dutch Catholic
immigrants.

FISH, NELLIE
UNIONVILLE, ONT.
Interviewed on 21 June 1977; 1 hr.;
1 tape; English; by Nancy Jones.
Dutch war bride.

FORD, JACOBA
TORONTO, ONT.
Interviewed on 23 Aug. 1977; 1 hr.;
1 tape; English; by Nancy Jones.
Dutch war bride.

FRY, IDA
TORONTO, ONT.
Interviewed on 12 Aug. 1977; 1 hr.;
1 tape; English; by Nancy Jones.
Dutch war bride.

GALLAGHER, MARIA
TORONTO, ONT.
Interviewed on 24 Aug. 1977; 1 hr.;
1 tape; English; by Nancy Jones.
Dutch war bride.

GEORGE, MRS. LLOYD
AGINCOURT, ONT.
Interviewed on 14 June 1977; 1 hr.;
1 tape; English; by Nancy Jones.
Dutch war bride.
De Nederlands Courant. 7 Oct.
1976. 15pp.

GLAZEMA, SAM
MOOREFIELD, ONT.
Personal certificates, and immigration documents, 1951-55 (4 items).
Photographs. Taped interview. 8
photographs: the Glazema family; and
employment in brickyard in Holland
and Milton, 1951. Interviewed on 28
June 1978; 1.5 hrs.; 2 tapes; English;
by E. Hietkamp. Post-WWII immigrant.

GRANDY, NINA
TORONTO, ONT.
Interviewed on 20 July 1977; 1 hr.;
1 tape; English; by Nancy Jones.
Dutch war bride.

GROL, LINI
FONTHILL, ONT.
5 scrapbooks containing clippings of
articles, and poems by Lini Grol,
artwork, photographs, certificates,
and various books by donor, 1970-76.
1 reel of microfilm.

GROOTSCHOLTEN, REV. MARTIN
LONDON, ONT.
Interviewed on 4 May 1979; 3 hrs.;
3 tapes; English; by E. Murphy.
Immediate post-WWII immigrant.

HARKEMA, GERALDINE
THUNDER BAY, ONT.
 Personal papers include certificates, letters, and a membership booklet of the Ladies' Orange Benevolent Association of British America. 3 cm (27 items). Photographs. Taped interview.
 10 photographs: the Harkema and Fruchwick families in Holland, Ont., 1920-76.
 Interviewed on 14 Dec. 1978; 2 hrs.; 2 tapes; English/Dutch; by Henry Kamphof. WWI immigrant.

HARTMANS, REV. R. A.
TORONTO, ONT.
 Pioneer Christian Monthly. 1959. 10th anniversary issue; 1 Dec. 1960 - Dec. 1972; Feb. 1977. 2 cm.

HASKVITZ, ALAN
GLENGARRY, ONT.
 Personal file, map of Glengarry and bulletins of Christian Farmers' Federation, 1970-77. 1 cm (5 items).

HAVEMAN, MICHIEL
MOOREFIELD, ONT.
 11 photographs: the Havemann family in Holland, Drayton, and Moorefield, 1900-77; "Klompendansers" celebrations in Drayton, 1977; and religious ceremony at the Reformed Church, Drayton. Taped interview.
 Interviewed on 12 June 1978; 2 hrs.; 2 tapes; Dutch; by E. Hietkamp. Arrived in 1952.
 Calvinist Contact. 23 June 1978. 350th anniversary of the Reformed Church in America. .5 cm.

HEEREMA, HENRY
THUNDER BAY, ONT.
 Personal documents, including passenger list of *S.S. Zuiderkruis*, 1952 (2 items). Photographs. Taped interview.
 20 photographs: portraits and dwellings of Heerema family in Holland and Thunder Bay, 1948-77.
 Interviewed on 23 Aug. 1979; 1.5 hrs.; 2 tapes; English; by Henry Kamphof.
Discusses immigration to Canada, settlement in Port Arthur and dairy farming.

HEERGAARDEN, HARRY
BRAMPTON, ONT.
 Personal documents (photographed), c. 1920s (4 items). Taped interview.
 Interviewed on 5 April 1977; 1 hr.; 1 tape; English; by Mark Boekelman. Immigrated to Canada in 1927.

HEERINGA, J.
STONEY CREEK, ONT.
 Personal certificates (some photographed, 20 items). Photographs. Taped interview.
 4 photographs: the Heeringa family; and dwellings in Chatham and Stoney Creek, 1952.
 Interviewed on 25 April 1977; 2 hrs.; 2 tapes; English; by Mark Boekelman. Arrived in Canada in 1952.

HENSBERGER, J.
TORONTO, ONT.
 Passport and C.N. Railway identification card, 1927. Photographs. Taped interview.
 22 photographs: J. D. Hensbergen, 1927-30; religious life at the New Apostolic Church in Toronto, n.d.; and employment in agriculture in Manitoba, 1927-28.
 Interviewed on 25 March 1977; 1 hr.; 1 tape; English; by Mark Boekelman. Arrived in Canada in 1927.

HESSELINK, JOHN
DRAYTON, ONT.
3 photographs: the Hesselink family in Drayton, 1951-54. Taped interview.
Interviewed on 17 April 1978; 1 hr.; 1 tape; Dutch; by E. Hietkamp. Emigrated in 1952.

HIRSCH, ALBERT
TORONTO, ONT.
Interviewed on 13 July 1977; 1 hr.; 1 tape; English; by Nancy Jones. Dutch war bride.

HOLLAND, F.
TORONTO, ONT.
Interviewed on 1 June 1977; 1 hr.; 1 tape; English; by Nancy Jones. Dutch war bride.

HOOGSTRATEN, MR.
TORONTO, ONT.
Membership list of the Netherlands Luncheon Club, 1974. .25 cm.

ISHWARAN, WOBINT
TORONTO, ONT.
Interviewed on 28 Feb. 1977; 1 hr.; 1 tape; English; by Mark Boekelman. Post-WWII immigrant.

JAMES, GRETA
THUNDER BAY, ONT.
Perpetual diary, and daily reminder, n.d. 1 cm. Photographs. Taped interview.
40 photographs: unidreentified, n.d.
Interviewed on 22 March 1978; 1 hr.; 1 tape; English; Henry Kamphof.

JONES, NANCY
TORONTO, ONT.
Horn, M. "The Liberators and the Liberated: Some Preliminary Observations on the Relations Between Canadian Soldiers and Dutch Civilians, 1944-46." n.d. Typescript, 15pp.
Jones, Nancy. "Summary of Interviews of Dutch War Brides Residing in Ontario." 1977. Typescript. 12pp.

JORDAN, GEESJA
SHELBOURNE, ONT.
Interviewed on 28 June 1977; 1 hr.; 1 tape; English; by Nancy Jones. Dutch war bride.

KAEMINGH, GRADA
EMO, ONT.
Family records, n.d. 2 cm. Photographs. Taped interview.
12 photographs: the Kaemingh family in Holland, Manitoba, and Emo, 1931-68.
Interviewed on 30 July 1978; 1 hr.; 1 tape; English; by Henry Kamphof.

KAEMINGH, TED
EMO, ONT.
Interviewed on 1 Aug. 1978; 1 hr.; 1 tape; English; by Henry Kamphof.

KAMERBEEK, TEUNIS
SUDBURY, ONT.
Interviewed on 9 June 1982; 1 hr.; 1 tape; English; by G. Schinko. Immigrated to Canada in 1953.

KAMSTRA, CECIL
SOUTH GILLIES, ONT.
Personal documents, and 1 scrapbook, 1925-53. 3 cm (19 items). Photographs. Taped interview.
40 photographs: the Kamstra family in Holland, and South Gillies, 1924-41; and farming activity and construction of a house in South Gillies, 1939-41.
96 photographs: 1903-50, schools, religious life, dwellings, and work in

farming and logging in South Gillies.
Interviewed on 29 March 1978; .75
hr.; 1 tape; English; by Henry
Kamphof.

KAMSTRA, JACK
SOUTH GILLIES, ONT.
4 photographs: houses in South Gillies, 1941. Taped interview.
Interviewed on 3 June 1978; 1 hr.; 1
tape; English; by Henry Kamphof.

KAMSTRA, KLAAS
SOUTH GILLIES, ONT.
Personal papers, 1953-72, including
a land title certificate, 1906. 2 cm (25
items). Photographs. Taped interview.
23 photographs: members of the
Kamstra family; and cattle farming in
South Gillies, 1937-71.
Interviewed on 28 Feb. 1978; 1 hr.;
1 tape; English; by Henry Kamphof.
Arrived in Canada in 1923.

KEMPTON, CORRIE
TORONTO, ONT.
Interviewed on 11 May 1977; 1 hr.;
1 tape; English; by Nancy Jones.
Dutch war bride.

KENNER, MARIA
TORONTO, ONT.
Interviewed on 12 July 1977; 1 hr.;
1 tape; English; by Nancy Jones.
Dutch war bride.

KIDD, MARGUERETHA
TORONTO, ONT.
Interviewed on 25 July 1977; 1 hr.;
1 tape; English; by Nancy Jones.
Dutch war bride.

KINCZAL, JOHANNA
TORONTO, ONT.
Personal documents (some photo-
graphed), 1910-44 (6 items). Photo-

graphs. Taped interview.
2 photographs: Johanna Kinczal, n.d.
Interviewed on 16 May 1977; 1 hr.;
1 tape; English; by Mark Boekelman.
Arrived in 1951.

KLEINGELD, LEO
ALMA, ONT.
Interviewed on 20 June 1978; 2 hrs.;
2 tapes; English; by E. Hietkamp.
Immigrated to Canada in 1930.

KLOMP, WILLIAM
THUNDER BAY, ONT.
Interviewed on 8, 26 June 1978; 2
hrs.; 2 tapes; English; by Henry
Kamphof.

KNIGHT, KEITH (CALVIN COLLEGE,
GRAND RAPIDS, MICHIGAN)
ST. CATHARINES, ONT.
44 photographs: used in *Calvinist
Contact*, showing religious ceremony
in Dutch Reformed churches; Dutch
immigrants on board ship; celebration
of St. Nicholas; exhibitions and business enterprises in St. Catharines,
1927-77.
*Church and Nation for Reformed
Faith and Action.* 1956-69. 2 reels of
microfilm.

KOESLAG, GERRIT-WILLEM
CLIFFORD, ONT.
Scrapbook containing material related
to family; and local and international
news, n.d. 2 cm. Photographs. Taped
interview.
15 photographs: the Koeslag family,
1939-57.
Interviewed on 13 June 1978; 1.5
hrs.; 2 tapes; English; by E.
Hietkamp. Immigrated to Canada in
1948.

KOK, LOUIE C.
THUNDER BAY, ONT.
10 photographs: dwellings of the Kok family in Holland, Winnipeg, and Thunder Bay, 1950-74; and religious life in churches constructed by the Kok family in Thunder Bay, 1967. Taped interview.
Interviewed on 19, 21 Sept. 1978; 2 hrs.; 2 tapes; English; by Henry Kamphof.

KONING, MR. AND MRS. RAY
CHATHAM, ONT.
"25th Anniversary Booklet of the Dutch-Canadian Credit Union, 1976."
Hollandia News. Feb. 1976 - July 1977.
Home and Family. Nov. 1953 - July 1956. Incomplete.
The Banner: Official Publication of the Christian Reformed Church. 3 Dec. 1976 - 26 May 1978. Incomplete.
The Christian Reader. Feb., March 1964.
The Outlook. March 1978. (Devoted to the exposition and defence of the reformed faith). 24 pp.

KOOY, LEN
TORONTO, ONT.
A collection of photographs, calendars, programmes, and posters relating to the Toronto Dutch community, c. 1970s (38 items). 1 reel of microfilm.

KORTEWEG, LAURENS
THUNDER BAY, ONT.
Personal documents and correspondence, 1949-59 (10 items). Photographs. Taped interview.
42 photographs: portraits and dwellings of the Korteweg family in Holland, Leamington, Hamilton, and

Thunder Bay, 1918-74.
Interviewed on 25 Oct., 15 Jan. 1978; 2 hrs.; 2 tapes; English; by Henry Kamphof. Post-WWII immigrant.

KRABBE, MR. AND MRS.
ELORA, ONT.
Personal documents, 1934-54 (12 items). Photographs. Taped interview.
15 photographs: the Krabbe family in Holland, and Rothsay, 1952-53; Dutch immigrants en route to Canada, 1952; farming in Pilkington Township, 1952-54; and religious activity at the Dutch Reformed Church in Drayton, 1952-57.
Interviewed on 18 April 1977; 1 hr.; 1 tape; English; by Mark Boekelman. Arrived in Canada in 1952.
25th Anniversary Brochure of the Drayton Reformed Church. 1977. .5 cm.
25th Anniversary Programme of the Drayton Reformed Church. 1977. .5 cm.

KRIENER, JACK
TORONTO, ONT.
Personal documents (some photographed-8 items), 1953-60. Taped interview.
Interviewed on 5 April 1977; 2 hrs.; 2 tapes; English; by Mark Boekelman. Immigrated to Canada in 1954.

KROFT, MAGDALENA
SUDBURY, ONT.
7 photographs, n.d. Taped interview.
Interviewed on 13 July 1982; 1.5 hrs.; 2 tapes; English; by G. Schinko. Arrived in Canada in 1950.

KROL, JOHN
GLENGARRY, ONT.
Interviewed on 28 July 1977; 1 hr.;
1 tape; English; by Alan Haskvitz.

LANDMAN, JOHN
DRAYTON, ONT.
8 photographs: the Landman family
in Holland and Drayton, 1951-76;
Dutch immigrants en route to Canada,
1951, 1958. Taped interview.
Interviewed on 3 July 1978; 1 hr.; 1
tape; English; by E. Hietkamp.
Post-WWII immigrant.

LLOYD, GRETA
GUELPH, ONT.
Interviewed on 20 June 1977; 1hr.; 1
tape; English; by Nancy Jones. Dutch
war bride.

LONEY, GRACE
EMO, ONT.
2 personal scrapbooks, consisting
largely of newsclippings, 1951-56. 2
cm.

LOPERS, HANK
DRAYTON, ONT.
6 photographs: the Lopers family in
Holland, 1940-51. Taped interview.
Interviewed on 1 May 1978; 1 hr.; 1
tape; English; by E. Hietkamp.
Post-WWII immigrant.

LUYKX, ANTONIUS AND JOHANNA
SIMCOE, ONT.
1 photograph: the family in Holland,
1950.
Interviewed on 1 Aug. 1979; 1 hr.; 1
tape; English; by E. Murphy.

MAAT, DICK
THUNDER BAY, ONT.
The collection contains donor's per-
sonal documents, and associational

records, specifically from the Christian Society for Culture and Social
Development, the Thunder Bay Christian School Society, the Immigration
Committee for Canada of the Christian Reformed Church, and the Fort
William Christian Reformed Church,
1947-67. 4.5 cm. Photographs.
19 photographs: family and dwellings; and employment in agriculture,
n.d.
Films from the Netherlands. 1955.
Booklet. 14 pp.

MACRITCHIE, MRS. H.
TORONTO, ONT.
Interviewed on 18 July 1977; 1 hr.;
1 tape; English; by Nancy Jones.
Dutch war bride.

MADDEROM, P.
ZUID SCHARWOUDE, THE NETHER-
LANDS
Wereld-Contact. 1962-1971. 1 reel
of microfilm.

MAERVEE, REV. CORNELIUS
CALEDONIA, ONT.
Interviewed on 3 March 1979; 2
hrs.; 2 tapes; English; by E. Murphy.
Activities in Dutch Canadian Catholic
parish life.

MARJERISON, HOARSE
APPLE HILL, ONT.
Interviewed on 30 July 1977; .75
hr.; 1 tape; English; by Alan
Haskvitz.

MCLAREN, DUNCAN
TORONTO, ONT.
1 poster, and 1 flyer of Netherlands
Bazaar, 1977, and 1 advertisement of
Dutch language programme.

MELNICK, LOUISE
KEEWATIN, ONT.
 Biography of Louise Melnik, 1979.
.25 cm. Photographs. Taped inter-
view.
 6 photographs: the Melnick family in
Holland, 1928-65.
 Interviewed on 23 Aug. 1981; 1hr.;
1 tape; English; by Henry Kamphof.
Dutch war bride.

MOESKER, ADOLF
DRAYTON, ONT.
 1 photograph: Dutch immigrants en
route to Canada, 1954. Taped interview.
 Interviewed on 23 June 1978; 1 hr.;
1 tape; English; by E. Hietkamp.
Post-WWII immigrant.

MOL, MARTEN
TORONTO, ONT.
 Memoirs of Mol Marten, 1952;
correspondence, 1959-77; file of
Dutch immigrants to Canada,
1968-71; 1 flyer, n.d.; and commemorative booklets, 1975. 2 cm (5
items). Photographs.
 4 photographs: taken at the First
Reformed Church in Toronto,
1949-62.
 *25th Anniversary of the First Chris-
tian Reformed Church of Toronto.*
Toronto, 1975. Booklet.

MORRISON, JEAN
THUNDER BAY, ONT.
 Personal accounts of Fort William.
.25 cm (3 items).

MULDER, ALBERTUS AND JEANETTE
HAMILTON, ONT.
 Personal papers, 1948-75. 1 cm.
Photographs. Taped interview.
 38 photographs: the DeWeerd, and
Mulder families in Holland, Zurich,

and Ancaster, 1935-77; and agricultural work in Ancaster, Ont.,
1948-52.
 Interviewed on 3 Feb. 1979; 1 hr.; 2
tapes; Dutch; by F. Boonstra.
Post-WWII immigrants.

MURDOCH, KIEK
TORONTO, ONT.
 Interviewed on 19 May 1977; tran-
script; English; by Nancy Jones.
Dutch war bride.

MYDERWYK, JOHANNES
MURILLO, ONT.
 Personal documents, c. 1970s. 1 cm
(7 items). Photographs. Taped interview.
 16 photographs: portraits and dwellings of the Myderwyk family in Holland and Murillo, 1956-79.
 Interviewed on 20 Jan. 1981; 2 hrs.;
2 tapes; English; by Henry Kamphof.
Ontario Milk Producer. July 1980.
46 pp.

NIEZEN, HARRY
TORONTO, ONT.
 Immigration papers, c. 1950s. 1 cm
(9 items). Photographs. Taped interview.
 10 photographs: Dutch immigrants
en route to Canada, 1951.
 Interviewed on 14 March 1977; 1
hr.; 1 tape; Dutch/English; by A.
Niezen. Post-WWII immigrant.

NORTHCOTE, TRUSS
TORONTO, ONT.
 Interviewed on 4 May 1977; 1 hr.; 1
tape; English; by Nancy Jones. Dutch
war bride.

OLIVIER, LAWRENCE
THUNDER BAY, ONT.
 21 photographs: the Olivier family;

employment in drilling, 1918-75.
Taped interview.
Interviewed on 3 Jan. 1979; 1 hr.; 1
tape; English; by Henry Kamphof.
Pre-WWII immigrant.

OOSTERHOFF, ANIETA
WELLANDPORT, ONT.
1 photograph: Klompen Dancers in
Drayton, 1976.
Interviewed on 5 July 1978; .5 hr.; 1
tape; English; by E. Hietkamp.
Community News. 6 June 1977. Clipping about Klompen dancers.

OOSTERHUIS, WILMA S.
NEWMARKET, ONT.
Immigration papers, c. 1920s (2
items). Photographs. Taped interview.
5 photographs: Dutch immigrants
aboard ship, 1929; employment in
agriculture, 1934-45; and Dutch
Ladies' Aid picnic in Burlington,
1931.
Interviewed on 2 May 1977; 1 hr.; 1
tape; English; by Mark Boekelman.
Arrived in Canada in 1929.

OOSTING, JAN
GLENGARRY, ONT.
Interviewed on 22 July 1977; .5 hr.;
1 tape; English; by Alan Haskvitz.
Post-WWII immigrant.

PARKS, A. H.
TORONTO, ONT.
Interviewed on 17 May 1977; 1 hr.;
1 tape; English; by Nancy Jones.
Dutch war bride.

PARSONS, MRS. M.
LONDON, ONT.
Questionnaire regarding background
and war time experience (1 item).

PETERS, JOHN
GLENGARRY, ONT.
Interviewed on 7 July 1977; 1 hr.; 1
tape; English; by Alan Haskvitz.
Post-WWII immigrant.

POLAK, S.
TORONTO, ONT.
Interviewed on 19 July 1977; 1 hr.;
1 tape; English; by Nancy Jones.
Dutch war bride.

POOT, CORNELIS
GOWANSTOWN, ONT.
Wartime documents, and emigration
papers, 1942-60. 1 cm (8 items).
Taped interview.
Interviewed on 2 June 1978; 1 hr.; 1
tape; English; by E. Hietkamp.
Arrived in Canada in 1951.

POTHOF, FRANS
TORONTO, ONT.
Immigration identification card, n.d.
Photographs. Taped interview.
5 photographs: the Pothof family in
Holland, and Toronto, 1953-57; and
immigrants en route to Canada, Holland, 1953.
Interviewed on 29 March 1977; 2
hrs.; 2 tapes; English/Dutch; by Mark
Boekelman. Immigrated to Canada in
1953.

PUL, MARINUS
PALMERSTON, ONT.
20 photographs: portraits, dwellings,
and business enterprises of the Pul
family in Holland, and Inwood,
Listowel, and Orillia, 1938-77. Taped
interview.
Interviewed on 8 Jan. 1979; 2.5 hrs.;
3 tapes; English; by E. Hietkamp.
Immediate post-WWII immigrant.

REEMEYER, EGBERDINA
HAMILTON, ONT.
 Personal documents (photographed),
n.d. .5 cm (4 items). Photographs.
Taped interview.
 11 photographs: the Reemeyer family
in Holland, and Hamilton, 1920-44;
Dutch immigrants on board ship,
1930; and groups of people at the
First Reformed Church. 1938-39.
 Interviewed on 25 March 1977; 1hr.;
1 tape; English; by Mark Boekelman.
Immigrated to Canada in 1929.

REIJENGA, JOHANNA
TORONTO, ONT.
 Personal documents (photographed),
1920s (4 items). Taped interview.
 Interviewed on 19 April 1977; 1 hr.;
1 tape; English; by Mark Boekelman.
Immigrated to Canada in 1926.

REINDERS, JAN
DRAYTON, ONT.
 11 photographs: 1952-75, the
Reinders family in Holland, and
Drayton; employment in agriculture;
and Dutch immigrants arriving in
Canada, 1952. Taped interview.
 Interviewed on 26 May 1978; 1 hr.;
1 tape; English; by E. Hietkamp.
Post-WWII immigrant.
 Ons Tweede Thuis. Publication of the
Emigration Commission of the Neth-
erlands Women's Committee, 1959.
108 pp.

RHYZAK, C.
TORONTO, ONT.
 Interviewed on 10 Aug. 1977; 1 hr.;
1 tape; English; by Nancy Jones.
Dutch war bride.

ROES, ADRIAN AND BERNADETTE
LAMBETH, ONT.
 Interviewed on 4 May 1979; 1 hr.; 1
tape; English; by E. Murphy.

ROMYN, ELDERT
EMO, ONT.
 1 family register. .25 cm. Photographs. Taped interview.
 22 photographs: the Romyn family in
Holland, Manitoba, and Emo,
1927-78.
 Interviewed on 31 July 1978; 1 hr.;
1 tape; English; by Henry Kamphof.

ROODZANT, N.
TORONTO, ONT.
 11 photographs: the Roodzant family, 1952-53.

RUPKE, JOHN
KETTLEBY, ONT.
 Immigration and other personal
papers, 1929-54 (10 items). Taped
interview.
 Interviewed on 6 May 1977; 2 hrs.;
2 tapes; English; by Mark
Boekelman. Arrived in Canada in
1929.

SALEMIK, JOSEPH
HANMER, ONT.
 Interviewed on 25 June 1982; 1 hr.;
1 tape; English; by G. Schinko.
Arrived in Canada in 1951.

SAYERS, MR.
TORONTO, ONT.
 3 membership booklets of the Netherlands Luncheon Club, 1954-64,
1966-67, 1967-68. 1 cm.

SCHRYER, THEODORA
SCARBOROUGH, ONT.
 Interviewed on 4 March 1977; 1 hr.;
1 tape; English; by Mark Boekelman.

SCHRYER, THEODORA
TORONTO, ONT.
 180 photographs: from the *De Nederlandse Courant*, including celebrations and entertainment, business enterprises, and sports in Toronto, c. 1950-70.
 Der Nederlandse Courant., 1953-72. Incomplete. 1974-79. Scattered issues. 20 cm.
 Der Nederlandse Post. 1952-60. Incomplete. 4 cm.

SCHRYER, THEODORA
TORONTO, ONT.
 Bulletins, annual reports, and newsclippings of various Dutch-Canadian organizations, most notably, the Holland Club of Guelph, and the Dutch Canadian Society of London, Ont. 7 cm (14 items). Photographs.
 3 photographs: Hans Melis in Unionville, n.d.

SCHUT, EDWARD (EVERT)
VAL THERESE, ONT.
 Interviewed on 14 July 1982; 2 hrs.; 2 tapes; English; by G. Schinko. Arrived in Canada in 1957.

SCHURINGA, HERMAN
TORONTO, ONT.
 Immigration and other personal papers, 1948-50. 2 cm. Photograph. Taped interview.
 Interviewed on 25 April 1977; 1 hr.; 1 tape; Dutch; by Mark Boekelman. Immigrated to Canada in 1948.
 25th Anniversary Booklet of the First Christian Reformed Church of Toronto. .5 cm.

SIEBERT, HENRIETTE
CAMBRIDGE, ONT.
 Interviewed on 2 Aug. 1977; 1 hr.; 1 tape; English; by Nancy Jones. Dutch war bride.

SIEDERS, BILL
FORT FRANCES, ONT.
 14 photographs: the Sieders family in Holland, Manitoba, Emo, and Fort Frances, 1935-71. Taped interview.
 Interviewed on 31 July 1978; 1 hr.; 1 tape; English; by Henry Kamphof.

SKINNER, WILHEMINA M.
TORONTO, ONT.
 Interviewed on 6 June 1977; 1 hr.; 1 tape; English; by Nancy Jones. Dutch war bride.

SMIT, KLAAS
MISSISSAUGA, ONT.
 Immigration papers, 1949. .25 cm. Photographs. Taped interview.
 6 photographs: the Smit family; and employment in agriculture in Holland, Arthur, and Walkerton, 1949-57.
 Interviewed on 28 March 1977; 1 hr.; 1 tape; English; by Mark Boekelman. Post-WWII immigrant.

SMITS, LENARD
LANCASTER, ONT.
 Interviewed on 24 July 1977; .75 hr.; 1 tape; English; by Alan Haskvitz. Arrived in Canada in 1950.

SPAANS, G. E.
UNIONVILLE, ONT.
 Interviewed on 1 March 1977; 1 hr.; 1 tape; English; by Mark Boekelman. Post-WWII immigrant.
 20th Anniversary of the Dutch-Canadian Association of Greater Toronto. n.d. Pamphlet.

SPEELMAN, P.
TORONTO, ONT.
 The Speelman papers, 1954-76,
cover the following organizations:
Toronto District Christian High
School Association, National Union
of Christian Schools, Christian
Labour Association of Canada, Asso-
ciation for Reformed Scientific
Studies, Church and Nation for
Reformed Faith in Action, the Second
Toronto Christian Reformed Church,
the Canadian Christian Culture
Society, and the Dutch-Canadian
Association of Greater Toronto. 5
reels of microfilm.
 *Church and Nation for Reformed
Faith and Action.* 1956-70. 4 reels of
microfilm.

SPIKMAN, RALPH
MOOREFIELD, ONT.
 5 photographs: the Spikman family
and their dwellings, 1947-49. Taped
interview.
 Interviewed on 8 May 1978; 2 hrs.;
2 tapes; English; by E. Hietkamp.
Immediate post-WWII immigrant.

STAALSTRA, CORNELIUS
SUDBURY, ONT.
 2 photographs: taken at the Dutch
Entertainment Club in Sudbury, 1974.
Taped interview.
 Interviewed on 8 July 1982; 3.5 hrs.;
4 tapes; English; by G. Schinko.
Post-WWII immigrant.

STEENHOF, C.
BURLINGTON, ONT.
 Family register, 1894, and birth
certificates. 1 cm (5 items). Taped
interview.
 Interviewed on 1 April 1977; 1 hr.;
1 tape; English; by Mark Boekelman.
Arrived in Canada in 1927.

The Banner. 5 Nov. 1976, 10 Dec.
1976.

STEVENS, HILCO
MOOREFIELD, ONT.
 Documents of the Netherlands Emigration Service, and other personal
papers. 1 cm (13 items). Photographs. Taped interview.
 8 photographs: dwellings of the
Stevens family in Holland, and
Ingersoll, 1959; and Dutch immigrants en route to Canada, 1959.
 Interviewed on 28 April 1978; 1 hr.;
1 tape; English; by E. Hietkamp.
Arrived in 1959.

STEVENS, RALPH
DRAYTON, ONT.
 7 photographs: Dutch immigrants on
ship en route to Canada, 1950; and
farming in Peel, and Drayton, 1958.
Taped interview.
 Interviewed on 19 June 1978; 1.5
hrs.; 2 tapes; English; by E.
Hietkamp. Immigrated in 1950.

STEWART, T.
TORONTO, ONT.
 Interviewed on 19 May 1977; 1 hr.;
1 tape; English; by Nancy Jones.
Dutch war bride.

STILETTO, GRETA
THUNDER BAY, ONT.
 Personal diary and papers of Dirk
Nyman, 1924-62 (8 items). Photographs. Taped interview.
 11 photographs: the Nyman family;
and dwellings, and business enterprises in Upsala, 1924-58.
 Interviewed on 19 April 1978; 1 hr.;
1 tape; English; by Henry Kamphof.

ST. NICOLAAS, ARNOLD
TORONTO, ONT.
 Membership book of DUCA Credit
Union. .25 cm. Photograph. Taped
interview.
 1 photograph: a Dutch document,
n.d
Interviewed on 25 March 1977; 1
hr.; 1 tape; English/Dutch; by Mark
Boekelman.

STRYBOSH, JOHN
LONDON, ONT.
 Interviewed on May 3 1979; 2 hrs.;
2 tapes; English; by E. Murphy.
Post-WWII immigrant.

STURKENBOON, WILLIAM
GLENGARRY, ONT.
 Interviewed on 10 July 1977; 1.5
hrs.; 2 tapes; English; by Alan
Haskvitz. Post-WWII immigrant
farmer.

SWANINK, BILL
TORONTO, ONT.
 Newsclippings regarding Dutch
immigrants, and programmmes of
plays performed by *Fama*,
Dutch-Canadian Dramatic Society,
1954-74 (8 items).

TAEKEMA, ALBERT
DRAYTON, ONT.
 Interviewed on 18 April 1978; 1 hr.;
1 tape; English; by E. Hietkamp.
Immigrated to Canada in 1958.

TEKLENBURG, ANTONIUS
SUDBURY, ONT.
 12 photographs: Teklenburg's Sea-
food Restaurant in Sudbury, 1974-80.
Taped interview.
 Interviewed on 13 July 1982; 1.5
hrs.; 2 tapes; English; by G. Schinko.
Post-WWII immigrant.

TEN HAVE, ROELOF
THUNDER BAY, ONT.
 2 family registers and newsclippings,
n.d. .25 cm. Photographs. Taped
interview.
 44 photographs: the Ten Have family
in Holland, and Canada, 1905-63;
and parish and and farming activity at
Fort William (Thunder Bay).
 Interviewed on 7 Oct. 1978; 1 hr.; 1
tape; English/Dutch; by Henry
Kamphof. Post-WWII immigrant.

TIGCELAAR, KLAAS.
WATERDOWN, ONT.
 Newsclippings and telegrams, 1962.
.5 cm. Photographs. Taped interview.
 24 photographs: the Tigchelhaar
family; and farming activity in Holland and Waterdown, 1910-62.
 Interviewed on 15 Jan. 1979; .5 hr.;
1 tape; English; by F. Boonstra. Emigrated in 1930.

TIMMERMANS, THEODORA
LAMBETH, ONT.
 Interviewed on 5 May 1979; 2 hrs.;
2 tapes; English/Dutch; by E.
Murphy. Post-WWII immigrant.

TOMBS, C.
CAMBRIDGE, ONT.
 Interviewed on 6 June 1977; 1 hr.; 1
tape; English; by Nancy Jones. Dutch
war bride.

TORBROEK, MR.
NETHERLANDS
 Wereld Contact. Sept. 1971 - Jan.
1979. 1 reel of microfilm.

TURKSTRA, PETER
BURLINGTON, ONT.
 Interviewed on 17 May 1977; 2 hrs.;

2 tapes; English; by Mark Boekelman. Arrived in Canada in 1927.

TUYL, REV. CARL D.
TORONTO, ONT.
Link. Dec. 1974-May 1977. 1 reel of microfilm.
25th Anniversary of the First Christian Church of Toronto. 1975. 53 pp.

VAN ANKUM, AREND
ALMA, ONT.
 Interviewed on 30 May, 12 June 1978; 2.5 hrs.; 3 tapes; Dutch; by E. Hietkamp. Immediate post-WWII immigrant.

VAN DE LIGT, THEODORUS
BLEZARD VALLEY, ONT.
 Interviewed on June 22 1982; 3 hrs.; 3 tapes; English; by G. Schinko. Immigrated to Canada in 1952.

VAN DEN HAZEL, WIENIK
WALLENSTEIN, ONT.
 Immigration and other personal papers, 1949-50. .25 cm. Photographs. Taped interview.
 19 photographs: the Van Den Hazel family and dwellings in Holland, Alberta, Wallestein, and Fordwich, 1909-76.
 Interviewed on 11 July 1978; 2 hrs.; 2 tapes; English; by E. Hietkamp. Post-WWII immigrant farming family.

VAN DEN HURK, JOSEPH AND HERMIONE
STRATFORD, ONT.
 Interviewed on 18 July 1979; 2 hrs.; 2 tapes; English; by E. Murphy. Immediate post-WWII immigrant.

VAN DER BIJLAARD, GERHARD
BRAMPTON, ONT.
 Immigration documents, c. 1960s. 1 cm (3 items). Photograph. Taped interview.
 1 photograph: donor, n.d.
 Interviewed on 17 March 1977; 1 hr.; 1 tape; English/Dutch; by Mark Boekelman. Post-WWII immigrant.

VAN DER ELST, A.
TORONTO, ONT.
 Interviewed on 17 March 1977; 1 hr.; 1 tape; English/Dutch; by Mark Boekelman. Post-WWII immigrant.

VAN DER EYK, JACOB
TORONTO, ONT.
 Interviewed on 15 April 1977; 1 hr.; 1 tape; English; by Mark Boekelman. Post-WWII immigrant.

VAN DER KNAAP, ADRIAAN
SUDBURY, ONT.
 Interviewed on 9 July 1982; 4 hrs.; 4 tapes; English; by G. Schinko. Post-WWII immigrant.

VAN DER KNAAP, TRUUS
SUDBURY, ONT.
 Interviewed on 30 June 1982; 1 hr.; 1 tape; English; by G. Schinko. Post-WWII immigrant.

VAN DER LEE, ADRIAN
WATERFORD, ONT.
 2 photographs: the Van der Lee family in Holland, and Waterford, n.d. Taped interview.
 Interviewed on 24 Jan 1933; 1 hr.; 1 tape; English; by E. Murphy. Post-WWII immigrant.

VAN DER OECTELAAR, MARINUS
ALEXANDRIA, ONT.
 Interviewed on 17 July 1977; .75

hr.; 1 tape; English; by Alan
Haskvitz. Post-WWII immigrant.

VANDERPOST, JACK AND MARY
PORT DOVER, ONT.
2 photographs: the Vanderpost fam-
ily in British Columbia, and Port
Dover, Ont., n.d. Taped interview.
Interviewed in April 1979; 1 hr.; 1
tape; English; by E. Murphy.
Post-WWII immigrant.

VANDER VECHTE, ANTONIUS AND
ANTONIA
COLLINGWOOD, ONT.
9 photographs: the Vander Vetche
family, 1951-76; and Dutch immi-
grants leaving for Canada, 1951-76.
Taped interview.
Interviewed on 7 March 1979; 2
hrs.; 2 tapes; English; by E. Murphy.
Immigrated to Canada in 1951.

VAN DER WEY, HARRY
THUNDER BAY, ONT.
2 photographs: the Van Der Wey
family, 1930-45.
Interviewed on 9, 19 June 1978; 2
hrs.; 2 tapes; English; by N.
Kamphof.

VAN DERWIELEN, ANTOON
GLENGARRY, ONT.
Interviewed on 13 July 1977; 1 hr.;
1 tape; English; by Alan Haskvitz.
Post-WWII immigrant farming fam-
ily.

VAN DER WOUDEN, CONNIE
HARRISTON, ONT.
4 photographs: Dutch business enterprises, and a rest home in Harriston,
1959-61. Taped interview.
Interviewed on 12 Oct. 1978; 1.5
hrs.; 2 tape; English; by E.
Hietkamp. Post-WWII immigrant.

VAN DONKERSGOED, ELBERT
GORRIE, ONT.
16 photographs: the family, 1951-76;
dwellings, 1951-52; and agricultural
work, 1951-76. Taped interview.
Interviewed on 26 Sept. 1978; 2
hrs.; 2 tapes; Dutch; by E. Hietkamp.
Post-WWII immigrant.

VAN EMPEL, MICHAEL
SUDBURY, ONT.
Interviewed on 12 July 1982; 2 hrs.;
2 tapes; English; by G. Schinko.
Arrived in Canada in 1953.

VAN GALEN, RITA AND RIES
SIMCOE, ONT.
6 photographs: the Van Galen family
in Holland, Germany, and Simcoe,
1953-66. Taped interview.
Interviewed on 1 March 1979; 1 hr.;
1 tape; English; by E. Murphy.
Arrived in Canada in 1966; Roman
Catholic.

VAN HEMERT, JOCOBUS
NEWMARKET, ONT.
Interviewed on 5 May 1977; 1 hr.; 1
tape; English; by Mark Boekelman.
Arrived in Canada in 1947.
Calvinist Contact. 24, 31 July 1972.
Hollandia News. 5, 19 July 1976.

VAN HEZEWIJK, JOHN G.
UNIONVILLE, ONT.
4 postcards of hotels, and taverns in
Gravenhurst, Ont., n.d. Taped inter-
view.
Interviewed on 11 April 1976; 1 hr.;
1 tape; English; by Mark Boekelman.
Arrived in Canada in 1926.

VAN HOREN, PETER
SUDBURY, ONT.
Immigration papers, c. 1950s (8
items). Photographs. Taped interview.

10 photographs: farming on Calumet Island, Quebec, 1952.
Interviewed on 8 June 1982; 1 hr.; 1 tape; English; by G. Schinko. Emigrated in 1951.

VAN KOOTEN, REV. T. C.
LYNDEN, WASHINGTON
Van Kooten, T. C. *Living in a New Country*. Hamilton, 1959. 157 pp.

VAN KUIKEN, REV. J.
AMSTELVEEN, HOLLAND
A collection of pamphlets on the Christian Reformed Church, 1951-74; and passenger lists, memos, and bulletins from various Dutch ships, 1952-53. 9 cm (71 items). Photograph.
1 photograph: donor in Toronto, 1974.

VAN LOON, CORNELIUS
GLENGARRY, ONT.
Interviewed on 7 July 1977; 1 hr.; 1 tape; English; by Alan Haskvitz. Post-WWII immigrant farmer.

VAN PASSEN, PETER AND DORA
PORT DOVER, ONT.
Immigration documents and printed items, 1945-59 (7 items). Photographs. Taped interview.
8 photographs: the Van Passen and Gubbels families, n.d.
Interviewed on 4 Dec. 1978; 1 hr.; 1 tape; English; by E. Murphy. Post-WWII immigrants.

VAN RAADSHOOVEN, WILHELM H.
FALCONBRIDGE, ONT.
Interviewed on 22 June 1982; 2.5 hrs.; 3 tapes; English; by G. Schinko. Immigrated to Canada in 1953.

VAN RAMSHORST, H.
TORONTO, ONT.
Personal documents, family history, and clippings, 1914-73. 2 cm (6 items). Photographs. Taped interview.
25 photographs: family; employment in agriculture; and religious activity at the Dutch Reformed Church in Saskatchewan, n.d.
Interviewed on 21 March 1977; 2 hrs.; 2 tapes; English/Dutch; by Mark Boekelman. Arrived in Canada in 1914.

VAN SETERS, HUGO
TORONTO, ONT.
Immigration documents (photographed), c. 1960s (3 items). Taped interview.
Interviewed on 16 May 1977; 1.5 hrs.; 2 tape; English; by Mark Boekelman. Arrived in Canada in 1924.

VAN SLEEVEN, MARTIN
WILLIAMSTOWN, ONT.
Interviewed on 29 July 1977; .75 hr.; 1 tape; English; by Alan Haskvitz. Post-WWII immigrant farmer.

VAN SPRUNDEL, PIET
SUDBURY, ONT.
Interviewed on 24 June 1982; 1 hr.; 1 tape; English; by G. Schinko. Post-WWII immigrant.

VAN WEZEL, FATHER JAN
DOMMELER, THE NETHERLANDS
Interviewed on 7, 23 Aug. 1979; 3 hrs.; 3 tapes; Dutch; by Henry Van Stekelnburg.

VAN WEZEL, REV. JOHN
DELAWARE, ONT.
Interviewed on 5 Dec. 1978; 2 hrs.;

2 tapes; English; by E. Murphy.
Immediate post-WWII immigrant.

VANZEYL, ALBERT
MISSISSAUGA, ONT.
 Personal documents, c. 1920s (4
items). Photographs. Taped interview.
 11 photographs: employment in agriculture, 1928-29; Dutch immigrants
on board ship en route to Canada,
1928; and Albert Vanzeyl during
military service, 1944; in Holland,
and Georgetown.
 Interviewed on 23 Feb. 1977; 1 hr.;
1 tape; English; by Mark Boekelman.
Arrived in Canada in 1928.

VEENSTRA, REV. JOHN
TORONTO, ONT.
 The collection contains Agenda and
Acts of Synod, 1971-74, and Index of
Synodical Decisions, 1857-72. 3 reels
of microfilm.
 *Mensen in Canada--Over
Ontdekkers, Pioniers en Immigranten.*
Hamilton, 1959. 38 pp.

VERHOEVAN, JOHN
SIMCOE, ONT.
 1 photograph: donor in Haliburton,
1973. Taped interview.
 Interviewed on 5 Jan. 1979; 1 hr.; 1
tape; English; by E. Murphy. Arrived
in Canada 1926.

VERKUILEN, MARTIN
LANCASTER, ONT.
 Interviewed on 22 July 1977; 1 hr.;
1 tape; English; by Alan Haskvitz.
Arrived in 1957.

VERMEY, WILLIAM
TORONTO, ONT.
 8 photographs: the Vermey family,
1944-47; and parish activities at various Dutch Reformed churches in Ger-

many, and Toronto.
 Interviewed on 22 March 1977; 1
hr.; 1 tape; English; by Mark
Boekelman. Arrived in Canada in
1954.

VISSCHER, FRANK
DRAYTON, ONT.
 Personal papers include emigration
documents, family register, speech
and personal notes, and letters,
1949-75; and minutes of the Drayton
Immigration Committee, 1950-60. 2
cm (20 items). Photographs. Taped
interview.
 9 photographs: portraits and dwellings of the Visscher family, 1949-55.
 Interviewed on 9 May 1978; 4 hrs.;
4 tapes; English; by E. Hietkamp.
Arrived in Canada in 1949. *Newsletter of the Christelijke
Emigratie-Centrale.* 1949. 8 pp.
 Pioneer. Vol. 2, no. 23, 1952.

VOS, JAN
DRAYTON, ONT.
 Personal papers, 1947-51. 1 cm (8
items). Photographs. Taped interview.
 11 photographs: the Vos family in
Holland, and Drayton, 1934-39;
employment in agriculture; and Dutch
immigrants en route to Canada.
 Interviewed on 24 April 1978; 1 hr.;
1 tape; Dutch; by E. Hietkamp.
Arrived in 1953.

WAGENAAR, MARTEN
KENORA, ONT.
 Personal documents, 1952-67 (4
items). Photographs. Taped interview.
 13 photographs: the Wagenaar family
in Holland, Manitoba, and Kenora,
1931-36.
 Interviewed on 25 Aug. 1981; 2
hrs.; 2 tapes; English; by Henry
Kamphof. Post-WWII immigrant.

WALRAVE, JOHN
THUNDER BAY, ONT.
8 photographs: dwellings, and farming in Holland, Rosslyn, and Kakabeka Falls, 1951-78. Taped interview.
Interviewed on 21 June 1974; 1.5 hrs.; 2 tapes; English; by Henry Kamphof. Post-WWII immigrant.
Banner. North American publication of the Christian Reformed Church, n.d. (1 issue).

WARK, ROSE
THUNDER BAY, ONT.
17 photographs: family and dwellings of the Sweep and Wark families in Holland, South Gillies, and Thunder Bay, 1918-71. Taped interview.
Interviewed on 19 Oct. 1978; 1 hr.; 1 tape; English; by Henry Kamphof. Post-WWII immigrant.

WELTER, R. P.
THUNDER BAY, ONT.
Interviewed on 5 Sept., 17, 24 Oct. 1979; 2 hrs.; 2 tapes; English; by Henry Kamphof.

WESTERHOF, HARRY
TORONTO, ONT.
Vanguard. Aug./Sept. 1972, Jan. 1971, Feb. 1971, Dec. 1970, May, June, July, Aug. 1977.

WESTRA, MR. AND MRS. ROEL
THUNDER BAY, ONT.
Personal documents, 1939-56. 1 cm (9 items). Photographs. Taped interview.
26 photographs: family and dwellings of Westra family; employment in agriculture; Holland and Ont., 1928-80.
Interviewed on 22 Sept. 1981; 2

hrs.; 2 tapes; in Dutch/English; by Henry Kamphof. Post-WWII immigrant.

WHEELER, LUCY
LAUREL, ONT.
Interviewed on 29 May 1977; 1 hr.; 1 tape; English; by Nancy Jones. Dutch war bride.

WIERZEMA, HENK
TORONTO, ONT.
2 handbooks for new Canadians, 1950, 1954, and bulletin of Second Christian Reformed Church of Toronto, 1958. 2 cm. 7 photographs. Taped interview.
7 photographs: the Wierzma family, 1936-53; and Dutch immigrants en route to Canada, 1952.
Interviewed on 28 March 1977; 1 hr.; 1 tape; English; by Mark Boekelman. Arrived in Canada in 1952.
Calvin Spark. Dec. 1970.
Calvinist Contact. 1976 (4 issues).
Conversation Newsletter. Fall 1976.
De Nederlanse Courant. 1976 (2 issues).
Holland Herald. n.d. (3 issues).
Hollandia News. 6 Dec. 1976.
The Sower. Feb. 1977.

WILLIMS, PETER AND NELLIE
MOUNT BRIDGES, ONT.
1 photograph: family, n.d. Taped interview.
Interviewed on 5 May 1979; 3 hrs.; 3 tapes; English; by E. Murphy. Post-WWII immigrants.

WIMMENHOVE, HENRY
DRAYTON, ONT.
Interviewed on 2 May 1978; 2 hrs.; 2 tapes; English; by E. Hietkamp. Arrived in Canada in 1951.

WISMAN, TOM
KESWICK, ONT.
 Interviewed on 17 May 1977; 1 hr.;
1 tape; English; by Mark Boekelman.
Immigrated to Canada in 1928.

WOODFORD, GLADYS
THUNDER BAY, ONT.
 Autograph book, 1900-06. 1 cm.
Photographs. Taped interview.
 16 photographs: the Klomp family in
Holland, and Thunder Bay; farming,
and business activity, 1908-70.
 Interviewed on 14 Sept. 1978; 1 hr.;
1 tape; English; by Henry Kamphof.
Pre-WWI immigrant family.

WYGERGANGS, JOHANNA
LANCASTER, ONT.
 Interviewed on 22 July 1977; 1 hr.;
1 tape; English; by Alan Haskvitz.

YFF, REV. P. Y.
HAMILTON, ONT.
 Pioneer Christian Monthly. 1951-77.
10 reels of microfilm.

YPMA, GEORGE
THUNDER BAY, ONT.
 13 photographs: the Ypma family,
and farming activity in Port Arthur,
1945-76. Taped interview.
 Interviewed on 25 Feb. 1978; 2 hrs.;
2 tapes; English; by Henry Kamphof.

YPMA, JACOB S.
THUNDER BAY, ONT.
 34 photographs: the Ypma family in
Argentina, Pearl, and Slate River;
Dutch immigrants on board ship en
route to Canada; and farming and
religious activity at Slate River, n.d.
Taped interview.
 Interviewed on 27 Sept. 1978; 1 hr.;
1 tape; Dutch/English; by Henry
Kamphof.

YPMA, LOUIE
THUNDER BAY, ONT.
 Personal documents, 1941-50 (3
items). Photographs. Taped interview.
 8 photographs: the Ypma family in
Holland and Port Arthur, 1954.
Taped interview.
 Interviewed on 21, 25 July 1978; 2
hrs.; 2 tapes; English; by H.
Hietkamp.

ZANTINGE, JOHN
DRAYTON, ONT.
 Personal papers, including immigra-
tion documents, 1946-54 (6 items).
Photographs. Taped interview.
 2 photographs: John Zantinge in
Holland, 1949.
 Interviewed on 6 May 1978; 2 hrs.;
2 tapes; English; by E. Hietkamp.
Post-WWII immigrant.

ZONNENBERG, MARY
TORONTO, ONT.
 1 poem: "Een Emigrant pas in
Canada," n.d. Poem. .25 cm. Photographs. Taped interview.
 11 photographs: the Zonnenberg
family; and dwellings in Toronto,
1951-55.
 Interviewed on 17 March 1977; 1
hr.; 1 tape; English; by Mark
Boekelman. Arrived in Canada in
1951.

ALDERSHOT CHRISTIAN REFORMED
CHURCH
BURLINGTON, ONT.
 Bulletins, 1974-77. 1 reel of micro-
film.

ANCASTER CHRISTIAN REFORMED
CHURCH
ANCASTER, ONT.
*A Quarter Century in a New Land:
Anniversary Booklet of Classis
Hamilton.* 1978. 1 cm.
Newsletter. 1977-78. 2 cm.

ATHENS CHRISTIAN SCHOOL
ATHENS, ONT.
A Christian Alternative in Education.
Brochure.
Newsletter. Jan. 1969-Dec. 1977.
Scattered issues. 1 cm.

BELLEVILLE DISTRICT CHRISTIAN
SCHOOL
BELLEVILLE, ONT.
Records, 1956-77, which include
minutes, constitution, correspondence,
financial statements, newsletters, and
pamphlets. 4 reels of microfilm.

BELVOIR CENTRE SACRED HEART
SEMINARY
DELAWARE, ONT.
Cards and a flyer, n.d. .25 cm.
Photograph.
1 photograph: taken at the Sacred
Heart Seminary, 1954.

BENELUX CLUB
SAULT STE. MARIE, ONT.
Unity and Friendship. Dec. 1972 -
Nov. 1977. Incomplete. 1 reel of
microfilm.

BETHEL CHRISTIAN REFORMED
CHURCH
BROCKVILLE, ONT.
6 photographs: parish activity; and
buildings occupied by congregation,
n.d.
Bonekamp G. *Authority: Behind the
Classroom Door.* Association of
Christian School Administrators.

1973. 26 pp.
Scholland, M. *Children of the Refor-
mation.* 1958. 142 pp.
Voor Litchings Blad. Uitgave de
Christian Reformed Immigration
Society. 1953. 16 pp.
25th Anniversary Booklet. 1975. 20
pp.
*Burlington Christian Reformed
Church Directories.* 1968, 1969. 40
pp.

BETHLEHEM CHRISTIAN REFORMED
CHURCH
THUNDER BAY, ONT.
Bulletins, 1973-77. 1 reel of micro-
film.

BLYTH CHRISTIAN REFORMED
CHURCH
BLYTH, ONT.
Brief history of church, calendars,
and bulletins, 1970-78. 1 cm.
Church Directory. 1972. .25 cm.

BURLINGTON CHRISTIAN REFORMED
CHURCH
BURLINGTON, ONT.
25th Anniversary Booklet. 1978. 40
pp.

CALVARY CHRISTIAN REFORMED
CHURCH
CHATHAM, ONT.
Bulletins, 1975-78. 1 reel of micro-
film.

CALVIN CHRISTIAN REFORMED
CHURCH
DUNDAS, ONT.
Records, 1955-78, which include
constitution, minutes, financial
reports, newsletters, and yearbooks. 4
reels of microfilm.
Anniversary Booklet. 1978. 1 cm.

CALVIN CHRISTIAN REFORMED
CHURCH
OTTAWA, ONT.
*25th Anniversary Booklet of the
C.C.R. Church.* 1978. 1 cm.
Church Yearbooks. 1956, 1958-63,
1965-68. 4 cm.
*One Hundred Years in the New
World.* 1957. 220 pp.

CALVIN CHRISTIAN SCHOOL
DRAYTON, ONT.
Records, 1949-78, which include
constitution, board minutes, financial
statements, correspondence, and
newsclippings. 3 reels of microfilm.
Photographs.
26 photographs: religious and school
activities at Calvin Christian School
and Christian Reformed Church in
Drayton, 1958-75.

CALVIN CHRISTIAN SCHOOL
DRAYTON, ONT.
Recorded on 9 June 1978; 2 hrs.; 2
tapes; English/Dutch; by E.
Hietkamp. Church sermon.

CALVIN CHRISTIAN SCHOOL
DUNDAS, ONT.
Included are policy handbook, commemorative booklet, and bulletins,
1967-69. 1 reel of microfilm. Photographs.
19 photographs: activities at the
Calvin Christian School, 1962-72.

CALVIN COLLEGE (KEITH KNIGHT)
ST. CATHARINES, ONT. & GRAND
RAPIDS, MICHIGAN
Calvinist Contact. 1949-76. 17 reels
of microfilm.

CAMBRIDGE DISTRICT CHRISTIAN
HIGH SCHOOL
WATERLOO, ONT.
Newsletter. 1976-78. 1 cm.

CANADIAN CHRISTIAN EDUCATION
FOUNDATION
BURLINGTON, ONT.
Christian Home and School. Dec.
1977. 32 pp.

CANADIAN REFORMED SCHOOL
SOCIETY
CHATHAM, ONT.
Records, 1950-78. 1 reel of micro-
film. Photographs.
7 photographs: students and staff at
Ebenezer Christian School in
Chatham, 1975.

CAN TRAVEL
MILTON, ONT.
Papers of the Hollanda Canada Club,
c. 1970s. 7 cm (70 items).

CATHOLIC IMMIGRATION SERVICE
TORONTO, ONT.
Correspondence, newsclippings,
pamphlets, and leaflets. 3 cm. Photo-
graphs.
20 photographs: the Peeters and Van
der Steen families, 1959-60; and
Dutch contract farm workers, the
"Young Farmers, " 1967; 7 photo-
graphs: stained glass church windows,
n.d.
*De Nederlandse Emigratie Gezien
Vanuit Canada.* n.d. Typescript. 25
pp.
*Katholiek Hulpboekje voor
Emigranten.* 1957. 50 pp.
Ons Boerenerf. 1954. 48 pp.

CATHOLIC NETHERLANDS ORGANIZ-
ATION
DUNDAS, ONT.
Records, 1945-70, which include
constitution, minutes, correspondence,
financial statements, membership
lists, and miscellaneous papers. 5 cm.
Photographs.
23 photographs: parades, parties and
exhibitions sponsored by the Catholic
Netherlands Organization in Dundas,
and Hamilton, 1959-70.
Alliance News. Sept. 1972, April,
July 1973. 1 cm.
Circuit. 1967-69. Scattered issues. 1
cm.
Compass onder ons. 1960-62. Scat-
tered issues. 2 cm.
*Globe and Mail Reader's Guide for
New Canadians.* n.d. 25 pp.

CHANNEL (BEN VANDERZANDE)
ST. CATHARINES, ONT.
Channel. Oct. 1975-Aug. 1977. 1
cm.
National Union of Christian Schools.
1975-76. Directory. 251 pp.

CHRISTIAN FARMERS' FEDERATION
DRAYTON, ONT.
Records, 1954-77, which include
minutes, constitution, by-laws, financial statements, correspondence, and
pamphlets. 4 cm. 1 reel of microfilm.
Photographs.
Bulletin. 1965-76 (incomplete), June
1969-Dec. 1970. 5 cm.
The Christian Farmer. 1974-75. 2
cm.

CHRISTIAN LABOUR ASSOCIATION OF
CANADA
TORONTO, ONT.
A collection of pamphlets, and
essays commenting on labour and
industrial conflict, 1967-77; and

minutes, 1952-55. 15 cm. 1 reel of
microfilm.

CHRISTIAN REFORMED CHURCH
AYLMER, ONT.
Minutes and correspondence,
1949-52; and bulletins, 1953-78. 3
cm. 2 reels of microfilm. Photograph.
1 photograph: the Christian
Reformed Church in Aylmer, 1968.

CHRISTIAN REFORMED CHURCH
EMO, ONT.
Minutes and financial records,
1959-77. 1 reel of microfilm. Taped
interview.
*25th Anniversary Booklet of Emo
C.R.C.* 1978. 18 pp.

CHRISTIAN REFORMED CHURCH
KITCHENER, ONT.
The collection contains minutes,
financial records, yearbooks,
scrapbooks, bulletins, newsletters,
membership lists, and miscellaneous
paper items, 1972-78. 15 cm. Photograph.
1 photograph: religious ceremony at
Kitchener Reformed Church, n.d.

CHRISTIAN TRADE UNIONS OF
CANADA
HAMILTON, ONT.
De Gids. 1952-57. 1 reel of micro-
film.

COMMITTEE FOR JUSTICE AND LIB-
ERTY
TORONTO, ONT.
Newsletter. Aug. 1972-April 1977. 2
cm.
Political Service Bulletin. 1974-75 (3
issues).

DAMES CONTACT CLUB
TORONTO, ONT.
Included are minutes, constitution, correspondence, annual reports, and membership lists, 1973-77. 1 reel of microfilm.

DRAYTON CHRISTIAN REFORMED CHURCH
DRAYTON, ONT.
Records, 1950-73, which include minutes, correspondence, financial statements, annual reports, membership lists, bulletins, and miscellaneous papers. 9 cm. 2 reels of microfilm. Photographs.
2 photographs: taken at the Christian Reformed Church, 1950.

DUCA CHOIR
TORONTO, ONT.
Scrapbook containing correspondence, programmes, newsclippings, photographs, and posters, 1964-77. 1 reel of microfilm.

DUCA CREDIT UNION OF PETERBOROUGH
PETERBOROUGH, ONT.
Records, 1963-72, which include minutes, correspondence and newsclippings. 8 cm. Photographs.
22 photographs: folk dancing, n.d., and a group at DUCA Credit Union in Peterborough, n.d.
Newsletter. 1963-72. 4 cm.

DUCA CREDIT UNION OF HAMILTON
HAMILTON, ONT.
Minutes, correspondence, annual reports, and newsletters. 1956-77. 2 cm. Photographs.
8 photographs: taken at DUCA Hamilton Credit Union, n.d.; and celebration of St. Nicholas in Hamilton, n.d.

Netherletter. Vol. 1, 1972. 1 reel of microfilm.

DURHAM CHRISTIAN HIGH SCHOOL
BOWMANVILLE, ONT.
Records, 1962-78, include minutes, correspondence, financial statements, membership lists, yearbooks, and booklets. 3 reels of microfilm.

DUTCH BURIAL SOCIETY
THUNDER BAY, ONT.
Regulations and minutes, 1954-78. 2 cm. Photographs. Taped interview.

DUTCH CANADIAN CLUB
KINGSTON, ONT.
Records, 1973-77, include minutes, constitution, correspondence, financial statements, and miscellaneous papers. 1 reel of microfilm. Photographs.
2 photographs: folk dancing at the Dutch Canadian Club, n.d.

DUTCH CANADIAN CREDIT UNION
(BERT KRUITHOF)
TORONTO, ONT.
Programmes and annual report, 1970-74. 2 cm. Photographs.
41 photographs: from the *DUCA Post*, showing folk dancing, theatrical productions, exhibitions, celebrations, and storefronts, 1967-76.
DUCA Post. 1963-76. 2 reels of microfilm.

DUTCH CANADIAN CREDIT UNION
CHATHAM, ONT.
Photograph album and scrapbook, n.d. 1 reel of microfilm.
DUCA Chatham, *25th Anniversary*. 1976. 20 pp.
Newsletter. 1969-77. 1 reel of microfilm.

DUTCH CANADIAN CREDIT UNION
TORONTO, ONT.
Records, 1954-76, which include
minutes, constitution, financial statements, and clippings. 2 reels of
microfilm.

DUTCH CANADIAN CULTURE CLUB
CHATHAM, ONT.
Records, 1955-71, which include
constitution, minutes, correspondence,
financial reports, and miscellaneous
papers. 3 cm. Photograph.
1 photograph: the Dutch Canadian
Culture Club, n.d.

DUTCH CANADIAN FEDERATION
TORONTO, ONT.
Records, 1945-76, which include
minutes, correspondence, financial
statements, and bulletins. 1 reel of
microfilm.

DUTCH CANADIAN SOCIETY OF LON-
DON
LONDON, ONT.
Includes regulations, minutes, correspondence, bulletins, scrapbook, and
clippings, 1961-72. 2 reels of microfilm. Photographs.
2 photographs of Dutch Canadian
Society members, n.d.

DUTCH CREDIT UNION OF OSHAWA
OSHAWA, ONT.
Kenyan, Rod. *To the Credit of the
People.* n.d. 310 pp.
Annual Report. 1963-65, 1967-75. 2
cm.
Insight. Feb., March, May 1977. 33
pp.

DUTCH CULTURAL SOCIETY OF
BRANTFORD
BRANTFORD, ONT.
Constitution and miscellaneous

papers, 1975-77. 1 cm. Photographs.
12 photographs: entertainment organized by the Dutch Cultural Society,
1976-77.
Newsletter. 1976. .25 cm.

DUTCH LADIES' SOCIETY
FORT WILLIAM, ONT.
Minutes, membership list, and pro-
gramme, 1935-55. 1 cm.

DYKEHOPPERS CARNIVAL SOCIETY
LONDON, ONT.
Papers, 1954-76. 2 cm.

FIRST CHRISTIAN REFORMED CHURCH
CHATHAM, ONT.
*50th Anniversary Booklet of the
F.C.R.C. of Chatham.* 1977. 60 pp.

FIRST CHRISTIAN REFORMED CHURCH
OF BARRIE
BARRIE, ONT.
Bulletins, 1966-77. 1 reel of micro-
film.

FIRST CHRISTIAN REFORMED CHURCH
THUNDER BAY, ONT.
Bulletins and financial records,
1957-78. 3 reels of microfilm.

FIRST CHRISTIAN REFORMED CHURCH
THUNDER BAY, ONT.
The collection contains minutes of
Classis Minnesota North, by-laws,
bulletins, treasurer's reports, programmes, and membership lists,
1950-78. 6 reels of microfilm.
*25th Anniversary Booklet of Classis
Minnesota North.* 1975. 79 pp.

FREE REFORMED CHURCH
CHATHAM, ONT.
Included are by-laws of the Canadian
Reformed School Society of Chatham
and District, financial statements, and

miscellaneous items, 1974-78. 4 cm. Photographs.
25th Anniversary of the Reformed Church in Chatham. 1976. 13 pp.
Yearbook of the Free Reformed Church of North America. 1976-78 (2 issues). 102 pp.

FREE REFORMED CHURCH OF NORTH AMERICA
THORNHILL, ONT.
Yearbooks of the Free Reformed Church of North America, 1974-77. 8 cm.

FRIESIAN CULTURE CLUB
JARVIS, ONT.
Photograph albums, and programmes, 1972-78. 1 reel of microfilm.
25th Anniversary of Ebenezer Christian Reformed Church. 1978. 78 pp.

GEZELLIGHEID KENT GEEN TIJD CLUB
TORONTO, ONT.
Correspondence, annual report, and clippings, 1972-77. 1 cm.

GIRLS' CLUB "BLOSSOM"
TORONTO, ONT.
Minutes, and annual reports, 1956-78. 1 reel of microfilm.

GOLDEN TRIANGLE DUTCH CANADIAN CLUB
CAMBRIDGE, ONT.
Included are Club's constitution, minutes, financial records, correspondence, programmes, and bulletins, 1970-78. 2 reels of microfilm.

GRACE CHRISTIAN REFORMED CHURCH
COBOURG, ONT.
Bulletins and newsletters, 1973-76. 1 reel of microfilm.

HAMILTON HOLLAND CLUB
HAMILTON, ONT.
Bulletins, announcements, invitations, and miscellaneous cards. 1975-77. 1 reel of microfilm.
De Nederalndse Courant. 14 Nov. 1974. 12 pp.
Newsletter. Sept. 1975-Aug. 1977. 1 cm.

HOLLAND-CANADA ASSOCIATION (WINDSOR DISTRICT)
WINDSOR, ONT.
Holland Canada Newsletter. 1974-76. Scattered issues. 4 cm.

HOLLAND CANADA CLUB OF GUELPH
GUELPH, ONT.
Records, 1970-77, which include constitution, minutes, correspondence, and bulletins. 1 reel of microfilm.

HOLLAND CANADA CLUB OF MILTON
MILTON, ONT.
Correspondence, financial records, and membership cards, 1973. 6 cm.

HOLLAND CHRISTIAN HOMES INC.
TORONTO, ONT.
Correspondence and brochures. 2 cm.

"HOLLANDSE DAG" (DUTCH DAY)
MOOREFIELD, ONT.
Brief history of annual event and songbook. .25 cm. Photographs.
2 photographs: the celebration of Hollandse Dag, 1978.

9TH "HOLLANDSE DAG" (DUTCH DAY)
MOOREFIELD, ONT.
 Recorded on 14 June 1978; 4 hrs.; 4 tapes; Dutch; by E. Hietkamp. Recording of the day's events, and ceremonies.

IMMANUEL CHRISTIAN REFORMED CHURCH
BRAMPTON, ONT.
 Church bulletins, 1953-73. 2 reels of microfilm.

IMMIGRATION COMMITTEE FOR CANADA OF THE CHRISTIAN REFORMED CHURCH
TORONTO, ONT.
 Included are records of the ICC, the Canadian Netherlands Immigration Council, the ICC-CNIC Young Farmers' Movement, and scattered records of the Aurora and District Chamber of Commerce, 1955-71. 1 meter. Photographs.
 90 photographs: Dutch immigrants work on Canadian farms, "Young Farmers," 1958-69.

JOHN KNOX CHRISTIAN SCHOOL
BRAMPTON, ONT.
 13 photographs: taken at John Knox Christian School in Brampton, 1972-73.
 News Reel. 1973-77. School newsletter. reels of microfilm.

JOHN KNOX CHRISTIAN SCHOOL
BROCKVILLE, ONT.
 25th anniversary booklet. 1977. 10 pp.
 "Christian Education." n.d. 2 pp.

JOHN KNOX MEMORIAL SCHOOL
FRUITLAND, ONT.
 Included are minutes, correspon-

dence, financial statements, and miscellaneous items, 1954-78. 1 reel of microfilm.

KITCHENER-WATERLOO CHRISTIAN SCHOOL SOCIETY
KITCHENER, ONT.
 Minutes and membership list, 1962-74. 1 reel of microfilm.

LASTING FRIENDSHIP GROUP
ALMA, ONT.
 Constitution of club and minutes, 1968-75. 2 cm. Photographs. Taped interview.
 5 photographs: the Christian Reformed Church, Drayton in 1977.
 5th anniversary booklet. 1977. 14 pp.
 Pioneer. March 1977. 32 pp.

LAURENTIAN HILLS CHRISTIAN SCHOOL
KITCHENER, ONT.
 Constitution, minutes, and poster and brochures, 1964-66. 2 cm. 1 reel of microfilm.

LIMBURGSE IMMIGRATIE STICHTING
HEERLEN (LIM), THE NETHERLANDS
 Promotional material, 1970-77. 3 cm.
 Holland: Treasures of Limburg. n.d. 24 pp.

LUS DEO CHOIR AND GIRLS' CLUB "LYDIA"
THUNDER BAY, ONT.
 Minutes, 1952-75. 1 reel of microfilm.

MAPLE LEAF REFORMED CHURCH
TORONTO, ONT.
 11 letters relating to mediatory attempts among Dutch church communities, 1962-68. .25 cm.

MARANATHA CHRISTIAN REFORMED
CHURCH OF BOWMANVILLE
BOWMANVILLE, ONT.
 Records, 1966-78, which include
minutes, financial statements, and
church programmes. 2 reels of microfilm. Photographs.
 8 photographs: religious life at
Maranatha Christian Reformed
Church, including construction of new
building, 1969.

MARANATHA CHRISTIAN REFORMED
CHURCH (REV. J. KOOLE)
CAMBRIDGE, ONT.
 Includes parish registers, bulletins,
and letters. 1 reel of microfilm. Pho-
tographs.
 2 photographs: taken at Marantha
Christian Church, 1972.

MARANATHA CHRISTIAN REFORMED
CHURCH, YORK AND HOLLAND
LADIES' SOCIETY, HOLLAND MEN'S
SOCIETY
CAYUGA, ONT.
 Minutes, 1957-1973. 1 reel of microfilm. Photographs.
 11 photographs: the Elgersma family, 1948-57; and parish activity at
various Christian Reformed churches,
1949-70.
 1976 Directory of Christian Reformed
churches in Hamilton area. 190 pp.
MARANTHA CHRISTIAN REFORMED
CHURCH (B. NYMEYER)
CAMBRIDGE, ONT.
 Announcements, financial reports,
membership list, and church programmes, 1957-58. 2 cm.

MULTICULTURAL NEWSPAPER
MICROFILM PROJECT
TORONTO, ONT.
 Dutch Free Press. 15 July 1954 - 28
Feb. 1968. 4 reels of microfilm.

Hollandia News. 9 Sept. 1954 - 6
June 1986. 13 reels of microfilm.
 De Nederlanse Courant. 9 Jan. 1975
- 15 Dec. 1987. 10 reels of microfilm.

NEDERLANDIA SOCCER CLUB
TORONTO, ONT.
 Records, 1962-67, include constitution, minutes, correspondence, annual
reports, regulations, and membership
lists. 3 reels of microfilm. Photographs.
 6 photographs: the Neerlandia Soccer
Club, and the Toronto Dutch Biljiard
Fan Club in Toronto, 1962-67.

NETHERLANDS CATHOLIC IMMIGRA-
TION SERVICE
OTTAWA, ONT.
 Compass: Onder Ons. 1954-57. 1
reel of microfilm.

NETHERLANDS CENTER CHARITABLE
FOUNDATION INC.
TORONTO, ONT.
 Handwritten statistical survey of
assistance given to Dutch immigrants,
1958-77, and miscellaneous items. 2
cm.
 *Handleiding Voor Nederlandse
Immigranten.* Toronto: Catholic Netherlands Immigrants Service, 1959. 32
pp.

NETHERLANDS CLUB
ST. CATHARINES, ONT.
 10th Anniversary Booklet of Club
Netherlands, 1965-75. 28 pp.
 *Monthly Bulletin of Netherlands
Club.* 1971-77. 1 reel of microfilm.

NETHERLANDS EMIGRATION SERVICE
GRAND RAPIDS, MICHIGAN
 Ganzevoort Collection. Primary

material for research by Herman Ganzevoort, n.d. 20 reels of microfilm.

NETHERLANDS LUNCHEON CLUB
TORONTO, ONT.
 Records, 1964-78, include list of members, annual reports,and circulars. 1 reel of microfilm.
 Toronto Cricket, Skating and Curling Club News Bulletin. April 1971.

ONTARIO ALLIANCE OF CHRISTIAN SCHOOLS
DUNDAS, ONT.
 Records, 1972-77, include minutes, annual reports, financial statements, and miscellaneous items. 1 reel of microfilm.
 Posthumous, K. "Historical Background and Implication." 1977. A typescript history of the Calvinist Dutch in Canada. 1977. 4 pp.

ONTARIO CHRISTIAN TEACHERS' ASSOCIATION
GUELPH, ONT.
 Records, 1967-81, include constitution, financial reports, correspondence, minutes, and brochures and flyers. 4 cm.
 Ontario Alliance of Christian Schools. *Newsletter.* 1966-67. 4 cm.
 Ontario Christian Teachers Association. *Newsletter.* Nov. 1975-June 1977. 1 cm.
 Christian Home and School. Sept. 1977. 31 pp.
 John Calvin Christian School Community Handbooks. 1977. 18 pp.

ONTARIO SOCIETY OF CHRISTIAN SCHOOL ADMINISTRATORS
GEORGETOWN, ONT.
 Records, 1969-77, include constitution, minutes, correspondence, and

memoranda. 1 reel of microfilm.
 Newsletter. 1971-73. Scattered issues.

PATMOS GALLERY
TORONTO, ONT.
 Newsclippings, leaflets, flyers, and press releases, 1973. 1 cm.
 Bulletin. 1972-73. 1 cm.
 Institute for Christian Art. n.d. Pamphlet.
 Patmos Quarterly Bulletin. 1969-76. 1 cm.

PRO REGE PUBLISHING COMPANY
TORONTO, ONT.
 Records, 1958-77. 1 reel of microfilm.

QUINTE COMMUNITY CREDIT UNION
BLOOMFIELD, ONT.
 Minutes, annual reports, and provincial charter, 1960-77. 2 cm. Photographs.

REHOBOTH CHRISTIAN REFORMED CHURCH
BOWMANVILLE, ONT.
 Records, 1950-78, include annual reports, minutes, and a weekly church bulletin. 3 reels of microfilm. Photographs.
 2 photographs: taken at Rehoboth Christian Reformed Church, n.d.
 25th Anniversary Directory of Rehoboth Church. 1974. 36 pp.

ROYAL NETHERLANDS EMBASSY
TORONTO, ONT.
 2 emigration manuals, n.d. 1 reel of microfilm.
 Van Banning, C. "Statistical Report on Dutch in Canada." n.d. Typescript.
 "Reiswijzer voor Emigranten Naar Canada." n.d. Typescript.

Elders: maandblad over emigratie.
Nos. 4-12. 1978. 2 cm.

SACRED HEART FATHERS, ST.
PATRICK'S RECTORY
CALEDONIA, ONT.
Letters and manuscript by Rev. G.
Wubbels on immigration to Canada,
1975-77. 2 cm.

ST. WILLIBROD CREDIT UNION
LONDON, ONT.
Records, 1965-76, include constitution and by-laws, correspondence,
financial reports, and miscellaneous
printed items. 1 reel of microfilm.
25 Years of Service, 1950-75. 1 cm.
Bulletin. July 1974, June 1975, Sept.
and Oct. 1976. .5 cm.
News Reports. Dec. 1976, March
1977. .5 cm.
Success. May 1976. .25 cm.

THE ASSOCIATION FOR THE
ADVANCEMENT OF CHRISTIAN
SCHOLARSHIP
TORONTO, ONT.
Curriculum, pamphlets, books, and
announcements. 10 cm.
ICS Update. Spring 1977. .25 cm.
Perspective. Dec. 1967-77. 5 cm.
Christian Reformed Church
yearbooks. 1975, 1976. 4 cm.

THE INSTITUTE OF CHRISTIAN
STUDIES
TORONTO, ONT.
Papers, n.d. 1 cm.

THE NETHERLANDS FOLKLORE
GROUP
TORONTO, ONT.
Scrapbooks, 1963-74. 1 reel of
microfilm.

THUNDER BAY CHRISTIAN SCHOOL
ASSOCIATION
THUNDER BAY, ONT.
Minutes, letters, and financial state-
ments, 1951-68. 1 reel of microfilm.

TIMOTHY CHRISTIAN SCHOOL
BARRIE, ONT.
Collection contains constitution,
financial reports, memoranda, and
miscellaneous printed items. 18 cm.
Photographs.
6 photographs: Timothy Christian
School building under construction,
1962-65.
Christian Home and School.
1964-72. Scattered issues. 6 cm.
*First Christian Reformed Church of
Barrie Bulletin.* 16 April 1961. 10
pp.
The Christian School Herald.
1961-70. Scattered issues, 6 cm.
The Voice of the School. 1961-69.
Scattered issues. 2 cm.
Timothy Christian School Bulletin.
n.d. 2 cm.

TORONTO-AMSTERDAM TWIN CITIES
ASSOCIATION
TORONTO, ONT.
Records, 1976-78, include minutes,
constitution, newsletters, and mem-
bership lists. 1 reel of microfilm.

TORONTO DISTRICT CHRISTIAN
HIGHSCHOOL
WOODBRIDGE, ONT.
Constitution and by-laws, and bull-
etins. 3 cm.

TRENTON CHRISTIAN SCHOOL
TRENTON, ONT.
Records, 1953-78, include
scrapbooks, minutes, constitution,
correspondence, and newsletters. 4
reels of microfilm.

TRINITY CHRISTIAN SCHOOL
BURLINGTON, ONT.
 Records, 1954-77, include minutes, correspondence, scrapbook, and miscellaneous items. 2 reels of microfilm. Photographs.
 10 photographs: children, classrooms, and sports at Trinity Christian School, 1976-77.
 Three in One: the Trinity Newsletter. 1963-78. Scattered issues.

WEDGE PUBLISHING FOUNDATION
TORONTO, ONT.
 Vanguard. 1970-77. Scattered issues. 10 cm.

YOUNG PEOPLE OF YESTERDAY
(JONGEREN VAN VROEGER)
LONDON, ONT.
 2 books of minutes, 1971-76. 2.5 cm. Photographs.
 9 photographs: activities at the Senior Citizens' Club in London, n.d.

ESTONIAN COLLECTION

GRIMM, WOLDEMAR
TORONTO, ONT.
 Interviewed on 16, 21 April 1978;
5.5 hrs.; 6 tapes; Estonian; by Endel
Aruja. Post-WWII immigrant.

KOLLMAN, ROMAN A.
DETROIT, MICHIGAN
 Scrapbook, c. 1940s. 1 reel of
microfilm.
 Linnutee. n.d. Microfilm.
 Loomine. n.d. Microfilm.
 Sissejuhatuseks. n.d. Microfilm.

LINKRUS, JAAN
TORONTO, ONT.
 Passenger list of ship crossing, n.d.
.25 cm. Photograph. Taped interview.
 1 photograph: the *S.S. Victory*,
which brought Estonian immigrants to
North America, 1949.
 Interviewed on 2 Aug. 1978; 6 hrs.;
6 tapes; Estonian; by Endel Aruja.
Post-WWII Immigrant.

MARTIN, JAAN
LINDSAY, ONT.
 Personal papers, n.d. 2 cm. Photo-
graphs.
 23 photographs: the Martin family in
Estonia and Ont.; and traditional
Estonian dress, 1924-76.

MATKAR, ATSO
SUDBURY, ONT.
 Self–interview of 24 Feb. 1978; 12.5
hrs.; 13 tapes; Estonian.

NELBERG, AGU
TORONTO, ONT.
 Personal papers, 1963-75. 14 cm.
Photographs.
 13 photographs: family and friends,
1959-75.

OLBREI, RAHEL
TORONTO, ONT.
 Interviewed on 27 March, 9 April
1980; 6 hrs.; 6 tapes; Estonian; by
Endel Aruja. Post-WWII immigrant.

PAAS, OSKAR
TORONTO, ONT.
 Interviewed on 23 Jan., 3 Feb. 1978;
3 hrs.; 3 tapes; by Endel Aruja.
Post-WWII immigrant.

PAAS, PRIIT
TORONTO, ONT.
 Personal papers, c. 1940s. 1 cm.
Photographs. Taped interview.
 19 photographs: 1915-77;
the Estonian Women's Society of
Toronto, 1973.
 Interviewed on 25 Aug., 6 Sept., 17
Nov. 1977; 6 hrs.; 6 tapes; Estonian;
by Endel Aruja.

SCHÖNBERG, ARTHUR
TORONTO, ONT.
 Personal papers, n.d. 2 cm. Taped
interview.
 Interviewed on 11 July 1978; 3 hrs.;
3 tapes; Estonian; by Endel Aruja.
Post-WWII immigrant.

TORK, JUHAN
TORONTO, ONT.
Personal papers, 1958-70. 1 cm.
Photograph. Taped interview.
1 photograph: Juhan Tork and his
wife, 1977.
Interviewed on 24 Oct. 1977-17 July
1978; 17 hrs.; 17 tapes; Estonian; by
Endel Aruja.

ESTONIAN SUMMER CAMP SOCIETY
(CAMP SEEDRIORU)
ELORA, ONT.
Seedrioru, 1955-80. 1980. 141 pp.

MULTICULTURAL HISTORY SOCIETY
OF ONTARIO
TORONTO, ONT.
Kareda, Endel. *East and West.* 1947.
Estonia. New York: Estonian-Ameri-
can National Council, n.d. Pamphlet.
Estonian Bibliography. 1 cm.

MULTICULTURAL NEWSPAPER
MICROFILM PROJECT
TORONTO, ONT.
Meie Elu. 7 Jan. 1977-31 Dec. 1987
(weekly). 9 reels of microfilm.
Vaba Eestlane. Toronto, 6 Jan.
1977-30 Dec. 1987 (semi–weekly). 16
reels of microfilm.

ST. JAMES ESTONIAN CHURCH (REV.
T. NÕMMIK)
TORONTO, ONT.
Church announcements, pro-
grammes, and Psalm readings,
1976-77. 1 cm.
*20th Anniversary Booklet of the
Swedish Lutheran Church Toronto.*
1953-73. 23 pp.
Newsletter. 1977 (5 issues).

ACOSTA, TERESA T.
TORONTO, ONT.
 Interviewed on 15 Aug. 1979; 1 hr.;
1 tape; English; by G. P. Espinosa.
Post-WWII immigrant.

ARENA, EULOGIO
TORONTO, ONT.
 Interviewed on 30 Aug. 1979; 1.5
hrs.; 2 tapes; English; by G. P.
Espinosa. Discusses the Folklorico
Dance Troupe.

BELEN, SEVERO
TORONTO, ONT.
 Interviewed on 29 June 1980; 1 hr.;
1 tape; English; by R. E. Bustamante.
Discusses Silayon Drop-in, and
Filipino integration.

BILLIONES, MARIO
TORONTO, ONT.
 Interviewed on 22 Feb., March
1980; 1.5 hrs.; 2 tapes; English; by
G. P. Espinosa. Discusses the history
of the club Circulo Ilongo.

BUSTAMANTE, ROSALINA E.
TORONTO, ONT.
 15 photographs: Filipino dishes and
costumes, n.d.

CAJILIG, ANGEL G.
TORONTO, ONT.
 Interviewed on 10 March 1980; 1.5
hrs.; 2 tapes; English; by G. P.
Espinosa. Discusses the activities of
the club Circulo Ilongo.

CASTILLO, JULIE
TORONTO, ONT.
 Interviewed on 4 July 1980; 1 hr.; 1
tape; English; by R. E. Bustamante.
Discusses the history of the Filipino
Parents' Association.

DE COSTRO, NORMA
TORONTO, ONT.
 Interviewed in June 1980; 1 hr.; 1
tape; English; by R. E. Bustamante.
One of the earliest members of the
Filipino group in Toronto.

DE GUZMAN, BABY
TORONTO, ONT.
 Interviewed on 16 April 1980; 1 hr.;
1 tape; English; by R. E. Bustamante.
Television producers of Filipino cul-
tural programmes in Toronto.

FARROL, CECILIA AND BERNARDO
TORONTO, ONT.
 9 photographs: the Farrol family;
and store fronts in Toronto, 1965-80.
Taped interview.
 Interviewed on 15 June 1980; 1.5
hrs.; 2 tapes; English; by R. E.
Bustamante. Arrived in Canada in late
the 1950s.

FERNANDEZ, FREDERICO
(PHILIPPINE TRADE COMMISSIONER)
TORONTO, ONT.
n of pamphlets, and two albums of
photographs on Philippine exports to
Canada. 1970s. 5 cm.
 23 photographs: Philippine Trade
Commission, exhibition of Filipino
products in Toronto, 1979.

GUARIN, FERNANDO M.
TORONTO, ONT.
on 30 Aug. 1979; 1.5 hrs.; 2 tapes;
English; by G. P. Espinosa. Dancer
in Folklorico ensemble.

HALILI, LELICIA
TORONTO, ONT.
2 photographs: Filipino children in a
heritage class Christmas celebration,
n.d. Taped interview.
Interviewed on 28 July 1980; 1 hr.;
1 tape; English; by R. E. Bustamante.
Discusses Filipino heritage classes.

HERNANDEZ, CECILIA E.
TORONTO, ONT.
Interviewed on 15, 16 Aug. 1979; 1
hr.; 1 tape; English; by G. P.
Espinosa. Dancer in Folklorico
ensemble.

JAVIER, EMILIA
TORONTO, ONT.
Interviewed on 18 June 1980; .5 hr.;
1 tape; English; by R. E. Bustamante.
Discusses the Pillars-Silayan Drop-In.

JEW, TACIANA
MISSISSAUGA, ONT.
Interviewed on 28 Aug. 1980; 1 hr.;
1 tape; English; by R. E. Bustamante.
Discusses Filipino costumes and cul-
tural values.

NABOR, DORIS AND GRACE
TORONTO, ONT.
Interviewed on 27 July 1980; .5 hr.;
1 tape; English; by R. E. Bustamante.
Discusses the Block Rosary brought
to Canada from the Philippines.

PALOMERA, PETER V.
TORONTO, ONT.
Interviewed on 30 Aug. 1979; 1.5
hrs.; 2 tapes; English; by

G. P. Espinosa. Discusses the
Folklorico Dance Troupe.

RENOUF, ALLAN
TORONTO, ONT.
Interviewed on 28 Aug. 1979; 1 hr.;
1 tape; English; by G. P. Espinosa.
Discusses the Folklorico Dance
Troupe.

ROJO, OSCAR
TORONTO, ONT.
Articles of incorporation, agenda of
meetings, statement of objectives,
correspondence, and miscellaneous
printed items, 1977-80. 2 cm.
The Recorder. Jan. 1978 - March
1980. A Filipino-Canadian newspaper. 1 cm.

VALENCIA, FATHER THADDEUS
TORONTO, ONT.
Interviewed on 5 July 1980; 1 hr.; 1
tape; English; by R. E. Bustamente.
Discusses his involvement in associations, problems of early Filipino
immigrants, and North American
conceptions of Filipinos.

=====

BLOCK ROSARY (ROSE OCAMPO)
TORONTO, ONT.
Recording of religious group proceedings of 24 July 1980; .5 hr.; 1
tape; English; by R. E. Bustamante.

CIRCULO ILONGO (A. CAJILIG)
TORONTO, ONT.
This collection, 1974-80, includes a
constitution, by-laws, minutes, files
of letters, financial statements,
reports, membership lists, flyers,
invitations, and programmes. 9.5 cm.
Photographs. Taped interview.
7 photographs: Circulo Ilongo activ-

ities in Toronto, 1975-80.
10th Anniversary Programme. 1979.
14 pp.
Philippine Cultural Show Programme. 1977-79 (3 issues).

FILIPINO PARENTS' ASSOCIATION OF
METRO TORONTO
TORONTO, ONT.
Constitution, 1980. .25 cm. See Julie
Castillo.

FILIPNESCA TV VARIETY SHOW
TORONTO, ONT.
Programme information, 1979. .25
cm.

FOLKLORICO FILIPINO CANADA
TORONTO, ONT.
The collection, 1974-79, contains a
constitution, minutes, correspondence,
contracts, performance applications,
repertoires, membership lists, clippings, and a guide and historical
sketch of the various dances performed by the Folklorico ensemble. 5
cm. See also, Peter Palomera. Photographs.
27 photographs: folk dancing
perfomances, n.d.
Anniversary Booklet of Folklorico.
1979. 1 cm.
Philippines. 1979. .25 cm.
The Filipino Santacruzan Programme. 1978. .25 cm.

FOLKLORICO FILIPINO OF CANADA
(PETER PALOMERA)
TORONTO, ONT.
Recorded in July 1979; 6 hrs.; 6
tapes; Filipino; by G. P. Espinosa.
Filipino folk music.

KABABAYAN COMMUNITY SERVICE
CENTRE
TORONTO, ONT.
Includes a constitution, minutes, brochure, and a list of Board members,
1977-80. 3 cm. See Taciana Jew.

MULTICULTURAL NEWSPAPER
MICROFILM PROJECT
TORONTO, ONT.
Atin Ito. Toronto, Dec. 1976 - May
1980. 2 reels of microfilm.

SILAYON FILIPINO COMMUNITY
CENTRE
TORONTO, ONT.
Constitution, programme, and annual
report, 1971-80. 3 cm. Photographs.
See B. Severo.
14 photographs: annual
"Santacruzon" celebrations; and activities of Silayon, n.d.
Silahis. Vol. 1, Dec. 1975; vol. 5,
1980. 4 cm.

AHVENNIEMI, EERO
SUDBURY, ONT.
 Interviewed on 21 Nov. 1977; .5
hr.; 1 tape; Finnish; by A. Lahtinen.
Immigrated to Canada in 1952.

AHVENNIEMI, KAARINA
SUDBURY, ONT.
 Interviewed on 21 Nov. 1977; .25
hr.; 1 tape; Finnish; by A. Lahtinen.
Immigrated to Canada in 1952.

ÄIJÖ, SULO AND AINO
N.A.
 Interviewed on 18 March 1983; 2.5
hrs.; 3 tapes; Finnish; by K.
Lindström.

ÅKERVALL, HENRY
THUNDER BAY, ONT.
 Interviewed in 1976; .5 hr.; 1 tape;
English; by J. Päiväläinen. A former
professional hockey player and coach.

ALA, MR. AND MRS.
THUNDER BAY, ONT.
 Interviewed on 23 June
1976; .5 hr.; 1 tape; English; by R.
Puiras. Discusses their involvement
with the Kuhnus Athletic Club in
Nipigon, Ont. in the 1920s.

ALANEN, W. AND N. MÄKI
THUNDER BAY, ONT.
 Interviewed on July 1976; .5 hr.; 1
tape; English; by J. Päiväläinen. Discusses their involvement with the
Ponteva Club in Nolalu, Ont. in the
1930s.

ALANEN, WILHO
THUNDER BAY, ONT.
 Interviewed on 10 April 1979; .75
hr.; 1 tape; English; by H. Doherty.
Born in Port Arthur, Ont., involved
the in Bushworkers' Union movement.

ALOPAEUS, JORMA
SAULT STE. MARIE, ONT.
 2 Finnish passports, 1929, 1944, and
3 family tree documents, n.d. 1 cm.
Photographs. Taped interview.
 14 photographs: the Alopaeus family
in Finland, Lapland, and Sault Ste.
Marie, 1910-77.
 Interviewed on 16 Oct. 1980; 1 hr.;
1 tape; Finnish; by H. Vuorimies.
Immigrated to Canada in 1949.

ANDERSON, GEORGE A.
THUNDER BAY, ONT.
 Interviewed on 13 Aug. 1981; 1 hr.;
1 tape; English; by A. Tolvanen. Dis-
cusses his early life in Port Arthur,
Ont., in the 1920s.

ANDERSON, HELEN
THUNDER BAY, ONT.
 Interviewed in Jan. 1978; 1 hr.; 1
tape; English; by C. Budner. Discusses life in Port Arthur at the turn
of the century.

ANDERSON (TYRVÄNEN), YRJÖ A.
THUNDER BAY, ONT.
 Interviewed on 13 Aug. 1981; 1 hr.;
1 tape; Finnish; by A. Tolvanen. Discusses Old World experiences.

ANTTILA, HENRY
THUNDER BAY, ONT.
Collection of Finnish songs (words and music), 1937-52. 1 cm (22 items). Photographs. Taped interview. 3 photographs: a choir; and stores in Fort William, 1937.
Interviewed on 28 April 1979; 1 hr.; 1 tape; Finnish; by R. Nieminen. Immigrated to Canada in 1923, was member of the L.W.I.U.

ANTTILA, WILHO
THUNDER BAY, ONT.
Interviewed in July 1976; .75 hr.; 1 tape; English; by Tuija Puiras. Discusses Finnish sports in the 1920s.

BECK, ARNOLD
THUNDER BAY, ONT.
Interviewed in Sept. 1978, May 1979; 2 hrs.; 2 tapes; English; by E. Nordström. Active in the northwestern Ont. Finnish socialist movement in the 1920s.

BERGLUND, WILLIAM
THUNDER BAY, ONT.
Interviewed on 23 March 1979; .75 hr.; 1 tape; English; by H. Doherty. Immigrated to Canada in 1922.

BERTILS, AINO
SOUTH PORCUPINE, ONT.
Interviewed on 19 July 1977; 1 hr.; 1 tape; Finnish; by Lennard Sillanpaa.

DARCIS, IRENE
THUNDER BAY, ONT.
Interviewed in 1976, re-recorded on 26 Aug. 1982; .25 hr.; 1 tape; by C. Budner. Discusses Finnish-Canadian athletics.

DUSTIN, ELVIRA
THUNDER BAY, ONT.
Interviewed on 29 Dec. 1976; .25 hr.; 1 tape; English; by Tuija Puiras. Discusses her career in bowling.

EILOMAA, LAURA AND TAISTO
SUDBURY, ONT.
Interviewed on 30 Oct., 28 Dec. 1977; 1 hr.; 1 tape; Finnish; by A. Lahtinen.

EKLUND, W. AND E. SUKSI
SUDBURY, ONT.
Interviewed on 9 May 1980; 2.5 hrs.; 3 tapes; English; by V. Lindström, and Ian Radforth. Editor of *Vapaus*, and union organizer.

EKLUND, WILLIAM
SUDBURY, ONT.
Interviewed on 3 Sept. 1977; 2 hrs.; 2 tapes; English; by Lennard Sillanpaa. Former editor of *Vapaus*, and union organizer.

ERICKSON, MARY
NOLALU, ONT.
Interviewed on 31 May 1979; .5 hr.; 1 tape; Finnish; by R. Nieminen and H. Doherty. Immigrated to Canada in 1911.

FINNILÄ, MRS. I
SUDBURY, ONT.
See Elinä Sytelä.

FISKAR, CARL
THUNDER BAY, ONT.
Interviewed on 18 July 1976; .5 hr.; 1 tape; English; by J. Päiväläinen. Discusses his hockey career.

FLINK, NIKOLAI AND EMMA
TORONTO, ONT.
Interviewed on 13 June 1978; 1.25

hrs.; 2 tapes; Finnish; by V.
Lindström. Immigrated to Canada in
1904.

FREEMAN, MEERI
SUDBURY, ONT.
Interviewed on 15 Dec. 1977; .5 hr.;
1 tape; Finnish; by A. Lahtinen.
Immigrated to Canada in 1926.

GRENON, HELEN
SUDBURY, ONT.
14 photographs: theatrical productions in Sudbury, 1938-57. Taped
interview.
Interviewed on 20 Dec. 1977; .75
hr.; 1 tape; English; by Lennard
Sillanpaa. Discusses early life in
lumber camps and mines.

GREUS, ESTER
SAULT STE. MARIE, ONT.
Letter regarding the Finnish Pente-
costal Mission Building Fund in
Sudbury. .25 cm. Photographs. Taped
interview.
15 photographs: Ester Greus in Fin-
land, Toronto, and India, 1926-78.
Interviewed on 5 Feb. 1981; 1 hr.; 1
tape; Finnish; by H. Vuorimies.
Arrived in Canada in 1926.
Greus, E. *Indiasta Palmumaasta.*
1946. 56 pp..
Maailmanääret. 1980. 67 pp.
Todistaja. Vol. 55, no. 9, 1980. 35
pp.

GROENBERG, PAULA
TORONTO, ONT.
Aaltio, Tauri. "Finnish Immigra-
tion." 1979. 3 pp.
Karni, M.G., *et al.*, eds. *Migration
Studies C3: The Finnish Experience in
the Western Great Lakes Region.*
Turku: 1975. 234 pp.
Virtanen, Keijo. "Ameriikkalainen

Kulttuuri ja sen Leviäminen
Eurooppaan." n.d. 26 pp.
Vapaa Sana. Dec. 1976 - May 1977
(39 issues).

GRÖNROOS, GERTIE
THUNDER BAY, ONT.
Interviewed on 9 Aug. 1982, and
re-recorded; .75 hr.; 1 tape; English;
by H. Doherty. Born in Port Arthur,
Ont. in 1917.

GUSTAFSON, GUNNAR
TORONTO, ONT.
Interviewed on 11 June 1980; 1.5
hrs.; 2 tapes; Finnish; by R.
Hammaren. Immigrated to Canada in
1927.

GUSTAFSON, GUNNAR AND AINO
BURLINGTON, ONT.
Newsclippings, articles, and programmes about the Finnish Organization of Canada musical activities;
and 4 festival ribbons, 1957-77. 4 cm
(27 items). Photographs. Taped interview.
42 photographs: FOC (Finnish
Organization of Canada) musical and
theatrical activities in Sudbury and
Toronto, 1948-56.
Interviewed on 30 Aug. 1978; 2.5
hrs.; 3 tapes; English; by V.
Lindström. Immigrated in 1927.

HAAPALA-TUURI, TOIVO J.
THUNDER BAY, ONT.
Interviewed on 22 July 1981; 1 hr.;
1 tape; Finnish/English; by A.
Tolvanen. Immigrated to Canada in
1929.

HAKOLA, ELLI AND EERO
TIMMINS, ONT.
12 photographs: entertainment at the
Finnish Song Festival, including folk

dancing and gymnastics in Timmins, 1950; and employment in the lumber industry in Timmins, Cochrane, Grassy River, 1925-44. Taped interview.
Interviewed on 14 July 1977; 1.5 hrs.; 3 tapes; Finnish; by Lennard Sillanpaa. Discusses the Finnish Lutheran Church.

HALL, ALFREDA
TORONTO, ONT.
Rissanen, Esther. *Use My Skis, Lord!* 1977. The story of Esther Rissanen, a Baptist Missionary to the Finnish settlers at the Lakehead, 1939-75. 63 pp.
The Link and Visitor. Vol. L, no. 10, Dec. 1977. Baptist Women's Missionary Society of Ontario and Quebec. 15 pp.

HALONEN, HILJA
SAULT STE. MARIE, ONT.
15 photographs: the Halonen family in Finland, and Thunder Bay, 1923-57. Taped interview.
Interviewed on 20 Jan. 1981; 1 hr.; 1 tape; Finnish; by H. Vuorimies. Discusses boarding house activity.

HALONEN, JORMA
THUNDER BAY, ONT.
List of newspapers, periodicals, pamphlets, and books, 1905-74, and 66 articles on labour conditions and struggles in northwestern Ont.
Daily News. Port Arthur, Ont. 30 April 1906 - 22 May 1914. 24 articles about Harry Bryan, a prominent labour leader.
Daily News. 1908-11.
News Chronicle. 1943. 3 obituaries of Oscar Sundin.
News Chronicle. 1937. 20 articles and ads of Thunder Bay

co-operatives.
News Chronicle. 1951-58. Documentation on the Pike Lake Study Circle. 12 cm.
Remember When. 1978. Bay-Secord residents' newsletter. 2 pp.
Times Journal. 1902-08.

HANNI, MATTI
THUNDER BAY, ONT.
Interviewed on 8 March 1979; .5 hr.; 1 tape; Finnish; by R. Nieminen.

HANNI, MATTI
THUNDER BAY, ONT.
Interviewed on 24 July 1978; 1 hr.; 1 tape; Finnish; by Satu Repo. Immigrated to Canada in 1926.

HARD, RAIMO
SUDBURY, ONT.
Interviewed on 5 April 1978; 1 hr.; 1 tape; Finnish; by V. Lindström. Arrived in Canada in 1951.

HARD, RAIMO
SUDBURY, ONT.
Interviewed on 5 April 1978; 1 hr.; 1 tape; Finnish; by A. Lahtinen. Immigrated to Canada 1951.

HARJU, MIINI
ST. CATHARINES, ONT.
1 passport, 1930, and a socialist Christmas card. .25 cm. Photographs. Taped interview.
13 photographs: military service during the Finnish Civil War, 1917-20; and Finnish social gatherings in Ont., 1930-43.
Interviewed on 14 Sept. 1978; 2 hrs.; 2 tapes; Finnish; by V. Lindström. Immigrated to Canada in 1930.

HARJU, UUNO
ST. CATHARINES, ONT.
Passports, programmes, books, clippings, and certificates, 1921-71. 2 cm. Photographs. Taped interview.
9 photographs: the Harju family, including sports activity in Finland, and Canada, 1923-32.
Interviewed on 14 Sept. 1978; 1 hr.; 1 tape; Finnish; by V. Lindström. Arrived in Canada in 1927.
Davies, Joseph E. *Mission to Moscow*. New York, 1941. 494 pp.
Jääskeläinen, Kaapro. *Iloisia Juttuja* (Funny Stories). Sudbury: Vapaus, 1951. 175 pp.
Lindewall, Arvo. *Suomesta Hawaiin* (From Finland to Hawaii). Sudbury: Vapaus, 1941. 173 pp.
Minz, I. *The Army of the Soviet Union*. Moscow: Foreign Language Pub., 1942. 172 pp.
Ruissalo, Annie. *Päivälahden Tarina* (The Story of Päivälahti). Sudbury: Vapaus, 1943. 120 pp.
_____. *Sisarukset*. Sudbury: Vapaus, 1945. 164 pp.
Voyetekhov, Boris. *Sevastopolin Viime Päivät* (The Last Days of Sevastopol). Superior, Wisconsin: Työväen Lehtiliikkeiden Kustannuskomitea, 1943. 176 pp.

HENDRIKSON, I.
THUNDER BAY, ONT.
Papers on Intola School, 1910-60. 1 cm. Photographs. Taped interview.
RESTRICTED
5 photographs: Intola School, c. 1926-27.
Interviewed in Summer 1974; .5 hr.; 1 tape; Finnish; by M. Metsäranta. Discusses his work experiences in the bush camps.

HERNESHUHTA, VIRMA
THUNDER BAY, ONT.
Interviewed on 1978; 2 hrs.; 2 tapes; English; by C. Budner. Discusses her father's writing career.

HIETALAHTI, TOIVO AND SALMINEN KAUKO
TIMMINS, ONT.
Interviewed on 11 July 1977; 2 hrs.; 2 tapes; Finnish; by Lennard Sillanpaa.

HIETANEN, HANNU
SOUTH PORCUPINE, ONT.
Interview on 15 July 1977; 1 hr.; 1 tape; Finnish; by Lennard Sillanpaa. Immigrated to Canada in 1927.

HIETAPAKKA, ARVO JOEL
THUNDER BAY, ONT.
23 photographs: work in farming, logging, construction, and mining at Onion Lake, Tarmola, Gorham, Port Arthur, and Cobalt, 1912-47. Taped interview.
Interviewed on 23 July 1981; .75 hr.; 1 tape; Finnish/English; by A. Tolvanen. Grew up in Port Arthur, father immigrated to Canada in 1907.

HILL, A. T.
THUNDER BAY, ONT.
Interviewed in 1974; 1 hr.; 1 tape; English; by A. Tolvanen. Active member of the Finnish Socialist Organization, organizer of the Bushworkers' Union.

HIRVI, ANTTI
SUDBURY, ONT.
1 photograph: the donor in Sudbury, 1978. Taped interview.
Interviewed on 28 March 1978; 1 hr.; 1 tape; Finnish; by A. Lahtinen. Immigrated to Canada in 1927.

HIRVI, TYYNE
SUDBURY, ONT.
1 photograph: Tynne Hirvi in
Sudbury, 1978. Taped interview.
Interviewed on 28 March 1978; .25
hr.; 1 tape; Finnish; by A. Lahtinen.
Born in Whitefish, Ont. in 1921.

HIRVONEN, PENTTI AND P. JUNNI
THUNDER BAY, ONT.
Interviewed on 24 April 1980; 1.5
hrs.; 2 tapes; Finnish; by R.
Hammaren. Discusses the activities of
the Finnish male choir.

HJORTH, JENNY AND LENNART
TORONTO, ONT.
2 scrapbooks including clippings,
sheet music, poems, personal papers,
and lists of F.O.C. plays and casts,
1924-71. 5.5 cm. Photographs. Taped
interview.
350 photographs: Finnish theatre
groups, orchestras, and family gatherings in Ont. and Finland, 1903-30.
Interviewed on 13 June 1978; 1 hr.;
1 tape; Finnish; by V. Lindström.
Immigrated to Canada in the late
1920s.

HOLLI, MATTI
WINDSOR, ONT.
Scrapbook, 1943–59, and music programmes, biographical sketch, and
clippings, 1954–80. 2 cm. 1 reel of
microfilm. Photographs.
4 photographs: Matti Holli conduct-
ing a symphony orchestra in Windsor,
1949-76.

HOLMA, HILDA
TORONTO, ONT.
Immigration papers, 1928, and ten
postcards. 2 cm. Photographs. Taped
interview.
24 photographs: the Holma family,

1908-35.
Interviewed on 7 Aug. 1978; .5 hr.;
1 tape; Finnish; by V. Lindström.
Arrived in Canada in 1928.

HORMAVIRTA, IRENE
TORONTO, ONT.
Personal documents, 1912-69. 3 cm.
Photographs. Taped interview.
302 photographs: 1887-1967, genesis
of the Finnish community in Toronto;
the Lindala and Hormavirta families;
entertainment and business enterprises; and farming and logging in
Sault Ste. Marie, and Sudbury.
Interviewed on July 1978; 3 hrs.; 3
tapes; English/Finnish; by V.
Lindström. Arrived in the early
1900s.
*Canadan Suomalainen Järjestö 25
Vuotta, 1911-36.* Sudbury: Vapaus,
1936. 183 pp.

HORMAVIRTA, SAIMI
TORONTO, ONT.
57 photographs: northern Ont. lumber camps, 1930-45; and the Algoma
Central Railway in northern Ont.
Taped interview.
Interviewed on 28 April 1980; 1.5
hrs.; 2 tapes; English; by V.
Lindström and I. Radforth. Discusses
her experiences in the lumber camps
north of Sault Ste. Marie in the
1920s.

HUITIKKA, ONNI
FORT FRANCES, ONT.
Interviewed on 9 May 1979; .5 hr.;
1 tape; Finnish; by R. Nieminen and
H. Doherty. Arrived in Canada in
1930.

HUJANEN, VILHO
RICHMOND, BRITISH COLUMBIA
Correspondence between the Finnish

Democratic League, and the Finnish Advancement Association regarding Finnish-Canadian aid to the Soviet Union, 1942; and two adjusters' Daily Performance Reports, n.d. .5 cm (4 items). Photographs.
23 photographs: Finns in the Timmins area; and theatre and sports activities, 1930-51.

HUNNAKKO, WALTER
NOLALU, ONT.
Interviewed on 31 May 1979; .5 hr.; 1 tape; Finnish; by R. Nieminen and H. Doherty. Arrived in Canada in 1928.

HUNTUS, OTTO
NIPIGON, ONT.
Interviewed on 7 June 1979; .5 hr.; 1 tape; Finnish; by R. Nieminen and H. Doherty. Arrived in 1923.

HUUKI, EELI
SAULT STE. MARIE, ONT.
11 photographs: the Huuki family in Timmins, and Finland, 1912-33; and work in the logging industry in northen Ont., 1928-30. Taped interview.
Interviewed on 19 Jan. 1981; 1 hr.; 1 tape; Finnish/English; by H. Vuorimies. Arrived in Canada in the 1920s.

IKONEN, AATU
TORONTO, ONT.
13 personal letters and postcards, 1924-62; personal documents, passports, deeds, report cards, and a landing card, 1906-65, and programmes regarding sports and musical events, 1939-67. 6 cm (28 items). Photographs. Taped interview.
9 photographs: the Ikonen family; and sports activities in Finland and

Toronto, 1916-47.
Interviewed on 24, 27 July 1978; 2 hrs.; 2 tapes; Finnish; by V. Lindström. Arrived in Canada in the 1920s.

ILKKA, MRS.
NOLALU, ONT.
Interviewed on 11 June 1975; .5 hr.; 1 tape; English; by C. Kouhi and L. Tolvanen. Arrived in Canada in 1902.

INKILÄINEN, ERKKI
PORCUPINE, ONT.
Interviewed on 14 July 1977; .25 hr.; 1 tape; English; by Lennard Sillanpaa. Arrived in Canada in 1951.

INKILÄ, NILS
THUNDER BAY, ONT.
Interviewed on Oct. 1976; .25 hr.; 1 tape; English; by Tuija Puiras. Discusses the Reipas Club.

JAAKKOLA, LILY
SAULT STE. MARIE, ONT.
23 photographs: employment in the lumber industry, and on railway construction in Algoma, 1926-39. Taped interview.
Interviewed on 7 Nov. 1980; 1 hr.; 1 tape; Finnish; by H. Vuorimies. Arrived in Canada in 1923.

JAAKKOLA, LILY
SAULT STE. MARIE, ONT.
18 photographs: military service in Finland, 1931-43; and a dwelling in Sault Ste. Marie, 1953.

JACKSON, JOHN E
THUNDER BAY, ONT.
Interviewed on 12 June 1979; 1.75 hrs.; 2 tapes; Finnish; by R. Nieminen. Arrived in Canada in 1910.

JACOBSON, LAURA
LAKE PENAGE, ONT.
Interviewed on 26 Sept. 1987; 2
hrs.; 2 tapes; Finnish; by V.
Lindström. Arrived in Canada in
1924.

JALAVA, MAURI
TORONTO, ONT.
Interviewed on 1 Feb. 1980; 1 hr.; 1
tape; English; by V. Lindström.
Founded the Finnish Toronto Credit
Union.

JÄRVINEN, IRMA
SOINTULA, BRITISH COLUMBIA
Matti, Halminen. *Sointula—Kalevan
Kansan ja Kanaden Suomalaisten
Historiaa* (The history of Kalevan
Kansa and the Canadian Finns).
Helsinki: Mikko Ampuja, 1936. 140
pp.

JOHNSON, EINO H.
TORONTO, ONT.
4 letters, 1902-66. .25 cm. Photographs. Taped interview.
22 photographs: 1903-16, lumber
camps and homestead life in the Port
Arthur area, 1905; and 3 Johnson
children upon arrival to Port Arthur,
1903.
27 postcards: 1907–66, early impressions of northwestern Ont., such as a
street in Cobalt, 1908; and a col-
lapsed grain elevator in Fort William,
1906.
Interviewed on 18 July 1978; .5 hr.;
1 tape; English/Finnish; by V.
Lindström. Arrived in Canada in
1903.

JOHNSON, TAIMI
THUNDER BAY, ONT.
Personal documents and correspon-
dence. Photographs. Taped interview.

47 photographs: n.d.
Interviewed in July 1976; .5 hr.; 1
tape; English; by Tuija Puiras. Discusses Finnish athletic activities.

JOKIMÄKI, URHO EMIL
SAULT STE. MARIE, ONT.
Interviewed on 26 Nov. 1980; 1 hr.;
1 tape; Finnish; by H. Vuorimies.
Active in the Pentecostal Church.

JOKIMÄKI, VEIKKO AND MRS. HELMI
AMHERSTBURG, ONT.
Interviewed on 1 June 1980; .5 hr.;
1 tape; English/Finnish; by R.
Nikander. Parents of Mr. Jokimäki
arrived in 1924.

JUHALA, ANNIE
EMO, ONT.
Interviewed on 8 May 1979; .5 hr.;
1 tape; English; by H. Doherty.
Arrived in North America in 1914.

JUNKA, VILPAS
TIMMINS, ONT.
Interviewed on 14 July 1977; 1.25
hrs.; 2 tapes; Finnish; by Lennard
Sillanpaa. Arrived in the 1920s.

JUSSILA, EERO
SAULT STE. MARIE, ONT.
18 photographs: the Jussila family in
Finland, Algoma, and South Porcu-
pine, 1928-78; and mining in South
Porcupine, 1928. Taped interview.
Interviewed on 21 Jan. 1981; 1 hr.;
1 tape; Finnish/English; by H.
Vuorimies. Arrived in Canada in
1927.

JUURINEN, ERKKI
WINDSOR, ONT.
Interviewed on 20 May 1980; 1 hr.;
1 tape; English; by R. Nikander. Discusses the Finnish church.

KAIHLA, MAUNO O.
SAULT STE. MARIE, ONT.
 Collection of papers from Juho A.
Palokangas, 1898-1961, which
includes a play and role book collection; handwritten manuscript for
Nouseva Voima, a Kanadan Teollisuus
Kannatuksen Liitto newspaper in Sault
Ste. Marie, 1925, 1926, 1931, 1936;
and literature from the Finnish Canadian Historical Society. Collection
also includes manuscripts of poems,
short stories, novels, scrapbooks,
calendars, diaries, minutes, and
reports of organizations such as the
Työväen Opiston Kannatus Yhdistys,
1916; the Algoma Line Strikers Committee minutes, 1919; and personal
documents. 17 reels of microfilm.
Photographs.
 331 photographs: festivals, mining,
logging, and Finnish organizations in
Finnish–Canadian communities of
Ont., 1898–1961, all taken by Juho
A. Palokangas.

KALLIO, LAINA
WALDEN, ONT.
 Interviewed on 28 Dec. 1977; .5 hr.;
1 tape; Finnish; by A. Lahtinen. Born
to Finnish parents who arrived in
Canada in the early 1900s.

KALLIO, VÄINÖ
WALDEN, ONT.
 Interviewed on 28 Dec. 1977; 1.5
hrs.; 2 tapes; Finnish; by A.
Lahtinen. Donor's parents arrived in
Canada in the early 1900s.

KANERVA, IMPI
SCHUMACHER, ONT.
 Interviewed on 18 July 1977; .75
hr.; 2 tapes; Finnish; by Lennard
Sillanpaa. Arrived in Timmins, Ont.
in 1913.

KANGAS, KATHY
THUNDER BAY, ONT.
 Interviewed on Feb. 1978; 1 hr.; 1
tape; English; by C. Budner. Discusses her athletic activities.

KARILA, ELLEN
THUNDER BAY, ONT.
 Interviewed in June 1976; 1 hr.; 1
tape; English; by Tuija Puiras. Active
member of the Nahjus Club, a Finnish sports organization.

KÄRKI, ARMAS
SUDBURY, ONT.
 Interviewed on 15 Dec. 1977; 1 hr.;
1 tape; Finnish; by A. Lahtinen.
Arrived in Canada in 1928.

KARNI, AINI
COOK, MINNESOTA
 24 religious pamphlets, 1892-1956.
Kirkollinen Kalenteri. 1903-62. 43
calendars.
Raittiuskansan Kalenteri. 1921-69.
21 calendars.
Siirtokansan Kalenteri. 1919-73. 22
calendars.

KATILA, KIRSTI
TORONTO, ONT.
 Transcript of an interview with Otto
Katila, 1974. Discusses his emigration, and early days in Canada. 5 pp.
Photographs.
 7 photographs: Otto Katila; and as a
member of Lord Byng's staff,
1924-26.

KAUKOLA, SYLVI
THUNDER BAY, ONT.
 1 article about local history by A. T.
Hill, c. 1970s; and the history of
labour movement, and rise of socialism in Finland and Russia. 9 pp.
Photographs. Taped interview.

25 photographs: various F.O.C. theatrical and choir productions; and trade-union activities in the lumber industry, c. 1920-40.
Interviewed on 14 March 1979; 1 hr.; 1 tape; English; by H. Doherty. Arrived in Canada in 1912.

KAUPPI, ANNA
SAULT STE. MARIE, ONT.
42 photographs: the Kauppi family at sporting events, theatrical porductions, stagings, businesses, and work in the logging industry in Sault Ste. Marie, 1913-55. Taped interview.
Interviewed on 8 May 1981; 1 hr.; 1 tape; Finnish; by H. Vuorimies. Born in 1905 in Sault Ste. Marie.

KEKKI, MARTTA
SUDBURY, ONT.
Interviewed on 10 Nov. 1977; 1 hr.; 1 tape; Finnish; by A. Lahtinen. Immigrated to Canada in 1924.

KENTALA, OLAVI
THUNDER BAY, ONT.
Interviewed on 12 March 1979; .5 hr.; 1 tape; Finnish; by R. Nieminen. Landed in Halifax, Nova Scotia in 1926.

KENTALA, VELI
THUNDER BAY, ONT.
Interviewed on 22 May 1980; 1 hr.; 1 tape; Finnish; by R. Hammaren. Immigrated to Canada in 1952.

KENTALA, VELI
TORONTO, ONT.
Viikkosanomat. 3 July 1974 - 21 Dec. 1981. 8 reels of microfilm.

KERKKO, CHARLES
TORONTO, ONT.
Honorary certificates from the Spanish Civil War, 1938, and membership cards and books from organizations and sports clubs, Brigades Internacionales, Octubre 1936 - Octubre 1938. 3 cm. Photographs. Taped interview.
11 photographs: Finnish lumber workers in Kirkland Lake, 1931; and C. Kerkko, Toivo Suni, and William Lahti as Spanish Civil War soldiers in Madrid, 1938.
Interviewed on 21 Oct. 1978; 1.5 hrs.; 2 tapes; Finnish; by V. Lindström. Discusses the turn of the century Finnish immigrants in Toronto.
Joulu. 1973. 48 pp.
Liekki. June 1972 - June 1974. 3 cm.
Vapaus. Dec. 1973 - June 1974. 1 cm.

KESKINEN, OIVA
AMHERSTBURG, ONT.
Interviewed on 24 May 1980; 1 hr.; 1 tape; Finnish; by O. Nikander. Immigrated to Canada in 1952.

KETO, REINO
TORONTO, ONT.
Personal papers and Spanish Civil War documents, and a notebook kept by Mr. Keto in Spain, 1938. 6 cm. Photographs. Taped interview.
70 photographs: Finnish-Canadian volunteers fighting in the Spanish Civil War, 1936-39.
Interviewed on 10 Nov. 1978; 4 hrs.; 4 tapes; Finnish; by V. Lindström. Union organizer in northern Ont. lumber camps, recounts his role in the Spanish Civil War.
Lahtinen, William. *50 Vuoden Varrelta* (After 50 Years). Superior,

Wisconsin: American Finnish Publishing and Työmies Society, 1953. 255 pp.
Luoto, Lauri. *Kamaran Sankarit* (The Heroes of Kamara). Superior, Wisconsin: Amerikan Suomalaisten Sos. Kustannusliikkeiden Liitto, 1927.
Pulli, E. A. *Ja Setä Sami Avasi Ovensa* (And Uncle Sam Opened his Doors). Duluth: Finnish Pub. Co., 1947. 253 pp.
Joulu 1975. Sudbury, Ont.: Vapaus, 1975. 52 pp.
Volunteer. Vol. 1, no. 8, 1978. Organ of the Abraham Lincoln Brigade, a Spanish Civil War veterans' magazine. 12 pp.

KETOLA, NIILO
THUNDER BAY, ONT.
Interviewed on 12 March 1979; 1 hr.; 1 tape; Finnish; by R. Nieminen. Immigrated to Canada in 1923.

KILPONEN, REINO
THUNDER BAY, ONT.
Interviewed on 1976; .5 hr.; 1 tape; English; by J. Päiväläinen. Discusses his athletic career.

KINNUNEN, AARO
TORONTO, ONT.
Personal documents, 1914-24. 1 cm (6 items). Taped interview. Interviewed on 21 Aug. 1978; .5 hr.; 1 tape; Finnish; by V. Lindström. Immigrated in the early 1920s.

KIVILUOMA, KAUKO
THUNDER BAY, ONT.
Interviewed on 25 July 1980; .5 hr.; 1 tape; Finnish; by R. Hammaren. Arrived in Canada in 1951.

KIVINEN, ARMAS
THUNDER BAY, ONT.
Interviewed on 6 March 1979; .5 hr.; 1 tape; Finnish; by R. Nieminen. Born in Port Arthur, Ont. in 1917.

KIVINEN, FRED
SUDBURY, ONT.
Interviewed on 28 Feb. 1978; 1 hr.; 1 tape; Finnish; by A. Lahtinen. Arrived in Canada in 1926.

KIVISTÖ, TOIVO
NIPIGON, ONT.
Interviewed on 10 July 1976; .5 hr.; 1 tape; English; by A. Jokelainen and J. Päiväläinen. Member of the Kuhnus Sports Club in Nipigon, Ont.

KNUTILA, VILHELMINA
PORCUPINE, ONT.
36 photographs: Finnish Canadians; parish; and businesses in Timmins, Porcupine, and South Porcupine, 1977. Taped interview. Interviewed on 19 July 1977; 1.5 hrs.; 3 tapes; Finnish; by Lennard Sillanpaa. Discusses early 20th century life in Porcupine.

KOIVISTO, SUOMA
SAULT STE. MARIE, ONT.
12 photographs: the Koivisto family; and employment in logging in Algoma, and Sault Ste. Marie, 1926-37. Taped interview. Interviewed on 17 April 1981; 1 hr.; 1 tape; Finnish/English; by H. Vuorimies. Arrived in Canada in 1921.

KOIVISTO, WEIKKO
THUNDER BAY, ONT.
Interviewed on 3 June 1976; 1.5 hr.; 2 tapes; English; by A. Jokelainen. Discusses his athletic activities.

KOIVU, AARNE
SUDBURY, ONT.
Interviewed on 6 April 1980; 1 hr.;
1 tape; Finnish; by R. Hammaren.
Arrived in Canada in 1929.

KOIVU, ANNA
THUNDER BAY, ONT.
Interviewed on 28 May 1975; .5
hrs.; 1 tape; Finnish; by L. Tolvanen
and C. Kouhi. Arrived in Intola in
1910.

KOIVURANTA, ALPO
THUNDER BAY, ONT.
Programmmes of Finnish-Canadian
sports organizations. 2 cm (3 items).
Photographs.
32 photographs: sports, mainly
wrestling and gymnastics in Toronto,
Timmins, and South Porcupine,
1920-31; F.O.C. theatrical productions; Camp Tarmola in Toronto,
1937; and co-operative store in South
Porcupine, n.d.

KOIVURANTA, MARY
THUNDER BAY, ONT.
Interviewed on 29 May 1979; .5 hr.;
1 tape; Finnish; by R. Nieminen.
Landed in Halifax, Nova Scotia in
1928.

KOKKOLA, OSMO LEO
WINDSOR, ONT.
Interviewed on 5 June 1980; 1 hr.; 1
tape; English; by R. Nikander.
Landed in Halifax, Nova Scotia in
1926.

KOLJONEN, JUHANI
LIVELY, ONT.
Interviewed on 15 Feb. 1978; .5 hr.;
1 tape; Finnish; by A. Lahtinen.
Arrived in Canada in 1926.

KORKALAINEN, AUGUSTI
THUNDER BAY, ONT.
7 photographs: employment in railway yards in Fort William, 1913; and
trapping in northern Ont., c. 1930s.
Taped interview.
Interviewed on 15 Aug. 1981; 1 hr.;
1 tape; Finnish; by A. Tolvanen. Discusses his employment with the
railroad, and in the lumber camps at
the beginning of this century.

KORPI, ELI
NOLALU, ONT.
Interviewed on 31 May 1979; 1 hr.;
1 tape; Finnish; by R. Nieminen.
Immigrated to Canada in 1924.

KORPI, YRJÖ
THUNDER BAY, ONT.
"Brigadas Internacionales—Carnet
Militar," military passbook from
the Spanish Civil War, 1937; and a
combat certificate of the Brigadas
Internacionales, 1939. 1 cm (2 items).

KORPI, YRJÖ
THUNDER BAY, ONT.
Interviewed in March 1979; .25 hr.;
1 tape; Finnish; by E. Nordström.
Arrived in Port Arthur in 1930.

KORRI, ALVA
PORCUPINE, ONT.
Interviewed on 19 July 1977; .25 hr.;
1 tape; English; by Lennard
Sillanpaa. Recollections of life in
lumber camps in the Porcupine area
during the 1930s and 1940s.

KORRI, LINNE
TIMMINS, ONT.
28 photographs: a funeral following
a mining accident, 1928; and recreational activities such as parades,
sports, theatre stagings, and picnics in

Timmins, Schumacher, and Matagami River, 1917-35. Taped interview. Interviewed on 18 July 1977; 2 hrs.; 2 tapes; Finnish; by Lennard Sillanpaa. Discusses activities in Workers' Co-op, the Finnish Organization Hall, and the Finnish Canadian labour movement.

KOSKI, HILJA
FORT FRANCES, ONT.
Interviewed on 9 May 1979; 1 hr.; 1 tape; English/Finnish; by R. Nieminen and H. Doherty. Arrived in Canada in 1912.

KOTANEN, MR. AND MRS. ARVID
THUNDER BAY, ONT.
Interviewed on 3 June 1975; .5 hr.; 1 tape; English; by C. Kouhi and L. Tolvanen. They recount their early experiences in the community of Ostola, and their involvement in the Lutheran Church.

KOTANEN, DICK
THUNDER BAY, ONT.
Interviewed on July 1976; .5 hr.; 1 tape; English; by Tuija Puiras. Discusses his amateur hockey career.

KOTANEN, RAY
THUNDER BAY, ONT.
Interviewed in July 1976; .5 hr.; 1 tape; English; by Tuija Puiras. Involved in the Finnish Athletic Club Nahjus.

KOVALAINEN, ELVI
AMHERSTBURG, ONT.
15 photographs: Finns and work in the lumber industry in Port Arthur, and Kirkland Lake, 1930-35; and 1 newspaper clipping of Finland's 37th Independence Day celebrations in Windsor, 1954. Taped interview.

Interviewed on 24 May 1980; .5 hr.; 1 tape; English; by R. Nikander. Arrived in Canada in 1930.

KUHMO, EDITH
GORHAM (LAPPE), ONT.
Interviewed on 25 July 1981; 1 hr.; 1 tape; English; by A. Tolvanen. Arrived in Lappe, Ont. in the late 1920s.

KUHMO, TOIVO
GORHAM (LAPPE), ONT.
Interviewed on 25 July 1981; 1 hr.; 1 tape; Finnish; by A. Tolvanen. Homesteader in Jacques Township, Ont.

KUIKKA, VÄINÖ
LIVELY, ONT.
Interviewed on 15 Feb. 1978; 1 hr.; 1 tape; Finnish; by A. Lahtinen. Immigrated to Canada in 1928.

KUJANPÄÄ, KAARLO
TORONTO, ONT.
Personal documents, 1918-53; F.O.C. choir and orchestral material, 1908-20; theatre and sports material, 1945-68; 6 booklets regarding the Soviet Union, marriage, and other socialist themes, 1911-59. 1 meter. Photographs. Taped interview. 76 photographs: the Kujanpää family in Finland and Canada; and F.O.C. theatre performances from the 1930s. Interviewed on 1, 16 June 1978; 3 hrs.; 3 tapes; Finnish; by V. Lindström. Arrived in Canada in 1922.
Ikinuorten Sanomat. Oct. 1973 - March 1978 (22 issues).
Joulu. 1960-76 (8 issues).
Kevät. 1950-76 (7 issues).
Northern Neighbours. July 1976 - April 1977 (8 issues).

Punalippu. 1971. 1974 (5 issues).
Vappu. 1960-68 (5 issues).

KUJANPÄÄ, MARTHA
TORONTO, ONT.
Personal documents, 1913-49. 1 cm.
Photographs. Taped interview.
25 photographs: F.O.C. theatre and
choir activities in Toronto, 1916-30;
and Finnish women working as servants and seamstresses, 1914-15.
Interviewed on 1, 16 June 1978; 4
hrs.; 4 tapes; Finnish/English; by V.
Lindström. Arrived in Canada in
1913.

KUOKKANEN, OLAVI
TIMMINS, ONT.
Interviewed on 12 July 1977; .5 hr.;
1 tape; Finnish; by Lennard
Sillanpaa. Active in the Finnish
Lutheran Church of Timmins.

KURKI, HELMI
SAULT STE. MARIE, ONT.
Personal papers, 1948-69. 2 cm.
Photographs. Taped interview.
13 photographs: the life of Helmi
Kurki in Finland and Montreal, Que-
bec, 1921-56.
Interviewed on 23 Oct. 1980; 1 hr.;
1 tape; Finnish; by H. Vuorimies.
Immigrated to Canada in 1929.

KYLLÖNEN, YRJÖ
SUDBURY, ONT.
Interviewed on 21 Feb. 1978; 1 hr.;
1 tape; Finnish; by A. Lahtinen.
Arrived in Canada in 1926.

LAAKSO, H.
SUDBURY, ONT.
See Helen Nevala.

LAAKSO, WÄINÖ
THUNDER BAY, ONT.
Interviewed on 17 June 1976; 1 hr.;
1 tape; English; by A. Jokelainen. A
long-time member of the Finnish Athletic Club Nahjus.

LAAMANEN, AILEEN
SOUTH PORCUPINE, ONT.
1 photograph: donor in South Porcu-
pine, 1977. Taped interview.
Interviewed on 22 June 1977; 1 hr.;
1 tape; English; by Lennard
Sillanpaa. She has lived in South
Porcupine, Ont. since 1912.

LAARI, ANTON
PORT WELLER, ONT.
Personal documents, 1918-62;
handwritten book of poetry, n.d.; and
guestbook of Hilda Laari, 1946. 4
cm. Photographs.
17 photographs: 1930s, a chicken
farm near St. Catharines, camp life
and quarters in northern Ont., and a
Finnish picnic in St. Catharines, c.
1950.
Jalkanen, Hilma. *Naisvoimistelua*
(Gymnastics for Women). Helsinki:
Kustannusosakeyhtio Otava, 1938.
Koskimies, Airi. *Iloa Voimisteluun*
(Joy in Exercise). Porvoo: Werner
Soderström Osakeyhtio, 1938. 87 pp.
Laherma, Väinö. *Vapaaliikkeitä*
(Gymnastic Movements). Helsinki:
Työväen Urheilulehti Osakeyhtio,
1923. 51 pp.
_____. *Sauwaliikkeitä* (Gymnastic
Movements with Rods). Helsinki:
Työväen Urheilulehti Osakeytio,
1923. 48 pp.
_____. *Urheilupoikain Opas* (Ath-
letic Boys' Guide). Helsinki: Työväen
Urheilulehti Osakeyntiö. 1924. 130
pp.
_____. *Voimisteluryhmiä Pyramiideja*

(Group Gymnsatics, Pyramids).
Helsinki: K. J. Gummerus
Osakeyhtiö, 1935. 71 pp.
 Luoto, Lauri. *Ikuiset Uhritulet* (The
Eternal Fires of Sacrifice). Superior,
Wisconsin: Amerikan Suom. Sos.
Kustannusliikkeiden Liitto, 1929. 364
pp.
 Potti, Kalle. *Iloinen Harbori* (The
Happy Harbour). Duluth, Minnesota:
Päiväleht: Kustannusyhtiö, 1924. 130
pp.
 Reaman, George E. *English for New
Canadians.* Toronto, 1930.
 Ruissalo, Annie. *Sisarukset* (Sisters
or Siblings). Sudbury: Vapaus, 1945.
164 pp.
 Savela, Evert. *Vanha Perintötalo*
(The Old Inherited House). U.S.A.
Kansallinen Kustannuskomitea, 1941.
127 pp.
 Väisönen, Yrjö. *Kisapirtti Sävelmistö*
(Music for 125 Finnish National
Dances). Porvoo: Werner Söderström
Osakeyhtiö, n.d. 64 pp.
 _____. *Työläisnaisten Urheilulehti*
(Working Women's Sports Maga-
zine). No. 1, 1923. 166 pp.; no. 1,
1928. 228 pp.
 _____. *Liikuntaleikkejä* (Exercise
Games). Porvoo: Werner Söderström
Osakeyhtiö, 1933. 168 pp.
 _____. *Naisen Urheilukirja*
(Women's Sports Book). Porvoo:
Werner Söderström Osakeyhtiö,
1933. 147 pp.
 _____. *TUL: Toimitsija-Opas*
(Workers' Sports Federation
Managers' Guide). Helsinki: Työväen
Urheiluliitto, 1937. 154 pp.
 Frontier College of Canada. *A
Primer for Adults: Elementary English
for Foreign Born Workers in Camps.*
Toronto, 1930.

LAGERBOM, EINARI
SUDBURY, ONT.
 1 photograph: the donor in Sudbury,
1978. Taped interview.
 Interviewed on 2 Feb. 1978; 1 hr.; 1
tape; Finnish; by A. Lahtinen. Discusses his participation in Finnish
choirs.

LAHTI, GEORG AND HELEN
SUDBURY, ONT.
 2 photographs: mining in Sudbury,
1913-16. Taped interview.
 Interviewed on 31 Oct. 1977; 1 hr.;
1 tape; Finnish; by A. Lahtinen.
Migrations to and from Canada, the
U.S., and Finland.

LAHTI, LAURI
THUNDER BAY, ONT.
 Interviewed on 10 June 1976; 1 hr.;
1 tape; English; by A. Jokelainen.
Athlete with the Finnish Athletic Club
Nahjus.

LAHTI, LEO
SUDBURY, ONT.
 Interviewed on 5 Jan. 1978; .5 hr.; 1
tape; Finnish; by A. Lahtinen.
Arrived in Canada in 1930.

LAHTINEN, A. M.
SUDBURY, ONT.
 22 photographs: Finnish Canadians
in Sudbury, 1978.

LAHTI, TYYNE
SAULT STE. MARIE, ONT.
 Personal documents, programmes,
poems, and calendars. 5 cm. Photographs. Taped interview.
 27 photographs: friends and choir
performances in Sault Ste. Marie,
1905-49.
 Interviewed on 20 March 1981; 1

hr.; 1 tape; Finnish/English; by H.
Vuorimies. Arrived in Canada in
1923.

LAIN, TOIVO
WINDSOR, ONT.
 Interviewed on 28 May 1980; .5 hr.;
1 tape; English; by R. Nikander.
Post-WWII immigrant.

LAINE, MARI
KAMINISTIQUIA, ONT.
 Interviewed on 17 Aug. 1981; 1 hr.;
1 tape; Fin-Karelian dialect; by A.
Tolvanen. Arrived in the early 1920s.

LAKE, TED
THUNDER BAY, ONT.
 Interviewed on 21 June 1976; 1 hr.;
1 tape; English; by M. Kraft.
Recounts his affiliation with the Fin-
nish Athletic Club Nahjus.

LÄNKINEN, AIRA
SUDBURY, ONT.
 1 photograph: Aira Lankinen in
Sudbury, 1978. Taped interview.
 Interviewed on 22 Feb. 1978; 1 hr.;
1 tape; Finnish; by A. Lahtinen.
Post-WWII immigrant.

LÄNKINEN, ERIK
SUDBURY, ONT.
 1 photograph: E. Lankinen in
Sudbury, 1978. Taped interview.
 Interviewed on 22 Feb. 1978; .5 hr.;
1 tape; Finnish; by A. Lahtinen.
Arrived in Canada in 1930.

LATVA, TYYNE
TORONTO, ONT.
 52 photographs: Kitchener Street
School, 1920s; the C.N. Railroad
bridge construction in Ont., 1930s;
and family, F.O.C. choirs, and theatrical productions, 1911-65. Taped

interview.
 Interviewed on 4 June 1978; 4 hrs.;
4 tapes; Finnish; by V. Lindström.
Arrived in Canada in 1911.
 Aaltonen, E. *Vanhan Forssan
Elämä, 1846-1899.* Forssa: Forssan
Kirjapaino O.Y. Vol. 1, 1932. 202
pp.; vol. 2, 1933. 318 pp.
 Toveritar Kymmenvuotias, 1911-21.
Astoria, Oregon: Toveri Press, 1921.
112 pp. Tenth anniversary publication
of the history of *Toveritar*, Finnish
socialist newspaper for women which
includes articles, short stories, and
poems.
 *Canadan Suomalaisten Sotilaiden
Muistoalbumi* (Finnish Canadian
Soldiers' Memorial Album). Sudbury:
Vapaus, 1946. 69 pp.

LAUKKA, JUSSI E.
THUNDER BAY, ONT.
 Interviewed on 14 Aug. 1981; 2
hrs.; 2 tapes; Finnish; by A.
Tolvanen. Took a homestead at
Kaministiquia in 1917, involved in
building the Labour Temple, and
opened a co-op restaurant.

LEHTINEN, VIHTORI
THUNDER BAY, ONT.
 Interviewed on 18 Aug. 1981; 1 hr.;
1 tape; Finnish; by A. Tolvanen.
Pre-WWI immigrant.

LEHTO, ANNA
THUNDER BAY, ONT.
 4 photographs: unidentified Finnish
women; and a funeral in Thunder
Bay, 1932. Taped interview.
 Interviewed on 17 April 1979; 1 hr.;
1 tape; Finnish; by R. Nieminen.
Immigrated to Canada in 1924.

LEHTOLA, AMANDA
SAULT STE. MARIE, ONT.
 1 Finnish passport, n.d. Photographs. Taped interview.
 13 photographs: the Lehtola family in Finland and Kirkland Lake, 1922-61.
 Interviewed on 31 Oct. 1980; 1 hr.; 1 tape; Finnish; by H. Vuorimies.

LEHTONEN, PIRKKO
SUDBURY, ONT.
 2 photographs: Pirkko Lehtonen in Sudbury, 1977. Taped interview.
 Interviewed on 6 Sept. 1977; .5 hr.; 1 tape; Finnish; by Lennard Sillanpaa. Post-WWII immigrant.

LILLO, ELLA
SUDBURY, ONT.
 Interviewed on 5 April 1980; 1 hr.; 1 tape; English/Finnish; by R. Hammaren. Discusses musical and choir activities.

LUKKARILA, FELIX
SUDBURY, ONT.
 Interviewed on 7 Feb. 1978; 1 hr.; 1 tape; Finnish; by A. Lahtinen. Discusses work experiences in logging.

LUMIALA, PAUL
THUNDER BAY, ONT.
 6 photographs: the Lundson and Lumiala families in Finland, Toronto, and Thunder Bay, 1928-59.

LUND, PENTTI
THUNDER BAY, ONT.
 Interviewed on 16 June 1976; .5 hr.; 1 tape; English; by A. Jokelainen. Recounts his professional hockey career.

LUOMA, GEORGE
TIMMINS, ONT.
 1 Finnish passport, 1915. Photographs. Taped interview.
 2 photographs: the Luoma family, 1915; and a funeral following a mining accident, 1928 in Timmins.
 Interviewed on 13 July 1977; .25 hr.; 1 tape; English; by Lennard Sillanpaa.

LUOMA, KAARIN
SAULT STE. MARIE, ONT.
 Personal documents, 1931-46. 2 cm (10 items). Photographs. Taped interview.
 12 photographs: family in Finland, Toronto, and South Porcupine, 1929-52.
 Interviewed on 18 Oct. 1980; .5 hr.; 1 tape; Finnish; by H. Vuorimies. Worked as a domestic in Toronto.

LUOTO, AARNE
EMO, ONT.
 12 photographs: work and strikes in the logging industry in Port Arthur, 1920-40. Taped interview.
 Interviewed on 8 May 1979; 2 hrs.; 2 tapes; Finnish; by R. Nieminen. Arrived in Canada in 1927.

LUUKKONEN, AINO
SUDBURY, ONT.
 25 photographs: business enterprises and theatrical productions in Finland and Sudbury, 1940-70. Taped interview.
 Interviewed on 2 Sept. 1977; 1 hr.; 1 tape; Finnish; by Lennard Sillanpaa. Worked as a domestic in Toronto.

LUUKONEN, TOIVO
SUDBURY, ONT.
 1 photograph: Toivo and Aino

Luukonen in Sudbury, 1977. Taped interview.
Interviewed on 2 Sept. 1977; 1.5 hrs.; 2 tapes; Finnish; by Lennard Sillanpaa. Discusses pre-WWII occupations, activities at Sampo Hall, and involvement with the Finnish Friendship Circle.

MACDONALD (NEE SEPPÄLÄ), MARY
THUNDER BAY, ONT.
Interviewed on 29 July 1977; .5 hr.; 1 tape; English; by C. Kouhi. Recollections of her family's involvement in the Finnish community of Port Arthur.

MAGNUSON, BRUCE
TORONTO, ONT.
The collection contains documents, correspondence, and clippings regarding WWII internment, the Lumber and Sawmill Workers' Union, the Canadian Union of Woodworkers, and Pat Walsh, 1940-62. Included are pamphlets of the Labour Progressive Party, 1938-59. 12 cm. Photographs.
181 photographs: working and living conditions in northern Ont.; bushcamp life; activities of the Lumber Workers' Industrial Union; and the Lumber Saw Mill Workers' Union, 1912-53.

MÄKI, BILL
THUNDER BAY, ONT.
Interviewed in 1976; .5 hr.; 1 tape; English; by J. Päiväläinen. Discusses his professional hockey, football, and baseball careers.

MÄKI, FRANKLIN
SOUTH PORCUPINE, ONT.
Interviewed on 13 July 1977; 1 hr.; 2 tapes; English; by Lennard Sillanpaa. Born in the Porcupine area.

MÄKI, HARVEY
WINDSOR, ONT.
1 newspaper photograph: burning of a mortgage at St. Mark's Lutheran Church in Windsor, 1960. Taped interview.
Interviewed on 23 May 1980; 1 hr.; 1 tape; English; by R. Nikander. Pre-WWII immigrant.

MÄKI, MARIA
TORONTO, ONT.
Personal documents, 1906-24. 1 cm. Photographs. Taped interview.
42 photographs: 1906-49, Finns working in the garment industry; and a celebration of the Amalgamated Clothing Workers of America at the Royal York Hotel Toronto, 26 Feb. 1949.
Interviewed on 17-21 July 1978; .5 hr.; 1 tape; Finnish; by V. Lindström. Arrived in Canada in 1924.

MÄKI, NIILO
THUNDER BAY, ONT.
Interviewed on 24 June 1976; .25 hr.; 1 tape; English; by J. Päiväläinen. Discusses his affiliation with the Ponteva Athletic Club of Nolalu, Ont.

MÄKYNEN, LAINA
TIMMINS, ONT.
Interviewed on 13 July 1977; .5 hr.; 1 tape; Finnish; by Lennard Sillanpaa. Pre-WWII immigrant.

MANNILA, MAINO
THUNDER BAY, ONT.
Interviewed in Aug. 1976; .25 hr.; 1 tape; English; by Tuija Puiras. Recounts his athletic activities.

MANNILA, ROY
THUNDER BAY, ONT.
Interviewed on 24 May 1979; 2 hrs.;
2 tapes; English; by E. Nordström.
Discusses the Finnish socialist move-
ment in the Red Rock area.

MANSIKKA, ARVI
TORONTO, ONT.
Interviewed on 29 Jan. 1980; 1 hr.;
1 tape; English; by V. Lindström.
Discusses role in the Finnish mixed
chorus "Sointu," and other Finnish
organizations.

MARKKANEN, KYLLIKKI
TORONTO, ONT.
47 photographs: Finnish Canadians
during official functions in Toronto,
Waterloo, and Ottawa, 1947-69.

MARTTILA, KAARLO
ARMSTRONG LAKE (SUDBURY), ONT.
Interviewed on 1 Dec. 1977; .5 hr.;
1 tape; Finnish; by A. Lahtinen. Discusses work in the railway, and in
logging camps.

MARTTILA, TYYNE
ARMSTRONG LAKE, ONT.
Interviewed on 1 Dec. 1977; .5 hr.;
1 tape; Finnish; by A. Lahtinen.
Worked as a maid in Toronto.

MATSON, ARVO
THUNDER BAY, ONT.
Interviewed on 21 Jan. 1979; 1 hr.;
1 tape; English; by H. Doherty. Discusses life in Fort William in the
1920s and 1930s.

MATSON, KATRI
THUNDER BAY, ONT.
7 photographs: sports activities,
Nakina, n.d. Taped interview.
Interviewed on 26 April 1979;

.5 hr.; 1 tape; Finnish; by R.
Nieminen. Immigrated to Canada in
1924.

MAUKONEN, BRET
TORONTO, ONT.
6 photographs: the Maukonen family
in Toronto, 1902-1917; and a
missionary, 1982.

MIKKELA, JULIA
THUNDER BAY, ONT.
Interviewed on 17 July 1974; 1 hr.;
1 tape; Finnish/English; by C. Kouhi.
Discusses mainly the Laestadian
Church.

MYNTTINEN, ANJA
TORONTO, ONT.
Aikamme. Vol. 4, no. 2, 1980. 26
pp.

NENONEN, IMPI
SAULT STE. MARIE, ONT.
Interviewed on 30 Oct. 1980; 1 hr.;
1 tape; Finnish; by H. Vuorimies.

NEVALA, HELLEN
SUDBURY, ONT.
Interviewed on 15 Oct. 1977; .5 hr.;
1 tape; Finnish; by A. Lahtinen. Discusses farming in the Sudbury area.

NIEMI, EINO
THUNDER BAY, ONT.
Interviewed on 27 July 1981; 1 hr.;
1 tape; Finnish; by A. Tolvanen.
Arrived in Canada in 1927.

NIKANDER, OIVA
WINDSOR, ONT.
1 Finnish passport belonging to Karl
Nikander, 1923. .25 cm. Photographs. Taped interview.
3 photographs: family in Holland,
and Cochrane, 1924, 1929, 1944.

Interviewed on 15 May 1980; 1 hr.;
1 tape; English; by R. Nikander.
Immigrated to Canada in 1923.

NISSILÄ, NIILO JOHANNES
ST. CATHARINES, ONT.
Personal documents, 1926, and
printed material. 11 cm. Photographs.
Taped interview.
21 photographs: 1916-32, sports;
theatre; mining strike; and Finnish
(I.W.W.) picnic in Astabula Harbour,
1918.
Interviewed on 8 Feb. 1979; .5 hr.;
1 tape; English/Finnish; by Allen
Seager and V. Lindström. Account of
the Noranda Strike in the 1930s.
Eklund, W. *Me Haluamme Elää—5
Vuotta V.E. Päivästä* (We Want to
Live—5 Years Ago V.E. Day).
Sudbury: Vapaus, 1950. 30 pp.
Engels, Friedrich. *Perheen,
Yksityisomaisuuden ja Valtion
Alkuperä* (The Origin of the Family,
Personal Wealth and the State).
Helsinki: Kansankulttuuri Oy., 1946.
238 pp.
Foote, E. B. *Kotilääkäri Kirja
Perheelle ja Yksityisille* (The Home
Doctor Book for Families and Indi-
viduals). Murray Hill, c. 1903. 904
pp.
Halme, Kaarlo, translator. *Sirpin ja
Vasaran Maasta* (From the Land of
the Hammer and Sickle). Superior,
Wisconsin: Työmies Society Print,
1930. 2 cm.
Halonen, A. *Suomen Luokkasota*
(Class War in Finland). Superior,
Wisconsin: Työmies Society Print,
1928. 526 pp.
Kivimaa, Arvi, and Rislakki, Ensio,
eds. *Suomen Kasvot—Suomalaista
Kulttuuria Kuvina* (The Face of Fin-
land—Finnish Culture in Pictures).
Helsinki: Kustannusosakeyhtiö Otava,

1948. 2 cm.
Leonov, Leonid. *Velikoshumskin
Valloitus* (The Invasion of
Velikoshumsk). Helsinki:
Kansankulttuuri Oy., 1946. 202 pp.
Luoto, Lauri. *Kamaran Sankarit*
(The Heroes of Kamara).
Mäkinen, Aili, Hertta Kuusinen, *et
al. S K P Taistelujen
Tiellä—Vuosikirja 1* (The Finnish
Communist Party in Battle, Yearbook
1). Oulu: Kansankulttuuri Oy., 1945.
100 pp.
Marx, K. and F. Engels.
Kommunistinen Manifesti (Communist
Manifesto). Sudbury: Vapaus, 1934.
126 pp.
Mattson, Helmi. *Aavikon Vaeltajat*
(Travellers of the Plain). Astoria,
Oregon: Pacific Development Society,
1928.
Pessi, Ville. *Yleinen Tilanne ja S K
P:n Politiikan Pääsunta* (The General
Situation and the Main Thrust of the
Politics of the Finnish Communist
Party). Helsinki: S K P:n
Valistusjaosto, 1945. 61 pp.
Stenberg, Elli, Ville Pessi *et al. Yrjö
Sirola, Muistelmia Suomalaisesta
Demokratian Esitaistelijasta* (Yrjö
Sirola, Memories of an Early Fighter
for Finnish Democracy). Helsinki:
Kansankulttuuri Oy., 1946. 102 pp.
Tanner, J. Alfred. *Humoristisia
Lauluja* (Humorous Songs). Lahti:
Aug. Kanerva, 1923. 16 pp.
Teräväinen, Aili. *Kuopuksen
Kengissä* (In My Little Brother's
Shoes). Sudbury: Vapaus, 1947. 235
pp.
Tshakovski, Aleksander. *Piirritetyssä
Leningradissa* (In Besieged
Leningrad). Helsinki: Kansankulttuuri
Oy., 1945. 171 pp.
Wilskman, Ivar. *Terveyden Opas* (A
Guide to Health). Helsinki: Yrjö

Weilin and Kumpp Oy., 1910. 143 pp.

_____. *Suomalais—Canadalaisen Amatööriurheiluliiton Vuosikirja 1946* (Finnish Canadian Amateur Sports Federation Yearbook, 1946). Toronto: FCASF, 1946. 37 pp.

_____. *Etelä—pohjanmaa Kuvissa.* Vaasa: Vaasa Oy., 1946. 183 pp.

_____. *Meidän Poikamme Espanjassa* (Our Sons in Spain). Finnish Workers' Federation, U.S., 1939.

NISSILÄ, NIILO J.
ST. CATHARINES, ONT.
Interviewed in Sept. 1978; 1.5 hrs.; 2 tapes; Finnish; by V. Lindström. Immigrated in 1916.

NORDSTRÖM, EINAR
THUNDER BAY, ONT.
People's Co-operative Store advertisment, Port Arthur, 1908. 1 pp. Taped interview.
Interviewed on 15, 19 March 1979; 4.25 hrs.; 5 tapes; English; by H. Doherty. Discusses the Finnish Left, and the trade union movement.

NORDSTRÖM, EINAR
THUNDER BAY, ONT.
Interviewed on 18, 19 May 1979; 6 hrs.; 7 tapes; English; by J. Holmberg. Discusses immigration, and work experiences in the lumber camps and unionism.

NOWAK, GÖTA
SOUTH PORCUPINE, ONT.
Interviewed on 19 July 1977; .5 hr.; 1 tape; Finnish; by Lennard Sillanpaa. A founding member of Porcupine Suomi Klubi.

NUMMI, TAIMI AND ALEX
TORONTO, ONT.
Personal papers, 1911-34. 2 cm.
Photographs.
97 photographs: Finns in various locations in Ont., 1910-32.

NUPPOLA, VEIKKO
TORONTO, ONT.
Interviewed on 9 March 1980; .5 hr.; 1 tape; Finnish; by R. Hammaren.

NUTTAL, EDITH
THUNDER BAY, ONT.
Interviewed in 1974; .5 hr.; 1 tape; English; by C. Kouhi. Discusses grandmother as one of the pioneer settlers in Port Arthur, Ont.

OJA, RONALD
THUNDER BAY, ONT.
Interviewed in 1976; .25 hr.; 1 tape; English; by C. Budner. Discusses his coaching activities in both hockey and baseball.

OKSANEN, AINO AND URHO
TORONTO, ONT.
Handwritten poems by donor, n.d.; scrapbook of published poems, and articles in newspapers, 1936-76. 2 cm. Taped interview.
Interviewed on 9 Oct. 1978; 2 hrs.; 2 tapes; Finnish; by V. Lindström. WWI immigrant.
Gershuni, G. *Vankiloissa ja Kidutuskammioissa* (In the Prisons and Torture Chambers). Helsinki: Kustannusosakeyhtiö Otava, 1907. 264 pp.
Lissagaray. *Pariisin Veripäivät eli Pariisin Kommunin Historia v. 1871* (Bloody Days in Paris or the History of the Paris Commune 1871). Pori: Osuuskunta Kehitys, 1908. 427 pp.

Rydberg, Kaisu M. *Katselin Amerikkaa* (I Looked at America). Helsinki: Kustannusosakeyhtiö Tammi, 1946. 301 pp.

Tarkiainen, V. *Suomalaisen Kirjallisuuden Historia* (The History of Finnish Literature). Helsinki: Kustannusosakeyhtiö Otava, 1934. 346 pp.

Tokoi, Oskari. *Lapsuuteni Muistoja* (Memories of My Childhood). Kokkola: Keski Pohjanmaan Kirjapaino Oy., 1953. 194 pp.

_____. *The Century Magazine*. Vol. 37, Nov. 1888 - April 1889. New York: The Century, 1889. 960 pp.

PAAVI, ONNI
THUNDER BAY, ONT.
Interviewed on 26 June 1976; 1 hr.; 1 tape; English; by J. Päiväläinen. Discusses his athletic activities, and the history of Nahjus sports club.

PAIVIO, JULES
TORONTO, ONT.
Poem by Aku Päiviö, "Pojalleni Espanjassa" (For My Son in Spain), 1938. An article by Isadore Tivin and Stephen Zak, "Spain Revisited-Canadian Style," (about the reunion in Spain of Canadian Mackenzie-Papineau Battalion/Lincoln Brigade veterans of the Spanish Civil War, 1979. .25 cm. Photographs. Taped interview.
6 photographs: J. Päiviö during military service in the Spanish Civil War, 1937-39.
Interviewed on 24 Jan. 1980; 2 hrs.; 2 tapes; English; by V. Lindström. Discusses his life as an artist, and his involvement in the Spanish Civil War.

PAJALA, TOIVO
SUDBURY, ONT.
1 photograph: Toivo Pajala in Sudbury, 1977. Taped interview. Interviewed on 4 Sept. 1977; .75 hr.; 1 tape; Finnish; by Lennard Sillanpaa. Started a ski manufacturing firm in the 1930s.

PAKKALA, TEUVO
TORONTO, ONT.
Interviewed on 23 Jan. 1980; 1 hr.; 1 tape; Finnish; by V. Lindström. Immigrated in 1958.

PARNEGA (NEE KAARELA), AILI
THUNDER BAY, ONT.
Interviewed in Summer 1976; .25 hr.; 1 tape; English; by Tuija Puiras. Recounts her athletic activities.

PELTO, LEMPI AND CHARLES
THUNDER BAY, ONT.
Interviewed on 14 June 1979; .5 hr.; 1 tape; English; by H. Doherty. Both lifetime residents of Nolalu, Ont.

PENNA, ANTTI
SUDBURY, ONT.
Interviewed on 6 Dec. 1977; .25 hr.; 1 tape; Finnish; by A. Lahtinen. Arrived in Canada in 1928; located in the U.S. in 1913.

PENNA, HILDA
SUDBURY, ONT.
Interviewed on 6 Dec. 1977; .5 hr.; 1 tape; Finnish; by A. Lahtinen. Arrived in Canada in 1911.

PENTTILÄ, OLLI
SUDBURY, ONT.
Interviewed on 8 Nov. 1977; 1 hr.; 1 tape; Finnish; by A. Lahtinen. Arrived in Canada in 1926.

PENTILLÄ, SALLI
SUDBURY, ONT.
Interviewed on 8 Nov. 1977; .5 hr.;
1 tape; Finnish; by A. Lahtinen.
Immigrated to Canada in 1929.

PENTTINEN, SETH AND
KAUKO PÖLKKI
THUNDER BAY, ONT.
Vitkala, Eva M. *Suomalainen Orjatyttö* (Finnish Slave-Girl).
Duluth, Minnesota: Finnish Daily, 1917. 222 pp.
_____. *Siirtokansan Kalenteri.* (Immigrant Peoples' Almanac). 1918. 187 pp.
Canadan Uutiset. 3 July 1928 (1 issue).
Industrialisti. 13 Jan. 1927; 3-5, 11 March 1927; 24 June 1940 (6 issues).
Työväen Osuustoimintalehti (Co-operative Weekly). 20 June 1940 (1 issue).

PETERSON, WALTER
SOUTH ALGOMA, ONT.
Interviewed on 15 April 1979; 1 hr.;
1 tape; English; by E. Nordström.
Immigrated to Canada in 1921.

PIETILÄ, OLIVER
TIMMINS, ONT.
Interviewed on 11 July 1977; 1 hr.;
1 tape; English; by Lennard Sillanpaa. Discusses his immigration, working conditions in the 1930s, and activities in Finnish organizations.

PIETILÄ, OLIVER
TIMMINS, ONT.
Papers pertaining to the Timmins Credit Union, 1948-78. 1 cm.

PITKÄNEN, AINO
THUNDER BAY, ONT.
44 photographs: employment in the

agriculture and logging industry, Tarmola, Kivikoski, 1925-30. Taped interview.
Interviewed on 17 April 1979; 1 hr.;
1 tape; Finnish; by R. Nieminen.
Arrived in Canada in 1920.

PITON, AILI
TORONTO, ONT.
15 photographs: Toronto's Finnish Society's Drama Club and Children's Orchestra, 1917, 1919, 1923; and the Lindala family. Taped interview.
Interviewed on 10-14 July 1978; 2 hrs.; 2 tapes; English/Finnish; by V. Lindström. Recollections of Toronto's Finnish in the early 1900s.

PÖLKKI, KAUKO
THUNDER BAY, ONT.
"Lappe, the Early Years." *Chronicle Journal.* 12 June 1981. 1 newsclipping about early Finnish settlement in Lappe, Ont.

PÖYHÖLÄ, TOIMI
THUNDER BAY, ONT.
Interviewed on 13 June 1979; .5 hr.;
1 tape; Finnish; by R. Nieminen.
Arrived in Canada in 1926.

PUKKALA, SAM
THUNDER BAY, ONT.
Interviewed on 12 March 1979; 1.5 hrs.; 2 tapes; Finnish; by R. Nieminen. Immigrated to Canada in 1923.

PUNKARI, MAIRE
SAULT STE. MARIE, ONT.
Personal papers, 1940s. 1 cm. Photographs. Taped interview.
41 photographs: the life of Arvi Iisakki Heinonen; and parish activity in Finnish communities, such as Copper Cliff, Timmins, Sudbury,

Saskatchewan, and the U.S., 1912-82.
Interviewed on 16 July 1982; 1 hr.;
1 tape; English; by M. Stefura. Rev.
Arvi Heinonen's daughter, Maire,
discusses his career.

PYNNÖNEN, ELLEN
SAULT STE. MARIE, ONT.
  Personal papers, 1942-78. .5 cm.
Photographs. Taped interview.
  12 photographs: the family in Fin-
land, 1902-39; a choir; and traditional
Finnish "Crown Wedding" in
Timmins, 1939.
  Interviewed on 27 Oct. 1980; 1 hr.;
1 tape; Finnish; by H. Vuorimies.
Arrived in Canada in 1929.

RAJILA, MAILA
AMHERSTBURG, ONT.
  Interviewed on 25 May 1980; 1 hr.;
1 tape; Finnish; by O. Nikander.
Arrived in Canada in 1953.

RAKETTI, HARRY
THUNDER BAY, ONT.
  Share certificates of the Finnish
Co-operative Store Company in Fort
William, 1910, and the Farmers'
Mercantile Association. Ltd., 1912.
.25 cm. Photographs. Taped inter-
view.
  2 photographs: Finnish co-operative
stores in Thunder Bay, n.d.
  Interviewed on 11 April 1979; 1 hr.;
1 tape; English; by H. Doherty.
Arrived in Canada in 1915.

RANTA, ESKO
TIMMINS, ONT.
  Interviewed on 11 July 1977; .25
hr.; 1 tape; Finnish; by Lennard
Sillanpaa. Post-WWII immigrant.

RANTA, LIISA C.
SUDBURY, ONT.
  1 photograph: the donor in Sudbury,
1978. Taped interview.
  Interviewed on 15 March 1978; 1
hr.; 1 tape; Finnish; by A. Lahtinen.
Discusses work as a domestic, and a
storekeeper.

RANTALA, GUSTAF
TIMMINS, ONT.
  Interviewed on 17 July 1977; .5 hr.;
1 tape; English; by Lennard
Sillanpaa. Arrived in Canada in the
1930s.

RAUTIO, MARTTI
THUNDER BAY, ONT.
  Interviewed on July 1976; .5 hr.; 1
tape; English; by J. Päiväläinen.
Discusees his skiing career.

REPO, SATU
TORONTO, ONT.
  1 article "Lakehead in the Thirties,"
1979, on the history of labour
struggles at Lakehead. .25 cm.

RINNE, AUGUSTI
THUNDER BAY, ONT.
  Interviewed on 17 Aug. 1981; .75
hr.; 1 tape; Finnish; by Ahti
Tolvanen. Homesteaders in Lappe,
Ont. in the late 1920s.

RINTA, EINO
THUNDER BAY, ONT.
  Interviewed in 1976; .75 hr.; 1 tape;
English; by C. Budner. Recounts his
participation in various sports.

RISSANEN, MAIRE M.
SAULT STE. MARIE, ONT.
  1 Finnish passport, 1974. 32 pp.
Photographs. Taped interview.

8 photographs: family in Finland, 1943-70.
Interviewed on 24 Oct. 1980; 1 hr.;
1 tape; Finnish; by H. Vuorimies.

RITA, ARNE
THUNDER BAY, ONT.
Interviewed on 11 June 1976; .5 hr.
1 tape; Finnish; by A. Jokelainen.
Discusses his career as an athlete.

RITA, AARNE AND VIENO
THUNDER BAY, ONT.
Interviewed on 19 June 1980; 1 hr.;
1 tape; Finnish; by Paul Lumiala.
Arrived in 1923, both involved in
Finnish choirs.

RITARI, AARNE
SUDBURY, ONT.
1 newsclipping, biography of A.
Ritari, n.d. Photographs. Taped
interview.
3 photographs: donor and his business enterprise, 1977.
Interviewed on 9 Sept. 1977; 1 hr.;
1 tape; English; by Lennard
Sillanpaa. Discusses early Finnish
community in Copper Cliff, Ont.

RUOHO, MARTHA
NIPIGON, ONT.
Interviewed on 7 June 1979; .5 hr.;
1 tape; Finnish; by R. Nieminen and
H. Doherty. Arrived in Canada in
1925.

RUOHONEN, KAARINA
SUDBURY, ONT.
1 photograph: donor in Sudbury,
1978. Taped interview.
Interviewed on 30 Jan. 1978; 1 hr.;
1 tape; Finnish; by A. Lahtinen.
Member of Voima choir.

SAARI, AUGUST
THUNDER BAY, ONT.
Interviewed on 31 July 1974; .5 hr.;
1 tape; Finnish; by M. Metsäranta.
Recounts the difficulties Finns
encountered in their unionization
efforts.

SAARI, SIRKKA
SUDBURY, ONT.
Interviewed on 20 Oct. 1977; 1 hr.;
1 tape; Finnish; by A. Lahtinen.
Arrived in Canada in 1961.

SAARINEN, JALMARI
BARBER'S BAY, ONT.
Interviewed on 18 July 1977; 1 hr.;
1 tape; Finnish; by Lennard
Sillanpaa. Recounts his participation
in left wing Finnish organizations.

SALMI, LYYLI
SOUTH PORCUPINE, ONT.
Essay on the founding of the church,
on its 30th Anniversary, by L. Salmi,
1976. 4 pp. Taped interview.
Interviewed on 15 July 1977; 1 hr.;
1 tape; Finnish; by Lennard
Sillanpaa. Discusses her participation
in the Finnish Pentecostal Church in
South Porcupine.

SALMIJÄRVI, SANNI
THUNDER BAY, ONT.
Interviewed on 7 June 1984; 2 hrs.;
2 tapes; Finnish; V. Lindström.

SALMIJÄRVI, SANNI
THUNDER BAY, ONT.
Share certificate of a Thunder Bay
Co-op dairy, 1952. 2 pp. Taped inter-
view.
Interviewed on 24 Feb. 1979; 1 hr.;
1 tape; Finnish; by R. Nieminen.
Immigrated to Canada in 1913.
Ruissalo, Annie. *Päivälahden*

Tarina. 1943. 120 pp.
Teräväinen, Aili. *Kuopuksen Kengissä*. 1947. 235 pp.

SALMINEN, EDITH
TORONTO, ONT.
18 photographs: 1927-40, skiing and theatrical events in the Sudbury and Timmins area.

SALMINEN, IVAR
THUNDER BAY, ONT.
Interviewed on 11 March 1979; .5 hr.; 1 tape; Finnish; by R. Nieminen. Landed at Halifax in 1928.

SALMINEN, KAUKO
TIMMINS, ONT.
Interviewded on 11 July 1977; 1.5 hrs.; 2 tapes; English; by Lennard Sillanpaa. Post-WWII immigrant.

SALMINEN, KERTTU
SAULT STE. MARIE, ONT.
2 Canadian passports, 1952, 1973; and 2 newsclippings, 1942. .5 cm. Photographs. Taped interview.
29 photographs: the Salminen family in Finland, and Sault Ste. Marie, 1920-70; and employment in the lumber industry, Regan, 1930.
Interviewed on 27 Nov. 1980; 1 hr.; 1 tape; Finnish; by H. Vuorimies. Arrived in the late 1910s or early 1920s.

SALO, OSCAR
THUNDER BAY, ONT.
Interviewed in July 1976; .5 hr.; 1 tape; Finnish; by Tuija Puiras. Early member of the Finnish Athletic Club "Nahjus," (q.v.).

SALONEN, KAARLO
HAMILTON, ONT.
Interviewed on 14 Nov. 1982; 2

hrs.; 2 tapes; Finnish; by I. Lindström. Account of the I.W.W. Labour Temple in Port Arthur, Ont.

SALONEN, REINO
PARRY SOUND, ONT.
Interviewed on 14 May 1980; 1 hr.; 1 tape; Finnish; by V. Lindström. Arrived in the late 1920s.

SAXBERG, GUS
THUNDER BAY, ONT.
Interviewed in Aug. 1976; .5 hr.; 1 tape; English; by J. Päiväläinen. He recounts his experiences as a professional hockey player.

SEPPÄLÄ, EINAR
NOLALU, ONT.
Interviewed on 11 July 1977; .5 hr.; 1 tape; English; by C. Kouhi. Discusses the Finnish community in Nolalu in the early 1900s.

SEPPÄLÄ, ELVINA
THUNDER BAY, ONT.
20 photographs: employment in the lumber industry; and dwellings in Thunder Bay, 1920-60.

SHEARE, LEO
THUNDER BAY, ONT.
Interviewed on 1 June 1976; 1 hr.; 1 tape; English; by A. Jokelainen. He was an active member of the Finnish Athletic Club Nahjus from 1925 to 1955.

SIIMES, ALBERT
WINDSOR, ONT.
Interviewed on 5 June 1980; 1 hr.; 1 tape; Finnish; by O. Nikander. Played flute for the Windsor Symphony for many years.

SIIRALA, KAISA
WATERLOO, ONT.
2 autobiographies of V. Koski, n.d.
2 cm.

SILJANDER, KALLE
THUNDER BAY, ONT.
7 photographs: work and strikes in
the logging industry in Port Arthur,
and Nipigon, 1930-35.

SILJANDER, KALLE
THUNDER BAY, ONT.
1 share certificate of Vigor Co-op
Society Limited, 1933. 2 pp. Taped
interview.
Interviewed on 8 March 1979; 1 hr.;
1 tape; Finnish; by R. Nieminen.
Arrived in Canada in 1926.

SILLANPAA, ELSA
SAULT STE. MARIE, ONT.
Personal documents, 1926-28. 1 cm.
Photographs. Taped interview.
19 photographs: the Sillanpaa family
in, Timmins, 1924-65; and employ-
ment in the logging industry in
Shillington, 1925-27.
Interviewed on 8 Nov. 1980; 1 hr.;
1 tape; Finnish; by H. Vuorimies.
Immigrated to Canada in 1930.

SILLANPAA, LENNARD
OTTAWA, ONT.
Handwritten autobiography of V.
Koski discussing life in the Porcupine
gold mining area in the 1920s;
newsclipping about Elsa Stortroen,
1977; and programme of the National
Festival of New Canadians, McIntyre
Arena, 1940. 1.5 cm. Photographs.
39 photographs: activities in the Finnish communities of Sudbury and
Timmins, including festivals, gymnastics, and business enterprise, 1933-50.
49 photographs: 1977, parish activity

at St. Matthew's Finnish Lutheran
Church in Sudbury, and St.
Timothy's Evangelical Lutheran
Church in Copper Cliff.
72 photographs: Finnish festivals,
including songs, folk dancing, and
gymnastics in Sudbury, Sault Ste.
Marie, and Copper Cliff, 1977-78.
Freed, Verna S. *Historical Bells.*
1978. 89 pp.
Sillanpaa, Lennard. "The Political
Behaviour of Canadians of Finnish
Descent in the District of Sudbury."
A licentiate thesis, University of
Helsinki, 1975. 145 pp.

SILLANPAA, SYLVIA
TIMMINS, ONT.
Interviewed on 9 July 1977; 1 hr.; 1
tape; English; by Lennard Sillanpaa.
Relates her involvement in the
Worker's Co-op and Finnish Hall
during the 1920s; and, the split
among Finns in 1931.

SIPILÄ, LYDIA
THUNDER BAY, ONT.
Interviewed in June 1976; 1 hr.; 1
tape; Finnish; by A. Jokelainen.
Member of the Finnish Athletic Club
Nahjus.

SIRKKA HOSTIKKA
HELSINKI, FINLAND
The collection contains 103 membership cards of various clubs, unions
and organizations, 1933-77, constitution of the I.W.W., 1929, constitutions and by-laws of the Finnish
Workers' and Farmers' League of
Canada, 1929-33, and letters, personal documents, and clippings,
1927-70. 8 cm (121 items). Photographs.
10 photographs: the family in
Toronto, 1927; and choirs sponsored

by the Finnish Social Club, 1940-60.
Kansallispuku Kuvasto. Lahti: Helmi
Vuorelma Oy., 1943. Picture collection of Finnish national dresses. 21
pp.

SNELLMAN, KARL
SUDBURY, ONT.
54 photographs: the Snellman and
Lehti families, 1908-22, mainly from
the Sudbury area; Finnish festivals;
and employment in farming, mining,
and logging.

SORA, EEVA
THUNDER BAY, ONT.
Interviewed on 25 April 1980; 1 hr.;
1 tape; Finnish; by R. Hammaren.
Immigrated to Canada in 1952.

ST. AMAND, LEMPI
THUNDER BAY, ONT.
Interviewed on 17 June 1977; .5 hr.;
1 tape; English; by M. Kraft. Arrived
in 1929, a gymnastic coach.

STENBACK, ORVAL
THUNDER BAY, ONT.
Interviewed in July 1976; .5 hr.; 1
tape; English; by J. Päiväläinen. Discusses his hockey carrer.

STEPHENSON, RICHARD
WHITEFISH, ONT.
9 assorted ledgers, journals, and cash
books, 1930-65. 34 cm. Donation
includes a number of publications for
which a finding aid is available.

STORTROEN, MAGNE ED
PORCUPINE, ONT.
64 photographs: paintings by Elsa
Stortroen in Porcupine, 1898-1930.

SUHONEN, HEIKKI K.
BARBER'S BAY, ONT.
Interviewed on 21 July 1977; 1 hr.;
1 tape; Finnish; by Lennard
Sillanpaa. Discusses working conditions in the lumber camps, and mines
in northern Ont.

SUKSI, EDWIN
SUDBURY, ONT.
Interviewed on 8 June 1979; 2 hrs.;
2 tapes; Finnish; by J. Halonen.
Immigrated to Canada in 1924.

SUKSI, EDWIN
SUDBURY, ONT.
2 photographs: Edwin Suksi in
Sudbury, 1977. Taped interview.
Interviewed on 7 Sept. 1977; 2 hrs.;
2 tape; English; by Lennard
Sillanpaa. Arrived in the 1920s,
involved in the Lumber Workers'
Industrial Union.

SUND, ELMA
THUNDER BAY, ONT.
Handwritten memoirs of E. Sund's
experiences as cook in the bushcamps
in northwestern Ont., 1921-WWII. 3
pp. Taped interview.
Interviewed on 26 July 1981; 1 hr.;
1 tape; Finnish; by A. Tolvanen.

SUOSMAA, AKLEX
TORONTO, ONT.
Interviewed on 11 June 1980; 2 hrs.;
2 tapes; Finnish; by R. Hammaren.
Arrived in Canada in 1952.

SVENSK, OIVA
WHITEFISH, ONT.
Personal documents, 1896-1903, and
1 roominghouse account book from
Toronto, 1903. 1 cm (9 items). Photographs. Taped interview.
35 photographs: a Temperance Asso-

ciation in Toronto; and buildings in Toronto, Whitefish, and Copper Cliff, 1906-30.
Interviewed on 19 March 1979; .5 hr.; 1 tape; English; by V. Lindström. Immigrated to Canada in 1903.

SYRJÄ, HELVI
SAULT STE. MARIE, ONT.
18 photographs: dwellings; and work in the lumber industry in Maher, Moose River, 1939-58. Taped interview.
Interviewed on 6 Nov. 1980; 1 hr.; 1 tape; Finnish; by H. Vuorimies. Arrived in the 1920s.

SYTELÄ, ELINÄ
SUDBURY, ONT.
Interviewed on 15 Nov. 1977; .5 hr.; 1 tape; Finnish; by A. Lahtinen. Arrived in Canada in 1929.

TAHVANA, AINO
SUDBURY, ONT.
Interviewed on 5 Jan. 1978; .5 hr.; 1 tape; Finnish; by A. Lahtinen. Arrived in 1927.

TARVAINEN, EINO
TORONTO, ONT.
History article on Finnish-Canadian, working-class theatre, n.d. 4 pp. Photographs.
19 photographs: F.O.C. theatrical productions in Toronto, 1930-45.

TARVAINEN, HELEN
TORONTO, ONT.
31 photographs: women's gymnastics; and athletic competition, probably of "Yritys" Athletic Club of Toronto in the 1930s. Taped interview.
Interviewed on 5 March 1979;

1.5 hrs.; 2 tapes; English; by V. Lindström. Arrived in 1927, worked as a domestic in Toronto.
Tarvainen, Helen. "History of Canada." *Vapaus*. 1967.

TENHUNEN, BRUNO
SUDBURY, ONT.
2 photographs: the donor in Sudbury, 1977. Taped interview.
Interviewed on 8 Sept. 1977; 2.5 hrs.; 3 tapes; English; by Lennard Sillanpaa. Immigrated to Canada in the late 1920s.

TIENHARA, TOIVO
SOUTH PORCUPINE, ONT.
Interviewed on 19 July 1977; 1 hr.; 1 tape; Finnish; by Lennard Sillanpaa. Describes Red-White Finnish rivalries in the lumber camps.

TIMBERG, KATRI
SUDBURY, ONT.
1 photograph: the donor in Sudbury, 1978. Taped interview.
Interviewed on 8 March 1978; 1 hr.; 1 tape; Finnish; by A. Lahtinen. Arrived in Canada in 1951.

TOIKKO, LYYLI
THUNDER BAY, ONT.
Interviewed on 12 March 1979; .25 hr.; 1 tape; Finnish; by R. Nieminen. Immigrated to Canada in 1925.

TUOMI, EINI
PIKE LAKE, ONT.
Interviewed on 5 Jan. 1979; .5 hr.; 1 tape; Finnish; by R. Nieminen. Arrived in Canada in 1923.

TUOMI, SARA
THUNDER BAY, ONT.
Interviewed on 11 June 1979; 1 hr.;

1 tape; Finnish; by R. Nieminen.
Immigrated to Canada in 1925.

TUOMINEN, HEIMO
KAMINISTIQUIA, ONT.
Interviewed in Jan. 1978; 1.5 hrs.; 2
tapes; English; by C. Budner. Parents
were pioneers of Kaministiquia and
Pohjola, Ont.

TURPELA, OLAVI
SAULT STE. MARIE, ONT.
Interviewed on 27 April 1980; 1 hr.;
1 tape; Finnish; by R. Hammaren.
Arrived in 1951.

TYNJÄLÄ, URHO
SOINTULA, BRITISH COLUMBIA
11 photographs: the bodies and
funeral of Rosvall and Voutilainen in
Thunder Bay, 1929-30; the Isku
Athletic Club in Port Arthur, 1930; a
lumber workers' picnic in Port
Arthur, 1929; and a band from Port
Arthur, c. 1930.

UITTO, EINO
N.A.
Interviewed on 27 Dec. 1982; 2 hrs.;
2 tapes; Finnish; by Karl Lindström.

VÄLIMAA, KALLE
SUDBURY, ONT.
Interviewed on 4 Feb. 1978; .5 hr.;
1 tape; Finnish; by A. Lahtinen.
Arrived in Canada in 1952.

VÄLIMAA, LILY
SUDBURY, ONT.
1 photograph: Kalle and Lily
Välimaa in Sudbury, 1978. Taped
interview.
Interviewed on 4 Feb. 1978; .5 hr.;
1 tape; Finnish; by A. Lahtinen.
Parents arrived in the early 1900s.

VALTONEN, AINO
SUDBURY, ONT.
Interviewed on 22 Feb. 1978; 1 hr.;
1 tape; Finnish; by A. Lahtinen.
Immigrated to Canada in 1930.

VANHATALO, HELMI
SAULT STE. MARIE, ONT.
1 letter, n.d. 2 pp. Photographs.
Taped interview.
11 photographs: Finnish in Regina,
Winnipeg, and Finland, 1907-40.
Interviewed on 17 Oct. 1980; 1 hr.;
1 tape; Finnish; by H. Vuorimies.

VEHKALA, TAUNO
BARBER'S BAY, ONT.
Interviewed on 20 July 1977; 2 hrs.;
2 tapes; Finnish; by Lennard
Sillanpaa. Post WWII immigrant.

VESIK, SAARA
SUDBURY, ONT.
Interviewed on 3 March 1978; 1 hr.;
1 tape; Finnish; by A. Lahtinen.
Immigrated to Canada in 1952.

VIITA, LEO AND ANNA
SUDBURY, ONT.
Interviewed on 17 June 1981 and
re-recorded; 1 hr.; 1 tape; Finnish;
by A. Lahtinen.

VIITANEN, TOIVO
THUNDER BAY, ONT.
Interviewed in 1976; 1 hr.; 1 tape;
English; by A. Jokelainen. Prominent
member of the Nahjus Athletic Club
from the 1940s to 1955.

VOUTILAINEN, PAAVO
THUNDER BAY, ONT.
Interviewed in 1976; .5 hr.; 1 tape;
Finnish/English; by J. Päiväläinen.
Discusses his athletic activities.

VOUTILAINEN, PAAVO
THUNDER BAY, ONT.
 Interviewed in Dec. 1975; .5 hr.; 1
tape; Finnish; by C. Budner. He was
director and coach of the Isku Athletic CLub.

WAINIO, GUS
THUNDER BAY, ONT.
 Interviewed in summer 1976; 1 hr.;
1 tape; English; by C. Budner. Discusses Finnish-Canadian hockey.

WÄYRYNEN, WALTER
THUNDER BAY, ONT.
 Article and poem on 22nd anniver-
sary of the deaths of Rosvall and
Voutailainen, union organizers in the
Port Arthur area, 1951; and poem,
"Jaakon Tarina," 1943. .25 cm.
Taped interview.
 Interviewed on 11 June 1979; .5 hr.;
1 tape; Finnish; by R. Nieminen.
Arrived in Canada in 1927; worked
on the railroad most of his life.

WICKSTRÖM, ELMA
THUNDER BAY, ONT.
 1 share certificate of Thunder Bay
Co-op Dairy Ltd., Nov. 4, 1929. 2
pp. Taped interview.
 Interviewed on 1 March 1979; .25
hr.; 1 tape; English; by H. Doherty.
Her mother arrived in 1902.

WIDGREN, ALFRED
THUNDER BAY, ONT.
 Interviewed on Aug. 1976; 1 hr.; 1
tape; English; by J. Päiväläinen. Discusses his athletic career.

WIDGREN, ALFRED
THUNDER BAY, ONT.
 Interviewed on 23 Aug. 1982 and
re-recorded; 1.25 hrs.; 1 tape; Eng-

lish; by H. Doherty. Parents arrived
in Canada in 1901

WILLFOR, AARNI
TORONTO, ONT.
 Diary of Juhannes Hännikäinen, n.d.
1 cm.

WILSON, ARLINE
THUNDER BAY, ONT.
 Interviewed in July 1976; .5 hr.; 1
tape; English; by Tuija Puiras. Mem-
ber of the Finnish Athletic Club
Nahjus.

WIRKKUNEN, JOE V.
THUNDER BAY, ONT.
 Interviewed in 1976; .5 hr.; 1 tape;
English; by J. Päiväläinen. Discusses
his hockey career.

WIRTA, MIINA
THUNDER BAY, ONT.
 Interviewed on 29 May 1979; .5 hr.;
1 tape; Finnish; by R. Nieminen.
Arrived in Canada in 1919.

═══════════════════════════

AGRICOLA FINNISH LUTHERAN
CHURCH (REV. LESLIE LURVEY)
WILLOWDALE, ONT.
 Parish records, 1931-81. 6 reels of
microfilm.
 *Agricola Finnish Lutheran Church
History, 1931-72.* 12 pp.
 Booklet of the International Lutheran
Youth Congress, 1968. 6 pp.
 The Messenger. 22 Jan. 1950. Sun-
day school paper. .25 cm.

AGRICOLA FINNISH LUTHERAN
CHURCH (REV. LESLIE LURVEY)
TORONTO, ONT.
 Records, 1931-72, which include
minutes, correspondence, financial

statements, and bulletins. 19 cm. Photographs.
8 photographs: in the Lutheran League Diary, 1935-80.

AMERICAN FINNISH SOCIALIST ORGANIZATION (HELEN TARVAINEN, FINNISH ORGANIZATION OF CANADA)
TORONTO, ONT.
22 Nov. - 1 Dec. 1914. Minute book of Fourth American Socialist Organization Delegates Meeting. 1 reel of microfilm.
Lahtinen, William. *50 Vuoden Varrelta*. Superior, Wisconsin: America Finland and Työmies Society, 1953.

ANDERSON'S DAIRY
CREIGHTON, ONT.
Financial records, 1930-65. 1 reel of microfilm.

APOSTOLIC LUTHERAN CHURCH
PORT ARTHUR, ONT.
Records, 1899-73, and land deeds, 1899, 1912. 3 cm.

CANADA-FINLAND CHAMBER OF COMMERCE
TORONTO, ONT.
By-laws, 1971. .25 cm.

CANDAN TEOLLISUUS KANNATUKSEN LIITTO (ALICE NIEMI)
SAULT STE. MARIE, ONT.
Minutes and membership lists, 1933-73. 2 reels of microfilm.

CANADIAN FRIENDS OF FINLAND: FOUNDING SYMPOSIUM LECTURES
TORONTO, ONT.
Recordings of lectures and founding meeting, 16 Oct. 1982; 2 hrs.; 2 tapes; English; by Paula Groenberg.

CEDAR CLUB (PERTTI LEHTO)
UDORA, ONT.
Minutes, correspondence, and miscellaneous items, 1953-78. 1 reel of microfilm.

CENTRAL ORGANIZATION OF LOYAL FINNS IN CANADA
LIVELY, ONT.
By-laws and membership card, 1935. .25 cm.

CONSUMERS' CO-OPERATIVE SOCIETY LTD.
TIMMINS, ONT.
Records, 1951-66. 2 reels of microfilm.

FINLANDIA CLUB
ST. CATHARINES, ONT.
Minutes and scrapbooks, 1939-78. 2 reels of microfilm. 2 cm. Photographs.
23 photographs: men, women and children building power station, 1929; and Finlandia Club activities in St. Catharines, c. 1978.

FINNISH ANGLERS AND HUNTERS CLUB
TORONTO, ONT.
Club records, 1955-77. 2 reels of microfilm. Photographs.
11 photographs: activities of the Finnish Anglers and Hunters Club of Ont., 1958-77.

FINNISH ARTS AND CRAFTS SOCIETY (KAY SALOMAA)
TORONTO, ONT.
Constitution, minutes, and miscellaneous printed items, 1972-75. 1 cm. Photographs.
9 photographs: exhibitions of the Finnish Arts and Crafts Society in Toronto, 1975-77.

FINNISH ASSOCIATION OF PORT
ARTHUR
PORT ARTHUR, ONT.
 Minutes, 1918-25, and a list of
founding members, 1918. 6 cm.

FINNISH ATHLETIC CLUB *NAHJUS*
THUNDER BAY, ONT.
 Interviews conducted in 1976 with
club members Leo Sheare, Toivo
Viitanen, and Weikko Koivisto; 2
hrs.; 2 tapes; English; by A. Budner.
Discuss the history of the Nahjus
Clubs.

FINNISH ATHLETIC CLUB *SISU*
TORONTO, ONT.
 Club records, 1949-77. 1 reel of
microfilm. Photographs.
 8 photographs: the Finnish Athletic
Club "Sisu," mainly gymnastics,
1970-80.

FINNISH ATHLETIC CLUB *STAR*
ST. CATHARINES, ONT.
 Records, 1933-67, which include
constitution, minutes, general corre-
spondence, reports, and programmes.
24 cm.
Finnish Canadian sports books:
 F.A.C. Yritys 40th anniversary cel-
ebration programme, 1946. 20 pp.
 F.C.A.S.F. 25 Year History, 1943.
68 pp.
 F.C.A.S.F. 40 Year History, 1943.
68 pp.
 F.O.C. and F.C.A.S.F. United 15th
Grand Festival programme, 1971. 12
pp.

FINNISH ATHLETIC CLUB *VOIMA*
SUDBURY, ONT.
 Records, 1954-71. 1 reel of micro-
film.

FINNISH BETHLEHEM LUTHERAN
CHURCH
TORONTO, ONT.
 Records, 1927-76, which include
records of the Hebron Finnish Evangelical Lutheran National Church of
Toronto. 3 reels of microfilm. Photographs.
 45 photographs: religious life at
Bethlehem Lutheran Church,
1931-59; and 2 documents of incorporation.
 *50th Anniversary of Finnish
Bethlehem Lutheran Church.* 20 pp.
Booklet.

FINNISH CANADIAN ART SOCIETY
TORONTO, ONT.
 Minutes, 1977. .25 cm.

FINNISH CANADIAN GYMNASTIC
CLUB FOR WOMEN
TORONTO, ONT.
 Scrapbooks, 1968-77. 1 reel of
microfilm. Photographs.
 43 photographs: sports activities at
the Finnish Athletic Club "Sisu," and
the Finnish Canadian Gymnastics
Club for Women.
 "Mari-Girls." Toronto, 1950-77.

FINNISH CANADIAN HISTORICAL
SOCIETY
SUDBURY, ONT.
 First founded in 1944, the Society's
goal was "in all ways possible to preserve the memory of Finnish Canadians, and their descendants." The
collection covers all aspects of Finnish immigrant life. Series A deals
with church, and congregational
activities; Series B deals mainly with
branch life of the U.C.L.A.; Series C
with temperance societies' activities;
and Series D with Finnish-Canadian
writers and speakers, and contains an

important section on the Central
Organization of Loyal Finns in
Canada, including samples of early
handwritten newspapers. This series
also contains records of the Workers'
and Farmers' Association, South
Porcupine, and the Finnish Canadian
League for Democracy in Toronto.
Series E includes general information
about the Sudbury, Copper Cliff,
Toronto, Sault Ste. Marie, Kirkland
Lake, and Thunder Bay regions.
Series F and G consist of the
Society's own records, minutes,
correspondence, financial accounts,
and membership lists. Finally, Series
H, I, and J cover the
Finnish-Canadian newspapers and
publishing industry. 35 reels of
microfilm.

A collection of 2,000 photographs,
which range from studio portraits to
snapshots, and spans the period from
the 1890s to the 1970s. Finnish communities in both British Columbia and
Ont. are covered. In Ont., the photographs are pictorial records of
churches, weddings, funerals, labour
movements, the lumber industry, picnics, and storefronts. Of particular
relevance are the photographs of the
Hollinger Mine strike, 1912, and the
Hollinger Mine accident funeral of
those worker's involved in the accident at the mine.

FINNISH CREDIT UNION
TORONTO, ONT.
Financial records, 1962-73, and mis-
cellaneous paper items, 1971-78. 3
cm.
Newsletters. 1963-77, in Finnish,
1971-75, in English. 1 cm.
Tähdenväleyä. n.d. .25 cm.

FINNISH EVANGELICAL LUTHERAN
NATIONAL CHURCH
PORT ARTHUR, ONT.
Records, which include handwritten
by-laws (1903), land deeds, and a list
of church officers (1908-43). 5 cm.

FINNISH GOLDEN AGE CLUB
TORONTO, ONT.
Constitution, minutes, and programmes, 1963-75. 1 reel of microfilm. Photographs.
4 photographs: the Finnish Golden
Age Club, 1967-70.

FINNISH MALE CHOIR
SUDBURY, ONT.
Records, 1960-76, which include
programmes, membership lists, and a
scrapbook. Photographs.
9 photographs: performances by the
Finnish Male Choir in Sudbury,
1963-75.

FINNISH MALE SINGERS OF NORTH
AMERICA
TORONTO, ONT.
Records, 1971-76, which include
minutes, correspondence, and miscel-
laneous printed items. 2 cm.

FINNISH MIXED CHOIR
THORNHILL, ONT.
Records, 1971-78, covering Choir's
membership, and activities. 12 cm.
Photographs.
6 photographs: performances in
Toronto and Sudbury, 1974-78.

FINNISH ORGANIZATION OF CANADA
(F.O.C.)
SAULT STE. MARIE, ONT.
F.O.C. Sault Local minutes, 1969,
and lists of members, n.d. 1 cm.

FINNISH ORGANIZATION OF CANADA
LOCAL 79
McINTOSH SPRINGS, ONT.
 Minutes of labourers and farmers meetings, and McIntosh Springs Section's meetings, 1932-55, and an account book, 1932-37. 1 reel of microfilm.

FINNISH ORGANIZATION OF CANADA
TORONTO, ONT.
 Finnish-Canadian play and manuscript collection. 51 sheets of microfiche (51 items).

FINNISH SENIOR CITIZENS' CLUB
SUDBURY, ONT.
 Club records, 1971-77. 1 reel of microfilm. Photograph.
 1 photograph: Finnish seniors on an excursion in Sudbury, 1972.

FINNISH SENIOR CITIZENS FRIENDSHIP CIRCLE
SUDBURY, ONT.
 Records, 1975-77. 1 reel of microfilm.

FINNISH SOCIAL CLUB
TORONTO, ONT.
 Minutes of annual general meetings, 1957-78; expense and income summary, 1977; and lists of members, programmes, and miscellaneous paper items, 1970s. 2 cm. Photographs.
 16 photographs: theatrical productions, Toronto, 1932-77.

FINNISH SOCIALIST LOCAL (SSO)
N.A.
 Pre-1914 membership list. .25 cm.

FINNISH UNITED CHURCH (REV. R. HEPOLEHTO)
TORONTO, ONT.
 Minutes, ledgers, membership register, church service records, Ladies' Auxilliary notebook, and Young People's Association records, 1907-78. 5 reels of microfilm. Photographs.
 21 photographs: religious life at the Finnish United Church in Toronto, 1925-74.
 35th Anniversary Booklet, Church of all Nations. n.d. 1 cm.
 Kanadan Viesti. 1955-57. Microfilm.

FINNISH WAR VETERANS IN CANADA
TORONTO, ONT.
 Constitution, minutes, membership lists, and scrapbook, 1971-77. 1 reel of microfilm. Photographs.
 11 photographs: activities of the Finnish War Veterans in Canada, n.d.

GORHAM AND WARE UNION SCHOOL
NO. 2
N.A.
 Annual school reports, 1913, 1914. .5 cm.

HEBRON FINNISH EVANGELICAL LUTHERAN NATIONAL CHURCH
TORONTO, ONT.
 See Bethlehem Lutheran Church.

INSTITUTE OF GENERAL HISTORY
TURKU, FINLAND
 The American Letter collection contains correspondence from Finnish immigrants in Canada and the U.S., to residents of Satakunta and Varsinais (Suomi provinces in Finland), 1876-1966. Text in Finnish. 6,000 letters sent to Satakunta province, 1880-1964, 5,500 letters constitute those sent to Varsinais-Suomi province, 1876-66. 41 reels of microfilm.

LADIES OF KALEVA
SUDBURY, ONT.
Minutes of founding meeting of the
club Sinijärvien Tupa, 1966-77. 1 reel
of microfilm.

LOYAL FINNS IN CANADA
SUDBURY, ONT.
Records, 1930-76, which include
those of Finnish Senior Citizens'
Club. 4 reels of microfilm. Photographs.
10 photographs: activities of the
Loyal Finns in Canada, including
parades, and folk dancing in Sudbury,
1935-44.

MALE CHORUS *KALEVA*
SAULT STE. MARIE, ONT.
Records, annual reports, programmes, and clippings. 1 reel of
microfilm. Photographs.
4 photographs: male choirs in Sault
Ste. Marie, 1963.

MULTICULTURAL HISTORY SOCIETY
OF ONTARIO
TORONTO, ONT.
Bulletin. No. 19. French Canadian
Historical Society. 32 pp.
Byerly Bag. Vol. 7, no. 12, Dec.
1977. 24 pp.
Co-operative Builder. Vol. 53, no.
27, July 1978. 2 pp.
Minnesotan. Vol. 2, no. 4, Winter
1974. 14 pp.
Suomi-U.S.A. No. 1, 1977. 46 pp.

Newspapers:
Canadan Uutiset. 3 Jan. 1918 - 29
Dec. 1927. 10 reels of microfilm.
Liekki. Sudbury, 4 Jan. 1958 - 29
June 1974. 17 reels of microfilm.
New Voice. Nov. 1946 - Nov. 1947.
1 reel of microfilm.

Vapaus. Toronto, 2 Jan. 1958 - 26
June 1974. 17 reels of microfilm.

NEW ATTEMPT TEMPERANCE
SOCIETY
N.A.
Membership list, 1905. .25 cm.

NORTH STAR ATHLETIC CLUB
SAULT STE. MARIE, ONT.
Constitution, minutes of Club executive, and scrapbook, 1964-79. 1 reel
of microfilm.

ONTARIO ETHNIC NEWSPAPER
MICROFILM PROJECT
TORONTO, ONT.
Aika. Nov. 1903 - 15 July 1904. 1
reel of microfilm.
Liekki. 7 Dec. 1935 - 28 Dec. 1957.
22 reels of microfilm.
Vapaus. Jan. 1921 - Dec. 1957. 27
reels of microfilm.

ONTARIO FINNISH REST HOME ASSO-
CIATION
SAULT STE. MARIE, ONT.
Records, 1971-77. 1 reel of micro-
film. Photographs.
15 photographs: the Ontario Finnish
Rest Home, 1974-78.
RESTRICTED

PIKE LAKE STUDY CIRCLE
THUNDER BAY, ONT.
Minutes, 1932-34, attendance record,
1933-34, and black list, 1933. 1 cm.

PORCUPINE SUOMI KLUBI (OLLI
HOVILA)
SOUTH PORCUPINE, ONT.
Records, 1953-65. 1 reel of micro-
film.

ST. JOHN'S EVANGELICAL LUTHERAN
CIRCLE
TIMMINS, ONT.
 Church and marriage registers,
1935-70. 1 reel of microfilm. Photo-
graphs.
 4 photographs: religious life at St.
John's Evangelical Lutheran Circle in
Timmins, n.d.

ST. JOHN'S LUTHERAN CHURCH
SOUTH PORCUPINE, ONT.
 Records, 1935-76. 3 reels of micro-
film. **RESTRICTED**

ST. MARK'S LUTHERAN CHURCH
(VILPAS JUNKA)
TIMMINS, ONT.
 Financial records, minutes, corre-
spondence, members lists, and mis-
cellaneous items, 1938-70. 9 reels of
microfilm.
 Positive Programme for Peace.
1948. Microfilm.
 Joulukellot. 1970-74. Microfilm.
 Soviet American Relations. 1946.
Microfilm.

ST. MARY'S LUTHERAN CHURCH
SAULT STE. MARIE, ONT.
 Church records, 1905-78. 7 reels of
microfilm. **RESTRICTED**
 Kylväjä (The Organ of the Friends of
Temperance). 1900-01. Microfilm.

ST. MATTHEW'S FINNISH LUTHERAN
CHURCH (REV. JUKKA JOENSUU)
SUDBURY, ONT.
 Parish records, 1932-76. 8 reels of
microfilm. Photographs.
 62 photographs: religious life at St.
Matthew's Finnish Lutheran Church
in Sudbury, 1933-72.

ST. TIMOTHY'S LUTHERAN CHURCH
COPPER CLIFF, ONT.
 Parish records, 1896-1969, including
first director's meeting, 1896, and
membership book, 1898. 24 reels of
microfilm. Photographs.
RESTRICTED
 186 photographs: religious life at St.
Timothy's Lutheran Church in Cop-
per Cliff, 1903-71.
 Pikkussaari, Rev. L. T. "New Light
on Indo-European Languages." 1956.
Booklet. 72 pp.
 Kevään Airut. 1953. Microfilm.
 Isien Usko. 1962, 1971-73. Micro-
film.
 Seimen Joulu. 1943. Microfilm.
 Suomalainen. 1962-64. Microfilm.
 The Church Servant. 1941-47, 1949.
Microfilm.
 Vesan Kronikks. 1944-46. Microfilm.
 Uusi Lansi. 1967. Microfilm.

SUOMI SEURA KALEVALA
TORONTO, ONT.
 Records and programmes, 1955-63.
2 cm.

THE FINNISH PENTECOSTAL CHURCH
OF TORONTO/SAALEM (REV. LEEVI
A. HAIKONEN)
TORONTO, ONT.
 The collection contains by-laws,
n.d.; minutes, 1954-82; correspondence, 1947-82; financial records,
1931-81; 1 Church annual report,
1963-64; and sermons, programmes,
membership information, certificates,
letters of recommendation, and trans-
fers. 40 cm. 3 reels of microfilm.
Photographs.
 53 photographs: 1931-79, church
activities; and founding church members, 1931.
 *Toronto Saalem-Seurakunta,
1930-80.* 50th anniversary publica-

tion. 1.5 cm.
Totuuden Todistaja. 1928–59.
Saalem church articles. 2 cm.
Totuuden Todistaja. Toronto ed.,
1977-82. 1 cm.

THUNDER BAY FINNISH CANADIAN
HISTORICAL SOCIETY
THUNDER BAY, ONT.
 The bulk of the collection is comprised of capsule histories of Thunder
Bay (Port Arthur/Fort William)
region settlements: Alppila, Devon,
Intola, Kivikoski, Kamimistiquia,
Nolalu, Ostola, Suomi and Silver
Mountain, and Tarmola. Accompanied by land registers, lists of
settlers, maps, school records, and
resident interviews, these concise
histories provide a first-hand account
of settlement in northwestern Ont.,
1909-74. It also includes papers from
Nahjus Sports Club, 1920-58. 26 cm.
Photographs. **RESTRICTED**
 350 photographs: rural Finnish community activities, mostly farming and
logging, in the Thunder Bay region,
n.d.
Industrialisti. 1921-1930. .5 cm.,
excerpts with English translations.
Siirtokansan Kalenteri. 1954–58.
Directory of families and organizations in Thunder Bay. 3 cm.

TIMMINS WORKERS' AND FARMERS'
LEAGUE (EERO HAKOLA)
TIMMINS, ONT.
 Records; 1931-61, which include
minutes on Progressive Society and
Harmony Hall meetings. Incomplete.
1 reel of microfilm.

TORONTO FINNISH ADVANCEMENT
ASSOCIATION
TORONTO, ONT.
Leaflet on the anniversary of Finnish
independence, 1977. .25 cm.

TORONTO FINNISH MALE CHORUS
(RAIMO NUTTIKA)
TORONTO, ONT.
 Records, 1956-75, covering Choir's
membership and activities. 2 reels of
microfilm. Photographs.
 4 photographs: performances by the
Toronto Finnish Male Choir, n.d.

TORONTO SUOMI LIONS CLUB
TORONTO, ONT.
 Club records, 1971-77. 1 reel of
microfilm. Photographs.
 21 photographs: activities of the Finnish Lions Club in Toronto, 1971-77.

VAPAA SANA PRESS LTD
TORONTO, ONT.
 61 photographs: belonging to the late
Lydia Gronroos-Dufva. Finnish Song
Festival in Sault Ste. Marie, 1949;
the Unhola family in Toronto,
1920-60; and Finns during social
gatherings.

WORKINGMEN'S ASSOCIATION
IMATRA NO. 9
PORT ARTHUR, ONT.
Membership list, 1906-10. .25 cm.

FRANCO-ONTARIAN COLLECTION

BEAULIEU, EMILIENE
MONTREAL, QUEBEC
 Interviewed on 25 July 1985; 1 hr.;
1 tape; French; by Anne Schooley.

BOUCHARD, FLORIDA
SUDBURY, ONT.
 Interviewed on 19 July 1982; 1 hr.;
1 tape; French; by Diane Landry.

BOUGIE, MGR. HENRI
CORNWALL, ONT.
 Interviewed on 25 July 1977; 1 hr.;
1 tape; English; by Patricia Kulick.
Discusses their lives on the farm in
Fraserfield, Ont.

CHALIFOUX, SIMONE
SUDBURY, ONT.
 Interviewed on 20 July 1982; .5 hr.;
1 tape; French; by Diane Landry.
Active member of various
Franco-Ontarian associations in
Sudbury.

CREVIER, LAURENT
GLENGARRY, ONT.
 Interviewed on 19 Oct. 1977; 1 hr.;
1 tape; English; by Patricia Kulik.
Discusses his business ventures in the
Glengarry district.

D'AMOURS, ROLAND
MOONBEAM, ONT.
 6 photographs: employment in the
logging industry in Moonbeam,

1920-45. Taped interview.
 Interviewed on 31 Dec. 1980; 1 hr.;
1 tape; French; by Michel D'Amours.

DANCAUSE, ALEXANDER
APPLE HILL, ONT.
 Interviewed on 6 July 1977; 1 hr.; 1
tape; English; by Patricia Kulick.
Discusses work and business enter-
prise in Apple Hill.

DESBIENS, ARMAND
MOONBEAM, ONT.
 Interviewed on 3 July 1980; .5 hr.; 1
tape; French; by Michel D'Amours.
Comments on the Union des
Cultivateurs Catholiques.

DESCHENAUX, REV. DONAT
MOONBEAM, ONT.
 Interviewed on 20 July 1980; 2 hrs.;
2 tape; French; by Michel D'Amours.
Comments on church involvement in
the local farming communities.

DESGRANGES, RAOULE
SUDBURY, ONT.
 Interviewed on 7 July 1982; 2 hrs.; 2
tapes; French; by Diane Landry.

DUCHARME, JEAN-BAPTISTE
SUDBURY, ONT.
 4 photographs: business enterprise,
and funeral home in Sudbury, c.
1950. Taped interview.
 Interviewed on 12 Aug. 1982; 2
hrs.; 2 tapes; French/English; by
Diane Landry. Discusses his work,

business enterprise, and involvement in civic politics.

ETHIER, DENIS
GLEN ROBERTSON, ONT.
 Interviewed on 29 Aug. 1977; 1 hr.; 1 tape; English; by Patricia Kulick. Comments on Franco-Anglo ethnic, and cultural differences.

FAUBERT, ALBERT
ALEXANDRIA, ONT.
 Interviewed on 28 July 1977; 2 hrs.; 2 tapes; English; by Patricia Kulick. Commentary on Franco-Anglo tensions and prejudices.

GADBOIS, ADRIAN
CORNWALL, ONT.
 Interviewed on 30 Aug. 1977; 2 hrs.; 2 tapes; English; by Patricia Kulick. Comments on government's treatment of Franco-Ontarians.

GADBOIS, CLIFFORD
GLENGARRY, ONT.
 Interviewed on 27 Nov. 1977; 1 hr.; 1 tape; English; by Patricia Kulick.

GAUTHIER, CATHERINE T.
GLENGARRY, ONT.
 Interviewed on 4 July 1977; 2 hrs.; 2 tapes; English; by Patricia Kulick. A commentary on being a "mixed Canadian."

GAUTHIER, GÉRALD
SUDBURY, ONT.
 Interviewed on 6 July 1982; .75 hr.; 1 tape; French; by Diane Landry. A biographical sketch.

GOSSELIN, FRANCOIS X.
KAPUSKASING, ONT.
 Interviewed on 2 July 1980; 1 hr.; 1 tape; French; by Michel D'Amours.

GUÉNETTE, CHARLES
MATTICE, ONT.
 Interviewed on Oct. 1980; 2 hrs.; 2 tapes; French; by Michel D'Amours.

GUINDON, REV. BERNARD
GLENGARRY, ONT.
 Interviewed on 11 July 1977; 1 hr.; 1 tape; English; by Patricia Kulick. Discusses English prejudices, and politics within the Church.

HUOT, REAL
GLENGARRY, ONT.
 Interviewed in July 1977; 1 hr.; 1 tape; English; by Patricia Kulick. Discusses enterprise and the local economy.

LAFAVE, AMBROSE
CORNWALL, ONT.
 Interviewed on 22 July 1977; 1 hr.; 1 tape; English; by Patricia Kulick. His feelings on French Canadianism.

LANTHIER, GEORGE
ALEXANDRIA, ONT.
 Interviewed in July 1977; 1 hr.; 1 tape; English; by Patricia Kulick. Discusses his bakery business.

LAPOINTE, RAYMOND
GLENGARRY, ONT.
 Interviewed on 29 July 1977; 1 hr.; 1 tape; English; by Patricia Kulick. Gives some statistics on the local counties.

LARABIE, LUDGER
KAPUSKASING, ONT.
 Personal papers, 1932-74. 1 reel of microfilm. Taped interview. Interviewed on 15 Oct. 1980; .5 hr.; 1 tape; French; by Michel D'Amours. Discusses his work history, and business enterprise.

LEFEBVRE, GERARD
GLENGARRY, ONT.
 Interviewed on 16 July 1977; 1 hr.;
1 tape; English; by Patricia Kulick.
Talks about the family business.

LÉONARD, ERNEST
MOONBEAM, ONT.
 Interviewed on 29 Dec. 1980; 1 hr.;
1 tape; French; by Michel D'Amours.
One of the early homesteaders in the
area.

MACDONNEL, KATHLEEN
GLENGARRY, ONT.
 Interviewed on 13 July 1977; 1 hr.;
1 tape; English; by Patricia Kulick.
Comments on the harmonious rela-
tions between French and English
Canadians in the region.

MASSIE, BRUNO
ALEXANDRIA, ONT.
 Interviewed on 28 July 1977; 1 hr.;
1 tape; English; by Patricia Kulick.
Discusses the school system in the
area.

MÉNARD, MARIE L.
GREEN VALLEY, ONT.
 Interviewed in July 1977; 1 hr.; 1
tape; English; by Patricia Kulick.
Discusses French-English ralations.

MICHAUD, GILBERT
SUDBURY, ONT.
 Interviewed on 19 Aug. 1982; 1 hr.;
1 tape; French; by Diane Landry.
One of the early homesteaders in the
Sudbury district.

PICHÉ, EMERELDA
SUDBURY, ONT.
 6 photographs: the Bonin family in

Sudbury, 1938-55. Taped interview.
 Interviewed on 13 July 1982; .75
hr.; 1 tape; French; by Diane Landry.

PROULX, GILBERTE
SUDBURY, ONT.
 Interviewed on 19 July 1982; 1 hr.;
1 tape; French; by Diane Landry.

ROULEA, PAUL
ALEXANDRIA, ONT.
 Interviewed on 10 Nov. 1977; 1 hr.;
1 tape; English; by Patricia Kulick.
Discusses his grandmother's campaign to get French taught in the
school system.

ROZON, JOSEPH S.
GLENGARRY, ONT.
 Interviewed on 7 July 1977; 1 hr.; 1
tape; English; by Patricia Kulick.

ROZON, RUDOLPH
ALEXANDRIA, ONT.
 Interviewed on 29 July 1977; 1 hr.;
1 tape; English; by Patricia Kulick. A
discussion on farm and family life in
the Glengarry district.

THÉRIAULT, ALPHEGE
SUDBURY, ONT.
 Interviewed on 26 Oct. 1982; 2 hrs.;
2 tapes; French; by Diane Landry.

TOUCHETTE, JEAN PAUL
LANCASTER, ONT.
 Interviewed on 15 Aug. 1977; 1 hr.;
1 tape; English; by Patricia Kulick.

VILLENEUVE, OSIE
GLENGARRY, ONT.
 Interviewed on 15 Aug. 1977; 2
hrs.; 2 tapes; English; by Patricia
Kulick. A commentary on
French-English relations.

VILLENEUVE, FATHER RUDOLPH
CORNWALL, ONT.
Interviewed on 15 Aug. 1977; 1 hr.;
1 tape; English; by Patricia Kulick.
Comments on French-English rela-
tions.

═══════════════════

ARCHIVES OF THE JESUIT FATHERS
SUDBURY, ONT.
60 photographs: religious life; the
railroad; mining; and logging in
Sudbury, and surrounding region,
1883-1957.

MULTICULTURAL HISTORY SOCIETY
OF ONTARIO
TORONTO, ONT.
Courrier Sud. 6 Jan. 1974 - 12 Nov.
1976. 4 reels of microfilm.
Cri de L'Est. 1912. 1 reel of micro-
film.
L'Ami du Peuple. 11 June 1942 - 14
Nov. 1968. 8 reels of microfilm.
Le Corrier d'Outaoauais. n.d. 1 reel
of microfilm.
Le Cultivateur. n.d. 1 reel of micro-
film.
Le Rempart. Windsor, 5 Jan. 1983 -
19 Dec. 1984. 1 reel of microfilm.

ONTARIO ETHNIC NEWSPAPER
MICROFILM PROJECT
TORONTO, ONT.
L'Alliance de Toronto. Nov. 1954 -
Nov 1955. 1 reel of microfilm.
Le Revue Ontarienne. Dec. 1963 -
Dec. 1966. 1 reel of microfilm.

GERMAN COLLECTION

ABICHT, HELGA
WATERLOO, ONT.
 Interviewed on 27 July 1977; 2 hrs.;
2 tapes; English; by E. Ruge. Orig-
inally from Saskatchewan, moved to
Germany, and immediately after
WWII immigrated back to Canada.

ALTMAR, GEORGE
TORONTO, ONT.
 Travel documents, 1927-28. .5 cm.
Photographs.
 8 photographs: the Altmar family;
employment in agriculture, trucking,
and the restaurant business in
Hungary, Saskatchewan, and Ont.,
1926-56.

AMBERG, LUCY
MISSISSAUGA, ONT.
 Interviewed on 22 March 1979; .75
hr.; 1 tape; English; by H. Martens.
Post-WWII immigrant.

ANDRESEN, HELGA
TORONTO, ONT.
 Interviewed on 21 Nov. 1978; 1.5
hrs.; 2 tapes; English; by K. Lundy.
Arrived in Canada in 1952.

ANDRESEN, HEIDI
TORONTO, ONT.
 Interviewed on 9 Nov. 1978; 1.25
hrs., 2 tapes; English; by K. Lundy.
Born in Toronto.

ANTLER, WILHELMINE B.
PEMBROKE, ONT.
 Interviewed on 14 Feb. 1981; .5 hr.;

1 tape; English/German; by Peter
Hessel.

ARMIN, JAY
TORONTO, ONT.
 Interviewed in June 1980; 1.5 hrs.; 2
tapes; English; by K. Michael.
Pre-WWI immigrant.

BAEHR, HANS AND ERICA
TORONTO, ONT.
 Newsclippings on donors 1966-72.
.25 cm. Taped interview.
 Interviewed on 10 Oct. 1978; 2 hrs.;
2 tapes; English/German; by K.
Lundy. Post-WWII immigrants.

BAETZ, J. H.
KITCHENER, ONT.
 A biographical sketch of J. H. Baetz,
and a history of the Young Men's
Club of WWI, 1978. .5 cm. Taped
interview.
 Interviewed on 1 Dec. 1977; 2 hrs.;
2 tapes; English; by B. Dandyk.
Post-WWI immigrant.

BARTELS, KLAUS R.
TORONTO, ONT.
 Personal papers, documents, and
certificates, 1944-61 (correspondence,
circulars, minutes, and members lists
from the Deutscher Automobil Club,
1959-78); and a biography of the
Bartels family. 2 cm. Photographs.
Taped interview.
 28 photographs: Bartels family in
Germany, and Toronto, 1909-56; and
Deutscher Automobil Club Inc.,
1960-70.

Interviewed on 14 March 1978; 1.75 hrs.; 2 tapes; English; by B. Dandyk. Arrived in Canada in 1956.

BAUER, RUDOLF
MISSISSAUGA, ONT.
Interviewed on 26 Feb. 1979; 1.25 hr.; 2 tapes; English; by K. Lundy. Post-WWII immigrant.

BENZINGER, MICHAEL
WINDSOR, ONT.
Scrapbook of minutes and statutes of the Synod Diocese of London, 1956-66; and a Mouillon family tree, newsletters, circulars, and pro- grammes from St. Michael's Church in Windsor. 1 reel of microfilm. 1.5 cm. Photographs. Taped interview.
24 photographs: parish activity, and 20th anniversary dinner at St. Michael's Church in Windsor, 1953- 66.
Kontakt. Autumn 1976. .25 cm.

BENZINGER, MICHAEL
WINDSOR, ONT.
Interviewed on 15 March 1978; 1 hr.; 1 tape; English; by T. Bozek. Post-WWII immigrant.

BERENCZ, FERDINAND
TORONTO, ONT.
Immigration documents, 1953-54, and miscellaneous papers from the Vereinigung der Donauschwaben (Association of Danube Swabians) in Toronto, 1972-78. Photographs. Taped interview.
27 photographs: the Berencz family in Yugoslavia, and Austria, 1939-51; immigrants en route to Canada, 1953; costume parties, and beauty contest in Toronto, 1959-74.
Interviewed on 15 Feb. 1978; 1.25

hrs.; 2 tapes; English/German; by B. Dandyk. Arrived in Canada in 1953.

BERNARD, RUTH
TORONTO, ONT.
Interviewed in June 1980; 1.25 hrs.; 2 tapes; English; by K. Michael. Post-WWII immigrant.

BINKLE, ROY AND HELEN
NEUSTADT, ONT.
Interviewed on 20 Feb. 1978; 1 hr.; 1 tape; English; by E. Ruge. Third generation immigrant.

BITZER, WILFRIED
KITCHENER, ONT.
6 photographs: the Bitzer family, 1903-36. Taped interview.
Interviewed on 2, 18 May, 10 June 1977; 3 hrs.; 3 tapes; Eng- lish/German; by E. Ruge. Interwar immigrant, active in German-Cana- dian organizations.

BOEKELMAN, MARK
TORONTO, ONT.
Leibbrandt, Gottlieb. *"A Little Para- dise": Aus der Geschichte und Leben der Deutschkanadier in der County Waterloo, 1800-75*. Kitchener: Allprint Co., 1977. 416 pp.

BOLLENACH, ERNST
KITCHENER, ONT.
Interviewed on 2 Aug. 1977; 2 hrs.; 4.5 tapes; German; by E. Ruge. Immediate post-WWII immigrant.

BONGART, KLAUS H.
KITCHENER, ONT.
Interviewed on 30 Sept. 1977; 3 hrs.; 3 tapes; English; by E. Ruge. Post-WWII immigrant, was active in

Kitchener's German community affairs, particularly in the Canadian Society for German Relief.

BRANDT, MATHIAS
KITCHENER, ONT.
 Romanian identification card, certificate of nationality, and travel document, 1947-49; Canadian immigration certificate, 1949; and German passport, 1953. 2 cm. Photographs. Taped interview.
 11 photographs: the Brandt family in Romania, 1929-50; and activities of Schwaben Club in Kitchener, 1956.
 Interviewed on 7 Dec. 1977; 2 hrs.; 2 tapes; English; by B. Dandyk. WWI immigrant.

BRAUN, GEORGE
DELHI, ONT.
 Interviewed on 12 July 1977; 1 hr.; 1 tape; English; by David Judd. Discussion includes anecdote of O.P.P. raid, searching for spies, on the German Club in WWII.

BRAUN, OLGA
KITCHENER, ONT.
 Interviewed on 29 June 1977; 1 hr.; 1 tape; English; by E. Ruge.

BREITHAUPT, JAMES
KITCHENER, ONT.
 Brief histories of the Breithaupt family, n.d., 1977. Taped interview.
 Interviewed on 27 April 1977; 2 hrs.; 2 tapes; English; by E. Ruge. Discusses his political career.

BROWN, HOWARD B.
NEUSTADT, ONT.
 Interviewed on 10 April 1978; 2 hrs.; 2 tapes; English; by E. Ruge. Discusses influential Germans in Neustadt.

BRUM, HENRY
ALICE TOWNSHIP, ONT.
 Interviewed on 14 Feb. 1981; 1 hr.; 1 tape; German/English; by P. Hessel. Born in 1887 in Alice Township, founded Brum Dairy.

BRUMM, DONALD W.
PEMBROKE, ONT.
 Interviewed on 14 Feb. 1981; .5 hr.; 1 tape; English/German; by P. Hessel. Fourth generation German Canadian.

BUDENZ, CARL
WESTON, ONT.
 Interviewed on 27 June 1979; 1.5 hrs.; 2 tapes; English; by H. Martens. Post-WWII immigrant.

BUTZ, WALTER
KITCHENER, ONT.
 1 passport, n.d. .25 cm. Taped interview.
 Interviewed on 27 June 1977; 1 hr.; 1 tape; English; by E. Ruge. Post-WWII immigrant.

CĀLĪTIS, REV. J. (ST. ANDREW'S EVANGELICAL LUTHERAN LATVIAN CHURCH)
TORONTO, ONT.
 Correspondence, lists of immigrants, and identification cards from the Canadian Lutheran World Relief in Winnipeg, and the Evangelical Lutheran Immigration and Service Centre in Toronto, 1954-69. 14 cm.

CHRISTL, RUDI
TORONTO, ONT.
 Interviewed on 16 April 1980; 1.25 hrs.; 2 tapes; English; by K. Michael. Arrived in Canada in 1965.

COGHLAN, CHRISTINA
TORONTO, ONT.
 Interviewed on 16 Nov. 1978; 1.25
hrs.; 2 tapes; English/German; by K.
Lundy. Born in Toronto.

COLLIER, MARIA
WILLOWDALE, ONT.
 Interviewed on 30 Nov. 1978; 1.5
hrs.; 2 tapes; English; by K. Lundy.
Arrived in Canada in 1963.

CONRAD, JOHN
KITCHENER, ONT.
 Immigration documents, 1928-29. .5
cm. Photograph. Taped interview.
 1 photograph: group, n.d.
 Interviewed on 9 Sept. 1977; 2 hrs.;
2 tapes; English/German; by B.
Dandyk. Arrived in Canada in 1930.

DANDYK, FRANZ
KITCHENER, ONT.
 Birth, marriage, and death certifi-
cates, 1921-57. .25 cm. Photographs.
Taped interview.
 12 photographs: family, 1940-1960.
 Interviewed on 22, 23 March 1977;
.5 hr.; 1 tape; English; by B.
Dandyk. Emigrated in 1948.

DANDYK, MARIA
KITCHENER, ONT.
 34 photographs: the Dandyk family
in Germany, and Kitchener, 1935-57;
German immigrants en route to
Canada, 1957; and personal docu-
ments. Taped interview.
 Interviewed on 16 March 1977; .5
hr.; 1 tape; English; by B. Dandyk.
Arrived in Canada in 1948.

DANECKE, MARGARETE
KITCHENER, ONT.
 Immigration certificate and identifi-
cation card, 1960; German passport,
1967; and diploma, 1957. .25 cm.
Taped interview.
 Interviewed on 5 April 1977; 1 hr.;
1 tape; German; by E. Ruge.
Post-WWII immigrant.

DERTINGER, VINCE
DELHI, ONT.
 Brief history of the Dertinger family,
n.d. .25 cm.

DICKEY, LARRY
SIMCOE, ONT.
 Doughtery, R. and Wilf Pong. "The
German Ethnic Group in Norfolk
County." n.d. 1 cm.
 Drayson, V. "The German
Mennonite from Mexico." n.d. .5
cm.

DINSPEL, ANTON
GRAND RIVER, ONT.
 Interviewed on 5 July 1977; 1 hr.; 1
tape; German; by E. Ruge.
Post-WWII immigrant.

DREGER, E. J.
BRESLAU, ONT.
 Biography and documents of H. L.
Janzen, 1845-1927, and exerpt from
the minutes of the Economical Mutual
Insurance Co.'s Board of Director's
meeting, 1927. .5 cm. Photographs.
 11 photographs: the Janzen family,
and enterprises c. 1885-1930.
 Busy Berlin. 1897. Jubilee souvenir.
1 cm.

EBERDT, FRANK
KITCHENER, ONT.
 Interviewed on 15 Aug. 1977; 1 hr.;
1 tape; English; by E. Ruge.
Post-WWII immigrant.

FIALA, KARL
TORONTO, ONT.
Interviewed on 12 Feb. 1979; 1.25
hrs.; 1 tape; English; by K. Lundy.
Post-WWII immigrant.

FIEDLER, BERNIE
TORONTO, ONT.
Interviewed in July 1980; 1 hr.; 1
tape; English; by K. Michael.
Arrived in Canada in 1957.

FISCHER, ADOLF
KITCHENER, ONT.
Interviewed on 16 Nov. 1977; 2
hrs.; 2 tapes; English; by B. Dandyk.
Post-WWII immigrant.
FISCHER, ANNEMARIE
OAKVILLE, ONT.
Interviewed on 8 May 1979; 1 hr.; 1
tape; German; by K. Lundy. Arrived
in Canada in 1976.

FODOR, MARGARET
TORONTO, ONT.
2 news releases on illustrator, Walter
Trier, 1980. .25 cm. Taped interview.
Interviewed in July 1980; 1.5 hr.; 2
tapes; English; by K. Michael. Immigrated to Canada in 1947.

FRAPPIER, ANDREA
SUDBURY, ONT.
A Schraer-Schryer family tree,
1851-75, n.d. .25 cm. Taped interview.
Interviewed on 2 Sept. 1982; 1 hr.;
1 tape; English; by G. Schinko.
Sudbury's German immigrants at the
turn of the century.

FUNCKEN, EUGENE
WATERLOO, ONT.
Emigrated from the Netherlands to
Canada in 1864, a Roman Catholic

doctor in theology, and founder of St.
Jerome's College in Waterloo, Ont.,
1866. Donation includes correspondence, personal diaries, manuscripts,
and poems belonging to Ludwig and
Eugene Funcken, 1856-88. 8 reels of
microfilm. See St. Jerome's College.

GANZER, I.
DUNDAS, ONT.
"Brantforder Narrernspiegel."
1977-78. 1 cm.
Festival Calendars. 1977-78, 1978-79
(2 items).
"Germania Post." 1970-78. 1 cm.
Germania 100 Jahre. n.d. 216 pp.
"Hamiltoner Narrenspiegel" 1966-79
(1967 missing). 1 cm.

GLEASON, H. A.
TORONTO, ONT.
"Church Distribution as Evidence for
Settlement Patterns—Germans in the
Niagara Peninsula." n.d. .25 cm.

GLEBE, DELTON
WATERLOO, ONT.
Interviewed on 18, 25 Sept. 1977; 2
hrs.; 2 tapes; English; by E. Ruge.
Discusses his work as Reverend of
Lutheran Church, and Dean of Water-
loo Lutheran Seminary.
The First 60 Years. Waterloo
Lutheran University, 1971. .5 cm.

GOETZE, REV. JOHN
KITCHENER, ONT.
Interviewed on 17 May 1977; 1 hr.;
1 tape; German; by E. Ruge. Dis-
cusses the foundation of the Central
Baptist Church in the 1940s.

GOTTHARDT, ARNO
TORONTO, ONT.
Personal resumes and promotional
photographs. .25 cm.

Taped interview.
Interviewed in April 1980; 1.5 hrs.;
2 tapes; German/English; by K.
Michael. Arrived in Canada in 1952.

GÖTZE JR., JOHANNA
BRESLAU, ONT.
Interviewed on 18 June 1977; 1 hrs.;
1 tape; German; by E. Ruge. Post-
WWII immigrant.

GÖTZE SR., JOHANNA
KITCHENER, ONT.
Personal documents, mainly certifi-
cates, pertaining to Rev. Boleslaus
Götze, 1841-1956. 5 cm. Taped inter-
view.
Interviewed on 18, 20, 22 June
1977; 2 hrs.; 5 tapes; German; by E.
Ruge. Post-WWII immigrant.

GRIFE, ANNA
RANKIN, ONT.
1 photograph: n.d. Taped interview.
Interviewed on 6 June 1981; 1 hr.; 1
tape; English/German; by P. Hessel.
Recollections of the German community in Renfrew County.

GRIFE, LOLA
PEMBROKE, ONT.
Material pertaining to the Grace
Lutheran Church in Green Lake; list
of founding members, 1868; a brief
history of Lutherans in Wilberforce
Township (Renfrew County, Ont.),
1976; church leaflets, 1963-76; and
clippings. 1 cm.

GSCHAIDER, ADOLF
TORONTO, ONT.
Interviewed on 24 Feb. 1979; 1.5
hrs.; 2 tapes; English; by K. Lundy.
Post-WWII immigrant.

HARNEY, R. F.
TORONTO, ONT.
A circular letter from "Concerned
Parents of German Descent" protest-
ing TV show, "Holocaust." .25 cm.

HARTEL, HANS
BRANTFORD, ONT.
Deutscher Klub von Brantford. 1978.
25th anniversary booklet. 65 pp.

HAUSER, TONY V.
TORONTO, ONT.
Catalogue of donor's portraits on
exhibition in Los Angeles, booklet of
his photos, and 2 newsclippings,
1980. .5 cm. Taped interview.
Interviewed in Sept. 1980; 2 hrs.; 3
tapes; English; by K. Michael.
Arrived in Canada in 1967, discusses
his career as portrait photographer in
Toronto.

HEICK, OTTO W.
WATERLOO, ONT.
Interviewed on 24 July 1977; 1 hr.;
1 tape; English; by E. Ruge. Immigrated to Canada in 1947.

HEINZE, ANNEMARIE
TORONTO, ONT.
Interviewed on 27 Jan. 1979; 1.5
hrs.; 2 tapes; English; by K. Lundy.
Arrived in Canada in 1952.

HENKEL, AGATHE
TORONTO, ONT.
Interviewed on July 1980; 1.25 hrs.;
2 tapes; English; by K. Michael.
Arrived in Canada in 1952.

HERZBERG, GERHARD
TORONTO, ONT.
Interviewed on 19 May 1978; 1 hr.;
1 tape; English; by A. M. Nicholson.

HESS, ALBERT
KITCHENER, ONT.
2 brief histories of German immigration to Waterloo County; a transcript on the Pennsylvania Dutch, 1974; and printed items. 1.5 cm. Taped interview.
Interviewed on 7, 17, 28 April 1977; 4 hrs.; 4 tapes; German; by E. Ruge. Discusses involvement with the "House of Friendship," and the "Canadian Society for German Relief."
200 Jahre Deutsche Siedlung in Kanada, 1752-1952, Canadian-German Alliance, 1952. 30 pp.
"Early Days of Insemination."
Kitchener-Waterloo Record, 1977. .25 cm.

HESSEL, PETER
OTTAWA, ONT.
Consular reports from Prussian Embassy in London, to Prussian Minister of External Affairs in Berlin, March 1863, in German, and passenger lists (1858-1863) from the port of Hamburg to the Port of Quebec, in German. 2 reels of microfilm. Photographs.
7 photographs: German Canadians in Renfrew County, 1981.
Labudde, H. J. "Die deutsche Auswanderung nach Kanada." Dissertation, n.d., in German. 1 reel of microfilm.

HOLZAEPFEL, GEORG
KITCHENER, ONT.
3 newsclippings on Kabel's Tailoring Department and G. Holzaepfel, a tailor in Kitchener, 1970. .25 cm. Photograph. Taped interview.
1 photograph: the Holzaepfel family in Kitchener, 1937.
Interviewed on 25 May 1977; 1 hr.;

1 tape; German/English; by E. Ruge. Arrived in Canada in 1927.

HUETHER-WEPPLER, ANNA
NEUSTADT, ONT.
Papers, 1850-77, which include the history of the Huether and Wiegand families, correspondence, newsclippings, and a register book of baptisms, marriages, and burials of St. Paul's Church in Neustadt, 1870-1954. 1 reel of microfilm. Taped interview.
Interviewed on 10 Dec. 1977; 2 hrs.; 2 tapes; English; by E. Ruge. A pioneer of Neustadt, Ont.

JAKOBS, REV. J.
AYLMER, ONT.
3 photographs: a German Saturday School; and a picnic in Aylmer, 1976.
"Der Missionsbote." n.d. .25 cm.
"Evangeliums Posaune." n.d. .25 cm.
"Freuden Aere." n.d. .25 cm.

JANOTTA, ERIC
TORONTO, ONT.
Interviewed on 25 May 1979; .75 hr.; 1 tape; English; by H. Martens. Discusses involvement with the German congregation of St. Patrick on McCaul Street in Toronto.

JESSAT, GÜNTER
LINWOOD, ONT.
Interviewed on 25 Aug. 1977; 2 hrs.; 2 tapes; German; by E. Ruge. Former president of Concordia Club.

JOISTEN, BERNHARD P.
TORONTO, ONT.
Biography of donor, immigration papers, 1952, 1962; certificates, 1927-62; an article written by B.

Joisten; and a family book, 1951-52.
2 cm. Photographs. Taped interview.
5 photographs: the Joisten family in
Germany, France, and Toronto,
1941-65.
Interviewed on 2 March 1978; 1.75
hrs.; 2 tapes; English; by B. Dandyk.
Post-WWII immigrant.

JOISTEN, WALTER
OSHAWA, ONT.
Immigration documents, 1953-58;
funeral announcements, 1951-57; clippings on the Deutsch-Kanadischer
Saengerbund in Ottawa, 1975-78; a
labour card, 1932; a certificate of
apprenticeship, 1957; the Joisten
family book, 1930; and the Kolping
family book, 1955. 2 cm. Photographs. Taped interview.
37 photographs: the Joisten family in
Germany, and Toronto, 1930-74;
Edelweiss Choir, and the
Deutsch-Kanadischer Sängerbund in
Toronto, 1972-74.
Interviewed on 3 Aug. 1978; 1 hr.; 1
tape; English; by B. Dandyk. Arrived
in Canada in 1953.

KAEFER, REV. KARL
KITCHENER, ONT.
Personal documents, 1940-50s. 1
cm. Taped interview.
Interviewed on 17 Nov. 1977; 3
hrs.; 3 tapes; English/German; by B.
Dandyk. Discusses experiences in
Germany during WWII.

KARG, OSCAR
WATERLOO, ONT.
Interviewed on 10, 20 Dec. 1977; 2
hrs.; 2 tapes; English/German; by E.
Ruge. Post-WWII immigrants, active
in the Transylvania Club.

KELP, ROBERT
KITCHENER, ONT.
5 photographs: the Kelp family,
1906-48. Taped interview.
Interviewed on 2, 5, 7, 9 March
1977; 5 hrs.; 5 tapes; German; by E.
Ruge. Post-WWII immigrant.

KEMPE, FRANK
DELHI, ONT.
Immigration identification cards,
1928. .25 cm. Photographs.
1 photograph: Frank Kempe with
friends in a tobacco field in Delhi;
and Frank Kempe at the Romanian
church in Hamilton, 1934-39.

KEPPLER, CASPAR
KITCHENER, ONT.
Immigration documents, 1927, and a
brochure of the Canadian Schwaben
Sick Benefit Association Inc., 1947. 1
cm. Taped interview.
Interviewed on 13 Sept., 17 Nov.
1977; 2 hrs.; 2 tapes; Ger-
man/English; by B. Dandyk. Arrived
in Canada in the late 1920s.

KIEFER, OTTO
KITCHENER, ONT.
3 Kiefer family trees and correspondence, 1870-72. .25 cm. Taped interview.
Interviewed on 4 Aug. 1977; 1 hr.; 1
tape; German; by B. Dandyk. Arrived
in Canada in 1955.

KLEIN, LOTHAR
TORONTO, ONT.
Interviewed on 13 June 1980; 1.75
hrs.; 2 tapes; English; by K. Michael.
Post-WWII immigrant.

KNIPL, ELISABETH
TORONTO, ONT.
Interviewed on 26 April 1979; .5

hr.; 1 tape; English; by H. Martens. Arrived in Canada in 1953.

KOPRIVA, KARL
HAMILTON, ONT.
 Agenda of first meeting of German Association in Hamilton, 1929, leaflet of the Germania Club in Hamilton, 1976, a newsletter of the German Canadian Benevolent Society for Aged Persons in Hamilton, 1978, and a membership fee card, 1977. .25 cm. Photographs. Taped interview.
 4 photographs: donor in Austria, and in Yugoslavia, on board ship, 1918-33.
 Interviewed on 25 Oct. 1978; 2 hrs.; 2 tapes; German/English; by R. Neumann. Immigrated to Canada in 1927, founded the German Society in 1929.

KRAEMER, FRANK
KITCHENER, ONT.
 Historical sketches of the Kraemer and Spetz families, who were early settlers to Waterloo County, 1961, 2 notices, 1975, and a newsclipping on Rev. Dr. Theobald Spetz, 1850-1921. .25 cm.

KRAMER, EUGEN O.
KITCHENER, ONT.
 Interviewed on 2, 7 Oct. 1977; 2 hrs.; 2 tapes; German; by E. Ruge. Post-WWII immigrant.

KRAUSHAAR, HEINZ
KITCHENER, ONT.
 Interviewed on 3 Aug. 1977; 1 hr.; 1 tape; German; by E. Ruge. Immigrated to Canada in 1928.

KRIENER, LEONIE (BRAMM)
HANMER, ONT.
 The G. Bramm collection contains commemorative booklets, baptismal and confirmation certificates, 1895-1914, financial records of Niagara Pressed Brick Co. Ltd. Concordia Club and Berlin Piano Co., 1877-1905, correspondence of Bramm Bros., 1892-1908, and miscellaneous notes and clippings, 1908-72. 23 cm. Photographs.
 13 photographs: the Bramm and Kreiner families in Berlin, 1896-1913; employment in furniture manufacturing, 1900; and class photographs from schools in Kitchener, 1912-13.
 Baird, Sandy. *Tale of the Twin Cities: Kitchener-Waterloo.* n.d. 20 pp.
 Potter, Alex O. "Let's Reminisce." Kitchener-Waterloo Record, 1954. 36 pp.
 Rev. Frank Malinsky Committee. *Grace and Blessing.* Ontario District of the Lutheran Church Missouri Synod, 1954. 104 pp.
 Uttley, W. V. *A History of Kitchener, 1807-1916.* 1937. 12 pp.
 _____. *125th Anniversary, 1835-1960.* 26 pp.
 _____. *90th Anniversary of Ladies' Aid, 1865-1955.* 16 pp.
 Berlin Today. Aug. 1906. 88 pp.
 Here We Live. Dow Kingsbeer Brewery Ltd. Late 1950s. 20 pp.
 Kitchener Centennial, 1854-1954. 112 pp.
 "The Story of a Busy City." *Kitchener-Waterloo Record.* 1962, 23 pp.
 News Record of Berlin. 1908. 46 pp. Special industrial souvenir numbers of this newspaper.
 St. Paul's Evangelical Lutheran Church. 100th Anniversary, 1835-1935.

Souvenir of Hamilton, Canada.
1891. 66 pp.
Waterloo Country. Aug. 1914. 68
pp.

KROEG, STEFAN
TORONTO, ONT.
 Interviewed on 1 June 1978; 1.5
hrs.; 2 tapes; English; by B. Dandyk.
Arrived in Canada in 1948.

KROMER, PAUL
TORONTO, ONT.
 Interviewed on 15 Oct. 1979; 1.5
hrs.; 1 tape; English; by H. Martens.
Arrived in Canada in 1953.

KUMBERG, HANS-JÜRGEN
TORONTO, ONT.
 Personal papers, which include German school and army certificates,
immigration documents and clippings,
1935-77, and documents pertaining to
the Canadian Baltic Society in
Toronto, 1975. 2 cm. Photographs.
Taped interview.
 18 photographs: donor during military service in Italy, 1944-45; and
immigrants en route to Canada, 1951.
 Interviewed on 21 Feb. 1978; 2 hrs.;
2 tapes; English; by B. Dandyk.
Immigrated to Canada in 1951.

KUNTZ, TOM
WATERLOO, ONT.
 Clippings, documents, and a brief
history of Kuntz Brewery, 1936-56.
.5 cm. Photograph.
 1 photograph: Kuntz brothers at
Kuntz Brewery, 1894.

KUPRATH, FRIEDERIKE
TORONTO, ONT.
 Interviewed on 21 Feb. 1979; 1.75
hrs.; 2 hrs.; German; by K. Lundy.
Post-WWII immigrant.

LACHKNER, HENRY A.
WATERLOO, ONT.
 Family tree and article on H. G.
Lackner (1861-1925), n.d. .5 cm.
Taped interview.
 Interviewed on 16 Nov. 1977; 1 hr.;
1 tape; English; by B. Dandyk.
Pre-WWI immigrant.

LACKNER, NORBERT
TORONTO, ONT.
 A biography of the donor, immigra-
tion documents, 1950, 19 postcards
and letters written by donor in a
Russian prisoner-of-war camp,
1946-1950, and certificate from the
"Gottscheer Relief Association" in
Toronto, n.d. 3 cm (42 items). Photo-
graphs. Taped interview.
 22 photographs: activities of the
Gottscheer Verein, conventions.
 Interviewed on 15 March 1978; 3
hrs.; 3 tapes; English/German; by B.
Dandyk. Immigrated to Canada in
1952.
 Gotscheer Gedenkstaette. Dec. 1976;
Feb., Aug. 1977. 40 pp.
 Gottscheer Zeitung. 1977. 76 pp (9
issues).

LANGEN, LISELOTTE
TORONTO, ONT.
 Interviewed on 10 March 1979; 1.25
hrs.; 2 tapes; German; by K. Lundy.
Arrived in Canada in 1950.

LANGHOR, MARIE
TILLSONBURG, ONT.
 Interviewed on 26 July 1977; .75
hrs.; 1 tape; English; by David Judd.
Discusses tobacco farming in south-
western Ont.

LANG, MONIKA
PICKERING, ONT.
 Correspondence and clippings per-

taining to German Publications Ltd. in Pickering, c. 1960-80. .5 cm. Photographs.
48 photographs: German Publications Ltd. in Toronto, 1969-78.

LAUTENSCHLAGER, FRIEDRICH AND ERIKA
MISSISSAUGA, ONT.
Interviewed on 28 Oct. 1978; 2 hrs.; 2 tapes; English/German; by K. Lundy. Post-WWII immigrants.

LAUTENSCHLAGER, GERHARDT
TORONTO, ONT.
Interviewed on 11 April 1979; 1 hr.; 1 tape; English; by K. Lundy. Post-WWII immigrant.

LEIB, OTTO
TORONTO, ONT.
Interviewed on 5 Oct. 1978; 1.5 hrs.; 2 tapes; English/German; by K. Lundy. Immigrated to Canada in 1953.

LICKER, MATHEW
KITCHENER, ONT.
Romanian passports and certificates, and a Canadian immigration identification card, 1928-40. .5 cm. Photographs. Taped interview.
2 photographs: the Licker family in Romania, and Kitchener, 1904-34.
Interviewed on 27 July 1977; 2 hrs.; 2 tapes; English/German; by B. Dandyk. Arrived in Canada in 1928.

LÖFFLER, ALBERT
NEW HAMBURG, ONT.
20th anniversary booklet of the Canadian Baltic Immigrant Aid Society, 1968. 1 cm. Taped interview.
Interviewed on 20 Sept. 1977; 1 hr.;

1 tape; German; by E. Ruge. Post-WWII immigrant.

LOSEREIT, HEINRICH
KITCHENER, ONT.
Interviewed on 7, 19 Feb. 1978; 1 hr.; 1 tape; English/German; by E. Ruge. Post-WWII immigrant.

LOWE, GERTRUDE MARIA
SUDBURY, ONT.
Interviewed on 10 Aug. 1982; 1.5 hr.; 1 tape; German; by G. Schinko. German war bride.

LUBINSKI, BARBARA M.
TORONTO, ONT.
Interviewed on 3 Oct. 1978; 1 hr.; 1 tape; English/German; by K. Lundy. Arrived in Canada in 1939.

LUTKENHAUS-MUTHING, ALMUTH
OAKVILLE, ONT.
Interviewed in April 1980; 1.25 hrs.; 2 tapes; English; by K. Michael. Immigrated to Canada in 1966.

MAJOR, LEON
TORONTO, ONT.
Letters by German in Kapuskasing, Ont., translated and censored, 1917-22. 1 cm. Photographs.
3 photographs: unidentified, n.d.

MARTENS, HILDEGARD M.
TORONTO, ONT.
4 anniversary booklets. 2 cm. Photographs.
5 photographs: Mary Lake pilgrimage to commemorate the escape of Donau-Schwaben from Hungary, Romania, and Yugoslavia, 1979.

MASON, HILDE
TORONTO, ONT.
Interviewed on 26 Nov. 1978;

1.5 hrs.; 2 tapes; English; by K. Lundy. German war bride.

MATHES, DAVID
KITCHENER, ONT.
Interviewed on 3, 10 Feb. 1978; 1 hr.; 1 tape; German/English; by E. Ruge. Active in Transylvania Club, and German-Canadian organizations.

MATROSOVS, URSULA
TORONTO, ONT.
Curriculum vitae of donor who is an artist, 1977. .25 cm. Taped interview.
Interviewed on 3 Feb. 1979; 1.25 hrs.; 2 tapes; English; by K. Lundy. Post-WWII immigrant.

McCOY, DORIS
DELHI, ONT.
Interviewed on 26 July 1977; 1 hr.; 1 tape; English; by David Judd. Discusses tobacco farming and community life in the Delhi region.

McKINNON, MR.
WATERLOO, ONT.
Spetz, Theobald. *The Catholic Church in Waterloo County.* 1916. Diamond Jubilee History of the Diocese of Hamilton. 1 reel of microfilm.

McLAREN, DUNCAN
TORONTO, ONT.
1 poster of a German concert in Toronto, 3 Feb. 1980; and German concerts in Toronto, Niagara Falls, and Cambridge, Feb. and March 1980. With 4 posters of social events of the Germania Club in Hamilton, 1976-77; and a circular, "Holocaust Course Stirs Controversy," issued by Concerned Parents of German Descent in Toronto, n.d. .25 cm.

MEISSNER, EKKEHARD AND BEATRIX
AURORA, ONT.
Interviewed on 3 March 1979; 2 hrs.; 2 tapes; English; by K. Lundy. Post-WWII immigrants.

MERSCH, HUBERT
WATERLOO, ONT.
German passport and clipping, 1966-79. .25 cm. Photographs. Taped interview.
11 photographs: choir performances in Germany, and Kitchener, 1965-76.
Interviewed on 24 Nov. 1977; 2 hrs.; 2 tapes; English/German; by B. Dandyk. Post-WWII immigrant, discusses his Old World experiences.

METTLER, JOHN
KITCHENER, ONT.
Leaflets and 2 constitutions of the Canadian-Schwaben Sick Benefit Association in Kitchener, 1947-60, and printed items. 3 cm. Taped interview.
Interviewed on 18 Oct. 1977; 2 hrs.; 2 tapes; English; by B. Dandyk. Arrived in Canada in 1928, discusses socialist and Nazi associations in Kitchener in the 1930s.
German-Hungarian Family Calendar. 1938-40, 1947, 1951, 1953. Not published during WWII. 3 reels of microfilm.
Summerfest. 29-30 June 1956, 3-5 July 1959, 17-19 July 1964 (3 issues). 1 cm.
Tag der Deutsch-Kanadier. 30 June, 1-2 July 1961, 5-7 July 1963 (2 booklets).

MIKULA, MR. AND MRS. J.
DELHI, ONT.
Apprenticeship certificate as a wagon builder, 1928. .25 cm. Photograph.

1 photograph: work on railroad in Langenburg, Saskatchewan, 1928.

MILLER, JOHN ADAM
SUDBURY, ONT.
Interviewed on 12 Aug. 1982; 1.5 hrs.; 2 tapes; English; by G. Schinko. Immigrated to Canada in 1930.

MITTELSTAEDT, REV. KURT
KITCHENER, ONT.
Passport and diary, 1951. .5 cm. Photographs. Taped interview.
10 photographs: donor; and employment in agriculture and logging in Bremen, Saskatchewan, Alberta, and London, Ont., 1951-71.
Interviewed on 8 Sept. 1977; 2 hrs.; 2 tapes; English; by B. Dandyk. Arrived in Canada in 1951.

MORSCHER, EDDA
KITCHENER, ONT.
Personal travel documents and postcards, 1959-69. .5 cm. Photographs. Taped interview.
6 photographs: the Moscher family; and dwellings of the Krische and Morscher families in Yugoslavia, Austria, and Kitchener, 1940-70.
Interviewed on 15 June 1977; 1 hr.; 1 tape; German; by E. Ruge. Post-WWII immigrant, discusses her deeply-rooted, traditional German values and customs.

NEHELI, F.
NIAGARA FALLS, ONT.
Constitution, charter, letters, programmes, and calendars of Club Rheingold in Port Colborne, Ont., 1960-79. 1.5 cm (15 items).
Anniversary Yearbook of Club Rheingold. 1952-77. 1 cm.

NEURENBERG, W.
GRAVENHURST, ONT.
Constitution, clippings, and membership list of the German Canadian Country Club, 1977-78. .5 cm. Photographs.
16 photographs: social activities at the German Canadian organization, and the Old Country Club in Gravenhurst, Ont., 1970-76.

NIEMEYER, REV. H. W.
OTTAWA, ONT.
Brochure and reports, 1965-75. Photographs.
9 photographs: religious life at Martin Luther German Evangelical Church in Ottawa, c. 1965-75.

OESTERLE, LEONHARD
TORONTO, ONT.
Interviewed in April 1980; 2 hrs.; 2 tapes; English; by K. Michael. Arrived in Canada in the 1950s, discusses his art work, and political background.

PASTERNAK, PEGGY
TORONTO, ONT.
Interviewed on 8 Nov. 1978; 1.25 hrs.; 2 tapes; English; by K. Lundy. Born in Toronto, emphasizes his strong ties with the German language, and culture.

PENTEKER, JOHN
KITCHENER, ONT.
Interviewed on 22 June 1977; 1 hr.; 1 tape; German; by E. Ruge. Post-WWII immigrant.

PÉQUEGNAT, MARCEL
KITCHENER, ONT.
2 newsclippings on the

Swiss-Canadian Pequegnat family of watchmakers, 1967. .25 cm. Taped interview.
Interviewed on 4 Aug. 1977; 1 hr.; 1 tape; English; by B. Dandyk. WWI immigrant.

PITZER, SISTER MARY AGNES
TORONTO, ONT.
Interviewed on 27 Jan. 1979; 1.5 hrs.; 2 tapes; English; by H. Martens. Interwar immigrant, discusses social activities at the German-Catholic Congregation at St. Patricks's on McCaul Street in Toronto.

PLESCHINGER, ANTON
KITCHENER, ONT.
Interviewed on 30 Nov., 14 Dec. 1977; 3 hrs.; 3 tapes; by B. Dandyk. Arrived in Canada in 1948.

POSEL, WALLI
TORONTO, ONT.
Interviewed on 13 Oct. 1978; .5 hr.; 1 tape; English/German; by K. Lundy. She immigrated to Canada in 1952.

PRAWZICK, GÜNTHER MAX
SUDBURY, ONT.
Interviewed on 25 Aug. 1982; 1 hr.; 1 tape; German; by G. Schinko. Arrived in Canada in 1956.

PRUEFER, REV. HELMUTH
KITCHENER, ONT.
Clippings concerning the Lutheran Church in Kitchener, 1953-74. .25 cm. Taped interview.
Interviewed on 24 June 1977; 1 hr.; 1 tape; English; by E. Ruge. Discusses the founding of the Bethel Lutheran Church.

PUCHTA, ZIGGY
TORONTO, ONT.
Interviewed in Sept. 1980; 1.5 hrs.; 2 tapes; English; by K. Michael. Immigrated to Canada in 1953.

RATTEL, REV. JOHANNES
KITCHENER, ONT.
Interviewed on 7 Oct. 1977; 1 hr.; 1 tape; German; by E. Ruge. Discusses Lutheran Church in Kitchener.

REPPERT, LIESELOTTE
TORONTO, ONT.
Rolf Reppert personal papers, 1932-54, documents, clippings, and correspondence. 5 cm. See Club der Freunde Berlins.

RICHTER, BARBARA
MISSISSAUGA, ONT.
Interviewed on 2 April 1979; 1.25 hrs.; 2 tapes; English; by K. Lundy. Arrived in Canada in 1963.

RICHTER, JURGEN AND THOMAS
TORONTO, ONT.
Interviewed on 18 Feb. 1979; 1 hr.; 1 tape; English; by K. Lundy. Post-WWII immigrants.

RICHTER, KLAUS AND SIGRID
TORONTO, ONT.
Interviewed on 25 Jan. 1979; 1.5 hrs.; 2 tapes; English; by K. Lundy. Arrived in Canada in 1969.

RICKER, GOTTLOB
KITCHENER, ONT.
Immigration documents, 1945-56; and Russian certificates and letters of reference, 1937-39. A biographical sketch of donor. 1 cm. Photographs. Taped interview.
11 photographs: the Ricker family at a funeral; and in the military in Rus-

sia, Germany, and Kitchener,
1941-73.
 Interviewed on 1 Dec. 1977; 2 hrs.;
2 tapes; English; by B. Dandyk.
Immigrated to Canada in 1956.

RIMROTT, FREDERICK P.
THORNHILL, ONT.
 Flyer and booklet concerning German school, n.d. 1 cm. Taped interview.
 Interviewed on 12 Oct. 1978; 1.5
hrs.; 2 tapes; English/German; by K.
Lundy. Post-WWII immigrant.

RINCK, AKSEL
MISSISSAUGA, ONT.
 Correspondence pertaining to the
German Canadian Council for the
Arts, 1974-76. .25 cm. Photographs.
Taped interview.
 2 photographs: the donor in Germany, 1941-45.
 Interviewed on 26 Aug. 1978; 1 hr.;
1 tape; English; by B. Dandyk. Discusses involvement with German-Canadian associations, and as editor
of *Toronto Zeitung*.
 Contacta. 1973. 50 pp.
 Globus. 1973 (German-Canadian
issue). 16 pp.
 This Town Is Wide Open. No. 11,
Nov. 1972 (German Cultural Festival
Week). 16 pp.

RINGWELSKI, HILLA
TORONTO, ONT.
 Interviewed on 20 Oct. 1978; 1 hr.;
1 tape; German/English; by K.
Lundy. Post-WWII immigrant.

RIST, WILLY
OTTAWA, ONT.
 Minutes of the founding meeting of
the German Karneval Association of
Ottawa, 1966; and 2 letterheads and

programme of the German Mardi
Gras Society in Ottawa. .25 cm.
Photographs.
 2 photographs: activities of the German Mardi Gras Society in Ottawa, c.
1965-75.
 Faschingsheft. 1974-75.
 The Nutty Town Cryer. 1969. Booklet.

ROESELER, PAUL H.
TORONTO, ONT.
 Interviewed on 26 March 1979; 1.25
hrs.; 2 tapes; English; by H. Martens. Post-WWII immigrant.

ROTHSCHILD, JOHANNA
TORONTO, ONT.
 Interviewed in June 1980; 1.25 hrs.;
2 tapes; English; by K. Michael. The
donor was a German war bride.

RUDT, KURT H.
PEMBROKE, ONT.
 Writings of personal experiences in
Canada, and East Germany, 1967,
1981. 1 cm. Photograph.
 1 photograph: 1981.

SACCÉ, EDGAR
THORNHILL, ONT.
 Printed items pertaining to Lutheran
Missouri Synod Credit Union,
1952-60, and an application for the
Deutsche Sprachschuke, n.d. .5 cm.
 *Zehn Jahre Sprachschulen für
Deutsch, 1956-66*. 39 pp.

SALB, STEVE
TORONTO, ONT.
 Records pertaining to the Kolping
Society of Canada, and the Kolping
family in Toronto: constitution and
amendments, 1955-64; minutes,
1955-74; financial reports, 1956-74;
correspondence, 1961-64; member-

ship lists and application forms, 1961-64; miscellaneous items: press releases, notes, memoranda, letterheads, circulars, 1955-64. .5 meters. Taped interview.

Interviewed on 29 May 1979; 1.5 hrs.; 2 tapes; English; by H. Martens. One of the founders of the Kolping Society in Toronto.

SAUER, ANTON
TORONTO, ONT.

Interviewed on 26 April 1979; .75 hr.; 1 tape; English; by H. Martens. Arrived in Canada in 1948.

SCHAEFFER, PETER
DELHI, ONT.

Interviewed on May 22 1985; 2.5 hrs.; 3 tapes; English; by Anne Schooley. Discusses woman's role on tobacco farm.

SCHEUNEMANN, ALFRED
RANKIN, ONT.

Interviewed on 6 June 1981; 1 hr.; 1 tape; English/German; by P. Hessel. Recollections of his childhood in a predominantly German community in Renfrew County.

SCHIKETANZ, MARGARETE
KITCHENER, ONT.

Clippings about donor in Kitchener, 1968. .25 cm. Taped interview.
Interviewed on 5, 13 Oct. 1977; 2 hrs.; 2 tapes; German; by E. Ruge. Post-WWII immigrant.

SCHMALZ, W. H. E.
KITCHENER, ONT.

W. H. E. Schmalz, whose father was mayor of Berlin, Ont. in 1911-12, was an architect and a practising historian who wrote regional histories, and a biography of a local,

wealthy German family. The collection includes personal papers, school material, musical memorabilia, and ancestors' family documents, 1851-1911. It also contains Waterloo County souvenir albums and records relating to the history of Kitchener and W. H. E. Schmalz's involvement in the Kitchener Musical Society, 1950-75, and in St. Paul's Lutheran Church, Kitchener, 1921-69. 11 cm. 4 reels of microfilm. Photographs. Taped interview.

Over 200 photographs: the Schmalz family, 1870-1924; entertainment, 1886-1923; and the Kitchener Musical Society Band, 1907-69, all taken in Kitchener along with buildings throughout Ont. such as schools, houses, and churches, designed by W. H. E. Schmalz.
Interviewed on 21 April 1977, 20 June 1978; 2 hrs.; 2 tapes; English; by B. Dandyk. Early member of the German community in Berlin, Ont.

SCHMIDT, ADAM AND MARIE
KITCHENER, ONT.

Immigration papers, 1929-50. 1 cm. Photographs. Taped interview.
11 photographs: the Gossmann and Schmidt families in Romania, Austria, and Germany, 1918-49; and immigrants at point of departure, Bremen, 1949.
Interviewed on 28 Sept. 1977; 2 hrs.; 2 tapes; English/Germany; by B. Dandyk. Post-WWII immigrant.

SCHMIDT, ADAM
KITCHENER, ONT.

Interviewed on 5 Aug. 1977; 1 hr.; 1 tape; English; by B. Dandyk. Interwar immigrant.

SCHMIDT, EVA
MILTON, ONT.
Interviewed on 4 April 1979; 1.5
hr.; 2 tapes; English/German; by K.
Lundy. Arrived in Canada in 1954.

SCHMIDT, HERMINIO P.
WATERLOO, ONT.
Interviewed on 10 July 1977; 1 hr.;
1 tape; German; by E. Ruge.
Post-WWII immigrant.

SCHNEIDER, NORMAN
CAMBRIDGE, ONT.
Interviewed on 6 Sept. 1977; 1 hr.;
1 tape; English; by B. Dandyk.
Founding family of J. M. Schneider
meatpacking plant, 1890.

SCHNEIDER, WALTER
NEW HAMBURG, ONT.
Travel documents, 1940, 1950. .5
cm. Taped interview.
Interviewed on 22 June 1977; 1 hr.;
1 tape; German; by E. Ruge.

SCHOEPKE, SIEGFRIED W.
BRESLAU, ONT.
1 floor plan of Siegfried Schoepke's
house in Breslau, Ont. .25 cm. Photographs. Taped interview.
2 photographs: members and dwellings of the Schoepke family in
Breslau, 1955-76.
Interviewed on 28 April, 14 May
1977; 3 hrs.; 3 tapes; German; by E.
Ruge. Post-WWII immigrant.

SCHROEDER, BERNARD J.
SUDBURY, ONT.
1 birth certificate of B. C.
Schroeder, 1951. Photograph. Taped
interview.
1 photograph: the Schroeder family
in Massey, 1959.
Interviewed on 30 Aug. 1982; 1 hr.;

1 tape; English; by G. Schinko. Third
generation German Canadian.

SCHWARTZ, HEBERT
KITCHENER, ONT.
Interviewed on 28 March 1978; 1
hr.; 1 tape; English; by E. Ruge.
Second generation German Canadian,
parents arrived in 1930.

SCHWARTZ, VERNER JULIUS
OTTAWA, ONT.
Interviewed on 24 Feb. 1981; .75
hr.; 1 tape; English; by P. Hessel.
Son of German immigrants who
arrived in 1869.

SEIZ, CHRISTINE
TORONTO, ONT.
Interviewed on 2 Nov. 1978; 1.5
hrs.; 2 tapes; English; by K. Lundy.
Arrived in Canada in the mid-1970s.

SERTL, ELSA
TORONTO, ONT.
Interviewed on 19 Oct. 1978; 1.5
hrs.; 2 tapes; English/German; by K.
Lundy. Immigrated to Canada in
1959.

SIEBER, FRANK
KITCHENER, ONT.
Interviewed on 14 Nov. 1977; 2
hrs.; 2 tapes; English/German; by B.
Dandyk. Arrived in Canada in 1951.

SIMON, ERNIE J.
KITCHENER, ONT.
Interviewed on 6 Dec. 1977; 2 hrs.;
2 tapes; English; by B. Dandyk.
Immigrated to Canada in 1928.

SINKINS, JACK
WATERLOO, ONT.
Military papers of Lieutenant Colo-
nel William M. O. Lochead, Com-

mander of the 118th Battalion in Kitchener, Ont., 1915-16. 5 reels of microfilm.

SNYDER, FRED
WATERLOO, ONT.
Genealogical material pertaining to the Groff family, 1958-76. .25 cm. Photographs.
2 photographs: the Snyder reunion, Doon, 1909; and Berlin Junior Farmers' Association in Kitchener, 1916. File contains biography of the Groff and Snyder families.

STAATS, HERBERT
TORONTO, ONT.
Interviewed on 27 July 1978; 1.75 hrs.; 2 tapes; English/German; by B. Dandyk. Arrived in Canada in 1953.

STEIN, WERNER O.
KITCHENER, ONT.
Interviewed on 27 April 1977; 1 hr.; 1 tape; English; by B. Dandyk. Immediate post-WWII immigrant.

STICHMANN, MATTHEW
PORT PERRY, ONT.
6 photographs: the Trenz family in Yugoslavia, and Ont. 1918-32; Danau Schwaben in traditional costume; a passion play in Toronto, 1934, 1936; and a funeral in Windsor, Ont., 1932.
Das erste Jahrzehnt der deutsch-katholischen Gemeinde (The first ten years of the German-Catholic parish). 1939. 1 reel of microfilm.

STIEGER, RAIMUND
TORONTO, ONT.
Stieger family papers, 1949-50; which include clippings, posters, letters, and tickets pertaining to Edelweiss Children's Choir in Toronto, and the Johann Strauss Gesellschaft in

Richmond Hill, 1949-78. Also includes a biography of Raimund Stieger. 2 cm. Photographs. Taped interview.
11 photographs: Austria, and Toronto, 1935-60; and executive of Johann Strauss Gesellschaft, n.d.
Interviewed on 15 March 1978; 1.75 hrs.; 2 tapes; English; by B. Dandyk. Arrived in Canada in 1954.
Litera. 1959-69 (5 issues). 80 pp.

STORK, FRIEDRICH J.
KITCHENER, ONT.
Interviewed on 5 Nov., 7 Dec. 1977; 2 hrs.; 2 tapes; German; by E. Ruge. Post-WWII immigrant.

TELIPASA, MARY
TORONTO, ONT.
1 photograph: the Telipasa family in Yugolsavia, 1930. Taped interview. Interviewed on 28 March 1979; 1 hr.; 1 tape; English; by H. Martens. Immigrated to Canada in 1949.

TIDMAN, CHRISTINE
TORONTO, ONT.
2 photographs: the Hansen family in Halifax, 1954; and immigrants en route to Canada, 1954. Taped interview.
Interviewed on 10 Nov. 1978; 1.5 hrs.; 2 tapes; English; by K. Lundy. Post-WWII immigrant.

TRIESELMAN, RICHARD
OTTAWA, ONT.
Concordia Anniversary Brochure, 1958-78.
Hofbräuhaus News. 1973-78. 1 reel of microfilm.
Ottawa Herald. 1973-78.

TUERR, PAUL
KITCHENER, ONT.
 Interviewed on 5 March 1978; 1 hr.;
1 tape; German; by E. Ruge.
Pre-WWII immigrant.

VON AESCH, CHRISTINE
TORONTO, ONT.
 Interviewed on 23 Oct. 1978; 1.5
hrs.; 2 tapes; English; by K. Lundy.
Post-WWII immigrant.

VON HARPE, ULRICH
WATERLOO, ONT.
 Von Harpe family papers, 1934-71,
which include autobiographies, family
tree, proof of "Aryanship," and other
Nazi certificates. Various certificates
regarding Ulrich von Harpe's career
as a naval officer, 1950-63. 1 reel of
microfilm. Taped interview.
 Interviewed on 15 Dec. 1977; 1 hr.;
1 tape; German; by E. Ruge.
Post-WWII immigrant.

VON HERTZENBERG, WOLDEMAR
AND HILDEGARD
PICKERING, ONT.
 Interviewed on 24 March 1979; 2
hrs.; 2 tapes; German/English; by K.
Lundy. Post-WWII immigrants.

WAGNER, HELEN (CANADA TRUST)
KITCHENER, ONT.
 A Guide to Waterloo Region. 1973.
48 pp.

WAGNER, MARTIN
SIMCOE, ONT.
 Interviewed on 26 July 1977; 1.5
hrs.; 1 hr.; English; by Hilda Schenn.
Discusses tobacco farming and com-
munity life in southern Ont.

WALLIS, WALTER
SIMCOE, ONT.
 Records of family tobacco farm business, 1928-46. 1 cm. 1 reel of microfilm. Taped interview with T. Youse.
 "100 Years with Christ for Christ,
1854-1954." St. Peter's Lutheran
Church, Delhi. 26 pp.

WARWAS, HANS AND HELGA
TORONTO, ONT.
 Immigration documents, 1938-59,
and records relating to Sportclub "'64
" (Toronto), 1965-75. 6 cm. Photographs. Taped interview.
 22 photographs: the Warwas and
Kostorz families, and business in
Upper Silesia, Germany, 1928-45;
immigrants en route to Canada, 1951;
and dwellings, and sports in Toronto,
1951-78.
 Interviewed on 9 March 1978; 3.5
hrs.; 4 tapes; English; by B. Dandyk.
Post-WWII immigrants.

WEBER, ELDON
WATERLOO, ONT.
 Interviewed on 20 Oct., 10 Nov.
1977; 1 hr.; 1 tape; English; by E.
Ruge. Third generation German
Canadian.
 Weber, Eldon D. "Descendents of
Henry B. Steckle." 1967. 1 cm.
"Waterloo-Wellington Branch
Genealogical Society." Vol. 5, no. 5
1977. 1 cm.

WEICKER, SAMUEL
KITCHENER, ONT.
 Weicker family album and records
pertaining St. Matthew's Lutheran
Church in Kitchener, 1910-77. 1 reel
of microfilm. 5 cm.
 Jubilaeums Buechlein, 1861-1911,

Festschrift zur Feier des 50 jaehrigen Jubilaeums der evang.—Lutherischen Synode von Canada, 1911. 115 pp.

WEISBACH, HENRY
TORONTO, ONT.
 Interviewed on 2 June 1978; 1.75 hrs.; 2 tapes; English; by B. Dandyk. Arrived in Canada in 1939.
 Weisbach, Henry. "The Story of the German People." .5 cm.
 _____. "Politische Parteien in Kanada." .5 cm.
 Anniversary booklets of the Sudeten German Club, 1965-77. 3 cm.
 "Jahrestag der Sudeteneinwanderer in Kanada." *New Yorker Staats-Zeitung und Herold.* No. 126, 13 Aug. 1974. 1 cm.
 VorWärts, 1956-78. Originals. Incomplete. 20 cm.

WEISBACH, HERMINE AND HENRY
TORONTO, ONT.
 Interviewed on 2, 13 April 1984; 3.5 hrs.; 4 tapes; German; by E. Hussmann. Arrived in Toronto in 1941, after migration from British Columbia.

WEISE, KURT
HAMILTON, ONT.
 Immigration papers and certificates of the Weise family, 1956 .5 cm. Photographs. Taped interview.
 3 photographs: activities of the organization "Fidelio 65," a branch of the German Mardi Gras Society, n.d.
 Interviewed on 4 Oct. 1978; 2 hrs.; 2 tapes; German/English; by R. Neumann. Immigrated to Canada in 1956.

WEISS, FATHER WOLFGANG
KITCHENER, ONT.
 Interviewed on 29 June 1977; 1 hr.;

1 tape; German; by E. Ruge. Discusses his travels and work at St. Mary's Rectory.

WEKERLE, ANTON
THORNHILL, ONT.
 Interviewed on 10 March 1979; 1.25 hrs.; 2 tapes; English; by H. Martens. Immigrated to Canada in 1947.

WENDLER, LINDA W.
SUDBURY, ONT.
 Interviewed on 19 Aug. 1982; 1.5 hrs.; 2 tapes; German; by G. Schinko. Pre-WWII immigrant.

WENTZLAFF, REV. WALTER
WINDSOR, ONT.
 Evangelical Lutheran Church collection includes directories, anniversary booklets, and programmes, c. 1930-77; and proceedings of the Ont. district conventions, 1946-66. Ordination certificate, and other items belonging to Rev. Wentzlaff, 1925-75. 1 reel of microfilm. Photographs.
 3 photographs: the family in Vancouver, British Columbia, and Kingsville, Ont. 1925-77.
 The Lutheran Witness. 1946-67. (Ont. district edition). 1 reel of microfilm.

WERNECKE, HEINZ
KITCHENER, ONT.
 Includes Oktoberfest material, 1972-77, booklets and papers of Concordia Brass Band, 1968-72; miscellaneous papers pertaining to the Waterloo County Police Band, 1968-70, and donor's biography. 3 cm. Photographs. Taped interview.
 14 photographs: music bands that H. Wernecke was involved with, most of which participated in the

Oktobermusikfest in Kitchener, 1968-76.
Interviewed on 10, 22 Aug. 1978; 1.75 hrs.; 2 tapes; English; by B. Dandyk. He arrived in Canada in 1951.
Anniversary of Canadian German Society, 1947-72. 43 pp.

WERNER (SENIOR), JOHN
KITCHENER, ONT.
Interviewed on 12 May, 19 June 1977; 2 hrs.; 2 tapes; German; by E. Ruge. Discusses traditions of Transylvanian Society.

WERNER, OTTO
KITCHENER, ONT.
Interviewed on 5 June 1977; 2 hrs.; 2 tapes; German; by E. Ruge. Former president of Concordia Club.

WERTHEIMER, LEONARD
TORONTO, ONT.
Interviewed on 30 Jan. 1979; 1.25 hrs.; 2 tapes; English/German; by K. Lundy. Post-WWII immigrant.

WIESE, MARGARETE
KITCHENER, ONT.
2 letters and receipts, 1970-71. .25 cm. Photograph. Taped interview.
1 photograph: German immigrants en route to Canada, 1952.
Interviewed on 3 July 1977; 2 hrs.; 2 tapes; German; by R. Ruge.
Post-WWII immigrant.

WOLF, MARIA AND GEORGE
DELHI, ONT.
Austrian immigration papers and certificates, 1938-52 (6 items). Photograph.
1 photograph: the Wolf family, c. 1931.

WULKAN, DAVID
TORONTO, ONT.
Interviewed on 6 June 1980; 1 hr.; 1 tape; English; by K. Michael. Immigrated to Canada in 1951.

YANKE, ALBERT
KITCHENER, ONT.
Clipping regarding the renaming of Berlin, Ont., 1966, and 2 family trees. .25 cm. Photographs. Taped interview.
3 photographs: the Yanke family in Kitchener, 1860(?).
Interviewed on 12 Oct. 1977; 2 hrs.; 2 tapes; English; by B. Dandyk. Ancestors arrived in the late 19th century.
"Name Change Approved by Scant 81 Votes." *Kitchener-Waterloo Record.* 2 Sept. 1966. .25 cm.

YOUSE, EDITH
TILLSONBURG, ONT.
3 photographs: construction of Rhineland Church, c. 1917.

YOUSE, THOMAS H.
TILLSONBURG, ONT.
Interviewed on 26 July 1977; 1 hr.; 1 tape; English; by David Judd. Discusses anti-German sentiments during WWI.

YUNGBLUT, EARL
NEUSTADT, ONT.
Interviewed on 21 Feb. 1978; 1 hr.; 1 tape; English; by E. Ruge. Third generation German Canadian.

YUNGBLUT, ELEDA L.
NEUSTADT, ONT.
Interviewed on 21 Feb. 1978; 1 hr.; 1 tape; English/German; by E. Ruge. Third generation German Canadian.

ZEIDLER, EBERHARD
TORONTO, ONT.
 Interviewed in June 1980; 2 hrs.; 2
tapes; English; by K. Michael.
Post-WWII immigrant.

ZILLINGER, MAGDALENA
TORONTO, ONT.
 Interviewed on July 1980; 1.25 hrs.;
2 tapes; English; by K. Michael.
Post-WWII immigrant.

═══════════════════

BENTON BAPTIST CHURCH
(B. CLUBINE)
KITCHENER, ONT.
1931, which include church council
minutes, Sunday School minute book,
cash book, marriage register, lease of
burial lots, and clippings. 1 reel of
microfilm (18 pages).
 Baptist Church. Anniversary issues
of 1901-66. 65 pp.
 Baptist Herald. 1967. 28 pp.

BETHEL LUTHERAN CHURCH
KITCHENER, ONT.
 Record book with minutes and
founding constitution, n.d., membership lists, 1949-77, and clippings
about the Church, 1953-74. 1 reel of
microfilm. .5 cm. Photographs.
Taped interview with Rev. Helmuth
Pruefer. Photographs.
 4 photographs: religious activity; and
clergymen at Bethel Lutheran Church,
c. 1970s.
 *10th Anniversary Booklet of the
Evangelical Lutheran Church.* 1959.
Microfilm.
 *25th Anniversary Booklet of Bethel
Lutheran Church.* 1949-74. 2 cm., in
German.
 Festschrift zur EinWeihung. 23 June
1963. 1 cm., in German/English.

CANADIAN SOCIETY FOR GERMAN
RELIEF
WATERLOO, ONT.
 The collection includes constitution,
cashbooks, minutes, correspondence,
annual and press reports, membership
lists, and records pretaining to specific fund-raising drives, 1947-76. 11
reels of microfilm. 2 cm. Taped
interview with K. Bongart.
 *25th Anniversary Book of the Cana-
dian Society for German Relief.* 1972.
2 cm.
 *Anniversary Book of 200 Years of
German Settlement in Canada,
1752-1952.* 1952. Microfilm.
 Bulletin. 1951-53. Microfilm.
 The Canadian-German Yearbook.
n.d. Microfilm.

CATHOLIC KOLPING SOCIETY OF
CANADA
KITCHENER, ONT.
 "5th National Convention, 1975." 26
pp.
 "Die Liturgie der Kirche." 1964. 12
pp.
 Kolping Messenger. June 1964. 16
pp.

CENTRAL BAPTIST CHURCH
KITCHENER, ONT.
 Written report by, and taped inter-
view with Rev. J. Götze.
 *20th Anniversary of Central Baptist
Church, 1953-73.* .5 cm.

CHURCH OF GOD
KITCHENER, ONT.
 Marriage register, old and new
constitution, minutes, bulletins, and
reports, 1971-77, and Rev. Karl
Kaefer's personal documents,
1940-59. 5 cm. Photographs.
 2 photographs: dedication at
Gemeindeg Gottes in Kitchener,

1975; and immigrants en route to Canada, Bremén, 1929.

CHURCH OF THE GOOD SHEPHERD (NEW JERUSALEM SOCIETY) KITCHENER, ONT.
Records, 1843-1903, which include minutes and account book of the New Jerusalem Society, correspondence, financial statements, marriage registers, land deeds, and lists of burial plots belonging to the Church of the Good Shepherd, and an historical sketch of the Swedenborgian congregation in Kitchener, 1939. 1 reel of microfilm. Photographs.
15 photographs: Swedenborgians, 1860-1932; and New Church Convention, U.S., 1932.

CLUB DER FREUNDE BERLINS TORONTO, ONT.
The collection contains a constitution, minutes, financial records, pamphlets, clippings, posters, tickets, members lists, and leaflets, 1963-76. 1 meter. Photographs. See Lieselotte Reppert.
44 photographs: activities of the Club der Freunde Berlins in Toronto, 1958-70.
Berliner Baer. 1969-75. Club newsletter. 6 cm.
Berliner Leben. 1971-72 (5 issues).
Berliner Magazin. 1972 (2 issues).
Die Vereinswelt 1961 U.S. German clubs and societies (2 issues). 2 cm.
West Berliner Illustrierte Zeitschrift. 1952.

CLUB LORELEY (O. HELLER) OSHAWA, ONT.
Records, 1968-78, which include by-laws, minutes, correspondence, statements of revenue and expenses, membership list, bulletins, posters,

flyers, tickets, calendars, and clippings. 1 reel of microfilm. 32 loose pages and 1 scrapbook. Photographs.
12 photographs: activities of the Club Loreley Oshawa, 1962-76.
Loreley Nachrichten. 20 Oct. 1975. 13 pp.
Newsletter. 1970-79. 15 cm.
"Trans-Kanada Vereinigung." 1974. 1 cm.

CONCORDIA CLUB KITCHENER, ONT.
Records of the German Language School Concordia, 1970-73, which include constitution and amendments, 1971, annual reports, 1970-72, correspondence, 1971-73, financial statements, 1973-75, circulars, course outline, and clippings. 3.5 cm. Photographs. Taped interviews with Herminio Schmidt and O. Werner.
95 prints and photographs: documents, letters and clippings pertaining to the Concordia Club, 1870-1980.
Centennial Anniversary of Concordia Club. 1973. 220 pp.
Nachrichten. No. 98, Feb. 1977. 1 cm.

CONCORDIA SCHOOL PARENT TEACHER ASSOCIATION WATERLOO, ONT.
Interviewed on 10 July 1977; 1 hr.; 1 tape; German; by E. Ruge. Meeting and student Christmas festivities.

DEUTSCHER AUTOMOBIL CLUB TORONTO, ONT.
Records, bulletins, and newsletters, 1959-78. 3 reels of microfilm. 1 cm. Photographs. Taped interview with K. Bartels.
5 photographs: Deutscher Automobil

Club Inc. in Toronto, 1944-78.
Newsletter. 1974-75. 1 reel of microfilm.

EMMANUEL LUTHERAN CHURCH
PETERSBURG, ONT.
 Records, 1851-1961, which include
constitution, 1869, minutes, cash
book, membership lists, and parish
registers. 2 reels of microfilm.
*35th Anniversary Booklet of
Emmanuel Lutheran Church.* 1937.
.25 cm
 100th Anniversary Booklet of Congregation. 1951. 16 pp.

GERMAN CANADIAN CLUB OF
AYLMER (O. SCHNEIDER)
SPARTA, ONT.
 Records, 1949-78, include constitution, by-laws, minutes, cash ledgers,
notices, tickets, and programmes. 1
reel of microfilm. 1 cm. Photographs.
 3 photographs: documents and activities of German Canadian Club in
Aylmer, 1954.

GERMAN CANADIAN CLUB OF SARNIA
(W. VOGT)
SARNIA, ONT.
 Records, 1960-78, include charter of
incorporation, minutes of
shareholder's and general meetings,
correspondence, financial statements
reports, membership lists, programmes, and flyers. 1 reel of microfilm. 1.5 cm. Photograph.
 1 photograph: clubhouse of the German Canadian Club, 1968.
Carnival Season. 1972-73. Booklet.
66 pp.
German Pension in Canada. 1972.
Booklet 79 pp.
Morgen Tomorrow Sarnia, 1973-78.

Microfilm.
*Trans-Canada Union of German
Canadians.* 1973. 118 pp.

GERMAN CANADIAN CLUB
(S. SCHREIBER)
MIDLAND, ONT.
tch of Club, membership lists, applications, and a flyer, 1978-79. 1 cm.

GERMANIA CLUB
HAMILTON, ONT.
 Flyers of social events of the
Germania Club, 1976-77 (4 items).
Germania 100 Jahre, 1864-1964.
1964. 216 pp.
*Germania post-Centennial Edition
Heft.* July 1967. 104 pp.

HARFENTOENE MALE CHOIR
TORONTO, ONT.
 Minutes of executive and general
meetings, 1961-77; correspondence,
1977; membership list, 1977-78; celebration of the Deutsch-Kanadischer
Sängerbund, 1967; brief history of
the choir, 1929-39; and concert programmes and announcements,
1939-78. Photographs. Taped interviews with B. Joisten and W. Joisten.
 20 photographs: performances by the
Harfentoene Male Choir in Ont.,
Montreal, and Germany, 1955-74.

HARMONIE
TORONTO, ONT.
"Sprachschulen fuer Deutsch." 1966.
Yearbook. 39 pp.

HISTORICAL SOCIETY OF
MECKLENBURG UPPER CANADA
(P. A. PRAXMARER)
TORONTO, ONT.
tches of the following personalities:
Alvensleben, Helmcken, Hespeler,
Beck, Schwedtfeger, Arnoldi,

Zeisberger, and Berczy, 1965,
1972-76; biography of William Moll
Berczy, 1744-1813; booklets, pamph-
lets, flyers, and 2 copies of Kanada
Kalender dated 1910 and 1916. 3 cm.
Mitteilungsblaetter. Oct. 1974 -
April 1978. Newsletter (15 pieces).

IMMANUEL PENTECOSTAL CHURCH
KITCHENER, ONT.
 Church record books, 1952-67; historical sketch of Church, 1977; and
bulletins and pamphlets, 1974-78. 1
reel of microfilm. 1 cm (15 items).
See Rev. K. Mittelstaedt.
Bethel Park Anniversary Brochure.
25 years, n.d. .5 cm.
"Missionsnachrichten." 1977-78. .5
cm.

J. M. SCHNEIDER INC.
KITCHENER, ONT.
 Includes programmes, clippings, and
biographical sketches of N. C.
Schneider and J. M. Schneider Ltd.,
1900-76. 2 cm. Photographs. Taped
interview with N. Schneider.
 86 photographs: the J. M. Schneider
meatpacking plant, including staff,
work and recreational activity,
1910-53.
Dutch Girl News. 1960-67 (8 issues).
J. M. Schneider Ltd. Anniversary
issues. 1936-65. 1.5 cm.
Schneider News. 1947, 1950 (4
issues).
The Voice. 1942-48 (11 issues).

KITCHENER-WATERLOO REGIONAL
FOLK ARTS COUNCIL
KITCHENER, ONT.
 A brochure, list of members, 1977,
and a president's report, 1976. .25
cm.

MARTIN LUTHER KIRCHE
(PASTOR J. RATTEL)
KITCHENER, ONT.
 and documents of Pastor J. Rattel,
1971-72, church board minutes,
1975-77, and treasurer's report, 1975.
1 cm. Taped interview.

MULTICULTURAL HISTORY SOCIETY
OF ONTARIO
TORONTO, ONT.
 Barbier, L. *The Story of the First
Lutheran Church, 1851-1976.* 1976. 1
cm.

MULTICULTURAL NEWSPAPER
MICROFILM PROJECT
TORONTO, ONT.
 Heimatbote. June 1961 - Dec. 1987.
6 reels of microfilm.
 Kitchener Journal. 15 Jan. 1968 - 12
Sept. 1989. 13 reels of microfilm.
 Mitteilungs-Blatt. 3 Sept. 1970 - 1
Nov. 1970. 1 reel of microfilm.
 Ottawa Herald. Oct. 1977 - Dec.
1982. 2 reels of microfilm.

ONTARIO ETHNIC NEWSPAPER
MICROFILM PROJECT
TORONTO, ONT.
 Berliner Journal. Jan. 1880 - Dec.
1916. 36 reels of microfilm.
 Canada Museum. 27 Aug. 1835 - 20
Oct. 1836; 22 Dec. 1838 - 18 Dec.
1840. 1 reel of microfilm.
 Kanadisches Volksblatt. 5 Jan. 1865
-18 Dec. 1872; 12 April 1876 - 24
Dec. 1879; 4 Jan. 1882 - 26 Dec.
1884; 2 Jan. 1889 - 2 Dec. 1908. 30
reels of microfilm.
 Der Deutsche Canadier. 5 Jan. 1844
- 11 Aug. 1864. 18 reels of micro-
film.
 Der New-Hamburger Neutrale. 19
Jan. 1855 - 25 Sept. 1857. 1 reel of
microfilm.

Der Morgenstern. 6 June 1839 - 16 Sept. 1841. 1 reel of microfilm.

Der Perth Volksfreund. 22 July 1881 - 22 Dec. 1882. 1 reel of microfilm.

Deutsche Zeitung. 3 Nov. 1891 - 27 Sept. 1899. 3 reels of microfilm.

Die Ontario Glocke. 3 Jan. 1883 - 16 Sept. 1886; 2 Jan. 1889 - 28 Dec. 1898; 5 Jan. 1910 - 28 Dec. 1910. 15 reels of microfilm.

Freie Presse. 6 Aug. 1886 - 5 Aug. 1887. 1 reel of microfilm.

Hamburger Beobachter. 9 Feb. 1855 - 22 Feb. 1856. 1 reel of microfilm.

Ontario Journal. 10 Jan. 1917 - Dec. 1918. 2 reels of microfilm.

PEACE LUTHERAN CHURCH
(REV. W. WENTZLAFF)
WINDSOR, ONT.
Volksblatt. 1871-1908. Newsletters. 5 reels of microfilm.

SAXONIA CLUB (H. KIRSCHT)
TORONTO, ONT.
 Minutes of executive meetings, reports, and announcements, 1977-78. 1 cm. Taped interview with H. Staats. **RESTRICTED**

SCHWABEN CLUB
KITCHENER, ONT.
 Interviewed on 25 July 1977; 1 hr.; 1 tape; English/German; by B. Dandyk. Discusses the history of the Club with members.

ST. JEROME'S COLLEGE
WATERLOO, ONT.
 This collection includes correspondence, minutes, account books, Catholic publications, membership lists, and documents on the history of the following parishes: Congregation of the Resurrection Corporation in Kitchener, 1864-1967, Roman Cath-

olic School Board in Berlin, Ont., 1883-1907, St. Mary's Parish in Kitchener, 1858-1966, St. Mary's College in Kentucky, U.S., 1872-1973, Provincial Chapter of Ontario-Kentucky Province, 1967-70, St. Agatha Church in Waterloo, Ont., 1834-87, St. Louis Church in Waterloo, 1916-66, and Church of the Holy Family in New Hamburg, 1899-1928. 30 reels of microfilm. See Ludwig Funcken.

Catholic Resurrection. 1947-57. Newsletter. Microfilm.

Resurrection. 1959-63. Bulletin. Microfilm.

ST. JOHN EVANGELICAL LUTHERAN CHURCH
OTTAWA, ONT.
 Includes service programmes, 1959-65; anniversary booklets, 1945, 1965, 1970; and church records, 1894-1978. 1 reel of microfilm. 1 cm. Photographs.
 37 photographs: religious life at St. John Evangelical Lutheran Church, 1900-70.

61st Anniversary of St. John Evangelical Lutheran Church, 1895-1956. 1 cm.

ST. MARY'S RECTORY
KITCHENER, ONT.
 Records, 1921-75, which include correspondence, bank statements, and brochures. 1 reel of microfilm.

ST. MATHEW'S EVANGELICAL LUTHERAN CHURCH
KITCHENER, ONT.
 Includes correspondence, annual reports, membership lists, and dues, n.d. 2 cm. Photograph.
 1 photograph: the bell of St. Matthew's Lutheran Church, c. 1930.

"70 Years of Service." 1974. Anniversary booklet. 11 pp.
Jubilaeums Buechlein, 1861-1911, 50th Anniversary of Lutheran Synod in Canada. 1911. 122 pp.
"Kirche Daheim." c. 1930s. Booklet. 19 pp.

ST. MICHAEL'S CHURCH
(REV. J. HALTER)
WINDSOR, ONT.
" 1951-78, church bulletins, and 3 letters on former prisoners of Russian prison camp, 1950, 1979. 3 reels of microfilm. 2 cm.
25 Years of St. Michael: The German Catholic's Parish, 1949-74. Booklet.
Prayer Book. 1958. 72 pp.
The Fate of the Germans. Vol. 5. n.d. Documentation of the banishment of the Germans from East-German Europe. .25 cm.

ST. PATRICK'S CATHOLIC CHURCH
TORONTO, ONT.
Bulletin. 1972 (2 issues).
Der Deutsche Katholik in Kanada. 1976-77 (2 issues).

ST. PAUL'S LUTHERAN CHURCH
KITCHENER, ONT.
Constitution, 1869, minute books, and parish registers, 1834-1932. 1 reel of microfilm.
100th Anniversary of St. Paul's Evangelical Lutheran Church. 1935. 72 pp.
Grace and Blessing: A History of the Ontario District of the Lutheran Church. 1954. 104 pp.

ST. PAUL'S LUTHERAN CHURCH
(REV. R. W. HURAS)
BRIDGEPORT, ONT.
Includes constitution and minutes, 1859-1935; congregational member-

ship records, 1874-1942; financial records, 1884-1934; and baptismal, marriage, and burial registers, 1858-1942. 2 reels of microfilm.

ST. PAUL'S LUTHERAN CHURCH
(REV. T. PFOTENHAUER)
OTTAWA, ONT.
The collection includes constitution and by-laws of St. Paul's and the Lutheran Laymen's League, minutes of congregational meetings, Deacon's meetings and voter's meetings, as well as financial records, annual reports, and scrapbooks, 1888-1948. 3 reels of microfilm. Photographs. **RESTRICTED**
107 photographs: religious life at St. Paul's Lutheran Church, including buildings, clergy, and services in Ottawa, 1875-1968.
St. Paul's Anniversry Booklet. 1934. Microfilm.
St. Paul's Messengers. 1930-1950. Church bulletins. Microfilm.

SUDETEN KLUB "VORWAERTS"
TORONTO, ONT.
The collection includes constitution; minutes of annual Klub meetings and the Toronto Multicultural Centre Association; correspondence; circulars; and invitations of social events; membership lists, 1947-78; and miscellaneous papers from Trans-Canada Alliance in Hamilton, 1972-73. 34 cm. Taped interview with H. Weisbach.
VorWärts. 1948-78. Complete. 6 reels of microfilm.

TEUTONIA CLUB
WINDSOR, ONT.
Includes by-laws, 1968; minutes of membership mettings, 1935-75; minutes of board meetings, 1954-76;

minutes of Ladies' Club, 1935-47;
minutes of Youth Groups, 1944-48;
minutes of Girls' Club, 1935-41;
financial records, 1935-50; and miscellaneous membership material
including lists of members, 1935-66.
Photograph. 4 reels of microfilm. 1
cm. Photograph. **RESTRICTED**
  1 photograph: Executive Committee
of the Teutonia Club in Windsor,
1968.
  Club Book. 1935-70.
  "Club Messenger." Nos. 99, 100.
  "Homeland Messenger." Nos. 213,
222, 223.
  "Pacific's Reviewer." No. 279.

THE WATERLOO LUTHERAN SEM-
INARY
WATERLOO, ONT.
*Jubilaeums Buechlein, Synode von
Canada*. 1911. Jubilee. 1.5 cm.
  "The Evangelical Lutheran Seminary
of Canada." 1923-24. .5 cm.
  "The First 60 Years." 1971. Anni-
versary of Waterloo Lutheran Univer-
sity. 1 cm.
  "The Lutheran Theological Seminary
at Waterloo, 50th Anniversary Cata-
logue, 1960-61." 22 pp.
  "The Waterloo Lutheran Seminary
Catalogue, 1961-62." 22 pp.
  "The Waterloo Lutheran Seminary
Calendar." 1962-66 (4 issues).
  "Waterloo College at Waterloo,
Ontario, Annual Catalogue." 1921-22.
.5 cm.
  "Waterloo College School,
Announcement." 1927-28. .5 cm.

TRANS-CANADA ALLIANCE OF GER-
MAN CANADIANS
KITCHENER, ONT.
  The Trans-Canada Alliance of Ger-
man Canadians was formed in
Kitchener in 1973 as an umbrella

organization for German-Canadian
associations in Ont. and as part of the
nationwide T.C.A. Records, 1975-77,
include minutes, correspondence,
membership lists, clippings of the
T.C.A., and member organizations,
T.C.A. scrapbook, historical sketches
of the Transylvania Club, and the
Sickness and Deaths Fund, by-laws
and minutes of the Benevolent Society
Black Forest, 1976. 1 reel of microfilm. 1.5 cm. Taped interview with
H. Schmidt.
  "Schulrundbriefe." 1974. 1 cm.

TRANSYLVANIA CLUB
KITCHENER, ONT.
  Records include statutes and minutes,
1953-78; correspondence, 1954-77;
and financial statements and reports,
1951-75. Miscellaneous items of the
Saxons and German school of
Transylvania Club ouchas membership lists, Oktoberfest material, permits and contracts, clippings, programmes, and invitations. In addition,
there are financial records, and correspondence of the Deutsche
Sprachschule in Kitchener, 1961-73.
49 reels of microfilm. Taped interview with David Mathes.
  Transylvania Club Nachrichten.
1968-78. Bulletin. Microfilm.

TRINITY EVANGELICAL LUTHERAN
CHURCH
WINDSOR, ONT.
  The collection consists of a constitution, by-laws, minutes of various congregations and committees, including
the Men's Club and Ladies' Aid
Society, correspondence, and financial statements from the Trinity Evangelical Lutheran Church, baptismal,
marriage, and communion registers,
lists of Officers and Pastors, and

clippings regarding Church, 1922-79. It also contains records from the German Evangelical Lutheran St. Paulus Congregation in Windsor, 1930-73. 4 reels of microfilm. Photographs.

12 photographs: religious life at Trinity Evangelical Lutheran Church, c. 1965-75.

50th Anniversary Book. 1972. 4 cm.

WEST GERMAN CONSULATE
(W. BITZER)
KITCHENER, ONT.

between Kitchener and Toronto consulates, and Germany, 1962-77, and government forms and brochures regarding pensions, family inheritance, and declarations, 1957-76. 6.5 cm.

"Merkblätter fü Auslandtätige und Auswanderer." Kanada Merkblatt. June 1971. 60 pp.

WINDSOR SAXON CLUB
WINDSOR, ONT.

Constitution of the First Transylvanian Saxon Sick Assistance Union, 1929, programmes, invitations, circulars, and Christmas song booklet from the Windsor Saxon Club, 1968-79. 1 cm.

Matthiae, Andreas. "Siebenbürgen." 1967. 125 pp.

"A History of the Saxon Club." n.d. .25 cm.

Newsletters. 1969-72. .5 cm.

Saxon Year Book, 1902-77. 1977. 99 pp.

WOODSTOCK GERMAN CANADIAN CLUB (CHRIS GROSS)
WOODSTOCK, ONT.

Records, 1969-76, which include Club constitution, amendments, minutes, correspondence, financial reports, membership dues, various newsletters, and bulletins, 1967-77. The collection contains records pertaining to the Trans-Canada Alliance of German Canadians in Kitchener, 1966-78. 3 reels of microfilm.

ADAM, STELIOS
TORONTO, ONT.
 Interviewed on 27 July 1977; .5 hr.;
1 tape; Greek; by C. Haralabopoulos.
Post-WWII immigrant.

AGELAKOS, DEMOS
TORONTO, ONT.
 Interviewed on 16 July 1977; .5 hr.;
1 tape; Greek; by C. Haralabopoulos.
Post-WWII immigrant.

ALEXOPOULOS, CAROL
TORONTO, ONT.
 2 photographs: Kalliorri Liatskou
receiving award at Greek school,
Toronto, 1954. Taped interview.
 Interviewed on 18 March 1978; .5
hr.; 1 tape; English; by L. Polyzoi.
Post-WWII immigrant.

ANDRIKOPOULOS, ALEX
TORONTO, ONT.
 Promotional material describing
activities of Greek travel agency,
Atlas Tours. 1 cm. Taped interview.
Interviewed on 19 Jan. 1978; .5 hr.;
1 tape; Greek; by C. Haralabopoulos.
Post-WWII immigramt.

ANGELAKOS, LEFKI
TORONTO, ONT.
 4 photographs: the Angelakos family
in Greece, Toronto, 1962. Taped
interview.
 Interviewed on 6 Sept. 1977; .5 hr.;
1 tape; Greek; by C. Haralabopoulos.
Post-WWII immigrant.

ANTONIADIS, BILL
WILLOWDALE, ONT.
 Inspection cards, Oct. 1921. .25 cm.
Photographs.
 5 photographs: family including a
block of store, Toronto, 1905-35; and
St. George's Hellinic Young Ladies'
Association, Toronto, 1934-35.
 AHEPA Convention Souvenir Book.
Toronto, 1953. .5 cm.

ANTONOPOULOS, THEODOSIA
TORONTO, ONT.
 Interviewed on 15 Nov. 1978; .5
hr.; 1 tape; Greek; by C.
Haralabopoulos. Immigrated to
Canada in the mid-1970s.

APOSTALAKOS, LYKOURGOS
TORONTO, ONT.
 1 Greek passport, 1966. .25 cm.
Photographs. Taped interview.
 3 photographs: family, c. 1950-60.
Interviewed on 2 Aug. 1978; .5 hr.;
1 tape; Greek; by C. Haralabopoulos.
Arrived in Canada in 1951.

APOSTOLAKOS, MATA
TORONTO, ONT.
 1 Greek passport, 1951; and 1 court
notice, 1960. .25 cm. Photographs.
Taped interview.
 9 photographs: M. Apostolakos
during her early years in Toronto, c.
1951-60.
 Interviewed on 10 Sept. 1978; 1 hr.;
1 tape; Greek; by C. Haralabopoulos.
Immigrated to Canada in 1951.

ARVANITIS, GERRY
TORONTO, ONT.
 Interviewed on 18 Sept. 1977; .5
hr.; 1 tape; Greek; by C.
Haralabopoulos. Post-WWII immigrant, discusses relationship between
the community and clergy.

ATHANASIADIS, DEMETRIOS
TORONTO, ONT.
 Interviewed on 20 Oct. 1977; .5 hr.;
1 tape; Greek; by C. Haralabopoulos.
Post-WWII immigrant.

ATHANASOPOULOS, TOM AND
IOANNIS
WINDSOR, ONT.
 Interviewed on 9 Aug. 1980; 1 hr.; 1
tape; Greek; by Ross Valdis.
Post-WWII immigrant.

AVGERIS, TOM
TORONTO, ONT.
 Interviewed on 15 Oct. 1977; .5 hr.;
1 tape; Greek; by C. Haralabopoulos.
Arrived in Canada in 1962.

BAILLIE, HELEN
TORONTO, ONT.
 Interviewed on 23 July 1977; 1 hr.;
1 tape; English/Greek; by S.
Petrolekas.

BAKA, KANELLA
TORONTO, ONT.
 Interviewed on 16 Aug. 1978; 1 hr.;
1 tape; Greek; by C. Haralabopoulos.
Post-WWII immigrant.

BAKAS, DEMETRIOS
TORONTO, ONT.
 Interviewed on 25 Aug. 1978; .5 hr.;
1 tape; Greek; by C. Haralabopoulos.
Post-WWII immigrant.

BASIL, STEELE
TORONTO, ONT.
 Menu and clippings of Steele's Tav-
ern, c. 1974. .25 cm. Photographs.
 8 photographs: the Basil family,
Smyrna, Toronto, 1900-39; activities
of AHEPA, 1937, and the St.
George's Greek Orthodox Young
Men's Association, 1939; also, the
Lantern Tea Room, Toronto, 1928.
 AHEPA Convention Year Book. Syra-
cuse, New York, 1937. 2 cm.
 AHEPA pamphlet, 1939. .25 cm.

BOOTH, CHARLES
SUDBURY, ONT.
 8 photographs: Greek Canadians and
restaurants, Sudbury, 1911-45.

BOTTEAS, EVELYN
TORONTO, ONT.
 Transcript; 5 pages; of interview of
30 Jan. 1978; by L. Polyzoi. She
describes her experiences as a former
student in Toronto's Greek Communal School, 1930-33 (includes a letter
by E. Botteas providing additional
information).

BUCKTHOUGHT, P.
OTTAWA, ONT.
 A collection of yearbooks and sou-
venir programmes:
 *150th Anniversary of Independence,
1821-1971.* Hellenic Community of
Ottawa, 1971. 96 pp.
 Hellenic Independence, 1821-1978.
Hellenic Community of Ottawa, 1978.
1 cm.
 Hellenic Independence, 1821-77.
Hellenic Community of Ottawa, 1977.
.5 cm.

BURNETT, MARGARET
SUDBURY, ONT.
Clippings, n.d. Photograph. Taped interview.
1 photograph: a grocery store, Sudbury, 1907.
Interviewed on 29 June 1982; 1 hr.; 1 tape; English; by Steve Moutsatsos. Describes early Greek community in Sudbury.

CARRAS, PETER
TORONTO, ONT.
Interviewed on 18 Sept. 1978; .5 hr.; 1 tape; Greek; by C. Haralabopoulos. Greek Orthodox priest.

CHALTAS, GEORGE
ORILLIA, ONT.
Interviewed on 8 Oct. 1978; .5 hr.; 1 tape; Greek; by C. Haralabopouslos. Arrived in the late 1950s.

CHECKERIS, ERNIE
TORONTO, ONT.
Interviewed on 3 Aug. 1982; 1 hr.; 1 tape; English; by S. Moutsatsos. Involved in Toronto's Greek associational life.

CHRISTAKOS, ANASTASIA
SUDBURY, ONT.
10 photographs: 1900-40, Greek Canadians in Sudbury, including hunting, 1911; a picnic, 1919; and military service during WWII.

CHRISTAKOS, KATIE
SUDBURY, ONT.
14 photographs: photographs: Greek Canadians in Greece, Sudbury, 1910-34, including a grocery store and a Greek community picnic, Sudbury, 1934.

DALLAS, TESS
TORONTO, ONT.
Membership list of the Lord Byron Chapter of AHEPA (American Hellenic Educational Progressive Association) in Toronto, 1945; wedding invitation, 1929; scrapbook of correspondence, clipplings, and newsletters belonging to Eleftherios Dallas, 1922-58; biographical statement of E. Daugounas (Dallas) , 1892; and certificate of naturalization, 1926. 3 cm. Photographs.
26 photographs: mostly of Dallas and Misseyanni family members, Mytelene, Toronto, 1910-58; and Greek banquet in Toronto, 1926; and Lord Byron Chapter of AHEPA in Toronto, 1932.
Vlassis, G. D. "The Glory that is Greece." Ottawa: Royal Greek Embassy, 1959. 25 pp.
"The Cyprus Question." Athens: Greek Government Information Department, 1956. 24 pp.
The AHEPAN. Vol. 5, nos. 7, 9, 1931; vol. 6, no.7, 1932.
Greek Community Yearbook. Toronto, 1934. 1 cm.
Eighth Annual Convention of the Order of AHEPA in Boston Massachusetts. Washington, D.C.: AHEPA National Headquarters, 1930. 150 pp.
Order of AHEPA Yearbook. Washington, D.C., 1930. 122 pp.
Order of AHEPA constitution with a supplement of the policies, acts and practices of the Order, U.S., 1937. 190 pp.

DASKALAKI, VASSY
TORONTO, ONT.
Interviewed on 11 Aug. 1977; .5 hr.; 1 tape; Greek; by C. Haralabopoulos. Post-WWII immigrant.

DASKALAKI, V.
TORONTO, ONT.
 Correspondence with
Hellenic-Canadian Cultural Society;
and papers from the Greek Protypa
School, n.d. 1 cm.
 Periodicals of Greek Protypa School,
n.d. 1 cm.

DECOVICH, ARTA
TORONTO, ONT.
 Interviewed on 23 Oct. 1977; 1 hr.;
1 tape; Greek; by C. Haralabopoulos.

DEMAKAKOS, KOSTA
TORONTO, ONT.
 Interviewed on 12 Sept. 1978; .5
hr.; 1 tape; Greek; by C.
Haralabopoulos.

DEMEROUTIS, KALLIOPE
OTTAWA, ONT.
 4 photographs: Hellenic Community
picnics, 1945-53; Greek school, 1949;
and Independence Day festivity, 1948
in Ottawa. Taped interview.
 Interviewed on 18 Aug. 1977; .5 hr.;
1 tape; Greek; by D. Liakakos.
Arrived in Canada in the late 1930s.

DENNISON, NICK
TORONTO, ONT.
 Register of Lord Byron Chapter of
AHEPA (American Hellenic Educa-
tional Progressive Association),
Toronto, 1928-34; and AHEPA Chap-
ter certificate of meritorious service,
1978. 1 cm. Photographs.
 5 photographs: activities of AHEPA,
1931-71, including international
AHEPA picnic, Queenston Heights,
1931; N. Dennison during military
service in WWII, 1942; dances at St.
George's Greek Orthodox Church,
Toronto, 1945-50; and Daughters of
Penelope, 1968-70.

*AHEPA Yearbook: 48th Supreme
Convention.* Athens, 1970. 2 cm.

DIAKOPOULOS, NIKOLAS
TORONTO, ONT.
 Interviewed in Summer 1977; 1.5
hrs.; 1 tape; English; by S.
Petrolekas. Arrived in Toronto in
1912.

DIAMADAKOS, LOUIS
TORONTO, ONT.
 Interviewed on 25 Aug. 1978; .5 hr.;
1 tape; Greek; by C. Haralabopoulos.
Immigrated to Canada in 1955.

DIMAS, CHRISTOS
TORONTO, ONT.
 Immigration documents and corre-
spondence, 1946-76. 1 cm. Photo-
graphs. Taped interview.
 2 photographs: family in Toronto, c.
1970s.
 Interviewed on 28 May 1978; 1 hr.;
1 tape; Greek; by C. Haralabopoulos.
Arrived in Canada in 1966.
 Lambros, Apostolos M. "Annals of
Greeks of Mansoura." Alexandria,
1957. 15 pp., in Greek.
 Article on Ioannis Dimas,
Tachydromos. Jan. 1950. .25 cm.

DIMSON, BILL
TORONTO, ONT.
 22 photographs: the B. Dimson family, Greece, Toronto, 1924-42; choirs
at at St. George's Greek Orthodox
Church, celebrations, sports and a
restaurant, Toronto, 1935-48; and B.
Dimson during military service in
WWII.

DOURAMAKOU, LIA
TORONTO, ONT.
 Papamanoli, E. N. *Perileptike istoria
tou Kanada Kai Elleno-Kanadikos*

Odigos (Short History of Canada and Greek-Canadian Guide). Montreal, 1921. 1 reel of microfilm.

DOUROS, SOPHIE
TORONTO, ONT.
5 photographs: Greek community school, 1928; the Marmon family, 1917; members of the Daughters of Penelope, 1950; and a play of the Greek Orthodox Youth of America, 1936.

DRATSIDIS, PETROS
TORONTO, ONT.
Personal documents, 1965-77. 1 cm. Taped inteview.
Interviewed on 10 Sept. 1977; 1 hr.; 1 tape; Greek; by C. Haralabopoulos. Post-WWII immigrant.

ECONOMIDES, PERRY
TORONTO, ONT.
Interviewed on 26 Jan. 1978; 1 hr.; 1 tape; Greek; by C. Haralabopoulos. Politically active in Toronto's Greek community.

ECONOMOPOULOS, PETER
TORONTO, ONT.
8 photographs: tracing the immigration to Toronto of P. Economopoulos, Greece, Toronto, 1947-53; includes work in lumber industry in Thunder Bay, 1951-53.

FATSIS, BILL
TORONTO, ONT.
Ta Nea. Nos. 1-7, March, June 1976. .5 cm.

FOURIEZOS, PATRA
SUDBURY, ONT.
Interviewed on 7 June 1982; 1 hr.;

1 tape; Greek; by S. Moutsatsos. Arrived in the 1910s, initially worked as domestic.

FUNDOS, ANTHONY
THORNHILL, ONT.
1 photograph: the Fundos family, Thornhill, 1975. Taped interview.
Interviewed on 18 Aug. 1977; .5 hr.; 1 tape; Greek; by C. Haralabopoulos. Discussion on his alienating experience in Canada.

GEORGANAS, HARRY
OTTAWA, ONT.
2 photographs: Ottawa: executive members of the Council of the Hellenic Community, 1955; and Easter celebration, 1952. Taped interview.
Interviewed on 24 Aug. 1977; 1 hr.; 1 tape; Greek; by D. Liakakos.

GEORGOULIS, DEMETRIOS
TORONTO, ONT.
28 photographs: political demontrations, including protests against the Vietnam War and the Greek Junta, Toronto, 1967-68. Taped interview.
Interviewed on 10 July 1977; .5 hr.; 1 tape; Greek; by C. Haralabopoulos. Arrived in 1967; discusses failure of adjusting to Canada and plans of returning to Greece.

GIOULOS, THEODORE
TORONTO, ONT.
Interviewed on 23 Sept. 1977; .5 hr.; 1 tape; Greek; by C. Haralabopoulos. Discusses differences in Canadian and Greek social life and his reasons for wanting to return to Greece.

GLINOS, HELEN
LONDON, ONT.
1 photograph: George Vlassis, Toronto, c. 1930-35.
Vlassis, George D. "Comparitive Study of Secondary Education in the United States, Canada, and Greece." M.A. thesis, 1932. 1 cm.
The Hellenic Directory. London, Ont., 1978. 28 pp.
Youth Planbook, 1977-78. Greek Orthodox Archdiocese of North and South America. 1 cm.

GONIDOU, DESPINA
TORONTO, ONT.
Material sent by Archdiocese concerning Greek schools in Toronto, 1959-61. .5 cm. Photographs. Taped interview.
4 photographs: Greek school celebration of Christmas, 1959, celebration of New Year's Day, 1960, and a dance group, 1961, all taken in Toronto.
Interviewed on 11 Oct. 1977; 10-page transcript; English; by L. Polyzoi. Arrived in 1953, discusses her work as Greek school teacher in Toronto.

HADJIS, NICK
TORONTO, ONT.
Interviewed on 28 Jan. 1978; .5 hr.; 1 tape; English; by L. Polyzoi. Arrived in Canada in the 1930s.

HATZIS, COSTA
SUDBURY, ONT.
4 photographs: visit of the Greek Ambassador to the Greek community in Sudbury, 1978. Taped interview.
Interviewed on 23 June 1982; 1 hr.; 1 tape; Greek; by S. Moutsatsos.

Describes his leading role in the development of the Greek community organization in Sudbury.

JANETAKES, POLITIME
TORONTO, ONT.
Handwritten speech presented at 50th Anniversary of Ladies' Auxiliary Society, Toronto, n.d. .25 cm. Photographs. Taped interview.
17 photographs: activities of the American Hellenic Educational Progressive Association, the St. George's Hellenic Young Ladies' Association, the Greek Orthodox Ladies' Philoptochos Society, religious life at St. George's Greek Orthodox Church, Toronto, Queenston, 1926-54, and parades for the Greek War Relief Fund, 1941, and Independence Day, 1950-52.
Interviewed on 30 Jan. 1977; 1.5 hrs.; 1 tape; Greek; by A. Douramakou. Very active in the Ladies' Auxiliary Society of Toronto's Greek community.

KABOURIS, JOHN
TORONTO, ONT.
6 theatre programmes, 1974-76. 1.5 cm. Photographs. Taped interview.
44 photographs: mostly of his theatrical perfomances and his paintings; and Greek folk dancing, c. 1970-80.
Interviewed on 20 Aug. 1977; .5 hr.; 1 tape; Greek; by C. Haralabopoulos. Talks about his career as an artist.

KADIDAKIS, EMMANUEL
TORONTO, ONT.
Interviewed on 7 Aug. 1977; .5 hr.; 1 tape; Greek; by C. Haralabopoulos. Discusses his preferences for Greek village life.

KALOGEROPOULOS, NICK
TORONTO, ONT.
Interviewed on 2 Oct. 1977; .5 hr.;
1 tape; Greek; by C. Haralabopoulos.
Post-WWII immigrant.

KANARELLIS, MYRSINE
TORONTO, ONT.
Interviewed on 18 Oct. 1977; .25
hr.; 1 tape; Greek; by C.
Haralabopoulos. Post-WWII immi-
grant.

KARACOSTAS, CHRISTOS
TORONTO, ONT.
Personal documents, 1957-78. .5 cm
(9 items). Taped interview.
Interviewed on 20 May 1978; 1 hr.;
1 tape; Greek; by C. Haralabopoulos.
Arrived in Canada in 1960.

KARANTJAS, FAY
TORONTO, ONT.
Personal documents, 1882-1933. .5
cm. Photograph.
1 photograph: a theatrical production
at the Greek Community School,
Toronto, 1933.

KARASAVIDIS, SAVVAS
TORONTO, ONT.
10 Nov. 1978; 1 hr.; 1 tape; Greek;
by C. Haralabopoulos. Arrived in
Toronto in 1970.

KARDARAS, ALEX
BRACEBRIDGE, ONT.
Interviewed on 17 Nov. 1978; .25
hr.; 1 tape; Greek; by C.
Haralabopoulos. Arrived in 1959,
ventured into the restaurant business.

KARRY, GEORGE
WINDSOR, ONT.
8 photographs: the G. Karry family,
Greece, London, 1916-62; and picnic

of the Hellenic Educational Progressive Association, Niagara Falls, 1931.

KELESIDES, CHRISTOS
TORONTO, ONT.
Interviewed on 15 Aug. 1978; 1 hr.;
1 tape; Greek; by C. Haralabopoulos.
Immigrated to Canada in 1968.

KIRIKOPOULOS, GEORGE
TORONTO, ONT.
Interviewed on 27 July 1977; 1 hr.;
1 tape; Greek; by C. Haralabopoulos.
Discusses the educational system both
in Canada and in Greece.

KONTOPIDIS, JOHN
TORONTO, ONT.
Interviewed on 23 June 1978; 1 hr.;
1 tape; Greek; by C. Haralabopoulos.
Arrived in Canada in 1973.

KOSTOPOULOS, DENIS
TORONTO, ONT.
1 letter from Greece describing life
in Canada. .25 cm. Photographs.
Taped interview.
37 photographs: mostly of dancers,
business enterprises, and Greek community activities, Toronto, c. 1970s.
Interviewed on 25 Aug. 1977; .5 hr.;
1 tape; Greek; by C. Haralabopoulos.
Post-WWII immigrant.

KOSTOPOULOS, JOHN
TORONTO, ONT.
Interviewed on 14 Jan. 1978; .25
hr.; 1 tape; Greek; by C.
Haralabopoulos. Arrived in Canada in
the 1970s.

KOUVELA, KATIA
TORONTO, ONT.
Interviewed on 22 Sept. 1977; 1 hr.;
1 tape; Greek; by C. Haralabopoulos.
Post-WWII immigrant.

LAGGES, GUS
SUDBURY, ONT.
1 Greek passport, 1925; 1 AHEPA members card, n.d. .25 cm. Photograph. Taped interview.
1 photograph: Gus Lagges during military service in Greek army, Greece, 1924.
Interviewed on 14 June 1982; 2 hrs.; 2 tapes; English; by S. Moutsatsos. Immigrated to Canada in 1925.

LAGGES, NICK, MARIA ILTSOPOLOS, AND SHIRLEY MOUTSATSOS
SUDBURY, ONT.
11 photographs: Greek Canadians, business enterprise, and a restaurant, Sudbury, 1954-60. Taped interview.
Interviewed on 8 July 1982; 2 hrs.; 2 tapes; Greek; by S. Moutsatsos. Arrived in Canada in 1952.

LEVINE, KAREN
TORONTO, ONT.
Scrapbook of clippings from various Greek (American and Canadian) newspapers, 1912-45. 1 reel of microfilm.

LIAKAKOS, D.
OTTAWA, ONT.
"Greek Pioneers in Ottawa." Aug. 1977. 8 pp.

LIAKAKOS, MARIA
WINDSOR, ONT.
Interviewed on 27 July 1980; 1 hr.; 1 tape; Greek; by Ross Valdis. Immigrated from Greece to Canada (Quebec), married and then moved to Windsor.

LIATIRAS, NICKY
TORONTO, ONT.
Interviewed on 15 May 1978; .5 hr.;

1 tape; Greek; by C. Haralabopoulos. Arrived in Canada in 1977.

LIKOKAPIS, HARRY
TORONTO, ONT.
1 Greek passport, 1968, and a Greek Naval Student passbook, 1965. 1 cm. Taped interview.
Interviewed on 28 July 1977; .5 hr.; 1 tape; Greek; by C. Haralabopoulos. Post-WWII immigrant.

LIKOKAPIS, KATERINA
TORONTO, ONT.
3 photographs: the Likokapis family, Toronto, Athens, c. 1970. Taped interview.
Interviewed on 12 Aug. 1979; .25 hr.; 1 tape; Greek; by C. Haralabopoulos. Arrived in Canada in the early 1970s.

LIKOKAPIS, SOPHIA
TORONTO, ONT.
Interviewed on 10 Aug. 1977; .5 hr.; 1 tape; Greek; by C. Haralabopoulos. Arrived in Canada in the 1970s.

LIOUNIS, CONSTANTINE
TORONTO, ONT.
Interviewed on 5 Oct. 1977; 1 hr.; 1 tape; Greek; by C. Haralabopoulos. Post-WWII immigrant.

LISKAKOS, MARIA
WINDSOR, ONT.
Interviewed on 27 July 1980; 1 hr.; 1 tape; Greek; by Ross Valdis. Arrived in Canada in 1934.

LOGOTHETOPOULOS, JOHN
TORONTO, ONT.
Interviewed on 15 Sept. 1978; .5 hr.; 1 tape; Greek; by C. Haralabopoulos. Left Greece after Civil War, graduate work in England

and then immigrated to Toronto on being offered a research position at the University of Toronto.

LOLAS, CHRIS
SUDBURY, ONT.
Interviewed on 7 July 1982; 1 hr.; 1 tape; Greek; by S. Moutsatsos. Arrived in Canada in 1957.

LOUKIDELIS, SPYROS
SUDBURY, ONT.
Interviewed on 24 June 1982; 1 hr.; 1 tape; Greek; by S. Moutsatsos. Turn of the century Greek immigrants to Sudbury.

MANIATES, SOPHIE
TORONTO, ONT.
Transcript of Greek Radio programme concerning Greek Communal School, Toronto, 1956. .25 cm. Photographs. Taped interview.
4 photographs: celebration of Independence Day, and a theatrical production, Toronto, 1956-57.
Interviewed on 15 Aug. 1977; 1 hr.; 1 tape; English; by L. Polyzoi. Family arrived in 1930s.
"True Education." *AHEPA Year Book*. 1939. .25 cm.

MARINI, VASSO
TORONTO, ONT.
Interviewed on 10 Aug. 1978; .5 hr.; 1 tape; Greek; by C. Haralabopous. Arrived in 1970.

MARMON, GUS
TORONTO, ONT.
A collection of documents relating to the "Blythewood Affair," 1953-58; immigration papers, 1912-50; and miscellaneous items from the organization, the Daughters of Penelope, 1950s. 3 cm. Photographs. Taped interview.
43 photographs: G. Marmon and his parents who immigrated to Toronto in the early 1900s; Mary Marmon (nee Kartoli) and her relatives, Egypt, Smyrna, Toronto, 1909-35; also, activities of organizations such as the American Hellenic Educational Progressive Association, 1964, the Daughters of Penelope, 1968-70, and dances at St. George Greek Orthodox church, 1945-50, Toronto, London.
Interviewed on Aug. 1977, 11 June 1978; 4 hrs.; 4 tapes; English; by S. Petrolekas and L. Polyzoi. Parents arrived in the early 1900s.
The Ahepan. July-Aug. 1940, Aug.-Oct. 1970. 1 cm.
Ahepa Convention Yearbook. 1976. 1 cm.
Daughters of Penelope 25th Anniversary Ball. 1975. .5 cm.
Hellenic Yearbook. Ontario, 1939. 153 pp.

MAVRAGANIS, PANTELIS
TORONTO, ONT.
Interviewed on 30 May 1978; .5 hr.; 1 tape; Greek; by C. Haralabopoulos. Post-WWII immigrant.

MEFSUT, PAUL
OTTAWA, ONT.
5 photographs: members of the American Hellenic Educational Progressive Association, 1962; Greek folk dancing, 1966; Hellenic Community Centre, 1967; Greek Orthodox Church, 1976 all taken in Ottawa. Taped interview.
Interviewed on 1 Sept. 1977; 1 hr.; 1 tape; Greek; by D. Liakakos. Arrived in Canada in 1952.

MERGELAS, BOJM
TORONTO, ONT.
 2 photographs: Bojm Mergelas and friends, Toronto, 1916-18. Taped interview.
 Interviewed in Aug. 1977; 2 hrs.; 2 tapes; English; by S. Petrolekas. Recollections of activities in the Greek and Macedonian communities of Toronto in the early 1900s.

MILIONIS, TASOS
TORONTO, ONT.
 Greek Telephone Directory, Toronto. 1978, 1979. 3 cm

MINIOTIS, NICK
TORONTO, ONT.
 Interviewed on 12 June 1978; .75 hr.; 1 tape; Greek; by C. Haralabopoulos. Arrived in Canada in 1967.

MITCHELL, NETA
SUDBURY, ONT.
 Interviewed on 20 June 1982; 1 hr.; 1 tape; English; by S. Moutsatsos. Discusses her parents' immigrant and settlement experiences in Sudbury.

MOUTSATSOS, PETER
SUDBURY, ONT.
 2 photographs: family in Sudbury, 1959-62. Taped interview.
 Interviewed on 25 June 1982; 1 hr.; 1 tape; English; by S. Moutsatsos. Recounts early years in Sudbury's Greek community.

MOUTSATSOS, STEVE
SUDBURY, ONT.
 6 photographs: fishing operation, Goulais Bay, 1905-15.

NICOPOULO, BILL
BRACEBRIDGE, ONT.
 Interviewed on 22 Nov. 1978; .25 hr.; 1 tape; Greek; by C. Haralabopoulos. Post-WWII immigrant.

PALAKAS, CONSTANTINE
TORONTO, ONT.
 Interviewed on 9 July 1977; .25 hr.; 1 tape; Greek; by C. Haralabopoulos. Post-WWII immigrant.

PALMER, PETER
TORONTO, ONT.
 Interviewed on 13 Oct. 1977; 1 hr.; 1 tape; English; by L. Polyzoi. Arrived in Canada in 1928.

PAPAGEORGE, ATHENA
TORONTO, ONT.
 Interviewed on 14 Aug. 1977; .5 hr.; 1 tape; Greek; by C. Haralabopoulos. Post-WWII immigrant.

PARASKEVOPOULOS, MR. P.
TORONTO, ONT.
Annual Choir Festival programme, Toronto, 7 May 1950. 15 pp.

PARASKEVOPOULOS, TED
TORONTO, ONT.
 2 Y.M.C.A. membership cards, 1913; constitution of Greek Ladies' Philanthropic Organization, "Enosis," 1925; AHEPA meeting invitation and officers list, 1930; candidate list, Hellenic Community of "St. George" elections, 1948; and theatre programme, "Golpho," 1949. 1 cm. Photographs. Taped interview.
 4 photographs: 1912-46.
 Interviewed on 26 July 1977; 3.75

hrs.; 4 tapes; English/Greek; by S.
Petrolekas. Recollections of the Greek
community in Toronto at the turn of
the century.

PATITSAS, THANASIS
SUDBURY, ONT.
 1 photograph: Tom Patitsas,
Sudbury, 1974. Taped interview.
 Interviewed on 14 June 1982; 1 hr.;
1 tape; English; by S. Moutsatsos.
Post-WWII immigrant.

PAVLAKIS, SMARO
TORONTO, ONT.
 Constitution of Greek Ladies' Philanthropic Association "Enosis," 1921;
report of the Hellenic Community of
Ontario, 1950; list of priests at St.
George Greek Orthodox Church,
Toronto, 1926-78; correspondence
and certificates regarding Greek
teachers, 1913-76; and clippings
dealing with Toronto Greek commun-
ity, 1934-49. 3 cm. Photograph.
Taped interview.
 1 photograph: the First Masquerade
Ball of St. George Ladies' Philan-
thropic Society, Toronto, 1926.
 Interviewed on 24 Aug. 1977; 1 hr.;
1 tape; English/Greek; by L. Polyzoi.
Immigrated to Canada in 1925.
 Fotinos, D. *New Reader*. New York,
1942. 1 cm.
 Kyriakopoulos, D. *Geography of
Greater Greece*. Athens, 1932. 1 cm.
 Makrinos, A. *Public School Gram-
mar*. Athens, 1924. 1 cm.
 Pappas, Christos. *Bedtime Stories*.
Boston, 1934. .5 cm.
 Papamicheal, E. *ABC Reader* (part
2). Athens, 1926. 1 cm.
 Polyzoidis, G. *Reader of Church
History*. New York, n.d. .5 cm.
 Sakellarides, C. *Holy History of the*

New Testament. New York, 1927. .5
cm.
 *128th Celebration of Greek Indepen-
dence Day*. March 1949. 17 pp.
 Children's Hymn Book. Chicago,
1934. .5 cm.
 *Detailed Programme of the Greek
Schools of the Archdiocese of North
and South America*. New York, 1935.
.5 cm.
 The Greek Teacher. Vols. 1, 2, 3,
1945-47. Putman, Connecticut. 3 cm.
 Hellenic Yearbook. 1937. Coronation
issue, Ontario. .5 cm.
 The Orthodox Observer. Feb. 1969,
March 1970. 32 pp.
 St. George's Church Yearbook.
Toronto, 1937. .25 cm.

PERROS, ANGELO
TORONTO, ONT.
 Interviewed on 18 May 1978; .5 hr.;
1 tape; Greek; by C. Haralabopoulos.
Arrived in Canada in 1967.

PETROLEKAS, STAVROS
WILLOWDALE, ONT.
 Clippings and printed items. 2.5 cm.
Photograph.
 1 photograph: youths from the St.
George's Greek Orthodox Church in
Toronto's Centennial Parade, 1934.
 Bourboulis, G. M. *The Temptation*.
Oshawa, Ont., 1952. Poetry collec-
tion. 80 pp.
 Papadakis, C. *Canada, First Year*.
Toronto, 1969. .5 cm.

PEZOULAS, GUS
OTTAWA, ONT.
 Clippings, 1959-60. .25 cm. Photographs. Taped interview.
 8 photographs: Greek school, 1958;
activities of the American Hellenic
Educational Progressive Association,
1960-64; members of Greek Orthodox

Youth of America, 1958, all taken in Ottawa.
Interviewed on 10 Aug. 1977; 1 hr.; 1 tape; Greek; by D. Liakakos.

PHILLIPS, STEPHANIE (NEE MAVROU)
TORONTO, ONT.
Certificates and biographical statement belonging to Vassilios Mavrou, 1928-80. .25 cm. Photographs.
5 photographs: family including Greek traditional dress, Greece, Toronto, 1912-37.

POLYMENAKOS, LEONIDAS
TORONTO, ONT.
Personal documents, 1944-77. .5 cm. Taped interview.
Interviewed on 31 Oct. 1977; .5 hr.; 1 tape; Greek; by C. Haralabopoulos. Immediate post-WWII immigrant.

POLYZOI, LOUESA
TORONTO, ONT.
Partial records of the Greek Ladies' Philanthropic Association and graduation certificates from the Greek Communal School of Toronto, 1958, 1960. 1 cm (15 items).
Transcripts of two interviews (anonymous) conducted by L. Polyzoi: 19 March 1978; 6 pages; English; discussion of early years of Greek settlement in Toronto and 6 Nov. 1977; 7 pages; English; experiences of a Greek teacher in contemporary Greek community schools.
Kofsifou, Anthony. *The Unfulfilled Dream of a Dead Immigrant.* New York, 1960. 176 pp., in Greek.
Kourides, Peter T. *The Evolution of the Greek Orthodox Church in America and Its Present Problems.* New York, 1959. 1 cm.
Leber, George J. *The History of the Order of AHEPA, 1922-72.* 1972. 3 cm.
Price, C. A. *Report on the Greek Community in Toronto.* 1958. 17 pp.
Zei, Martha. *Hope for Freedom.* Athens, 1975. 80 pp.
"AHEPA: Fifty Years in Canada." Nov. 1978. 8 pp.
"Greeks Claim Ill-Treatment." *Globe and Mail.* 2 March 1918. 2 pp.
AHEPA 42nd Supreme Convention Yearbook. Aug. 1964. 1 cm.
AHEPA Yearbook. Lord Byron Chapter, Toronto, 1945. 2 cm.
Community Voice. Vol. 1, no. 1, Oct. 1977; vol. 1, no. 4, May 1978; Sept. 1979. .5 cm.
Cosmos. Nos., 1-3, April-June 1978 (Greek-Canadian monthly). .5 cm.
Greek American Progressive Association Convention Yearbook. 1964. 1 cm.
The Greek Orthodox Archdiocese of North and South America Yearbook. New York, 1976. 2 cm.
Greek Telephone Directory of Toronto. 1965, 1966, 1974, 1977, 1978. 4 cm.
Instructions Concerning the Military Obligations and the Special Privileges to Greeks Living Abroad. Athens, 1973. 62 pp.
Our Hellenic Home. Toronto, 1978. .25 cm.
Makedonomachos. Dec. 1978. 12 pp.
Pan-Macedonian Association 32nd National Convention Yearbook. July 1978. .5 cm.
5 Greek Public School Texts: Grade 6 History, Athens, 1956; grades 3 and 4 Mythology, New York, 1945; Classical History Reader, New York, 1957; New Testament Reader, New York, 1949; grade 5 Church History, Athens, 1952. 5 cm.

PONTIKIS, TOM
WINDSOR, ONT.
Greek Unemployment Insurance record book, 1955; Greek Merchant Navy Mechanics Union constitution, 1961; "Memories of My Childhood," handwritten collection of Greek songs, 1948. 1.5 cm. Photograph.
1 photograph: unidentified people on boat, 1966.

RAMPHOS, PHILIP
OTTAWA, ONT.
1 photograph: a Greek Orthodox Primate with Anglican Bishop, Ottawa, 1955. Taped interview.
Interviewed on 12 Aug. 1977; 1 hr.; 1 tape; Greek; by D. Liakakos. Discusses his involvement in Greek church and community activities.

RETSAS, JOHN
TORONTO, ONT.
Interviewed on 24 Sept. 1978; .5 hr.; 1 tape; Greek; by C. Haralabopoulos. Arrived in Canada in 1972.

RIZAKOS, PETER
TORONTO, ONT.
Interviewed in Summer 1978; 1 hr.; 1 tape; Greek; by C. Haralabopoulos. Post-WWII immigrant.

ROUMANAS, REV. VASILIOS
TORONTO, ONT.
11 photographs: religious ceremony at St. Demetrios Greek Orthodox Church, Toronto, 1972-76. Taped recording.
Recorded in Summer 1976; 1 hr.; 1 tape; Greek; by Peter Belesis. Part of the Greek Orthodox Sunday liturgy conducted by the late Rev. Vasilios

Roumanas with Orpheus Choir, at St. Demetrios Greek Orthodox Church, Toronto.

SCOPIS, SYLVIA
TORONTO, ONT.
42 photographs: 1905-80, 2 postcards, 1912, 1914; members and friends of the P. Scopis family, Greece, U.S.A., Cobourg, Toronto; and a number of very early impressions, including a billiard hall and a restaurant of Brantford and Owen Sound, 1920-32.

SKILARIS, KOSTAS
TORONTO, ONT.
Interviewed on 1 March 1978; 1 hr.; 1 tape; Greek; by C. Haralabopoulos. Post-WWII immigrant.

SPANOS, CHRISTOS
TORONTO, ONT.
Interviewed on 15 July 1977; .25 hr.; 1 tape; Greek; by C. Haralabopoulos. Post-WWII immigrant.

SPANOS, JOHN
TORONTO, ONT.
Interviewed on 23 July 1977; .5 hr.; 1 tape; Greek; by C. Haralabopoulos. Post-WWII immigrant.

STATHIS, REV. GEORGE
ST. CLAIR, MICHIGAN
20 Aug. 1980; 1 hr.; 1 tape; Greek; by Ross Valdis. Discusses the establishment of the Greek Orthodox Church in Windsor, Ont.

STAVRINOS, DEMETRIOS
TORONTO, ONT.
15 June 1978; 1 hr.; 1 tape; Greek; by C. Haralabopoulos. Arrived in Canada in 1967.

STRATAS, JOHN
TORONTO, ONT.
Certificate of service, Canadian
Armed Forces, 1932; naturalization
card, 1932; AHEPA initiation certifi-
cate, 1931. .5 cm. Photographs.
Taped interview.
6 photographs: J. Stratas during mili-
tary service in WWI, 1918; a grocery
store, 1916; Greek school, 1939;
religious ceremony at St. George's
Greek Orthodox Church, 1917; and
organization, the Daughters of
Penelope, 1946, all taken in Toronto.
Interviewed on 30 March 1978/11
May 1978; 1 hr.; 1 tape; English; by
L. Polyzoi. Recollections of J.
Stratas' business and family life in
Toronto in the 1920s and 1930s.

THERIOS, CHRISTOS
TORONTO, ONT.
Interviewed on 14 July 1977; .25
hr.; 1 tape; Greek; by C.
Haralabopoulos. Post-WWII immi-
grant.

THERIOS, STAVROULA
TORONTO, ONT.
Interviewed on 25 Sept. 1977; .5
hr.; 1 tape; Greek; by C.
Haralabopoulos. Post-WWII immi-
grant.

TROHATOS, GEORGE
TORONTO, ONT.
Interviewed on 8 Sept. 1978; .5 hr.;
1 tape; Greek; by C. Haralabopoulos.
Immigrated to Canada in 1962.

TSABUKOS, CONSTANTINE
TORONTO, ONT.
Interviewed on 20 Aug. 1978; .75
hr.; 1 tape; Greek; by C.
Haralabopoulos. Post-WWII immi-
grant.

TSATSOS, NICHOLAS
TORONTO, ONT.
Personal correspondence, 1972-76.
.5 cm. Photographs. Taped interview.
3 photographs: unidentified, n.d.
Interviewed on 11 Sept. 1977; .75
hr.; 1 tape; Greek; by C.
Haralabopoulos. Post-WWII immigrant.

TSIRBA, MARIA
TORONTO, ONT.
Interviewed on 18 June 1978; .5 hr.;
1 tape; Greek; by C. Haralabopoulos.
Arrived in Canada in 1973.
Unpublished paper on Greek and
Italian immigrants in Canada, c.
1970s. 63 pp.

TZIKOULIS, ALEKA
TORONTO, ONT.
Interviewed on 15 Oct. 1977; 1 hr.;
1 tape; Greek; by C. Haralabopoulos.
Arrived in Canada in the early 1970s.

VAFIADES, PANAGIOTIS
TORONTO, ONT.
Interviewed on 24 July 1977; .25
hr.; 1 tape; Greek; by C.
Haralabopoulos. Post-WWII immi-
grant.

VAGIANAS, GREGORY
TORONTO, ONT.
Interviewed on 21 May 1978; .5 hr.;
1 tape; Greek; by C. Haralabopoulos.
Arrived in Canada in 1972.

VARELIS, PHILIPP
TORONTO, ONT.
Interviewed on 23 June 1978; .5 hr.;
1 tape; Greek; by C. Haralabopoulos.
Post-WWII immigrant.

VASILIADIS, MARY
WINDSOR, ONT.
Interviewed on 31 Aug. 1980; 1 hr.;
1 tape; Greek; by Ross Valdis.
Post-WWII immigrant.

VAZINTARIS, ANTHONY
TORONTO, ONT.
Toulipes. Athens, 1972. Poetry
collection. .5 cm. Taped interview.
Interviewed on 14 Sept. 1977; .5
hr.; 1 tape; Greek; by C.
Haralabopoulos. Post-WWII immi-
grant.

VAZINTARIS, NICK
TORONTO, ONT.
Interviewed on 8 Jan. 1978; 1 hr.; 1
tape; Greek; by C. Haralabopoulos.
Post-WWII immigrant, intends to
return to Greece.

VAZINTARIS, TOULA
TORONTO, ONT.
Interviewed on 15 Jan. 1978; .5 hr.;
1 tape; Greek; by C. Haralabopoulos.
Post-WWII immigrant.

VICHOS, EMMANUEL
WINDSOR, ONT.
Interviewed on 7 Sept. 1980; 1.5
hr.; 2 tapes; English; by Ross Valdis.
Post-WWII immigrant.

VLASTOS, GEORGE
TORONTO, ONT.
Interviewed on 16 Jan. 1978; .5 hr.;
1 tape; Greek; by C. Haralabopoulos.
Arrived in Canada in the 1970s.

WILSON, GINA (NEE BOUKYDIS)
TORONTO, ONT.
Canadian passport, 1957; "Diana
Sweets" menus, 1931, 1947; wedding
invitation, 1920; and clippings about
"Diana Sweets," 1962-75. Photo-
graphs.
19 photographs: the Boukydis and
Matalas families, Toronto, Chicago,
1912-65; and a sweets shop, "Diana
Sweets," 1915-54.
Karyatika. New York, 1951. 2 cm
(selections from book).

ZAFIRIOUS, STAVROS
OTTAWA, ONT.
Correspondence concerning immigration, 1951-52, and immigration documents, 1950-55. .5 cm (12 items).
Photographs.
5 photographs: the S. Zafirious family, Greece, Halifax, Ottawa,
1951-53; and Greek immigrants,
Greece, Halifax, 1951.

ZIATAS, CHRISTOS
TORONTO, ONT.
Interviewed on 10 June 1978; .5 hr.;
1 tape; Greek; by C. Haralabopoulos.
Post-WWII immigrant.
Baconsky, A. E. *Eleven Poems.*
Toronto, 1977. 14 pp.
Ziatas, Christos. *Gestures.* 1975. 1
cm.

AHEON ASSOCIATION (C. MAGAFAS)
TORONTO, ONT.
Constitution, 1967. .25 cm. Photo-
graph.
1 photograph: ceremony at cenotaph,
Toronto, c. 1970-80.

ALEXANDER THE GREAT ASSOCI-
ATION
TORONTO, ONT.
Constitution, n.d., and programmes
regarding activities of the Alexander
the Great Association and the Pan
Macedonian Association, Toronto, c.
1970s. 1.5 cm. Photograph.

1 photograph: members of the Alexander the Great Association, c. 1970s.

AMERICAN HELLENIC EDUCATIONAL PROGRESSIVE ASSOCIATION, LORD BYRON CHAPTER
TORONTO, ONT.
Newsletter. 3 April 1978. .25 cm.

AMERICAN HELLENIC EDUCATIONAL PROGRESSIVE ASSOCIATION, LORD NELSON CHAPTER
LONDON, ONT.
Minutes and miscellaneous records, 1929-78. 1 reel of microfilm. Photographs.
5 photographs: activities of the American Hellenic Educational Progressive Association, London, 1929-37.

AMERICAN HELLENIC EDUCATIONAL PROGRESSIVE ASSOCIATION
OTTAWA, ONT.
AHEPA Yearbook. 1970, 1977. 1 cm.

ANNUNCIATION OF THE VIRGIN MARY, GREEK ORTHODOX CHURCH
TORONTO, ONT.
Baptismal register, 1961-67. 1 reel of microfilm.

ARGO ELECTRONICS
TORONTO, ONT.
Financial records and miscellaneous items, 1977-78. 1 cm.

ASSOCIATION OF KATALINON AND ITHAKISION
TORONTO, ONT.
Constitution, n.d. .25 cm.

ASSOCIATION OF TORONTO'S ZARAKITON PROFETES ELIAS
TORONTO, ONT.
Constitution and miscellaneous items, 1975-76. .5 cm.

ATHENS TRAVEL SERVICE
TORONTO, ONT.
A passport cover, dance invitation, and business cards, c. 1970-80. .25 cm. Photographs.
10 photographs: folk dancers, travel agency, and the Greek ambassador and bishop, c. 1965-75.

ATLAS TOURS
TORONTO, ONT.
Promotional material, c. 1970s. 1 cm. See A. Andrikopoulos

BENEVOLENT ASSOCIATION KRATERON OF FLORINA
TORONTO, ONT.
Constitution, minute book, members list and telephone directory, 1948-70. 2 cm. Photographs.
RESTRICTED
2 photographs: activities of the Hellenic Benefit Association, Toronto, c. 1935-40.
Hellenic Benefit Association, 1934-64. 30th Anniversary Souvenir Album, Toronto, 1964. 1 cm.
Benevolent Association of Krateron and Florina. Toronto, 1970. .5 cm.

CANADIAN ARCADIAN ASSOCIATION
HAMILTON, ONT.
Constitution, brochures, and flyers, 1963-71. 2 cm.
The Greek War of Independence 150th Anniversary. 1976. 1 cm.

CHRISTIAN DEMOCRATIC ASSOCI-
ATION OF CANADA
TORONTO, ONT.
 Flyers and stationery of the Associ-
ation, c. 1970s. .5 cm.
 News Horizons. Nos. 1-5, 1974.
Newsletter. 1 cm.

COSMOS GREEK-CANADIAN MAGA-
ZINE (G. KOTSIKAS)
TORONTO, ONT.
 4 photographs: folk dancing and par-
ade, Toronto, c. 1970-80.
 Cosmos. No. 3, June 1978. .5 cm.

CRETAN ASSOCIATION, M.
PAPADAKIS
HAMILTON, ONT.
 21 photographs: activities of the
Cretan Association, including celebrations, folk dancing and demonstrations, Hamilton, 1964-74.

CRONOS TRAVEL
TORONTO, ONT.
 Promotional material, 1976-77. 2
cm.

ESTIA
TORONTO, ONT.
 Estia. 1968-69 (14 issues). 3 cm.

FEDERATION OF STEREA HELLAS
TORONTO, ONT.
 Constitution, 1953. 1 cm.

GREEK-CANADIAN ASSOCIATION
"TRIPOLIS"
TORONTO, ONT.
 Constitution, 1975. .25 cm.

GREEK CANADIAN DEMOCRATIC
ORGANIZATION
TORONTO, ONT.
 Minutes and correspondence,
1976-79. 7 cm.

"W.P.C. Peace Courier." Feb. 1979.
.25 cm.
 Continuing Education. Toronto
Board of Education, 1979. .25 cm.
 Greek Canadian Monthly Review.
Feb. 1979. .25 cm.

GREEK CANADIAN SENIOR CITIZENS'
CLUB
TORONTO, ONT.
 Constitution, correspondence, financial budget, and membership applications, 1977-79. 1 cm. Photographs.
 2 photographs: executive and parade
of Greek Canadian Senior Citizens
Club, Toronto, c. 1978.

GREEK CANADIAN SOCIETY AGIOS
CEORGIOS
TORONTO, ONT.
 Constitution and by-laws, 1977. .25
cm.

GREEK COMMUNITY OF METROPOLI-
TAN TORONTO INC.
TORONTO, ONT.
 The collection contains correspondence, constitution, regulations and
resolutions, financial statements and
other miscellaneous items, 1973-78. 1
reel of microfilm. 2 cm. See N.
Tsatsos.
 Community Voice. Dec. 1977, April
1978, Feb. 1979. .5 cm.

GREEK COMMUNITY OF WINDSOR
WINDSOR, ONT.
 Minutes, 1954-64; financial records,
1967-76; and membership dues book,
1958-60. 1 reel of microfilm. Taped
interview with E. Vichos, president
of Club.

GREEK GOSPEL CHURCH
TORONTO, ONT.
 Church service programme, 1978-79,

and convention programme, 1979. 1.5
cm. Photograph.
1 photograph: religious activity at
Greek Gospel Church, Toronto, c.
1978.

GREEK LADIES' PHILOPTOCHOS
SOCIETY OF OTTAWA
OTTAWA, ONT.
Constitution booklet, 1944, minutes
and financial accounts, 1952-79, and
miscellaneous items, n.d. 3 cm.

GREEK ORTHODOX ARCHDIOCESE OF
NORTH AND SOUTH AMERICA
TORONTO, ONT.
Records, 1974-78, include minutes,
correspondence, and clippings. 2 cm.
Yearbook. 1966, 1979. 1 cm.
2 calendars, 1966, 1979. 1 cm.

GREEK ORTHODOX LADIES'
PHILOPTOCHOS SOCIETY OF LONDON
LONDON, ONT.
Constitution booklet, 1974, and his-
torical sketch of Society, 1975. .5
cm.

GREEK ORTHODOX LADIES'
PHILOPTOCHOS SOCIETY
TORONTO, ONT.
1 photograph: members of the Greek
Orthodox Ladies' Philoptochos
Society, Toronto, c. 1970.
Clergy-Laity Conference Yearbook.
1975. 1 cm.

GREEK ORTHODOX YOUTH OF
AMERICA (REV. PETER VASILIADIS)
WINDSOR, ONT.
Constitution, 1976, and minutes,
1968-80. 1 reel of microfilm. See
also taped interview with Mary
Vasiliadis. Photograph.

1 photograph: membership certificate
for the Greek Orthodox Youth of
America, Toronto, 1965.

GREEK SCHOOL OF WINDSOR (REV.
P. VASILIADIS)
WINDSOR, ONT.
Enrolment records, 1967-78, and
marks books. 3 cm.

GREEK WAR RELIEF (MR. AND MRS.
H. LUKOS)
WINDSOR, ONT.
Correspondence and clippings. 2
reels of microfilm.

GREEK WOMEN'S PLATO ASSOCI-
ATION (MR. AND MRS. H. LUKOS)
WINDSOR, ONT.
Records, 1938-80, include member-
ship list and dues, minutes, and finan-
cial statements. 3 reels of microfilm.
Photographs.
3 photographs: the Lukos family,
Windsor, 1948-54.

HELLENIC ASSOCIATION OF HELION
HERMES
TORONTO, ONT.
Minutes, membership list, correspon-
dence, flyers, and dance souvenir
albums, 1966-79. 1 reel of microfilm.
Photographs.
4 photographs: activities of the Ilian
Association, Toronto, 1964-72.
The Voice of Ilians. Dec. 1972. 1
issue. 12 pp.

HELLENIC CANADIAN PROFESSIONAL
AND BUSINESSMEN'S ASSOCIATION
TORONTO, ONT.
Constitution, 1979. .25 cm.

HELLENIC COMMUNITY OF
HAMILTON AND DISTRICT
HAMILTON, ONT.
 Minutes of annual conventions,
1952-69; marriage records, 1957-68;
members lists, 1953-60; and bulletins
from St. Demetrius Greek Orthodox
Church, 1976-78; also, a collection of
AHEPA yearbooks and convention
programmes. 1 reel of microfilm. 16
cm. Photographs.
 15 photographs: activities organized
by AHEPA and religious life at St.
Demetrius Greek Orthodox Church,
Hamilton, 1950-70.
 *10th Anniversary of the St.
Demetrios Hellenic Community of
Hamilton and District.* 1960.
Yearbook. .5 cm.
 25th Anniversary Yearbook. 1978. .5
cm.
 Greek School Yearbook. 1975. .5
cm.
 *AHEPA 43rd Annual District Con-
vention.* Hamilton, Ont., 19-22 May
1978. 1 cm.

HELLENIC COMMUNITY OF OTTAWA
OTTAWA, ONT.
 Included are minutes, general correspondence, membership fees, and
yearbooks, 1950-80. 9 cm.
 Diamond, Xenophon. "Curriculum of
the Greek Orthodox Sunday Schools."
45 pp.
 50th Anniversary 1929-1979. Hellenic Community of Ottawa
Yearbook, 1979. 1.5 cm.
 *Birth of Hellenic Independence,
1821-1965.* Hellenic Community of
Ottawa. 27 March, 1965. .5 cm.
 *Hellenic Community Voice of
Ottawa.* 1976-77. Scattered newspaper issues). 1 cm.
 *Hellenic Independence Day,
1821-1980.* Hellenic Community of

Ottawa Yearbook, 1980. 1.5 cm.
 Yearbook. 1971, 1976, 1977, 1978.
6 cm.

HELLENIC COMMUNITY OF ST.
DEMETRIOS
HAMILTON, ONT.
 School Yearbook. 1975. .5 cm.

HELLENIC FREE PRESS
TORONTO, ONT.
 Correspondence regarding 1974
Cyprus conflict, and letters to the
editor, 1975-76. .25 cm. Photographs.
 15 photographs: organizations such
as the Pan Macedonian Association
and Society of Florina, n.d.; schools
and business enterprise, n.d.; folk
dancing, 1975; and religious life at
St. George's Greek Orthodox Church,
Toronto,1976-77.

HELLENIC PHARMACY
TORONTO, ONT.
 Promotional material, 1978. 1 cm.

HELLENIC TRIBUNE (D. ZOTOS)
TORONTO, ONT.
 Correspondence, list of early sub-
scribers, flyers, and clippings,
1959-67. 1 cm. Photographs. 43
photographs: 1958-68, various Greek
community activities in Toronto,
including Greek Independence Day
celebrations, activities of AHEPA, the
Pan Macedonian Association, the
Greek Orthodox Youth of America,
the Kastorian Association, and religious life at St. Demetrios Greek
Orthodox Church.
 Bouqueto. 1971. .5 cm.
 Clergy-Laity Conference. Toronto,
28-31 May 1975. Yearbook, 208 pp.

Greek Community of Metro Toronto Special Issue. 1977. Magazine. .25 cm.

Hellenic Tribune. 1961-76. Scattered issues. 1 cm.

The Immigrant. 1968. .5 cm.

Pan Arcadian Federation of America and Canada. 1961. .5 cm.

Pontiaki Estia. 1976-78. Scattered issues. 1 cm.

Soccer Canada. 1977. .5 cm (4 issues).

Toronto Society of Epirus. 1974. .5 cm.

HOLY CROSS GREEK ORTHODOX CHURCH AND GREEK COMMUNITY OF WINDSOR
WINDSOR, ONT.

Consecration Yearbook of the Holy Cross Greek Orthodox Church. Sept. 1975. 60 pp.

Greek Community of Windsor Bulletin. Oct. 1967 - June 1980. 122 publications. 4 cm.

HOLY TRINITY, GREEK LADIES' PHILOPTOHOS SOCIETY OF ST. DEMETRIOS GREEK ORTHODOX CHURCH
HAMILTON, ONT.

Historical sketch of Society, n.d. .25 cm.

10th Anniversary Yearbook. 1960. .5 cm.

25th Anniversary Yearbook, 1978. .5 cm.

HOLY TRINITY GREEK ORTHODOX CHURCH
TORONTO, ONT.

Baptismal and marriage registers, 1974-79. 1 reel of microfilm.

HOLY TRINITY GREEK ORTHODOX PARISH
LONDON, ONT.

Included are correspondence, financial report, certificates, and bulletins concerning Greek schools, 1976-78. 1 cm. Photographs.

3 photographs: activities at Holy Trinity Greek School, London, 1963-78.

First Grade Primer. 1978. .5 cm.

First Grade Exercise Book. 1961. .5 cm.

Greek Orthodox Archdiocese Yearbook. 1977. 1 cm.

London Greek Community Telephone Directory. 1976. .5 cm.

KASTORIA SOCIETY AND SUBURBS INC.
TORONTO, ONT.

15th Anniversary Yearbook. 1975. .5 cm.

LADIES' PLATO SOCIETY OF WINDSOR (ZOIRA FITZIOS)
WINDSOR, ONT.

Books of minutes, 1954-62, and financial statements, 1956-60. 1 cm.

MULTICULTURAL HISTORY SOCIETY OF ONTARIO
TORONTO, ONT.

Evdomada. Nos. 1-89, Oct. 1976-Sept. 1978 (missing nos. 31-34, 49). Weekly newspaper. 1 reel of microfilm, 16 cm.

To Vima. (Detroit Greek Tribune) and *Ethnikon Vima* (National Greek Tribune), 11 Feb. 1934 - 7 Nov. 1980. 7 reels of microfilm.

MULTICULTURAL NEWSPAPER MICROFILM PROJECT
TORONTO, ONT.

Eleutheros Typos (Hellenic Free

Press). Jan. 1978 - 31 March 1982. 4
reels of microfilm.
Ellenike Estia. June 1966 - Dec.
1969. 1 reel of microfilm.
Ellenokanadika Chronika
(Hellenic-Canadian Chronicles). 20
May 1981 - 29 Dec. 1987. 7 reels of
microfilm.

NAFPAKTION ASSOCIATION
TORONTO, ONT.
Constitution, 1977. .25 cm.

NEOI KAIROI (NEW TIMES)
TORONTO, ONT.
General correspondence, 1967-68.
.25 cm.

NESTNIOTON ASSOCIATION
TORONTO, ONT.
Constitution, 1958. .25 cm.

ONTARIO ETHNIC NEWSPAPER
MICROFILM PROJECT
TORONTO, ONT.
Neoi Kaipoi. 25 March 1967 - 29
Nov. 1968. 1 reel of microfilm.
Neos Kosmos. 12 Aug. 1967 - 12
March 1970. 1 reel of microfilm.

PALLESVIAKOU ASSOCIATION ARION
TORONTO, ONT.
Constitution, 1974. .25 cm.
Lesviaka. No. 18 (April 1979). .25
cm.

PANEPIROTIC FEDERATION OF
AMERICA
TORONTO, ONT.
Convention books, 1965, 1973. 1
reel of microfilm.

PAN-MACEDONIAN ASSOCIATION OF
CANADA
TORONTO, ONT.
37th National Pan-Macedonian Con-

vention. Toronto, July 5-10, 1983.
125 pp.
Macedonian Defender. June 1975 -
March 1978 (4 issues). 60 pp.
Macedonian Echo. Dec. 1976. 60
pp.
*Pan-Macedonian Association 31st
National Convention Yearbook.* 1977.
208 pp.

PAN PELOPONNISIAKI FEDERATION
TORONTO, ONT.
Constitution, n.d. .25 cm.

PARNON ASSOCIATION
TORONTO, ONT.
Constitution and by-laws, 1972. .25
cm.

PARNASSOS SOCIETY INC., THE
OTTAWA, ONT.
Included are reports, letters of patent
and flyers, 1974-78. .5 cm.
Paranssos Bulletin. 1976-79. Scat-
tered issues. 1 cm.

PONTION BROTHERHOOD
TORONTO, ONT.
Constitution, 1963, flyers and other
miscellaneous items, 1970s. 1.5 cm.
Taped interview with S. Karasavidis.
Lost Fatherland. 1975. Yearbook. .5
cm.
Pontiaki Estia. June 1974-July 1978.
21 scattered issues. 2.5 cm.

SOCIETY OF AMYTEON AND SUBURBS
TORONTO, ONT.
Constitution, minutes, and members
list of Amyntas Ladies' Society,
1970-79. .5 cm.

SOCIETY OF EPIRUS
TORONTO, ONT.
Constitution, correspondence and
printed items, 1964-80. 2 cm. Photo-

graph.
1 photograph: activity of the Society of Epirus, Toronto, 1974.
10th Anniversary Yearbook. 1974. .5 cm.
Panepirotic Struggle. No. 30, June 1973. Newspaper. .25 cm.
Youth Chapter First Anniversary Yearbook. 1974. .5 cm.

SOCIETY OF FLORINA
TORONTO, ONT.
Records, 1963-79, include constitution, correspondence, minute book, and flyers. 1 reel of microfilm.
27th Pan Macedonian Convention Souvenir Book. 1973. 106 pp.

SOCIETY OF KALYVIA SOHAS
TORONTO, ONT.
Constitution, n.d. .25 cm.

SOCIETY OF KASTORIANS
"OMONOIA," LADIES BRANCH
TORONTO, ONT.
Included are constitution, correspondence, minutes, and invitations, 1954-79. 1 reel of microfilm. Photographs.
6 photographs: activities of the Society of Kastorians, Toronto, 1974-78.
20th Anniversary Souvenir Booklet. 1974. On microfilm.

SOCIETY OF MILEA
TORONTO, ONT.
Souvenir Journal of the Society of Milea. Jan. 1977. 40 pp.

SPARTAN SOCIETY
TORONTO, ONT.
Flyers and programmes issued by the Spartan Society. 2 cm. Photographs.
5 photographs: members and activ-

ities of the Spartan Society, Toronto, c. 1970-80.
Evdomada. Toronto, Feb. 1979. Newspaper. 4 pp.
Hellenic Free Press. Toronto, Nov. 1977 - Feb. 1979. 1 cm.
Laconic Herald. Sept. 1976 - March 1977. 13 scattered issues. Greek newspaper .5 cm.
O Xenichtis. July 1975 - Nov. 1976. 16 scattered issues. Greek newspaper. 1 cm.
Spartan News. Jan 1979. Greek newspaper. 4 pp.

ST. GEORGE'S GREEK ORTHODOX
CHURCH
TORONTO, ONT.
Minutes, correspondence and miscellaneous records, including birth, baptismal and marriage certificates, 1964-75. 1 reel of microfilm. Photographs.
10 photographs: religious services and parish activity at St. George Greek Orthodox Church, Toronto, c. 1970s.

ST. IRENE CHRISOVALANTOU GREEK
ORTHODOX CHURCH
TORONTO, ONT.
Baptismal and marriage registers, 1976-78. 1 reel of microfilm.

ST. NEKTARIOS GREEK ORTHODOX
CHURCH
TORONTO, ONT.
Orthodox Life. 1970-78. Church bulletin. 1 reel of microfilm.

ST. NICHOLAS GREEK ORTHODOX
CHURCH
TORONTO, ONT.
 Flyers, announcements, bulletins,
and 1 wall calendar, 1975-79. 1 cm.
 Clergy-Laity Conference Yearbook.
1975. 1 cm.

ÁGOSTON, MR.
DELHI, ONT.
 3 photographs: Saskatchewan, c.
1928.

AXFORD, MADGE
OAKVILLE, ONT.
 Immigration papers, and a land deed,
c. 1920-30. .5 cm. Photographs.
Taped interview.
 20 photographs: Madge Axford in
Welland, and Oakville, c. 1928-80.
 Interviewed on 23 April 1982; 1 hr.;
1 tape; English; by Susan
Papp-Zubrits. Recollections of grow-
ing up in Welland, Ont.
*50th Anniversary Book of Our Lady
of Hungary R.C. Church*. Welland,
Ont., n.d. 40 pp.

BALÁSZ, ANDY
DELHI, ONT.
 Interviewed on 27 July 1977; 1 hr.;
1 tape; English; by Susan Gálos.
Discusses life in Transylvania, and
business enterprise in Tillsonburg
where father was mayor.

BÁLINT, GABRIELLA
TORONTO, ONT.
 Included are correspondence,
flyers,name lists, and clippings
regarding events surrounding the
"Hungarian Revolution" (1956), the
Hungarian Relief Fund, and the spon-
soring of Hungarian immigrants
1954-77. Also, material pertaining to
the *Magyar
Becsület Mozgalom* (Hungarian Honour Movement): founding resolution,
fundemental principles (for the establishment of a Hungarian government
in exile), and flyers, 1952-53; minutes and notes of the Canadian Hungarian Federation, 1952; by-laws of
the Toronto Hungarian House; flyers,
1955-77; and personal papers of the
the Bálint family. The collection also
contains an array of newspaper issues
and periodicals. .5 meters.
Amerikai-Kanadai Magyar Élet. Chicago, 28 Aug. 1976 (weekly). 20 pp.
Kanadai Magyar Újság. Winnipeg, 2
Nov. 1956, 26 July 1974, 13 June
1975, 12 March 1976 (bi-weekly, 4
issues).
Képes Világhíradó (Illustrated World
News). Dec. 1958 - April 1969 (105
issues).
Katolikus Magyarok Vasárnapja.
Youngstown, 18 Sept. 1977 (weekly).
8 pp.
Magyar Élet (Hungarian Life). 28
June 1958, 13 March 1971, 1978-79
(loose sheets). .5 cm.
Magyar Hírek. Budapest, 15 May
1958; 28 Jan., 25 March 1978. (bi-
weekly, 3 issues).
Magyar Nők Lapja. Toronto, 1958
(bi-weekly, 3 issues).
Menora—Egyenlőseg. Toronto, 6
Sept. 1975, 24 Sept. 1977 (Jewish
weekly, 2 issues).
Sporthírádo (Sports News). Vol. 8,
1960 (weekly, 50 issues).
Tanú—Irodalmi és Kulturalis Szemle.
Vol. 1, no. 1. Toronto, March 1978
(monthly). 8 pp.

*Új Garia—Szabad Magyarok
Független Hetilapja.* Munich, 9 Nov.
1956 (weekly). 8 pp.

BAYER, JULIA
TORONTO, ONT.
 Immigration cards, clippings, and
flyers, 1925-67. 2 cm. Photographs.
Taped interview.
 27 photographs: portraits and personal documents of the Bayer family
in Toronto, 1925-49; and religious
life at the Hungarian United Church
and at St. Elizabeth of Hungary Catholic Church in Toronto, 1931-37.
 Interviewed on 20 Nov. 1976; 1 hr.;
1 tape; English; by Carmela Patrias.
Arrived in Canada in 1926, discusses
congregation of St. Elizabeth of
Hungary Roman Catholic Church and
relationship between "old" and "new"
immigrants.
 *25th Anniversary of the Toronto
Hungarian House.* Dec. 1967. 8 pp.
 Az Otthon. Winnipeg, Dec. 1935
(monthly). 16 pp.
 Tárógato. Toronto, Sept. 1941, 1981
(monthly). 3 cm.

BÉKÉSI, FATHER ISTVÁN
TORONTO, ONT.
 Interviewed on 27 Feb. 1979; 1 hr.;
1 tape; Hungarian; by S.
Papp-Zubrits. Immigrated to Cananda
in 1947, discusses history of St.
Elizabeth of Hungary Roman Catholic
Church, and work with Catholic
Youth organization.

BIRINYI, JULIANA
TORONTO, ONT.
 Interviewed on 8 Dec. 1976; 1 hr.; 1
tape; Hungarian; by Carmela Patrias.
Immigrated to Canada in the late
1920s.

BIRINYI, SÁNDOR
TORONTO, ONT.
 Interviewed on 8 Dec. 1976; 1 hr.; 1
tape; Hungarian; by Carmela Patrias.
Arrived in Canada in 1926, discusses
employment history in construction
and with the Swift Co., his wife
operated a boarding house.

BISZTRAY, GEORGE
TORONTO, ONT.
 Interviewed on 12 Jan. 1979; 1.5
hr.; 2 tapes; English; by S.
Papp-Zubrits. Post-WWII immigrant.

BLASKO, MRS.
TORONTO, ONT.
 4 photographs: activities of the
Kossuth Sick Benefit Society and the
Independent Mutual Benefit Feder-
ation in Toronto, 1930-40. Taped
interview.
 Interviewed in Feb. 1977; 1 hr.; 1
tape; English; by Carmela Patrias.
Member of the Independent Mutual
Benefit Federation.

BRIETENBACH, S.
WELLAND, ONT.
 Balogh, Jozsef. *Uj
Magyarorszag—Egy Kanadai Magyar
Szemuvegenat.* Toronto, 1947. 86 pp.

CHOROS, JOE
SIMCOE, ONT.
 Interviewed on 12 July 1977; .5 hr.;
1 tape; English; by David Judd.
Owned a tobacco farm for 19 years.

CSELENYI, JOSEPH
TORONTO, ONT.
 Personal papers, scrapbook, programmes, flyers, and clippings,
1967-76. 2 cm. Taped interview.
 Interviewed on 3 March 1978; .75
hr.; 1 tape; English; by M. Zalan.

Discusses career in theatre, and interior designing.

CSOK, ELIZABETH
TORONTO, ONT.
6 photographs: parish activity at the First Hungarian Presbyterian Church, and St. Elizabeth of Hungary Catholic Church in Toronto, 1933-43. Taped interview.
Interviewed on 29 Nov. 1976; 1 hr.; 1 tape; English; by Carmela Patrias.
Arrived in Canada in 1928; discusses work history, Hungarian Catholic congregation, and regionalism among Hungarians.

CZEGLÉDY-NAGY, NINA
TORONTO, ONT.
Interviewed on 28 March 1978; .75 hr.; 1 tape; English; by M. Zalan.
She and her husband landed at Montreal in 1956.

CZERLAU, JOE
SIMCOE, ONT.
Interviewed on 26 July 1977; .5 hr.; 1 tape; English; by Susan Gálos.

CZERLAU, JOE AND ELIZABETH
VIENNA, ONT.
Interviewed on 28 July 1977; 1 hr.; 1 tape; English; by Susan Gálos.
They discuss status of tobacco farmers and ethnic composition of the Simcoe, Ont. area.

CZUKAR, HELEN
HAMILTON, ONT.
4 photographs: the Czukar family; and employment in agriculture in Brantford, 1940-50.

DE NAGAY, MÁRIA
TORONTO, ONT.
Booklets on home and garden design-

ing, biographical sketch of donor and newsclippings, 1964-77. .5 cm. Photograph. Taped interview.
1 photograph: sculpture by Mária De Negay, Toronto, 1977.
Interviewed on 3 Jan. 1978; .75 hr.; 1 tape; English; by M. Zalan.
Post-WWII immigrant. Arrived in Toronto in 1951.

DÉNES, LÁSZLO
TORONTO, ONT.
39 photographs: Hungarian refugees en route to Canada, 1956.

DE PEDERYT, DORA
TORONTO, ONT.
2 letters and 5 drawings, 1957-67; and a brief biography of donor. .5 cm. Photographs. Taped interview.
6 photographs: studio and sculptures of D. De Pederyt in Toronto, 1950-71.
Interviewed on 5 Jan. 1978; .75 hr.; 1 tape; English; by M. Zalan.
Post-WWII immigrant.
Dedication Booklet of St. David and St. Patrick Church. 1967. .5 cm.

DOKA, REV. KÁLMÁN
TORONTO, ONT.
Interviewed on 4 March 1983; 2 hrs.; 2 tapes; English; by S. Zubrits.

DUDÁS, MARY
TORONTO, ONT.
1 photograph: the first Hungarian St. Stephen's Day celebration in Toronto, 1937. Taped interview.
Interviewed in Fall 1976; 1 hr.; 1 tape; English; by Carmela Patrias.

DUROVEC, ANDREW R.
UNIONVILLE, ONT.
Calendars, poems, articles, flyers, and newsclippings, 1954-77. 3 cm.

Tima, L. J. "A Short History of the Hungarian People in Canada." Toronto, 1957. 19 pp.

A Nő (Woman). 1948-52. Scattered issues. 1 reel of micofilm.

Calendar of the Canadian Hungarian Worker (Kanadai Magyar Munkás, Naptára). 1936. 1 reel of microfilm.

Calendar of the Hungarian Home Association. 1968. 1 reel of microfilm.

Dictionary of Foreign Words (Idegen Szavak Szótára), c. 1930. 1 reel of microfilm.

Kanadai Kis Ujság (Canadian Little Paper). 14 April 1939. 14 pp.

Magyar Canadians. July 1939. 12 pp.

Newsletter. 1969. The Anti-Bolshevist League. 7 pp.

EGRI, GEORGE
TORONTO, ONT.
Interviewed on 28 March 1978; .5 hr.; 1 tape; English; by M. Zalan. Discusses career as a journalist and editor of an ethnic newpaper, *Menora*, in Toronto.

ELEK, MICHAEL
SCARBOROUGH, ONT.
Interviewed on 29 March 1978; .5 hr.; 1 tape; English; by M. Zalan. Arrived in Canada in 1956, discusses career as a physician.

ENDES, LESLIE
TORONTO, ONT.
Leaflet issued by the Hungarian Canadian Cultural Centre, n.d. .25 cm. Taped interview.
Interviewed on 16 Aug. 1978; .5 hr.; 1 tape; English; by S. Papp-Zubrits. Discusses differences and relationship between pre- and post-WWII Hungarian immigrants.

Kronica. 8 Aug. 1975. The Hungarian Canadian Cultural Centre in Toronto. 24 pp.

EPPEL, JOHN
COURTLAND, ONT.
Interviewed on 26 July 1977; 3.5 hrs.; 4 tapes; English; by Hilda Schenn. Arrived in Canada in 1932.

FALUDY, GEORGE
TORONTO, ONT.
Interviewed on 11 Jan. 1978; .5 hr.; 1 tape; English; by M. Zalan. Fled Hungary in 1956, discusses his career as a writer.
Faludy, George. *Levelek az utókorhoz*. Toronto, 1975. 206 pp.
_____. *Francois Villon Balladai*. Tel Aviv, 1978. 96 pp.

FAY, EDMUND DE
TORONTO, ONT.
Interviewed on 15 May 1979; 3 hrs.; 3 tapes; English; by S. Papp-Zubrits. Post-WWII immigrant.

FELD, FRANK
THUNDER BAY, ONT.
Interviewed on 28 Dec. 1977; .75 hr.; 1 tape; English; by Cairine Budner. Parents immigrated to Canada in the 1920s.

FERENTZY, TIBOR
TORONTO, ONT.
Interviewed on 14 March 1979; .5 hr.; 1 tape; English; by S. Papp-Zubrits. Discusses his association with the Tansylvanian community in Toronto.
Haraszti, Endre. *Ethnic History of Transylvania*. Florida: Danubian Press, 1971. 218 pp.
Documented Facts and Figures on Transylvania. Compiled by the

Danubian Research Center and the
Transylvanian World Federation.
Florida: The Danubian Press, 1977.
80 pp.

FEUER, GEORGE
TORONTO, ONT.
 Newspaper articles regarding Hun-
garian Chair at University of
Toronto, 1971, and biographical
sketch of donor. .5 cm. Photographs.
Taped interview.
 2 photographs: G. Feuer in Toronto,
c. 1970-80.
 Interviewed on 9 Jan. 1978; .75 hr.;
1 tape; English; by M. Zalan.
Fled Hungary in 1956, worked for
the University of Toronto Banting
Institute.

FORBÁTH, PÉTER
TORONTO, ONT.
 Interviewed on 30 Jan. 1978; .75
hr.; 1 tape; English; by M. Zalan.
Immigrated to Canada in 1956, dis-
cusses his profession as a surgeon.

FORGÁCH, WALTER
TORONTO, ONT.
 Interviewed on 25 August 1978; 2
hrs.; 2 tapes; English; by S.
Papp-Zubrits and Carmela Patrias.

FÜLÖP, GEORGE
TILLSONBURG, ONT.
 Interviewed on 26 July 1977; 1.75
hrs; 2 tapes; English; by Susan
Gálos. Discussion traces family business from tobacco farming to motel
operations.

GÁBOR, ÁGOTA
TORONTO, ONT.
 Four newspaper articles regarding
Ágota Gábor, 1977. .25 cm. Taped
interview.

Interviewed on 3 March 1978; .5
hr.; 1 tape; English; by M. Zalan.
She fled Hungary in 1956, discusses
her career in acting and dancing.

GÁBORI, ÉVE
TORONTO, ONT.
 Interviewed on 7 March 1978; .75
hr.; 1 tape; English; by M. Zalan.
Fled Hungary in 1956, employed in
Toronto as a librarian.

GABURA, MRS.
TORONTO, ONT.
 Passport, 1926. .25 cm. Photo-
graphs. Taped interview.
 8 photographs: activities of the Fed-
eration of Democratic Hungarian
Canadians, 1944, Petofi Youth Club,
n.d., Independent Mutual Benefit
Federation, n.d., and Kossuth Sick
Benefit Society in Toronto, and
Hamilton, c. 1926-44.
 Interviewed in Winter 1977; 1 hr.; 1
tape; English; by Carmela Patrias.
Arrived in Canada in the 1920s.

GÁLOS, CHARLES AND ÉVA
DELHI, ONT.
 Interviewed on 1 Aug. 1977; .75 hr.;
1 tape; English; by Susan Gálos.
Arrived in Canada in 1928.

GÁL, SÁNDOR
DELHI, ONT.
 Interviewed on 21 July 1977; .75
hr.; 1 tape; Hungarian; by P. Pandy.
Arrived in Canada in 1928.

GERVERS, VERONICA
TORONTO, ONT.
 Interviewed on 8 Feb. 1978; .5 hr.;
1 tape; English; by M. Zalan. Post-
WWII immigrant.

GILVESY, GEORGE
TILLSONBURG, ONT.
Interviewed on 22 Aug. 1979; 2
hrs.; 2 tapes; Hungarian; by S.
Papp-Zubrits. Recounts the establish-
ment of community organizations—the
Munkás movement, Delhi Hungarian
House, and *Székely.*

GIRHINY, FATHER JOHN
HAMILTON, ONT.
20 photographs: activities in the
Welland Hungarian community,
including religious life, parades and
theatrical productions, c. 1970-80.
Taped interview.
Interviewed on 8 Aug. 1979; 2 hrs.;
2 tapes; English; by S. Papp-Zubrits.
Provides history of St. Michael's
Greek Catholic Church in Hamilton.

GYALLAY-PAP, DONALD
TORONTO, ONT.
Interviewed on 6 Nov. 1978; 2 hrs.;
2 tapes; Hungarian; by S.
Papp-Zubrits. Post-WWII immigrant,
discusses early life in Transylvania,
and his work in the Canadian Hungarian Federation.

HABE, GNACZ AND KATHERINE
DELHI, ONT.
4 photographs: tobacco farming in
Simcoe, Walsingham, and Scotland,
Ont., 1930-39.

HALÁSZ DE BEKY, IVÁN
TORONTO, ONT.
Hungarian Canadian Church period-
ical collection, 1951-76; also, records
from the Hungarian Canadian Federation, 1965, and the Toronto Hungarian House, 1956. 2 reels of microfilm. Taped interview.
Interviewed on 18 Sept. 1981; .75

hr; 1 tape; English; by Jung-gun
Kim.
Tanú. Toronto, March 1978 - July
1979 (weekly). 1 reel of microfilm.
Tiszakerecsenytől Kanadáig. Buda-
pest, 1963. 414 pp.

———.
TORONTO, ONT.
This collection consists of papers
related to the establishment of the
Hungarian Chair at University of
Toronto, c. 1970s; Hungarian Consu-
lar correspondence from Winnipeg
and Montreal, 1920-40; papers related
to Nemeth Laszlo, and the Hungarian
Cultural Association, c. 1970-81; and
1 file of memoranda belonging to
Hebert O. Frind, c. 1955-56. 12 cm.
Taped interview.
Interviewed on 24 Feb. 1978; .75
hr.; 1 tape; English; by Magda Zalan.
Post-WWII immigrant.

———.
TORONTO, ONT.
Hungarian-Canadian pamphlet collec-
tion (23 items). 1 reel of microfilm.
Taped interview.
Interviewed on 1 March 1979; 1 hr.;
1 tape; English; by S. Papp-Zubrits.
Halasz de Beky, I. *Arccal a Falnak.*
Toronto: Amerikai Magyar Irok,
1972. Poems. 47 pp.
———. *Rab ës Börtonőr.* Toronto,
1975. Poems. 96 pp.
———. *Korai Dér.* Toronto, 1981.
Poems. 27 pp.
Várnay, Nándor. *Gyakorlati Angol
Nyelvkőnyv Bevándorló magyaroknak*
(A Practical English Language Course
for Hungarian Immigrants).
Vancouver: Mitchell Press Ltd.,
1957. 79 pp.
Kanada Tőrténelme. Winnipeg,
Manitoba, 1941. 265 pp.

HARASZTI, ENDRE
HAMILTON, ONT.
Collection consists mostly of written works by Endre Haraszti, satirical cartoons of an immigrant, and souvenir booklets, 1961-79. 2 reels of microfilm.

HASILO, MATHIAS
TILLSONBURG, ONT.
Interviewed on 16 May 1982; .75 hr.; 1 tape; Hungarian; by S. Papp-Zubrits. Discusses community life, and work in the tobacco growing district of Tillsonburg.

HERTEL, ANDREW
DELHI, ONT.
1 photograph: Hertel family in Hungary, 1910. Taped interview. Interviewed on 11 July 1977; .5 hr.; 1 tape; English; by Piri Pandy.

HIDY-DUVRAK, MARTHA
TORONTO, ONT.
Interviewed on 24 Jan. 1978; .5 hr.; 1 tape; English; by M. Zalan. Arrived in Canada in 1956, discusess her career as a concert master.

HIRSCH, JOHN
TORONTO, ONT.
Scrapbooks containing newsclippings, programmes, and letters, 1952-56. 1 cm. Taped interview.
Interviewed on 13 March 1978; .5 hr.; 1 tape; English; by M. Zalan. Arrived in Canada in the 1950s, discusses his career as a theatre director.

HORDOS, JOSEPH AND OLLINGA
SASKATCHEWAN
Interviewed in 1973; 1.5 hrs.;

1 tape; Hungarian; by Eugene Boday. Arrived in Canada in 1906.

HORVÁTH, FRANCESKA
TORONTO, ONT.
Clippings, mostly on Frances Tallarom Horváth in various acting roles, 1950-80. .25 cm. Photographs. Taped interview.
84 photographs: Horváth family; and parish activity at St. Elizabeth of Hungary Catholic Church, including theatrical productions, picnics, and schools in Toronto, 1940-78.
Interviewed on 26 April 1978; .75 hr.; 1 tape; English; by S. Papp-Zubrits.

ILLÉS, BÁLINT
TORONTO, ONT.
Immigration documents, 1 flyer and a collection of mostly left-wing Hungarian publications. 3 reels of microfilm. 20 cm. Photographs.
3 photographs: monuments and memorials to Hungarian heroes in Niagara Falls, and Pickering, 1967-68.
Balogh, Jozsef. *Hitler Titkos Fegyvere* (The Secret Weapon of Hitler). Toronto, 1943. 80 pp.
Buck, Tim. *Kanada*. Budapest, 1950. 173 pp. Microfilm.
Gross, Rev. Laszlo A. *A Vegső Harc* (The Final Struggle). Chicago, 1944. A collection of articles. 160 pp. Microfilm.
Hollos, Jozse. Collection of speeches by Jozse Hollos, 1926-36. 64 pp. Microfilm.
Kostya, Sandor. *Édes Anyanyelvünk* (Our Beloved Mother Tongue). Toronto, 1959. 110 pp.
Kovács, Erzsi. *Apróságok* (Trifles/Odds and Ends). New York, 1967. A collection of articles. 160 pp.
Rácz, Lászlo. *Porszem a Viharban*

(Dust in the Storm). New York, 1965. 194 pp. Microfilm.

Szőke, Istran. *A Magyarság Történelme* (The History of 's). Toronto, 1937. 220 pp. Microfilm.

'48—as Kossuth Évkönyv (Calendar of the Independent Smallholders' Party). Budapest, 1948. 200 pp. Microfilm.

A Magyar Nép Küzdelme (The Struggle of the Hungarian People). Toronto, 1944. 78 pp. Microfilm.

A Szociálizmushoz Vezető Út Kanadában (The Way Toward Socialism In Canada). Toronto: Communist Party of Canada, 1960. 36 pp. Microfilm.

Békéért, Haladásért, Szociálizmusért (For Peace, Progress and Socialism). Speeches by Tim Buck, Toronto, 1946. 48 pp. Microfilm.

Egy Jobb Kanadát (A Better Canada). Campaign literature of the Labour Progressive Party. Toronto, 1940s. 30 pp. Microfilm.

Kanadai Függetlenség és Népi Demokrácia. Toronto: Labour Progressive Party, 1952. 30 pp. Microfilm.

Kanadai Függetlenség és Népi Parlament (Canadian Independence and People's Parliament). Toronto: Labour Progressive Party, 1954. 32 pp.

Két Világháboru Között (Between Two World Wars). New York, 1936.

Legyünk Urai Saját Házunknak (Let Us Be Masters of Our Own House). n.d. National Committee of the Communist Party of Canada.

Öt Magyar Költő (Five Hungarian Poets: Csokonai, Batsanui, Katona, Petőfi, and Ady). Toronto, n.d. 80 pp. Microfilm.

ISAAC, MEDY
TORONTO, ONT.
Interviewed on 4 Sept. 1979; .5 hr.; 1 tape; English; by S. Papp-Zubrits. Reminiscences of life in Saskatchewan, and subsequent move to Toronto.

JÁGER, JOSEPH
TORONTO, ONT.
A collection of drama scripts used by Hungarians in Toronto in presenting amateur plays, such as *Gyrus Zsidó, Őrmester úr Jelentem Alássan, Az Ördög Párnája, Mari Esete, Mihok,* and *Samu.* 10 cm. Photographs. Taped interview.
17 photographs: theatrical productions at St. Elizabeth of Hungary Catholic Church, Toronto, 1930-60; and employment in construction in Black River, Quebec, 1928-29.
Interviewed on 13 Sept. 1978; 3 hrs.; 3 tapes; English; by S. Papp-Zubrits. Immigrated to Canada in 1928, member of the Brantford Hungarian Mutual Benefit Society.

JONÁS, GEORGE
TORONTO, ONT.
Interviewed on 23 Jan. 1978; .75 hr.; 1 tape; English; by M. Zalan. Discusses his writing career.

JUHÁSZ, FRANK
RICHMOND HILL, ONT.
50th Anniversary of St. Elizabeth of Hungary Roman Catholic Church. Toronto, 1978. 40 pp.

JURETIC, FRANK
TORONTO, ONT.
Interviewed on 11 Feb. 1980; .75 hr.; 1 tape; Hungarian; by

S. Papp-Zubrits. Discussion on life as part of Hungarian minority in Yugoslavia.

KAMAN, ALFRED
SIMCOE, ONT.
Interviewed on 21 July 1977; .75 hr.; 1 tape; Hungarian; by P. Pandy and Rev. Pandy. Immigrated to Canada in 1957.

KATONA, JOHN
DELHI, ONT.
1 photograph: work on the farm, Delhi, 1959.

KÉKKŐ, GÁBOR
TORONTO, ONT.
3 catalogues of the Gábor Kékkő Gallery, Luzern, Germany, n.d. 1 cm. Taped interview.
Interviewed on 19 Jan. 1978; .25 hr.; 1 tape; English; by M. Zalan. Discusses emigration, and career as an art dealer.

KEMENES-KETTNER, BÉLA
ST. CATHARINES, ONT.
1 photograph: group of political leaders with representatives of the St. Catharines Multicultural Centre, 1978. Taped interview.
Interviewed on 28 Feb. 1981; 1 hr.; 1 tape; Hungarian; by S. Papp-Zubrits. Post-WWII emigrant.

KERTÉSZ, GÉZA
WELLAND, ONT.
G. Kertész immigrated to Canada in 1929 at the age of sixteen. He found employment in a textile mill in Welland, and later ventured unsuccessfully into growing tobacco in Delhi, Ont. He was past president, and longtime member of the Hungarian Welland Self-Culture Society, and

a reporter for the inter-war newspaper, *Welland Kisújság* (Little Hungarian News of Canada).
The G. Kértsz collection consists of personal papers—correspondence (between donor and brother in Hungary), travel documents, clippings, and invitations, 1935-77; miscellaneous material (constitution and by-laws, membership lists, minutes, correspondence, invitations, and programmes) from the following organizations and institutions: Welland Hungarian Self-Culture Society, Delhi and Tobacco District Hungarian House, Canadian Hungarian Christian Association (Niagara Falls), Hungarian Veterans, *Magyar Munkás* (Hungarian Workers Movement), St. Catharines Hungarian Cultural Society, and both Hungarian churches in Welland, Our lady of Hungary Roman Catholic Church and the Welland Hungarian Presbyterian Church, 1932-77. Included is a selection of Hungarian-language books, pamphlets, and souvenir albums, published mostly in Budapest, Winnipeg, Toronto, Welland, and Delhi, 1939-79. .5 meters. Photographs.
17 photographs: activities of the Hungarian Self-Culture Society, 1940-58; weddings, 1930-40; and Emery Orosz, all taken in Welland.
25 Ev Jubileumi Emlékkönyve. Silver Jubilee of Our Lady of Hungary Church, Welland, 1953. 39 pp. *A Kanada Dohányvidéki Magyar Ház Emlékalbuma*. Dedication album of the Delhi and Tobacco District Hungarian House, 1949. 35 pp.
A Kanadai Magyar Ujság Képes Nagy Naptára (Yearbook of the Canadian Hungarian News). 1946-49. 6 cm.

KERTÉSZ, PAULINA
WELLAND, ONT.
Interviewed on 22 Oct. 1979; .5 hr.;
1 tape; Hungarian; by S.
Papp-Zubrits. Discusses personal
history, and that of her husband,
Geza Kertész.

KERTÉSZ, SÁNDOR
TORONTO, ONT.
Interviewed on 28 Nov. 1978; 1 hr.;
1 tape; Hungarian; by S.
Papp-Zubrits. Discusses his involvement in Hungarian theatre in Toronto.
Torontoi Művész Szinház. 16 programmes of the Hungarian Art Theatre, Toronto, 1968-78. 4 cm.

KISH, COLUMBA
TORONTO, ONT.
Interviewed on 15 June 1978; 1 hr.;
1 tape; English; by S. Papp-Zubrits.
Reminiscences of early life in
Saskatchewan, migration to Toronto,
and her work at the St. Elizabeth of
Hungary Church Rectory.

KOHÁRI, JOSEPH
TORONTO, ONT.
Interviewed on 23 March 1979; 1
hr.; 1 tape; English; by S.
Papp-Zubrits. Immigrated to Canada
in the late 1950s.

KOPÁCSI-GELBERGER, JUDITH
TORONTO, ONT.
Interviewed on 8 Dec. 1982; 2.5
hrs.; 3 tapes; English; by S.
Papp-Zubrits.

KORPONAY, MIKLOS
TORONTO, ONT.
Scrapbooks, chiefly on events sur-
rounding the "Hungarian Revolution,"
1956, and the subsequent exodus of
Hungarian political refugees. 1 reel of

microfilm. Taped interview.
Interviewed on 8 Nov. 1978; 2 hrs.;
2 tapes; English; by S. Papp-Zubrits.
Arrived in Canada in 1951.

KOVÁCS, LAWRENCE
WELLAND, ONT.
Constitution and by-laws of the Inde-
pendent Mutual Benefit
Federation in Toronto, 1941; and
calendars published by the *Amerikai
Magyar Szó*, 1958. 6 cm.
Szőke, Istvaá. *We Are Canadians.*
Toronto: The National Group of the
Hungarian-Canadians, n.d. 96 pp.
Bethlen Naptár 1967 (Bethlen
Yearbook). Ligonier, Penna.: Hun-
garian Reformed Federation of
America, 1967. .5 cm.
The Hungarian ABC and Reader.
Toronto: Canadian Federation of
Democratic Hungarians, 1943. 50 pp.
Kanadai Magyar Munkás Yearbook.
1945-57, 1959 (including the special
edition of 1949 commemorating the
centennial of 1848, and the War of
Independence of 1848-49). 24 cm.

KUKUCSKA, KÁROLY
DELHI, ONT.
2 photographs: Mr. and Mrs.
Charles Kukucska, 1926; and employment in farming in Saskatchewan,
n.d. Taped interview.
Interviewed on 13 July 1977; .75
hr.; 1 tape; Hungarian; by P. Pandy.
Discusses Hungarian community and
tobacco farming in Delhi, Ont.

KURELY, M.
TORONTO, ONT.
Számadás. 15 Aug. 1975 - 15 April
1977. 1 reel of microfilm.

LENTE, MIKLOS
TORONTO, ONT.
Personal documents and clippings, 1965-77. 1 cm (10 items). Photographs. Taped interview.
12 photographs: Miklos Lente while shooting various films in Bahamas, Missouri, and Hungary, 1958-77. File contains a brief biography of Miklos Lente.
Interviewed on 3 April 1978; .75 hr.; 1 tape; English; by M. Zalan. Arrived in Canada in 1956, discusses career in photography.

MAJORCSAK, MIKLOS
TILLSONBURG, ONT.
Interviewed on 24 July 1977; 1 hr.; 1 tape; English; by Susan Gálos. Immigrated to Canada in the late 1930s.

MAKSZIM, JOHN
COURTLAND, ONT.
3 photographs: John Makszim in Aylmer, Ont., 1930-44.

MARCIN, A.
TILLSONBURG, ONT.
3 photographs: family in Hungary, and Ont., c. 1960s.

MAYORCSAK, STEVE
TILLSONBURG, ONT.
Interviewed on 22 July 1977; .25 hr.; 1 tape; English; by Susan Gálos.

MIKLOS, KOI
DELHI, ONT.
Interviewed on 7 July 1977; .5 hr.; 1 tape; Hungarian; by P. Pandy. Immigrated to Canada in 1929.

MINACS, STEVE
OSHAWA, ONT.
Orbán Sándor scrapbook, 1910-28,

and 3 playscripts, 1916. 1 reel of microfilm. Photographs. Taped interview.
49 photographs: the Minacs family; and entertainment in the Hungarian community of Oshawa, including folk dancing and theatrical productions, some held at the Hungarian Cultural Club, 1929-78.
Interviewed on 2 Aug. 1979; 2 hrs.; 2 tapes; English; by S. Papp-Zubrits.

MOOS, VERA
TORONTO, ONT.
4 photographs: the Klein, Kennedy and Korányi families in Toronto, 1922-39.

MORE, ANDREW
DELHI, ONT.
Interviewed on 11 July 1977; .75 hr.; 1 tape; English; by David Judd. Discusses farming, and fertilizer business in the Delhi tobacco district.

MUSTONEN, GYÖRGYI
TORONTO, ONT.
Interviewed on 21 Feb. 1978; .25 hr.; 1 tape; English; by M. Zalan. She arrived in Canada with her husband in 1972.

NAGY, GEORGE
TORONTO, ONT.
Interviewed on 6 May 1978; 3 hrs.; 3 tapes; English; by S. Papp-Zubrits. Post-WWII immigrant.

NÉMETH, ALEX
DELHI, ONT.
2 photographs: the Németh family upon arrival in Delhi, 1927-34.

NYAKAS, NÁNDOR
TORONTO, ONT.
Interviewed on 26 March 1978; .5

hr.; 1 tape; English; by M. Zalan.
Arrived in Canada in 1971.

PANDY-SZEKERES, P.
DELHI, ONT.
 Miscellaneous printed items from the
Hungarian community in Delhi, Ont.,
c. 1960-80. 2.5 cm. Photograph.
 1 photograph: Women's Group of
Delhi, and Tobacco District Hungari-
an House, Delhi, Ont.

PAPP-ZUBRITS, SUSAN
TORONTO, ONT.
 Miscellaneous papers covering the
following Hungarian organizations:
Hungarian Helicon Society, Rakoczi
Foundation, Canadian Hungarian Cul-
tural Centre, Hungarian Scout Associ-
ation, St. Elizabeth of Hungary
Roman Catholic Church, 1979-81,
and the Canadian Ethnic Girl Guide
Council, 1972-80. 2.5 cm. Photo-
graphs.
 10 photographs: activities at the
Hungarian Canadian Cultural Centre,
including a Hungarian School in
Toronto, 1978-79.
 Kronika. Toronto, Nov. 1979
(monthly). 48 pp.
 Menorah—Egyenlőség. 19 Jan. 1980.
Hungarian Jewish weekly. .25 cm.

PATRIAS, CARMELA
TORONTO, ONT.
 Anonymous interview recorded on
23 Nov. 1976; 1 hr.; 1 tape; Hungarian; by Carmela Patrias. Interviewee
immigrated to Canada in the late
1920s.

POKOLY, LÁSZLO
TORONTO, ONT.
 Interviewed on 13 Sept. 1977; 2
hrs.; 2 tapes; English; by Alexander
Nicholson.

POLYOKA, MARY
HAMILTON, ONT.
 Identification card from C.P. Railway, Department of Colonization,
issued to Mary Polyoka, 1929. .25
cm. Photographs.
 10 photographs: the Polyoka family
in Hungary, 1913-29; and activities of
the Canadian Hungarian Workers and
Farmers Club, mostly theatrical productions, Hamilton, 1913-63.

PORTER, ANNA
TORONTO, ONT.
 Interviewed on 11 April 1979; .75
hr.; 1 tape; English; by S.
Papp-Zubrits. Post-WWII political
refugee.

PUSKAS, J. (HUNGARIAN ACADEMY
OF SCIENCES)
BUDAPEST, HUNGARY
 This collection contains mostly
records of the Independent Mutual
Benefit Federation, Toronto—letters
patent, constitutions, minute books,
correspondence, history of the
I.M.B.F. by J. Blasko, and other
writings, 1927-56; and minutes of the
Toronto Hungarian Worker Club,
1934 and the Welland Chapter of the
Canadian Hungarian Benefit Federation, 1928-40. Also included are
Hungarian-language plays and
left-wing pamphlets, c. 1930-50, and
miscellaneous paper items, including
proceedings from the General Assembly of the Presbyterian Church in
Canada, 1920-82. .5 meters.

PUTOTSKI, GEORGE
DELHI, ONT.
 3 photographs: the Putotski family in
Hungary, and Delhi, 1915-43.

RADOCZ, ANDY
DELHI, ONT.
1 photograph: farming with horses in Delhi, 1946.

RAPAI, PAUL
DELHI, ONT.
Records of the Delhi and Tobacco District Hungarian House, 1947-49; membership booklet with constitution of Toronto Hungarian House, 1947; and programmes and flyers, 1948-49. 2 cm. Photographs. Taped interview.
22 photographs: executives, exhibitions and parades (and documents) of the Delhi and Tobacco District Hungarian House in Delhi, Ont., 1947-48,
Interviewed on 21 Aug. 1979; 4 hrs.; 4 tapes; Hungarian; by S. Papp-Zubrits. Discusses tobacco farming in Delhi.
Élet—Dohányvidéki Kisújság. 1958. Souvenir Album of Canada Tobacco District Hungarian House. 38 pp.

RÉKAI, JOHN
TORONTO, ONT.
1 photograph: John Rékai (including biographical sketch), 1977. Taped interview.
Interviewed on 7 Jan. 1978; 1 hr.; 1 tape; English; by M. Zalan. Arrived in Toronto in 1950, discusses his career as a surgeon.
The Spark. Vol. 8, nos. 2, 4. Toronto, 1977. Bulletin of the Central Hospital. .25 cm.

RIEGER, BÉLA
GUELPH, ONT.
Constitution of the Hungarian Home Club, 1962, 1968; and 1 letter, n.d. .25 cm.

SCHVARCZ KOPF, HELEN
SUDBURY, ONT.
5 photographs: 1952-69, Hungarian picnic, 1953; children in traditional costume, 1953; folk dancing, 1952; table of food fair and congregation, n.d., all taken in Sudbury. Taped interview.
Interviewed in June 1981; 2 hrs.; 2 tapes; English; by Mary Stefura. Arrived in Canada in 1929, member of the Hungarian Cultural Society.

SERESS, REV. EDMUND
TORONTO, ONT.
Interviewed on 16 Nov. 1978; 1.5 hrs.; 2 tapes; Hungarian; by S. Papp-Zubrits. Historicaccount of the First Hungarian Presbyterian Church.

SIMON, JIMMY
WELLAND, ONT.
Statutes and membership booklet of the Welland Hungarian Self-Culture Society, 1940; and flyers pertaining to Our Lady of Hungary Church of Welland, n.d. 1 cm. Taped interview.
Interviewed on 25 Oct. 1979; .5 hr.; 1 tape; Hungarian; by S. Papp-Zubrits. Co-founder of the Hungarian Self-Culture Society in Welland.
Gorham, Beth and E. Krupta. "The Hungarians of Welland: An Analysis of the Hungarian Community in Welland." 1979. Welland Heritage Council and Multicultural Centre. 40 pp.
40th Anniversary of the Welland Hungarian Self-Culture Society. 1961. 28 pp.
50th Anniversary of the Our Lady of Hungary Church of Welland. 1978. 44 pp.

SIMON, JOSEPH
DELHI, ONT.
Interviewed on 12 July 1977; 1 hr.;
1 tape; Hungarian; by P. Pandy. Discusses farming in the Delhi tobacco
district.

SOJNOCKI, PEARL; AND EUGENE AND
HELEN RUZSA
HAMILTON, ONT.
Membership book of the Hungarian
Presbyterian Funeral Benefit Society,
1945; and papers relating to Rev.
Eugene Rusza, 1969, 1976. 1 cm.
Photographs. Taped interview.
4 photographs: Rev. Eugene Rusza
at the American Hungarian Federation
Convention Banquet, Hamilton, 1941,
and Hungarian Soccer Team, 1948.
Interviewed on 23 Aug. 1979; 2
hrs.; 2 tapes; English; by S.
Papp-Zubrits. Reminiscences about
Rev. Eugene Ruzsa and the Presby-
terian Hungarian congregation in
Hamilton.

SŐMJÉN, JOHN
TORONTO, ONT.
Personal documents, 1938-57. .5 cm.
Taped interview.
Interviewed on 10 Feb. 1978; .5 hr.;
1 tape; English; by M. Zalan.
Arrived in Canada in 1951, discussion
on family life, work experiences, and
ethnic retention.

STEINMETZ, BEATRICE
CAMPBELLFORD, ONT.
Interviewed on 15 May 1977; 1 hr.;
1 tape; English; by Carmela Patrias.
Arrived in Canada in 1928.

STEINMETZ, REV. CHARLES
CAMPBELLFORD, ONT.
Interviewed on 28 March 1979;
2.5 hrs.; 3 tapes; English; by
S. Papp-Zubrits and Carmela Patrias.

STEINMETZ, REV. CHARLES
CAMBELLFORD, ONT.
Scrapbook of clippings from largely
Hungarian newspapers in Ont.,
1937-75; records of the First Hungarian Presbyterian Church, and personal
papers, 1931-81. 2 reels of microfilm. 12 cm. Photographs. Taped
interview.
120 photographs: Ethnic Press Association visit to Ottawa, 1957; parish
activity, including construction and
dedication at the Free Magyar
Reformed Church in Toronto,
1943-53; Sunday school, choirs,
marriages and confirmations at the
First Hungarian Presbyterian Church
in Toronto, 1932-52; and celebration
of National Day in Welland, 1935.
Interviewed on 30 Aug. 1977; 1 hr.;
1 tape; English; by Carmela Patrias.
Gyertyafény (Candlelight). 28 July
1935 - 26 Jan. 1936 (Presbyterian
weekly). 1 reel of microfilm.

SÜLE, HELEN
TORONTO, ONT.
Interviewed on 6 Dec. 1976; 1 hr.; 1
tape; English; by Carmela Patrias.
Husband arrived in Canada in 1927.

SÜLE, JOSEPH
TORONTO, ONT.
Membership certificate of Toronto
Hungarian House, 1967. .25 cm.
Photographs. Taped interview.
4 photographs: the Sule family;
plays at Toronto Hungarian House;
and excutive of the Canadian Cultural
Centre, Toronto, 1925-67.
Interviewed on 26 Nov. 1976; 1 hr.;
1 tape; Hungarian; by Carmela
Patrias.

SZABAD, P.
DELHI, ONT.
 2 photographs: wedding, 1928; and
hunting, 1948 in Ont.

SZAKÁLY, ZOLTÁN
CAMBRIDGE, ONT.
 Interviewed on 3 Dec. 1979; .75 hr.;
1 tape; Hungarian; by S.
Papp-Zubrits. Discusses involvement
in Hungarian-Canadian Club, and
general observations on 1956 Hungarian refugees.

SZATHARY, CHARLES
TORONTO, ONT.
 Records and diaries of "Árpád
Vezér" Boy Scout Troops, 1949-50.
1 reel of microfilm.

SZEGŐ, JOSEPH
TORONTO, ONT.
 2 photographs: the Szegő family in
Toronto, 1981. Taped interview.
 Interviewed on 13 May 1981; 1.5
hrs.; 2 tapes; Hungarian; by S.
Papp-Zubrits. Father arrived in
Canada at the turn of the 20th cen-
tury.

SZILÁGYI, GEORGE
TILLSONBURG, ONT.
 Interviewed on 21 July 1977; 1 hr.;
1 tape; English; by Susan Gálos.

SZKIBA, BÁLINT, ANDRÁS BALÁZS,
AND JÁNOS DROTOS
TILLSONBURG, ONT.
 Interviewed on 22 Aug. 1979; 1 hr.;
1 tape; English; by S. Papp-Zubrits.
Members of Székely-Magyar
Szövetség.

TAKÁCS, HELEN
SCOTLAND, ONT.
 2 photographs: tobacco farming in
Delhi, 1950.

TARR, JOHN
SIMCOE, ONT.
 Interviewed on 25 July 1977; 2 hrs.;
2 tapes; English; by Susan Gálos.

TELEKI, SAM
TORONTO, ONT.
 Interviewed on 21 March 1978; .5
hr.; 1 tape; English; by M. Zalan.
Family arrived Canada in 1954.

TESSENYI, JÁNOS
TORONTO, ONT.
 Opera programmes, 1968-78. 1 cm.
Photograph. Taped interview.
 1 photograph: János Tessenyi in
Toronto, c. 1975. File includes bio-
graphical sketch of donor.
 Interviewed on 27 Feb. 1978; .25
hr.; 1 tape; English; by M. Zalan.
Arrived in Canada in 1974, discusses
her career as an opera singer.

TOTH, MRS.
DELHI, ONT.
 5 photographs: family in Hungary,
and Delhi, n.d.

TUZ, REV. TOMAS
TORONTO, ONT.
 Interviewed on 16 March 1979; .5
hr.; 1 tape; Hungarian; by S.
Papp-Zubrits. Post-WWII immigrant,
discusses his work with 1956 Hungarian refugees, and his activities as a
writer.

VÁGO, BÉLA
TORONTO, ONT.
 Interviewed on 25 Nov 1976; 1 hr.;

1 tape; Hungarian; by Carmela Patrias. Arrived in Canada in 1928.

VASTAGH, JOSEPH
TORONTO, ONT.
Független Magyarország. Vol 1. no.1, April 1968 - June 1969. 1 reel of microfilm.

VATAI, REV. LÁSZLO
TORONTO, ONT.
Souvenir book of the Hungarian United Church, 1978. .5 cm. See Halász de Beky Collection for list of congregation, and annual reports of the Hungarian United Church, 1963, 1964. Taped interview.
Interviewed on 18 Aug. 1979; 1 hr.; 1 tape; Hungarian; by S. Papp-Zubrits.

VERES, HELEN
DELHI, ONT.
Interviewed on 12 July 1977; .5 hr.; 1 tape; English; by P. Pandy.

VÖRÖSVÁRY-WELLER, ISTVÁN
TORONTO, ONT.
Donor's journalist certificate, Budapest, 1933; and printed material from *Kanadai Magyarság*, Toronto, 1955, 1965. Photographs. Taped interview.
10 photographs: from *Kanadai Magyarság* newspaper, including interior/exterior views of building and Hungarian Boy Scouts in Toronto, 1955-75.
Interviewed on 19 Sept. 1978; 1 hr.; 1 tape; Hungarian; by S. Papp-Zubrits. He established two Hungarian-language newspapers in Toronto—*Magyar Élet* (Hungarian Life), and *Kanadai Magyarság* (Canadian Hungarians); he also

assisted many newly arrived Hungarian immigrants in Toronto in the 1950s.

WAPPEL, MARAGARET
TORONTO, ONT.
Interviewed on 17 Jan. 1977; 2 hrs.; 2 tapes; English; by Carmela Patrias.

WERLE, C.
TORONTO, ONT.
7 photographs: religious life at the First Hungarian Baptist Church in Toronto, c. 1930-40. Taped interview.
Interviewed on 10 May 1977; 1 hr.; 1 tape; English; by Carmela Patrias.

WESZELY, TSTRAN
BURLINGTON, ONT.
30 photographs: activities, mainly social gatherings and theatrical productions of the Canadian Hungarian Workers and Farmers Club in Hamilton, c. 1930-50.

ZADUBÁN, GEORGE
NORTH YORK, ONT.
Interviewed on 24 March 1979; 1.5 hrs.; 2 tapes; Hungarian; by S. Papp-Zubrits.

ZALAN, MAGDA
TORONTO, ONT.
Letters, certificates, and clippings, n.d. 1 cm. Photographs. Taped interview.
7 photographs: Magda Zalan (including brief autobiography) in Romania, Budapest, Cannes, and Venice, n.d.
Self-interviewed on 21 Feb. 1978; .75 hr.; 1 tape; English. Arrived in Toronto in 1975, she has worked as journalist.

ZEND, ROBERT
TORONTO, ONT.
Interviewed on 28 March 1978; .5
hr.; 1 tape; English; by M. Zalan.
He and his wife arrived in Canada in
1956.

ZSIGMOND, ANDREW
TORONTO, ONT.
Interviewed on 9 Aug. 1978; .75 hr.;
1 tape; Hungarian; by S.
Papp-Zubrits. Discusses difficulties of
Hungarian minority in Romania, and
immigration to Canada in the 1970s.

=================

BRANTFORD HUNGARIAN MUTUAL
BENEFIT SOCIETY (J. JAGER)
TORONTO, ONT.
Records 1935-52, of the Brantford
Hungarian Mutual Benefit Society,
Toronto Branch, and a collection of
Hungarian plays, 1930s. 1 reel of
microfilm. 2 cm. See J. Jager.

BRANTFORD HUNGARIAN MUTUAL
BENEFIT SOCIETY (MIKE PETIS)
HAMILTON, ONT.
Minutes and financial records of the
Brantford Hungarian Mutual Benefit
Society, Hamilton Branch, 1927-78. 1
reel of microfilm. See J. Jáger.

CANADIAN HUNGARIAN FEDERATION
TORONTO, ONT.
Records, 1956-76, include constitution, minutes, correspondence, financial accounts, and miscellaneous
papers: resolutions, briefs, memoranda, and programmes. 7 reels of
microfilm. Taped interview with
George Nagy. Finding aid avilable.
RESTRICTED

CHURCH OF THE ANCIENT MAGYAR
FAITH
TORONTO, ONT.
Küldetés. Jan., April 1977 (month-
ly). .5 cm.

DÉLVIDÉK CLUB
TORONTO, ONT.
Minutes, by-laws, and miscellaneous
items, 1962-79. 1.5 cm. Taped interview with F. Juretic.

ELSŐ MAGYAR REFORMÁTUS EGYHAZ
(FIRST HUNGARIAN PRESBYTERIAN
CHURCH, REV. E. SERESS)
TORONTO, ONT.
Constitution, minutes, and correspondence, 1930-54; annual reports,
1936-63; marriage register, 1937-78;
and church publications. 3 reels of
microfilm. 3 cm. See Halász de Beky
and Rev. C. Steinmetz.
Tárogató. Toronto: United Church of
Canada, 1942 (3 issues). In Hungari-
an/English.

FIRST HUNGARIAN BAPTIST CHURCH
TORONTO, ONT.
Records, 1928-67, including mem-
bership list, flyers, and church bull-
etins. 1 reel of microfilm. 2 cm.
RESTRICTED
23 photographs: parish activity at the
First Hungarian Baptist Church,
including camping and ecumenical
service in Toronto, c. 1970-77.
Viczian, John. "The Background,
Beginnings and Growth of Hungarian
Baptists in Toronto, 1929-76."
Toronto, 1978. 67 pp.
Bibliamagyarázó (Bible Expositor).
Cleveland: Hungarian Baptist Union
of America, 1972-77 (quarterly). 1
reel of microfilm.

Emlékkönyv. 1929-39. Hungary
Baptist Church of Toronto, 1939. 42
pp.

HUNGARIAN CANADIAN CLUB OF
WATERLOO-WELLINGTON
CAMBRIDGE, ONT.
Minutes, reports, correspondence,
financial records, and lists of Hungarians in the Guelph-Kitchener region.
1 reel of microfilm. Taped interview
with Zoltán Szakály.
RESTRICTED

HUNGARIAN CANADIAN CULTURAL
CENTRE
TORONTO, ONT.
Minutes, flyers, and miscellaneous
papers, 1977-81. 1 cm.

HUNGARIAN CANADIAN ENGINEERS'
ASSOCIATION
TORONTO, ONT.
Report by president and invitations,
1981. .25 cm.
Együttmüködés. Jan. 1981. .25 cm.

HUNGARIAN CULTURAL CLUB
OSHAWA, ONT.
Constitution, financial records,
flyers, and clippings. 1935-55. 1 reel
of microfilm. See S. Minacs.

HUNGARIAN CULTURAL SOCIETY
ST. CATHARINES, ONT.
Miscellaneous papers, 1978-81. .5
cm.

HUNGARIAN FREEDOM FIGHTERS
FEDERATION
TORONTO, ONT.
Constitution, minutes, and list of
candidates for various posts, 1958.
.5 cm. See Rákoczi Society.

HUNGARIAN HELIKON BALL COMMITTEE
TORONTO, ONT.
Records, 1961-79, include correspondence, minutes, financial statements, and miscellaneous items:
programmes, flyers, invitations, and
clippings; also, scrapbooks, 1974-78.
2 reels of microfilm. Photographs.
22 photographs: Helicon Ball in
Toronto, 1975-77.

HUNGARIAN HOME ASSOCIATION
ANNUAL
WINDSOR, ONT.
Miscellaneous documents, 1968. 1
reel of microfilm.

HUNGARIAN PRESBYTERIAN CHURCH
DELHI, ONT.
Dedication Album. 22 July 1951. 1
reel of microfilm.

HUNGARIAN READERS' SERVICE
TORONTO, ONT.
Review. 1976-79. .25 cm.

HUNGARIAN SCOUTS ASSOCIATION
TORONTO, ONT.
Papers, 1978-80. .5 cm.

HUNGARIAN SELF-CULTURE SOCIETY
WELLAND, ONT.
Minutes, 1924-34. 1 reel of microfilm. Photographs. See J. Simon and
P. Kertész.
20 photographs: activities of the
Hungarian Self-Culture Society (Magyar Önképzőkör); members, Welland,
1930-58.
Fortieth Anniversary Booklet. 1961.
1 cm.

HUNGARIAN TURUL SOCIETY
TORONTO, ONT.
Napjaink (Our Days). Sept. - Dec.
1980. .25 cm.

JOHN CALVIN HUNGARIAN PRESBY-
TERIAN CHURCH
HAMILTON, ONT.
Church register, 1926-80, and annual
reports, 1971-79. 1 reel of microfilm.
Photographs.
20 photographs: parish activity,
including parades and theatrical productions, 1932-79.
*25th Anniversary of John Calvin
Hungarian Presbyterian Church.*
1958. 32 pp.
*50th Anniversary of John Calvin
Hungarian Presbyterian Church.*
1976. 40 pp.

KODALY ENSEMBLE
TORONTO, ONT.
Letter of incorporation, scrapbook,
and 2 posters, 1960-75. 1 reel of
microfilm. 1 cm. Photographs. Taped
interview with G. Zabudan.
68 photographs: entertainment by the
Kodaly Ensemble, including choirs
and folk dancing, 1960-75 Toronto.
File contains a brief history of the
Kodaly Ensemble.
Ritmus. 1966-77. 9 scattered issues.

MULTICULTURAL HISTORY SOCIETY
OF ONTARIO
TORONTO, ONT.
Egységes Magyarság (United Hun-
garians). 9 Oct. 1959 - 1 July 1961. 2
reels of microfilm.
Uj Szo. Toronto, 3 Jan. 1976 - June
1987. 4 reels of microfilm.

MULTICULTURAL NEWSPAPER
MICROFILM PROJECT
TORONTO, ONT.
Menor Egyenlőség. 8 Jan. 1977 - 1
Oct. 1985. 11 reels of microfilm.

NATIONAL HUNGARIAN CONFERENCE
IN AID OF THE HUNGARIAN PEOPLE
TORONTO, ONT.
Records, 1945-47, including letters,
telegrams, and newsletters. 1 reel of
microfilm.

ONTARIO ETHNIC NEWSPAPER
MICROFILM PROJECT
TORONTO, ONT.
Kanadae Kis Ugság. 20 June 1935 -
28 March 1941. 1 reel of microfilm.
Kanadai Magyar Munkás. 16 July
1929 - 28 Dec. 1967. 39 reels of
microfilm.

RÁKOCZI SOCIETY (MIKLOS
KORPONAY)
TORONTO, ONT.
Records of the Rákoczi Society,
1960-76, include ground and oper-
ational rules, minutes, correspondence, and miscellaneous papers:
clippings, news releases, and programmes, many of which pertain to
the Hungarian Freedom Fighters'
Federation, the Antibolshevist Friends
Association, and the Hungarian Educational Committee. 1 reel of microfilm. Photographs.
17 photographs: exhibition of the
Rákoczi Foundation in Toronto, 1976.

ST. ELIZABETH OF HUNGARY ROMAN
CATHOLIC CHURCH
TORONTO, ONT.
Minutes, correspondence, financial
records, parish bulletins, and reports,
1942-52. Also, papers from the Catholic Church Council, and the Catholic

Man's Society, 1979-81. 2 reels of
microfilm. 1 cm. Taped interview
with Rev. I. Bekesi. Photographs.
209 photographs: parish activity at
St. Elizabeth of Hungary Catholic
Church, including exterior and
interior views of church, clergymen,
festivals schools, social gatherings,
and theatrical productions in Toronto,
1932-78.
Bulletins. 1950-74. 5 reels of microfilm.

ST. MICHAEL'S HUNGARIAN GREEK
CATHOLIC CHURCH
HAMILTON, ONT.
Church bulletins, pamphlets, and
correspondence, 1949-79. 3 cm.
Photographs. Taped interview with
Father J. Girhiny.
17 photographs: parish activity at St.
Micheal's Church, 1958-74, including
services, clergymen, social gather-
ings, and building. File contains brief
history of this church.
Dedication Album. St. Michael Hun-
garian Greek Catholic Church of
Hamilton, 1974. .25 cm.
Magyar Kultúra. Hamilton, 1 Dec.
1968 (1 issue).
Magasztalja az én lelkem az Urat.
Toronto: St. George Missionary
Association, 1952. Prayer and Psalm
booklet. 96 pp.

SZÉKELY-MAGYAR SZÖVETSÉG
TILLSONBURG, ONT.
Records, 1950-78, include minutes,
correspondence, monthly financial
reports, and membership lists,
1950-78. 1 reel of microfilm. Photographs. Taped interview with B.
Szkiba.
14 photographs: Association's activities, 1950-78, including sports and
folk dancing, 1950-76.

TORONTO HUNGARIAN HOUSE
TORONTO, ONT.
Constitution and by-laws, 1944, minutes of the Canadian Hungarian Federation, 1977, and flyers and postcards. 1 cm.
Newsletter. 1976-80. 6 pp.

UNITED HUNGARIAN FUND
TORONTO, ONT.
Papers pertaining to the Toronto
Hungarian House and the Canadian
Hungarian Foundation. 1 cm. Photo-
graphs. Taped interview with J.
Kohari.
35 photographs: activities including
demonstrations, and exhibitions of the
Hungarian Canadian Federation,
related to the United Hungarian Fund,
Toronto, 1970-78.
Hungarian Business Directories.
1969-78. 2 cm.

VICTORIA PLASTIC INDUSTRIES LTD.
HAMILTON, ONT.
Minutes, general agenda, business
letters, newsclippings, and financial
statements, 1954. 1 reel of microfilm.

WORLD TRANSYLVANIAN FEDER-
ATION (ISTVAN ZOLCSAK)
SÃO PAULO, BRAZIL
Correspondence of International
Relations Divisions of the World
Transylvanian Federation, 1975-77;
and essay, "Rumania's Violations of
the Helsinki Final Act Provisions,
1980," prepared by the W.T.F. 19
cm.

ANDREW, ANNE
TORONTO, ONT.
Interviewed on 24 April 1979; 1.75 hrs.; 2 tapes; English/Gaelic; by Louis Manning. Discussion of life in Ireland, Co. Tipperary, before immigrating in 1972 and life in Toronto since immigration.

BONNER, ROBERT
TORONTO, ONT.
Interviewed on 7 Dec. 1978; 2 hrs.; 2 tapes; English; by Louis Manning. Immigrated from Belfast in 1953.

BOYD, CATHAL
TORONTO, ONT.
Interviewed on 20 March 1978; 1 hr.; 1 tape; English; by Louis Manning. Immigrated to Canada (Toronto) in 1975 from Co. Mayo, Ireland.

BROWN, BRIDGET
WILLOWDALE, ONT.
Interviewed on 10 Feb. 1978; .25 hr.; 1 tape; English; by Donald Brown. Immigrated to the United Kingdom in 1948 and from there she came to Canada in 1957.

CAMPBELL, MIKE
TORONTO, ONT.
Interviewed on 11 March 1978; 2 hrs.; 2 tapes; English; by Louis Manning. Immigrated to Canada in 1957.

CASEY, MICK AND COLLETTE
TORONTO, ONT.
Immigrated to Canada in the 1960s and discuss both their backgrounds in Ireland and their experiences as immigrants.

CASSIDY, MARY AND GERARD
TORONTO, ONT.
Interviewed on 7 March 1978; 2 hrs.; 2 tapes; English; by Louis Manning. Both interviewees immigrated in 1973, discuss their background in Ireland and reasons for immigrating to Canada.

CROWE, GERARD M.
TORONTO, ONT.
Immigrated to Canada in the 1960s; discusses role of catholicism and various Irish groups and societies in Toronto.

CULLEN, BETTY AND PADDY
TORONTO, ONT.
Interviewed on 13, 15 May 1978; 3 hrs.; 3 tapes; English; by Louis Manning. Memories of life in Ireland to 1973 and their subsequent experiences as immigrants in Canada.

DELAYNEY, PEGGY
TORONTO, ONT.
Interviewed on 31 March 1979; 2.5 hrs.; 2 tapes; English/Gaelic; by Louis Manning. Irish background and immigrant experiences in Canada from 1952.

DUANE, ANDREW
TORONTO, ONT.
Interviewed on 19 Nov. 1978; 2 hrs.; 2 tapes; English; by Louis Manning. Immigrated to Canada in 1948, discusses experiences living in Montreal and Toronto.

DUFFIN, JOE
SCARBOROUGH, ONT.
Interviewed on 10 June 1978; 3 hrs.; 3 tapes; English; by Louis Manning. Immigrated to Canada in 1960.

FAHY, ROBERT
TORONTO, ONT.
Interviewed on 26 Jan. 1978; 1 hr.; 1 tape; English; by Louis Manning. Immigrated to Canada in 1962 from a farm in Co. Galway, Ireland.

FITZPATRICK, P.
TORONTO, ONT.
Interviewed on 24 Nov., 3 Dec. 1978; 2 hrs.; 2 tapes; English; by Louis Manning. Immigrated to Canada in 1954, describes his experiences in the Old Country and in Canada.

GALLAGHER, GERRY
TORONTO, ONT.
Interviewed on 4 Feb. 1978; 2 hrs.; 2 tapes; English; by Louis Manning. Post-WWII immgrant, discusses his work with construction unions in Ontario.

HARNETT, MAUREEN
TORONTO, ONT.
Interviewed on 9 April 1979; 1.5 hrs.; 2 tapes; English; by Louis Manning. Immigrated from Ireland in 1954, settled first in Newfoundland and then in Ontario in 1964.

GORMLEY, KEVIN
TORONTO, ONT.
Interviewed on 19 April 1978; 2 hrs.; 2 tapes; English; by Louis Manning. Left Ireland in 1966, worked first in U.K. as airline agent and then Chicago, U.S.A. in same capacity before transferring to Toronto in 1974. Discusses Canadian Irish Cultural and Immigrant Aid Society.

HEFFERNON, MICHAEL AND EITHNE
TORONTO, ONT.
Interviewed on 2 April 1979; 2 hrs.; 2 tapes; English; by Louis Manning. They immigrated to Canada in the 1970s, he as a veterinary surgeon and she as a harpist.

HUNT, PATRICK
TORONTO, ONT.
Interviewed on 6 Dec. 1978; 2 hrs.; 2 tapes; English; by Louis Manning. Immigrated to Canada, Quebec, in the 1950s and then moved to Toronto in the 1960s.

KEARNEY, BRIAN O'CONOR
MISSISSAUGA, ONT.
Interviewed on 11 April 1979; 1.75 hrs.; 2 tapes; English; by Louis Manning. Arrived in Canada in 1948, moved to Toronto in 195.

KELLY, SEÁN
TORONTO, ONT.
Interviewed on 9 Jan. 1979; 1.5 hrs.; 2 tapes; English; by Louis Manning. Post-WWII immigrant, arrived in Canada in 1953 after two years in U.K.

KENNEDY, EOIN AND CLARE
TORONTO, ONT.
Interviewed on 20, 21 April 1978; 1.5 hrs.; 2 tapes; English; by Louis

Manning. They immigrated to Canada in the early 1970s.

LANGAN, CHRIS
TORONTO, ONT.
Interviewed on 20 Feb. 1978; 1 hr.; 1 tape; English; by Louis Manning. Immigrated to Canada in the 1950s.

LYNN, JONATHAN
TORONTO, ONT.
Interviewed on 30 March 1978; 1 hr.; 1 tape; English; by Louis Manning. Discusses his background in Ireland and his life in Canada since his immigration in 1968.

LYONS, DENNIS
TORONTO, ONT.
Interviewed on 3 May 1978; 1.75 hrs.; 2 tapes; English; by Louis Manning. Arrived in Canada in 1968, discusses involvement with Irish traditional music.

MANNING, AIDAN
TORONTO, ONT.
Interviewed on 18 Nove. 1979; 1.75 hrs.; 2 tapes; English; by Louis Manning. Discusses background in Ireland and sojourns in U.K. and immigration to Canada in 1967.

McCOOEY, SIOBÁN
TORONTO, ONT.
Interviewed on 5 April 1978; 1.5 hrs.; 2 tapes; English; by Louis Manning. She immigrated to Canada in 1962, discusses childhood poverty in Ireland and struggles as an artist in Old Country and Canada.

MOLLOY, TOM AND EILEEN
TORONTO, ONT.
Interviewed on 2 June 1979; 2 hrs.; 2 tapes; English; by Louis Manning.

The Molloys immigrated to Canada in the late 1950s, they discuss their pre-migration experiences, their marriage and their lives as immigrants in Canada.

MULCAHY, SEÁN
TORONTO, ONT.
Interviewed on 23, 24 March 1979; 1.75 hrs.; 2 tapes; English; by Louis Manning. Moved to Canada in 1957, discusses his career in radio, the theatre and so forth.

MURPHY, BRÍD
TORONTO, ONT.
Interviewed on 18 April 1978; .75 hr.; 1 tape; English; by Louis Manning. Immigrated to Canada in 19348, discusses her experiences in Ireland, U.K. and her emigration to Canada.

MURPHY, RICHARD
SCARBOROUGH, ONT.
Interviewed on 1 April 1979; 1 hr.; 1 tape; English; by Louis Manning. Emigrated to Canada in 1949 and describes marriage and work experiences here.

O'BRIEN, BETTY AND JOHN
TORONTO, ONT.
Interviewed on 1 Feb. 1978; 2 hrs.; 2 tapes; English; by Louis Manning. Discusses their experiences in Ireland and their immigration to Canada in the 1950s.

O'RIORDAN, MARY
TORONTO, ONT.
Interviewed on 20, 21 Jan. 1979; 1.25 hrs.; 2 tapes; English; by Louis Manning. Recounts her Irish background and moves to various countries overseas and immigration to Canada in 1962.

RAE, RALPH
GLENGARRY, ONT.
 Interviewed on 8 Dec. 1977; 2 hrs.;
2 tapes; English; by Patricia Kulick.
Reminiscences about family's Irish
roots via the immigration to Canada
of a great-grandfather.

REILLY, MICHAEL J.
TORONTO, ONT.
 Interviewed on 18 Dec. 1978; 2 hrs.;
2 tapes; English; by Louis Manning.
Immigrated to Canada in 1957, discusses activities with unions as stew-
ard and business agent.

ROONEY, MICHAEL
TORONTO, ONT.
 Interviewed on 25 Nov. 1978; 2
hrs.; 2 tapes; English; by Louis Manning. Describes background in Ireland
and experience in Canada (from 1961)
as musician with R.C.A.F. (sergeant)
and subsequent career in Toronto.

SLATTERY, PAT
TORONTO, ONT.
 Interviewed on 17 Oct. 1978; 1.25
hr.; 2 tapes; English; by Louis Manning. After five-year stay in U.K.
(from Ireland) immigrated to Canada
in 1968.

STOKES, SEÁMUS M.
TORONTO, ONT.
 Interviewed on 26 June 1978; 2 hrs.;
2 tapes; English; by Louis Manning.
Describes sojourning in U.K. from
Ireland and eventual immigration to
Canada in 1972, life as a mature stu-
dent at University of Toronto and so
forth.

WALSHE, VERA, JOHN AND
GERALDINE ELLIOT, AND HELEN
RAFTER
TORONTO, ONT.
 Recording of round-table discussion
of 23 Jan. 1978; 1 hr.; 1 tape; by
Louis Manning. Discussion focusses
on life in Ireland and emigration to
Canada in the 1960s.

=====================

GAELIC SYMPOSIUM, ROMAN CATH-
OLIC MASS
TORONTO, ONT.
 Recording of 12 Feb. 1978; .75 hrs.;
1 tape; Gaelic/English;; recorded by
Louis Manning. Proceedings of
Roman Catholic Mass held for Gaelic
Symposium in Toronto.

UNIVERSITY OF TORONTO RADIO
TORONTO, ONT.
 Recording of 16 March 1979, St.
Patrick's Day, broadcast by Univer-
sity of Toronto radio on the Irish in
Canada, 1795-1979.

ARGENTIN, ELIZABETTA
SUDBURY, ONT.
 Interviewed on 8 July 1984; .75 hr.;
1 tape; Italian; by D. Visentin.
Pre-WWII immigrant.

ARTUSO, EMILIA
SUDBURY, ONT.
 Interviewed on 4 July 1984; 1.25
hrs.; 2 tapes; Italian; by D. Visentin.
Post-WWII immigrant.

AUGIMERI, MARIA C.
TORONTO, ONT.
 6 photographs: traditional costume,
and women baking, and sewing, c.
1940-80.

BAAR, ELLEN
TORONTO, ONT.
 Transcript of taped interview with
Lena Turonni of Welland, Ont. 16
pp.

BACCARI, MICHELE
THUNDER BAY, ONT.
 Interviewed on 22 March 1978; 1
hr.; 1 tape; Italian; by A. Pucci.
Recounts events of the C.P. Railway
Freight Handlers' Strike, 1909, and
the Port Arthur Coal Handlers'
Strike, 1912.

BACCEGA, ANGELINA
COPPER CLIFF, ONT.
 Interviewed on 31 July 1984; .75
hr.; 1 tape; Italian; by D. Visentin.
Discusses boardinghouse practices,
and husband's work at INCO in the
early 1900s.

BACCI, RUGGERO
TORONTO, ONT.
 Correspondence regarding Ruggero
Bacci's internment in Petawawa
Internment Camp, and camp in
Fredericton, New Brunswick,
1940-42; and letters about his subse-
quent employment, 1943. 42 letters.
Photographs. Taped interview.
 4 photographs: interned Italians in
Fredericton, New Brunswick, 1942; 2
pencil sketches of donor at Petawawa
Internment Camp, 1940-41; and a
music band, "La fanfare degli italiani
giovani del littorio all'estero," in
front of the Casa d'Italia, Beverly and
Dundas Streets in Toronto, c. 1930s.
 Interviewed on 1 Aug. 1978; 1.5
hrs.; 2 tapes; Italian; by J. Zucchi.
Arrived in Canada in 1922, a leading
member of the Toronto Fascio.

BADANAI, HUBERT
THUNDER BAY, ONT.
 Interviewed on 15 June 1978; 1 hr.;
1 tape; English; by A. Pucci. Immigrated to Canada in 1913, became a
politician in Fort William.

BARATTA, GIUSEPPE
THUNDER BAY, ONT.
 Interviewed on 11 Nov. 1978; 1.5
hrs.; 2 tapes; Italian; by A. Pucci.
Immigrated to Canada in 1912.

BARBIERI, PAOLO
DOWNSVIEW, ONT.
 Interviewed on 13 Feb. 1980; 1 hr.;
1 tape; Italian; by M. Augimeri.

BARDEGGIA, ALDO
SUDBURY, ONT.
 Interviewed on 2 Aug. 1984; .75 hr.;
1 tape; English; by D. Visentin.
Immigrated to Canada in 1927.

BASSANO, BRIGIDA
TORONTO, ONT.
 Interviewed on 18 June 1987; 2 hrs.;
2 tapes; Italian/Molisan dialect; by
Nick Forte. Arrived in 1923, a pioneer immigrant among the Molisani
from Guglionesi, celebrated her
102nd birthay in 1987.

BASSI, EVELYN
TORONTO, ONT.
 Immigration papers, 1914-19. Photographs. Taped interview.
 1 photograph: Lorenzo and Maria
Christante, 1919; and a passport picture of Maria Cristofoli.
 Interviewed on 17 Nov. 1977; 1 hr.;
1 tape; English; by F. Zucchi.

BERTOIA, PAUL
TORONTO, ONT.
 Interviewed on 23 May 1978; 2 hrs.;
2 tapes; Italian/English; by J. Zucchi.

BERTULLI, ADRIANO
COPPER CLIFF, ONT.
 Interviewed on 4 Aug. 1984; 1 hr.; 1
tape; Italian; by D. Visentin.

BILLOKI, VELDA
SUDBURY, ONT.
 Interviewed on 10 April 1981; .25
hr.; 1 tape; English; by A. Taverna.

BIONDI (NÉE GIMPOLI), GEORGINA
SUDBURY, ONT.
 10 photographs: the John Gimpoli
family, 1921-55. Taped interview.
 Interviewed on 31 Jan. 1982; 1 hr.;
1 tape; English; by A. Taverna.

She immigrated to Connecticut,
U.S.A. with her first husband in the
early 1900s, re-settled in Creighton,
Ont.

BISCEGLIA, OLIVERIO
TORONTO, ONT.
 Interviewed on 10 March 1980; .75
hr.; 1 tape; Italian; by J. Di Nardo.

BORG, FRANCES
TORONTO, ONT.
 Interviewed on 18 April 1983; 1 hr.;
1 tape; English; by Enrico Cumbo.
Arrived in Canada in 1912.

BORSELLINO, ALFRED
HAMILTON, ONT.
 16 photographs: family picnics; and
the Royal Marine Band of Hamilton,
1930-55. Taped interview.
 Interviewed on 11 Dec. 1979; 1 hr.;
1 tape; English; by L. Cellini.

BOSA, PETER
TORONTO, ONT.
 Interviewed on 22 Aug. 1977; 1.5
hrs.; 2 tapes; English; by J. Zucchi.
Arrived in Canada in 1948.

BRANCA, MARIA
TORONTO, ONT.
 Order book, 1926-27; bank receipts
of remittances to Italy 1927-56; immigration documents, c. 1920s; letters,
1936, 1944; and an Italian diary,
1950-62. Photographs. 3 reels of
microfilm.

BRESCIA, VINCENZO
THUNDER BAY, ONT.
 Interviewed on 14 Sept. 1978; 3.75
hrs.; 4 tapes; Italian; by A. Pucci.
Post-WWI immigrant.

BRESSAN, OTTORINO
TORONTO, ONT.
 Interviewed on 22 June 1977; 2.5
hrs.; 3 tapes; English; by J. Zucchi.
Arrived in Canada in 1957.
 Bressan, Ottorino. *Non dateci
lenticchie* (Don't Give Us Lentils):
*esperienze, commenti, prospettive di
vita italo-canadese.* Toronto:
Gagliano Printing, 1962.

BULFON, REV. ERMANNO
TORONTO, ONT.
 Immigration documents, 1960-67
(4 items). Taped interview.
 Interviewed on 23 July 1977; 1.75
hrs.; 2 tapes; English; by J. Zucchi.
Immigrated to Canada in 1967.

CAICCO, EUGENIO
SUDBURY, ONT.
 Interviewed on 26 Aug. 1977; 1.75
hrs.; 2 tapes; English; by N. Cotrupi.

CAMILUCCI, ENIO
COPPER CLIFF, ONT.
 Interviewed on 30 July 1984; .75
hr.; 1 tape; Italian/English; by D.
Visentin. Arrived in Canada in 1923.

CAMPAGNARO, MR.
GUELPH, ONT.
 Interviewed on 7 April 1977; .75
hr.; 1 tape; English; by S. Traplin.
Arrived in Canada in 1912.

CANELLA, MIRANDA ROMANA
TORONTO, ONT.
 Immigration Department occupational
profile, 1955; statement of repayment
of assisted passage loan, 1955; and
letter acknowledging payment of loan,
1960. .5 cm. Taped interview.
 Interviewed on 30 June 1977;
1.5 hrs.; 2 tapes; English; by

J. Zucchi. Immigrated to Canada in
the late 1950s.

CARERE, DR.
GUELPH, ONT.
 A genealogy compiled by Dr.
Carere, son of Giacomo Carere, who
was an influential member of
Guelph's Italian community. 1 cm.

CARNIATO, ANITA
THUNDER BAY, ONT.
 1 photograph: the first Italian picnic
in Port Arthur in 1931, sponsored by
the Italian Mutual Benefit Society of
Port Arthur, which was formed in
1929. Taped interview.
 Interviewed on 17 March 1978; 1
hr.; 1 tape; Italian/English; by A.
Pucci.

CARNIATO, MARIA
THUNDER BAY, ONT.
 Interviewed on 28 March 1978; 1.5
hrs.; 2 tapes; Italian; by A. Pucci.
Arrived in Canada in 1908.

CARNOVALE, JOHN
TIMMINS, ONT.
 Hostess Committee telephone instructions, 1954, Nativity of Our Lord
Parish Combined Funds Canvass in
Timmins, 1959; "Sacred Heart
Church Combined Funds canvass,"
1958, and 22 newsclippings, c.
1930s. 2 cm. Photographs. Taped
interview.
 14 photographs: interior and exterior
of Carnovale barbershop in Timmins,
c. 1910s; John Carnovale's arena and
"bank saloon," 1920s; Carnovale in
military uniform in Petawawa, 1918;
his wedding ceremony; and Carnovale
family, n.d.
 6 photographs: Italo Balbo and the
squadron of airplanes he escorted on

a 1933 transatlantic voyage destined for the Chicago World's Fair, which re-fueled in Newfoundland. Taped interview.
Interviewed on 10 May 1977; 2.5 hrs.; 3 tapes; English; by Angela Lucchetta McPeek.

CASAGRANDE, FRANCESCO
SUDBURY, ONT.
Interviewed on 28 July 1984; .5 hr.; 1 tape; English/Italian; by D. Visentin. Arrived in Canada in 1927.

CASELLA, ANNA
TORONTO, ONT.
Interviewed on 28 March, 17 April 1980; 4 hrs.; 4 tapes; Italian/English; by J. Di Nardo. Immigrated to Canada in 1910.

CASSALOTO, MRS.
GUELPH, ONT.
Interviewed on 1 April 1977; .75 hr.; 1 tape; English; by S. Traplin. Discusses life of her father, John Tantardini, a prominent Italian in Guelph.

CASTELLI, SAVERIO
TORONTO, ONT.
Interviewed on 3 April 1980; 1.75 hrs.; 2 tapes; Italian; by J. Di Nardo.

CECHETTO, ELENA
SUDBURY, ONT.
13 photographs: the Cechetto family and friends, 1905-43.

CECILIONI, VITTORIO
HAMILTON, ONT.
3 Italian passports, 1904, 1913. Photograph. Taped interview.
1 photograph: family, n.d.
Interviewed on 20 May 1977; 1.5 hrs.; 1 tape; English; by L. Cellini.

CECUTTI, NORMA
SUDBURY, ONT.
5 photographs: the Cecutti family, 1909-59.

CELLINI, LEO
HAMILTON, ONT.
Catalogue of United Steelworkers of America, Local 1005, a Stelco billet, n.d., brochure from the opening of St. Anthony of Padua Convent, 1961; Rev. Sardo's curriculum vitae. 2 cm. Photographs. Taped interviews.
4 photographs: Hamilton Steelworkers Council (with Italian member, Di Francesco), n.d.; traditional women's dress; "Brightside Hotel;" early Italian business, 1934; and Rev. Sardo.
Seven taped interviews with interviewees who preferred to remain anonymous; 1977-1979; 7 tapes; Italian/English; by L. Cellini.

CELOTTI, TEO
TORONTO, ONT.
Italian passport, 1950; marriage certificate, 1951; Italian military discharge, 1951; and family certificate, 1958. Taped interview.
Interviewed on 25 July 1977; .5 hr.; 1 tape; English; by J. Zucchi. Arrived in Canada in 1951.

CESCHIA, DINO AND MARIO VENIR
TORONTO, ONT.
Notebook containing poems by D. Ceschia, 1954. Photographs. Taped interview.
11 photographs: working life and Sunday diversions of Italian railway navvies at Sioux Lookout, 1954.
Interviewed on 16 July 1977; 2.5 hrs.; 3 tapes; Italian; by J. Zucchi. Immigrated to Canada in the mid-1950s.

CILIO, GINO
TORONTO, ONT.
 Interviewed on 17 Aug. 1977; 1.5
hrs.; 2 tapes; English; by J. Zucchi.
Arrived in Canada in 1953.

CIMICATA, CARMELA
DOWNSVIEW, ONT.
 Interviewed on 28 Jan. 1980; .5 hr.;
1 tape; Italian; by M. Augimeri.
Discusses Calabrian folklore and
festivities.

CIMICATA, FRANCESCA
DOWNSVIEW, ONT.
 Interviewed on 29 Jan. 1980; .5 hr.;
1 tape; Italian; by M. Augimeri.
Discusses Calabrian folklore and
festivities.

COLANGELO, BERLINO
HAMILTON, ONT.
 Newsclipping, n.d. Photographs.
Taped interview.
 12 photographs: Italian social gatherings in Hamilton, and Gagliano, Italy,
most of them dating from the 1940s
and 1950s.
 Interviewed on 9 May 1977; 2 hrs.;
3 tapes; Italian/English; by L. Cellini.
Describes life in internment camps
during WWII.

COLANGELO, URBANO
HAMILTON, ONT.
 Interviewed on 9 May 1977; .5 hr.;
1 tape; Italian; by L. Cellini.

COMAR, ENZO
TORONTO, ONT.
 Italian passport, 1953, and Canadian
immigration identification card, 1954.
Taped interview.
 Interviewed on 26 June 1977; 1.5
hrs.; 2 tapes; English; by J. Zucchi.
Arrived in Canada in 1954.

COMISSO, ANITA
SUDBURY, ONT.
 Interviewed on 10 July 1984; 1 hr.;
1 tape; Italian/English; by D.
Visentin. Arrived in Canada in 1926.

CONTE, ANTONIETTA
SUDBURY, ONT.
 Interviewed on 19 June 1984; .75
hr.; 1 tape; Italian; by D. Visentin.
Immigrated to Canada in 1954.

CONTINI, FIORAVANTE
TORONTO, ONT.
 9 photographs: mainly of WWI military service in Italy, 1914-18. Taped
interview.
 Interviewed in March 1982; 2 hrs.; 2
tapes; English; by V. Tullo.

CORDONE, MARIA G.
TORONTO, ONT.
 Italian military certificates, 1908;
Italian passports, technical school
graduation certificate, and report
card, 1904-05; religious article written by a Franciscan, 1909; and correspondence, and typescript memoirs of
Antonina Larosa. 2 cm (11 items).
Photographs. Taped interview.
 3 photographs: the Larosa family,
1900-60.
 Interviewed on 10 June 1977; 1.5
hrs.; 2 tapes; English; by J. Zucchi.
Immigrated to Canada in 1919.

CORDONE, MARIA
HAMILTON, ONT.
 Interviewed on 1 July 1977; 2 hrs.; 2
tapes; English; by L. Cellini.

CREMASCO, PETER
HAMILTON, ONT.
 Interviewed on 1 July 1977; 2 hrs.; 2
tapes; English; by L. Cellini. Development of Italian-Canadian commun-

ity of Hamilton, Ont., and life
through the WWII period.

CRENNA, MR. AND MRS.
GUELPH, ONT.
 Interviewed on 13 April 1977; 1 hr.;
1 tape; English; by S. Traplin.
Arrived in Canada in 1904.

D'ALOISIO, MARY
SUDBURY, ONT.
 1 photograph: the interior of Fera
Bros., and Celestini Store in
Creighton, Ont., 1914. Taped inter-
view.
 Interviewed on 3 April 1981; .25
hr.; 1 tape; English; by A. Taverna.
Immigrated to Canada in 1910.

DEL BIANCO, ANTONIA
THUNDER BAY, ONT.
 Interviewed on 26 May 1978; .75
hr.; 1 tape; English; by A. Pucci.
Immigrated to Canada in 1910.

DEL BIANCO, VITTORIO
THUNDER BAY, ONT.
 44 photographs: social gatherings in
Fort William; and Vittorio del
Bianco, 1913-41. Taped interview.
 Interviewed on 7 June 1978; .75 hr.;
1 tape; Italian/English; by A. Pucci.
Immigrated to Canada in 1913.

DE LUCA, ALFREDO
TORONTO, ONT.
 Interviewed on 12 June 1977; 1 hr.;
1 tape; English; J. Zucchi. Arrived in
Canada in 1949.

DE MARCO, ANTONIETTA
NORTH BAY, ONT.
 Passenger declaration, landing card,
and identity card, n.d. .5 cm. Photographs. Taped interview.
 16 photographs: the De Marco fam-

ily in Italy, and North Bay, 1900-40;
elementary school classroom, n.d.;
and bugle band organized by Figli di
Colombo, c. late 1930s.
 Interviewed on 24 Aug. 1977; 1 hr.;
1 tape; Italian/English; by N.
Cotrupi.

DE MARSICO, GIOVANNI
TORONTO, ONT.
 Travel documents and marriage
certificate, n.d. .5 cm (7 items).
Taped interview.
 Interviewed on 21 June 1979; 1 hr.;
1 tape; English; by R. Healey.

DEOTTO, BRUNO
TORONTO, ONT.
 Italian newspaper article, 1963.
Photograph. Taped interview.
 1 photograph: Coro Santa Cecilia in
its first year, 1954.
 Interviewed on 19 July 1977; 2 hrs.;
3 tapes; English; by J. Zucchi.
Arrived in Canada in 1954.

DE SANCTIS, NICK
TORONTO, ONT.
 Interviewed on 9 July 1987; 2 hrs.; 2
tapes; Italian; by Nick Forte. Discusses the Molisan post-WWII community of Toronto, and Montreal,
Quebec.

DESANDO, EUGENIO
THUNDER BAY, ONT.
 Interviewed on 4 Oct. 1978; 1.5
hrs.; 2 tapes; Italian; by A. Pucci.
Immigrated to Canada in 1927.

DESANTIS, CARMINE
ST. CATHERINES, ONT.
 1 photograph: Carmine De Santis,
1979. Taped interview.

Interviewed on Jan. 1979; 1.5 hrs.; 2 tapes; English; by L. De Santis.

DE ZORZI, MARIA
TORONTO, ONT.
 Registry certificate, n.d.; Italian wedding certificate, 1913; Italian birth certificate, 1951; and naturalization certificate, 1909. Photographs. Taped interview.
 11 photographs: the De Zorzi family, 1892-1914.
 Interviewed on 18 Nov., 10 Dec. 1977; 2.75 hrs.; 3 tapes; English; by J. Zucchi and F. Zucchi. Immigrated to Canada in 1910.

DI GIULIO, DONALD
TORONTO, ONT.
 D. di Giulio co-founded the newspaper *Il Messagero*, and the Pisticci Club. Collection Includes papers from Pisticci Club: statute, c. 1960; financial statements and letters of incorporation, 1960-62; Pisticci Club programme, July 1965; notices of Club meetings and dances, 1960, 1974; and correspondence from Rocco Lofranco, 1965, and the Department of Provincial Secretary and Citizenship, 1960-64. 3 cm (9 items). Taped interview.
 Interviewed on 13, 20 June 1979; 3 hrs.; 3 tapes; English/Italian; by R. Healey.
 Di Giulio, D. "Tramorito della cultura italiana." *Il Messagero.* Toronto, 1932. .25 cm.
 "Al nido di natale col premier dell'Ontario." Toronto, Sept. 1974. Booklet.
 "Programma del Pisticci Club." Toronto, July 1965. Booklet.

DI IORIO, GIUSEPPE
TORONTO, ONT.
 Interviewed on 11 April 1980; 1.5 hrs.; 2 tapes; Italian; by J. Di Nardo. Immigrated to Canada in the 1950s.

DI MANNO, BENNY
THOROLD, ONT.
 Sons of Italy pass book, Loggia Gabriele D'Annunzio, n.d., and certificate of naturalization, n.d. Taped interview.
 Interviewed on 23 Aug. 1977; 3 hrs.; 3 tapes; English; by P. Jones. Arrived in Canada in 1912.

DI SALVATORE, PIETRO
HAMILTON, ONT.
 Interviewed on 6 Sept. 1977; 1 hr.; 1 tape; English/Italian; by L. Cellini.

DI STEFANO, SERGIO
TORONTO, ONT.
 Interviewed on 25 June 1977; 1 hr.; 1 tape; English; by J. Zucchi. Arrived in Canada in 1950.

DI VALENTIN, DONINO
TORONTO, ONT.
 Interviewed on 13 June 1977; 1 hr.; 1 tape; English; by J. Zucchi. Arrived in Canada in 1948.

DI VALENTIN, MARIANNA
TORONTO, ONT.
 Italian army discharge, 1921. Photograph.
 1 photograph: n.d. Taped interview.
 Interviewed on 18 Oct. 1977; .75 hr.; 1 tape; English; by F. Zucchi. Immigrated to Canada in 1936.

DOZZI, MARIA
SUDBURY, ONT.
 Interviewed on 5 July 1984; .75 hr.;

1 tape; Italian; by D. Visentin.
Arrived in Canada in 1932.

DRI, MARIO AND RENATA
TORONTO, ONT.
Immigration documents, n.d., postcard of ship *Giulio Cesare,* n.d., and
letter to Mario Dri from Forum Construction Co., c. 1950s. .5 cm. Taped
interview.
Interviewed on 29 Aug. 1977; 1.25
hrs.; 2 tapes; English; by J. Zucchi.
Arrived in Canada in 1957.

D'URZO, MARIA ANTONIETTA
TORONTO, ONT.
Interviewed on 31 Jan. 1980; 1.5
hrs.; 2 tapes; Italian; by M.
Augimeri.

ELY, BRIGIDA
TORONTO, ONT.
Italian passport, ship boarding card,
and landing card, 1924. Photograph.
Taped interview.
1 photograph: Brigida Ely and Family in Toronto, 1927.
Interviewed on 12 July 1977; 1 hr.;
1 tape; English; by J. Zucchi. Immigrated to Canada in the 1920s.

EMBRO, LOUIS AND ANGELA
GUELPH, ONT.
Italian passport, ship identity card,
n.d., and 3 letters, 1961. .25 cm.
Photographs. Taped interview.
8 photographs: the Embro family in
Italy and Guelph, 1910-50; and front
of Embro's fruit store, c. 1910s.
Interviewed on 21 April 1977; 1 hr.;
1 tape; English; by S. Traplin.

FABBRO, ROSE
SUDBURY, ONT.
Biographical sketch, 1918-70. Photo-
graphs. Taped interview.

24 photographs: the life of Joseph
Fabbro, a long-time mayor of
Sudbury.
Interviewed on 15 June 1981; .75
hr.; 1 tape; Italian/English; by A.
Taverna. Discusses the political
career of Joseph Fabbro.

FARANO, JIM
TORONTO, ONT.
Interviewed on 18 Dec. 1978; 1 hr.;
1 tape; Italian/English; by J. Zucchi.

FAVA, GIUSEPPE
NORTH BAY, ONT.
1 photograph: gold and jewellery
donated to the motherland by Italian
immigrants in North Bay, c. 1930s.
Taped interview.
Interviewed on 23 July 1977; 1.5
hrs.; 2 tapes; English; by N. Cotrupi.

FAVA, MARIO
TORONTO, ONT.
Certificato di Patriota, 1945; immigration identification card, 1956;
work card for the Council of Carpenters and Joiners of America, 1959;
and dues book for the United Brotherhood of Carpenters and Joiners of
America, 1958. Taped interview.
Interviewed on 16 Aug. 1977; 1.5
hrs.; 2 tapes; English; by J. Zucchi.
Arrived in Canada in 1956.

FEDERICO, RAFFAELLA
TORONTO, ONT.
Interviewed on 27 Jan. 1980; 1.5
hrs.; 2 tapes; Italian; by M.
Augimeri.

FEDERICO, SALVATORE
THUNDER BAY, ONT.
Interviewed on 6 April 1978; 1 hr.;
1 tape; Italian; by A. Pucci.
Post-WWII immigrant.

FERRI, FRANK
HAMILTON, ONT.
Interviewed on 10 April 1983; 2 hrs.; 2 tapes; English; by Enrico Cumbo.

FOGOLIN, TONY
THUNDER BAY, ONT.
Interviewed on 20 Sept. 1978; 1.75 hrs.; 2 tapes; Italian; by A. Pucci. Immigrated to Canada in 1913.

FORTE, NICK
TORONTO, ONT.
2 anti-strike posters issued by the Toronto Metro Home Builders' Association during the 1960-61 residential construction work stoppages in Toronto.
Il Lavoratore. Vol. 1, no. 1, Sept. 1959 - vol. 3, no. 16, March 1961. Toronto (12 issues). 5 cm.

FOURNIER, L.
HAMILTON, ONT.
Interviewed on 16 Nov. 1977; .75 hr.; 1 tape; English; by L. Cellini.

FRACASSO, LUIGI
NORTH BAY, ONT.
Interviewed on 20 Aug. 1977; 1.5 hrs.; 2 tapes; Italian/English; by N. Cotrupi.

FREDIANI, FRANK
TORONTO, ONT.
Certificato penale, 1912, 1922; steamship tickets, 1922; identity card, 1922; medical certificate, 1922; handwritten sponsorship and note concerning insured passage, 1922; letter from mayor approving passport, 1922; Italian consulor documents, 1921; English-Italian notebook; and lists of names of Italians interned in Camp Petawawa, n.d. Photographs.

Taped interview.
16 photographs: the Frediani family, 1905-40; theatrical production, 1916; front of Florentine Shop building, 1939; the Fascio Femminile organization, 1934; photocopies of a photo album; and a sketch of Frank Frediani made by an inmate at Camp Petawawa, 1940.
Interviewed on 24 May, 5 July 1978; 3 hrs.; 3 tapes; Italian/English; by J. Zucchi. Discusses his involvement in the Toronto Fascio movement in the 1930s.

FUSCO, VINCENZA
TORONTO, ONT.
Interviewed on 22 March, 14 April 1983; 1 hr.; 1 tape; English/Italian; by Enrico Cumbo. Arrived in Canada in 1922.

GATTO, GRADY
TORONTO, ONT.
Interviewed on 23 March 1979; 1 hr.; 1 tape; English; by J. Zucchi.

GENIOLE, AUDREY
TORONTO, ONT.
Italian army document, naturalization certificate, entrance examination, Italian textbook, and notes, n.d. Photographs. Taped interview.
22 photographs: the Geniole and Trauzzi families, 1930-38.
Interviewed on 20 Sept. 1977; 1 hr.; 1 tape; English; by A. McPeek.

GENNARO, JOSEPH
TORONTO, ONT.
Interviewed on 30 March 1983; 2 hrs.; 2 tapes; English; by Enrico Cumbo. Arrived in Canada in 1920.

GHETTI, DOMENICA
SUDBURY, ONT.
Interviewed on 27 July 1984; .75 hr.; 1 tape; Italian; by D. Visentin.

GIOVANNIELLI, LUCY
TORONTO, ONT.
Interviewed on 31 Aug. 1978; 1.25 hrs.; 2 tapes; English; by J. Zucchi.

GLIONNA, MICHAEL
TORONTO, ONT.
Interviewed on 19 Feb. 1979; 5 hrs.; 5 tapes; English/Italian; by J. Zucchi. Describes Toronto's Italian district in St. John's Ward in the early 1900s.

GOLINI, ROCCO
HAMILTON, ONT.
2 photographs: donor's father in British Columbia, 1907; and women making tomato sauce in Hamilton, n.d.

GRANZOTTO, GIUSEPPE AND ANGELA
TORONTO, ONT.
3 photographs: baptisms and a wedding, 1954-56. Taped interview. Interviewed on 18 June 1977; 1.5 hrs.; 2 tapes; English; by J. Zucchi. Arrived in Canada in 1951.

GRI, DANIEL
TORONTO, ONT.
Interviewed on 5 July 1977; 1 hr.; 1 tape; English; by J. Zucchi. Arrived in Canada in 1949.

GRIMALDI, ANGELO G.
TORONTO, ONT.
3 photographs: 1930-1950, first reunion to obtain the Casa d'Italia, 1949.

GRITTANI, ELENA
TORONTO, ONT.
Joseph and Elena Grittani were actively involved in the Italian Immigrant Aid Society in the 1950s and 1960s. The collection includes a scrapbook of newsclippings and photographs dating from 1919 to the 1970s, and personal documents, letters, announcements, and a list of contributors to the "Collection in Aid of Destitute Italian Children, 1947." 1 reel of microfilm. 2 cm. Photographs. 9 photographs: Italian pavilion at National Exhibition in Toronto, 1934; "Knights of Columbus Bowling," n.d.; dinner for the "Collection in Aid of Destitute Italian Children," 1947; and J. Grittani, family and friends.

GRITTANI, GIANBATTISTA
HAMILTON, ONT.
Interviewed on 31 March 1983; 2 hrs.; 2 tapes; Italian/English; by Enrico Cumbo.

GRITTANI, RON
TORONTO, ONT.
Italian penal certificate, 1903, emigration documents, including memo from Lloyd Sabaudo to Ron Grittani regarding payment for transatlantic passage, 1921, and naturalization certificate, 1927. Photographs. 15 photographs: the Grittani family and friends in Toronto, 1930-1950.

GROSSO, JOHN
HAMILTON, ONT.
2 photographs: of the Anglo Canadian Concert Band of Huntsville, 1915, 1925; and the Grosso family in Italy in the early 1900s.

GROSSO, JOHN
HAMILTON, ONT.
 Interviewed on 14 July 1977; .75
hr.; 1 tape; English; by L. Cellini.

GUARASCI, GIUSEPPE
THUNDER BAY, ONT.
 Interviewed on 29 Sept. 1978; 1.5
hrs.; 2 tapes; Italian; by A. Pucci.
Immigrated to Canada in 1912.

HARNEY, R. F.
TORONTO, ONT.
 1 photograph: coat of arms of the
Societá Italo-Canadese, 1919.

IANNARELLI, CHIARA
TORONTO, ONT.
 Interviewed on 6 March 1980; 1 hr.;
1 tape; Italian; by J. Di Nardo.
Arrived in Canada in 1964.

IATI, PAOLO
NORTH BAY, ONT.
 Interviewed on 30 July 1977; 1 hr.;
1 tape; English/Italian; by N.
Cotrupi.

IGLESIAS, MRS.
TORONTO, ONT.
 1856 Papal certificate; Italian army
discharge certificate; military certificate and regulations, 1897; passport
"Umberto I Passaporto per l'Interno,"
1938. 1 cm (5 items). Photographs.
Taped interview.
 2 photographs: H. Corti, father of
donor, n.d.; and Ward 3 Conservative
Party picnic, 1922.
 Interviewed on 9 May 1978; 1 hr.; 1
tape; English/Italian; by J. and F.
Zucchi. Discusses Enrico Corti, her
father.

INNEO, FATHER ANTHONY
WELLAND, ONT.
 Interviewed on 25 May 1977; 1 hr.;
1 tape; English; by P. Jones.

IPPOLITO-FICK, SARAH
TORONTO, ONT.
 4 photographs: St. Joseph's Day
block party, 1940; Italian students at
Cathedral Girls High School, n.d.;
and two boys wearing Sardo Bros.
T-shirts, n.d. Taped interview.
 Interviewed on 23 June 1977; 1 hr.;
1 tape; English; by L. Cellini.

JONES, CLARE P.
WELLAND, ONT.
 Handwritten Italian marriage records
of Welland parishes, 1900-25. 2 cm.

JULIAN, ANTHONY
TORONTO, ONT.
 23 photographs: ceremonies and
activities at St. Anthony of Padua
Church, 1933-58; parades and processions, 1937-59; work on railway
sites, 1931; and building of the Sons
of Italy, n.d. Taped interview.
 Interviewed on 26 Nov. 1977; .75
hr.; 1 tape; English; by L. Cellini.

LALAMA, PASQUALE.
TORONTO, ONT.
 Interviewed on 27 July 1977; 1 hr.;
1 tape; Italian; by P. Jones.

LASOTA, TERESA
WELLAND, ONT.
 2 photographs: Plymouth Cordage
(house and field), c. 1920-25. Taped
interview
 Interviewed on 16 July 1977; 1 hr.;
1 tape; English; by P. Jones.

LOFRANCO, ROCCO
TORONTO, ONT.
Al nido di natale col premier dell'
Ontario. Toronto, n.d. 20 pp.
Interviewed on 14 June, 4 July, 25
Sept. 1979; 5 hrs.; 5 tapes; English;
by R. Healey.

LOMBARDI, REV. MASSEY, IMMACU-
LATE CONCEPTION CHURCH
TORONTO, ONT.
1 photograph: Toronto Fascio
leaders: M. Missori, T. Mari, A.
Gatto, R. Davidiata, G. Tomasicchio,
and F. Perullo, c. 1930s; and nega-
tive of an Italian document, n.d.

LONGO, MRS.
GUELPH, ONT.
2 Italian birth certificates, n.d. Italian army certificate, 1913, immigration declaration, 1912, Certificato
Penale, 1913, naturalization certificate, 1934, and Canadian citizenship
certificate, 1951. Photographs. Taped
interview.
10 photographs: personal documents
of the Valerioti and Longo families,
1903-51.
Interviewed on 11 April 1977; 1 hr.;
1 tape; English; by S. Traplin.
Arrived in Canada in 1912.

LUCCHETTA, JOSEPH
TORONTO, ONT.
Personal documents, Italian military
certificates, emigration papers, 1910s,
and account book, 1920s. Photographs.
15 photographs: 1914-1940s,
Lucchetta family; Alfonso Volonte,
the donor's father, who served at St.
Agnes Church; wedding ceremonies;
first Communion; and Confirmation.

LUCCHETTA, JOSEPH
TORONTO, ONT.
Interviewed on 23 May 1977; 3 hrs.;
3 tapes; English; by A. McPeek.

LUCENTI, ROCCO
NORTH BAY, ONT.
A warrant for presentation for examination in Italian, n.d. .25 cm. Photograph. Taped interview.
1 photograph: the North Bay Premier
Band, comprised largely of Italians,
1926; and the Societá Cristoforo
Colombo, 1919.
Interviewed on 25 Aug. 1977; 1.5
hrs.; 2 tapes; English; by N. Cotrupi.

MACEROLLO, JOSEPH
GUELPH, ONT.
Interviewed on 3 Aug. 1977; .5 hr.;
1 tape; English; by S. Traplin.

MAINELLA, ANTOINETTE
TORONTO, ONT.
Italian passport, 1920, certificate of
military decoration, 1926, marriage
certificate, 1928, house mortgage,
1942, and 2 American border crossing identity cards, 1944. 2 cm (9
items). Taped interview.
Interviewed on 20 April 1977; 1 hr.;
1 tape; English; by A. McPeek.

MARANDO, ANTONIA
WELLAND, ONT.
Interviewed on 5 July 1977; 1 hr.; 1
tape; English; by P. Jones. Immigrated to Canada in 1921.

MARCHI, OTTAVIO
TORONTO, ONT.
2 passports (Italian and Argentine),
1959, 1966; 2 Argentine identity
cards, 1958; 2 Italian identity cards,
1948, 1952; 2 certificates of good
conduct, Argentine, 1959; work

certificate, Argentine, 1959; Italian driver's license, 1948; and English course certificate, 1960. 2 cm (35 items). Photographs. Taped interview. 3 photographs: a factory in Buenos Aires that Ottavio Marchi partially owned, c. 1950s.
 Interviewed on 28 July 1977; 1.5 hrs.; 2 tapes; English; by J. Zucchi. Immigrated to Canada in 1959.

MARCHIORI, JULIA
THUNDER BAY, ONT.
 58 photographs: the Italian immigrant experience in Fort William's East End, 1903-1930s. Taped interview.
 Interviewed on 7 Nov. 1978; 1.5 hrs.; 2 tapes; English/Italian; by A. Pucci.

MARCHIORI, SATURNO
THUNDER BAY, ONT.
 Interviewed on 4 May 1978; 1 hr.; 1 tape; Italian/English; by A. Pucci. Immigrated to Canada in 1914.

MARINI, ORESTE
HAMILTON, ONT.
 9 photographs: Oreste Marini and friends; farming and delivery trucks in Hamilton, and Saskatchewan, 1917-30. Taped interview.
 Interviewed on 18 Feb. 1978; 1.5 hrs.; 2 tapes; Italian/English; by L. Cellini. Arrived in Canada in 1915.

MARUCCI, PETER
GUELPH, ONT.
 Interviewed on 14 June 1977; 1 hr.; 1 tape; English; by S. Traplin.

MASCIOLI, ELIO
NORTH BAY, ONT.
 Interviewed on 31 July 1977; 1 hr.;

1 tape; English; by N. Cotrupi. Discusses immigration history of family, and settlement in the U.S. and Canada in the early 1900s.

MAZZOCATO, FINIZIA
TORONTO, ONT.
 Interviewed on 7 March 1980; .5 hr.; 1 tape; Italian; by J. Di Nardo.

MESCHINO, ARMAND, TOM AND JOE
DOWNSVIEW, ONT.
 15 photographs: 1925-48, business activities; peddling of bananas on Clinton Street; work at Meschino Banana warehouse; and First Communion ceremony at St. Agnes Church. Taped interview.
 Interviewed on 22 Aug. 1978; 1.5 hrs.; 2 tapes; English; by J. Zucchi. Discusses the banana wholesale business, 1930s.

MICHELON, ANGELO
SUDBURY, ONT.
 Interviewed on 16 July 1984; 1 hr.; 1 tape; English; by D. Visentin. Immigrated to Canada in the 1920s.

MOLLICA, ANTHONY
WELLAND, ONT.
 Ministry of Education memo regarding Heritage Language Programme; unpublished articles, "The Teaching of Italian in the High Schools of Ontario," and "Italian in the Secondary Schools of Ontario." 2 cm. Taped interview.
 Interviewed on 28 June 1977; 1 hr.; 1 tape; English; by P. Jones. Arrived in Canada in 1950.

MONTEMURRO, STANLEY NATALE
NORTH BAY, ONT.
 Interviewed on 27 Aug. 1977; 1.5 hrs.; 2 tapes; English; by N. Cotrupi.

MURATORI, JOHN
THOROLD, ONT.
 Interviewed on 22 Aug. 1977; 1 hr.;
1 tape; English; by P. Jones. Arrived
in Canada in 1911.

NERO, DOMENICO
WELLAND, ONT.
 Interviewed on 22 June 1977; 1 hr.;
1 tape; English; by P. Jones. Arrived
in Canada in 1912.

NOONAN, REV. JAMES (HOLY
ROSARY CHURCH)
THOROLD, ONT.
 Handwritten list of assistant Italian
priests for the Church, n.d. and a
50th anniversary programme of the
Holy Rosary Church, 1925-75. .5
cm. Taped interview.
 Interviewed on 16 Aug. 1977; 1 hr.;
1 tape; English; by P. Jones.

ORLANDO, ROSINA
TORONTO, ONT.
 Passport, n.d.; document entitled
"Atto di Espatrio," n.d.; certificate of
naturalization, 1921; birth certificate,
1965. Taped interview
 Interviewed on 1 May 1980; 1 hr.; 1
tape; English; by J. Di Nardo.
Post-WWI immigrant.

PACECCA, LUCY
HAMILTON, ONT.
 5 photographs: the Pacecca family;
grocery store, c. 1944; home which
they built n.d.; and Father Mascari
baptising their son, 1955. Taped
innterview.
 Interviewed on 18 May 1977; 1 hr.;
1 tape; English; by L. Cellini.

PALMA, DON
WELLAND, ONT.
 Interviewed on 30 June 1977; 3 hrs.;
3 tapes; English; by P. Jones.

PANCARO, LUIGI
TORONTO, ONT.
 1 photograph: Luigi Pancaro, 1958.

PANTALEO, IRENE
TORONTO, ONT.
 Interviewed on 6 Dec. 1978; 2 hrs.;
2 tapes; Italian/English; by J. Zucchi.

PAPA, VITO
TORONTO, ONT.
 Vito Papa's book of poems, 1976. 1
cm, in Italian.

PARISSI, LUCY
TORONTO, ONT.
 Interviewed on 27 April 1983; .75
hr.; 1 tape; English; by Enrico
Cumbo.

PASCUZZO, ANTONIO
THUNDER BAY, ONT.
 Interviewed on 15 Oct. 1978; 2 hrs.;
2 tapes; Italian; by A. Pucci. Immigrated to Canada in 1924.

PASQUALE, DONNA
HAMILTON, ONT.
 Interviewed on 13 April 1983; 1 hr.;
1 tape; Italian/English; by Enrico
Cumbo.

PAUTASSO, LUIGI
TORONTO, ONT.
 Text of lecture given at the Ladies of
Loggia Regina Elena, Ordine Figli
d'Italia, 1935; also, various Italian-
Canadian printed materials. 4 cm.
 Gualteri, Francesco M. *We Italians:
A Study in Italian Immigration in
Canada.* Toronto: Italian World War

Veterans Association, 1928. 78 pp.
Annuario italiano. Toronto: Italian
Information Bureau, 1935. 96 pp.

PAVAN, EUGENIO
SUDBURY, ONT.
 Interviewed on 2 July 1984; 1 hr.; 1
tape; Italian/English; by D. Visentin.
Arrived in Canada in 1920.

PECILE, PIETRO
TORONTO, ONT.
 Immigration documents, 1950s;
union letter, 1958; correspondence
with the Italian-Canadian Institute of
Public Opinion, 1959; embassy correspondence, 1958-59; bank correspondence, 1961-62; and newsclippings,
n.d. Photographs. Taped interview.
 2 photographs: Italian immigrants en
route to Canada; and house under
construction in Toronto, 1964.
 Interviewed on 9 Aug. 1977; 1 hr.; 1
tape; English; by J. Zucchi. Arrived
in Canada in 1955.

PELLEGRINA, RINO
TORONTO, ONT.
 Collection includes record book of
work expenses, 1953-56, 1957-60;
record book of household expenses,
1945-63; record book of work, 1947;
miscellaneous employment records,
1951; expense sheets and invoices for
R. F. Welsh Ltd., 1953;
newsclippings, 1953; electoral notice,
1953, 1957-60; correspondence
between C.N. Railway, C. Caccia
and R. Pellegrina, 1970; Italian military draft papers; vocational training
and language certificates; and an
international Labourers' Union membership book, 1960. 5 cm (16 items).
1 reel of microfilm. Photographs.
Taped interview.
 9 photographs: Rino Pellegrina on a

construction site, n.d.; a group of
Friulans, 1959; an Italian choir,
1954; Italian immigrants on the ship
Conte Biancamano, 1953; Italian
railway navvies, 1953; and the donor
at Christmas, 1954.
 Interviewed on 6 Aug. 1977; 2 hrs.;
2 tapes; English; by J. Zucchi.
Arrived in Canada in 1953.

PENNACHIETTI, MARIA
THOROLD, ONT.
 Certificate from Club Roma, n.d.,
certificate of naturalization, n.d., souvenir programmes from Club Roma,
1967, blessing from the Pope, golden
wedding anniversary booklet of Mr.
and Mrs. Pennachietti, 1922-72. 2 cm
(11 items). Taped interview.
 Interviewed on 8 Aug. 1977; 1 hr.; 1
tape; English; by P. Jones. Arrived in
Canada in 1922.

PERUSINI, PALMIRA
SUDBURY, ONT.
 Interviewed on 20 June 1984; .75
hr.; 1 tape; Italian; by D. Visentin.
Immigrated to Canada in 1930.

PERUZZI, GIUSEPPE
TORONTO, ONT.
 Italian identification card and passport, 1951, and "Dues Book of Brick-
layers, Masons and Plasterers International Union of America," 1957. 1
cm. Photographs. Taped interview.
 3 photographs: donor working as a
mason, 1960; a group of Friulans in
front of "fogolar," 1958; and an Ital-
ian/Friulan choir directed by M.
Zanini, 1958.
 Interviewed on 10 Aug. 1977; 1.5
hrs.; 2 tapes; English; by J. Zucchi.
Arrived in Canada in 1952.

PIANOSI, GIOVANNI
COPPER CLIFF, ONT.
 Interviewed on 1 Aug. 1984; .5 hr.;
1 tape; English; by D. Visentin.

PICCININNI, JOE
TORONTO, ONT.
 Interviewed on 19 April 1983; 1 hr.;
1 tape; English; by Enrico Cumbo.
Arrived in Canada in 1902.

PICHELLI, GABRIELE
WELLAND, ONT.
 Interviewed on 9 July 1977; 2 hrs.; 2
tapes; English; by P. Jones. Arrived
in Canada in 1928.

PIEROBON, LUCIA
SUDBURY, ONT.
 Interviewed on 21 June 1984; 2 hrs.;
2 tapes; Italian; by D. Visentin.
Arrived in Canada in 1958.

PIETROPAOLO, VINCENZO
TORONTO, ONT.
 18 photographs: Calabrian folklore
and traditions in Toronto; and processions, 1970-85.

PIOTTO, LINO
SUDBURY, ONT.
 Interviewed on 11 July 1984; 1.5
hrs.; 2 tapes; Italian/English; by D.
Visentin.

PISSOLANTE, JOE
HAMILTON, ONT.
 Historical sketch of St. Enoch's
Presbyterian Church, n.d. Photo-
graphs. Taped interview.
 Interviewed on 27 Sept. 1977; 1 hr.;
1 tape; English; by L. Cellini.

PIZZOFERRATO, JEAN
TORONTO, ONT.
 Interviewed on 4 Feb. 1978; .75 hr.;
1 tape; English/Italian; by L. Cellini.

POLITICCHIA, RICCARDO
TORONTO, ONT.
 Interviewed on 15 Dec. 1977; 1 hr.;
1 tape; English/Italian; by J. Zucchi.
Arrived in Canada in 1936.

POLLO, REV. E.
TORONTO, ONT.
 La voce della domenica. Toronto,
Jan. 1971 - April 1974. 2 reels of
microfilm.

POLTICCHIA, REV. R.
TORONTO, ONT.
 *The Franciscan Fathers' Silver Jubi-
lee Commemoration, St. Agnes
Church.* 1934-59. Toronto, 1959. 1
reel of microfilm.
 *60th Anniversary of Rev. Polticchia's
Ordination.* Toronto, St. Agnes
Church, 1970.
 *Golden Jubilee of Fr. Riccardo's
Ordination to the Priesthood.*
Toronto, St. Agnes Church, 1961. .5
cm.

PRIOLO, VINCENZO
NORTH BAY, ONT.
 Certificate of discharge from active
service, 1940, Canadian passport,
n.d., and honourary certificate for
Italian WWI veteran, 1934. Photographs. Taped interview.
 9 photographs: Priolo family in
North Bay, Italy, and West Virginia,
some of which date back to the 1880s
and 1890s; and the Figli di Colombo
organization, n.d.
 Interviewed on 6 Aug. 1977; 2 hrs.;
2 tapes; Italian/English; by N.
Cotrupi.

PUCCINI, BERT
TORONTO, ONT.
7 photographs: family and friends of Abramo Puccini in Toronto, and Italy, 1918-48; and funeral of Mrs. J. Puccini at Mount Hope Cemetery, 1922. Taped interview.
Interviewed on 10 Aug. 1978; 1.5 hrs.; 2 tapes; English; by J. Zucchi.

RANIERI, ANTOINETTE
TORONTO, ONT.
Interviewed on 21 March 1980; 1.5 hrs.; 2 tapes; English; by J. Di Nardo.

RAY, JOHN
SUDBURY, ONT.
89 photographs: the Ray family; and family documents, 1905-81. Taped interview.
Interviewed on 24 Oct. 1981; .75 hr.; 1 tape; Italian; by A. Taverna. Arrived in Canada in 1919.

REALE, VENUSTA
WELLAND, ONT.
Interviewed on 29 July 1977; 1 hr.; 1 tape; English; by P. Jones. Arrived in Canada in 1916.

RELIC, JOSEPHINE
HAMILTON, ONT.
4 photographs: the Di Vincent family in Hamilton, c. 1900-60.

REMIGIO, GEORGE
WELLAND, ONT.
Immigration and military papers, including a *Januarius Costagliola* certificate, c. 1910-20s. Taped interview.
Interviewed on 6 Sept. 1977; 1 hr.; 1 tape; English; by P. Jones. Arrived in Canada in 1913.

RICCI, MICHELE
NORTH BAY, ONT.
Interviewed on 26 Aug. 1977; .75 hr.; 1 tape; English; by N. Cotrupi.

RIGATO, VIRGINIO
THUNDER BAY, ONT.
Interviewed on 9 May 1978; 1 hr.; 1 tape; Italian; by A. Pucci. Arrived in Canada in 1912.

ROBSON, ANN MARIE
HAMILTON, ONT.
Interviewed in Jan. 1979; 1 hr.; 1 tape; English; by L. Cellini. An account of growing up as an Irish-German ethnic in a predominantly Italian-Canadian environment.

ROSART, WILLIAM
HAMILTON, ONT.
60 photographs: the Rosart family and friends; and store fronts and porches, taken mainly in the 1910s and 1920s.

ROSINI, GENOEFFA
SUDBURY, ONT.
Interviewed on 8 July 1984; .75 hr.; 1 tape; Italian; by D. Visentin.

ROTONDO, SANTO
SUDBURY, ONT.
Interviewed on 13 July 1984; 1 hr.; 1 tape; English/Italian; by D. Visentin.

SABUCCO, DANTE
WELLAND, ONT.
Personal documents, c. 1910s. 1 cm (8 items). Taped interview.
Interviewed on 12 July 1977; 1 hr.; 1 tape; English; by P. Jones. Arrived in Canada in 1914.

SABUCCO, LUCIA
WELLAND, ONT.
Interviewed on 12 July 1977; 1 hr.;
1 tape; English; by P. Jones. Arrived
in Canada in 1907.

SALATINO, MICHELE
THUNDER BAY, ONT.
Interviewed on 20 Oct. 1978; 1.5
hrs.; 2 tapes; Italian; by A. Pucci.
Immigrated to Canada in 1906.

SALVO, ANTHONY
HAMILTON, ONT.
Interviewed in 1977; 1 hr.; 1 tape;
English; by L. Cellini.

SANGALI, ROSA MARIA
TORONTO, ONT.
A manuscript from Rosa Sangali,
1976. 141 pp. Taped interview.
Interviewed on 8 March 1980; .75
hr.; 1 tape; Italian; by J. Di Nardo.
Arrived in Canada in 1975.

SANTAGAPITA, RINA
TORONTO, ONT.
Interviewed on 28 Jan., 22 April
1978; 1.5 hrs.; 2 tapes; English; by
J. Zucchi and F. Zucchi.

SARDO, REV. STEPHEN
HAMILTON, ONT.
Clippings and a souvenir booklet.
1.5 cm (6 items). Taped interview.
Interviewed on 4 Sept. 1977; 1 hr.;
1 tape; English; by L. Cellini.
St. Anthony of Padua Church.
Hamilton, 1954. .5 cm.

SCAGNETTI, LILLIAN
SUDBURY, ONT.
31 photographs: various family and
social gatherings; the interior and
exterior of the Scagnetti store; the
Scagnetti restaurant; and boarding in

Garson, Ont. 1916-73. Taped interview.
Interviewed on 13 Oct. 1981; .75
hr.; 1 tape; English; by A. Taverna.

SCHIAVO, ROCCO
NORTH BAY, ONT.
1 photograph: a threatrical production by the Figli di Colombo, late
1930s. Taped interview.
Interviewed on 23 Aug. 1977; 2
hrs.; 2 tapes; Italian; by N. Cotrupi.

SCINTO, LUCIETTA
SUDBURY, ONT.
Interviewed on 24 July 1984; 1 hr.;
1 tape; English/Italian; by D.
Visentin.

SERAFINI, AUGOSTO
TORONTO, ONT.
5 photographs: Immigrant Day celebration, Earlscourt Park, 1974;
Canada Day Celebration at Ontario
Place, n.d.; and printing press of *Il
Tevere*, the newspaper edited by A.
Serafini. Taped interview. Interviewed on 11 Oct. 1978; 1 hr.; 1
tape; English; by W. Mraz. Arrived
in Canada in 1951.

SERIANNI, JULIE
WELLAND, ONT.
*Golden Jubilee Celebration of St.
Mary's Church.* Welland, c. 1962.

SIGNORINI, ANTONIO
TORONTO, ONT.
*Aprimi e ti aiuteró: guida
informativa per la comunitá italiana.*
Toronto: Metro Social Service Directory for Italians, 1974. 27 pp., in Ital-
ian/English.

SILVESTRO, MRS.
GUELPH, ONT.
 Interviewed on 3 April 1977; .5 hr.;
1 tape; English/Italian; by S. Traplin.
Arrived in Canada in 1920.

TANEL, GIUSEPPE AND ANTONIETTA
TORONTO, ONT.
 Immigration documents, c. 1940s (5
items). Taped interview.
 Interviewed on 7 June 1977; 1 hr.; 1
tape; Italian; by J. Zucchi. Arrived in
Canada in 1949.

TEMELINI, ANTONIO
SUDBURY, ONT.
 Interviewed on 21 June 1984; .5 hr.;
1 tape; Italian; by D. Visentin.
Arrived in Canada in 1950.

TESSARO, MIGLIO
COPPER CLIFF, ONT.
 Interviewed on 28 July 1984; 1 hr.;
1 tape; English; by D. Visentin.
Arrived in Canada in 1913.

TODERO, ANGELO MICHELE
THUNDER BAY, ONT.
 Interviewed on 14 Nov. 1978; .75
hr.; 1 tape; Italian; by A. Pucci.
Immigrated to Canada in 1911.

TONINI, MARIA
SUDBURY, ONT.
 Interviewed on 17 July 1984; .75
hr.; 1 tape; Italian; by D. Visentin.
Arrived in Canada in 1915.

TOPPAN, MARINO
TORONTO, ONT.
 Actively involved in organizing and
defending the rights of Italian immigrant workers, particularly in the construction industry, since late 1950s.
Papers include transcripts of radio
programme *La voce del lavoro*,

1965-70; minutes and newsletters
1966-67; and miscellaneous file,
including transcripts of Construction
Safety Association messages, 1970.
14 cm.

TOPPAZZINI, GINA
COPPER CLIFF, ONT.
 9 photographs: the Secco family and
friends, 1911-18; first Communion
and Confirmation, 1920; the Italian
Copper Cliff Club, 1951; Ladies'
Auxiliary of the Italian Club in Copper Cliff; and children at elementary
school, n.d. Taped interview.
 Interviewed on 17 June 1981; 1 hr.;
1 tape; English; by M. Stefura and A.
Celli.

TULUMELLO, PETER
WELLAND, ONT.
 Immigration papers and documents
from Italian Consul in Welland, n.d.
(10 items). Taped interview.
 Interviewed on 21 June 1977; 1 hr.;
1 tape; English; by P. Jones.

TURRONI, ELENA
WELLAND, ONT.
 Land deed, flour bills, mortgages,
1910-1938, "Sante Lettere" (holy let-
ters), 1890, and membership list of
Order of Sons of Italy Mutual Benefit
Society, 1940, 1951. 2 cm (27 items).
Photographs. Taped interview.
 13 photographs: personal documents
of the Di Martile family, 1912-51.
 Interviewed on 1 June 1977; 2 hrs.;
2 tapes; English; by P. Jones.

UBRIACO, GRAZIA
THUNDER BAY, ONT.
 Interviewed on 19 May 1978; 1 hr.;
1 tape; Italian; by A. Pucci.

VALERI, MARIA
HAMILTON, ONT.
3 photographs: a railway gang of
Italian workers in British Columbia,
1907. Taped interview.
Interviewed on 7 April 1977; 1.5
hrs.; 2 tapes; Italian; by L. Cellini.
Immigrated to Canada in 1907.

VALERIOTE, DOMINIC
GUELPH, ONT.
Interviewed on 24 July 1977; 1 hr.;
1 tape; English; by S. Traplin.

VALERIOTI, MICHAEL
GUELPH, ONT.
Dominion Express Company, Guelph
office: receipt book for money sent to
Italy, 1912-28; and passport and
certificates of donor, 1901-14. 1 cm.
1 reel of microfilm.

VELTRI, GIOVANNI
THUNDER BAY, ONT.
In 1918 Veltri formed the R. F.
Welch Co., which maintained the
railway. He recruited hundreds of
male workers directly from Italy. *The
Memoirs of Giovanni Veltri*, his auto-
biography, was published by the
Multicultural History Society of
Ontario in 1987.

VENDITTI, LIDIA
TORONTO, ONT.
Interviewed on 22 March 1980; 1
hr.; 1 tape; Italian; by M. Augimeri.

VENDRUSCOLO, LEO AND WANDA
DOWNSVIEW, ONT.
Work contract with R. F. Welsh
Limited., n.d.; vaccination certificate,
1952; Department of Labour dis-
charge from contract employment,
n.d.; and Italian identity card, 1952.
Photographs. Taped interview.

10 photographs: Leo Vendruscolo on
board ship *Argentina* en route to
Canada, 1952; donor with fellow
workers on C.P. Railway site in
Thompson, Manitoba, 1952-53;
boarding house in Toronto, 1953; and
Wanda Vendruscolo with classmates,
1936.
Interviewed on 3 June 1977; 2 hrs.;
2 tapes; English; by J. Zucchi.
Arrived in Canada in 1935.

VENIER, AGOSTINO
TORONTO, ONT.
Agostino Venier immigrated to
Canada in 1954. Since his arrival he
has been a prominent member of
community organizations such as the
Italo-Canadian Recreation Club, and
the Italian Costume and Folklore
Ballet of Canada which he helped to
found. During the late 1960s he participated in Liberal election campaigns, and subsequently, ran in
provincial and municipal elections.
The collection includes personal
papers, n.d., financial records of
Venier's business enterprises,
1961-80; material on cultural and
recreational activities from organizations such as Famee Furlane, ICRC,
Community Folk Arts Council, Santa
Cecilia Folk Choir, and sports clubs,
c. 1965-80; miscellaneous leaflets and
pamphlets pertaining to local political
elections, 1965-75; copies of Legisla-
ture of Ontario Debates, 1969-81; and
issues of various Italian-Canadian
newspapers and magazines. (9
meters). **RESTRICTED**

VICKERS, DANIEL
TORONTO, ONT.
Italian Week Brochure. Toronto,
1978.

VIDOTTO, ANTONIO
THUNDER BAY, ONT.
 Interviewed on 26 April 1978; .5 hr.; 1 tape; Italian; by A. Pucci.

VIDOTTO, PIERINA
THUNDER BAY, ONT.
 Interviewed on 17 April 1978; 1 hr.; 1 tape; Italian; by A. Pucci.

VIOLA, CESIRA
HAMILTON, ONT.
 Interviewed on 11 Feb. 1978; .75 hr.; 1 tape; English/Italian; by L. Cellini. Describes her sheltered life due to her marriage at an early age.

VIRDÒ, MARIA
DOWNSVIEW, ONT.
 Interviewed on 29 Jan. 1980; .5 hr.; 1 tape; Italian/English; by M. Augimeri. Discusses Calabrian folk medicine, folklore and superstition.

VIRDÒ, RAFFAELE
DOWNSVIEW, ONT.
 Interviewed on 29 Jan. 1980; 1 hr.; 1 tape; Italian; by M. Augimeri. Discusses Calabrian folktales.

VISENTIN, GIOVANNI
SUDBURY, ONT.
 Interviewed on 19 July 1984; 1 hr.; 1 tape; Italian; by D. Visentin. Discusses community life in Coniston, Ont. in the post-WWI years, including military service, boardinghouse practices, and business enterprises.

VITALI, ADOLFO
COPPER CLIFF, ONT.
 Interviewed on 26 July 1984; 1.25 hrs.; 2 tapes; Italian/English; by D. Visentin. Discusses employment, and parish life in Copper Cliff.

WATSON (NÉE CECCHETTO), ELENA
SUDBURY, ONT.
 Interviewed on 7 Feb. 1982; 1 hr.; 1 tape; English; by A. Taverna. Provides family and community history in Copper Cliff, Ont., in the early 1900s.

YOUNDER, L.
TORONTO, ONT.
 1 photograph: the Dezorzi family on farm in Vineland, Ont., 1925; the Della Stua family in front of house on Lansdowne Avenue in Toronto, 1917.

ZAFFIRO, F.
HAMILTON, ONT.
 3 Italian Canadian pamphlets: *Lodge Roma*. 1936; programme for Dopolavoro Society festival. 1938; and souvenir booklet of Sons of Italy Temple opening, 1932. 1 reel of microfilm.

ZANATTA, AMABILE
SUDBURY, ONT.
 Interviewed on 9 July 1984; .75 hr.; 1 tape; Italian; by D. Visentin. Arrived in Canada in 1925.

ZANINI, RENZO
TORONTO, ONT.
 2 immigration identification cards and 2 Italian passports, 1949, 1951; family certificate, 1950; 2 income tax returns, 1950-51; and a letter to R. Zanini. Photograph. Taped interview.
 1 photograph: a group of Italian passengers on the ship *Conte Biancamano* en route to Canada, 1951.
 Interviewed on 4 Aug. 1977; 1 hr.; 1 tape; English; by J. Zucchi. Arrived in Canada in 1949, worked as a bricklayer, and later for a sub—contracting construction firm.

ZAVAGNO, VITTORIO
TORONTO, ONT.
 Italian passport, 1946; immigration
identity card, 1951; landing card,
n.d.; and international certificate of
vaccination, 1951. 1 cm. Photographs. Taped interview.
 13 photographs: Zavagno's bakery,
his delivery trucks; and his family,
1956-69.
 Interviewed on 7 July 1977; 1.25
hrs.; 2 tapes; English; by J. Zucchi.
Immigrated to Canada in the 1950s.

ZORZZI, JOSEPH
SUDBURY, ONT.
 Interviewed on 18 July 1984; .75
hr.; 1 tape; Italian; by D. Visentin.
Arrived in Canada in 1950.

ZUCCHI, JOHN
TORONTO, ONT.
 Handwritten note on Loggia Galileo
Galilei, 1938. .25 cm. Photographs.
 4 photographs: Italian navvies on
C.N. Railway line in Kamloops,
British Columbia, 1911, and musi-
cians, 1921.
 Settimana italiana di Ottawa '77.
Ottawa, 1977. Booklet. 33 pp.

ZULIANI, GIUSEPPE
THUNDER BAY, ONT.
 Interviewed on 2 Nov. 1978; 1 hr.;
1 tape; Italian; by A. Pucci. Immigrated to Canada in 1911.

———————————

CATHEDRAL BOYS HIGH SCHOOL
HAMILTON, ONT.
 2 photographs: Cardinal Sincero at
school opening, c. 1940s.

COMPAGNIA DEI GIOVANI (THEATRE
YOUTH COMPANY)
TORONTO, ONT.
 24 photographs: theatrical productions, n.d.

COSTI (CENTRO ORGANIZZATIVO
SCUOLE TECNICHE ITALIANE)
TORONTO, ONT.
 First established in 1961 as an
English-language school and vocational training centre for newly
arrived Italian immigrants. By the
1970s COSTI was assisting newcomers from many other sending
countries. The collection contains
applicants' files, class lists, minutes
of meetings, financial and adminis-
trative records, and correspondence.
It includes scattered issues of *Il Ponte*
and *Il Notizario*, and items about the
aims and purpose of COSTI,
1961-74. 20 meters.
RESTRICTED

DANTE ALIGHIERI SOCIETY
TORONTO, ONT.
 Statute, n.d.; minutes, 1970-78; list
of members, n.d.; correspondence,
n.d.; reports, announcements, bur-
saries and cultural exchanges,
1971-78; printed matter, and a
scrapbook of newsclippings. 2 reels
of microfilm.

DOFASCO NEWS
HAMILTON, ONT.
 16 photographs: Italian workers at
Dofasco plant, 1940-45.

FACI (FEDERAZIONE DELLE
ASSOCIAZIONI E CLUB
ITALO-CANADESI)
TORONTO, ONT.
 Records, 1971-78, include statute,

minutes, reports, and correspondence. 1 reel of microfilm.

ITALIAN CANADIAN BENEVOLENT CORPORATION (GIANNI A. GROHOVAZ)
TORONTO, ONT.
ICBC report to donors, 1975; flyers, newsletter and concert programmes from Villa Colombo, 1977; and newsletter from the Italo-Canadian Club Toronto, 1975. Also, financial statements and reports, interview transcripts and miscellaneous clippings, 1975-85. 20 cm. Photographs. Taped interviews with over 150 founders and promoters of the ICBC.
The interviews were conducted by Mr. Gianni Grohovaz in 1984 through 1985. **RESTRICTED*
Grohovaz, Gianni A. *"...e con rispetto parlando é al microfono Gianni Grohovaz"*. Toronto: Sono Me, 1983.
_____. *Per ricordar le cose che ricordo*. Toronto: Dufferin Press, 1976.
_____. *Strada Bianca*. Toronto: Sono Me, 1989. Book of poems.

ITALIAN CANADIAN CLUB
GUELPH, ONT.
Constitution and by-laws, 1952, minutes, 1961-70, aims and objectives of Club. 3 cm. Taped interview.

ITALIAN IMMIGRANT AID SOCIETY
TORONTO, ONT.
First founded in 1951, the IIAS played a leading role in assisting needy and newly arrived Italian immigrants of the post-WWII period. IIAS records include Society's incorporation and by-laws, 1956; minutes of committee and general meetings, 1956-58, 1959, 1966; correspon-

dence, 1961; financial statements, 1955-65; and annual reports, 1962-68, COSTI (Centro Organizzativo Scuole Tecniche Italiane) statistical records, 1961-64; minutes of House of Commons proceedings on immigration, 1958; and scrapbook of photographs, pamphlets, telegrams, invitations, menu, newsclippings. Women's Auxiliary of the IIAS: minutes of general and executive meetings, 1961-64, 1965; correspondence, 1962-64; financial records and report, 1955-64; executive and membership lists, 1955-62, 1964-65. 3 reels of microfilm.

LA COMPAGNIA DEI GIOVANI
TORONTO, ONT.
Correspondence, minutes, financial statements, programmes, and announcements, 1972-78. 1 reel of microfilm.

MULTICULTURAL HISTORY SOCIETY OF ONTARIO
TORONTO, ONT.
4 photographs from *Hamilton Spectator,* Hamilton, Ont.: men of St. Anthony of Padua, 1912; Sartorio's Band, n.d.; and the building of the Rocamutese Society, 1935.
4 photographs: Italian grocery store and its delivery trucks in Toronto, 1977.
Consular reports of Italian Fascist government in Canada. c. 1936-45. 3 reels of microfilm.
Bolletino dell'emigrazione. Italian Ministry of Foreign Affairs: Rome, 1902-27. The bulletin is one of the most important sources of information on Italian immigration around the world. It includes articles and monographs written by consular officials, special investigators, and others. In

addition to immigration statistics and laws, it provides data on working and living conditions in receiving societies, and on their respective Italian communities. Finally, it documents the debate on immigration that occurred within Italy. 15 reels of microfilm.

Newspapers:

Attenzione. New York. Dec. 1977 - May 1983. Incomplete. 6 cm.

Comunitá viva. Toronto. May 1973 - Dec. 1989. 15 cm.

Il Congresso. 1977-78. District bulletin of the National Congress of Italian Canadians. .5 cm.

Emigrato. Vol. 2, no. 5. Toronto, 30 March 1932. 1 reel of microfilm.

Famiglia italiana. 1978 (3 issues).

La Gazzetta. Windsor, 14 Jan. 1983-12 Dec. 1986. 1 reel of microfilm.

Il Giornale di Toronto. Toronto, 10 Feb. 1967 - 26 Dec. 1975; 2 Jan. 1976 - 5 Oct. 1979 (weekly). 13 reels of microfilm.

Il Laghetto. Toronto (198 issues) Incomplete. 3 cm.

Il Lavoratore. Toronto, 19 March 1936 - 17 Sept. 1938. 1 reel of microfilm.

Insieme. Montreal, July 1984 - June 1989. 10 reels of microfilm.

Progresso Italo-Canadese. Toronto, 21 Dec. 1929 - 22 Oct. 1931. Incomplete. 1 reel of microfilm.

Rossato. Italy, 1972. Scattered issues. 3 cm.

Mosaico. Toronto, 1975-76. Incomplete. 7 cm.

La Vittoria. Toronto, 18 April 1942 - 16 Oct. 1943. 1 reel of microfilm.

La Voce. Toronto, 1973. Scattered issues. 2 cm.

La Voce degli Italo-Canadesi. Toronto, 1 Oct. 1938 - 30 April 1940 (weekly). 1 reel of microfilm.

Monographs:

Campanella, Mary, ed. *Symposium '77: On the economic, social and cultural conditions of the Italian Canadian in the Hamilton-Wentworth region*. Hamilton: The Italian Canadian Federation of Hamilton, 1977. 70 pp.

Conte, V.R. *Raccolta di poesie*. Toronto, 1977. Booklet of poems.

Dobrzensky, Leopolda L. *They Worked and Prayed Together: Italians in Haliburton County*. Haliburton, Ont., 1988. 53 pp.

Grohovaz, G.A., ed. *Famee Furlane: The First Half Century, 1932-1982*. Toronto: Town Press, 1982.

Grohovaz, G.A., ed. *To Friuli, from Canada with Love*. Ottawa: Foundation of the National Congress of Italian Canadians, 1983.

Souvenir Booklets and Programmes:

Chiaroscuro. Toronto: La Voce Publishing., 1978.

Riganelli, Co. ed. *Club Roma: 25 Years of Dedication to the Community, 1961-1986*. Toronto: Webcom Ltd., 1987.

Coro Santa Cecilia: 25 Years of Italian Voices in Canada, 1961-86. Toronto: Toma Publishing Inc., 1986.

Italian Festival of the 12th Annual Caruso Club. Sudbury, 1984. 65 pp.

La Nostra Storia, 1938-88. Toronto: Societá Femminile Friulana, 1988. 218 pp.

MULTICULTURAL NEWSPAPER MICROFILM PROJECT TORONTO, ONT.

Domenica. Toronto, 1 Dec. 1968 - 7 Sept. 1969. 1 reel of microfilm.

Forze Nuove. Toronto, Sept. 1972 - Jan. 1977. 1 reel of microfilm.

Messaggero Oratinese. Port Colborne, Ont., Oct. 1977 - Dec. 1987. 1 reel of microfilm.
L'Ora di Ottawa. Ottawa, 14 July 1980 - 14 Dec. 1987. 8 reels of microfilm.
Panorama. Toronto, 4 Nov. 1955 - 24 May 1957. 1 reel of microfilm.
La Settimana. Toronto, 10 March 1975 - 14 Jan. 1977. 1 reel of microfilm.
Il Sole. Toronto, 21 June 1969 - 20 May 1972. 4 reels of microfilm.
Lo Specchio. Toronto. Aug. 1984 - 20 Nov. 1987. 1 reel of microfilm.
Il Tevere. Toronto, 30 Dec. 1972 - 3 Oct. 1985. 12 reels of microfilm.

NATIONAL CONGRESS OF ITALIAN CANADIANS
TORONTO, ONT.
 Minutes, memos, and objectives, 1972-78. 1 reel of microfilm.

ONTARIO MULTICULTURAL THEATRE ASSOCIATION
TORONTO, ONT.
 Minutes, correspondence, financial statements, members lists, brochures, and announcements, 1971-78. 2 reels of microfilm.

PISTICCI CLUB
TORONTO, ONT.
 Records, 1964-79, comprise statute, minutes, correspondence, and misccellaneous printed items including newsclippings; regarding the Pisticci Youth Club. 5 cm, 1 reel of microfilm. Taped interview with Rocco Lofranco. See Donald di Giulio.

SOCIETÁ CARUSO
SUDBURY, ONT.
 The collection consists of minutes of general and Board of Directors' meet-ings, 1967-75; 24 letters concerning Flood Relief for Italy, 1951-52; 36 letters concerning Club business, 1971-78; and a scrapbook containing constitutions, members lists, bulletins, letters, advertisements, newsclippings, 1947-81. Ladies' Auxiliary of the Societá Caruso: 4 general membership meetings, 1948-63; 1 file of publicity correspondence, 1962-69; 1 book of membership dues, 1950-57; 1 roll book of executive, 1966-73; and 2 scrapbooks of newsclippings, photographs, membership list, and bulletins, 1948-81. 3 reels of microfilm. Photograph.
 1 photograph: the first executive representing Cristoforo Colombo and his crew, in costume, 1948; 1 film of 1975 Caruso Club Italian Festival.

SOCIETÁ ITALIANA DI BENEVOLENZA FORT WILLIAM (THUNDER BAY), ONT.
 The Italian Benevolent Society of Fort William was first established in 1909 in Fort William's "East End." Records include regulation booklet of Italian Benevolent Society, and constitution of female section of Society, n.d.; minute book with ledger entries, 1908-43; membership books including minutes, 1909-27, 1933-39; sick benefit forms of the Society, 1926, 1928; and scrapbook with membership and ledger entries, 1933-37. 2 reels of microfilm.

SOCIETÁ ITALIANA DI BENEVOLENZA "PRINCIPE DI PIEDMONTE"
THUNDER BAY, ONT.
 Minutes, 1944-61. 1 reel of microfilm. See the Societa' Italiana di Benevolenza, Fort William.

SOCIETÁ ITALIANA DI COPPER CLIFF
COPPER CLIFF, ONT.
 Records, 1934-76, comprise minutes,
financial ledger, membership dues
lists, and material from the female
members of the Society. 6 reels of
microfilm. Photographs.
 43 photographs: Club activities, (theatre, sports, social gatherings) and
buildings, 1948-63. Included are 4
films, n.d.

SOCIETÁ ITALO-CANADESE
TORONTO, ONT.
 1 photograph: the Societá
Italo-Canadesse Band, c. 1910s.

ST. ANTHONY OF PADUA CHURCH
HAMILTON, ONT.
 Correspondence, 1948-49; financial
statements of St. Anthony Building
Fund, 1948-54; church bulletins,
1951, 1960; married couples club
rules, 1947; and newsclippings, 1966.
In addition, notebook of minutes and
letters concerning arrangements for
spring and fall festival dances,
1955-65; statements of expenses for
dances, 1955-65; notebooks of various committees, 1962-71; and members lists, 1973-74. 2 reels of microfilm. Taped interviews with L.
Pacecca and A. Julian. See J. Julian.

ST. ANTHONY'S ROMAN CATHOLIC
CHURCH
THUNDER BAY, ONT.
 Bulletins. 1952-76. 4 reels of micro-
film.

JAPANESE COLLECTION

AMEMORI, MITSUO
TORONTO, ONT.
 Interviewed on 23, 24 June 1982;
4.5 hrs.; 5 tapes; Japanese; by M.
Koizumi. Arrived in Canada in 1912.

FUJITA, MACHI
BEAMSVILLE, ONT.
 Interviewed on 12 April, 10 May
1980; 5.5 hrs.; 6 tapes; Japanese; by
Tomoko Makabe. Immigrated to
Canada in 1913.

FUJIWARA, MITSUMORI
TORONTO, ONT.
 Interviewed on 27 Jan. 1978; 3 hrs.;
3 tapes; English; by G. Shikatani.
Donor's parents arrived in Canada at
the turn of the century.

GOTO, TERUJI
TORONTO, ONT.
 Interviewed on 19 Feb. 1978; 1.5
hrs.; 2 tapes; English; by G.
Shikatani. Discusses history of Japan-
ese Buddhist congregation in Toronto.

HIRAMATSU, TOYOSHI
TORONTO, ONT.
 Interviewed on 4 Nov. 1977; 1.75
hrs.; 2 tapes; English; by G.
Shikatani.
 Worked in lumber mill in British
Columbia, interned during WWII,
migrated to Ont.
 Hiramatsu, Toyoshi. "Biography of
Yasutaro Yamaga." 1977. 4 pp.

IMAI, REV. PAUL
TORONTO, ONT.
 Interviewed on 16 Feb. 1978; 1.5
hrs.; 2 tapes; English; by G.
Shikatani. Arrived in Toronto in
1953.

IROMOTO, NOBUO
TORONTO, ONT.
 Interviewed on 8 Aug. 1981; 1 hr.; 1
tape; English; by Jung Kim. Editor of
Nikka Times.
 Nikka Times. Vol. 1, no. 1, 17 Oct.
1979 - 7 Aug. 1981. 1 reel of micro-
film.

ISHIKAWA, SHOZO
TORONTO, ONT.
 Interviewed on 17 May 1982; 2.5
hrs.; 3 tapes; Japanese; by Shinichiro
Kawai. Arrived in British Columbia
in 1935, moved to Toronto in 1949.

IWASAKI, YORIKI
TORONTO, ONT.
 Interviewed on 12 Oct. 1977; 1 hr.;
1 tape; English; by G. Shikatani.
Arrived in Vancouver, British Columbia in the 1920s, moved to Toronto in
1946.

KADONAGA, KO
TORONTO, ONT.
 Interviewed on 27 Feb., 22 April
1980; 7 hrs.; 7 tapes; Japanese; by
Tomoko Makabe. She immigrated to
Canada in 1919.

KAJIOKA, TERUKO
TORONTO, ONT.
Interviewed on 23 Aug. 1977; 1.75 hrs.; 2 tapes; English/Japanese; by G. Shikatani. Moved from British Columbia to Toronto in 1925.

KASHIMA, FRANK K.
TORONTO, ONT.
Interviewed on 10 April 1978; 1.75 hrs.; 2 tapes; English; by G. Shikatani. Moved from British Columbia to Ont. after WWII.

KASHIMA, FRANK K.
TORONTO, ONT.
Interviewed on 28 May 1982; 3.5 hrs.; 4 tapes; Japanese; by S. Kawai. Arrived in British Columbia in 1931, moved to Ont. in 1947.

KIMURA, MASUITSU
TORONTO, ONT.
Interviewed on 17 Nov. 1977; 2 hrs.; 2 tapes; Japanese; by G. Shikatani. Worked in British Columbia, interned during WWII. Travelled extensively through British Columbia and Ont.

KIMURA, YOSHIKAZU
TORONTO, ONT.
7 photographs: the Kimura family, in British Columbia, 1918-20; and internment of Japanese Canadians, Angler, 1942-45. Taped interview.
Interviewed on 20, 25 Oct. 1977; 3 hrs.; 3 tapes; English; by G. Shikatani. Discusses extreme prejudice toward Japanese during the 1920s, internment in WWII, and migration to Toronto the after war.

KITAGAWA, MURIEL
TORONTO, ONT.
Collection of documents from Nisei Affairs 1946; the National Japanese Canadian Citizens' Association, 1924-58; the Canadian Japanese Association 1940; the Japanese Catholic Church, 1954-64; the Co-operative Committee on Japanese Canadians, 1946; and the National Citizenship Seminar, 1952-58. Collection also includes Kitagawa's personal papers and scrapbook, 1933-72. 2 reels of microfilm. Photographs.
44 photographs: Kitagawa and Fujiwara families; Japanese localities in Vancouver, 1900-44; Japanese Public School, 1929; sports organizations such as a tennis club, a rugby team, and the Asahi Baseball Team, 1915-30.
Kitagawa, Muriel. *Go East!* n.d. 27 pp. Microfilm.
_____. *Baiting the Bull.* n.d. 4 pp. Microfilm.
Bulletin. 1949. National Canadian Citizens' Association. 62 pp.
Citizen. n.d. 33 pp. Microfilm.
Lumen. 1955-58. Japanese Catholic Church. 86 pp. Microfilm.
The New Age. 1932-33. 48 pp. Microfilm.

KITAMURA, TAKAAKI
TORONTO, ONT.
Interviewed on 26 May 1982; 5.5 hrs.; 6 tapes; Japanese; by Maya Koizumi. Worked in British Columbia, interned during WWII, migrated to Ont. in the 1940s.

KONDO, DENSAKU
TORONTO, ONT.
Interviewed on 8 Feb. 1979;

1.5 hrs.; 2 tapes; English; by G. Shikatani. Discusses his career as an artist.

KUMANO, HARRY
TORONTO, ONT.
Interviewed on 7 May 1982; 2 hrs.; 2 tapes; Japanese; by S. Kawai. Born in Vancouver in 1907.

MAYEDA, KAZUYE AND TSUKANE
TORONTO, ONT.
164 photographs: Japanese-Canadian families; Japanese Canadians while interned during WWII; employment, schools, and religious events in British Columbia and Ont., 1920-1950. Taped interview.
Interviewed on 19 Jan. 1978; 2.25 hrs.; 3 tapes; English; by G. Shikatani. Discusses turn of the century immigration, work in British Columbia, WWII evacuation and internment, and migration to Ont. in 1946.
Mayeda, Harold. *My Life Is Message: The Akagawa Story*. 1972. 350 pp.

NAKAJIMA, REV. TAKEO
TORONTO, ONT.
Interviewed on 26 Aug. 1977; 1 hr.; 1 tape; English; by G. Shikatani. Discusses occupation as Methodist minister.

NAKAMICHI, SEIICHIRO
TORONTO, ONT.
Interviewed on 20 May 1982; 2 hrs.; 2 tapes; Japanese; by S. Kawai. Immigrated to British Columbia with father in early 1920s, moved to Toronto in 1947.

NAKASHIMA, TSUTAYO
KINGSVILLE, ONT.
Interviewed on 23, 24 May, 20, 21 June 1980; 4.5 hrs.; 5 tapes; Japanese; by T. Makabe. Immigrated to British Columbia in 1916, was evacuated and interned in 1942, moved to Leamington, Ont. in 1953.

NOBUOKA, RYOTARO
TORONTO, ONT.
Notebook of memoirs, 1940s, and documents, 1930s. 1 cm. Photographs. Taped interview.
12 photographs: the Nobuoka family, 1916-73; Japanese Language School in Vancouver, 1937; and the Japanese-Canadian Citizens' Association in Toronto, 1952-62.
Interviewed on 7 Dec. 1977; 2 hrs.; 2 tapes; English; by G. Shikatani. Immigrated to British Columbia in the early 1920s, was interned during WWII, and later moved to Toronto.

OGAKI, MAKI
TORONTO, ONT.
Interviewed on 5, 20 Feb. 1980; 2 hrs.; 2 tapes; Japanese; by T. Makabe. She arrived in British Columbia in 1915.

OHTAKE, FRANK
TORONTO, ONT.
3 registration cards from WWII, 1942; and a licence to acquire property for Japanese in Canada. Taped interview.
Interviewed on 7 Jan. 1978; 3 hrs.; 3 tapes; English; by G. Shikatani. Migrated to Alberta in 1923, was displaced and interned in WWII, and moved to Toronto after the war.

OHTAKE, MIYOKO
TORONTO, ONT.
9 photographs: internment of Japanese Canadians; and Tashme Re-location Camp in British Columbia, 1942-43.

OKADA, KAYO
TORONTO, ONT.
Interviewed on 28, 29, 30 June 1982; 6.5 hrs.; 7 tapes; Japanese; by M. Koizumi. Moved to Toronto from British Columbia in the early 1950s.

OKIHIRO, KOICHIRO
TORONTO, ONT.
Interviewed on 27 May 1982; 5.5 hrs.; 6 tapes; Japanese; by Maya Koizumi. Arrived in British Columbia in 1926, moved to Toronto in 1944, after internment.

OKIHIRO, KOICHIRO
TORONTO, ONT.
Scrapbook, personal diary, and correspondence, report from a New Westminister Committee on wartime evacuation, inventories of personal properties, and miscellaneous items, 1942. 1 reel of microfilm. Photograph. Taped interview.
1 photograph: the Okihiro family, n.d.
Interviewed on 25 April 1978; 2.25 hrs.; 3 tapes; English; by G. Shikatani. Discusses workplace discrimination, and internment in WWII.

SASAKI, MIDORI AND SHUICHI
TORONTO, ONT.
Interviewed on 19 April 1978; 1.75 hrs.; 2 tapes; English/Japanese; by G. Shikatani. Arrived in British Columbia immediately after the anti-Oriental riot of 1907.

SASAKI, TAKI
TORONTO, ONT.
Interviewed on 24 March, 2 May 1980; 5 hrs.; 5 tapes; Japanese; by T. Makabe. She arrived in Canada in 1919.

SHIBUYA, HARRY KIYOSHI
TORONTO, ONT.
Interviewed on 9 Jan. 1978; 1.75 hrs.; 2 tapes; English; by G. Shikatani. Donor's father arrived in 1906, was evacuated and interned during WWII, and later moved to Toronto in 1947.

SHIMIZU, HIDE
TORONTO, ONT.
British Columbia Security Commission card, 1942. .25 cm. Photographs. Taped interview.
103 photographs: the family; internment and re-location camps, schools in British Columbia, 1943-50; and religious activity at the Japanese United Church in Toronto, 1950-73.
Interviewed on 5 Oct. 1977, 22 Jan. 1979; 5 hrs.; 5 tapes; English; by G. Shikatani. Donor's father arrived at the turn of century, was displaced during WWII, settled in Toronto immediately after the war.
McFadden, Isobel. *The Man Who Knew the Difference*. 1965. 46 pp.

TAKAHASHI, KOH
TORONTO, ONT.
1 photograph: Koh Takahashi in Japan, 1927; and Japanese Canadians at farewell party, Church of the Nations in Toronto, 1935. Taped interview.
Interviewed on 2 June 1978; 1.25 hrs.; 2 tapes; English; by G. Shikatani. Arrived in Toronto in the early 1920s.

TAKATA, KENSUKE AND TOYO
TORONTO, ONT.
Interviewed on 12 Dec. 1977; 2.25 hrs.; 3 tapes; English/Japanese; by G. Shikatani. Immigrated in 1910s, worked in British Columbia, was displaced during WWII, moved to Toronto immediately after the war.

TAKEMURA, UME
TORONTO, ONT.
Interviewed on 12 Feb., 5 April 1980; 5 hrs.; 5 tapes; Japanese; by T. Makabe. Arrived in British Columbia in 1918, was displaced in 1942, settled in Toronto after WWII.

TANAKA, GEORGE
MISSISSAUGA, ONT.
Interviewed on 12 Oct. 1977; 3 hrs.; 3 tapes; English; by G. Shikatani. Discusses early life in Vancouver, internment, and incidents of discrimination in British Columbia and Ont. A founding member of the Japanese Canadian Citizens' Association.

TANAKA, GEORGE
TORONTO, ONT.
Interviewed on 17 May 1978; 2.25 hrs.; 3 tapes; English; by G. Shikatani. Involved in the founding of the Japanese Canadian Citizens' Association in 1940.

TANAKA, YAYE
TORONTO, ONT.
Interviewed on 24 March 2 May 1980; 5 hrs.; 5 tapes; Japanese; by T. Makabe. Arrived in Canada as a "picture bride" in 1911.

UMEHARA, HANA
KING CITY, ONT.
30 photographs: dwellings, including a Japanese teahouse and garden belonging to the Umehara family in Japan Temperanceville, 1906-80. Taped interview.
Interviewed on 19 Oct. 1977; 1.25 hrs.; 2 tapes; English; by G. Shikatani. Arrived in Canada as a Methodist missionary.

UMEZUKI, CHIYO
TORONTO, ONT.
Interviewed on 5 March 1979; 3 hrs.; 3 tapes; English; by G. Shikatani. Discusses early life in British Columbia, evacuation and internment, and the move to Montreal, Quebec, and Toronto.

UMEZUKI, TAKAICHI
TORONTO, ONT.
Personal papers, 1930-77. 1 cm (8 items). Taped interview.
Interviewed on 4 Feb. 1978; 2.5 hrs.; 3 tapes; English/Japanese; by G. Shikatani.

WATANABE, SUMIYE
TORONTO, ONT.
Interviewed on 23 Nov. 1977; 1.5 hrs.; 2 tapes; English/Japanese; by G. Shikatani. Discusses WWII internment and move to Toronto after the war.

YOKOTA, REV. STANLEY
TORONTO, ONT.
Interviewed on 27 Jun 1978; 1.5 hrs.; 2 tapes; English; by G. Shikatani. Discusses history of the Canadian Japanese Mission.

YOSHIDA, HIDEO
TORONTO, ONT.
Recorded in 1978; .5 hr.; 1 tape; English. Teenage group in Sunday Dharma (Buddhist) class.

YOSHIDA, TAKEO
TORONTO, ONT.
25 prisoner-of-war postcards from
Japanese-Canadian inmates of intern-
ment camps in Ont., 1943. .5 cm.
Taped interview.
Interviewed on 6 June 1978; 2.5
hrs.; 3 tapes; English; by G.
Shikatani. Discusses early life in
British Columbia, WWII internment,
and move to Toronto after the war.

CANADIAN JAPANESE MISSION
TORONTO, ONT.
Records, 1959-70, which include a
financial account book, minutes,
retreat files, and a constitution of the
Nisei Gospel Church. 1 reel of micro-
film. Taped interview with Rev. S.
Yokota (q.v.).

JAPANESE-CANADIAN CENTENNIAL
SOCIETY
TORONTO, ONT.
Pamphlet collection, press releases,
calendars, and posters, 1977. 1 cm.

JAPANESE GOSPEL CHURCH
TORONTO, ONT.
Records, 1959-74, which include a
constitution, correspondence, minutes
and financial statements, 1959-74,
and a collection of church service
programmes, 1969-75. 1 reel of
microfilm. Photographs. Taped interview with Rev. S. Yokota.
2 photographs: religious life at the
Japanese Gospel Church, 1959-73.
*The Canadian Japanese Mission
Courier.* 1966-77. Scattered issues.
Microfilm.
*A Historical Sketch of the Canadian
Japanese Mission, 1942-78.* Booklet.
56 pp.

MULTICULTURAL HISTORY SOCIETY
OF ONTARIO
TORONTO, ONT.
Canada Times. Toronto, 2 April
1982 - 19 Dec. 1987. 13 reels of
microfilm.
Continental Times. 3 Dec. 1948 - 30
March 1982. 35 reels of microfilm.
The New Canadians. Jan. 1939 -
Jan. 1985. 47 reels of microfilm.
Nisei Affairs. July 1945 - June 1947.
1 reel of microfilm.

NIPPONIA HOME
BEAMSVILLE, ONT.
Twenty-One Years of Service. 1980.
Anniversary booklet. 75 pp.

ST. ANDREW'S JAPANESE CON-
GREGATION
TORONTO, ONT.
Annual reports and programmes,
1975-78. 2 cm. Photographs. Taped
interview with Rev. K. Imai (q.v.).
RESTRICTED
6 photographs: church life at St.
Andrew's Japanese Congregation in
Toronto, 1969-77.

TORONTO BUDDHIST CHURCH
TORONTO, ONT.
Minutes, c. 1950, certificate of
incorporation for Credit Union, 1951,
and miscellaneous items. 1 cm. Taped
interview with T. Goto (q.v.) and
other church members.
Interviewed on 5 Feb. 1978; 1.5
hrs.; 2 tapes; English; by G.
Shikatani. Discussion with various
members.
With Amida's Guidance We Build.
1954. 20 pp.
In Gassho, We Support. 1958. 12
pp.

TORONTO JAPANESE UNITED CHURCH
RECORDS
TORONTO, ONT.
 Collection includes minutes, correspondence, financial records, and
parish registers, 1951-71. 1 reel of
microfilm.

JEWISH COLLECTION

ABRAMOVITZ, ALBERT
TORONTO, ONT.
 Pamphlet collection, including publications by the following: Communist Party of Canada, Labour Progressive Party of Canada, Canadian Labour Defense League, Canadian League Against War and Fascism, "Der Kampf," "Morning Freiheit" (U.S.), United Jewish People's Order, and All Canadian Congress of Labour. 1920-59. 1 reel of microfilm. 2 cm. Photographs.
 3 photographs: Jewish involvement in labour unions such as the Amalgamated Clothing Workers of America, and the All Canadian Congress of Labour, 1940.

ABRAMS, GOLDA
TORONTO, ONT.
 5 photographs: activities of the Toronto Jewish Folk Choir, and the Montreal Jewish Choir, 1953-55.

ADLER, HILDA AND LOU
TORONTO, ONT.
 Theatre and concert programmes, and souvenir booklets, 1936-59. Photographs.
 12 photographs: grocery store, 1923-24; activities of the United Jewish People's Order, 1950-56; religious life as represented by the graduating class of the Brunswick Talmud Torah in Toronto, 1932.

ADLER KAGAN, ANNE
TORONTO, ONT.
 Issues of *Der Jiddisher Journal* (The Daily Hebrew Journal), 1960-62, each containing articles by Yossel Adler. 4 cm (29 issues).

ALLEN, GURSTON
TORONTO, ONT.
 Allen family papers, 1921-53, consist of scrapbooks, clippings, letters, and booklets. 6 cm. Photographs.
 81 photographs: the Allen, Fauman, and Birnbaum families in Pennsylvania, Brantford, Cobourg, and Toronto, 1890-1963; business enterprise (a theatre) in Brantford, and Kitchener, 1907-52; members of the Allen family during military service at Camp Borden, Toronto, 1939-44; dwelling of the Allen family in Cobourg, 1915; and members of the fraternity, Pi Lambda Phi, 1926-34.

AMZALAG, HANNAH
TORONTO, ONT.
 Interviewed on 27 Oct. 1977; 2 hrs.; 2 tapes; French/English; by Raphael Bendahan. Discusses Jewish life in Mogador, Morocco.

ANDREWS, D. (Y.M.H.A., NORTHERN BRANCH)
TORONTO, ONT.
 Programme and brochure advertising Jewish Book Fair, 1977. .5 cm.

ARNOLD, ORO
TORONTO, ONT.
 Interviewed on 5 Oct. 1977; 1 hr.; 1 tape; English; by Raphael Bendahan.

ARTHURS, ELLEN
TORONTO, ONT.
Dorothy Dworkin papers consist of correspondence, 1909-28, souvenir booklets, and paper items, n.d. The collection also contains miscellaneous books on North American Jewry, which were donated by Ellen Arthurs, daughter of D. Dworkin. 1 reel of microfilm. .3 meters. Photographs.
36 photographs: the Dworkin family in Toronto, and Montreal, 1910-70; activities of organizations such as the Workmen's Circle, Women's Auxiliary of the Mount Sinai Hospital, and the Jewish Labour Committee, 1910-57.
50th Anniversary of the Jewish Daily Forward. New York, 1947.
Forty Years Workmen's Circle: A History in Pictures. New York, 1940, in English/Yiddish.
Silver Jubilee of the Toronto Cloakmakers Union, I.L.G.W.U. 1911-36, in English/Yiddish.
Twentieth Anniversary Reunion of the 1910 Cloakmakers General Strike. New York, 1930, in English/Yiddish.

BACH, JEAN
TORONTO, ONT.
Interviewed on 20 July 1977; .5 hr.; 1 tape; English; by Gitta Wallen. Arrived in Canada in 1954.

BALMEA, LORE
TORONTO, ONT.
Interviewed on 12 July 1977; .5 hr.; 1 tape; English; by Gitta Wallen. Immigrated to Canada in 1939.

BASKIN, RABBI BERNARD
HAMILTON, ONT.
Interviewed on 7 Dec. 1977; 1 hr.;

1 tape; English; by Sheldon Levitt. Discusses the congregation and community activities.

BASMAN, BASHE
TORONTO, ONT.
The Label Basman collection consists of personal documents and correspondence (mostly from Lithuania) 1920-32; speeches, greetings, and eulogies by Label Basman, 1940-75; plays by Label Basman, 1937-70; educational and related material from the Sholem Aleichem School in Winnipeg, I. L. Peretz School in Vancouver and the Morris Winchevsky School in Toronto; and an assortment of printed items from the Labour League and its successor, the United Jewish People's Order, 1930-76. .3 meters. Photographs.
15 photographs: Label Basman with friends, and colleagues in Toronto, Winnipeg, and Montreal, 1922-70, includes Jewish-Canadian schools.

BAUER, WERNER
OTTAWA, ONT.
Immigration papers, including Palestine passport, 1940s. .25 cm (10 items). Taped interview.
Interviewed on 17 Aug. 1977; 2.5 hrs.; 3 tapes; English; by Zvia Schwartz. Post-WWII immigrant.

BENAIM, JACQUE AND MARCELLE
TORONTO, ONT.
Interviewed on 16 Oct. 1977; 1.75 hrs.; 2 tapes; English/French by Raphael and Sydney Bendahan. Discusses cultural differences between Canadian, and Moroccan way of life.

BENCHETRIT, ALBERT
TORONTO, ONT.
Interviewed on 1 Nov. 1977; 2 hrs.;

2 tapes; French/Spanish; by Raphael and Sydney Bendahan.

BENDAHAN, SYDNEY AND MIRIAM
TORONTO, ONT.
Interviewed on 21 Aug. 1977; 2 hrs.; 2 tapes; English; by Raphael Bendahan. Compares attitudes toward Jews in Gibraltar, and Canada.

BENDAHAN, SYDNEY
TORONTO, ONT.
The diaspora of North African Jews in Canada is thoroughly documented in this wide-ranging collection which encompasses numerous Sephardic institutions and organizations in the cities of Toronto, Montreal, and Ottawa/Hull. Included are Sydney Bendahan's personal papers, 1945-74, consisting largely of letters, speeches, certificates, and identification cards; clippings pertaining to the Farband Labour Zionist Order, 1963-71; records of the Magen David Sephardic Congregation, 1958-75; correspondence, minutes and reports of the Jewish Immigrant Aid Services of Canada, 1966-73; miscellaneous papers of the Canadian Sephardic Federation and B'nai B'rith Lodge, 1965-74; and general clippings. 1 meter. Photographs. (Finding aid available).
6 photographs: 1940s.
Frontier News. 1971. .5 cm.
JIAS News. March 1969 - Dec. 1970.
The Alliance Review. n.d. .5 cm.
The Jewish Standard. 1973-76. Scattered issues. 2 cm.

BENOLIEL, SARAH
TORONTO, ONT.
Personal papers, n.d. .25 cm. Photographs. Taped interview.

11 photographs: n.d.
Interviewed on 6 Aug. 1977; 2 hrs.; 2 tapes; French/Spanish; by Raphael Bendahan.

BENZACAR, MAURICE
TORONTO, ONT.
Interviewed on 16 Aug. 1977; 1.5 hrs.; 2 tapes; English/Spanish; by Raphael and Sydney Bendahan.

BERMAN, SENTO
TORONTO, ONT.
Interviewed on 22 Feb. 1978; 1.5 hrs.; 2 tapes; English; by Beverly Stern. Immigrated to Canada in 1921.

BERNSTEIN, BELLA
HALIBURTON, ONT.
Interviewed on 10 Nov. 1977; .75 hr.; 1 tape; English; by Sheldon Levitt. Father arrived in Canada in 1905.

BERNSTEIN, MAX
TORONTO, ONT.
Interviewed on 2, 4 March 1979; 1.5 hr.; 2 tapes; English; by Lisa Weintraub. Personal history with special emphasis on living in Kensington Market in Toronto.

BIDERMAN, DAISY
TORONTO, ONT.
Hart, Arthur D. *The Jews in Canada: A Complete Record of Canadian Jewry from the Days of the French Regime to the Present Time.* Toronto, 1926. 1 reel of microfilm.
Dedication booklet of the Jewish Folklore School Building. 1954. .5 cm. Programme of the Jewish National Workers' Alliance. 18 Dec. 1943. .25 cm.

BIDERMAN, MORRIS
TORONTO, ONT.
 Biderman's report to inner meeting
of Montreal members of the National
Executive of the United Jewish
People's Order, Montreal 1958-59;
and correspondence regarding
U.J.P.O. affairs, 1958-59. .5 cm.
 1 photograph: the Biderman family
in Toronto in the early 1940s.

BIRNBAUM, EDITH AND FRANK
TORONTO, ONT.
 Personal papers, 1920s, and photographs. .5 cm.
 7 photographs: group portrait of the
Jewish National Workers Alliance
(Farband), c. 1920s; the Savlov family in Toronto, 1922; and Hebrew and
public schools in Toronto, 1917-52.

BITTON, SHALON AND EMMA
TORONTO, ONT.
 Interviewed on 12 Oct. 1977; 1.5
hrs.; 2 tapes; Spanish/French; by
Raphael and Sydney Bendahan.

BLAZER, PEARL
TORONTO, ONT.
 Scrapbook of clippings, programmes,
leaflets, and scripts of the New Dance
Theatre (United Jewish People's
Order), c. 1940-60; includes script
"No Time to Cry" (1951) written by
members, which is about struggles
and layoffs in the needle trade in
Toronto. 5 cm. Photographs.
 10 photographs: youth group and
New Dance theatre of the United
Jewish People's Order, 1950; and
Morris Winchevsky School, Toronto
in 1945-50.

BLOOM, MORRIS
TORONTO, ONT.
 Included are records of the

Workmen's Circle, and the Peretz
School, n.d. 1 reel of microfilm. Pho-
tograph. Taped interview.
 1 photograph: Camp Yungvelt of the
Workmen's Circle in Toronto, 1931.
 Interviewed on 13 June 1977; .75
hr.; 1 tape; English; by Karen
Levine. Immigrated to Canada in
1921.
 Jubilee Programme of Branch 670 of
Workmen's Circle. 1944. Microfilm.

BLUMENSTEIN, HERLICH
TORONTO, ONT.
 4 letters from a relative in New
York, 1906-07; and a Holy Blossom
Temple membership card, 1977. .25
cm.

BOCKNEK, HY
TORONTO, ONT.
 12 photographs: sports, mostly basketball and baseball, different teams,
several associated with the Hebrew
Literary and Athletic Club, 1915-26;
Duke School cooking class, 1914; the
Bocknek family in Toronto, 1946-69.
 Third anniversary dinner booklet of
the B'nai B'rith Toronto Chapter,
1917. 25 pp.

BOMGARD, MAX
TORONTO, ONT.
 Interviewed on 23 Feb. 1978; 1.5
hrs.; 2 tapes; English; by Beverly
Stern. Arrived in Canada in the early
1920s.

BRONSTEIN, ROSE
TORONTO, ONT.
 6 left-wing pamphlets, Toronto,
1940s. 3.5 cm. Photograph.
 1 photograph: scene at the United
Jewish People's Order, Camp
Naivelt, 1944.

BULLER, ANNIE
TORONTO, ONT.

Annie Buller-Guralnick, (1896-73) was a founding member of the Communist Party of Canada. She managed the Party newspaper, *The Worker*, from 1925 to 1929. She played a leading role in work with the unemployed, and the Workers' Unity League in the early 1930s, especially as an organizer of the Dressmakers' Union of the W.U.L. Jailed many times during the thirties, she is particularly remembered for her role in the miners' strike in Estevan, Saskatchewan, in 1931. In the 1940s she served as managing editor of the *Canadian Tribune*, and sat on the Central Committee of the C.P.C., while devoting much of her time to speaking and writing on women's issues. Included are scrapbooks and notebooks, 1941-42; speeches, lectures, and articles on women's issues, 1930-1970; C.P.C. documents, 1940-68; and biographical material. 1 reel of microfilm. Photographs.

66 photographs: activists in the Communist Party of Canada in Alberta, Toronto, and Winnipeg, 1920-70; and scenes from a communist-utopian Finnish settlement at Sointula, British Columbia, 1920-30.

BURTON, SUSAN
TORONTO, ONT.

Burton family papers, 1921-42, which include letters, cablegrams, certificates, and clippings. 1 reel of microfilm. Photographs.

83 photographs: members and business enterprise of the Budabin (Burton) family in Romania and Vienna, 1930-39.

BURTON, SUSAN
TORONTO, ONT.

Burton family correspondence, 3 Romanian passports, and other immigration documents, 1939-42. 1 cm. Photographs. Taped interview.

29 photographs: the trade-union movement including activists, and demonstrations, 1915-45. The Industrial Union of Needle Trades Workers, and the United Jewish People's Order figure prominently. Interviewed on 10 June 1977; .5 hr.; 1 tape; English; by Gitta Wallen. Arrived in Canada in 1939.

CHAIKOFF, J.
TORONTO, ONT.

1 photograph: executive members of the Young Socialist Club of Toronto, 1915.

CHUD, HY AND PEARL
TORONTO, ONT.

11 photographs: labour union activities including social events, and sports in Montreal and Toronto, 1931-69. The Workmen's Circle, and the United Jewish People's Order are represented. Also, Jewish Canadians during military service in WWII in England, 1945.

CLAVIR, MARIA
TORONTO, ONT.

Interviewed on 5 June 1977; .5 hr.; 1 tape; English; by Gitta Wallen. Post-WWII immigrant.

COHEN, JACQUES AND ELIANE
TORONTO, ONT.

Interviewed on 23 Nov. 1977; 2.5 hrs.; 3 tapes; French/English; by Raphael and Sydney Hamouth Bendahan.

COHEN, MAX
TORONTO, ONT.
Minute book of Ezras Noshem Society (founding group of Mount Sinai Hospital in Toronto), and 2 pamphlets from the Folks Farein (Jewish retirement home in Toronto), n.d. 2 cm. Photograph.
1 photograph: members of the Ezras Noshem Society in Toronto, 1923.
Cohen, Pauline. *Each Generation Launches a New One.* Anti-Jewish Pro-Nazi newspaper, 1937, Toronto. .25 cm.

COHEN, OSCAR
TORONTO, ONT.
A collection of Nazi and pro-Nazi publications, n.d. 1 reel of microfilm.

CORCOS, SOLY AND DENISE
TORONTO, ONT.
Interviewed on 6 Sept. 1977; 1.5 hrs.; 2 tapes; English/French; by Raphael Bendahan.

COWAN, ELSIE
TORONTO, ONT.
Interviewed on 26 July 1977; .75 hr.; 1 tape; English; by Gitta Wallen. Arrived in Canada in 1939.

DABOUS, M.
SUDBURY, ONT.
5 photographs: 8 newsclippings, mostly of Sam Rothchild's hockey career, 1925-38.

DE PINTO, DENISE AND ROGER
TORONTO, ONT.
Interviewed on 21 Dec. 1977; 2.5 hrs.; 3 tapes; English/French by Raphael Bendahan. Discussed Egyptian life before, and after foundation of the state of Israel, and their immigration experience.

DISENHOUSE, SAM
TORONTO, ONT.
1 photograph: the choir, the Freiheit Gezangs Farein, performing at the Jewish Workers' Cultural Centre in Toronto, 1934.

DOLGOY, MAX
TORONTO, ONT.
Miscellaneous papers from the International Ladies' Garment Workers' Union, including membership book, n.d. 1.5 cm. Photographs.
19 photographs: theatrical production and group of children at the Morris Winchevsky School, 1940-45; and activities at Camp Kinderland and Camp Naivlet of the Labour League, and the United Jewish People's Order in Brampton, and Rouge Hill, 1930-46.

DORDICK, FAGEL
TORONTO, ONT.
Polish certificates, 1922, and a poem written by Lil Illomaki in honour of the 75th birthday of J. Dordick, n.d. .5 cm. Photographs.
6 photographs: members of the Fur and Leather Workers Union, and the Jewish Arts Circle (Labour League), Toronto, 1920-54.

DORN, MYER (SHAAREI SHOMAYIM)
TORONTO, ONT.
Bulletins in honour of the 50th Anniversary of Shaarei Shomayin, 1977-78. .5 cm.

DUCOVE, ROSE
TORONTO, ONT.
Interviewed in 1977; 1 hr.; 1 tape; English; by Barbara Swimmer. Arrived in Canda in 1921.

DUNCAN, MCLAREN
TORONTO, ONT.
 Poster advertising demonstration by
the United Garment Workers, Local
253, to be held in Toronto May 16
1960.

EASSER, SARAH
TORONTO, ONT.
 2 photographs: the Easser and
Feschter families in Toronto, c. 1913;
C.C.F. Discussion-Picnic, Toronto,
1940. Taped interview.
 Interviewed on 6 June 1977; 1.5
hrs.; 1 tape; English; by Karen
Levine. Moved to Toronto in 1909,
early member of Workmen's Circle.

EGIER, ARTHUR
TORONTO, ONT.
 23 photographs: Jewish Canadians,
in particular the Eisenberg, Eiger,
and Turner families in Toronto,
1915-60; and the interior of Goel
Tzedec Synagogue, n.d.

EGIER, NAN
TORONTO, ONT.
 Included are personal papers of the
Egier family; scrapbooks of letters to,
and about Dr. D. A. Turner; miscellaneous papers from Mount Sinai
Hospital, the Holy Blossom Temple,
and the Board of Jewish Education;
biography of Sol Eisen; and an assortment of leaflets programmes, bulletins, and clippings, 1940s-1970s. 15
cm. Photographs.
 12 photographs: Mount Sinai Hospital; and religious life at Minsher
Synagogue in Toronto, c. 1970-80.
 Fields, Rabbi Harvey. *Echoes of
Anguish.* n.d. 35 pp.
 100th Anniversary of Holy Blossom
Temple Bulletin, 1856-1956. 72 pp.
 Canadian Zionist. Nov. 1977 -

April 1978.
 Orah. Hadassah-Wizo, Dec. 1977 -
Jan. 1978, 63 pp.
 Reporter. Hadassah-Wizo, Nov.,
Dec. 1977; March, April 1978. .5
cm.
 Hamilton and District Jewish Tele-
phone Directory. 1975-77. 136 pp.
 Souvenir Booklet of Negev Dinner
for Rabbi W. G. Plaut. 1975. 120 pp.
 Reform Judaism. Jan., Feb. 1978.
.25 cm.

EISENBERG, JOSEPH
TORONTO, ONT.
 Papers relating to Joseph Eisenberg's
work for the Progressive Conserva-
tive Party of Canada, 1956-74. 1 cm.
Photographs.
 2 photographs: Hy Bossin and Joseph
Eisenberg in Toronto, c. 1962-74.
 Jewish Standard. 14 March, 4 April
1974. .25 cm.
 *Yearbook of the Canadian Motion
Picture Industry, 1952-53.* 224 pp.

EISENBERG, SADIE
TORONTO, ONT.
 *50th Anniversary Booklet of Pioneer
Women of Toronto.* 1975. .25 cm.

EISEN, DAVID
TORONTO, ONT.
 Scrapbook of articles by Dr. Eisen, 2
volumes of Eisen diaries, and a list of
doctors practising in Toronto,
1900-56. 1.5 cm. Photographs.
 6 photographs: Jewish-Canadian
members of the medical profession,
including Phi Delta Epsilon at the
University of Toronto, 1926-57.

EISEN, MORTON
TORONTO, ONT.
 Diary and scrapbooks of Solomon
Eisen, 1915-20. 2 reels of microfilm.

EISEN, VERA
TORONTO, ONT.
 Programme of Palmerston Home
Association, 1947. .25 cm. Photographs.
 4 photographs: business enterprise in
the form of theatres, 1916-23; and
religious life in the Holy Blossom
Temple Sisterhood in Toronto,
1957-66.

ENGLANDER, HARRY
TORONTO, ONT.
 1 photograph: the Canadian Confer-
ence of the Ontario Fur Workers'
Union, King Edward Hotel in
Toronto, 1925.

FAGAN, SAUL
TORONTO, ONT.
 17 photographs: activities of the
United Hat, Cap, and Millinery
Workers Union in Toronto and New
York, 1936-61.

FIELD, ROSE
TORONTO, ONT.
 Programme of the Spring Music
Festival of the Mandolin Symphony
Orchestra, and the Freiheit Gezangs
Farein choir, May 14, 1939. .5 cm.,
in English/Yiddish.

FIELD, VIVIAN
SUDBURY, ONT.
 Personal correspondence, 1920s, and
scrapbook of newsclippings on Joe
Ironstone, 1966. 1 cm. Photograph.
 1 photograph: an advertisement for a
store in Sudbury, 1915.

FINE, IZZY
TORONTO, ONT.
 4 photographs: committees and blues
band of Labour League in Toronto,
1934-42.

FINKELSTEIN, P.
TORONTO, ONT.
 Immigration documents, 1948-51. 2
cm.

FISHER, J.
TORONTO, ONT.
 2 photographs: opening ceremony of
Hebrew Men of England Synagogue,
1922; and the Canadian Jewish
Legion Bugle and Drum band, 1933.

FOX, MILLIE
TORONTO, ONT.
 50th Anniversary History of McCaul
St. Synagogue, 1937. .5 cm.

FREED, MRS. R.
TORONTO, ONT.
 Interviewed on 16 Oct. 1977; .5 hr.;
1 tape; English; by Sheldon Levitt.
Grew up on Chestnut Street in
Toronto; father was the first Ortho-
dox Rabbi in Toronto.

FRIEDBERG, RABBI BENJAMIN
TORONTO, ONT.
 Interviewed on 11 Nov. 1977; 1 hr.;
1 tape; English; by Sheldon Levitt.
Chief Rabbi of Beth Tzedec Syna-
gogue.

FROLIC, HERTA
TORONTO, ONT.
 Interviewed on 14 June 1977; .75
hr.; 1 tape; English; by Gitta Wallen.
Immigrated to Canada in the late
1930s.

FRUMHARTZ, MUNI
OTTAWA, ONT.
 Scrapbook containing clippings and
letters on the life of Paul Frumhartz,
founder of the Workmen's Circle,
Peretz Shule in Toronto, n.d. 2 cm.,
in English/Yiddish. Photographs.

5 photographs: Jewish-Canadian schools, including the Workmen's Circle, Peretz Shule in Toronto, 1911-31.

FUTERMAN, BENNY
TORONTO, ONT.
25th jubilee programme of the Toronto Hebrew Peddlars Protective Association, 1913-38. .5 cm. Photograph.
1 photograph: of 25th anniversary banquet of the Montreal Junk Peddlers Union, 1948.

GALINSKY, SAM
TORONTO, ONT.
Interviewed on 12, 24 Aug. 1977; 2.75 hrs.; 3 tapes; English; by Karen Levine. Father arrived in Canada in 1907.

GELLER, IRVING
TORONTO, ONT.
Interviewed on 24 Feb. 1978; 1.5 hrs.; 2 tapes; English; by Beverly Stern. Father arrived in Toronto in 1909.

GELLER, MAX
TORONTO, ONT.
Interviewed on 1 Feb. 1978; 1 hr.; 1 tape; English; by Beverly Stern. Arrived in Toronto in 1909.

GERSHMAN, JOSHUA
TORONTO, ONT.
Joshua Gershman was national organizer of the Industrial Union of Needle Trade Workers (W.U.L.) in the early 1930s, then Canadian representative of the Fur and Leather Workers' Union. In that same decade he became the editor of the Jewish-Canadian progressive newspaper, *Der Kampf* (The Struggle), later succeeded

by the *Der Veg* (The Road). In 1940 he founded the *Vochenblatt/Canadian Jewish Weekly,* of which he was editor until 1978. The collection includes his personal and business correspondence, particularly that pertaining to the *Vochenblatt* office, 1936-80. It also contains records covering numerous organizations: Canadian Jewish Congress, 1942-77, World Jewish Congress, 1944-75, Labour Progressive Party/Communist Party of Canada, National Jewish Committee (LPP-CP), 1945-80, and the United Jewish People's Order, 1939-78. Finally, there are substanial runs of serials, political pamphlets, and clippings. 3 meters, mostly in English/Yiddish.
SOME RESTRICTIONS

GIBBS, THELMA KOPLAND
TORONTO, ONT.
Interviewed on Aug. 1977; .5 hr; 1 tape; English; by Barbara Swimmer. Father arrived in Canada in 1914.

GITLEMAN, BARBARA AND CAROL
TORONTO, ONT.
1 letter discussing immigration to Canada, n.d., and a genetic family tree of the Gitleman and Lesser families. .5 cm.

GLICKMAN, JACOB
TORONTO, ONT.
"Toronto Jewry 1971: A Demographic Profile" 1 chapter of Ph.D. thesis (University of Toronto, 1976). 45 pp.

GOLDMAN, JEFFREY
TORONTO, ONT.
2 photographs: n.d., and 3 postcards from Palestine, 1898-89.

GOLDMAN, MERLE
TORONTO, ONT.
 Interviewed in Aug. 1977; .5 hr.; 1
tape; English; by Barbara Swimmer.
Mother arrived in the early 1910s.

GOLDSMITH, KATHE
TORONTO, ONT.
 Interviewed on 18 June 1977; 2 hrs.;
2 tape; English; by Gitta Wallen.
WWII immigrant.

GOLLOM, JOSEPH
TORONTO, ONT.
 Gollom, J. "History of the Mount
Sinai Hospital." 1974. .5 cm.

GORD, GOLDIE
TORONTO, ONT.
 Membership dues card of the International Jewelry Worker's Union,
Local 33, Toronto, 1939, and an
invitation in Russian. n.d. Photographs.
 14 photographs: Jewish-Canadian
involvement in organizations such as
the Berdichever Sick Benefit Society,
Canada Workmen's Circle, Labour
League, and the United Jewish
People's Order in Toronto, 1913-60.

GORD, IDA
TORONTO, ONT.
 2 photographs: of Muni Erlich,
Communist Party organizer, veteran
of Mac-Pac Battalion in Spain, killed
in action in France, 1944.

GRANT, ESTHER
TORONTO, ONT.
 1 Toronto Labour Lyceum Stock
certificate, 1925. .25 cm.

GREEN, RABBI S.
HAMILTON, ONT.
 Interviewed on 7 Dec. 1977;

.75 hrs.; 1 tape; English; by Sheldon
Levitt. Discusses his congregation in
Hamilton.

GREENBAUM, SYLVIA
TORONTO, ONT.
 14 photographs: United Jewish
People's Order Bowling League, and
the Toronto Jewish Folk Choir,
Toronto, 1945-50.

GREENSPOON, IRVING
TORONTO, ONT.
 1 photograph: Irving Greenspoon,
1936. Taped interview.
 Interviewed on 11 Aug. 1980; .5 hr.;
1 tape; English; by Derald Field.
Born in Toronto in 1914; father
started Greenspoon Bros. Wreckers.

GREENSPOON, MRS. S.
SUDBURY, ONT.
 2 photographs: Greenspoon brothers
in military service, 1940-45. Taped
interview.
 Interviewed on 8 June 1982; .5 hr.;
1 tape; English; by Dina Abramson.
Discusses early life in Sudbury.

GROSSMAN, IRVING
TORONTO, ONT.
 Interviewed on 5 Jan. 1978; 1.5 hrs.;
2 tapes; English; by Sheldon Levitt.
Discusses the architecture, and con-
struction of four Toronto synagogues.

HAMOUTH, SOL, SARAH BENOLIEL,
AND MIRIAM BENDAHAN
TORONTO, ONT.
 Interviewed on 12 Sept. 1974; 1 hr.;
1 tape; French/Spanish; by Miriam
and Raphael Bendahan. Post-WWII
immigrants.

HARNICK, LOUIS
TORONTO, ONT.
Family papers which consist of poems, letters, and clippings, 1918-25; and correspondence and financial records pertaining to Louis Harnick Fur Co., 1924-39. 2 reels of microfilm. Photographs.
12 photographs: the Harnick family, 1913-23.

HARTMAN, JOE
TORONTO, ONT.
49 photographs: activities, mostly gymnastics, of the Workers Sport Association, Camp Tarmola, Toronto, Timmins, 1930s.

HEICHELHEIM, GERTA
TORONTO, ONT.
Interviewed on 13 July 1977; .5 hr.; 1 tape; English; by Gitta Wallen. Arrived in Toronto in 1948 after migrating to England in 1933.

HERSCHFIELD, BABE (JEWISH HISTORICAL SOCIETY OF WESTERN CANADA)
WINNIPEG, MANITOBA
1 certificate granting land to Samuel Crawford, 1832. .25 cm.

HERSHKOVITZ, AL
TORONTO, ONT.
A collection of trade-union leaflets, Toronto, 1957-60. Photograph. Taped interview.
1 photograph: employees of S. Kelman Fur Co. in Toronto, c. 1930-40.
Interviewed on 29 Sept. 1977; 5 hrs.; 5 tapes; English; by Karen Levine. Discusses involvement in the Canadian labour movement and the Left.

ISAAC, BELLA
TORONTO, ONT.
Interviewed 18 July 1977; .25 hr.; 1 tape; German; by Gitta Wallen. Arrived in Canada in 1954.

ISACOFF, JACK
TORONTO, ONT.
5 photographs: manual training classes at Winchester Street Public School in Toronto, 1920; employees of the C.N. Telegraph Office in Toronto, 1921. Taped interview.
Interviewed on 11 Aug. 1977; .75 hr.; 1 tape; English; by Karen Levine. Discusses involvement in union movement.

KAGAN, SAM
TORONTO, ONT.
A collection of Yiddish literary journals, poetry, and music sheets, 1920-29, mostly from Montreal, Toronto, and New York. Included are titles such as *Canada, In Zich, Der Naiye Dor, Noentkeit, Shir Hshirim,* and *Dos Folk Zingt.* 1 reel of microfilm. Photographs. Taped interview.
22 photographs: individual and group portraits of Jewish-Canadian artists; activities of various organizations such as the Jewish Arts Circle, Freiheit Gezangs Farein choir, Labour League, and the United Jewish People's Order, Toronto, 1920-51.
Interviewed on 28 Feb., 7 March 1978; 3 hrs.; 3 tapes; English; by Karen Levine. Discusses his involvement in the Canadian labour movement in the 1920s.

KAHEN, MR. AND MRS. GORDON
TORONTO, ONT.
1 marriage certificate (photographed), 1932. .25 cm., in Hebrew.

KAHN, CAROLA
TORONTO, ONT.
 Interviewed on 27 July 1977; 1 hr.;
1 tape; English; by Gitta Wallen.
Arrived in the late 1930s.

KAMERLING, MARGARET
TORONTO, ONT.
 Interviewed on 25 Aug. 1977; .5 hr.;
1 tape; English; by Gitta Wallen.
Arrived in Canada in 1944.

KASHTAN, DAVE
TORONTO, ONT.
 Records of the National Committee
to Save the Rosenbergs; which
include some correspondence,
1953-54, leaflets issued by committee, clippings regarding its activities,
petitions, press releases, and
speeches. Also, several leaflets and
bulletins relating to Morton Sobell
case, n.d. 4 cm. Photograph.
 1 photograph: vigil in front of
American Consulate in support of
clemency for the Rosenbergs in
Vancouver, 1953.

KATZ, RALPH
TORONTO, ONT.
 Records pertaining to the Toronto
Workmen's Circle: minutes of the
School Building Committee, 1953-55
and of the City Committee, 1952-72;
accounts and receipt books, 1948-55;
and file of correspondence, mostly
between Toronto Workmen's Circle,
and *Jewish Daily Forward,* New
York, 1947-79. 9 cm. Photographs.
 61 photographs: activities of the
Toronto Workmen's Circle, 1915-71.
Topics include committees, Camp
Yungvelt, Peretz School, and demon-
strations protesting Soviet
Anti-Semitism (mid-1960s).

KATZ, W.
TORONTO, ONT.
See Conference of the United Jewish
People's Order.

KELMAN, RABBI JOSEPH
TORONTO, ONT.
 Interviewed on 15 Dec. 1977, 12
Jan. 1978; 1.25 hrs.; 2 tapes; Eng-
lish; by Sheldon Levitt. Discusses
history of his congregation.

KENNY, ROBERT S.
TORONTO, ONT.
 Pamphlet and broadside collection
largely related the Communist Party
of Canada and affiliated organizations, 1935-60; and 2 fascist leaflets,
and CN liner poster. 1 reel of microfilm. Photographs.
 2 photographs: posters advertising
transatlantic ship passenger service,
1911-12.

KIRSH, GERALD
TORONTO, ONT.
 1 photograph: the Turner family,
1903.

KIRSH, H. J.
TORONTO, ONT.
 Kirsh, H.J. "Conflict Resolution and
the Legal Culture: A Study of Rab-
binical Court." Osgoode Hall Law
Journal, 1971. 23 pp.
 _____. "Select Bibliography of the
modern Influence of Jewish Law in
England and in North America." May
1975. 4 pp.
 Sohn, H.A. "Human Rights Law in
Ontario: The Role of the Jewish
Community." CJHS. June 1980. 29
pp.

KLEIN, JACK AND LEO SNOW
TORONTO, ONT.
Interviewed on 28 Feb. 1978; 1.5
hrs.; 2 tapes; English; by Beverly
Stern. They arrived in Canada in the
1920s.

KNIGHT, NORMAN
OTTAWA, ONT.
2 photographs: N. Knight, Maurice
Spector with his wife, Trotsky's
secretary, and Leon Trotsky, Norway, 1935.

KOGAN, OSCAR
TORONTO, ONT.
Interviewed on 21 June-15 Sept.
1977; 5.5 hrs.; 6 tapes; English; by
Karen Levine. Discusses involvement
in the trade union movement and
left-wing political activities in the
1920s through the 1940s.

KOPYTO, ISRAEL
TORONTO, ONT.
Interviewed on 3 Sept. 1977; 1 hr.;
1 tape; English; by N. Egier. Dis-
cusses his return visit to Poland in
1976.
Kopyto, Israel. "Poland Erases
Memory of Jews." *Toronto Daily
Star,* 29 Aug. 1977. .25 cm.

KRAISMAN, LILLIAN
TORONTO, ONT.
File of correspondence of Sam
Kraisman dealing with
trade-unionism, includes clippings, a
speech, minutes and a "scab" list
from Guelph, 1934; also, souvenir
booklets, 1960s, and correspondence
concerning Sam Kraisman's 70th
birthday, and the 20th anniversary of
Local 199 of the International Ladies'
Garment Workers' Union. 8 cm., in
English/Yiddish. Photographs.

11 photographs: Sam Kraisman,
including his address to workers in
Lowell, Massachusetts, 1955-65; and
activities of the International Ladies'
Garment Workers' Union, Local 199
in Toronto, 1965.

KRAPIFKO, ELLEN
TORONTO, ONT.
Certificate of naturalization for Joe
Krapifko, Lithuanian, 1911. .25 cm.
Photograph.
1 photograph: business enterprise
(ice cream parlour) in Toronto, 1912.

KROVIS, J.
TORONTO, ONT.
3 photographs: immigrants on board
ship, 1924.

KUESSOUS, ELIE
TORONTO, ONT.
Interviewed on 14 Dec. 1977; 2 hrs.;
2 tapes; English; by Raphael and
Sydney Bendahan. Post-WWII immi-
grant.

LADOWSKY, KEVE
TORONTO, ONT.
Interviewed on 8 April 1978; 2 hrs.;
2 tapes; English; by Beverly Stern.
Arrived in Canada in 1920.

LANG, SELMA
TORONTO, ONT.
Interviewed on 20 June 1977; 1 hr.;
1 tape; English; by Gitta Wallen.
Post-WWII immigrant.

LAPEDES, BECKY
CAMP NAIVELT, ONT.
Interviewed on Sept. 1980; 1 hr.; 1
tape; English. This is a recording of
Becky Lapede's birthday party at
Camp Naivelt.

LAPEDES, BECKY
TORONTO, ONT.
32 photographs: activities of the
Labour League in Brampton, Rouge
Hill, and Toronto, 1925-45; activists
in various organizations including the
Communist Party of Canada, the
United Jewish People's Order, and
the Canadian Congress of Women,
Toronto, 1928-55. Taped interview.
Interviewed on 7 June 1978; 3 hrs.;
3 tapes; English; by Karen Levine.
Family arrived in 1905; she was very
active in trade unionism and women's
groups; recounts Eaton's strike in
1910.

LESSER, JOSEPH
SUDBURY, ONT.
Interviewed on 29 June 1982; .5 hr.;
1 tape; English; by Dina Abramson.
Discusses early life in Sudbury.

LEVANT, ANNE
TORONTO, ONT.
62 photographs: the Levant, Sacks,
and Smith families in England,
Winnipeg, and Toronto, 1902-52,
including military service in WWI
and WWII.

LEVINE, FANNIE
TORONTO, ONT.
9 photographs: the Levine family, c.
1915, including view of a drygoods
store, Toronto, c. 1930-40. Taped
interview.
Interviewed on 17 May 1977; 1.75
hrs.; 2 tapes; English; by Karen
Levine. Arrived in Canada in 1913.

LEVINE, GILBERT
OTTAWA, ONT.
The collection contains labour news
of the 1940s and 1950s; papers on
Jewish schools, 1937-57; correspon-

dence, 1944-45 **RESTRICTED**;
and miscellaneous paper items. 2
reels of microfilm.

LEVINE, GORDON
DURHAM, ONT.
Interviewed on 9 June 1982; .5 hr.;
1 tape; English; by Dina Abramson.
About early life in Sudbury.

LEVINE, HELEN
OTTAWA, ONT.
2 photographs: Hillel Foundation
Executive at Queen's University,
Kingston, 1945; and Jewish girls'
Sunday school class, Ottawa, 1945.

LEVINE, KAREN
TORONTO, ONT.
Newsclippings dealing with the trial
of 8 Communist leaders in Winnipeg,
1931; transcript of trial of John
Navizowski (Navis) who was a founding member of Ukrainian section of
the Communist Party of Canada,
Winnipeg, 1931; and miscellaneous
printed items, 1955-69. 3.5 cm.
Photograph.
1 photograph: membership certificate
for the Jewish National Workers
Alliance of America in Toronto,
1921.

LEVINE, MRS. F.
TORONTO, ONT.
Included are personal papers and
membership list of Workmen's
Circle, 1956-65. 1 reel of microfilm.

LEVITT, SHELDON
TORONTO, ONT.
The Shuls pictorial project, 1977,
was designed to document Jewish
religious life in synagogues, their
architecture, art, and artifacts. It
consists of over 1000 photographs and

slides, most of them from Toronto but also from Brantford, Hamilton, London, and Niagara Falls.

LEVKOE, RUTH
OAKVILLE, ONT.
A collection of letters written by Charles Rosen while posted with Canadian Army in Canada and overseas, 1943-46. 1 reel of microfilm. Photographs.
5 photographs: the Rosen family in Toronto, 1933-45.

LEWIS, BERNARD G.
THORNHILL, ONT.
5 photographs: high school, military service, and work at a mining camp in Sudbury, 1927-43. Taped interview.
Interviewed on 10 Aug. 1980; .5 hr.; 1 tape; English; by D. Field. Born in Copper Cliff in 1904(?).

LIBERBAUM, HARRY
TORONTO, ONT.
Interviewed on 4 July 1977; 1 hr.; 1 tape; English; Gitta Wallen. Arrived in Canada in 1923.

LIEBERMAN, SADIE
TORONTO, ONT.
3 photographs: Hadassah and the Zion Benevolent Association in Toronto, 1915; and picnic of the Zion Benevolent Association, n.d.

LIEBGOTT, ESTHER
TORONTO, ONT.
1 photograph: Freiheit Gezangs Farein (predecessor of the Toronto Jewish Folk Choir), Toronto, 1925-35. A film of labour picnic at Camp Naivelt, c. 1948. Includes footage of Tim Buck delivering speech; visual only, no audio.

LITVAK, NATHAN
TORONTO, ONT.
Interviewed on 4 Aug. 1977; 1.25 hrs.; 1 tape; English; by Karen Levine. Arrived in the early 1920s, worked in garment industry, and participated in 27-week strike at Crown Tailors in 1924-25.

LOEB, JUSTIN
TORONTO, ONT.
Interviewed on 9 Aug. 1977; .25 hr.; 1 tape; English; by Gitta Wallen.

MADGER, BEACHIE
TORONTO, ONT.
Account book of father's tobacco/magazine store in Toronto, 1948-51; and school records from Yiddishe Folks Shule-Farband, Toronto, 1937-38. 5 cm., in English/Yiddish Photographs.
4 photographs: Yiddishe Folks Shule-Farband (school), 1942, and tobacco/magazine store in Toronto, 1920-40.

MAGERMAN, ASIE
TORONTO, ONT.
Souvenir booklets from the Cloackmakers' Union (I.L.G.W.U.) and clippings, c. 1944-70. 2 cm. Photographs.
2 photographs: committees of the International Ladies' Garment Workers' Union, 1937.

MAGERMAN, A.
TORONTO, ONT.
10 photographs: activists in the Left Poale Zion, Toronto, 1920-30; and activities of the International Ladies' Garment Workers' Union, 1936-63.

MAGNUSON, MARION
TORONTO, ONT.
Personal papers: contact book which mother of donor brought from Russia, 1911; father's English vocabulary book, n.d.; series of postcards and letters (translated) exchanged between father and mother, 1910-11; also, 1915 Jewish yearbook published by the Jewish Socialist Federation of America, New York as well as certificates, and souvenir convention badges, n.d. 7 cm. Photographs.
33 photographs: the Nodelman family in Russia, and Toronto, 1908-40; business enterprise, a delicatessen/ice cream parlor, Toronto, c. 1919-40; activists in various organizations and labour unions, such as the Workers' Sport Association, Fur Workers Union, Workmen's Circle, and Jewish Socialist Territorialist Labour Party, 1915-49.

MANDELBAUM, PERCY
TORONTO, ONT.
Jewish newsclippings, 1930s. .25 cm.
The Mezryczer Wochenblat. 23 Oct. 1931. .25 cm.

MANDEL, SHOSHKE
TORONTO, ONT.
6 photographs: Shoshke Mandel reflecting her involvement in various Jewish, and labour organizations in Toronto, and Helsinki, 1927-55.

MARKUS, LOUIS
TORONTO, ONT.
1 Tenaim (engagement contract), 1877; and 1 Ketuba (marriage contract), 1977. .25 cm.

MENDELBAUM, PERCY
TORONTO, ONT.
88 photographs: Mezritcher Orphans brought from Poland to Canada, 1924-29; including employment in agriculture in Georgetown, 1928.

MENDELOVITZ, JOE
TORONTO, ONT.
2 photographs: Labour League conference, Rouge Hill, 1930; and Labour League Mandolin Orchestra, Toronto, 1932-33.

MESLIN, DIANA
TORONTO, ONT.
Minute books of United Jewish People's Order committee, and executive, 1947-48. 4 cm. Taped interview. Interviewed on 26 Jan. 1978; 1.5 hrs.; 1 tape; English; by Karen Levine. Born in 1909 in Montreal, then moved to Toronto; participated in Workmen's Circle.

MESLIN, JOE
TORONTO, ONT.
4 photographs: activities of the Workmen's Circle, including Camp Yungvelt, the Peretz Shule Choir, and a mandolin orchestra in Toronto, 1932-38.

MEYER, ELSA
TORONTO, ONT.
Interviewed on 11 May 1977; 1 hr.; 1 tape; English; by Gitta Wallen. Arrived in Canada in 1939.

MILGROM, MRS. R.
TORONTO, ONT.
Recorded on 4 Sept. 1977; 1 hr.; 1 tape; by N. Egier. Yiddish songs.

MONSON, RABBI DAVID
TORONTO, ONT.
 Interviewed on 11, 15 Nov. 1977; 9
Jan. 1978; 1.5 hrs.; 2 tapes; English;
by Sheldon Levitt. Discusses the
foundation of the Beth Shalom Synagogue.

MORYOUSSEF, MAURICE AND SIMONE
TORONTO, ONT.
 Interviewed on 7 Dec. 1977; 2.5
hrs.; 3 tapes; French/English; by
Raphael and Sydney Bendahan.

MOSES, DOROTHY
SUDBURY, ONT.
 9 photographs: business enterprises
(newspaper, and tobacco store) in
Sudbury, c. 1930-40.

MOSES, ELEANOR
TORONTO, ONT.
 Smith family papers, 1880-1957. 2
reels of microfilm. Photographs.
 60 photographs: the Pullan and Smith
families, 1909-43; organizations such
as the Girl Guides, and the University
of Toronto Menorah Society,
1917-43; and orphans at the Jewish
Nursery and Children's Home, c.
1927.

MOSES, FRED
TORONTO, ONT.
 Interviewed on 8 June 1977; .75 hr.;
1 tape; English; by Karen Levine.
Arrived in 1928; member of the
capmakers union.

MUKAMEL, SALEH
TORONTO, ONT.
 3 Iraqui scrolls Kamiah on parch-
ment to ward off evil spirits or death.
.25 cm.

MUNZ, HELEN
TORONTO, ONT.
 Interviewed on 13 June 1977; 1 hr.;
1 tape; English; by Gitta Wallen.

MUNZ, JARO
TORONTO, ONT.
 Interviewed on 13 June 1977; 1 hr.;
1 tape; English; by Gitta Wallen.

MYERS, MOLLY
TORONTO, ONT.
 1 photograph: laying of foundation at
the U.J.P.O. Morris Winchersky
Centre in Toronto, 1961.

NADEL, CHAIM
HAMILTON, ONT.
 Interviewed on 15 June 1977; 1.75
hrs.; 2 tapes; English; by Karen
Levine. Immediate post-WWII immi-
grant.

NAHMAN, MIRIELLE AND LEON
TORONTO, ONT.
 Interviewed on 20 Dec. 1977; 2 hrs.;
2 tapes; French/English; by Raphael
Bendahan.

NDELBERG-RAPP, ANNE
TORONTO, ONT.
 Naturalization papers, 1879, and
obituary, n.d. .25 cm. Photograph.
 1 photograph: Mr. and Mrs. Sam
Rapp, Toronto, 1923.

NESBITT, MORAY
TORONTO, ONT.
 Abraham Nisnevitz (1877-1955) was
a working-class Jewish poet and
political activist. His collection
includes original writings, 1906-55; a
run of magazines—*ICOR News* and
Masses of the Progressive Arts Club,
1930s; and printed materials from the
Labour League, the Y.K.U.F. and

I.C.O.R., n.d. 2 reels of microfilm.
Photographs.
 5 photographs: including one taken at
the founding congress of the Jewish
Socialist Party of America and
Canada in Rochester, New York,
1911.

NEUFELD, OTTO
TORONTO, ONT.
 Interviewed on 18 Aug. 1977; 1 hr.;
1 tape; English; by Gitta Wallen.
Post-WWII immigrant.

NIKELSKY, ANNE
TORONTO, ONT.
 9 photographs: activists in the organization Paole Zion, Poland, 1930-40;
and Camp Naivelt of the United
Jewish People's Order, Toronto,
1940.

OCKRANT, MR. AND MRS.
TORONTO, ONT.
 Birth certificate, 1908 (issued in
1966), Jewish marriage certificate,
1935, and British passport, 1965. 1
cm.

ORBACH, CARL
TORONTO, ONT.
 26 photographs: Jewish Canadian
families, 1912-65; organizations such
as the Workmen's Circle, Young
Judea Group, Young Workers' Club,
and fraternities at the University of
Toronto, 1913-50; and immigrants en
route to Canada, 1925.

ORLAN, AL
TORONTO, ONT.
 Souvenir programmes of the Toronto
Jewish Folk Choir, 1943-78; and
Silver Jubilee Souvenir Journal of the

Toronto Cloakmakers Union, 1936.
(15 items). 6.5 cm, in English/ Yiddish.

PAPE, MORLEY
TORONTO, ONT.
 Autobiography of Morley Pape,
Regional Director of Canadian Coun-
cil of Liberal Congregations, n.d. .5
cm.

PAPERNICK, SAMUEL
HAMILTON, ONT.
 Interviewed on 16 June 1977; 1.25
hrs.; 2 tapes; English; by Karen
Levine. Discusses his involvement in
the International Ladies' Garment
Union and the United Jewish People's
Order.

PENCINER, BERNICE
TORONTO, ONT.
 1 photograph: the Shendalman family
in Toronto 1923.

PENNER, NORMAN
TORONTO, ONT.
 1 photograph: Norman Penner speaking at the National Federation of
Labour Youth Conference, Toronto,
1948.

PEREL, SHLOIME
TORONTO, ONT.
 The Lazar Zaidman collection
includes correspondence and documents related to the communist
parties of Canada, Great Britain, and
U.S., and to the Jewish question, c.
1940-60. 2 cm.

PEREZ, JACK AND ESTER
TORONTO, ONT.
 Interviewed on 23 Sept. 1977; 2
hrs.; 2 tapes; French/English; by
Raphael and Sydney Bendahan.

PERLMUTTER, HELEN
TORONTO, ONT.
Interviewed on 26 June 1977; .5 hr.;
1 tape; English; by Gitta Wallen.

PHILLIPS, ART
TORONTO, ONT.
Personal papers, 1919-35, consisting
largely of letters. 1 cm.

PLISKOW, MORT
SUDBURY, ONT.
Minutes of B'nai B'rith and the
Hadassah, 1959- ; documents on the
Aid to Israel campaign, Sudbury
Lodge, 1946; certificate of member-
ship given to J. Lesser allowing him
to join Grand Lodge, 1946; and
miscellaneous clippings about the
Sudbury Jewish community, n.d. 3.5
cm. Photographs.
12 photographs: religious life in the
Shaar Hashomayim Synagogue in
Sudbury, and Sault Ste. Marie, c.
1965-70.

PLISKOW, RUTH
SUDBURY, ONT.
Interviewed on 9 June 1982; .5 hr; 1
tape; English; by Dina Abramson.
Involved in the B'nai B'rith.

POSEN, MOLLY
TORONTO, ONT.
Papers from the Canadian Panel of
Women, 1969, and Molly Posen's
memoirs, n.d. 1 cm.

POSNER, CHARLES
TORONTO, ONT.
Interviewed on 1 Feb. 1978; .25 hr.;
1 tape; English; by Beverly Stern.
Arrived in Toronto in 1927.

ROBIN, LEO
TORONTO, ONT.
6 photographs: Leo Robin in
Toronto, Winnipeg, and Montreal,
1930-70. Taped interview.
Interviewed on 18 Jan. 1978; 8.25
hrs.; 9 tapes; English; by Karen
Levine.

ROSENBLATT, JOE
TORONTO, ONT.
Printed items, 1967-79. 2.5 cm.

ROSEN GRANATSTEIN, DINA
TORONTO, ONT.
1 Romanian passport, and Canadian
immigration identification card, 1925.
Photographs.
2 photographs: the Rosen family, in
Romania, and Canada, 1925-30.

ROSEN, LEO
TORONTO, ONT.
1 flyer from Darcy Street Talmud
Torah, 1939; 1 letter from donor's
father in Poland, 1938. .25 cm.

ROSENTHAL, HENRY
VANCOUVER, BRITISH COLUMBIA
Writings of the late Morris
Rosenthal, activist in the Workmen's
Circle and writer, n.d. .5 cm., in
Yiddish.

ROTHCHILD, FREDERIC
TORONTO, ONT.
Interviewed on 9 Aug. 1977; 1 hr.; 1
tape; English; by Gitta Wallen.
Post-WWII immigrant.

ROTHSCHILD, SAMUEL
SUDBURY, ONT.
Interviewed on 15 June 1982; 1 hr.;
1 tape; English; by Dina Abramson.
Discusses his immigration and activity
in sports.

ROTHSCHILD, SAMUEL
SUDBURY, ONT.
 Interviewed on 24 July 1980; 2.5
hrs.; 3 tapes; English; by D. Field.
About early life in Sudbury.

ROTSTEIN, ABRAHAM
TORONTO, ONT.
 1 photograph: of the Furriers'
Branch of the Independent
Workmen's Circle in Toronto,
1970-75. Taped interview.
 Interviewed on 25 April 1978; 1.5
hrs.; 2 tapes; English; by Karen
Levine. Discusses his work as a
tailor, cloakmaker, and furrier, and
his subsequent participation in the
International Fur and Leather
Workers' Union.

RUDERMAN, ROBERT
TORONTO, ONT.
 Eisen, David. *Toronto's Jewish Doc-
tors*, 1960, 15 pp.

SABLE, JEAN
TORONTO, ONT.
 Interviewed on 6 Feb. 1978; 1 hr.; 1
tape; English; by Beverly Stern.
Arrived in Toronto in 1913.

SAIGER, PERCY
TORONTO, ONT.
 Immigration documents, letters, and
a certificate of Ministerial Registra-
tion empowering Rev. Saiger to
perform marriages, 1922-41. 1 cm.
Photographs.
 4 photographs: Cantor Harry Siger,
n.d.; activities of the Workmen's
Circle, including a mandolin orches-
tra, and the Hirsch Lekert Club,
Toronto, 1935-37.
 A Sense of Spadina. Canadian Jewish
Congress. 1974. .5 cm.

SALSBERG, JOSEPH B.
TORONTO, ONT.
 Index of R. Kenny Collection, which
includes campaign, and miscellaneous
material pamphlets by Salsberg; and
newsclippings of Salsberg's column in
Daily Hebrew Journal, 1969-70. 2
cm. Taped interview.
 Interviewed on 2 June 1978 to 22
Jan. 1979; 14 hrs.; 18 tapes.; by A.
MacLennan and P. Kligman. Interviews cover most of his life, particularly his involvement in the Canadian
labour movement.
 "Spadina, Heart of a Riding." *The
Canadian Tribune.* 26 Sept. 1955. 25
cm.

SALSBERG, JOSEPH B.
TORONTO, ONT.
 Interviewed on 23 Sept. 1977; .5
hr.; 1 tape; English; by K. Troy.
Reminiscences of early period of
Kensington Market.

SCHECHTER, LEE
TORONTO, ONT.
 1 photograph: the Children's Mandolin Orchestra of the United Jewish
People's Order, Toronto, 1935.

SCHWARTZ, SYLVIA
TORONTO, ONT.
 209 photographs: leading members
of the Communist Party of Canada,
and other left-wing political and
cultural activists in Toronto, 1949-58.
All photographs taken by donor, and
accompanied by short biographical
sketches.

SEDEROWSKY-ROSENBLUT, AMELIE
TORONTO, ONT.
 Interviewed on 18, 25 July 1977; 2
hrs.; 2 tapes; English; by Gitta
Wallen. Arrived in Canada in 1953.

SHEK, SOL
TORONTO, ONT.
Sol Shek's diary written in Poland, 1916-20; unfinished memoirs (1967) on immigration to Canada and involvement in the Labour League in the 1930s. 1 reel of microfilm. Photographs.
4 photographs: Sol Shek, n.d.; committee of the Labour League, 1943; and Winchevsky Shule (school), 1945-50.

SHELLEY, KATHERINE
TORONTO, ONT.
Interviewed on 13 July 1977; .25 hr.; 1 tape; English; by Gitta Wallen. Arrived in Canada in 1939.

SHENDROFF, SAMUEL
TORONTO, ONT.
Interviewed on 3 Aug. 1977; 1 hr.; 1 tape; English; by Barbara Swimmer. Immigrated to Canada in 1907.

SILBERT, MORRIS
HAMILTON, ONT.
Interviewed on 16 June 1977; 1.25 hr.; 2 tapes; English; by Karen Levine. Parents arrived in 1905, discusses involvement in the United Jewish People's Order and ideological tensions in the Jewish community of Hamilton.

SILBURT, BETH
TORONTO, ONT.
3 photographs: young Jewish immigrant boys in Vancouver, 1908; picnic of the Warsawer Ladzer (Lodge) in Toronto in the late 1920s; Mr. and Mrs. A. Gorback, pioneers of Hirsch Settlement, Saskatchewan, taken in Jewish Home for the Aged, Winnipeg, 1940s.

SIMMS, MRS. F.
DUNDAS, ONT.
Letters (1939), a Polish document Wyciag Zaktu Slubu (1938), and a 1927 Jewish newspaper (no title). .5 cm. Photograph.
1 photograph: Toronto Cloak Manufacturers' Association, Royal York Hotel, 1943.

SIMON, GAIL
TORONTO, ONT.
2 photographs: the Simon family in Brantford, c. 1865.

SIMON, HARRY
TORONTO, ONT.
3 trade-unionist and anti-Nazi articles written by Harry Simon, and 60th jubilee souvenir book of the Bakery and Confectionary Workers' Union, Local 181 in Toronto, 1972. 3 cm. Photographs.
6 photographs: activities of the Jewish Labour Committee, Montreal, 1950-70, and of labour unions including Fur Workers' Union dinner in Toronto, 1947, Amalgamated Meat Cutters and Butcher Workmen of North Amercia conference, Toronto, 1952, Canadian Labour Congress conference, Montreal, 1957, and a Labour Day parade in Toronto, 1947.

SINGER, MORRIS
TORONTO, ONT.
7 photographs: employment for a clothing manufacturer in Toronto, c. 1970-80.

SLONIM, RABBI REUBAN
TORONTO, ONT.
Interviewed in Nov. 1977; 1 hr.; 1 tape; English; by Sheldon Levitt.

SMITH, HARRY
TORONTO, ONT.
1 photograph: the Joint Board of the Cloak, Suit and Dresmakers' Union, International Ladies' Garment Workers' Union in Toronto, 1936. Taped interview.
Interviewed on 18 July 1977; 1.75 hrs.; 2 tapes; English; by Karen Levine. Landed at Ellis Island in 1907.

SOKOL, MRS. N.
TORONTO, ONT.
Papers from Sokol's Hebrew School, c. 1940s. 1 cm.

SPRACHMAN, MANDEL
TORONTO, ONT.
Interviewed on Nov. 1977; 1.25 hrs.; 2 tapes; English; by Sheldon Levitt.

STEINBERG, BEN
TORONTO, ONT.
Scrapbook, mostly newsclippings, programmes, and ads for services and concerts conducted by Cantor Steinberg. 1 reel of microfilm.

STEINBERG, ELISE
TORONTO, ONT.
Various publications by the founders of Holy Blossom Temple and others (9 items).

STREN, SADIE
BRANTFORD, ONT.
Stren family papers, 1911-61, consist of documents and letters relating to the first Jewish families in Brantford; records of the Brantford Hebrew Association, and miscellaneous items, such as a land registry book, and papers from the first movie theatre in Brantford. 1 reel of microfilm. Photo-graphs.
170 photographs: depicting all aspects of the Jewish community of Brantord and surrounding region, 1907-77. Topics include family portraits, business enterprises, religious life, schools, military service, organizations, and recreation. 5 of these represent the Simon family, the first Jewish settlers in Brantford, 1881.

STROM, HAROLD
TORONTO, ONT.
2 photographs: activists in the Amalgamated Clothing Workers' of America, 1935; and classroom at Essex Street Public School, 1941, in Toronto.

SUGARMAN, JACK
TORONTO, ONT.
Interviewed on 14 Nov. 1977; 2 hrs.; 2 tapes; English; by Sheldon Levitt.

TAUB, MUNI
TORONTO, ONT.
2 letters from Dr. Norman Bethune in China, 1939; file of material concerning the trial and activities of Max Federman, and others of the Fur Workers' Union, Toronto, 1936-40. 2.5 cm. Photograph.
1 photograph: Norman Bethune and co-workers in Spain, mid-1930s.

TAUB, SADIE
TORONTO, ONT.
Button to welcome home the men of the Mackenzie-Papineau Battalion, 1939. Photographs.
5 photographs: embroidery shop, 1925; Mount Royal School, 1926; and Jewish Canadians in military service in WWI, all taken in Montreal.

TOHN, MAX
TORONTO, ONT.
129 photographs and postcards:
(Russian, American, Japanese, Yiddish, and Canadian) collected in
Toronto, showing historical figures,
Canadian farm scenes, classical sculptures, and romance, 1913-19.

TORONTOW, JOSEPH
OTTAWA, ONT.
1 photograph: marriage certificate,
n.d. Taped interview.
Interviewed on 4 Aug. 1977; 2 hrs.;
2 tapes; English; by Zvia Schwartz.
Highlights his participation in the
"Chevre Kaddisha," (men responsible
for burial rites).

TRACK, A.
TORONTO, ONT.
2 photographs: softball teams in
Toronto, 1929-32.

TROSTIN, IZZY
TORONTO, ONT.
Membership dues card of the
I.L.G.W.U., Local 72, Toronto,
1937; souvenir programmes of jubilee
concerts of the Jewish Workers Cultural Centre (including Freiheit
Gezangs Farein choir and the Mandolin Symphony Orchestra), 1935,
1936. 2.5 cm. Photographs.
15 photographs: sports activities,
parades, processions, and theatrical
productions of various organizations,
including Camp Naivelt of United
Jewish People's Order, Freiheit
Gezangs Farein choir, and the
Workers Sport Association in
Toronto, 1926-50.

TULCHINSKY, ANNE
TORONTO, ONT.
Minutes and miscellaneous papers of

the Canadian Hadassah, 1932-68,
including poems, prayers, and
newsclippings. 2 cm. Photographs.
22 photographs and contact sheets:
Anne and Harry Tulchinsky in
Greece, and Brantford, 1924-51;
members of organizations such as the
Hadassah, Zionist Organization of
Canada, and the Canadian Jewish
Congress in Toronto, and Brantford,
1933-51.
The Canadian Zionist. Vol. 2, No.
4, June 1935. .25 cm.
The Expositor. 1932, 1936. .25 cm.

TURLEY, EVE
TORONTO, ONT.
16 photographs and postcards: the J.
Blugerman family and friends in
Toronto, 1910-35; Jewish-Canadian
left-wing activists, including views of
Labour Day parade, 1934, and demonstration by Toronto Dance Centre
group (off-shoot of the Labour
League, later the United Jewish
People's Order), Toronto, 1935.

TURNER, MRS. CHARLES
TORONTO, ONT.
Documents and papers about Dr.
David, Turner and the Holy Blossom
Temple, 1929-78. 2 cm.
Bulletin. Holy Blossom Temple, 21
April 1978. .25 cm.

VINE, GOLDIE
TORONTO, ONT.
The Harry Price collection consists
of minutes, in Yiddish of the
Hamilton Chapter of the I.C.O.R.
(Association for Jewish Colonization
in the Soviet Union), 1930-37; and
minutes, in Yiddish of open and
executive meetings of the Jewish
Workers' Conference Against War,
Fascism and Anti-Semitism in

Hamilton, 1935. In addition, there are pamphlets and leaflets, most of them issued by I.C.O.R. (New York) and the Labour Progressive Party (Toronto), 1935-31. 12 cm.

WAGMAN, MORRIS
TORONTO, ONT.
 Interviewed on 1 Feb. 1978; .5 hr.; 1 tape; English; by Beverly Stern. Arrived in Canada in 1917.

WALSH, ESTHER AND BILL
TORONTO, ONT.
 The Steele/Walsh collection contains correspondence, the bulk of which is from Dick Steele while interned under the Defence of Canada Regulations, and while in Canadian Army overseas, 1942-44; also letters between Bill Walsh, while interned, and his wife; miscellaneous items: personal documents and clippings. 3 reels of microfilm. Photographs.
 27 photographs: demonstrations of the Young Communist League, 1930, and demonstrations against nuclear proliferation, 1946, in Toronto; labour union activity in Hamilton and Kitchener, 1936-52; and portraits of Dick Steele during military service, 1942-44.

WATSON, RAE
TORONTO, ONT.
 7 photographs: Rae Watson in Russia, and Toronto, 1907-41.

WAXMAN, AL
TORONTO, ONT.
 1 photograph: autographed portrait of Al Waxman, Toronto, 1978.

WEIL, SYBIL
TORONTO, ONT.
 Interviewed on 27 June 1977; 1 hr.;

1 tape; English; by Gitta Wallen. Post-WWII immigrant.

WEINBERG, ERNA
TORONTO, ONT.
 Interviewed on 9 June 1977; 1 hr.; 1 tape; English; by Gitta Wallen. Arrived in Canada in 1939.

WEINRIB-FREED, RUTH
TORONTO, ONT.
 Marriage announcement, n.d. .25 cm.

WEISMAN, ELLIS
NORTH BAY, ONT.
 Newsclippings, c. 1949. .25 cm. Photographs. Taped interview.
 8 photographs: the Weisman and Ironstone families in Sudbury, 1919, including children and a fur trading company, c. 1910-20.
 Interviewed on 6 July 1980; 1 hr.; 1 tape; English; by D. Field. About turn of the century Jewish life in Copper Cliff, Ont.

WIENER, ABE
TORONTO, ONT.
 Interviewed on 13 Feb. 1978; 1.5 hrs.; 2 tapes; English; by Beverly Stern. Father arrived in Canada in 1905.

WOLFF, REGINA
TORONTO, ONT.
 Interviewed on 29 June 1977; 1 hr.; 1 tape; English; by Gitta Wallen. Immigrated to Canada in 1947.

YAFFE, BEN
TORONTO, ONT.
 Price lists from J. Yaffe Raw Furs, 1907, 1917; Shulman-Vinusky family tree, 1942-46. .5 cm. Photographs.
 8 photographs: the J. Yaffe family,

plus portraits of fur merchants, and social events of organizations formed by fur merchants, Toronto, 1923-37.

YOLLES, EISEN
TORONTO, ONT.
Papers from the Independent Order of Foresters, n.d.; an historical sketch of the Associated Hebrew Schools, 1947; and 2 files of clippings, 1900-20. 1.5 cm. Photograph.
1 photograph: of Pride of Israel Sick Benefit Society certificate, n.d.

ZARETSKY, ISADORE
TORONTO, ONT.
Interviewed on 13 Feb. 1978; 2 hrs.; 2 tapes; English; by Beverly Stern. Left Russia for Toronto in 1920.

ZIGER, JACK
TORONTO, ONT.
Interviewed on 14 July 1977; 1.5 hrs; 2 tapes; English; by Karen Levine. Arrived in Toronto in 1909.

ZUCKER, PHIL
NIAGARA FALLS, ONT.
Interviewed on Nov 1977; .5 hr.; 1 tape; English; by Sheldon Levitt. Arrived in 1932; discusses incidents of anti-Semitism in Niagara Falls.

AGUDATH ISRAEL SYNAGOGUE
OTTAWA, ONT.
Programmes and bulletins, 1958-74. 1 cm (10 items).

ANSCHE MINSKER CONGREGATION
(MORRIS BLOOM)
TORONTO, ONT.
Records, 1930-70, include minute books, financial reports, flyers, membership, and address lists. 8 cm.

Photograph.
1 photograph: mortgage burning celebration at the school, "Minsher Shul," Toronto, 1937.

ASSOCIATION OF NEW CANADIANS FROM THE U.S.S.R. (M. LEFEL)
TORONTO, ONT.
Invitation for the first concert of the Russian Jewish Association, n.d.; a letter issued by the Committee of Soviet Political Prisoners about writer G. Svisky, n.d.; and a bulletin, no.1, n.d. .5 cm.

BAYCREST CENTRE FOR GERIATRIC CARE
TORONTO, ONT.
Board of Director's minutes, 1953-70. 1 reel of microfilm. Photographs.
2 photographs: taken at the Jewish Old Folks Home in Toronto, 1917-30.
Baycrest News. March, May, Nov. 1977. .5 cm.
Honour Roll (Baycrest Men's Service Club), 1971-77. 2 cm.

BETH ISRAEL CONGREGATION
PETERBOROUGH, ONT.
Diamond Jubilee of Beth Israel Congregation. 1900-64, 97 pp.

BETH JACOB SYNAGOGUE
HAMILTON, ONT.
Minute books, 1924-61, including financial records. 1 reel of microfilm. "History of Beth Jacob Congregation, 1896-1969." 97 pp.

BETH SHOLOM SYNAGOGUE
TORONTO, ONT.
Records, 1946-71, and scrapbooks,

1946-61. 2 reels of microfilm. Photographs.
 28 photographs: n.d.

BETH TIKVAH SYNAGOGUE
TORONTO, ONT.
 Scrapbooks, 1966-77. 1 reel of microfilm. Photographs.
 7 photographs: religious life at Beth Tikvah Synagogue, 1967-71.

BETH TZEDEC SYNAGOGUE
TORONTO, ONT.
 Communique no. 10 issued by the Canadian Committee for Soviet Jewry, 1977.
 Information Bulletin on Soviet Jewry. Vol. 3, no. 4; and House of Commons Debates, 21 March 1977. 1 cm.
 Dedication Booklet of Beth Tzedec Synagogue, 1955. .5 cm.

B'NAI B'RITH GIRLS DEBORAH CHAPTER
TORONTO, ONT.
 2 scrapbooks, 1961-64. 1 cm.

B'NAI JACOB CONGREGATION
NIAGARA FALLS, ONT.
 Records, 1920-55. 1 reel of microfilm. Photographs.
 2 photographs: n.d.

CANADIAN CLOTHIERS
TORONTO, ONT.
 Material dealing with labour relations at Tip Top Tailors Ltd. and Toronto's garment industry, 1922-66. .5 meters. Photograph.
 1 photograph: interior of Tip Top Tailors in Toronto, 1931.

CANADIAN COUNCIL OF LIBERAL CONGREGATIONS
TORONTO, ONT.
 Minutes, 1961-77. 1 reel of microfilm.

CHEVRE KADISHA AGUDAS ACHIM CONGREGATION
TORONTO, ONT.
 Constitution and by-laws, correspondence, 1924-25. .5 cm. Photograph.
 1 photograph: Max Safer in Toronto, 1978.

CONFERENCE OF THE UNITED JEWISH PEOPLE'S ORDER
TORONTO, ONT.
 6 photographs: probably of the W. Katz family; and members of the United Jewish People's Order, Toronto, 1972.
 Recorded in 1972 3.5 hrs.; 4 tapes; in English/Yiddish. Proceedings in which activities of organization and policy problems are discussed.

CONGREGATION ANSHE SHOLOM
HAMILTON, ONT.
 The collection contains minutes of Deborah Sisterhood, Deborah Verein and board meetings, ledger sheets of Anshe Sholom, marriage registers, souvenir programmes, and newclippings, 1870-1968. 1 reel of microfilm. Photograph.
 1 photograph: *Old Anshe Sholom* newspaper, n.d.

FUR AND LEATHER WORKERS' UNION (MAX FEDERMAN)
TORONTO, ONT.
 A collection of leaflets related to activities of the Fur and Leather

Workers' Union, 1938-62. 2 cm (19 items). Photograph.
1 photograph: furriers annual picnic in Port Dalhousie, 1923.

HAMILTON CARHARTT MANUFACTURING CO.
TORONTO, ONT.
Company records, 1901-60; and union material, 1920-41. 1 reel of microfilm.

HAMILTON JEWISH COMMUNITY CENTRE
TORONTO, ONT.
25th Anniversary Booklet. 1975. 70 pp.

HOLY BLOSSOM TEMPLE SISTERHOOD
TORONTO, ONT.
Minutes, correspondence, and yearbooks, 1927-74. 2 reels of microfilm.
1 photograph: n.d.

HOLY BLOSSOM TEMPLE
TORONTO, ONT.
Records, 1974-78, include constitution and proposed amendments, correspondence, financial statements, and programmes. 3.5 cm. Photographs.
4 photographs: religious life at the Holy Blossom Temple in Toronto, c. 1938-66.
Holy Blossom Temple Bulletin. Dec. 1977 - March 1978. 1 cm.

HUTNER, MURRAY
TORONTO, ONT.
Canadian Jewish Review. Montreal, 4 Nov. 1921 - 16 Dec. 1966 (some gaps 1931-41; Sept. 1952-58). 35 reels of microfilm.

INTERNATIONAL LADIES' GARMENT WORKERS' UNION
TORONTO, ONT.
Included in the collection are minute books of various garment union locals and committees, 1930-70; correspondence (largely with S. Kraisman, Union Manager), 1934-71; and miscellaneous records relating to various activities of the I.L.G.W.U. 16 reels of microfilm. Photographs.
7 photographs: I.L.G.W.U. banquets and conventions in Boston, Toronto, and Hamilton, 1936-47; and General Strike Committee in Toronto, 1919.
Souvenir albums, 1936, 1938, 1949, 1961. 1 reel of microfilm.

JEWISH COMMUNITY CENTRE
OTTAWA, ONT.
The collection includes the first minute book of Adath Jeshuran Synagogue, 1892, and assorted publications including yearbooks, anniversary programmes, and bulletins, 1958-70. 6 cm.

JEWISH HISTORICAL SOCIETY OF WESTERN CANADA
WINNIPEG, MANITOBA
5 photographs: Manitoba Hebrew School, 1920, B'nai B'rith House, Synagogue, Purim Carnival, 1912, banquet, 1948, taken in Fort William (Thunder Bay).

JUDEAN BENEVOLENT AND FRIENDLY SOCIETY (ZENA SHAPIRO)
TORONTO, ONT.
Book of Ritual. 1924. 29 pp.

KAPLAN AND SPRACHMAN LTD.
ARCHITECTS
TORONTO, ONT.
Project list and drawings of Toronto

and Sudbury synagogues, 1920-50. 1 reel of microfilm.

KENORA JEWISH COMMITTEE
KENORA, ONT.
 Included are minutes of general members meetings, 1941-45; financial reports and cash books, 1945-54; and 18 letters regarding Kenora Synagogue, 1941-48. 1.5 cm.

LUBAVITCH YOUTH ORGANIZATION
TORONTO, ONT.
 Invitation sent to Russian immigrants for Pidyon Haben Ceremony, 1977. .25 cm
 "Hostages." *Globe and Mail* article about Gregory Svirsky, n.d., .25 cm.

MULTICULTURAL HISTORY SOCIETY
OF ONTARIO
TORONTO, ONT.
 Numerous clippings related to Canadian Jewry, 1976-78. 1.5 cm.
 Canadian Jewish Outlook. Oct. 1963 - Dec. 1978. 4 reels of microfilm.
 Canadian Jewish News. 1 Jan. 1960 - 21 Dec. 1989. 39 reels of microfilm.

MOUNT SINAI HOSPITAL
TORONTO, ONT.
 Included are minutes, correspondence, annual reports, capsule history of Mount Sinai, and miscellaneous paper items, 1937-78. 7 cm.
 Dworkin, Dorothy. "History of Mount Sinai Hospital." n.d. .5 cm.

M. STONE CLOTHING LTD.
TORONTO, ONT.
 Order book, 1929-70. 1 reel of microfilm.

SECULAR JEWISH ASSOCIATION
TORONTO, ONT.
 Constitution and by-laws, statement of objectives, pamphlets, and flyers. 1 cm.

SHOMRAI SHABBOTH CONGREGATION
TORONTO, ONT.
 Testimonial Dinner Booklet. 1972. 105 pp.

SMITH TRANSPORT
TORONTO, ONT.
 Clippings and programmes, 1962-75. 1 cm. Photographs.
 24 photographs: the Philip Smith family and business enterprise in Oshawa, and Toronto, 1935-70.

TORONTO CLOAKMAKERS' UNION
TORONTO, ONT.
 44 photographs: the International Ladies' Garment Workers' Union, activities including social events, conventions, and demonstrations in Toronto, 1919-72.
 Souvenir journals, n.d. 1 reel of microfilm.

TORONTO JEWISH FOLK CHOIR
TORONTO, ONT.
 72 photographs: entertainment provided by the Toronto Jewish Folk Choir, Toronto, 1948-75.
 Souvenir programmes, 1942-43, 1946-48, 1950. 1 reel of microfilm.

TORONTO WORKMEN'S CIRCLE COLONY
TORONTO, ONT.
 Records, 1969-78, include minute book of Branch 680E, original constitution, 1926; and revised constitution, 1971. 1 reel of microfilm.

UNITED GARMENT WORKERS OF
AMERICA, LOCAL 253
TORONTO, ONT.
 Records, 1947-66, include minutes,
collective agreements, financial statements, correspondence, and leaflets. 2
reels of microfilm.

UNITED HATTERS' CAP AND MIL-
LINERY WORKERS' UNION
TORONTO, ONT.
 Records, 1940-70, include collective
agreements, minutes, membership
lists, correspondence, financial statements, and newsletters. 2 reels of
microfilm. Photographs.
 26 photographs: union activities,
including strikes in Toronto, and New
York, 1930-75.

UNITED JEWISH PEOPLE'S ORDER
TORONTO, ONT.
 The collection includes records,
correspondence, and policy statements
of the U.J.P.O, 1930s-1970s. It also
contains minutes of the Aid to Russia
Committee, 1942; and miscellaneous
leaflets and bulletins issued by various Jewish organizations such as the
Jewish Defence League, 1960-72. 1
reel of microfilm. 9 cm. Photographs.
 256 photographs: activities of the
United Jewish People's Order and its
predecessor, the Labour League in
Toronto, 1915-80. Subjects include
committees, entertainment, sports,
schools, and camps.

WORKMEN'S CIRCLE OF CANADA
TORONTO, ONT.
 Scrapbook, 1939-49. 1 reel of micro-
film.
 2 photographs: committees of the
Workmen's Circle for the annual
Masquerade Ball in Toronto, 1913;
and membership certificate for
Kropotkin Publication Society in
Toronto, 1916.

KOREAN COLLECTION

AHN, REV. SANDY
TORONTO, ONT.
Interviewed on 10 June 1978; 1 hr.;
1 tape; Korean; by Jung-gun Kim.
Discusses difficulty and conflict in
adjusting to Canadian ways.

CHAE, REV. IN-WHAN
TORONTO, ONT.
Interviewed on 39 Sept. 1978; 1.5
hrs.; 2 tapes; Korean; by Jung-gun
Kim. Sermon preached by Rev. Chae
In-Whan.

CHOI, DUCK SIN
TORONTO, ONT.
Interviewed on 22 April 1978; 2
hrs.; 2 tapes; Korean; by Jung-gun
Kim. Discusses the political conspir-
acies and intrigue of the Park Chung
Hee administration.

CHUN, CHOONG-LIM
TORONTO, ONT.
Interviewed on 9 Dec. 1978; 3.5
hrs.; 4 tapes; Korean; by Jung-gun
Kim. Arrived in Canada in 1962,
pioneer immigrant in building the
Korean community in Toronto.

CHUNG, CHUL KI
TORONTO, ONT.
Interviewed on 7, 12, March 1978;
4.5 hrs.; 5 tapes; Korean; by Jung-
gun Kim. Discusses his political
involvement in Korea and Canada.

HAHN, REV. TAE-KYUNG
TORONTO, ONT.
Interviewed on 24, 25 Feb. 1979;

3.5 hrs.; 4 tapes; Korean; by Jung-
gun Kim. 2 lectures by Rev. Hahn on
the state of Koreans in Manchuria,
held at the Toronto Korean United
Church.

HAM, SOK HON
TORONTO, ONT.
Interviewed on 16, 18, 21 Sept.
1979; 8 hrs.; 10 tapes; Korean; by
Jung-gun Kim. 2 lectures (with ques-
tion and answer sessions) by Teacher
Sok Hon Ham during his visit to
Toronto.

HONG, JOON-SOO
TORONTO, ONT.
Interviewed on 2 April 1978; 3.5
hrs.; 4 tapes; Korean; by Jung-gun
Kim. Immigrated sometime in the
1960s.

HONG, REV. S. K. AND REV. M. C.
YO
TORONTO, ONT.
Interviewed on 10 Feb. 1979; 2 hrs.;
2 tapes; Korean; by Jung-gun Kim. A
discussion on Christian education in
immigrant churches.

HOOK, S. W., H. C. CHO, AND S. C.
CHANG (TORONTO KOREAN
Y.M.C.A)
TORONTO, ONT.
Interviewed on 17 Nov. 1978; 1.5
hrs.; 2 tapes; Korean; by Jung-gun
Kim. A panel discussion on the future
role of the Korean Canadian Associ-
ation in Toronto.

HUH, YOUNG-SIK
TORONTO, ONT.
 Interviewed on 28 Oct. 1978; 3.5
hrs.; 4 tapes; Korean; by Jung-gun
Kim. Forum on Korean Language
Programmes in Toronto Area, held at
Toronto Korean Catholic Church.

IM, CHANG-BIN
TORONTO, ONT.
 Interviewed on 1 April 1978; 2 hrs.;
2 tapes; Korean; by Jung-gun Kim.
Discusses Korean community politics,
among other things.

JO, JUNG WHAN
TORONTO, ONT.
 Interviewed on 25 March 1979; 1.25
hrs.; 2 tapes; Korean; by Jung-gun
Kim. A commentary on Korean poli-
tics.

KIM, MR. AND MRS. BYUNG WOOK
TORONTO, ONT.
 Interviewed on 16, 29 Dec. 1978; 6,
7 Jan. 1979; 7.25 hrs.; 8 tapes; Korean; by Jung-gun Kim. Life histories
and settlement in Canada.

KIM, CHAI CHOON
TORONTO, ONT.
 Interviewed on 10 Feb. 1979; 2 hrs.;
2 tapes; Korean; by Jung-gun Kim.
On ethnic nationalism abroad as it
pertains to the Koreans.

KIM, REV. CHAND-KIL (ANNUAL
CONFERENCE OF THE KOREAN
SCHOOL TEACHERS' ASSOCIATION)
TORONTO, ONT.
 Interviewed on 26 May 1979; .5 hr.;
1 tape; Korean; by Jung-gun Kim.
Rev. C. Kim speaking on the import-
ance of church school activities in the
Korean immigrant community.

KIM, CHANG-YULL, ET AL.
(TORONTO KOREAN Y.M.C.A.)
TORONTO, ONT.
 Interviewed on 16 Sept. 1978; 2.5
hrs.; 3 tapes; Korean; by Jung-gun
Kim. Forum on Korean language pro-
grammes in the Toronto area.

KIM, CHANG-YULL
TORONTO, ONT.
 Interviewed on 19 Jan., 1978; 1 hr.;
1 tape; Korean; by Jung-gun Kim.
Recounts his activity in administering
Korean immigration to Toronto.

KIM, CHANG-YULL
TORONTO, ONT.
 Interviewed on 10 June 1978; 1 hr.;
1 tape; Korean; by Jung-gun Kim.
History and significance of children's
summer camp activities.

KIM, REV. DAI-KYUN
TORONTO, ONT.
 Interviewed on 10 June 1978; 1.25
hrs.; 2 tapes; Korean; by Jung-gun
Kim. Discusses his research and find-
ings on Korean church schools.

KIM, DUK YOL
TORONTO, ONT.
 Interviewed on 10, 11 Feb. 1979; 2
hrs.; 2 tapes; Korean; by Jung-gun
Kim. 2 talks by Dr. D. Kim entitled
"A Vision of Immigrant Church" and
"Church Mission for the Second
Generation Immigrants."

KIM, REV. ECK-SUN (ANNUAL CON-
FERENCE OF TORONTO KOREAN
CHURCH SCHOOL TEACHERS' ASSOCI-
ATION)
TORONTO, ONT.
 Interviewed on 26 May 1979; 1 hr.;
1 tape; Korean; by Jung-gun Kim.
Rev. Kim speaking on "The Philos-

ophy of Immigrant Church School."

KIM, REV. ECK-SUN
TORONTO, ONT.
 Interviewed on 23 Sept. 1978; 26
Aug. 1979; 1.25 hrs.; 2 tapes; Kore-
an; by Jung-gun Kim. 2 sermons
preached by Rev. E. Kim at the
Toronto Korean United Church.

KIM, REV. ICK-SUN
TORONTO, ONT.
 Interviewed on 10 June 1978; 1.25
hrs.; 2 tapes; Korean; by Jung-gun
Kim. 3 talks on church school activ-
ities at Sae-Hahn Korean Presbyterian
Church.

KIM, IN SOOK
TORONTO, ONT.
 Correspondence mostly between
Toronto and North Korea, 1977-78. 1
cm.

KIM, J.
BRANTFORD, ONT.
 Documents related to the Kims' con-
tract managership with Bantam
Stores, Division of Royal Oak Dairy
Ltd., 1975-76. 8 cm.

KIM, JUNG
TORONTO, ONT.
 Assorted documents of early Korean
students in Canadian colleges and
universities, 1915-47. 2 cm.
 "Korea Town Thriving on Bloor St.
W." *Toronto Star*. 27 Sept. 1977. .25
cm.

KIM, KYUNG JAE (COUNCIL FOR
DEMOCRACY IN KOREA)
TORONTO, ONT.
 15 Aug. 1979; 1.75 hrs.; 2 tapes;
Korean; by Jung-gun Kim. K. Kim
speaking of "The Meaning of the Sec-

ond Liberation of Korea."

KIM, LAWRENCE
TORONTO, ONT.
 Canada News. 7 Oct. 1971 - 30 May
1981. 4 reels of microfilm.

KIM, MOON-RYANG (KOREAN CANA-
DIAN CULTURAL ASSOCIATION)
TORONTO, ONT.
 Interviewed on 20, 21 March 1978;
3.5 hrs.; 4 tapes; Korean; by Jung-
gun Kim. Immigrated to Canada in
1971.

KOH, WON
TORONTO, ONT.
 Interviewed on 2 Dec. 1978; 1.75
hrs.; 2 tapes; Korean; by Jung-gun
Kim. Dr. W. Kohn speaking on
Korean poets involved in the protest
movement against the South Korean
regime.

LEE, REV. SANG CHUL
TORONTO, ONT.
 Interviewed on 7, 13 April 1979;
1.25 hrs.; 8 tapes; Korean; by Jung-
gun Kim. Life history of Rev. S.
Lee.

LEE, REV. SANG CHUL
TORONTO, ONT.
 Recorded on 9 Sept. 1979; .75 hr.; 1
tape; Korean; by Jung-gun Kim. A
sermon preached by Rev. S. Lee at
the Toronto Korean United Church.

LEE, REV. SUNG-KAP
TORONTO, ONT.
 Interviewed on 10 June 1978; 1.25
hrs.; 2 tapes; Korean; by Jung-gun
Kim. Bible Instruction and Language
in Immigrant Church School, a panel
discussion with participation by Rev.

S. K. Lee, K. T. Hahn and E. W. Kim, at the Annual Conference of the Toronto Church School Teachers' Association, Sae-Hahn Church.

MOON, REV. CHAIRIN
TORONTO, ONT.
 Interviewed on 3, 22 Dec. 1977; 9 hrs.; 9 tapes; Korean; by Jung-gun Kim. An historical account of Manchuria.

MOON, REV. CHAIRIN
TORONTO, ONT.
 2 photographs: graduating class of 1931, Emmanuel College in Toronto; and Rev. Moon, 1973. Taped recording.
 Recorded on 2 April 1978; 1 hr.; 1 tape; Korean; by Jung-gun Kim. Sermon preached by Rev. Moon before his return to Korea.
 "Minister Faced Prison Camp Death Three Times." *Toronto Star*. 2 May 1973. .25 cm.

NAM, CHUNG-SOOK
TORONTO, ONT.
 Interviewed on 30 Sept., 1 Oct. 1978; 3.5 hrs.; 4 tapes; Korean; by Jung-gun Kim. Revival sermons.

OGLE, GEORGE
TORONTO, ONT.
 Interviewed on 27 May 1978; .75 hr.; 1 tape; Korean; by Jung-gun Kim. A discussion on the Urban Industrial Mission in South Korea.

PARK, CHAN-UNG
TORONTO, ONT.
 Interviewed on 4 March 1978; 2 hrs.; 2 tapes; Korean; by Jung-gun Kim. Discussion on the South Korean 1960s student democracy movement, immigration in 1975, and Canadian nativism and prejudice as perceived and encountered by the interviewee.
 Chongryonghoe yonpo (Blue Dragon Family Annals). Nos. 1-12, 1965-76. 2 cm.
 Sungchonko (Victory Drum), 1977, 102 pp.; 1978, 107 pp.

————.
TORONTO, ONT.
 Recorded in 1975-76; 7.5 hrs.; 8 tapes; Korean; by Jung-gun Kim. Manuscripts tape recorded by the author, C. Park.

PARK, REV. KYU-BONG (KOREAN CHURCH SCHOOL TEACHERS' ASSOCIATION)
TORONTO, ONT.
 Recorded on 26 May 1979; 1 hr.; 1 tape; Korean; by Jung-gun Kim. Rev. K. Park speaking on Immigrant Church School and Music.

RO, YOON KEU
TORONTO, ONT.
 Interviewed on 10 Feb. 1978; 3.75 hrs.; 4 tapes; Korean; by Jung-gun Kim. Arrived in late 1960s, later president of the Korean Canadian Cultural Association

SCOTT, WILLIAM
BRANTFORD, ONT.
 Interviewed on 17 Nov. 1977; 1 hr.; 1 tape; English; by Jung-gun Kim. Account of various Korean "seed" immigrants.
 Scott, William. *Canadians in Korea: Brief Historical Sketch of Canadian Mission Work in Korea*. 1975. 243 pp.

SEO, REV. KEUM CHA
BRAMALEA, ONT.
62 photographs: religious activities at
the East Manchurian Presbytery,
Manchuria, 1939. Taped interview.
Interviewed on 18 Sept. 1978; 4
hrs.; 4 tapes; Korean; by Jung-gun
Kim. Arrived in Canada in 1975.
*Jubilee Album of the East
Manchurian Presbytery.* 1939. 1 cm.

SONG, JOONG-GOO
TORONTO, ONT.
Interviewed on 11 Oct. 1978; 3.75
hrs.; 4 tapes; Korean; by Jung-gun
Kim. Immigrated to Canada in 1968.

SUH, CHUNG-KYUN
TORONTO, ONT.
Interviewed on 7 Oct. 1978; 1.5
hrs.; 2 tapes; Korean; by Jung-gun
Kim. A presentation on the prospect
of Korean unification.

SUK, REV. KWANG-OK
TORONTO, ONT.
Interviewed on 16 Aug. 1978; 2
hrs.; 2 tapes; Korean; by Jung-gun
Kim. Immigrated to Canada in 1977,
discusses her training as Buddhist
nun, and the founding of Pulkwang-sa
Temple.

SUNOO, HAROLD HAKWON
TORONTO, ONT.
Interviewed on 27 May 1978; .75
hr.; 1 tape; Korean; by Jung-gun
Kim. On the question of desired
Korean unification.

SURH, WILLIAM
TORONTO, ONT.
Clippings, 1950-55, and 1 telegram
regarding immigration, 1953. .25 cm.
Photographs. Taped interview.
21 photographs: W. Surh's life in

Toronto, 1953-1970.
Interviewed on 20 Jan. 1978; .5 hr.;
1 tape; English; by Jung-gun Kim.
Immigrated to Canada in 1953.

WHANG, TAI YUN
TORONTO, ONT.
Interviewed on 8 Nov. 1977; 4 hrs.;
4 tapes; Korean; by Jung-gun Kim.
Arrived in Canada in 1947.

YIM, SANG-DAE
TORONTO, ONT.
Interviewed on 1 Oct. 1978; .25 hr.;
1 tape; Korean; by Jung-gun Kim. A
prayer offered at a revival meeting.

═══════════════════════

ASSOCIATION OF KOREAN CHRISTIAN
SCHOLARS IN NORTH AMERICA
TORONTO, ONT.
Financial records, 1978, and bro-
chures. .25 cm. See Toronto Korean
United Church.
Hoeji (News and Views). No. 4,
Jan. 1978. 26 pp.

ASSOCIATION OF KOREAN CHRISTIAN
SCHOLARS IN NORTH AMERICA
WALTHAM, MASSACHUSSETS
Recorded from 31 May to 2 June
1979; 11 hrs.; 14 tapes; Kore-
an/English; by Jung-gun Kim. 9 pres-
entations on Korean immigration and
ethnicity.

ASSOCIATION OF KOREAN SCHOLARS
IN CANADA (CHAI SHIN YU)
TORONTO, ONT.
Membership list with annual confer-
ence programme, 1974. .5 cm.

BECKER MILK COMPANY LTD (K.Y. KANG)
PORT CREDIT, ONT.
 Contract manager manual, 1975. .25 cm.

CANADA ASIA WORKING GROUP
TORONTO, ONT.
 "Human Rights Are Being Trampled Upon Somewhere in Asia." 1978. .25 cm.
 Canada Asia Currents. Vol. 1, nos. 1-2, 1979. .5 cm.
 Made in Korea: Cheap Clothing at Whose Expense. 1978. .25 cm.

CANADA NEWS PUBLICATIONS
TORONTO, ONT.
 21 photographs showing various activities (sports, entertainment, religious ceremony, schools) within Toronto's Korean community, 1970s.
 American News. March 1972 - Jan. 1975. Microfilm.
 Hanin opso chonwhabu (Korean Business and Organization Directory). June 1977, Oct. 1977, Jan. 1979, May 1979. .25 cm.
 Hankookilbo Overseas Edition. 7 Jan. 1972 - 2 Nov. 1973. Microfilm.
 Local News. Dec. 1971 - Dec. 1972. Microfilm.

COUNCIL FOR DEMOCRACY IN KOREA
TORONTO, ONT.
 Included are a series of lectures on Korean unification (4 of which have been recorded on audio cassettes) and newsclippings, 1977-79. 3 cm.

DONG WOO MUTUAL ASSOCIATION
TORONTO, ONT.
 Dong Woo Chusorok (Membership Directory). 1978. 1 cm.

EAST TORONTO KOREAN PRESBYTERIAN CHURCH
TORONTO, ONT.
 Kyohoe yoram (Church Handbook). 1977. 24 pp.
 Kyou chusorok (Membership Directory). 1979. 43 pp.
 Pogoso. 1978. A Report on Starting a Korean Language School. 11 pp.
 Saop pogoso. 1974, 1975, 1977, 1978. Annual report. 1.5 cm.

FIRST KOREAN PRESBYTERIAN CHURCH
TORONTO, ONT.
 Purun chochang (Green Pasture). Nos. 1-18, Jan. 1977 - Aug. 1978. (No. 4 missing). .25 pp.

HANMAN KOREAN LANGUAGE SCHOOL
TORONTO, ONT.
 Samples of instructional materials, n.d. 1 cm. See Y. S. Huh.

KOREAN ASSOCIATION OF HAMILTON
HAMILTON, ONT.
 Constitution, annual reports, membership lists, and flyers, 1977-78. 1 cm.
 Hanin hoebo. Nos. 1-3, May, July, Dec. 1978. Bulletin. .25 cm.

KOREAN BUDDHIST ASSOCIATION
TORONTO, ONT.
 Newsclippings and 6 introductory brochures on the Toronto Korean Buddhist Association and the Son (Zen) Lotus Society, n.d. 1 cm.
 Taped recording.
 Recorded on 17 Jan. 1979; 1.5 hrs.; 2 tapes; English; by Jung-gun Kim. Korean Buddhist chant followed by a sermon preached by Samu Sunin.

KOREAN CANADIAN ASSOCIATION OF
METROPOLITAN TORONTO
TORONTO, ONT.
 The collection includes constitution,
financial records, annual reports,
correspondence, an address book, and
programmes, 1972-79; also list of 800
petitioners sent to the president of the
Republic of Korea, 1977. 3 cm.
 Hanin Hoebo. Dec. 1969 - Aug.
1979. Scattered issues of bulletin. 2
cm.

KOREAN CANADIAN CULTURAL ASSO-
CIATION
TORONTO, ONT.
 *Canadian-Korean Youth Orchestra:
Concert 3.* 1989. 20 pp.
 *Directory of Korean-Canadians in
Metropolitan Toronto. 1979-80.* 257
pp.
 *Directory of Korean-Canadians in
Metropolitan Toronto. 1984.* 260 pp.
 *Directory of Korean-Canadians in
Ontario.* 1987, 144 pp.; 1989, 300
pp. 4 cm.
 Korean Business Directory, Toronto
region. 1985-86. 177 pp.
 *Koreans in Ontario: A Community
Conference.* 1986. 58 pp.
 The Korean Buddhist News. 1987.
Exhibition of 100 Kinds of Dal-Ma
Zen Drawing and Calligraphy by
Korean Senior Monks. 20 pp.

KOREAN-CANADIAN PEN CLUB
TORONTO, ONT.
 Imin munhak (Immigrants' Litera-
ture). 1979. .5 cm.

KOREAN CANADIAN SCHOLARSHIP
FOUNDATION
TORONTO, ONT.
 1 brochure explaining the purpose
and activities of the Foundation.
1979. .25 cm.

KOREAN CATHOLIC COMMUNITY OF
LONDON
LONDON, ONT.
 46 photographs: activities of Korean
Catholics in London, Ontario, c.
1960-80.
 Chubo. Jan. 1977 - Dec. 1978.
Church bulletin. 400 pp.
 Yaksa (A Short History). Jan. 1979.
.25 cm.

KOREAN CENTRAL PRESBYTERIAN
CHURCH
TORONTO, ONT.
 Membership directory and 1 flyer,
1979. .25 cm.
 Kyoin chusorok Membership Direc-
tory. 1979. 4 pp.
 Pulkidung Pillar of Fire. Vol. 1, no.
1, Sept. 1973; no. 2, Feb. 1974. 1
cm.

KOREAN CHRISTIAN SCHOOL
LONDON, ONT.
 Church pamphlets, 1970s. 2 cm. See
Rev. S. K. Lee:
 Haengsa kyehoekpyo (Church Activ-
ities). 1977. 5 cm.
 Kanaan. Nos. 6, 7, 9; March, June,
Oct. 1978. 1 cm.
 Kil (The Way). Nos. 1-5, April
1974-Dec. 1975. 1 cm.
 Yonye saop pogoso (Annual Report).
1972, 1973, 1976, 1977. 1 cm.

KOREAN CHURCH OF TORONTO
ISLINGTON, ONT.
 Chubo. 4 Dec. 1977; 8, 29 Jan.
1978. Church bulletin. .25 cm.
 Kolkoda. No. 1, Oct. 1977. .25 cm.
 Kyohoe sosik. (Pastoral Epistle).
No.3, Jan. 1978. .25 cm.
 Songchang kyehoeg-an (Church
Development Plan). 1978. .25 cm.

KOREAN DEMOCRACY AND UNIFICA-
TION SOCIETY OF CANADA
TORONTO, ONT.
 Constitution, 1977, and taped lec-
ture, "Contemporary Korean National
Poets and Their Role in Fighting
against the Dictatorship," by Dr. Won
Koh, 1978.

KOREAN EDUCATION SOCIETY OF
TORONTO
TORONTO, ONT.
 Records, 1977-78, include constitution, minutes, correspondence, financial statements, membership and mailing lists, reports, and flyers. 2 cm.

KOREAN HUMAN RIGHTS COUNCIL IN
ONTARIO
TORONTO, ONT.
 Constitution and by-laws and miscel-
laneous paper items, c. 1977. .5 cm.

KOREAN JOURNAL (YOUNG RIN YU)
TORONTO, ONT.
 The Korean Journal. Toronto, 26
Nov. 1972 - 19 March 1978. News-
paper (weekly). 5 reels of microfilm.

KOREAN PRAYER MEETING
TORONTO, ONT.
 Interviewed on 10, 17, 24 Nov., 1
Dec. 1978; 3.5 hrs.; 4 tapes; Korean;
by Jung-gun Kim.

KOREAN PUBLIC FORUM (TORONTO
KOREAN Y.M.C.A.)
TORONTO, ONT.
 Interviewed on 4 Feb. 1978; 2.5
hrs.; 3 tapes; Korean; by Jung-gun
Kim. Public forum on the future
direction for the Korean community
in Canada, with Dr. Sang Whay
Kooh, Rev. Samu SunimFirst Korean,
Rev. P. Lee, Mr. Taik K. Chun, and
Mr. Chan Do Park participating.

KOREAN SENIOR CITIZEN'S ASSOCI-
ATION
TORONTO, ONT.
 Noin hoebo (The Voice of Korean
Senior Citizens). Jan.-Oct. 1975.

KOREAN SOCIETY OF LONDON
LONDON, ONT.
 Minutes, membership list (in news-
letters), and leaflets, 1970-77. 2 cm.
Photographs.
 5 photographs: activities of the Kore-
an Society of London, Ont., c. 1970s.
 Hanin chusorok (Address book).
1978. 60 pp.
 Sosik. 1970-78. Newsletter. 3 cm.

KOREAN SOCIETY OF METROPOLITAN
WINDSOR
WINDSOR, ONT.
 Newsletter. Jan., Feb., April 1976.
.25 cm.

KOREAN UNIVERSITY STUDENTS'
ASSOCIATION
SCARBOROUGH, ONT.
 Maetdol (Millstone). 1978-79. 1 cm.

"KOREAN VOICE OF HOPE"
TORONTO, ONT.
 Recorded on 7, 8, 15, 22 Nov.; 6,
13, 20 Dec. 1977; 3 Jan. 1978; 3
hrs.; 3 tapes; Korean; by Jung-gun
Kim. 30-minute weekly radio programme broadcast by CHIN 101 FM.

MULTICULTURAL HISTORY SOCIETY
OF ONTARIO
TORONTO, ONT.
 Kang, S. B. *Saem gurigo namu.*
1977. 167 pp.
 Lee, Sang Mook. *Purun chot-ui
ch'onyo* (The Virgin with Blue
Nipples). 1976. 120 pp.
 Stiles, John. "Canadian-Korean Rela-
tions." A lecture given at the

Inter-University Seminar on Modern East Asia, Glendon College, 24 Nov. 1978. 10 pp.
Che samil (The Third Day). Nos. 1-41, Oct. 1974-Aug. 1979 (nos. 6, 7, 16 missing). 2 cm.
Korea Times. 1 June 1981 - 31 Dec 1987. 20 reels of microfilm.
Minjoong Shinmoon. 23 Feb. 1979 - 25 Dec. 1987. 14 reels of microfilm.
Tong Il Munye. No. 1, March 1979; No. 2, June 1979. .5 cm.

MULTICULTURAL NEWSPAPER MICROFILM PROJECT
TORONTO, ONT.
Korean Journal. Toronto, 26 Nov. 1972 - 27 Dec. 1987. 11 reels of microfilm.
Korea Times. Toronto, 1 Jan. 1988 - 30 Dec. 1989. 7 reels of microfilm.

ONTARIO ETHNIC NEWSPAPER MICROFILM PROJECT
TORONTO, ONT.
Korean Canada Times. 19 March 1971 - 17 July 1972. 1 reel of microfilm.

ONTARIO KOREAN BUSINESSMEN'S ASSOCIATION
TORONTO, ONT.
Silhyop: News Magazine for Ontario Korean Businssmen. No. 1, Dec. 1978; No. 2, March 1979. .5 cm.

RADIO HANKOOK, KOREAN RADIO PROGRAMME
HANKOOK, KOREA
Recorded on 27 Nov., 11 Dec. 1977; 15, 22 Jan. 1978; 2 hrs.; 2 tapes; Korean; by Jung-gun Kim. 30-minute weekly programmes.

SAE-HAHN KOREAN PRESBYTERIAN CHURCH
TORONTO, ONT.
3 brochures related to Church activities, n.d. .5 cm
Kyou chusorok (Membership Directory). 1978. 28 pp.
Sae-Hahn Sosik (Newsletter). No. 1, Jan. 1977 - No. 9, Feb 1978. 1.5 cm.

SEOUL NATIONAL UNIVERSITY ALUMNI-CANADA
NEWMARKET, ONT.
Hoewon myongpu (Address Book). 1979. 37 pp.
Sangrok (Evergreen). No. 1 June 1978. 40 pp.
Tongchang hoebo (Alumni News). May 1979. .25 cm.

THE COUNCIL OF KOREAN UNITED CHURCH LEADERS IN CANADA
TORONTO, ONT.
Bijon (Vision). Nos. 1 - 5, June 197? - Nov. 1976. 5 cm.

THURSDAY EVENING PRAYER MEETING
TORONTO, ONT.
2 books of minutes, March-Dec. 1977; and taped prayer and discussion.

TORONTO KOREAN BIBLICAL SEMINARY
TORONTO, ONT.
3 brochures introducing Toronto Korean Biblical Seminary, n.d. .25 cm.
Yoram. 1978-79. Bulletin. .25 cm.

TORONTO KOREAN CATHOLIC CHURCH
TORONTO, ONT.
Financial reports, membership directories, and flyers, 1977-79. 1 cm.

Hanman chapji (Hanman Church Magazine). Nos. 2-5, 1972-78. 4 cm.

Hanman chubo (Hanma Church Bulletin). Jan. 4-Dec. 1976. 4 cm.

TORONTO KOREAN CHURCH SCHOOL TEACHERS' ASSOCIATION (ELEMENTARY SECTION)
TORONTO, ONT.
Constitution, annual reports, financial records, members list, and flyers, 1977-79. 1 cm. See Korean Teachers' Association.

TORONTO KOREAN METRO UNITED CHURCH (REV. CHAI-SHIN YU)
TORONTO, ONT.
Brochures related to Church activities, 1979. 3 cm. See Rev. Duk-yul Kim.

Hanin kyohoe sosik. Nos. 11-50, Nov. 1974-Aug. 1979 (nos. 16-21, 29 missing). Newsletter. 3 cm.

Karam (River). Nos. 16-18, Oct. 1975-Jan. 1978. .5 cm.

Kyoin chusorok. 1978. Membership directory. 71 pp.

TORONTO KOREAN MINISTERS' ASSOCIATION
TORONTO, ONT.
Membership Directory. 1978. .25 cm.

TORONTO KOREAN MISSION CHURCH
TORONTO, ONT.
1 photograph: members of the Mission, 1978.

Kwangyaui sori (A Voice in the Wilderness). Nos. 36-38, April, June 1977, April 1978. .5 cm.

Saop mit haengsa kyehoekpyo (Business and Activities). 1979. 13 pp.

TORONTO KOREAN PRESBYTERIAN CHURCH
TORONTO, ONT.
Church Bulletins, 1968-70; church school curriculum and budget; 1978-79; and leaflets, 1976-79. 1 reel of microfilm. 2 cm. See C. K. Kim.

Kim, Rev. Chang-Kim. "New Perspectives in the Relationship Between Mother-in-law and Daughter-in-law within the Korean Family." A paper prepared for his doctor of ministry programme, McCormick Theological Seminary, Chicago, n.d. .5 cm.

_____. "Toronto Korean Biblical Seminary." A paper prepared for his doctor of ministry programme, McCormick Theological Seminary, Chicago, n.d.

Chu ane hana (One in God). Sept. 1975. .25 cm.

Chubo. 1968-70. Church bulletin. 1 reel of microlm.

Chusorok. 1978, 1979. Membership directory. 1 cm.

Joshua. Nos. 2-3, 1976, 1977. 2.5 cm.

Kaech okcha (The Pioneer). Nos. 1-30, Jan. 1976-June 1979. 3 cm.

Kyohoe illam. 1977, 1978, 1979. Church Handbook. .5 cm.

Saop pogo. 1976, 1977, 1978. Annual report. 1.5 cm.

Wolbo. Vol. 1, no. 1, Jan. 1968; Vol. 2, no. 9, Dec. 1970 (monthly). 1 reel of microfilm.

Wolpo. June 1968-Dec. 1969 (monthly). 1 cm.

TORONTO KOREAN UNITED CHURCH (REV. SANG-CHUL LEE)
TORONTO, ONT.
Brochures related to church activities, choir membership list and a guide for newcomers, 1975-78. 1 cm.

Kim, Yu Rak. *Insul-ui sado.* (The

activities of Dr. F. Murray in Korea.)
Seoul: Korean Christian Literature
Society, 1973. 187 pp.
Kyoin chusorok. 1976, 1978. (Mem-
bership directory). 1.5 cm.
Pyonji. Nov. 1977 - Sept. 1979.
Newsletter. 3 cm.
Sado (Disciple). No. 1, 1976. 56 pp.
Saop pogoso. 1974, 1975, 1977
1978. Annual report. 2 cm.
Sonkuja (The Pioneer). Nos. 1-17,
April 1970-Nov. 1975; and scattered
issues from Feb. 1976 to July 1979.

TORONTO KOREAN Y.M.C.A.
TORONTO, ONT.
22 leaflets related to the activities of
the Toronto Korean YMCA, 1977-78.
*Growing Koreans: A Survey on the
Built-up Areas of Koreans in Metro
Toronto*. Prepared by John Kang, in
Sook Cho and Joanne Lee, sponsored
by the Korean Service Centre of
YMCA, and funded by the Ministry
of Culture and Recreation, Summer
1978. .5 cm.
Hangul Kyobon. n.d. Korean Heri-
tage Language Text. 1 cm.
Sosik. Sept. 1977, March 1979.
Newsletter. .5 cm.

YOUNG-NAK KOREAN PRESBYTERIAN
CHURCH OF TORONTO
TORONTO, ONT.
Membership directory, 1978. .5 cm.
Young-Nak (Eternal Joy). No. 1, July
1978; no. 2, Nov 1978. .5 cm.

AGÜERO, MARCELINO
TORONTO, ONT.
Interviewed on 4 April 1979; 1.5 hrs.; 2 tapes; Spanish; by Ruth Lee. Discusses objectives and activities of the Encuentro de Organizaciones Latinoamericanas.

AGUILAR, SONIA
TORONTO, ONT.
Interviewed on July 1987; 1.5 hrs.; 2 tapes; English; by Michael Le Desma. Emigrated from Ecuador to Canada in the 1970s, discusses her acculturation, and ethnic identity.

ARANGO, CAROLINA
TORONTO, ONT.
Correspondence and clippings related to donor's book, *Fantasias*. 1 cm (9 items). Taped interview.
Interviewed on 29 May 1979; 2.5 hrs.; 3 tapes; Spanish; by Ruth Lee. Emigrated from Columbia, discusses her poetry, and involvement in the Colombian Cultural Association of Toronto.

ARANGO, CAROLINA
TORONTO, ONT.
Recorded on 29 May 1979; 2.5 hrs.; 3 tapes; Spanish; by Ruth Lee. Colombian conference held at the University of Toronto. Discusses Bogota City, its geography, culture and festivities, and the "Birth and Development of America."

ARANGO, WILLIAM
TORONTO, ONT.
Interviewed on 7 July 1979; .5 hr.; 1 tape; Spanish; by Ruth Lee. Born in Colombia, arrived in 1944, a leading member of the Colombian Cultural Association.

BORJA, LUIS EDUARDO
TORONTO, ONT.
Interviewed on 13 Feb. 1978; 1 hr.; 1 tape; English; by Beatrice Traub-Werner. A Colombian immigrant, worked as a journalist for *El Popular*.
Borja, Lalo. "Latin Americans in Canada in the First Decade: A Proposal for a Photographic Study." 1978. 5 pp.

BORJAS, LALO
TORONTO, ONT.
Interviewed on 28 Feb. 1981; 1 hr.; 1 tape; English; by L. Rojas. Arrived in Canada as an illegal immigrant. Illustrated book on Latin Americans in Toronto, c. 1970s.

BOUCH, JORGE AND ELENA
TORONTO, ONT.
Interviewed on 14 Nov. 1977; 1 hr.; 1 tape; Spanish; by Beatrice Traub-Werner. Emigrated from Chile after the overthrow of the Allende government.

CARCAMO BRUCH, MARGARITA
TORONTO, ONT.
Interviewed on 4 May 1979; 1.5 hrs.; 2 tapes; Spanish; by Ruth Lee. Arrived in Canada in 1949, founding member of the Spanish-Speaking Parents' Association. in Toronto.

CASS, OLGA
TORONTO, ONT.
Interviewed in Aug. 1987; 1.5 hrs.; 2 tapes; English; by Michael Le Desma. Political refugee from El Salvador, discusses his involvement in St. Peter's Immigration Centre.

DELIA, MARIA
TORONTO, ONT.
Interviewed in Aug. 1987; 1 hr.; 1 tape; English/Spanish; by Michael Le Desma. Emigrated from Uruguay, involved with St. Peter's Immigration Centre.

DURAN, MARCELA AND CLAUDIO
TORONTO, ONT.
Articles and clippings. Taped interview.
Interviewed on 4 March 1977; 1 hr.; 1 tape; English; by Beatrice Traub-Werner. Chilean political refugees during the overthrow of the Allende government.
Duran, Claudio. "Chile: Revolution and Counter-Revolution." *Social Praxis*. 1973.
_____. "Psycho War of the Media in Chile Under Allende." *Media Probe*. n.d.
Duran, Marcela. "Values of Education : A Study of the Spanish-Speaking Latin American Children in the Junior Schools of Metro Toronto." Masters thesis, University of Toronto, 1975.

ELMIR, ALBERTO
TORONTO, ONT.
Interviewed on 7 July 1987; 1.5 hrs.; 2 tapes; English; by Michael Le Desma. Emigrated from Ecuador, editor of *El Popular* newspaper.

FORBES RUEDA, AMADA AND JOSE
TORONTO, ONT.
19 postcards received from relatives, n.d. Taped interview.
Interviewed on 1 Nov. 1977; 1 hr.; 1 tape; Spanish; by Beatrice Traub-Werner. Arrived in Canada in 1968.

GATICA, JORGE AND GILDA
TORONTO, ONT.
Interviewed on 12 Dec. 1977; 2 hrs.; 2 tapes; Spanish; by Beatrice Traub-Werner. Chilean immigrants, 1970s; Gilda works for Instituto Latinoamericano de Educacion y Cultura.

GOULLIVER, ROSA
TORONTO, ONT.
Interviewed on 28 Nov. 1977; 1 hr.; 1 tape; Spanish; by Beatrice Traub-Werner. Arrived from Ecuador in 1972.

HACKEMBRUCH, HENRI AND BLANCA
MISSISSAUGA, ONT.
Interviewed on 9 July 1979; 3.5 hrs.; 4 tapes; Spanish; by Ruth Lee. They emigrated from Uruguay in 1969.

HUMERES, EUGENIA
TORONTO, ONT.
Interviewed on 28 Oct. 1977; .5 hr.; 1 tape; Spanish; by Beatrice Traub-Werner. Emigrated from Chile in 1973.

JIMENEZ, MANUEL
TORONTO, ONT.
Interviewed on 14 May 1979; 2 hrs.;
2 tapes; Spanish; by Ruth Lee. Emigrated from Peru in 1969.

LAZCANO, DAVID
TORONTO, ONT.
Interviewed on 28 Feb. 1978; 2 hrs.;
2 tapes; English/Spanish; by Beatrice
Traub-Werner. Originally from
Bolivia, arrived in Canada, via
Argentina in 1970.

LE DESMA, MICHAEL
TORONTO, ONT.
Assorted material from the
Cross-Cultural Communications
Centre, press releases by *International Hispanic Fiesta*, feasibility
study of Atkinson College Outreach
Programme for the Latin American
community, list of numerous Latin
American clubs and localities in
Metro Toronto, as well as miscel-
laneous articles, pamphlets, and clip-
pings, c. 1980-87. 12 cm. Photo-
graphs.
29 photographs: Latin American
store fronts, churches, and people in
Toronto. 10 photographs: multi-eth-
nic, c. 1980-85; and "El Rincon" bar,
n.d.
Anonymous interview with "Pedro";
recorded in Aug. 1987; 1 hr.; 1 tape;
English; by Michael Le Desma. Interview with a political refugee who fled
Guatemala.
Jofre, Manuel A. "Bibliography of
Latin American Literature in English
Translation." York University, 1978.
El Pregonero Hispano. Sept., Dec.
1984; March, Oct. 1985; May, June
1987. 4 cm.
Gráfico L. Toronto, July 1987
(monthly) .25 cm.

Guía Hispana, Toronto-Montreal.
1986. 1987. 3 cm.
International Hispanic Fiesta. Sept.
1986 (special issue).
Jornada. Vol. 1, no. 1, Oct. 1986,
July 1987 (2 issues).
La Razón. Toronto, Aug. 1987.
(weekly, 1 issue).
*Latin American Working Group
Bookstore Catalogue.* 1986. .5 cm.
"Latin-American Newcomers: Issues
Affecting the Adaptation of Immi-
grants from Chile, Nicaragua,
Guatemala, and El Salvador." Alberta
Manpower Settlement Services, 1983.
Nuevo Diario. Toronto, Aug. 1987.
(weekly, 1 issue).
*Segundo Anuario Fotográfico
Chileno.* Santiago: Inst. Chileano
Canadiense de Cultura, 1982.
"Select Bibliography on
Spanish-Speaking Immigrants in
Canada, 1500-77." Canadian Ident-
ities Programme, Office of the Secre-
tary of State, 1977.
"Socio-economic Profile Needs and
Gaps of the Hispanic Community in
Metropolitan Toronto." Hispanic
Social Development Council, 1983.
Tiempo. Toronto, July 1987 (1
issue).

LEE, RUTH
TORONTO, ONT.
Includes pamphlets, flyers, and
newsclippings, many from the Centro
Para Gente de Habla Hispana,
Toronto, c. 1975-80. 3 cm.
Boletin Informativo. 1979. Centro
Para Gente de Habla Hispana. 1 cm.
Crítica. 17 Feb. 1979; 24, 31 March
1979.
Correo Hispano Americano (3 issues).

El Popular. 21 March 1979; 16, 18 April 1979 (3 issues).
Toronto Latino. 19-23 Feb. 1979 (1 issue).

MACARI, RAQUEL
TORONTO, ONT.
Interviewed on 9 May 1979; 1 hr.; 1 tape; Spanish; by Ruth Lee. Discusses his work with mentally handicapped children, and the founding of the organization "Nueva Esperanza" (New Hope).

MARZIALI, HEBER
MISSISSAUGA, ONT.
Biographical sketch letters from family in Montevideo, Uruguay, Jan.-June 1968. The letters detail the family's preparation for emigration. 2 cm (83 items). Photographs. Taped interview.
26 photographs: Latin American community activities in Toronto, 1960-70.
Interviewed on 7 Nov. 1977; 3 hrs.; 3 tapes; Spanish; by Beatrice Traub-Werner. Originally from Uruguay, arrived in the 1960s.
Spanish Directory, 1977-78. .5 cm.

MARZIALI, HEBER
TORONTO, ONT.
Interviewed on 16 March, 23 April 1979; 2.25 hrs.; 3 tapes; Spanish; by Ruth Lee. Founding member of Centro Latinoamericano, and Club Uruguay, discusses their histories.

MARZIALI, RAQUEL
TORONTO, ONT.
Interviewed on 3 March, 30 April 1979; 2 hr.; 2 tape; Spanish; by Ruth Lee. Worked at the Centre for Spanish-Speaking Peoples, initially called the Asociación Mujeres Hispanas.

MCHUGH, GERMANIA AND WILSON NAVARETTE
TORONTO, ONT.
Interviewed on 16 March 1978; 2 hrs.; 2 tapes; Spanish/English; by Beatrice Traub-Werner.

MEDINA, AIDA
TORONTO, ONT.
Deportation papers, c. 1970s. 1 cm.
Photographs. Taped interview.
16 photographs: unidentified, c. 1970s.
Interviewed on 2 Jan. 1978; 2 hrs.; 2 tapes; Spanish; by Beatrice Traub-Werner. Originally from Peru.

MILUY, JACQUELINE
TORONTO, ONT.
Interviewed on 2 Feb. 1978; 1 hr.; 1 tape; English/Spanish; by Beatrice Traub-Werner. Emigrated from Uruguay in 1970.

MONTERO, GLORIA
TORONTO, ONT.
Interviewed on 30 Nov. 1977; 1 hr.; 1 tape; Spanish; by Beatrice Traub-Werner. Peruvian, immigrated to Canada, via London, England.

MURIALDO, EVELYN
TORONTO, ONT.
Interviewed on 23 Oct. 1977; 1 hr.; 1 tape; English; by Beatrice Traub-Werner. Emigrated from Chile in 1967.

NAVARRO, OSCAR
TORONTO, ONT.
Interviewed on 9 Jan. 1978; 2 hrs.; 2 tapes; English; by Beatrice

Traub-Werner. Arrived from Peru in 1973, member of the Peruvian Canadian Association.

NINIHUEYLCA, LUISA
TORONTO, ONT.
Interviewed in Aug. 1987; 1.5 hrs.; 2 tapes; English; by Michael Le Desma. Originally from Peru.

PEREZ, BELISARIO
TORONTO, ONT.
Interviewed on 9 March 1981; 1 hr.; 1 tape; English; by L. Rojas. Originally from Guatemala.

PICK, ZUZANA
TORONTO, ONT.
Interviewed on 2 April 1981; 1 hr.; 1 tape; English; by L. Rojas. A Colombian immigrant.

PIEDRAHITA, MARIA S.
TORONTO, ONT.
Interviewed on 11 Nov. 1977; 1 hr.; 1 tape; Spanish; by Beatrice Traub-Werner. A Colombian immigrant.

PINEDA, OLGA
TORONTO, ONT.
Interviewed on 10 March 1981; 1 hr.; 1 tape; Spanish; by L. Rojas. Discusses the Canadian educational system vis-a-vis Latin American students.

PIRIZ, WILSON
TORONTO, ONT.
Interviewed on 27 April 1979; 2.5 hrs.; 3 tapes; Spanish; by Ruth Lee. Discusses involvement in Club Uruguay.

ROJAS, RAUL
TORONTO, ONT.
Interviewed on 6 March 1981; 1 hr.; 1 tape; English; by L. Rojas. Commentary on the degree of cohesion within Toronto's Latin American community.

RUIZ, WILSON
TORONTO, ONT.
Interviewed on 5 March 1981; 1 hr.; 1 tape; English; by L. Rojas. Discusses his immigration, and his career as a T.V., and radio broadcaster.

SMITH, MARIA LUISA
TORONTO, ONT.
Interviewed on 19 Dec. 1977; 2 hrs.; 2 tapes; Spanish; by Beatrice Traub-Werner. Originally from Ecuador, recounts her immigration to Canada.

TABAK, ENRIQUE
TORONTO, ONT.
Collection of assorted material from the Latin-American Institute of Culture and Education, "Dia del Chidrens" (1977), Centre for Spanish-Speaking Peoples, Bloor-Bathurst Information Centre, Sadra Day Care Centre, Centro Hispanoamericano de Cultura, and Centro Ecumenico Pastoral Latinoamericano, 1976-77; and documents regarding the Toronto Board of Education's Heritage Language Programme, 1977. 12 cm. Taped interview.
Interviewed on 12 March 1977; 1 hr.; 1 tape; English; by Beatrice Traub-Werner. Discusses the history of the Group for the Defence of Human Rights in Argentina.
La Tribuna. Nov. 1976; March, April 1977.

TRAUB-WERNER, BEATRICE
TORONTO, ONT.
 Collection of bulletins, flyers,
pamphlets, and book lists from the
Centre for Spanish-Speaking Peoples,
Latin American Working Group,
Latin American Community Centre,
Cross-Cultural Communications
Centre, Group for the Defence of
Human Rights in Argentina, and
Encounter of Latin American Organ-
izations, c. 1970-80. 9 cm.
 Rojas, Raul. "Latin American Immi-
grants in Toronto." Prepared by
IMPACT Toronto, a project funded
by the Secretary of State through
Summer Job Corps., Ottawa, 1978.
64 pp.
 Club de Seniors Hispano-Americano.
March 1978. Newsletter.
 Guia de los recien llegados.
Toronto: Ministry of Culture and
Recreation, 1976.
 *La emigracion europa a la America
Latina: Fuentes y estado de
investigacion.* Colloquium Verlag
Berlin, 1975.
 "Latin Americans In North York: An
Exploratory Study Submitted to the
Latin American Community Centre."
Spanish Speaking Peoples in Weston,
Nov. 1980.
 Migracion. Vol. 4, nos. 9-10, 1974.
Buenos Aires: Comision Catolica
Argentina de Immigracion. .5 cm.
 Snippets. Community newspaper
monitoring project, 1977. .5 cm (3
issues).
 *Two Thirds: A Journal of Under-
development Studies.* Vol. 1. no. 1,
1978. .5 cm.
 We Are One People. c. 1977.
Encounter of Latin American Organ-
izations in Toronto. 67 pp.

UHALDE, JUAN JOSE
TORONTO, ONT.
 Interviewed on 6 May 1979; 2 hrs.;
2 tapes; Spanish; by Ruth Lee. Discusses the history of the Uruguayian
dance ensemble "Abriendo
Horizontes."

UREÑA, EDUARDO
TORONTO, ONT.
 Interviewed on 15 March 1981; 1
hr.; 1 tape; English; by L. Rojas.
Interview deals with the history of the
Latin American press in Toronto.

VARGAS, PEDRO
TORONTO, ONT.
 Interviewed on 23 Feb. 1981; 1 hr.;
1 tape; English; by L. Rojas. Discusses the prejudice he has experi-
enced in Canada.

VILLARROEL, MARIO
TORONTO, ONT.
 Interviewed on 17 Feb. 1978; 1 hr.;
1 tape; English; by Beatrice
Traub-Werner. Emigrated from
Bolivia in 1964 as a seminarian.

===

"ABRIENDO HORIZONTE"
TORONTO, ONT.
 6 photographs: folk dance
perfomances in Uruguay, 1960s. See
Juan Jose Uhalde.

ASSOCIATION CULTURAL
COLOMBIANA DE TORONTO
TORONTO, ONT.
 Includes letter of incorporation,
correspondence, and pamphlets,
1978-79. 1.5 cm.

BALLET FOLCLORICO COLOMBIANO
TORONTO, ONT.
7 letters regarding the performance of the dance group, c. 1970s. Taped interview with W. Arango.

CENTRE FOR SPANISH-SPEAKING
PEOPLES
TORONTO, ONT.
Includes minutes, financial records, annual reports, bulletins, and newsclippings, 1976-77; and the Heritage Language Programme, 1977. 3 cm. See taped discussion of women's group meeting at the Centre, Raquel Marziali.
Annual Report. 1976-77. .5 cm.
Newsletter. 1975, 1976. 3 cm.

CLUB URUGUAY'S ANNUAL GENERAL
ASSEMBLY
TORONTO, ONT.
Recorded on 17 March 1979; .5 hr.; 1 tape; Spanish; by Ruth Lee. Reports from the president and treasurer.

EL POPULAR (LATIN AMERICAN
NEWSPAPER)
TORONTO, ONT.
Physical distribution study on the newspaper, 1980. .5 cm. Taped interview with E. Ureña, editor of paper.

GROUP FOR THE DEFENCE OF CIVIL
RIGHTS IN ARGENTINA (E. TABAK)
TORONTO, ONT.
Collection of pamphlets, letters, posters, and announcements issued by the Group for Defence of Civil Rights in Argentina, Toronto, c. 1970-80. 6 cm. Taped interview with M. and C. Durah.
Argentina '76: A Dossier on Political Repression and the Violation of Human Rights. .5 cm.

GRUPO JUVENIL OF CLUB URUGUAY
TORONTO, ONT.
2 photographs: n.d. See F. Piritz and Heber Marziali.

LATIN-AMERICAN COMMUNITY
CENTRE
TORONTO, ONT.
Information sheets, 1977. .25 cm.

MULTICULTURAL HISTORY SOCIETY
OF ONTARIO
TORONTO, ONT.
Anderson, Grace M. "A Fragile Unity: Spanish-Speaking Immigrants in Anglophone Cities." 1982. Unpublished. 298 pp.

MULTICULTURAL NEWSPAPER
MICROFILM PROJECT
TORONTO, ONT.
Correo Hispano Americano. Toronto, 8 Jan. 1977 - 14 1978. 1 reel of microfilm.
El Popular. Toronto, 11 Sept. 1970 - 31 Dec. 1987. 37 reels of microfilm.

"NUEVA ESPERANZA" (NEW HOPE)
TORONTO, ONT.
See Raquel Macari.

PERUVIAN CANADIAN ASSOCIATION
TORONTO, ONT.
Internal regulations and letters of incorporation, 1975. .25 cm. Taped interview with M. Jimenez.

WOMEN OF LATIN AMERICAN
DESCENT
TORONTO, ONT.
Recorded on 27 Oct. 1977; 1 hr.; 1 tape; Spanish; by Beatrice Traub-Werner. A taped session of evening meetings.

LATVIAN COLLECTION

AUNS, D.
OTTAWA, ONT.
13 photographs: family gatherings; and picnics in Ottawa, 1959-52. Taped interview.
Interviewed in April 1978; 2 hrs.; 2 tapes; Latvian; by I. P. Taylor.

BABRIS, JANINA
ILLINOIS, U.S.
Babris, Janina. *Friendship on the Wing*. Grand Haven, Michigan: Raven Printing 1975. A children's story in English.
_____. *In Human Touch*. Houston: Lumen Christi Press, 1975. Poetry, in English.

BATRAKS, ILMĀRS
TORONTO, ONT.
Atbalss (Echo). Toronto, 10 June 1948 - 29 April 1949. 1 reel of microfilm.
Kanadas Vēstnesis (Canadian Latvian Herald). 4 March 1949 - 22 April 1949. 1 reel of microfilm.

BAUMANIS, EDMUNDS
TORONTO, ONT.
Minutes of the Toronto Latvian Centre, 1976, and clippings, 1978. 2 cm. Taped interview.
Interviewed in July 1978; 2 hrs.; 2 tapes; Latvian; by I. P. Taylor.

BELAGLAZOVS, ARVĪDS
TORONTO, ONT.
Interviewed on 21 Jan. 1977; 2 hrs.; 2 tapes; Latvian; by I. P. Taylor. Arrived in Canada in 1951.

BELAGLAZOVS, JĀNIS
OTTAWA, ONT.
Literātūra un Māksla. 1978. Newspaper from Latvia, U.S.S.R. 1 reel of microfilm.

BENCONS, MR.
TORONTO, ONT.
Daugavas Vanagi. Münster, Germany, June 1954 - Dec. 1962 (monthly). 2 reels of microfilm. See Latvian Relief Organization, DV reels.

BRAUNS, MRS.
TORONTO, ONT.
1 photograph: sailing vessel used by Latvian refugees for illegal entry into Canada, 1949. Taped interview.
Interviewed on 16 Feb. 1977; 1 hr.; 1 tape; Latvian; by I. P. Taylor. Fled to Canada in 1948.

BRUNOUS, PAULS
TORONTO, ONT.
Interviewed on 22 Feb. 1977; 2 hrs.; 2 tapes; Latvian; by I. P. Taylor.

CĀLĪTIS, REV. J.
TORONTO, ONT.
Material covering early years of St. Andrew's Church, 1953-56. 1 reel of microfilm.

CĒBERS, GUSTE
TORONTO, ONT.
Interviewed on 3 July 1977; 1 hr.; 1 tape; Latvian; by I. P. Taylor. Arrived in Canada, via the U.S. in 1968.

ČIPĀNS, JĀNIS
HAMILTON, ONT.
Interviewed on 30 March 1978;
3 hrs.; 3 tapes; Latvian; by I. P. Taylor. Fled Latvia during WWII.

ČULĪTIS, M.
TORONTO, ONT.
18 photographs: people involved in
publishing *Latvija*, Germany, c. 1952.
Bavārijas Latviešu Vēstnesis. 25
Aug. 1945 - 30 March 1946. Latvian
refugee newspaper. Part of 7 reels of
microfilm.
Latviešu Vēstnesis. 22 Dec. 1945 -
23 Nov. 1946. News bulletin. Part of
7 reels of microfilm.
Latvija. 1946-51. Latvian newspaper.
Part of 7 reels of microfilm.

DAMBERGS, CENSIS
TORONTO, ONT.
Scrapbook, 1950-70, which includes
photographs and clippings of prominent Latvian musicians, artists,
scholars, and clergy in Canada. 1 reel
of microfilm. Photographs. Taped
interview.
4 photographs: Latvian dance troupe;
play; Latvian Community Centre, and
wedding, 1963-73.
Interviewed on 25 Jan 1977; 2 hrs.;
2 tapes; Latvian; by I. P. Taylor.
Immigrated to Canada in 1951.

DOBELIS, KONRADS
HAMILTON, ONT.
Konrads Dobelis arrived in Canada
in 1927. While in Edmonton, Alberta
he founded the Edmonton Latvian
Society "IMANTA." In 1948 he
assisted in the foundation of the
Latvian National Federation in
Canada and became its first president,
as he also worked to promote Latvian
emigration from displaced persons

camps in Germany. The weekly
publication of *Brīvais Latvietis* was
produced through his efforts. Included
are documents regarding the donor's
role in aiding Latvian immigrants,
including correspondence with the
Latvian Relief Organization, c. 1947.
Collection also includes miscellaneous
papers covering the history of early
Latvian immigrants and the formation
of various Latvian organizations
across Canada, 1947-75. 3 reels of
microfilm. See Latvian Relief Association. Photographs.
20 photographs: Latvian refugees in
D.P. camps in Germany, c. 1945-50;
farming in Alberta, n.d.; and Latvian
immigrants en route to Canada, c.
1945-50.
Universitas. 1954-77. Latvian Fraternity Magazine. 5 reels of microfilm.

DUMPIS, ROBERTS
SUDBURY, ONT.
Interviewed on 11 April 1981; .5
hr.; 1 tape; Latvian; by Leonids
Grasis. Immigrated to Canada in
1947.

FEIZAKS, VELTA
TORONTO, ONT.
Interviewed on 8 Feb. 1977; 1 hr.; 1
tape; Latvian; by I. P. Taylor.
Arrived in Canada in the early 1950s.

GABRĀNS, MR.
TORONTO, ONT.
Church bulletins issued by the Canadian Latvian Catholic Association,
1964-74. 4 cm. Photographs.
Photographs: a Catholic Church service in Latvia, 1972.

GRASIS, LEONIDS
SUDBURY, ONT.
33 photographs: social gatherings in

Sudbury's Latvian community,
1967-77. Taped interview.
Interviewed on 1 May 1981; .5 hr.;
1 tape; Latvian; by Leonids Grasis.
Discusses the beginning of Sudbury's
Latvian theatre.

JANITENS, AINA
SUDBURY, ONT.
Interviewed on 24 May 1981; .5 hr.;
1 tape; Latvian; by Leonids Grasis.
Immigrated to Canada in 1949.

JĒGERIS, E.
HAMILTON, ONT.
Interviewed on 29 March 1978; 2
hrs.; 2 tapes; Latvian; by I. P. Taylor. WWII displaced person.

KĀRKLIŅŠ, VITOLDS
SUDBURY, ONT.
2 scrapbooks, clippings reflecting the
Latvian community in Sudbury and
international political events; and
posters, poetry, letters, programmes,
and invitations, 1950-79. 1 reel of
microfilm. 7.5 cm.

KĀRKLIŅŠ, VITOLDS
SUDBURY, ONT.
Interviewed on 5 April 1981; .25
hr.; 1 tape; Latvian; by Leonids
Grasis. Immigrated in the late 1940s.

KĀRKLIŅŠ, VITOLDS
SUDBURY, ONT.
Sadberijas Latviešu 25 Gadi. 1977.
The 25 Years of Sudbury's Latvians.
.5 cm.
Sadberijas Latviesu Skola 25 Gados.
1977. 25 Years of Sudbury's Latvian
School. .5 cm.

KARPOUS, IDA
OTTAWA, ONT.
Interviewed on 23 Feb. 1977; 1 hr.;

1 tape; Latvian; by I. P. Taylor.
Arrived in Canada in 1970.

LANGE, REV. EDGARS
OTTAWA, ONT.
48 photographs: refugees in a displaced persons camp in Lübeck, Germany, 1949-51. Photographs. Taped
interview.
6 photographs: the Lange family.
Interviewed on 25 Jan. 1977; 1.5
hrs.; 2 tapes; Latvian; by I. P. Taylor. Moved to Canada in the early
1950s.

LŪSIS, ARNOLDS ARCHBISHOP
TORONTO, ONT.
Scrapbooks, 1965-74. 5 reels of
microfilm.

MEŽAKS, JĀNIS
TORONTO, ONT.
Brīvais Latvietis. Edmonton, June
1948 - May 1949. 1 reel of microfilm.

MIKLAŠEVICS, VILIS
TORONTO, ONT.
Personal documents and correspondence regarding the formation of the
Latvian Catholic Association,
1930-65. 1 reel of microfilm. Photographs. Taped interview.
3 photographs: religious activity
represented by the Canadian Latvian
Catholic Association in Toronto,
1968-77.
Interviewed on 10 May 1977; 2 hrs.;
2 tapes; Latvian; by I. P. Taylor.
Immigrated to Canada in 1948,
founding member of the Latvian
Catholic Association in Canada.

MILLERS, ARMINS
OTTAWA, ONT.
Interviewed on 17 Feb. 1977; 1 hr.;

1 tape; Latvian; by I. P. Taylor.
Immigrated to Canada in 1951.

MILLERS, KĀRLIS
OTTAWA, ONT.
Interviewed on 22 March 1977; 2
hrs.; 2 tapes; Latvian; by I. P. Taylor. Arrived in Canada in the early
1950s.

OZOLIŅŠ, ANDREJS
TORONTO, ONT.
33 photographs: Latvian Guides and
Scouts in Germany, and Toronto,
1946-65. Taped interview.
Interviewed on 11 May 1977; 1 hr.;
1 tape; Latvian; by I. P. Taylor.
Arrived in Canada in 1956.
*Gaujas Gaidu un Rīgas Skautu
Vienības Toronto, Kanadā* (Gaujas
Guides and Rigas Scout Troups in
Toronto, Canada). 1966, 1971.

PĀRUPS, EDVINS
OTTAWA, ONT.
Scrapbook, 1945-76, which includes
photographs letters, documents, and
clippings on the Pārups family in
Canada. 1 reel of microfilm. Photographs. Taped interview.
4 photographs: the Baltic Federation,
1974; and the Latvian Fraternity
founding celebration in Ottawa, n.d.
Interviewed on 3 Feb. 1977; 2 hrs.;
2 tapes; Latvian; by I. P. Taylor.
Immigrated to Canada in 1948.

PAUKŠENS, JĀNIS
OTTAWA, ONT.
4 photographs: the Paukšens family
in Siberia, Latvia, and St. Catharines,
Ont. 1930-60. Taped interview.
Interviewed on 20 Jan. 1977; 2 hrs.;
2 tapes; Latvian; by I. P. Taylor.
Arrived in Canada in 1948.

PĒTERSONS, E.
THORNHILL, ONT.
10 photographs: choir performances
in Toronto, 1930-60, and construction
in hydro, Mattawa, 1949.

PĒTERSONS, V.
TORONTO, ONT.
6 photographs: activities of the
Fraternitas Academica in Toronto,
1970-75.
*50th Anniversary Programme of the
Fraternitas Academica* .5 cm.
Architekts. Nos. 19-23, 1959-65. .5
cm.
Ceļinieks (Traveller). Nos. 27-34,
38, 1958-60. 2 cm.
Latviešu Skautu Priekšnieks (Latvian
Chief Scouter). 1961-66. .5 cm.

PURVS, INTA (LNAK CULTURAL
BRANCH)
TORONTO, ONT.
453 photographs: Latvian theatrical
productions in Toronto, 1950-75.

RASA, ARNOLDS
KARS (OTTAWA), ONT.
Interviewed on 10 March 1977; 1
hr.; 1 tape; Latvian; by I. P. Taylor.
Arrived in 1951.

ROZENTĀLS, MR. AND MRS.
TAURĪTIS
HUNTSVILLE, ONT.
Interviewed on 13 Aug. 1977; 2
hrs.; 2 tapes; Latvian; I. P. Taylor.
Immediate Post-WWII immigrants.
Laiks. 1954-74. Newspaper. .25
meters.
Latvija Amerikā 1959-74. Newspaper. 5 meters.

RUPNERS, EGONS
OTTAWA, ONT.
War diary, 1945-46, which describes

his experiences in a POW camp in Italy. 1 reel of microfilm. Photographs. Taped interview.
2 photographs: the Rupners family in Gock River in Toronto, 1950, 1975. Interviewed on 27 Jan. 1977; 2 hrs.; 2 tapes; Latvian; by I. P. Taylor. Immigrated in the late 1940s.

SAKSS, IMANTS
HAMILTON, ONT.
44 photographs: Latvia and Germany, 1928-65; and Latvian musical activities in Hamilton, Ont., 1953-65. Taped interview.
Interviewed on 19 Nov. 1977; 2 hrs.; 2 tapes; Latvian; by I. P. Taylor. Emigrated in the late 1940s, discusses Latvian music and musicians.

SĪPOLIŅŠ, LEOPOLDS
OTTAWA, ONT.
Interviewed on 23 March 1977; 3 hrs.; 3 tapes; English; by I. P. Taylor. Immigrated to Canada in the late 1940s.

ŠĶIDRA, VIESTURIS
OTTAWA, ONT.
86 photographs: Latvian refugees in D.P. camps in Germany, 1946-50; employment with Ontario Hydro in Rolphton, Ont., 1950-51; and Latvian festivities, including choirs and folk dancing, in Hamilton and Niagara Falls, 1952-55. Taped interview.
Interviewed in Nov. 1977; 3 hrs.; 3 tapes; Latvian; by I. P. Taylor. Immediate post-WWII immigrant.

SLAVIETIS, VERA
TORONTO, ONT.
Interviewed on 12 April 1977; 2 hrs.; 2 tapes; Latvian; by

I. P. Taylor. Immigrated to Canada in the early 1950s.

SPRUDŽS, ALEKSANDRS
OTTAWA, ONT.
5 photographs: students in schools and institutions in Latvia, 1914-43. Taped interview.
Interviewed on 23 March 1977; 2 hrs.; 2 tapes; English; by I. P. Taylor. Arrived in 1951.

TAYLOR, ILZE PĒTERSONS
TORONTO, ONT.
6 photographs: Latvian schools, church services, and activities of the Sorority Imeria, 1960-62.
Invalidu Vēstis (Invalid News). Nos. 7-9, 1975-77. 1 cm.
Jāņi. 24 June. Pamphlet of John's Day. .5 cm.
Kultūras Dienas Montrealā. n.d. Pamphlet announcing Ottawa Choir singing in Montreal, Quebec, n.d. .5 cm.
Kaŗa Invalids (War Invalids). Nos. 14-22, 1969-77. Latvian War Invalid Association. 2.5 cm.
Latvian National Federation in Canada. c. early 1950s. 1 cm.
Latviešu Dziesmu Svētki un Latviešu Dienas Kanadā. 1976. Booklet on Latvian Song Festival in Canada. .5 cm.
Mūsu Latvija: Zeme, kas palika ugunīs (Our Latvia: The Land Left in Flames). Nürnberg, Germany: UNRRA, 1946.
Vēstis. Oct 1976. Newsletter of St. John's Church. 1 cm.

TREILONS, EGONS
TORONTO, ONT.
Interviewed on 31 Aug. 1978; 1 hr.; 1 tape; English; by Wally Mraz. Immediate post-WWII immigrant.

UPESLĀCIS, VIKTORS
TORONTO, ONT.
Interviewed on 15 March 1977; 3
hrs.; 3 tapes; English; by I. P. Taylor. Immigrated to Canada in 1949.
Photographs.
7 photographs: the Upelacis family,
1953-75; associational life, including
the Latvian Federation in Canada,
1958-70; Toronto Latvian High
School, c. 1955-60; and the interior
of printing firm, 1963.

VĪKSNE, INGRIDA
TORONTO, ONT.
Interviewed on 30 June 1977; 2 hrs.;
2 tapes; Latvian; by I. P. Taylor.
Immigrated to Canada in the early
1950s.

ZARIŅŠ, JĀNIS
HAMILTON, ONT.
"Freedom Fighters," and aphorisms
by J. Zariņš. Unpublished essays on
Strēlnieks, n.d. 2 cm., in Latvian,
with translation.
Photographs. Taped interview.
13 photographs: the Zariņš family;
and a Latvian school in Hamilton,
1920-60.
Interviewed on 30 March 1978; 2
hrs.; 2 tapes; Latvian; by I. P. Taylor. Fled Latvia during WWII.

=====

AMBER PRESS (K. SIDARS)
TORONTO, ONT.
2,474 photographs: from the files of
Amber Press, covering social, politi-
cal and cultural activities among
Latvians in Canada and abroad, c.
1940-80. Publications:
Dangavs, Tālivaldis. *Strandējušo
Sala.* Toronto: Daugavas Vanags,
1967. 599 pp.

Freimanis, Eduards. *Divas Pasaules*
(Two Worlds). Toronto, 1976.
Freivalds, Osvalds. *De internerade
balternas and ragedi i Sverige ar
1945-46.* Stockholm: Daugavas
Vanagi, 1967. 432 pp.
Hāzners, Vilis. *Laiks, Telpa, Ļaudis*
(History of Latvian Relief Society).
Toronto: Daugavas Vanagi, 1974. 3
volumes.
Ozoliņš, Krišjānis. *Celies Augšā*
(Rise Up). Toronto, 1976. 277 pp.
Zariņš, Jānis. *Cepure ar Zelta Vārpu*
(Hat with the Golden Stalk of Wheat).
Toronto: Amber Press, 1975. 390 pp.
Ozoliņa, A. E. *Atmiņu Ziedi* (The
Blossoms of Memory). Toronto:
Amber Press, 1976.
No Kalpaka priedes lidz Minsterei
(From the pine of Kalpaks to
Münster). Ziemeļblāzma, Sweden,
1969.
Latvia 1968. American Latvian
Association, Washington, U.S.
Lettonie. American Latvian Associ-
ation, 1968. U.S., in French.

ASSOCIATION OF LATVIAN ENGINEERS
ABROAD
OTTAWA, ONT.
The Association of Latvian Engineers was founded in 1948 in West
German D.P. camps, and with subsequent emigration, local branches were
established in Canada, Australia, and
the United States of America. Papers
consist of minutes, correspondence,
annual reports, and miscellaneous
printed items regarding conventions,
1947-78. 2 reels of microfilm.

CANADIAN LATVIAN CATHOLIC ASSO-
CIATION
TORONTO, ONT.
Minutes, correspondence, newslet-

ters, and clippings, 1950-77. 5 reels of microfilm.

LATVIAN CANADIAN CULTURAL
CENTRE
TORONTO, ONT.
Miscellaneous papers regarding the foundation of the Centre, 1974-76. 1 reel of microfilm.

LATVIAN EVANGELICAL LUTHERAN
CHURCH
SUDBURY, ONT.
Records, 1951-80, which include minutes, and correspondence. 2 reels of microfilm. Taped interview with V. Karkliņš.

LATVIAN LUTHERAN PEACE CHURCH
OTTAWA, ONT.
Parish register, c. 1952-76. 1 reel of microfilm. Photographs.
25 Years of Ottawa's Latvian Church. n.d. Booklet.
Baznīcas Vēstis. 1953-77. Parish newsletter. 2 reels of microfilm.
Ottawa's Latvian Public School. n.d. Booklet.

LATVIAN NATIONAL FEDERATION IN
CANADA (LNAK)
TORONTO, ONT.
The collection includes statutes, members' papers and minutes of LNAK meetings, 1949-50, correspondence, and annual summaries and circulars pertaining to Latvian schools across Canada, 1951-77. 4 reels of microfilm.
Annual Report. 1962-77. 1 reel of microfilm.

LATVIAN NATIONAL YOUTH FEDER-
ATION OF CANADA (A. UPESLĀCIS)
TORONTO, ONT..
Akka. Nos. 2-4, 1976. Literary

periodicals .5 cm.
Kaskākāpēckurkamko. Nos. 1-2, 1969. Bulletin. .5 cm.
LNJAK Apkārtraksts. Nos. 7-22, 1972-75. Newsletter. 1 cm.
Sešikā. Nos. 5-11, 1969-72. Bi-annual news bulletin. 1 cm.

LATVIAN PUBLIC SCHOOL
TORONTO, ONT.
25th Anniversary of Latvian Public School. 1975. .5 cm.
Ausekltīis (Little Morning Star). Nos. 2-11, 1967-76. 10 scattered issues.
Mazputniņš (Little Bird). Nos. 7-144, 1959-70. 60 scattered issues.

LATVIAN RELIEF SOCIETY,
"DAUGAVAS VANAGI"
SUDBURY, ONT.
Minutes, correspondence, financial records, commemorative booklets, and members' attendance book, 1952-81. 2 reels of microfilm. Photographs. Taped interview with R. Dumpis, and A. Janitens.
2 photographs: Daugavas Vanagi, 1978-81.

LATVIAN RELIEF SOCIETY OF
CANADA, "DAUGAVAS VANAGI" (MR. BENCONS)
TORONTO, ONT.
The Latvian Relief Society, "Daugavas Vanagi," was founded in 1945 in Belgium. The following year, numerous chapters were established in D.P. camps in West Germany. The subsequent immigration of Latvians to North America and Australia made the Society a global organization, with the city of Münster serving as headquarters by 1948. Though initially a relief organization, the Society soon broadened its scope to preserving Latvian heritage, and to

regain Latvian national independence. The collection contains minutes of general and director's meetings, correspondence, newsletters, and miscellaneous records, 1951-67. 4 reels of microfilm. .5 meters. Photographs. See Konrads Dobelis and the DP Sudbury Branch. Photographs.

213 photographs: initially gathered for use in the book, *Laiks, Telpa, Ļaudis,* which reflects the relief work done by "Daugavas Vanagi." Photographs: taken in Hamilton, Kitchener, Niagara Falls, St. Catharines, Sudbury, and Toronto, 1950-75.

Annual Reports. 1968-77. 1 reel of microfilm.

Laiks, Telpa, Ļaudis. Toronto: Daugava Vanagu Apgāds, 1974. 3 volumes.

LATVIAN SUNDAY SCHOOL
SUDBURY, ONT.

Constitution, minutes, correspondence, and daily journals of classes, 1953-67. 2 reels of microfilm. Photographs.

2 photographs: n.d.

ONTARIO ETHNIC NEWSPAPER
MICROFILM PROJECT
TORONTO, ONT.

Brīvā Balss. 15 May 1949 - 8 Sept. 1951. 1 reel of microfilm.
Jaunais Apskats. Feb. 1955 - Sept. 1956. 1 reel of microfilm.

PHILYRONIA (LATVIAN FRATERNITY)
HAMILTON, ONT.

Correspondence and bulletins, late 1940s, early 1950s. 1 reel of microfilm.

ST. ANDREW'S EVANGELICAL
LUTHERAN LATVIAN CHURCH
TORONTO, ONT.

Parish register, 1952-77, service and concert programmes, 1966-76, and papers, newsletters, leaflets on the early history of the church. 3 reels of microfilm. Photographs.

9 photographs: theatrical productions and Christmas parties at St. Andrew's Church, c. 1950s.

Newsletter. 1971-77. 1 reel of microfilm.

Sidrabene. 1957. .5 cm.

The Baltic Peoples Want to Exist. No. 1, 1950. .5 cm.

ST. JOHN'S EVANGELICAL LUTHERAN
LATVIAN CHURCH
TORONTO, ONT.

Founded in 1948 by post-WWII Latvian emigrants. The Church presently has a membership of about 1,700. The first pastor, Rev. Arnold Lūsis, served the congregation for 25 years. Included are general correspondence, 1949-54; minister's notes and correspondence, 1952-59; church register, 1965; and miscellaneous records, 1948-63. In addition, newsletters, correspondence, annual reports, and hymnal sheets, 1950-77. 5 reels of microfilm. 30 cm. Photographs.

91 photographs: religious and community activities at St. John's Evangelical Lutheran Latvian Church, 1950-76.

SUDBURY LATVIAN THEATRE
(LEONIDS GRASIS)
SUDBURY, ONT.

26 photographs: scenes from Latvian plays, 1942-79.

"TECHNIKAS APSKATS" (N.
ZOLDNERS)
OTTAWA, ONT.
As the official organ of the Association of Latvian Engineers in Canada since 1954, the journal carries engineering articles, book reviews, and some biographical sketches. Papers, 1953-74, include correspondence, articles, and subscription lists. 1 meter.
Technikas Apskats. 1954-78 (78 issues).

TORONTO LATVIAN HIGH SCHOOL
(MRS. SLAVIETS)
TORONTO, ONT.
School scrapbooks, 1967-74. 2 reels of microfilm. Photographs.
Photographs: album containing over 70 images of school activities, including graduation pictures, and folk dancing, 1957-75.

TORONTO LATVIAN PENSIONERS'
SOCIETY
TORONTO, ONT.
Society statutes and minute book, 1974-77, and correspondence and clippings. 1 reel of microfilm.

TORONTO LATVIEŠU BIEDRĪBA
TORONTO, ONT.
Apkārtraksts. Nos. 13-15; 17-19; 21-27; 30-31; 34-36, 1969-77. Newsletters (18 issues).
Toronto Latviešu Biedrība. 1973. 72 pp.

LEBANESE COLLECTION

BOUSHY, K.
TORONTO, ONT.
 Recorded in May 1973; 1 hr.; 1
tape; English; by Mark Boekelman.
Radio programme.

DABLIZ, A. W.
SUDBURY, ONT.
 Interviewed on 1 Aug. 1984; .5 hr.;
1 tape; English; by Kareem Toni.
Arrived in Canada in 1968.

DABLIZ, MAHA
SUDBURY, ONT.
 Interviewed on 31 July 1984; .5 hr.;
1 tape; English; by Kareem Toni.
Pre-WWII immigrant.

DABOUS, MORRIS
SUDBURY, ONT.
 Interviewed on 23 July 1984; .5 hr.;
1 tape; English; by Kareem Toni.
Father arrived at the turn of this
century.

GUIBEAULT, ARTIMISIA
SUDBURY, ONT.
 3 photographs: candy store facade in
Sudbury, 1941; Grade 9 class,
Sudbury Mining and Technical
School, 1933; and the Guibeault
family, n.d. Taped interview.
 Interviewed on 8 Aug. 1984; .5 hr.;
1 tape; English; by Kareem Toni.
Recollections of Sudbury in the 1930s
and 1940s, and father's occupation as
a peddlar.

HADDAD, F.
SUDBURY, ONT.
 Interviewed on 25 July 1984; .5 hr.;
1 tape; English; by Kareem Toni.

KARAM, PHILIP
OTTAWA, ONT.
 22 photographs: ice cream parlour in
Ottawa, 1911; parades and processions in Kirkland Lake, 1937;
social and religious activities at the
Lebanese parishes in Ottawa,
1915-74; and Lebanese people in
Kirkland Lake, 1907-50.

MARCHIONI, NASIMA
SUDBURY, ONT.
 Interviewed on 24 July 1984; .5 hr.;
1 tape; English; by Kareem Toni.
Started dressmaking business with her
mother.

MENSOUR, CAMILLIA FAY
SUDBURY, ONT.
 Interviewed on 9 Aug. 1984; .5 hr.;
1 tape; English; by Kareem Toni.
Parents worked as peddlars on the
railway, and in lumber camps.

PRUSILA, GEORGE
SUDBURY, ONT.
 4 postcards: the Syrian float in the
1937 Coronation Parade in Kirkland
Lake.

SHAMESS, MARY
SUDBURY, ONT.
 2 photographs: Mary Shamess at the
age of 25 in Espanola, c. 1920s;
Shamess Bros. store in Kapuskasing,

1927. Taped interview.
Interviewed on 3 Aug. 1984; .5 hr.;
1 tape; English; by Kareem Toni.
Family arrived in Canada in 1908.

SKAFF, MR.
TORONTO, ONT.
 Circular letters, 1977-78. .25 cm.

═══════════════

LEBANESE CANADIAN ASSOCIATION
(KA'MEL BOUSHY)
OTTAWA, ONT.
 Minutes, 1960-78, a constitution, and
a membership application form. 1 reel
of microfilm.

MARONITE ASSOCIATION OF OTTAWA
(G. RITCHIE)
OTTAWA, ONT.
 Minute book, correspondence, and
programmes, 1970-76. 1 reel of
microfilm. Photograph.
 1 photograph: a family gathering, c.
1970s.

MULTICULTURAL HISTORY SOCIETY
OF ONTARIO
TORONTO, ONT.
 The Mercury. Toronto, 7 Sept. 1936
- 25 Feb. 1938. 1 reel of microfilm.

ST. ELIJAH EASTERN ORTHODOX
CHURCH (REV. E. HANNA)
OTTAWA, ONT.
 Church constitution, community
directory, and pamphlets, c. 1969-77.
3 cm.
 *A Tribute ... to the Old Church in
the New World*. c. 1977. Commemorative issue by St. Nicholas Orthodox
Church of 31st Antichian Archdiocese
convention. 295 pp.
 Can-Am Soyo. Feb. 1978. Newsletter
.25 cm.

Community Directory. 1969. 102 pp.
Soyo: Parish Life Conference. 1977.
.5 cm.

STS. PETER AND PAUL LEBANESE
CATHOLIC CHURCH
OTTAWA, ONT.
 Correspondence, community direc-
tory, Lebanese identity card,
newsclippings, and post cards,
1949-71. 4 cm. Photographs.
 The Light. 1970-71. St. Elijah Ortho-
dox Church Ottawa. 1 cm.
 *St. Elijah Parish and Community
Directory*. 1964. .5 cm.

STS. PETER AND PAUL LEBANESE
MELKITE CHURCH (REV. ECONOMOS
HABIB KWAITER)
OTTAWA, ONT.
 Correspondence, financial statements, and miscellaneous printed
items such as notices, invitations, and
parish booklets, 1961-76. 7 cm.
Photographs.
 3 photographs: social and religious
activities at Sts. Peter and Paul Parish
in Ottawa, 1970-76.
 Haddad, A. C. *The Melkite Hymnal*.
1975. Melodies adapted from Greek
and Melkite traditions. 226 pp.
 The Lebanese in Ottawa. 1977-78.
120 pp.
 St. Peter and Paul. 1975 Plan booklet of parish centre. 5 cm.
 *Tenth Anniversary of Cathedral of
Our Lady of the Annunciation*. 1975.
172 pp.

ANDRATIS, ANTHONY
DELHI, ONT.
Interviewed on 29 July 1977; .5 hr.;
1 tape; English; by B. Povilaitis.
Recounts parents' emigration and
father's tobacco farming in Delhi,
Ont.

AUGAITIS, PETRAS
DELHI, ONT.
Interviewed on 13 July 1977; 1 hr.;
1 tape; Lithuanian; by B. Povilaitis.
Immediate post-WWII immigrant;
started as a sharegrower in tobacco
farming.

AUGUSTINAVIČIUS, ALBERTAS
LASALETTE, ONT.
Interviewed on 22 July 1977; 1 hr.;
1 tape; English; by B. Povilaitis.
Tobacco farmer in the Delhi region.

BALČIŪNAS, STANLEY
TORONTO, ONT.
Stanley Balčiūnas emigrated to
Manitoba in 1927, where he was
briefly employed as a farm labourer,
and then moved to Toronto. A devout
Catholic and strong anti-Communist,
he worked hard to promote
Lithuanian language and culture. In
1933 he organized a children's choir
at St. John's Roman Catholic
Lithuanian Parish, and then ventured
to establish the first Lithuanian school
in Toronto, which held semi-weekly
evening classes during the 1935-44
years. Later, Mr. Balčiūnas also
organized an orchestra and a drama
group at St. John's parish and, more

recently, founded the Lithuanian
Saturday School, *Maironio Mokykla
Toronto*. The S. Balčiūnas book collection consists of Catholic and
Lithuanian nationalist works, published c. 1903-74; it also includes
periodicals from pre-WWII Lithuania,
such as *Aidai* and *Ūkininkas*, and
some non-political material (art
books, poetry, dictionaries, and phonograph records) from Soviet
Lithuania. .5 meters. Taped interview.
Interviewed on 25 March, 10 April,
25 Aug. 1976; 4 hrs.; 4 tapes; English; by E. H. Kuechmeister. Discusses history of St. John's Benevolent Society.

BATAITIS, JUOZAS
SUDBURY, ONT.
Immigration documents, n.d., 1
dinner menu, 1949, and Woods
payroll, 1952. 1 cm. Photographs.
4 photographs: INCO Triangle,
1974; Steelworkers Union Local 6500
striking against INCO in 1970; and
social gatherings, 1954.

BELLIS, JOE
TORONTO, ONT.
Interviewed on 18 Nov. 1977; 1 hr.;
1 tape; English; by Algirdas Stankus.
Parents arrived in 1910; recounts
work at Massey Harris, his first
house with 11 boarders; divisions
within Toronto's Lithuanians; prejudice encountered; and union organizing.

BRUZAS, VALYS
SUDBURY, ONT.
Passage contract ticket and identification card, n.d. .5 cm. Photographs.
3 photographs: F. Valys in Wales, Abitibi Lake, c. 1950-65s.
Keleivis (Calendar). 1956, 1968. 158 pp.

ČEBATORIUS, JONAS
SUDBURY, ONT.
1 Unemployment Insurance card, 1952; 1 personal identification card issued in Lithuania, 1945; a "Certificate of Training for Employment at the Coal Face," 1950; and a steamship and rail ticket to Canada. .25 cm. Photographs. Taped interview.
8 photographs: 1926-54; picnic at Ramsey Lake near Sudbury, 1954.
Interviewed on 10 March 1981; 1.25 hrs.; 2 tapes; Lithuanian; by Sigute Rudis. Arrived in 1952.

ČESKAUSKAS, ROKAS
SUDBURY, ONT.
12 photographs: 1928-40, mostly of donor and family members in Sudbury, and Fort William.

ČINČIUS, KAZYS
TORONTO, ONT.
Assorted material: programmes, ads, tickets for various events (plays, concerts, commemorations, and demonstrations) in the Toronto Lithuanian community, 1966-81; leaflets from the Lithuanian Pavillion at Caravan and about the *Vasario 16ta* Lithuanian high school in the Federal Republic of Germany; typewritten journal put out by the Toronto *Ateitininkai*, a Catholic youth group, n.d.;
anti-communist leaflets, booklets and clippings, n.d.; correspondence and notes from Toronto's Lithuanian

"Saturday School" (Maironis School), c. 1970s; and various booklets published by the Lithuanian Engineers in Exile Association, late 1940s. 17.5 cm. Photographs.
4 photographs taken in Trakai, c. 1960.
Inžinieriaus Kelias. Feb. 1946 - Dec. 1948. A typewritten journal published by the Lithuanian Engineers in Exile Association. 2 cm (8 issues).
Yearbook of Lithuanian Refugees in Seligenstadt DP Camp, 1949. 1 cm.

ČIRŪNA, BRONĖ
TORONTO, ONT.
Overseas passport of Lithuanian Republic (Independence period), 1927; immigration identification card, 1927; Acme Screw and Gear Employee identification card and Employees' Mutual Benefit Society membership card, 1945. 1.5 cm. Photographs. Taped interview.
9 photographs: Čirūna family gatherings, 1930-66; and funeral at St. John the Baptist Lithuanian Church, 1966.
Interviewed on 13 Feb. 1978; 2 hrs.; 2 tapes; Lithuanian; by Algirdus Stankus. Immigrated to Canada in the 1920s.

DAGYS, JOKŪBAS
TORONTO, ONT.
7 photographs: family and school days in Lithuania, 1920s-40; D.P. camp in Germany, 1946; and Dagy's sculptures. Taped interview.
Interviewed on 8 Dec. 1977; 1 hr.; 1 tape; Lithuanian; by Algirdus Stankus. Immigrated to Canada in 1951.
Dagys Dejuoja ir Dainuoja. n. d. A poetry collection with photographs of his sculptures, in Lithuanian

Dagys—Sculptures and Paintings,
n.d. An illustrated album, in English.

DANYS, J. V.
OTTAWA, ONT.
 3 programmes for shows of
Lithuanian artists' work, 1975-76. 1.5
cm.

DAVEIKIS, VINCAS
AZILDA, ONT.
 Immigration documents, employment
contract, and 2 maps, 1942-49. 2 cm.
Photographs. Taped interview.
 5 photographs: donor working in the
bush near Timmins, 1947-48.
 Interviewed on 23 March 1982; .5
hr.; 1 tape; Lithuanian; by Nijole
Paulaitis. Immigrated to Canada in
1947.

DIRSĖ, BIRŪTĖ
WALSHINGHAM, ONT.
 Interviewed on 21 July 1977; 1 hr.;
1 tape; English; by B. Povilaitis.
Immediate post-WWII immigrant.

DIRSĖ, BRONIUS
WALSHINGHAM, ONT.
 Interviewed on 18 July 1977; .5 hr.;
1 tape; Lithuanian; by B. Polivaitis.
On tobacco farming in Delhi region.

GAIDA, REV. PRANAS
MISSISSAUGA, ONT.
 Interviewed on 26 April 1977; 2
hrs.; 2 tapes; English; by Marion
Kunstler. Discusses ill feeling
between prewar and post-war immigrants in parish of St. John the Baptist in Toronto.

GARBENS, AL
TORONTO, ONT.
 Interviewed on 7 April 1976; .5 hr.;

1 tape; English; by E. H.
Kuechmeister.

GUSTAINIS, JONAS
TORONTO, ONT.
 Minutes, statutes and financial lists
from the Resurrection Par-
ish—Prisikelimo Parapijos scholarship
and loan fund, 1962-64; minutes and
other material of the organizing com-
mittee of a convention of former
pupils of Ausra high school in
Kaunas, 1971; minutes and statutes of
Prisikelimo Parapija Catholic Man's
Society; minutes, correspondence and
financial statements of the Society of
Lithuanian Doctors in Canada,
1962-65. 11.5 cm. Photographs.
Taped interview.
 28 photographs: 1947-64, various
Lithuanian conventions in Toronto,
Detroit, and Cleveland; social gather-
ings and sport meets in Toronto and
Hamilton; work with the railway in
Kenora; and the ship *S.S. Sobieski*,
Genoa, 1948.
 Interviewed on 8 Feb. 1978; 2 hrs.;
2 tapes; Lithuanian; by Algirdus
Stankus. Arrived immediately after
WWII.

GUTAUSKAS, JOHN
WASAGA BEACH, ONT.
 Interviewed on 11 Aug. 1977; .5 hr.;
1 tape; Lithuanian; by B. Povilaitis.
Priest of Lithuanian Roman Catholic
Church in Delhi, Ont.

IMBRAS, TADAS
SUDBURY, ONT.
 Immigration papers, 1928, and miscellaneous certificates, 1919-22. 2 cm
(15 items). Photographs.
 5 photographs: of Tadas Imbras as a
soldier in Lithuania and with siblings
in Canada, 1919-31.

JAKUBICKAS, STEPAS
DELHI, ONT.
Laisvoji Lietuva (Free Lithuania). 18
May 1950 - 19 Aug. 1952. 1 reel of
micːofilm.

JUOZAPAVIČIUS, ANTANAS
SUDBURY, ONT.
1 certificate, 1947. Photographs.
Taped interview.
10 photographs: mostly from D.P.
camps in Germany, 1946, 1949.
Interviewed on 3 March 1981; .5
hrs.; 1 tape; Lithuanian; by N.
Paulaitis. Arrived in Canada in 1949.
Lithuania. n.d. Monograph. 152 pp.

JUŠKA, POVILAS
SUDBURY, ONT.
Statement of wages and deductions
from INCO, 1943. Photographs.
Taped interview.
2 photographs: P. Juška in
Edmonton, 1929, and in
Peterborough, 1934; and donor's
uncle in Chicago (1922).
Interviewed on 11 Feb. 1981; 1 hr.;
1 tape; Lithuanian; by Joe Bataitis.
Immigrated to Canada in 1928.

KALINAUKAS, ANNE
TORONTO, ONT.
Interviewed on 7 April 1976; .5 hr.;
1 tape; English; by E. H.
Kuechmeister.

KARPIS, JONAS
TORONTO, ONT.
Information booklet, including stat-
utes and list of members of
Lithuanian House., 1973. 1 cm.
Taped interview.
Interviewed on 22 Feb. 1978; 3 hrs.;
3 tapes; Lithuanian; by Algirdus
Stankus. Immediate post-WWII immi-
grant.

*25th Anniversary of Toronto
Lithuanian House.* 1976. .5 cm.
Lietuvis. No. 1, Feb. 16 1972; no.
2, Feb. 16 1973. Newsletter.
Lietuviai. 15 March 1977. Newslet-
ter contains 2 articles on the
Lithuanian community in Toronto. .5
cm.
KLB Toronto Apylinkės Biuletenis
(publication of the Canadian
Lithuanian Community Association,
Toronto Branch).
*Newsletter of the North American
Lithuanian Physical Education and
Sports Union.* Nos. 1-2, 1976-77. .5
cm.

KASLAVIČIUS, JUOZAS
TILLSONBURG, ONT.
Passport of the Republic of
Lithuania, 1926. .25 cm.

KEVĖZA, JOE AND STEPHANIE
TORONTO, ONT.
Interviewed on 9, 10 March 1977;
2.5 hrs.; 3 tapes; English; by M.
Kunstler. Immigrated to Canada in
1926.

KEVĖZA, JOE
TORONTO, ONT.
Joe Keveza immigrated to Alberta in
1926 (the year of a right-wing coup in
Lithuania) where he worked as a farm
labourer. After settling in Toronto he
became a member of the United
Brotherhood of Carpenters and
Joiners of America, a co-founder and
president of the Sons and Daughters
of Canadian Lithuanian Mutual Benefit Society, and was also involved in
the New Horizon Program (a renova-
tion campaign for the Sons and
Daughters Society's Lithuanian Hall
on Claremont Street in Toronto.
Personal papers: identification and

immigration card, 1926; Russian army document, 1909; copy of C.N. Railway identification card for J. Keveza as a colonist under the $350 farmer scheme, n.d.; dues book of the United Brotherhood of Carpenters' and Joiners' of America, 1961-63. Also, handwritten financial accounts pertaining to the collection of funds for the renovation of the Lithuanian Hall on Claremont Street in Toronto, 1957-59. 9 cm. Photographs. Taped interview. Finding aid available.
9 photographs: 1931-61, activities of the Sons and Daughters Society (including Bangos Choir); family gatherings; and 1 postcard of ship *S.S. Estonia,* 1926.
Interviewed on 9 March 1977; 1 hr.; 1 tape; English; by M. Kunstler.
Liaudies Balsas. 17 Nov. 1972; 2 Feb. 1973. Articles about Joe Keveza's life. .25 cm.

KIBICKAS, JONAS
SUDBURY, ONT.
1 photograph: immigrants en route to Canada, 1927. Taped interview.
Interviewed on 1 March 1981; 1 hr.; 1 tape; Lithuanian; by N. Paulaitis. Arrived in Canada in 1927.

KOLYČIUS, VINCAS
TORONTO, ONT.
Interviewed on 27 Jan. 1978; 2 hrs.; 2 tapes; English; by Algirdus Stankus. Immediate post-WWII immigrant.

KRIAUČELIŪNAS, JURGIS
SUDBURY, ONT.
Immigration documents, 1936-48, and 1 miner's certificate from Sudbury, 1974 (9 items). Photographs. Taped interview.

2 photographs: donor's parents, n.d. Interviewed on 2 April 1981; .5 hr.; 1 tape; Lithuanian; by J. Labuckas. Immigrated to Canada in 1948.

KRUČAS, JUOZAS
SUDBURY, ONT.
2 navigation certificates, 1947; 2 Industrial Mechanic's Certificates, n.d.; Department of Labour Certificate, n.d.; 2 letters, a map, last issue of *Keleivis* newspaper and 2 booklets, n.d. 2 cm (11 items).

KVIKLYS, BRONIUS
CHICAGO, ILLINOIS
Canadian Lithuanian Union
(Kanados Lietuviu Sajunga, a forerunner of the Kanados Lituviu Bendruomene). No. 1, 1949. .25 cm.

LAURAS, FRANK AND ELSIE
TORONTO, ONT.
Interviewed on 22 April 1977; 1 hr.; 1 tape; English; by M. Kunstler. Discusses work in Sons and Daughters Society in drama and choir.

MARTIŠIUS, JUOZAS
SUDBURY, ONT.
Immigration documents, 1947-51. .5 cm. Taped interview.
Interviewed on 18 March 1981; .5 hr.; 1 tape; Lithuanian; by N. Paulaitis. Arrived in Canada in 1951.

MATULAITIS, VITALIUS
TORONTO, ONT.
Immigration papers, 1948, pay slips from Toronto Carpet Mfg., 1948-56; and membership cards of Textile Workers' Union of America. 1 cm. Photographs. Taped interview.
9 photographs: 1946-48 D.P. camp in Germany, work in a textile mill and on a lumber camp in Ont.

Interviewed on 5 Oct 1977; 2 hrs.; 2 tapes; Lithuanian; by Algirdus Stankus. Immediate post-WWII immigrant.
15th Anniversary of Aušra Sports Club. 1970. 80 pp.
25th Anniversary of Toronto Lithuanian House. 1976. 128 pp.
Prisikelimo Parapija--Resurrection Parish Yearbook. 1956, 1960. 2 cm.

MAZAITIS, AGOTA
SUDBURY, ONT.
Interviewed on 8 Feb. 1981; 1.5 hrs.; 2 tapes; Lithuanian; by N. Paulaitis. Immigrated to Canada in 1950.

MAZAITIS, PETRAS
SUDBURY, ONT.
Interviewed on 8 Feb. 1981; 1 hr.; 1 tape; Lithuanian; by N. Paulaitis. Landed at Halifax in 1950.

MAŽEIKA, S.
DELHI, ONT.
Contract for passage on Canadian ship for Antanas Mazeika, 1928; immigration identification card and Canadian Pacific health certificate, 1928. .5 cm.

MIKŠTAS, ANTANAS
SUDBURY, ONT.
Certificates of emigration and citizenship, n.d. .5 cm. Taped interview.
Interviewed on 13 April 1981; 1 hr.; 1 tape; Lithuanian; by N. Paulaitis. Immigrated to Canada in 1947.

MIKŠYS, JONAS
HAMILTON, ONT.
5 photographs: taken at Bishop V. Valancius Lithuanian Saturday School, Hamilton, 1955-76.
Interviewed on 25 May 1978; 1 hr.;

1 tape; Lithuanian; by Algirdus Stankus. Arrived in Canada in 1949.
25 Anniversary Yearbook of the Vysk M. Valančius Lithuanian School in Hamilton. 1974. 1 cm.

MINIOTA, STEFANIJA
TORONTO, ONT.
Lithuanian passport, 1946; documents from the International Refugee Organization, 1950; and an information sheet, "Welcome to Canada," issued on board passenger ship, n.d. 1 cm (5 items). Taped interview.
Interviewed on 26 Sept. 1977; 2 hrs.; 2 tapes; Lithuanian; by Algirdus Stankus.

MORKIS, ANTHONY
TORONTO, ONT.
Interviewed on 18 Nov., 21 Dec. 1977; 4 hrs.; 4 tapes; English; by M. Kunstler. Arrived in the 1910s.

MOTEJŪNAS, MARY
KESWICK, ONT.
9 photographs: Lithuanian social and religious activities (the Ausra Choir, clergymen at St. John the Baptist Lithuanian Church) in Toronto, 1921-46; included is a 1921 photograph of Lithuanian picnic in High Park in Toronto. Taped interview.
Interviewed on 3 Nov. 1977; 1 hr.; 1 tape; English; by Algirdus Stankus. Family arrived in 1912.
Ausra Choir of Toronto. n.d. Programme of performance in Detroit, with photograph of choir. .5 cm.
Kanados Lietuvis. Vol. 1, no. 1, n.d. The Canadian Lithuanian (monthly). .5 cm.

NORKUS, MEČYS
DELHI, ONT.
Interviewed on 19 July 1977; 1 hr.;

1 tape; Lithuanian; by B. Povilaitis. Discusses his experiences in tobacco farming, among other things.

PAULAITIS, NIJOLĖ
SUDBURY, ONT.
Personal papers, including immigration documemts, 1948- . .5 cm (13 items). Photographs.
17 photographs: 1916-49; actvities at Lithuanian Saturday School; and ship *S.S. Sobieski* en route to Canada, 1948.

PETRĖNAS, GRACE
SUDBURY, ONT.
Agreement of Tenancy, 1949, calendar and miscellaneous documents, 1944-52. .5 cm.
Children's Happiness. n.d. 92 pp.

POVILAITIS, BRONIUS
TILLSONBURG, ONT.
Interviewed on 28 July 1977; 1 hr.; 1 tape; Lithuanian; by B. Povilaitis. Discusses tobacco farming.

PRANCKUS, JONAS VAL
CARON, ONT.
Interviewed on 18 Jan. 1981; 1 hr.; 1 tape; Lithuanian; by J. Labuckas. Landed at Halifax in 1951.

RAŠKEVIČIUS, IDA
SUDBURY, ONT.
Vaccination certificate, 1937; and passenger list from the "R.M.S. Samaria," 1950. .5 cm.
Vydunas, W. St. *Life in Lithuania in 1770*. n.d. 50 pp.
Lietuvos Keleivis. 1930. .25 cm.

RATAVIČIUS, KSAVERAS
OTTERVILLE, ONT.
4 photographs: a wedding; and school children, 1920-30.

Taped interview.
Interviewed on 25 July 1977; 1 hr.; 1 tape; Lithuanian; by B. Povilaitis. Settled in southwestern Ont.'s tobacco farming district immediately after WWII.

RINKŪNAS, ANTANAS
TORONTO, ONT.
Interviewed on 2 Nov. 1977; .5 hr.; 1 tape; Lithuanian; by Algirdus Stankus. Arrived in 1948.
Rinkunas, A. *Kregždutė II*. n.d. Lithuanian school primer. 1 cm.
_____. *Kregždutė III*. n.d. 1 cm.
Teviskes Ziburiai. No. 43. Toronto, 1977. Article by A. Rinkūnas summarizing history of Lithuanian immigration to Canada and the founding of the Lithuanian Community Association. .25 cm.

RUDIS, SIGUTĖ
HANMER, ONT.
Personal papers, including immigration documents, 1936-57. 1 cm (17 items).

RUKŠYS, ANDRIUS
NAUGHTON, ONT.
5 photographs: donor in refugee camp in Velbert, Germany, 1946; and on the *S.S. Carintia* en route to Halifax, 1957. Taped interview.
Interviewed on 27 March 1981; 1 hr.; 1 tape; Lithuanian; by N. Paulaitis. Landed at Halifax in 1957.

SABAS, REV. ANTANAS
SUDBURY, ONT.
7 photographs: religious life at Christ the King Church, 1950-74. Taped interview.
Interviewed on 30 Dec. 1981; .5 hr.; 1 tape; Lithuanian; by N. Paulaitis. Immigrated to Canada in 1950.

SABAS, REV. AUGUSTINAS
SUDBURY, ONT.
Interviewed on 6 April 1981; 1 hr.;
1 tape; Lithuanian; by N. Paulaitis.
Arrived in Canada in 1959.

SAMULEVIČIUS, J.
TORONTO, ONT.
10 photographs: choir groups at St.
John the Baptist Lithuanian Curch in
Toronto, 1930s, 1940s; and a
Lithuanian picnic, May 1934.

SENKEVIČIUS, ČESLOVAS
TORONTO, ONT.
Interviewed on 25 April 1978; 2
hrs.; 2 tapes; Lithuanian; by Algirdas
Stankus. Arrived in 1950.

SHINKUNAS, JOSEPH
TORONTO, ONT.
Immigration documents, 1927-28,
including Canadian Pacific immigrant
contract and identification cards. .5
cm. Photographs. Taped interview.
18 photographs: Bangos Choir in
Toronto, 1931-38, 1956-60,
Interviewed on 19 Jan. 1978; 1 hr.;
1 tape; English; by M. Kunstler.
Pre-WWII immigrant.

STANKUS, ANTANAS
TORONTO, ONT.
Algirdus Stankus book collection:
commemorative post-WWII publications of Catholic parishes, sports
clubs, and cultural organizations—most of them from the
Toronto and Hamilton Lithuanian
communities. Also included are programmes, periodicals, newsletters,
maps and posters. .5 meters (70
items).
Michelsonas, S. *Lietuvių Išeivija
Amerikoje, 1868-1961*. Boston:
Keleivis Press, 1961. Photocopy of

the chapter on Canadian Lithuanian
organizations (pp. 415-29).
*25th Anniversary of Resurrection
Parish*. Toronto, Franciscan Fathers,
1978. 128 pp., in Lithuanian.
Aukuras. 1975. 25th anniversary of
Hamilton Lithuanian Theatre Group.
40 pp., in Lithuanian/English).
Canadian Lithuanian Day. 1954,
1960. Souvenir booklets containing
descriptions of community and activ-
ities. (2 issues). 2 cm., in Eng-
lish/Lithuanian.
Gyvenimas Viešpaciui (Life for the
Lord). 1965. Published by Sisters of
the Immaculate Conception of the
Virgin Mary.
Kalendorius. 1976, 1977. Collection
of short stories, poems, photographs,
and ads published by Resurrection
Parish (2 issues) in Lithuanian.
Kregždutė (The Sparrow). n.d.
Lithuanian school primer. 1 cm., in
Lithuanian.
Lietuvių Namai. 1961. 10th Anniver-
sary of Toronto Lithuanian House. .5
cm., in Lithuanian.
Lithuanians in Hamilton. 1975.
Commemorating the 25th anniversary
of the Lithuanian community in
Hamilton. 111 pp., in
Lithuanian/English.
Mano Katekizmas. 1959. Children's
catechism. .5 cm., in Lithuanian.
Marionis Lithuanian School.
Toronto, 1974. 25th anniversary
publication. .5 cm., in Lithuanian.
Mūsų Pasaulis (Our World). 1977-
78. Yearbook of Maironis Lithuanian
School. 104 pp., in Lithuanian.
Parama Credit Union. 1962, 1977.
10th and 25th anniversary booklets. 1
cm., in Lithuanian with copy of
charter in English.
Prisikėlimo Parapijos Credit Union.
1972. 10th anniversary booklet of the

Resurrection Parish Credit Union. .5
cm., in Lithuanian with copy of
charter in English.
Sportas. Nos. 16-19, 1966-69. Jour-
nal of the American Lithuanians'
Athletic Union. 1 cm., Lithuanian.
Tauta Budi. 1953. Lithuanian Scouts
calendar. 302 pp., in Lithuanian.
Vytis Sports Club, 1948-73. 1973.
Commemorative yearbook. .5 cm., in
Lithuanian.
PERIODICALS:
Gairė. No. 1, April 1978. Publica-
tion of the Lithuanian-Venezuelan
Community. .5 cm., in Lithuanian.
Lithuanian Sports Review. Vol. 1,
nos. 1, 2, 1965. .5 cm., in English.
Pasaulio Lietuvis. No. 42, June
1978. Journal of Lithuanian World
Community Association. 32 pp., in
Lithuanian.
Švietimo Gaires. No. 5, May 1978.
Journal of the U.S.-Lithuanian Com-
munity Association Education Com-
mission. 23 pp., in Lithuanian.
NEWSLETTERS:
Lietuvis. No. 2, Feb. 1973. Newslet-
ter of the Canadian Community,
Toronto Branch. .5 cm., in
Lithuanian.
Vytis Sports Club. Nos. 1, 2, 1978.
Members' newsletter. .5 cm., in
Lithuanian.

STANKUS, STASĖ
SUDBURY, ONT.
Interviewed on 5 April 1981; 1 hr.;
1 tape; Lithuanian; by N. Paulaitis.
Immigrated to Canada in 1947.

STAŠKUS, JUOZAS
SUDBURY, ONT.
Interviewed on 13 Feb. 1981; 1 hr.;
1 tape; Lithuanian; by N. Paulaitis.
Arrived in Canada in 1948.

STEPŠYS, VACLOVAS
SUDBURY, ONT.
Interviewed on 30 March 1981; 1
hr.; 1 tape; Lithuanian; by Sigute
Rudis. Immigrated to Canada in
1952.

ŠTREITAS, VICTORAS
TORONTO, ONT.
5 photographs: of the Lithuanian
Volunteer Veteran Society and St.
John the Baptist Benefit Society,
1967-72; and the ship *I.V. Streitas,*
1947. Taped interview.
Interviewed on 8 Oct. 1977; 1 hr.; 1
tape; Lithuanian; by Algirdus
Stankus. Arrived in Canada in 1947.
Tėviškės Žiburiai. n.d. Article on
Lithuanians in Vancouver.

STRODOMISKIS, A.
DELHI, ONT.
Lithuanian passport, contract for
passage on Canadian Pacific ship,
1928, and lapel button, "C.P.O.s to
Canada," n.d. 1.5 cm (5 items).

STRODOMSKIS, JULIUS
DELHI, ONT.
Interviewed on 20 July 1977; 1 hr.;
1 tape; Lithuanian; by B. Povilaitis.
Discusses, among other things, work
in tobacco farming.

VENSKUS, MARIA
SUDBURY, ONT.
Employment card and map of
Europe, n.d. .25 cm. Taped interview
with A. Sapoka.
Interviewed on 1 Feb. 1981; 1 hr.; 1
tape; Lithuanian; by N. Paulaitis.
Arrived in Canada in 1948.
Sapoka, Adolfas. *Lithuania Through
the Ages*. 1948. 100 pp.

VERIKAITIS, VACLOVAS
TORONTO, ONT.
 Opera contract for V. Verikaitis with Canadian Opera Co., 1962. .25 cm. Photographs. Taped interview.
 4 photographs: German D.P. camps, 1946-47; and a lumber camp at Sioux Lookout, 1947.
 Interviewed on 3 Feb. 1978; 1 hr.; 1 tape; Lithuanian; by Algirdus Stankus. Immediate post-WWII immigrant.

VISOCKAS, BIRUTE
SUDBURY, ONT.
 Interviewed on 3 Feb. 1973; 1 hr.; 1 tape; Lithuanian; by Siguete Rudis. Father arrived in 1927.

YLA, ADELE
TORONTO, ONT.
 3 union cards from the Dressmakers' Union of Toronto, 1936; list of contributors to *Darbiniko Zodis* newspaper, n.d.; book listings from the Lithuanian Literary Society, 1952, 1977; and miscellaneous papers belonging to the Sons and Daughters Benefit Society. 4 cm. Photograph. Taped interview.
 1 photograph: Canadian Lithuanians on visit to homeland, 1957.
 Interviewed on 17 Feb., 21 April 1977; 6 hrs.; 6 tapes; English; by M. Kunstler. Discusses her union activities in the inter-war years; also a participant in the Women's Circle, Bangos Choir, Lithuanian Language School, the Sons and Daughters Sick Benefit Society, and Red Cross war work.

YLA, JONAS
TORONTO, ONT.
 Jonas Yla emigrated to Saskatchewan in 1927 where he worked as a farm labourer; then moved to Ont. in 1929 to work in lumber camps, on the railway and in a factory in Toronto. Both he and his wife were actively involved in the Canadian-Lithuanian labour movement. In the 1930s he belonged to the Canadian Lithuanian Freethinkers Youth Group and was a long time member of the Sons and Daughters of Canadian Lithuanian Mutual Benefit Society. For many years he was national secretary of the Cananadian Lithuanian Literary Society, a left-wing educational and publication association. And, most important, in 1932 he founded the *Liaudies Balsas*, a progressive Lithuanian newspaper which he operated until 1975. Material includes minutes of the 4th National Canadian Lithuanian Congress, Toronto, 1946, and a substantial book collection consisting of the following: Marxist-Leninist pamphlets; textbooks on Lithuanian language, literature and history; guidebooks to Lithuanian towns and its countryside; anti-religious works and satires of Christianity; as well, novels with specifically socialist themes. Publication dates c. 1927-75, title list available. Taped interview with Jonas and Adele Yla.
 Interviewed on 22 Nov. 1977; 1 hr.; 1 tape; English; by M. Kunstler. Discusses the history of the Sons and Daughters Society and of the "Literary Society."
Janauskas, Zigmos, ed. *Už Lietuvos Laisve* (For the Freedom of Lithuania). Toronto: Lithuanian Can. National Committee, 1944. .5 cm.
_____. *Taikos ir Gerbuvio Klausimais* (A Question of Peace and Welfare). Canadian Lithuanian Literary Society, 1956. .5 cm.

Yla, Jonas. *Slaptasis Ginklas*. 1953.
Script of one-act play. .5 cm., in
Lithuanian.
_____. *Salaputris*. n.d. Script of a
comic play. .5 cm., in Lithuanian.
Ar Taika Yra Galima (Is Peace Poss-
ible). Toronto: Lithuanian Canadian
National Committee, 1949. .5 cm.
Liaudies Balsas (The People's
Voice). Nos. 586-638. Toronto. 1
Jan. - 31 Dec 1943. 1 reel of micro-
film.
_____. 28 June 1946 - 20 Dec.
1974. Incomplete. 1 meter.

YOKUBYNAS, MARIA
TORONTO, ONT.
Papers, 1935-77, include correspondence (particularly on efforts to aid
post-WWI Lithuanian D.P.s); notes
on the history of "Daina" (Lithuanian
women's charitable group);
newsclippings from Lithuanian newspapers as well as Toronto
English-language dailies, all of which
relate to Lithuanians in Canada; also,
miscellaneous items: a comic skit,
programme of the Ausros Choir and a
Delegate pin for SLA (Lithuanian
Alliance of America) convention. 7
cm. Photographs. Taped interview.
6 photographs: M. Yokubinas at
school, 1918; Toronto Lithaunian
picnic, High Park, 1934 ; and
Lithuanian Catholic church groups,
1929-53.
Interviewed on 19 Jan. 1977; 3 hrs.;
3 tapes; English; by M. Kunstler.
Discusses journalism career, the
history of the St. John Society and
Daina Society, and her antipathy for
Canadian Lithuanian communists.

BALTIJA FOLK AND DANCE
ENSEMBLE
LONDON, ONT.
Collection contains financial records,
correspondence, programmes, flyers,
and clippings, 1966-78. 1 reel of
microfilm. Photographs.
16 photographs: folk dancing in London, 1966-78.

"BIRUTE" LITHUANIAN WOMENS'
MUTUAL BENEFIT SOCIETY
TORONTO, ONT.
Minutes, 1920-23; plus accounts of
dues payments and membership lists
of Sons and Daughters of Canadian
Lithuanian Mutual Benefit Society,
1927-28. 1 reel of microfilm. See
also collection of Adele Yla.

CANADIAN LITHUANIAN COMMUNITY
(S. BALIŪNAS)
LONDON, ONT.
Records, 1949-75, include minutes,
accounts of expenditures and income,
members' lists, and a file concerning
"Lithuanian Day in Canada," festival
in London, Ont., 1969. 1 reel of
microfilm. Photographs.
RESTRICTED
5 photographs: Lithuanians in tradi-
tional costume, London, 1970-75.
Pasaulio Lietuvis. Sept.-Oct. 1974.
Serial publication of Canadian
Lithuanian Community. 1 reel of
microfilm.

CANADIAN LITHUANIAN FUND
TORONTO, ONT.
Letter and receipt acknowledging
donation by the St. John the Baptist
Benefit Society. .25 cm. See St.
John's Benevolent Society.

CANADIAN LITHUANIAN NATIONAL
COMMITTEE
TORONTO, ONT.
1 photograph: 1947. See Jonas Yla.

CHRIST THE KING CHURCH
(LITHUANIAN ROMAN CATHOLIC
CONGREGATION)
SUDBURY, ONT.
Included are marriage, baptismal,
and burial records (1930-81), history
of Church, newsclippings, church
bulletins, and Roman Catholic publications. 5 cm. Taped interview with
A. Sabas. Photographs.
6 photographs: church ceremonies
and picnics, 1953-74; and A. Sabas
on ship *Samaria* en route to Canada,
1950.

CONNAUGHT PROJECT (ROBERT F.
HARNEY)
TORONTO, ONT.
57 photographs: Lithuanian Canadians and activities of various organizations, such as the Bangos Choir,
the Sons and Daughters Canadian
Lithuanian Mutual Benefit Society,
the Lithuanian Canadian Youth Association, and the Lithuanian Canadian
Congress. In addition, there are photographs of religious life at St. John
the Baptist Lithuanian Church, and a
family/church picnic at St. Augustine
Seminary in the early 1930s, taken in
Montreal, Niagara Falls, and
Toronto, 1926-63.
Burė, K. "Toronto Lietuviu Praeitis
ir Dabartis." Four part article in
Vienybe. 22 June-July 1939.

HAMILTON LITHUANIAN PENSIONERS'
CLUB (P. ENSKAITIS)
HAMILTON, ONT.
Constitution of Hamilton Lithuanian
Pensioners' Club, 1975. Photographs.

24 photographs: from Club's
scrapbook, social events, lists of
members, and newsclippings, 1970.
1.5 cm.

"IRON WOLF" LITHUANIAN GAME
AND FISH CLUB
SUDBURY, ONT.
Includes 1 book of financial records,
Club minutes, letters from solicitors,
1 letters patent, 2 membership cards,
and files with lists of members and
miscellaneous items, 1963-82, 4 cm.
Photographs.
4 photographs: hunting activities,
1965-74.

KANADOS LIETUVIŲ BENDRUOMENĖ
(LITHUANIAN CANADIAN COMMUN-
ITY)
ST. CATHARINES, ONT.
Letters patent incorporating this
organization, plus 3 sets of revised
by-laws, 1963-66. .5 cm.

KANADOS LIETUVIŲ KATALIKŲ
KULTUROS DARUGIJA "ŽIBURIAI"
TORONTO, ONT.
Minutes, 1952; 2 letters, n.d.;
receipt and certificate for donation
made to *Teviskes Žiburiai*, 1967,
1976. 2.5 cm. (Part of St. John's
Benevolent Society collection).

LITHUANIAN CANADIAN COMMUNITY
(JOE BATAITIS)
SUDBURY, ONT.
The collection contains revised constitutions, minutes, correspondence,
financial records, annual reports, and
miscellaneous papers, 1950-76. 3
reels of microfilm.

LITHUANIAN CANADIAN COMMUNITY
(K. BARONAS)
HAMILTON, ONT.

The Lithuanian-Canadian Community, succeeding the Lithuanian League of Canada and the Lithuanian Association of Canada, drafted its first constitution in 1950. Records, 1948-75, include statutes, minute books, financial reports, correspondence, lists of Lithuanians in Hamilton area, commemorative booklets, and miscellaneous documents. 1 meter. Photographs. See collections of the London and Sudbury Branches.
23 photographs of choirs, folk dancing, and sports during the "First Canadian-Lithuanian Days, Hamilton, 1953-63.

Gudelis, P. *Bolševikų valdžios atsiradimas Lietuvoje 1918-1919 metais ju pačių dokumentu šviesoje*, n.d.

Jurgėla, C. R. *Tannberg, 15 July 1410*. New York, 1961.

Krivickas, D. *Soviet-German Pact of 1939 and Lithuania*. Hamilton, 1959.

Simutis, A. *Pasulio Lietuvių Žinynas*. New York, 1953. Lithuanian World Directory.

SPORTS PUBLICATIONS:

Sulaitis, Ed. *Lietuviškasis Krepšinis* (Lithuanian Basketball). Chicago, 1957.

Programmes of North American Lithuanian Games, 1956-63. 2 cm.

Programme of North American Baltic Soccer Championship, 1958.

Sportas. Nos. 112-14, 119-120, 1968. Lithuanian S.S.R. Sports News. .5 cm.

Sporto Žinios. Nos. 8-12, 1958; no. 1, 1959. .5 cm.

CULTURAL PUBLICATIONS:

Hamilton Lithuanian House. 1960, 1962. 4th and 6th anniversary booklets. 1 cm.

Vienybe (Unity). No. 39, 1965; nos. 2, 6, 1966.

LITHUANIAN LITERARY SOCIETY
TORONTO, ONT.

Catalogue of books available from the Lithuanian Literary Society, 1952. .25 cm.

LITHUANIAN SATURDAY SCHOOL OF LONDON
LONDON, ONT.

Brochure, diplomas and report cards from the Lithuanian Saturday School of London. 3.5 cm. Photographs.
4 photographs: Folk Arts Council, 1975-76.

LITHUANIAN SATURDAY SCHOOL
SUDBURY, ONT.

Records, 1950-80, include minutes, books of attendance and marks, history of School, correspondence, newsclippings, exercise books and a play. 7 cm. Photographs.
11 photographs: Saturday School related activities, 1962-81.

LITHUANIAN SOCIAL DEMOCRATIC FEDERATION OF CANADA
TORONTO/OAKVILLE, ONT.

Constitution and by-laws, minutes of Oakville and Toronto Branches, and correspondence, 1952-60. 1 cm.

LOVERS OF THE FATHERLAND SOCIETY
TORONTO, ONT.

Booklet with constitution and history of the Draugija, 1930. .5 cm. See St. John's Benevolent Society.

MULTICULTURAL HISTORY SOCIETY
OF ONTARIO
TORONTO, ONT.
Darbininkų Žodis. Oct. 1932 - 19
Nov. 1936. 2 reels of microfilm.

PARAMA CREDIT UNION
TORONTO, ONT.
Report on holdings of the St. John
the Baptist Benevolent Society, 1966.
.25 cm. See St. John's Benevolent
Society.

SONS AND DAUGHTERS OF CANADIAN
LITHUANIAN MUTUAL BENEFIT
SOCIETY
TORONTO, ONT.
The collection includes minutes,
1937-75; membership lists, 1938-49;
and miscellaneous items: revised
by-laws, certificates, speech by J. Yla
at 65th anniversary banquet, letters,
and clippings. 3 reels of microfilm. 1
cm. Photographs.
2 photographs: Toronto picnic of the
Canadian Lithuanian Freethinkers
Youth Association, 1930; and branch
charter for the Sons and Daughters
Canadian Lithuanian Mutual Benefit
Society, 1936.
*40th Anniversary of the Sons and
Daughters.* 1952. 20 pp.

ST. JOHN THE BAPTIST BENEVOLENT
SOCIETY (REV. P. GAIDA)
TORONTO, ONT.
St. John's Benevolent Society was
established by Roman Catholic
Lithuanians to provide benefits in
times of illness and death, to organize
social and cultural events, and to
maintain religious life. The first
meetings were held in the basement of
St. Agnes Church, an Italian parish at
Dundas and Grace Streets The collection, 1920-74, includes minutes of

meetings, treasurer's reports,
comptroller's reports for 1933, 1934,
several receipt books, history of the
society, and miscellaneous material:
membership lists and applications,
certificates, and clippings. 2 reels of
microfilm. Finding aid available. See
S. Balciunas. **RESTRICTED**

SUSIVIENYJIMAS LIETUVIU
AMERIKOJE (LITHUANIAN ALLIANCE
OF AMERICA)
TORONTO, ONT.
Delegate pin for convention in
Scranton, Pa., showing crest of
Alliance, 1938.

THE LITHUANIAN VETERAN GUARD
ASSOCIATION OF CANANDA
(SUDBURY BRANCH "MAIRONIS")
SUDBURY, ONT.
Records, 1975-81. 1 reel of microfilm. Photographs. Taped interview
with A. Juozapavicius.
5 photographs: various commemorative ceremonies, 1976-80.

TORONTO LITHUANIAN CULTURE
CHOIR
TORONTO, ONT.
Concert programme of perfomance at
Anapilis Lithuanian Centre in
Mississauga on 11 April 1976. .25
cm.

TORONTO LITHUANIAN WOMEN'S
CLUB
TORONTO, ONT.
Club minutes, 1949-71. 1 reel of
microfilm.

WORLD LITHUANIAN DAYS
TORONTO, ONT.
The World Lithuanian Days were
held in Toronto, 26 June - 6 July
1978, and hosted by the

Lithuanian-Canadian Community. The
Days consisted of three main events:
the First World Lithuanian Games,
the Fifth Lithuanian Song Festival,
and the Fifth Lithuanian World Congress (the "Seimas" of the World
Lithuanian Community). The collection includes souvenir booklets, programmes, bulletins, maps, a lapel
button and posters. 4 cm (12 items).
See Lithuanian-Canadian Community,
Hamilton Branch.

MACEDONIAN COLLECTION

DUKE, STOYAN
TORONTO, ONT.
10 photographs: the Duke family, taken at a farm near Port Hope, 1908-45; and in the village of Bešina, Macedonia, 1932.

ELIA, DANA
TORONTO, ONT.
Turkish passport, 1912; christening invitation, 1923; wedding invitation, 1922; business card of the hotel and restaurant "Macedonia," n.d.; and 2 telegrams regarding arrival of mail-order bride; and 2 letters between bride and groom. 2 cm (8 items).

EVANS, D.
TORONTO, ONT.
Interviewed on 2 Aug. 1975; 2 hrs.; 2 tapes; English; by Lillian Petroff.

EVANS, T.
TORONTO, ONT.
Stoichev, Gorgie. *Prikazka Za Bapchor* (Story of Bapchor). Toronto, 1977. 131 pp.

EVANS, VASSA
TORONTO, ONT.
Macedonian proverbs, expressions, and clippings, n.d. Photographs.
2 photographs: St. George's Macedonian Bulgarian Eastern Orthodox Church and bazaar, c. 1950s.

FLORINOFF, LAZAR
TORONTO, ONT.
5 photographs: Macedonian Patriotic Organization parade in Detroit, Michigan, 1930s; Ladies' Conference of M.P.O. in Toronto, 1957; traditional play, "Kcrvava Svadba" (the Bloody Wedding) in Detroit, 1940; and a postcard of St. Cyril's grave in the church of St. Clement in Rome, Italy.

FLORO, PARA
TORONTO, ONT.
2 photographs: a tractor at a farm in Port Hope, Ont., 1920s.

FRANGO, D.
TORONTO, ONT.
3 photographs: Salonica coffee shop, 1935; house built by Mr. Frango in Nevoliany, 1935; and Mr. Frango on horseback, n.d.

GEORGE, JEAN
TORONTO, ONT.
Programme of the 13th Annual Ladies' Section Conference of the Macedonian Patriotic Organization, 1970. 1 cm. Photographs.
2 photographs: "Grads Restaurant" in Toronto, 1940s.
2 photographs: the Young Macedonian Patriotic Organization dance group in Toronto, 1955; and St. George's "Vardar" dancers, Toronto Caravan Festival, 1972.

GRUDEFF, JOHN
TORONTO, ONT.
Scrapbook, correspondence, 1913-64, an unpublished manuscript, clippings, programmes, and photographs of daughter Marian Grudeff, a concert pianist, n.d. 1 reel of microfilm.

HARNEY, R. F.
TORONTO, ONT.
28 photographs: activities of the Skopje (Nevoliany) Benevolent Association, the Macedonian Patriotic Organization, 1935-56; and religious ceremonies at Sts. Cyril and Methody Macedonian Orthodox Church, 1911.
Benefit Society Oshchima: 75th Anniversary, 1907-82. Toronto, 1982. Illustrated. 1.5 cm.
The Children of 1948. The Association of Refugee Children from Aegean Macedonia, 1988. 43 pp.
The Miladinov Brothers: A Miscellany. Toronto: Macedonian Historical Society of Canada, 1982.

LECHTMAN, BEN
TORONTO, ONT.
1 photograph: Gina Petroff, 1977.

MARKOFF, BLAZHE
TORONTO, ONT.
1 photograph: parade of Macedonian Patriotic Organization in Toronto, 1927.

PANDOFF, SOPHIE
TORONTO, ONT.
10 photographs: the Pandoff family at their farm in Port Hope, 1924; Nick Pandoff in front of butcher store, 1948; activities of the Macedonian Patriotic Organization, 1940-46; and activities at St. George's Macedonian Bulgarian Eastern Orthodox Church such as the laying of cornerstone, a theatrical production, a soccer team, and a Bulgarian school, 1941-47.

PAPPAS, ROBERT
TORONTO, ONT.
"Health Rules" issued by the Department of Public Health, Toronto, 1928. 1 cm.

PAVLOVICH, MRS.
TORONTO, ONT.
1 photograph: the Pavlovich family in Macedonia, 1937.

PETROFF, A.
TORONTO, ONT.
Interviewed on 6 Dec. 1975; 1 hr.; 1 tape; English; by Lillian Petroff.

PETROFF, GEORGE
TORONTO, ONT.
A selection of Bulgarian-language books. Granite City, Illinois, 1894-1920, from Naroden Glas Bulgarian Bookstore. 6 cm.
Naroden Glas: Jubilee Almanac, 1908-33. Granite City, Illinois: Naroden Glas Publishing, 1933, in Bulgarian. 1 reel of microfilm.

PETROFF, GINA
TORONTO, ONT.
Interviewed in 1976; 1 hr.; 1 tape; English; by R. F. Harney. Discusses Macedonian society, and the status of women.

———.
TORONTO, ONT.
Interviewed on 15 Jan. 1976; 1 hr.; 1 tape; English; by R. F. Harney. Discusses the transatlantic crossing from Macedonia.

PETROFF, GINA
TORONTO, ONT.
 Interviewed on 21 Jan. 1976; 1.5
hrs.; 2 tapes; English; by R. F.
Harney.

———.
TORONTO, ONT.
 Interviewed in Feb., Oct. 1976; 4
hrs.; 4 tapes; English; by R. F.
Harney.

———.
TORONTO, ONT.
 Interviewed on 12 Oct. 1976; 1 hr.;
1 tape; English; by R. F. Harney.

———.
TORONTO, ONT.
 Interviewed on 13 Oct. 1976; 1 hr.;
1 tape; English; by R. F. Harney.
Discusses political unrest and guerilla
warfare in Macedonia; buying a car;
and Macedonian music.

PETROFF, LILLIAN
TORONTO, ONT.
 List of prominent Macedonians in the
Toronto area, 1977; printed items
from the Canadian Macedonian Place,
1977-78; and Macedonian almanacs
and immigrant guidebooks. 5 cm. 4
reels of microfilm. Photographs.
 11 photographs: family and friends
of Noel Petroff, 1910-30; and the
interior of an ice cream parlour, c.
1930s.
 Malincheff, D. G. and J.
Theophilact. *The First
Bulgarian-English Pocket Dictionary.*
Toronto, 1913. 1 reel of microfilm.
 Nedielkov, Khristo. *Bulgarian and
Bulgarian-English Phrasebook.* Granite City, Illinois, 1911. 2 cm.
 Youcheff, A. *Macedonian-Bulgarian
Phrase Book and Letter Writer.* Chi-

cago, 1917. In English/Macedonian. 1
reel of microfilm.
 Macedonie Album—Almanach. 1931.
Illustrated, maps. 1 reel of microfilm,
in French/Macedonian.
 Macedonian Almanac, 1940.
Indianapolis: Macedonian Tribune
Co., 1940. 474 pp. In Macedonian/
English. Microfilm

PHILLIPS, ANNABELLE
TORONTO, ONT.
 1 photograph: Macedonian Soccer
Club at St. George's Macedonian
Bulgarian Eastern Orthodox Church,
1945.
 Krvava Svadba. n.d. Traditional
Macedonian play. 77 pp.
 Selo Buf (Story of the Village Buf).
Bushola, 1976. 15 pp.

PHILLIPS, MICHAEL
TORONTO, ONT.
 5 photographs: convention of the
Macedonian Patriotic Organization,
1936; interior of donor's restaurant,
1946; and donor's family and friends,
1930-46.

RALLEY, D.
TORONTO, ONT.
 4 photographs: the Zagorichene (Village) Benefit Society, 1907; wedding
of D. N. Ralley, 1922; and personal
documents, 1927.

RISTICH, HELEN
TORONTO, ONT.
 Turkish passport and naturalization
certificate of Bojin Nikoloff, 1920;
and Greek passport of Mara Bojin
Cole, n.d. .5 cm

SPERO, DONNA
TORONTO, ONT.
1 photograph: funeral in Macedonia, 1943.

STAVROFF, WILLIAM B.
TORONTO, ONT.
By-laws of the Gabresh Benevolent Society "Napreduk," 1911, and invitations to Ilinden picnics, 1968, 1970, 1972. 2 cm. Photographs.
19 photographs: activities (school, choir, conventions) of the Sts. Cyril and Methody Macedonian-Bulgarian Eastern Orthodox Church, and the Macedonian Patriotic Organization, 1925-63; and the Gabresh Benevolent Society, 1927.

THOMAS, D. K.
TORONTO, ONT.
7 photographs: the Thomas family in Macedonia and Toronto, 1900-35.

TOMEV, FOTO
TORONTO, ONT.
By-laws of the Macedono-Bulgarian Orthodox Parish of Sts. Cyril and Methody Cathedral in Toronto, 1959; poster announcing "Ilinden" picnic in Toronto, 1966; and leaflet announcing Macedonian concert and dance in Toronto, 1977. 2 cm. Photographs.
51 photographs: Macedonian Turkish personal documents, c. 1920-1930.
Christowe, Stoyan. *New Macedonia.* Detroit: Macedonian-American People's League, c. 1945. Pamphlet, in English.
Tomev, Foto. *Short History of Zhelevo Village Macedonia.* Toronto: Zhelevo Brotherhood, 1971. 163 pp., in English/Bulgarian.
_____. *Macedonian Folktales.* n.d. Original handwritten copy and typed manuscript. 2 cm.

La Broderie Nationale Macedonienne. Skopje: Institut de Folklore, 1975. Illustrated.

TRENTON, VASIL
TORONTO, ONT.
Application for naturalization of Naso Vasiloff; statutory declaration of Lambro G. Lantzakis, 1932; historical brief, "The Name of Macedonia," n.d.; bill of sale of restaurant, 1929; and address and expense book, n.d. 2 cm. Photographs.
47 photographs: mainly of family and friends in Macedonia and Toronto, 1907-63.

ZABKA, FATHER J. (STS. CYRIL AND METHODIUS CHURCH)
TORONTO, ONT.
25 Years of Sts. Cyril and Methodius Parish, 1934-59. Toronto, 1959. Illustrated. 79 pp., in English/Macedonian.

━━━━━━━━━━

BANITZA BENEVOLENT SOCIETY
TORONTO, ONT.
Financial records of Society, 1911-49. In Macedonian. 1 reel of microfilm.
Brief History of the Village Banitza and Its People. Toronto: Banitza Benevolent Society, 1986.

CANADIAN MACEDONIAN PLACE
TORONTO, ONT.
Minutes and agendas of meetings, 1978. 5 cm.
Newsletter. May, June, Sept. 1978. 1 cm.

INDEPENDENT MUTUAL BENEFIT
SOCIETY
TORONTO, ONT.
 Constitution, by-laws, and member-
ship records, 1941-50. 1 reel of
microfilm.

MACEDONIAN CANADIAN SENIOR
CITIZEN'S CLUB
TORONTO, ONT.
 *Brief History of Canadian
Macedonian Immigrants and their
Background.* Toronto: Macedonian
Canadian Senior Citizen's Club,
1980. 160 pp.
 Newsletter. Vol. 1, nos. 1-3, 1978. 1
cm.

MACEDONIAN PATRIOTIC ORGANIZ-
ATION
TORONTO, ONT.
 By-laws of M.P.O., Macedonian
newspapers, and miscellaneous publi-
cations dealing with the Macedonian
national question. .5 meters. 3 reels
of microfilm. Photographs.
 1 photograph: M.P.O. convention in
Toronto, 1940.
 Anastasoff, Christ, ed. *The Case for
an Autononous Macedonia.* St. Louis,
Missouri: Central Committee of the
Macedonian Political Organization of
the U.S. and Canada, 1945. 205 pp.
Microfilm.
 Mihailoff, Ivan. *Macedonia: A
Switzerland of the Balkans.* St. Louis,
Missouri, 1950. 134 pp. Microfilm.
 *16th Annual Convention of the
Macedonian Political Organizations
of the U.S.A. and Canada.*
Indianapolis, 1937. 188 pp.
 Ilinden, 1903-58. Indianapolis:
Macedonian Patriotic Organization.
Booklet. Microfilm.
 Macedonia. Vol. 1, no. 1, Jan.
1932; vol. 1, no. 10, Dec. 1910.

Indianapolis. 2 cm.
 Macedonia. Vol. 1, no. 2, 1949; no.
3, Jan. 1950; vol. 2, no. 1, May
1950; no. 5, April 1951; nos. 1-29,
Aug. 1954 - Oct. 1958. Newspaper.
In English/Macedonian/
French/German/Italian. Microfilm.
 *Macedonia's Rise for Freedom,
1903: The Great Insurrection.* Micro-
film.
 Macedonian Illustrated. Sofia, Bul-
garia, 1919. Original. Microfilm.

PAN-MACEDONIAN ASSOCIATION
TORONTO, ONT.
 Minutes, 1965, and flyers. 1 cm. 1
reel of microfilm.
 *32nd National Convention, Toronto,
Canada, July 4th-July 9th, 1978.* The
Pan-Macedonian Association of
Ontario, 1978. 1 cm., in Eng-
lish/Macedonian.
 The Royal Canadian Legion. Greek
Veterans (Ont. no. 626) Branch,
Toronto, 1979. .5 cm

SELYANI MACEDONIAN FOLKLORE
GROUP
TORONTO, ONT.
 Correspondence and promotional
material—programmes, flyers, clippings, announcements—regarding
Group's activities, 1971-78. 1 reel of
microfilm. 2 cm. Photographs.
 14 photographs: folk dancing by the
Selyani Macedonian Folklore Group,
1971-76.

ST. CLEMENT OF OHRID
MACEDONIAN ORTHODOX (REV. D.
KOSTADINOVSKI)
TORONTO, ONT.
 Miscellaneous parish records, includ-

ing marriage service book, n.d., and
church bulletins, 1970s. 2 cm.

St. Clement of Ohrid. 1972. Convention booklet. .5 cm.

ST. NAUM MACEDONIAN ORTHODOX
CHURCH (REV. J. BOSEOVSKI)
HAMILTON, ONT.

Macedonian calendars, bank flyers,
convocation yearbooks, baptismal and
marriage certificates, invitation, greeting card, newsclippings, flyers, and
posters regarding social and church
events, 1972-78. 3 cm. Photographs.

4 photographs: religious life at St.
Naum Church in Hamilton, 1971-78.

Macedonian Word. 1977-78. 3
issues.

STS. CYRIL AND METHODY CATHE-
DRAL
TORONTO, ONT.

Minutes and parish records, 1910-46.
1 reel of microfilm. Photographs.

14 photographs: religious activities at
Sts. Cyril and Methody Cathedral,
1911-35; and personal documents,
1915-23.

*50th Anniversary of Sts. Cyril and
Methody Macedono-Bulgarian Orthodox Cathedral, 1910-1960*. Toronto,
1960. 118 pp.

BONAVIA, LAWRENCE O.
MISSISSAUGA, ONT.
 Over 50 photographs: religious activities at St. Paul the Apostle Church,
including clergy and ceremonies,
1946-70; the Maltese Canadian
Society of Toronto; and immigrants
en route to Canada, 1940s. Taped
interview.
 Interviewed on 17, 24 Feb. 1978; 2
hrs.; 2 tapes; English; by Richard
Cumbo. Arrived in 1948 as a member
of the Order of Franciscan Minors;
an active leader within Toronto's
Maltese community.
 Bonavia, George. *Focus on Cana-
dian Immigration.* 1977.
 _____. *Maltese in Canada.* Ottawa:
Multiculturalism Directorate, 1980.
 *New Directions: A Look at Canada's
Immigration Act and Regulations.*
April 1978. 28 pp.

BORG, JESSIE
MARYLAND, U.S.
 Maltese passport, and a clipping,
"Maltese Society 50 Years Old." .25
cm. Photographs.
 4 photographs: religious ceremony at
St. Paul the Apostle Church, c. 1940;
the Borg family, 1940-69; and activities of the Maltese Canadian Society
of Toronto, 1969, all taken in
Toronto.

BORG, JOAN
TORONTO, ONT.
 Immigration documents, 1910s; and
a letter from Workmen's Compensa-
tion Board, 1947. 1 cm. Photographs.

Taped interview.
 6 photographs: the Borg family,
1916-17; and religious life at St. Paul
the Apostle Church in Toronto,
1931-51.
 Interviewed on 19 Feb. 1978; 1 hr.;
1 tape; English; by Richard Cumbo.
Father arrived in Toronto in 1913.

BORG, JOSEPHINE P.
TORONTO, ONT.
 British passport, 1922, including
non-resident alien's border crossing
identification, n.d. .25 cm. Photographs. Taped interview.
 6 photographs: the Borg family
1922-65; and activities of the Maltese
Canadian Society of Toronto,
1960-65.
 Interiewed on 20 Feb. 1978; 1 hr.; 1
tape; Maltese/English; by Richard
Cumbo. Arrived in Toronto in 1922
where her husband had settled in
1916.

CACHIA, MARIA CARMELA
TORONTO, ONT.
 Immigration papers, including correspondence between the Cachia family,
and the Canadian government
1912-17; and diary of Joseph Cachia,
1924-39. 2 cm. Photographs. Taped
interview.
 Over 50 photographs: the Cachia and
Sciberras families in Malta and
Toronto, 1920-76.
 Interviewed on 10 Feb. 1978; 1 hr.;
1 tape; English; by Richard Cumbo.

She arrived in Canada in 1926, a decade after her father and husband had immigrated.

CALLEJA, J.
TORONTO, ONT.
1 map of Malta. Photograph.
1 photograph and 2 post cards: Maltese beaches and coastline, 1978.

CAMILLERI, CARMELA AND FRANCIS
TORONTO, ONT.
British Malta passport, 1927. .25 cm. Photographs. Taped interview.
4 photographs: the Camilleri family, 1928-34; and activities of the Maltese Canadian Society of Toronto, 1962-65.
Interviewed on 23 Feb. 1978; 1 hr.; 1 tape; English; by Richard Cumbo. Immigrated to Canada in 1927.

CAMILLERI, JOSEPH AND VINCENT
TORONTO, ONT.
Interviewed on 10 March 1978; 2 hrs.; 2 tapes; English/Maltese; by Richard Cumbo. Both immigrated to Canada in the 1910s.

CARUANA, C. (ED. *FORUM MELITENSE)*
TORONTO, ONT.
Open letter of petition regarding immigration of Maltese, 1956; and various Maltese-Canadian publications, 1969-77. 12 cm. See Institute of Maltese Canadian Affairs. Photographs.
12 photographs: presentation ceremonies for the flags of Malta and Canada, 1963-77.
Malta Handbook, 1976. Malta: Department of Information, 1976. Illustrated, 170 pp., in English.

COLEIRO, SALVATORE AND CARMELA
TORONTO, ONT.
Immigration documents and marriage certificates, 1920-21. .5 cm. Photographs. Taped interview.
Photographs: Carmela Coleiro and her 3 children, 1927; and St. Paul the Apostle Church in Toronto, 1930.
Interviewed on 13 March 1978; 1 hr.; 1 tape; Maltese/English; by Richard Cumbo. They ar-rived in Canada in the late 1910s.

CUMBO, RICHARD
TORONTO, ONT.
Minutes, correspondence, and other records of various Maltese Canadian organizations: the Federation of Maltese Organizations, the Maltese Falcon Co., the Maltese Canadian Association of Malta, and the Maltese-Canadian Society of Toronto, 1987-89. Collection also includes correspondence with Canadian politicians and the Maltese consul, clippings, newspapers, and newsletters. .5 meters. Photographs.
17 photographs: social events and exhibitions of the Maltese Canadian Society of Toronto, 1971-75.
Bonavia, George, comp. and ed., *1988 Maltese Directory, Canada.* 35 pp.
Association of Maltese Communities of Egypt. London, England, March - Sept. 1988, March 1989 (3 newsletters).
L-Ahbar. Toronto, June 1987 - Jan. 1989 (14 issues).
Lil Hutna. Sept. 1987, Jan. 1988, July 1988 (3 issues). In Maltese.
Maltese Canadian Club Newsletter. London, Ont., May 1987 - May 1989 (6 issues).
Melita Soccer Club Inc. Newsletter. Toronto, 1988-89 (4 issues). Maltese

Soccer Club.
St. Paul the Apostle. Toronto,
1987-88. Bulletin of Franciscan Friars
of Malta (10 issues).

DE BATISSE, ROBERT
TORONTO, ONT.
 Immigration documents, 1920s, and
military papers from the Canadian
army, 1940s. 1 cm (14 items). Photographs.
 14 photographs: the Cachia and De
Batisse families in Malta and
Toronto, 1914-70; and Anthony De
Batisse in military, and musical band
uniforms, 1930-45.

DE BATTISTA, ANTHONY AND
XAVERIA
TORONTO, ONT.
 British Malta passport, 1927. .5 cm.
Photographs. Taped interview.
 2 photographs: Anthony De Battista
in Malta and Toronto, c. 1925-45.
 Interviewed on 12 April 1978; 1 hr.;
1 tape; Maltese/English; by Richard
Cumbo. The donor's father arrived in
1913, and his children followed in
1927.

FENECH, JOHN AND MARY
TORONTO, ONT.
 Birth and marriage certificate, 1905,
1932. Photographs. Taped interview.
 9 photographs: the Fenech and Aguis
families in Malta and Toronto,
1925-70; and religious activity at St.
Paul the Apostle Church in Toronto,
1930-55.
 Interviewed on 26 Feb. 1978; 1 hr.;
1 tape; Maltese/English; by Richard
Cumbo. He arrived in 1917, and was
followed by his wife in 1929.

FRENDO-CUMBO, PRIOR JOSEPH
OSHAWA, ONT.
 6 photographs: Maltese National Day
celebration in Toronto, 1977.

GOGGI, ALF
TORONTO, ONT.
 1 photograph: the executive committee of the Maltese Canadian Society
of Toronto, 1951-52.

KIOMALL, DOMINIC AND LUCY
TORONTO, ONT.
 Immigration papers, programmes,
and clippings on the Maltese Toronto
community, 1948-74. 2 cm. Photographs. Taped interview.
 29 photographs: the Kiomall and
Falzon families, occasionally shown
in Maltese costume, 1924-65; D.
Kiomall working as a truck driver,
1936, 1961; ship *Vulcania*, 1948; and
social gatherings and religious ceremonies at St. Paul the Apostle Church
in Toronto, 1950-60.
 Interviewed on 10 March 1978; 1
hr.; 1 tape; Maltese/English; by
Richard Cumbo. Immigrated to
Canada in 1948.

MICALEFF, JOSEPH
TORONTO, ONT.
 1 file of correspondence and flyers
regarding a Maltese radio programme
in Toronto, 1971-76; a biography of
the donor, n.d.; and clippings. 2 cm.
Photograph.
 1 photograph: Joseph Micaleff in
Toronto, 1975.

PRATTIS, M.
TORONTO, ONT.
 Brochures and flyers from St. Paul
the Apostle parish in Toronto,
1960-76. 3 cm.

SAPIANO, LAWRENCE AND PAULINE
TORONTO, ONT.
 Interviewed on 6 March 1978; .75
hr.; 1 tape; English; by Richard
Cumbo. He arrived in 1925, and
arranged for his wife's immigration in
1938.

VALENZIA, EMMANUELA
MALTA
 1 photograph: Maltese emigrants
prior to their departure from Valetta,
Malta, bound for Ont., 1952.

VELLA, MICHAELINA
TORONTO, ONT.
 Souvenir booklets and printed items
from St. Paul the Apostle Maltese
Catholic parish in Toronto. 5 cm.
Photographs.
 14 photographs: the Vella and
Debono families in Malta and
Toronto, 1905-76; and religious
activity at St. Paul the Apostle
Church in Toronto, 1958-60.
 *1st Anniversary Souvenir of St. Paul
the Apostle New Church*. Toronto:
Franciscan Fathers, 1957.
 *25th Anniversary of St. Paul the
Apostle Church*. Toronto: Franciscan
Fathers, 1955.

———————————————

GOZITAN SOCCER CLUB (GOZO
CLUB)
TORONTO, ONT.
 4 photographs: the Gozitan Soccer
Club in Toronto, and Malta, 1967-76.

INSTITUTE OF MALTESE CANADIAN
AFFAIRS
TORONTO, ONT.
 Forum Melitense. Toronto, Winter
1968 - Spring 1978. 1 reel of micro-
film.

MALTA BAND CLUB (J. GATT)
TORONTO, ONT.
 Records, 1971-77, which include a
constitution, correspondence, Club
minutes, member's lists, and miscellaneous items. 4 cm. Photographs.
 58 photographs: performances of the
Malta Band Club, including parades
and processions, 1970-76.

MALTA DRAMATIC CIRCLE (E.
BONNELLO)
TORONTO, ONT.
 5 newsclippings regarding the Circle,
1975-76. .25 cm. Photographs.
 5 photographs: the Malta Dramatic
Circle in Toronto, 1975-78.

MALTA FALCONS SOCCER CLUB
OSHAWA, ONT.
 Constitution, correspondence, financial statements, and clippings,
1947-77. 2 cm.

MALTA UNITED SOCIETY
WINDSOR, ONT.
 List of executive members, 1978.
.25 cm.

MALTESE CANADIAN SOCIAL CLUB
(S. MAGRI)
ST. THOMAS, ONT.
 Constitution, correspondence of the
executive and members, minutes of
meetings, membership lists, and programmes, 1973-77. 4 cm.

MALTESE CANADIAN SOCIAL CLUB
(V. CASSAR)
GUELPH, ONT.
 Constitution, correspondence, min-
utes, and miscellaneous printed items
including menus, programmes, and
clippings. 1 reel of microfilm. 2 cm.
Photographs.

5 photographs: activities of the Maltese Canadian Social Club in Guelph, Ont., c. 1976-78.

MALTESE CANADIAN SOCIETY OF TORONTO
TORONTO, ONT.
Constitution and rules, 1967; minutes, 1975, 1982-89; guest books, 1962-77; financial reports, 1974-76; and printed items, 1972-77. 12 cm. 2 reels of microfilm. Photographs.
19 photographs: activities and committees of the Maltese Canadian Society of Toronto, some taken at St. Paul the Apostle Church, 1934-71; and Maltese historical documents, 1970-71.
Cumbo, Richard. *60th Anniversary of the Maltese-Canadian Society of Toronto, 1922-82*. Toronto, 1982. Illustrated. .5 cm.
Malta Herald. Toronto, May 1968 - May 1969. 2 cm.
Lil Hutna. 1974, 1975, 1976, 1979 (4 issues).

MALTESE PROGRAMME FAN CLUB
TORONTO, ONT.
Correspondence, and various records, 1972-77. 1 reel of microfilm. Photographs.
3 photographs: social gatherings organized by the Club, c. 1970-75.

MELITA SOCCER CLUB
TORONTO, ONT.
Records, 1973-76, which include correspondence, Club minutes, and programmes. 1 reel of microfilm. Photographs.
32 photographs: sports and social gatherings, including the Calypso Carnival of the Melita Soccer Club in Toronto, 1965-77.

MULTICULTURAL HISTORY SOCIETY OF ONTARIO
TORONTO, ONT.
Bloor West Villager. Toronto, 1972-74. Articles written by Richard Cumbo. 1 reel of microfilm.
The Maltese Journal. New York, Jan. 1935 - Nov. 1946. 1 reel of microfilm.

ONTARIO ETHNIC NEWSPAPER MICROFILM PROJECT
TORONTO, ONT.
Maltese News. April 1954 - Nov. 1965. 1 reel of microfilm.

ST. PAUL THE APOSTLE CHURCH
TORONTO, ONT.
Parish announcements, 1939-77, and Holy Name Society minutes, 1953. 2 reels of microfilm. Photographs.
7 photographs: interior and exterior of St. Paul the Apostle Church., c. 1977-76.

BARRAK, EVELYN
TORONTO, ONT.
 3 photographs: Our Lady of
Assumption Melkite Catholic
Mission, Toronto, 1922, 1927, and
Lebanon, 1914.

GENABRY, REV. B.
TORONTO, ONT.
 Assorted records and newsletters
from Our Lady of Assumption
Melkite Catholic Church, 1914-77. 5
cm. Photographs.
 3 photographs: religious activities at
Our Lady of Assumption Melkite
Catholic Mission, 1972-75.

GENADRY, MSGR. A. (MELKITE
CHURCH)
TORONTO, ONT.
 *Golden Dedication of Our Lady of
the Annunciation Church*. Boston,
1942. 185 pp., in Akron/English
 *Golden Jubilee of St. Elias Church,
1908-58*. Cleveland, 1958. 104 pp.,
in English.
 St. Basil's Souvenir Program. Utica,
New York, 1941. 2 cm., in
Akron/English.
 *Sts. Peter and Paul Church: History
of Foundation*. Ottawa, 1962. 121
pp., in English.

GENADRY, MSGR. ANTOINE
TORONTO, ONT.
 Commemorative booklets and serials.
10 cm.
 *A Souvenir from Boston and New
England in Honor of His Beatitude
Our Lady of Purgatory Church*

Golden Jubilee, 1971-67. New Bed-
ford, Massachusetts, 1967.
 *Golden Jubilee of Atlanta Maronite
Community, 1962*. Atlanta: St.
Joseph's Maronite Church, 1962. 109
pp., in English.

MEOUCHI, PAUL PETER, MARONITE
PATRIARCH
BOSTON, 1962
 *St. Anthony's Maronite Church 50th
Anniversary, 1903-53*. Lawrence,
Massachusetts, 1953.
 Trait d'Union. 1964-79. Bulletin of
St. Sauveur Parish of Montreal.
Incomplete. 5 cm.

OUR LADY OF THE ASSUMPTION
MELKITE CATHOLIC MISSION
TORONTO, ONT.
 Parish registers of births, marriages,
and deaths among Greek-Melkite
catholic community of Toronto,
1967-79. 1 reel of microfilm.
 Weekly Bulletin. 1968-69. 1 cm., in
English/Akron.

OUR LADY OF THE ASSUMPTION
MELKITE CATHOLIC MISSION
TORONTO, ONT.
 Constitution, 1975, correspondence,
1914, 1958; first annual report, 1968-
69; and statistics of Melkite community in Toronto, 1976. 1.5 cm.

ANDRES, WILLIAM
ST. CATHARINES, ONT.
Interviewed on 20 Nov. 1966; 2
hrs.; 2 tapes; English; by T. Funk.
Discusses the Mennonite Niagara
Peninsula community.

BAAR, ELLE
TORONTO, ONT.
Genealogy of Peter and Anna Epp,
n.d.; and transcriptions of interviews
with Russian Mennonites who immigrated in the 1920s. 6 cm.
Baar, Ellen. "Mennonites of
Niagara: An Inventory of Materials."
1977. Unpublished essay. 1 cm.
*15th Anniversary of the Niagara
Christian Fellowship Chapel,
1954-1969.* 20 pp.

BAER, OSCAR
NEW HAMBURG, ONT.
Interviewed on 5 June 1980; .75 hr.;
1 tape; English; by R. Neff. General
discussion on early family life, and
changes within the Mennonite church
and its different ecclesiastical bodies.

BAERG, REV. W.
NIAGARA FALLS, ONT.
Interviewed in 1976; 1 hr.; 1 tape;
English; by T. Funk. Member of the
Niagara Falls Mennonite Brethren
Fellowship.

BANMAN, HENRY
AYLMER, ONT.
Printed items pertaining to Old Colony Mennonites of Mexico, 1950s (5
items). See Conrad Grebel Project.

Taped interview.
Interviewed on 17 May 1979; 1.75
hrs.; 2 tapes; German; by R.
Sawatsky. Discusses family migra-
tions between Mexico, Manitoba and
Ont.; and the differences between
Mexican and Ontarian Old Colony
Mennonites.

BANMAN, REV. JOHN
LONDON, ONT.
Interviewed on 11 June 1979; 2.5
hrs.; 3 tapes; English; by R.
Sawatsky. Memories of childhood in
Mexico, and subsequent dislocation to
Manitoba, and Ont.

BAST, MATTIE
CAMBRIDGE, ONT.
Interviewed on 9 July 1979; .5 hr.; 1
tape; English; by R. Neff. A discussion on early local Mennonite and
Amish congregations in the Kitchener
area.

BAUMAN, DANIEL AND PEARL
ELMIRA, ONT.
Interviewed on 10 July 1980; 1.25
hrs.; 2 tapes; English; by R. Neff.
Discusses the history of the Bauman
family in Europe and locally.

BAUMAN, JAMES
WALLENSTEIN, ONT.
Interviewed on 22 July 1980; 2 hrs.;
2 tapes; English; by Carolyn
Musselman. A discussion on the
Mennonite educational system.

BAUMAN, REBECCA
KITCHENER, ONT.
Interviewed on 9 May 1980; 1.75
hrs.; 2 tapes; English; by R. Neff.
Discusses her Russian family background; Old Order church services;
and its resistance towards conscription
and technological changes.

BAUMAN, SALOME
CAMBRIDGE, ONT.
Interviewed on 17 July 1980; 1.25
hrs.; 2 tapes; English; by R. Neff.
Discussion on her religious faith and
education as a Mennonite youth, and
an evaluation of local, past, and
present church leadership.

BEARINGER, HOWARD AND JESSIE
PETERSBURG, ONT.
Interviewed on 14 July 1981; .5 hr.;
1 tape; English; by L. Friesen. Both
belong to the Ontario Mennonite Conference. They comment on the differences and relationship between the
different Mennonite ecclesiastical
bodies in Ont., such as the Ontario
Mennonite Conference, Mennonite
Brethren in Christ, Old Order
Mennonite, United Mennonite, and
the Western Ontario Mennonite Conference.

BEATTY, PERRIN
FERGUS, ONT.
Interviewed on 14 July 1980; 1 hr.;
1 tape; English; by Carolyn
Musselman. Discusses involvement in
Old Older, and its disputes with
government.

BOWMAN, JESSE
ST. JACOBS, ONT.
Collection of scripture verses which
clarify the Mennonite position on
insurance, n.d.; and a summary of
interview with Bowman, 1980. .5 cm.

BROWN, KATIE
LEAMINGTON, ONT.
Interviewed on 6 Aug. 1981; .5 hr.;
1 tape; English; by L. Friesen. Parent
emigrated from Russia. Comments on
the Inter-Mennonite Conference, and
the possibility of future amalgamation
among the different Mennonite conferences in Ont.

BRUBACHER, AMZIE
NEW HAMBURG, ONT.
Interviewed on 23 July 1981; .75
hr.; 1 tape; English; by L. Friesen.
Of Swiss background, discusses eth-
nic variations, and the different
Mennonite church conferences in Ont.

BRUBACHER, EZRA
ELMIRA, ONT.
Interviewed on 14 July 1980; .5 hr.;
1 tape; English; by R. Neff. General
discussion on childhood, strict
segragated upbringing, the cleric sys-
tems, and an evaluation of Old Order
social scriptures.

BRUBACHER, LYDIA
ELMIRA, ONT.
Interviewed on 7 July 1980; .5 hr.; 1
tape; English; by R. Neff. The history of Steiner and Brubacher families, both Old Order Mennonites.

BRUBACHER, STANLEY
CAMBRIDGE, ONT.
Interviewed on 11 July 1979; 1 hr.;
1 tape; English; by R. Neff. Recollections of the founding of Rockway
Mennonite School in Kitchener; his
family; and his early years on the
farm.

BRUBACKER, STANLEY
PRESTON, ONT.
Interviewed on 24, 25 Nov. 1977; 2
hrs.; 2 tapes; English; by J. Nyce.
Discussion on religion, superstition,
folk medicine, customs, and conventions at the turn of the century.

COFFMAN, BARBARA
ST. CATHARINES, ONT.
Records from the United Mennonite
Church of Ontario in St. Catharines,
1970s; and printed matter largely
from the Canadian Mennonite Pub-
lishing Association, 1960s, 1970s. 4
cm. Taped interview.
Interviewed on 6 Nov. 1976; 1 hr.;
1 tape; English; by T. Funk. Member
of the First Mennonite Church of
Vineland.
Agape. May-June, 1977.
Christian Living. June 1977.
Gospel Herald. 14 June 1977.
Mennonite Reporter. 13 June 1977.
Provident, Highlights. Spring-Sum-
mer 1977.
The Glory and the Shame. May
1968.

COFFMAN, DAVID
BEAMSVILLE, ONT.
Printed items on Mennonite teach-
ings, 1970s. 5 cm. Taped interview.
Interviewed on 23 June 1977; 1.25
hrs.; 2 tapes; English; by A.
Marshall. Father was born in Vir-
ginia, and in the early 1900s migrated
to Vineland, Ont. where he was
summoned to preach by the
Mennonite Church.
Epp, Frank H. *The Glory and the
Shame.* Winnipeg: Canadian
Mennonite Pub. Association, 1968.
79 pp.
Christian Living. Vol. 24, no. 6,

June 1977. 47 pp.
Gospel Herald. 14 June 1977. 16 pp.

CRESSMAN, ABNER
NEW HAMBURG, ONT.
Interviewed on 21 May 1980; 2.75
hrs.; 3 tapes; English; by R. Neff.
Outlines family background in Europe
and locally, and comments on the
present schisms whithin the
Mennonite church.

CRESSMAN, BARBARA
KITCHENER, ONT.
Interviewed on 22 May 1980; .75
hr.; 1 tape; English; by R. Neff.
Dicusses family background, contact
with Russian-Mennonite immigrants,
and changing mores within the
Mennonite community.

CRESSMAN, CLARENCE AND
MARGARET
PLATTSVILLE, ONT.
Interviewed on 20 May 1980; 1.25
hrs.; 2 tapes; English; by R. Neff.
Discusses the history of the Cressman
and Ferguson families; comments on
Mennonite courting practices; wed-
dings; and local voting procedures.

CRESSMAN, HANNAH
ELMIRA, ONT.
Interviewed on 16 July 1980; .5 hr.;
1 tape; English; by R. Neff. Dis-
cusses reasons for leaving Old Order
Mennonite Church.

CRESSMAN, JACOB
PRESTON, ONT.
Interviewed on 19 Oct. 1977; 1 hr.;
1 tape; English; by J. Nyce. Discusses his early life in a Mennonite
community.

CRESSMAN, JOHN
CAMBRIDGE, ONT.
 Interviewed on 12 July 1979; 1 hr.;
1 tape; English; by R. Neff. Recol-
lections of the arrival of Russian
Mennonites in the 1920s; and com-
ments on schisms within the
Mennonite Church.

CRESSMAN, JOHN
PRESTON, ONT.
 Interviewed on 24 Oct. 1977; .75
hr.; 1 tape; English; by J. Nyce.
Discusses growing up in a Mennonite
home.

CRESSMAN, JOSEPH AND IDA
CAMBRIDGE, ONT.
 Interviewed on 5 July 1979; 1 hr.; 1
tape; English; by R. Neff. Discusses
the arrival and settlement of Russian-
Mennonite immigrants in Cambridge
in the 1920s.

CRESSMAN, JOSEPH
PRESTON, ONT.
 Interviewed on 9, 10 Nov. 1977; 1.5
hrs.; 2 tapes; English; by J. Nyce.
Discusses his family background, life
on the farm, and raising horses.

CRESSMAN, LLOYD AND ALICE
WATERLOO, ONT.
 Interviewed on 29 Aug. 1979; .75
hr.; 1 tape; English; by R. Neff.
Daughter of Scottish immigrant father
and Mennonite mother. Discusses
Mennonite church discipline.

CRESSMAN, SAMUEL AND VIOLA
CAMBRIDGE, ONT.
 Interviewed on 21 July 1980; .75
hr.; 1 tape English; by R. Neff.
Discusses her Old Order Mennonite
background.

CRESSMAN, ZENAS
BADEN, ONT.
 Interiewed on 28 May 1980; 1.25
hrs.; 2 tapes; English; by R. Neff.
Discusses history of the Cressman
family; and comments on revival
meetings, Mennonite social scriptures, and Old Order intransigence
towards military service.

DICK, HENRY
RUTHVEN, ONT.
 Interviewed on 5 Aug. 1981; .5 hr.;
1 tape; English; by L. Friesen. His
parents were from the Ukraine,
arrived after WWII.

DICK, JACOB
CHATHAM, ONT.
 Interviewed on 6 Aug. 1981; 1.25
hrs.; 2 tapes; English; by L. Friesen.
Emigrated from Russia in 1924, dis-
cusses pre-migration conditions of
Russian Mennonites.

DICK, JOHN
LEAMINGTON, ONT.
 Interviewed on 4 Aug. 1981; .5 hr.;
1 tape; English; by L. Friesen. Parents emigrated from Russia in 1924.

DICK, VICTOR AND MARIE
LEAMINGTON, ONT.
 Interviewed on 5 Aug. 1981; .5 hr.;
1 tape; English; by L. Friesen. Old
Colony Russian Mennonites who
arrived in Saskatchewan in 1922.

DICK, WILLIAM
WATERLOO, ONT.
 Interviewed on 24 June 1981; .5 hr.;
1 tape; English; by L. Friesen. Of
Russian background, discusses the
prospect of amalgamation of the vari-
ous Mennonite church conferences in
Ont.

DORSCHT, ROSE
KITCHENER, ONT.
Interviewed on 6 Dec. 1977; 1.5 hrs.; 2 tapes; English; by J. Nyce. Mainly a discussion on the problems of health and healing, folk medicine, and religious belief.

DRIEDGER, CORNELIUS
LEAMINGTON, ONT.
Interviewed on 4 Aug. 1981; .5 hr.; 1 tape; English; by L. Friesen. Of German and Russian descent, parents arrived in the early 1920s.

DRIEDGER, ELFRIEDA
LEAMINGTON, ONT.
Interviewed on 9 July 1979; .75 hr.; 1 tape; English; by R. Sawatsky. Recollections of first contacts with Mexican Mennonites.

DRIEDGER, HENRY
LEAMINGTON, ONT.
Interviewed on 6 Aug. 1981; 1 hr.; 1 tape; English; by L. Friesen. Originally from Siberia, relates trials and tribulations prior to, and during his emigration.

DRIEDGER, JACOB
LEAMINGTON, ONT.
Interviewed on 5 Aug. 1981; .75 hr.; 1 tape; English; by L. Friesen. Emigrated from Russia in 1924.

DRIEDGER, SUSIE
LEAMINGTON, ONT.
Interviewed on 6 Aug. 1981; .5 hr.; 1 tape; English; by L. Friesen. Originally from Russia, discusses restriction of religious practices there.

DUECK, REV. CORNELIUS
AYLMER, ONT.
Interviewed on 30 May 1979; .5 hr.; 1 tape; English; by R. Sawatsky. Discusses his personal history, and that of the Ontarion Sommerfelder Church.

DUECK, HENRY
LEAMINGTON, ONT.
Interviewed on 4 Aug. 1981; .5 hr.; 1 tape; English; by L. Friesen. Parents emigrated from Russia in 1925.

DYCK, CORNELIUS
PORT ROWAN, ONT.
Interviewed on 29 May 1979; 2 hrs.; 2 tapes; German; by R. Sawatsky. Discusses immigration to Mexico, and its Mennonite community.

DYCK, PETER
WHEATLEY, ONT.
Interviewed on 12 July 1979; 1.25 hrs.; 2 tapes; German; by R. Sawatsky. Discusses his personal history, including emigration to Mexico, and a Mennonite community in Wheatly, Ont.

EBY, FOSTER
BADEN, ONT.
Interviewed on 13 July 1978; 3 hrs.; 3 tapes; English; by J. Nyce. Foster Eby is the son of Gordon C. Eby, whose diary has been published by the Multicultural History Society of Ontario; interview provides contextual information on the diary.

ECKHART, JOHN
ST. CATHARINES, ONT.
Interviewed on 18 Jan. 1977; 1 hr.; 1 tape; English; by T. Funk. Member of the Grantham Mennonite Brethren.

ELVEN, SHANTZ
KITCHENER, ONT.
Interviewed on 18 June 1980; 1 hr.;

1 tape; English; by S. Musselman. Discussion on involvement in the Conscientious Objectors movement during WWI and WWII.

ENNS, HERBERT
WATERLOO, ONT.
 Interviewed on 9 July 1981; .75 hr.; 1 tape; English; by L. Friesen. Russian Mennonite who immigrated to Canada in 1924.

EPP, FRANK
ST. CATHARINES, ONT.
 7 photographs: the F. Epp family, and their dwelllings in Saskatchewan, 1912-65.

EPP, REV. H. P.
ST. CATHARINES, ONT.
 Interviewed on 6 July 1977; 1 hr.; 1 tape; English; by A. Marshall. Originally from Russia, the family arrived in 1925. Detailes the differences in religious practices and ceremonies between the various Mennonite ecclesiastical groups.
 Jahrbuch der vereinigten Mennoniten Gemeinden in Ontario, Canada, 1954. Yearbook. 1 cm.

EPP, HENRY
KITCHENER, ONT.
 Interviewed on 31 July 1979; 1 hr.; 1 tape; English; by R. Sawatsky. Personal history donor, describes congregational life among Mennonites in Leamington and Kitchener, Ont.

EPP, HENRY
LEAMINGTON, ONT.
 Interviewed on 3 Aug. 1981; .5 hr.; 1 tape; English; by L. Friesen. Originally from Russia, he arrived in

1925, describes the Mennonite community (mainly Russian) in Leamington, Ont.

EPP, PETER
BLYSEWOOD, ONT.
 Interviewed on 4 Aug. 1981; 1 hr.; 1 tape; English; by L. Friesen. Describes life of Mennonite farming communities in Soviet Russia during the collectivization years of the early 1930s.

EPP, WALTER
ST. CATHARINES, ONT.
 Interviewed on 7 June 1977; 1 hr.; 1 tape; English; by A. Marshall. Born in Saskatchewan, moved to the Niagara Peninsula, Ont. in 1941.

ERB, EMMA AND FANNIE BAUMAN
WATERLOO, ONT.
 Interviewed on 15 Aug. 1979; .75 hr.; 1 tape; English; by R. Neff. Parents were Old Order Mennonites. The donors compare their childhood Mennonite community to their present-day one.

FLAMING, HENRY
LEAMINGTON, ONT.
 Interviewed on 18 July 1979; 1 hr.; 1 tape; English; by R. Sawatsky. Family originally from Russia, discusses his experiences as a teacher, particularly among Mexican Mennonite children in Ont.

FRANSEN, NICK
VINELAND, ONT.
 Interviewed on 1 Jan. 1977; 2 hrs.; 2 tapes; English; by T. Funk. Member of the United Mennonite Church of Vineland.

FRETZ, WINFIELD
WATERLOO, ONT.
 Interviewed on 6 June 1980; 1 hr.; 1 tape; English; by Carolyn Musselman. Involved with Conrad Grebel College.

FRIESEN, CORNY
PORT ROWAN, ONT.
 Interviewed on 24 Aug. 1979; 1 hr.; 1 tape; German; by R. Sawatsky. Born in Manitoba, moved to Ont. in 1956.

FRIESEN, REV. DAVID
AYLMER, ONT.
 Interviewed on 4, 12 June 1979; 2.5 hrs.; 3 tapes; English; by R. Sawatsky. Represents the Ontario Mennonite Immigrant Advisory Committee, discusses his personal history and work with immigration and citizenship concerns among Mexican Mennonites in Ont.

FRIESEN, REV. ISAAC
VINELAND, ONT.
 Interviewed on 8 Aug. 1979; 1 hr.; 1 tape; German; by R. Sawatsky. Discusses history of United Mennonite Church in Vineland, Ont.

FRIESEN, NETTIE
WHEATLEY, ONT.
 Interviewed on 5 July 1979; 1.25 hrs.; 2 tapes; German; by R. Sawatsky. Born in Mexico. Discusses early memories of Mennonite community in Mexico. Immmigrated to Clear Water, Ont. in 1957.

FROESE, DIEDRICH
LEAMINGTON, ONT.
 Interviewed on 5 Aug. 1981; .5 hr.; 1 tape; English; by L. Friesen. Russian Mennonite, arrived in Canada in 1926.

FROESE, HELEN
NIAGARA FALLS, ONT.
 Interviewed on 8 Feb. 1977; 1 hr.; 1 tape; English; by T. Funk. Members of the Niagara Christian Church.

GIESBRECHT, PETER
AYLMER, ONT.
 Interviewed on 20 June 1979; .75 hr.; 1 tape; German; by R. Sawatsky. Discusses memories of childhood in Mexico and Manitoba, and the founding of the Old Colony church in Ont.

GIESBRECHT, REV. PETER
KITCHENER, ONT.
 Interviewed on 25 July 1979; 1 hr.; 1 tape; English; by R. Sawatsky. Recounts his experiences as a teacher in Manitoba, Belize, Ont., and Mexico.

GIESBRECHT, WILLIAM
LEAMINGTON, ONT.
 Interviewed on 4 July 1979; 1 hr.; 1 tape; English; by R. Sawatsky. Originally from Steinbach, Manitoba, moved to Ont. in 1968.

GIMBEL, ANNIE
CAMBRIDGE, ONT.
 Interviewed on 4 June 1980; 1 hr.; 1 tape; English; by R. Neff. Reminisces of contacts with Russian-Mennonite immigrants, discusses reasons why she left the Old Order Mennonite Church.

GINGERICH, AMOS
WATERLOO, ONT.
 Interviewed on 30 May 1980; .5 hr.; 1 tape; English; by R. Neff. Outlines

the history of the Gingerich and Bauman families.

GINGERICH, ANGUS
CAMBRIDGE, ONT.
 Interviewed on 11 July 1979; .75 hr.; 1 tape; English; by R. Neff. Discussion on changing values and traditions within the Mennonite community of Cambridge.

GOERTZ, HENRY
ST. CATHARINES, ONT.
 Interviewed on 11 June 1977; 1.75 hrs.; 2 tapes; English; by A. Marshall. Emigrated from Russia in 1926.

GOOD, ABNER
CAMBRIDGE, ONT.
 Interviewed on 25 July 1979; 1 hr.; 1 tape; English; by R. Neff. Russian-Mennonite immigrant, reminiscences of Mennonite and German community in St. Jacobs during WWI.

GOOD, ABNER
PRESTON, ONT.
 Interviewed on 25 Oct. 1977; 2 hrs.; 2 tapes; English; by J. Nyce. General discussion on the Mennonite faith, and traditional life.

GOOD, GERALD
NEW HAMBURG, ONT.
 Interviewed on 23 July 1981; .75 hr.; 1 tape; English; by L. Friesen. Of Swiss-German background, discusses the prospect of amalgamation of the different Mennonite church groups in Ont.

GOOD, MELINDA
PRESTON, ONT.
 Interviewed on 17 Oct. 1977; .5 hr.; 1 tape; English; by J. Nyce. Dis-

cusses traditional Mennonite life the role of women within it.

HALLMAN, LEAH
NEW DUNDEE, ONT.
 Interviewed on 28 Aug. 1979; 1.75 hrs.; 2 tapes; English; by R. Neff. Recollections of her first encounters, and shared experiences with Russian-Mennonite immigrants in the 1920s.

HALLMANS, ANSON
PRESTON, ONT.
 Interviewed on 26 Oct. 1977; .5 hr.; 1 tape; English; by J. Nyce. Discusses growing up in a traditional Mennonite home, and conflict regarding careers.

HAMM, DIEDRICH
LANGTON, ONT.
 Interviewed on 29 May 1979; 1 hr.; 1 tape; Low German; by R. Sawatsky. Was a member of Old Colony Church in Mexico. Relates personal memories of early life in Mexico and Manitoba.

HARMS, JOHN B.
AYLMER, ONT.
 Interviewed on 16 May 1979; 1.25 hrs.; 2 tapes; German; by R. Sawatsky. Born in Manitoba, moved to Ont. in 1958. Discusses early life and influences of the Kleine Gemeinde and Old Colony in Mexico.

HIGH, ISAAC
ST. CATHARINES, ONT.
 2 photographs: Mennonite Canadians in Kitchener, and Pennsylvania, 1913-43. Taped interview.
 Interviewed on 7 July 1977; 2 hrs.; 2 tapes; English; by A. Marshall. Born in St. Catharines in 1910, and acted as sponsor for several

Russian-Mennonite immigrant families. Comments on the gradual dissolution of cohesion within his Mennonite community.

HUNSBERGER, MARY
BADEN, ONT.
Interviewed on 18 June 1980; 1.25 hrs.; 2 tapes; English; by R. Neff. Provides history of the Cressman and Hallman families, and their neighbourly relations with Russian-Mennonite immigrants.

HUNSBERGER, MINNIE
CAMBRIDGE, ONT.
Interviewed on 10 July 1979; 1 hr.; 1 tape; English; by R. Neff. Discussion on the changing (and vanishing) traditional way of life among Mennonites of Cambridge.

HUNSBERGER, VERA
CAMBRIDGE, ONT.
Interviewed on 6 July 1979; .75 hr.; 1 tape; English; by R. Neff. Attended Toronto Bible College, mission work in Kansas City, discussion on Young People's bible meetings, Literary Society meetings, and revival meetings.

HUNSBERGER, VERA
PRESTON, ONT.
Interviewed on 26 Oct. 1977; 1 hr.; 1 tape; English; by J. Nyce. Recollections of life as a young girl, farming, and labour hiring practices.

HURST, NOAH
ST. JACOBS, ONT.
Interviewed on 17 July 1980; .75 hr.; 1 tape; English; by R. Neff. Provides family history and reasons for leaving the Old Order Mennonite Church.

JACOBSH, REV. JOSEPH
AYLMER, ONT.
Interviewed on 26 June 1979; .75 hr.; 1 tape; English; by R. Sawatsky. Discusses personal history, and the founding of Gottes Gemeinde Church in Aylmer.

JANZEN, BILL
WATERLOO, ONT.
Interviewed on 25 Aug. 1979; 1.75 hrs.; 2 tapes; English; by R. Sawatsky. Personal history of Bill Janzen.

JANZEN, JACOB
LEAMINGTON, ONT.
Interviewed on 7 Aug. 1981; 1 hr.; 1 tape; English; by L. Friesen. Russian Mennonites, arrived in 1924. Discuss conditions, and religious life in Mennnonite colonies of Soviet Russia.

KAUFFMAN, ED
ST. AGATHA, ONT.
Interviewed on 10 July 1981; .75 hr.; 1 tape; English; by L. Friesen. Of Swiss-German background, belongs to Ontario Mennonite Conference, comments optimistically on the prospect of almalgamation of the various Mennonite conferences in Ont.

KEHL, JOHN
CAMBRIDGE, ONT.
Interviewed on 1 Aug. 1979; 1 hr.; 1 tape; English; by R. Neff. Provides history of the First Mennonite Church in Kitchener.

KENNELL, ELKANNAH
WELLESLEY, ONT.
Interviewed on 29 July 1981; .75 hr.; 1 tape; English; by L. Friesen. Of Amish background, member of

Mapleview Church, comments on the increasing liberalization and secularization of the Mennonite church.

KINZIE, EDWIN AND LINEAN
CAMBRIDGE, ONT.
 Interviewed on 27 Aug. 1979; .75 hr.; 1 tape; English; by R. Neff.

KINZIE, ISAIAH
CAMBRIDGE, ONT.
 Interviewed on 13 July 1979; .5 hr.; 1 tape; English; by R. Neff. Provides personal history, and the history of Hagey's Mennonite Church (presently Preston Mennonite Church).

KLASSEN, ISAAC
LANGTON, ONT.
 Interviewed on 13 July 1979; 1.25 hrs.; 2 tapes; English; by R. Sawatsky. Provides history of the Klassen family, members of the Ontario Old Colony Church.

KLASSEN, PETER
QUEENSTON, ONT.
 Interviewed on 7 Oct. 1977; 1 hr.; 1 tape; German; by T. Funk.

KNARR, GARY
ELMIRA, ONT.
 Interviewed on 14 July 1981; .75 hr.; 1 tape; English; by L. Friesen. Of Swiss background, member of the Ontario Mennonite Conference, feels close to the United Mennonites (some cultural differences, but no theological differences between the two).

KOCH, EARL
NEW HAMBURG, ONT.
 Interviewed on 15 July 1980; 1 hr.; 1 tape; English; by Carolyn Musselman. Discusses contentious

issues between Old Order, conservative Mennonites and the government.

KOLB, PRISCILLA
KITCHENER, ONT.
 Interviewed on 30 Aug. 1979; .5 hr.; 1 tape; English; by R. Neff. Anecdotes about Russian-Mennonite immigrant families and the Blenheim Mennonite Church.

KONRAD, BILL
WHEATLEY, ONT.
 Interviewed on 6 Aug. 1981; .5 hr.; 1 tape; English; by L. Friesen. Parents immigrated to Canada in the 1920s, members of the Western Ontario Mennonite Conference.

KONRAD, GEORGE B.
WHEATLEY, ONT.
 Interviewed on 26 July 1979; .75 hr.; 1 tape; English; by R. Sawatsky. Russian Mennonites, discussion on Mennonite community in Leamington, Ont.

KONRAD, GEORGE
BLYSEWOOD, ONT.
 Interviewed on 3 Aug. 1981; .5 hrs.; English; by L. Friesen. A farmer of Dutch-German descent; discusses life lived in Russian-Mennonite enclaves.

KOOP, ELSA
WHEATLEY, ONT.
 Interviewed on 26 July 1979; 1 hr.; 1 tape; English; by R. Sawatsky. Discusses involvement in programmes of South Essex community council.

KOOP, WALTER
LEAMINGTON, ONT.
 Interviewed on 3 Aug. 1981; .5 hr.; 1 tape; English; by L. Friesen. Of German Mennonite background,

although parents born in Russia, feels close to Old Older and Amish Mennonites.

KROEKER, DAVE
WATERLOO, ONT.
Interviewed on 30 June 1981; 1 hr.; 1 tape; English; by L. Friesen. Of Russian-Mennonite background, member of the General Conference and Rudnerweider Mennonite Church.

LEIS, ALVIN
WELLESLEY, ONT.
Interviewed on 20 May 1981; .5 hr.; 1 tape; English; by L. Friesen. Of Amish-Mennonite background, disapproves of future amalgamtion of the various Ont. conferences.

LICHTI, MARY
NEW HAMBURG, ONT.
Interviewed on 23 July 1980; .5 hr.; 1 tape; English; by R. Neff. Provides history of the Beck and Roth families.

LOEWEN, ABE
AYLMER, ONT.
Interviewed on 15 May 1979; 1 hr.; 1 tape; German; by R. Sawatsky. Born in Mexico, immigrated to Ont., via Manitoba in 1952.

LOEWEN, VIC
NIAGARA-ON-THE-LAKE, ONT.
Interviewed in Nov. 1976; 1 hr.; 1 tape; English; by T. Funk. Member of Orchard Park Bible Church.

LUTHY, DAVID
AYLMER, ONT.
Brochures on contentious issues between government and Old Order Amish and Mennonites, c. 1960s. 3 cm.
Stoll, Joseph. *Who Shall Educate*

Our Children?. Aylmer, Ont.: Pathway Pub. Corp., 1965. 80 pp.
Family Life. June 1980. 35 pp.

MARTENS, JOHN
LEAMINGTON, ONT.
Interviewed on 5 Aug. 1981; .75 hr.; 1 tape; English; by L. Friesen. Born in Ukraine in 1911, immigrated to Canada in 1925.

MARTENS, VICTOR
KITCHENER, ONT.
Interviewed on 25 June 1981; .25 hr.; 1 tape; English; by L. Friesen. Of Russian-Mennonite background, Mennonite Brethen, member of Rockway Church, believes amalgamation of the various Ont. conferences is possible.

MARTIN, AMOS
KITCHENER, ONT.
Interviewed on 9, 12, 20, 30 June 1978; 6 hrs.; 6 tapes; English; by J. Nyce. Personal history of Amos Martin.

MARTIN, AMSEY
FLORADALE, ONT.
Personal papers, n.d. .25 cm.

MARTIN, CATHERINE NAOMI
CAMBRIDGE, ONT.
Interviewed on 21 Aug. 1979; 1 hr.; 1 tape; English; by R. Neff.

MARTIN, ENOCH
ST. JACOBS, ONT.
Interviewed on 3 June 1980; .75 hr.; 1 tape; English; by R. Neff. Provides history of the Martin and Bauman families.

MARTIN, JESSE
PRESTON, ONT.
 Interviewed on 24 Oct. 1977; .75
hr.; 1 tape; English; by J. Nyce.
Recounts her life as a wife of a
Mennonite pastor, and her relation-
ship with her husband.

MARTIN, LEIGHTON
WATERLOO, ONT.
 Interviewed on 16 June 1980; .75
hr.; 1 tape; English; by Carolyn and
Karey Musselman. Discusses issues
taken up by conservative Mennonites
against government--from military
service and education, to jury duty
and immigration.

MARTIN, LYDIA ANN
CAMBRIDGE, ONT.
 Interviewed on 12 July 1979; .5 hr.;
1 tape; English; by R. Neff. Discusses split in the Old Order Church,
and formation of the Martin
Mennonites.

MARTIN, SAMUEL AND ELMEDA
ELMIRA, ONT.
 Interviewed on 15 July 1980; 1.25
hrs.; 2 tapes; English; by R. Neff.
Provides history of the Martin and
Riest families, comments on the
"charismatic movement" and
lay-participation in the Mennonite
church.

MARTIN, SIMEON
ST. JACOBS, ONT.
 Interviewed on 3 June 1980; 1.75
hrs.; 2 tapes; English; by R. Neff.
History of the A. Martin family, and
anecdotes of Russian-Mennonite
immigrants.

MCKEGNEY, J.
KITCHENER, ONT.
 Interviewed on 30 Nov. 1977; 1 hr.;
1 tape; English; by J. Nyce. Discusses her research on Christian Eby,
and folk medicine.

MCLOUGHRY, ELLIOT IRWIN
KITCHENER, ONT.
 Interviewed on 30 May, 18 June
1980; 2 hrs.; 2 tapes; English; by
Carolyn Musselman. Discusses con-
tentious issues between the govern-
ment and Old Order Amish and
Mennonites.

METZGER, GEORGE
ST. JACOBS, ONT.
 Interviewed on 20 May 1980; 1 hr.;
1 tape; English; by R. Neff. Provides
history of the Metzger family, and
disputes between Old Order and
Ontario Conference Mennonites.

METZGER, WESLEY
ELMIRA, ONT.
 Interviewed on 9 July 1980; 1.25
hrs.; 2 tapes; English; by R. Neff.
Provides history of the Metzger and
Shantz families.

MILLAR, ANNE
KITCHENER, ONT.
 Interviewed on 26 April 1978; .5
hr.; 1 tape; English; by J. Nyce.
Discussion on her experiences with
the Sixth and Seventh Book of Moses,
and on her grandfather, Christian
Eby.

MILLAR, ANNE
KITCHENER, ONT.
 Diary and letters of Gordon C. Eby,
1911-13; 1914-19. 24 cm. 1 reel of
microfilm. Photographs. Taped interview.

Over 150 photographs: people, farming, picnics, dwellings, and automobiles among the Mennonite community of Kitchener, 1906-13.
Interviewed on 17 Feb. 1978; .5 hr.; 1 tape; English; by J. Nyce. Memories of grandfather, Christain Eby.

MILLAR, DOUGLAS
KITCHENER, ONT.
Interviewed on 23 June 1981; 1 hr.; 1 tape; English; by L. Friesen. Of Pennsylvania-German background, belongs to both the Ont. and United Mennonite Conferences.

MUSSELMAN, BEULAH
ELMIRA, ONT.
Interviewed on 14 July 1980; 1.25 hrs.; 2 tapes; English; by R. Neff. Provides history of the Snyder and Weber families.

MUSSELMAN, CAROLYN AND KAREY
CAMBRIDGE, ONT.
Correspondence pertaining to project among Old Order Mennonites around Kitchener-Waterloo. 1 cm.

NEUFELD, AGATHA
LEAMINGTON, ONT.
Interviewed on 7 Aug. 1981; .5 hr.; 1 tape; English; by L. Friesen. Born in Russia in 1923, immigrated to Canada in 1924.

NEUFELD, C.
NIAGARA FALLS, ONT.
Interviewed on 3 March 1977; 2 hrs.; 2 tapes; English; by T. Funk. Member of the Niagara United Church.
NEUKAMM, EMIL
AYLMER, ONT.
Interviewed on 5 June 1979; .75 hr.; 1 tape English; by R. Sawatsky. History of the Emil family, and their tobacco farming operation.

PENNER, JACOB AND GEORGE EPP
ST. CATHARINES, ONT.
Interviewed on 12 Feb. 1977; 1 hr.; 1 tape; Phattdeutsch; by T. Funk. Member of the St. Scott Mennonite Brethren Church.

PENNER, MARTIN
AYLMER, ONT.
Interviewed on 22 May 1979; 1.75 hrs.; 2 tapes; German; by R. Sawatsky. Memories of early life in Mennonite settlements in Mexico.

PETERS, CORNELIUS
AYLMER, ONT.
4 diaries of Jacob Peters, n.d. 6 cm. (Part of Conrad Grebel College Archives). Taped interview.
Interviewed on 16 May 1979; 2 hrs.; 2 tapes; German; by R. Sawatsky. Recounts experiences in Mennonite colonies of Manitoba, Saskatchewan, and Mexico.

PETERS, CORNELIUS
AYLMER, ONT.
Interviewed on 13 June 1979; 2 hrs.; 2 tapes; English/German; by R. Sawatsky. Recounts early life experiences in Mexico, migration to Manitoba, and farming and tortilla businesses in Aylmer in the 1970s.

PETERS, HEINRICH
MAPLETON, ONT.
Interviewed on 27 June 1979; 2 hrs.; 2 tapes; German; by R. Sawatsky. Provides history of the Peters family which belonged to the Kleine Gemeinde church.

PETERS, JAKE
LANGTON, ONT.
Interviewed on 3 July 1979; 1 hr.; 1 tape; English; by R. Sawatsky. Memories of early life in Mexico, immigration to Ont. in 1961, and participation in the Aylmer EMMC Church.

QUIRING, REV. CORNELIUS
LEAMINGTON, ONT.
Interviewed on 10 July 1979; 1.75 hr.; 2 tapes; German; by R. Sawatsky. Memories of childhood in Mexico, attendance in Colony schools, immigration to Ont., and appointment as minister in the Old Colony Church.

RAMSEYER, WILLIAM AND GLADYS
BADEN, ONT.
Interviewed on 3 July 1980; .75 hr.; 1 tape; English; by R. Neff. Provides history of the Ramseyer family, and its encounters with Russian immigrant Mennonites in the 1920s.

REESOR, JAMES
KITCHENER, ONT.
Interviewed on 12 May 1981; .5 hr.; 1 tape; English; by L. Friesen. Of Swiss-German background, mother of Amish descent, member of the Ontario Mennonite Conference.

REGIER, ED
VIRGIL, ONT.
Interviewed on 9 June 1977; 2 hrs.; 2 tapes; English; by A. Marshall. Born in Russia in 1895, moved to the Niagara Peninsula, via Manitoba, in 1943.

REIMER, GERHART
VINELAND, ONT.
Interviewed in Jan. 1977; 1 hr.; 1 tape; German; by T. Funk. Member of the Vineland Mennonite Brethren Church, discussion on the Mennonite community of the Niagara Peninsula.

REIMER, REV. PETER
PORT ROWAN, ONT.
Interviewed on 14 June 1979; .75 hr.; 1 tape; German; by R. Sawatsky. Born in in Russia, arrived in Canada in 1926.

REMPEL, HANS
ST. CATHARINES, ONT.
Interviewed on 22 Jan. 1977; 2 hrs.; 2 tapes; German; by T. Funk.

ROPP, IVAN
WELLESLEY, ONT.
Interviewed on 30 July 1981; .5 hr.; 1 tape; English; by L. Friesen. Of German background, family moved to Ont. in the 1970s, members of the Western Ontario Mennonite Conference.

ROTH, MATILDA
NEW HAMBURG, ONT.
Interviewed on 23 July 1980; .75 hr.; 1 tape; English; by R. Neff. Provides history of the Schwartzentruber family.

RUDY, JACOB AND ADA
CAMBRIDGE, ONT.
Interviewed on 23 Aug. 1979; .75 hr.; 1 tape; English; by R. Neff. Discussion on the way of life of Russian-Mennonite immigrants.

SAUDER, AARON
WATERLOO, ONT.
Interviewed on 9 June 1980; .75 hr.; 1 tape; English; by R. Neff. Discussion on the way of life of Russian-Mennonite immigrants.

SAWATSKY, REV. BEN
WATERLOO, ONT.
 Interviewed on 20 Aug. 1979; 1.5
hrs.; 2 tapes; English; by R.
Sawatsky. Memoir of the interviewee.

SAWATZKY, REV. NEIL
AYLMER, ONT.
 Interviewed on 19 June 1979; .75
hr.; 1 tape; English; by R. Sawatsky.
A detailed commentary on theological
issues seaparating the numerous
Mennonite church conferences.

SCHLEGEL, RAY
KITCHENER, ONT.
 Interviewed on 23 May 1980; 1 hr.;
1 tape; English; by Carolyn
Musselman. Discusses contentious
issues between government and Old
Order Amish and Mennonites.

SCHROEDER, AARON
LEAMINGTON, ONT.
 Interviewed on 5 July 1979; .75 hr.;
1 tape; German; by R. Sawatsky.
Bitter memories of his early life in
Mexico, moved to a Matheson, Ont.
settlement in 1958; discusses his
occupational history, and involvement
in the Mennonite church.

SCHROEDER, ALEX
VIRGIL, ONT.
 Interviewed on 10 June 1977; 1 hr.;
1 tape; English; by A. Marshall. Born
in Poland, arrived in Canada in 1950.

SCHUTZ, REV. ALLEN JOHN
PRESTON, ONT.
 Interviewed on 3 Nov. 1977; 1.5
hrs.; 2 tapes; English; by J. Nyce.
Discusses his early life, and conver-
sion to an Evangelist.

SCHWARTZENTRUBER, GERALD
WELLESLEY, ONT.
 Interviewed on 20 May 1981 .75 hr.;
1 tape; English; by L. Friesen. Of
Swiss-Amish background, member of
the Western Ontario Mennonite Conference.

SCHWARTZENTRUBER, IDA
NEW HAMBURG, ONT.
 Interviewed on 25 July 1980; .5 hr.;
1 tape; English; by R. Neff. Provides
local family history and description of
ancestors' occupations.

SHANTZ, ELVEN
KITCHENER, ONT.
 Interviewed on 28 May 1980; 1.5
hrs.; 2 tapes; English; by Carolyn
Musselman. Discusses contentious
issues between government and Old
Order Amish and Mennonites.

SHANTZ, ELVEN
KITCHENER, ONT.
 Interviewed on 8 Aug. 1979; 1.5
hrs.; 2 tapes; English; R. Neff. Discussion on changing Mennonite attitudes toward conscription from WWI
to WWII.

SHANTZ, ELVEN
KITCHENER, ONT.
 Interviewed on 9, 12 Dec. 1977; 2.5
hrs.; 3 tapes; English; by J. Nyce.
Discusses gardening, folk medicine,
his attempts at healing, and general
everyday prosaic life on the farm.

SHANTZ, IVAN
ELMIRA, ONT.
 Interviewed on 8 July 1980; 1.25
hrs.; 2 tapes; English; by R. Neff.
Relates reasons for leaving Old Order
Mennonite Church.

SHANTZ, JUNIA
CAMBRIDGE, ONT.
 Interviewed on 6, 13 Aug. 1979; 2.5
hrs.; 3 tapes; English; by R. Neff.
Brief accounts of the people buried at
Wanner Mennonite Church cemetary.

SHANTZ, LORNE AND ADA
BADEN, ONT.
 Interviewed on 18 June 1980; 1.25
hrs.; 2 tapes; English; by R. Neff.
Retells history of the Shantz family,
and of local church leadership.

SHANTZ, MYRA
CAMBRIDGE, ONT.
 Interviewed on 28 Aug. 1979; 1 hr.;
1 tape; English; by R. Neff. Stories
about Russian-Mennonite immigrant
neighbours, and Mennonite church
activities in the Cambridge community.

SNIDER, HANNAH
CAMBRIDGE, ONT.
 Interviewed on 17 July 1979; .25
hr.; 1 tape; English; by R. Neff.
Recollections of Russian-Mennonite
immigrants, and of church activities
in the Mennonite community of Cambridge.

SNIDER, LEONARD
ST. JACOBS, ONT.
 Interviewed on 29 May 1980; 1.5
hrs.; 2 tapes; English; by R. Neff.
Provides history of the Weber and
Snider families.

SNIDER, NORMAN
CAMBRIDGE, ONT.
 Interviewed on 19 July 1979; 1.5
hrs.; 2 tapes; English; by R. Neff.
Outlines history of the establishment
of the Mennonite church in Elmira,
Ont., and of the breaking away of the
Old Order group from it.

SNIDER, STANLEY
CAMBRIDGE, ONT.
 Interviewed on 27 July 1979; 1 hr.;
1 tape; English; by R. Neff. Anecdotes about Russian-Mennonite immigrants, and the Mennonite community
of Cambridge during WWI.

SNYDER, DOUG
WATERLOO, ONT.
 Interviewed on 20 July 1981; .5 hr.;
1 tape; English; by L. Friesen. Of
Swiss-Mennonite (Old Order) background, member of the Ontario
Mennonite Conference, comments on
the role of the Inter-Mennonite Conference in bringing the various
Mennnonite church conferences
together.

SNYDER, DOUGLAS
WATERLOO, ONT.
 Interviewed on 3 July 1980; 1 hr.; 1
tape; English; by Carolyn
Musselman. On contentious issues
between Old Order Amish and
Mennonites, and government.

SNYDER, EDWARD AND EMMA
CAMBRIDGE, ONT.
 Interview on 22 Aug. 1979; 1 hr.; 1
tape; English; by R. Neff. Stories
about Russian-Mennonite immigrants.

SNYDER, FRED
WATERLOO, ONT.
 Graf-Groof family papers and clip-
pings, 1835-1976 (7 items). Photo-
graphs.
 2 photographs: Snyder reunion,
Doon, 1909; Berlin Junior Farmers'
Association, 1916.

SNYDER, LILLIAN
CAMBRIDGE, ONT.
 Interviewed on 30 July 1979; .75
hr.; 1 tape; English; by R. Neff.
Recollections of Russian-Mennonite
immigrant families, and the Cambridge Mennonite community in
general.

SNYDER, PERCY
BADEN, ONT.
 Interviewed on 17 June 1980; .75
hr.; 1 tape; English; by R. Neff.
Provides history of Snyder family.

SNYDERS, ORLAN
PRESTON, ONT.
 Interviewed on 4 Nov. 1977; .75
hr.; 1 tape; English; by J. Nyce.
Discussion on Mennonite gardening,
technique, and form.

STECKLY, JOSEPH
PRESTON, ONT.
 Interviewed on 18 Oct. 1977; .75
hr.; 1 tape; English; by J. Nyce.
Discussion on farming family life,
and on the Mennonite faith.

STEINGART, FRANK
ST. CATHARINES, ONT.
 1 photograph of Russian-Mennonite
immigrants en route to Canada, 1924.
Taped interview.
 Interviewed on 31 May 1977; 1 hr.;
1 tape; English; by A. Marshall. Of
Russian-Mennonite background,
immigrated to Canada, c. 1920s.

STOBBE, BERNHARD
WATERLOO, ONT.
 Interviewed on 24 July 1981; 1.25
hrs.; 2 tapes; English; by L. Friesen.
Description of Mennonite evacuation

from war-torn Poland in 1939; and a
commentary on the role of the
Inter-Mennonite Conference in
Ontario.

TOEWS, JOHN
LEAMINGTON, ONT.
 Interviewed on 12 July 1979; 1 hr.;
1 tape; English; by R. Sawatsky.
Description of vegetable farming
operation using Mexican Mennonite
work-force.

TOMAN, KATIE
NEW HAMBURG, ONT.
 Recorded on 15 July 1978; 1 hr.; 1
videotape; English; by K. Lamb and
J. Nyce. These videotapes are rough
footages of a traditional Pennsylvania
German-Mennonite home and garden.

VOTH, HEINRICH
COPENHAGEN, ONT.
 Interviewed on 5 June 1979; 1 hr.; 1
tape; German; by R. Sawatsky. Born
in Manitoba, of Russian-Mennonite
background. Discusses migration to
Mexico, settlement in Ont., 1966, and
involvement in the founding of the
Sommerfelder Church in Ont.

VOTH, JOHN
AYLMER, ONT.
 Interviewed on 12 June 1979; 1.5
hrs.; 2 tapes; German; by R.
Sawatsky. Memories of early life in
Mexican Mennonite colonies, moved
to Ont. in 1969, discusses beginnings
of Sommerfelder Church in Ont.

WALL, A.
ST. CATHARINES, ONT.
 Interviewed on 25 Jan. 1977; 2 hrs.;
2 tapes; English; by E. Baar. Member of the United Mennonite Church.

WALL, ABRAM
ST. CATHARINES, ONT.
 3 photographs: farming in Namaka,
Ont., 1926-29. Taped interview.
 Interviewed on 8, 11 July 1977; 3.5
hrs.; 4 tapes; English; by A.
Marshall. Emigrated from Russia in
1926. Travelled to Alberta, and finally settled in Ont. in 1938; provides
accounts of early church leaders in
the Niagara Peninsula, Ont.

WALL, AARON
ELMIRA, ONT.
 Interviewed on 30 July 1979; 1 hr.;
1 tape; German; by R. Sawatsky.
Born in Mexico, moved to Ont., c.
1960s. Discusses employment history
and activities of Old Colony Church
in the Kitchener area.

WARKENTIN, PETER
LEAMINGTON, ONT.
 Interviewed on 7 Aug. 1981; 1 hr.; 1
tape; English; by L. Friesen. Russian
Mennonites, immigrated to Canada in
the 1920s.

WEBER, CATHERINE
CAMBRIDGE, ONT.
 Interviewed on 6 July 1979; .75 hr.;
1 tape; English; by R. Neff. Recounts
social and religious activities at the
Ontario Mennonite Bible School in
Kitchener, Ont.

WEBER, ERVIN
CAMBRIDGE, ONT.
 Interviewed on 19 July 1979; 1.5
hrs.; 2 tapes; English; by R. Neff.
Recollections of Mennonite community in the Berlin (Kitchener) area
during WWI.

WEBER, ERVIN
PRESTON, ONT.
 Interviewed on 11, 14 Nov. 1977; 3
hrs.; 3 tapes; English; by J. Nyce.
Memories of his early childhood
years, and commentary on Christian-
ity, and morality with reference to the
Mennonite Church.

WEBER, HOWARD
KITCHENER, ONT.
 Interviewed on 10 Aug. 1979; .75
hr.; 1 tape; English; by R. Neff.
Discussion on his Mennonite faith,
and the diminishing central role of the
church in Mennonite community of
Kitchener.

WEBER, JOHN
PETERSBURG, ONT.
 Interviewed on 20 July 1981; .5 hr.;
1 tape; English; by L. Friesen. Of
Swiss-German background, member
of the Ontario Mennonite Conference,
discusses the prospect of amalgamation of the several Ont. Mennonite
conferences.

WEBER, JOSEPH
WATERLOO, ONT.
 Interviewed on 14 Aug. 1979; 1 hr.;
1 tape; English; by R. Neff. Discussion on the "new charismatic
movement," and growth of the
Mennonite community of Waterloo.

WEBER, MR. AND MRS. ORPHAN
PRESTON, ONT.
 Interviewed on 17, 18, 21 Nov.
1977; 3 hrs.; 3 tapes; English; by J.
Nyce. They describe their childhood
at the turn of the century, life within
their Mennonite community, and folk
medicine.

WIEB, AARON
EDEN, ONT.
Wieb family register, n.d. 1 cm.
Taped interview.
Interviewed on 28 May 1979; 1.5
hrs.; 2 tapes; German; by R.
Sawatsky. Memories of childhood in
Mexico, migration to Ont., involve-
ment in Old Colony church.

WIEB, REV. JACOB
AYLMER, ONT.
Interviewed on 18 June 1979; 2.75
hrs.; 3 tapes; German; by R.
Sawatsky. Memories of early life in
Mexico, and beginnings of the Old
Colony Church in Ont.

WIEBE, BERNHARD.
PORT BURWELL, ONT.
Interviewed on 6 June 1979; 1.5
hrs.; 2 tapes; German; R. Sawatsky.
Recollections of early life in Mexico
and Belize, moved to Ont., c. 1960s.

WIEBE, H.
ST. ANN'S, ONT.
Interviewed on 21 Jan. 1977; 1 hr.;
1 tape; English; by E. Baar. Member
of St. Ann's Community Church.

WIEBE, HENRY
LOWBANKS, ONT.
4 photograhs: wedding reception and
activities at Old Colony Sunday
School, 1959-62. Taped interview.
Interviewed on 26 June 1979; 1 hr.;
1 tape; English/German; by R.
Sawatsky. Discusses first contacts
with Mexican Mennonites, and the
beginnings of the Old Colony church
in Ont.

WIEBE, JACOB
LEAMINGTON, ONT.
Interviewed on 17 July 1979; .75

hr.; 1 tape; German; by R. Sawatsky.
Emigrated from Mexico, via
Manitoba in 1952; discusses the
beginnings of the Old Colony church
in Ont.

WIEBE, JACOB
TILLSONBURG, ONT.
Interviewed on 28 June 1979; 1.5
hrs.; 2 tapes; German; by R.
Sawatsky. Memories of early life in
Mexico and Manitoba; moved to Ont.
in 1955, and worked in Aylmer
tobacco factory for 15 winters.

WIEBE, RAMON
AYLMER, ONT.
Interviewed on 25 June 1979; .75
hr.; 1 tape; English; by R. Sawatsky.
Memories of early life in Mexico,
employment history, and discussion
on congregation of the Gottes
Gemeinde in Ont.

WIEB, REV. JACOB
AYLMER, ONT.
Interviewed on 18 June 1979; 2.75
hrs.; 3 tapes; German; by R.
Sawatsky. Memories of early life in
Mexico, and beginnings of the Old
Colony Church in Ont.

WIENS, ERWIN
BRESLAU, ONT.
Interviewed on 28 May 1980; 1.25
hrs.; 2 tapes; English; by Carolyn
Musselman. Comments on contentious
issues between government and Old
Order Amish and Mennonites.

WIENS, ERWIN
BRESLAU, ONT.
Interviewed on 22 July 1981; .5 hr.;
1 tape; English; by L. Friesen. Of
Russian-Mennonite background,
immigrated to Canada in 1948.

WIENS, WERNER
ST. WILLIAMS, ONT.
Interviewed on 28 June 1979; .75 hr.; 1 tape; English; by R. Sawatsky. Description of farming operation in Port Rowan area: recruitment of Mennonites from Mexico for the tomato and cucumber harvest, difficulties in procuring "stoop workers" locally, and problems of Wiens with Mexican Mennonite workers.

WILLIAMS, RUDY
ST. CATHARINES, ONT.
Interviewed on 1 March 1977; 1 hr.; 1 tape; English; by T. Funk. Member of Grace Mennonite Church.

WILLMS, DANIEL
VIRGIL, ONT.
Interviewed in April 1977; 2 hrs.; 2 tapes; English; by T. Funk. Member of Mennonite Brethren Church of Virgil.

WISMER, HENRY
CAMBRIDGE, ONT.
Interviewed on 3 Aug. 1979; 1 hr.; 1 tape; English; by R. Neff. Personal history of H. Wismer.

WITMER, LESLIE
BADEN, ONT.
Interviewed on 28 May 1980; 1.75 hrs.; 2 tapes; English; by R. Neff. Personal history of L. Witmer.

WOELK, PETER
PORT ROWAN, ONT.
Interviewed on 31 May 1979; 2 hrs.; 2 tapes; German; by R. Sawatsky. Recollections of early life in Mennonite colonies in Mexico, immigrated to Ont. in 1974.

WOOLNER, VERNON
CAMBRIDGE, ONT.
Interviewed on 20 July 1979; .75 hr.; 1 tape; English; by R. Neff. Stories on Russian-Mennonite immigrant families.

WRAASE, LOVINA
ELMIRA, ONT.
Interviewed on 15 May 1980; .75 hr.; 1 tape; English; by R. Neff. Provides history of the Wraase and Horst families, members of the Old Order church.

ZEHR, VERNON
NEW HAMBURG, ONT.
Interviewed on 23 July 1981; .5 hr.; 1 tape; English; by L. Friesen. Of Swiss-German Amish background, member of the Western Ontario Mennonite Conference.

ZIEGLER, MARY
FLORADALE, ONT.
Interviewed on 8 May 1980; .75 hr.; 1 tape; English; by R. Neff. Provides history of the Ziegler and Shoemaker families.

ZIEGLER, PHYANNA
ELMIRA, ONT.
Interviewed on 8 May 1980; 1 hr.; 1 tape; English; by R. Neff. Provides history of the Ziegler, Bauman, and Bearinger families.

———————————————

CONFERENCE OF MENNONITES IN CANADA
WINNIPEG, MANITOBA
Flyers and brochures from conference, 1979-80. .5 cm.

CONRAD GREBEL PROJECT
WATERLOO, ONT.
 Papers from various churches in the
Kitchener-Waterloo area, dating from
the mid-19th century to the present.
29 reels of microfilm. Finding aid
available.

HAGEY-PRESTON MENNONITE
CHURCH
CAMBRIDGE, ONT.
 Brochures, 1967. 1 cm.

MULTICULTURAL HISTORY SOCIETY
OF ONTARIO
TORONTO, ONT.
 Fretz, J. Winfield. *The Mennonites
in Ontario*. Waterloo, Ont.:
Mennonite Historical Society of
Ontario, 1967. 43 pp.
 Mennonite Historian. Vol. 1, no. 1,
Sept. 1975 - vol. 15, no. 4, Dec.
1989. 8 cm.
 Mennonite Life. March 1986 - Dec.
1989. Incomplete. 6 cm.

NIAGARA UNITED MENNONITE
CHURCH
VIRGIL, ONT.
 *50th Anniversary of Niagara United
Mennonite Church, 1938-1963*. 1 cm.

BLACK, MARIE A.
SUDBURY, ONT.
 30 photographs: buildings, parades,
groups of people, soldiers, and logging industry in Sudbury, c. 1900-20.

FLIS, JESSE
TORONTO, ONT.
 Board of Education reports on heritage languages for the City of
Toronto, and the Ministry of Education; and information for school
principals, policy and procedures,
1977-78. 1 cm. See Jesse Flis, Polish
Collection. **RESTRICTED**

HARTMAN, JOE
TORONTO, ONT.
 49 photographs: activities of the
Workers Sport Association in
Toronto, Timmins, and Palermo,
1930s.

KAZOR, FRED
TORONTO, ONT.
 17 photographs: activities (mainly
gymnastics) of the Workers Sports
Association in Toronto, and
Winnipeg, 1935-40.

LEVINE, DAVID
TORONTO, ONT.
 15 photographs: ethnic groups on the
street, and in a billiard hall in
Toronto, 1978-79.

MAGNUSON, BRUCE
TORONTO, ONT.
 Scrapbooks, 1935-58, containing
documents, leaflets, and clippings
related to the lumber, sawmill, and
bushworkers' unions, labour
struggles, and working conditions in
northern Ont., and the Communist
Party of Canada. 3 reels of microfilm. Photographs.
 181 photographs: employment in the
logging industry, labour unions,
strikes, and forest fires in northern
Ont., Alberta, and British Columbia,
1912-53.
 Ontario Timber Worker. Sudbury, 4
July 1947 - May 1951. 1 reel of
microfilm.

McLAREN, DUNCAN
TORONTO, ONT.
 1 immigrant newsletter written on
board the *U.S.A.T. General M.B.
Stewart*, 1-14 Nov. 1947. 16 pp., in
Ukrainian, Polish, Lithuanian, Yugoslavian, Estonian, Latvian, and English. Photographs.
 20 photographs: ethnic storefronts in
Hamilton, 1972-78.

RINELLA, JOSEPH
TORONTO, ONT.
 2 photographs: St. Lawrence Market
in Toronto, c. 1900, 1950.

BAPTIST WOMEN'S MISSIONARY
SOCIETY OF ONTARIO AND QUEBEC
HAMILTON, ONT.
 Canadian Christian Fellowship:
material used in teaching English to
immigrants, n.d. 1 reel of microfilm.

CANADIAN ETHNIC JOURNALISTS'
CLUB
TORONTO, ONT.
 Statute, 1977, a press release, and
menu from the Ethnic Journalists'
Award Dinner, 1980. .5 cm.

COUNCIL OF ETHNOCULTURAL
ORGANIZATIONS OF CANADA
VANCOUVER, BRITISH COLUMBIA
 Vokser Sammen. 1981. .5 cm., in
Danish.

ETHNIC PRESS ASSOCIATION OF
ONTARIO
TORONTO, ONT.
 Records, including by-laws, minutes,
and correspondence of the Ethnic
Press Association and the Ontario
Inter-Group Committee on Aging
which was a centennial project of the
Ethnic Press Association, 1965-78. 3
meters. Photographs.
 11 photographs: party held in honour
of Allan Grossman by the Ethnic
Press Association in Toronto 1961;
and a Karsh portrait of Arthur
Maloney, n.d.

KITCHENER-WATERLOO REGIONAL
FOLK ARTS COUNCIL
KITCHENER, ONT.
 List of members and directors,
annual report, and pamphlets, 1976-77.

Newsletter. Multicultural Centre,
Nos. 1-36, April 1974 - March 1980.
2 cm.

LABOUR PROGRESSIVE PARTY
TORONTO, ONT.
 Recorded in 1954; 1 hr.; 1 tape;
English. Speech delivered at an inner
party meeting by Paul Phillips, Secretary of L.P.P. in charge of national
groups in Toronto, c. 1954. Speech at
same meeting by Tim Buck, General
Secretary of L.P.P.

MULTICULTURAL COUNCIL OF
WINDSOR AND ESSEX COUNTY
WINDSOR, ONT.
 Multicultural publications, ethnic
pavilions represented at the Carousel
of Nations in Windsor, Ont., 1980,
1981, includes brochures, leaflets,
and news releases issued by the
Multicultural Council of Windsor and
Essex County, 1976-1980. 5.5 cm.
 Carousel of the Nations '80. 1980.
5th anniversary programme. 32 pp.
 Monthly News. Sept.-Dec. 1980, Jan.
1981. .5 cm.

ONTARIO ETHNIC NEWSPAPER
MICROFILM PROJECT
TORONTO, ONT.
 The Citizen's News. Sept. 1961 -
Jan. 1962. 1 reel of microfilm.
 The New Canadians. 2 Dec. 1937 -
Dec. 1939. 1 reel of microfilm.

ST. LAWRENCE PARKS COMMISSION
OLD FORT HENRY
KINGSTON, ONT.
 Over 100 photographs: internment of
enemy aliens at Fort Henry during
WWI.

WOMEN'S BAPTIST HOME MISSION-
ARY SOCIETY OF ONTARIO WEST
HAMILTON, ONT.
 Teaching aids, n.d. 1 reel of micro-
film.

WOMEN'S BAPTIST HOME MISSION-
ARY SOCIETY OF ONTARIO WEST
HAMILTON, ONT.
 Minute books of New Canadian
Committee, 1934-55. 1 reel of micro-
film.

WOMEN'S BAPTIST HOME MISSION-
ARY SOCIETY OF ONTARIO WEST
HAMILTON, ONT.
 Minute books of Slavic Committee,
1916-39. 2 reels of microfilm.

NATIVE PEOPLES COLLECTION

ACKABEE, LEO
EAGLE RIVER, ONT.
 Interviewed on 18 Jan. 1978; .75
hr.; 1 tape; English; by Adeline
Shaw. A re-telling of various experi-
ences in his life.

ANDERSON, WILLIAM
WALPOLE ISLAND, ONT.
 Interviewed on 31 Jan. 1979; .75
hr.; 1 tape; English; by Gladys
Tooshkenig and Burton Jacobs. A
customs officer on Walpole Island.

BLACKBIRD, JENNIE
WALPOLE ISLAND, ONT.
 Interviewed on 9 Nov. 1978; .5 hr.;
1 tape; English; by Gladys
Tooshkenig and Burton Jacobs. Dis-
cusses her 4-year attendance at
Mohawk Institute in Brantford, Ont.

BLACKBIRD, SIMON
WALPOLE ISLAND, ONT.
 Interviewed on 27 Feb. 1978; 2 hrs.;
2 tapes; English/Indian; by Patricia
Soney and Burton Jacobs. Discusses
his life history, and Indian farming
practices.

BROWN, BUSTER
BURLEIGH FALLS, ONT.
 Interviewed on 28 Nov, 4 Dec.
1977; 1.75 hrs.; 2 tapes; English; by
Fay Tilden. Discusses personal history, work in guiding and trapping,
and court cases for hunting and land
rights.

CHRISTENSEN, MARGARET
WALPOLE ISLAND, ONT.
 Interviewed on 11 Jan. 1979; .5 hr.;
1 tape; English; by Gladys
Tooshkenig and Burton Jacobs. Dis-
cusses her work as a Public Health
Nurse on Walpole Island.

COLWELL, WILLIAM
WALPOLE ISLAND, ONT.
 Interviewed on 30 Nov. 1978; .5
hr.; 1 tape; English; by Gladys
Tooshkenig and Burton Jacobs. Discusses his work as a police constable
on the Walpole Island reserve.

COOK, PAUL
WALPOLE ISLAND, ONT.
 Interviewed on 29 Nov. 1978; .75
hr.; 1 tape; English; by Gladys
Tooshkenig and Burton Jacobs. Discusses the history, and functions of
the Walpole Island Alternate Education Programme.

DAY, WILLIAM
WALPOLE ISLAND, ONT.
 Interviewed on 20 March 1978; 1
hr.; 1 tape; English; by Patricia
Soney and Burton Jacobs. Discusses
business and professional activities on
Walpole Island, including a saw mill
operation.

DEAN, GRANT
WALPOLE ISLAND, ONT.
 Interviewed on 11 Jan. 1979; .5 hr.;
1 tape; English; by Gladys
Tooshkenig and Burton Jacobs. Dis-
cusses his ferry service business,

which runs between Walpole Island and Algonac, Michigan.

DODGE SR., ELDRON
WALLACEBURG, ONT.
 Interviewed on 10 Jan. 1979; .5 hr.; 1 tape; English; by Gladys Tooshkenig and Burton Jacobs. Discusses the history of Walpole Island Evangelistic Centre where he was pastor for 7 years.

FISHER, ARTHUR
WALPOLE ISLAND, ONT.
 Interviewed on 23 March 1978; .75 hr.; 1 tape; English; by Burton Jacobs. Discusses his work aboard boats and tugs.

FORBES, DOUGLAS
WALPOLE ISLAND, ONT.
 Interviewed on 7 Dec. 1978; 1 hr.; 1 tape; English; by Gladys Tooshkening and Burton Jacobs. Discusses his work as principal of the Walpole Island Day School.

HASKINS, GAY (INDIAN COMMUNITY SECRETARIAT)
TORONTO, ONT.
 Dimensions. Vol. 5, nos. 3, 4, (April, May/June 1977). Newsletter of OMNSIA. .5 cm.

HILL, DAN
TORONTO, ONT.
 Ontario Native Experience. Sept. 1974, Feb. 1975, March 1975. 1 cm.
 Toronto Native Time. Sept. 1973, Dec. 1974, Feb. 1975, March 1976, May 1976, Feb. 1977. 6 cm.

IRONS, ROSE
BURLEIGH FALLS, ONT.
 Interviewed on 18 Nov. 1977; .5 hr.; 1 tape; English; by Fay Tilden.

Describes settlement at Burleigh Falls, and her work history.

ISAAC, ELIZABETH M.
WALPOLE ISLAND, ONT.
 Interviewed on 24 Jan. 1978; .5 hr.; 1 tape; English; by Patricia Soney. Recollections of her early life on the Island.

JACOBS, BURTON
WALLACEBURG, ONT.
 10 photographs: ferries, basketmakers, and officials opening Tecumseh Road on Walpole Island, 1920-78.

JACOBS, DEAN M.
WALLACEBURG, ONT.
 9 photographs: community members, a ferry, and a storefront on Walpole Island, 1937-49.
 Jacobs, Dean M., comp. *Land Claims Research Paper: Walpole Island Indian Reserve.* Association of Iroquois and Allied Indians, 1973. 182 pp.

JACOBS, HARRIET
WALLACEBURG, ONT.
 3 photographs: children at a nursery school; and Girl Guides on Walpole Island, 1952. Taped interview.
 Interviewed on 29 Nov. 1978; .5 hr.; 1 tape; English; by Gladys Tooshkenig. Provides history and functions of the Day Nursery on the Walpole Island Reserve.

JACOBS, ISABEL
BURLEIGH FALLS, ONT.
 17 photograhs: campgrounds, dwellings, and guiding parties during fishing expeditions in Burleigh Falls, 1940-60.

JACOBS, JOHN
BURLEIGH FALLS, ONT.
 15 photographs: guiding parties during fishing expeditions in Burleigh Falls, 1920-60.

JACOBS, REV. LAVERNE
WALPOLE ISLAND, ONT.
 Interviewed on 10 Jan. 1978; .5 hr.; 1 tape; English; by Gladys Tooshkenig. Discusses the history and activities of St. John's Anglican Church on Walpole Island.

JACOBS, RUFUS
WALPOLE ISLAND, ONT.
 Interviewed on 17 Jan. 1979; .5 hr.; 1 tape; English; by Gladys Tooshkenig and Burton Jacobs. Discusses the history of the Walpole Island Fire Department, where he worked as Fire Chief.

JACOBS, SANDY
BURLEIGH FALLS, ONT.
 Interviewed on 10 Jan. 1978; 1 hr.; 1 tape; English; by Fay Tilden. Discusses the socio-economic disadvantages of "non-status" Indians.

JAMES, NELSON
WALPOLE ISLAND, ONT.
 Interviewed on 8 March 1978; 1 hr.; 1 tape; Indian; by Patricia Soney and Burton Jacobs. Memories of early life on the Island.

JOHNSON, DALLAS
BURLEIGH FALLS, ONT.
 7 photographs: the Johnson family; donor in WWII military uniform; and a guiding party for a fishing expedition in Burleigh Falls, c. 1940-50.

JOHNSON, GERALD
BURLEIGH FALLS, ONT.
 Interviewed on 24 Nov. 1977; 1 hr.; 1 tape; English; by Fay Tilden. Discusses history of settlement at Burleigh Falls.

KELLY, JANE AND J. MEAWASIGE
EAGLE RIVER, ONT.
 1 photograph: donor at Eagle River, c. 1978. Taped interview.
 Interviewed on 9 Jan. 1978; 1 hr.; 1 tape; Ojibway; by Adeline Shaw. Discusses local Indian customs, religion, and medicine.

KEWAYOSH, ROSIE E.
WALPOLE ISLAND, ONT.
 Interviewed on 24 Jan. 1978; .5 hr.; 1 tape; English/Ojibway; by Patricia Soney. Discusses personal history.

KEWAYOSH, ROSIE
WALLACEBURG, ONT.
 1 photograph: *Tashmoo* boat that landed on Walpole Island, 1930-40.

KIYOSHK, ROBERT
WALPOLE ISLAND, ONT.
 Interviewed on 4 Jan. 1979; .75 hr.; 1 tape; English; by Gladys Tooshkenig and Burton Jacobs. Description of the Walpole Island Fair.

KORZINSKI, JAKE
EAGLE RIVER, ONT.
 23 photographs: people, dwellings, and storefronts at Eagle River, 1920-60. Taped interview.
 Interviewed on 8 Dec. 1977; 1 hr.; 1 tape; English; by Adeline Shaw. Recollections of the difficult years during his childhood, and an outline of the many jobs held as an adult.

LACOSSE, ROSE
EAGLE RIVER, ONT.
 Interviewed on 30 Nov. 1977; .5
hr.; 1 tape; English/Ojibway; by
Adeline Shaw.

LUDWIG, GLEN
WALPOLE ISLAND, ONT.
 Interviewed on 14 Dec. 1978; .75
hr.; 1 tape; English; by Gladys
Tooshkenig and Burton Jacobs.
 Discussion on farming enterprises on
the Island.

MCIVOR, ROSE
EAGLE RIVER, ONT.
 Interviewed on 25 Nov. 1977; .5
hr.; 1 tape; English; by Adeline
Shaw. Discusses personal history,
including many years of privation and
poverty.

MCRAE, VIOLET
SOMBRA, ONT.
 11 photographs: activities on
Walpole Island, 1952-61, including a
parade. Taped interview.
 Interviewed on 16 Nov. 1978; .25
hr.; 1 tape; English; by Gladys
Tooshkenig and Burton Jacobs.
Speaks of the years she spent as a
Public Health Nurse on Walpole
Island.

MEAWASIGE, CATHERINE
EAGLE RIVER, ONT.
 1 photograph: the family at Eagle
River, 1970. Taped interview.
 Interviewed on 10 Jan. 1978; .5 hr.;
1 tape; Indian; by Adeline Shaw. Discusses personal history.

MISKOKOMON, FRANCES
WALPOLE ISLAND, ONT.
 9 photographs: the Miskokomon
family on Walpole Island, c. 1900-40.

Taped interview.
 Interviewed on 7 Dec. 1978; .75 hr.;
1 tape; English; by Gladys
Tooshkenig and Burton Jacobs. An
account of school years in the late
1920s.

NAHDEE, LILLIAN
WALPOLE ISLAND, ONT.
 Interviewed on 23 March 1978; 1
hr.; 1 tape; English; by Patricia
Soney and Burton Jacobs. She ran a
store on the Island, reminisces about
social events on the Island.

NEWBERRY, EDWARD
SUDBURY, ONT.
 1 photograph: the first student at the
Native Studies Programme at the University of Sudbury, c. 1969. Taped
interview.
 Interviewed on 14 June 1982; .5 hr.;
1 tape; English; by Barbara Cooke.
Discusses the founding of an Amerindian Studies Programme at Laurentian
University.

NOBLE, KEN
SUDBURY, ONT.
 Interviewed on 11 Aug. 1982; .5 hr.;
1 tape; English; by Barbara Cooke.
An account of the life of the Burwash
Native Peoples Project.

OLIVER, CLARENCE
WALPOLE ISLAND, ONT.
 Interviewed on 9 March 1978; 1.5
hr.; 2 tapes; English; by Patricia
Soney and Burton Jacobs. Discussion
on the ferry service, and Henry
Ford's plans for the Island.

PINNANCE, MITCHELL
WALLACEBURG, ONT.
 Interviewed on 9 March 1978; .5
hr.; 1 tape; English; by Patricia

Soney and Burton Jacobs. Discusses farming operations on Walpole Island.

RECOLLET, BOB
SUDBURY, ONT.
Interviewed on 12 July 1982; .75 hr.; 1 tape; English; by Barbara Cooke. Discusses the history of the Nickel Belt Indian Club.
Challenge Cup 1982. 1983. The Nickel Belt Indian Club souvenir booklet.

RILEY, HENRY
WALPOLE ISLAND, ONT.
Interviewed on 20 March 1978; 1 hr.; 1 tape; English; by Patricia Soney and Burton Jacobs. Describes the tourism industry on the Island.

SAMPSON, CHARLES
WALLACEBURG, ONT.
4 photographs: two women dancing; a man in a rowboat; cowboys, and the Anglican Church, Walpole Island, c. 1900-40.

SAMPSON, IDA
WALLACEBURG, ONT.
Interviewed on 21 Dec. 1978; .5 hr.; 1 tape; English; by Gladys Tooshkenig and Burton Jacobs. Her memories of the Walpole Island Fair.

SANDS, CLAYTON
WALPOLE ISLAND, ONT.
Interviewed on 25 Jan. 1979; .5 hr.; 1 tape; English; by Gladys Tooshkenig and Burton Jacobs. Discusses the hunting and fishing industry on the Island.

SANDS, PRISCELLA
WALPOLE ISLAND, ONT.
Interviewed on 16 Nov. 1978; .5 hr.; 1 tape; English; by Gladys

Tooshkenig and Burton Jacobs. Commentary on the Walpole Island Health Centre.

SANDS, RITA
WALLACEBURG, ONT.
Interviewed on 18 Jan. 1979; .75 hr.; 1 tape; English; by Gladys Tooshkenig and Burton Jacobs. A discussion on hockey tournaments.

SANDS, TERRY E.
WALLACEBURG, ONT.
4 photographs: fairs and a school on Walpole Island, Ont., c. 1900-10.

SHIPMAN, EVA
WALPOLE ISLAND, ONT.
1 photograph: horse racing on Walpole Island, 1931. Taped interview.
Interviewed on 30 Nov. 1978; .5 hr.; 1 tape; English; by Gladys Tooshkenig and Burton Jacobs. Memories of Walpole Island Fair, and fairs of nearby centres.

SHOGNOSH, DANIEL
WALPOLE ISLAND, ONT.
Interviewed on 13 April 1978; 1 hr.; 1 tape; Ojibway; by Patricia Soney and Burton Jacobs. Discusses farming with oxen.

SKYE, ALBERT
EAGLE RIVER, ONT.
Interviewed on 13 March 1978; 1 hr.; 1 tape; English; by Adeline Shaw. Discusses his early life, and his belief in Indian religion and medicine.

SNAKE, SANDRA
WALPOLE ISLAND, ONT.
Interviewed on 15 Nov. 1978; .5 hr.; 1 tape; English; Gladys

Tooshkenig and J. Burton. Discusses the history of the Walpole Island Day Nursery.

SONEY, AARON
WALPOLE ISLAND, ONT.
 Interviewed on 24 Jan. 1979; .5 hr.; 1 tape; English; by Gladys Tooshkenig and Burton Jacobs. Discusses the history and functions of the Walpole Island Band Office.

SONEY, ALFRED
WALPOLE ISLAND, ONT.
 Interviewed on 12 April 1978; 1 hr.; 1 tape; English; by Patricia Soney and Burton Jacobs. Discusses the tourist invasion of the Island.

SONEY, AMYLINE
WALPOLE ISLAND, ONT.
 Interviewed on 6 Dec. 1978; .75 hr.; 1 tape; English; by Gladys Tooshkenig and Burton Jacobs. Discusses early school years in the 1920s and 1930s.

SONEY, PRISCILLA
WALPOLE ISLAND, ONT.
 Interviewed on 30 Jan. 1978; 1 hr.; 1 tape; English; by Patricia Soney. Memories of life on the Island.

SONEY, RANDY
WALLACEBURG, ONT.
 Interviewed on 21 Dec. 1978; .5 hr.; 1 tape; English; by Gladys Tooshkenig and Burton Jacobs. Discusses the history of the Walpole Island Police Department.

TAYLOR, HORACE
BURLEIGH FALLS, ONT.
 Interviewed on 28 Nov. 1977; 1 hr.; 1 tape; English; by Fay Tilden. Discusses work as a guide, and details the hunting and fishing industry.

TAYLOR, RUSSELL
BURLEIGH FALLS, ONT.
 Interviewed on 11, 15 Nov., 16 Dec. 1977; 2.5 hrs.; 3 tapes; English; by Fay Tilden. Detailed description of donor's enlistment in the Canadian army, his injuries, and his work in lumber camps and guiding at Burleigh Falls.

TOOSHKENIG, MYRTLE
WALPOLE ISLAND, ONT.
 2 photographs: children at the Day School on Walpole Island, 1930; and Girl Guides at a residential school in Brantford, Ont., 1943.

TOOSHKENIG, WILLIAM
WALLACEBURG, ONT.
 Interviewed on 30 Dec. 1978; 1 hr.; 1 tape; English; by Gladys Tooshkenig and Burton Jacobs. Band Councillor and Economic Development Officer of Walpole Island.

WILLES, J.
LAKEFIELD, ONT.
 7 photographs: local Indians canoeing, and cutting ice blocks in Lakefield, Ont., 1940-60.

WILLIAMS, HARRY
WALPOLE ISLAND, ONT.
 Interviewed on 28 Jan. 1978; .5 hr.; 1 tape; English; by Patricia Soney. Discussion focusses on his experiences during WWII.

WILLIAMS, HARRY
WALPOLE ISLAND, ONT.
 Interviewed on 20 Dec. 1978; .5 hr.; 1 tape; English; by Gladys

Tooshkenig and Burton Jacobs. Outlines history of the Brass Band of
Walpole Island.

WILLIAMS, ROBERT
WALPOLE ISLAND, ONT.
 Interviewed on 24 Jan. 1979; .5 hr.;
1 tape; English; by Gladys
Tooshkenig and Burton Jacobs. Dis-
cusses his work with the Public
Works Department on the Island.

===============

BURWASH NATIVE PEOPLE'S PROJECT
SUDBURY, ONT.
 Bylaws of Project Committee, n.d.,
and development and budget reports,
1979. 1.5 cm. Photograph. Taped
interview with Ken Noble.
 1 photograph: the Project's Board of
Directors in Sudbury, 1980.

NORWEGIAN COLLECTION

HOGSTAD, HAROLD
THUNDER BAY, ONT.
Recorded on 4 March 1978; .25 hr.;
1 tape; English; by Harold Hogstad.
An historical sketch of the Norwegian
Lodge "Nordstjernen" (North Star).

KAYS, LUCILE
THUNDER BAY, ONT.
1 resumé from donor, 1938. .25 cm.
Photographs. Taped interview.
7 photographs: the Antonisen family
in Norway and Germany, 1860-1935.
Interviewed on 4 Oct. 1978; .5 hr.;
1 tape; English; by Harold Hogstad.
Family immigrated to Canada in
1905.

NESS, OLAF
THUNDER BAY, ONT.
Interviewed on 31 Jan. 1978; .5 hr.;
1 tape; English; by Harold Hogstad.
A summary of the donor's life in
Norway, his immigration to Canada,
and his work experiences.

STYFFE, JOHN R.
THUNDER BAY, ONT.
9 photographs: lumbercamp and
pulpwood mill in Thunder Bay,
1935-55. Taped interview.
Interviewed in 1978; .5 hr.; 1 tape;
English; by Harold Hogstad. Interview is about the donor's father,
Oscar Styffe.

OUR SAVIOUR'S LUTHERAN CHURCH
THUNDER BAY, ONT.
Souvenir booklets, and church bro-
chures, 1969-77. 2 cm. Photograph.
Taped interview.
1 photograph: a male choir at
Saviour's Lutheran Church in Port
Arthur, 1914.
Recorded on 4 March 1978; .5 hr.; 1
tape; English; by Harold Hogstad. A
summary of the history of the first
Norwegian Church of Port Arthur.

MULTICULTURAL HISTORY SOCIETY
OF ONTARIO
TORONTO, ONT.
Lille Norge Avisen. April 1944 -
Feb. 1945. 1 reel of microfilm.

POLISH COLLECTION

ADACH, EDWARD AND CZESŁAWA
TORONTO, ONT.
 Interviewed on 4 July 1980; 1 hr.; 1
tape; Polish; by Roman Bielski. They
arrived in Canada in 1964.

ADUCKIEWICZ, MARIAN
HAMILTON, ONT.
 Newspaper article about donor's
wartime activities, in *Hamilton Spectator*. 5 Nov. 1976. .25 cm. Taped
interview.
 Interviewed on 23 Nov. 1978; 1 hr.;
1 tape; Polish; by Roman Bielski.
Immediate post-WWII immigrant.

ANDRES, JOZEF AND ANNA
TORONTO, ONT.
 Interviewed on 13 Oct. 1979; 1.5
hrs; 2 tapes; Polish/English; by
Roman Bielski. Immigrated to Canada
in 1947.

ANDRUSZKIEWICZ, ZYGMUNT
BRANTFORD, ONT.
 Interviewed on 28 June 1981; 2 hrs.;
2 tapes; Polish; by Josef Sieramski.
Immediate post-WWII immigrant.

ANTONOWICZ, HENRYK
SUDBURY, ONT.
 Interviewed on 4 Dec. 1977, 9
March 1978; 1.5 hrs.; 2 tapes; Polish; by Roman Bielski. Immediate
post-WWII immigrant.

ASCIUKIEWICZ, BOLESŁAW
TORONTO, ONT.
 Interviewed on 15 May 1981;

1.5 hrs.; 2 tapes; Polish; by Roman
Bielski. Arrived in Canada in 1971.

BABICZ, INRENA
TORONTO, ONT.
 Interviewed on 16 Aug. 1982; .5 hr.;
1 tape; Polish; by Roman Bielski.
Arrived in Canada in 1962.

BACH, FELICJAN
TORONTO, ONT.
 Interviewed on 14 Jan. 1978; 1 hr.;
1 tape; English; by Roman Bielski.

BACH, FELIX
TORONTO, ONT.
 Interviewed on 10 Jan. 1978; 1 hr.;
1 tape; Polish; by Roman Bielski.

BAJACZYK, ANTONINA
TORONTO, ONT.
 Interviewed on 12 Nov. 1981; 2
hrs.; 2 tapes; Polish; by A. Pietrus.
Arrived in Canada in 1971.

BAKA, VICTORIA
TORONTO, ONT.
 Interviewed on 2 June 1982; .5 hr.;
1 tape; Polish; by Roman Bielski.
Immigrated to Canada in 1930.

BALCERZAK, LUCJAN AND HALINA
TORONTO, ONT.
 Interviewed on 2 July 1981; 1.5 hrs;
2 tapes; Polish; by Roman Bielski.
Post-WWII immigrants.

BALEWICZ, STEFAN
TORONTO, ONT.
Interviewed on 18 Dec. 1977; 3 hrs.;
3 tapes; Polish; by Roman Bielski.

BANDROWSKI, STEFAN
OTTAWA, ONT.
Papers on the forestry industry, c.
1970s. .5 cm. Taped interview.
Interviewed on 27 Dec. 1979; 1.5
hrs.; 2 tapes; Polish; by Roman
Bielski. Arrived in 1953.

BARABASZ, JAN AND HELENA
TORONTO, ONT.
Interviewed on 31 Aug. 1981; .75
hr.; 1 tape; Polish; by Roman Bielski.
Arrived in Canada in 1949.

BARAN, JOSEF
OSHAWA, ONT.
Interviewed on 20 June 1981; .75
hr.; 1 tape; Polish; by Roman Bielski.
Immigrated to Canada in 1926.

BARANKIEWICZ, TEODOR
TORONTO, ONT.
Interviewed on 20 Dec. 1978; 1 hr.;
1 tape; Polish; by Roman Bielski.

BARANOWSKI, JÓZEF
SUDBURY, ONT.
Personal papers, including morality
certificate and immigration card,
1926. .25 cm (8 items). Taped interview.
Interviewed on 8 Feb. 1980; 2 hrs.;
2 tapes; Polish; by I. Dembek.

BARANOWSKI, STANISŁAW
TORONTO, ONT.
Interviewed on 24 March 1981; 2
hrs.; 2 tapes; Polish; by Josef
Sieramski.

BARLOG, JAN
TORONTO, ONT.
Interviewed on 5 July 1982; 1 hr.; 1
tape; Polish; by Roman Bielski.
Arrived in Canada in 1926.

BARSZCZEWSKI, MARY
SUDBURY, ONT.
Polish passport, birth certificate, and
army book, n.d. .5 cm. Photographs.
Taped interview.
7 family photographs:, 1906-55.
Interviewed on 10 Sept. 1980; 1.75
hrs.; 2 tapes; Polish/English; by I.
Dembek.

BARTEL, JACEK AND HANNA
TORONTO, ONT.
Interviewed on 10 May 1979; 1.5
hrs.; 2 tapes; Polish; by Roman
Bielski.

BARTOSZ, WALTER
TORONTO, ONT.
Interviewed on 5 April 1981; 2 hrs.;
2 tapes; Polish; by Josef Sieramski.
Arrived in Canada in 1927.

BARYLUK, MARIAN
THUNDER BAY, ONT.
2 photographs: the Baryluk family in
Thunder Bay, 1949-74. Taped interview.
Interviewed on 2 Aug. 1978; 1 hr.; 1
tape; Polish; by G. Kokocinski. The
son of a Polish immigrant who came
to Canada in 1902.

BAS, WIKTOV
WINDSOR, ONT.
Interviewed on 19 June 1987; 1 hr.;
1 tape; Polish; by Roman Bielski.

BECK, JÓZEF
TORONTO, ONT.
Interviewed on 6 Dec. 1978; 1 hr.; 1 tape; Polish; by Roman Bielski.

BEDNARCZYK, TADEUSZ
BRANTFORD, ONT.
Interviewed on 27 June 1981; 2 hrs.; 2 tapes; Polish; by Josef Sieramski. Immigrated to Canada in 1952.

BEJGER, MARIAN
TORONTO, ONT.
Interviewed on 12 March 1981; .75 hr.; 1 tape; Polish; by Roman Bielski. Arrived in Canada in 1967.

BELINA-BRZOZOWSKI, ADAM
RANDON, QUEBEC
Interviewed on 9 Aug. 1978; 1 hr.; 1 tape; Polish; by Roman Bielski.

BELINA-BRZOZOWSKI, ADAM AND MARIA
RANDON, QUEBEC
Interviewed on 5 Aug. 1979; 1.5 hrs.; 2 tapes; Polish; by Roman Bielski.

BELINA-PRAŻMOWSKI, LECH
OSHAWA, ONT.
Interviewed on 21 Nov. 1981; .5 hr.; 1 tape; Polish; by Roman Bielski. Arrived in Canada in 1947.

BENEDA, WŁADYSŁAW
TORONTO, ONT.
Interviewed on 20 Dec. 1977; 1 hr.; 1 tape; Polish; by Roman Bielski.

BETOWSKI, LEON
TORONTO, ONT.
Interviewed on 25 March 1981; 2 hrs.; 2 tapes; Polish; by Josef Sieramski.

BIALEK, PAWEL
OSHAWA, ONT.
Interviewed on 21 Nov. 1981; .75 hr.; 1 tape; Polish; by Roman Bielski. Immigrated to Canada in 1926.

BIALY, WLADYSLAW
TORONTO, ONT.
5 photographs: military service in England, and France, 1940; and newly arrived Polish immigrants in Toronto, 1949. Taped interview. Interviewed on 20 March 1981; 2 hrs.; 2 tapes; Polish; by Josef Sieramski. Moved to Canada in 1949.

BIDAS, JAN
TORONTO, ONT.
Interviewed on 21 April 1981; 2 hrs.; 2 tapes; Polish; by Josef Sieramski. Immigrated to Canada in 1949.

BIELECKA, LOTTA
TORONTO, ONT.
Interviewed on 4 July 1978; 2 hrs.; 2 tapes; English; by Roman Bielski. Immediate post-WWII immigrant.

BIELSKA-GEBETHNER-GIEDROYC, JANINA
MONTREAL, QUEBEC
Interviewed on 12 Aug. 1978; 1 hr.; 1 tape; Polish; by Roman Bielski. Immediate post-WWII immigrant.

BIELSKI, CASIMIR
TORONTO, ONT.
Interviewed on 11 Sept. 1980; 1.5 hrs.; 2 tapes; Polish/English; by Roman Bielski. Former president of the Canadian Polish Congress.

BIELSKI, ROBERT
TORONTO, ONT.
Interviewed on 9 July 1978; 1.5 hrs.;

1 tape; English; by Roman Bielski. Immediate post-WWII immigrant.

BIELSKI, ROMAN
TORONTO, ONT.
Interviewed on 31 Jan. 1980, 18 Feb. 1980; 15 hrs.; 13 tapes; English/Polish; by K. Gebhard.

BIELSKI, ROMAN
TORONTO, ONT.
Interviewed on 9 Jan. 1977; 2 hrs.; 2 tapes; English; by P. Colagiovanni and R. F. Harney.

BIELSKI, ROMAN
TORONTO, ONT.
Personal papers, including poems and genealogy of Bielski line, 1929-60. .5 cm. Photographs. Taped interview.
14 photographs: family and friends of Roman Bielski, 1928-60.
Self-interview of 1 July 1978; 1 hr.; 1 tape; English.
30th Anniversary of the First and Second Polish Armoured Regiment Association. 1978. 38 pp., in Polish.
Notrum Polishonii w Oshawie, 1953-61. St. Hedwig's Church and Parish. 74 pp., in Polish/English.
Silver Jubilee Parish of St. Hedwig, 1952-77. Oshawa, 1977. Booklet. 41 pp., in Polish.

BIENIASZ, JÓZEF AND ALFREDA
TORONTO, ONT.
Interviewed on 11 Nov. 1979; 1.25 hrs.; 2 tapes; Polish; by Roman Bielski. Post-WWII immigrant.

BIEKO, JAN
TORONTO, ONT.
Interviewed on 12 March 1979; .75 hr.; 1 tape; English; by Roman Bielski.

BIEŃKOWSKI, MIROSŁAW
TORONTO, ONT.
Interviewed on 22 Oct. 1981; 2 hrs.; 2 tapes; Polish; by A. Pietrus. Immigrated to Canada in 1951.

BIEKOWSKI, TADEUSZ
TORONTO, ONT.
Interviewed on 1 July 1978; 1 hr.; 1 tape; English; by Roman Bielski. Immediate post-WWII immigrant.

BIERNACIK, MARIAN AND SANDRA
TORONTO, ONT.
Interviewed on 6 July 1980; 1 hr.; 1 tape; English; by Roman Bielski. Arrived in Canada in 1949.

BIEROZO, VIKTOR
TORONTO, ONT.
Interviewed on 1 Oct. 1978; 1 hr.; 1 tape; Polish; by Roman Bielski.

BIEROZO, VIKTOR
TORONTO, ONT.
Interviewed on 18 Jan. 1978; 1.5 hrs.; 2 tapes; Polish/Russian; by Roman Bielski.

BILAWAJDER, JOZEF
TORONTO, ONT.
Interviewed on 23 Nov. 1977; 1 hr.; 1 tape; English; by Roman Bielski.

BIRLASKI, JÓZEF AND MARIA
TORONTO, ONT.
Interviewed on 28 Feb. 1982; 1 hr.; 1 tape; Polish; by Roman Bielski. Immigrated to Canada in 1971.

BITTNER-KRAJEWSKA, JANINA
WILLOWDALE, ONT.
Interviewed on 12 Jan. 1980; 1 hr.; 1 tape; Polish; by Roman Bielski. Arrived in Canada in 1951.

BŁACHUT, TEODOR
OTTAWA, ONT.
 Interviewed on 17 June 1980; 1 hr.;
1 tape; Polish; by Roman Bielski.

BŁASIAK, MICHAŁ
SUDBURY, ONT.
 4 photographs: picnics of the Polish
Club, and a concert at the Polish
School, Sudbury, 1935-39. Taped
interview.
 Interviewed on 4 Feb. 1980; 2.5
hrs.; 3 tapes; Polish; by I. Dembek.

BŁASZYK, CZESŁAW
TORONTO, ONT.
 Interviewed on 18 Sept. 1981; 1 hr.;
1 tape; Polish; by A. Pietrus. Immigrated to Canada in 1956.

BLOCK-BOLTEN, ISABELLA
TORONTO, ONT.
 Interviewed on 8 April 1979; 1.5
hrs.; 2 tapes; Polish; by Roman
Bielski. Immediate post-WWII immi-
grant.

BLOK-GŁÓWCZYSKA, VERONIKA
TORONTO, ONT.
 Interviewed on 4 May 1979; 1.5
hrs.; 2 tapes; Polish; by Roman
Bielski.

BLONDOWSKI, JÓZEF
HAMILTON, ONT.
 Interviewed on 29 Nov. 1978; 1 hr.;
1 tape; Polish; by Roman Bielski.

BŁOSKI, JADWIGA
TORONTO, ONT.
 Interviewed on 23 Jan. 1979; .75
hr.; 1 tape; Polish; by Roman Bielski.

BŁOSKI, MICHAŁ
TORONTO, ONT.
 Interviewed on 23 Jan. 1979;

1.5 hrs.; 2 tapes; Polish; by Roman
Bielski.

BŁOSKI, STANISŁAW AND MARY
TORONTO, ONT.
 Interviewed on 23 July 1981; .75
hr.; 1 tape; Polish; by Roman Bielski.
Immigrated to Canada in 1941.

BOBROWSKI, STANISŁAW
TORONTO, ONT.
 Information bulletin of the Polish
Government in exile, London, Eng-
land, 1979. .25 cm. Photograph.
Taped interview.
 1 photograph: S. Bobrowski,
Toronto, 1979.
 Interviewed on 31 May 1978; 3 hrs.;
3 tapes; Polish; by Roman Bielski.

BODZICZ, OLIMPIA
TORONTO, ONT.
 Interviewed on 24 Jan. 1980; 1.5
hrs.; 2 tapes; Polish; by Roman
Bielski. Immigrated to Canada in
1958.

BOHDAN, EIBICH
TORONTO, ONT.
 Interviewed on 8 Nov. 1978; 2 hrs.;
2 tapes; Polish; by Roman Bielski.

BOHDANOWICZ, ANDRZEJ AND
MARIA
TORONTO, ONT.
 Interviewed on 20 June 1979; 1.5
hrs.; 2 tapes; Polish; by Roman
Bielski.

BOHDANOWICZ, KONRAD
TORONTO, ONT.
 Interviewed on 17 July 1979; 1 hr.;
1 tape; Polish; by Roman Bielski.

BOJARCZUK, SISTER MARY ARCH-
ANGEL
TORONTO, ONT.
Interviewed on 24 July 19; 1 hr.; 1
tape; English/Polish; by J. Stanley.

BOLEK, JÓZEF AND NATALIA
TORONTO, ONT.
Interviewed on 21 Jan. 1981; .75
hr.; 1 tape; Polish; by Roman Bielski.
Arrived in Canada in 1948.

BORCZON, CZESLAW AND GENOWEFA
TORONTO, ONT.
Interviewed on 19 Jan. 1982; 1 hr.;
1 tape; Polish; by Roman Bielski. He
arrived in 1927; she arrived in 1947.

BORKOWSKI, TEODOR
TORONTO, ONT.
Bulletins of the Royal Canadian Air
Force, 430 Warsaw Wing, 1964-65;
and clippings related to St. Stanislaus
Parish Credit Union, n.d. .5 cm. (16
items). Taped interview.
Interviewed on 7 Nov. 1979; 1 hr.;
1 tape; Polish; by Roman Bielski.
Moved to Canada in 1948.

BOWERS, FRANK
COPPER CLIFF, ONT.
Interviewed on 10 Aug. 1977; .5 hr.;
1 tape; English; by Theresa
Stankiewicz.

BOWERS, PAUL
SUDBURY, ONT.
Assessment notice, 1918, 1919;
receipts, 1913, 1917; ticket, Grand
Draw, 1913; prayer, 1892; "In
Memorian," 1921-1980; baptismal
certificates, 1957; and newsclippings,
1930s-1940s. 4 cm (30 items). Photographs. Taped interview.
40 photographs: Bower family and
friends, including a wedding ceremony, Sudbury, Copper Cliff, 1910-65.
Interviewed on 12 April 1980; 1 hr.;
1 tape; English; by I. Dembek.

BOZEK, ALEKS
DELHI, ONT.
8 photographs: activities of the Polish Alliance of Canada, Branch 17,
Delhi, c. 1960-80. Taped interview.
Interviewed on 30 Sept. 1981; 1 hr.;
1 tape; Polish; by A. Pietrus. Immigrated to Canada in 1958.

BOZYK, ADAM
TORONTO, ONT.
Interviewed on 17 Feb. 1981; 1 hr.;
1 tape; Polish; by Roman Bielski.
Arrived in 1947.

BRACZKA, FRANK AND MARIA
TORONTO, ONT.
Interviewed on 13 March 1982; 1
hr.; 1 tape; Polish; by Roman Bielski.
They arrived in Canada in 1974.

BRODZKI, MARIA
TORONTO, ONT.
Interviewed on 12 Dec. 1978; 1 hr.;
1 tape; Polish; by Roman Bielski.

BRODZKI, STANISLAW
TORONTO, ONT.
Interviewed on 12 Dec. 1978; 1 hr.;
1 tape; Polish; by Roman Bielski.

BRUDNICKI, IRENA
DON MILLS, ONT.
Interviewed on 5 Aug. 1978; 1 hr.; 1
tape; English; by Roman Bielski.

BRUDNICKI STANISLAW
DON MILLS, ONT.
13 Aug. 1978; 1 hr.; 1 tape; English; by Roman Bielski.

BRYK, MARIA
TORONTO, ONT.
 Interviewed on June 1981; 2 hrs.; 2
tapes; Polish; by Josef Sieramski.
Arrived in Canada in 1933.

BRYK, STANISŁAW AND ZOFIA
TORONTO, ONT.
 Interviewed on 14 July 1982; .75
hr.; 1 tape; Polish; by Roman Bielski.

BRZOZOWICZ, PETER
TORONTO, ONT.
 Papers related to C. P. Brzozowicz
Engineering Firm, 1951-75. 1 cm.

BRZOZOWSKI, MAX
HAMILTON, ONT.
 Interviewed on 30 Nov. 1978; 1 hr.;
1 tape; Polish; by Roman Bielski.
Immediate post-WWII immigrant.

BUDREWICZ, ANTONI
TORONTO, ONT.
 Interviewed on 12 Dec. 1977; 1.5
hrs.; 2 tapes; Polish; by Roman
Bielski.

BUDZYSKI, JAN
OSHAWA, ONT.
 Interviewed on 21 Nov. 1981; .75
hr.; 1 tape; Polish; by Roman Bielski.

BUGAJ, ANDRZEJ
TORONTO, ONT.
 Interviewed on 1 Nov. 1977; 1 hr.;
1 tape; English; by Roman Bielski.

BUKOWSKI, LECH
TORONTO, ONT.
 Interviewed on 10 Aug. 1981; 1.25
hrs.; 2 tapes; Polish; by Roman
Bielski. Arrived in Canada in 1967.

BULKOWSKI, FRANK
KITCHENER, ONT.
 Interviewed on 23 April 1977; .5
hr.; 1 tape; English; by Roman
Bielski.

BUOZIAK, KAZIMIERA
TORONTO, ONT.
 Interviewed on 10 Feb. 1982; 2 hrs.;
2 tapes; Polish; by A. Pietrus.
Arrived in Canada in 1958.

BURATYSKI, L.
SUDBURY, ONT.
 Invitations and newsclippings,
1956-66. .5 cm. Photographs.
 4 photographs: Polish Christmas and
of Millenium celebrations, Sudbury,
1963-64.

BURCZYK, ALOYZY
TORONTO, ONT.
 Interviewed on 26 Oct. 1978; 2 hrs.;
2 tapes; Polish; by Roman Bielski.

BURNY, ZUZANNA
TORONTO, ONT.
 Interviewed on 26 Oct. 1979; .75
hr.; 1 tape; Polish; by Roman Bielski.

BUSZKIEWICZ, ANNA WĄSIK
DELHI, ONT.
 Interviewed on 30 Sept. 1981; 1 hr.;
1 tape; Polish; by A. Pietrus. Immigrated to Canada in 1930.

BYSTRAM, EUGENIUSZ
OTTAWA, ONT.
 Interviewed on 30 Nov. 1979; 1
hr.; 1 tape; Polish; by Roman Bielski.
Arrived in Canada in 1954.

BYSTRY, TADEUSZ
TORONTO, ONT.
 Interviewed on 28 Sept. 1981; 2

hrs.; 2 tapes; Polish; by A. Pietrus. Arrived in Canada 1949.

BYSZEWSKI, ZBIGNIEW
OTTAWA, ONT.
Interviewed on 8 Aug. 1978; 1 hr.; 1 tape; English; by Roman Bielski.

CACKOWSKI, TADEUSZ
OTTAWA, ONT.
Interviewed on 18 June 1980; 2 hrs.; 2 tapes; Polish; by Roman Bielski.

CALIK, REV. JÓZEF
OSHAWA, ONT.
Interviewed on 21 Nov. 1981; .75 hr.; 1 tape; Polish; by Roman Bielski.

CAPUTA, ANTONI
KITCHENER, ONT.
Interviewed on 23 Sept. 1977; .5 hr.; 1 tape; English; by Roman Bielski.

CERSKI, JAN AND KATARZYNA
TORONTO, ONT.
Interviewed on 22 May 1980; 1.5 hrs.; 2 tapes; Polish; by Roman Bielski.

CESIOR, MIECZYSŁAW AND ADELA
TORONTO, ONT.
Interviewed on 20 Nov. 1982; 1.25 hrs.; 2 tapes; Polish; by Roman Bielski.

CHECKO, TADEUSZ AND MARIA
TORONTO, ONT.
Interviewed on 18 Nov. 1979; 1 hr.; 1 tape; Polish; by Roman Bielski. Immediate post-WWII immigrant.

CHMIELEWSKI, JAN AND WŁADYSŁAWA
TORONTO, ONT.
Interviewed on 14 Nov. 1980; .75

hr.; 1 tape; Polish; by Roman Bielski. Arrived in the early 1950s.

CHOROSTECKI, JOSEF
TORONTO, ONT.
Interviewed on 19 May 1981; 3 hrs.; 3 tapes; Polish/English; by J. Siermaski.

CHUBA, BOLESŁAW AND JADWIGA
TORONTO, ONT.
Interviewed on 9 Oct. 1979; 1 hr.; 1 tape; Polish; by Roman Bielski.

CHUCHRA, ZBIGNIEW
TORONTO, ONT.
Interviewed on 23 April 1979; 2 hrs.; 2 tapes; Polish; by Roman Bielski.

CHUDOBA, FRANCISZEK
TORONTO, ONT.
5 photographs: most of them from military service, c. 1940-45. Taped interview.
Interviewed on 15 Nov. 1977; 1 hr.; 1 tape; English; by Roman Bielski.

CHUDOBA, FRANK AND ANIELA
TORONTO, ONT.
Interviewed on 23 March 1981; 12 hr.; 1 tape; Polish; by Roman Bielski.

CHYBICKI, WŁADYSŁAW
TORONTO, ONT.
Interviewed on 13 July 1982; .75 hr.; 1 tape; Polish; by Roman Bielski.

CHYKA, NORMA
SUDBURY, ONT.
Newsclippings, a programme and photographs. .5 cm.
22 photographs: the Yankowski family, Cobalt, Sudbury, Copper Cliff, 1898-1910; a general store and hotel in Niagara-on-the-Lake, c. 1910-50;

military service in Polish Blue Army, 1917-18; and White Eagles soccer team, Sudbury, 1950-55.

CIECIUCH, B.
KITCHENER, ONT.
Interviewed on 23 Sept. 1977; .5 hr.; 1 tape; English; by Roman Bielski.

CIESIELSKI, ZBIGNIEW
TORONTO, ONT.
Interviewed on 27 April 1979; 2 hrs.; 2 tapes; English; by Benedykt Heydenkorn.

CIOSK, JAN
OSHAWA, ONT.
Interviewed on 21 Nov. 1981; .75 hr.; 1 tape; Polish; by Roman Bielski.

CISZEWSKI, ZYGMUNT AND JULIA
TORONTO, ONT.
Interviewed on 29 Nov. 1981; 1 hr.; 2 tapes; Polish; by Roman Bielski. They immigrated to Canada in 1946.

CISZEWSKI, ZYGMUNT
TORONTO, ONT.
Interviewed on 16 Jan. 1978; 1 hr.; 1 tape; Polish; by Roman Bielski.

CWINAR, CZESŁAW AND NADZIEJA
TORONTO, ONT.
Interviewed on 11 Oct. 1980; 1.5 hrs.; 2 tapes; Polish; by Roman Bielski. Immigrated to Canada in 1953.

CWYNAR, CZESŁAW
TORONTO, ONT.
Interviewed on 13 April 1981; 1.5 hrs.; 2 tapes; Polish; by Roman Bielski. Arrived in Canada in 1947.

CWYNAR, JAN
TORONTO, ONT.
Interviewed on 11 April 1981; .75 hr.; 1 tape; Polish; by Roman Bielski.

CWYNAR, JAN AND ZOFIA
TORONTO, ONT.
Interviewed on 6 April 1981; 1.5 hrs.; 2 tapes; Polish; by Roman Bielski.

CYBULKO, IRENA
TORONTO, ONT.
Interviewed on 16 April 1981; .5 hr.; 1 tape; Polish; by Roman Bielski.

CYGAN, WALDEMAR AND STEFANIA
TORONTO, ONT.
Interviewed on 2 March 1981; 1 hr.; 1 tape; Polish; by Roman Bielski. They arrived in Canada in 1966.

CYNBERG, DAWID
RANDON, QUEBEC
Interviewed on 7 Aug. 1978; 2 hrs.; 2 tapes; English; by Roman Bielski. Mora, Sylwester and Piotr Zwierniak. *Sprawiedliwosc Sowiecka* (Soviet Justice). Italy, 1945. 275 pp.

CZAJKA, MARY
SUDBURY, ONT.
Interviewed on 7 Aug. 1978; .5 hr.; 1 tape; English; by Theresa Stankiewicz.

CZAJOR, WŁADYSŁAW AND JANINA
TORONTO, ONT.
Interviewed on 25 Oct. 1979; 1 hr.; 1 tape; Polish; by Roman Bielski.

CZAPRAN, FRANCISZEK
TORONTO, ONT.
Interviewed on 10 May 1978; 1 hr.; 1 tape; English; by Roman Bielski.

CZARNECKI, JÓZEF AND JOYCE
TORONTO, ONT.
Interviewed on 8 July 1980; 1 hr.; 1
tape; Polish; by Roman Bielski.

CZARNECKI, ZENOBIA
TORONTO, ONT.
Interviewed on 3 Aug. 1978; .5 hr.;
1 tape; Polish; by Roman Bielski.
Arrived in Canada in 1974.

CZERECHOWICZ, ANTONI
HAMILTON, ONT.
Interviewed on 29 Nov. 1978; 1 hr.;
1 tape; Polish; by Roman Bielski.

CZERNIEC, JAN
TORONTO, ONT.
Diploma for fulfilling duty toward
Poland by serving with the Polish
Armed Forces during WWII, London,
England, 1945. .25 cm. Photographs.
Taped interview.
3 photographs: unidentified, taken in
Italy, Jerusalem, and Toronto, c.
1943-53.
Interviewed on 30 Nov. 1977; .5
hr.; 1 tape; English; by Roman
Bielski.

CZERWISKI, JAN AND MARIA
TORONTO, ONT.
Interviewed on 23 Nov. 1980; .75
hr.; 1 tape; Polish; by Roman Bielski.

CZUBAK, MARIA
TORONTO, ONT.
Interviewed on 30 Jan. 1979; .75
hr.; 1 tape; Polish; by Roman Bielski.

CZUBAK, TADEUSZ
TORONTO, ONT.
Interviewed on 30 Jan. 1979; 1.5
hrs.; 2 tapes; Polish; by Roman
Bielski.

CZYCZYRO, FRANK
SUDBURY, ONT.
Interviewed on 3 Dec. 1977; .5 hr.;
1 tape; English; by Roman Bielski.

CZYŻ, FRANCISZEK
BRANTFORD, ONT.
Interviewed on 15 June 1981; .75
hr.; 1 tape; Polish; by Les Wawrow.

DĄBROWSKA, ANNA
TORONTO, ONT.
Interviewed on 1 Nov. 1979; .5 hr.;
1 tape; Polish; by Roman Bielski.

DACA, FRANCES
TORONTO, ONT.
Interviewed on 7 May 1981; .5 hr.;
1 tape; Polish; by Josef Sieramski.

DASZKIEWICZ, HALINA
TORONTO, ONT.
Interviewed in Jan. 1979; 1 hr.; 1
tape; Polish; by D. Rogacki.

DASZKIEWICZ, JÓZEF AND HALINA
TORONTO, ONT.
Interviewed on 9 Jan. 1980; 1 hr.; 1
tape; Polish; by Roman Bielski.

DMUCHOWSKI, FRANCISZEK
TORONTO, ONT.
Interviewed on 6 Sept. 1981; 1 hr.;
1 tape; Polish; by A. Pietrus. Immi-
grated to Canada in 1946, joined the
Polish Alliance of Canada in 1959.

DOBROWOLSKI, J.
OTTAWA, ONT.
1 manuscript, "Grupa Taneczana
Polishonii Ottawskiej, 1956-81," by
J. A. Dobrowolsk. .5 cm.

DOBROWOLSKI, WŁADYSŁAWA AND
JANINA
TORONTO, ONT.
Interviewed on 6 Jan. 1981; 1 hr.; 1
tape; Polish; by Roman Bielski.

DOBRZASKI, JERZY
TORONTO, ONT.
Interviewed on 9 April 1981; 2 hrs.;
2 tapes; Polish; by Josef Sieramski.

DOLHAN, HELENA
TORONTO, ONT.
Interviewed on 10 Oct. 1981; .5 hr.;
1 tape; Polish; by Roman Bielski.

DOLIK, JOZEF AND HELENA
TORONTO, ONT.
Interviewed on 16 May 1979; .5 hr.;
1 tape; Polish; by Roman Bielski.

DOMALEWSKI, JAN
SUDBURY, ONT.
Interviewed on 3 Dec. 1977; 1 hr.; 1
tape; English; by Roman Bielski.

DOMASKA, JADWIGA AND LUDOGIERD
OTTAWA, ONT.
Interviewed on 22 Feb. 1980; 1.5
hrs.; 2 tapes; Polish; by Roman
Bielski.

DRAŻBA, JAN AND JÓZEFA
TORONTO, ONT.
Interviewed on 14 Oct. 1980; 1 hr.;
1 tape; Polish; by Roman Bielski.

DROZDOWSKI, WACŁAW AND
STANISŁAWA
TORONTO, ONT.
Interviewed on 23 April 1980; 1.25
hrs.; 2 tapes; Polish; by Roman
Bielski.

DROZD, WINCENTY
TORONTO, ONT.
Interviewed on 3 Dec. 1980; .75 hr.;
1 tape; Polish; by Roman Bielski.

DRYGAŁA, JAN
OSHAWA, ONT.
Personal papers and clippings,
1970s. .5 cm (7 items). Taped interview.
Interviewed on 20 June, 21 Nov.
1981, and 23 Jan. 1982; 3 hrs.; 3
tapes; Polish; by Roman Bielski.

DUBICKA, MARIA
TORONTO, ONT.
Interviewed on 11 May 1981; 2 hrs.;
2 tapes; Polish; by Josef Sieramski.
Immigrated to Canada in 1952.

DUBICKI, PAWEŁ
TORONTO, ONT.
Interviewed on 12 May 1981; 2 hrs.;
2 tapes; Polish; by Josef Sieramski.

DUBISKI, STANISŁAW
TORONTO, ONT.
Interviewed on 1 Nov. 1978; 1 hr.;
1 tape; English; by Roman Bielski.

DUBOWSKI, JAN
SUDBURY, ONT.
Interviewed on 3 March 1978; 1 hr.;
1 tape; Polish; by Roman Bielski.

DUBOWSKI, JAN
SUDBURY, ONT.
Interviewed on 2 Dec. 1977; .75 hr.;
1 tape; English; by Roman Bielski.

DUCHNICKA, STEFANIA
TORONTO, ONT.
Interviewed on 9 Aug. 1982; .5 hr.;
1 tape; Polish; by Roman Bielski.

DUDA, EDWARD
SUDBURY, ONT.
 Interviewed on 3 Dec. 1977; .5 hr.;
1 tape; English; by Roman Bielski.

DUDA, KAZIMIERZ AND WŁADYSŁAWA
TORONTO, ONT.
 Interviewed on 2 Feb. 1980; 1.5
hrs.; 2 tapes; Polish; by Roman
Bielski.

DUDA, STEFAN AND STEFANIA
TORONTO, ONT.
 Interviewed on 27 Sept. 1979; 1.5
hrs.; 2 tapes; Polish; by Roman
Bielski.

DUDAREWICZ STANISŁAWA AND
CZESŁAW
TORONTO, ONT.
 Interviewed on 17 Sept. 1979; 1.5
hrs.; 2 tapes; Polish; by Roman
Bielski.

DUDZISKI, STEFAN
KAKABEKA FALLS, ONT.
 Personal papers, including military
documents, 1943-77. .5 cm. Photographs. Taped interview.
 12 photographs: WWII military campaign and family portraits, Poland,
Gaza, Iraq, 1935-71; including a
motor hotel in Kakabeka Falls.
 Interviewed on 9 July 1978; 2 hrs.; 2
tapes; Polish; by G. Kokocinski.
Immediate post-WWII immigrant.

DUKSZTA, JANUSZ (M.P.)
TORONTO, ONT.
 Election campaign papers and clippings, 1971-76; also, a 1973-74
directory of language and citizenship
classes. 14 cm.

DULNA, STANISŁAWA
OSHAWA, ONT.
 Interviewed on 23 Jan. 1982; .75
hr.; 1 tape; Polish; by Roman Bielski.

DYL, JAN W.
TORONTO, ONT.
 Interviewed on 6 May 1981; 1 hr.; 1
tape; Polish; by Josef Sieramski.
Immigrated to Canada in 1926.

DZEWIECKI, JÓZEF AND JÓZEFA
OTTAWA, ONT.
 Interviewed on 28 Dec. 1979; 1 hr.;
1 tape; Polish; by Roman Bielski.

DZIĘCIOŁOWSKA, ANNA
TORONTO, ONT.
 Various documents pertaining to
military service in the U.S.S.R., Italy
and England. 1 cm. Photographs.
Taped interview.
 2 photographs: unidentified group, c.
1940s.
 Interviewed on 19 Jan. 1982; 1 hr.;
1 tape; Polish; by A. Pietrus. Arrived
in 1960; active in the Polish Alliance
of Canada.

DZIENDZIOŁA, MIKOŁAJ AND MARIA
TORONTO, ONT.
 Interviewed on 21 May 1979; 2 hrs.;
2 tapes; Polish; by Roman Bielski.
DZIURKA, JOHN
HAMILTON, ONT.
 Interviewed on 30 March 1981; 2
hrs.; 2 tapes; Polish; by Josef
Sieramski. Parents immigrated to
Canada before WWII.

DZWONKOWSKI, ZYGMUNT
TORONTO, ONT.
 List of donor's military awards,
1946; and letter to same from the
Canadian Department of Mines and
Resources regarding immigration to

Canada, 1948. .5 cm. Photographs.
Taped interview.
3 photographs: portraits and personal
documents of donor, 1940-45.
Interviewed on 15 April 1978; 3
hrs.; 3 tapes; Polish; by Roman
Bielski. Arrived in Canada in the late
1940s.

EZMAN, JULIAN AND FRANCISZKA
TORONTO, ONT.
Interviewed on 3 May 1981, 1 Nov.
1979; 2.5 hrs.; 3 tapes; Polish; by
Roman Bielski. Immigrated to Canada
in 1952.

FAFISKI, MAXYMILJAN
TORONTO, ONT.
Interviewed on 20 July 1979; 1 hr.;
1 tape; Polish; by Roman Bielski.

FALKOWSKA, ANNA
OSHAWA, ONT.
Interviewed on 21 Nov. 1981; .75
hr.; 1 tape; Polish; by Roman Bielski.

FALKOWSKA, BARBARA
TORONTO, ONT.
Interviewed on 20 Feb. 1978; 1 hr.;
1 tape; Polish; by Roman Bielski.

FALKOWSKI, STEFAN
TORONTO, ONT.
Interviewed on 20 Feb. 1978; hr.; 1
tape; Polish; by Roman Bielski.

FARYNIARZ, FRANK AND KAZIMIERA
TORONTO, ONT.
Interviewed on 4 Sept. 1979; 1.25
hrs.; 2 tapes; Polish; by Roman
Bielski. Immigrated to Canada in
1952.

FEDEC, J.
SUDBURY, ONT.
6 photographs: the White Eagle
soccer team, Sudbury, 1949-50.

FEDOROWICZ, KAZIMIERZ
TORONTO, ONT.
Interviewed on 5 Feb. 1978; 3 hrs.;
3 tapes; Polish; by Roman Bielski.

FIGIEL, MIECZYSŁAW
TORONTO, ONT.
Interviewed on 28 Nov. 1977; 1 hr.;
1 tape; English; by Roman Bielski.

FIJAŁKOWSKI, BOLESŁAW
TORONTO, ONT.
Interviewed on 1 March 1979; 2
hrs.; 2 tapes; English; by Roman
Bielski.

FIJAŁKOWSKI, MARIA-TERESA
TORONTO, ONT.
Interviewed on 1 March 1979; .75
hr.; 1 tape; English; by Roman
Bielski.

FILIPIUK, KRYSTYNA
TORONTO, ONT.
Interviewed on 5 Aug. 1982; .75 hr.;
1 tape; Polish; by Roman Bielski.
FILIPIUK, ZENONA
TORONTO, ONT.
Interviewed on 4 Aug. 1982; .75 hr.;
1 tape; Polish; by Roman Bielski.
Arrived in 1961.

FISCHER, JÓZEF
TORONTO, ONT.
Interviewed on 17 July 1979; .75
hr.; 1 tape; Polish; by Roman Bielski.

FITKOWSKI, S.
WELLAND, ONT.
Immigration documents (photo-
graphed), including 2 parental permits

for emigration, 1929. .5 cm (13 items). Photographs.
2 photographs: Polish theatrical productions, Poland, Welland, 1927, 1949.

FLIS, JESSE
TORONTO, ONT.
Papers regarding heritage languages at the Toronto Board of Education, 1977-78. .5 cm. Taped interview.
Interviewed on 29 May 1981; 2 hrs.; 2 tapes; English; by Josef Sieramski.

-----.
TORONTO, ONT.
Interviewed on 27 Sept. 1978; 1 hr.; 1 tape; English; by J. Stanley.

FLIS, WALTER AND ANNA
TORONTO, ONT.
Interviewed on 1 July 1979; 1.5 hrs.; 2 tapes; Polish; by Roman Bielski.

FOLTYNSKI, LYDIA AND JANUSZ
TORONTO, ONT.
Interviewed on 13 Nov. 1979; 1.25 hr.; 2 tapes; Polish; by Roman Bielski.

FOLTYNSKI, STELLA
TORONTO, ONT.
Interviewed on 13 Nov. 1979; 1 hr.; 1 tape; Polish; by Roman Bielski.

FUDALA, RYSZARD
TORONTO, ONT.
"A brief historical account of the activities of the 7th Horse Artillery Regiment," London, England, 1977. 13 pp., in Polish. Taped interview.
Interviewed on 27 March 1978; 1 hr.; 1 tape; Polish; by Roman Bielski.

FURMANIAK, SERGIUSZ
TORONTO, ONT.
Interviewed on 10 May 1978; 1 hr.; 1 tape; Polish; by Roman Bielski.

GAC, JAN AND HONORATA
TORONTO, ONT.
Interviewed on 2 Feb. 1981; 1 hr.; 1 tape; Polish; by Roman Bielski.

GAGAT, ZOFIA
TORONTO, ONT.
Interviewed on 8 May 1981; .75 hr.; 1 tape; Polish; by Roman Bielski. Immigrated to Canada in 1977.

GAJEWSKI, TADEUSZ
WINDSOR, ONT.
Interviewed on 19 June 1982; .75 hr.; 1 tape; Polish; by Roman Bielski. Post-WWII immigrant.

GALICA, JAN
TORONTO, ONT.
Interviewed on 18 Sept. 1978; 2 hrs.; 2 tapes; Polish; by Roman Bielski. Post-WWII immigrant.

GAŁKA, JÓZEF AND HELENA (WITH TADEUSZ, EDWARD AND DANUTA)
TORONTO, ONT.
Interviewed on 5 Jan. 1981; 1.5 hrs.; 2 tapes; Polish; by Roman Bielski. Immigrated to Canada in 1949.

GAŁOMB, JULIA
THUNDER BAY, ONT.
Immigration documents, 1929-30. .5 cm. Photographs. Taped interview.
7 photographs: J. Galomb, family and friends, Poland, Port Arthur, 1926-51.
Interviewed on 24 June 1978; 1 hr.; 1 tape; Polish; by G. Kokocinski.

GAŁUSZA, MICHAŁ
TORONTO, ONT.
 Interviewed on 7 Sept. 1978; 1 hr.;
1 tape; Polish; by Roman Bielski.
Post-WWII immigrant.

GAŁUSZKA, JÓZEF
TORONTO, ONT.
 Interviewed on 26 March 1979; 1
hr.; 1 tape; Polish; by Roman Bielski.
Immigrated to Canada in the late
1940s.

GAŁUSZKA, WANDA
TORONTO, ONT.
 Interviewed on 26 March 1979; 1.5
hrs.; 2 tapes; Polish; by Roman
Bielski. Post-WWII immigrant.

GARBOWSKI, EWA
TORONTO, ONT.
 Interviewed on 25 March 1981; 2
hrs.; 2 tapes; Polish; by I. Dembek.
Post-WWII immigrant.

GARLICKI, ANDRZEJ AND WANDA
OTTAWA, ONT.
 Personal papers, 1923-79. .5 cm.
Taped interview.
 Interviewed on 29 Dec. 1979; 1.5
hrs.; 2 tapes; Polish; by Roman
Bielski. Post-WWII immigrant.

GARNICKI, STANISŁAW AND ZOFIA
TORONTO, ONT.
 Interviewed on 17 Dec. 1979; 1.5
hrs.; 2 tapes; Polish; by Roman
Bielski. Immigrated to Canada in
1950.

GAWEŁCZYK, MAXYMILIAN
TORONTO, ONT.
 Interviewed on 19 Aug. 1978; 1 hr.;
1 tape; Polish; by Roman Bielski.
Post-WWII immigrant.

GAWLIK, CECYLJA
TORONTO, ONT.
 Interviewed on 29 March 1979; .5
hr.; 1 tape; English; by Roman
Bielski. Immigrated to Canada in
1968.

GAWLIK, STEFAN
TORONTO, ONT.
 Interviewed on 29 March 1979; .75
hr.; 1 tape; English; by Roman
Bielski. Post-WWII immigrant.

GAWOLEWICZ, MIECZYSŁAWA
OTTAWA, ONT.
 Interviewed on 2 Dec. 1979; 1 hr.; 1
tape; Polish; by Roman Bielski.
Immigrated to Canada in 1960.

GAWORECKI, JÓZEF AND MARIA
TORONTO, ONT.
 Interviewed on 8 June 1981; 2.25
hrs.; 3 tapes; Polish; by Roman
Bielski. Immigrated to Canada in
1960.

GAWORECKI, TADEUSZ AND MARIA
TORONTO, ONT.
 Interviewed on 25 May 1981; 1.5
hrs.; 2 tapes; Polish; by Roman
Bielski. Arrived in Canada in 1972.

GAZDA, ELIZABETH
DELHI, ONT.
 1 photograph: Jan and Sophia Gazda,
Poland, 1919. Taped interview.
 Interviewed on 30 Sept. 1981; 1 hr.;
1 tape; Polish; by A. Pietrus. Immigrated to Canada in the 1960s; member of the Polish Alliance of Canada.

GEBHARD, K.
TORONTO, ONT.
 Papers (members' guide, flyers,
reports, bulletins and newsclippings)
concerning St. Stanislaus Credit

Union, St. Casimir Parish and the Canadian Polish Congress, 1970s. 4 cm.
Bulletin of St. Stanislaus Parish Credit Union Ltd. Nos. 2-6, 119, 127, 129, 130, 133-135, 137, 139, 141-156, 158-164, 166, 167, 172-174, 176, 178 (1958-78) 2 cm.
Kurier Polishsko-Kanadyjski. 13 Feb. 1979. Newspaper. .25 cm.

GĘBSKI, ANTONI
TORONTO, ONT.
Interviewed on 27 Jan. 1978; 3 hrs.; 3 tapes; Polish; by Roman Bielski. Immigrated to Canada in 1950.

GERTLER, WŁADYSŁAW
TORONTO, ONT.
Interviewed on 8 Sept. 1978; 1.5 hrs.; 2 tapes; English; by Roman Bielski. Post-WWII immigrant.

GIEDROYĆ, ANDRZEJ
MONTREAL, QUEBEC
Interviewed on 14 April 1979; 1.75 hrs.; 2 tapes; Polish; by Roman Bielski. Post-WWII immigrant.

GIERA, ZBIGNIEW
TORONTO, ONT.
7 Canadian newsclippings concerning Polish immigrants, 1930s, 1940s; a typescript of speech made on the occassion of the arrival in Canada of the Polish merchant ship *Piłsudski*, 1936; postcards, 1930s; and 1 business card belonging to Society of Friends (Quakers) Anglo-American Mission for Aid to Poland, c. 1930s. .5 cm (13 items). Photographs. Taped interview.
21 photographs: various social events and receptions of Polish organizations in Winnipeg, Edmonton and Fort William, 1930-40; 2 of them show

Polish-Canadians visiting Warsaw. Interviewed on 7 Oct. 1978; 1 hr.; 1 tape; Polish; by Roman Bielski. Post-WWII immigrant.

GIERLACH, MIECZYSŁAW AND HELEN
TORONTO, ONT.
Interviewed on 8 Sept. 1979; 1.5 hrs.; 2 tapes; Polish; by Roman Bielski. Immigrated to Canada in the 1950s.

GITNER, ALOYZY
SUDBURY, ONT.
Interviewed on 3 Dec. 1977; .5 hr.; 1 tape; English; by Roman Bielski. Post-WWII immigrant.

GŁADKI, FRANCISZEK
TORONTO, ONT.
Interviewed on 15 May 1978; 1 hr.; 1 tape; Polish; by Roman Bielski. Post-WWII immigrant.

GŁADU, JANINA
ST. CATHARINES, ONT.
Janina Gladu was a teacher in Polish language schools in St. Catharines. Her collection contains printed material—grammar and literature text books, brochures and pamphlets—published during the 1960s and 1970s. It also includes daily progress records from "Maria Kouopnicka School," 1962-75; and 1 folder containing correspondence, statutes, history of Polish school in St. Catharines, and list of parents who sent their children to Polish schools, 1955-78. 30 cm. Title list available.

GLICA, STANISŁAW AND IRENA
TORONTO, ONT.
Interviewed on 18 March 1980; 1 hr.; 1 tape; Polish; by Roman Bielski. Immigrated to Canada in 1952.

GLINICKI, TADEUSZ
SUDBURY, ONT.
 Interviewed on 3 Dec. 1977; .5 hr.;
1 tape; English; by Roman Bielski.
Post-WWII immigrant.

GOŁĄB, MICHAŁ
THUNDER BAY, ONT.
 Personal documents of donor and
spouse tracing their immigration to
Canada. .5 cm. Photographs. Taped
interview.
 12 photographs: M. Gołąb, family
and friends, Poland, Thunder Bay,
1919-77.
 Interviewed on 23 June 1978; 3 hrs.;
3 tapes; Polish; by G. Kokocinski.
Arrived in Canada in 1927.

GOLEN, STEFAN AND HELENA
TORONTO, ONT.
 Interviewed on 29 Feb. 1980; 1 hr.;
1 tape; Polish; by Roman Bielski.
Arrived in Canada in 1961.

GOLOMB, JULIA
THUNDER BAY, ONT.
 Interviewed on 24 June 1978; 2 hrs.;
1 tape; Polish; by G. and Janina
Kokocinski.

GOLONKA, STANISLAW AND ANNA
TORONTO, ONT.
 Interviewed on 27 Jan. 1981; 1.5
hrs.; 2 tapes; Polish; by Roman
Bielski. Post-WWII immigrant.

GONCIARZ, PIOTR
TORONTO, ONT.
 Interviewed on 25 Jan. 1978; 1.5
hrs.; 2 tapes; Polish; by Roman
Bielski. Immigrated to Canada in
1946.

GONSIK, TADEUSZ
TORONTO, ONT.
 Interviewed on 6 Feb. 1979; 1.5
hrs.; 2 tapes; Polish; by Roman
Bielski. Post-WWII immigrant.

GÓRAL, IGNACY
TORONTO, ONT.
 Interviewed on 14 Aug. 1981; 2
hrs.; 2 tapes; Polish; by A. Pietrus.
Immigrated to Canada in 1949.

GORLEWSKI, WŁADISŁAW AND LUCJA
TORONTO, ONT.
 Interviewed on 2 Sept. 1980; .75
hr.; 1 tape; Polish; by Roman Bielski.
Immigrated to Canada in 1948.

GÓRSKA, IRENA
TORONTO, ONT.
 Interviewed on 15 March 1981; 1
hr.; 1 tape; Polish; by Roman Bielski.
Immigrated to Canada in 1949.

GÓRSKA, MARGARETE
WINDSOR, ONT.
 Interviewed on 16 June 1982; 1.5
hrs.; 2 tapes; Polish; by Roman
Bielski.

GÓRSKA, MARJA
OSHAWA, ONT.
 Interviewed on 23 Jan. 1982; .75
hr.; 1 tape; Polish; by Roman Bielski.
Immigrated to Canada in 1949.

GORYCKI, JAN
OSHAWA, ONT.
 Interviewed on 17 Feb., 1982; 1.5
hrs.; 2 tapes; Polish; by A. Pietrus.
Immigrated to Canada in 1930.

GORZELANY, JAN AND MARIA
TORONTO, ONT.
 Interviewed on 12 Dec. 1981; 1.5

hrs.; 2 tapes; Polish; by Roman
Bielski. Immigrated to Canada in
1928.

GORZELANY, JAN
TORONTO, ONT.
 Interviewed on 21 March 1981; 2
hrs.; 2 tapes; Polish; by Josef
Sieramski. Immigrated to Canada in
1928.

GRABOWSKI, JAN
SUDBURY, ONT.
 Interviewed on 4 March 1978; 2
hrs.; 2 tapes; Polish; by Roman
Bielski. Post-WWII immigrant.

GRABOWSKI, JAN
SUDBURY, ONT.
 Interviewed on 2 Dec. 1977; .5 hr.;
1 tape; English; by Roman Bielski.
Post-WWII immigrant.

GRANAT, FRANCISZKA
TORONTO, ONT.
 Interviewed on 5 April, 20 May
1982; 1.5 hrs.; 2 tapes; Polish; by
Roman Bielski. Immigrated to Canada
in 1927.

GREGOROWICZ, JAN
TORONTO, ONT.
 Interviewed on 24 March 1981; 2
hrs.; 2 tapes; Polish; by Josef
Sieramski. Post-WWII immigrant.

GRIGENCZA, ADOLF AND JULIA
TORONTO, ONT.
 Interviewed on 21 Jan. 1982; 1.5
hrs.; 2 tapes; Polish; by Roman
Bielski. Arrived in Canada in 1948.

GROBELNY, JOSEPH
THUNDER BAY, ONT.
 Immigration documents, 1919-38,
and C.P.R. nomination papers, 1928.

.5 cm. Photographs. Taped interview.
 7 photographs: the Grobenly family,
including military service, Poland,
Thunder Bay, 1920-76.
 Interviewed on 7 Sept. 1978; 1 hr.;
1 tape; Polish; by G. Kokocinski.
Arrived in Canada in 1928.

GROCHOWSKI, PIOTR
TORONTO, ONT.
 Interviewed on 15 May 1978; 1.5
hrs.; 2 tapes; English; by Roman
Bielski. Post-WWII immigrant.

GRODZIEJKO, STANLEY AND MARY
TORONTO, ONT.
 Interviewed on 24 June 1979; 1.5
hrs.; 2 tapes; Polish; by Roman
Bielski. Post-WWII immigrant.

GRUCHAŁA, JOE
TORONTO, ONT.
 6 photographs: J. Gruchala during
WWII military service, Italy, Poland.
Taped interview.
 Interviewed on 6 Nov. 1977; 1 hr.;
1 tape; English; by Roman Bielski.
Post-WWII immigrant.

GRUCHAŁA-WIESIERSKI, ALBIN
TORONTO, ONT.
 Interviewed on 8 Oct. 1978; 2 hrs.;
2 tapes; Polish; by Roman Bielski.
Post-WWII immigrant.

GRUDZIE, MARY
THUNDER BAY, ONT.
 Naturalization certificates of donor
and spouse, 1926, 1939. .25 cm.
Photographs. Taped interview.
 6 photographs: family, 1930-70.
 Interviewed on 3 July 1978; 1 hr.; 1
tape; Polish/English; by G.
Kokocinski.

GRUDZISKI, ANTONI
LONDON, ENGLAND
 Article by donor, "Wojny Akt Ostani" (Last act of war), n.d. .25 cm. Taped interview.
 Interviewed on 6 Sept. 1978; 2 hrs.; 2 tapes; Polish; by Roman Bielski. Post-WWII immigrant.

GRUSZKA, IZYDOR AND HELENA
TORONTO, ONT.
 Interviewed on 7 April 1981; 1 hr.; 1 tape; Polish; by Roman Bielski. Immigrated to Canada in 1948.

GRUZIEWICZ, HENRY AND IZABELA
TORONTO, ONT.
 Interviewed on 23 March 1980; 1.5 hrs.; 2 tapes; Polish; by Roman Bielski. Immigrated to Canada in 1957.

GRYGATOWICZ, MICHAŁ AND JULIA
TORONTO, ONT.
 Interviewed on 1 Dec. 1982; .75 hr.; 1 tape; Polish; by Roman Bielski. Arrived in Canada in 1965.

GRYGIER, TADEUSZ
OTTAWA, ONT.
 Interviewed on 26 Dec. 1979; 1.5 hrs.; 2 tapes; Polish; by Roman Bielski. Immigrated to Canada in 1960.

GRYGUĆ, WANDA
TORONTO, ONT.
 Assorted printed material, mostly text books and pamphlets, related to activities of St. Casimir's Polish School, 1968-78. 12 cm (38 items). List of titles available. Taped interview.
 Interviewed on 25 Sept. 1978; 1 hr.; 1 tape; English/Polish; by J. Stanley.

GRYKA, PIOTR, BRONISŁAWA AND STEFAN
TORONTO, ONT.
 Interviewed on 10 Feb. 1981; 1.5 hrs.; 2 tapes; Polish; by Roman Bielski. Immigrated to Canada 1952.

GRZESŁO, LUDWIK
SUDBURY, ONT.
 Interviewed on 3 March 1978; 1 hr.; 1 tape; Polish; by Roman Bielski. Post-WWII immigrant.

GRZESŁO, LUDWIK
SUDBURY, ONT.
 Interviewed on 3 Dec. 1977; 1 hr.; 1 tape; English; by Roman Bielski. Post-WWII immigrant.

GRZESZCZUK, STANISŁAW AND ANIELA
TORONTO, ONT.
 Interviewed on 20 Nov. 1979; 1.5 hrs.; 2 tapes; Polish; by Roman Bielski. Post-WWII immigrant.

GRZYBEK, ANIELA
TORONTO, ONT.
 Interviewed on 21 Oct. 1981; 1 hr.; 1 tape; Polish; by Roman Bielski.

GRZYBER, ADAM AND ZOFIA
TORONTO, ONT.
 Interviewed on 18 Oct. 1981; 1.5 hrs.; 2 tapes; Polish; by Roman Bielski. Post-WWII immigrant.

GURSKI, JÓZEF
TORONTO, ONT.
 Interviewed on 3 July 1978; 1 hr.; 1 tape; English; by Roman Bielski. Post-WWII immigrant.

GUTKOWSKI, ZENON
TORONTO, ONT.
 Interviewed on 17 Jan. 1979; 1 hr.;

1 tape; English; by Roman Bielski. Post-WWII immigrant.

HABERLING, JÓZEF
TORONTO, ONT.
Interviewed on 25 April 1979; 1.5 hrs.; 2 tapes; Polish; by Roman Bielski. Post-WWII immigrant.

HAHN, EDMUND
OTTAWA, ONT.
Interviewed on 3 Dec. 1979; 1.5 hrs.; 2 tapes; Polish; by Roman Bielski. Post-WWII immigrant.

HAJDUK, WŁADYSŁAW AND STANISŁAWA
TORONTO, ONT.
Interviewed on 23 Aug. 1982; .75 hr.; 1 tape; Polish; by Roman Bielski. Post-WWII immigrant.

HALIK, JÓZEF
OSHAWA, ONT.
Personal papers, n.d. .25 cm. Taped interview.
Interviewed on 20 June 1981; 1 hr.; 1 tape; Polish; by Roman Bielski. Arrived in Canada in 1912.

HALINA, FRANKOWSKA AND PAWEŁ SZUMSKI
TORONTO, ONT.
Interviewed on 15 Nov. 1981; 1 hr.; 1 tape; Polish; by Roman Bielski. Immigrated to Canada in 1962.

HAŁKO, LECH A.
TORONTO, ONT.
Curriculum vitae of donor, n.d. .25 cm.

HALUCHA, JOHN
WAWA, ONT.
WWII military documents, 1943-48. .25 cm. Photographs. Taped interview.
4 photographs: family in Wawa, c. 1950-80.
Interviewed on 1 Nov. 1978; 1 hr.; 1 tape; Polish; by G. Kokocinski. Arrived in Canada in 1947.

HAMULECKI, JÓZEF
BRANTFORD, ONT.
20 photographs: largely group portraits from conventions or special events in the Polish Canadian community, Toronto, Oshawa, Brantford, 1953-70. Taped interview.
Interviewed on 28 June 1981; 1 hr.; 1 tape; Polish; by Josef Sieramski. Arrived in Canada in 1950.

HANUS, STANISŁAW AND MARIA
TORONTO, ONT.
Interviewed on 17 March 1980; 1 hr.; 1 tape; Polish; by Roman Bielski. Immigrated to Canada in 1947.

HAPONIK, STANLEY AND JANINA
TORONTO, ONT.
Interviewed on 5 Nov. 1981; .75 hr.; 1 tape; Polish; by Roman Bielski. Immigrated to Canada in 1948.

HARBULIK, B.
SUDBURY, ONT.
Interviewed on 3 Dec. 1977; .5 hr.; 1 tape; English; by Roman Bielski.

HARNEY, ROBERT F.
TORONTO, ONT.
Pamphlet from the Warsaw Pavillion, Metro International Caravan, 1970. .25 cm.

HAUSER, EUGENIUSZ
TORONTO, ONT.
Interviewed in Aug. 1978; 1 hr.; 1 tape; English; by Roman Bielski. Post-WWII immigrant.

HEWNER, WACŁAW AND JANINA
TORONTO, ONT.
Interviewed on 11 May 1982; 1.5
hrs.; 2 tapes; Polish; by Roman
Bielski. Immigrated to Canada in
1948.

HEYDENKORN, BENEDYKT
TORONTO, ONT.
The Benedykt Heydenkorn collection
consists in part of printed materials,
mostly almanacs and jubilees,
records, souvenirs, and leaflets from
a number of Polish organizations in
Toronto and Hamilton. Some of these
include miscellaneous items on Polish
language schools, 1970s; reports and
bulletins of various Polish credit
unions, 1920s-1970s; leaflets issued
by Polish anti-communist groups,
1960s, and articles on Wladyslas
Dutkiewicz, editor of the *Polish
Communist* newspaper in Canada,
1981; and a report on the religious
state of Poles in Canada, 1964
RESTRICTED
In addition, there are minutes of St.
Stanislaus Credit Union, 1945-49;
resolutions and members' files of the
Polish Alliance in Canada, 1943-61;
and papers on the St. Stanislaus
Kostka Mutual Aid Society, 1912-21.
.5 meter. Finding aid.
ALMANACS AND JUBILEES:
*15th Anniversary of the Polish
National Catholic Church of the Holy
Trinity.* Hamilton, 1964. 31 pp.
*20th Anniversary of the Polish Evan-
gelical Church in Toronto.* 1973. 53
pp.
*25th Anniversary of the Polish
National Union in Canada.* Toronto,
1955. 175 pp.
*25th Anniversay of the St. Stanislaus
Kostka Fraternal Aid Society.*
Hamilton, 1937. 8 pp.

*Commemorative Booklet of the Bless-
ing of the Church of Our Lady of
Czestochowa.* London, 1954. 72 pp.
*Fifty Years of Polish Scouts in
Canada.* Toronto, 1960. 78 pp.
*Forty Years of St. Stanislaus Mutual
Benefit Society in Hamilton, 1912-42.*
Toronto, 1952. 43 pp.
*Golden Jubilee of St. Stanislaus Par-
ish.* Toronto, 1961. 181 pp. Micro-
film.
*Golden Jubilee of the Polish Alliance
in Canada.* Toronto, 1957. 286 pp.
*Golden Jubilee of the Polish National
Association.* London, Ont. 128 pp.
*Jubilee Book of St. Stanislaus
Church.* Hamilton, 1968. 166 pp.
Polski kalendarz dla Kanady, 1915
(Polish Canadian Calendar). 66 pp.
*Remembrance Book of the Poles in
Kitchener.* 1966. 243 pp.
*Silver Anniversary of the Polish
Canadian Alliance Youth, Branch 20.*
Windsor, 1977. 6 pp.
*The Mutual Aid Society of the Polish
Alliance in Canada, 1907-55.*
Toronto, 1955. 30 pp.
*BOOKS, PAMPHLETS, AND
ESSAYS:*
Cyrankiewicz, Jósef and W.
Gomułka. *Na Drodze do Polski
Ludowej* (On the Road to a People's
Poland). Toronto, 1947. 48 pp.
Dekowski, J. J. *Błękitini i inne
wiersze* (The Blueblooded and Other
Poems). St. Catharines, 1948. 24 pp.
Iwicki, John. *Resurrectionist Studies:
The First Hundred Years.* Rome,
1966. 298 pp.
Ketrzynski, Wojciech. *Tysiąclecie
Polski* (Thousand Years of Poland).
Toronto, 1960. 16 pp.
Kytchowski, T. "The Polish Cana-
dian Research Institute: Its Aims and
Achievements." Toronto, 1967. 7
pp.

Sznuk, S. M. "Special Report on Communist Ideology and Communism: A Selected Annotated Bibliography." Ottawa, 1962. .25 cm.
Wolniak, Zygfryd. "Tysiąclecie sprawa wszystkich Polaków" (The Millennium as a Concern of all Poles). Toronto, 1962. 21 pp.
A Manual for Teaching in Polish Schools in Canada. Toronto: Educational Committee of the Polish Alliance, 1970. 168 pp.
Ku Jedności (Towards Unity). Toronto, 1964. 16 pp.
Zawsze z Bogiem (Always with God). Toronto, 1969. 341 pp.
Zbior konspektów lekcyjnych (Collection of Lecture Summaries). Toronto: Association of Polish Teachers in Canada, 1975. 231 pp.
PERIODICALS:
Bulletin of the Canadian Polish Congress. Nos. 1-3, 1953. 2 cm.
Poland Today. No. 1, Nov. 1977. Published by the Polish Students of Ottawa University, 32 pp.
Przewodnik Miłosierdzia (Guide to Mercy). Vol. 4, no. 1. Toronto, 1975. 20 pp.
Związkowiec (The Alliancer). Toronto, 1933-35. Newsletter (monthly). 1.5 cm.

HOLUBOWICZ, STANLEY
KITCHENER, ONT.
Report on the activities of the Polish Canadian Millennium Fund, 1976; Polish Legion Octoberfest programme, Kitchener, 1977. .5 cm. Taped interview.
Interviewed on 15, 22 Oct. 1977; 1.5 hrs.; 2 tapes; English; E. Ruge. Post-WWII immigrant.

HRECZUK, ANNA
SUDBURY, ONT.
Interviewed on 4 Aug. 1977; 1 hr.; 1 tape; English; by E. Sawicki.

HRUSZCZAK, ANTONI
TORONTO, ONT.
Interviewed on 4 Jan. 1979; 2 hrs.; 2 tapes; Polish; by Roman Bielski. Post-WWII immigrant.

HRYCAK, MARCIN AND ZOFIA
TORONTO, ONT.
Interviewed on 22 Aug. 1980; .75 hr.; 1 tape; Polish; by Roman Bielski. Post-WWII immigrant.

HUL, JAN
TORONTO, ONT.
Interviewed on 26 March 1981; 1 hr.; 1 tape; Polish; by Josef Sieramski. Immigrated to Canada in 1928.

HUNDR, ALEXY
SUDBURY, ONT.
Interviewed on 3 Dec. 1977; .5 hr.; 1 tape; English; by Roman Bielski. Post-WWII immigrant.

IGNAKIEWICZ, STANISLAW AND LIDIA
TORONTO, ONT.
Interviewed on 22 Nov. 1982; .5 hr.; 1 tape; Polish; by Roman Bielski. Post-WWII immigrant.

ILNICKI, DIONIZY
TORONTO, ONT.
Interviewed on 13 Nov. 1978; 1 hr.; 1 tape; Polish; by Roman Bielski. Immigrated to Canada in the 1950s.

IMIOTO, MRS.
WELLAND, ONT.
Photograph: the *Ascania* (Cunard

White Star), ship on which donor migrated to Canada, c. 1950.

IVES, TADEUSZ
TORONTO, ONT.
Interviewed on 10 June 1978; 1 hr.; 1 tape; English; by Roman Bielski. Post-WWII immigrant.

IZEWSKI, ZDZISŁAW
TORONTO, ONT.
Interviewed on 5 July 1978; 1 hr.; 1 tape; Polish; by Roman Bielski. Post-WWII immigrant.

JACHIMOWICZ, JULIAN
TORONTO, ONT.
Interviewed on 21 March 1982; .5 hr.; 1 tape; Polish; by Roman Bielski. Immigrated to Canada in the 1950s.

JĄCZEK, STANISŁAW
TORONTO, ONT.
Interviewed on 7 Feb. 1979; 2 hrs.; 2 tapes; English; by Roman Bielski. Arrived in Canada in 1963.

JANIEC, ANTONI AND STANISŁAWA
TORONTO, ONT.
Interviewed on 14 April 1980; 1.5 hrs.; 2 tapes; Polish; by Roman Bielski. Immigrated to Canada in 1928.

JANKOWSKI, G.
TORONTO, ONT.
Memorial article on Jan Zubko, 1889-75; obituary of Antoni Rosciszewski, 1897-74, printed in 1976. .25 cm.

JANKOWSKI, LEON
TORONTO, ONT.
Interviewed on 31 May 1979; 1.5 hrs.; 2 tapes; Polish; by Roman Bielski. Post-WWII immigrant.

JANOTA, EUGENIUSZ
TORONTO, ONT.
Interviewed on 16 Dec. 1977; 1 hr.; 1 tape; Polish; by Roman Bielski. Post-WWII immigrant.

JANOTA, HALINA
TORONTO, ONT.
Interviewed on 18 Dec. 1977; 1 hr.; 1 tape; Polish; by Roman Bielski. Post-WWII immigrant.

JAREM, WILHELM AND JANINA
TORONTO, ONT.
Interviewed on 5 Dec. 1982; 1.5 hrs.; 2 tapes; Polish; by Roman Bielski. Arrived in Canada in 1952.

JASISKI, BRONYSŁAW AND EMILIA
TORONTO, ONT.
Interviewed on 18 July 1979; 1.5 hrs.; 2 tapes; Polish; by Roman Bielski. Post-WWII immigrant.

JASISKI, ZYGMUNT
TORONTO, ONT.
Interviewed on 4 Jan. 1979; 1 hr.; 1 tape; Polish; by Roman Bielski. Post-WWII immigrant.

JAŚKIEWICZ, CZESŁAW AND ZOFIA
TORONTO, ONT.
Interviewed on 5 June 1979; 2.5 hrs; 3 tapes; Polish; by Roman Bielski. Post-WWII immigrant.

JAŚLAN, WŁADYSŁAW
TORONTO, ONT.
Interviewed on 13 March 1981; 2.5 hrs.; 3 tapes; Polish; by Josef Sieramski. Arrived in Canada in 1947.

JASŁOWSKI, FELIKS
HAMILTON, ONT.
Interviewed on 29 Nov. 1978; 1 hr.;

1 tape; English; by Roman Bielski.
*Echa Konferencji "Polonia
78—Polishonia Jutra. "* Toronto,
1978. Bulletin. 16 pp.

JASTRZĘBSKI, JÓZEF AND OLGA
TORONTO, ONT.
Interviewed on 7 June 1979; 2 hrs.;
2 tapes; Polish; by Roman Bielski.

JASZCZUK, WŁADYSŁAW AND ZOFIA
TORONTO, ONT.
Interviewed on 9 Sept. 1979; 1.5
hrs.; 2 tapes; Polish; by Roman
Bielski. Immediate post-WWII immi-
grant.

JAWORSKI, JÓZEF AND ANNA
TORONTO, ONT.
Interviewed on 15 April 1980; 1.5
hrs.; 2 tapes; Polish; by Roman
Bielski. Immigrated to Canada in
1948.

JAWORSKI, ZDZISŁAW
OTTAWA, ONT.
Interviewed on 30 Nov. 1977; .5
hr.; 1 tape; Polish; by Roman Bielski.

JERUZALSKI, JANINA
WILLOWDALE, ONT.
Interviewed on 1 May 1978; 1 hr.; 1
tape; Polish; by Roman Bielski.
Immediate post-WWII immigrant.

JESIONEK, E.
WELLAND, ONT.
2 photographs: refugees in a displaced persons camp in Germany, c.
1947; and immigrants en route to
Canada, 1947.

JOCZYS, BARBARA
TORONTO, ONT.
Interviewed on 8 Oct. 1981; .5 hr.;

1 tape; Polish; by Roman Bielski.
Immigrated to Canada in 1967.

JORDAN, HELENA
TORONTO, ONT.
Interviewed on 13 May 1981; 1 hr.;
1 tape; Polish; by Josef Sieramski.
Arrived in Canada in 1942.

JÓZEFÓW, PAUL
SUDBURY, ONT.
Personal documents; poster announcing "Polish Soldier Day," c. 1939-45;
flyer advertising Canadian Government Victoria Loan, 1943; and concert programme of Witol Malcużyski,
1963. 6 cm. Photograph. Taped
interview.
1 photograph: the Sixth Annual Convention of the Polish Alliance Friendly Society of Canada, 1942.
Interviewed on 12 April 1980; .75
hr.; 1 tape; Polish; by Theresa
Stankiewicz. Worked for C.P.R. in
Sudbury; also, active member of the
"Polish Alliance Friendly Society of
Canada, " 1923-75.
*40th Anniversary of the Polish
Alliance in Canada.* 1946. 176 pp.

JUDEK, STANISŁAW
OTTAWA, ONT.
Interviewed on 17 June 1980; .75
hr.; 1 tape; Polish; by Roman Bielski.

JURALEWICZ, JERZY
TORONTO, ONT.
Interviewed on 3 Dec. 1978; 2 hrs.;
2 tapes; Polish; by Roman Bielski.
Immediate post-WWII immigrant.

JURKIEWICZ, BOLESLAW
TORONTO, ONT.
Interviewed on 25 Jan. 1981; 1.5

hrs.; 2 tapes; Polish; by Roman
Bielski. Immigrated to Canada in
1947.

JURKOWSKI, LEONARD
TORONTO, ONT.
 Interviewed on 23 March 1981; 1
hr.; 1 tape; Polish; by Josef
Sieramski. An inter-war immigrant,
discusses involvement in the Canadian
Polish Congress.

JURKOWSKI, LEONARD
TORONTO, ONT.
 Interviewed on 26 April 1977; 1 hr.;
1 tape; Polish; by Benedykt
Heydenkorn.

KACPERSKA, WERONIKA
SCARBOROUGH, ONT.
 Interviewed on 2 Sept., 21 Oct.
1981; 4 hrs.; 4 tapes; Polish; by A.
Pietrus. Arrived in Canada in 1948.

KACZMAREK, LUDWIK
TORONTO, ONT.
 Interviewed on 11 Oct. 1978; 2 hrs.;
2 tapes; Polish; by Roman Bielski.

KACZMARSKI, ANDRZEJ
TORONTO, ONT.
 Interviewed on 24 Feb. 1980; .75
hr.; 1 tape; Polish; by I. Dembek.

KALECKI, BOHDAN
TORONTO, ONT.
 Interviewed on 22 May 1978; 2 hrs.;
2 tapes; English; by Roman Bielski.

KALINOWSKA, WANDA
TORONTO, ONT.
 Interviewed on 14 March 1979; .75
hr.; 1 tape; English; by Roman
Bielski.

KALINOWSKI, ZENON
WINDSOR, ONT.
 Interviewed on 19 June 1982; .5 hr.;
1 tape; Polish; by Roman Bielski.

KALINOWSKI, TADEUSZ
TORONTO, ONT.
 Interviewed on 14 March 1979; 1
hr.; 1 tape; Polish; by Roman Bielski.

KALMYKOW, MIKOŁAJ AND VIOLETTA
TORONTO, ONT.
 Interviewed on 17 Sept. 1980; 1 hr.;
1 tape; Polish/English; by Roman
Bielski.

KALUCKI, MAXYMILIAN
TORONTO, ONT.
 Interviewed on 18 March 1978; 1
hr.; 1 tape; English; by Roman
Bielski.

KAŁWA, JÓZEFA
TORONTO, ONT.
 Interviewed on 22 Nov. 1979; 30
min.; 1 tape; Polish; by Roman
Bielski.

KAŁWA, LESZEK AND WIKTORIA
TORONTO, ONT.
 Interviewed on 22 Nov. 1979; 1 hr.;
1 tape; Polish; by Roman Bielski.

KAMISKI, ANTONI AND CZESŁAWA
TORONTO, ONT.
 Interviewed on 16 Aug. 1981; 1 hr.;
1 tape; Polish; by Roman Bielski.

KAMISKI, WALTER
TORONTO, ONT.
 Interviewed on 25 Sept. 1978; 1 hr.;
1 tape; English; by Roman Bielski.

KANCZEWSKI, LESZEK
TORONTO, ONT.
 Interviewed on 18 Nov. 1981; .75

hr.; 1 tape; Polish; by Roman Bielski.

KARGOL, ADOLF
HAMILTON, ONT.
 Interviewed on 23 March 1981; 2
hrs.; 2 tapes; Polish; by Josef
Sieramski.

KARLO, LEONARD
TORONTO, ONT.
 Interviewed on 22 March 1978; .75
hr.; 1 tape; English; by Roman
Bielski.

KAROLEWSKI, EUGENIUSZ
SUDBURY, ONT.
 Interviewed on 3 Dec. 1977, 3
March 1978; 1.5 hrs.; 2 tapes; Eng-
lish/Polish; by Roman Bielski.

KARPACZ, CECYLJA
TORONTO, ONT.
 Interviewed on 2 June 1982; .75 hr.;
1 tape; Polish; by Roman Bielski.

KARWACKA, MARIA
TORONTO, ONT.
 Interviewed on 9 May 1981; 2 hrs.;
2 tapes; Polish; by Josef Sieramski.
Arrived in Canada in 1929.

KASPRZYK, TOMAN
HAMILTON, ONT.
 Interviewed on 28 Nov. 1978; 1 hr.;
1 tape; Polish; by Roman Bielski.

KASZUBA, JAN
HAMILTON, ONT.
 Interviewed on 28 March 1981; 1
hr.; 1 tape; Polish; by Josef
Sieramski.

KASZUBA, JAN
TORONTO, ONT.
 Interviewed on 23 Nov. 1978; 1 hr.;
1 tape; Polish; by Roman Bielski.

KASZUBA, WŁADYSŁAWA
HAMILTON, ONT.
 Interviewed on 23 March 1981; 2
hrs.; 2 tapes; Polish; by Josef
Sieramski. Arrived in Canada in
1951.

KAZIMIEROW, PIOTR
SUDBURY, ONT.
 Interviewed on 3 Dec. 1977, 3
March 1978; 2 hrs.; 2 tapes; Polish;
by Roman Bielski.

KĘDZIERSKI, KAZIMIERZ
TORONTO, ONT.
 Interviewed on 1 March 1978; 1.5
hrs.; 2 tapes; Polish; by Roman
Bielski.

KĘDZIOR, ZYGMUNT AND
KATARZYNA
TORONTO, ONT.
 Interviewed on 8 May 1979; 1.5
hrs.; 2 tapes; Polish; by Roman
Bielski. Immediate post-WWII immi-
grants.

KENDZIOR, STANSŁAW
TORONTO, ONT.
 Interviewed on 5 Nov. 1977; 1.5
hrs.; 2 tapes; Polish; by Roman
Bielski.

KĘSIK, JAN
SUDBURY, ONT.
 Interviewed on 2 Dec. 1977, 3
March 1978; 1.75 hrs.; 2 tapes; Eng-
lish/Polish; by Roman Bielski.

KEY-KWIECISKI, TADEUSZ AND
ELŻBIETA
TORONTO, ONT.
 Interviewed on 24 May 1979; 1.5
hrs.; 2 tapes; Polish; by Roman
Bielski.

KICZMA, MARIA
HAMILTON, ONT.
 Interviewed on 2 April 1981; 1 hr.;
1 tape; Polish; by Josef Sieramski.

KIDERES, STANLEY
THUNDER BAY, ONT.
 Immigration and military papers,
1942-65. .5 cm (23 items). Photographs. Taped interview.
 10 photographs: Kideres family
members, England, Poland, Mara-
thon, including military service,
1944-72.
 Interviewed on 19 Nov. 1978; 1 hr.;
1 tape; Polish; by G. Kokocinski.
Immigrated to Canada in 1949.

KINASTOWSKI, ANNA
TORONTO, ONT.
 Interviewed on 28 Sept. 1980; 1 hr.;
1 tape; Polish; by Roman Bielski.

KINASTOWSKI, WŁADYSŁAW
TORONTO, ONT.
 Interviewed on 9 Sept. 1980; 1 hr.;
1 tape; Polish; by Roman Bielski.

KIRKWOOD, KRYSTYNA
OTTAWA, ONT.
 Interviewed on 23 Feb. 1980; 1.5
hrs.; 2 tapes; Polish; by Roman
Bielski.

KIRPA, JÓZEF
TORONTO, ONT.
 Interviewed on 18 April 1982; 1 hr.;
1 tape; Polish; by Roman Bielski.

KIRPA, WŁADYSŁAW
TORONTO, ONT.
 Interviewed on 18 April 1982; .5
hr.; 1 tape; Polish; by Roman Bielski.

KISIEL, ELŻBIETA
TORONTO, ONT.
 Interviewed on 1 May 1978; 1 hr.; 1
tape; Polish; by Roman Bielski.

KISIELEWSKI, ALEXANDER
SCARBOROUGH, ONT.
 Interviewed on 1 Nov. 1978; 1 hr.;
1 tape; Polish; by Roman Bielski.

KISIELEWSKI, FRANK
TORONTO, ONT.
 Interviewed on 24 Aug. 1980; 1 hr.;
1 tape; Polish; by Roman Bielski.

KLACZYSKA, LUDMILLA
TORONTO, ONT.
 Family history, various records and
programmes from the Sprawozdanie
and Polish Veterans conventions,
1921-74. 3 cm. Taped interview.
 1 photograph: Polish Canadian participation in a parade, U.S.A., c.
1956-70.
 Interviewed on 28 April 1982; 1 hr.;
1 tape; Polish; by Roman Bielski.

KLAMANN, JÓZEF
TORONTO, ONT.
 Interviewed on 1 Feb. 1978; 1 hr.; 1
tape; Polish; by Roman Bielski.

KLEMANSIEWICZ, WOJCIECH AND
WERONIKA
TORONTO, ONT.
 Interviewed on 2 July 1980; 1 hr.; 1
tape; Polish; by Roman Bielski.

KLEMENSOWICZ, ZENON AND
KRYSTYNA
TORONTO, ONT.
 Interviewed on 8 Sept. 1980; 1.5
hrs.; 2 tapes; Polish; by Roman
Bielski.

KLIBER, ZYGMUNT
OSHAWA, ONT.
Interviewed on 21 Nov. 1981; .75
hr.; 1 tape; Polish; by Roman Bielski.

KLICH, ALEXANDER, LEOKADIA,
BEATA AND BOGUSŁAW
TORONTO, ONT.
Interviewed on 22 Nov. 1980; 1.5
hrs.; 2 tapes; Polish/English; by
Roman Bielski.

KLIMEK, B.
SUDBURY, ONT.
3 photographs of work in mining,
including Polish miners, at Kirkland
Lake, and Sudbury, 1948-75.

KLIN, STANISŁAW AND KRYSTYNA
TORONTO, ONT.
Interviewed on 13 May 1981; .75
hr.; 1 tape; Polish; by Roman Bielski.
Arrived in Canada in 1965.

KLOTECKI, STEFAN
KITCHENER, ONT.
Interviewed on 23 Sept. 1977; .5
hr.; 1 tape; English; by Roman
Bielski.

KMIETOWICZ, FRANCISZEK
TORONTO, ONT.
Interviewed on 25 Jan. 1982; 2 hrs.;
2 tapes; Polish; by A. Pietrus. Immigrated to Canada in 1977.

KNAPP, STANLEY AND HELEN
TORONTO, ONT.
Interviewed on 29 May 1979; 1.5
hrs.; 2 tapes; Polish; by Roman
Bielski.

KOBAK, MICHAEL
THUNDER BAY, ONT.
Interviewed on 3 July 1978; 1 hr.; 1

tape; Polish; by G. Kokocinski.
Arrived in Canada in 1923.

KOBYLANSKI, CZESLAW
TORONTO, ONT.
Interviewed on 16 Dec. 1977; 2 hrs.;
2 tapes; English; by Roman Bielski.

KOCIOK, MARIOLA
TORONTO, ONT.
Interviewed on 5 Oct. 1978; 1 hr.; 1
tape; English; by J. Stanley.

KOCIOK, WOJCIECH AND MARIA
TORONTO, ONT.
Interviewed on 8 July 1982; 1 hr.; 1
tape; Polish; by Roman Bielski.

KOCISZEWSKI, JAN
TORONTO, ONT.
Interviewed on 5 April 1981; 1 hr.;
1 tape; Polish; by Roman Bielski.

KOCMIEL, JÓZEF AND KRYSTYNA
TORONTO, ONT.
Interviewed on 3 Aug. 1981; 1 hr.; 1
tape; Polish; by Roman Bielski.

KOCZOROWSKI, JANUSZ
TORONTO, ONT.
Interviewed on 12 Nov. 1981; 1 hr.;
1 tape; Polish; by A. Pietrus. Arrived
in Canada in 1965.

KOCZOROWSKI, JANUSZ AND
STANISŁAWA
TORONTO, ONT.
Interviewed on 10 Dec. 1980; 1 hr.;
1 tape; Polish; by Roman Bielski.

KOGLER, RUDOLF
TORONTO, ONT.
Interviewed on 21 Sept. 1978; 1 hr.;
1 tape; English; by Roman Bielski.

KOGUT, ADAM
BRANTFORD, ONT.
4 photographs: activities of the Polish Alliance of Canada, 1943-49, and A. Kogut in Poland.
Interviewed on 20 June 1981; 1 hr.; 1 tape; Polish; by Les Wawrow.
Post-WWI immigrant.

KOHAR, ANNA
THUNDER BAY, ONT.
Personal documents, 1940-50. Photographs. Taped interview.
12 photographs: the Kohar family, Saskatchewan, Fort William, 1910—77.
Interviewed on 3 May 1978; 2 hrs.; 2 tapes; Polish; by G. Kokocinski.
Immigrated to Canada in 1907.

KOKOCINSKI, GEORGE AND JANINA
THUNDER BAY, ONT.
Personal papers, including immigration documents and newsclippings, 1939-76. .5 cm. Photographs. Taped interview.
23 photographs: Kokocinski family members, Poland, Port Arthur, Dryden, Toronto, including their stay in a displaced persons camp in Germany, 1946-47; also, theatre and choir activities in a Polish Saturday School in Port Arthur, 1962-66.
Interviewed on 28 Feb. 1979; 3 hrs.; 3 tapes; Polish/English; by G. Kokocinski. Arrived in Canada in 1949.

KOLANOWSKI, STANISŁAW AND JANINA
TORONTO, ONT.
Interviewed on 31 Jan., 1 Feb. 1982; 1 hr.; 2 tapes; Polish/English; by Roman Bielski.

KOLBUSZEWSKI, HALINA
HAMILTON, ONT.
A review of eighteen years of activity of the Women's section S.P.K, No. 23 Hamilton, 1971; information bulletins of the Polish Combatants' Association, Hamilton, April 1963 - Jan. 1965, and historical sketch of same; also, handwritten account of the Polish scouting movement in Hamilton, n.d. 4 cm. Taped interview.
1 photograph of Polish National Day celebration, Hamilton, 1964.
Interviewed on 27 Nov. 1978; 1 hr.; 1 tape; Polish; by Roman Bielski.
Dziedzictwo (Heritage). No. 2. Hamilton, Feb., March 1979. Bulletin of the St. Stanislaus Kostka Mutual Aid Benefit Society, Hamilton. .25 cm.
SPK W Kanadzie. Vols. 64-65, 1977, 1978 (3 issues). 1 cm.

KOLBUSZEWSKI, LEON
HAMILTON, ONT.
Interviewed on 28 Nov. 1978; 2 hrs.; 2 tapes; Polish; by Roman Bielski.

KOŁODZIEJ, JÓZEF AND LUDWIKA
TORONTO, ONT.
Interviewed on 21 March, 1 Nov. 1982; 1.75 hrs.; 2 tape; Polish; by Roman Bielski.

KOLODZIEJ, WINCENTY
OSHAWA, ONT.
Interviewed on 21 Nov. 1981; .75 hr.; 1 tape; Polish; by Roman Bielski.
Immigrated to Canada in 1927.

KOMAR, HENRYK
SUDBURY, ONT.
Interviewed on 3 Dec. 1977; .75 hr.; 1 tape; English; by Roman Bielski.

KOMOROWSKA, IRENA
TORONTO, ONT.
Interviewed on 13 Sept. 1978; 3 hrs.; 3 tapes; English; by Roman Bielski.

KOMOROWSKI, JERZY
TORONTO, ONT.
Interviewed on 6 July 1978; 1 hr.; 1 tape; Polish; by Roman Bielski.

KONIECZNY, BRONISŁAWA
TORONTO, ONT.
Interviewed on 10 June 1980; 1 hr.; 1 tape; Polish; by Roman Bielski. Immigrated to Canada in 1956.

KONOPKA, CZESŁAW AND BRONISŁAWA
TORONTO, ONT.
Interviewed on 5 July 1981; 1.5 hrs.; 2 tapes; Polish; by Roman Bielski.

KONOPKA, STANISLAUS
TORONTO, ONT.
Interviewed on 2 March, 14 May 1981; 5 hrs.; 5 tapes; Polish; by Josef Sieramski. Arrived in Canada in 1924.

KOPCIONEK, IGNACY
TORONTO, ONT.
Interviewed on 13 Jan. 1978; 1 hr.; 1 tape; Polish; by Roman Bielski.

KOPEC, STANISŁAW
TORONTO, ONT.
Interviewed on 20 April 1978; 1 hr.; 1 tape; Polish; by Roman Bielski.

KOPERA, JÓZEF
TORONTO, ONT.
Interviewed on 19 March 1981; 2 hrs.; 2 tapes; Polish; by Josef Sieramski. Immigrated to Canada in 1926.

KOPROWSKI, MICHAŁ
SCARBOROUGH, ONT.
Interviewed on 27 May 1978; 1 hr.; 1 tape; Polish; by Roman Bielski.

KORBUT, CZESŁAW
HAMILTON, ONT.
Interviewed on 30 Nov. 1978; 1 hr.; 1 tape; Polish; by Roman Bielski.

KORZENIECKI, B.
SUDBURY, ONT.
Interviewed on 3 Dec. 1977; .5 hr.; 1 tape; English; by Roman Bielski.

KORZENIECKI, JÓZEF
SUDBURY, ONT.
Interviewed on 4 Dec. 1977; .75 hr.; 1 tape; English/Polish; by Roman Bielski.

KORZENIOWSKI, WALENTY AND KAROLINA
TORONTO, ONT.
Interviewed on 28 Feb. 1982; 1.5 hrs.; 2 tapes; Polish; by Roman Bielski. Arrived in Canada in 1946.

KORZINIECKI, JÓZEF
SUDBURY, ONT.
Interviewed on 4 March 1978; 1 hr.; 1 tape; Polish; by Roman Bielski.

KOS, JAN
SUDBURY, ONT.
Interviewed on 3 Dec. 1977; .5 hr.; 1 tape; English; by Roman Bielski.

KOS, JULIAN AND REGINA
TORONTO, ONT.
Interviewed on 4 March 1980; 1.5 hrs.; 2 tapes; Polish; by Roman Bielski. Immigrated to Canada in 1947.

KOŚCIELNIAK, JAN
KAPUSKASING, ONT. Immigration and
I.R.O. documents, 1948. 1 cm. Pho-
tographs. Taped interview.
7 photographs: family in Poland and
Germany, 1934-52.
Interviewed on 24 Aug. 1978; 2
hrs.; 2 tapes; Polish; by G.
Kokocinski. Immigrated to Canada in
1948.

KOSIAN, FATHER RYSZARD
TORONTO, ONT.
Interviewed on 28 Jan. 1980; 1.5
hrs.; 2 tapes; Polish; by Roman
Bielski.
"The Church in Polish Canadian
Life." Toronto, 1978. Brochure. 10
pp.

KOSIOREK, VINCENT
KITCHENER, ONT.
Interviewed on 23 Sept. 1977; .5
hr.; 1 tape; English; by Roman
Bielski.

KOSSECKI, FRED
TORONTO, ONT.
Interviewed on 21 Sept. 1981; 2
hrs.; 2 tapes; Polish; by A. Pietrus.
Immigrated to Canada in 1959.

KOSSOWSKI, JANUSZ
TORONTO, ONT.
Interviewed on 22 April 1979; 1.5
hrs.; 2 tapes; French/English; by
Roman Bielski.

KOSTKA, HENRYK AND STANISŁAWA
TORONTO, ONT. Interviewed on 26
May 1981; .75 hr.; 1 tape; Polish; by
Roman Bielski. Immigrated to Canada
in 1967.

KOSTKA, JAN AND JOANNA
TORONTO, ONT.
Interviewed on 28 April 1981; .75
hr.; 1 tape; Polish; by Roman Bielski.
Arrived in Canada in 1947.

KOSTOWSKI, ANASTAZJA
HAMILTON, ONT.
Interviewed on 20, 26 April 1977; 1
hr.; 1 tape; Polish; by Benedykt
Heydenkorn.

KOSTRZEWSKI, STEFAN
CAMBRIDGE, ONT.
Interviewed on 14 Feb. 1979; 1.5
hrs.; 2 tapes; Polish; by Roman
Bielski.

KOSTRZEWSKI, TADEUSZ AND
STANISŁAWA
TORONTO, ONT. Interviewed on 9
Feb. 1982; 1 hr.; 1 tape; Polish; by
Roman Bielski. Immigrated to Canada
in 1958.

KOTT, JAN AND TERESA
TORONTO, ONT.
Interviewed on 18 Oct. 1982; 1 hr.;
1 tape; Polish; by Roman Bielski.
Arrived in Canada in 1957.

KOVELL, PETER
TORONTO, ONT.
Interviewed on ⸱J May 1981; 2 hrs.;
2 tapes; Polish; by Josef Sieramski.
Arrived in Canada in 1949.

KOWAL, JERZY
TORONTO, ONT.
Interviewed on 15 March 1982; .75
hr.; 1 tape; Polish; by Roman Bielski.

KOWACZYK, BOLESLAW
TORONTO, ONT.
Interviewed in Aug. 1978; 2 hrs.; 2
tapes; English; by Roman Bielski.

KOWALEWSKI, HENRYK AND HALINA
TORONTO, ONT.
Interviewed on 15 March 1982; 1
hr.; 1 tape; Polish; by Roman Bielski.
They arrived in Canada in 1950.

KOWALEWSKI, JAN
TORONTO, ONT.
Interviewed on 7 Nov. 1977; .5 hr.;
1 tape; Polish; by Roman Bielski.

KOWALSKA, JADWIGA
TORONTO, ONT.
Interviewed on 31 Oct. 1979; 1.5
hrs.; 2 tapes; Polish; by Roman
Bielski.

KOWALSKA, LUDOMIRA
TORONTO, ONT.
Interviewed on 31 July 1978; 1 hr.;
1 tape; Polish; by J. Stanley.
Polish Voice. Aug. 1977, July 1978.
.5 cm.
*Thirty Years of Women's Clubs of the
Polish National Association.* Toronto,
1967. 84 pp., in Polish.

KOWALSKI, STEFAN
TORONTO, ONT.
Interviewed on 10 Dec. 1981; .75
hr.; 1 tape; Polish; by Roman Bielski.
Arrived in Canada in 1967.

KOWALSKI, WACLAW
HAMILTON, ONT.
Interviewed on 27 Nov. 1978; 1 hr.;
1 tape; Polish; by Roman Bielski.

KOZAKOWSKI, ROMA
TORONTO, ONT.
Interviewed on 16 Jan. 1979; 1 hr.;
1 tape; Polish; by Roman Bielski.

KOZAKOWSKI, ANDRZEJ
TORONTO, ONT.
Interviewed on 16 Jan. 1979; 1 hr.;
1 tape; Polish; by Roman Bielski.

KOZERA, STEFAN
TORONTO, ONT.
Interviewed on 5 Feb. 1979; .75 hr.;
1 tape; English; by Roman Bielski.

KOZIEL, JAN AND HELENA
TORONTO, ONT.
Interviewed on 18 Aug. 1981; .5 hr.;
1 tape; Polish; by Roman Bielski.
Arrived in Canada in 1979.

KOZIEL, RYSZARD
TORONTO, ONT.
Interviewed on 3 Oct. 1981; .75 hr.;
1 tape; Polish; by Roman Bielski.
Immigrated to Canada in 1967.

KOZLOWSKI, ANASTAZJA
HAMILTON, ONT.
10 photographs: Polish Canadians,
including activities and theatrical productions of the Alliance of Canada,
Hamilton, 1900-52. Taped interview.
Interviewed on 30 March 1981; 2
hrs.; 2 tapes; Polish; by Josef
Sieramski. Pre-WWII immigrant.

KOZLOWSKI, ANASTAZJA
HAMILTON, ONT.
Interviewed on 7 April 1981; 2 hrs.;
2 tapes; Polish; by Josef Sieramski.

KOZLOWSKI, ANASTAZJA
HAMILTON, ONT.
Interviewed on 20, 26 April 1977; 1
hr.; 1 tape; Polish; Benedykt
Heydenkorn.

KRAJEWSKI, BOLESLAW
OSHAWA, ONT.
Interviewed on 20 June 1981; .75

hr.; 1 tape; Polish; by Roman Bielski. Arrived in Canada in 1969.

KRAJEWSKI, W.
TORONTO, ONT.
Resumé of donor, n.d. .25 cm.

KRAJEWSKI, WOJCIECH
TORONTO, ONT.
Interviewed on 10 March 1981; 2 hrs.; 2 tapes; Polish; by Josef Sieramski. Arrived in Canada in 1948.

KRAJEWSKI, WOJCIECH
TORONTO, ONT.
Interviewed on 16 Jan. 1980; 1 hr.; 1 tape; Polish; by Benedykt Heydenkorn.

KRAWCZYK, WANDA
TORONTO, ONT.
Interviewed on 29 Sept. 1978; 1 hr.; 1 tape; English; by J. Stanley.

KRAWCZYK-KRANE, WANDA
TORONTO, ONT.
Interviewed on 20 Oct. 1981; 2 hrs.; 2 tapes; Polish; by A. Pietrus.

KRAWCZEK, JAN AND WERONIKA
TORONTO, ONT.
Interviewed on 29 March 1982; 1 hr.; 1 tape; Polish; by Roman Bielski. Arrived in Canada in 1949.

KRAWCZYSKI, JAN AND IRENA
TORONTO, ONT.
Interviewed on 8 Aug. 1980; 1.5 hrs.; 2 tapes; Polish; by Roman Bielski.

KRECHOWICZ, STEFAN
OSHAWA, ONT.
Interviewed on 20 June 1981;

.75 hr.; 1 tape; Polish; by Roman Bielski. Immigrated to Canada in 1947.

KRÓL, IGNACY
TORONTO, ONT.
Interviewed on 15 Jan. 1981; 1.5 hrs.; 2 tapes; Polish; by A. Pietrus. Immigrated to Canada in 1972.

KRÓL, STANLEY
TORONTO, ONT.
Interviewed on 2 Nov. 1980; .75 hr.; 1 tape; Polish; by Roman Bielski. Arrived in Canada in 1953.

KROLEWICZ, MIECZYSŁAW AND ZDZISŁAWA
TORONTO, ONT.
Interviewed on 25 Oct. 1982; 1 hr.; 1 tape; Polish; by Roman Bielski. Arrived in Canada in 1953.

KUCZYSKI, B.
SUDBURY, ONT.
Interviewed on 3 Dec. 1977; .75 hr.; 1 tape; English; by Roman Bielski.

KRUKOWSKI, PAWEŁ AND MARIA
TORONTO, ONT.
Interviewed on 14 July 1982; .5 hr.; 1 tape; Polish; by Roman Bielski. Immigrated to Canada in 1949.

KRUPA, STANISŁAW
THUNDER BAY, ONT.
Military passport, 1926, Polish passport, 1930, naturalization certificate, 1939. .5 cm. Photographs. Taped interview.
2 photographs: 1 passport picture and donor in military uniform, c. 1920-45..
Interviewed on 14 June 1978; 2 hrs.; 2 tapes; Polish; by G. Kokocinski. Immigrated to Canada in 1930.

KRUPOWICZ, WŁADYSŁAW
TORONTO, ONT.
Interviewed on 20 March 1978; 2
hrs.; 2 tapes; Polish; by Roman
Bielski.

KRYLA, JÓZEF AND ELEONORA
TORONTO, ONT.
Interviewed on 3 Dec. 1981; 1 hr.; 1
tape; Polish; by Roman Bielski.
Arrived in Canada in 1948.

KRYNICKI, JAN
KITCHENER, ONT.
Interviewed on 23 Sept. 1977; .5
hr.; 1 tape; English; by Roman
Bielski.

KRZYŻANOWSKI, ANTONI
TORONTO, ONT.
2 passports and other travel documents, c. mid-1920s. .5 cm.
2 photographs: family in Poland in
1927 prior to immigration to Canada;
and in Vanguard, Saskatchewan,
1927.

KRŻYZANOWSKI, ANTONI
TORONTO, ONT.
Interviewed on 9 March 1981; 1.5
hrs.; 2 tapes; Polish; by Roman
Bielski. Immigrated to Canada in
1927.

KRZYŻEK, STANISŁAW
TORONTO, ONT.
Interviewed on 13 Nov. 1977; .75
hr.; 1 tape; English; by Roman
Bielski.

KUBERSKI, WŁADYSŁAW
TORONTO, ONT.
Interviewed on 2 Sept. 1981; 2 hrs.;
2 tapes; Polish; by A. Pietrus. Immigrated to Canada in 1950.

KUBIK, FLORIAN AND JADWIGA
TORONTO, ONT.
Interviewed on 20 Oct. 1982; 1 hr.;
1 tape; Polish; by Roman Bielski.
Immigrated to Canada in 1962.

KUFEL, ADOLF AND BRONISŁAWA
TORONTO, ONT.
Interviewed on 28 Oct. 1980; .75
hr.; 1 tape; Polish; by Roman Bielski.
Arrived in Canada in 1951.

KULESZA, PAWEŁ
TORONTO, ONT.
Interviewed on 12 Nov. 1978; 2
hrs.; 2 tapes; Polish; by Roman
Bielski.

KULIK, EFREM
HAMILTON, ONT.
Interviewed on 29 March 1981; 1
hr.; 1 tape; Polish; by Josef
Sieramski.

KULISKI, RYSZARD AND ANNA
TORONTO, ONT.
Interviewed on 16 Nov. 1981; .75
hr.; 1 tape; Polish; by Roman Bielski.
Arrived in Canada in 1968.

KULIS, MAREK
TORONTO, ONT.
Interviewed on 9 March 1981; 1 hr.;
1 tape; Polish; by Roman Bielski.
Arrived in Canada in 1974.

KUNICKI, FRANCISZEK AND
WERONIKA
TORONTO, ONT.
Interviewed on 14 June 1982; 1 hr.;
1 tape; Polish; by Roman Bielski.
Arrived in Canada in 1966.

KURBAT, TOMASZ AND HELENA
TORONTO, ONT.
Interviewed on 14 July 1980;

1.5 hrs.; 2 tapes; Polish; by Roman
Bielski.

KURCZ, ANNA
TORONTO, ONT.
Interviewed on 10 June 1980; .5 hr.;
1 tape; Polish; by Roman Bielski.
Arrived in Canada in 1976.

KURDYBELSKI, JÓZEF
TORONTO, ONT.
Interviewed on 14 July 1981; 1.5
hrs.; 2 tapes; Polish; by Roman
Bielski. Arrived in Canada in 1971.

KUŚNIERCZYK, JOHN AND MICHALINA
SUDBURY, ONT.
5 photographs: members of the Ituna
and Kusnierczyk families, Sudbury,
1928-61; and Polish Club picnic in
1934. Taped interview.
Interviewed on 28 Jan. 1980; 1.25
hrs.; 2 tapes; Polish/English; by I.
Dembek. Immigrated to Canada in
1913.

KUSZELEWSKI, WŁADYSŁAW AND
WANDA
TORONTO, ONT.
Interviewed on 9 June 1982; 1.5
hrs.; 2 tapes; Polish; by Roman
Bielski.

KUZIORA, STANLEY
THUNDER BAY, ONT.
Army book, 1923, and documents
concerning donor's immigration to
Canada, 1920s. .5 cm. Photographs.
Taped interview.
2 photographs: the Kuziora family,
Thunder Bay, 1936-69.
Interviewed on 1 Aug. 1978; 2 hrs.;
2 tapes; Polish; by G. Kokocinski.
Arrived in Canada in 1926.

KWAPIE, MIECZYSŁAW
TORONTO, ONT.
Interviewed on 10 Oct. 1978; 2 hrs.;
2 tapes; English; by Roman Bielski.

KWIECIE, ALEX
TORONTO, ONT.
Interviewed on 1 Sept. 1981; 2 hrs.;
2 tapes; Polish; by A. Pietrus. Immigrated to Canada in 1927.

LACHOWSKI, CELESTYN
TORONTO, ONT.
Interviewed on 19 Jan. 1981; .5 hr.;
1 tape; Polish; by Roman Bielski.
Arrived in Canada in 1947.

LADOSZ, JÓZEF
DELHI, ONT.
Interviewed on 30 Sept. 1981; 2
hrs.; 2 tapes; Polish; by A. Pietrus.
Immigrated to Canada in 1926.

LANGNER, ZDZISLAW AND JANINA
TORONTO, ONT.
Interviewed on 10 March 1980; 1.5
hrs.; 2 tapes; Polish; by Roman
Bielski.

ŁAPISKA, ANNA
TORONTO, ONT.
Interviewed on 28 Jan. 1979; 1 hr.;
1 tape; English; by Roman Bielski.

LAROCQUE, HELEN
WAHNAPITAE, ONT.
Land Titles Act, certificate of owner-
ship, 1912; contract for conveying
His Majesty's mail, 1903. .5 cm.
Photographs. Taped interview.
8 photographs: portraits and personal
documents of Suzsek family,
Sudbury, 1910-45.

Interviewed on 7 March 1980; 2
hrs.; 2 tapes; English; by I. Dembek.
Early 20th century homesteaders in
northen Ont.

LASEK, STANISLAW
TORONTO, ONT.
Interviewed on 17 Oct. 1981; 2 hrs.;
2 tapes; Polish; by A. Pietrus. Immigrated to Canada in 1960.

LASKOWSKI, ADAM
TORONTO, ONT.
Interviewed on 23 Sept. 1982; .75
hr.; 1 tape; Polish; by Roman Bielski.
Arrived in Canada in 1958.

LASKOWSKI, ADAM
TORONTO, ONT.
Interviewed on 1 June 1978; 1 hr.; 1
tape; English/Polish; by Roman
Bielski.

LASKOWSKI, ADAM AND KAZIMIERA
TORONTO, ONT.
Interviewed on 28 April 1982; 1.5
hrs.; 2 tapes; Polish; by Roman
Bielski. Arrived in Canada in 1958.

LASKOWSKI, LEON
TORONTO, ONT.
Interviewed on 23 March 1981; .75
hr.; 1 tape; Polish; by Roman Bielski.
Immigrated to Canada in 1949.

LĄTKIEWICZ, BOHDAN
TORONTO, ONT.
Interviewed on 10 Dec. 1978; 1 hr.;
1 tape; Polish; by Roman Bielski.

LATOCHA, JAKOB
TORONTO, ONT.
Interviewed on 23 June 1982; .75
hr.; 1 tape; Polish; by Roman Bielski.
Immigrated to Canada in 1928.

LATOWIEC, SŁAWOMIR
HAMILTON, ONT.
Interviewed on 29 Nov. 1978; 2
hrs.; 2 tapes; Polish; by Roman
Bielski.

LAUBIC, MIECZYSŁAW
TORONTO, ONT.
Interviewed on 17 April 1982; 1.5
hrs.; 2 tapes; Polish; by Roman
Bielski. Arrived in Canada in 1942.

LAUBITZ, MIECZYSŁAW
TORONTO, ONT.
Correspondence from the Polish
Alliance in Toronto and the Polish
Canadian Congress; Identification
card "Congress de la Route," n.d. .25
cm. Photographs. Taped interview.
2 photographs: members of the
Polish Alliance of Canada, meeting
held in honour of General Anders,
Toronto, 1915.
Interviewed on 12 March 1981; 2
hrs.; 2 tapes; Polish; by Josef
Sieramski.

LEADER, HENRYK AND FELLA
TORONTO, ONT.
Interviewed on 7 Dec. 1981; 2 hrs.;
2 tapes; Polish; by Roman Bielski.
Immigrated to Canada in 1949.

LEJA, ANNA
TORONTO, ONT.
Interviewed on 8 Feb. 1982; .5 hr.;
1 tape; Polish; by Roman Bielski.
Immigrated to Canada in 1948.

LEJA, JAN AND ZOFIA
TORONTO, ONT.
Interviewed on 15 Feb. 1982; .75
hr.; 1 tape; Polish; by Roman Bielski.
Arrived in Canada in 1965.

LEJA, STANISŁAW AND ZOFIA
TORONTO, ONT.
 Interviewed on 4 June 1981; 1 hr.; 1
tape; Polish; by Roman Bielski.
Arrived in Canada in 1974.

LEJCH, ADAM
TORONTO, ONT.
 Interviewed on 30 April 1978; 1 hr.;
1 tape; Polish; by Roman Bielski.
Arrived in Canada in 1949.

LEPARSKA, DANUTA
TORONTO, ONT.
 Interviewed on 2 July 1982; .75 hr.;
1 tape; Polish; by Roman Bielski.
Arrived in Canada in 1949.

LEPPEK, WITOLD H.
TORONTO, ONT.
 Witold H. Leppek, a post-WWII
Polish immigrant who died in 1981,
combined his many activities in
Toronto's Polish community with his
avid interest in photography to create
a good career for himself. The
demand for his photographs came
primarily from local Polish organizations and newspapers, although he
did accept private assignments like
weddings and portraits. The collection
totals 15,906 black and white negatives, 1,353 black and white prints,
11,228 colour negatives and 1,655
colour prints, and it spans the period
from 1968 to 1981. Some of the
general themes covered by the photographs range from folk festivals and
church life to the workplace and
human disasters. Most, if not all, of
Toronto's post-WWII Polish-Canadian
organizations are represented in this
pictorial collection. Some of these are
the Canadian Polish Congress, the

Polish Alliance of Canada and the
Polish National Union of Canada.
Finding aid available.

LETKI, WŁADYSŁAW AND IRENA
TORONTO, ONT.
 Interviewed on 29 Sept. 1981; .75
hr.; 1 tape; Polish; by Roman Bielski.
Immigrated to Canada in 1961.

LEWALSKI, ZDZISŁAW
THUNDER BAY, ONT.
 Interviewed on curriculum vitae and
covering letter, n.d. .25 cm.

LEWICKI, STANISŁAW
TORONTO, ONT.
 Interviewed on 16 March 1978; 2
hrs.; 2 tapes; Polish; by Roman
Bielski.

LEŻANSKI, JÓZEF
TORONTO, ONT.
 Interviewed on 15 April 1981; 3.5
hrs.; 4 tapes; Polish; by Josef
Sieramski. Immigrated to Canada in
1948.

LIS, JÓZEF
TORONTO, ONT.
 Interviewed on 4 April 1982; 1.5
hrs.; 2 tapes; Polish; by Roman
Bielski. Arrived in Canada in 1928.

LISIECKI, MARIANNA
SUDBURY, ONT.
 Polish passport, and Canadian Pacific
Identification, n.d. 1 cm. Photo-
graphs. Taped interview.
 4 photographs: family prior to emi-
gration, Poland, 1929-38.
 Interviewed on 31 Jan. 1980; .25
hr.; 1 tape; Polish; by I. Dembek.
Arrived in Canada in 1938.

LISOWSKA, ELŻBIETA
TORONTO, ONT.
Interviewed on 26 March 1981; .75
hr.; 1 tape; Polish; by Roman Bielski.
Arrived in Canada in 1977.

LISOWSKI, HALINA
TORONTO, ONT.
Interviewed on 19 May 1978; 1 hr.;
1 tape; Polish; by Roman Bielski.

LISOWSKI, JAN AND ZOFIA
TORONTO, ONT.
Interviewed on 29 Oct. 1980; 1.5
hrs.; 2 tapes; Polish; by Roman
Bielski. Immigrated to Canada in
1952.

LISOWSKI, JERZY
TORONTO, ONT.
Interviewed on 19 May 1978; 1 hr.;
1 tape; Polish; by Roman Bielski.

LITOWISKI, PIOTR AND MARIA
TORONTO, ONT.
Interviewed on 5 Jan. 1982; .75 hr.;
1 tape; Polish/English; by Roman
Bielski. Arrived in Canada in 1961.

LITWICKI, ZBIGNIEW AND DANUTA
TORONTO, ONT.
Interviewed on 10 Nov. 1982; .75
hr.; 1 tape; Polish/English; by Roman
Bielski. Arrived in Canada in 1974.

LIZEWSKA, JANINA AND JÓZEF
TORONTO, ONT.
Interviewed on 29 March 1982; 1
hr.; 1 tape; Polish; by Roman Bielski.
Immigrated to Canada in 1928.

ŁOMNICKI, ZYGMUNT
TORONTO, ONT.
Interviewed on 10 Jan. 1979; 2 hrs.;
2 tapes; English; by Roman Bielski.

ŁOPISKI, HENRYK MIECZYSŁAW
TORONTO, ONT.
Interviewed on 19 Aug. 1981; 2
hrs.; 2 tapes; Polish; by A. Pietrus.
Arrived in Canada in 1949.

LOTTAMOZA, EMILIA
TORONTO, ONT.
Interviewed on 9 Oct. 1979; 1.5
hrs.; 2 tapes; Polish; by Roman
Bielski.

LUBNIEWSKI, EUGENIUSZ AND JANINA
TORONTO, ONT.
Interviewed on 20 Oct. 1980; 1.5
hrs.; 2 tapes; Polish; by Roman
Bielski. Immigrated to Canada in
1948.

ŁUCKI, JERZY
TORONTO, ONT.
Clipping of donor's article about the
Polish Parachute Brigade, in
Związkowiec newspaper, 1978. .25
cm. Taped interview.
Interviewed on 11 Feb. 1978; 2 hrs.;
2 tapes; English; by Roman Bielski.

ŁUCZAK, LUDWIK
HAMILTON, ONT.
Interviewed on 29 Nov. 1978; 1 hr.;
1 tape; Polish; by Roman Bielski.

LUDCZYK, MIECZYSŁAW
OSHAWA, ONT.
Interviewed on 23 Jan. 1982; 1.5
hrs.; 2 tapes; Polish; by Roman
Bielski. Arrived in Canada in 1953.

LUDKOWSKI, PIOTR
TORONTO, ONT.
Interviewed on 17 Nov. 1977; 1 hr.;
1 tape; English; by Roman Bielski.

LUDWISKI, WŁADYSŁAW AND MARIA
TORONTO, ONT.
Interviewed on 21 April 1980; 2
hrs.; 2 tapes; Polish; by Roman
Bielski. Arrived in Canada in 1951.

LUDWISKI, WŁADYSŁAW
TORONTO, ONT.
1 article on autonomy for Poland and
Finland, n.d.; clipping from Press
Agency of Free Poland, 1979, Lon-
don, England. .5 cm. Taped inter-
view.
Interviewed on 28 April 1980; 3
hrs.; 3 tapes; Polish; by Roman
Bielski.

ŁUKASIEWICZ, HALINA
OTTAWA, ONT.
Interviewed on 31 Dec. 1979; 1 hr.;
1 tape; Polish; by Roman Bielski.

ŁUKASIEWICZ, JULIUSZ
OTTAWA, ONT.
Resume and business, 1978-79; and
a series of science articles, 1970s. 1
cm. Taped interview.
Interviewed on 29 Dec. 1979; 1.25
hrs.; 2 tapes; Polish; by Roman
Bielski.

ŁUKASIEWICZ, MARIAN
TORONTO, ONT.
Interviewed on 8, 9 Jan. 1982; 3.5
hrs.; 4 tapes; Polish; by A. Pietrus.
Arrived in Canada in 1967.

ŁUKASIEWICZ, STANISŁAW AND
MARIA
TORONTO, ONT.
Interviewed on 10 March 1981; 1
hr.; 1 tape; Polish; by Roman Bielski.
Arrived in Canada in 1958.

LUKOWSKI, PETER
DRYDEN, ONT.
Personal documents, 1960s. Photographs. Taped interview.
5 photographs: family in Dryden,
1944-77.
Interviewed on 12 Oct. 1978; 1 hr.;
1 tape; Polish; by G. Kokocinski.
Arrived in Canada in 1946.

LUKOWSKI, WALTER
CAMBRIDGE, ONT.
Interviewed on 14 Feb. 1979; .75
hr.; 1 tape; Polish; by Roman Bielski.

LUNSKI, EDWARD
KAPUSKASING, ONT.
Polish passport, 1928; Canadian
certificate of naturalization, 1935; and
immigration Indentification card,
1928. .5 cm. Photographs. Taped
interview.
2 photographs: including a family
wedding, 1939-58.
Interviewed on 25 Aug. 1978; 2
hrs.; 2 tapes; Polish; by G.
Kokocinski. Pre-WWII immigrant.

LUPINSKI, STANISLAW AND OLGA
TORONTO, ONT.
Interviewed on 30 Sept. 1979; 2
hrs.; 2 tapes; Polish/English; by
Roman Bielski.

MADERA, ANDRZEJ
TORONTO, ONT.
Interviewed on 6 Aug. 1981; 2.5
hrs.; 3 tapes; Polish; by A. Pietrus.
Arrived in Canada in 1947.

MADOWA, MICHAŁ AND STEFANIA
TORONTO, ONT.
Interviewed on 18 Feb. 1982; .75
hr.; 1 tape; Polish; by Roman Bielski.
Arrived in Canada in 1950.

MAGDA, MICHAŁ AND ZOFIA
TORONTO, ONT.
Interviewed on 26 March 1980; 1
hr.; 1 tape; Polish; by Roman Bielski.
Arrived in Canada in 1966.

MAGDA, PAWEŁ AND ZOFIA
TORONTO, ONT.
Interviewed on 13 March 1980; 1
hr.; 1 tape; Polish; by Roman Bielski.
Immigrated to Canada in 1962.

MAJEWSKA, ANNA
TORONTO, ONT.
Interviewed on 1 July 1978; 1 hr.; 1
tape; Polish; by Roman Bielski.

MAKOWSKI, WILLIAM BOLESŁAW
TORONTO, ONT.
Interviewed on 23 Sept. 1977; 2
hrs.; 2 tapes; English; by Roman
Bielski.

MAKSYMOWICZ, ALEXANDER
SUDBURY, ONT.
Interviewed on 3 Dec. 1977; .5 hr.;
1 tape; English; by Roman Bielski.
Arrived Canada in 1947.

MAKURAT, KAZIMIERZ AND HELENA
TORONTO, ONT.
Interviewed on 21 Dec. 1980; 1.5
hrs.; 2 tapes; Polish; by Roman
Bielski. Arrived in Canada in 1973.

MALATYSKI, ANTONI
TORONTO, ONT.
The Malatyski collection, 1934-76,
contains personal papers (private
correspondence, rough drafts of his
writing, newsclippings) as well as
minutes, reports, correspondence,
constitutions and by-laws from various organizations to which he
belonged. These include the Canadian
Polish Congress, Polish Unity in
Germany (British Zone), Millenium
Fund and Celebrations, Polish Political Ex-Prisoners' Association, Polish
Combatants' Association, Polish
National Fund, Polish National Union
in Canada, Polish Teachers' Association, Adam Mickiewicz Foundation,
Wawel Villa Inc. (Polish Home for
Senior Citizens), Fund for the Blind
Children in Laski, and Alliance of the
Polish Eastern Provinces. The
remainder of the collection has no
direct connection to his associational
participation. However, as an ardent
member of the Canadian Polish
Research Institute, Malatyski collected material that reflected the
cultural and social life of Toronto's
Polish community. This consists
largely of Polish periodicals,
1929-75; books, 1911-77; pamphlets
and bulletins, 1944-75, the bulk of
which was published in Toronto and
London, England. Finding aid is
available. 2 meters. Photographs.
12 photographs: mostly of the Polish
Combatants' Association, 1931-70.

MALINOWSKI, PAWEŁ
TORONTO, ONT.
Interviewed on 3 Nov. 1977; 1 hr.;
1 tape; English; by Roman Bielski.

MALINOWSKI, STANISŁAW AND MARIA
TORONTO, ONT.
Interviewed on 4 Oct. 1981; 1 hr.; 1
tape; Polish; by Roman Bielski.
Arrived in Canada in 1950.

MALINOWSKI, STEFAN, HELENA AND
ELŻBIETA
TORONTO, ONT.
Interviewed on 28 May 1981; 1.5
hrs.; 2 tapes; Polish; by Roman
Bielski. Immigrated to Canada in
1960.

MARGULEWSKI, MIECZYSŁAW AND
JADWIGA
TORONTO, ONT.
 Interviewed on 8 March 1982; 1 hr.;
1 tape; Polish; by Roman Bielski.
Arrived in Canada in 1971.

MARKOWICZ, HANNA
TORONTO, ONT.
 Interviewed on 12 Aug. 1978; 1 hr.;
1 tape; English; by J. Stanley.

MARKS, MARIA AND STANISŁAW
TORONTO, ONT.
 Interviewed on 6 Sept. 1979; 1 hr.;
1 tape; Polish; by Roman Bielski.
Immigrated to Canada in 1951.

MARSZAŁEK, ROMUALD
TORONTO, ONT.
 Interviewed on 28 March 1979; 1
hr.; 1 tape; Polish; by Roman Bielski.

MARSZAŁEK, STEFANIA
TORONTO, ONT.
 Interviewed on 29 March 1979; .5
hr.; 1 tape; Polish; by Roman Bielski.

MARYBOWICZ, BARBARA
HAMILTON, ONT.
 Interviewed on 21 March 1979; 1.5
hrs.; 2 tapes; Polish; by Roman
Bielski.

MARYNOWICZ, WALERIAN
TORONTO, ONT.
 Interviewed on 5 Aug. 1982; 1 hr.; 1
tape; Polish; by Roman Bielski.
Immigrated to Canada in 1944.

MARZEC, JÓZEF AND LUDWIKA
TORONTO, ONT.
 Interviewed on 12 Jan. 1982; 1 hr.;
1 tape; Polish; by Roman Bielski.
Arrived in Canada in 1947.

MASLACH, MICHAEL
DRYDEN, ONT.
 Personal documents, 1920-60 (10
items). Photographs. Taped interview.
2 photographs: Maslach family,
Dryden, c. 1930.
 Interviewed on 18 May 1978; 1.5
hrs.; 2 tapes; Polish/English; by G.
Kokocinski.

MASLONA, EDWARD AND MARIA
GRIMSBY, ONT.
 Interviewed on 15 Oct. 1979; 1.5
hrs.; 2 tapes; Polish; by Roman
Bielski. Immigrated to Canada in
1948.

MATEJUK, MIKOŁAJ
OSHAWA, ONT.
 Interviewed on 23 Jan. 1982; .5 hrs.;
1 tape; Polish; by Roman Bielski.
Immigrated to Canada in 1953.

MATTEN, IRENA
TORONTO, ONT.
 Interviewed on 1 May 1978; 1 hr.; 1
tape; Polish; by Roman Bielski.

MATULANIS, JERZY
TORONTO, ONT.
 Interviewed on 21 Oct. 1978; 2 hrs.;
2 tapes; Polish; by Roman Bielski.

MATULEWICZ, ALEXANDER
TORONTO, ONT.
 Interviewed on 11 June 1979; 1.5
hrs.; 2 tapes; Polish; by Roman
Bielski. Arrived in Canada in 1952.

MAZIERSKI, FELIX
HAMILTON, ONT.
 Interviewed on 29 Nov. 1978; .5
hr.; 1 tape; Polish; by Roman Bielski.

MAZUR, FATHER JAN
TORONTO, ONT.
Interviewed on 18 Jan. 1980; 1.5 hrs.; 2 tapes; Polish; by Roman Bielski.
Dziedzictwo (Heritage). Nov 1957, March 1958, Aug. 1961, Jan. 1965, Nov. 1978, Dec. 1978, Jan. 1979 Bulletin of the St. Stanislaus Kostka Mutual Aid Benefit Society, Hamilton (7 issues).
Golden Jubilee of the Hamilton St. Stanislaus Benefit Society, 1912-62. 104 pp.
Silver Jubilee Oblate Fathers, 1935-60. Toronto, 89 pp.

MCLAREN, DUNCAN
TORONTO, ONT.
1 poster/notice of annual meeting of Polish-Canadian Librarians' Association

MCCLOSKEY, RAYMOND
MISSISSAUGA, ONT.
Scrapbook of newsclippings, programmes, correspondence, and ribbons documenting the career of Andrezej Waclawski. Also, 82 letters from A. Waclawski in Belgium and in Ont. to his fiance, later his wife, 1930s. 6 cm. Photographs.
20 photographs: tracing the life of A. Waclawski, as a Sunday School teacher in the 1920s and his internment, n.d., Toronto, 1929-60; includes a funeral in 1937.

MENKIS, SIEGRFRIED
TORONTO, ONT.
Army discharge certificate, 1948. .25 cm. Taped interview.
Interviewed on 12 Oct. 1978; 1 hr.; 1 tape; English; by Roman Bielski.

"The Poles who Fight under Britain's Flag." *News of the World*, 4 March 1945. .25 cm.

MIAZGA, DOMINIK AND JÓZEFA
TORONTO, ONT.
Interviewed on 6 March 1980; 1 hr.; 1 tape; Polish; by Roman Bielski.

MICEK, PIOTR AND ANNA
TORONTO, ONT.
Interviewed on 27 March 1980; 1.5 hrs.; 2 tapes; Polish; by Roman Bielski. Immigrated to Canada in 1951.

MICEK, STAN AND KATARZYNA
TORONTO, ONT.
Interviewed on 12 May 1980; 1 hr.; 1 tape; Polish; by Roman Bielski.

MICHALSKI, JAN
TORONTO, ONT.
Polish passport, 1920; constitution of Polish Alliance Friendly Society, 1950; and miscellaneous paper items, 1926-40s. 1 cm. Photographs. Taped interview.
6 photographs: donor while in Polish Army, 1920s; group photos of opening of Tadeusz Kosciusko language school, c. 1950-55; and the executive of the Polish Alliance of Canada, 1952-53.
Interviewed on 3 March 1981; 2 hrs.; 2 tapes; Polish; by Josef Sieramski. Arrived in Canada in 1923.

MIECZKOWSKI, ANTONI AND BARBARA
TORONTO, ONT.
Interviewed on 11 May 1981; .75 hr.; 1 tape; Polish; by Roman Bielski.

MIECZKOWSKI, KAZIMIERZ AND
HELENA
TORONTO, ONT.
 Interviewed on 14 Jan. 1981; 1 hr.;
1 tape; Polish; by Roman Bielski.
Immigrated to Canada in 1963.

MIEDZISKI, JERZY
OTTAWA, ONT.
 Interviewed on 17 June 1980; 2 hrs.;
2 tapes; Polish; by Roman Bielski.
Arrived in Canada in 1953.

MIELCAREK, JAN
TORONTO, ONT.
 Interviewed on 10 May 1981; 1 hr.;
1 tape; Polish; by Josef Sieramski.

MIKLUSZKA, JÓZEF AND ANNA
TORONTO, ONT.
 Interviewed on 3 Sept. 1980; 1 hr.;
1 tape; Polish; by Roman Bielski.
Arrived in Canada in 1962.

MIKOCKI, JAKOB
TORONTO, ONT.
 Interviewed on 2 Sept. 1981; 1 hr.;
1 tape; Polish; by Roman Bielski.
Immigrated to Canada in 1951.

MIKOŁAJCZYK, ALBION
TORONTO, ONT.
 Interviewed on 4 June 1978; 1 hr.; 1
tape; Polish; by Roman Bielski.

MIKOLAJEWICZ, BRONISŁAW
TORONTO, ONT.
 Interviewed on 25 April 1978; 1.5
hrs.; 2 tapes; English; by Roman
Bielski.

MINKOWSKI, EDMUND
TORONTO, ONT.
 20 photographs: the Minkowski family, Poland, France, Toronto,
1950-65; military service in a civilian
guard brigade on a U.S. army base in
France, c. 1950-55.

MINKOWSKI, IRENE
TORONTO, ONT.
 17 photographs: the Jarmasz family,
most taken while refugees in a camp
for displaced persons in Germany.
Topics include folk dancing, theatrical
productions and activities in a summer Scout camp, 1945-60.

MIODOSKI, EUGENIUSZ
TORONTO, ONT.
 Interviewed on 14 Nov. 1978; 1 hr.;
1 tape; Polish; by Roman Bielski.
Arrived in Canada in 1961.

MIRECKI, BOGUSŁAW
TORONTO, ONT.
 Interviewed on 6 Oct. 1978; 1 hr.; 1
tape; Polish; by Roman Bielski.

MISTAKA, STANISŁAW AND STEFANIA
TORONTO, ONT.
 Interviewed on 14 Dec. 1981; 1.5
hrs.; 2 tapes; Polish; by Roman
Bielski. Arrived in Canada in 1965.

MISZTAL, STANISŁAW
TORONTO, ONT.
 Interviewed on 4 June 1978; 1.5
hrs.; 2 tapes; Polish; by Roman
Bielski.

MISZTAL, STANISŁAW
TORONTO, ONT.
 Interviewed on 9 Feb. 1978; 2 hrs.;
2 tapes; Polish; by Roman Bielski.

MŁODZISKI, WALDEMAR AND
DANUTA
TORONTO, ONT.
 Interviewed on 14 Jan 1980; 1 hr.; 1
tape; Polish; by Roman Bielski.

MONID, LEON AND JULIA
TORONTO, ONT.
Interviewed on 19 Sept. 1979; 1.5 hrs.; 2 tapes; Polish; by Roman Bielski.

MORAWIEC, JAN
TORONTO, ONT.
Interviewed on 6, 19 Oct. 1978; 3.5 hrs.; 5 tapes; English; by Roman Bielski.

MOŚCICKI, WACŁAW AND STANISŁAWA
TORONTO, ONT.
Interviewed on 12 June 1979; 1 hr.; 1 tape; Polish; by Roman Bielski. Immigrated to Canada in 1930.

MOSKAL, STANISŁAW
TORONTO, ONT.
Interviewed on 28 Oct. 1977; 1.5 hrs.; 2 tapes; English; by Roman Bielski.

MOTYKA, STAN AND STANISŁAWA
TORONTO, ONT.
Interviewed on 16 Oct. 1980; 1.5 hrs.; 2 tapes; by Roman Bielski. Arrived in Canada in 1951.

MROCHEK, STEVEN
SUDBURY, ONT.
Interviewed on 4 March 1980; .5 hr.; 1 tape; English; by I. Dembek.

MUCHA, ROMAN AND LEOKADIA
TORONTO, ONT.
Interviewed on 22 April 1980; 3 hrs.; 3 tapes; Polish; by Roman Bielski. Immigrated to Canada in 1961.

MUNIAK, LEONARD AND JULIA
TORONTO, ONT.
Interviewed on 2 July 1979; 1.5 hrs.;

2 tapes; Polish; by Roman Bielski. Arrived in Canada in 1951.

MUSIAL, STANISŁAW AND HELENA
TORONTO, ONT.
Interviewed on 29 Nov. 1979; 1.5 hrs.; 2 tapes; Polish; by Roman Bielski.

MUSSAKOWSKI, ZBIGNIEW
SUDBURY, ONT.
Interviewed on 3 Dec. 1977; .5 hr.; 1 tape; English; by Roman Bielski.

MYHER, LEO AND ROSE
SUDBURY, ONT.
16 photographs: portraits and dwellings of family and friends of the Myher family, Wilno, Barry's Bay, Sudbury, Copper Cliff, 1900-33. Taped interview.
Interviewed on 4 May 1981; 1.25 hrs.; 2 tapes; English; by I. Dembek. Immigrated to Canada in 1901.

MYŚLISKI, JÓZEF
SUDBURY, ONT.
Army book, marriage and baptismal certificates, records of earnings, and a building premit, n.d. .5 cm. Photographs. Taped interview.
4 photographs: Polish church life in Coniston, Ont., 1929-36.
Interviewed on 15 Oct. 1980; 1 hr.; 1 tape; Polish; by I. Dembek.

NADOLSKI, JÓZEF AND CZESŁAWA
TORONTO, ONT.
Interviewed on 15 July 1980; 1 hr.; 1 tape; Polish; by Roman Bielski. Immigrated to Canada in 1959.

NAGRODZKI, ZDZISŁAW AND JANINA
TORONTO, ONT.
Interviewed on 10 April 1980; 1.5

hrs.; 2 tapes; Polish; by Roman Bielski. Immigrated to Canada in 1950.

NAJDER, ANTONI AND KAZIMIERA
TORONTO, ONT.
Interviewed on 15 May 1979; 1.5 hrs.; 2 tapes; Polish; by Roman Bielski.

NAROŻASKI, JOHN
SUDBURY, ONT.
Immigration and military documents, 1929-43. 1 cm. Taped interview.
Interviewed on 14 March 1980; 1 hr.; 1 tape; Polish/English; by I. Dembek.

NAWROCKI, TADEUSZ
TORONTO, ONT.
Interviewed on 20 Jan. 1978; 1.5 hrs.; 2 tapes; Polish; by Roman Bielski.

NĘDZA, ALICJA AND MICHAŁ
TORONTO, ONT.
Interviewed in Jan. 1979; 1.5 hrs.; 2 tapes; Polish; by D. Rogacki.

NĘDZA, MICHAŁ AND ALICJA
TORONTO, ONT.
Interviewed on 19 April 1982; 1.5 hrs.; 2 tapes; Polish; by Roman Bielski. Immigrated to Canada in 1930.

NĘDZA, MICHAŁ
TORONTO, ONT.
8 photographs: activities of various organizations such as the Federation of Polish Societies in Canada, the Polish Canadian Youth Congress and the Polish Alliance of Canada, Toronto, Hamilton, 1930-45. Taped interview.
Interviewed on 4 Aug. 1981;

1.5 hrs; 2 tapes; Polish; by Les Wawrow and by A. Pietrus. Immigrated to Canada in 1927.

NEJGEBAUER, TADEUSZ AND TERESA
TORONTO, ONT.
Interviewed on 13 Dec. 1982; .75 hr.; 1 tape; Polish; by Roman Bielski.

NEJMARK, MAGDALENA
TORONTO, ONT.
Interviewed on 3 June 1980; 2.5 hrs.; 3 tapes; Polish; by Roman Bielski.

NIEWADA, MARIAN AND JANINA
TORONTO, ONT.
Interviewed on 3 March 1980; 1 hr.; 1 tape; Polish; by Roman Bielski. Immigrated to Canada in 1963.

NIZE, STANISLAW
WINDSOR, ONT.
Interviewed on 18 June 1982; .75 hr.; 1 tape; Polish; by Roman Bielski.

NOCO, WACŁAW
TORONTO, ONT.
Interviewed on 13 April 1978; 2 hrs.; 2 tapes; Polish; by Roman Bielski.

NOGAS, FELIKS AND JÓZEFA
TORONTO, ONT.
Interviewed on 21 Oct. 1980; 1 hr.; 1 tape; Polish; by Roman Bielski. Immigrated to Canada in 1955.

NOGA, WIKTORIA AND HENRYK
TORONTO, ONT.
Interviewed on 21 Sept. 1980; 1.5 hrs.; 2 tapes; Polish; by Roman Bielski. Immigrated to Canada in 1964.

NORBETT, BOGDAN
TORONTO, ONT.
Interviewed on 18 Nov. 1981; 1.5
hrs.; 2 tapes; Polish; by A. Pietrus.
Arrived in Canada in 1965.

NOWAK, DOMINIK
HAMILTON, ONT.
Interviewed on 29 Nov. 1978; 1 hr.;
1 tape; Polish; by Roman Bielski.
*Thirteenth International Convention
of the Polish Army Veterans Association of America.* Hamilton, 1958. 78
pp.

NOWAK, HENRYK AND LIDIA
TORONTO, ONT.
Interviewed on 15 April 1981; .75
hr.; 1 tape; Polish; by Roman Bielski.
Immigrated to Canada in 1971.

NOWAKOWSKI, MARIAN
TORONTO, ONT.
Interviewed on 12 Feb. 1979; 1.5
hrs.; 2 tapes; English; by Roman
Bielski.

NYTKO, SZCZEPAN AND ZOFIA
TORONTO, ONT.
Interviewed on 2 May 1982; 1.5
hrs.; 2 tapes; Polish; by Roman
Bielski. Arrived in Canada in 1948.

OCHOCISKI, ALOYZY
SCARBOROUGH, ONT.
Interviewed on 10 April 1978; 1 hr.;
1 tape; English; by Roman Bielski.

OGÓREK, MARIAN
WINDSOR, ONT.
Interviewed on 19 June 1982; 1 hr.;
1 tape; Polish; by Roman Bielski.

OLASZ, TADEUSZ AND MARIA
TORONTO, ONT.
Interviewed on 6 July 1980; 1 hr.; 1

tape; Polish; by Roman Bielski.
Arrived in Canada in 1965.

OLECH, WOJTEK
TORONTO, ONT.
Interviewed on 3 April 1978; 2 hrs.;
2 tapes; Polish; by Roman Bielski.

OLEJARZ, JÓZEF
TORONTO, ONT.
Interviewed on 6 June 1978; 1 hr.; 1
tape; Polish; by Roman Bielski.

ONIAZK, CZESŁAW
SUDBURY, ONT.
Interviewed on 3 Dec. 1977; .25 hr.;
1 tape; Polish; by Roman Bielski.

OPIC, ZDZISŁAW
TORONTO, ONT.
Interviewed on 22 April 1978; 1 hr.;
1 tape; English; by Roman Bielski.

ORLIK-RUCKEMANN, WILHELM AND
KAZIMIERZ
OTTAWA, ONT.
An account of battles in Sept. 1939,
by General Orlik-Ruckemann, n.d.;
map showing military operations in
Sept. 1939, n.d. .5 cm. Taped inter-
view.
Interviewed on 2 Dec. 1979; 2 hrs.;
2 tapes; Polish; by Roman Bielski.

ORŁOWSKI, STANISŁAW
TORONTO, ONT.
Interviewed on 7 Nov. 1978; 1 hr.;
1 tape; English; by Roman Bielski.

ORŁOWSKI, STANISŁAW
TORONTO, ONT.
Interviewed on 18 Oct. 1978; 1 hr.;
1 tape; English; by Roman Bielski.

OZEWICZ, ANDREW
TORONTO, ONT.
Interviewed on 1 May 1980; .5 hr.;
1 tape; English; by Roman Bielski.

PAJDO, RYSZARD
TORONTO, ONT.
Interviewed on 21 Sept. 1982; .75
hr.; 1 tape; Polish; by Roman Bielski.
Arrived in Canada in 1948.

PALCZEWSKI, JÓZEF
TORONTO, ONT.
Interviewed on 21 Jan. 1978; 2 hrs.;
2 tapes; English; by Roman Bielski.

PALKA, BOLESŁAW
TORONTO, ONT.
Interviewed on 8 April 1981; 3.5
hrs.; 4 tapes; Polish; by Josef
Sieramski. Arrived in Canada in
1948.

PALINKIEWICZ, STEFAN AND MARY
TORONTO, ONT.
Interviewed on 21 Jan. 1980; 1 hr.;
1 tape; Polish; by Roman Bielski.

PALUCH, KAZIMIERZ
SUDBURY, ONT.
Interviewed on 15 Oct. 1980; .5 hr.;
1 tape; Polish; by I. Dembek.
Arrived in Canada in 1952.

PALYS, JADWIGA
SUDBURY, ONT.
Polish passport, n.d. Photographs.
Taped interview.
12 photographs: portraits and dwell-
ings of Palys family, including a wed-
ding and a Creighton mine, 1936-63.
Interviewed on 25 Oct. 1980; 1 hr.;
1 tape; Polish; by I. Dembek.
Pre-WWII immigrant.

PALYS, JÓZEF AND MARIAN
TORONTO, ONT.
Interviewed on 16 March 1981; 1
hr.; 1 tape; Polish; by Roman Bielski.
Immigrated to Canada in 1957.

PANAK, MICHAŁ
TORONTO, ONT.
Interviewed on 28 Oct. 1978; 2 hrs.;
2 tapes; Polish; by Roman Bielski.
Immigrated to Canada in 1951.

PANASOW, JAKUB
HAMILTON, ONT.
Handwritten autobiographical sketch,
in Polish, n.d. .25 cm. Photographs.
Taped interview.
2 photographs: J. Panasow during
military service, Poland, 1922-24.
Interviewed on 29 Nov. 1978; 1 hr.;
1 tape; Polish; by Roman Bielski.
Immigrated to Canada in 1952.

PANEK, WŁADYSŁAWA AND JOANNA
TORONTO, ONT.
Interviewed on 13 Jan. 1981; 1 hr.;
1 tape; Polish; by Roman Bielski.
Arrived in Canada in 1960.

PANKOWSKI, JOSEPH
TORONTO, ONT.
107 photographs: J. Pankowski
during participation in activities of
several Polish organizations, particularly the Polish Alliance of Canada,
Toronto, 1916-77.

PARFINOWICZ, ALFRED
TORONTO, ONT.
Interviewed on 8 Jan. 1982; 1.5 hrs.;
2 tapes; Polish; by A. Pietrus. Immigrated to Canada in 1951.

PARTYKA, JOHN
WINDSOR, ONT.
Interviewed on 19 June 1982; .5 hr.;
1 tape; English; by Roman Bielski.

PASLAWSKI, HENRYK
SCARBOROUGH, ONT.
2 postcards sent to donor from relatives in the Soviet Union, 1949.
Photographs. Taped interview.
68 photographs: Polish Flying
Squadrons 303 and 307, England,
1940-45.
Interviewed on 10 April 1978; 1 hr.;
1 tape; English; by Roman Bielski.

PASON, BOLESLAW AND GERTRUDA
TORONTO, ONT.
Interviewed on 22 June 1981; 1.5
hrs.; 2 tapes; Polish; by Roman
Bielski. Immigrated to Canada in
1966.

PASTERNAK, JAN
SUDBURY, ONT.
2 photographs: Polish Alliance of
Canada meetings, Sudbury, 1943,
1955; and Polish school, Sudbury,
1938. Taped interview.
Interviewed on 6 Feb. 1980; 1 hr.; 1
tape; Polish; by I. Dembek.

PATRZALEK, TADEUSZ AND ZOFIA
TORONTO, ONT.
Interviewed on 15 Nov. 1982; .75
hr.; 1 tape; Polish/English; by Roman
Bielski. Arrived in Canada in 1951.

PATYNA, LEON
TORONTO, ONT.
Interviewed on 13 Feb. 1978; 1 hr.;
1 tape; Polish; by Roman Bielski.

PAWLIKOWSKI, KASPER
OTTAWA, ONT.
Interviewed on 3 Dec. 1979; 1.5

hrs.; 2 tapes; Polish; by Roman
Bielski. Arrived in Canada in 1953.

PAWLOWSKI, ADOLF AND DANUTA
TORONTO, ONT.
Interviewed on 25 Nov. 1981; 1 hr.;
1 tape; Polish; by Roman Bielski.
Arrived in Canada in 1946.

PEC, EDMUND
TORONTO, ONT.
Interviewed on 7 Nov. 1980; 1 hr.;
1 tape; Polish; by Roman Bielski.
Immigrated to Canada in 1948.

PEJKO, JÓZEF AND ELŻBIETA
TORONTO, ONT.
Interviewed on 16 Aug. 1982; .75
hr.; 1 tape; Polish; by Roman Bielski.
Arrived in Canada in 1960.

PIASKOWSKI, STANLEY
SUDBURY, ONT.
Interviewed on 27 Feb. 1980; 1 hr.;
3 tapes; English; by I. Dembek.
Immigrated to Canada in 1927.

PIATAS, IRENE
TORONTO, ONT.
Interviewed on 20 April 1979; 1 hr.;
1 tape; Polish; by Roman Bielski.

PIATAS, WACLAW
TORONTO, ONT.
Donor's (and his mother's) summons
to the German Court in Lublin, June
1942. .25 cm. Taped interview.
Interviewed on 20 April, 3 May
1979; 2.75 hrs.; 3 tapes; Polish; by
Roman Bielski.

PIĄTEK, JÓZEF
DELHI, ONT.
Interviewed on 30 Sept. 1981; 2
hrs.; 2 tapes; Polish; by A. Pietrus.
Immigrated to Canada in 1928.

PIECZORA, LUDOMIRA
TORONTO, ONT.
Interviewed on 22 Feb. 1979; .75
hr.; 1 tape; Polish; by Roman Bielski.

PIECZORA, STEFAN
TORONTO, ONT.
Interviewed on 22 Feb. 1979; 1 hr.;
1 tape; Polish; by Roman Bielski.

PIEKARSKI, JÓZEF AND STANISŁAWA
TORONTO, ONT.
Interviewed on 24 May 1982; 1 hr.;
1 tape; Polish; by Roman Bielski.
Arrived in Canada in 1976.

PIEKARSKI, JÓZEF AND STANISŁAWA
TORONTO, ONT.
Interviewed on 16 May 1980; 1 hr.;
1 tape; Polish; by Roman Bielski.
Immigrated to Canada in 1976.

PIELA, JOSEPH
THUNDER BAY, ONT.
Donor's identification and immigration papers, 1920s; plus a handbook
for Polish emigrants to Canada published by the Polish Government in
Warsaw, 1927. 1 cm. Photographs.
Taped interview.
2 photographs: J. Piela, peeling bark
from a spruce log, c. 1935.
Interviewed on 10 May 1978; 2 hrs.;
2 tapes; Polish; by G. Kokocinski.
Arrived in Canada in 1928.

PIETRUNIAK, JAN AND ZOFIA
TORONTO, ONT.
Interviewed on 23 July 1980; 1 hr.;
1 tape; Polish; by Roman Bielski.
Immigrated to Canada in 1958.

PISKI, MARIANNA
THUNDER BAY, ONT.
Immigration documents, 1927-28.
Photographs. Taped interview.

5 photographs: the Pinski family,
Thunder Bay, 1923-73.
Interviewed on 7 Nov. 1978; 1 hr.;
1 tape; Polish; by G. Kokocinski.
Pre-WWII immigrant.

PIÓRKO, JÓZEF AND SALOMEA
TORONTO, ONT.
Interviewed on 5 May 1980; 1 hr.; 1
tape; Polish; by Roman Bielski.
Immigrated to Canada in 1949.

PIOTROWICZ, RYSZARD AND ALICJA
TORONTO, ONT.
Interviewed on 7 July 1979; 1 hr.; 1
tape; Polish; by Roman Bielski.

PIOTROWSKI, ANTONI
TORONTO, ONT.
Interviewed on 2 March 1978; 1 hr.;
1 tape; Polish; by Roman Bielski.

PIOTROWSKI, JULIA
FORT FRANCES, ONT.
Austrian and Polish passports, 1912,
1923; inspection card for immigration, 1912, and certificate (authoriz-
ation) to display Polish Legion
emblem, 1922; 2 Dan. Citizenship
Certificates, 1939, 1949. .5 cm.
Taped interview.
Interviewed on 12 Sept. 1978; 1 hr.;
1 tape; Polish; G. Kokocinski.

PŁACHCISKA, ALEKSANDRA
TORONTO, ONT.
Interviewed on 17 Aug. 1981; .5 hr.;
1 tape; Polish; by Roman Bielski.
Arrived in Canada in 1965.

PLESNAR, FRANK AND MARIA
TORONTO, ONT.
Interviewed on 6 Sept. 1981; 1.25
hrs.; 2 tapes; Polish; by Roman
Bielski. Arrived in Canada in 1951.

POCHWAŁOWSKI, JÓZEF
TORONTO, ONT.
Interviewed on 8 June 1978; 1 hr.; 1
tape; Polish; by Roman Bielski.

PODGÓRSKI, MARIA
FORT FRANCES, ONT.
Interviewed on 13 Sept. 1978; 1 hr.;
1 tape; Polish; by G. Kokocinski.
Arrived in Canada in 1923.

PODKOWISKI, STANISŁAW
TORONTO, ONT.
Interviewed on 26 Feb. 1979; 1.5
hrs.; 2 tapes; Polish; by Roman
Bielski.

PODKOWISKI, ZOFIA
TORONTO, ONT.
Interviewed on 27 Feb. 1979; .5 hr.;
1 tape; Polish; by Roman Bielski.

POHRANYCHNY, ANASTASIA
NIAGARA FALLS, ONT.
Lives of Saints. Poland, 1895. 1,262
pp.

POLENSKA, EMILA
WINDSOR, ONT.
Interviewed on 20 June 1982; 1 hr.;
1 tape; Polish; by Roman Bielski.

POLENSKI, WITOLD
WINDSOR, ONT.
Interviewed on 19 June 1982; 1 hr.;
1 tape; Polish; by Roman Bielski.

POLKOWSKI, JÓZEF
OTTAWA, ONT.
Interviewed on 3 April 1980; .75
hr.; 1 tape; Polish; by Roman Bielski.

PÓŁŚWIĄTEK, FRANK
TORONTO, ONT.
23 photographs: mostly from military
service in Italy, 1940-45. Taped

interview.
Interviewed on 19 Dec. 1977; 1 hr.;
1 tape; English; by Roman Bielski.

POPEK, ZBIGNIEW AND EWA
TORONTO, ONT.
Interviewed on 19 Aug. 1981; .75
hr.; 1 tape; Polish; by Roman Bielski.
Immigrated to Canada in 1969.

POPŁAWSKI, ZYGMUNT
HAMILTON, ONT.
Interviewed on 30 Nov. 1978; 1 hr.;
1 tape; Polish; by Roman Bielski.
Wing Report, 1977. Hamilton, May
1978. Royal Canadian Air Force
Association. .25 cm.

POPRAWA, MIECZYSŁAW
TORONTO, ONT.
Interviewed on 4 July 1978; 2 hrs.; 2
tapes; Polish; by Roman Bielski.

PÓRCZYSKI, JÓZEF
TORONTO, ONT.
Interviewed on 20 Nov. 1978; 2
hrs.; 2 tapes; Polish; by Roman
Bielski.

PORTKO, JANINA
TORONTO, ONT.
Interviewed on 7 April 1981; 2 hrs.;
2 tapes; Polish; by Josef Sieramski.
Immigrated to Canada in 1929.

POSPIESZYNSKI, CZESLAW
TORONTO, ONT.
Interviewed on 11 June 1981; 1 hr.;
1 tape; Polish; by Josef Sieramski.
Immigrated to Canada in 1947.

POTOCKA, EVA
MONTREAL, QUEBEC
Interviewed on 6 Aug. 1979; 1.5
hrs.; 2 tapes; Polish; by Roman
Bielski.

POTOCKI, PETER
MONTREAL, QUEBEC
 Interviewed on 14 Aug. 1978; 1 hr.;
1 tape; English; by Roman Bielski.

POTRZEBOWSKA, IRENA
TORONTO, ONT.
 Interviewed on 5 June 1981; 2 hrs.;
2 tapes; Polish; by Josef Sieramski.
Immigrated to Canada in 1951.

POTWOROWSKI, EDMUND
KRAKOW, POLAND
 Interviewed on 22 Aug. 1979; 3
hrs.; 3 tapes; Polish; by Roman
Bielski.

POWAŁA, FRANCISZEK
SUDBURY, ONT.
 Interviewed on 3 Dec. 1977; .75 hr.;
1 tape; English; by Roman Bielski.

POWĘSKA, JOSEPHINE
BRANTFORD, ONT.
 Interviewed on 22 June 1981; .75
hr.; 1 tape; English; by Les
Wawrow.

PREIBISH, ANDRE
OTTAWA, ONT.
 Curriculum vitae and autobiography,
1980. .25 cm. Taped interview.
 Interviewed on 3 April 1980; 1.5
hrs.; 2 tapes; Polish; by Roman
Bielski. Arrived in Canada in 1963.

PROKOP, LEON AND ANNA
TORONTO, ONT.
 Interviewed on 6 Feb. 1981; .75 hr.;
1 tape; Polish; by Roman Bielski.
Arrived in Canada in 1956.

PROKSA, VIKTOR
SUDBURY, ONT.
 Interviewed on 3 Dec. 1977; .5 hr.;
1 tape; English; by Roman Bielski.

PROSZEK, ROMAN
CAMBRIDGE, ONT.
 The Roman Proszek collection consists largely of souvenir booklets from
the Polish Combatants' Association,
the First Polish Armoured Division
and the National Polish Falcons,
mostly published in the 1970s. (See
title listing under Publications). Also
included are a minute book of the
16th General Convention of the Polish
Combatants' Association in Canada,
1975; list of soldiers from the First
Polish Armoured Division who died
in battle during WWII, 1964; and a
programme of a banquet of the occa-
sion of the 30th anniversary of the
Great Battles of the Second World
War, 1974. 7 cm (15 items). Taped
interview.
 Interviewed on 14 Feb. 1979; 1.5
hrs.; 2 tapes; Polish; by Roman
Bielski.
 20th Anniversary Polish Combatants'
Association. Buffalo, New York,
1974. 29 pp.
 30th Anniversary of the Association
of the First and Second Armoured
Division, Canada, 1948-78. Toronto,
1978. 38 pp.
 Bulletin of the Association of the
First Polish Armoured Division. Nos.
3, 6, 15, 1971-78. 88 pp.
 First Polish Armoured Division Con-
vention. Buffalo, 1975. 12 pp.
 National Polish Falcons of America
Convention. New Britain,
Connecticut, 1976. 80 pp.
 Nicholaus Rej Polish Library,
1908-72. Kitchener, Ont. 36 pp.
 Polish Armoured Division: 35th
Anniversary Convention. Toronto,
1977. 13 pp.
 Polish National Relief Fund Conven-
tion. Chicago, 1974. 80 pp.

PROSZEK, ZOFIA
CAMBRIDGE, ONT.
Interviewed on 15 Feb. 1979; 3 hrs.;
3 tapes; Polish; by Roman Bielski.
*80th Anniversary of the Sacred Heart
Polish Saturday School*. Kitchener,
1975. 104 pp.

PRZEDBORSKI, STANISLAW
HAMILTON, ONT.
Oświęcim Concentration Camp docu-
ment, n.d., in German. .25 cm.
Photographs. Taped interview.
19 photographs: concetration camp,
Poland, 1940-45.
Interviewed on 29 Nov. 1978; 1 hr.;
1 tape; Polish; by Roman Bielski.

PRZYBYŁO, M.
TORONTO, ONT.
Army discharge document, 1946. .25
cm. Taped interview.
Interviewed on 27 Oct. 1977; 1 hr.;
1 tape; English; by Roman Bielski.
Głos Tobruku, 8 Dec. 1941. News-
letter issued to Polish soldiers in
Tobruk. .25 cm.

PRZYBYSLAWSKI, FRANK AND JANINA
TORONTO, ONT.
Interviewed on 25 Nov. 1980; 1.5
hrs.; 2 tapes; Polish; by Roman
Bielski. Arrived in Canada in 1947.

PRZYBYSZEWSKA, ANIELA
TORONTO, ONT.
Interviewed on 2 June 1981; 1 hr.; 1
tape; Polish; by Josef Sieramski.
Immigrated to Canada in 1952.

PRZYCHODZKA, BARBARA
TORONTO, ONT.
Interviewed on 18 Sept. 1982; .75
hr.; 1 tape; Polish; by Roman Bielski.
Arrived in Canada in 1981.

PRZYGODA, ZDZISŁAW
TORONTO, ONT.
Papers related to the erection of the
Casimir Gzowski Memorial, 1968;
and brief autobiography of George
W. Janowski, 1897-1978. 2 cm.
Photographs.
21 photographs and one 16 mm
colour film on the erection of the
Casimir Gzowski Memorial, May
1968.
Przygoda, Zd Z. *W Słuzbie Polonii
Kanadyjskiej* (In Service for the
Polish-Canadian). Toronto, 1969. 147
pp.
Turek, Wictor. *Sir Casimir S.
Gzowski*. Toronto, 1957. 109 pp.

PTASZYSKI, P.
SUDBURY, ONT.
Personal documents of late Mr.
Kremer: 1 Polish passport; 1 military
book; 2 school certificates; 1 Canadian passport; letters and clippings,
n.d. 1 cm.

PUACZ, TADEUSZ
SUDBURY, ONT.
Army service certificate and various
cards of Identification, 1944-74. .5
cm. Tape interview.
Interviewed on 30 June 1977; 1 hr.;
1 tape; English; E. Sawicki.

PUCIŁOWSKI, STANLEY
TORONTO, ONT.
Interviewed on 30 Nov. 1977; .5
hr.; 1 tape; English/Polish; by Roman
Bielski. Arrived in Canada in 1946.

PUKLICZ, MIECZYSLAW
WINDSOR, ONT.
Interviewed on 19 June 1982; .75
hr.; 1 tape; Polish; by Roman Bielski.

PUSTKOWSKI, ANTONI
TORONTO, ONT.
Interviewed on 18 Feb. 1978; 2 hrs.;
2 tapes; English; by Roman Bielski.

PYRA, FRANK
OSHAWA, ONT.
Interviewed on 17 Feb. 1982; 2 hrs.;
2 tapes; Polish; by A. Pietrus.
Arrived in Canada in 1949.

PYRA, STEFANIA
OSHAWA, ONT.
Interviewed on 17 Feb. 1982; 1.5
hrs.; 2 tapes; Polish; by A. Pietrus.
Immigrated to Canada in 1949.

PYZIK, TADEUSZ
TORONTO, ONT.
9 photographs: taken during military
service, c. 1940-45. Taped interview.
Interviewed on 3 Jan. 1978; 1 hr.; 1
tape; English; by Roman Bielski.
*Organization of Veterans of the Sec-
ond Polish Corps., 1961-71.* 63 pp.
Jednodniówka, 1961-71. Commemorative publication on the history of
the 2nd Polish Corps. 63 pp.

RABCZAK, WŁADYSŁAW AND HALINA
TORONTO, ONT.
Interviewed on 3 July 1980, 9 Dec.
1982; 1.75 hrs.; 2 tapes; Polish; by
Roman Bielski. Arrived in Canada in
1966.

RĄCZKA, WŁADYSŁAW AND PELAGIA
TORONTO, ONT.
Interviewed on 14 Aug. 1980; 1 hr.;
1 tape; Polish; by Roman Bielski.
Immigrated to Canada in 1947.

RADECKI, FRANK AND EMILIA
TORONTO, ONT.
Interviewed on 14 May 1979; 1.5

hrs.; 2 tapes; Polish; by Roman
Bielski.

RADOMSKI, FELIKS
SUDBURY, ONT.
Interviewed on 18 Aug. 1981; 2
hrs.; 2 tapes; Polish; by A. Pietrus.
Arrived in Canada in 1951.

RADZIMISKI, HENRYK
TORONTO, ONT.
Interviewed on 30 April 1979; 1.5
hrs.; 2 tapes; Polish; by Roman
Bielski.

RAKOWSKA-HARMSTONE, TERESA
OTTAWA, ONT.
Interviewed on 19 June 1980; 1.5
hrs.; 2 tapes; Polish; by Roman
Bielski.,

RAS, WŁADYSŁAW
HAMILTON, ONT.
Interviewed on 31 March 1981; 1
hr.; 1 tape; Polish; by Josef
Sieramski. Immigrated to Canada in
1969.

REZAK, ALEKSANDER
TORONTO, ONT.
Interviewed on 6 April 1981; 2 hrs.;
2 tapes; Polish; by Josef Sieramski.
Immigrated to Canada in 1955.

ROBAK, MICHAŁ
THUNDER BAY, ONT.
Interviewed on 3 July 1978; 2 hrs.; 1
tape; Polish; by G. Kokocinski.

RODAK, JÓZEF
GERALDTON, ONT.
Interviewed on 13 July 1978; 1 hr.;
1 tape; Polish; by G. Kokocinski.
Arrived in Canada in 1949.

ROGACKI, RICHARD AND DONATA
TORONTO, ONT.
Recorded on 29, 31 Jan. 1976; 2
hrs.; 2 tapes; Polish/English; by
Richard and Donata Rogacki. Anony-
mous interview with Polish-Canadian.

ROGÓŻ, STANISŁAW
TORONTO, ONT.
Interviewed on 15 Aug. 1981; 2
hrs.; 2 tapes; Polish; by A. Pietrus.
Arrived in Canada in 1953.

RONIKIER, IRENA
OTTAWA, ONT.
Interviewed on 2 April 1980; 1.5
hrs.; 2 tapes; Polish; by Roman
Bielski.

ROSIEK, TADEUSZ AND CZESŁAWA
TORONTO, ONT.
Interviewed on 7 May 1979; 1.5
hrs.; 2 tapes; Polish; by Roman
Bielski.

ROSISKI, ZBIGNIEW
HAMILTON, ONT.
Interviewed on 29 Nov. 1978; 1 hr.;
1 tape; Polish; by Roman Bielski.

ROSISKI, JAN AND MAŁGORZATA
TORONTO, ONT.
Interviewed on 25 Oct. 1982; .75
hr.; 1 tape; Polish; by Roman Bielski.

ROZWADOWSKY, JERZY
TORONTO, ONT.
Interviewed on 15 Dec. 1978; 1 hr.;
1 tape; Polish; by Roman Bielski.

RUDNICKA, MARIA
HAMILTON, ONT.
Interviewed on 20 March 1979; 2
hrs.; 2 tapes; Polish; by Roman
Bielski.

RUDNICKI, LUDWIK
TORONTO, ONT.
82 photographs: fund-raising event
and ceremonies regarding the monuments and memorials to the Katyn
Massacre, Toronto, 1978. Taped
interview.
Interviewed on 2 Nov. 1978; 1 hr.;
1 tape; Polish; by Roman Bielski.

RUDNICKI, SABINA
TORONTO, ONT.
Interviewed on 2 Nov. 1978; 1 hr.;
1 tape; Polish; by Roman Bielski.

RUDOWICZ, S.
TORONTO, ONT.
Interviewed on 6 Jan. 1978; 1 hr.; 1
tape; Polish; by Roman Bielski.
Arrived in Canada in 1949.

RUPIK, STANISŁAW AND BOŻENA
TORONTO, ONT.
Interviewed on 18 Nov. 1980; 1.5
hrs.; 2 tapes; Polish; by Roman
Bielski.

RUS, HENRYK AND HELENA
TORONTO, ONT.
Interviewed on 10 Nov. 1981; .75
hr.; 1 tape; Polish; by Roman Bielski.
Arrived in Canada in 1949.

RUSIN, JÓZEF
SUDBURY, ONT.
Interviewed on 12 March 1980; 1.5
hrs.; 2 tapes; Polish/English; by I.
Dembek. Immigrated to Canada in
1927.
*Directory of Polish Societies in
Canada.* 1938. 76 pp.

RUSZATA, EDWARD
SUDBURY, ONT.
Interviewed on 12 June 1980; .75

hr.; 1 tape; Polish; by I. Dembek.
Immigrated to Canada in 1959.

RUSZCZYC, BARBARA
TORONTO, ONT.
Interviewed on 14 Jan. 1979; 1 hr.;
1 tape; Polish; by Roman Bielski.

RUSZCZYC, BOGDAN
TORONTO, ONT.
Interviewed on 14 Jan. 1979; 1 hr.;
1 tape; English; by Roman Bielski.

RUSZKOWSKI, ANDRZEJ AND IRENA
OTTAWA, ONT.
Miscellaneous clippings and articles,
1976-79. 1 cm. Taped interview.
Interviewed on 23 Feb. 1980; 2.5
hrs.; 3 tapes; Polish; by Roman
Bielski.

RUTA, CHRISTINA AND MIECZYSŁAW
TORONTO, ONT.
Interviewed on 10 Oct. 1981; 1 hr.;
1 tape; Polish; by Roman Bielski.
Immigrated to Canada in 1974.

RUTKOWSKI, FRANK
TORONTO, ONT.
Interviewed on 20 April 1978; 1.5
hrs.; 2 tapes; Polish; by Roman
Bielski.

RUTKOWSKI, IRENA
SUDBURY, ONT.
Immigration documents, 1947-48,
and newsclippings. .5 cm. Photographs. Taped interview.
32 photographs: Rutkowskis' wedding reception, family parties, as well
as various social functions of the
Polish Combatants' Association, the
Canadian Polish Congress and the
Polish Youth Group, Sudbury,
1940-79.
Interviewed on 28 Feb. 1981;

1.5 hrs.; 2 tapes; Polish; by I.
Dembek.
*Sixth Annual Convention of Polish
Combatants' Association.* 1955. 12
pp.

RYBACZEK, FELIKSA
TORONTO, ONT.
Interviewed on 8 May 1981; 1 hr.; 1
tape; Polish; by Josef Sieramski.
Immigrated to Canada in 1931.

RYBACZEK, STANISŁAW
TORONTO, ONT.
Interviewed on 8 May 1981; 1 hr.; 1
tape; Polish; by Josef Sieramski.
Immigrated to Canada in 1931.

RYBAK, FRANCISZEK
TORONTO, ONT.
Interviewed on 7 Jan. 1978; 1 hr.; 1
tape; Polish; by Roman Bielski.

RYCHLICKI, FELICJA
TORONTO, ONT.
Interviewed on 1 Sept. 1981; 2 hrs.;
2 tapes; Polish; by A. Pietrus. Immigrated to Canada in 1948.

RYCHLICKI, HENRYK
TORONTO, ONT.
Interviewed on 2 Jan. 1978; 2 hrs.; 2
tapes; Polish; by Roman Bielski.

RYCHLIK, BOLESLAW AND HELENA
TORONTO, ONT.
Interviewed on 28 July 1981; 1.5
hrs.; 2 tapes; Polish/English; by
Roman Bielski. Arrived in Canada in
1964.

RYTWISKI, GEORGE
TORONTO, ONT.
Interviewed on 23 Nov. 1978; 1 hr.;
1 tape; Polish; by Roman Bielski.

RZESZUT, S.
THUNDER BAY, ONT.
Interviewed on 31 Dec. 1978; 1 hr.;
1 tape; Polish; by G Kokocinski.
*Golden Jubilee of the Pilsudski
Mutual Benefit Society, 1928-78.*
Thunder Bay, 1978. 29 pp.
*Silver Jubilee of the Polish Mutual
Benefit Society, 1928-53.* Fort
William, 1953. 56 pp.

SADŁOWSKI, JAN
TORONTO, ONT.
Interviewed on 3 Feb. 1982; 2 hrs.;
2 tapes; Polish; by A. Pietrus. Immigrated to Canada in 1951.

SADOWSKI, STANISŁAW
TORONTO, ONT.
Interviewed on 10 Oct. 1978; 1.5
hrs.; 2 tapes; English; by Roman
Bielski.

SADOWSKI, WŁADYSŁAW
TORONTO, ONT.
Interviewed on 2 Feb. 1978; 2 hrs.;
2 tapes; English; by Roman Bielski.

SAKOWSKI, FRANK
TORONTO, ONT.
Carte de membre of the Polish
Alliance in Belgium, 1948-56. Photographs. Taped interview.
3 photographs: Polish Alliance members in Belgium, c. 1945-50.
Interviewed on 20 March 1981; 2
hrs.; 2 tapes; Polish; by Josef
Sieramski. Arrived in Canada in
1951.

SAMBORSKI, EUGENIUSZ
TORONTO, ONT.
Interviewed on 11 June 1978; 1 hr.;
1 tape; English; by Roman Bielski.

SAMULSKI, MARY
SUDBURY, ONT.
Interviewed on 15 July 1977; .25
hr.; 1 tape; Polish; by Theresa
Stankiewicz.

SAMULSKI, SEWERYN AND MARIA
SUDBURY, ONT.
Constitution and by-laws of the
Polish Club, Sudbury, 1935; and
newsclippings pertaining to Polish
· activities in Sudbury, n.d. .5 cm.
Photographs. Taped interview.
Photographs: Germany Graduating
Class and of Polish Club rule book,
n.d.
Interviewed on 14 Jan. 1981; 2 hrs.;
2 tapes; Polish; by I. Dembek.

SAMULSKI, SEWERYN
SUDBURY, ONT.
21 photographs: activities of Polish
refugees in a displaced person's
camp, Germany, 1945-50; most of
Girl Guides. Taped interview.
Interviewed on 8 July 1977; 1 hr.; 1
tape; Polish; by Theresa Stankiewicz.

SAMULSKI, S.
SUDBURY, ONT.
21 photographs: activities of Polish
refugees in a displaced persons'
camp, Germany, 1945-60.

SAS-KORCZYSKI, ALFRED
TORONTO, ONT.
Interviewed on 5 July 1978; 2 hrs.; 2
tapes; Polish; by Roman Bielski.

SAS-KORCZYSKI, LUDWIKA
TORONTO, ONT.
Interviewed on 9 Aug. 1978; 1 hr.; 1
tape; Polish; by Roman Bielski.

SAWICKI, ALEXANDER
FORT FRANCES, ONT.
 Typewritten autobiography of donor, n.d. .25 cm. Photographs. Taped interview.
 6 photographs: members of the Sawicki family, Poland, Fort Frances, 1927-76.
 Interviewed on 11 Sept. 1978; 1 hr.; 1 tape; Polish; by G. Kokocinski. Immigrated to Canada in 1930.

SAWKO, ARKADIUSZ
TORONTO, ONT.
 Interviewed on 10 March 1981; 2 hrs.; 2 tapes; Polish; by Josef Sieramski. Post-WWII immigrant.

SAWKO, MARIA
TORONTO, ONT.
 2 letters of reference, 1939; demobilization letter, 1954, and certificates of military service, n.d. .5 cm. Photographs. Taped interview.
 14 photographs: Mr. Sawko in army, Mrs. Sawko as young girl in Poland, and Mrs. Sawko with family in Canada, 1930-65.
 Interviewed on 10, 13 March 1981; 4 hrs.; 4 tapes; Polish; by Josef Sieramski. Post-WWII immigrant.

SAWOSZCZUK, KAZIMIERZ
TORONTO, ONT.
 Interviewed on 1 March 1978; 2 hrs.; 2 tapes; Polish; by Roman Bielski.

SAWULA, KAROL
TORONTO, ONT.
 Interviewed on 16 May 1981; 2 hrs.; 2 tapes; Polish; by Josef Sieramski. Arrived in Canada in 1929.

SCHABOWSKA, LEOKADIA
TORONTO, ONT.
 Interviewed on 29 April 1980; .75 hr.; 1 tape; Polish; by Roman Bielski. Immigrated to Canada in 1947.

SCHIPPKE, CZESŁAW AND ERYKA
TORONTO, ONT.
 Interviewed on 22 April 1981; 1.5 hrs.; 2 tapes; Polish; by Roman Bielski. Arrived in Canada in 1965.

SCHNAJDER, WŁADYSŁAWA
TORONTO, ONT.
 Interviewed on 4 June 1982; .75 hr.; 1 tape; Polish; by Roman Bielski. Immigrated to Canada in 1952.

SENICA, PIOTR
TORONTO, ONT.
 Interviewed on 6 Jan. 1978; .75 hr.; 1 tape; Polish; by Roman Bielski.

SERGIEJ, BOLESŁAWA
THUNDER BAY, ONT.
 Immigration documents, 1927-29. .5 cm. Photographs. Taped interview.
 8 photographs: the Sergiej family, Poland, Port Arthur, 1928-56.
 Interviewed on 25 May 1978; 1 hr.; 1 tape; Polish; by G. Kokocinski.

SIECZKOWSKI, JÓZEF
TORONTO, ONT.
 Congratulatory letter from G. Legge on the 35th anniversary of the formation of the First Polish Armoured Division, 1977; and newsclipping about the battles of the Polish Armed Forces, 1978. .25 cm. Taped interview.
 Interviewed on 14 June 1978; 2 hrs.; 2 tapes; Polish; by Roman Bielski.

SIEDLECKI, PIOTR
TORONTO, ONT.
Interviewed on 12 Sept. 1977; .5
hr.; 1 tape; English; by Roman
Bielski.

SIELSKI, ELJASZ
RED LAKE, ONT.
Personal papers and photographs,
1946-49. .5 cm. Taped interview.
14 photographs: the Sielski family,
Poland, Germany, Red Lake,
1937-77; and former prisoners of war
and refugees in a displaced persons
camp, Germany, 1942-48.
Interviewed on 15 Oct. 1978; 1 hr.;
1 tape; Polish; by G. Kokocinski.
Immigrated to Canada in 1949.

SIEMIESKI, MARIA
MONTREAL, QUEBEC
Interviewed on 9 Aug. 1978; 1 hr.; 1
tape; Polish; by Roman Bielski.

SIEMIESKI, STANISŁAW
MONTREAL, QUEBEC
Interviewed on 9 Aug. 1978; 1 hr.; 1
tape; English; by Roman Bielski.

SIEMIESKI, WILHELM AND ROZA
MONTREAL, QUEBEC
Interviewed on 2 Aug. 1979; 2.5
hrs.; 3 tapes; Polish; by Roman
Bielski.

SIMON, SOFI
TORONTO, ONT.
Interviewed on 12 June 1981; 1 hr.;
1 tape; Polish; by Josef Sieramski.
Arrived in Canada 1952.

SISCOE, ANNASTASIA
SUDBURY, ONT.
5 photographs: members of the
Polish Association "Sokol," Timmins,
1915, 1972; the Siscoe family, Cisco

Island, 1923. Taped interview.
Interviewed on 5 Oct. 1980; 1.75
hrs.; 2 tapes; Polish; by I. Dembek.
Immigrated to Canada 1914.

SISCOE, JOE
SUDBURY, ONT.
Interviewed on 5 July 1977; .25 hr.;
1 tape; English; by Theresa
Stankiewicz.

SIUDA, FRANK AND JANINA
TORONTO, ONT.
Interviewed on 28 March 1980; 1.5
hrs.; 2 tapes; Polish; by Roman
Bielski. Immigrated to Canada in
1952.

SIUDA, TADEUSZ AND IRENA
TORONTO, ONT.
Interviewed on 4 Feb. 1980; 1.5
hrs.; 2 tapes; Polish; by Roman
Bielski. Immigrated to Canada in
1952.

SKARŻYSKI, ANTONI
MONTREAL, QUEBEC
Interviewed on 10 Aug. 1978; 2
hrs.; 2 tapes; English; by Roman
Bielski.

SKIBISKI, MIKOŁAJ
TORONTO, ONT.
Interviewed on 25 Aug. 1982; .75
hr.; 1 tape; Polish; by Roman Bielski.
Arrived in Canada in 1954.

SKIKIEWICZ, TADEUSZ
TORONTO, ONT.
Interviewed on 16 Jan. 1978; 1 hr.;
1 tape; English; by Roman Bielski.

SKLAZESKI, PETRONELA
THUNDER BAY, ONT.
Personal documents, 1923-39. .5 cm.
Photographs. Taped interview.

6 photographs: family in Thunder Bay, c. 1923-60.
Interviewed on 6 May 1978; 2 hrs.; 2 tapes; Polish; by G. Kokocinski. Immigrated to Canada in 1923.

SKOBKOWICZ, JÓZEF AND ANNA
TORONTO, ONT.
Interviewed on 8 Aug. 1982; .75 hr.; 1 tape; Polish; by Roman Bielski. Immigrated to Canada in 1978.

SKOMRA, BOLESLAW
TORONTO, ONT.
Interviewed on 20 April 1979; 1.5 hrs.; 2 tapes; Polish; by Roman Bielski.

SKOWRONEK, JULIAN AND ANNA
TORONTO, ONT.
Interviewed on 17 Aug. 1980; .75 hr.; 1 tape; Polish; by Roman Bielski. Immigrated to Canada in 1963.

SKRZYPKOWSKI, HENRY
HAMILTON, ONT.
Interviewed on 15 June 1981; 1 hr.; 1 tape; Polish; by Josef Sieramski. Arrived in Canada in 1956.

SKRZYPKOWSKI, HENRYK
HAMILTON, ONT.
Interviewed on 30 March 1981; 2 hrs.; 2 tapes; Polish; by Josef Sieramski. Arrived in Canada in 1956.

SLAWEK, JAN
BRANTFORD, ONT.
Interviewed on 22 June 1981; 1.75 hrs.; 2 tapes; Polish; by Les Wawrow.

ŚLĄZAK, WLADYSLAW AND JANINA
TORONTO, ONT.
Interviewed on 24 May 1982; .5 hr.;

1 tape; Polish; by Roman Bielski. Arrived in Canada in 1982.

SLOMIANY, MIECZYSLAW
OSHAWA, ONT.
Interviewed on 20 June 1981; .75 hr.; 1 tape; Polish; by Roman Bielski. Arrived in Canada in 1960.

SLOMIANY, WLADYSLAW
OSHAWA, ONT.
Interviewed on 20 June 1981; .75 hr.; 1 tape; Polish; by Roman Bielski. Immigrated to Canada in 1955.

SLOWIK, TADEUSZ AND MARIA
TORONTO, ONT.
Interviewed on 2 Dec. 1980; 1 hr.; 1 tape; Polish; by Roman Bielski. Immigrated to Canada in 1956.

SMAGALA, JANUSZ AND BARBARA
TORONTO, ONT.
Interviewed on 6 Jan. 1982; 1.5 hrs.; 2 tapes; Polish; by Roman Bielski. Immigrated to Canada in 1972.

SMAGATA, B.
WELLAND, ONT.
2 photographs: wedding portrait, Poland, 1915; employees of Page Hersey Tubes Ltd., Welland, 1931.

SMOLKA, ANDRZEJ AND NADIA
TORONTO, ONT.
Interviewed on 3 Nov. 1980; .75 hr.; 1 tape; Polish; by Roman Bielski. Immigrated to Canada in 1952.

SMULSKI, MICHAEL
THUNDER BAY, ONT.
Interviewed on 16 June 1978; 2 hrs.; 2 tapes; Polish; by G. Kokocinski. Arrived in Canada in 1928.

SOBOLEWSKI, B.
THUNDER BAY, ONT.
Papers, including historical sketch, on Polish Combatants' Association (S.P.K.) in Thunder Bay, c. 1979s. .5 cm. Photographs. Taped interview.
19 photographs: Branch activity of the Polish Combatants' Association, Thunder Bay, 1961-78.
Interviewed on 20 March 1979; 1 hr.; 1 tape; Polish; by G. Kokocinski.

SOCHA, CZESŁAW AND LEONIA
TORONTO, ONT.
Interviewed on 11 Jan. 1982; 1.5 hrs.; 2 tapes; Polish; by Roman Bielski. Arrived in Canada in 1946.

SOFOREK, ROMAN AND TERESA
TORONTO, ONT.
Interviewed on 12 July 1979; 1.5 hrs.; 2 tapes; Polish; by Roman Bielski.

SOJA, ZDZISŁAW AND MARIA
TORONTO, ONT.
Interviewed on 29 Jan. 1980; 1.5 hrs.; 2 tapes; Polish; by Roman Bielski. Immigrated to Canada in the late 1940s.

SOKOŁOWSKI, TADEUSZ
TORONTO, ONT.
Interviewed on 18 Oct. 1977; 1.5 hrs.; 2 tapes; English; by Roman Bielski.

SOLODZIAK, JÓZEF AND MARIA
TORONTO, ONT.
Interviewed on 18 May 1981; 1.5 hrs.; 2 tapes; Polish; by Roman Bielski. Immigrated to Canada in the 1950s.

SOLSKI, MICHAEL
CONISTON, ONT.
Personal documents and minutes of town council, n.d. .5 cm. Photographs. Taped interview.
3 photographs: opening of St. Stanislaus Church, Copper Cliff, 1900; and men at work in a smelter, Coniston, 1925; "Polish Town," Coniston, c. 1930.
Interviewed on 15 June 1980; .75 hr.; 1 tape; English; by I. Dembek. Immigrated to Canada in 1911.

SOMMERFELD, LEONARD
TORONTO, ONT.
Donor's military papers, 2 Identification documents, 1937, 1946, and stock certificate, 1949. Taped interview.
Interviewed on 5 May 1978; 2 hrs.; 2 tapes; Polish; by Roman Bielski.

SOSIEWICZ, ADOLF AND JANINA
TORONTO, ONT.
Interviewed on 17 Nov. 1980; 1 hr.; 1 tape; Polish; by Roman Bielski. Arrived in Canada in 1948.

SOSIEWICZ, ADOLF AND JANINA
TORONTO, ONT.
Interviewed on 24 Oct. 1979; 1.5 hrs.; 2 tapes; Polish; by Roman Bielski. Arrived in Canada in 1948.

SOSIEWICZ, ADOLF
TORONTO, ONT.
Interviewed on 5 Sept. 1981; 2.5 hrs.; 3 tapes; Polish; by A. Pietrus. Arrived in Canada in 1949.

SOWISKI, STANLEY
TORONTO, ONT.
Interviewed on 30 March 1978; 2 hrs.; 2 tapes; Polish; by Roman Bielski.

SPIWAK, HENRYKA
SUDBURY, ONT.
Interviewed on 4 July 1977; .5 hr.; 1
tape; Polish; E. Sawicki.

SROKA, CZESŁAWA AND BARBARA
TORONTO, ONT.
Interviewed on 5 Sept. 1980; 1 hr.;
1 tape; Polish; by Roman Bielski.

STACHNIUK, MICHAŁ
SUDBURY, ONT.
Interviewed on 3 Dec. 1977; .25 hr.;
1 tape; English; by Roman Bielski.

STACHOWSKI, LEON
TORONTO, ONT.
Interviewed on 3 April 1978; 2 hrs.;
2 tapes; Polish; by Roman Bielski.

STANCLIK, LEOPOLD
TORONTO, ONT.
Interviewed on 14 June 1978; 1.5
hrs.; 2 tapes; English; by Roman
Bielski.

STANKIEWICZ, CASIMIR
TORONTO, ONT.
Interviewed on 15 Dec. 1980; 1 hr.;
1 tape; Polish; by Roman Bielski.
Arrived in Canada in 1952.

STANKIEWICZ, MATILDA
SUDBURY, ONT.
Military and immigration documents,
1940s; also, savings account book and
shares of stock market, 1930-43. .5
cm. Photographs. Taped interview.
5 photographs: Dengler wedding
portrait, Sudbury, 1897; and the
Dengler family, Colbat, Uxbridge,
Sudbury, 1913-47.
Interviewed on 6 July 1977; .25 hr.;
1 tape; English; by Theresa
Stankiewicz.

STANKIEWICZ, MATILDA
TORONTO, ONT.
Interviewed on 12 Dec. 1980; .5 hr.;
1 tape; Polish; by I. Dembek. Immigrated to Canada in 1921.

STARO, MIKOŁAJ
TORONTO, ONT.
Interviewed on 4 May 1981; 2 hrs.;
2 tapes; Polish; by Josef Sieramski.
Arrived in Canada in 1928.

STARUSZKIEWICZ, TADEUSZ AND
KRYSTYNA
TORONTO, ONT.
Interviewed on 19 Aug. 1982; 1.5
hrs.; 2 tapes; Polish; by Roman
Bielski. Arrived in Canada in 1963.

STARZYSKA, ALISIA
TORONTO, ONT.
Interviewed on 29 June 1978; 1 hr.;
1 tape; English/Polish; by J. Stanley.

STARZYSKA, A.
TORONTO, ONT.
The A. Starzyska collection includes
Polish grammar texts; children's
schoolwork and school curricula
material, 1970s; also, records from
M. Curie-Skłodowska School,
1970-77, and theatre material from
M. Kopernik School, 1966-69. .5
meters. Photographs.
15 photographs: activities and exhibitions of Polish schools in Toronto,
1976-77.
Bibliotelczka Nauczyciela. Toronto,
1973. 47 pp.
Elementarz. Warsaw, 1974. 168 pp.
Informator Nauczyciela. Toronto,
1975, 1976. 64 pp.
Język Polski dla Klasy IV. Warsaw,
1969. 212 pp.
Materiały do Inscenizacji. Toronto,
1976. .5 cm.

Polska Mowa. Chicago, 1965. 175 pp.
Pomysl i Zgadnij. Toronto, 1977. 34 pp.
Słownik Tematyczny. Toronto, 1977. 26 pp.
Teacher's Guide, n.d. 168 pp.
Umiem Czytać. Chicago, 1953. 104 pp.

STASZAK, TED AND MARY
TORONTO, ONT.
Interviewed on 4 June 1980; 1 hr.; 1 tape; Polish; by Roman Bielski.
Immigrated to Canada in 1953.

STASZCZYSZYN, JAN AND ZENOBIA
TORONTO, ONT.
Interviewed on 30 June 1981; .75 hr.; 1 tape; Polish; by Roman Bielski.
Arrived in Canada in 1946.

STELMASZYSKI, TADEUSZ AND ALEXANDRA
NIAGARA FALLS, ONT.
Interviewed on 16 Oct. 1979; 2 hrs.; 2 tapes; Polish; by Roman Bielski.

STEMPIE, MIKOŁAJ
SUDBURY, ONT.
Polish passport, 1928, and ship ticket folder, n.d. .25 cm. Photographs. Taped interview.
3 photographs: St. Casimiri's Church, 1957; Polish Club reception, 1957; and visit of Polish airmen, 1941.
Interviewed on 8 Feb. 1980; 1.25 hrs.; 2 tapes; Polish; by I. Dembek.
Immigrated to Canada in 1928.

STOCZAN, PIOTR
TORONTO, ONT.
Interviewed on 18 Feb. 1978; 1 hr.; 1 tape; English; by Roman Bielski.

STOHANDEL, KAZIMIERZ
TORONTO, ONT.
Interviewed on 10 Jan. 1979; 1 hr.; 1 tape; Polish; by Roman Bielski.
Ethnic Link. April 1978. Publication of Canadian Ethnic Scouts. 27 pp.
Our World. Notes about the Polish Scouting Movement in Canada, U.S.A., Australia, and France. 107 pp.

STOHANDEL, ZOFIA
TORONTO, ONT.
Interviewed on 10 Jan. 1979; 1 hr.; 1 tape; Polish; by Roman Bielski.
Wici Harcerskie Kanady. Nos. 112, 113, 1978. 88 pp.
Ethnic Scout Jamboree. Kaszuby, Ontario, 1967. 29 pp.

STOLARSKI, JANINA
TORONTO, ONT.
Interviewed on 14 March 1979; .75 hr.; 1 tape; Polish; by Roman Bielski.

STOLARSKI, LESZEK
TORONTO, ONT.
Interviewed on 14 March 1979; .75 hr.; 1 tape; Polish; by Roman Bielski.
Immigrated to Canada in 1962.

STRASZAK, JERZY AND ELZBIETA
OTTAWA, ONT.
Interviewed on 27 Dec. 1979; 1.5 hrs.; 2 tapes; Polish; by Roman Bielski.

STROJEK, ŁUKASZ AND MARIA
TORONTO, ONT.
Interviewed on 11 Nov. 1980; 1 hr.; 1 tape; Polish; by Roman Bielski.
Immigrated to Canada in 1929.

STROJEK, WŁADYSŁAW AND MARIA
TORONTO, ONT.
Interviewed on 3 March 1981; 1 hr.;

1 tape; Polish; by Roman Bielski.
Arrived in Canada in 1959.

STROJEK, WOJTEK AND HILDEGARD
TORONTO, ONT.
 Interviewed on 3 Nov. 1980; 1.5
hrs.; 2 tapes; Polish/English; by
Roman Bielski. Arrived in Canada in
1951.

STYSISKI, JÓZEFAT
HAMILTON, ONT.
 24 photographs and post cards: concentration camps at Birkenau and
Auschwitz, 1940-45. Taped interview.
 Interviewed on 29 Nov. 1978; 1 hr.;
1 tape; Polish; by Roman Bielski.

SUBDA, ANTONI
TORONTO, ONT.
 Interviewed on 3 June 1981; 1.5
hrs.; 2 tapes; Polish; by Roman
Bielski. Arrived in Canada in 1960.

SUSKA, ANDRZEJ
TORONTO, ONT.
 Interviewed on 8 Nov. 1981; 3 hrs.;
3 tapes; Polish; by A. Pietrus. Immigrated to Canada in 1970.

SWERNIK, ADELIA
SUDBURY, ONT.
 Life story of Joseph Czaja (by Mrs.
Czaja), n.d. .25 cm. Taped interview.
 Interviewed on 18 Feb. 1980; .75
hr.; 2 tapes; English/Polish; by I.
Dembek. Pre-WWI immigrant.

ŚWIDERSKI, EUGENIUSZ AND ZOFIA
TORONTO, ONT.
 Interviewed on 11 July 1981; 1 hr.;
1 tape; Polish; by Roman Bielski.
Immigrated to Canada in 1946.

ŚWIDERSKI, STANISŁAW AND ANNA
TORONTO, ONT.
 Interviewed on 3 Feb. 1982; .75 hr.;
1 tape; Polish; by Roman Bielski.
Arrived in Canada in 1963.

ŚWIDERSKI, TADEUSZ AND
MAŁGORZATA
TORONTO, ONT.
 Interviewed on 12 Sept. 1979; 2
hrs.; 2 tapes; Polish; by Roman
Bielski. Arrived in Canada in 1948.
 Polish Voice. 1979. Newsletter. 12
pp.

ŚWIERCZEK, MARIOLA
TORONTO, ONT.
 Interviewed on 8 July 1982; .5 hr.; 1
tape; Polish; by Roman Bielski.

SWIETOR, ZECKI SZYMON
TORONTO, ONT.
 Interviewed on 9 Feb. 1982; .5 hr.;
1 tape; Polish; by Roman Bielski.
Arrived in Canada in 1976.

SWISTARA, ANNA
TORONTO, ONT.
 Interviewed on 7 April 1981; 2 hrs.;
2 tapes; Polish; by Josef Sieramski.
Immigrated to Canada in 1931.

SYNOWIEC, JÓZEF
TORONTO, ONT.
 Interviewed on 9 Jan. 1978; 2 hrs.; 2
tapes; Polish; by Roman Bielski.

SZARŁOWSKI, STANISŁAW
TORONTO, ONT.
 Interviewed on 24 Nov. 1977, 14
Feb. 1978; 2.75 hrs.; 2 tapes; Polish;
by Roman Bielski.

SZASZEK, RYSZARD
TORONTO, ONT.
Interviewed on 2 Oct. 1978; 1 hr.; 1
tape; Polish; by Roman Bielski.

SZATKOWSKI, TADEUSZ
SUDBURY, ONT.
Interviewed on 3 Dec. 1977; .5 hr.;
1 tape; English; by Roman Bielski.

SZAWIOLA, STANISŁAW
TORONTO, ONT.
Interviewed on 1 Feb. 1978; 2 hrs.;
2 tapes; Polish/Russian; by Roman
Bielski.

SZCZASIUK, BERNARD
TORONTO, ONT.
Interviewed on 7 Nov. 1977; .75
hr.; 1 tape; English; by Roman
Bielski. Arrived in Canada in 1946.

SZCZEPANIK, WERONIKA
HAMILTON, ONT.
Interviewed on 23 March 1981; 1
hr.; 1 tape; Polish; by Josef
Sieramski.

SZCZEPASKI, BRONISŁAW
TORONTO, ONT.
Interviewed on 25 June 1978; 1 hr.;
2 tapes; Polish; by Roman Bielski.

SZCZYGŁOWSKI, ROMAN AND MARIA
TORONTO, ONT.
Interviewed on 9 Feb. 1981; .75 hr.;
1 tape; Polish; by Roman Bielski.
Arrived in Canada in 1950.

SZCZYGŁOWSKI, TADEUSZ
TORONTO, ONT.
Album of printed photographs
covering the activities of the 2nd
Warsaw Armoured Division, Rome,
1946. 300 pp. Taped interview.

Interviewed on 13 Nov. 1977; .75
hr.; 1 tape; English; by Roman
Bielski.

SZELĄŻEK, STANISŁAW AND IRENA
TORONTO, ONT.
Interviewed on 1 April 1982; 1.5
hrs.; 2 tapes; Polish; by Roman
Bielski. Arrived in Canada in 1948.

SZLACHTA, STAN AND JANINA
TORONTO, ONT.
Interviewed on 1 Dec. 1982; .75 hr.;
1 tape; Polish; by Roman Bielski.
Arrived in Canada in 1948.

SZLICHCISKI, ZDIZISŁAW
TORONTO, ONT.
Interviewed on 21 Nov. 1977; 1 hr.;
1 tape; English; by Roman Bielski.

SZNUK, STEFAN
OTTAWA, ONT.
Interviewed on 3 Dec. 1979; 1.5
hrs.; 2 tapes; Polish; by Roman
Bielski.

SZOPIAN, TADEUSZ
TORONTO, ONT.
Interviewed on 4 Dec. 1978; 1 hr.; 1
tape; Polish; by Roman Bielski.

SZPONARSKI, GEORGE
SUDBURY, ONT.
Interviewed on 19 Aug. 1977; 1 hr.;
1 tape; Polish; by L. Sawicki.

SZTRUMF, JADWIGA
TORONTO, ONT.
Interviewed on 17 July 1978; 1 hr.;
1 tape; English/Polish; by J. Stanley.

SZTUKOWSKI, STANISLAW
TORONTO, ONT.
Interviewed on 1 March 1978; 1 hr.;

1 tape; English; by Roman Bielski. Immigrated to Canada in the 1950s.

SZUMILAS, MICHAŁ
TORONTO, ONT.
Interviewed on 5 July 1982; .75 hr.; 1 tape; Polish; by Roman Bielski. Immigrated to Canada in 1928.

SZUMSKI, WŁADYSŁAW AND BARBARA
TORONTO, ONT.
Interviewed on 19 June 1979; 1.5 hrs.; 2 tapes; Polish; by Roman Bielski.

SZWAJKOWSKI, BRONISŁAW AND ZOFIA
TORONTO, ONT.
Interviewed on 19 Jan. 1980; 1 hr.; 1 tape; Polish; by Roman Bielski.

SZYDŁOWSKI, KAZIMIERZ AND ZENONA
TORONTO, ONT.
Interviewed on 21 May 1980; 1.5 hrs.; 2 tapes; Polish; by Roman Bielski. Immigrated to Canada in the late 1950s.

SZYMASKI, H.
TORONTO, ONT.
20th Anniversary of Battle of Monte Casino. Toronto: Ninth Heavy Artillery Division, 1944-64, Polish Veterans, 1964. 68 pp.

SZYMASKI, LESZEK
TORONTO, ONT.
A brief historical sketch of the 4th Polish Regiment of Field Artillery, n.d. Typewritten, in Polish. .25 cm. Taped interview.
Interviewed on 2 Nov. 1977; 1 hr.; 1 tape; English; by Roman Bielski.

SZYMCZUK, MR.
SIMCOE, ONT.
1 photograph: employment in tobacco farming, 1950.

SZYNGIEL, RYSZARD AND WŁADYSŁAWA
TORONTO, ONT.
Interviewed on 26 Oct. 1979; 1.5 hrs.; 2 tapes; Polish; by Roman Bielski.

SZYPKIE, TADEUSZ AND STANISLAWA
TORONTO, ONT.
Interviewed on 8 Dec. 1980; 1.5 hrs.; 2 tapes; Polish; by Roman Bielski. Immigrated to Canada in 1951.

SZYRYSKI, VICTOR
OTTAWA, ONT.
Interviewed on 17 June 1980; 1 hr.; 1 tape; Polish; by Roman Bielski.

TABACZYSKI, JOHN
KITCHENER, ONT.
Pesonal papers and church records from various Roman Catholic parishes in Kitchener and Hamilton, 1847-75. 1 reel of microfilm. Photographs. Taped interview.
16 photographs: Tabaczynski's life in Poland, England and Canada, 1933-52.
Interviewed on 14, 28 March, 30 April 1978; 2 hrs.; 3 tapes; English; by E. Ruge.

TABAKA, WŁADYSŁAW
OTTAWA, ONT.
Interviewed on 2 April 1980; 2 hrs.; 2 tapes; Polish; by Roman Bielski. Immigrated to Canada in 1952.

TARAS, TADEUSZ AND AGNIESZKA
TORONTO, ONT.
Interviewed on 10 Nov. 1979; 1.5
hrs.; 2 tapes; Polish; by Roman
Bielski. Immigrated to Canada in
1961.

TARNOWSKI, KAZIMIERZ
WINDSOR, ONT.
Interviewed on 19 June 1982; .75
hr.; 1 tape; Polish; by Roman Bielski.

TAYLOR, HALINA AND ELŻBIETA
TORONTO, ONT.
Interviewed on 7 May 1980; 1 hr.; 1
tape; Polish; by Roman Bielski.
Immigrated to Canada in 1961.

TEBINKA, A.
THUNDER BAY, ONT.
Programme of the Polish Women's
Club, 1974; 2 congratulatory letters
from the city of Thunder Bay, 1974;
and newsclippings, 1964, 1973, 1974.
.5 cm. Photographs. Taped interview
with A. Tebinka, president of club.
5 photographs: activities of the Polish Women's Club in Thunder Bay,
c. 1954-74.
Interviewed on 25 March 1979; 1
hr.; 1 tape; Polish; by G. Kokocinski.

TEBINKA, STANISŁAW
THUNDER BAY, ONT.
Military certificates and
newsclippings, 1946-51. .5 cm. Photographs. Taped interview.
6 photographs: Tebinka family members, Italy, Thunder Bay, 1943-76.
1 photograph: the 7th General Convention of the Canadian Polish Congress, 29-30 Oct. 1955, Brantford.
Interviewed on 23 Jan. 1979; 2 hrs.;
2 tapes; Polish; by G. Kokocinski.
Arrived in Canada in 1946.

TEHMAN, WŁADEK AND ANNA
TORONTO, ONT.
Interviewed on 10 Oct. 1979; 1.5
hrs.; 2 tapes; Polish; by Roman
Bielski. Immigrated to Canada in
1949.

TELESZ, HALINA
TORONTO, ONT.
Interviewed on 6 April 1979; .75
hr.; 1 tape; Polish; by Roman Bielski.

TELESZ, TADEUSZ
TORONTO, ONT.
Interviewed on 6 April 1979; .75
hr.; 1 tape; Polish; by Roman Bielski.

TERKA, CZESŁAW AND JADWIGA
TORONTO, ONT.
Interviewed on 16 Feb. 1981; 1 hr.;
1 tape; Polish; by Roman Bielski.

TODKULSKI, JÓZEF
SUDBURY, ONT.
Interviewed on 3 Dec. 1977; .5 hr.;
1 tape; English; by Roman Bielski.

TOLLOCZKO, IGOR
TORONTO, ONT.
Interviewed on 18 March 1978; 2
hrs.; 2 tapes; English; by Roman
Bielski.

TOMCZYK, MARIAN
SUDBURY, ONT.
Interviewed on 3 Dec. 1977; .25 hr.;
1 tape; English; by Roman Bielski.
Arrived in Canada in 1953.

TOPOLNICKI, JULIAN
TORONTO, ONT.
The Julian Topolnicki collection
spans the period from the 1930s
through the 1970s, and its
wide-ranging material covers numerous Polish organizations in major

cities across Canada. These include the Canadian Polish Congress, Friends of the Polish Sea, Federation of Polish Societies, National Defence Fund Committee, Holy Trinity Church in Montreal, and the Canadian Polish Welfare Institute. Complementing the books of minutes, annual reports, financial records, bulletins, and correspondence are photographs. 1.5 meter. Finding aid available.

110 photographs: 1932-52, mostly of people, organizations and festivities. Montreal, Toronto, Windsor, and Edmonton are the principal settings. Numerous organizations are covered: Association of Poles Abroad, Polish Section of the Red Cross, Polish Catholic League, Polish National Trust, Sons of Poland, Polish Relief and Defence Committee, White Eagle Society, and Polish War Veterans Society. Two photographs are of particular historical significance—the Convention at which the Canadian Polish Congress was formed, Toronto, 1944; and the Third Convention of the Federation of Polish Societies in Canada, Hamilton, 1934.

TOPOLSKI, BOGUSŁAW
OTTAWA, ONT.
 Interviewed on 2 Dec. 1979; .5 hr.; 1 tape; Polish; by Roman Bielski. Arrived in Canada in 1957.

TRZCISKI, J.
RANDON, QUEBEC
 Interviewed on 23 Aug. 1979; 1.5 hrs.; 2 tapes; Polish; by Roman Bielski. Arrived in Canada in 1951.

TUKALSKI, BERLACH AND MARIA
OTTAWA, ONT.
 Interviewed on 30 Dec. 1979; 1 hr.;

1 tape; Polish; by Roman Bielski. Arrived in Canada in 1948.

TULECKI, KAZIMIERZ
TORONTO, ONT.
 Interviewed on 20 July 1978; 2 hrs.; 2 tapes; Polish; by Roman Bielski.

TUMANOWSKI, JAN
SUDBURY, ONT.
 2 Millenium programmes, 1966; concert programme, 1965; newsclippings, 1959, 1966, 1971, 1974, 1977; Polish Combatants' Association diploma, n.d., and a membership card, 1953. 1 cm. Photographs. Taped interview.
 14 photographs: Polish soccer in Sudbury, 1955; Polish veterans working on farms, 1949; Polish Combatants' Association, No. 24, 1954; Polish dance group, Syrena, 1959; and Paderewski Choir, Ottawa, 1965.
 Interviewed on 3 Dec. 1977, 4 March 1978; 1.5 hr.; 2 tapes; English/Polish; by Roman Bielski.

TURCZYNIAK, FRANCISZEK
TORONTO, ONT.
 Interviewed on 24 Sept. 1981; 1.5 hrs.; 2 tapes; Polish; by A. Pietrus. Arrived in Canada in 1964.

TURCZYSKI, STANISŁAW
TORONTO, ONT.
 Interviewed on 14 Aug. 1981; 2.5 hrs.; 3 tapes; Polish; by A. Pietrus. Arrived in Canada in 1947.

TURZASKÍ, WŁADYSŁAW
TORONTO, ONT.
 Interviewed on 21 Oct. 1977; 2 hrs.; 2 tapes; English; by Roman Bielski.

TWARÓG, FRANCISZEK AND KRYSTYNA
TORONTO, ONT.
2 photographs: with Pope John Paul II, Rome, c. 1970-80. Taped interview.
Interviewed on 9 Feb. 1982; 1 hr.; 1 tape; Polish; by Roman Bielski. Immigrated to Canada in 1948.

TWOREK, JAN AND ANIELA
TORONTO, ONT.
Interviewed on 23 Sept. 1979; 1 hr.; 1 tape; Polish; by Roman Bielski.

TYBURA, MICHAŁ
SUDBURY, ONT.
Interviewed on 3 Dec. 1977; .5 hr.; 1 tape; English; by Roman Bielski.

TYRSZ, STANISŁAW
TORONTO, ONT.
Interviewed on 21 Nov. 1982; .75 hr.; 1 tape; Polish; by Roman Bielski. Immigrated to Canada in 1965.

TYSIĄCZNY, LEON
TORONTO, ONT.
Interviewed on 7 Dec. 1982; 1.5 hrs.; 2 tapes; Polish/English; by Roman Bielski. Arrived in Canada in 1951.

TYSZKIEWICZ, ANDRZEJ
RANDON, QUEBEC
Interviewed on 8 Aug. 1978; 1 hr.; 1 tape; Polish; by Roman Bielski.

TYSZKIEWICZ, ELŻBIETA
RANDON, QUEBEC
Interviewed on 8 Aug. 1978; .5 hr.; 1 tape; Polish; by Roman Bielski.

UFNAL, ZBIGNIEW AND ELŻBIETA
TORONTO, ONT.
Interviewed on 14 Oct. 1981;

.75 hr.; 1 tape; Polish; by Roman Bielski. Immigrated to Canada in 1963.

UIBERALL, JANUSZ
TORONTO, ONT.
Krzyk (Outcry). Sept. 1974 - March 1978 (monthly, 32 issues). Complete. 1 reel of microfilm.

UJEJSKA, WANDA
TORONTO, ONT.
Interviewed on 14 Dec. 1978; 2 hrs.; 2 tapes; English; by Roman Bielski.

UJEJSKI, JERZY
TORONTO, ONT.
Interviewed on 5 Jan. 1979; 1 hr.; 1 tape; English; by Roman Bielski.

UJEJSKI, STANISŁAW
TORONTO, ONT.
Interviewed on 14 Oct. 1978; 1.5 hrs.; 2 tapes; Polish; by Roman Bielski. Arrived in Canada in 1957.

URBANOWICZ, MARIAN
TORONTO, ONT.
Interviewed on 14 Dec. 1978; 1 hr.; 1 tape; English; by Roman Bielski.

URBASKA, PAULINA
TORONTO, ONT.
Interviewed on 2 Sept. 1981; 1 hr.; 1 tape; Polish; by A. Pietrus. Arrived in Canada in 1969.

VORONICH, HELTIA
SUDBURY, ONT.
Interviewed on 29 June 1977; 1.5 hrs.; 2 tapes; Polish; E. Sawicki.

WACH, JAN
TORONTO, ONT.
 Interviewed on 24 March 1981; 2
hrs.; 2 tapes; Polish; by Josef
Sieramski.

WACHNIK, EMILIA
TORONTO, ONT.
 Interviewed on 10 Aug. 1982; .5 hr.;
1 tape; Polish; by Roman Bielski.
Arrived in Canada in 1965.

WACKO, JAN
TORONTO, ONT.
 Interviewed on 20 July 1981; .75
hr.; 1 tape; Polish; by Roman Bielski.
Arrived in Canada in 1963.

WACYK, EDWARD AND ZUZANNA
TORONTO, ONT.
 Interviewed on 16 July 1980; 1 hr.;
1 tape; Polish; by Roman Bielski.
Arrived in Canada in 1948.

WACYK, JÓZEF
TORONTO, ONT.
 Interviewed on 20 Feb. 1979; 1.5
hrs.; 2 tapes; Polish; by Roman
Bielski.

WALCZAK, STEFAN
TORONTO, ONT.
 Interviewed on 10 June 1979; 1.5
hrs.; 2 tapes; Polish; by Roman
Bielski.
 *Thirty Years of the Auxiliary Air
Force in England, 1943-73.* Toronto,
1973. 57 pp.

WALCZAK, WINCENTY
TORONTO, ONT.
 Interviewed on 14 April 1981; 2 hrs;
2 tapes; Polish; by Josef Sieramski.
Immigrated to Canada in 1948.

WALENSKA, COLONNA
RANDON, QUEBEC
 Interviewed on 19 Aug. 1979; 1 hr.;
1 tape; Polish; by Roman Bielski.

WANTOTA, W.
WELLAND, ONT.
 Ship card, *S.S. Megantic*, 1928;
Immigration Identification card, 1928;
and health certificate, 1926. .25 cm.
Photographs.
 11 photographs: pre- and
post-emigration, portraits and personal documents of the Wantota
family, Poland, Welland, 1926-50.

WANTUCH, ANDRZEJ
SUDBURY, ONT.
 Interviewed on 9 Dec. 1977; 1 hr.; 1
tape; English; by Roman Bielski.

WARDACH, ROCH
OSHAWA, ONT.
 Interviewed on 21 Nov. 1981; .75
hr.; 1 tape; Polish; by Roman Bielski.
Arrived in Canada in 1950.

WARENDA, JAN
SUDBURY, ONT.
 Army book, 1919; health certificate,
1933; and 2 identification cards, n.d.
. 5 cm. Photographs.
 2 photographs: donor upon arrival in
Canada, n.d.

WARJAS, ZYGMUNT AND STEFANIA
TORONTO, ONT.
 Interviewed on 31 Aug. 1982; .75
hr.; 1 tape; Polish; by Roman Bielski.
Arrived in Canada in 1953.

WAROCZEWSKI, ALEXANDER
TORONTO, ONT.
 Interviewed on 7 April 1978; 3 hrs.;
3 tapes; Polish; by Roman Bielski.

WARSZAWSKA, DANUTA
TORONTO, ONT.
A collection of students' question-
naires on why they chose to study
Polish, 1976-78. 2 cm. Taped inter-
view.
Interviewed on 6 Oct. 1978; 1 hr.; 1
tape; English; by J. Stanley.

WASIUK, JOSEPHINE AND KRYSTYNA
TORONTO, ONT.
Interviewed on 5 Aug. 1982; 1 hr.; 1
tape; English; by Roman Bielski.

WAWROW, LES
TORONTO, ONT.
The bulk of the Les Wawrow collection is comprised of printed material:
Polish grammar texts, most of them
pulished by the Association of Polish
Teachers in Canada; Polish history
books published in Warsaw and London, England; as well as Polish periodicals and com-memorative booklets
from Toronto and Hamilton as listed
below. In addition, there are papers
pertaining to the 1978 municipal election in Ward 11, Parkdale, Toronto;
pamphlets, clippings, and financial
statements from 1976-79 elections; as
well as miscellaneous items from the
Polish (Toronto) Credit Union,
1970s. 20 cm. Photograph.
1 photograph: S. Januszko, Toronto,
1980.
*25 Rocznica Założenia Polskiej
Y.M.C.A.* (25th Anniversary of the
Polish Y.M.C.A.). Toronto, 1947. 48
pp.
*25th Anniversary of the Pastorate of
Father Capiga.* Hamilton, 1974.
.5 cm.
*Biuletin Nauczycielstwa Polskiego w
Kanadzie.* No. 46, 1973; no. 50,
1978. .5 cm.
Ćwiczenia z gramatyki i pisowni

Polskiej na kl. VI.. St. Casimiri's
Polish School. n.d. 24 pp.
Echo Magazine. Vol. 1, no. 1, 1970
- vol. 5, no. 26, 1976 (24 issues). 9
cm.
Książka o Polisce. Association of
Polish Teachers in Canada. 1966. 489
pp.
*Informator Nauczyciela Szkół
Polskich w Kanadzie.* No. 1, 1973;
no. 2, 1975; no. 3, 1977.
Pomyśl i zgadnij. Toronto, 1977.
Association of Polish Teachers in
Canada. 34 pp.
Słownik Tematyczny. Toronto, 1977.
Association of Polish Teachers in
Canada. 26 pp.
Spółdzielca. No. 1, March 1979.
Polish Alliance (Toronto) Credit
Union Ltd. (quarterly). .5 cm.
Twoje Dziecko. Toronto, 1975.
Toronto Board of Education. 14 pp.

WAWROW, WINCENTY
TORONTO, ONT.
Interviewed on 5, 17 March 1981; 4
hrs; 4 tapes; Polish; by Josef
Sieramski. Post-WWII immigrant.

WAWRZONEK, CZESŁAW
TORONTO, ONT.
Interviewed on 1 Sept. 1981; 2 hrs.;
2 tapes; Polish; by A. Pietrus. Immigrated to Canada in 1962.

WAWRZONEK, KAZIK
TORONTO, ONT.
Over 1300 photographs and contact
prints: depicting areas, activities, and
prominent members of the Polish
Toronto community, c. 1960-80.
Topics include street scenes, artists
and entertainment, the publication
Echo and the group Arabeska.

WĘGLARZ, BRUNO AND IRENA
TORONTO, ONT.
 Interviewed on 21 Sept. 1982; 1 hr.;
1 tape; Polish; by Roman Bielski.
Arrived in Canada in 1963.

WIECZOREK, FELIX
TORONTO, ONT.
 Interviewed on 27 Oct. 1977; 1 hr.;
1 tape; English; by Roman Bielski.

WIECZOREK, TOMASZ
WELLAND, ONT.
 Canadian immigration documents
(photographed) and medical certifi-
cates related to donor's stay at D.P.
camps in Germany, 1945-48; also, a
public notice for school meeting,
1915. .5 cm (15 items).
 Walpole, Hugh R. *Foundations of
English for Foreign Students*. Chica-
go, 1946. 55 pp.
 Fakty o Kanadzie (Facts about
Canada). Ottawa, 1947. 19 pp.
 Learning the English Language.
Canada, 1948. 32 pp.
 Trzydzieści Lekcyj (Thirty Lessons).
Nos. 11, 12, 13, 15, n.d. 39 pp.

WIEJAK, WALTER
THUNDER BAY, ONT.
 Personal documents 1939-47, including certificate of contract completion
from Department of Labour, Canada,
1949; and membership card of Canadian Legion of B.E.S.L., 1949. .5
cm. Photographs. Taped interview.
 22 photographs: W. Wiejak in Polish
army, 1937; as D.P. worker in Germany, 1945; in a bush camp in
Canada, 1947; and wedding and
family pictures, 1950s-1970s.
 Interviewed on 19 Nov. 1978; 2
hrs.; 2 tapes; Polish; by G.
Kokocinski. Immigrated to Canada in
1947.

WIENCEK, STANISŁAW
LEVACH, ONT.
 Assorted paper items: list of Poles in
Sudbury, 1969; material related to
Poland's Millenium of Christianity
(appeal, list of donors, clippings, and
leaflets), 1966; Steelworkers' leaflet,
1965; papers from St. Casimir
Church in Sudbury (regulations,
bulletins, clippings, correspondence,
programmes, and announcements),
1959, 1960s; records from the Canadian Polish Congress (minutes,
report, announcements, and invitations) 1963, 1964, 1969; bulletins,
report and clippings from the Polish
Combatants' Association, 1969-73;
correspondence and list of donors
from the "White Eagle" Polish Sports
Club. Also, miscellaneous items:
parody of Red Army programme,
1970, brochure on Exchance Programme KUL and U.L., 1979, and
poster of Malcuzynski's concert, n.d.
5 cm. Photographs. Taped interview.
 7 photographs: activities of the
"White Eagle" Sports Club, 1953-68;
Polish school, 1963-66; a Polish
Alliance of Canada Christmas party,
1969, all taken in Sudbury.
 Interviewed on 27 Feb. 1980; .5 hr.;
1 tape; Polish; by I. Dembek.
Arrived in Canada in 1950.

WIESZCZYCKI, JERZY
HAMILTON, ONT.
 Interviewed on 29 Nov. 1978; 1 hr.;
1 tape; Polish; by Roman Bielski.

WIESZCZYCKI, G.
HAMILTON, ONT.
 Material pertaining to Warsaw Royal
Castle Reconstruction Fund organized
by the Polish Congress in
Hamilton—reports, list of donors,
appeals for donations, correspon-

dence, and by-laws, 1972-78. 1 cm.
"The Royal Castle in Warsaw."
Hamilton, n.d. .5 cm.

WIJAC, ALBIN
TORONTO, ONT.
Interviewed on 25 July 1978; 1 hr.;
1 tape; English; by Roman Bielski.

WILCZYSKI, JAN
TORONTO, ONT.
Interviewed on 8 Nov. 1977; .75
hr.; 1 tape; English; by Roman
Bielski.

WILK, ANTONI
SUDBURY, ONT.
Interviewed on 3 Dec. 1977; .5 hr.;
1 tape; English; by Roman Bielski.

WILK, STEFANIA
TORONTO, ONT.
Interviewed on 30 June 1982; 1 hr.;
1 tape; Polish; by Roman Bielski.
Arrived in Canada in 1929.

WILL, ALFONS
TORONTO, ONT.
Interviewed on 29 Oct. 1980; 1 hr.;
1 tape; Polish; by Roman Bielski.
Immigrated to Canada in 1968.

WILOWSKI, JAN AND EMILIA
TORONTO, ONT.
Interviewed on 29 Aug. 1981; 1 hr.;
1 tape; Polish; by Roman Bielski.
Arrived in Canada in 1964.

WINIARZ, TADEUSZ AND MARIA
TORONTO, ONT.
Interviewed on 6 Sept. 1982; 1.5
hrs.; 2 tapes; Polish; by Roman
Bielski. Immigrated to Canada in
1959.

WINISZEWSKI, FRANK
TORONTO, ONT.
Interviewed on 5 Nov. 1977; 1 hr.;
1 tape; Polish; by Roman Bielski.

WIŚNIEWSKI, STANISŁAW
TORONTO, ONT.
Interviewed on 21 Sept. 1981; 2
hrs.; 2 tapes; Polish; by A. Pietrus.
Immigrated to Canada in 1965.

WISNIEWSKI, STANISLAW
TORONTO, ONT.
Interviewed on 1 March 1978; 1 hr.;
1 tape; Polish; by Roman Bielski.

WITAMBORSKI, LONGIN AND
ANTONINA
TORONTO, ONT.
Interviewed on 11 Nov. 1981; 1 hr.;
1 tape; Polish; by Roman Bielski.
Arrived Canada in 1952.

WITKOWSKI, JOHN
WELLAND, ONT.
5 photographs: family and friends of
J. Witkowski, Hamilton, Boston
Creek, Kirkland Lake; and employment in mining at Kirkland Lake,
1934.

WŁADYCZASKI, WACŁAW
TORONTO, ONT.
Interviewed on 13 Oct. 1981; 2 hrs.;
2 tapes; Polish; by A. Pietrus.
Arrived in Canada in 1967.

WŁODARCZYK, STEFAN AND WANDA
TORONTO, ONT.
Interviewed on 13 Aug. 1980; 2
hrs.; 2 tapes; Polish; by Roman
Bielski. Arrived in Canada in 1956.

WNUK, LAWRENCE
WINDSOR, ONT.
Interviewed on 18 June 1982; 2 hrs.;
2 tapes; Polish; by Roman Bielski.

WOJCIECHOWSKI, JERZY ANTONI
OTTAWA, ONT.
Miscellaneous paper items, 1975-80.
.5 cm. Taped interview.
Interviewed on 3 April 1980; 2 hrs.;
2 tapes; Polish; by Roman Bielski.
Arrived in Canada in 1949.

WOJCIECHOWSKI, KLIM AND
BRONISŁAWA
TORONTO, ONT.
Interviewed on 3 June 1982; 1 hr.; 1
tape; Polish; by Roman Bielski.
Arrived in Canada in 1960.

WOJCIECHOWSKI, WŁADYSŁAW
AZILDA, ONT.
Immigration papers and I.R.O. let-
ter, 1950. .25 cm. Taped interview.
Interviewed on 23 Jan 1980; 1 hr.; 1
tape; Polish; by I. Dembek.

WOJCIESZEK, JÓZEF
TORONTO, ONT.
Interviewed on 1 July 1978; 1 hr.; 1
tape; English; by Roman Bielski.

WÓJCIK, JÓZEF AND ZOFIA
TORONTO, ONT.
Interviewed on 26 Oct. 1981; 1.5
hrs.; 2 tapes; Polish; by Roman
Bielski. Arrived in Canada in 1947.

WOJDA, STANISŁAW AND KATARZYNA
TORONTO, ONT.
Interviewed on 7 Sept. 1981; 1.5
hrs.; 2 tapes; Polish; by Roman
Bielski. Arrived in Canada in 1948.

WOJNAR, ANNA
OSHAWA, ONT.
Interviewed on 21 Nov. 1981; .75
hr.; 1 tape; Polish; by Roman Bielski.
Arrived in Canada in 1948.

WOJS, JÓZEF AND CECYLIA
TORONTO, ONT.
Medical statements, 1946; letter to
the military government in Heilbronn,
1946; and certificate from the Polish
Department in Heilbronn, 1947. .5
cm. Taped interview.
Interviewed on 1 May 1979; 2 hrs.;
2 tapes; Polish; by Roman Bielski.

WOJTALA, BRONSIŁAWA
HAMILTON, ONT.
Interviewed on 30 March 1981; 2
hrs.; 2 tapes; Polish; by Josef
Sieramski. Arrived in Canada in
1929.

WOJTASIK, STANISŁAW
TORONTO, ONT.
2 army identification papers, 1939,
1942. .25 cm. Taped interview.
Interviewed on 14 Nov. 1977; 1 hr.;
1 tape; English/Polish; by Roman
Bielski.

WOJTKOWIAK, REV. WOJCIECH
TORONTO, ONT.
Interviewed on 10 Jan. 1980; 1.5
hrs.; 2 tapes; Polish; by Roman
Bielski. Arrived in Canada in 1977.
*Sunday Bulletin of St. Casimir's Par-
ish.* Toronto, 1979, 1980. .25 cm.

WOJTOWICZ, WŁADYSŁAW
TORONTO, ONT.
Interviewed on 15 May 1981; 2 hrs.;
2 tapes; Polish; by Josef Sieramski.
Arrived in Canada in 1948.

WOLAK, J.
WELLAND, ONT.
Interviewed on 2 photographs: members of the Wolak family, Welland, c. 1930-40.

WOLICKI, ANTONI AND JADWIGA
TORONTO, ONT.
Interviewed on 10 May 1980; 1 hr.; 1 tape; Polish; by Roman Bielski. Immigrated to Canada in 1966.

WOŁNIK, BRONISLAW
OSHAWA, ONT.
Interviewed on 20 June 1981; .75 hr.; 1 tape; Polish; by Roman Bielski. Arrived in Canada in 1949.

WOLNIK, MICHAEL
TORONTO, ONT.
Interviewed on 15 April 1978; 1 hr.; 1 tape; English; by Roman Bielski.

WOLNIK, MICHALINA
TORONTO, ONT.
Interviewed on 20 Jan. 1982; 2 hrs.; 2 tapes; Polish; by A. Pietrus. Immigrated to Canada in 1949.

WOLNIK, MICHALINA
TORONTO, ONT.
Interviewed on 15 April 1978; 1 hr.; 1 tape; Polish; by Roman Bielski.

WOLNIK, MICHALINA
TORONTO, ONT.
Interviewed on 23 June 1978; 1 hr.; 1 tape; English/Polish; by J. Stanley.

WOLNIK, MICHALINA
TORONTO, ONT.
The collection includes textbooks used in Polish language classes, school notebooks, Polish short plays, books printed in Poland before WWII, and files on Invalids' Com-

mission, the Polish Teachers' Association and the Polish Scouts' Association, 1920s-1970s. .5 meters. Photographs.
21 photographs: activities in Toronto's post-WWII Polish language schools.
Maskoff, Józef. *W. Dąbrowie Górniczej.* Lwow, 1920. 3 pp. play.
Popiel, Zofia. *Szopka Polskiego Tułacza.* Toronto, 1958. A play written for Polish evening schools. 14 pp.
Wrzos, Bonifacy. *Strażacy.* n.d. 7 pp.
Aby nasze dzieci mówiły po polsku. London, 1951. 12 pp.
Bulletin of the Polish Teachers' Association. Nos. 6, 11, 12, 1963-67 (3 issues).
Dziatwa (Children). 1952-70. 5 cm.
Wiselka. Nos. 7-8, 1963. 21 pp.
Wychowanie Ojczyste. London, 1952-72. 4 cm.

WOLNIK, MICHAŁ
TORONTO, ONT.
Personal documents and correspondence, c. 1940s. 1 cm (42 items). Taped interview.
Interviewed on 4 March and 10 April 1981; 4 hrs.; 4 tapes; Polish; by Josef Sieramski. Arrived in Canada in 1948.

WOŁOSZCZAK, STEFAN AND ANIELA
TORONTO, ONT.
Interviewed on 9 Dec. 1981; .75 hr.; 1 tape; Polish; by Roman Bielski. Immigrated to Canada in 1947.

WOŁOSZCZAK, WŁADYSŁAW
TORONTO, ONT.
12 photographs: group portraits of members of the Polish Alliance of Canada, folk dancers and children in

public and Polish schools, Toronto,
1935-65. Taped interview.
Interviewed on 5 March 1981; 2
hrs.; 2 tapes; Polish; by Josef
Sieramski.

WOTAWA, KAZIMIERZ
HAMILTON, ONT.
Interviewed on 29 Nov. 1978; 1 hr.;
1 tape; Polish; by Roman Bielski.

WOYZBUN, JERZY AND HANNA
TORONTO, ONT.
Interviewed on 11 July 1979; 1.5
hrs.; 2 tapes; Polish; by Roman
Bielski.

WOZNICZKA, FRANK
TORONTO, ONT.
Interviewed on 9 Sept. 1980; 1 hr.;
1 tape; Polish; by Roman Bielski.
Arrived in Canada in 1946.

WRÓBEL, JERZY
TORONTO, ONT.
Interviewed on 9 Feb. 1982; 2 hrs.;
2 tapes; Polish; by A. Pietrus. Parents emigrated in 1946.

WRÓBEL, STANISŁAW
SUDBURY, ONT.
Interviewed on 16 Aug. 1981; 1 hr.;
1 tape; Polish; by A. Pietrus. Immigrated to Canada in the 1940s.

WRÓBLEWSKI, ANTONI
TORONTO, ONT.
2 brief accounts regarding the activities of the Polish Uhlans during
WWII, n.d. .25 cm., in Polish.
Taped interview.
Interviewed on 9 Jan. 1978; 2 hrs.; 2
tapes; English; by Roman Bielski.

WRZODAK, KAZIMIERZ
TORONTO, ONT.
Interviewed on 14 June, 19 July
1978; 4 hrs.; 4 tapes; Polish; by
Roman Bielski.

WUR, JULIA
TORONTO, ONT.
Interviewed on 3 June 1981; 1 hr.; 1
tape; Polish; by Josef Sieramski.
Arrived in Canada in 1928.

WYGNANIEC, BOLESŁAW AND LILA
TORONTO, ONT.
Interviewed on 11 Aug. 1980; 1.5
hrs.; 2 tapes; Polish; by Roman
Bielski. Immigrated to Canada in
1952.

WYKURZ, WŁADYSŁAW
SUDBURY, ONT.
Interviewed on 3 Dec. 1977; .25 hr.;
1 tape; English; by Roman Bielski.

WYPIEWSKI, WOJCIECH
TORONTO, ONT.
Interviewed on 24 Nov. 1978; 1 hr.;
1 tape; Polish; by Roman Bielski.

WYPYCH, ZBIGNIEW AND URSZULA
TORONTO, ONT.
Interviewed on 18 May 1982; 1.5
hrs.; 2 tapes; Polish; by Roman
Bielski. Arrived in Canada in 1976.

WYRZYKOWSKI, ZENON
TORONTO, ONT.
Interviewed on 1 Nov. 1978; 3 hrs.;
3 tapes; Polish; by Roman Bielski.

WYSOCKA, STANISŁAWA
TORONTO, ONT.
Interviewed on 26 Feb. 1981; .75
hr.; 1 tape; Polish; by Roman Bielski.
Arrived in Canada in 1953.

YANKOWSKI, J.
SUDBURY, ONT.
Newsclippings, 1940s-1960s. .5 cm.

YAVORSKI, O.
TORONTO, ONT.
 Passport and marriage certificate of
Franciszka Mazurkiewicz, 1922;
Polish bonds, 1920; and letter from
Customs and Excise, Canada, permit-
ting John Kuzyk to brew beer, 1927.
.5 cm. Photographs.
 5 photographs: including 1 wedding
picture of Frances Mazurkiewicz and
J. Kuzyk, Fort Frances, 1922-30.

YEDLINSKA, BARBARA
WINDSOR, ONT.
 Interviewed on 19 June 1982; .5 hr.;
1 tape; Polish; by Roman Bielski.

ZABORSKI, BOGDAN
OTTAWA, ONT.
 Interviewed on 2 Dec. 1979; 1.5
hrs.; 2 tapes; Polish; by Roman
Bielski.

ZAHARYASZ, ALBIN AND GIZELA
TORONTO, ONT.
 Interviewed on 2 June 1981; 1 hr.; 1
tape; Polish; by Roman Bielski.
Arrived in Canada in 1964.

ŻAK, JAN
TORONTO, ONT.
 Interviewed on 9 Nov. 1981; 1.5
hrs.; 2 tapes; Polish; by A. Pietrus.
Immigrated to Canada in 1949.

ZALESKA, STANISŁAWA
TORONTO, ONT.
 Interviewed on 24 Aug. 1982; .5 hr.;
1 tape; Polish; by Roman Bielski.
Immigrated to Canada in 1959.

ZALEWSKI, EDWARD AND LEONIDA
OSHAWA, ONT.
 Interviewed on 21 Nov. 1981; 1 hr.;
1 tape; Polish; by Roman Bielski.
Arrived in Canada in 1955.

ZALUTYSKA, WANDA
TORONTO, ONT.
 Interviewed on 25 Aug. 1978; 2
hrs.; 2 tapes; Polish; by Roman
Bielski.

ZAMOYSKA, JADWIGA
RANDON, QUEBEC
 Interviewed on 8 Aug. 1979; 1.5
hrs.; 2 tapes; Polish; by Roman
Bielski. Immigrated to Canada in
1948.

ZAPIOR, WINCENTY
THUNDER BAY, ONT.
 Personal documents of donor and
spouse, 1920-35. .25 cm. Photographs. Taped interview.
 3 photographs: Zapior family,
Poland, Thunder Bay, c. 1930-42.
 6 photographs: activities of the Polish Alliance of Canada in Thunder
Bay, Branch 19, 1965-78.
 Interviewed on 12 June 1978, 23
March 1979; 3 hrs.; 3 tapes; Polish;
by G. Kokocinski. Arrived in Canada
in 1930.

ZAREMBA, JAN
TORONTO, ONT.
 Donor's memoirs from service in the
14th Division Horse Artillery in Sept.
1939 campaign, 1977. .25 cm. Taped
interview.
 Interviewed on 12 Dec. 1977; .75
hr.; 1 tape; English; by Roman
Bielski.

ZAREMBA, ROMAN
TORONTO, ONT.
Interviewed on 3 Aug. 1981; 1 hr.; 1
tape; Polish; by Roman Bielski.
Arrived in Canada in 1966.

ZARYCKA, REGINA
TORONTO, ONT.
Interviewed on 24 Feb. 1981; 1 hr.;
1 tape; Polish; by Roman Bielski.
Arrived in Canada in 1947.

ZASOWSKI, JAN AND KAROLINA
TORONTO, ONT.
Interviewed on 22 Oct. 1979; 1 hr.;
1 tape; Polish; by Roman Bielski.
Immigrated to Canada in the 1950s.

ZAWADZKI, SZCZĘSNY
TORONTO, ONT.
Letter warning those who would sup-
port Juliusz Sokolnicki, a "pretender"
to the Presidency of the Polish Gov-
ernment in Exile, 1977. .25 cm, in
Polish. Taped interview.
Interviewed on 7 Feb. 1978; 3 hrs.;
3 tapes; English; by Roman Bielski.
*25th Anniversary of the 18th Lwów
Batallion.* London, 1977. 60 pp., in
Polish.

ZAWISZA, ZOFIA AND ELŻBIETA
TORONTO, ONT.
Interviewed on 5 May 1982; .75 hr.;
1 tape; Polish; by Roman Bielski.
Arrived in Canada in 1970.

ZDANCEWICZ, JÓZEF AND
KATARZYNA
TORONTO, ONT.
Brief family history and 1 copy of
family Coat of Arms, n.d. .25 cm.
Photographs. Taped interview.
3 photographs: copy of family Coat
of Arms, J. Zdancewicz in uniform of
Royal Canadian Legion, c. 1970-80,
and Polish expedition to Alaska,
1974.
Interviewed on 25 Nov. 1982; 1.5
hrs.; 2 tapes; Polish; by Roman
Bielski. Immigrated to Canada in
1958.

ZELINSKI, EDWARD
THUNDER BAY, ONT.
4 photographs: the Zelinski family,
Thunder Bay, 1929-48; and members
of an amateur theatrical group, 1929.
Taped interview.
Interviewed on 12 Feb. 1979; 1 hr.;
1 tape; Polish/English; by G.
Kokocinski.

ZEMBSKI, EDMOND
TORONTO, ONT.
Interviewed on 12 Nov. 1981; 1 hr.;
1 tape; Polish; by A. Pietrus. Arrived
in Canada in 1956.

ZIELISKA, P.
OTTAWA, ONT.
*Grupa Taneczna Polonii Ottawskiej,
1956-81.* 22 pp.

ZIELISKI, EDMUND
HAMILTON, ONT.
Interviewed on 29 Nov. 1978; 1 hr.;
1 tape; Polish; by Roman Bielski.
*Bulletin of the Polish Combatants'
Association, Hamilton Branch,
1961-77.* 4 cm. Incomplete.

ZIELISKI, STEFAN
TORONTO, ONT.
Interviewed on Aug. 1978; 1 hr.; 1
tape; English; by Roman Bielski.

ŻÓŁTOWSKA, MARIA
RANDON, QUEBEC
Interviewed on 10 Aug. 1978; 1 hr.;
1 tape; Polish; by Roman Bielski.

ŻÓŁTOWSKI, GEORGE
RANDON, QUEBEC
Interviewed on 14 Aug. 1979; 1.5
hrs.; 2 tapes; Polish; by Roman
Bielski.

ZUBKOWSKI, RABCEWICZ
OTTAWA, ONT.
Interviewed on 28 Dec. 1979; 2 hrs.;
2 tapes; Polish; by Roman Bielski.

ŻUKOWSKI, WŁADYSŁAW
TORONTO, ONT.
Interviewed on 15 June 1981; .75
hr.; 1 tape; Polish; by Roman Bielski.

ŻUROWSKI, ADAM
OTTAWA, ONT.
Interviewed on 2 April 1980; 2 hrs.;
2 tapes; Polish; by Roman Bielski.
Arrived in Canada in 1942.

ZYGMONT, JOHN
CHELMSFORD, ONT.
2 Polish passports, 1927, 1929; marriage and birth certificates, 1922; and
Identification card, 1929. .5 cm. Photographs. Taped interview.
5 photographs: family and friends on
Zygmont farm, 1930-42.
Interviewed on 20 Feb. 1980; 1.25
hrs.; 2 tapes; Polish/English; by I.
Dembek. Immigrated to Canada in
1927.

ZYTKA, STANISŁAW
SUDBURY, ONT.
Interviewed on 3 Dec. 1977; .75 hr.;
1 tape; English; by Roman Bielski.

ZYWERT, ZGYMUNT
TORONTO, ONT.
Interviewed on 5 May 1981; 2 hrs.;
2 tapes; Polish; by Josef Sieramski.
Arrived in Canada in 1948.

ŻYWOT, BOLESŁAW
TORONTO, ONT.
Interviewed on 13 March 1981; 2.5
hrs.; 3 tapes; Polish; by Josef
Sieramski.

═══════════════

CANADIAN POLISH CONGRESS,
HAMILTON DISTRICT
HAMILTON, ONT.
The collection contains constitution,
Hamilton Branch, 1944; correspon-
dence and minutes, 1944-79; financial
records and reports, 1958-78. Also,
miscellaneous items from the
Millenium of Christianity, the
Copernicus Committee, Royal Castle
Fund, and Hamilton Festival of
Nations, c. 1970s. 5 reels of micro-
film.

CANADIAN POLISH CONGRESS (K.
BŁASZCZYK)
SUDBURY, ONT.
Records include annual reports,
1956-65; financial statements of
Millenium Fund, 1962-66; minutes of
Millenium Committee, 1956-80;
membership lists and correspondence,
1956-63. 2 reels of microfilm.

CANADIAN POLISH CONGRESS (S.
TEBINKA)
THUNDER BAY, ONT.
Papers include 2 president's reports
on general activities, 1976-78; correspondence, programmes and
president's reports from the
Millenium Committee, 1965-67; also,
historical sketches of the following
organizations: Canadian Polish Congress (1977), the Polish Youth Club
(1946-50), Polish Dancing Group
(1939-50), St. Casimiri's Church,
Polish Youth Association (1971-76),

the Polish Alliance Society (1977), First Polish Hall (1976), and Polish Parish—all of them in Thunder Bay and surrounding region. 5 cm. Photograph.

1 photograph: the 7th General Convention of the Canadian Polish Congress, Brantford, 29-30 Oct., 1955.

CANADIAN POLISH CONGRESS: THE SUDBURY COPERNICUS QUINCENTARY COMMITTEE
SUDBURY, ONT.

Records, 1973-74, comprise correspondence, minutes, programmes, communiques, and lists of Poles in Sudbury. 1 reel of microfilm. Photographs.

2 photographs: executive members of Copernicus Committee, 1973.

CANADIAN POLISH CONGRESS, TORONTO DISTRICT
TORONTO, ONT.

The collection contains general correspondence, 1948-72; minutes of Executive Committee meetings, 1950-75; minutes of general meetings, 1951-71; announcements, appeals, and communiques, 1951-62. Also included are miscellaneous records covering the following Polish-Canadian organizations: Invalid's Commission, 1955-72; Veteran's Commission, 1951-71; Welfare Commission, 1951-70; Polish School Committee, 1951-71; Polish Scouts Committee, 1953-71; Millenium Committee, 1959-71; 3rd of May Celebrations C'tee, 1951-63; 11th of November Celebrations Committee, 1950-72. 1.25 meters.
RESTRICTED

CANADIAN POLISH TEACHERS' ASSOCIATION
TORONTO, ONT.

Records, 1970-78, include minutes, reports, regulations, and correspondence; also, manuscript of memoirs (from the Canadian Polish Research Institute writers' contest), lists of Polish schools and teachers, curricula packages and teaching aids. In addition, there are miscellaneous papers (membership lists, programmes, reports) from the Polish Teachers' Association Conventions, Montreal, 1971, and Toronto, 1973. 1 meter.

FEDERATION OF POLISH WOMEN IN CANADA (W. GLINICKA)
SUDBURY, ONT.

Included are statutes and minutes from Women's Federation, 1966-71; also, serials issued by Women's Federation, 1956-77, and newsclippings. 5 cm. Photographs.

4 photographs: Polish Women's Federal receptions, Sudbury, c. 1964-70.
Głos Kobiet (Women's Voice). No. 85, 1976. 25 pp.
Informator Federacji Kobiet w Kanadzie. Nos. 1-108, 1956-77. Incomplete (missing nos. 15, 16, 35, 36, 37, 44, 45, 46, 59, 67, 94, 97, 104). 1.5 cm.
People's Poland and Poles Abroad. London, 1976. .5 cm.

FRIENDS OF CANADIAN POLISH YOUTH (POLISH CANADIAN RESEARCH INSTITUTE)
TORONTO, ONT.

The collection includes by-laws and list of members, 1956; minutes of meetings, 1953-56; correspondence and communiques, 1952-66; financial statements and reports, 1953-63; also, correspondence with organizations of

Z.H.P. (Polish Scouting in Canada).
30 cm. Photographs.
3 photographs: the executive of
Friends of Canadian Polish Youth,
Toronto, n.d.

FRIENDS OF GIRL AND BOY SCOUTS
SUDBURY, ONT.
Minutes, 1971-78, as well as finan-
cial and membership records. 2 cm.

HOLY TRINITY CHURCH
SUDBURY, ONT.
Historical sketch of the parish, n.d.,
list of founders of parish, n.d., and
church contributions, 1944. 1 cm. See
I. Dembek.

JESUIT MISSION IN SUDBURY
SUDBURY, ONT.
Status Animorum of the Jesuit
Mission in Sudbury, 1914. .5 cm.

KOŁO MŁODZIEŻY "SYRENA" (P.
TELECKI)
SUDBURY, ONT.
Minutes, 1959-62. 3 cm.

MULTICULTURAL HISTORY SOCIETY
OF ONTARIO
TORONTO, ONT.
Biekowska, Danuta. *Meeting Polish
Writers: An Annotated Reader and
Glossary.* 286 pp.
Jurszus, Jadwiga and A.
Tomaszewski. *Toronto Trana.*
Toronto, 1967. 188 pp.
Turek, Viktor. *The Polish Past in
Canada.* Toronto, 1960. 138 pp.
Wakowicz, Melchior. *Three Gener-
ations.* Toronto, 1973. 418 pp.
*Golden Jubilee of the Polish
Alliance, 1907-1957.* 286 pp.
Kronika Tygodniowa, 9 Jan. 1988 -
27 Jan. 1989. 2 reels of microfilm.
Parkdale Citizen. Toronto, Oct. 1971

- Dec. 1974. 1 reel of microfilm.
Slavica Canadiana. Winnipeg, 1961,
1963, 1965, 1966, 1967, 1968, 1969,
1970, 1971 (annual).
Studies. Nos. 2, 4, 5, 7, 9, 10,
1958-75. Polish Research Institute in
Canada.
*Silver Jubilee of the Oblate Fathers,
1935-1960.* 89 pp.
Topics on Poles in Canada. Toronto,
1976. 3 reprints: "Prejudice and
Polish-Canadian High School Students
in Windsor" by A.
Dunin-Markiewicz; "The Ethnic
Parish" by M. Smith; and "The Pol-
ish Community in Canada" by R.
Kogler. 3 booklets.

MULTICULTURAL NEWSPAPER
MICROFILM PROJECT
TORONTO, ONT.
Echo Tygodnia. Toronto, 15 Dec.
1983 - 6 Jan. 1988. 8 reels of microfilm.
Kurier Polski. Toronto, 29 Dec.
1972 - 22 Dec. 1987. 6 reels of
microfilm.

ORGANIZATION OF THE VETERANS OF
THE POLISH SECOND CORPS OF THE
EIGHTH ARMY
TORONTO, ONT.
Proposed statute, by-laws, regulations, and liquor licence, 1966-76;
minutes, 1963-76; correspondence,
communiques, 1967-79; financial
reports, 1968-75; membership lists
and attendance book, 1969-79; file on
co-operation with the Canadian Polish
Congress, 1969-79; and miscellaneous
paper items—invitations, clippings,
receipts, pamphlets. 8 cm. Taped
interview with Stefan Duda.
Jednodniówka, 1961-71. 1971. Anniversary publication. .5 cm.

POLISH ALLIANCE OF CANADA, 29TH
GENERAL CONVENTION
GRIMSBY, ONT.
  Recorded on 26, 27 Oct. 1979; 5
hrs.; 5 tapes; Polish; by Les
Wawrow.

POLISH ALLIANCE OF CANADA,
BRANCH 10
BRANTFORD, ONT.
  Minute books, 1930-77. 1 reel of
microfilm.

POLISH ALLIANCE OF CANADA,
BRANCH 13 (BORYS HARBULIK)
SUDBURY, ONT.
  Included are 1 book of minutes,
1961-80, and a certificate of the
United Polish Relief Fund. 3 cm.

POLISH ALLIANCE OF CANADA,
BRANCH 13
THUNDER BAY, ONT.
  Records include minutes and correspondence, 1977, annual reports,
1975-77, clippings from anniversary
book, 1906-46, and transcript of
Christmas greetings broadcasted in
1976. 1 cm. Photographs. Taped
interview with W. Zapior.
  4 photographs: Polish Alliance banquets, c. 1970s.
  *70th Anniversary of the Polish
Alliance of Canada, 1907-77.* .5 cm.

POLISH ALLIANCE OF CANADA,
BRANCH 17 (A. BOZEK)
DELHI, ONT.
  The collection consists of minutes of
Branch 17, 1967-78; minutes of
Ladies' Circle, 1962-80; correspondence, 1976-80; financial records and
reports, 1973-79. As well, miscellaneous items: programmes, newsletters, a scrapbook with photographs,
and 1 delegate ribbon, 1970s. 1 reel

of microfilm. Photographs.
  8 photographs: Polish Alliance activities in Delhi, Ont., n.d.
  Nowinki. 1976-80. Newsletter of
Polish Alliance of Canada, Branch
17, Delhi. Microfilm.

POLISH ALLIANCE OF CANADA,
BRANCH 21
OSHAWA, ONT.
  Minutes, 1960-76. 1 reel of micro-
film. Taped interview with Jan
Gorycki.

POLISH ALLIANCE OF CANADA,
BRANCH 7, NEW TORONTO
TORONTO, ONT.
  Included are 5 books of minutes
(1930-74) and 1 book of correspondence (1945-59) dealing mostly with
the Youth Branch. 1 reel of microfilm.

POLISH ALLIANCE OF CANADA,
BRANCH NO. 10
BRANTFORD, ONT.
  Minutes, 1930-77. 1 reel of micro-
film.
  18 photographs: conventions and
leadership of the Polish Alliance of
Canada, 1957-67.

POLISH ALLIANCE OF CANADA,
GROUP 13 (JAN KOSCIUSZKO)
SUDBURY, ONT.
  Financial records: dues paid by
members, 1951-52; monthly statements, 1937-56; members burial
insurance dues, 1956; membership
file, including applications, 1935-52;
and 2 Identification cards. 4 cm.

POLISH ALLIANCE OF CANADA
TORONTO, ONT.
  Correspondence, 1961-62. 1 cm.

Photographs. Taped interview with S. Konopka.
44 photographs: activities of the Polish Alliance of Canada, including conventions, celebrations, and Miss Polonia contests, Toronto, 1930-73; also, 600th anniversary celebration of Jagiellonian University, Poland, c. 1966.

POLISH ALLIANCE PRESS
TORONTO, ONT.
Związkowiec (Alliancer). Toronto, 1935-78. Complete. 44 reels of miicrofilm.

POLISH CANADIAN AGRARIAN ASSOCIATION (Z.W.P.)
SUDBURY, ONT.
Minutes of Z.P.W.P., 1955-1965; and miscellaneous paper items: speeches, programmes, an invitation, and newsclippings, 1955-57. 5 cm. Photographs. Taped interview with E. Ruszata.
9 photographs: mostly of banquets and members of the Polish-Canadian Agrarian Association, Sudbury, 1955-57.

POLISH CANADIAN CLUB
OTTAWA, ONT.
Records, 1936-79, include minutes, correspondece and miscellaneous papers on "Millenium of Christianity." 6 reels of microfilm. Photographs.
32 photographs: Polish Canadians, 1938-42; and activities of the Polish Canadian Club, 1972-74.

POLISH CANADIAN RESEARCH INSTITUTE
TORONTO, ONT.
Most of this collection is made up of records from the Polish Canadian

Youth Congress: resolutions (1969), correspondence (1970-72), financial statements (1970-73), and miscellaneous paper items pertaining to the Polish-Canadian Youth Conventions (1969, 1971). It also contains calendars and souvenir booklets, a file on various Polish-Canadian activities, and an essay on the Polish Youth Congress by Peter Taraska (1938). 14 cm.
115 photographs: Polish communities across Canada, particularly Barry's Bay, Saskatchewan, Alberta, and British Columbia, 1919-77.
Kogler, R. *The Polish Community in Canada.* Toronto, 1976. 46 pp.
Turek, Victor. *Polonica Canadiana.* Toronto, 1958. 138 pp.
25 Rocznica Założenia Polskiej Y.M.C.A. Toronto, 1947.
25th Anniversary of the Pastorate of Fr. Capiga, C.R. n.d. .5 cm
Echo Magazine. 1970-74. Scattered issues. 3 cm.
Slavica Canadiana, Annual, 1969. Winnipeg, Manitoba, 1970. 63 pp.

POLISH CLUB OF SUDBURY
SUDBURY, ONT.
Constitution and by-laws, 1935; charter of Club, 1936; minutes of Club meetings (handwritten in Polish), 1952-54, 1956-58, 1969-80; minutes of Ladies' Circle meetings, 1959-80; minutes and by-laws of shareholders, 1936-70; financial reports, 1969-70; and miscellaneous items—newsclippings, lists of shareholders, letters to Club. 1 reel of microfilm. 4 cm. Photograph.
1 photograph: the celebration of the Festival of the Sea at the Polish Club, 1937.

POLISH COMBATANTS' ASSOCIATION,
NO. 23, LADIES AUXILIARY
HAMILTON, ONT.
 Regulations of Combatants' Association, n.d.; minutes with a report on 18 years of activity, 1953-67; correspondence (including notices, communiques, announcements), 1958-66; financial records, 1953-73; and clippings about the Combatants' Association, 1961-62. 8 cm. Taped interview with H. Kolbuszewska.

POLISH COMBATANTS' ASSOCIATION,
BRANCH 23
HAMILTON, ONT.
 Bulletin, 1952-79. 1 reel of microfilm.

POLISH COMBATANTS' ASSOCIATION,
BRANCH 24
SUDBURY, ONT.
 Records, 1952-81, include minutes, financial reports and bulletins; also, regulations and minutes of the Polish Combatants' Association, No. 24, Credit Union; and miscellaneous papers such as list of scholarship awards, diplomas and newsclippings. 2 reels of microfilm. Photographs.
 5 photographs: parades and banquets involving organizations like the Polish Combatants' Association and the Canadian Polish Congress, Sudbury, 1954-78.
 3 photographs: activities of the Ladies' Auxiliary of the Polish Combatants' Association, Sudbury, 1962-63.

POLISH ETHNIC RETENTION PROJECT
TORONTO, ONT.
 Conducted during the summer of 1982 by E. Kania, R. Smolak and M. Węgierski, the more than 110 hours of oral interviews with 89 Toronto Polish immigrants focus on factors influencing the maintenance of ethnic identity within their community. Polish is the language used in most interviews. Interview log forms are available for these recordings.

POLISH NATIONAL RELIEF AND
DEFENCE COMMITTEE IN CANADA
WINNIPEG, MANITOBA
 Correspondence, 1944-50; financial records (cash received, disbursements, and statements), 1939-46; and 6 annual reports, 1939-46. 1 reel of microfilm.

POLISH PARISH OF ST. STANISLAUS
TORONTO, ONT.
 Jubilee histories of Polish organizations in Toronto and London, Ont., 1907-1970. 1 reel of microfilm.
 7 photographs: church life at St. Stanislaus, including first communion groups and Christmas parties, Toronto, 1948-64.
 Golden Anniversary of the Polish Alliance of Canada, 1907-57. Microfilm.
 Polish National Association, 1920-70. London, Ont. Microfilm.
 St. Stanislaus Parish in Toronto, 1911-61. Microfilm.

POLISH WHITE EAGLES
SUDBURY, ONT.
 Financial records, 1950-61; and history of Polish soccer in Sudbury, 1980. 2 cm.

SIR CASIMIR GZOWSKI POLISH SATURDAY SCHOOL
SUDBURY, ONT.
 List of children, 1962-70; correspondence, 1963-80; minutes of general

meetings, 1973-78; and minutes of Parents' Committee meetings, 1962-73. 1 reel of microfilm. 2 cm.

ST. ANNES CHURCH
SUDBURY, ONT.
  List of parish members, n.d. .25 cm. See I. Dembek.

ST. CASIMIR PARISH COUNCIL (REV. E. WAWRYK)
SUDBURY, ONT.
  1 book of minutes, 1967-80. 2 cm. See St. Casimir's Church.

ST. CASIMIR'S CHURCH (REV. J. B. STANKIEWICZ)
THUNDER BAY, ONT.
  Deeds and agreements, 1929; list of members, provisory rules, n.d.; early chronicles, 1922, bulletins and historical notes. 1 cm. Photographs.
  4 photographs: religious services at St. Casimir's Church, Thunder Bay, 1942-70.
  Bulletins, 1956, 1958, 1977. 1 cm.
  Fiftieth Anniversary of St. Casimir's Church. Thunder Bay, 1972. .25 cm.

ST. CASIMIR'S POLISH ROMAN CATHOLIC CHURCH (FATHER E. WAWRZYK)
SUDBURY, ONT.
  Included in this collection are lists of income and expenses dealing with the erection of St. Casimir Church Rectory, 1954-65; financial records of parish, 1958-69; list of donations from parishoners, n.d.; correspondence and invoices, 1955-60; church register, 1956-80; bulletins and annual reports, 1964-80; minutes of St. Casimir Catholic Women's League, 1966-77; and miscellaneous items--historical sketch, speeches, and reports on parish activity. 2 reels of

microfilm. Photographs.
  6 photographs: church construction, early 1950s.

ST. CASIMIR'S POLISH YOUTH GROUP (MONICA JABLONSKI)
SUDBURY, ONT.
  Minutes, correspondence and members lists, 1975-80. 3 cm. See St. Casimir's Church, Sudbury.

ST. CASIMIR'S POLISH YOUTH GROUP
SUDBURY, ONT.
  Minutes and correspondence, 1975-80. 2 cm.

ST. JACQUES CHURCH
HANMER, ONT.
  List of Polish names from church register of birth, marriages, 1906-60. .25 cm.

ST. MARY'S POLISH ROMAN CATHOLIC CHURCH (REV. J. GURKA)
THUNDER BAY, ONT.
  Souvenir booklet. 1 cm. Photographs. Taped interview.
  6 photographs: parish activities at St. Mary's, 1963-66.
  Newsletter, Dec. 1978-April 1979. .5 cm.
  Souvenir Booklet of the Dedication of St. Mary's Roman Catholic Church. Aug. 1965. .5 cm.

ST. STANISLAUS CHURCH
COPPER CLIFF, ONT.
  Church registers of births and marriages, 1901-07; plus church bulletins, 1979. 1.5 cm.

WHITE EAGLE DANCE ENSEMBLE
TORONTO, ONT.
 Scrapbooks, 1966-77. 1 reel of
microfilm. Photographs.
 19 photographs: entertainment as
provided by the White Eagle Dance
Ensemble, Toronto, Poland, 1967-72.

PORTUGUESE COLLECTION

ALVIS, BOBBY
SCARBOROUGH, ONT.
 Interviewed on 1 Feb. 1979; 2 hrs.;
2 tapes; English; by S. Sugunasiri.
Arrived in Canada in 1967.

ANDRADE, MARIA
CAMBRIDGE, ONT.
 1 photograph: the Andrade family in
Galt, c. 1970s. Taped interview.
 Interviewed on 20 June 1977; 1 hr.;
1 tape; English; by S. de Britto
Costa-Pinto.

ARRUDA, MESSIAS
CAMBRIDGE, ONT.
 14 photographs: the Arruda family;
and religious ceremonies in Nipigon,
Kitchener, and Toronto, 1957-70.

BORGES, ÁLVARO MANUEL
GALT, ONT.
 1 photograph: a religious procession
in Portugal, c. 1955-60. Taped interview.
 Interviewed on 19 July 1977; 1 hr.;
1 tape; Portuguese; by S. de Britto
Costa-Pinto. Arrived in Canada in
1959.

CABRAL JR., MANUEL
CAMBRIDGE, ONT.
 6 photographs: business enterprises
Galt, Cambridge, and Ayr, 1957-74.
Taped interview.
 Interviewed on 3 June 1977; 1 hr.; 1
tape; English; by S. de Britto
Costa-Pinto.

CÂMARA, MARIANO RAPOSO
GALT, ONT.
 2 photographs: the Câmara family,
1960. Taped interview.
 Interviewed on 20 Sept. 1977; 1 hr.;
1 tape; Portuguese; by S. de Britto
Costa-Pinto.

CAMPION, ARLETE
TORONTO, ONT.
 Interviewed on 23 July 1980; 1 hr.;
1 tape; English; by A. Lopes-Silver.

COELHO, JOSE ASSUNÇÃO
GALT, ONT.
 4 photographs: Portuguese immi-
grants on arrival in Toronto, 1957;
and views of Santa Maria, Azores,
n.d. Taped interview.
 Interviewed on 1 July 1977; 1 hr.; 1
tape; Portuguese; by S. de Britto
Costa-Pinto.
 Figueiredo, de Jaime. *Ilha de
Gonçalo Velho*. Lisboa: c. de
Oliveira, 1954. 207 pp.

CORREIA DA SILVA, JOSÉ
GALT, ONT.
 Interviewed on 18 Aug. 1977; 1 hr.;
1 tape; Portuguese; by S. de Britto
Costa-Pinto.

COSTA, RAUL
TORONTO, ONT.
 20 photographs: Portuguese immi-
grants en route to Canada; and the
Costa family in Toronto, 1958-61.
Taped interview.

Interviewed on 10 June 1980; 1 hr.; 1 tape; English; by A. Lopes-Silver.

DA ROSA DA SILVEIRA, JOSÉ
GALT, ONT.
Interviewed on 2 Dec. 1977; 1 hr.; 1 tape; Portuguese; by S. de Britto Costa-Pinto.

DA SILVA, ILISA
TORONTO, ONT.
1 photograph: Portuguese men disembarking at Halifax, Nova Scotia from the *S.S. Roma,* 1956; and a birthday party, 1957. Taped interview.
Interviewed on 29 July 1980; .5 hr.; 1 tape; Portuguese; by A. Lopes-Silver.

DA SILVA FERREIRA, ANTÓNIO
GALT, ONT.
1 photograph: the da Silva family, 1956. Taped interview.
Interviewed on 22 Oct. 1977; 1 hr.; 1 tape; Portuguese; by S. de Britto Costa-Pinto.

DE ANDRADE, JOSÉ RICARDO
GALT, ONT.
34 photographs: Portuguese immigrants en route to Canada, 1957; dwellings of the de Andrade family in the Azores and Galt, Ont. 1954-59; and railway work in British Columbia, 1957-58. Taped interview.
Interviewed on 25 July 1977; 1 hr.; 1 tape; Portuguese; by S. de Britto Costa-Pinto. Arrived in Canada in 1957.

DE FREITAS, JUVENAL
TORONTO, ONT.
Interviewed on 14 Aug. 1980; 1 hr.; 1 tape; English; by A. Lopes-Silver.

DE PINHO, MANUEL
SUDBURY, ONT.
Interviewed on 19 July 1984; .5 hr.; 1 tape; English; by A. Teixeira. Arrived in Canada in 1956.

DE VARGAS, ODÍLIO
CAMBRIDGE, ONT.
18 photographs: Portuguese immigrants en route to Canada, 1956; dwellings of the de Vargas family, 1956-58; employment in a factory, n.d.; and activities of the Portuguese Club, 1962-71. Taped interview.
Interviewed on 24 June 1977; 1 hr.; 1 tape; Portuguese; by S. de Britto Costa-Pinto.
Canada: Instruções Para Uso Dos Emigrantes. Portugal: Ministerio do Interior, Junta da Emigração, 1955. 103 pp.

DIAS, JOSÉ
CAMBRIDGE, ONT.
Interviewed on 11 June 1977; 1 hr.; 1 tape; Portuguese; by S. de Britto Costa-Pinto.

DIAS, JOSÉ
BRAMPTON, ONT.
44 photographs: Portuguese immigrants en route to Canada, c. 1957; the Dias family in the Azores, and Galt, 1951-73; religious ceremonies, 1957-62; and work on the railway, and in a factory in Galt, 1958-61.

DIAS, MANUEL
GALT, ONT.
7 photographs: work on the railway in Galt, 1957; and religious ceremonies, 1960-63. Taped interview.
Interviewed in 1977; 1 hr.; 1 tape; Portuguese; by S. de Britto Costa-Pinto.

DOS SANTOS CORDEIRO, JOSÉ
GALT, ONT.
8 photographs: the Cordeiro family, and work in a factory in Edmonton, Winnipeg, and Galt, Ont., 1957-65. Taped interview.
Interviewed on 30 Oct. 1977; 1 hr.; 1 tape; Portuguese; by S. de Britto Costa-Pinto.

DOS SANTOS CORDEIRO, VIRGILIO
GALT, ONT.
Interviewed on 7 Aug. 1977; 1 tape; Portuguese; by S. de Britto Costa-Pinto. Discusses Azorean immigration to Galt, Ont.

DUARTE, MANUEL
GALT, ONT.
8 photographs: work in a factory in Guelph, 1958; and a religious festival, "Espírito Santo," at Our Lady of Fátima Church, 1958-62. Taped interview.
Interviewed on 24 Sept. 1977; 1 hr.; 1 tape; Portuguese; by S. de Britto Costa-Pinto.

EMÍDIO, JOAQUIM
TORONTO, ONT.
Interviewed on 28 June 1980; 1 hr.; 1 tape; Portuguese; by A. Lopes-Silver.

EVANGELHO, MARIE JUDITE
TORONTO, ONT.
4 photographs: a religious feast in Portugal, 1952. Taped interview.
Interviewed on 25, 30 Oct. 1978; 1.5 hrs.; 2 tapes; English; by H. Fisher.

FERNANDES, ÂNGELO
CAMBRIDGE, ONT.
9 photographs: Portuguese immi-

grants en route to Canada, n.d.; the Fernandes family; and their dwellings, 1955-65.

FERNANDES, MANUEL
GALT, ONT.
8 photographs: Portuguese immigrants en route to Canada, c. 1955; the Fernandes family; and farming in Galt, 1955-65. Taped interview.
Interviewed on 17 Oct. 1977; 1 hr.; 1 tape; Portuguese; by S. de Britto Costa-Pinto.

FREIRE, ANTÓNIO
CAMBRIDGE, ONT.
6 photographs: Portuguese immigrants, 1947; and Portuguese landmarks, n.d.

GREENHILL, PAULINE AND JOHN JUNSON
TORONTO, ONT.
116 photographs and slides: Portuguese house facades showing statues, and icons of saints in the Bellwoods district of Toronto, c. 1987.

JORGE, BENJAMIN AVILA
GALT, ONT.
7 photographs: the Portuguese community in Galt; parades and processions; and the Portuguese Club, 1962-70. Taped interview.
Interviewed on 11 July 1977; 1 hr.; 1 tape; Portuguese; by S. de Britto Costa-Pinto.

LINDO, MANUEL
CAMBRIDGE, ONT.
17 photographs: the Lindo family in Kitchener, 1957; and panoramic scenes in the Azores, n.d.

MADRUGA, JOSÉ
GALT, ONT.
Interviewed on 23 July 1977; 1 hr.;
1 tape; Portuguese; by S. de Britto
Costa-Pinto.

MAIA, DELKAR NAPOLEÃO
TORONTO, ONT.
10 photographs: Portuguese immigrants aboard the *S.S. Hellas,* 1953;
the Maia family in Toronto, 1953-55;
and a picnic at Niagara Falls, 1955.
Taped interview.
Interviewed on 2 July 1980; .75 hr.;
1 tape; English; by A. Lopes-Silver.

MARTINS, MANUEL
GALT, ONT.
Interviewed on 3 Oct. 1977; 1 hr.; 1
tape; Portuguese; by S. de Britto
Costa-Pinto.

MARTINS, MANUEL
CAMBRIDGE, ONT.
6 photographs: the Martins family;
and a general store in Galt, Ont., and
Quebec, 1960-70.

MILLS, TOM
CAMBRIDGE, ONT.
5 photographs: activities, a band, and
a folk dancing group of the Portuguese Club in Galt, 1970-75.

MOSES, WILLIAM
SCARBOROUGH, ONT.
Interviewed on 20 Feb. 1979; 2 hrs.;
2 tapes; English; by S. Sugunasiri.
Arrived in Canada in 1971.

PEDROSA, JOSÉ
CAMBRIDGE, ONT.
32 photographs: the Pedrosa family
in Portugal, Newfoundland, and
Kitchener, 1947-75; cod fishing in
Newfoundland, 1947; and music and

folk dancing at the Portuguese Club
in Galt, 1970-71.

PEREIRA, ALEX
SUDBURY, ONT.
Interviewed on 21 Aug. 1984; 1 hr.;
1 tape; Portuguese; by A. Teixeira.
Arrived in Canada in 1958.

PEREIRA, FRANCISCO
CAMBRIDGE, ONT.
12 photographs: Portuguese immigrants en route to Canada, 1957;
religious ceremonies in the Azores,
and Hamilton, 1957-61; and the
Pereira family in Galt, 1959.

PEREIRA, FRANCISCO
GALT, ONT.
Interviewed on 8 July 1977; 1 hr.; 1
tape; Portuguese; by S. de Britto
Costa-Pinto.

PEREIRA, MANUEL
SUDBURY, ONT.
Interviewed on 13 July 1984; .5 hr.;
1 tape; Portuguese; by A. Teixeira.
Immigrated to Canada in 1958.

PINHEIRO, GIL
GALT, ONT.
Interviewed on 19 June 1977; 1 hr.;
1 tape; Portuguese; by S. de Britto
Costa-Pinto.

PINHEIRO, GIL
CAMBRIDGE, ONT.
4 photographs: Gil Pinheiro and his
dwellings; processions in the Azores,
and Galt, c. 1959-70.

RAMALHO, FERNANDO
TORONTO, ONT.
Interviewed on 14 June 1980; 1.25
hrs.; 2 tapes; English; by A.
Lopes-Silver.

RAPOSO, FERNANDO
TORONTO, ONT.
Interviewed on 15 July 1980; 1.25
hrs.; 2 tapes; English; by A.
Lopes-Silver.

RIBEIRO, ANTÓNIO
TORONTO, ONT.
Interviewed on 25 July 1980; 1 hr.;
1 tape; English; by A. Lopes-Silver.

ROQUE DIAS, ANTÓNIO
SUDBURY, ONT.
Interviewed on 25 July 1984; 1 hr.;
1 tape; Portuguese; by A. Teixeira.
Arrived in Canada in 1955.

SANTO CORDEIRO, VIRGÍLIO
GALT, ONT.
Interviewed on 7 Aug. 1977; 1 hr.; 1
tape; Portuguese; by S. de Britto
Costa-Pinto.

SILVA, MARIA DE FÁTIMA
SUDBURY, ONT.
4 photographs: wedding and family
(photocopies), 1965-1970. Taped
interview.
Interviewed on 14 July 1984; .5 hr.;
1 tape; Portuguese; by A. Teixeira.
Arrived in Canada in 1970.

SIMÕES, JOSÉ CARLOS
TORONTO, ONT.
Interviewed on 26 Sept. 1977; 1 hr.;
1 tape; Portuguese; by S. de Britto
Costa-Pinto.

SOARES DOS REIS, JOÃO
GALT, ONT.
7 photographs: work on the railway
in Galt, Ont., 1958. Taped interview.
Interviewed on 21 Oct. 1977; 1 hr.;
1 tape; Portuguese; by S. de Britto
Costa-Pinta. Arrived in Canada in
1960.

SOUSA, J. C.
TORONTO, ONT.
Miscellaneous material such as bro-
chures, flyers, and bulletins, from
Toronto's Portuguese organizations,
1970s. 4 cm.
Sousa Lara, António de. *Linhagens
de Portugal.* Moreiras Pessanha de
Canavezes. 1977. Pamphlet, in Portu-
guese.
Boletim do Sport Agrense of Toronto.
Vol. 1, nos. 2-4, 1978. 1 cm.
Boletim Informativo. Clube
Transmontano. Toronto, May 1978.
.25 cm.
Contacto, Journal de Informação.
First Portuguese Canadian Club. Nos.
1-4. Toronto, 1978. 1 cm.
The Kensington. Oct. 1976, Summer
1978. .5 cm, in Portuguese.

TEIXEIRA, ANA
SUDBURY, ONT.
4 photographs: family; and wedding, 1958-63. Taped interview.
Interviewed on 9 July 1984; .75 hr.;
1 tape; Portuguese; by A. Teixeira.
Arrived in Canada in 1966.

TEIXEIRA, MARIA
SUDBURY, ONT.
Clippings on Sudbury's Portuguese
community, 1979-83. 1 cm. Photo-
graphs.
Over 40 photographs: (photocopies)
Portuguese activities such as folk
dancing, soccer, and theatre in
Sudbury, 1979-83.

TOMAZ, MÁRIO COELHO
TORONTO, ONT.
Interviewed on 16 June 1980; 1 hr.;
1 tape; Portuguese; by A.
Lopes-Silver. Arrived in Canada in
1955.

VIEIRA, SAMUEL
TORONTO, ONT.
Immigration papers, correspondence from Portugal, notes, diary, and personal financial records, 1958-60.
1 reel of microfilm. Photographs. Taped interview.
19 photographs: the Vieira family in Portugal, and Toronto, 1959-68.
Interviewed on 12 June 1980; 1.75 hrs.; 2 tapes; English; by A. Lopes-Silver.

CAMBRIDGE DAILY REPORTER
CAMBRIDGE, ONT.
Reports and clippings. 1 cm. Photographs.
3 photographs: Portuguese Information Centre, and the Portuguese Sport Club, 1970-76.

CLUBE PORTUGUES DE SUDBURY
SUDBURY, ONT.
Minutes and financial records, 1978-84. 7 cm.

KITCHENER PORTUGUESE CLUB
KITCHENER, ONT.
14 photographs: entertainment and sports at the Club, 1970-75.

MULTICULTURAL HISTORY SOCIETY OF ONTARIO
TORONTO, ONT.
Martins, Luís A. *Emigração Portuguesa no Canadá*. Lisbon, 1971. Pamphlet, in Portuguese.
Comunidade. Vol. 1 - 11. Toronto, July 1975. 1 reel of microfilm.
Guia Comercial Português. 1975, 1978, 1980, 1982, 1983, 1984, 1985. Portuguese Business Directory for Toronto, Mississauga, Oakville, Brampton, Hamilton, Cambridge, and Kitchener. 30 cm.
Lista Telefónica Portuguesa. 1982, 1983, 1984, 1985. Portuguese Telephone Directory for Toronto, Mississauga, and Brampton. 10 cm.
Papers on the Portuguese Community. Ministry of Culture and Communications, n.d. 3 short essays.
Portuguese Directory for the Metropolitan Area of Toronto. International Institute of Metropolitan Toronto, c. 1970s.
Yupa (Voice). Dec. 1983-86. York University Portuguese Students' Association (5 issues).

MULTICULTURAL NEWSPAPER MICROFILM PROJECT
TORONTO, ONT.
Correio Português. Toronto, 15 Jan. 1978-21 Dec. 1982 (semi-monthly).
O Jornal Português. Toronto, 8 March 1986-27 May 1975 (semi-monthly). 6 reels of microfilm.
O Lusitano. Cambridge, 21 July 1978-23 Dec. 1987. 4 reels of microfilm.

OUR LADY OF FÁTIMA CHURCH
CAMBRIDGE, ONT.
Bulletin. 1972-77. 1 reel of microfilm.

BALAŞA, GEORGE
HAMILTON, ONT.
An anti-communist flyer denouncing alleged communist infiltration into Romanian religious congress in Kitchener, 1974. In addition, ribbons, a button, a badge, and annual convention brochures from the Romanian Cultural Association, and the Union and League of American Societies of America in Hamilton, c. 1970s. 15 cm.

Dima, Nicolae. *Amintiri din Închisoare.* Hamilton: Biblioteca Asociaţia Culturală Română, 1974. 272 pp., in Romanian.

Novac, Nicolae. *Cetăţi Sfărâmate.* Hamilton: Biblioteca Asociaţia Culturală Română, 1973. Short stories. 120 pp., in Romanian.

Posteuca, Vasile. *Cantece din fluier.* Cleveland, Ohio, 1960. Poems. 36 pp., in Romanian.

_____. *Catapeteasma Bucovineană.* Mexico, 1963. 1 poem. 29 pp., in Romanian.

Smultea, Ilie. *Romania: the State at the Danube's Mouth.* Chicago: Middle West Romanian American Committee, 1961. 63 pp.

6th Annual Convention of the Ladies' Auxiliary of the Union and League of R.S.A.. Hamilton, 1971. Booklet. 25 pp.

10th Annual Convention of the Ladies' Auxiliary of the Union and League of R.S.A.. Montreal, 1975. 79 pp.

43rd Convention of the Union and League of Romanian Societies of America, 1970. Hamilton: Asociaţia Culturală Română, 1970. Booklet. 49 pp.

Istoria Uniunii şi Ligii Societăţilor Româneşti din America. Cleveland, Ohio: Union and League of Romanian Societies of America, 1956. 416 pp., in Romanian.

Zece Ani de Activitate, 1957-67. Hamilton: Asociaţia Culturală Română, 1967. 13 pp.

BARBU, GEORGE
BURLINGTON, ONT.
Immigration identification card, 1929. .5 cm. Taped interview. Interviewed on 5 Dec. 1978; 1.5 hrs.; 2 tapes; English; by John Omorean. Pre-WWII immigrant.

BARBU, TRAIAN
HAMILTON, ONT.
Interviewed on 11 Oct. 1978; .5 hr.; 1 tape; Romanian; by John Omorean. Arrived in Canada in 1928.

BEZUSKO, VERONICA
HAMILTON, ONT.
Interviewed on 17 Nov. 1978; 1 hr.; 1 tape; Romanian/English; by John Omorean. Immigrated to Canada in the 1920s.

BODNARIUK, VICTORIA
HAMILTON, ONT.
Interviewed on 6 Nov. 1978; .75 hr.; 1 tape; English/Romanian; by John Omorean. Immigrated to Canada in 1925, co-founder of "Reuniuea," Romanian Ladies' Auxiliary.

BUIA, EUGENE
TORONTO, ONT.
Queen Marie of Romania. *Ode to Romania*. Paris, 1923. 1 reel of microfilm, includes:
Jonnesco, T. "Foreign Policy of Romania." n.d.
_____. "In Silence of Monasteries." n.d.
Iorga, N. "Romania." n.d.

CAZAC, AVRAM
HAMILTON, ONT.
Interviewed on 15 Dec. 1978; 1 hr.; 1 tape; Romanian/English; by John Omoream. Family moved to Canada in 1902.

CIUREA, REV. NICOLAE
HAMILTON, ONT.
Interviewed on 13 Dec. 1978; 1 hr.; 1 tape; Romanian; by John Omorean. Post-WWII immigrant, active in formation of Orthodox Church in Romanian community of Hamilton.
Cuvânt-Bun. Vol. 7, nos. 1-2, 15 Jan. 1934. Bucureşti, Creştine Ortodoxe (1 issue).

CLIM, SOFIA
HAMILTON, ONT.
"Gloria." Romanian Society of Hamilton members pin, c. 1915-25, calendars, and booklets. 14 cm. Photographs. Taped interview.
10 photographs: the Clim family and friends, 1910-1920s; Gloria Romanian Society of Hamilton, 1916; and Romanian Church Choir, 1935.
Interviewed on 9 Nov. 1978; 1 hr.; 1 tape; Romanian/English; by John Omorean. She arrived in Canada in 1913, active in Romanian organizations in Montreal, Quebec, and Hamilton.
Alte Aventuri ale lui Sherlock Holmes

(Adventures of Sherlock Holmes). Bucharest, 1908. 96 pp., in Romanian.
Calendarul Bisericesc: "Creştin Ortodox." Detroit, 1926. Booklet. 48 pp.
Calendarul Solia. Romanian Orthodox Episcopate of America. 1936, 1938, 1939, 1949, 1967, 1978. 16 cm.
Doine Lacrămi şi Suspine. Gherla, 1905.
Untitled booklet of Romanian plays, short stories, and poems, n.d. 30 pp.

CUPCIC, NICOLAI
HAMILTON, ONT.
7 photographs: family and friends of donor, 1915-38; religious ceremonies at the Romanian Orthodox Church, 1928, 1936; and Romanian picnic at park near Westinghouse Co. in Hamilton, 1938.

DANCIU, PERŞA
HAMILTON, ONT.
Interviewed on 17 Nov. 1978; .5 hr.; 1 tape; Romanian/English; by John Omorean. Arrived in the early 1900s.

DIMITRU, JOHN AND ELENA
BURLINGTON, ONT.
Interviewed on 4 Nov. 1978; 2 hrs.; 2 tapes; Romanian/English; by John Omorean. Arrived in the 1920s.

DOBREA, SILVIA
HAMILTON, ONT.
Canadian passport and naturalization certificate, 1938; memorial records (funeral guestbook), 1957; and yearbooks. 14 cm. Photographs. Taped interview.
42 photographs: tobacco farming; and reunions among the Popaiov and

Dobrea families in Delhi, Ont.,
1938-61.
Interviewed on 6 Dec. 1978; .5 hr.;
1 tape; Romanian; by John Omorean.
Father arrived in Delhi in 1929.
Calendarul Credinţa. Romanian
Orthodox Church of America. 1953,
1976. 144 pp., 260 pp., in Roma-
nian/English.
*Calendarul Jubiliar al Ziarului
America, 1906-56.* Cleveland, Ohio:
Union and League of Romanian
Societies of America, 1956. 336 pp.,
in Romanian.
*Calendarul Jubiliar America,
1906-66.* Cleveland, Ohio: Union and
League of Romanian Societies of
America, 1966. 292 pp., in Roma-
nian.
Calendarul Solia. Romanian Ortho-
dox Episcopate of America. 1968,
1973. 276 pp., 256 pp., in Roma-
nian/English.
*The Fifty-Third Anniversary of St.
George's Romanian Orthodox Parish,
1918-71.* Windsor, Ont.: St. George's
Romanian Orthodox Cathedral, 1971.
Booklet. 40 pp., in Roma-
nian/English.

DUMITRU, ANDRONACHE
TORONTO, ONT.
Interviewed on July 1978; .75 hrs.; 1
tape; Romanian; by Radu Toma.

DUMITRU, JOHN
HAMILTON, ONT.
Interviewed on 6 July 1978; 1 hr.; 1
tape; Romanian; by Radu Toma.

FLUTUR, LEON
PUSLINCH, ONT.
Interviewed on 15 Nov. 1978; 1.5
hrs.; 2 tapes; Romanian/English; by
John Omorean. His father arrived in
1911.

HERTEL, ANDREW
DELHI, ONT.
Romanian school report card, 1921;
Romanian passport, n.d.; and landing
vaccination card, n.d.

HORTOPAN, GEORGE
TORONTO, ONT.
Personal documents, and clippings,
1902-42. 1 cm. Photographs. Taped
interview.
6 photographs: 100th birthday celebration of Teofil Hortopan, 1976.
Interviewed on 26 Sept. 1977; .5
hr.; 1 tape; English; by Eugene Buia.
Discusses the life of his father, who
arrived in 1906.

IAPEC, ANGHILENA
HAMILTON, ONT.
Interviewed on 4 Dec. 1978; 1 hr.; 1
tape; Romanian; by John Omorean.
Father moved to Canada at the begin-
ning of the 20th century.

KEPPLER, CASPAR
KITCHENER, ONT.
Romanian passport and immigration
identification card; military certifi-
cate, 1923; and a brochure of the
Canadian-Schwaben Sick Benefit
Association, 1956. 1 cm.

LATA, PETER
PRINCETON, ONT.
Interviewed on 11 Nov. 1978; 1 hr.;
1 tape; Romanian; by John Omorean.
Arrived in Canada in 1929.

LUPU, T. (WITH REV. N. TANASE)
TORONTO, ONT.
1 invitation to baptism, 1947; 1
invitation to Romanian Cultural Centennial in Kitchener, 1972; 1 bulletin
of St. George's Romanian Orthodox
Church, n.d.; and a commemorative

booklet of the union of Bessarabia and Romania, n.d. 2 cm. Taped interview.
Interviewed on 4 July 1978; 1 hr.; 1 tape; English; by Radu Toma.
Comemorează Unirea Basarabiei cu România. Asociatia Culturală Romana Hamilton. n.d. Commemorative booklet of the union of Bessarabia and Romania. 14 pp.

MARIONCU, CUSMAN
HAMILTON, ONT.
2 Yugoslavian passports, 1927, 1928; and 1 immigration identification card, 1928. Photographs. Taped interview.
17 photographs: Romanian immigrants in Winnipeg, Edmonton, and Hamilton, 1918-43; and funeral of Ion Marioncu (father of donor) in 1918 in Hamilton.
Interviewed on 11 Dec. 1978; 1 hr.; 1 tape; Romanian; by John Omorean. Father arrived in 1914.

MELNECIUC, VASILE
DUNDAS, ONT.
Interviewed on 7 Oct. 1978; .5 hr.; 1 tape; English; by John Omorean. Immigrated to Canada in 1912.

MIKA, TRAIAN
HAMILTON, ONT.
1 banquet poster, 1970; and 10 *Credința* calendars, 1968-77. 8 cm. Taped interview.
Interviewed on 16 Nov. 1978; .5 hr.; 1 tape; Romanian; by John Omorean. Arrived in Canada in 1928.

MOLOCI, DAMIAN
HAMILTON, ONT.
Interviewed on 6 July 1978; 1 hr.; 1 tape; Romanian; by Radu Toma.

MOLOCI, DAMIAN
HAMILTON, ONT.
Interviewed on 30 Nov. 1978; 1.5 hrs.; 1 tape; Romanian; by John Omorean. Immigrated to Canada in 1923.

MIHAELESCU-NASTURAL, PRINCE MONYO
TORONTO, ONT.
Biographical sketch, list of works in galleries and private collections, and a self-promotional brochure, n.d. Taped interview.
Interviewed on 9 Aug. 1977; .5 hr.; 1 tape; English; by Eugene Buia. Discusses his art in relation to the Romanian-Canadian experience.

OMOREAN, JOHN
COPETOWN, ONT.
1 poster for Romanian picnic, c. 1959; lists of members and supporters at Holy Resurrection Church, n.d.; and Romanian Orthodox Church bulletin and anniversary booklets. 5 cm. Photographs.
38 photographs: mostly of Romanian "Doina" Dancers; and some of the Romanian Orthodox Church Choir in Hamilton, and Montreal, 1935-77; and immigrants en route to Canada from Yugoslavia, 1956.
13 photographs: farming in Romania; military service; and group portraits, c. 1910-55.
Adevărul (The Truth). Vol. 5, no. 1. Hamilton, 1974. Invierea Domnului Parish. 20 pp.
Holy Resurrection Romanian Orthodox Church: 60th Anniversary, 1916-76. Hamilton, 1976. 64 pp.

PASCALUȚA, IOAN
TORONTO, ONT.
Interviewed on 4 July 1978; .5 hr.; 1

tape; Romanian; by Radu Toma.
Pascaluţa, Ioan. "Conferinta pentru
Securitatea Europei si Graniţele
Romaniei." *Acţiunea Românească*.
New York, 1975. 8 pp.
  Petrovici, O. M. "60 de Ani de la
Unirea Basarabiei." Toronto, 1978.
Unpublished essay with copies of
documents. 74 pp.
  Europa şui Neamul Românesc.
Milan, Italy; April and June 1977 (2
issues). 17 pp.

PENTIA, NICOLAE
BURLINGTON, ONT.
  Immigration identification card,
1929. .5 cm. Taped interview.
  Interviewed on 5 Dec. 1978; 1.5
hrs.; 2 tapes; English; by John
Omorean. Pre-WWII immigrant.
  *Monografia: Vladimirovac,
1808-1908*. Burlington, Ont.:
Hamilton Screen Print, 1967. 113
pp., in Romanian.

PODETZ, DORA
HAMILTON, ONT.
  1 statute of the Organization of the
Romanian Orthodox Church, 1935;
and 1 Austro-Hungarian passport,
1914. Taped interview.
  Interviewed on 8 Nov. 1978; .5 hr.;
1 tape; English; by John Omorean.
Member of the Romanian Ladies'
Auxiliary Committee.
  *Statutul: Pentru Organizarea
Bisericei Ortodoxe Romane in
America*. Episcopia Misionară
Ortodoxă Romana, 1938. 83 pp.

PODETZ, ILEN
PRINCETON, ONT.
  Interviewed on 12 Oct. 1978; 1 hr.;
1 tape; English; by John Omorean.

Arrived in 1914, recounts activities in
Hamilton's Romanian community
since the 1920s.

RADIA, NICK
HAMILTON, ONT.
  1 photograph: Sofia Radia as "Miss
Romania," Hamilton, 1968. Taped
interview.
  Interviewed on 5 Dec. 1978; 1.5
hrs.; 2 tapes; Romanian; by John
Omorean. Family arrived in 1928,
conversation highlights the traditional
Romanian "Petrovician" picnic in
Hamilton.
  Calendarul Oastea Domnului. Sibiu:
Oastea Domnului, 1936, 1938. 236
pp., in Romanian.

RILL, JOSEPH
DELHI, ONT.
  1 Romanian passport, 1928. 11 pp.

ZELEA, FATHER AND FATHER
TANASE
HAMILTON, ONT.
  Recorded on 14 Sept. 1977; 1 hr.; 1
tape; English-Romanian; by Eugene
Buia. Chants and wedding vows, followed by interviews with Father
Tanase about Romanian Orthodox
tradition, and how Romanian Canadians retained their religious practices
and beliefs. Also, interviews with
bride and groom, and parishioners on
the meaning of marriage in the Romanian Orthodox tradition.

SOMODOLEA, AUREL
HAMILTON, ONT.
  Interviewed on 6 July 1978; 1 hr.; 1
tape; Romanian; by Radu Toma.

ŞOMODOLEA, AUREL
HAMILTON, ONT.
  Interviewed on 11 Oct. 1978; .5 hr.;

1 tape; English; by John Omorean. Moved to Canada in 1922, involved in the United Romanian Society, an immigrant aid organization.

TANASE, REV. NICOLAE (ROMANIAN ORTHODOX CHURCH)
KITCHENER, ONT.
 Interviewed in July 1978; 1 hr.; 1 tape; English; by Radu Toma.

TAPEC, IOSIF
HAMILTON, ONT.
 2 Austrian passports for Mr. and Mrs. Tapec, 1955. 48 pp.

TODOREL, VICTORIA
HAMILTON, ONT.
 Interviewed on 2 Dec. 1978; 1 hr.; 1 tape; English; by J. Omarean. Early arrival, worked 31 years at Dofasco, participated in Ladies' Auxiliary Committee.

VACARCIUC, MARIA
HAMILTON, ONT.
 Interviewed on 14 Oct. 1978; 1 hr.; 1 tape; Romanian; by John Omorean. Joined husband in Canada in 1927.

WAGNER, MARTIN
SIMCOE, ONT.
 Immigration papers, including documents stating the Wagners' intention to retain Romanian citizenship, 1928-29. 1 cm (24 items). Taped interview with Martin and Katharine Wagner.
 Interviewed on 26 July 1977; 1 hr.; 1 tape; English; by Hilda Shenn. Immigrated to Canada in 1928.

WASHNUK, JOHN AND VERA
HAMILTON, ONT.
 11 photographs: family and Romanian festive traditions in Hamilton, and Manitoba, 1918-75. Taped interview.
 Interviewed on 6 Dec. 1978; 1 hr.; 1 tape; English; by John Omorean. Parents arrived in the early 1900s, donor worked at Dofasco for 33 years.
 Calendarul Solia. Romanian Orthodox Episcopate of America. 1958. 231 pp.

ZAMFIR, HELEN
COPETOWN, ONT.
 20 photographs: the Omorean family in Hamilton, Princeton, and Yugoslavia, 1928-50; and the Romanian picnic in Dundurn Park in Hamilton, 1938. Taped interview.
 Interviewed on 8 Dec. 1978; 1.5 hrs.; 2 tapes; English; by John Omorean. Parents arrived in 1929.

ZELINSKY, ILEANA
HAMILTON, ONT.
 Interviewed on 8 Dec. 1978; 1 hr.; 1 tape; Romanian; by John Omorean. Joined husband in Canada in 1928.

ZIVAN, NICOLAI
HAMILTON, ONT.
 Immigration identification card, 1926, and calendars and bulletins. Photographs. Taped interview.
 9 photographs: the Zivan's at church ceremonies and home in Hamilton; and pre-migration, Yugoslavia, 1905-46.
 Interviewed on 27 Nov. 1978; 1.5 hrs.; 2 tapes; Romanian; by John Omorean. Immigrated to Canada in 1926.
 Calendar Bisericesc. 1972, 1973, 1974, 1975, 1976. Vicariatul Ortodox Roman din Banatul iugoslav. 2 cm, in Romanian.
 Lumina. Vol. 8, no. 4. Varset: Libertatea, 1954. .5 cm.

Romanian Orthodox Church of the Resurrection Bulletin. Dec. 1969, Hamilton. 12 pp., in Romanian.

DACIA ROMANIAN CULTURAL ASSOCIATION
TORONTO, ONT.
1 affidavit of eligibility for office in Union and League of Romanian Societies of America, 1975; also, flyers and an issue of *America*. 1 cm. Photographs.
7 photographs: folk dancing sponsored by Dacia Society in Toronto, 1977-78.

MULTICULTURAL HISTORY SOCIETY OF ONTARIO
TORONTO, ONT.
Toma, Radu. *Românii din America*. Bucureşti: Editată de Asociaţia România, 1978. 234 pp., in Romanian.
Romanian American Heritage Center Information Bulletin. Vol. 1, no. 4, Summer 1984; vol. 3, no. 3, Spring 1986. 2 cm.

MULTICULTURAL NEWSPAPER MICROFILM PROJECT
TORONTO, ONT.
Ecouri Romaneşti. Toronto, Oct. 1974-Nov. 1984. 2 reels of microfilm.

ROMANIAN CANADIAN ASSOCIATION
TORONTO, ONT.
Charter, 1972. .5 cm.
Ecouri Romaneşti (Romanian Echoes). Oct. 1974 - Feb. 1979. 8 cm.

ROMANIAN CANADIAN FOLK AND ARTS SOCIETY
TORONTO, ONT.
Clippings from *Romanian Voice* on Romanian culture, n.d., and texts (illustrations) on Romanian museography, art, and culture. 7 cm.
Georgescu, Forian, ed. *Muzeul de Istorie al Republicii Socialiste Romania*. Bucarest, 1975. 140 pp., in English.
Musicescu, Maria A. and G. Ionescu, eds. *Bierica Domnească din Curtea de Argeş*. Bucarest: Editura Meridiane, 1976. 55 pp., in Romanian.
Nicolescu, Corina, ed. *Icoane Vechi Româneşti*. 3rd edition. Bucureşti: Editura Meridiane, 1976. 69 pp., in Romanian.
Voroneţ. 2nd edition, introduction by M. Musicescu. Bucureşti: Editura Meridiane, 1971. 60 pp., in Romanian.

ROMANIAN CULTURAL ASSOCIATION
HAMILTON, ONT.
Records include by-laws of R.C.A. and Football League, 1957-67; minutes of general and joint meetings with Montreal, Quebec, Toronto, Kitchener, Windsor, and Hamilton, 1957-77; correspondence, 1970-77; and financial reports, and statements, 1957-74. Miscellaneous items include camp and soccer club records, papers from radio programme, assorted newsletters, flyers, invitations, and clippings. 2 reels of microfilm. Photographs.
7 photographs: Romanian National Day celebration in Hamilton, 1973.
Tribuna Română. 1951-52. Romanian Cultural Association. 123 pp. (9 issues, monthly).

ROMANIAN DOINA CLUB
HAMILTON, ONT.
 Club minutes, journal, and accounts,
n.d.; and Doina Dance Group Presentation programme, 1976. 3 cm. Photographs.
See John Omorean.

ROMANIAN ORTHODOX CHURCH
TORONTO, ONT.
 Yearbooks, including a bi-centennial
edition, and annual reports from
selected pages of Episcopal annual
calendars, 1971-76. 6 cm.
 Calendarul America. Detroit:
Uniunea si Liga (Societăţilor
Romaneśti din Statele Unite si
Canada), 1973. Yearbook. 217 pp, in
English.
 *Calendarul: Naţional-Ilustrat al
Românilor Americani pe anul 1976.*
Detroit: Uniunea si Liga, 1976. 1 cm,
in English.
 Calendarul Solia. Detroit: Romanian
Orthodox Episcopate of America,
1976. Yearbook. 215 pp., in English.

ROMANIAN ORTHODOX CHURCH OF
THE HOLY RESURRECTION
HAMILTON, ONT.
 The collection contains financial
journals, 1938, 1951; funeral, birth,
and christening records, 1937-75;
membership books, 1942-51; and
minutes and financial accounts of
church choir, 1958-68. Along with
membership books of the ladies'
auxiliary "Reuniunea," and financial
report, 1936-48, the *United Society of
Romanians* journals, 1932-51. 3 reels
of microfilm. Photographs. Taped
interviews with V. Bodnariuk and J.
Dimitru. See Nicolai Cupcic.
 Holy Resurrection Romanian Ortho-

*dox Church: 60th Anniversary,
1916-1976.* Hamilton, 1976. 64 pp.,
in English/Romanian.

ROMANIAN ORTHODOX EPISCOPATE
OF AMERICA
DETROIT, MICHIGAN
 *Historical Anniversary Album,
1929-1979.* Jackson, Michigan:
Romanian Orthodox Episcopate of
America, 1979. llustrated. 128 pp., in
English.

ROMANIAN ORTHODOX MISSION
TORONTO, ONT.
 Troiţa: The Holy Cross. Toronto,
June 1953, Oct. 1968. Newsletter.
Romanian Orthodox Mission in
Toronto. 1 cm, in Romanian.

ST. GEORGE'S ORTHODOX CHURCH
TORONTO, ONT.
 Interviewed on 23 Oct. 1977; 1.5
hrs.; 2 tapes; English; by Eugene
Buia. Discussion with parishioners on
30-year history of church during a
two-day festival of the burning of the
church mortgage.

RUSSIAN COLLECTION

ABRAMOVICH, JACOB
ROCKFORD, ONT.
 Interviewed on 28 Feb. 1978; 1 hr.;
1 tape; Russian; by A. Mostovoy.
Immigrated to Canada in 1974.

ABRAMOVICH, LEONID
TORONTO, ONT.
 Interviewed on 20 April 1977; 1 hr.;
1 tape; Russian; by A. Mostovoy.

AIZIN, SELMA AND HINDY FRIDMAN
TORONTO, ONT.
 Interviewed on 6 Sept. 1977; 1 hr.;
1 tape; English; by A. Mostovoy.

ANDERSON, NIEL
TORONTO, ONT.
 Ontario Welcome House brochure on
Russian immigrants, 1977-78. .5 cm.
Taped interview with director of
Ontario Welcome House.
 Interviewed on 8 Dec. 1977; 1 hr.; 1
tape; English; by A. Mostovoy. Dis-
cusses activities of Ontario Welcome
House.

BAKICH, GERRY
THUNDER BAY, ONT.
 Russian Orthodox Messenger. New
York, Feb., June, Sept. 1902. 2 cm.

BALATOVSKY, SIMEON
TORONTO, ONT.
 Interviewed on 29 March 1977; 1
hr.; 1 tape; Russian; by A.
Mostovoy. Arrived in Canada in
1975.

BERKOVICH, IDA
TORONTO, ONT.
 Interviewed on 18 April 1978; 1 hr.;
1 tape; Russian; by A. Mostovoy.

BERKOVICH, RAYA
TORONTO, ONT.
 Interviewed on 20 April 1978; 1 hr.;
1 tape; Russian; by A. Mostovoy.

BIBERSHTEIN, NAILYA
TORONTO, ONT.
 Newspaper articles and correspondence dealing with Boris Bibershtein's
fight for re-union of his family,
1976-77. 1 cm, in English/Russian
(26 items). Taped interview.
 Interviewed on 6 June 1977; 1 hr.; 1
tape; Russian; by A. Mostovoy.

BRAT, MIKHAIL
HAMILTON, ONT.
 2 newsclippings about donor, violinist of Hamilton Symphony Orchestra,
immigrant from the U.S.S.R.,
1976-77. .25 cm. Taped interview.
 Interviewed on 4 Aug. 1977; .5 hr.;
1 tape; Russian; by M. Swoboda.

BRAUNSHTEIN, RAISA AND SULY
HAMILTON, ONT.
 Interviewed on 24 June 1980; 2 hrs.;
2 tapes; English; by Hana Cipris.

BUKHMAN, ALEX
HAMILTON, ONT.
 Interviewed on 8 July 1980; 1 hr.; 1
tape; English; by Hana Cipris.

CARMELLY, FELICIA
TORONTO, ONT.
 4 photographs: Russian immigrants in Toronto, c. 1970s. Taped interview.
 Interviewed on 15 Sept. 1977; 1 hr.; 1 tape; English; by A. Mostovoy.
 Arrived in Canada in 1963.

CHECHIK, MIRIAM
TORONTO, ONT.
 2 letters to donor, n.d. Photographs. Taped interview.
 8 photographs: Miriam Chechik's ancestors in Russia; and her school years in Toronto, 1900-76.
 Interviewed on 21 June 1977; 1 hr.; 1 tape; English; by A. Mostovoy.
 Arrived in Canada in 1973.

CIPRIS, HANA
HAMILTON, ONT.
 3 clippings from the newspaper *Federation News*, 1979-80, regarding Jewish-Russian immigrants in Hamilton.

COHERVA-CURTIS, STEPHEN
TORONTO, ONT.
 Scrapbook, 1925-57, containing correspondence, a financial statement, pamphlets, programmes, invitations, announcements, and clippings. Most of the material is related to the Russian Orthodox Christ the Saviour Cathedral in Toronto. 1 reel of microfilm. Photographs. Taped interview.
 9 photographs: parish activities; and ceremonies at the Russian Orthodox Christ the Saviour Cathedral in Toronto, c. 1957-70.
 Interviewed in Sept. 1977; 1 hr.; 1 tape; English; by A. Mostovoy.
 Arrived in Canada in 1921.

CROLL, DAVID
TORONTO, ONT.
 Interviewed on 4 Oct. 1977; 1 hr.; 1 tape; English; by A. Nicholson.

DJACHINA, MARY
TORONTO, ONT.
 Correspondence and certificates documenting the appointment and work of Rev. John Djachina, 1929-73. 1 reel of microfilm. Photographs. Taped interview.
 14 photographs: religious and cultural activities at Christ the Saviour Russian Orthodox Church in Toronto, 1930-73.
 Interviewed on 9 May 1977; 1 hr.; 1 tape; English; by A. Mostovoy.
 Russian Orthodox Calendars. 1953, 1956, 1962. Metropolitan Council of the Russian Orthodox Church in North America. 342 pp. Microfilm.
 Troitsky Calendar, 1943. St. Troitsky Monastery, Jordanville, New York. Includes "Rules for Carphagen and Konstantinopol Cathedrals" and "Troitsky Book." 224 pp. Microfilm.

DJUSIM, MICHAIL
TORONTO, ONT.
 Interviewed on 28 Sept. 1977; 1 hr.; 1 tape; Russian; by A. Mostovoy. Immigrated to Canada in 1972.

DOVENMAN, ALEX
TORONTO, ONT.
 Newsclippings and personal letter from the Soviet Union, c. 1970s. Taped interview.
 Interviewed on 26 March 1977; 1 hr.; 1 tape; English; by A. Mostovoy.
 Arrived in Canada in 1974.

FABRICIUS, LEO
TORONTO, ONT.
 13 photographs: Russian immigrants

at social gatherings, n.d.; and theatrical productions, 1960-65 in Toronto. Taped interview.
Interviewed on 9 Aug. 1977; 1 hr.; 1 tape; Russian; by A. Mostovoy. Immigrated to Canada in 1951.

FERDMAN, VLADIMIR
TORONTO, ONT.
Interviewed on 11 Feb. 1978; 1 hr.; 1 tape; Russian; by A. Mostovoy.

FLEISCHER, YUMA
TORONTO, ONT.
1 photograph: the Fleischer family in Toronto, 1975. Taped interview.
Interviewed on 8 Aug. 1977; 1 hr.; 1 tape; Russian; by A. Mostovoy.

FLEITMAN, EUGENIA
TORONTO, ONT.
Interviewed on 23 Jan. 1978; 1 hr.; 1 tape; Russian; by A. Mostovoy.

FRAJDENRAJCH, RAISA
HAMILTON, ONT.
Interviewed on 17 July 1980; 1 hr.; 1 tape; English; by Hana Cipris.

GARBER, BORIS AND YELENA
HAMILTON, ONT.
Interviewed on 9 June 1980; 1 hr.; 1 tape; Russian; by Hana Cipris.

GIL, VICTOR
HAMILTON, ONT.
Interviewed on 6 Aug. 1977; .5 hr.; 1 tape; Russian; by V. Swoboda.

GOLD, NATHAN
TORONTO, ONT.
Interviewed on 31 May 1977; 1 hr.; 1 tape; English; by A. Mostovoy. Immigrated to Canada in 1903.

GOLOVKO, YEKATERINA
TORONTO, ONT.
Interviewed on 4 June 1977; 2 hrs.; 2 tapes; Russian; by A. Mostovoy.

GREEN, RABBI MORTON
HAMILTON, ONT.
Interviewed on 9 July 1980; 1 hr.; 1 tape; English; by Hana Cipris. Immigrated to Canada in the 1970s.

GRESSEROV, PETER
TORONTO, ONT.
Personal papers, mostly military certificates from 6th Kazan Regiment, 1910s-1920s (18 items). Photographs. Taped interview.
8 photographs: the Gresserov family in Russia, Turkey, Yugoslavia, Italy, and Toronto, 1913-66.
Interviewed on 24 Aug. 1977; 2 hrs.; 2 tapes; Russian; by A. Mostovoy. Arrived in Canada in 1952.

GRODZEVSKY-HAIT, ZOYA
TORONTO, ONT.
Interviewed on 27 March 1977; 1 hr.; 1 tape; English; by A. Mostovoy.

GROSSMAN, GEORGINA
TORONTO, ONT.
Bulletins, flyers and letters on Russian Jewry in Canada, issued by the National Council of Jewish Women. 1 cm (13 items). Photographs. Taped interview.
3 photographs: activities of National Council of Jewish Women in Toronto, 1970s.
Interviewed on 5 April 1977; 1 hr.; 1 tape; English; by A. Mostovoy.

GRUCH, MRS.
TORONTO, ONT.
File containing pamphlet,

newsclippings, and announcements on Soviet Jewish immigration, c. 1970s. 2 cm.
Megillath Esther Kol Yisroel Chaverim (To bring a closer relationship between American, Canadian, and Russian Jewry). Elizabeth, New Jersey: Mohir, c. 1970. Pamphlet, in Russian.

GRUSH, SHEIVA
TORONTO, ONT.
Interviewed on 25 April 1978; 1 hr.; 1 tape; Russian; by A. Mostovoy.

GURSKY, OLGA
TORONTO, ONT.
Personal papers of Olga Gursky, including documents of identity and passport, 1955-67; and reminiscences of Russian Army, and testimonial from Tzar Alexander, Yugoslavia belonging to George Gursky, 1919-64. 1 cm (15 items). Photographs. Taped interview.
9 photographs: Colonel George and Olga Gursky, most taken with groups of Russian Legionnaires in Toronto, c. 1955-75.
Interviewed on 20 June 1977; 2 hrs.; 2 tapes; Russian; by A. Mostovoy. Immigrated to Canada in 1957.

GURVITZ, INNA
HAMILTON, ONT.
Interviewed on 10 June 1980; 1 hr.; 1 tape; English; by Hana Cipris.

HARJU, UUNO
ST. CATHARINES, ONT.
Minz, I. *The Army of the Soviet Union.* Moscow: Foreign Languages Publishing House, 1942. 172 pp.

HAROUTIOUNIAN, ELEONORA
HAMILTON, ONT.
Baggage label issued by Hebrew Immigrant Aid Society to new immigrants, n.d., and article from *Spectator* about donor, 19 March 1977. Photographs. Taped interview.
Interviewed on 16 June 1980; 1 hr.; 1 tape; Russian; by Hana Cipris.

ILIVITSKY, DORA
HAMILTON, ONT.
Interviewed on 23 July 1980; 2 hrs.; 2 tapes; Russian; by Hana Cipris.

ILIVITSKY, ZINA
HAMILTON, ONT.
5 letters from friends of the Ilivitski who were considered dissidents and "refuseniks" when the letters were written, 1980. .5 cm, in Russian. Photographs. Taped interview.
3 photographs: the Ilivitski family in Hamilton, 1980.
Interviewed on 11 July 1980; 2 hrs.; 2 tapes; English; by Hana Cipris.

INTRATOR, GLENYA
TORONTO, ONT.
Interviewed on 8 Sept. 1977; 1 hr.; 1 tape; English; by A. Mostovoy. Arrived in Canada in 1950.

KAUFMAN, ARKADY
TORONTO, ONT.
Certificates for valour during WWII; and passport for entry into Austria, n.d. .5 cm. Taped interview.
Interviewed on 12 Aug. 1977; 1 hr.; 1 tape; Russian; by A. Mostovoy.

KAUFMAN, PEPI
TORONTO, ONT.
Interviewed on 7 March 1978; 1 hr.; 1 tape; English; by A. Mostovoy.

KAVALERCHIK, LEIB
HAMILTON, ONT.
7 photographs: the Kavalerchik family, U.S.S.R., and Toronto, 1955-80.
Taped interview.
Interviewed on 4 July 1980; 2 hrs.; 2 tapes; English; by Hana Cipris.

KAZAKOV, SASHA AND ALLA
BURLINGTON, ONT.
Interviewed on 9 July 1980; 2 hrs.; 2 tapes; English; by Hana Cipris.

KERLER, OLEG
HAMILTON, ONT.
Interviewed on 19 June 1980; 1 hr.; 1 tape; English; by Hana Cipris.

KERNES, IRINA
BURLINGTON, ONT.
Interviewed on 9 July 1980; 1 hr.; 1 tape; Russian; by Hana Cipris.

KLIMOV, ANDREW
TORONTO, ONT.
Interviewed on 21, 27 July 1977; 2 hrs.; 2 tapes; English; by A. Mostovoy. Immigrated to Canada in 1948.

KOSAROW, IRENE
TORONTO, ONT.
Interviewed on 17 June 1977; 1 hr.; 1 tape; English; by A. Mostovoy.

KOTLYAR, BELLA
TORONTO, ONT.
13 photographs: Bella Kotlyar and her family, U.S.S.R., 1940-56.
Taped interview.
Interviewed on 26 Nov. 1977; 1 hr.; 1 tape; Russian; by A. Mostovoy.

KRAMES, CAROL
HAMILTON, ONT.
Interviewed on 14 Aug. 1980; 1 hr.; 1 tape; English; by Hana Cipris.

KRASNER, LEONID
TORONTO, ONT.
Interviewed on 11 May 1977; 1 hr.; 1 tape; Russian; by A. Mostovoy.
Arrived in Canada in 1971.

KRASNOV, SIMON
TORONTO, ONT.
Military distinctions and newsclipping, 1973; and letter from United Jewish Appeal, n.d. Photographs. Taped interview.
10 photographs: mostly of Major S. Krasnov in Soviet Army in Russia, and Germany, 1945-76; and Soviet immigrants en route to Canada, 1975.
Interviewed on 8 July 1977; 1 hr.; 1 tape; Russian; by A. Mostovoy.

KRUGLYAK, BELLA
TORONTO, ONT.
2 letters from friends and relatives in the Soviet Union, 1977. Photograph. Taped interview.
1 photograph: B. Kruglyak in Toronto, 1977.
Interviewed on 22 April 1977; 1 hr.; 1 tape; Russian; by A. Mostovoy.

KUCHINSKY, TATIANA
TORONTO, ONT.
Letters and notices concerning the foundation of a Russian club by members of the Joseph E. and Minnie Wagman Centre; lists of Russian members of Wagman Centre; and schedule of events from same, c. 1970s. Taped interview.
Interviewed on 14 Feb. 1978; 1 hr.; 1 tape; English; by A. Mostovoy.

KUPERMAN, IRA
TORONTO, ONT.
Papers tracing the Kuperman
family's immigration to Canada, c.
1960s-1970s. 1 cm. Photographs.
Taped interview.
4 photographs: pre-migration, Danil
Kuperman and family members,
Odessa, 1960-75.
Interviewed on 18 April 1977; 1 hr.;
1 tape; Russian; by A. Mostovoy.

KUPERMAN, MIRON
TORONTO, ONT.
Interviewed on 13 Dec. 1977; 1 hr.;
1 tape; Russian; by A. Mostovoy.
Immigrated to Canada in the 1970s.

LEFEL, MICHAEL
TORONTO, ONT.
Interviewed on 13 Nov. 1977; 1 hr.;
1 tape; Russian; by A. Mostovoy.

LEIDERMAN, EFIM
TORONTO, ONT.
Interviewed on 11 Feb. 1978; 1 hr.;
1 tape; Russian; by A. Mostovoy.

LESHCHINSKAYA, ELENA
TORONTO, ONT.
16 photographs: donor's family,
U.S.S.R., Italy, and Toronto,
1922-72. Taped interview.
Interviewed on 8 Feb. 1978; 1 hr.; 1
tape; Russian; by A. Mostovoy.

LIPOVETSKY, E.
TORONTO, ONT.
Interviewed on 21 March 1978; 1
hr.; 1 tape; Russian; by A.
Mostovoy.

LITSKY, LARISA
TORONTO, ONT.
Daughter's school report cards and
certificates of advancement, c. 1950s.

Photographs. Taped interview.
21 photographs: the Litsky family in
Odessa, Leningrad, Rome, and
Toronto, 1946-74.
Interviewed on 3 April 1978; 1 hr.;
1 tape; Russian; by A. Mostovoy.

LUCIUK, LUBOMYR
KINGSTON, ONT.
Lenin, V.I. *Proletarskaia Revoliutsia
i Renegat Kautskii.* 1920. 150 pp., in
Russian (photocopy).
*Kalendar' popovskii i Kalendar'
sovetskii.* 120 pp., in Russian (photo-
copy).
*Kommerscheskiia, rekomendatel'nyia
i prositel'nyia pisma.* 60 pp., in Rus-
sian/English (photocopy).
*Noveishii i Poln'ii Russko-Angliiskii i
Angliisko-Russkii Pis'monik.* New
York, 1918. 64 pp. (photocopy).

MALCHENKO, REV. VLADIMIR
TORONTO, ONT.
Interviewed on 6 Oct. 1977; 1 hr.; 1
tape; Russian; by A. Mostovoy.

MANDELSHTAM, BENJAMIN
TORONTO, ONT.
Interviewed on 11 July 1977; 1 hr.;
1 tape; Russian; by A. Mostovoy.
Arrived in Canada in 1976.

MARKUS, ROBERTA
TORONTO, ONT.
Interviewed on 2 Nov. 1977; 1 hr.;
1 tape; English; by A. Mostovoy.
Arrived in Canada in 1947.

MATIKAINEN, ALEXANDER AND
LEMPI
HAMILTON, ONT.
Interviewed on 21 Aug. 1977; 1 hr.;
2 tapes; Russian; by M. Swoboda.

MILKIS, YAKOV
TORONTO, ONT.
Soviet exit visa and announcement
for a concert of Yakov Milkis, and
his wife Mariana Rosenfeld, c. 1970s.
Photographs. Taped interview.
14 photographs: Y. Milkis, family
members, and fellow musicians,
U.S.S.R., and Toronto, 1960-77.
Interviewed on 26 July 1977; 1 hr.;
1 tape; Russian; by A. Mostovoy.

MIRKIN, EUGENIYA
HAMILTON, ONT.
1 photograph: the Mirkin family,
1979. Taped interview.
Interviewed on 16 June 1980; 1 hr.;
1 tape; English; by Hana Cipris.

MOCHORUK, NATALIA
TORONTO, ONT.
Interviewed on 16 April 1978; 1 hr.;
1 tape; Ukrainian/English/
Russian; by A. Mostovoy.

MORANIS, ANN
TORONTO, ONT.
Letters and report pertaining to the
Jewish Vocational Service, 1973-74;
and minutes of meetings of the Advisory Committee for Russian Engineers. 1 cm (7 items). Taped interview.
Interviewed on 20 Oct. 1977; 1 hr.;
1 tape; English; by A. Mostovoy.

MOSTOVOY, ALEX
TORONTO, ONT.
Pamphlets and job offer documents
from the Jewish Immigrant Aid
Society, c. 1976-77. 2 cm. Photograph. Taped interview.
1 photograph: taken at Camp
Northland-B'nai Brith, where children
of Russian immigrants rest in summer.

MOSTOVOY, ANNA
TORONTO, ONT.
Documents tracing family's immigration to Canada, brief personal file on
recent Russian Jewish immigration,
and pamphlets dated from 1977. 4
cm. Photographs.
3 photographs: degrees issued by
Russian universities, n.d.
Dorogie Druzia (Dear Friends). 1977
(12 issues).
Jews in the U.S.S.R.. 6, 27 May; 3
June 1977. .5 cm.

NAUMOV, HELLENE
TORONTO, ONT.
Interviewed on 16 July 1977; 1 hr.;
1 tape; English; by A. Mostovoy.

NEUSHUL, LEON
TORONTO, ONT.
Interviewed on 23 Aug. 1977; 1 hr.;
1 tape; English; by A. Mostovoy.
Immigrated to Canada in 1952.

PAPINIAN, SONIA
HAMILTON, ONT.
Interviewed on 23 June 1980; 1 hr.;
1 tape; Russian; by Hana Cipris.

PEKAR, EVA
TORONTO, ONT.
Letters and documents recording the
family's immigration to Canada;
certificates and diploma of Eva Pekar,
and correspondence ragarding her
father's release, n.d. Photograph.
Taped interview.
1 photograph: tombs and sepulchral
monuments, U.S.S.R, c. 1965.
Interviewed on 16 April 1977; 1 hr.;
1 tape; Russian; by A. Mostovoy.

PEKAR, SOLOMON
TORONTO, ONT.
Interviewed on 5 Feb. 1978; 1 hr.; 1
tape; Russian; by A. Mostovoy.

PENNER, DAWN
ST. CATHARINES, ONT.
Printed items from Niagara Credit
Union, 1976-78. 1 cm.

PEREL, MINDEL
TORONTO, ONT.
Interviewed on 9 Dec. 1977; 2 hrs.;
2 tapes; Russian; by A. Mostovoy.
Immigrated to Canada in 1976.

PERLAMUTROV, SEMYON
TORONTO, ONT.
Interviewed on 27 Nov. 1977; 1 hr.;
1 tape; Russian; by A. Mostovoy.

PLATONOVA, ELENA
TORONTO, ONT.
6 photographs: the Platonova family,
U.S.S.R., and Toronto, 1900-51.
Taped interview.
Interviewed on 19 March 1978; 1
hr.; 1 tape; Russian; by A.
Mostovoy.

POCH, LOUIS
TORONTO, ONT.
Interviewed on 23 Aug. 1977; 1 hr.;
1 tape; English; by A. Mostovoy.
Arrived in Canada in 1924.

RAEVSKY, DMITRY
TORONTO, ONT.
Interviewed on 22 Oct. 1977; 1 hr.;
1 tape; Russian; by A. Mostovoy.
Arrived in Canada in 1952.

RAYTSINA, GALINA
HAMILTON, ONT.
10 photographs: the Raytsina family,
U.S.S.R., 1922-76. Taped interview.

Interviewed on 16 June 1980; 2 hrs.;
2 tapes; Russian; by Hana Cipris.

REIMER, RUTH
PORT ROWAN, ONT.
2 Russian passports, identity cards,
medical certificates, and railway cards
of Aron and Marie Pauls, 1926. 1 cm
(8 items).

REITER, DORA
TORONTO, ONT.
Soviet student's record book, 1921.
Taped interview.
Interviewed on 15 Feb. 1978; 1 hr.;
1 tape; Russian/Yiddish/English; by
A. Mostovoy. Immigrated to Canada
in 1925.

RESNIK, SAMUEL
TORONTO, ONT.
Interviewed on 26 Sept. 1977; 1 hr.;
1 tape; English; by A. Mostovoy.

ROZLER, GARRY
TORONTO, ONT.
Interviewed on 12 March 1978; 1
hr.; 1 tape; Russian; by A.
Mostovoy. Arrived in Canada in
1975.

SADOFF, RAISKE
TORONTO, ONT.
Interviewed on 18 July 1977; 1 hr.;
1 tape; English; by A. Mostovoy.
Immigrated to Canada in the 1920s.

SADOWSKI, DAVID
TORONTO, ONT.
Interviewed on 22 Nov. 1977; 1 hr.;
1 tape; English; by A. Mostovoy.

SALMON, FRIDA
TORONTO, ONT.
Interviewed on 21 March 1978; 1
hr.; 1 tape; Russian; by A.
Mostovoy.

SCHMALZ, W. H. E.
KITCHENER, ONT.
Hiebert, Henry. *Recollections of My
Life in Russia, 1896-24*. Kitchener,
n.d. 34 pp.

SELESHKO, MIKHAILO
TORONTO, ONT.
Interviewed on 25 June 1977; 1 hr.;
1 tape; Ukrainian; by A. Mostovoy.
Immigrated to Canada in 1948.

SHAFIROVITCH, ARKADY
TORONTO, ONT.
Letters describing the difficulties in
obtaining Soviet exit visa for donor's
mother; and copies of House of Commons Debates, c. 1970s. Taped interview.
Interviewed on 15 Oct. 1977; 1 hr.;
1 tape; Russian; by A. Mostovoy.
Arrived in Canada in 1971.

SHERMAN, BENJAMAN
TORONTO, ONT.
Copy of congratulatory messages
from the Prime Minister on donor's
103rd birthday. Taped interview.
Interviewed on 6 Feb. 1978; 1 hr.; 1
tape; Russian/Ukrainian/English; by
A. Mostovoy. Arrived in Canada in
1905.

SHERMAN, SAM
TORONTO, ONT.
Recorded in Sept. 1982; 1 hr.; 1
tape; music; by A. Mostovoy. A
recording of Sam Sherman, 107 years
old, playing the drums with his
daughter on the piano.

SHINDELMAN, LUCIA
TORONTO, ONT.
Collection of letters, diplomas, and
newsclippings on the musical career
of Arkady Shindelman beginning
1954. Taped interview.
Interviewed on 6 Nov. 1977; 1 hr.;
1 tape; Russian; by A. Mostovoy.

SHKOLNIK, LEONID AND ANNA
HAMILTON, ONT.
School papers and certificates of
members of the Shkolnik family,
1978-1980. Photographs. Taped interview.
5 photographs: the Shkolnik family,
1978-80.
Interviewed on 7 July 1980; 2 hrs.; 2
tapes; English; by Hana Cipris.

SHLYONSKY, ZINORY
HAMILTON, ONT.
Interviewed on 4 Aug. 1977; 1 hr.; 1
tape; Russian; by M. Swoboda and
V. Swoboda.

SHTERENBERG, ALEXANDER
TORONTO, ONT.
Interviewed on 14 Aug. 1977; 1 hr.;
1 tape; Russian; by A. Mostovoy.

SHTERENBERG, MARK
TORONTO, ONT.
Interviewed on 24 Nov. 1977; 1 hr.;
1 tape; Russian; by A. Mostovoy.

SHTERENBERG, NAVA
TORONTO, ONT.
Diplomas and newsclippings on
donor's chess-playing career, c.
1975-80. Photographs. Taped interview.
Interviewed on 14 Aug. 1977; 1 hr.;
1 tape; Russian; by A. Mostovoy.

SHTERN, BORIS
HAMILTON, ONT.
Interviewed on 8, 11, 22 June 1980; 3 hrs.; 3 tapes; Russian; by Hana Cipris.

SIRKIS, ARKADY
TORONTO, ONT.
Interviewed on 5 March 1978; 1 hr.; 1 tape; Russian; by A. Mostovoy.

SITNIK, TAISA
HAMILTON, ONT.
Interviewed on 8 Aug. 1977; 1 hr.; 1 tape; Russian; by M. Swoboda.

SOKOLINSKY, POLINA
TORONTO, ONT.
9 photographs: the Sokolinsky family, U.S.S.R., 1933-50. Taped interview.
Interviewed on 19 Jan. 1978; 1 hr.; 1 tape; Russian; by A. Mostovoy.

STUDIN, YURI
TORONTO, ONT.
4 photographs: the Yuri Studin in Italy, and Toronto, 1976-78. Taped interview.
Interviewed on 25 Jan. 1978; 1 hr.; 1 tape; Russian; by A. Mostovoy.

SUMBERG, JESSIE
TORONTO, ONT.
Interviewed on 21 Feb. 1978; 1 hr.; 1 tape; Russian/English/Yiddish; by A. Mostovoy.

SWOBODA, LUDMILLA
HAMILTON, ONT.
Donor's personal documents, mostly from the Soviet Union, 1940-49; including covering letter from Canada's Deputy Minister of Labour, stating that Ludmilla Swodoba has agreed to the immigration require-

ments imposed prior to embarkation. Photographs. Taped interview.
32 photographs: the Swoboda family in Russia, Germany, Gravenhurst, and Hamilton, 1894-1960; activities at Russian School in the Russian Orthodox Church, 1954; and ship of donor's crossing to Canada.
Interviewed on 11 Aug. 1977; 1 hr.; 1 tape; English; by M. Swoboda.

SWOBODA, V. AND M.
HAMILTON, ONT.
Two interviews with anonymous interviewees 25 July 1977; 1 hr.; 2 tapes; Russian; by V. Swoboda and M. Swoboda and 15 July 1977; 1 hr.; 1 tape; Russian/English; by V. Swoboda.
Awake. Vol. 54, no. 11. Toronto, June 1973. Watchtower Bible and Tract Society, Jehovah Witness. 32 pp.

TABACK, TOBBI
TORONTO, ONT.
Interviewed on 28 Aug. 1977; 1 hr.; 1 tape; English; by A. Mostovoy.

TOOLIVETRO, MARIA
HAMILTON, ONT.
5 photographs: Maria Toolivetro, U.S.S.R., and Copenhagen, 1918-19. Taped interview.
Interviewed on 4 July 1977; .5 hr.; 1 tape; Russian; by M. Swoboda. Arrived in Canada in 1919.
Kiwanis Club of Hamilton Inc. Centennial Project Programme, 24 Oct. 1967. A celebration of elderly immigrants, "Canadians All," donor included. .5 cm, in English.

TOPOLSKI, WANDA
TORONTO, ONT.
Interviewed on 22 Oct. 1977; 1 hr.;
1 tape; English; by A. Mostovoy.

TSIMBERG, ISAAK
TORONTO, ONT.
Interviewed on 5 May 1977; 1 hr.; 1
tape; Russian; by A. Mostovoy.
Arrived in Canada in 1976.

VAISMAN, BORIS AND MARIANA
HAMILTON, ONT.
Interviewed on 20 Aug. 1977; 2
hrs.; 2 tapes; Russian; by Hana
Cipris.

VEKSLER, NADYA
TORONTO, ONT.
Interviewed on 6 Dec. 1977; 1 hr.; 1
tape; Russian; by A. Mostovoy.

YANIVKER, ARKADY
TORONTO, ONT.
Interviewed on 14 June 1977; 1 hr.;
1 tape; Russian; by A. Mostovoy.

YANKIVER, STEVE
TORONTO, ONT.
Interviewed on 11 June 1977; 1 hr.;
1 tape; English; by A. Mostovoy.

YARIS, LUBOV
TORONTO, ONT.
Student book of Lubov Yaris,
Odessa, and U.S.S.R., 1917. .5 cm.
Photographs. Taped interview.
22 photographs: the Yaris family,
taken mostly in Odessa, U.S.S.R.,
1902-75.
Interviewed on 1 April 1978; 1 hr.;
1 tape; Russian; by A. Mostovoy.

YOPIN, ARON
TORONTO, ONT.
Interviewed on 2 April 1978; 1 hr.;
1 tape; Russian; by A. Mostovoy.

ZAJDNER, SUSAN
TORONTO, ONT.
Papers from National Council of
Jewish Women concerning Russian
Jewry in Canada. 2 cm (5 items).
Taped interview.
Interviewed on 26 April 1977; 1 hr.;
1 tape; English; by A. Mostovoy.

ZEIN, MUSYA
TORONTO, ONT.
Communique regarding Soviet Jewry
and newspaper article about donor,
1978. Photographs. Taped interview.
3 photographs: Musya Zein,
U.S.S.R., Israel, and Toronto,
1969-76.
Interviewed on 30 March 1978; 1
hr.; 1 tape; Russian; by A.
Mostovoy. Immigrated to Canada in
1971.

ASSOCIATION OF NEW CANADIANS
FROM THE U.S.S.R.
HAMILTON, ONT.
Members' meeting recorded on 9
April 1978; 2.5 hrs.; 3 tapes; Russian/English; by A. Mostovoy.

ASSOCIATION OF NEW CANADIANS
FROM THE U.S.S.R.
TORONTO, ONT.
Records, 1977-78, comprise letters
patent, by-laws, and structure of the
Association; agendas and minutes of
Associational meetings, and protocols
of the Executive Committee; letters
and communiques to members and
from other organizations; and leaflets,

newsclippings, and assorted notes concerning the activities of Association. 3 cm. Taped interviews with members, S. Grush, M. Lefel, H. Naumov, and audio recordings of meetings.

ASSOCIATION OF NEW CANADIANS FROM THE U.S.S.R., MUSIC SCHOOL
TORONTO, ONT.
Recorded on 12 April 1978; 1 hr.; 1 tape; Russian; by A. Mostovoy.

CANADIAN COMMITTEE FOR SOVIET JEWRY
TORONTO, ONT.
Communiques, bulletins, and programmes issued by the Canadian Committee for Soviet Jewry, 1977. 6 cm. Taped interview with S. Reznik and D. Sadowsky, national directors.

CHRIST THE SAVIOUR CATHEDRAL RUSSIAN ORTHODOX CHURCH
TORONTO, ONT.
Church registers off births, marriages, and deaths; and applications, 1922-75; correspondence about church events, 1940-76; appointment certificates for rector and priest, 1929, 1956; statute and by-laws, 1954, 1977; and church calendars. See Mary Djachina. 3 reels of microfilm. 15 cm.
Canadian Greek-Orthodox Calendar. Vol. 4 - vol. 23. Toronto-Montreal, 1955-74 Diocesan Council of the Russian Greek Orthodox Church. Incomplete. 15 books, in Russian/Ukranian.
Jubilee Book of the Russian Orthodox Christ the Saviour Cathedral in Toronto, 1915-1965. Toronto, 1965. 48 pp. Illustrated, in Russian.

HOLY BLOSSOM TEMPLE
TORONTO, ONT.
Papers pertaining to Programme Isaiah for integration of Russian-Jewish immigrants, 1973-79. They include programme and regulations, correspondence, a financial statement and brief report; also miscellaneous items—leaflets and announcements, membership list of Russian Youth Club, and list of Russian immigrants seeking employment. 3 cm. Taped interview with F. Carmelly, director of Programme Isaiah.

HOLY TRINITY RUSSIAN ORTHODOX CHURCH (REV. V. MALCHENKO)
TORONTO, ONT.
Leaflets issued by the Holy Trinity Church, n.d., and programme for Christmas play, 1962. Photographs. Taped interview with Rev. E. Malchenko.
44 photographs: "Fir-Tree" celebration, 1967-68; theatrical performance "Vasilia the Beautiful," 1962; and graduation ceremonies at Russian language school, 1970-71.
Obsor Russkoi Pechati (The Russian Press Digest). No. 1. New York, Jan. 1955. 72 pp., in Russian.
Pravoslavnoie Obozrenie (Orthodox Observer). Vol. 21, nos. 41, 42. Montreal: Monastery Press, 1977. 132 pp., in Russian.
Russian Word in Canada. No. 250 - no. 256. Toronto, Oct. 1976 - April 1977. 4 cm, in Russian.

JEWISH IMMIGRANT AID SERVICES OF CANADA
TORONTO, ONT.
Memoranda, a report, bulletins, and programmes, 1975-77. 2 cm. Taped interview with Louis Poch, executive director of J.I.A.S.

MULTICULTURAL HISTORY SOCIETY
OF ONTARIO
TORONTO, ONT.
Vestnik. Toronto, 9 Jan. 1988 - 30
Dec. 1989. 2 reels of microfilm.

NEW CANADIANS CONFERENCE
TORONTO, ONT.
Recorded on 19 Feb. 1978; 3 hrs.; 3
tapes; Russian; by A. Mostovoy.

NOVGOROD PAVILION-CARAVAN
TORONTO, ONT.
Interview in Summer 1977; 1 hr.; 1
tape; Russian/English; by A.
Mostovoy.

ODESSA PAVILION-CARAVAN
TORONTO, ONT.
Programme—the Odessa Group in
"Celebration," directed and chor-
eographed by Taras Shipowick, 1977.
.25 cm. Taped recording.
Recorded in Summer 1977; 1 hr.; 1
tape; Ukrainian/English; by A.
Mostovoy.

ONTARIO ETHNIC NEWSPAPER
MICROFILM PROJECT
TORONTO, ONT.
Kanadsky Gudok. April 1931 - 4
April 1940. 10 reels of microfilm.
Vestnik. Toronto, 6 Nov. 1941 - 26
Dec. 1987. 36 reels of microfilm.

RUSSIAN CANADIAN CULTURAL AID
SOCIETY
TORONTO, ONT.
The collection consists of constitution
and by-laws, 1950-51, 1971; financial
statements, 1950-51; letters to members of Society, and flyers, programmes, invitations concerning
Society activities, 1950-76; and 1
menu from Russian party/ball, 1972.
4 cm. Taped interview with A.

Klimov, vice-president of Society.
35 photographs: cultural activities
and entertainment—beauty contests,
theatrical productions, ballet, folk
dancing—organized by the Society,
Toronto, 1953-75.
10 Lithographs by Eugene Klimoff.
Toronto: Russian Culture Club of
Toronto, c. 1960s.
Russian Word in Canada. Vol. 26,
no. 251, Nov. 1976; vol. 27, no.
256, April 1977. 96 pp.

RUSSIAN CANADIANS AT BAYCREST
CENTRE
TORONTO, ONT.
Recorded on 2 April 1978; 1 hr.; 1
tape; Russian/English/Yiddish; by A.
Mostovoy.

RUSSIAN-CANADIAN T.V. NEWS
TORONTO, ONT.
Recorded Oct. 1977 - March 1978;
Russian/English; 8 recordings; by A.
Mostovoy.

RUSSIAN ORTHODOX CHURCH
HAMILTON, ONT.
Papers include financial records of
the Church, and records of the
Church Women's Group
"Sestrichesto," 1965-76. 3 reels of
microfilm.

RUSSIAN ORTHODOX CHURCH IN
CANADA DIOCESAN COUNCIL
TORONTO, ONT.
Canadian Greek-Orthodox Calendar,
1954. 1 reel of microfilm.

RUSSIAN ORTHODOX CHURCH OUT-
SIDE RUSSIA, DIOCESE OF MONTREAL
AND CANADA CHURCH
HAMILTON, ONT.
Records and church bulletins,
1952-64. 4 reels of microfilm.

RUSSIAN SCHOOL, CHRIST THE SAV-
IOUR RUSSIAN ORTHODOX CHURCH
TORONTO, ONT.
 School documents, including attendance register, 1963-68; programmes
and awards, 1965-77; and principal's
scrapbook, 1968-73. 4 cm. Photographs.
 15 photographs: musical activities at
the Russian School in Toronto,
1965-70.

GROENBERG, PAULA
TORONTO, ONT.
Modersmaale. Jan. 1978 (1 issue).
16 pp.

HARRIS, DANIEL
OTTAWA, ONT.
A founding member of the Canadian
Nordic Society. Collection includes
financial records, and annual reports
from the Nordic Society, 1963-77. 2
cm.

CANADIAN NORDIC SOCIETY
TORONTO, ONT.
Records, 1963-75, which include a
constitution and by-laws, minutes,
correspondence, financial journal, and
members' list. .5 meters. 1 reel of
microfilm. Photographs.
5 photographs: activities of the Nor-
dic Society of Ottawa, 1970.
Scan. Jan. - July 1972. New York:
American Scandinavian Foundation,
1972 (monthly). 1 cm.
Sixtieth Annual Report, 1971. New
York: The American-Scandinavian
Foundation, 1972. 51 pp.
*Styrelse-Och Revisionsberattelser for
ar 1962.* Stockholm: Sverige-Amerika
Stiftelsen, 1962. 32 pp.

MULTICULTURAL HISTORY SOCIETY
OF ONTARIO
TORONTO, ONT.
Mattson, Hans. *The Story of an Emi-
grant.* New York: Arno Press, 1979.
314 pp.

McNight, Roger. *Moberg's Emigrant
Novels and the Journals of Andrew
Peterson: A Study of Influences and
Parallels.* New York: Arno Press,
1979. 235 pp., in English.
Rumblom, Harald and Dag Blank,
eds. *Scandinavia Overseas: Patterns
of Cultural Transformation in North
America and Australia.* Uppsala
Multi-ethnic Papers 7, 1986. 145 pp.,
in English.
Scott, Franklin D. *Trans-Atlantica:
Essay on Scandinavian Migration and
Culture.* New York: Arno Press,
1979. 208 pp., in English.
The Icelandic Canadian. Winter
1985. 48 pp. in English.
*The Scandinavian Canadian Busi-
nessman.* Vol. 1, May 1969 - vol. 10,
Dec. 1977. Oakville. 4 reels of
microfilm.

NORDIC SOCIETY OF TORONTO
TORONTO, ONT.
The collection includes a constitution, 1970; minutes and agendas,
1970-71, 1977; correspondence,
1970-74; financial statements,
1971-77; membership records,
1971-77; and club newsletter,
1970-77. Incomplete. 1 reel of microfilm.

ONTARIO ETHNIC NEWSPAPER
MICROFILM PROJECT
TORONTO, ONT.
Scandinavian News. Oct. 1941 - 1
Sept. 1945. 1 reel of microfilm.

SCANDINAVIAN CANADIAN
BUSINESSMEN'S CLUB
TORONTO, ONT.
 Records, 1965-74, which include a
constitution, minutes, and agenda,
letters to membership, income and
expense statements, membership list,
and miscellaneous printed items such
as menus, carol sheets, circulars,
invitations, and clippings. 1 reel of
microfilm.
 *Scandinavian Canadian Business-
man.* 1976 (3 issues).

SCANDINAVIAN CLUB OF OSHAWA
AND DISTRICT
OSHAWA, ONT.
 Records, 1967-77, which include
minutes, members list, general correspondence, and Club newsletter,
1968-71, 1973-77. Incomplete. 1 reel
of microfilm.

SCANDINAVIAN HOME SOCIETY
THUNDER BAY, ONT.
 Minute book, 1923-26; financial
statements, 1926; letters, 1927; and a
menu, 1926. Photographs.
 2 photographs: building which
housed the Scandinavian Home
Society in Thunder Bay, 1931-42.
 Stadgar (Lover). 1926. 4 pp.

SCOTTISH COLLECTION

CRAWFORD, MARIE
RIPLEY, ONT.
 History of the McLeod and Murray families in Bruce County. Gaelic songs on cassette. 5 cm. Taped interview.
 Interviewed on 23 Aug. 1977; 1 hr.; 1 tape; English; by Lesley McAllister.

DUMBRILLE, DOROTHY
ALEXANDRIA, ONT.
 Interviewed on 3 May 1978; 2 hrs.; 2 tapes; English; by Patricia Kulick.

FRASER, CAMPBELL
ALEXANDRIA, ONT.
 Interviewed on 1 May 1978; 1 hr.; 1 tape; English; by Patricia Kulick.
 A Short History of the Glensandfield United Church, 1880-1975. In commemoration of the 50th anniversary of the founding of the United Church of Canada on 10 June 1925.

FUNSTEN, M.
RIPLEY, ONT.
 Family histories and clippings about Huron Township, Ont., n.d. 2 cm. Photograph.
 1 photograph: the Matheson family, c. 1900.

HOLDER, WILLIAM
DORION, ONT.
 Interviewed on 31 March 1977; 1 hr.; 1 tape; English; by Einar Nordstrom.

MACDONALD, SISTER MARY CLAIR
ALEXANDRIA, ONT.
 Interviewed on 5 Jan. 1978; 1 hr.; 1 tape; English; by Patricia Kulick.

MACKAY, GERTRUDE
RIPLEY, ONT.
 Interviewed on 24 Aug. 1977; .5 hr; 1 tape; English; by Lesley McAllister.

MACKAY, JOHN A.
RIPLEY, ONT.
 Interviewed on 6 Sept. 1977; .5 hr.; 1 tape; English; by Lesley McAllister.

MCDONALD, JAMES H.
GLENGARRY, ONT.
 Interviewed on 14 May 1978; 2 hrs.; 2 tapes; English; by Patricia Kulick.

MCDONALD, MARY
RIPLEY, ONT.
 1 photograph: 2 Lewis children in typical dress.
 The Centennial of Presbyterianism, 1856-1956. Knox Church, Ripley, Ont., 1956. 63 pp.

MCDONALD, NORMAN C.
GODERICH, ONT.
 Interviewed on 31 Aug. 1977; .5 hr.; 1 tape; English; by Lesley McAllister.

MCGREGOR, ANNIE
KINCARDINE, ONT.
 2 photographs: the McGregor family, Isle of Lewis, 1950-60. Taped inter-

view.
 Interviewed on 17 Aug. 1977; .25
hr.; 1 tape; English; by Lesley
McAllister.

MCKAY, JOHN H.
KINCARDINE, ONT.
 Interviewed on 4 Sept. 1977; .75
hr.; 1 tape; English/Gaelic; by Lesley
McAllister.

MCLEOD, SAMUEL
GLENGARRY, ONT.
 Interviewed on 8 May 1978; 2 hrs.;
2 tapes; English; by Patricia Kulick.

PICOT, CHRISTINA M.
RIPLEY, ONT.
 Personal papers, including family
history, n.d. 3 cm. Photographs.
Taped interview.
 5 photographs: Scottish pioneers in
Ripley, Ont.
 Interviewed on 20 Aug. 1977; 1.5
hrs.; 2 tapes; English; by Lesley
McAllister.

SHEILLS, STEWART
RIPLEY, ONT.
 Interviewed on 2 Sept. 1977; .5 hr.;
1 tape; English; by Lesley
McAllister.

_____

MULTICULTURAL HISTORY SOCIETY
OF ONTARIO
TORONTO, ONT.
 Haliburton, Gordon. "'For Their
God'—Education, Religion and the
Scots in Nova Scotia." *Ethnic Heri-
tage Series*. Vol. 1.
 Hanna, Charles A. *The Scots-Irish or
the Scot in North Britain, North Ire-
land, and North America*. New York:
G. P. Putnam's Sons, 1902.

 Landsman, Ned C. *Scotland and Its
First American Colony, 1683-1765*.
Princeton, New Jersey: Princeton
University Press, 1985.
 Reid, Stanford W., ed. *The Scottish
Tradition in Canada*. Toronto:
McClelland and Stewart, 1976.
 The Fiery Cross. Ottawa, Oct. 1895 -
Jan. 1896. 1 reel of microfilm.

ONTARIO ETHNIC NEWSPAPER
MICROFILM PROJECT
TORONTO, ONT.
 Canada Scotsman. 11 July 1868-28
Jan. 1871; 15 Oct. 1908 - 30 Nov.
1909. 2 reels of microfilm.
 The Scottish Canadian. 2 Oct. 1890 -
5 Nov. 1891; Jan. 1903-1905. 2 reels
of microfilm.
 Tourist of the Woods and *Emigrant's
Guide*. 17 Jan. - 31 May 1884. 1 reel
of microfilm.

SERBIAN COLLECTION

ASANIN, CEDOMIR
TORONTO, ONT.
 Self-interviewed on 5 Feb. 1979; 1
hr.; 1 tape; English. Discusses the
history of the group "Hajduk Veljko"
as prepared and narrated by C.
Asanin.

CICA, SAVA
SUDBURY, ONT.
 1 baptismal certificate, n.d. Taped
interview.
 Interviewed on 4 Aug. 1982; .75 hr.;
1 tape; Serbian; by S. Moutsatsos and
G. Vlahovich. Arrived in Canada in
the late 1920s.

IVANIŠEVIĆ, NIKOLA
BELGRADE, YUGOSLAVIA
 Interviewed on 23 April 1979; 1.5
hrs.; 2 tapes; Serbo-Croat; by Vic
Tomovich. Discusses life during the
Spanish Civil War, and his return to
Canada, and post-WWII Yugoslavia.

JOVANOV, ZARKO
WINDSOR, ONT.
 Interviewed on 27 April 1977; 1 hr.;
1 tape; Serbian; by Vic Tomovich.
President of the Serbian Soccer Club,
"The Windsor Serbs," comments on
the Clubs strengths, and its present
and future plans.

KAJGANIC, KATA
SUDBURY, ONT.
 Interviewed on 10 Aug. 1982;

.75 hr.; 1 hr.; Serbian; by S.
Moutsatsos. Arrived in Sudbury in
1937.

MALOBABIC, DJURAN
TORONTO, ONT.
 13 photographs: traditional Serbian
wedding ceremony, 1978. Taped
interview.
 Interviewed on 25 March 1980; 1
hr.; 1 tape; Serbian; by S.P.
Milojevic. Discusses wedding ceremony in Serbian Orthodox religion.

MARKOVICH, OLGA B.
TORONTO, ONT.
 Printed items. 5 cm, in Serbian.
 *35th Anniversary Kola Srpskish
Sestara "Kraljica Aleksandra,"
1941-1976.* Booklet of Women's Aux-
iliary, St. Sava's Serbian Orthodox
Church. Illustrated. 37 pp., in
Serbian.
 Calendar. The Serbian Orthodox
Church in the U.S. and Canada,
1975. 130 pp., in English/Serbian.

MILOSAVLJEVICH, STANKO V.
MISSISSAUGA, ONT.
 VUK. Vol. 1, no.1, Winter 1978 -
vol. 2, no.2, Spring 1978. Published
by Cult. Ed. University of "Vuk Stef.
Karadzic." Quarterly magazine for
culture, education, and entertainment.

MILOŠEVIĆ, SAVO
SUDBURY, ONT.
 Interviewed on 11 Aug. 1982; 1 hr.;

1 tape; Serbian; by S. Moutsatsos and G. Vlahovich. Immigrated to Canada in 1926.

MIOŠIĆ, STEVE
TORONTO, ONT.
 Interviewed on 23 Feb. 1979; 1 hr.; 1 tape; Serbo-Croat; by Vic Tomovich. Yugoslav history in Canada from the 1930s to the 1970s.

PROTICH, GEORGE
TORONTO, ONT.
 Miscellaneous printed items issued by St. Sava Serbian Orthodox Church, 1964-73. 6 cm.
 Voice of St. Sava Serbian Orthodox Church. Toronto, Dec. 1964 - Feb 1973. 46 bulletins, in Serbian.

PUPIN, MICHAEL
TORONTO, ONT.
 Personal papers, 1922-35. 1 reel of microfilm.

RADOJKOVIC, D.
TORONTO, ONT.
 50th Anniversary of "Plavi Jadran" Fraternal Lodge. Toronto, 1977. 30 pp., in Serbian.
 Glasnik (Herald). Nov. 1975 - Jan. 1978. 9 church bulletins, in Serbian.

RISTIC, DIRJANA
WINDSOR, ONT.
 Interviewed on 28 April 1977; .75 hr.; 1 tape; English; by Vic Tomovich. Recounts history of the Serbian Women's Heritage Club of Windsor.

SERDAR, STEVAN
BELGRADE, YUGOSLAVIA
 Interviewed on 23 April 1979; 1.5 hrs.; 2 tapes; Serbo-Croat; by

Vic Tomovich. Discusses involvement in Spanish Civil War.

SIAUS, MATE
ZAGREB, YUGOSLAVIA
 Interviewed in July 1978; 1 hr.; 1 tape; Serbo-Croat; by Vic Tomovich. Discusses the Yugoslav community in Vancouver, British columbia and labour movement amongst Yugoslav Canadians.

SLEPCEVIC, PAVLE
TORONTO, ONT.
 Correspondence, clippings, and accounts of donor's work experiences, and involvement in Serbian organizations in Sudbury, c. 1938-1960s. 1 reel of microfilm. Photographs. Taped interview.
 14 photographs: immigrants en route to Canada, 1938; dwellings of the Slepcevic family, 1948-79; religious activities at St. Peter and Paul Serbian Orthodox Church, 1963; and Serbian Hall in Sudbury, n.d.
 Interviewed on 16 March 1979; 1 hr.; 1 tape; English; by S.P. Milojevic. Discusses arrival in Canada, jobs held, life in Sudbury, Serbian ethnic organizations, war effort in WWII, and his difficulties in bringing his family to Canada.

STEVANOV, BOGOLJUB
TORONTO, ONT.
 Interviewed on 7 July 1978; 1 hr.; 1 tape; Serbo-Croatian; by Vic Tomovich. About Serbians and other Yugoslavs in Canada since 1938; and special remarks about the Yugoslav socialists in Canada and on returning immigrants.

TOMOVICH, ANTO M.
WINDSOR, ONT.
Papers, 1945-75, include manuscripts, biographical material, clippings, and correspondence with various prominent Serbians in Australia, U.S., and South Africa. 2 reels of microfilm.

TOMOVICH, NADA
ST. CATHARINES, ONT.
Material on Serbian inventor and writer, Michael Pupin: letters, book reviews, and editorial work, n.d. 4 cm.

TOMOVICH, RAJNA
WINDSOR, ONT.
Papers cover social life of Serbian immigrants in the U.S., Canada, Australia, and Argentina. Manuscripts are of a literary and political nature, and also include clippings from local Canadian Serbian newspapers in which A. Tomovich's articles appeared, 1945-75. 10 cm. Photographs.
 2 photographs: 1945-75.

VUKADINOV, MILAN
WINDSOR, ONT.
Interviewed on 29 April 1977; 1 hr.; 1 tape; Serbo-Croatian; by Vic A. Tomovich. Vukadinov is one of the top Canadian chess players, and as a participant in many competitions speaks of Canadian chess in the 1970s, and his personal experiences as an immigrant.

GRACHANICA SERBIAN ORTHODOX CHURCH
WINDSOR, ONT.
Records of births, baptisms, marriages, and deaths for the Serbians of Windsor, 1949-78. 1 reel of microfilm.
 Sparks of Faith. Oct. 1977 - July 1977. Bulletin of the Grachanica Serbian Orthodox Church. 8 cm.

HOLY TRINITY SERBIAN ORTHODOX CENTRE
HAMILTON, ONT.
Charter, minutes, annual financial statements, and list of donors and members of the Centre, 1973-79. 1 reel of microfilm.

MULTICULTURAL HISTORY SOCIETY OF ONTARIO
TORONTO, ONT.
 Halpern, B. K. and Joel M. Halpern, eds. *Selected Papers on a Serbian Village: Social Structure as Reflected by History, Demography and Oral Tradition.* Amherst: University of Massachusetts, Department of Anthropology, Report No. 17, 1977. A collection of articles, in English.
 Serbs in the United States and Canada: A Comprehensive Bibliography. Madison: Immigration History Research Center, 1976. 129 pp.
 Pravda. 6 Jan. 1937 - 14 Aug. 1940. 1 reel of microfilm.
 Srpski Glasnik. Toronto, 17 May 1941 - 10 June 1948. 4 reels of microfilm.

MULTICULTURAL NEWSPAPER MICROFILM PROJECT
TORONTO, ONT.
 Glas Kanadskih Srba. 7 Jan. 1981 - 31 Dec. 1987. 3 reels of microfilm.

ONTARIO ETHNIC NEWSPAPER MICROFILM PROJECT
TORONTO, ONT.
 Glas Kanade (Voice of Canada).

27 Dec. 1934 - 30 Jan. 1941; 6 Feb. 1942 - 23 Dec. 1943. 2 reels of microfilm.

RADIO PROGRAMME "SUMADIJA" TORONTO, ONT.
Recorded 1973 through 1974; 2 hrs.; 8 tapes; English/Serbian; by Bora Dragasevich. Provides history of Serbs and Serbian emigration.

SERBIAN BROTHERS HELP OF CANADA
TORONTO, ONT.
Constitution, minutes of the Main Board and annual meetings, financial records, annual reports, and clippings, 1950-79. 2 reels of microfilm. 2 cm.
Serbian Charitableness. Vol. 1, no. 1, Nov. 1967 - Dec. 1980. Toronto (monthly). Incomplete. (8 issues), in Serbian.
The Tenth Anniversary of Serbian Brothers Help Inc., 1960-1970. Chicago, 1960. 264 pp., in Serbian.

SERBIAN CHETNIKS OF CANADA STONEY CREEK, ONT.
Programmes from the Serbian Chetniks Veterans Organizations and various Serbian publications, mostly from the 1970s. 6 cm. Photographs.
Over 50 photographs. activities of the Serbian Chetniks of Canada, Hamilton, 1970-77. Included are celebrations such as Chetniks Day and Drazin Day, and opening ceremonies for the Serbian Chetniks War Veterans Centre in Canada.
Serbia. 1975-78. Newspaper (31 issues).
Serbian Calendar, 1977. Booklet, in Serbian.
The Path of Orthodoxy. Dec. 1975. 1 cm., in English.

SERBIAN EASTERN ORTHODOX DIOCESE
WINDSOR, ONT.
Records of births and baptisms, 1949-62. 1 reel of microfilm.

SERBIAN LEAGUE OF CANADA HAMILTON, ONT.
A collection of Serbian language books, most of them published by the Serbian League in Hamilton in the 1960s and 1970s. They include anniversary booklets, first grade reader of Serbian language, political and historical texts. .5 meters. Photographs.
Over 170 photographs: various aspects of the Serbian community in Ontario—religious practices, entertainment, and demonstrations, as well as leading members, c. 1955-70.
Kostic, L. M. *Illusions and Prevarication of Serbian and Croatian Relations.* Hamilton, 1960. 152 pp., in Serbian.
_____. *The Serbian Writer and His People.* Hamilton: Serbian League of Canada, 1963. 72 pp., in Serbian.
Popovic, M. Z. *Victory for Communism or Capitalism.* Hamilton: Serbian League of Canada, 1962. 31 pp., in Serbian.
Stojanovic, M. T. *Priests Against Jesus.* Hamilton: Serbian League of Canada, 1965. 55 pp., in Serbian.
50th Anniversary of the Serbian Orthodox Church St. Nicholas of Hamilton, 1917-67. 106 pp., in Serbian.

SERBIAN NATIONAL FEDERATION LODGE NO. 120
HAMILTON, ONT.
Lodge minute book, 1955-77. 117 pp.

ST. NICHOLAS SERBIAN ORTHODOX
CHURCH
HAMILTON, ONT.
 Parish registers, 1914-53, 1953-74;
treasurer's books, 1914-49; and minutes of Supervisory Committee and
Church Board, 1933-38. 2 reels of
microfilm. Photographs.
 8 photographs: religious activity at
St. Nicholas Serbian Orthodox
Church of Hamilton, c. 1965-70; and
a funeral at Kirkland Lake, n.d.
 *10th Anniversary of St. Nicholas
Orthodox Church, 1967-77.* 4 pp.
 *50th Anniversary of St. Nicholas
Orthodox Church of Hamilton,
1917-67.* 112 pp., in Serbian.
 *Commemoration Album of St.
Nicholas Serbian Orthodox Church,
1965-75.* Hamilton, 1975. Illustrated.
127 pp.
 Parish Messenger. Jan. 1978. Newsletter. 3 pp.
 Serbian A-B-C Book. n.d. 40 pp.

ST. SAVA SERBIAN ORTHODOX
CHURCH
LONDON, ONT.
 Records, 1966-71, include minutes,
financial book, and correspondence;
and printed items, 1931, 1970s. 1 reel
of microfilm.

ST. SAVA SERBIAN ORTHODOX
CHURCH
TORONTO, ONT.
 Parish register of births, baptisms,
marriages, and deaths, 1952-78. 3
reels of microfilm.

TESLA MEMORIAL SOCIETY OF
CANADA AND THE U.S.A. (N.
TOMOVICH)
ST. CATHARINES, ONT.
 Correspondence, 1972-81, by-laws

1980, minutes for 1981, and miscellaneous notes and reports. 6 cm.

THE CIRCLE OF SERBIAN SISTERS
"DUCHESS ZORKA"
TORONTO, ONT.
 Records, 1965-79, comprise minutes,
correspondence, annual reports, and
miscellaneous items. 1 reel of micro-
film. Photographs.
 38 photographs: exhibitions, and
"Slava" celebrations organized by the
Circle of Serbian Sisters, Toronto,
1972-76.
 Kolo. 1974-75 (11 issues, monthly).

THE SERBIAN FOLKLORE YOUTH
GROUP "HAJDUK VELJKO"
TORONTO, ONT.
 Constitution and correspondence,
1973-79. 3 cm. Photographs. Taped
interview with C. Asanin.
 11 photographs: folk dancing by the
Serbian Folklore ensemble, Toronto,
1974-77.

THE SERBIAN ORTHODOX CHURCH OF
ST. ARCHANGEL MICHAEL
TORONTO, ONT.
 Records, 1963-79, include charter,
minutes, correspondence, cash books,
ledgers; and a collection of Serbian
language books, 1970s. 3 reels of
microfilm. 10 cm. Photographs.
 3 photographs: an anti-Tito demonstration in Ottawa, 1971; and interior
and exterior view of the Church,
1976.
 History Reader for Sunday School.
1979. 78 pp., in Serbian.
 *Who Controls the Serbian Othodox
Church in Yugoslavia?.* Libertyville,
Illinois: Free Serbian Orthodox Diocese of the U.S.A. and Canada, 1977.
30 pp., in English.

WHITE EAGLES SERBIAN NATIONAL
SPORTS CLUB
TORONTO, ONT.
 Miscellaneous printed items issued
by Club, 1970s. 8 cm. Photograph.
 1 photograph: White Eagle Soccer
Team, Toronto, 1974.
 *Soccer Weekly: Official Voice of the
N.S.L.* 1975-76 (13 issues).

SLOVAK COLLECTION

BEDNARIK, GEORGE AND MARCELA
MISSISSAUGA, ONT.
 Interviewed on 6 Aug. 1979; 2 hrs.;
2 tapes; English/Slovak; by Greg Teal
and Marlene Kadar.

BEDNARIK, GEORGE
MISSISSAUGA, ONT.
 Interviewed on 22 July-12 Aug.
1979; 5 hrs.; 5 tapes; English/Slovak;
by Greg Teal. Pre-WWII immigrant.

BEDNARIK, MARCELA
MISSISSAUGA, ONT.
 5 photographs: Bednarik family
members and dwellings,
Czechoslovakia, Toronto, 1930-78.
Taped interview.
 Interviewed on 16 July-14 Aug.
1979; 3.5 hrs.; 4 tapes; Eng-
lish/Slovak; by Marlene Kadar and
Greg Teal. Pre-WWII immigrant.

CIMBA, JOHN
HAMILTON, ONT.
 Interviewed on 4 Jan. 1979; .5 hr.; 1
tape; Slovak; by Helen Messina.
Arrived in the late 1960s.

DOBOS, ZIGMUND
HAMILTON, ONT.
 Interviewed on 7 Dec. 1978; 1.5
hrs.; 2 tapes; Slovak; by Helen
Messina.

DRMAJ, PAVEL
CAMBRIDGE, ONT.
 Interviewed on 13 Oct. 1978; 1 hr.;
1 tape; Slovak; by Bernard Kadnar.

FILIČKO, JAKUB
THUNDER BAY, ONT.
 Interviewed on Oct. 1978; .5 hr.; 1
tape; Slovak; by Bernard Kadnar.

FUGA, MSGR. FRANCIS
HAMILTON, ONT.
 Interviewed on 28 Jan. 1979; 1 hr.;
2 tapes; Slovak; by Helen Messina.
Arrived in Canada in 1954.
 *Parish Bulletins from the Assumption
of the Blessed Virgin Mary Slovak of
the Byzantine Rite Catholic Church.*
Hamilton, 1978 (54 issues).

GOLIAN, MARTIN
SARNIA, ONT.
 Some newsclippings, n.d. .5 cm.
Photographs. Taped interview.
 8 photographs: the Golian family,
Slovakia, c. 1920s; celebrations in
Sarnia's Slovak community, including
folk dancing by children, c. 1960-70;
and convention of the Canadian
Slovak League, 1975.
 Interviewed on 17 Sept. 1978; 1 hr.;
1 tape; Slovak; Bernard Kadnar.
Immigrated to Canada in 1927.

GUZEI, MIKE
ST. CATHARINES, ONT.
 Interviewed on 7 Feb. 1977; 2 hrs.;
2 tapes; English; by Ellen Baar and
A. Marshall. Immigrated to Canada
in the 1920s.

HLATKY, JOHN
HAMILTON, ONT.
 Interviewed on 1 Nov. 1978;

1.5 hrs.; 2 tapes; Slovak; by
Helen Messina. Post-WWII immigrant.

HOVANEC, JOHN
SUDBURY, ONT.
Inteviewed on 29 Jul. 1982; .25 hrs.;
1 tape; English; by Steve Moutsatsos.
Immigrated to Canada in 1948, first
to Saskatchewan and then to Ontario.

HUDAK, JOHN PAUL
WELLAND, ONT.
19 photographs: some them of folk
dancing at celebration of Slovak Day,
Welland, c. 1970-75. Taped interview.
Interviewed on 15 Oct. 1978; 1 hr.;
1 tape; Slovak; by Bernard Kadnar.
Immigrated to Canada in 1951.
*40 rokov KSL: Perspektívny profil:
K. 40. výročiu Kanadskej Slovenskej
Ligy, 1932-1972.* Welland, 1972. 88
pp.
*35th Anniversary of the Branch 23 of
the Canadian Slovak League,
1940-75.* Welland, 1940. 51 pp.

IVAN, JAN
WELLAND, ONT.
Interviewed on 15 Oct. 1978; 1 hr.;
1 tape; Slovak; by Bernard Kadnar.
Arrived in Canada in 1929.

IVANČO, JOHN
OSHAWA, ONT.
Interviewed on 12 Oct. 1978; .5 hr.;
1 tape; Slovak; by Bernard Kadnar.
Immigrated to Canada in 1949.

JASENAK, STEFAN
OSHAWA, ONT.
1 photograph: participants at a conference on multiculturalism, Ottawa,
1978. Taped interview.
Interviewed on 17 Dec. 1978; 1 hr.;

1 tape; Slovak; by Bernard Kadnar.
Immigrated to Canada in 1926.

KADNAR, BERNARD
TORONTO, ONT.
Vnuk, Frantisek. *This is Dr. Josef
Tito.* Cambridge, Ont.: Friends of
Good Books, 1977.
47th Convention of the Slovak Catholic Federation of America. Toronto,
1973. Souvenir booklet.
Echo. Nos. 1, 2, 3, 1972; no. 13,
1976; no. 15, 1977. Galt, Ont. Catholic journal. 6.5 cm, in Slovak.
Fraternally Yours, Ženská Jednota.
Cleveland, Ohio, 1974-77. Official
organ of the First Catholic Ladies'
Association. Incomplete.
Jednota. Middletown, Pa., 1963,
1973. Catholic calendar
Kalendár Kanadskej Slovenskej Ligy
(Calendar of the Canadian Slovak
League). 1962, 1963, 1970, 1970.
*Literárny almanach Slováka u
Amerike* (Literary Almanac for
Slovaks in America). Middletown,
Pa., 1965, 1969, 1970 (annually).
Posal (Apostle). A monthly for
Slovak Catholics in Cambridge, Ont.,
1974-78.
The Slovakian. Ottawa, 1949. 66
pp., in English.
Slovenskí jezuiti v Kanade (Slovak
Jesuits in Canada). Galt, Ont., 1959,
1960, 1962, 1963, 1965-76. Slovak
Jesuit Fathers.

KIJOVSKY, MARY AND MIKE
TORONTO, ONT.
Interviewed on 8 Aug. 1979; .75 hr.;
1 tape; English/Slovak; by Marlene
Kadar and Greg Teal. Discusses
return visits to Czechoslovakia.

KIJOVSKÝ, MICHAL
TORONTO, ONT.
Interviewed on 17 July, 9 Aug.
1979; 5 hrs.; 5 tapes; English/Slovak;
by Greg Teal and Marlene Kadar.
Arrived in Canada in the 1920s.

KORMENDY, STEFAN
WINDSOR, ONT.
Interviewed on 22 Oct. 1978; 1 hr.;
1 tape; Slovak; by Bernard Kadnar.
Arrived in Canada in the 1930s.

KUCERAK, JAN
TORONTO, ONT.
45 rokov: Kalendár 1977. Toronto:
Kanadského Slovenského Podporného
Spolku, 1977. Illustrated. 128 pp., in
Slovak.
*Revised By-Laws and Constitution of
the Canadian Slovak Benefit Society.*
Windsor, 1973. 100 pp., in
Slovak/English.
Slovenský hlas. 1952-78 (monthly,
28 sets, some incomplete).

KURDELL, GABRIEL
TORONTO, ONT.
34 letters concerning G. Kurdell's
activities. 4 cm. Taped interview.
Interviewed on 26 Oct. 1977; 1 hr.;
1 tape; English; by Wally Mraz.
Arrived in Canada in 1925, became
editor of *Kanadsky Slovak.*
Kurdell, Gabriel. *Europe's Greatest
Exodus.* Toronto, 1962.
Domobrana (Home Guard). 1956,
1957 (3 issues).
Kotva (Slovak Anchor). Oct.
1972-Feb. 1978. 11 scattered issues.

KURIS, STEFAN J.
TORONTO, ONT.
Military service book, n.d. .5 cm.
Photographs. Taped interview.
10 photographs: mostly of family

members, Toronto, 1930-74.
Interviewed on 6 Jun. 1979; 1 hr.; 1
tape; Slovack; by Bernard Kadnar.
Migration to Canada via Argentina
and the U.S. to cola mining in Nova
Scotia.

LUKACKO JR., JOHN
TORONTO, ONT.
Collection of material belonging to
the late John Lukacko Sr., founder of
Branches Nos. 7, 9, 15, 27 of the
Canadian Slovak League. Records,
1932-67, trace primarily his activities
in the League. Constitution, minutes,
and financial documents are in
Slovak, whereas most of the corre-
spondence and the publications are in
English. 25 cm. Photographs.
10 photographs: taken at congresses
of the Canadian Slovak League,
Toronto, Hamilton, Montreal, and
Port Arthur, 1941-63.
First Freedom Festival. Toronto:
Canadian Folk Dancing Association,
1962. Illustrated.
Rím. Toronto, 1952. Slovak Cultural
Review (2 issues).
"Slovaks in Toronto." 2 directory
lists of Slovaks in Toronto dating
from 1962-63, probably compiled by
Joe Benko.
*The 1100th Anniversary Arrival of
Sts. Cyril and Methodius in Slovakia.*
Welland, Ont., 1963.
*The Sts. Cyril and Methodius Jubileè
Folk Festival, 1863-1963.* Toronto:
Canadian Slovaks, 1963.
Zapisnica (Calendar of Canadian
Slovak League). 1954-58, 1961-65,
1969, 1971-75. 15 cm.

MANDA, STEVE
HAMILTON, ONT.
A collection of printed material:
newspapers, 1962-78; calendars,

1953-76; yearbooks, n.d.; and church bulletins, n.d.; mostly from Hamilton, Ont. and the U.S., in Slovak. Title list available. 5 meters.

MANIK, KAROL
KITCHENER, ONT.
 Passport and army passport of K. Manik, n.d.; also biographical notes about his life in Slovakia. 1.5 cm. Photographs. Taped interview.
 18 photographs: including some of activities of the Slovak Jesuit Fathers, Galt, Guelph, Kitchener, 1952-78.
 Interviewed on 13 Oct. 1978; 1 hr.; 1 tape; Slovak; by Bernard Kadnar. Arrived in Canada in 1926.

MICHNA, ANNA
OSHAWA, ONT.
 Interviewed on 17 Dec. 1978; 1 hr.; 1 tape; Slovak; by Bernard Kadnar. Immigrated to Canada in 1928.

MIŠĚK, JOHN WITH ANTON VAŠKOR
ALVINSTON, ONTARIO
 Interviewed on 27 May 1979; 1 hr.; 1 tape; Slovak; by Bernard Kadnar. Immigrated to Canada via Germany, settled first in Windsor, Ont. before moving to a farm in Kingsville, Ont.

MOROVČIK, HELEN
TORONTO, ONT.
 A collection of assorted original documents belonging to donor and spouse. Documents include birth certificates, school reports and diplomas, certificates of achievement, identity papers, refugee documents, letters of recommendation and papers on donor's immigration to Canada, 1930s-1950s. Material is in Czech, Slovak, German, and English (43 items). Photographs. Taped interview.
 20 photographs: Slovak immigrants

en route to Canada, 1949; the Moravcik family, 1949; delegation of the Czechoslovak National Association, Ottawa, 1953; and conventions of the Canadian Slovak League, 1963-75.
 Interviewed on 4 Oct. 1978; 1 hr.; 1 tape; Slovak; by Bernard Kadnar. Arrived in Canada in 1949.
 Kalendár Jednota. 1966, 1969, 1970, 1975. Proceedings from the General Conventions of the Canadian Slovak League.
 Kalendár Kanadskej Slovenskej Ligy (Calendar of the Canadian Slovak League). Winnipeg, 1965, 1969, 1971, 1972, 1974, 1975.

MRAZ, W.
TORONTO, ONT.
 Memorandum on Violation of Human Rights in Slovakia. n.d.
 Slovak World Congress. Bulletin No. 29. n.d.

PARIČI, ANDREW
WINDSOR, ONT.
 Interviewed on 22 Oct. 1978; 1 hr.; 1 tape; Slovak; by Bernard Kadnar. Immigrated to Canada in the late 1920s.

PATUŠ, MARKO
WELLAND, ONT.
 Interviewed on 1 Apr. 1979; 1 hr.; 1 tape; Slovak; by Bernard Kadnar. Immigrated to Canada in the interwar period.

POTOCKÝ, ANDREJ
THUNDER BAY, ONT.
 Interviewed on 9 Oct. 1978; 1 hr.; 1 tape; Slovak; by Bernard Kadnar. Immigrated to Canada in 1910, leading member of the Canadian Slovak League.

REISTETTER, STEPHEN
ST. CATHARINES, ONT.
 Interviewed on 26 Jan. 1977; 2.5
hrs.; 3 tapes; English/Slovak; by E.
Baar. Former president of the Cana-
dian Slovak League.

SHUBA, REV. MICHAEL
TORONTO, ONT.
 Untitled autobiography of Rev.
Shuba, 1903-72. 1 reel of microfilm.

SHUHET, MARY
HAMILTON, ONT.
 13 photographs: Slovak Youth Club,
1945; Slovak beauty contests, 1946,
1967; Slovak Music School, 1939;
Slovak Drama Group, 1945; Slovak
weddings, n.d., and the World Youth
Festival held in Slovakia, n.d.

SILAJ, LADISLAV
ELLIOT LAKE, ONT.
 Interviewed in Oct. 1978; .5 hr.; 1
tape; Slovak; by Bernard Kadnar.
Arrived in Canada in 1948.

SINCHAK, JOHN
ST. CATHARINES, ONT.
 13 photographs: mostly of family
members and farming activities in the
Grimsby and St. Catharines area,
1923-59. Taped interview.
 Interviewed on 29 Oct. 1978; .5 hr.;
1 tape; Slovak; by Bernard Kadnar.
Immigrated to Canada in 1930.

SITAR, PAVEL
ST. CATHARINES, ONT.
 8 photographs: theatrical production
of the Canadian Slovak League, St.
Catharines, 1952; grocery store in
Montreal, c. 1928; and the P. Sitar
family, 1970. Taped interview.

Interviewed on 29 Oct. 1978;
.75 hr.; 1 tape; Slovak; by Bernard
Kadnar. Immigrated to Canada in
1926.

SPRUŠANSKÝ, REV. JAN
WINDSOR, ONT.
 Interviewed on Oct. 1978; 1 hr.; 1
tape; Slovak; by Bernard Kadnar.
Arrived in Canada 1952.

STARK, KAREL
KITCHENER, ONT.
 Assorted paper items tracing the
donor's immigration and first years in
Canada in 1950s (9 items).

STANIK, JOZEF
INWOOD, ONT.
 Interviewed on 27 May 1979; 1 hr.;
1 tape; Slovak; by Brnard Kadnar.
Immigrated to Canada in the interwar
period.

THOMSON, MARY
MARKHAM, ONT.
 2 photographs: the Peslar family,
Slovakia, Toronto, c. 1920
 *Kanada: Země, lid hospodářské
poměry.* Praha, 1927.
 Martyrs' Shrine Message. Vol. 18,
no. 3, Oct. 1954; vol. 20, no. 1,
March 1956.
 Rím. Vol. 6, no. 1, Jan. 1954.
 Slovenské pohl'ady. Vol. 44, no. 2,
Feb 1928.

URBAN, JOHN
SUDBURY, ONT.
 Interviewed on 24 Apr. 1982; 3 hrs.;
3 tapes; English; by Mary Stefura.
Describes his career in mining and
Slovak community in Sudbury.

VYROSTKO, PAVEL
WELLAND, ONT.
 Interviewed on 1 Apr. 1979; 1 hr.;
1 tape; Slovak; by Bernard Kadnar.
Immigrated to Canada in the early
1930s.

YANKOVIC, MARTIN
KINGSTON, ONT.
 Army passport and Czech National
Alliance membership card, n.d. 1 cm.
Photographs. For taped interview for
M. Yankovic see Ukrainian oral
history collection.
 24 photographs: personal documents,
1925-28; parades and processions, c.
1940; group portrait of the
Czechoslovak National Alliance, n.d.;
and work on highway construction,
1928.

═══════════════

CANADIAN SLOVAK LEAGUE,
BRANCH 17
SARNIA, ONT.
 Minute book of Branch 17, 1939-53;
financial records, 1929, 1938-42,
1954-57; and miscellaneous publica-
tions from the Slovak League, .5
meters. See M. Golian. Photographs.
 2 photographs: the Canadian Slovak
League, Sarnia Branch, 1938.
 Zápisnica (Kanadskej Slovenskej
Ligy). 1969, 1970, 1971, 1972, 1973.
Annual reports of the Canadian
Slovak League. 11 cm.

CANADIAN SLOVAK LEAGUE,
BRANCH 24
SMITHVILLE, ONT.
 Records, 1940-63, comprise minute
book, some correspondence and
financial statements. 1 reel of microfilm. Photograph.
 1 photograph: taken at the 9th Con-

gress of the Canadian Slovak League,
Hamilton, 1953.

CANADIAN SLOVAK LEAGUE,
BRANCH 25
TORONTO, ONT.
 Constitution and by-laws, 1932; minute books, 1946-75; some financial
records, 1952-53; and printed items,
1950s. 9 cm.
 *40 rokov KSL: Perspektívny profil k
40. výročiu Kanadskej Slovenskej
Ligy, 1932-72.* Welland, 1972. 87
pp., in Slovak.
 Slovenský spevokol. Toronto, 1977.
Souvenir Program. Illustrated. 48 pp.
 Zápisnica, 1946, 1949, 1954, 1960,
1975. 8 cm.

CANADIAN SLOVAK LEAGUE,
BRANCH 31
ST. CATHARINES, ONT.
 A collection of calendars, souvenir
booklets and serials, published mostly
in the 1950s and 1960s, in Slovak. 3
meters. Title list available.
 Ave Maria. Cleveland, Ohio,
1950-77. Scattered issues. 12 cm.
 Kalendár Kanadskej Slovenskej Ligy.
Winnipeg, 1953-77. Scattered issues.
3 cm.
 Kanadský Slovák (The Canadian
Slovak). Toronto, 1961-77 Incom-
plete. .5 meters.
 Posol. Cambridge, Ont., 1974-77
(monthly). Incomplete. 8 cm.
 Slovenská obrana (Slovak Defence).
Pennsylvania, 1960-62. Incomplete.
1.5 meters.
 Slovenskí Jezuiti v Kanade, 1959-74.
25th anniversary booklet. 1 cm.

CANADIAN SLOVAK LEAGUE,
BRANCH 68
INGERSOLL, ONT.
 Records, 1971-77, include corre-

spondence, financial statements, annual reports, and members lists. 5.5 cm.

CANADIAN SLOVAK LEAGUE
OSHAWA, ONT.
 Minutes and financial records, 1927-67; also, bulletin of the Slovak World Congress and miscellaneous printed items, c. 1970s. 1 reel of microfilm. 7 cm. Photographs.
 12 photographs: activities of the Canadian Slovak League in Oshawa, Ottawa, and St. Catharines, 1931-76.
 Kalendár (Canadian Slovak League Yearbook). 1965, 1969, 1970-77 (15 issues). 15 cm.

CLUB GENERAL STEFANIK SLOVAK CIRCLE
OSHAWA, ONT.
 Minutes, 1931-34, and ledger books, 1928-54. 5 cm.

DUNAJ DANCERS (MARY RAFFAY)
HAMILTON, ONT.
 Historical sketch of the Slovak-Canadian Dunaj Dancers. .25 cm. Photographs.
 6 photographs: folk dancing at festivals, Hamilton, 1968.

FIRST CATHOLIC SLOVAK UNION JEDNOTA (MICHAEL DOBIS)
TORONTO, ONT.
 Printed items issued by Jednota Catholic Slovak Union, 1970s. 4 cm.
 50th Anniversary Programme, 1927-77. Toronto. Jednota Catholic Slovak Union, Branch 785. 40 pp., in English/Slovak.

SLOVAK CATHOLIC LADIES' UNION
TORONTO, ONT.
 Minute book, 1947-63. 3 cm.
 Ženská Jednota, 1947-72. 25th anni-

versary brochure. 4 pp.
 Spolkový adresár. 1952. North American-Slovak directory. 31 pp.

SLOVAK CATHOLIC SOKOL ASSEMBLY (JAN JASENEK)
TORONTO, ONT.
 Minutes, 1927-63, souvenir booklets, and miscellaneous printed items, 1970s. 1 reel of microfilm. 5 cm. Photographs.
 14 photographs: activities of the Slovak Catholic Sokol, Toronto, 1937-59.

SLOVAK CREDIT UNION
TORONTO, ONT.
 Financial records and certificates, 1971-78. .5 cm.

SLOVAK CULTURAL CENTRE
CAMBRIDGE-GALT, ONT.
 Echo duchovného prúdenia dneška. Nos. 12, 13, 15; 1975, 1977, 1978. Journal from Cambridge, Ont. (3 issues).
 Posol. 1974-77 (monthly, 37 issues).
 Slovenský spevokol. 1977. Souvenir book of Slovak Jesuit Fathers in Canada, 1973 (1 issue).

SLOVAKOTOUR (J. BANIK)
TORONTO, ONT.
 Travel brochures and promotional items on Czechoslovakia. 12 cm.

SLOVAK WORLD CONGRESS
TORONTO, ONT.
 Slovak World Congress Bulletin. 1971-77. Incomplete. 11 cm.

STS. CYRIL AND METHODIUS PARISH (REV. E.G. FUZY)
HAMILTON, ONT.
 A letter to Rev. G. Stopko from Bishop Ryan of Hamilton, 1950.

Also, anniversary booklets, Slovak
language primers, and postcards,
1970s. 5 cm.

ST. MARY'S SLOVAK GREEK CATH-
OLIC CHURCH (BISHOP M. RUSNAK)
TORONTO, ONT.
Records, 1952-77, include church
register of baptisms, some correspondence, and miscellaneous printed
items: anniversary booklets, programmes, flyers, and clippings. 1 reel
of microfilm. 18 cm. Photographs.
84 photographs: mostly of religious
ceremonies at St. Mary's church,
1952-70; members of the Rusnak
family, n.d.; and 16 postcards.
Mária. Hamilton, Ont., 1956-77.
Incomplete. 12 cm.

ST. PAUL'S EVANGELICAL LUTHERAN
CHURCH
TORONTO, ONT.
Bulletin. 1971-76. 2 reels of micro-
film.
Pamätnica, 1942-72. Toronto. Anni-
versary booklet of St. Paul's Slovak
Evangelical Lutheran Church. 70 pp.,
in Slovak.

STS. CYRIL AND METHODIUS
CHURCH (FATHER J. ZABKA)
TORONTO, ONT.
Anniversary booklet, church bulletin,
and souvenir programmes from the
1970s. 1 reel of microfilm. 6.5 cm.
Bulletin. 1970-75. 1 reel of micro-
film.

SLOVENIAN COLLECTION

DOLENC, IVAN
TORONTO, ONT.
Dnevnik Diary Slovene Canadian.
Toronto, 1976-78 (5 issues, monthly),
in Slovenian.

KOPAČ, REV. JANEZ
TORONTO, ONT.
Oznanila (Weekly Herald). Vols.
1-10, 1959-78. Brezmadežna Parish,
Mississauga. 2 reels of microfilm.

MAUKO, VLADIMIR
TORONTO, ONT.
Interviewed on 6 Sept. 1978; 1 hr.;
1 tape; English; by Wally Mraz.
Immigrated to Canada in 1948.
Slovenska Država (Slovenian Coun-
try). Toronto, July 1950 - Dec. 1961
(April 1952 missing). 1 reel of micro-
film.
Slovenska Pravica. Toronto, Dec.
1949 - June 1950. 1 reel of micro-
film.

SENICA, JOHN
TORONTO, ONT.
Certificate of incorporation, 1953,
and annual reports of John Krek's
Slovenian Credit Union in Toronto,
1969-78. 6 cm.
Čuješ, Rudolf P. *Ninidjanissidog
Saiagiinagog: Most Rev. Friderik
Baraga Apostle of Indians.*
Antigonish, Nova Scotia: St. Francis
Xavier University Press, 1968. 114
pp., in English.
Mauko, Vladimir, ed. *This is
Slovenia: A Glance at the Land and
Its People.* Toronto: Slovenian

National Federation of Canada, 1958.
Illustrated. 221 pp.
Slovenska Država. 1954-78. Com-
plete. 5 meters.

BOZJA BESEDA SLOVENIAN SCHOOL
TORONTO, ONT.
Collection, which includes a constitution, minutes, and financial records,
1961-78, a historical sketch of school,
a biography of Bishop Baraga, bro-
chures, a business directory, and
other printed items. 1 reel of micro-
film. 4 cm. Photographs.
11 photographs: religious activity at
the Our Lady of the Miraculous
Medal Church; and youth groups and
theatre, 1961-69.
Mauser, Karel. *Le eno je potrebno.*
Toronto, 1972. Biography of Bishop
F. Baraga, first bishop of Sault Ste.
Marie, Ont. 190 pp.
Božja Beseda. 1977 (9 issues).
*Cerkev Brezmadežne s Čudodelno
Svetinjo.* Toronto, 1962.
Anniversary booklet of Our Lady of
the Miraculous Medal Church. 64
pp., in Slovenian.
Slovenski Gospdarski Imenik. 1970.
Business directory. 64 pp.

CANADIAN SLOVENE GROUP FOR
CULTURAL EXCHANGES
MISSISSAUGA, ONT.
Flyers, brochures, and programmes.
1 cm.

HOLIDAY GARDENS SLOVENIAN
COUNTRY CLUB (FRANK JERINA)
TORONTO, ONT.
 Collection includes a financial
ledger, 1961-64, a constitution, n.d.,
minutes, 1970-78, and flyers. 1 reel
of microfilm. Photographs.
 28 photographs: activities of the
Club, Pickering, Ont., 1961-76.

MULTICULTURAL HISTORY SOCIETY
OF ONTARIO
TORONTO, ONT.
 Molek, Ivan J. *Slovene Immigrant
History, 1900-50: Autobiographical
Sketches*. Dover, Delaware: M.
Molek Inc., 1979. 533 pp.
 *Slovenes in the United States and
Canada: A Bibliography*. Minnesota:
Immigration History Research Centre,
University of Minnesota, 1981. 196
pp.
 Slovenians in Canada. Prepared by
P. Urbanc and E. Tourtel. Toronto:
The Slovenian Heritage Festival
Committee. 231 pp.

NAGELJ FOLK DANCING GROUP
TORONTO, ONT.
 General correspondence with list of
officers, and social events, 1969-71,
1977-78, and printed items, 1977-78.
4.5 cm. Photographs.
 7 photographs: folk dancing by the
Nagelj ensemble in Toronto, 1975.
 Ave Maria. Nov. 1977. A monthly
publication of the Slovenian Francis-
can Fathers in Lemont, Illinois. 1 cm.
 *Festival Kanadasko Slovenskih
Ansamblov* (Canadian Slovene Polka
Bands Festival). Toronto, 1978. 1
cm.
 The Baraga Bulletin. Vol. 30, no. 1,
Oct. 1977. Official publication of the
Cause of Bishop Baraga in Marquette,
Michigan (1 issue), in English.

ONTARIO ETHNIC NEWSPAPER
MICROFILM PROJECT
TORONTO, ONT.
 Domobrana. March 1965. 1 reel of
microfilm.

OUR LADY HELP OF CHRISTIANS
PARISH
TORONTO, ONT.
 Minutes of church committee, and
financial reports, 1949-69, church
bulletins, and Slovenian school text-
books. 1 reel of microfilm. 4 cm.
 Materina Beseda. Toronto: Centen-
nial Project of Slovenian School of
Our Lady Help of Christians, 1966.
A Slovenian children's primer. 153
pp.
 Veseli Dom. Toronto: Slovenian
School of Our Lady Help of Chris-
tians, 1965. General school text. 223
pp.

OUR LADY OF THE MIRACULOUS
MEDAL SLOVENIAN CATHOLIC
CHURCH
TORONTO, ONT.
 Parish records, 1960-78. 2 reels of
microfilm.
 Božja Beseda (God's Word).
1949-59, Toronto Slovenian religious
monthly. Microfilm.

SIMON GREGORČIČ SLOVENIAN CUL-
TURAL ASSOCIATION (F. SELJAK)
TORONTO, ONT.
 Flyers, Slovenian school notebooks,
and camp records, c. 1960-1970s. 1
reel of microfilm. Photographs.
 10 photographs: activities of the
Gregorčič Cultural Association,
1965-72.
 Zrnec, Tone. *Po Baragovi Deželi*.
Toronto, 1969. 177 pp., in Slovenian.

SLOVENIAN ASSOCIATION "BARAGA"
(OTMAR MAUSER)
TORONTO, ONT.
 1 letter from donor, n.d. .25 cm.
Photographs.
 36 photographs: scenes from theatrical productions organized by the Baraga Slovenian Association in Toronto, 1955-75.
 Marija Pomagaj v Toronto. Toronto, 1954. Church dedication booklet. 32 pp.
 Slovenska Misel. June 1965. 1 newspaper issue.
 Slovenski Dan. 1969, 1970, 1977. 6 pp. Brochures.

SLOVENIAN COMMUNITY CENTRE
AND THE CHURCH OF ST. GREGORY
THE GREAT
HAMILTON, ONT.
 Cultural committee minutes, 1974-77, church announcements, 1960-71, church bulletins, and other printed items. 3 reels of microfilm.
Photographs.
 33 photographs: Slovenian theatre and language school activities at Church of St. Gregory the Great in Hamilton, 1972-77.
 Slovenian Community Centre and the Church of St. Gregory the Great. Hamilton, c. 1960s. Commemorative booklet.
 Vestnik (Herald). 1960-78. Bulletin of Slovenian Parish of St. Gregory the Great in Hamilton. 2 reels of microfilm.

SLOVENIAN CULTURE AND SOCIAL
CLUB
LONDON, ONT.
 Club's minute book, 1961-71, and social announcements. 2 cm.

SLOVENIAN MUTUAL BENEFIT
SOCIETY "BLED" (A. JELOVČAN)
STONEY CREEK, ONT.
 Records, 1970-78, which include minutes, general correspondence, financial statements, a mailing list, and programmes. 6 cm.

SLOVENIAN MUTUAL BENEFIT
SOCIETY "BLED"
KIRKLAND LAKE, ONT.
 Records, 1933-77, which include executive and convention minutes, correspondence, members' dues books, and flyers. 8 reels of microfilm.

SLOVENIAN PARISHES CREDIT UNION
TORONTO, ONT.
 Financial records, 1963-65, 1967, 1975-77; and annual meeting reports, 1962-74. 7.5 cm.
 Naša Moč. 1957-1970. Newsletter of Our Lady Help of Christians (Parish) Toronto Credit Union. 3 cm.

AGNEW, VIJAY
THORNHILL, ONT.
Collection includes constitution of
the Indian Students' Association,
n.d.; circular from Bharat Credit
Union Ltd., n.d.; advertisements and
newsletter from Sri Chinmay Centre,
c. 1977; papers from the conference,
"Role of Indians in Canada," 1978;
and North York Board of Education
curriculum literature, 1978. South
Asian-Canadian newspapers mainly
published in the 1970s. 16 cm.
  Mehta, S. and V. Goel. *East Indian
Community Information Directory.*
Toronto, 1975. 68 pp.
*Folk Tales and Proverbs of the
Punjabi People.* Toronto, 1975. 122
pp.
*South Asians in Canada: A Hand-
book for Indians in Ottawa-Hull.*
Including a Telephone Directory,
1977-78. 72 pp.
  Asia Times. Toronto, 1973-78. Near-
ly complete (35 issues, semi-month-
ly). In English/Panjabi.
Fortnightly Crescent. 1 Nov. 1976,
15 Dec. 1977. 1 cm.
Gulrang. Toronto, 1978 (1 issue).
India Abroad. 1976-77. Scattered
issues.
India Calling. Toronto, 1977-78 (9
issues). 3 cm.
India Digest. 1976, 1977. Scattered
issues.
Lok Awaz. Vancouver, 1976-79.
Scattered issues. 4 cm.
New India Bulletin. Nov. - Dec.
1976. 18 pp.
News and Cine India. 6, 20 Jan.

1978. 24 pp.
The Canadian India Times. Ottawa,
1977-79. Scattered issues. 3 cm.
The Canadian Indian Star. Dec.
1973 - Dec. 1976 (24 issues).
The Link. Winnipeg, 1977, 1981.
Scattered issues.
The Canadian Times. Toronto, fore-
runner of *Canadian India Times,*
1976-77. Scattered issues. 3.5 cm.

AHSAN, TAQI
TORONTO, ONT.
Interviewed on 18 Oct. 1977; 1 hr.;
1 tape; English; by Vijay Agnew.
Immigrated to Canada in 1976.

AHUJA, SUSHMA
TIMMINS, ONT.
Interviewed on 19 Aug. 1978; .5 hr.;
1 tape; English; by Krishna Gupta.
Arrived in Canada in 1975.

ALI, MIR MAQSUD
TIMMINS, ONT.
Interviewed on 15 July 1978; 1 hr.;
1 tape; English; by Krishna Gupta.
Immigrated to Canada in 1970.

AMBIKE, S.
TORONTO, ONT.
Interviewed on 20 Aug. 1977; 1 hr.;
1 tape; English; by Vijay Agnew.
From Maharashtra, immigrated to
Canada in 1974.

BAGGA, URMIL
TORONTO, ONT.
Interviewed on 1 June 1977; 1 hr.;

1 tape; English; by Vijay Agnew.
Arrived in Canada in 1972.

BAKSHI, SUNITA
TORONTO, ONT.
 Interviewed on 16 May 1977; 1 hr.;
1 tape; English/Hindu; by Vijay
Agnew. Immigrated to Canada, via
Germany in 1976.

BANERJEE, KALYAN
TORONTO, ONT.
 Photographs: Bengali immigrant the-
atre productions used in *Polyphony:
The Bulletin of the Multicultural His-
tory Society of Ontario*. Vol. 5, no.
2, 1983, features a survey account of
Bengali theatre in Toronto.

BASU, SAMIR
TORONTO, ONT.
 Interviewed on 10 June 1977; 1 hr.;
1 tape; English; by Vijay Agnew.
Born in Calcutta, immigrated to
Canada in 1966.

BASVIAH, MR.
TORONTO, ONT.
 Interviewed on 10 April 1977; 1 hr.;
1 tape; English; by Vijay Agnew.
Immigrated to Canada, via the U.S.
in 1962.

BHARATENDU, DR.
TORONTO, ONT.
 Interviewed on 9 May 1977; 2 hrs.;
2 tapes; English; by Vijay Agnew.
Arrived in Canada in 1959.

BHARDWAJ, G.C.
TIMMINS, ONT.
 Interviewed on 12 Sept. 1978; 1 hr.;
1 tape; English; by Krishna Gupta.
Arrived in Canada in 1971.

BHOGAL, AVTAR SINGH
CAMBRIDGE, ONT.
 Interviewed on 7 Oct. 1979; 1 hr.; 1
tape; Panjabi; by T. Singh. From
Punjab, arrived in Canada in 1972.

CHAUHAN, MR. AND MRS.
TORONTO, ONT.
 Perdesi Panjab. Vols. 1-2. Toronto,
10 March 1977 - 15 Dec. 1978 (20
issues).

CHERA, SARDARA SINGH
MALTON, ONT.
 Interviewed on 9 Aug. 1979; 1 hr.; 1
tape; Panjabi; by T. Singh. From
Punjab, Pakistan, arrived in Canada
in 1976.

CHHATWAL, KULDEEP SINGH
KITCHENER, ONT.
 Interviewed on 17 Nov. 1979; 1 hr.;
1 tape; Panjabi/English; by T. Singh.
From Punjab, arrived in Canada in
1953.

DESAI, KAPPU
TORONTO, ONT.
 Interviewed on 28 Feb. 1977; .5 hr.;
1 tape; English; by Vijay Agnew.
From Madras, India, arrived in 1961.

DUTTA, PURISTOSH
TORONTO, ONT.
 Interviewed on 1 Feb. 1977; 1 hr.; 1
tape; English; by Vijay Agnew.
Bengali-Hindu, from Muzzafarpur,
Bihar, arrived in Canada in 1960.

FERNANDES, CHARLES
TORONTO, ONT.
 Interviewed on 22 March 1977; 1
hr.; 1 tape; English; by Vijay Agnew.
From Karachi, Pakistan, immigrated
to Canada, via England in 1968.

FRANCIS, STANLEY
TORONTO, ONT.
Interviewed on 22 March 1977; 1
hr.; 1 tape; English; by Vijay Agnew.
From Bombay, arrived in Canada in
1965.

GANGULI, RAMEN
BRAMALEA, ONT.
30 photographs: traditional Bengali
musicians, dance, and food preparation during festivities, such as the
Durga Puja, and the Rabindrajayanti,
c. 1970s.

GHOSH, RATIN
TORONTO, ONT.
Interviewed on 22 Feb. 1977; 2 hrs.;
2 tapes; English; by Vijay Agnew.
From Calcutta, arrived in Canada in
1965.

GILL, JIMMYAT SINGH
TORONTO, ONT.
Interviewed on 1 Oct. 1979; 1 hr.; 1
tape; Panjabi; by T. Singh. From
Punjab, immigrated to Canada in
1928.

GILL, M.
TORONTO, ONT.
Interviewed on 18 Jan. 1977; 1 hr.;
1 tape; English/Hindu; by Vijay
Agnew.

GILL, T.S.
TORONTO, ONT.
The Canadian India Star. Toronto, 1
Jan. - 16 Oct. 1978. 2 cm.
Panjabi Asia Times Fortnightly.
Toronto, 1 Jan. - 1 Nov. 1978. 2 cm.

GREWAL, HARCHARAN
MISSISSAUGA, ONT.
Interviewed on 1 Aug. 1979; 1 hr.;

1 tape; English; by T. Singh. Immigrated to Canada in 1965.

GUPTA, ARVIND
TIMMINS, ONT.
Interviewed on 10 July 1978; 1 hr.;
1 tape; English; by Krishna Gupta.
Arrived in Canada in 1967, relates
impressions of India—cultural, social,
and religious life.

GUPTA, H.K.L.
TIMMINS, ONT.
Interviewed on 7, 8, 9, 10 July
1978; 2 hrs.; 2 tapes; English; by
Krishna Gupta. Immigrated to Canada
in 1967.

GUPTA, KRISHNA
SOUTH PORCUPINE, ONT.
Constitution and flyers from the
Indian Immigrant Aid Service,
1977-78; lists of Indian organizations
in Toronto, 1978; draft constitution of
the Sudbury Prarthana Samaj, n.d.;
and issues from various South
Asian-Canadian newspapers, c.
1970s. 11 cm.
Hindu Vishwa. 1975, 1978. Scattered
issues.
India News. 1978. Scattered issues.
Pakistani Affairs. Ottawa, 1977,
1978, 1983. Scattered issues.
Subras. Toronto, 1978 (1 issue).

GUPTA, SUNIL
SOUTH PORCUPINE, ONT.
Interviewed on 18 Aug. 1978; .5 hr.;
1 tape; English; by Krishna Gupta.
Discusses visits to India and Indian
marriage ceremonies.

GUPTA, YUGESH
TIMMINS, ONT.
Interviewed on 22 July 1978; 1 hr.;
1 tape; English; by Krishna Gupta.

Arrived in Canada in 1974, discusses life history, marriage ceremony, and impressions of Canada.

GYANI, RANBIR SINGH
TORONTO, ONT.
 Interviewed on 9 July 1979; 1 hr.; 1 tape; English; by T. Singh. From Punjab, arrived in Canada in 1968.

HASTINGS, GLEN
TORONTO, ONT.
 Interviewed on 12 July 1977; 2 hrs.; 2 tapes; English; by Vijay Agnew. Arrrived in Canada in 1974, discusses student life and racism.

ISHWARAN, MR.
TORONTO, ONT.
 Interviewed on 17 March 1977; 1 hr.; 1 tape; English; by Vijay Agnew. Immigrated to Canada, via England in 1965.

JAIN, RAM
TORONTO, ONT.
 Nav Bharat. n.d. 21 scattered issues.

JOSHI, RAM
SOUTH PORCUPINE, ONT.
 Interviewed on 31 Aug. 1978; .75 hr.; 1 tape; English; by Krishna Gupta. Immigrated to Canada in 1972.
 Hindu Vishwa. July 1976; Feb., July, Sept., Oct. 1977; Feb. 1978. 1.5 cm.

KOTECHA, VIJAY
TIMMINS, ONT.
 Interviewed on 14 Sept. 1978; 1 hr.; 1 tape; English; by Krishna Gupta. Immigrated to Canada in 1975, comments on cultural differences between Canada and India.

KUMAR, MADAN
TORONTO, ONT.
 Interviewed on 1 June 1977; 1 hr.; 1 tape; English; by Vijay Agnew. Immigrated to Canada in 1971.

MALIK, DHARAM
TORONTO, ONT.
 Interviewed on 16 Jan. 1977; 1 hr.; 1 tape; English; by Vijay Agnew. Discusses the role of Indian women, the problem of readjustment after immigrating to India from Canada, and the difficulties in establishing cultural values to children.

McLAREN, DUNCAN
TORONTO, ONT.
 20 photographs: storefronts, restaurants, and East Indian cinemas in East Toronto's Gerrard-Woodbine Streets area, c. 1970s.

MENON, A.
TORONTO, ONT.
 Interviewed on 18 Jan. 1977; 1 hr.; 1 tape; English; by Vijay Agnew. Discusses religion.

MICHAEL, BERNADETTE
TORONTO, ONT.
 Interviewed on 21 Jan. 1977; 1 hr.; 1 tape; English; by Vijay Agnew. A Christian, immigrated to Canada in 1969.

MUIN, TALAT
TORONTO, ONT.
 Interviewed on 12 April 1977; 1 hr.; 1 tape; English; by Vijay Agnew. A Muslim, immigrated to Canada, via England in 1962.

MUKERJEE, SAMJEEV KUMAR
TIMMINS, ONT.
 Interviewed on 22 July 1978; 1 hr.;

1 tape; English; by Krishna Gupta. Arrived in Canada in 1968, discusses family history and comparisons between Canadian and South Asian culture.

Vivekananda, Swami. *My Master*. 1973. Booklet. 75 pp.

Star and Style. 8-21 April 1977. 51 pp.

The Statesman. 18 Feb. 1978. 20 pp.

MUKHERJEE, ALOK
TORONTO, ONT.
Interviewed on 23 May 1977; 1 hr.; 1 tape; English; by Vijay Agnew.

MURTY, MR.
TORONTO, ONT.
Interviewed on 18 May 1977; 1 hr.; 1 tape; English; by Vijay Agnew. Immigrated to Canada in 1970.

NANDA, NEENA
TORONTO, ONT.
Interviewed on 4 March 1977; 1 hr.; 1 tape; English; by Vijay Agnew. From Punjab, arrived in Canada in 1965.

NEFF, DAN
TORONTO, ONT.
India News. 3, 20 June 1977; 4 July 1977 (4 issues).

Overseas Hindustan Times. New Delhi, New York, 1975-77. 73 scattered issues.

OWAISI, L. (*CRESCENT INTERNATIONAL*)
TORONTO, ONT.
15 photographs: activities within the Pakistani community of Ont., including anti-racism demontrations at City Hall in Toronto, 1977; Pakistan Day celebration in Ottawa, 1974; and EID Prayer Festival at the Canadian National Exhibition in Toronto, 1976.

PANDA, RATAN
TORONTO, ONT.
Interviewed on 8 April 1977; 2 hrs.; 2 tapes; English; by Vijay Agnew. Describes transoceanic passage, family life, and community work.

PATEL, HARSHAD
TORONTO, ONT.
Interviewed on 13 Oct. 1977; 1 hr.; 1 tape; English; by Vijay Agnew. Hindu/Gujerati, immigrated to Canada in 1970.

PERIERA, CHERYL
TORONTO, ONT.
Interviewed on 16 May 1977; 1 hr.; 1 tape; English; by Vijay Agnew. Immigrated to Canada in 1972.

PIRBHAI, KALIM
TIMMINS, ONT.
Interviewed on 25 July 1978; 1 hr.; 1 tape; English; by Krishna Gupta. From Mombasa, Kenya, immigrated to Canada in 1973.

RAJAGOPAL, MOHAN
TORONTO, ONT.
Interviewed on 15 July 1977; 1 hr.; 1 tape; English; by Vijay Agnew. Hindu/Brahmin, immigrated to Canada in 1962.

RAJAGOPAL, R.
TORONTO, ONT.
Interviewed on 9 Jan. 1977; 1 hr.; 1 tape; English; by Vijay Agnew.

RAY, RATINDERA
TORONTO, ONT.

11 March 1977; 1 hr.; 1 tape; English; by Vijay Agnew. Hindu/Bengali, arrived in Canada in 1972.

REDDY, RINA
TORONTO, ONT.
Interviewed on 4 Feb. 1977; 1 hr.; 1 tape; English; by Vijay Agnew. Immigrated to Canada in 1965 after a 5-year stay in England.

SADIQ, NAZNEEN
TORONTO, ONT.
Interviewed on 6 May 1977; 1 hr.; 1 tape; English; by Vijay Agnew. A Muslim from Kashmir, immigrated to Canada in 1964.

SAYED, MEHBOOB
TORONTO, ONT.
Interviewed on 1 Nov. 1977; 1 hr.; 1 tape; English; by Vijay Agnew.

SENATHIRAJA, NALLA
TORONTO, ONT.
Interviewed on 13 April 1977; 2 hrs.; 2 tapes; English; by Vijay Agnew. Immigrated to Canada in 1966.

SHARMA, ROOP
TORONTO, ONT.
Interviewed on 6 March 1977; 2 hrs.; 2 tapes; English; by Vijay Agnew.

SINGH, AMARJIT
TORONTO, ONT.
Interviewed on 4 Aug. 1979; 1 hr.; 1 tape; Panjabi/English; by T. Singh. From Pakistan, arrived in Canada in 1975.

SINGH, ANANT
TORONTO, ONT.
Interviewed on 11 July 1977; 1 hr.; 1 tape; English; by Vijay Agnew. From Gujranwalla, Pakistan, immigrated to Canada in 1971.

SINGH, GERTRUDE
SOUTH PORCUPINE, ONT.
Interviewed on 8 Oct. 1978; .75 hr.; 1 tape; English; by Krishna Gupta. Immigrated to Canada in 1970.

SINGH, HARDEV
TORONTO, ONT.
Interviewed on 13 Jan. 1977; 2 hrs.; 2 tapes; English; by Vijay Agnew.

SINGH, ISHWAR AND RAVINDER KAUR
ANCASTER, ONT.
Interviewed on 4 July 1979; 1 hr.; 1 tape; Panjabi/English; by T. Singh. From Punjab, immigrated to Canada in 1962.

SINGH, VARA
TORONTO, ONT.
Interviewed on 10 Sept. 1979; 1 hr.; 1 tape; English; by T. Singh. Immigrated to Canada in 1967.

SUBHANI, MRS.
TORONTO, ONT.
Interviewed on 2 June 1977; 1 hr.; 1 tape; Hindu; by Vijay Agnew. A Muslim, arrived in Canada in 1973.

TRICHUR, SHIVRAM
TORONTO, ONT.
Interviewed on 11 May 1977; 1 hr.; 1 tape; English; by Vijay Agnew. Immigrated to Canada in 1962.

VENKATRAMAN, U.
TORONTO, ONT.
 Interviewed on 13 April 1977; 1 hr.;
1 tape; English; by Vijay Agnew. Ar-
rived in Canada via England in 1969.
Thyagaraja Music Festival. Toronto:
Bharathi Kala Manram, 1974. 3 cm.

ASSOCIATION OF WOMEN OF INDIA IN
CANADA
THORNHILL, ONT.
 Records, 1976-78, which include
constitution, minutes, correspondence,
and annual report, 1976-77, executive
members lists, newsletters, and
flyers. 3.5 cm.

BAHARATI KALA MANRAM
TORONTO, ONT.
 Records, 1969-78, which include
constitution, by-laws, correspondence,
financial reports, flyers, posters,
tickets, and members lists. 5.5 cm.
See U. Venkatraman.
RESTRICTED
 Anniversary *Celebrations Souvenir
Booklet.* 1973-74. 20 pp.
 Maram Letter. 1969-68. Bulletin (60
issues). 2 cm.

BANGLADESH ASSOCIATION OF
CANADA
TORONTO, ONT.
 Records, 1971-78, which include
constitutions, regulations, correspon-
dence, reports, and papers read at the
"National Symposium on Social and
Cultural Integration of Bangladesh in
Canada, 1978," newsletters, and mis-
cellaneous printed items. 1 reel of
microfilm. 2 cm.

CANADA-PAKISTAN ASSOCIATION
LONDON, ONT.
 Records, 1976-78, which include
constitution, minutes, correspondence,
membership list, flyers, and press
clippings. 1 reel of microfilm.
 *Proceedings of First
Canada-Pakistan Association's
National Multicultural Symposium.*
Ottawa, 30-31 July 1976. 64 pp.

CANADIAN SOCIETY FOR ASIAN
STUDIES
THORNHILL, ONT.
 Newsletter/bulletin, Nov. 1977;
Feb., April 1978. 1 cm.
 CASA-ACEA Revue. Nov. 1978. 40
pp.

CRESCENT INTERNATIONAL
TORONTO, ONT.
 1 photograph: *Crescent* newspaper
front page, 1977.
 Crescent. Toronto, 23 March 1973 -
1 March 1977. 1 reel of microfilm.
 Voice of Pakistan. Vol. 1, no. 1.
Toronto, March 1972 - March 1973,
forerunner of *Crescent.* 1 reel of
microfilm.

FEDERATION OF INDO-CANADIAN
ASSOCIATIONS
THORNHILL, ONT.
 Lists of membership associations,
executive, n.d.; correspondence,
1977, and invitations, tickets, and
flyers, 1977. 1.5 cm.

FEDERATION OF PAKISTANI CANA-
DIANS
TORONTO, ONT.
 Miscellaneous printed items: newspa-
pers, flyers, invitations, and a bro-
chure, 1978-79. 1.5 cm.
 Akhbar-I-Gulrng Fortnightly. 15
Aug. 1978. 12 pp.

Pakistan Time. 15 June 1978. 6 pp.
Viewpoint Fortnightly. 15 Oct. 1978.
8 pp.

GOLDEN TRIANGLE SIKH ASSOCI-
ATION
WATERLOO, ONT.
  Constitution, 1977; financial records,
1973-77; and announcements,
1978-79. 2 cm.

GUJARAT SAMAJ OF TORONTO
TORONTO, ONT.
  Constitution and by-laws, 1977; and
flyers, and programmes, 1975-78. 2
cm.

HERITAGE SIKH/HARMONY CANADA
TORONTO, ONT.
  General correspondence, background
paper to Harmony Canada, and
flyers, 1976-77. 1.5 cm.

HINDU PRATHANA SMAJ
TORONTO, ONT.
  Constitution, letters patent, correspondence, programmes, and flyers,
1969-77. 1 cm.

HINDU TEMPLE SOCIETY
TORONTO, ONT.
  Minutes to Charter Committee and
Board of Trustees meetings, letters
patent, circulars, and lists of Hindu
festivals, 1975-77. 1 cm.

INDIAN IMMIGRANT AID SERVICES
TORONTO, ONT.
  Papers, 1971-81, which include
constitution, minutes, annual reports,
correspondence (immigration policy),
I.I.A.S. special project reports, candi-
dates volunteer lists, and flyers. 1
reel of microfilm. 9 cm.
  Naidoo, Josephine. *The East Indian
Woman*. Toronto: I.I.A.S., 1976.

18 pp.
  Singh, Amarjit. *Adjustment in
Multicultural Canada: A Strategy*.
Toronto: I.I.A.S., 1978. 11 pp.
  India at a Glance. Toronto: Indian
Immigrant Aid Services, 1980. 45 pp.
  *Indians in Toronto Conference, May
14-15, 1977, Report*. Toronto, 1977.
72 pp.
  *Indian Community Information
Directory*. Toronto: I.I.A.S., 1978.
70 pp.
  Newsletter. 1972-78. Complete. 9
cm.
  *Proceedings of the Sikh Conference
1979*. Toronto, 24, 25 March 1979.
164 pp.

INDO-CANADA CHAMBER OF COM-
MERCE
TORONTO, ONT.
  By-laws, 1977, flyer and newsletter,
1978. .5 cm.

JAIN SOCIETY
TORONTO, ONT.
  Annual report and members lists,
1978; and 4 news bulletins from the
Association Women of India in
Canada, 1978. 1.5 cm.

MARATHI BHASHIK MANDAL (G.R.
DESHPANDE)
TORONTO, ONT.
  Initially, an informal organization of
Marathi-speaking immigrants, the
Marathi Bhaskik Mandal adopted a
formal constitution in 1974. Its aims
and objectives were to provide a
meeting place, and to promote the
Maharashtra culture in Canada.
Records, 1969-77, which include con-
stitution, correspondence, financial
statements, a newsletter, and miscel-
laneous printed items. 9 cm., in
Marathi/English.

Sahyardi. n.d. Magazine in Marathi. 50 pp.

Snehbandh. 1970-76. Newsletter. 3 cm.

Tera Hira. n.d. 220 pp., in Marathi.

METRO CARAVAN-NEW DELHI PAVILION
TORONTO, ONT.

Correspondence and flyers, 1978. .5 cm.

New Delhi Pavilion-Caravan '78. Toronto, 1978. 12 pp.

MULTICULTURAL HISTORY SOCIETY OF ONTARIO
TORONTO, ONT.

Awan, Sadiq Noor Alan. *The People of Pakistani Origin in Canada: The First Quarter Century*. Ottawa, 1976. 48 pp.

Buchignani, Norman and Doreen M. Indra with Ram Srivastava. *Continuous Journey: A Social History of South Asians in Canada*. Toronto, 1985. 250 pp.

Chandrasekhar, S., ed. *From India to America*. La Jolla, California, 1986. 111 pp.

Gundara, Jaswinder. *Splintered Dreams: Sikhs in Southern Alberta*. Calgary, 1985. 80 pp.

_____, comp. *They Tried to Rob Me of My Name*. Calgary, 1985. Cross-Cultural and Third World Literature for Social Change. 88 pp.

Irwin, Heather, comp. *South Asian Reader: Recent Articles from Newspapers and Magazines*. c. 1977-78.

Johnston, Hugh. *The East Indians in Canada*. Ottawa, 1984. 24 pp.

East Indians in the Caribbean: 150th Anniversary, 1838-1988. York-Indo Caribbean Sudies Conference, 6 - 10 July 1988, Toronto.

Mayer, Adrian C. *A Report on the East Indian Community in Vancouver*. Social and Economic Research, University of British Columbia, 1959. 37 pp.

McLeod, W. H., comp. *A List of Punjabi Immigrants in New Zealand, 1890-1939*. Hamilton: Country Section of the Central Indian Association, 1984. 82 pp.

Sandhu, Sukhdev S. *The Second Generation: Culture and the East Indian Community in Nova Scotia*. Ethnic Heritage Series, Vol. 2. Halifax, n.d. 34 pp.

Singh, Jarnail and Hardev Singh. *Proceedings of the Sikh Heritage Conference 1981*. Toronto, 1982.

Ubale, Bhansaheb. *Equal Opportunity and Public Policy. A Report on Concerns of the South Asian Canadian Community Regarding Their Place in Canadian Mosaic*. Toronto, 1977. 277 pp.

India, Pakistan, Bangladesh, and Sri Lanka Conference, Nov. 22, and 24, 1978. Toronto. North York Board of Education. 141 pp.

Indians in Ontario Conference, Nov. 17, 1974 Report. Toronto. 23 pp.

Papers on the East Indian Community. Government of Ontario, 1976. 34 pp.

Work Force Involvement of East Indian Immigrant Women in Western Canada. Department of Sociology, University of Alberta, 1980. 231 pp.

MULTICULTURAL NEWSPAPER MICROFILM PROJECT
TORONTO, ONT.

Canadian India Times. Ottawa, 2 Jan. 1975 - 7 Dec. 1981, in English. 3 reels of microfilm.

Gujarat Vartman. Toronto, 15 Aug. 1977 - 1 Oct. 1985, in Guajarati. 4 reels of microfilm.

The Messenger. Toronto, 3 March
1978 - 21 Oct. 1984, in Urdu. 2 reels
of microfilm.

NATIONAL ASSOCIATION OF CANA-
DIANS OF ORIGIN IN INDIA
OTTAWA, ONT.
 Draft constitution, by-laws, minutes,
correspondence, NACOI leaflets, and
publications, 1976-79. .5 meters.

NIRVAN BHAVAN FOR INDIANS IN
TORONTO
TORONTO, ONT.
 Chairperson's report, meeting notice,
and brochure about Nirvan Bhavan,
1978. .5 cm.

PAKISTAN ASSOCIATION OF
HAMILTON
HAMILTON, ONT.
 Constitution, minutes, correspon-
dence, financial statements, and a
calendar of events, 1975-78. 1 cm.

PAKISTANI CULTURAL AID CENTRE
TORONTO, ONT.
 Hal-E-Pakistan. Toronto, 1977.
Scattered issues, in Urdu.
 Pakistani Times Toronto, 1977-78. 9
scattered issues.

PRABASI
TORONTO, ONT.
 Records, 1975-79, which include
constitution, by-laws, financial
accounts, correspondence, flyers, and
circulars referring to race relations,
and racial incidents in Toronto. 24
cm.

PUBLIC FORUM
TORONTO, ONT.
 Recorded on 30 Oct. 1977; 2 hrs.; 2
tapes; English; by Vijay Agnew.
Recording of a public meeting held to

present "Equal Opportunity and Public Policy."

REFORM COMMITTEE—SIKH SANGAT
HAMILTON, ONT.
 Correspondence, and 2 newsletter
issues, 1978. .5 cm.

SOUTH ASIANS FOR EQUALITY
OTTAWA, ONT.
 Agendas and minutes of South Asian
Origins Liaison Committee meetings,
1977-78. 1cm.

SOUTH INDIA CULTURAL ASSOCI-
ATION
OTTAWA, ONT.
 Ads, posters, and flyers for
S.I.C.A.-sponsored functions, 1978,
and newclipings on cultural events,
1972, 1975, 1976. .5 cm.

SRI GURU SINGH SABHA CANADA
MISSISSAUGA, ONT.
 Club constitution, 1975, and a flyer,
"Gurpurb," n.d. .5 cm., in Panjabi.

THE CONTINUING COMMITTEE ON
RACE RALATIONS
TORONTO, ONT.
 2 copies of open letter concerning
the *Toronto Sun*, July, 1978; pamphlet, "Metropolitan Toronto Volunteers
in Confrontation with Racism," n.d.;
and ephemera. 1.5 cm.

THE EAST INDIAN DEFENCE COMMIT-
TEE
THORNHILL, ONT.
 Constitution of E.I.D.C., 1976, and
publications dealing with racism. 4
cm.

THE GOAN OVERSEAS ASSOCIATION
TORONTO, ONT.
 Newsletter. 1983-84. 5 scattered
issues.

THE INDIA CANADA SOCIETY OF
HAMILTON AND REGION
DUNDAS, ONT.
 Constitution, 1974; newsletter, 1978;
and poster for Society-sponsored
function, n.d. .5 cm.

VEDANTA SOCIETY OF TORONTO
TORONTO, ONT.
 Constitution, correspondence, advertisements, and agendas for Vedanta
functions, and newsletter, 1968-78.
12 cm.

SRI LANKAN COLLECTION

ABEYESEKERA, KIRTHIE
TORONTO, ONT.
 Interviewed on 24 May 1979; 2 hrs.;
2 tapes; English; by S. Sugunasiri.
Arrived in Canada in 1975.

ALI, MOHAMED S.
TORONTO, ONT.
 Interviewed on 26 May 1979; 1 hr.;
1 tape; English; by S. Sugunasiri.
Immigrated to Canada in 1975.

ALWIS, YVONNE
TORONTO, ONT.
 Interviewed on 29 May 1979; 1 hr.;
1 tape; English; by S. Sugunasiri.
Arrived in Canada in 1969, discusses
work, discrimination against women,
and ethnicity.

APPATHURAI, EDWARD
TORONTO, ONT.
 Interviewed on 29 Dec. 1978; 2 hrs.;
2 tapes; English; by S. Sugunasiri.
Arrived in Canada in 1963.

BELLANA, CHANDRARATNA
TORONTO, ONT.
 Interviewed on 7 Nov. 1978; 1 hr.;
1 tape; English/Sinhala; by S.
Sugunasiri. Arrived in Canada in
1973.

DE SILVA, EDWARD
TORONTO, ONT.
 Interviewed on 13 Nov. 1978; 2
hrs.; 2 tapes; English; by S.
Sugunasiri. Immigrated to Canada in
1966, involved in the Metro Toronto
Police Association.

DE SILVA, JANE
TORONTO, ONT.
 Interviewed on 6 July 1978; 1 hr.; 1
tape; Sinhala; by S. Sugunasiri. First
arrived in Canada in 1964, regular
participant at Buddhist gatherings.

DE SILVA, NEVILLE
MISSISSAUGA, ONT.
 Documents relating to the Ceylon
Club and Our Lady of Lanka Catholic
Guild, c. 1970s. .5 cm. Taped inter-
view.
 Interviewed on 27 April 1979; 2.5
hrs.; 3 tapes; English; by S.
Sugunasiri. Arrived in Canada in
1972, member of the Metro Police
Force, the Canada-Sri Lanka Associ-
ation, and Catholic organizations.

DE SILVA, P.
TORONTO, ONT.
 Interviewed on 7 Dec. 1978; 2 hrs.;
2 tapes; English; by S. Sugunasiri.
Immigrated to Canada in 1973,
disusses life in Sri Lanka.

DEVENDRA, MANIKKHAN
TORONTO, ONT.
 Interviewed on 13 July 1979; 2 hrs.;
2 tapes; English; by S. Sugunasiri.
Immigrated to Canada in 1972, active
member of Bharati Kala Manram.

DHAMMIKA, BHIKKHU KAHAGOLLE
TORONTO, ONT.
 Interviewed on 4 May 1979; 1.5
hrs.; 2 tapes; Sinhala; by S.

Sugunasiri. Arrived in Canada in the early 1970s, resident bhikkhu at the Toronto (Buddhist) Mahavihara.

EKANAYAKA, STANLEY
TORONTO, ONT.
 Interviewed on 22 Oct. 1978; 2 hrs.; 2 tapes; English; by S. Sugunasiri. Left for Canada in 1967, past president of the Canada-Sri Lanka Association and the Canadian Buddhist Vihara Society.

FERNANDO, KORUWAGE
TORONTO, ONT.
 Interviewed on 2 Nov. 1978; 1 hr.; 1 tape; English; by S. Sugunasiri. Arrived in Canada in 1972, former president, and active member of the Canadian Buddhist Vihara Society.

FERNANDO, PATRICK
HAMILTON, ONT.
 Interviewed on 21 Dec. 1978; 2 hrs.; 2 tapes; English; by S. Sugunasiri. Immigrated to Canada in 1972, former president of the Canada-Sri Lanka Assocation.

GAMAGE, LAKSHMAN
TORONTO, ONT.
 Interviewed on 24 Oct. 1978; 2 hrs.; 2 tapes; English; by S. Sugunasiri. Immigrated to Canada in 1971 via England, officer of the Canadian Buddhist Vihara Society.

HETTIARACHCHI, DAYA
TORONTO, ONT.
 Interviewed on 19 Nov. 1978; 3 hrs.; 3 tapes; English; by S. Sugunasiri. Immigrated to Canada in 1964.

JANSZ, WILHELM
TORONTO, ONT.
 Interviewed on 30 Jan. 1979; 2 hrs.; 2 tapes; English; by S. Sugunasiri. Left for Canada in 1975, trustee of Canada-Sri Lanka Association.

JAYASURIYA, SAM
TORONTO, ONT.
 Interviewed on 5 Nov. 1978; 1.5 hrs.; 2 tapes; English; by S. Sugunasiri. Immigrated to Canada in 1972, recounts prejudice he encountered in Toronto.

JEYANATHAN, PADMINI
MARKHAM, ONT.
 Interviewed on 1 Aug. 1979; 1 hr.; 1 tape; English; by S. Sugunasiri. Arrived in Canada in 1976, discusses Hindu activities at home, and in the community.

JOSEPH, DOROTHY
TORONTO, ONT.
 Interviewed on 5 June 1979; 2 hrs.; 2 tapes; English; by S. Sugunasiri. Left for Canada in 1971, discusses incidents of discrimination.

MADANAYAKA, BANDU
TORONTO, ONT.
 Interviewed on 26 Oct. 1978; 1 hr.; 1 tape; English; by S. Sugunasiri. Arrived in Canada in 1969, involved in the Toronto (Buddhist) Mahavihara.

OBEYESEKERE, SUSSANTHA
TORONTO, ONT.
 Interviewed on 18 Dec. 1978; 3 hrs.; 3 tapes; English; by S. Sugunasiri. Moved to Canada in 1971, played a prominent role in transforming the Ceylon Recreation Club to the Canada-Sri Lanka Association.

ORCHARD, THOMAS
TORONTO, ONT.
1 photograph: emigrants at point of departure from Sri Lanka, c. 1955. Taped interview.
Interviewed on 20 April 1979; 1.5 hrs.; 2 tapes; English; by S. Sugunasiri. Arrived in Canada in 1955, one of the first Sri Lankan immigrants in Toronto.

PEERIS, SUMITHRA
WATERFORD, ONT.
Interviewed on 18 Nov. 1978; 2 hrs.; 2 tapes; English; by S. Sugunasiri. Family immigrated to Canada in 1967, trustee of the Toronto (Buddhist) Mahavihara.

PEERIS, SUSANTHA GAMINI
WATERFORD, ONT.
Interviewed on 18 Nov. 1978; 1 hr.; 1 tape; English; by S. Sugunasiri. Immigrated to Canada in 1967, trustee and vice-president of the Toronto (Buddhist) Mahavihara.

PERERA, ALOY
OAKVILLE, ONT.
Interviewed on 1 Dec. 1979; 3 hrs.; 3 tapes; English; by S. Sugunasiri. Arrived in Canada in 1972, member of Lotus Club in Montreal, and the Canada-Sri Lanka Association in Toronto.

PERERA, BENET
TORONTO, ONT.
Interviewed on 18 Jan. 1979; 2 hrs.; 2 tapes; English; by S. Sugunasiri. Moved to Canada in 1972, discusses incidents of prejudice, and relations with other ethnic groups.

PERERA, HEMA
HAMILTON, ONT.
Interviewed on 5 June 1979; 1 hr.; 1 tape; English; by S. Sugunasiri. Arrived in Canada in 1974.

RAJANAYAGAM, SOLOMON
VELUPILLAI
TORONTO, ONT.
Interviewed on 26 Dec. 1978; 2 hrs.; 2 tapes; English; by S. Sugunasiri. Moved to Canada in 1958, first president of the Ceylon Recreation Club.

RAJAPAKSA, DEEPTHI
MISSISSAUGA, ONT.
Interviewed on 15 May 1979; 1.5 hrs.; 2 tapes; English; by S. Sugunasiri. Arrived in Canada in 1973.

SHERIFF, HASSAN
TORONTO, ONT.
Interviewed on 28 Dec. 1978; 3 hrs.; 3 tapes; English; by S. Sugunasiri. Immigrated to Canada in 1975, after working in England and Germany.

SIVALINGAM, NAGARATNAM
TORONTO, ONT.
Interviewed on 23 April 1979; 1 hr.; 1 tape; English; by S. Sugunasiri. Arrived in Canada in 1966, past president of the Hindu Temple Society, and the Tamil Eelam Society.

SUGUNASIRI, SUWANDA
TORONTO, ONT.
10 photographs: opening of the Sri Lankan Buddhist Temple in Toronto, 1976; and a family party, 1983. Taped interview.
Interviewed on 21 Feb. 1979; 2.5 hrs.; 3 tapes; English; by Vijay Agnew. Dr. Sugunasiri discusses his

life in Sri Lanka before emigrating and his subsequent career in Canada.

WANIGASEKARA, DIXON
TORONTO, ONT.
 Interviewed on 17 April 1979; 1.5 hrs.; 2 tapes; English; by S. Sugunasiri. Arrived in Canada in 1966.

WANIGASEKARA, GAMINI
TORONTO, ONT.
 Interviewed on 20 Oct. 1978; 2 hrs.; 2 tapes; English; by S. Sugunasiri. Left for Canada in 1971, past president of the Vihara Society.

WICKREMAARATCHI, TISSA
AGINCOURT, ONT.
 Interviewed on 22 Oct. 1978; 1 hr.; 1 tape; English; by S. Sugunasiri. Arrived in Canada in 1969.

WIJESENA, LALANI
TORONTO, ONT.
 Interviewed on 31 Oct. 1978; 1 hr.; 1 tape; English; by S. Sugunasiri. Arrived in Canada in 1976, involved in the Vihara Society.

CANADA-SRI LANKA ASSOCIATION
TORONTO, ONT.
 The Canada-Sri Lanka Association was formally established in 1968. Since then it worked to organize social activities within Toronto's Sri Lankan community—picnics, pilgrimages, cricket, tennis matches, and annual dances. Records, 1973-78, include a constitution, minutes, correspondence, historical sketch of the Association, and personal papers of the Tom Orchards family, the first Sri Lankan family in Toronto. 12 cm. See Thomas Orchards.

CANADIAN BUDDHIST VIHARA SOCIETY
TORONTO, ONT.
 Printed items, 1974-78. 1.5 cm.

TORONTO (BUDDHIST) MAHAVIHARA
TORONTO, ONT.
 Printed items, 1978. .5 cm.

TORONTO BUDDHIST TEMPLE OPENING
TORONTO, ONT.
 Recorded on 16 July 1978; 1 hr.; 1 tape; English; by S. Sugunasiri.

AHLBERG, EDWARD
TORONTO, ONT.
 Interviewed on 12 April 1978; 1 hr.;
1 tape; Swedish; by M.
Bolin.

AHLBERG, NILS
TORONTO, ONT.
 Interviewed on 1 May 1978; 1 hr.; 1
tape; English; by M. Bolin.

ALMQUIST, VIGGO
TORONTO, ONT.
 Interviewed on 10 Jan. 1978; 1 hr.;
1 tape; Swedish; by M. Bolin.
Arrived in Canada in 1975.

ANDERSSON, BERTIL
TORONTO, ONT.
 Interviewed on 4 Jan. 1978; 1 hr.; 1
tape; English; by M. Bolin.

ANDERSSON, GUMILLA
TORONTO, ONT.
 3 photographs: the Andersson family
in Sweden, 1947-57. Taped interview.
 Interviewed on 12 Jan. 1978; 1 hr.;
1 tape; English; by M. Bolin.

GÖRAN, ANTLÖV
TORONTO, ONT.
 Interviewed on 10 Jan. 1978; 1 hr.;
1 tape; English; by M. Bolin.

BERGENHOLZ, MARIANNE
TORONTO, ONT.
 Interviewed on 22 Jan. 1978; 1 hr.;
1 tape; Swedish; by M. Bolin.

BERGMAN, VALENTIN
TORONTO, ONT.
 Interviewed on 19 April 1979; .5
hr.; 1 tape; English; by E.
Nordström. Immigrated to Canada in
1928.

BOETTCHER, G.
TORONTO, ONT.
 Interviewed on 9 May 1978; 1 hr.; 1
tape; English; by M. Bolin.

BOLIN, MARGARETHA
TORONTO, ONT.
 Interviewed on 21 June 1978; 2.5
hrs.; 3 tapes; English; by D. Vickers
and V. Wilcox.

BRANDKVIST, JAN AND GUMMEL
TORONTO, ONT.
 Interviewed on 3 Feb. 1978; 1 hr.; 1
tape; English; by M. Bolin. Arrived
in Canada in the late 1960s.

CARLSSON, ANNICA
ST. THOMAS, ONT.
 4 photographs: donor with her
mother, and her sisters in Sweden, c.
1936-56.

CHARLES, KRISTINA
TORONTO, ONT.
 Interviewed on 10 April 1978; 1 hr.;
1 tape; English; by M. Bolin. Arrived
in Canada in 1968.

COLLINGS, BERIT
TORONTO, ONT.
 Interviewed on 9 March 1978; 1.5
hrs.; 2 tapes; English; by M. Bolin.

ELVIN, SUSANNE
TORONTO, ONT.
Interviewed on 7 Feb. 1978; 1 hr.; 1 tape; Swedish; by M. Bolin.

ENSTRÖM, JONAS
TORONTO, ONT.
Interviewed in 1977; .5 hr.; 1 tape; English; by Harold Hogstad.

ENSTRÖM, JONAS
THUNDER BAY, ONT.
Interviewed on 19 April 1979; .5 hr.; 1 tape; English; by E. Nordström. Immigrated to Canada in 1913.

ERIKSSON, EVA AND SIGURD
TORONTO, ONT.
1 photograph: donors on their wedding day in Sweden, 1961. Taped interview.
Interviewed on 11 Feb. 1978; 1 hr.; 1 tape; Swedish; by M. Bolin.

FORS, ARNE
TORONTO, ONT.
Interviewed on 21 April 1978; 1 hr.; 1 tape; English; by M. Bolin.

FUKUHARA, EVA
TORONTO, ONT.
Interviewed on 18 March 1978; 1 hr.; 1 tape; Swedish; by M. Bolin.

GROENBERG, PAULA
TORONTO, ONT.
Kronborg, Bo and T. Nilsson. *Stadsflyttare: Industrialisering, migration och socail mobilitet med utgangspunkt fran Halmstad, 1870-1910.* Studia Historica Upsaliensia 65, 1975. 298 pp.
Wester, Holger. *Innovationer i befolkningsrorligheten: En studie av spridningsforlopp i*

befolkningsrorligheten utgaende fran Petalax socken i Osterbotten. Studia Historica Upsaliensa 93, 1977. 220 pp.

GUSTAVSSON, BO
TORONTO, ONT.
Interviewed on 8 Feb. 1978; .5 hr.; 1 tape; English; by M. Bolin.

HANZON, MATS
TORONTO, ONT.
Interviewed on 4 April 1978; .75 hr.; 1 tape; English; by M. Bolin.

HASSELROT, KARL BERNT
TORONTO, ONT.
Interviewed on 27 Feb. 1978; 1 hr.; 1 tape; English; by M. Bolin.

IVANSSON, MARJA
TORONTO, ONT.
Interviewed on 1 March 1978; .75 hr.; 1 tape; English; by M. Bolin.

KALLNER, MAGNUS
TORONTO, ONT.
Interviewed on 31 Jan. 1978; 1 hr.; 1 tape; English; by M. Bolin

KALLNER, BRITT-MARIE AND MAGNUS
TORONTO, ONT.
Interviewed on 6 April 1978; 2 hrs.; 2 tapes; English; by M. Bolin.

KARLSSON, ANNIKA
TORONTO, ONT.
Interviewed on 8 Feb. 1978; 1 hr.; 1 tape; English; by M. Bolin.

KJALL, RUME
TORONTO, ONT.
Interviewed on 14 April 1978; 1 hr.; 1 tape; Swedish; by M. Bolin.

KLINT, INGER
AGINCOURT, ONT.
 Interviewed on 20 March 1978; 1
hr.; 1 tape; Swedish; by M. Bolin.

KÖHLER, MARGARETHA
TORONTO, ONT.
 Interviewed on 19 April 1978; .75
hr.; 1 tape; Swedish; by M. Bolin.

LAGERSTEN, ETHEL
TORONTO, ONT.
 4 photographs: the family in Estonia
1933-34; and the passenger ship,
Castlebianco. Taped interview.
 Interviewed on 8 May 1978; 2 hrs.;
2 tapes; English; by M. Bolin.

LEIGHT, MAUD
TORONTO, ONT.
 Interviewed on 8 Feb. 1978; 1 hr.; 1
tape; English; by M. Bolin.

LINDFORS, ARJA-MARIA
TORONTO, ONT.
 Interviewed on 10 May 1978; 1 hr.;
1 tape; English; by M. Bolin.

MAGNUSON, MARTIN
TIMMINS, ONT.
 Interviewed on 27 April 1979; .5
hr.; 1 tape; English; by E.
Nordström.

MAIL, JOHN
TORONTO, ONT.
 Interviewed on 12 April 1978; 1 hr.;
1 tape; English; by M. Bolin.

MOLIN, ELVIR
TORONTO, ONT.
 Interviewed on 3 March 1978; 1 hr.;
1 tape; English; by M. Bolin.

NÕMMIK, REV. T.
TORONTO, ONT.
 Interviewed on 10 May 1978; .5 hr.;
1 tape; English; by M. Bolin.
 *Svenka Lutherska Kyrkan i Toronto,
1953-1973.* Toronto: Swedish
Lutheran Congregation, 1973.

NORDAHL, ERIC
CONCORDE, ONT.
 4 photographs: the Nordahl family in
Sweden, British Columbia, and Ont.,
c. 1915-75. Taped interview.
 Interviewed on 11 March 1978; 2
hrs.; 2 tapes; English; by M. Bolin.

NORDAHL, PAUL
TORONTO, ONT.
 Interviewed on 12 May 1978; 1 hr.;
1 tape; English; by M. Bolin.

NORDLANDER, OSCAR
THUNDER BAY, ONT.
 20 photographs: work in northern
Ont. lumbercamps, c. 1923-40. Taped
interview.
 Interviewed on 2 March 1978; .5
hr.; 1 tape; English; by Harold
Hogstad.

OLSSON, BRITA
TORONTO, ONT.
 Interviewed on 5 March 1978; 1 hr.;
1 tape; English; by M. Bolin.

PALMQUIST, BHENDA
TORONTO, ONT.
 4 photographs: the Palquist family in
Stockholm, and Ont. 1920-23. Taped
interview.
 Interviewed on 26 Jan. 1978; 1 hr.;
1 tape; English; by M. Bolin.

PORTER, MARGARETHA
TORONTO, ONT.
Interviewed on 20 March 1978; .75 hr.; 1 tape; English; by M. Bolin.

REILITZ, SOLVEIG
TORONTO, ONT.
Interviewed on 10 Feb. 1978; 1 hr.; 1 tape; English; by M. Bolin.

RISBERG, ELIS
TORONTO, ONT.
Interviewed on 19 April 1979; .5 hr.; 1 tape; English/Swedish; by E. Nordström

SIMOLA, ASTRID
TORONTO, ONT.
Interviewed on 25 April 1978; 1 hr.; 1 tape; English; by M. Bolin.

SMITH, KAJSA GRETA
TORONTO, ONT.
6 photographs: the Wedin and Smith families in Saskatchewan, and Toronto, c. 1925-68. Taped interview.
Interviewed on 28 March 1978; 1.5 hrs.; 2 tapes; English; by M. Bolin.

SÖDERHOLM, HERBERT
TORONTO, ONT.
2 photographs: the city of Tallim; and interior of a church in Tallim, 1976. Taped interview.
Interviewed on 29 May 1978; 1 hr.; 1 tape; Swedish; by M. Bolin.

SÖDERSTRÖM, LARS
TORONTO, ONT.
Interviewed on 25 May 1978; 1 hr.; 1 tape; English; by M. Bolin.

SÖRMON, BENGT
TORONTO, ONT.
Interviewed on 10 April 1978; 1 hr.; 1 tape; English; by M. Bolin.

SVANTESSON, HARRY
TORONTO, ONT.
Interviewed on 1 June 1978; .5 hr.; 1 tape; English; by M. Bolin.

SVANTESSON, SVEN
TORONTO, ONT.
Interviewed on 15 May 1978; 2 hrs.; 2 tapes; Swedish; by M. Bolin.

SVENSK, OIVA
WHITEFISH, ONT.
Interviewed on 19 May 1979; .5 hr.; 1 tape; English; by V. Lindström.

SWANSSON, ANNA LISA
TORONTO, ONT.
Interviewed on 22 Jan. 1977; 1 hr.; 1 tape; English; by M. Bolin.

TRYGGVE, JOAN
TORONTO, ONT.
Interviewed on 26 March 1978; .75 hr.; 1 tape; English; by M. Bolin.

TUOMINEN, INGEGERD
TORONTO, ONT.
4 photographs: the Tuominen family in Toronto, 1930-54. Taped interview.
Interviewed on 15 May 1978; 1 hr.; 1 tape; Swedish; by M. Bolin.

VELJKOVIC, JENNY-LENA
TORONTO, ONT.
Interviewed on 14 March 1978; 1.5 hrs.; 2 tapes; English; by M. Bolin.

WALLENIUS, HAKAN
TORONTO, ONT.
Interviewed on 20 March 1978; 1
hr.; 1 tape; English; by M. Bolin.

WIIK, THORWALD
TORONTO, ONT.
Interviewed on 19 Jan. 1978; 1 hr.;
1 tape; English; by M. Bolin.

IMMANUEL LUTHERAN CHURCH
THUNDER BAY, ONT.
List of pastors, and a historical
sketch of the Church, 1946. .5 cm.
Taped recording.
Recorded on 3 March 1978; .25 hr.;
1 tape; English; by Harold Hogstad.

MULTICULTURAL HISTORY SOCIETY
OF ONTARIO
TORONTO, ONT.
Ander, F. O. *The Cultural Heritage
of the Swedish Immigrant: Selected
References*. New York: Arno Press,
1979. 185 pp.
Barton, H. A., ed. *Clipper Ship and
Covered Wagon: Essays from the
Swedish Pioneer Historical Quarterly*.
New York: Arno Press, 1979.
Broberg, G., H. Runblom, and M.
Tyden, eds. *Judiskt liv i Norden*.
Uppsala, 1988. 361 pp.
Capps, F. H. *From Isolationism to
Involvement: The Swedish Immigrant
Press in America, 1914-1945*. 231 pp.
Lejins, Janis. *Mana Dzimtene*.
Vasters, 1971. 333 pp.
Mattson, Hans. *The Story of an Emi-
grant*. Saint Paul, Minnesota: D. D.
Merrill Co., 1891. 314 pp.
Moberg, Vilhelm. *Unto a Good
Land*. New York: Simon and
Schuster, 1954. 306 pp.
Nans, N., Harold Runblom, et al.

Amerikaemigrationen. Uddevalla,
1980. 248 pp.
Runblom, Harold. "Internationell
migration—ettundervisnings
experiment." *Historiska Institutionens
Tidskrift*. No. 18, Dec. 1979. 52 pp.
_____. "Emigrationen som
Massfenomen." *Skoloversyrlsen*.
1979. 33 pp.
Runblom, Harold, and N. Hans, eds.
*From Sweden to America: A History
of the Migration*. Minneapolis: Uni-
versity of Minnesota Press, 1976. 390
pp.
Svanberg, Ingvar. "A Forest Lapp
Culture in Central Sweden in the 17th
and 18th Centuries." *Svenska
Landsmal och Svenskt Folkliv*. 1986.
17 pp.
Wicklund, Albin. *A Diamond Driller
Reminisces*. Duluth, Minnesota: Iron
Range Historical Society, 1977. 133
pp.
*Emigranterna och Kyrkan: Brev Fran
och Till Svenskar i Amerika
1849-1892*. Compilation by Gunnar
Westin. Stockholm, 1932. 612 pp.
Delegationen for Invandrarforkning.
*Framtida Invandrar och
Minoritiesforskning*. Rapport fran ett
seminarium i Sigtuna 12-13 februari
1985. 40 pp.
*Svenska Emigrationskommittens
Betankande*. Helsingfors, 1980. 109
pp.
*Swedish Immigration Research:
Introductory Survey and Annotated
Bibliography*. Stockholm: Commis-
sion on Immigration Research, 1979.
151 pp.
*The Swedish-American Historical
Quarterly*. Formerly the *Swedish
Pioneer Historical Quarterly*. Vol.
35, no. 1, Jan. 1984 - vol. 41, no. 2,
April 1990.
The Swedish Pioneer Historical

Quarterly. Vol. 32, no.1 (Jan. 1981) - vol. 34, no. 4 (Oct 1983).

MULTICULTURAL NEWSPAPER
MICROFILM PROJECT
TORONTO, ONT.
 Canada—Svensken. 15 Jan. 1961 - 31 Dec. 1978. 3 reels of microfilm.

NORSKENNET (SCANDINAVIAN SICK BENEFIT SOCIETY)
THUNDER BAY, ONT.
 Recorded on 3 March 1978; .25 hr.; 1 tape; English; by Harold Hogstad. A commentary on the role of the sick benefit society.

ROYAL SWEDISH EMBASSY (P. HAMMARSTRÖM)
OTTAWA, ONT.
 Printed items from the embassy, 1974. .5 cm.
 Olsson, N. W. *Tracing Your Swedish Ancestry*. Uppsala: Royal Ministry for Foreign Affairs, 1974. 27 pp.
 Publications on Sweden. Stockholm: Swedish Institute, 1987. 65 pp.

SCANDINAVIAN HOME SOCIETY
THUNDER BAY, ONT.
 Recorded on 3 Feb. 1978; .25 hr.; 1 tape; English; by Harold Hogstad. A brief historical commentary on the Home Society.

SWEDISH CHAMBER OF COMMERCE
TORONTO, ONT.
 Articles and constitution, n.d. .5 cm.

SWEDISH LUTHERAN CHURCH (REV. T. NÕMMIK)
TORONTO, ONT.
 Correspondence, 1961-77, financial statements, 1966-75, and parish direc-

tory and bulletins, 1964-77. 1 reel of microfilm.

ZION LUTHERAN CHURCH (F. EDSTRÖM)
THUNDER BAY, ONT.
 1977 Annual Report. .5 cm.

SWISS COLLECTION

BETTSCHEN, GOTTLIEB
NEW DUNDEE, ONT.
 Genealogical, biographical, and
pictorial history of the Bettschen
family, 1910. 1 reel of microfilm.

BOVAY, E. H.
NEW YORK, NEW YORK
 Clippings, 1977. .25 cm.
 Bovay, E. H. *The Swiss in Canada,
1604-1974*. Editions Universitaires
Fribourg, Suisee, 1974. 429 pp.
Fragments. Swiss Volksbank, 1973,
1974. .25 cm.

BURRI, E.
TORONTO, ONT.
 *Swiss Canadian Business Association
Inc., 10th Anniversary Issue*.
Toronto, 1967. 61 pp.

EGLI, WALTER
TORONTO, ONT.
 10 photographs: carnival celebration
in Toronto. 1977-78.
 Canadysli Toronto. 1976. .5 cm.
 Swiss Club Toronto, Zermatt. June
1978. .5 cm.

MUNZ, R.
MITCHELL, ONT.
 Personal diary, 1951, C.P. Railway
identification card, 1930, and a clipping, n.d. 1 cm.

PEQUEGNAT, MARCEL
KITCHENER, ONT.
 Biographical notes on Pequegnat

family, n.d. .5 cm. Taped interview.
Interviewed on 4 Aug. 1977; 1 hr.;
1 tape; English; by Bernard Dandyk.
Stories of Berlin and Kitchener, Ont.

STALDER, HENRI J.
TORONTO, ONT.
 2 photographs: donor in Toronto,
1978.

SWISS CANADIAN BUSINESS ASSOCI-
ATION
TORONTO, ONT.
 By-laws, 1973, membership lists,
1975-76, correspondence, 1976-78,
and reports, 1975-77. 3 cm. Photographs.
 2 photographs: activities of the Club
in Guelph, c. 1970-75.

SWISS CANADIAN CLUB OF GUELPH
GUELPH, ONT.
 Records, 1977-78, which include a
constitution, minutes, and Club bulletins. 2 cm.

SWISS CARNIVAL SOCIETY
TORONTO, ONT.
 Correspondence concerning various
Canadysli carnivals, clippings and
minutes, 1976-78. 2 cm. 1 reel of
microfilm.

SWISS CLUB INTERLAKE
OAKVILLE, ONT.
 Club constitution, minutes, financial

statements, and membership list, 1952-77. 1 reel of microfilm. Photograph.

1 photograph: picnic of the Swiss Club Interlake, Galnford Station, 1955.

SWISS CLUB OTTAWA VALLEY (A. J. BAER)
OTTAWA, ONT.

The collection includes a constitution, minutes, correspondence, ledger book, and membership lists, 1949-73. 24 cm. Photograph.

1 photograph: 2 members of the Club in Ottawa, 1955.

Frohe Festtage. Dec. 1974. .5 cm.

Pour les Suisses á l'Etranger. 1952. 51 pp.

Swiss Herald. Vancouver, 1954-55 (3 issues).

Swiss National Society, 1874-1949. Montreal, Quebec, 1949. Souvenir booklet. 80 pp.

SWISS CLUB THAMES VALLEY
MITCHELL, ONT.

Minutes of general meetings, 1960-78, minutes of Rifle Club meetings, 1974-78, and, miscellaneous correspondence, n.d. 1 reel of microfilm. Photographs.

38 photographs: Swiss immigrants en route to Canada, 1951; dwellings of the Munz family, 1951-71; and activities, such as farming, celebrations, parades, processions, and exhibitions in Mitchell, Ont., 1959-74.

The Mitchell Advocate. 2 Aug. 1973; 1 Aug. 1974; 8 Jan. 1976. 1 cm.

SWISS CLUB TORONTO
TORONTO, ONT.

Records, 1918-1960, which include a constitution, minutes, correspondence, financial reports, membership lists, memoranda, and miscellaneous printed items. 3 reels of microfilm. Photographs.

4 photographs: activities of the Club in Toronto, 1926-68.

Swiss Club Toronto, 1918-68. 50th anniversary booklet. 48 pp.

TURKISH COLLECTION

AKSAN, OKTAY
TORONTO, ONT.
1 photograph: donor, 1965-78.
Taped interview.
Interviewed on 27 March 1979; 1
hr.; 1 tape; English; by E.
Yilmazkaya. Arrived in Canada in
1967.

AKSOY, OZER
LONDON, ONT.
Letters to editors of magazine,
announcement of 1975
Turkish-Earthquake Relief Fund, and
3 flyers prepared for Turkish National
Day, n.d. .5 cm. Taped interview.
Interviewed on 22 Aug. 1979, 20
May 1982; 2 hrs.; 2 tapes; Turkish;
by E. Yilmazkaya. Immigrated to
Canada in 1956, involved in the
Turkish Association of London, Ont.

ALI, MUHSIN
TORONTO, ONT.
2 photographs: donor, 1978; and the
Turkish Cypriots Association in
Toronto, 1978. Taped interview.
Interviewed on 8 . 1979; 1 hr.; 1
tape; Turkish; by E. Yilmazkaya.
Moved to Canada in 1974.

ATLI, EROL
TORONTO, ONT.
1 photograph: donor in front of his
auto repair shop in Toronto, 1979.
Taped interview.
Interviewed on 16 July 1979; 1 hr.;
1 tape; Turkish; by E. Yilmazkaya.
Arrived in Canada in late 1960s.

AYBARS, OMER
TORONTO, ONT.
4 photographs: the Aybars family in
Turkey, 1955, 1975; donor as a cadet
in Turkish Military Academy, 1965;
and donor at Pickering Nuclear Station, 1976. Taped interview.
Interviewed on 4 April 1979; 1.25
hrs.; 2 tapes; English; by E.
Yilmazkaya. Moved to Canada in
1974.

AYKUL, MUZAFFER
TORONTO, ONT.
Interviewed on 5 Sept. 1979; 1.25
hrs.; 2 tapes; Turkish; by E.
Yilmazkaya. Arrived in Canada in
1975, member of the Turkish Canadian Friendship Association.

AYLIN, SEVINC
TORONTO, ONT.
Interviewed on 11 Jan. 1979; 1.5
hrs.; 2 tapes; Turkish; by E.
Yilmazkaya. She immigrated to
Canada in 1967.

AYLIN, TUNAY
TORONTO, ONT.
Photographs: the Aylin family in
Turkey and Toronto, 1963-75. Taped
interview.
Interviewed on 11 June 1979; 2 hrs.;
2 tapes; Turkish; by E. Yilmazkaya.
Immigrated to Canada with wife and
daughters in 1967.

BASCIFTCI, HÜSEYIN
TORONTO, ONT.
Interviewed on 26 Sept. 1979;

.5 hrs.; 1 tape; Turkish; by E.
Yilmazkaya. Immigrated to Canada in
1963, involved in Turkish Canadian
Friendship Association, and Turkish
Sunday School.

BENYES, YASAR
TORONTO, ONT.
 Interviewed on 30 Sept. 1979; 1.5
hrs.; 2 tapes; Turkish; by E.
Yilmazkaya. Moved to Canada in
1970.

BUYUKAKSOY, CEMIL
TORONTO, ONT.
 Interviewed on 7 Aug. 1979; 2.25
hrs.; 3 tapes; Turkish; by E.
Yilmazkaya. Arrived in Canada in the
mid-1960s.

CANDAN, AHMET
TORONTO, ONT.
 Interviewed on 3 Aug. 1979; 3.5
hrs.; 4 tapes; Turkish; by E.
Yilmazkaya. Arrived in Canada in
1966, co-founder and former president of the Turkish Canadian Friendship Association.

CELIK, HÜSEYIN
TORONTO, ONT.
 2 photographs: the Celik family,
1973-78. Taped interview.
 Interviewed on 6 July 1979; 1 hr.; 1
tape; Turkish; by E. Yilmazkaya.
Arrived in Canada in 1975.

CIMEN, MEMDUH A.
TORONTO, ONT.
 1 photograph: donor in Toronto,
1979. Taped interview.
 Interviewed on 7 June 1979; .5 hr.;
1 tape; English; by E. Yilmazkaya.
Immigrated to Canada in 1967,
involved in the Turkish Canadian
Friendship Association.

DILER, MECIT
TORONTO, ONT.
 5 photographs: the Diler family; a
Turkish banquet, and Turkish folk
dancing, 1954-77. Taped interview.
 Interviewed on 28 Feb. 1979; .5 hr.;
1 tape; English; by E. Yilmazkaya.
Arrived in the early 1970s, restaurant
operator in Turkey, and Canada.

DIREK, SELCUK
TORONTO, ONT.
 2 photographs: the Direk family,
1963-73. Taped interview.
 Interviewed on 9 March 1979; .5
hr.; 1 tape; English; by E.
Yilmazkaya. Arrived in Canada in
1970.

DONMEZ, ATILLA
KITCHENER, ONT.
 Interviewed on 12 June 1982; 1 hr.;
1 tape; Turkish; by E. Yilmazkaya.
Moved to Canada in 1971.

EREN, HÜSEYIN
WINDSOR, ONT.
 Interviewed on 30 Dec. 1982; 1.5
hrs.; 2 tapes; Turkish; by E.
Yilmazkaya. He arrived in Canada in
1972, involved in the Turkish Canadian Cultural Association of Windsor.

FIKRI, ERGUN M.
TORONTO, ONT.
 3 photographs: donor in Cyprus,
England, and Toronto, 1958-78.
Taped interview.
 Interviewed on 22 April 1979; 1.5
hrs.; 2 tapes; English; by E.
Yilmazkaya. Arrived in Canada in
1967.

GULER, HÜSEYIN
TORONTO, ONT.
 Interviewed on 28 July 1979; 2 hrs.;

2 tapes; Turkish; by E. Yilmazkaya.
Arrived in Montreal, Quebec in 1966
as a refugee.

HAYTAOGLU, FEVZI
TORONTO, ONT.
2 photographs: the Haytaoglus family
in Toronto, 1978. Taped interview.
Interviewed on 22 Sept. 1979; 1 hr.;
1 tape; Turkish; by E. Yilmazkaya.
Arrived in Canada in 1964, actively
involved in the Turkish Canadian
Friendship Association, and the Turkish Culture and Folklore Society.

HÜNER, MEHMET S.
TORONTO, ONT.
Interviewed on 26 May 1981; 2 hrs.;
2 tapes; Turkish; by E. Yilmazkaya.
Immigrated to Canada in 1969.

IKIZLER, HAYRETTIN
LONDON, ONT.
Interviewed on 14 May 1982; 2 hrs.;
2 tapes; Turkish; by E. Yilmazkaya.
Immigrated to Canada in 1965,
involved in the London Turkish Association.

ISIK, HÜSEYIN
TORONTO, ONT.
Interviewed on 7 June 1982; 2 hrs.;
2 tapes; Turkish; by E. Yilmazkaya.
He arrived Canada in 1980 seeking
refugee status.

ISKIN, ALP
TORONTO, ONT.
Interviewed on 13 March 1979, 27
Aug. 1980; 2.5 hrs.; 3 tapes; Eng-
lish; by E. Yilmazkaya. Immigrated
to Canada in 1977.

KARAKAZAN, YORGO
TORONTO, ONT.
1 photograph: donor in Turkey,

1968. Taped interview.
Interviewed on 16 Sept. 1979; 1 hr.;
1 tape; Turkish; by E. Yilmazkaya.
Immigrated to Canada in 1969.

KAIYLI, YILMAZ
TORONTO, ONT.
3 photographs: the donor in Turkey
and Ottawa, 1974-78. Taped interview.
Interviewed on 19 May 1979; 1 hr.;
1 tape; Turkish; by E. Yilmazkaya.
Arrived in Canada in 1971.

KAYMAKCIOGLU, PARSEL
TORONTO, ONT.
Interviewed on 15 April 1979; 2
hrs.; 2 tapes; Turkish; by E.
Yilmazkaya. Immigrated to Canada in
1961.

KEMAL, MUSTAFA
KITCHENER, ONT.
Interviewed on 13 June 1982; 1 hr.;
1 tape; Turkish; by E. Yilmazkaya.
Immigrated to Canada in 1978.

KESEBI, HASAN
TORONTO, ONT.
3 photographs: Hasan Kesebi with
friends and family in Turkey, and
Dartmouth, Nova Scotia, 1968-72.
Taped interview.
Interviewed on 17 April 1979; 1.5
hrs.; 2 tapes; Turkish; by E.
Yilmazkaya. Immigrated to Canada in
1970.

KISACIK, RECAI
LONDON, ONT.
Interviewed on 28 April 1982; 1 hr.;
1 tape; Turkish; by E. Yilmazkaya.
Moved to Canada in 1967.

KUZUCUOGLU, KORAY
KITCHENER, ONT.
  Interviewed on 12 June 1982; 2 hrs.;
2 tapes; Turkish; by E. Yilmazkaya.
Immigrated to Canada in 1965.
  Akisler. 1969. Dergisi, Turkish
Canadian Association. of
Kitchener-Waterloo. 2 bulletins, in
Turkish.
  Commemorative Issue. Aug. 1975.
First anniversary booklet of the Turk-
ish Peace Operation in Cyprus, issued
by the Turkish Cultural Association
of Kitchener. 19 pp., in English.

MEHMET, GUNAY
TORONTO, ONT.
  3 photographs: donor's wedding;
donor's parents, 1973; donor in
Cypriot-Turk militia; and donor in
1965. Taped interview.
  Interviewed on 21 April 1979; .75
hr.; 1 tape; Turkish; by E.
Yilmazkaya. Arrived in the late
1960s, co-organizer of the
Cypriot-Turks Association.

MEHMET, SEVKER
TORONTO, ONT.
  Photograph: Sevker Mehmet working
in his store, 1975. Taped interview.
  Interviewed on 25 Feb. 1979; .5 hr.;
1 tape; English; by E. Yilmazkaya.

MUHITTIN, AKDEMIR
TORONTO, ONT.
  Interviewed on 20 Feb. 1979; .5 hr.;
1 tape; English; by E. Yilmazkaya.
He immigrated to Canada in 1967.

MUSTAFA, YASAR
TORONTO, ONT.
  2 photographs: donor working as a
shoemaker in England, 1963-69.
Taped interview
  Interviewed on 15 Feb. 1979; 1 hr.;

1 tape; English; by E. Yilmazkaya.
Arrived in Canada in 1970.

ONAT, NECATI
TORONTO, ONT.
  Immigration papers and letters of
recommendation, 1973-76. Photo-
graph. Taped interview.
  Photograph: Necati Onat, 1973.
  Interviewed on 23 May 1979; 1 hr.;
1 tape; Turkish; by E. Yilmazkaya.
Arrived in Canada in 1974.

ONER, OZCAN
KITCHENER, ONT.
  Interviewed on 12 June 1982; 1 hr.;
1 tape; Turkish; by E. Yilmazkaya.
Moved to Canada in 1981.

OZARI, CENGIZ
TORONTO, ONT.
  Interviewed on 16 Feb. 1981; 2 hrs.;
2 tapes; Turkish; by E. Yilmazkaya.
Former board member of the Toronto
Turkish Canadian Association.

OZARI, SEVIM
TORONTO, ONT.
  6 photographs: the Ozari family,
1975-78; and dancers, singers, and
musicians of the Turkish Canadian
Friendship Association of Toronto,
1978. Taped interview.
  Interviewed on 12 July 1979; 2.5
hrs.; 3 tapes; Turkish; by E.
Yilmazkaya. She immigrated to
Canada in 1966.

OZEL, AYDIN
TORONTO, ONT.
  1 photograph: the Ozel family in
Cyprus, 1966. Taped interview.
  Interviewed on 19 June 1979; 1 hr.;
1 tape; Turkish; by E. Yilmazkaya.
Immigrated to Canada in 1967.

PARMAKSIZ, LATIF
TORONTO, ONT.
Interviewed on 13 Feb. 1981; 1 hr.;
1 tape; Turkish; by E. Yilmazkaya.
Arrived in the mid-1970s, discusses
the dissolution of the Toronto Turkish
Canadian Friendship Association.

PEKYAVUZ, EROL
TORONTO, ONT.
Interviewed on 13 . 1979; 1.5 hrs.; 2
tapes; Turkish; by E. Yilmazkaya.
Immigrated to Canada in 1963.

PINAR, HIKMET
TORONTO, ONT.
Interviewed on 5 . 1979; 1.5 hrs.; 2
tapes; Turkish; by E. Yilmazkaya.
Immigrated to Canada in 1971.

SEEDE, ALI KASSEM
LONDON, ONT.
Interviewed on 13 Nov. 1981; 1 hr.;
1 tape; English; by E. Yilmazkaya.
Immigrated to Canada in 1955.

SEEDE, GEMAL K.
LONDON, ONT.
Interviewed on 13 Nov. 1981; 2
hrs.; 2 tapes; English; by E.
Yilmazkaya.

SENER, YUCEL
TORONTO, ONT.
Personal diary recorded after Sener
left Turkey and came to Canada; and
lists and correspondence regarding
Sener's unsuccessful job search since
his arrival in Canada, n.d. 1 cm.
Photograph. Taped interview.
1 photograph: Yucel Sener, 1978.
Interviewed on 11 Sept. 1979; 2
hrs.; 2 tapes; Turkish; by E.
Yilmazkaya.

SEZEN, BEZMI
TORONTO, ONT.
2 photographs: the Sezen family in
Toronto, 1969-78. Taped interview.
Interviewed on 24 June 1979; 1.5
hrs.; 2 tapes; Turkish; by E.
Yilmazkaya. Immigrated to Canada in
1968.

SONKAYA, ERCAN
TORONTO, ONT.
3 photographs: the Sonkaya family in
Toronto, 1975-78. Taped interview.
Interviewed on 29 June 1979; 1 hr.;
1 tape; Turkish; by E. Yilmazkaya.
Immigrated to Canada in 1970.

SUNGUR, METE
TORONTO, ONT.
3 photographs: the Sungur family in
Turkey, and Toronto, 1945-78. Taped
interview.
Interviewed on 21 March 1979; .5
hr.; 1 tape; Turkish; by E.
Yilmazkaya.

TANACAN, ORMAN
TORONTO, ONT.
Interviewed on 6 March 1979; 1 hr.;
1 tape; Turkish; by E. Yilmazkaya.

TEKBAS, SÜKRÜ
TORONTO, ONT.
Interviewed on 22 July 1979; 1 hr.;
1 tape; Turkish; by E. Yilmazkaya.
Immigrated to Canada in 1963.

TEKIN, ONAL
TORONTO, ONT.
Interviewed on 18 Nov. 1980; 1 hr.;
1 tape; Turkish; by E. Yilmazkaya.
Moved to Canada in 1969; inter-
viewed when he was president of
Turkish-Canadian Frinedship Associ-
ation.

UCAR, MEHMET
TORONTO, ONT.
 Interviewed on 30 March 1979; .75
hr.; 1 tape; English; by E.
Yilmazkaya. Immigrated to Canada in
1970.

UGURSOY, MEHMET
TORONTO, ONT.
 Papers and a constitution from the
Turkish Canadian Culture Association
in Toronto, 1965-69, and announcements of activities, and meetings of
the Turkish Canadian Friendship
Association of Toronto, n.d. 2 cm.
Photographs. Taped interview.
 12 photographs: 1936-75, the
Ugursoy family in Turkey; the
donor's emigration in 1965; and the
donor refereeing games in the Nation-
al Soccer League in Toronto.
 1 photograph: celebration of the
Turkish Friendship Association.
 Interviewed on 28 April 1979; 1.5
hrs.; 2 tapes; Turkish; by E.
Yilmazkaya. Immigrated to Canada in
1965.
 Bulten. No. 1, March 1971 - no. 3,
July 1974. Bulletin of the Turkish
Canadian Friendship Association in
Toronto (3 issues). In Turkish.

UMUL, TUNCAY
TORONTO, ONT.
 Interviewed on 1 July 1979; 1 hr.; 1
tape; Turkish; by E. Yilmazkaya.
Arrived in Canada in 1972.

URAN, TAHSIN
TORONTO, ONT.
 Interviewed on 2 April 1979; .5 hr.;
1 tape; English; by E. Yilmazkaya.
Arrived in Canada in the mid-1970s.

YAYLALIER, YUKSEL
TORONTO, ONT.
 Interviewed on 12 April 1979; 1 hr.;
1 tape; Turkish; by E. Yilmazkaya.
Moved to Canada in the late 1960s,
former president of the Turkish Canadian Friendship Association.

YILMAZKAYA, E.
TORONTO, ONT.
 Dernek. No. 1, 1978 - no. 6, 1979.
Toronto. Turk-Kanada Dostluk
Cemiyetinin Malidir (5 issues). In
Turkish.

YONAR, BURHAN
TORONTO, ONT.
 1 photograph: Burhan Yonar in
Toronto, 1978. Taped interview.
 Interviewed on 24 Sept. 1979; 1.5
hrs.; 2 tapes; Turkish/English; by E.
Yilmazkaya. Immigrated to Canada in
1973.

ZORLU, HALIS
TORONTO, ONT.
 1 photograph: donor in Greece,
1974. Taped interview.
 Interviewed on 14 Aug. 1979; 1 hr.;
1 tape; Turkish; by E. Yilmazkaya.
Arrived in Canada in 1975.

========================

MULTICULTURAL HISTORY SOCIETY
OF ONTARIO
TORONTO, ONT.
 Svanberg, Ingvar. *Kazak Refugees in
Turkey: A Study of Cultural Persis-
tence and Social Change.* Studia
Multiethnica Upsaliensia No. 8.
Stockholm: Almqvist and Wiksell
International, 1989. 211 pp.
 "Muhterem Kardes." c. 1969. 1
flyer, in Turkish.
 "The Sick Man of Europe." *History*

of the 20th Century. No. 8, 1968. Issue focuses on Turkey and the Balkans.

TURKISH CANADIAN ASSOCIATION OF LONDON
LONDON, ONT.
 The collection includes a constitution, minute book, general correspondence, financial statements, and miscellaneous items: mailing list, resolutions, press releases, members' lists, and clippings, 1963-77. 6 cm. Photographs. Taped interview with O. Aksoy and H. Ikizler (q.v.).
 12 photographs: parties, exhibitions, and demonstrations of the Association, 1975-76.
 A Debate at the U.N.. Ankara: Directorate General of Press and Information, 1975. Pamphlet. 22 pp., in English.
 The Cyprus Question and its Evolution. Ankara: Ankara Academy of Economic and Community Sciences, 1975. Pamphlet. 27 pp., in English/Turkish.

TURKISH CANADIAN CULTURAL ASSOCIATION
OTTAWA, ONT.
 Includes Association's constitution, minute book, financial records, membership list, and newsclippings, 1971-77. 3 cm.

TURKISH CANADIAN CULTURAL ASSOCIATION OF WINDSOR
WINDSOR, ONT.
 Programme for the Association's 1980 general meeting, balance sheet for 1979 finances, newsletter, and leaflets. 2 cm. Taped interview with H. Eren (q.v.).

TURKISH CANADIAN FRIENDSHIP ASSOCIATION
TORONTO, ONT.
 Records, 1975-79, which include constitution, correspondence with Turkish Embassy, minutes and list of members present at 1977 general meeting, financial papers, guide for new immigrants, members' lists, literature on Turkish earthquake relief campaign, file on the Association's soccer team, and notice of dissolution of T.C.F.A. 1 reel of microfilm. Taped interview with A. Candan, H. Basciftci, M. Aykul, et al (q.v.).
 Dernek. Turk-Kanada Dostluk Dernegi'nin Yayin Organidir, 1979 (3 issues). In Turkish.

TURKISH CULTURAL ASSOCIATION
KITCHENER, ONT.
 21 photographs: Association's activities, and exhibitions, 1973-77.
 Merhaba. Turk-Kultur Derneginin Yayin Organi Olup, Parasizdir. No. 2, 1981 - no. 7, 1982 (6 issues, monthly). In Turkish.

TURKISH CULTURE AND FOLKLORE SOCIETY OF CANADA
TORONTO, ONT.
 Correspondence, 1976-78, rules of Society, 1977 report, announcements, and invitations. 1 reel of microfilm. 3 cm. Taped interview with F. Haytaoglu (q.v.). Photographs.
 22 photographs: folk dancing sponsored by Folklore Society, 1976-78.
 Sesimiz. 1978-79. Newsletter of Turk Kültür ve Folklor Dernegi Yayin Organi (3 issues, monthly). In Turkish.

TURKISH-CYPRIOT ASSOCIATION OF
TORONTO
TORONTO, ONT.
 Records, 1977-79, which include a
constitution, general correspondence,
financial statements, report on 1979
convention, membership list, programmes of national day commemorations, and notices of annual social
parties and meetings. 2 cm. Taped
interview with G. Mehmet (q.v.).

UKRAINIAN COLLECTION

ALBOSCHY, MIKE
SAULT STE. MARIE, ONT.
 Interviewed on 17 March 1978; 1
hr.; 1 tape; Ukrainian; by Mary
Stefura. Arrived in Canada in 1923.

ANAKA, FRED
SUDBURY, ONT.
 11 photographs: group and panoramic snapshots in the U.S.S.R.,
1913-1970. Taped interview.
 Interviewed on 1 June 1978; 1.5
hrs.; 2 tapes; English/Ukrainian; by
Ihor Dawydiak. Immigrated to
Canada in 1924.

ANDRIEVSKY, MITCH
KINGSTON, ONT.
 Personal documents, including
third-class berthing card issued by
Cunard Steam Ship Co., tracing the
emigration of Caroline Andrievsky
from the U.S.S.R. to Canada,
1914-25. 1.5 cm. Taped interview.
 Interviewed on 12 Feb. 1978; 1.5
hrs.; 2 tapes; English; by Lubomyr
Luciuk.

ANONYCHUK, JACOB
TORONTO, ONT.
 Interviewed on 1 Dec. 1977; 2 hrs.;
2 tapes; English; by Lubomyr
Luciuk.

ANTONOVYCH, MARKO
MONTREAL, QUEBEC
 Students'kyi Vistnyk (Student Her-
ald). Vol. 1, no. 1, 1923 - vol. 9,

nos. 8-10, 1931. Prague (monthly). In
French/Ukrainian. 2 reels of microfilm.

BABENKO, L.
TORONTO, ONT.
 Interviewed on 21 April 1982; 2.75
hrs.; 3 tapes; Ukrainian; by Lubomyr
Luciuk. Post-WWII political refugee.

BABIAK, STEFAN
TORONTO, ONT.
 Interviewed on 22 April 1982; 4
hrs.; 4 tapes; Ukrainian; by Lubomyr
Luciuk. Post-WWII political refugee.

BAKICH, GERRY
THUNDER BAY, ONT.
 Manual of treatment to diseases and
illnesses Ukrainian immigrants could
contract prior to and after arrival in
Canada. Untitled, n.d. 288 pp., in
Ukrainian.
 Hotovitzky, Rev. A., ed. *Russian
Orthodox American Messenger*. Feb.
- Sept. 1902. Monthly supplement.
179 pp.

BARDYN, IHOR
TORONTO, ONT.
 12 photographs: activities of the
Ukrainian Professional and Business
Club in Toronto, 1975-77.

BARYCKYJ, R.
SUDBURY, ONT.
 Interviewed on 14 May 1982; 1 hr.;
1 tape; Ukrainian; by Lubomyr
Luciuk. Post-WWII political refugee.

BAZYLEVYCZ, I.
TORONTO, ONT.
Papers, mostly correspondence and by-laws dealing with Rev. Josyph Slipyj, and the patriarchate of the Ukrainian Catholic Church. Also, miscellaneous printed material: church bulletins, souvenir booklets, programmes, and scattered issues from *Nasha Meta*, 1960-75; *Svoboda*, 1962-75; *Christelishe Stimme*, 1964, 1965; *Vil'ne Slovo*, 1965-76, and other Ukrainian-language newspapers. 11 cm. Photographs.

BENDICK, R.
SUDBURY, ONT.
6 photographs: activities of the Ukrainian National Youth Federation, including theatrical productions, 1946-55.

BESPALOV, DMYTRO
KITCHENER, ONT.
Interviewed on 29 May 1981; 1.5 hrs.; 2 tapes; Ukrainian; by I. Wynnyckyj.
Svitlo Evangely (Light of the Gospel). Nos. 39, 40, 1981. Official organ of the League of Christians of Evangelism in America (quarterly). Toronto: Kiev Printers, 1981.

BEY, WASYL
TORONTO, ONT.
Interviewed on 30 June 1981; 1 hr.; 1 tape; Ukrainian; by Halyna Benesh. Arrived in Canada in 1927.

BIDNIAK, PETRO
TIMMINS, ONT.
Interviewed on 12 June 1978; 1 hr.; 1 tape; Ukrainian; by M. Baryckyj. Immigrated to Canada in 1929.

BILENKI, ANNA
SCHUMACHER, ONT.
Interviewed on 12 June 1978; 1 hr.; 1 tape; Ukrainian; by Mary Stefura. Arrived in Canada in 1919.

BILYK, PARASKA
RED LAKE, ONT.
Interviewed on 3 . 1977; 1 hr.; 1 tape; Ukrainian; by Mary Stefura.

BISS, MICHAEL
BATH, ONT.
Interviewed on 7 Dec. 1977; 1 hr.; 1 tape; Ukrainian/English; by Lubomyr Luciuk. Immigrated to Canada in 1929.

BLAHEY, ANNA
TIMMINS, ONT.
49 grocery store bills from "Blahey and Cherwinka" in Timmins, Ont., 1920s. Photographs. Taped interview. 7 photographs: 1920-36, Ukrainian Labour Temple, 1922, and Prosvista Choir and Banquet, 1936 in Timmins. Interviewed on 29 Aug. 1977; 1 hr.; 1 tape; English/Ukrainian; by Mary Stefura. Immigrated to Canada in 1903.

BLASKO, B.
OSHAWA, ONT.
Knysh, Irene. "The Ukrainian Women's Organization of Canada, 1930-35." Article pertains to the Oshawa branch of Ukrainian Women, in Ukrainian. Microfilm.

BODNAR, ANASTAZIA
KITCHENER, ONT.
Interviewed on 15 Jan. 1980; 1 hr.; 1 tape; Ukrainian; by I. Wynnyckyj. Arrived in Canada in 1929.

BODNARCHUCK, IVAN
TORONTO, ONT.
4 photographs: activities at the M.
Hrushevsky Ukrainian School,
Toronto, 1969-81.

BOJCUN, ROMAN
TORONTO, ONT.
Interviewed on 24 March 1982; 3
hrs.; 3 tapes; Ukrainian; by Lubomyr
Luciuk.

BOJECZKO, OLGA
GUELPH, ONT.
First half of scrapbook, which
includes clippings from *The Guelph
Daily Mercury*, is related to the activities in the Ukrainian community of
Guelph, Ont., 1950-80. Second half
of scrapbook covers the Ukrainian
community in Acton, Ont. 1 reel of
microfilm. Taped interview.
Interviewed on 18 March 1980; .5
hr.; 1 tape; English; by I.
Wynnyckyj. Immigrated to Canada in
1934.

BONDAR, KATERYNA
SUDBURY, ONT.
13 photographs: members of the
Kateryna Bondar family, Ukraine,
1909-59. Taped interview.
Interviewed on 25 May 1978; .5 hr.;
1 tape; Ukrainian; by Ihor Dawydiak.
Immigrated to Canada in 1914.

BORENCKO, MICHAEL
KINGSTON, ONT.
Interviewed on 22 Nov. 1977; 1 hr.;
1 tape; Ukrainian; by Lubomyr
Luciuk. Immigrated to Canada in
1929.

BOROWYK, M.
OTTAWA, ONT.
Interviewed on 14 Sept. 1981;

2 hrs.; 2 tapes; Ukrainian; by
Lubomyr Luciuk. Post-WWII political
refugee.

BOSWICK, FRANCES
KINGSTON, ONT.
Interviewed on 1 Dec. 1977; 1 hr.; 1
tape; English; by Lubomyr Luciuk.
Immigrated to Canada in 1911.

BOYCHUK, STEVE
SAULT STE. MARIE, ONT.
Interviewed on 10 July 1978; .75
hr.; 1 tape; English/Ukrainian; by
Ihor Dawydiak.

BOYKO, PETRO; M. PROZAK AND J.
HUMENIUK
SAULT STE. MARIE, ONT.
Interviewed on 15 May 1982; .75
hr.; 1 tape; Ukrainian; by Lubomyr
Luciuk. Post-WWII immigrants.

BOYUK, IRENE
SUDBURY, ONT.
1 photograph: the Ukrainian Catholic
Women's League in Sudbury, 1971.

BROZINSKY, A.
HARROWSMITH, ONT.
2 Russian rouble notes, 1910, 1912,
and a Polish passport, 1925. Photographs.
28 photographs: the Brozinsky family, Ukraine, Kingston, and Deloro;
employment in smelting and refining,
Deloro, 1919.

BRYCZKA, DMYTRO
HAMILTON, ONT.
Interviewed on 17 May 1978; 1 hr.;
1 tape; Ukrainian; by R. Lupenec.
Immigrated to Canada in 1926.

BRYK, ALEXANDER
TORONTO, ONT.
 Interviewed on 8 July 1981; 1 hr.; 1
tape; Ukrainian; by Halyna Benesh.

BRYZHUN, LUDMYLA
HAKSTON, ONT.
 Interviewed in July 1979; 2 hrs.; 2
tapes; Ukrainian; by I. Wynnyckyj.
Arrived in Canada in 1948.

BUCHKOVSKY, YAVDOCHA
GUELPH, ONT.
 Interviewed on 18 March 1980; 1
hr.; 1 tape; Ukrainian; by I.
Wynnyckyj. Arrived in Canada in
1912.

BURAKOWSKI, MARY
TIMMINS, ONT.
 Interviewed on 13 June 1978; 1 hr.;
1 tape; Ukrainian; by Mary Stefura.

BURIANYK, WASYL
WINNIPEG, MANITOBA
 Interviewed on 30 May 1982; 2 hrs.;
2 tapes; Ukrainian; by Lubomyr
Luciuk.

CEBULA, WALTER
TORONTO, ONT.
 Interviewed on 19 May 1981; 1.5
hrs.; 2 tapes; English/Ukrainian; by
I. Wynnyckyj.

CHABAL, NICKOLAS
TORONTO, ONT.
 Papers, 1911-57, which include
Workmen's Records Book in German,
Polish, and Ukrainian, 1911, personal
memoir and correspondence, concert
programmes, minutes of the International Steamship Ticket Agency
(1921, 1931), federal election leaflets,
and posters announcing cultural
events in Toronto. 1 reel of microfilm. Photographs. Taped interview.
 10 photographs: wedding of Anna
and Nichola Chabal, 1915; Ukrainian
People's Home Association picnic, c.
1930s; concert sponsored by the
Ukrainian Canadian Committee, n.d.;
and interior/exterior of Provista
Booksellers and Printers, c. 1950s.
 Interviewed on 8 Feb. 1979; 1.75
hrs.; 2 tapes; Ukrainian; by Mary
Stefura. Immigrated to Canada in
1913.

CHARCHALIS, MYKOLA
TORONTO, ONT.
 Interviewed on 29 April 1982; 1 hr.;
1 tape; Ukrainian; by Lubomyr
Luciuk.

CHAYKA, REV. LEV
VAL D'OR, QUEBEC
 Interviewed on 10 July 1979; 1 hr.;
1 tape; Ukrainian; by Mary Stefura.
Arrived in Canada in 1948.

CHEPESIUK, MARTIN
TORONTO, ONT.
 Interviewed on 14 Feb. 1978; 2 hrs.;
2 tapes; Ukrainian/English; by
Lubomyr Luciuk.

CHEPIZAK, MIKE
KINGSTON, ONT.
 Interviewed on 23 March 1978; 1
hr.; 1 tape; Ukrainian/English; by
Lubomyr Luciuk. Immigrated to
Canada in 1928.

CHEREDAR, JAMES AND MARY
ST. CATHARINES, ONT.
 5 photographs: the Ukrainian
Prosvista Society, and the Lesia
Ukrayinka Ukrainian Women's Asso-
ciation in Thorold South, 1927-37.

CHRUSZCZ, ANDREW
TORONTO, ONT.
 Donor's immigration documents and army registration booklet, 1925-27. .5 cm. Taped interview.
 Interviewed on 27 March 1979; 1 hr.; 1 tape; Ukrainian; by O. Demianchuk. Immigrated to Canada in 1918.

CHYZ, REV. RUSSELL JOHN
KITCHENER, ONT.
 Personal documents, 1930; correspondence with clergymen, 1944-76; and miscellaneous Church Slavonic publications, Lviv, 1898, 1900, 1908. 2 reels of microfilm. Photographs. Taped interview.
 6 photographs: Rev. Chyz in Ukraine, Edmonton, and Fort William, 1913-50.
 Interviewed on 25 March 1979; 1 hr.; 1 tape; Ukrainian; by I. Wynnyckyj. Immigrated to Canada in 1930.

CIUCIURA, JOHN
CAMBRIDGE, ONT.
 Report card, 1910, and personal certificates, 1927-28. .5 cm. Photographs. Taped interview.
 10 photographs: weddings of family and friends in Ukraine, Preston, and Galt, 1911-32.
 Interviewed on 4 June 1979; 1 hr.; 1 tape; Ukrainian; by I. Wynnyckyj. Immigrated to Canada in 1928.

COPOR, O.
SUDBURY, ONT.
 Scrapbook of newsclippings, photographs, and programmes related to the Ukrainian community in Sudbury. Included is 1949 programme of the Ukrainian Bandurist under the direction of Hryhory Kytasty. 1 cm. Pho-

tograph.
 1 photograph: members of the United Hetman Organization in Sudbury, 1933.

CROUSE, KATHERINE
TORONTO, ONT.
 Katherine Crouse was involved in Ukrainian activities from 1948 to 1976. Her collection traces the growth of the Ukrainian-Canadian community, its concerns and direction since the Second World War. In addition to the records of the Ukrainian Catholic Women's League of Canada and other Ukrainian associations, her collection contains an array of printed material: 39 Ukrainian newspaper titles (from scattered issues to large runs), magazines, periodicals, calendars, and jubilee books. 3 meters. Finding aid available.

CYMBALITSY, PETRO
LONDON, ENGLAND
 Interviewed on 15 June 1982; 1.5 hrs.; 2 tapes; Ukrainian; by Lubomyr Luciuk.

CYMBALUK, FEDIR
TORONTO, ONT.
 Interviewed on 9 April 1982; 2.5 hrs.; 3 tapes; Ukrainian; by Lubomyr Luciuk. Post-WWII political refugee.

CZICH, MYKOLA
OTTAWA, ONT.
 Interviewed on 18 Sept. 1981; 2 hrs.; 2 tapes; Ukrainian; by Lubomyr Luciuk. Post-WWII political refugee.

DANYLIW, TEODOR
LONDON, ENGLAND
 Interviewed on 17 June 1982;

2.5 hrs.; 3 tapes; Ukrainian; by
Lubomyr Luciuk.

DAVIDOVICH, STEPHAN
TORONTO, ONT.
 Interviewed on 8 March 1982; 2
hrs.; 2 tapes; English/Ukrainian; by
Lubomyr Luciuk.

DAWYDIAK, W.
SUDBURY, ONT.
 Interviewed on 14 May 1982; 2 hrs.;
2 tapes; Ukrainian; by Lubomyr
Luciuk.

DIDIUK, WASYL
TORONTO, ONT.
 Interviewed on 29 Nov. 1977; 1 hr.;
1 tape; Ukrainian/English; by
Lubomyr Luciuk. Immigrated to
Canada in 1948.

DIDOWYCZ, REV. W.
MUNICH, GERMANY
 Interviewed on 22 July 1982; 2 hrs.;
2 tapes; Ukrainian; by Lubomyr
Luciuk.

DMYTRIW, ILLYA
LONDON, ENGLAND
 Interviewed on 16 June 1982; 1 hr.;
1 tape; Ukrainian; by Lubomyr
Luciuk.

DOBRIANSKY, MICHAEL
LONDON, ENGLAND
 Interviewed on 21 June 1982; 1 hr.;
1 tape; Ukrainian; by Lubomyr
Luciuk.

DOLOTOWITZ, PAUL AND
PETER SENYK
CAMBRIDGE, ONT.
 4 . 1979; 1 hr.; 1 tape; Ukrainian;
by I. Wynnyckyj. Arrived in Canada
in 1948.

DOSKOCH, SOPHIA
TORONTO, ONT.
 Interviewed on 24 July 1981; 1 hr.;
1 tape; Ukrainian; by Halyna Benesh.
Arrived in Canada in 1923.

DRAPAK, ANNIE
OSHAWA, ONT.
 Certificate of naturalization for
Harry Cymbaluk, 1926. .25 cm.
Photograph.
 1 photograph: wedding with mem-
bers of the Red Cross of the United
Hetman Organization in the back-
ground in Oshawa, c. 1930.

DROZDOWSKY, MYCHAILO
WATERFORD, ONT.
 Interviewed on 8 . 1980; 1 hr.; 1
tape; Ukrainian; by I. Wynnyckyj.

DUBYLKO, IVAN
TORONTO, ONT.
 Interviewed on 26 July 1981; 2 hrs.;
2 tapes; Ukrainian; by Lubomyr
Luciuk. Immigrated to Canada in
1948.

DUDA, BOHDAN
TORONTO, ONT.
 Interviewed on 14 Feb. 1982; .5 hr.;
1 tape; Ukrainian; by Lubomyr
Luciuk. Arrived in Canada in 1948.

DUVALKO, IVAN
TORONTO, ONT.
 Interviewed on 20 April 1982; 2
hrs.; 2 tapes; Ukrainian; by Lubomyr
Luciuk. Arrived in Canada in 1964.

ELIASHEVSKY, O.
TORONTO, ONT.
 Interviewed on 28 April 1982; 1.75
hrs.; 2 tapes; Ukrainian; by Lubomyr
Luciuk. Immigrated to Canada in
1948.

FARBATIUK, EWDOKIA
HAMILTON, ONT.
1 photograph: the Korpotnisky family in Saskatchewan, 1915. Taped interview.
Interviewed on 18 May 1978; .5 hr.; 1 tape; Ukrainian; by R. Lupenec. Arrived in Canada in 1900.

FEDAK, M.
TORONTO, ONT.
Interviewed on 9 April 1982; 2 hrs.; 2 tapes; Ukrainian; by Lubomyr Luciuk.

FEDOROWYCZ, WASYL
TORONTO, ONT.
Interviewed on 6 April 1982; 1.5 hrs.; 2 tapes; Ukrainian; by Lubomyr Luciuk. Post-WWII immigrant.

FIL, LEONID
TORONTO, ONT.
Interviewed on 28 April 1982; .75 hr.; 1 tape; Ukrainian; by Lubomyr Luciuk. Post-WWII immigrant.

FIRMAN, IVAN
TORONTO, ONT.
Interviewed on 30 April 1982; 2.25 hrs.; 3 tapes; Ukrainian; by Lubomyr Luciuk. Arrived in Canada in 1949.

FODCHUK, DMYTRO
TORONTO, ONT.
Bulletins and programmes from the Ukrainian Canadian Social Services, the World Congress of Free Ukrainians, the Ukrainian Democratic Youth Association, and the Ukrainian Dance Ensemble in Toronto, 1970s. Also, clippings on Patriarch Joseph Slipyj, 1976, and "Artists from U.S.S.R., the Republic of Ukraine," n.d. 6 cm. Photograph.
1 photograph: reunion of graduates

from the Teachers' College in Zaleshchki, 1959.

FROLICK, STANLEY
TORONTO, ONT.
Interviewed on 22 June, 30 Aug., 21 Sept. 1978; 7 hrs.; 7 tapes; Ukrainian/English; by Zoriana Sokolsky.

———.
TORONTO, ONT.
Interviewed from 1 July 1981; 35 hrs.; 42 tapes; Ukrainian/English; by Lubomyr Luciuk.

FUNDAK, O.
LONDON, ENGLAND
Interviewed on 4 Aug. 1982; 1.5 hrs.; 2 tapes; Ukrainian/English; by Lubomyr Luciuk.

FYSHKEVYTCH, J.
TORONTO, ONT.
Interviewed on 9 April 1982; 1 hr.; 1 tape; Ukrainian; by Lubomyr Luciuk. Post-WWII political refugee.

GADOWSKY, JOHN
KINGSTON, ONT.
Interviewed on 17 Nov. 1977; .75 hr.; 1 tape; Ukrainian; by Lubomyr Luciuk. Immigrated to Canada in 1927.

GALLAS-ANDREYEIW, MARY
OSHAWA, ONT.
Documents tracing the emigration of Maya Andreyeiw, 1920-23. .5 cm (10 items). Photographs.
2 photographs: Ukrainian bridal party, 1950.

GAWALDO, OLGA
SUDBURY, ONT.
Minute book of the Ukrainian "Sitch" Sporting Organization (also

known as the United Hetman Organ-
izations) in Sudbury, Ont., 1940-64.
Also, anniversary addresses,
speeches, and clippings pertaining to
the Hetman movement, 1940s-1950s;
and programmes commemorating
Ukrainian Independence Day,
1962-65. 1 reel of microfilm. 2 cm.
Photograph.
Esaiw, John comp. *Za Ukrainy (For*
Ukraine): The Tour of Hetman
Danylo Skoropadsky Through the
United States of America and
Canada, 1937-38. Edmonton: United
Hetman Organization, 1938. 1 reel of
microfilm.

GAWA, M.
TORONTO, ONT.
Interviewed on 10 Feb. 1982; 1.75
hrs.; 2 tapes; Ukrainian; by Lubomyr
Luciuk. Arrived in Canada in 1952.

GEMBATIUK, Y.
TORONTO, ONT.
Interviewed on 5 April 1982; 1.75
hrs.; 2 tapes; Ukrainian; by Lubomyr
Luciuk. Post-WWII political refugee.

GENYK-BEREZOWSKYJ, ROMAN
TORONTO, ONT.
A collection of bulletins, pro-
grammes, and newspapers, mainly
related to the Ukrainian Catholic
Church, and published in the
post-WWII period. .5 meters.
Fedynsky, A. "Bibliographical Indi-
cator of the Ukrainian Press Outside
the Boundaries of Ukraine." Cleve-
land, 1972. 80 pp.
Hladun, John. "I Am a Canadian."
Toronto, n.d. 16 pp.
Sixth Congress of Ukrainian
Catholics of Canada. Toronto, 1972.
72 pp., in English/Ukrainian.
Sviata Pokrova. Toronto, 1973,

1974, 1977 (3 issues). 156 pp.
Tserkovnyi Vistnyk. 1977. 25th anni-
versary. Herald of St. Nicholas
Ukrainian Catholic Church in
Toronto. .5 cm.
Vistnyk (Herald). Toronto, 1976,
1977. Bulletin of the World Congress
of Free Ukrainians (3 issues). 130 pp.

————.

TORONTO, ONT.
Kortschmaryk, F. B.
"Christianization of the European East
and Messianic Aspirations of Moscow
as the 'Third Rome'." Toronto:
Studium Research Institute, 1971. 56
pp.
Soltykevych, Iaroslav. *Saliut*
Ostann'oi Sotni. Toronto, 1964. 1.5
cm.
Kalendar Svitla 1970. Toronto,
1971. 192 pp.
Literatura i Mystetstvo (Literature
and Art), 1957-77 (monthly). Supple-
ment to *Homin Ukraini* (225 pieces).
Literatura, Mystetstvo, Rozvaha.
1953-72. Weekly supplement to
Swoboda (106 pieces).
My i Svit. Toronto, 1955-70. Scat-
tered issues (24 pieces). In Ukrainian.
St. Peter's and Paul Ukrainian Cath-
olic Church in Toronto. Dec. 1977,
Dec. 1978. Church bulletins, in
Ukrainian/English. .5 cm.
Svitlo, Katolyts'kyi Chasopys Dlia
Ukrains'koho Narodu. Toronto,
1950-66. Scattered issues (65 pieces).
In Ukrainian.
Visti z Rymu (News from Rome).
1964-76. Rome: Ukrainian Press
Bureau (131 pieces).

GERYCH, G.
OTTAWA, ONT.
Narod, Orhan Rus'ko-Ukrains'koii
Radykal'noii Partii (Organ of

Rus'-Ukrainian Radical Party). Vols.
1-6, 1890-1895. Lviv: Narodnia
Drukarnia. 1 reel of microfilm.

GRYSHCHUK, ALEC
TIMMINS, ONT.
 Interviewed on 12 June 1978; .5 hr.;
1 tape; Ukrainian; by M. Baryckyj.
Immigrated to Canada in 1928.

HABRUSEVICH, REV. J.
THUNDER BAY, ONT.
 Interviewed on 16 May 1982; 1 hr.;
1 tape; Ukrainian; by Lubomyr
Luciuk. Post-WWII political refugee.

HALUSCHAK, DMYTRO
ESPANOLA, ONT.
1 photograph: donor in Espanola,
1977. Taped interview.
 Interviewed on 9 Nov. 1977; 1 hr.;
1 tape; Ukrainian; by Mary Stefura.
Arrived in Canada in 1927.
 Kalendar-Almanach. Munich, 1948,
Hurtivnia Paperu, Yaroslav
Pastushenko. 208 pp.
 Zolotyi Kolos (Golden Head of
Wheat). 1930, 1932, 1936. Lviv:
Ivan Tyktor. Calendar-almanac (3
issues). 562 pp.

HANCHARYK, SAM
KENORA, ONT.
 The Sam Hancharyk collection consists of jubilee publications and almanacs, most of them from Winnipeg's
Ukrainian organizations, 1920s-1950s;
miscellaneous Ukrainian publications:
newspapers, bulletins, programmes,
and almanacs, from Toronto and
Ottawa, 1930s-1960s; and short plays
printed in Lviv, 1920s. 12 cm. Taped
interview.
 Interviewed on 29 Sept. 1977; 1 hr.;
1 tape; Ukrainian; by Mary Stefura.
Immigrated to Canada in 1912.

Svit Molodi (Youth's World). 1936,
1938. .5 cm.
Zhinocha Dolia (Woman's Fate).
1936-38. 3 cm.
Zhinocha Volia (Woman's Freedom).
1936-38. 2 cm.

HANSEN, MARY
SUDBURY, ONT.
 Personal documents of Sophia and
John Parchewski. Photographs. Taped
interview.
 13 photographs: a theatrical production at Worthington, Ont., 1916; families and weddings, Sudbury,
1912-38; and parish activity at St.
Mary's Ukrainian Catholic Church in
Sudbury, 1941-46.
 Interviewed on 4 Feb. 1978; 1 hr.; 1
tape; English; by Mary Stefura.

HARASYM, WILLIAM
TORONTO, ONT.
 Interviewed on 26 Jan. 1978; 1.5
hrs.; 2 tapes; English; by Lubomyr
Luciuk.

HARASYM, WILLIAM
TORONTO, ONT.
 Bulletins and programmes, 1950s,
and clippings, 1950, on the bombing
of the Ukrainian Hall on Bathurst
Street in Toronto. 2 cm. Photographs.
 7 photographs: Ukrainian
associational activities in Toronto,
1930s.
 *Chest', Shana Ukrains'kym
pioneram-budivnychym Kanady*.
Winnipeg, 1966. 80 pp.

HAWRYSCH, M.
TORONTO, ONT.
 Interviewed on 5 April 1982; 2.75
hrs.; 3 tapes; Ukrainian; by Lubomyr
Luciuk. Post-WWII political refugee.

HERCUN, FRANCISZEK
DRYDEN, ONT.
Immigration papers, 1920s. .5 cm.
Photographs. Taped interview.
2 photographs: Ukrainian Literary
Society building in Dryden, Ont,
1938.
Interviewed on 30 Sept. 1977; 1 hr.;
1 tape; Ukrainian; by Mary Stefura.
Immigrated to Canada in 1912.

HETHMAN, M.
TORONTO, ONT.
Interviewed on 25 Jan. 1978; 3 hrs.;
3 tapes; Ukrainian/English; by
Lubomyr Luciuk.

HETMANCZUK, MYKOLA
TORONTO, ONT.
Interviewed on 27 April 1982; .75
hr.; 1 tape; Ukrainian; by Lubomyr
Luciuk. Post-WWII immigrant.

HICKEY, D.
SUDBURY, ONT.
1 postcard; the Ukrainian Catholic
Church, Copper Cliff, 1925.

HILTZ, CARL
TORONTO, ONT.
Interviewed on 2 Dec. 1981; 1 hr.; 1
tape; English; by Lubomyr Luciuk.

HOLYNSKY, ROBERT
TORONTO, ONT.
Memoirs of Mykahilo Holynski,
n.d.; included are short stories, plays
and articles by Micheal Petrovsky. 10
cm. Photographs.
12 photographs: Ukrainian-language
school of the Ukrainian National
Federation in Toronto, 1928-40.

HORISHNYJ, IVAN
TORONTO, ONT.
Interviewed on 31 March, 7 April

1982; 3.75 hrs.; 4 tapes; Ukrainian;
by Lubomyr Luciuk. Post-WWII
political refugee.

HORLATSCH, STEPEN
TORONTO, ONT.
Interviewed on 1 May 1982; 1 hr.; 1
tape; Ukrainian; by Lubomyr Luciuk.
Post-WWII political refugee.

HOSHWA, MARIA
KENORA, ONT.
Interviewed on Personal documents
regarding immigration to Canada,
n.d. .5 cm.

HRAB, PEARL
TORONTO, ONT.
Interviewed on 24 July 1981; .5 hr.;
1 tape; Ukrainian; by Halyna Benesh.
Arrived in Canada in 1905.

HROBELSKY, J.
KENORA, ONT.
Cookbooks (manuscripts), 1940;
sewing book (manuscript), 1940;
collection of prose and poetry (manuscript) related to various occasions,
1940; and letter written by N.
Voloshyn about Christians and their
conduct, also prophecy, 1940. 2 cm.

HROBELSKY, REV. ROMAN
KENORA, ONT.
A collection of jubilees, bulletins,
and prayer books. 2 reels of micro-
film. 3 cm.
*Fiftieth Anniversary of St. Nicholas
Ukrainian Catholic Church.* Kenora,
Ont., 1967. 41 pp.
*Fiftieth Anniverary of Ukrainian
Pioneer Settlement in Canada.*
Yorkton, Saskatchewan, 1941. In
Ukrainian. History, biographies,
pictures of churches being built,
schools, and prominent Ukrainians.

1 reel of microfilm.
Liturgikon. Lviv, 1905. Religious handbook for Greek Catholic services, liturgy, and prayers. In Old Church Slavonic. 1 reel of microfilm.
Surma. 1928. Underground newspaper, organ of the Ukrainian Army Organization. 12 pp.

HRYCYSHYN, STEVE
KIRKLAND LAKE, ONT.
10 photographs: activities of the Ukrainian National Federation, and Ukrainian Women's Organization in Kirkland Lake, 1934-54. Taped interview.
Interviewed on 9 June 1978; 1.5 hrs.; 2 tapes; Ukrainian; by Mary Stefura. Immigrated to Canada in 1927.

HRYN, MYKOLA
TORONTO, ONT.
Interviewed on 19 April 1982; 1.5 hrs.; 2 tapes; Ukrainian; by Lubomyr Luciuk. Post-WWII political refugee.

HUMENIUK, THEODORE
TORONTO, ONT.
Interviewed on 20 June 1977; 2 hrs.; 2 tapes; Ukrainian; by Zoriana Sokolsky. Arrived in Canada in 1908.

HUMNISKI, NICK
TORONTO, ONT.
Interviewed on 16 Feb. 1978; 1 hr.; 1 tape; Ukrainian; by Lubomyr Luciuk. Immigrated to Canada in 1926.

HUNKEVICH, WILLIAM
TORONTO, ONT.
Hun'kevych (also spelled Hunkievich and Hunkevich) arrived in the U.S. from Lysvychi, Galicia in 1914 at the age of 18. He then moved to

Winnipeg, Manitoba, where along with his writing, he also developed a keen interest in politics. An energetic debater and businessman, he became an executive member of the Ukrainian Relief Association in 1929, and the Ukrainian Orthodox Church. After moving to Hamilton and then Windsor, Ont., he and his wife finally settled in Toronto until his death in 1953. The collection contains business records, most of Hun'kevych's works—plays, poems, novels, articles, and a loose scrapbook which includes election posters, handbills, and clippings, 1920s-1930s. Most of the material is in Ukrainian with some English and 1 piece in Esperanto. 3 reels of microfilm. Finding aid available.

ILLCHENKO, OLYA AND OLEXANDER
OTTAWA, ONT.
Interviewed on 6 Sept. 1981; 2 hrs.; 2 tapes; Ukrainian; by Lubomyr Luciuk. Immigrated to Canada in 1948.

IWACHNIUK, ANTIN AND NADIA
PROTON STATION, ONT.
The Iwachniuk collection is organized into four series (A, B, C, D).
Series "A" contains personal papers of both Nadia and Antin Iwachniuk, as well as private correspondence dating back to 1934.
Series "B" (1940s-1950s) is an archive of A. Iwachniuk's major community activities, in "PLAST" (Ukrainian Youth Organization), the Ukrainian Canadian Committee, "UHVR" (Ukrainian Supreme Liberation Council), miscellaneous Ukrainian organizations in Yugoslavia and Canada, and in various newspapers and journals (such as *Ukrains'ka*

*Trybuna, Homin Ukrainy, Vil'ne
Slovo, Hrvatska Smotra,* and
Omladina). Records include constitu-
tions, by-laws, minutes, reports,
clippings, and correspondence.
Series "C" (1961-81) contains docu-
ments related to the Iwachniuk Ukrai-
nian Studies and Research Fund at the
University of Ottawa.
Series "D" comprises three rare
Ukrainian (Lviv) publications of the
1935 to 1937 period—*Dazhboh,
Obrii,* and *Naperedodni.* 11 reels of
microfilm. Nos. 6, 7, 8, and 11 are
RESTRICTED

IWACHNIUK, ANTIN AND NADIA
PROTON STATION, ONT.
Interviewed on 9 Nov. 1981; 2 hrs.;
2 tapes; Ukrainian; by I. Wynnyckyj.
Arrived in Canada in 1948.

IWASYKIW, LEO
THUNDER BAY, ONT.
Interviewed on 17 May 1982; .75
hr.; 1 tape; Ukrainian; by Lubomyr
Luciuk. Post-WWII political refugee.

IZYK, REV. SEMEN
WINNIPEG, MANITOBA
Interviewed on 21 May 1982; 1.5
hrs.; 2 tapes; Ukrainian; by Lubomyr
Luciuk. Arrived in Canada in 1947.

JACENTY, A.
OSHAWA, ONT.
History of the Ukrainian Presbyterian Church and school for immigrants in Oshawa, 1912-59, in Ukrainian; and list of students attending
school in early years, 1912. .25 cm.
Photographs.
10 photographs: parish acitivity at

the Ukrainian Presbyterian Church;
interior and exterior views of the
church; the choir; and special services
in Oshawa, 1924-77.

JACKSON, ED
TORONTO, ONT.
Interviewed on 27 Jan. 1978; 2 hrs.;
2 tapes; English/Ukrainian; by
Lubomyr Luciuk.

JAWORSKYJ, V.
TORONTO, ONT.
Interviewed on 13 Feb. 1982; 4.5
hrs.; 5 tapes; Ukrainian; by Lubomyr
Luciuk. Post-WWII political refugee.

KACHNYCZ, WASYL
THUNDER BAY, ONT.
Interviewed on 16 May 1982; 1.5
hrs.; 2 tapes; Ukrainian; by Lubomyr
Luciuk.

KAPUSTA, MICHAEL
TORONTO, ONT.
Interviewed on 10 May 1982; 1 hr.;
1 tape; English; by Lubomyr Luciuk.

KARMANIN, OLGA
TORONTO, ONT.
Semen Kowbel was born in 1877, in
Borschiv, Western Ukraine. Fleeing
Austrian conscription, he immigrated
to Canada in 1909, and was soon followed by his wife. A
carpenter-builder by trade, he found
work and helped to build churches,
schools, and national halls wherever
Ukrainian immigrants set roots in
Canada. His literary production was
just as impressive—13 dramas, 5
plays, 3 volumes of poetry, 1 novel,
his own memoirs, and finally, the
lengthy memorial publication of the
National Home Association, 1950, for
which he was editor and a contri-

butor. Kowbel died in Toronto in 1965. This collection includes many of his works: memoirs, poetry, a dramatized Easter pageant, short stories, essays, biographical sketches, descriptions of homeland, one four-act drama, one fantasy drama, dramatized letters, and historical accounts of the immigration experience. The material is mainly in Ukrainian, with some English, 1910s-1950s. Title list is available. 3 reels of microfilm.

KARMANIN, OLGA
TORONTO, ONT.
A collection of manuscripts —speeches, debates, articles, and notes—written by S. Kowbel, 1937-50. Collection also includes plays, songs, and short stories by B. Lepkiy and S. Kowbel, c. 1918-40. 1 reel of microfilm. Title list available.

KAZOR, FRED
TORONTO, ONT.
Progress reports of gym students of the Ukrainian Labour Farmer Temple classes in Toronto, 1937; poster of gymnastic display at the Cosmopolitan Athletic Club, Toronto, 1936; and newsclippings, 1943. .5 cm. Photographs.
9 photographs: Workers' Sport Association in Kenora, and Toronto, 1936-55.

KEPKO, NICK
KIRKLAND LAKE, ONT.
Interviewed on 6 June 1978; .5 hr.; 1 tape; Ukrainian; by M. Baryckyj. Immigrated to Canada in 1925.

KIRKOSKI, C.
KENORA, ONT.
A collection of Ukrainian publications from Kenora, Ont., and Winnipeg, Manitoba: calendars, souvenir booklets, and periodicals, 1920s-1950s, some of which are from the Ukrainian Fraternal Society of Canada (30 items).

KIS, THEOFIL
OTTAWA, ONT.
Interviewed on 17 Sept. 1981; 1.5 hrs.; 2 tapes; Ukrainian; by Lubomyr Luciuk. Post-WWII political refugee.

KNYSH, Z.
TORONTO, ONT.
Interviewed on 10 March 1982; 3 hrs.; 3 tapes; Ukrainian; by Lubomyr Luciuk. Post-WWII political refugee.

KOCIJOWSKYJ, MYKOLA
SUDBURY, ONT.
Over 100 photographs: sports, camping, parties, parades, and demonstrations of the Ukrainian Cultural Centre, which also encompass the Canadian League for the Liberation of Ukraine, the Ukrainian Youth Association, and the Ukrainian School in Sudbury, 1950-77. Taped interview. Interviewed on 17 Sept. 1980; .5 hr.; 1 tape; Ukrainian; by O. Kupchak.

KOCIJOWSKY, MYKOLA
SUDBURY, ONT.
Interviewed on 14 May 1982; 1.5 hrs.; 2 tapes; Ukrainian; by Lubomyr Luciuk. Immigrated to Canada in 1952.

KOGAN, OSCAR
TORONTO, ONT.
Interviewed on 21 June, 15 Sept.

1977; 5.5 hrs.; 6 tapes; English; by K. Levine. Arrived in Canada in 1922.

KOLASKY, J.
TORONTO, ONT.
 Letters regarding donor's expulsion from the Association of United Ukrainian Canadians, and from the Communist Party of Canada, 1967-70. Also, souvenir booklets and programmes of various Ukrainian cultural organizations in Toronto, 1930s-1960s. 3 cm. Photograph.
 1 photograph: Ukrainian language school of the Association of United Ukrainian Canadians in Toronto, 1942.
 30th Anniversary of the Association of United Ukrainian Canadians, 1918-48. 56 pp.
 60th Anniversary of Ukrainian Life and Creative Work in Canada. Winnipeg: Ukrainian Slovo, 1951. 57 pp.
 1867-1967, Ukrainian Canadian Centennial Souvenir Book, 1967. 26 pp.
 Canadian Ukrainian National Music Festival. Toronto, 15-16 July 1939. 51 pp.
 Tribute to the Ukraine, Victory Festival. Toronto (Maple Leaf Gardens), 30 June 1945. 64 pp.

KOLOS, THEODORE
TORONTO, ONT.
 Interviewed on 3 May 1982; .75 hr.; 1 tape; Ukrainian; by Lubomyr Luciuk.

KOMAR, HILARY AND ANTONIA
CAMBRIDGE, ONT.
 2 photographs: concert sponsored by the Ukrainian National Federation (Galt Branch), Preston, 1962.

Taped interview.
 Interviewed on 18 June 1980; 1 hr.; 1 tape; Ukrainian; by I. Wynnyckyj. Immigrated to Canada in 1950.

KORDA, IVAN
THUNDER BAY, ONT.
 Interviewed on 18 May 1982; 2 hrs.; 2 tapes; Ukrainian; by Lubomyr Luciuk. Post-WWII political refugee.

KORDIUK, BOHDAN
MUNICH, GERMANY
 Interviewed on 13 July 1982; 2 hrs.; 2 tapes; Ukrainian; by Lubomyr Luciuk.

KOROLYSHYN, W.
TORONTO, ONT.
 Interviewed on 25 July 1981; 4 hrs.; 4 tapes; Ukrainian; by Lubomyr Luciuk.

KOSAK, I.
MUNICH, GERMANY
 Interviewed on 21 July 1982; 2 hrs.; 2 tapes; Ukrainian; by Lubomyr Luciuk.

KOSTECKI, STEVE
KIRKLAND LAKE, ONT.
 Interviewed on 6 June 1978; 1 hr.; 1 tape; Ukrainian; by Mary Stefura. Immigrated to Canada in 1921.

KOSTIUK, REV. ANDREW
LONDON, ENGLAND
 1 photograph: Rev. A. Kostiuk and a fellow parishoner taken at the Ukrainian Greek Orthodox Church of St. Sophia in Waterloo. Taped interview.
 Interviewed on 19 June 1982; 1 hr.; 1 tape; Ukrainian; by Lubomyr Luciuk.

KOSTIUK, ROMAN
TORONTO, ONT.
Interviewed on 27 April 1982; 1.75
hrs.; 2 tapes; Ukrainian; by Lubomyr
Luciuk. Arrived in Canada in 1948.

KOTOWICH, PETER
KINGSTON, ONT.
Interviewed on 29 Feb. 1978; 1 hr.;
1 tape; Ukrainian; by Lubomyr
Luciuk. Immigrated to Canada in
1928.

KOTOWICH, SYLVESTER
KINGSTON, ONT.
Interviewed on 10 Nov. 1977; 1 hr.;
1 tape; Ukrainian; by Lubomyr
Luciuk. Immigrated to Canada in
1925.

KOWALSKY, A.
TORONTO, ONT.
Interviewed on 22 April 1982; 1.75
hrs.; 2 tapes; Ukrainian; by Lubomyr
Luciuk. Post-WWII political refugee.

KOZLO, MARIA
ST. CATHARINES, ONT.
Immigration documents of Nick and
Maria Kozlo, 1927, 1934; also,
donors book, "Canadian Ukrainians
Help the Nations of the Soviet
Union," Toronto, 1941-43. 2 cm.
Photographs.
4 photographs: Ukrainian immigrants
on the Cunard ship *Auranaia*, 1934;
Labour Temple Ukrainian embroidery
display, Kirkland Lake, 1937; Ukrai-
nian Labour Temple Women's Choir,
Kirkland Lake, c. 1938-39; and
Ukrainian Labour Temple, National
Ukrainian Festival, 1938.

KOZYRA, ILKO
THUNDER BAY, ONT.
Interviewed on 18 May 1982;

3.5 hrs.; 4 tapes; Ukrainian; by
Lubomyr Luciuk. Post-WWII political
refugee.

KRAMARCHUK, SOFIA
KITCHENER, ONT.
5 photographs: family; and a wedding in Kitchener, 1917-29. Taped
interview.
Interviewed on 12 March 1979; 1
hr.; 1 tape; Ukrainian; by I.
Wynnyckyj. Arrived in Canada in
1923.

KRAWCHUCK, P.
TORONTO, ONT.
Borot'ba. 1 Jan. 1920 - 16 . 1920.
Vienna. (organ of Ukrainian workers)
1 reel of microfilm.
Nova Doba. 6 March 1920 - 22 .
1921. Vienna. (organ of Ukrainian
Communist Party in exile) 1 reel of
microfilm.

KREMYR, EVA
TIMMINS, ONT.
1 photograph: mining work in
Timmins, 1925. Taped interview.
Interviewed on 30 Aug. 1977; 1 hr.;
1 tape; Ukrainian; by Mary Stefura.
Arrived in Canada in 1907.

KREMYR, STANLEY
TIMMINS, ONT.
Over 90 photographs: unions,
strikes, theatre, orchestras, picnics,
and sports of the Association of
United Ukrainian Canadians, and its
socialist predecessor, the Ukrainian
Labour and Farmers' Temple Association in Timmins, and South Porcupine, 1910-58. Taped interview.
Interviewed in May 1978; 2 hrs.; 2
tapes; Ukrainian/English; by Mary
Stefura.

KRIL, M.
TORONTO, ONT.
Interviewed on 12 Feb. 1982; 1.75 hrs.; 2 tapes; Ukrainian; by Lubomyr Luciuk. Post-WWII political refugee.

KRUZELECKY, J.
TORONTO, ONT.
Interviewed on 24 April 1982; 2.75 hrs.; 3 tapes; Ukrainian; by Lubomyr Luciuk. Post-WWII political refugee.

KRYNYCKY, BOHDAN
OTTAWA, ONT.
Interviewed on 6 Sept. 1981; 1.5 hrs.; 2 tapes; Ukrainian; by Lubomyr Luciuk. Post-WWII political refugee.

KRYSAK, WASYL
TORONTO, ONT.
Interviewed on 21 April 1982; 2.5 hrs.; 3 tapes; Ukrainian; by Lubomyr Luciuk.

KRYSAK, WILLIAM
TORONTO, ONT.
Interviewed on 5, 19 April 1979; 3.5 hrs.; 4 tapes; Ukrainian; by O. Demianchuk.

KRYSTIA, WILLIAM
SUDBURY, ONT.
10 photographs: the Krystia family in Coniston, and Capreol, 1922-49; and, work in the railway. Taped interview. Interviewed on 30 Nov. 1981; 3 hrs.; 3 tapes; English; by Mary Stefura. Immigrated to Canada in 1908.

KRYVORUCHKO, ANATOL
OTTAWA, ONT.
Interviewed on 17 Sept. 1981; 1 hr.; 1 tape; Ukrainian; by Lubomyr Luciuk. Post-WWII political refugee.

KRYZANOWSKA, MR. AND MRS.
TORONTO, ONT.
Interviewed on 26 April 1982; 1 hr.; 1 tape; Ukrainian; by Lubomyr Luciuk. Post-WWII political refugee.

KUCHAR, MARVIN
ST. CATHARINES, ONT.
1 photograph: the Ukrainian National Youth Federation in Thorold, 1947. Taped interview. Interviewed on 18 June 1979; .75 hr.; 1 tape; Ukrainian/English; by Terry Pidzamecky. Immigrated to Canada in 1939.

KUCHMA, JULIA
KENORA, ONT.
Personal documents and photographs. .5 cm. 4 photographs: St. Nicholas Ukrainian Church parish celebration of Holy Sepulchre, 1921; Good Friday, 1923; Bishop's visit, 1952; and Mother's Day celebration in Kenora, 1958.

KULIK, MARY AND WALTER
TORONTO, ONT.
Interviewed on 13 Dec. 1977; 1 hr.; 1 tape; Ukrainian; by Lubomyr Luciuk. Immigrated to Canada in 1930.

KUNANEC, EMIL
TORONTO, ONT.
Interviewed on 25 Jan. 1978; 1.5 hrs.; 2 tapes; Ukrainian/English; by Lubomyr Luciuk.

KURYLIW, VASYL
SUDBURY, ONT.
Interviewed on 15 May 1982; 1.5 hrs.; 2 tapes; Ukrainian; by Lubomyr Luciuk. Post-WWII political refugee.

KUSHMELYN, WASYL
TORONTO, ONT.
Interviewed on 7 April 1982; 2.5
hrs.; 3 tapes; Ukrainian; by Lubomyr
Luciuk. Post-WWII political refugee.

KUSHNIR, O.
TORONTO, ONT.
Interviewed on 5 April 1982; 2.5
hrs.; 3 tapes; Ukrainian; by Lubomyr
Luciuk. Post-WWII political refugee.

KUZMA, STEPHANIA
TORONTO, ONT.
Interviewed on 21 July 1981; .5 hr.;
1 tape; Ukrainian; by Halyna Benesh.
Arrived in Canada in 1928.

KUZMYN, S.
KINGSTON, ONT.
Interviewed on 3 April 1978; 4 hrs.;
4 tapes; Ukrainian/English; Lubomyr
Luciuk. Post-WWII immigrant.

KUZYK, LAWRENCE
WOODSTOCK, ONT.
Interviewed on 23 June 1981; 1.5
hrs.; 2 tapes; Ukrainian; by I.
Wynnyckyj. Arrived in Canada in
1951, a member of the Studite monas-
tic order.

LACOSTA, JOHN
ST. CATHARINES, ONT.
Immigration documents, 1912,
1927-28. .5 cm. Photographs. Taped
interview.
4 photographs: the Lacosta family in
Bukovinia and Iroquois Falls,
1927-30.
Interviewed on 9 Sept. 1977; 1 hr.;
1 tape; Ukrainian; by Mary Stefura.
Immigrated to Canada in 1912.

LACUSTA, RAIFTA HRYÇIUK
ST. CATHARINES, ONT.
A collection of Ukrainian almanacs
and jubilees, mostly from Winnipeg
and Toronto, 1920s-1950s. Title list
available. Taped interview.
Interviewed on 9 Sept. 1978; 1 hr.;
1 tape; Ukrainian; Mary Stefura.
Arrived in Canada in 1928.

LAPCHINSKI, E.
SUDBURY, ONT.
1 photograph: family in Sudbury,
n.d.

LAWRENCE, MARY
OSHAWA, ONT.
Interviewed on 14 Dec. 1977; 1 hr.;
1 tape; English; by Lubomyr Luciuk.

LEBID, ANASTASIA
MONTREAL, QUEBEC
Interviewed on 2 Jan. 1982; 3 hrs.; 3
tapes; Ukrainian; by I. Wynnyckyj.
Arrived in Canada in 1949.

LENYK, VOLODYMYR
MUNICH, GERMANY
Interviewed on 20 July 1984; 2 hrs.;
2 tapes; Ukrainian; by Lubomyr
Luciuk.

LEWYCKYJ, OLGA
CAMBRIDGE, ONT.
Interviewed on 4 Aug. 1980; 1 hr.; 1
tape; Ukrainian/English; by I.
Wynnyckyj. Arrived in Canada in
1932.

LIBER, MICHAEL
TORONTO, ONT.
Kanads'ki Rusyny (Canadian
Ruthenian). Winnipeg, Manitoba,
1916-22. Contains religious matter,
photographs, schedules of services,
histories, poems, advertising and

calendars. 1 reel of microfilm.

Vira Ta Znannia (Faith and Knowledge). Vol. 1, nos. 1-10, June 1923 - March 1924. Toronto. Monthly evangelical paper for Ukrainian immigrants; Rev. P. C. Crath, editor and manager. 1 reel of microfilm.

Zamors'kyi Vistnyk (Trans-Oceanic Herald). Toronto, Jan. - 21 March 1920. Illustrated journal for adult education (14 issues), vol. 1, no. 2; vol. 2, nos. 1-2 missing. 1 reel of microfilm.

LIBER, MICHAEL (UKRAINIAN PEOPLE'S HOME ASSOCIATION) TORONTO, ONT.

The collection contains almanacs and jubilee booklets, 1930s-1950s; an evangelical monthly paper for Ukrainians, 1923-24; and a Ukrainian illustrated journal for adult education, 1920-21. Title list available.

Collection includes 1 scrapbook of clippings (from the Ukrainian People's Home Association) reflecting Ukrainian social events, political campaigns, and world affairs, 1925-38; and 9 scrapbooks of flyers and programmes of concerts, dances, picnics, lectures and other activities held at the Ukrainian National People's Home on Lippincott Street in Toronto, 1924-49. 7 reels of microfilm. Photographs.

17 photographs and 2 postcards: showing activities (choir, theatre, folk dancing, ballet) of the Ukrainian People's Home Association, Toronto, c. 1925-38, and picnics, 1933.

Nykoliak, D. *Korotkyi Istorychnyi Narys Ukrains'koho Narodn'oho Domu V Toronto* (A Short Historical Sketch of the Ukrainian People's Home in Toronto). Toronto, 1953. 38 pp., in Ukrainian.

60 Years in Canada, 1891-1951. Toronto, 1951. Jubilee book. 66 pp., in English/Ukrainian.

Vasile Auramenko's Ukrainian Folk Dance and Ballet. New York, 1931. 30 pp., in English.

Iuvileina Knyzhka Ukrainskoho Tovarystva—Vzaimna Pomich Jubilee book. Winnipeg: Ukrainian Relief Association, 1935. 114 pp.

LITWIN, ROMAN THOROLD, ONT.

11 photographs: cultural and political activities of the Ukrainian Prosvita Society (or Ivan Franko Society), Thorold South, 1926-32; employment in a foundry, Brantford, 1918. Taped interview.

Interviewed on 15 May 1979; 2 hrs.; 2 tapes; Ukrainian; by Terry Pidzamecky. Immigrated to Canada in 1912.

LITWINOW, W. TORONTO, ONT.

Interviewed on 29 April 1982; 2.5 hrs.; 2 tapes; Ukrainian; by Lubomyr Luciuk. Post-WWII political refugee.

LOZINSKY, TETIANA KENORA, ONT.

Interviewed on 28 May 1981; 2 hrs.; 2 tapes; Ukrainian; by Mary Stefura. Arrived in Canada in 1910.

LUCIUK, LUBOMYR KINGSTON, ONT.

Collection of correspondence between the Ukrainian Canadian Committee in Kingston, Ont. and that in Winnipeg, Manitoba, 1952-59. 193 pp.

Kropotkin, Peter. *Bread and Freedom.* Russian translation from French. New York: Union of Russian

Labourers, 1919. 217 pp.
Lenin, V. I. *Proletarskaia
revoliutsiia i renegat Kautskii*. Central
Executive Committee, R.F.K.P.A,
1920. 141 pp.
Pogin, A. P. *Noveishyi i Polnyi
russko-angliiskii i angliisko-russkii
pis'movnik*. Manual for letter writing.
New York, 1918. 63 pp.
Iuvileina Pamiatka, 1887-1937. 50th
jubilee commemorative book dedicated to Lieutenant-General Sikevitch,
his military service and work for
Ukrainian Independence. Published in
Canada in 1937. 112 pp., in Ukraini-
an/English.
*Iuvileina Pamiatka Vydana
zakhodamy Komitetu dlia
vshanuvannia iuvileiu heneral-
khorunzhoho V. Szykevicha v kil'kosti
1500*. Winnipeg, 1937. 100 pp., in
Ukrainian.
*Kalendar' popovskii i kalendar'
sovetskii* (Church and Soviet calendar). Issued in North America in
1921. 128 pp.
Interview recorded on 14 April 1982;
3.75 hrs.; 4 tapes; Ukrainian; by
Lubomyr Luciuk with a post-WWII
political refugee who wished to
remain anonymous.

LUCIUK, MARIA
KINGSTON, ONT.
Pamphlets, speeches, and bulletins
on Ukrainian national independence—all brought to Canada from
German D.P. camps. 2 cm (15
items). Photographs.
44 photographs: representing the
Ukrainian community in Kingston,
Ont. and surrounding region,
1951-80. Subjects include folk dancing, parades, organizations, and
religious ceremony.

*Kingston and District Folk Arts
Council, 1967-77*. Kingston, 1977.
176 pp.

LUCYK, MICHAEL
TORONTO, ONT.
2 photographs: group from the
Ukrainian Student Club in Toronto,
1939, and visit of Hetman
Skoropadsky, 1937.
*17th Anniversary of Ukrainian Grad-
uates in Detroit-Windsor*, 1956. 6
pp., in English.
*Bulletin of Ukrainian Canadian
Veterans' Association*. Canadian
Legion No. 360. Toronto, . 1954, 10
pp., in Ukrainian.

LUSYK, MICHAEL
TORONTO, ONT.
Interviewed on 15 April 1982; 2
hrs.; 2 tapes; English; by Lubomyr
Luciuk.

LUTYK, MICHALINA AND JOHN
SUDBURY, ONT.
Immigration documents of Michalina
Tys, 1927. Photographs. Taped interview with Michalina Lutyk. Photographs.
10 photographs: the Lutyk family,
Ukraine, Sudbury, including work in
agriculture, mining, and railway construction, 1925-38.
Interviewed on 10 May, 2 June
1977; 1 hr.; 1 tape; Ukrainian; by
Mary Stefura.

MAGA, MARY
TORONTO, ONT.
Interviewed on 4 Feb. 1979; 1 hr.; 1
tape; Ukrainian; by I. Wynnyckyj.
Immigrated to Canada in 1912.

MAJSTRENKO, IVAN
MUNICH, GERMANY
Interviewed on 9 July 1982; 2 hrs.; 2 tapes; Ukrainian; by Lubomyr Luciuk.

MAKAR, VOLODYMYR
TORONTO, ONT.
Interviewed on 23 March 1982; 3 hrs.; 3 tapes; Ukrainian; by Lubomyr Luciuk. Immigrated to Canada in 1950.

MAKOHON, PAVLO
TORONTO, ONT.
Interviewed on 24 April 1982; 2.75 hrs.; 3 tapes; Ukrainian; by Lubomyr Luciuk. Post-WWII political refugee.

MAKOWECKYJ, JAKIW
MUNICH, GERMANY
Interviewed on 12 July 1982; 2 hrs.; 2 tapes; Ukrainian; by Lubomyr Luciuk.

MAKSYMLIUK, A.
BARRIE, ONT.
Interviewed on 12 May 1982; 3.5 hrs.; 4 tapes; Ukrainian; by Lubomyr Luciuk. Post-WWII political refugee.

MALACHOWSKI, JACOB
OSHAWA, ONT.
Constitution and by-laws of the Oshawa Ukrainian Professional and Businessmen's Association (the Canuk Club) and newsclippings regarding same, 1955, 1958, 1963; Ukrainian currency bill, "1,000 griven," issued by Ukrainian State in 1918; as well, 1 large Ukrainian flag with Union Jack in one corner and printing "Tretii Sichovyi Kurin' Oshawa." 2 cm (5 items). Photographs.
8 photographs: Sitch members and Hetman Skoropads'ky, n.d; grand

opening of St. Georges Ukrainian Catholic Hall, 1928; mass at picnic of St. George Ukrainian Catholic Church, 1932; and Ukrainian student trip, Ottawa, 1955.

MALASCHUK, ROMAN
TORONTO, ONT.
Interviewed on 25 March 1982; 3.5 hrs.; 4 tapes; Ukrainian; by Lubomyr Luciuk. Immigrated to Canada in 1948.

MALETSKY, MYROSLAV
TORONTO, ONT.
Interviewed on 9 March 1982; 1.75 hrs.; 2 tapes; Ukrainian; by Lubomyr Luciuk. Post-WWII political refugee.

MANCHULENKO, SOPHIA
SAULT STE. MARIE, ONT.
Interviewed on 11 July 1978; .5 hr.; 1 tape; Ukrainian; by Ihor Dawydiak. Immigrated to Canada in 1924.

MARCHYN, ANDREW
ST. CATHARINES, ONT.
Interviewed on 18 June 1979; .75 hr.; 1 tape; Ukrainian/English; by Terry Pidzamecky. Arrived in Canada in 1911.

MARUNCHAK, M.
WINNIPEG, MANITOBA
Interviewed on 31 May 1982; 3 hrs.; 3 tapes; Ukrainian; by Lubomyr Luciuk.

MARUNIAK, V.
MUNICH, GERMANY
Interviewed on 23 July 1982; 2 hrs.; 2 tapes; Ukrainian; by Lubomyr Luciuk.

MARYGLAD, THOMAS
TORONTO, ONT.
Interviewed on 1 April 1982; 2.5
hrs.; 3 tapes; Ukrainian; by Lubomyr
Luciuk.

MARYGLAD, VICTORIA
TORONTO, ONT.
Interviewed on 3 April 1982; 4 hrs.;
5 tapes; Ukrainian; by Lubomyr
Luciuk.

MATIJASZ, MARIA
TIMMINS, ONT.
6 photographs: the Burak family,
Bukovyna, 1913-38. Taped interview.
Interviewed on 12 June 1978; .5 hr.;
1 tape; Ukrainian; by M. Baryckyj.
Immigrated to Canada in 1925.

MATLA, ALEXANDRA
TORONTO, ONT.
Interviewed on 24 March 1982; 3.5
hrs.; 4 tapes; Ukrainian; Lubomyr
Luciuk. Post-WWII political refugee.

MCLAREN, DUNCAN
TORONTO, ONT.
U.N.F. Organizational Fund,
1932-1957 card; Anniversary Banquet
and Great Musical Festival flyer,
1957; "In Memory of S. V. Petliura
and E. Konovalets'" card, n.d.; and 1
issue of *Zhyttia Slovo* (Life and
Word). 1977 (weekly newspaper). .5
cm, in Ukrainian.

MELNYK, PETRO
TORONTO, ONT.
Interviewed on 23 April 1982; 3
hrs.; 3 tapes; Ukrainian; by Lubomyr
Luciuk. Post-WWII political refugee.

MELNYK-KALUZYNSKA, H.
LONDON, ENGLAND
Interviewed on 6 Aug. 1982; 2 hrs.;

2 tapes; Ukrainian; by Lubomyr
Luciuk.

MIGUS, M.
TORONTO, ONT.
Interviewed on 2 April 1982; 2.75
hrs.; 3 tapes; Ukrainian; by Lubomyr
Luciuk. Post-WWII political refugee.

MOISIUK, ELI
HAMILTON, ONT.
3 photographs: members and dwellings of the Moisiuk family, Ukraine,
c. 1911-75. Taped interview.
Interviewed on 18 May 1978; .5 hr.;
1 tape; Ukrainian; by R. Lupenec.
Immigrated to Canada in 1912.

MOISIUK, OLGA
HAMILTON, ONT.
Interviewed on 18 May 1978; 1 hr.;
1 tape; English; by R. Lupenec.

MONCHAK, STEPHEN
ST. CATHARINES, ONT.
Biography of Stephen Monchak,
1976; and testimonial granted to S.
Monchak for the dedicated work with
the Ukrainian Peoples' Union, n.d. .5
cm. Photographs. Taped interview.
4 photographs: Choir Trancona,
1933; Ukrainian National Home,
1934; Ukrainian Credit Union, St.
Catharines, 25th anniversary, 1971;
and S. Monchak, n.d.
Interviewed on 1 March 1980; 1.25
hrs.; 2 tapes; Ukrainian; by Mary
Stefura. Arrived in Canada in 1929.

MOROS, H.
TORONTO, ONT.
Interviewed on 27 March 1982; 1.75
hrs.; 2 tapes; Ukrainian; by Lubomyr
Luciuk. Post-WWII political refugee.

MOSEWSKI, S.
OSHAWA, ONT.
3 photographs: a picnic and a folk dancing group, Oshawa, 1923-26.

MOSTOWAY, HARRY
TORONTO, ONT.
Personal letters from donor's hometown, Dmytriv, Ukrainian, 1929-38, and from Bishop Kyr Tsydor, 1958; bulletins from St, Basil's College in Toronto, 1959; pamphlet from the Ukrainian Canadian Committee to fund Ukrainian Studies, Toronto, 1953; and various Ukrainian concert programmes, 1950s. 2 cm. Taped interview.
11 photographs: family of H. Mostoway, 1920s; choir "Surma," 1934; Ukrainian Peoples' Home Choir, 1936; Drama Group of Ukrainian Peoples Home, 1944, 1946; and First Memorial Gathering of Ukrainian Parishes, 19 June 1932.
Interviewed on 14 June 1979; 4 hrs.; 4 tapes; Ukrainian; by Mary Stefura. Immigrated to Canada in 1928.

MOSTOWY, SEMEN
THOROLD, ONT.
Imprint from the official seal of Zhoda Ukrainian Co-operative Ltd., n.d. Photographs. Taped interview.
3 photographs: S. Mostowy's arrival to Canada, 1927, and his wedding, 1933.
6 photographs: Ukrainian organizational and cultural activities in Thorold, Ont., c. 1930s.
Interviewed on 23 May 1979; 2 hrs.; 2 tapes; Ukrainian/English; by Terry Pidzamecky. Arrived in Canada in 1926.

MOWCZKO, ANDREW
ST. CATHARINES, ONT.
Immigration documents, 1930. .5 cm. Photographs. Taped interview.
4 photographs: the Ukrainian Catholic Church, mainly Sts. Cyril and Methodius Ukrainian Catholic Church, 1947-48; and Ukrainian immigrants at port of Gdansk, 26 March 1930.
Interviewed on 13 Aug. 1979; 1 hr.; 1 tape; Ukrainian; by Terry Pidzamecky. Arrived in Canada in 1930.

MOZEWSKY, S.
OSHAWA, ONT.
2 photographs: congregation at George's Ukrainian Catholic Church, Oshawa, c. 1957.

MUCHA, M.
TORONTO, ONT.
Interviewed on 26 March 1982; 1.75 hrs.; 2 tapes; Ukrainian; by Lubomyr Luciuk. Post-WWII political refugee.

MUDRYK, STEPAN
MUNICH, GERMANY
Interviewed on 13 July 1982; 2 hrs.; 2 tapes; Ukrainian; by Lubomyr Luciuk.

MUZIK, MARY
OSHAWA, ONT.
1 photograph: a ballet school, Oshawa, 1932.

MYCHALCHUK, IVAN
OTTAWA, ONT.
Interviewed on 19 Sept. 1981; 2.75 hrs.; 3 tapes; Ukrainian; by Lubomyr Luciuk. Post-WWII political refugee.

MYHAL, BORIS
OTTAWA, ONT.
Interviewed on 7 Sept. 1981; 3.5
hrs.; 4 tapes; Ukrainian; by Lubomyr
Luciuk. Post-WWII political refugee.

MYKYTCZUK, KARPO
TORONTO, ONT.
Interviewed on 23 April 1982; 1 hr.;
1 tape; Ukrainian; by Lubomyr
Luciuk.

NACIUK, MICHAEL
KITCHENER, ONT.
3 photographs: the congregation at
the Ukrainian Catholic Church of the
Transfiguration, 1931; Naciuk's wedding, Kitchener, 1924; and Ukrainian
picnic, Kitchener, 1934. Taped interview.
Interviewed on 2 Feb. 1979; 1 hr.; 1
tape; Ukrainian; by I. Wynnyckyj.
Immigrated to Canada in 1912.

NAKLOWICZ, S.
VIENNA, AUSTRIA
Interviewed on 6 July 1982; 1 hr.; 1
tape; Ukrainian; by Lubomyr Luciuk.

NATZIUK, SOFIA
KITCHENER, ONT.
Interviewed on 31 May 1981; 2 hrs.;
2 tapes; Ukrainian; by I. Wynnyckyj.

NAZAR, MICHAEL
ST. CATHARINES, ONT.
Interviewed on 13 Aug. 1979; .75
hr.; 1 tape; English/Ukrainian; by
Terry Pidzamecky. Immigrated to
Canada in 1928.

OLAH, WASYL
TORONTO, ONT.
Interviewed on 3 May 1982; 1 hr.; 1
tape; Ukrainian; by Lubomyr Luciuk.
Post-WWII political refugee.

OLAR, MARIA
SEARCHMOUNT, ONT.
Interviewed on 15 March 1978; 1
hr.; 1 tape; Ukrainian; by Mary
Stefura. Immigrated to Canada in
1912.

ONYSCHUK, MICHEAL
TORONTO, ONT.
10 photographs: employment in agriculture, Cookstown, Wainfleet,
1931-50.

ORANSKI, BORIS
TORONTO, ONT.
Interviewed on 7 April 1982; 1 hr.;
1 tape; Ukrainian; by Lubomyr
Luciuk.

ORSHINSKY, PETER
FENWICK, ONT.
Immigration papers, 1938, and other
personal documentation. .5 cm (12
items). Photograph.
1 photograph: family in Alberta,
1922.

OZYMOK, PETER
TORONTO, ONT.
Interviewed on 21 July 1981; 1 hr.;
1 tape; Ukrainian; by Halyna Benesh.
Arrived in Canada in 1927.

PALADICHUK, WILLIAM
TORONTO, ONT.
Polish passport of donor issued in
Borszczow, 1922. Photographs.
Taped interview.
3 photographs: Paladichuk grocery
store in Lachine, Quebec, c. 1950;
store in Hamilton, Ont., c. 1952-60;
and front of Hotel Coulson, Sudbury,
1970, also partly owned by the
Paladichuck's; plus, 1 postcard of the
Paladichuk summer resort, Keswick,
Ont., c. 1960s.

Interviewed on 21 March 1979; 1.25 hrs.; 2 tapes; Ukrainian; by O. Demianchuk. Immigrated to Canada in 1922.

PALADIYCHUK, ROMAN
TORONTO, ONT.
Interviewed on 22 March, 4 April 1982; 4.5 hrs.; 5 tapes; Ukrainian; by Lubomyr Luciuk.

PALAHNUK, MIKE
SAULT STE. MARIE, ONT.
Interviewed on 11 July 1978; .5 hr.; 1 tape; Ukrainian; by I. Dawidiak. Immigrated to Canada in 1927.

PANCHUK, G. B.
MONTREAL, QUEBEC
The collection covers G. R. B. Panchuk's private and public life and the history of immediate post-WWII Ukrainian relief, and veteran organizations. As well as detailing the mass migration of Ukrainian refugees from Europe to Canada, it documents the following organizations: the Ukrainian Canadian Servicemen's Association, 1943-47; the Ukrainian Canadian Veterans' Association, 1946-75; the Central Ukrainian Relief Bureau, 1944-52; the Ukrainian Canadian Relief Mission and Fund, 1946-52; the Ukrainian Canadian Committee, 1947-68; Ukrainian Organizations in Europe, 1944-55; the Association of Ukrainians in Great Britain, 1946-52; the Federation of Ukrainians in Great Britain, 1950-52; and the 1st Division of the Ukrainian National Army (Divisia Halychyna), 1947-55. Panchuk's personal papers, mostly correspondence and his diaries, span a period from 1934 to 1973. Finally, included in the collection are miscellaneous records, newsclippings and souvenir booklets that reflect more closely the post-war Ukrainian experience in Canada, particularly parish life in Montreal. 20 meters. 1 reel of microfilm. Photographs. Taped interviews. Some of the personal correspondence is **RESTRICTED**
22 photographs: Divisia Halychyna (1st Division) Ukrainian National Army, Italy, 1947; activities of the Ukrainian Canadian Servicemen's Association, London, England, 1945-46.
Interviewed on 5 May, 1 June, 26 July 1981; 7.5 hrs.; 8 tapes; English/Ukrainian; by Lubomyr Luciuk.

PAPULAK, DAN
THUNDER BAY, ONT.
50th Anniversary of the Founding of Prosvita Society in Fort William, 1906-56. Thunder Bay, 1956. Golden Jubilee memoirs. 94 pp., in Ukrainian.
Canadian Orthodox Calendar.
Diocesan Council of the Russian Greek Orthodox Church in Canada. Toronto- Montreal, 1971. 145 pp.
Tochylo (Grindstone). Dec. 1945. Canada's Ukrainian national magazine of science, health, and humour. 20 pp., in Ukrainian.

PASNYK, JOHN
KITCHENER, ONT.
Some personal documents, membership book of the Ukrainian Sporting "Sitch" Association of Canada and miscellaneous items related to the Hetman movement, 1928-75. 3 cm (16 items). Taped interview.
Interviewed on 1 Nov. 1979; 1 hr.; 1 tape; Ukrainian; by I. Wynnyckyj. Arrived in Canada in 1923.

PAWLUK, STEPHAN
TORONTO, ONT.
 Interviewed on 25 Nov. 1981; 1.5
hrs.; 2 tapes; English; by Lubomyr
Luciuk. Arrived in Canada in 1934.

PECZENIUK, NESTOR
SUDBURY, ONT.
 Interviewed on 24 Jan. 1978; 1 hr.;
1 tape; English; by Mary Stefura.
Immigrated to Canada in 1954.

PETRASH, KONSTANTYN
OSHAWA, ONT.
 Interviewed on 29 Jan. 1978; 2 hrs.;
2 tapes; Ukrainian; by Lubomyr
Luciuk. Immigrated to Canada in
1926.

PETROWSKY, MICHAEL
TORONTO, ONT.
 Michael Petrowsky immigrated to
western Canada with his parents in
1912 and later moved to Ont.
Throughout his life he wrote as a
journalist, contributing articles to both
Ukrainian- and English-language
newspapers. He was publisher and
managing editor of the short-lived
periodicals, *Ukrainian Bazzar* (1934)
and *The New Canadian* (1938), published in Toronto. His interest in the
stage led him in 1930 to introduce
Ukrainian drama to the "Little Theatre" in Oshawa, Ont. Notable among
his plays and short stories are the
"Canadian Suitor" (1920), "O
Canada, My Canada" and "Dreams
are Sprinkled with Tears" (1973).
The Petrosky papers, 1918-77,
include donor's personal documents,
correspondence (English and Ukrainian), miscellaneous items from the
Oshawa Little Theatre (programmes,
notes, photographs, and playbills),
and clippings and articles, many

written by Petrowsky. 2 reels of
microfilm. 4 cm. Taped interviews.
 Interviewed on 25 April, 29 June
1977; 28 Feb. 1978; 5.5 hrs.; 6
tapes; English; by Mary Stefura.

PETRUCK, MYKOLA
TORONTO, ONT.
 Interviewed on 25 April 1982; 1.75
hrs.; 2 tapes; Ukrainian; by Lubomyr
Luciuk.

PETRYSHYN, A.
THUNDER BAY, ONT.
 Interviewed on 18 May 1982; 1 hr.;
1 tape; Ukrainian; by Lubomyr
Luciuk.

PIASECKY, MRS.
TORONTO, ONT.
 A collection of Ukrainian-Canadian
concert programmes, n.d., and
Toronto Ukrainian magazines,
1950-1970s. 1 reel of microfilm. 20
cm.
 Soltykewych, J. *Saliut Ostann'oi
Sotni* (Salute of the Last Company).
Toronto, 1964. On the 50th Anniver-
sary of the Military Order of
Ukrainski Sitchovi Striltsi. 64 pp., in
English/Ukrainian.
 My i Svit (We and the World).
Toronto, Sept. 1955 - Jan./Feb. 1970
(24 issues, monthly). Incomplete.
 Novi Dni (New Days). Dec. 1951 -
Sept. 1959 (110 issues, monthly).
Incomplete.
 Svitlo (The Light). Vol. XXXI,
1970. Basilian Fathers calendar. 192
pp.
 Svitlo (The Light). Toronto, 1 April
1950 - Nov. 1969. (128 issues,
monthly/bi-monthly). Incomplete.

PIDLISNY, MYKOLA
TORONTO, ONT.
Interviewed on 25 April 1982; 1.5
hrs.; 2 tapes; Ukrainian; by Lubomyr
Luciuk. Post-WWII political refugee.

PINIUTA, H.
FORT FRANCES, ONT.
"The Ukrainian in Fort Frances."
Manuscript covering period from
1920 to 1971. .5 cm.

PISOCKY, STEPAN
THUNDER BAY, ONT.
Interviewed on 18 May 1982; 1 hr.;
1 tape; Ukrainian; by Lubomyr
Luciuk.

POLOMANY, MICHAEL
KINGSTON, ONT.
9 photographs: Ukrainian Canadians
in Kingston, 1928-50, including mem-
bers of the Workingmen's Benevolent
Association and the Association of
United Ukrainian Canadians, 1945.
Taped Interview.
Interviewed on 9 Nov. 1977; 1 hr.;
1 tape; Ukrainian; by Lubomyr
Luciuk. Immigrated to Canada in
1926.

PORONIUK, MICHAEL
TORONTO, ONT.
Interviewed on 25 Jan. 1978; 1 hr.;
1 tape; Ukrainian/English; by
Lubomyr Luciuk. Immigrated to
Canada in 1952.
*Sixth Congress of the Ukrainian
Catholics of Canada.* Toronto, 1972.
72 pp., in English/Ukrainian.

PRIATKA, MARY
KAPUSKASING, ONT.
Interviewed on 11 June 1978; 1 hr.;
1 tape; Ukrainian; by Mary Stefura.
Immigrated to Canada in 1928.

PRYIMAK, LOUIS
WEST HILL, ONT.
Interviewed on 10-20 May 1977; 1.5
hrs.; 2 tapes; Ukrainian; by Zoriana
Sokolsky.

PRYMAK, LUKIAN
TORONTO, ONT.
Assorted material: report and
member's speech from the "Kish"
Hethman "Sitch" organization, 1929;
financial reports from the Ukrainian
weekly *Nasha Derzhava*, 1953-56;
financial statements related to P.
Hetman's trip to Canada, 1956; certificates of membership in the Prosvita
Organization, 1929; progammes of
anniversary concerts—Ukrainian Independence (1918), and Taras
Shevchenko, 1967-77; and brochures
on Ukrainian Canadian National
Fund, Ukrainian Heritage,
Centennary of Prosvita, meeting with
former political prisoner Leonid
Pliushch—all issued by the Ukrainian
Canadian Committee, 1968-78. 6 cm.
Photographs.
22 photographs: many of the Ukrainian United Hetman Organization in
Toronto and Grimsby, Ont., c. 1920-
50.

PYLYPIUK, MARY
HAMILTON, ONT.
Interviewed on 24 May 1978; 1 hr.;
1 tape; English; by R. Lupenec.

PYSKLYWEC, NICK
KIRKLAND LAKE, ONT.
C.P. Railway record of employment
booklet, 1928, and immigration
identification card, 1928. .5 cm.
Taped interview. Photographs.
17 photographs: members and
friends of the Pysklywec family,
including a funeral, Galicia, 1925-67;

convention to the Workingmen's Benevolent Association, Winnipeg, 1944; and groups and activities of the Ukrainian Labour and Farmers' Temple Association, Winnipeg, 1945-62.
Interviewed on 15 June 1977; 1 hr.; 1 tape; Ukrainian; by Mary Stefura. Arrived in Canada in 1928.

RADUL, MARIA
KIRKLAND LAKE, ONT.
29 photographs: family and friends of M. Radul in the Ukraine, Cobalt, Kirkland Lake, 1910-66; employment in mining in Cobalt, 1922-36; and activities of the Ukrainian National Federation and the Ukrainian Women's Organization of Canada, c. 1930-40. Taped interview.
Interviewed on 6 June 1978; 1 hr.; 1 tape; Ukrainian; by Ihor Dawydiak. Immigrated to Canada in 1914.

RADUL, MARIA
KIRKLAND LAKE, ONT.
Interviewed on 15 June 1977; 2 hrs.; 2 tapes; Ukrainian; by Mary Stefura.

RAISER, VIRA
HAMILTON, ONT.
Centennial Project Celebrating 'Canadians All'. Hamilton: Kiwanis Club, 1967. 35 pp.
Dumy i pisni (Thoughts and Songs). Toronto: Ukrainian Publishing, 1938. 101 pp.

RATUSHNIAK, SOPHIE
GERALDTON, ONT.
6 photographs: parish activity at St. Mary's Ukrainian Catholic Church, Geraldton, 1950-60.

RAWLUK, IVAN
LONDON, ENGLAND
Interviewed on 16 June 1982; 1.5 hrs.; 2 tapes; Ukrainian; by Lubomyr Luciuk.

REMEZA, SYLVESTER
OTTAWA, ONT.
Interviewed on 16 Sept. 1981; .75 hr.; 1 tape; Ukrainian; by Lubomyr Luciuk. Arrived in Canada in 1952.

RICHARD, MIKE
TORONTO, ONT.
Personal documents. Photographs. Taped interview.
2 photographs: donor and Ukrainian Canadians during military service in WWII, Kingston.
Interviewed on 23 Jan. 1978; 1.5 hrs.; 2 tapes; Ukrainian/English; by Lubomyr Luciuk. Arrived in Canada in 1928.

RODKEWYCZ, REV. J.
WINNIPEG, MANITOBA
Passenger list issued by C.P. Railway's Royal Mail Steamship Lines, Atlantic Service—*SS Empress of Britain*, 29 Nov. 1922. .25 cm.

ROHATYN, O.
SUDBURY, ONT.
20 photographs: mostly choirs and folk dancers in Sudbury, Toronto, 1948-77; members of the Ukrainian National Federation, Sudbury, 1968.

ROHOWSKY, K.
TORONTO, ONT.
Nowi Dni (New Days). Vol. 1 - vol. 30. Toronto, Feb. 1950 - Dec. 1979 (monthly magazine). 8 reels of microfilm.

ROJENKO, PETRO
(KIEV PRINTERS LTD.)
TORONTO, ONT.
1968-77, organ of the World Lemkos
Federation (for natives of
Lemkivshchyna territory). Toronto:
Canadian Lemko Association (68
issues, monthly) 4 cm.
  Beskyd, Julian. *Material Culture of
Lemko's Land.* Toronto: Kiev Printers
Ltd., 1972. 166 pp.
  Eliashevsky, Ivan, ed. *Lemko Alma-
nac.* Toronto: Organization for
Defence of Lemkivshchyna, 1970,
1973. Ukrainian calendar, historical
and literary items (2 books). 288 pp.
  Liubystok, 1975-78, Ukrainian maga-
zine of literature, arts, and critiques.
Toronto: P. Rojenko (9 magazines).
238 pp.

ROMAN, NESTOR
SUDBURY, ONT.
  Interviewed on 20 June 1977; 1 hr.;
1 tape; Ukrainian; by Mary Stefura.

ROMANIUK, MAKSYM
TORONTO, ONT.
  Interviewed on 21 July 1981; .75
hr.; 1 tape; Ukrainian; by Halyna
Benesh. Arrived in Canada in 1932.

ROMANOW, JOE
OTTAWA, ONT.
  Interviewed on 20 Sept. 1981; 2
hrs.; 2 tapes; English; by Lubomyr
Luciuk. Immigrated to Canada in
1911.

RONISH, JOSEPH AND ZOYA
SOUTH BOLTON, QUEBEC
  Interviewed on 17 Aug. 1981; 3
hrs.; 3 tapes; Ukrainian; by I.
Wynnyckyj.

ROSOCHA, STEFAN
TORONTO, ONT.
  Interviewed on 4 May 1982; 2.75
hrs.; 3 tapes; Ukrainian; by Lubomyr
Luciuk. Post-WWII immigrant.
  The Free Word Almanac (Kalendar
Slovo). 1961-78 (1963, 1971 miss-
ing).
  Toronto Free Press. 11 cm.

RUSAK, ONUFRY
KENORA, ONT.
  Army booklet, passport, and land
contract of donor, 1921, 1926, 1925,
respectively. .5 cm. Photograph.
  1 photograph: donor's uncle, Onufry
Hrychuk, 1910.

RUSZCZACK, O.
GUELPH, ONT.
  Newsclippings on the Ukrainian
Community in Acton, Ont. .5 reel of
microfilm.

RUTCHINSKI, MARY
TIMMINS, ONT.
  Interviewed on 29 Aug. 1977; .5 hr.;
1 tape; English; by Mary Stefura.

RYPALOWSKI, ALBINA
TIMMINS, ONT.
  Scrapbook: correspondence, letters,
financial records from bazaars,
announcements, and newsclippings,
198-74. Also, material dealing with
Timmins Ukrainian Radio Program,
"Sunday Bell," 1957- . Photographs.
1 reel of microfilm.
  3 photographs: wedding, n.d.;
Ukrainian Women's Organization,
n.d.; and Ukrainian language "Ridna
Shkola," Timmins, 1945.

SADOWSKY, ANELIA
KITCHENER, ONT.
  3 photographs: Hunchack weddings,

Kitchener, Welland, 1915-26. Taped interview.
Interviewed on 1 Dec. 1978; 1 hr.; 1 tape; Ukrainian; by I. Wynnyckyj. Arrived in Canada in 1913.

SADOWSKY, STEFAN
KITCHENER, ONT.
2 photographs: donor and friends, Guelph, 1914; and picnic of the Ukrainian Labour and Farmers' Temple Association, 1926. Taped interview.
Interviewed on 1 Dec. 1978; 1 hr.; 1 tape; Ukrainian; by I. Wynnyckyj. Arrived in Canada in 1913.

SAKALIUK, NIKOLA
TORONTO, ONT.
Interviewed on 14 Feb. 1978 and 5 Nov. 1980; 3.5 hrs.; 4 tapes; Ukrainian/English; by Lubomyr Luciuk. Immigrated to Canada in 1912, discusses his experiences in Fort Henry Internment Camp during WWI.

SALMERS, STEPHEN
OSHAWA, ONT.
Programmes from the Ukrainian Evangelic Reformed Church, 1970s, and newsclippings regarding Ukrainian community in Oshawa, n.d. 1 cm (17 items). Photographs.
9 photographs: the Salmers family, 1955-75; religious life at the Ukrainina Reformed Church, 1958; choirs of the Ukrainian National Federation, 1958-73; and celebration of "fiesta," including parades and processions, 1973-77, Oshawa.
1 photograph: picnic organized by the Ukrainian Presbyterian Church, Oshawa, c. 1940.

SALSKY, GEORGE
AYLMER, QUEBEC
Interviewed on 16 Sept. 1981; 1.75 hrs.; 2 tapes; English; by Lubomyr Luciuk. Immigrated to Canada in 1951.

SAMCHUK, ULAS
TORONTO, ONT.
Interviewed on 23 April 1982; 2.75 hrs.; 3 tapes; by Lubomyr Luciuk. Post-WWII political refugee.

SAWKA, JOHN
TORONTO, ONT.
Interviewed on 9 April 1979; 3 hrs.; 3 tapes; Ukrainian; by O. Demianchuk. Immigrated to Canada in 1929.

SAWKA, MARIA
TORONTO, ONT.
89 photographs: most of them from Toronto, showing scenes of numerous Ukrainian theatrical productions, and perfomances by Ukrainian choirs, 1928-68. Taped interview
Interviewed on 25 April 1979; 2 hrs.; 2 tapes; Ukrainian; by O. Demianchuk. Immigrated to Canada in 1929.

SELENKO, JULIA
TORONTO, ONT.
1 photograph: placing of wreath by the the Ukrainian National Federation, Toronto, 1938.

SELESHKO, MICHAILO
TORONTO, ONT.
Reiester Chleniv Ukranskoi Strilets'koii Hromady V Kanadi VID, 1929-40. 91 pp.
Ukrains'ka Strilets'ka Hromada V Kanadi, 1928-38. Almanac. Saskatoon, 1938. 160 pp.

SERBAN, STEVE
KENORA, ONT.
 Clippings on S. Serban's work as a
radio programmer on CJRL in Kenor,
Ont., serving the Ukrainian commun-
ity for 20 years, n.d. Taped inter-
view.
 Interviewed on 29 Sept. 1978; 1 hr.;
1 tape; Ukrainian; by Mary Stefura.
 Arrived in Canada in 1930.

SEROTIUK, RON AND SONJA
SEROTIUK-DUNN
SUDBURY, ONT.
 Volodymyr Serotiuk arrived in
Canada in 1926 from Mykulyntsi in
Western Ukraine. For twenty years
he taught "Ridna Shkola" (Ukrainian
Language School) and organized
instrumental ensembles and choirs
throughout Ont. The collection consists largely of 4 volumes of Ukrainian folk music, n.d. Included are
personal documents, 1897-1966;
theatre programmes and leaflets,
mostly Toronto, 1927-38; children's
and musical plays (all in Ukrainian,
published in the 1910s-1930s); as
well, various Ukrainian grammar,
music and history texts, 1911-48,
most of them printed in Lviv,
Toronto, New York, and
Kiev-Leipzig. 1 reel of microfilm. 13
cm. Photographs.
 19 photographs: the schools, orchestras, and choirs which Volodymyr
Serotiuk directed, c. 1920s-1940s.

SHANKOWSKY, L.
PHILADELPHIA, U.S.
 Interviewed on 3 Sept. 1981; 1.75
hrs.; 2 tapes; Ukrainian; by Lubomyr
Luciuk. Post-WWII political refugee.

SHARIK, MICHAEL
ST. CATHARINES, ONT.
 Interviewed on 5 June 1977; 2 hrs.;
2 tapes; Ukrainian; by Mary Stefura.
 Sharik, Michael. *Fifty Years Per-
spective.* Author's memoirs. Toronto:
Free Press, 1969. 432 pp.
 _____. *Thorny Trails across Canada.*
Continuation of memoirs. Toronto:
Free Press, 1971. 520 pp.

SHEBECH, M.
TORONTO, ONT.
 Interviewed on 23 March 1982; 1.5
hrs.; 2 tapes; Ukrainian/English; by
Lubomyr Luciuk.

SHELESTYNSKY, JOHN
KIRKLAND LAKE, ONT.
 Interviewed on 7 June 1978; 1 hr.; 1
tape; English; by Ihor Dawydiak.
Immigrated to Canada in 1929.

SHIPOSH, M.
SUDBURY, ONT.
 Interviewed on 13 May 1982; 1 hr.;
1 tape; Ukrainian; by Lubomyr
Luciuk. Post-WWII political refugee.

SHPAIUK, ELI
SUDBURY, ONT.
 Interviewed on 19 July 1978; 1 hr.;
1 tape; Ukrainian; by Mary Stefura.
Arrived in Canada in 1913.

SHTEPPA, PAUL
TORONTO, ONT.
 Shteppa, Paul. *Slovnyk Chuzhosliv*
(Dictionary of Foreign Words).
Toronto: I. Hladun and Sons, 1976.
38 pp.

SHTOGRYN, WILLIAM
THOROLD, ONT.
 2 photographs: members, including

orchestra, of the Farmers' Temple Association, Thorold, 1940.

SHULHA, PAUL
TORONTO, ONT.
 Interviewed on 27 . 1977; 1 hr.; 1 tape; Ukrainian; by Mary Stefura. Immigrated to Canada in 1927.

SIBLOCK, M.
OSHAWA, ONT.
 1 photograph: a softball team of the United Hetman Organization, Oshawa, 1935.

SIBLOCK, T.
OSHAWA, ONT.
 Immigration documents of Stefen Sebulak, 1910s. Photograph.
 1 photograph: wedding of Mr. and Mrs. Siblock, 1929.

SIRYK, GREGORY
FORT ERIE, ONT.
 Personal papers, 1941-46, including memoirs, "The Tragedy of My Family," covering the 1942-47 years, by G. Siryk, 1971; also, his diaries from 1970 to 1981. 10 cm.
 RESTRICTED Photographs.
 3 photographs: family, 1956-74.

SKOROCHID, WALTER
HAMILTON, ONT.
 Interviewed on 21 March 1982; 1.75 hrs.; 2 tapes; English; by Lubomyr Luciuk.

SKOROPAD, WASYL
SUDBURY, ONT.
 Interviewed on 17 May 1982; 2.75 hrs.; 3 tapes; Ukrainian; by Lubomyr Luciuk.

SMITH (CRAPLEVE), ANN
WINNIPEG, MANITOBA
 Interviewed in 1982; 1 hr.; 1 tape; English; by Lubomyr Luciuk. Recounts her activities in the Central Ukrainian Relief Bureau, 1946-52.

SMYK, REV. S.
TIMMINS, ONT.
 Scrapbook containing clippings of various newspapers; programmes of concerts, lectures, meetings, conferences; and applications and graduation certificates of schools; invitations, election flyers, and poems; schedules of church services and other activities; bulletins, annual reports, financial records. The material covers mostly Hamilton and Timmins, 1966-67; Windsor, Fort William and Red Lake, 1962-64. 1 reel of microfilm. Photographs.
 3 photographs: religious life, including First Communion at St. Georges's Ukrainian Catholic Church, Timmins, 1976.

SMYLSKI, PETER
TORONTO, ONT.
 Interviewed on 25 March 1982; 3 hrs.; 3 tapes; English/Ukrainian; by Lubomyr Luciuk.

SOKOLSKY, OSTAF
TORONTO, ONT.
 Programmes: concerts, plays, movies, and other activities of the Ukrainian community in Toronto, 1969, 1973-78 (57 items). 2 cm, in English/Ukrainian. Taped interview. Interviewed on 3 Dec. 1981; 2.75 hrs.; 3 tapes; Ukrainian; by Lubomyr Luciuk.
 Ukrainian Toronto. 1976. Directory of Ukrainian cultural groups, organiz-

ations, and institutions in Toronto, compiled by A. Gregorovich. 64 pp., in English.

SOKOLSKY, ZORIANA
TORONTO, ONT.
 Programmes of various activities sponsored by the Ukrainian Canadian Committee, 1977-78; pamphlets issued by the Ukrainian Art Foundation, 1972, 1978; booklets issued by the World Congress of Free Canadians and the Ukrainian Catholic of Toronto Eparchy, 1978; also, leaflets, clippings and posters on various Ukrainian social events, 1970s. 7 cm.
 "Easter Greetings." 2 collections of slides, including a teacher's manual and 2 audio cassettes with background information, which reflect Ukrainian Easter celebrations in Toronto.
 Bosiy, Volodymyr. *Forty Years at the Front of Ukrainian Activities, 1914-1954.* Toronto: Ukrainian Scientific Institute, 1954. 40 pp.
 Humeniuk, Ivan. *Moi Spomyny* (My Recollections). Toronto, 1957. Booklet dealing with the cultural and social development of Ukrainians in Eastern Canada. 61 pp.
 50th Anniversary of Military Service and 20th Anniversary of Activity for Ukrainian People by Lieutenant-General Sikevich. Toronto: Sikevich Fiftieth Anniversary Committee, 1937. 109 pp.
 Commemoration of the Most Rev. Bishop Rir Isidor Borecky. Toronto, 1978. .5 cm.
 Turning of Sod. 1968. Ceremony of St. Vladimir's Ukrainian Institute. 12 pp., in English/Ukrainian.
 Ukrainian Business and Professional Men's Almanac. Toronto: Ukrainian Business and Professional Men's Association, 1955. 58 pp.

Ukrainian Canadian Social Services Bulletin. Nos. 12, 13, 14, 15, 1976-78. 1 cm.

SOKOLSKY, ZORIANA
TORONTO, ONT.
 28 photographs: the "Feast of Jordan" celebration, Hawkestone, 1977.

SOLONYNKA, WASYL
TORONTO, ONT.
 Interviewed on 23 March 1982; 1.75 hrs.; 2 tapes; Ukrainian; by Lubomyr Luciuk.

SOLSKI, MIKE
CONISTON, ONT.
 7 photographs: the Osadchuk family, Ukraine, Copper Cliff, Coniston, North Bay, 1905-69; and theatrical production of the Ukrainian Labour and Farmers' Temple Association, Sudbury, 1927.

SOROCHAN, TEKLIA
KIRKLAND LAKE, ONT.
 Interviewed on 13 June 1977; 1 hr.; 1 tape; Ukrainian; by Mary Stefura. Arrived in Canada in 1912.

SOSNA, ALEXANDRA
OSHAWA, ONT.
 Interviewed on 16 April 1982; 3 hrs.; 3 tapes; Ukrainian; by Lubomyr Luciuk.

SPICOLUK, FRANK
NIAGARA FALLS, ONT.
 Interviewed on 15 Feb. 1978; 2 hrs.; 2 tapes; Ukrainian/English; by Lubomyr Luciuk.

STANKO, YAROSLAV
TORONTO, ONT.
 Interviewed on 14 April 1982; 2.75

hrs.; 3 tapes; by Lubomyr Luciuk. Post-WWII political refugee.

STEFANICH, LENA
TIMMINS, ONT.
Interviewed on 12 June 1978; .25 hr.; 1 tape; Ukrainian; by M. Baryckyj. Immigrated to Canada in 1913.

STEFURA, MARY
SUDBURY, ONT.
2 video cassettes: Cambrian Broadcasting of the "Today Show," 2 June 1978; and "They Came to Ontario: The Bukovinians," n.d. Photographs. 5 photographs: local Ukrainian organizations including literary societies, a school and businessmen, Espanola, Worthington, Sault Ste. Marie, 1912-28.
10th Anniversary of Ukrainian War Veterans' Association in Canada. Saskatchewan, 1938. 160 pp., in Ukrainian/English. Microfilm.
Jubilee Book of 50 Years of Army Service of General Sikevich. Toronto, 1937. 102 pp., in Ukrainian/English. Microfilm.

STEPANIUK, ARSEN
TORONTO, ONT.
Interviewed on 3 May 1982; .75 hr.; 1 tape; Ukrainian; by Lubomyr Luciuk. Post-WWII political refugee.

STEPANIUK, SOPHIA
TORONTO, ONT.
Some documents and articles from D.P. German camps, immediately following WWII. 1 cm. Taped interview.
Interviewed on 28 March 1981; 3.5 hrs.; 4 tapes; Ukrainian; by I. Wynnyckyj. Arrived in Canada in 1948.

STETSKO, SLAVA
MUNICH, GERMANY
Interviewed on 9 July 1982; .75 hr.; 1 tape; Ukrainian; by Lubomyr Luciuk.

STETSKO, YAROSLAV
MUNICH, GERMANY
Interviewed on 14 July 1982; 2 hrs.; 2 tapes; Ukrainian; by Lubomyr Luciuk.

STOS, PETER
SUDBURY, ONT.
2 photographs: wedding in Worthington, 1920.

STRATICHUK, JOHN
SAULT STE. MARIE, ONT.
Interviewed on 13 July 1978; .5 hr.; 1 tape; Ukrainian; by Ihor Dawydiak and Myron Baryckyj. Immigrated to Canada in 1913.

STRATICHUK, JOHN
SAULT STE. MARIE, ONT.
Interviewed on 15 May 1982; .75 hr.; 1 tape; Ukrainian; by Lubomyr Luciuk. Immigrated to Canada in 1913.

SUP, GEORGE AND STANLEY
VAL D'OR (LAC CASTAGNIER), QUEBEC
Some personal documents, 1907, 1937. .5 cm. Photographs.
31 photographs: most from the 1930s, documenting an experimental Ukrainian settlement in northeastern Quebec. Following Cardinal Andrij Sheptycky's visit to Canada in 1921, the decision was made to initiate a Ukrainian colony in Quebec appropriately called Sheptycky.

SWRYDENKO, REV. D.
SUDBURY, ONT.
Interviewed on 14 May 1982; 1.75 hr.; 2 tapes; Ukrainian; by Lubomyr Luciuk. Post-WWII political refugee.

SWYRYDENKO, PETER
THUNDER BAY, ONT.
Interviewed on 17 May 1982; 2.75 hrs.; 3 tapes; Ukrainian; by Lubomyr Luciuk. Post-WWII political refugee.

SYROID, WILLIAM
ESPANOLA, ONT.
Interviewed on 8 Nov. 1977; 2 hrs.; 2 tapes; Ukrainian; by Mary Stefura. Immigrated to Canada in 1912.

SZCZUR, RONIE
SAULT STE. MARIE, ONT.
Interviewed on 13 July 1978; .5 hr.; 1 tape; Ukrainin; by Ihor Dawydiak. Immigrated to Canada in 1923.

SZKRUMELAK, I. (IHOR YURKEWICH)
KINGSTON, ONT.
Exterior view of Davis Tannery, Kingston, 1978. Taped interview.
Interviewed on 29 March 1978; 1 hr.; 1 tape; Ukrainian/English; by Lubomyr Luciuk. Immigrated to Canada in 1951.

TELUK, DORIS
TORONTO, ONT.
Interviewed on 29 June 1981; .5 hr.; 1 tape; Ukrainian; by Halyna Benesh. Arrived in Canada in 1905.

TEMNYK, DARIA
TORONTO, ONT.
Records, 1952-71, from St. Josaphat's Ukrainian Catholic Cathedral and the League of Ukrainian Catholic Women, also at this parish. Included are clippings, a scrapbook, jubilee and anniversary booklets. 1 reel of microfilm. Photographs.
92 photographs: activities, mostly of women's groups, at St. Josaphat's Ukrainian Catholic Cathedral, Toronto, 1922-72.

TESLA, IVAN
OTTAWA, ONT.
Interviewed on 7 Sept. 1981; 3.5 hrs.; 4 tapes; Ukrainian; by Lubomyr Luciuk. Post-WWII political refugee.

TICKOLEZ, ANNE
ST. CATHARINES, ONT.
10 photographs: covering activities of various Ukrainian organizations in St. Catharines and surrounding region—the Ukrainian People's Home, Geraldton, 1937-39; the Ukrainian National Federation, 1943-60; Ukrainian Women's Organization, 1948; Ukrainian (St. Catharines) Credit Union, 1948; St. Cyril and Methodius Ukrainian parish, 1945.

TIMKO, WASYL
TORONTO, ONT.
Interviewed on 27 April 1982; 1.5 hrs.; 2 tapes; Ukrainian; by Lubomyr Luciuk. Immigrated to Canada in 1948.

TODORUK, PASTOR MICHAEL
ST. CATHARINES, ONT.
Immigration papers, 1928-30. 1 cm. Photographs. Taped interview.
5 photographs: Ukrainian Baptist Church activities in Hamilton and Toronto, 1948-59.
Interviewed on 16 July 1979; 1.25 hrs.; 2 tapes; Ukrainian; by Terry Pidamecky. Immigrated to Canada in 1928.
The Christian Herald. Sept. 1972 -

Feb. 1979. Ukrainian Evangelist-Baptist Union of Canada (7 issues). 2 cm.

TOMIUK, ELIZABETH
TIMMINS, ONT.
Interviewed on 12 June 1978; 2 hrs.; 2 tapes; Ukrainian; by Mary Stefura. Settled in Timmins in 1922.

TOWTRIVSKY, PETRO
KIRKLAND LAKE, ONT.
Interviewed on 6 June 1978; .75 hr.; 1 tape; Ukrainian; by Ihor Dawydiak. Immigrated to Canada in 1929.

TURESKI, FRED
OSHAWA, ONT.
8 photographs: religious ceremony and rites at St. George's Ukrainian Catholic Church; and choirs of the Ukrainian National Federation, Oshawa, 1942-61.

TURESKI, FRED
OSHAWA, ONT.
4 photographs: religious life at St. George's Ukrainian Catholic Church, 1942; and choirs of the Ukrainian National Federation, 1952-61.

TUROW, MICHAEL
CAMBRIDGE, ONT.
Personal documents of M. Turow and his wife Kathrine Turow (nee Mamotiuk). Taped interview.
3 photographs: Ukrainian language school, a choir and a picnic, Preston, 1920-31.
Interviewed on 17 Dec. 1979; 1 hr.; 1 tape; Ukrainian; by I. Wynnyckyj. Family arrived in the early 1910s.

URBAN, MARY
KIRKLAND LAKE, ONT.
Interviewed on 8 June 1978; .5 hr.;

1 tape; Ukrainian; by Ihor Dawydiak. Immigrated to Canada in in 1927.

VERYHA, WASYL
TORONTO, ONT.
Interviewed on 25 July 1981; 2.25 hrs.; 3 tapes; Ukrainian; by Lubomyr Luciuk. Imigrated to Canada in 1951.

WACHNA, ELIAS
TORONTO, ONT.
2 posters of Ukrainian sports activity, n.d. Photographs. Taped recording.
15 photographs: team sports, baseball and softball, Toronto, 1936-50.
Recorded on 15 June 1977; .5 hr.; 1 tape; English; by Zoriana Sokolsky. A monologue about Ukrainian sport activities.

WALER, MYKOLA
TORONTO, ONT.
Interviewed on 27 April 1982; 1.75 hrs.; 2 tapes; Ukrainian; by Lubomyr Luciuk. Post-WWII political refugee.

WALL (WOLOKHATIUK), ANNA
SUDBURY, ONT.
1 photograph: A. Wall, Sudbury, 1972. Taped interview.
Interviewed on 20 July 1977; 2 hrs.; 2 tapes; Ukrainian; by Mary Stefura. Arrived in Canada in 1896.

WANDZIAK, ANNIE
CONISTON, ONT.
Immigration documents, 1904-1913. .5 cm. Photographs.
20 photographs: mining activities in Coniston, Ont., 1920s, includes a 1925 Ukrainian picnic.

WASYLENKO, R.
OTTAWA, ONT.
Interviewed on 19 Sept. 1981; 1 hr.;

1 tape; Ukrainian; by Lubomyr
Luciuk. Post-WWII political refugee.

WASYLYSHEN, ANNE
WINNIPEG, MANITOBA
Interviewed on 30 May 1982; .75
hr.; 1 tape; English; by Lubomyr
Luciuk. Immigrated to Canada in
1915.

WERBOWECKI, PETER AND ANN
KITCHENER, ONT.
Personal papers of P. Werbowecki,
1926-36; some records of parishoners
at Ruthenian Catholic Parish,
Kitchener, 1913; also, membership
books, programmes and invitations
from the United Hetman Organization
of "Sitch" in Canada, 1933-36. 2 cm.
Photograph. Taped interview.
1 photograph: J. Wegera and P.
Werbowecki in "Sitch" uniform,
Kitchener, c. 1918.
Interviewed on 24 Jan. 1980; 1 hr.;
1 tape; Ukrainian; by I. Wynnyckyj.
Peter arrived first in 1926; Ann and
daughter followed the year after.

WEST, G.
TORONTO, ONT.
Interviewed on 14 Feb. 1978; .75
hr.; 1 tape; Ukrainian; by Lubomyr
Luciuk.

WINDJACK, SARA
ST. CATHARINES, ONT.
3 photographs: family in
Saskatchewan, 1910-1920.
6 photographs: taken at the Ukrainian Greek Orthodox Church, St.
Catharines, 1930-55. Taped interview.
Interviewed on 23 July 1979; 1.25
hrs.; 2 tapes; Ukrainian/English; by
Terry Pidzamecky. Family arrived in
1897.

*Dedication St. Vladimir's Ukrainian
Orthodox Church.* Toronto, 1948. 67
pp., in Ukrainian/English.
Nasha Kanada (Our Canada).
Ontario Government Immigration
Guidebook prepared by the Community Programme Branch, Department
of Education, Toronto, c. 1950. 48
pp., in Ukrainian.

WITYK, JOHN
KINGSTON, ONT.
13 photographs: activities of the
Canadian Ukrainian Committee,
including banquets and parades,
1940-51; parish activity at St.
Micheal's Ukrainian Catholic Church,
1951-54. Taped interview.
Interviewed on 24 Nov., 10 Dec.
1977; 4 hrs.; 4 tapes; Ukraini-
an/English; by Lubomyr Luciuk.
Immigrated to Canada in 1937.

WOLYNSKYJ, MYKOLA
VIENNA, AUSTRIA
Interviewed on 5 July 1982; 1 hr.; 1
tape; Ukrainian; by Lubomyr Luciuk.
Post-WWII political refugee.

WOWCZUK, EMILIAN
SIOUX LOOKOUT, ONT.
Some membership records from the
Ukrainian People's Home Association
at Sioux Lookout, Ont., 1936-39. 2
cm. Photographs. Taped interview.
6 photographs: the Wowczuk family,
1967-77; and activities of the Ukrainian People's Home, including folk
dancers and parades.
Interviewed on 30 Sept. 1977; 2
hrs.; 2 tapes; Ukrainian; by Mary
Stefura. Immigrated to Canada in
1907.

WOWK, RAYMOND
KINGSTON, ONT.
10 photographs: various Ukrainian
social gatherings (including folk dancing) in Kingston, c. 1930-70. Taped
interview.
Interviewed on 7 Nov. 1977; 1.75
hrs.; 2 tapes; English; by Lubomyr
Luciuk.

WOYCHUK, ANNA
SAULT STE. MARIE, ONT.
Interviewed on 13 July 1978; 1 hr.;
1 tape; English/Ukrainian; by Ihor
Dawydiak. Immigrated to Canada in
1929.

WOYNAROWSKY, WILLIAM
TORONTO, ONT.
Interviewed on 30 March 1982; 2.75
hrs.; 3 tapes; Ukrainian; by Lubomyr
Luciuk. Post-WWII political refugee.

WYNNYCKA, JAROSLAWA
TORONTO, ONT.
Interviewed on 15 Jan. 1982; 2.5
hrs.; 3 tapes; Ukrainian; by I.
Wynnyckya. Immediate post-WWII
immigrant.

WYNNYCKA, J.
TORONTO, ONT.
Bulletin of St. Nicholas Church.
Toronto. 1975-78 (9 issues). 168 pp.
*Bulletin of the Ukrainian Canadian
Committee.* 1975-78 (11 issues). 212
pp.
Novynky z Pansionu. Nos. 16-27,
1974-78. Bulletins from Ivan Franco
Senior Citizens' Home. 244 pp.
Ukrainian Toronto Directory. 1973.
33 pp., in English.
Ukrainka v sviti. 1966-76. Magazine
of the World Federation of Ukrainian
Women's Organizations (19 issues).
420 pp.

WYNNYCKYJ, IROIDA
KITCHENER, ONT.
A collection of programmes from
various Ukrainian organizations in
Kitchener, Waterloo, Cambridge,
Guelph, and Galt, dating from the
1940s to the 1980s. 7 cm. Photo-
graphs.
4 photographs: Ukrainian folk
dancers and choirs, Preston, Ont.,
1967.
Molytovnyk (Prayer Book).
Winnipeg, 1942. Prepared especially
for the soldiers, sailors, and airmen
of the Ukrainian Greek-Catholic
Church of Canada. 64 pp.
Pryvit Novoprybuvshym do Kanady
(For the Newcomers to Canada).
Winnipeg: Ukrainian Catholic Council
of Canada, 1948. Guidebook. 64 pp.

WYNNYCKYJ, J.
KITCHENER, ONT.
Documents (correspondence and
financial records) related to the 58th
anniversary of Ukrainian Independence celebrated in Kitchener, Ont.
on 4 Jan. 1976. 1.5 cm.

YAMKA, ANNA
KIRKLAND LAKE, ONT.
Interviewed on 8 June 1978; .5 hr.;
1 tape; Ukrainian; by Ihor Dawydiak.
Immigrated to Canada in 1926.

YANKOVIC, MARTIN
KINGSTON, ONT.
Interviewed on 14 Nov. 1977; 1 hr.;
1 tape; Ukrainian/English; by
Lubomyr Luciuk. Immigrated to
Canada in 1927.

YANKOWSKY, ZENON
OTTAWA, ONT.
Interviewed on 15 Sept. 1981; 2

hrs.; 2 tapes; Ukrainian; by Lubomyr
Luciuk. Post-WWII political refugee.

YAREMOVICH, ANTHONY
WINNIPEG, MANITOBA
Interviewed on 22 May 1982; 1.5
hrs.; 2 tapes; English/Ukrainian; by
Lubomyr Luciuk. Immediate
post-WWII immigrant.

YARMOLA, HERCIA
OSHAWA, ONT.
2 photographs: members of the
Ukrainian Prosvita Society, Oshawa,
c. 1920; and the St. John's Ukrainian
Credit Union, 1974.

YARYMOWICH, MICHAEL
TORONTO, ONT.
Diary of donor started on 17 March
1926, the day he left his hometown to
go to Ternopil' to "travel with the
transport" to Canada, and ended on
18 March 1927. Covers his work in
Canada and includes an accounting
his pay. 1 cm, in Ukrainian. Taped
interview.
Interviewed on 23 March 1979; 1.75
hrs.; 2 tapes; Ukrainian; by Olenka
Demianchuk. Immigrated to Canada
in 1926.

YASIUK, MARY
SUDBURY, ONT.
9 photographs: religious services at
St. Mary's Ukrainian Catholic
Church, Sudbury, 1950-58; and
orchestra of the Ukrainian National
Youth Federation, 1946.

YAWORSKY, A.
TORONTO, ONT.
Interviewed on 3 Feb. 1982; 3.5
hrs.; 4 tapes; Ukrainian; by Lubomyr
Luciuk. Post-WWII political refugee.

YAWORSKY, ALEXANDER
TORONTO, ONT.
Interviewed on 8 July 1977; 1.75
hrs.; 2 tapes; Ukrainian; by Zoriana
Sokolsky.

YAWORSKY, STEVE
OTTAWA-HULL, ONT.
Interviewed on 15, 17 Sept. 1981; 2
hrs.; 2 tapes; English/Ukrainian; by
Lubomyr Luciuk. Arrived in Canada
in 1948.

ZABAWA, ANNE
ESPANOLA, ONT.
2 photographs: picnic of women's
section of the Ukrainian Prosvista
Society, Espanola, 1935; and celebration of Ukrainian Youth Day, 1950.

ZALISCHUK, WILLIAM
TORONTO, ONT.
Interviewed on 13 July 1977; 1 hr.;
1 tape; English; by Zoriana Sokolsky.

ZAPARYNIUK, JACOB AND MARIA
SUDBURY, ONT.
Interviewed on 21 June 1978; 1 hr.;
1 tape; Ukrainian; by Ihor Dawydiak.
Immigrated to Canada in 1925.

ZAPARYNIUK, MARIA
SUDBURY, ONT.
7 photographs: orchestras of the
Ukrainian National Federation,
1937-39; religious services at St.
Volodymyr's Ukrainian Greek Orthodox Church, 1954-59; and donor,
1979. Taped interview.
Interviewed on 22 Nov. 1978; 1 hr.;
1 tape; Ukrainian; by Mary Stefura.

ZAPLOTINSKY, JOHN
KINGSTON, ONT.
Interviewed on 8 Nov. 1977; 2 hrs.;

2 tapes; Ukrainian; by Lubomyr Luciuk. Immigrated to Canada in 1928.

ZAPOTOSKI, GEO
VAL D'OR, QUEBEC
Interviewed on 9 June 1978; 1 hr.; 1 tape; Ukrainian; by M. Baryckyj. Emigrated in 1928.

ZARISKI, MARY
KIRKLAND LAKE, ONT.
4 photographs: work in mining, Sudbury, Timmins, 1930-40. Taped interview.
Interviewed on 14 June 1977; 2 hrs.; 2 tapes; Ukrainian; by Mary Stefura. Arrived in Canada in 1913.

ZAVARYCHYNE, YAROSLAV
TORONTO, ONT.
Concert flyers and leaflets of the Ukrainian Ballet Studio "Apollon," 2 April 1955, 22 April 1956, 14 June 1959, 12 June 1960. .5 cm.
3 photographs: "Apollon" Ukrainian Ballet Studio, Toronto, 1957-62.

ZAWERBNY, MICHAEL
TORONTO, ONT.
13 photographs: family in the Ukraine, Alberta, Toronto, 1927-47; and employment in housing construction, Alberta, 1930-47. Taped interview.
Interviewed on 10 April 1979; 4.75 hrs.; 5 tapes; Ukrainian; by O. Demianchuk. Immigrated to Canada in 1927.

ZAZULENCHUK, STEVEN
KIRKLAND LAKE, ONT.
Interviewed on 6 June 1978; .5 hr.; 1 tape; Ukrainian; by M. Baryckyj. Immigrated to Canada in 1930.

ZEBRUK, ANTON
KIRKLAND LAKE, ONT.
Interviewed on 14 June 1977; 2 hrs.; 2 tapes; Ukrainian; by Mary Stefura. Emigrated in 1912.

ZILINSKY, W.
OSHAWA, ONT.
8 photographs: choirs, orchestra, and folk dancers, many affiliated with the Ukrainian National Federation, Oshawa, 1928-35.

ZOLTANYCKY, ROMAN
TORONTO, ONT.
Interviewed on 12 July 1977; 1 hr.; 1 tape; English; by A. Sokolsky.

ZUPANSKI, DMITRO
GUELPH, ONT.
Interviewed on 12 March 1980; 1 hr.; 1 tape; Ukrainian; by I. Wynnyckyj. Arrived in Canada in 1926.

ZURKAN, ARTHUR
KENORA, ONT.
Interviewed on 26 Sept. 1977; 1 hr.; 1 tape; Ukrainian; by Mary Stefura. Immigrated to Canada in 1911.

ZYBYCK, JOHN
KINGSTON, ONT.
Interviewed on 7 Dec. 1977; 1 hr.; 1 tape; English; by Lubomyr Luciuk. Born to one of the first Ukrainian families in Kingston.

ZYMA, KARL
SUDBURY, ONT.
7 photographs: the Zyma family, Fort William, 1916-28; and employment in mining, Worthington, 1916.

Taped interview.
Interviewed on 18 Jan. 1978; 2 hrs.;
2 tapes; Ukrainian; by Mary Stefura.
Immigrated to Canada in 1913.

ASSOCIATION OF UNITED UKRAINIAN
CANADIANS
TORONTO, ONT.
Assorted printed matter—articles,
programmes, flyers, clippings, and
posters—dealing with the activities of
the A.U.U.C., the Ukrainian Labor-
Farmer Temple, the Canadian Council of National Groups, and various
Ukrainian cultural organizations, c.
1921-64. 7 cm. Photographs.
Over 150 photographs: covering the
activities of the Association and
related Ukrainian organizations,
1917-66. Some of these include the
Ukrainian Social Democratic Party,
the Ukrainian Labour Temple, the T.
Shevchenko Museum, and the
Bandura Choir. There are also photographs of picnics and dance groups,
as well as peace, strike and May Day
demonstrations.

BROTHERHOOD OF FORMER COMBAT-
ANTS OF THE 1ST UKRAINIAN DIVI-
SION OF THE UKRAINIAN NATIONAL
ARMY IN CANADA
TORONTO, ONT.
The collection contains correspon-
dence, bulletins and minutes from the
Toronto Division, 1952-76. It also
includes general correspondence from
outside Canada and records (mostly
correspondence and minutes) from the
other regional Divisions across
Canada. 10 reels of microfilm.

CANADIAN LEAGUE FOR THE LIBER-
ATION OF UKRAINE
KINGSTON, ONT.
Correspondence, 1956-71; and anni-
versary brochures, 1954, 1967. 2 cm.

CARPATHO-UKRAINIAN WAR
VETERANS' ASSOCIATION
TORONTO, ONT.
Minutes, correspondence, financial
ledgers, and clippings, 1967-81. 8
cm. Photographs.
29 photographs: various memorials
associated with the
Carpatho-Ukrainian War Veterans'
Association, 1971-78.

DELHI TOBACCO PROJECT
DELHI, ONT.
Ukrainian Softball League schedule,
1941. .25 cm.

FIRST UKRAINIAN PENTECOSTAL
CHURCH
TORONTO, ONT.
4 religio-political booklets, 1979-80.
2 cm. Taped interview with W.
Cebula.

HRUSHEWSKY UKRAINIAN SCHOOL
TORONTO, ONT.
Minute books, teacher's guidebook,
teaching programmes, and students'
report cards, 1968-81. 1 reel of
microfilm. Photographs.
20 photographs: School festivals,
picnics and graduations, 1969-81.

HRYHORIJ SKOVORODA SCHOOL OF
UKRAINIAN STUDIES
TORONTO, ONT.
Correspondence, teachers' journals,
final exams, and scrapbooks,
1959-76. 9 cm. Photographs.
30 photographs: students and activities, including theatre, at Hryhorij

Skovoroda School, 1957-76.
Problysky (Sunbeams). 1960-76.
Yearly student publication at Hryhorij
Skovoroda School. 5 cm.

KIEV PAVILION, CARAVAN
TORONTO, ONT.
Recorded in the summer of 1977; 1
hr.; 1 tape; by A. Mostovoy. A
concert performed at the pavilion.

KIEV PRINTERS
TORONTO, ONT.
A collection of Ukrainian pamphlets,
programmes, bulletins, flyers, and
posters printed by Kiev Printers, c.
1958-80 (50 items). Finding aid available.

LEMKO NEWS (PETRO ROJENKO)
TORONTO, ONT.
1 photograph: the executives of the
Canadian Lemko's Association at its
10th anniversary in 1971.

METROPOLITAN ANDREW
SHEPTYTSKY (A. BAZYLEVYCZ)
TORONTO, ONT.
Papers on the life and work of
Metropolitan Andrew Sheptytsky,
1862-1977. Included are published
articles dealing with pastoral messages at Metropolitan religious conferences; with church unity, social
affairs, Polish-Ukrainian relations; the
conception of the struggle for independence; and with the Metropolitan
in defence of Jews as well as defender
of the Orthodox churches. In addition, there are magazines, pamphlets,
memoirs, correspondence and
clippings—most of which is in Ukrainian with some English, French, German, Polish, and Latin. 2 reels of
microfilm.

MULTICULTURAL HISTORY SOCIETY
OF ONTARIO
TORONTO, ONT.
Ukrainian Canadian. 1 Sept. 1947 -
Dec. 1987. 30 reels of microfilm.
Zhyttia I Slovo. 3 Nov. 1965 - 28
Dec. 1987. 30 reels of microfilm.
Press kit on Natalka Husar, sculptor,
Ukrainian, Canadian/American 1980.
1 cm.

MULTICULTURAL NEWSPAPER
MICROFILM PROJECT
TORONTO, ONT.
Bat'kivshchyna. 7 Jan. 1976 - Feb.
1987. 2 reels of microfilm.

ONTARIO ETHNIC NEWSPAPER
MICROFILM PROJECT
TORONTO, ONT.
Boiova molod'. June 1930 - July
1932. 1 reel of microfilm.
Chervonyi prapor (The Red Flag).
15 Nov. 1907 - 8 Aug. 1908. 1 reel
of microfilm.
Emigrant. Lviv, Ukrainian. March
1910 - April 1911. 1 reel of micro-
film.
Farmers'ke zhyttia. 1 April 1925 - 3
July 1940. 16 reels of microfilm.
Holos Pratsi (Voice of Labour).
April 1922 - Feb. 1924. 1 reel of
microfilm.
Holos robitnytsi (Voice of Working
Women). Jan. 1923 - March 1924. 1
reel of microfilm.
Kadylo. May 1930 - 10 March 1918.
1 reel of microfilm.
Robochyi narod (The Working
People) 15 May 1912 - 28 Sept.
1918. 3 reels of microfilm.
Robitnyche slovo (Workers' Word).
6 Jan. 1917 - 29 Dec. 1917. 1 reel of
microfilm.
Robitnytsia. March 1924 - Aug.
1937. 7 reels of microfilm.

Svit Molodi. March 1927 - May 1930. 1 reel of microfilm.
Ukrainian Labor News. 22 March 1919 - 3 March 1920. 1 reel of microfilm.
Ukrains'ke zhyttia (Ukrainian Life). 7 Aug. 1941 - Oct. 1975. 25 reels of microfilm.

ONTARIO MODERN LANGUAGE TEACHERS' ASSOCIATION
KITCHENER, ONT.
OMLTA constitution, membership list, correspondence, programmes of conferences, list of attendees, and miscellaneous items, 1972-82. 1 reel of microfilm. See also audio recordings of conferences. Taped recordings.
A series of recordings of OMLTA Conference, Ukrainian Section proceedings 28 Apr. 1979, 11 Apr. 1982, and 13 Mar. 1982; 6 hrs.; 6 tapes; Ukrainian/English; by I. Wynnyckyj.

ORGANIZATION FOR DEFENCE OF LEMKIVSHCHYNA AND LEMKOS
TORONTO, ONT.
Mintues, 1970-72; financial reports, 1969-71; and membership card (American), 1972. 1 cm. See the P. Rojenko papers for Lemko publications.

OSHAWA UKRAINIAN PROSVISTA SOCIETY
OSHAWA, ONT.
2 photographs: choir, 1922, and picnic, 1928, of the Osahawa Ukrainian Prosvita Society.

PATRONAGE OF SHEVCHENKO SCIENTIFIC SOCIETY CENTRE
MONTREAL, QUEBEC
Correspondence, 1970-79. 4 cm.

"PLAST" UKRAINIAN YOUTH ASSOCIATION, MONTREAL BRANCH
MONTREAL, QUEBEC
Bulletin of Montreal Branch of "Plast". 1965-81. 5 cm.
Plastova Odnodnivka. 1953, 1956, 1957, 1962. Souvenir booklets. 2 cm.
Plast in Montreal. 1962. Souvenir booklet. 40 pp.

PONTIFICAL HIGH MASS
SUDBURY, ONT.
Recorded on 6 Nov. 1977; 1 hr.; 1 tape; Ukrainian; by Mary Stefura.

PROTECTION OF THE VIRGIN MARY UKRAINIAN CATHOLIC CHURCH
GUELPH, ONT.
Records, 1940-79, comprise council and congregation minutes, church correspondence, financial reports, and members lists; as well, baptismal, marriage and burial records, 1940-79. 1 reel of microfilm.

ST. ANDREW'S HOSPITAL ASSOCIATION
TORONTO, ONT.
Proposed constitution and by-laws, minutes, correspondence, financial reports, and newsclippings, 1958-74. 4 cm.

ST. GEORGE'S UKRAINIAN CATHOLIC CHURCH
TIMMINS, ONT.
Papers dealing with the erection of church, financial records, 10th anniversary booklet, and minutes of St. George's Catholic Church, 1948-63; also, membership books, minutes and cash books from the Ukrainian Catholic Women's League in Timmins, 1943-65. 1 reel of microfilm. Photographs.
4 photographs: activities, including

picnic, at St. George's Church, Timmins, and at Sacred Heart Ukrainian Catholic Church, Kirkland Lake, c. 1970-78.

ST. GEORGE'S UKRAINIAN CREDIT UNION
OSHAWA, ONT.
Books of recording secretary books, 1961-63. 3 cm, in English.

ST. GEORGE UKRAINIAN CATHOLIC CHURCH
OSHAWA, ONT.
Records comprise statute and minutes of Union of Ukrainian Brotherhoods, 1926, 1935-66; minutes of St. George's Church, 1914-76, and school, 1961-68; treasurer's books, 1946-73; and membership books, 1959-73. Photographs. 4 reels of microfilm.
3 photographs: Ukrainian School at St. George's Parish, 1923, 1942.
Year Book of Mount Mary Immaculate Academy. Ancaster, Ont., 1961. 60 pp.

ST. JOHN'S UKRAINIAN GREEK ORTHODOX CHURCH
OSHAWA, ONT.
3 anniversary booklets of St. John's Orthodox Church, 1955, 1960, 1975. 2 cm. Photographs.
3 photographs: membership cards of Church, n.d.
10th Anniversary of St. John's Ukrainian Greek Orthodox Church in Oshawa. 1955. 1 cm.

ST. JOSAPHAT'S UKRAINIAN CATHOLIC CATHERAL (REV. B. FILEWYCH)
TORONTO, ONT.
Book of minutes, list of parishoners, correspondence, and financial records from parish of St. Josaphat's Cathe-

dral, 1919-68; included are birth, marriage, and death registers, 1914-77, and baptismal records dating from 1911 to 1954. As well, minutes, members list and financial records of the Song and Drama Club and the Brotherhood of Ukrainian Canadians, 1927-58, at the same parish. 3 reels of microfilm.
Opening of the Church Home. Toronto: St. Vladimir's Greek-Orthodox Parish, 1938. Souvenir booklet. .5 cm.

ST. JOSAPHAT'S UKRAINIAN CATHOLIC SCHOOL (REV. B. FILEWYCH)
TORONTO, ONT.
24 photographs: school functions and parish activity at St. Josaphat's Ukrainian Catholic Cathedral, 1913-65.
Tenth Anniversary of St. Josaphat's Catholic School. Toronto, 1971. 146 pp.

ST. MARY'S CREDIT UNION
TORONTO, ONT.
Annual reports and brochures, 1961-75. 3 cm.

ST. MARY'S UKRAINIAN CATHOLIC CHURCH
CAMBRIDGE, ONT.
Council and congregation meetings, financial statements (including church building finances), and baptismal, marriage, and burial records, 1956-79. 1 reel of microfilm.

ST. MARY'S UKRAINIAN CATHOLIC CHURCH (M. PROCAK)
SAULT STE. MARIE, ONT.
I.M.P.A.C.T., Investigations into Multiculturalism: Practices, Attitudes and Citizenship Tendencies. A directory compiled by the Summer Job Corp Programme on all active

ethnocultural organizations in Sault Ste. Marie, including information about their histories and community involvement, 1978; list of Ukrainian students, and clippings of events and holidays held in the Ukrainian community of Sault Ste. Marie. 2 cm. Photographs.

6 photographs: schools affiliated with the Ukrainian Labour and Farmer's Temple Association and St. Mary's Ukrainian Catholic Church, Sault Ste. Marie, 1960-64; and Ukrainian Labour Temple, 1935.

ST. MARY'S UKRAINIAN CATHOLIC CHURCH
SUDBURY, ONT.
69 photographs: parish activity—religious services, camping, choirs, clergymen—at St. Mary's Church, 1929-80.

————.
SUDBURY, ONT.
Minutes, cash book, annual reports of the parish committee, and birth certificates, 1931-61; included are records of the Junior Catholic Women's League, 1929-32. 1 reel of microfilm. Photographs.
3 photographs: visit of Prince Danylo Skoropads'ky, 1937; and religious ceremony at St. Mary's Ukrainian Catholic Church, Sudbury.

ST. MARY'S UKRAINIAN CATHOLIC CHURCH
THOROLD, ONT.
Minutes of parish and Women's League, 1949-79; financial records for parish, church construction and Women's League, 1952-78; parish

records—baptismal, marriage, funeral, 1949-72; and miscellaneous items: list of donors, announcements, and clippings. 2 reels of microfilm.

ST. MARY'S UKRAINIAN CATHOLIC CHURCH
TORONTO, ONT.
Scattered isuues of journals and bulletins, 1967-77. 2 cm.

ST. MARY'S UKRAINIAN ORTHODOX CHURCH
FORT WILLIAM, ONT.
List of contributors from church construction, 1910-13; marriage records, 1938-48, birth and baptismal registry, 1938-52. 3 cm.

ST. MARY THE PROTECTRESS UKRAINIAN GREEK ORTHODOX CHURCH
WATERFORD, ONT.
Congregational minutes, correspondence, financial statements, and membership, baptismal, marriage, burial records, 1932-79. Photographs. 3 reels of microfilm.
11 photographs: parish activity, 1951-53.

ST. MICHAEL'S UKRAINIAN CATHOLIC CHURCH
KINGSTON, ONT.
Parish records, 1952-76. 3 cm.

ST. NICHOLAS SCHOOL OF UKRAINIAN STUDIES (KURSY UKRAYINOZNAVSTVA)
TORONTO, ONT.
Correspondence, 1966-79, and school journals, 1962-72; also scattered items: concert programmes, receipts, newsclippings, bulletins, and reports. 4 reels of microfilm.

ST. PETER AND PAUL UKRAINIAN
CATHOLIC CHURCH
TORONTO, ONT.
Annual report, bulletin and poster,
1979. .5 cm.

ST. VLADIMIR'S UKRAINIAN GREEK
ORTHODOX CHURCH
KIRKLAND LAKE, ONT.
Parish records, 1933-36. 1 reel of
microfilm.

ST. VLADIMIR'S UKRAINIAN ORTHO-
DOX CHURCH
TORONTO, ONT.
Ferensiw, Rev. H. "Lessons in the
History of the Ukranian Orthodox
Church." Toronto, 1966. 6 pp.
Ukrainian Orthodox Church. 1980.
Booklet. 7 pp.

ST. VOLODYMYR'S UKRAINIAN
GREEK ORTHODOX CHURCH
SUDBURY, ONT.
70 photographs: parish activity,
including school and entertainment, at
St. Volodymyr's Church, Sudbury,
1940-77.

STS. CYRIL AND METHODIUS UKRAI-
NIAN CATHOLIC CHURCH
ST. CATHARINES, ONT.
Correspondence, financial reports,
programmes, and newsletters,
1970-74. 1 reel of microfilm.
*25th Anniversary of Sts. Cyril and
Methodius Ukrainian Catholic
Church.* St. Catharines, 1969. 80 pp.
*Newsletters of Sts. Cyril and
Methodius Ukrainian Catholic
Church,* 1970-74 (251 issues). 1 reel
of microfilm.

SUDBURY CENTENNIAL PROJECT
SUDBURY, ONT.
Interviewed in Summer, 1980; 3

hrs.; 3 tapes; English; by A.
Kupchak, M. Walylycia and C. Susla.

SUDBURY REGIONAL
MULTICULTURAL CENTRE
SUDBURY, ONT.
Programmes and flyers, 1980. 1 cm.
Photographs.
7 photographs: activities at the
Centre, c. 1970s.

SUDBURY UKRAINIAN CO-OPERATIVE
SUDBURY, ONT.
Short history and excerpts from
annual meetings of Sudbury Ukrainian
Co-operative, 1935-75; records of net
income, 1934-70; and minutes of
members' and board of
directorss'meeting, 1935-72. 1 reel of
microfilm. Photographs. Taped interview with N. Peczeniuk.
RESTRICTED
6 photographs: the staff of the
Sudbury Ukrainian Co-operative Ltd.
and the Ukrainian (Sudbury) Credit
Union Ltd., 1955-75.
*40th Anniversary of the Ukrainian
Co-operative in Sudbury.* Sudbury,
1975. 16 pp., in Ukrainian.

THE CROSS AND THE FLAG
LOS ANGELES, CALIFORNIA
Articles related to the Hetman movement in North America, c. 1970s. .5
cm.

UKRAINIAN CATHOLIC WOMEN'S
LEAGUE, ST. GEORGE'S CATHOLIC
CHURCH
OSHAWA, ONT.
The collection contains minutes,
1941-71; correspondence, 1958,
1959, 1977; journal of finances,
1953-67; and miscellaneous items:
lists of members, programmes,
yearbooks, and historical sketch of

Women's League. 5 reels of microfilm. Photographs.

10 photographs: members of the Ukrainian Catholic Women's League, Oshawa, 1956-69.

UKRAINIAN ATHLETIC ASSOCIATION
KINGSTON, ONT.
Rules and regulations, minutes and assorted membership items, 1956. 2 cm. **RESTRICTED** Taped interview with I. Szkrumelak.

UKRAINIAN CANADIAN COMMITTEE
KINGSTON, ONT.
Records include constitution and resolution, financial reports correspondence and memos of the Ukrainian Canadian Committee, 1944-57; also, correspondence, financial statements, and reports from the Canadian Relief Fund, 1946-48; and finally, records and printed material—almanacs, pamphlets, newsletters—from the Ukrainian National Youth Federation of Canada, 1944-56. 2 reels of microfilm. Photographs. See Lubomyr Luciuk Collection.

12 photographs: activities of the Ukrainian Canadian Committee, 1940s, 1950s.

UKRAINIAN CANADIAN COMMITTEE
TORONTO, ONT.
Correspondence, 1976, and bulletins, 1963, 1976. 1 cm.

UKRAINIAN CATHOLIC CHURCH OF
TRANSFIGURATION
KITCHENER, ONT.
The collection, 1924-58, contains by-laws, congregational minutes, parish ledger and members' donations, baptismal and marriage records, and burial cards; also,

church bulletins, souvenir programmes, journals, flyers, and posters. 4 reels of microfilm. Photographs. Taped interview with P. Werbowski.

22 photographs: religious services and entertainment (drama groups, folk dancing, choirs) at the Ukrainian Catholic Church of Transfiguration, 1917-47.

UKRAINIAN CATHOLIC WOMEN'S
LEAGUE OF CANADA
TORONTO, ONT.
Records, 1944-79, include minutes, membership files, correspondence, miscellaneous documents, and branch reports; as well as thank-you letters for assistance, 1952-77. 17 reels of microfilm.
Outline of History of Ukrainian Catholic Women's League of Canada. Toronto: New Horizons, 1975. 360 pp.

UKRAINIAN CREDIT UNION
SUDBURY, ONT.
Minutes and annual reports, 1956-70. 1 reel of microfilm.
25th Anniversary of the Ukrainian Credit Union in Sudbury, 1969. .5 cm.

UKRAINIAN CULTURAL CENTRE
SUDBURY, ONT.
Letters patent and by-laws, 1961, and clippings, 1951-52. 1 cm. Photographs.

117 photographs: the Ukrainian community in Sudbury and Kirkland Lake, 1950s-1970s.

UKRAINIAN FRATERNAL SOCIETY OF
CANADA, BRANCH NO. 25
PRESTON, ONT.
Minutes, 1928-79. 1 reel of micro-
film.

UKRAINIAN FRATERNAL SOCIETY
ST. CATHARINES, ONT.
Records, 1929-79, comprise minutes,
charter and by-laws, correspondence,
and financial ledgers. Included is a
jubille book, 1935. 2 reels of microfilm.

UKRAINIAN GREEK ORTHODOX
CHURCH OF ST. VLADIMIR (REV. S.
SMYK)
KIRKLAND LAKE, ONT.
Records regarding the erection of
Church, 1933-35; marriage register,
1933-36; and manuscript, "History of
Ukrainian Catholic Parish in Kirkland
Lake, Ontario," by Rev. Smyk, 1978.
1 reel of microfilm. Photographs.
2 photographs: Ukrainian Catholic
Women's League, n.d., and Parish
Council, n.d.

UKRAINIAN GREEK ORTHODOX
CHURCH OF ST. SOPHIA
WATERLOO, ONT.
Minutes, 1969-71; financial records,
1961-69; and parish
records—baptismal, marriages, and
burials, 1970-78. 1 reel of microfilm.
Taped interview with Rev. A.
Kostiuk.
Izbornik. Lviv, 1914. 720 pp., in
church Slavonic. Microfilm.
Malyi Trebnuk. Warsaw, 1914.
Handbook in church Slavonic. 303
pp. Microfilm.

UKRAINIAN HETMAN ORGANIZATION
AND UKRAINIAN SPORTING "SITCH"
ASSOCIATION
TORONTO, ONT.
Records, 1923-71, include by-laws,
minutes, correpondence, financial
statements, and lists of members.
Also includes pamphlets published by
the United Hetman Organizations,
1933-39. 5 reels of microfilm. Photographs.
4 photographs: activities of the
United Hetman Organization, including a "Sitch" music band, Oshawa,
1918-33.

UKRAINIAN LITERARY SOCIETY
KENORA, ONT.
A library of Ukrainian publications,
most of them from Winnipeg and
Toronto, and some from Edmonton,
Kiev, Lviv, and Vienna. It includes 6
immigrant guidebooks, 1895-1910; 47
plays, 1910s-1930s; and 75 miscellaneous items—statutes, articles, short
stories, novels, speeches, and souvenir booklets, 1920s-1950s. Title list
available. .5 meters. 1 microfilm reel.

UKRAINIAN LITERARY SOCIETY OF T.
SHEVCHENKO
KENORA, ONT.
Minutes, 1923-66; financial statements, 1918-76; and membership
records, 1915-78. 2 reels of microfilm.

UKRAINIAN NATIONAL FEDERATION
TORONTO, ONT.
This vast collection contains the
records of the U.N.F. National
Executive, 1931-79, and those of the
Federation's 30 local branches, most
of them in Ont., Quebec and Alberta,
1917-76. It also documents the history of the Federation's ancillary

organizations: the U.N.F. Women's
Organization, Ont. branches only,
1935-76; the Ukrainian National
Youth Federation, Ont. and Quebec,
1936-77; the Ukrainian War
Veterans' Association, Ont. branches,
1929-79; as well as various other
groups, such as the Ukrainian Relief
Association. and Ukrainian Canadian
Committee, Timmins, Ont., 1933-39;
"Chaika" Dance Ensemble, Hamilton,
1959-78; and "Ridna Shkola,"
Sudbury branch, 1934-78. 391 reels
of microfilm.

UKRAINIAN NATIONAL YOUTH FED-
ERATION (M. KUCHAR)
ST. CATHARINES, ONT.
 Records, 1937-77, comprise minutes,
correspondence, and membership files
of the St. Catharines and Thorold
branches, 1937-77. 1 reel of microfilm. Photographs. See the Ukrainian
Canadian Committee Collection.
 7 photographs: recreational activities
organized by the Ukrainian National
Youth Federation, Sudbury, 1956-72.

UKRAINIAN ORTHODOX CHURCH OF
THE ASSUMPTION OF THE MOST
HOLY MOTHER OF GOD
THUNDER BAY, ONT.
 Baptismal and marriage registers,
1938-59, donors' list for church con-
struction, 1910-26, and church bull-
etins, 1977-78. 5 cm.

UKRAINIAN PEOPLE'S HOME ASSOCI-
ATION
TORONTO, ONT.
 Records, 1917-71, include minutes,
financial statements, reports, and general correspondence. Included are
dedication programmes in Ukrainian,
Toronto, 1920-54; a collection of
social science pamphlets in Ukrainian,

Toronto, 1917-38; and newsclippings,
Ukrainian and English, covering
Ukrainian activity in Toronto,
1920s-1950s. 8 reels of microfilm.
Photographs. See M. Liber Collec-
tion.
 10 photographs: group photographs:
of members of the United Hetman
Organization, Fort William, 1912;
parish activity at St. Vladimir's
Ukrainian Orthodox Church, Toronto,
Winnipeg, 1905-33; activities and
membership of the Ukrainian People's
Home Association, Toronto, 1926-31.

UKRAINIAN PEOPLE'S HOME OF IVAN
FRANKO
WATERFORD, ONT.
 Records, 1926-67, comprise
handwritten constitution, minutes of
trustees and general meetings, financial statements, and a short history of
the organization. 1 reel of microfilm.

UKRAINIAN PEOPLE'S HOME
PRESTON, ONT.
 Constitution, memo of agreement,
deeds of land, mortgages, and letters
patent; also, members' lists, memoirs,
and letters to Ukrainian Canadian
WWII soldiers, 1907-55. 1 reel of
microfilm. Taped interview with M.
Turow.

UKRAINIAN PROFESSIONAL AND BUSI-
NESS CLUB OF WATERLOO, WELLING-
TON AND PERTH
KITCHENER, ONT.
 Membership lists, minutes, press
releases, programmes, flyers, and
clippings, 1978-80. 2 cm.

UKRAINIAN PROFESSIONAL AND BUSI-
NESS CLUB
TORONTO, ONT.
 Records, 1937-79, include statute,

minutes of conventions and executive council, correspondence, annual reports, speeches, and programmes. 2 reels of microfilm. Photographs.
12 photographs: members of Ukrainian Businees Club, 1977-79.

UKRAINIAN PROFESSIONAL AND BUSINESSMEN'S ASSOCIATION
OSHAWA, ONT.
Minutes and financial accounts, 1952-78. 1 reel of microfilm.

UKRAINIAN PROSVITA ASSOCIATION
WINDSOR, ONT.
Minutes, 1932-33; financial records, 1932-41; and school attendance journal, 1953-57. 1 reel of microfilm.

UKRAINIAN PROSVITA SOCIETY
TIMMINS, ONT.
Cash book, 1934-37. 1 cm. Photograph.
1 photograph: Prosvita Timmins Choir, Timmins, 1933.

UKRAINIAN STUDENTS' CLUB OF THE UNIVERSITY OF WATERLOO
KITCHENER, ONT.
Minutes of general meetings, 1963-65; and general correspondence with members' lists, 1963-75; also, flyers and programmes of Ukrainian cultural events. 6 cm.

UKRAINIAN TEACHERS' ASSOCIATION OF CANADA
TORONTO, ONT.
Records, 1947-69, comprise minutes, constitution, financial reports, and membership lists and applications. 2 reels of microfilm. Photographs.
Over 100 photographs: Ukrainian Teachers' Association activities and school groups, mostly Toronto, 1958-62.

UKRAINIAN TECHNICAL SOCIETY IN CANADA
TORONTO, ONT.
Constitution and by-laws, minutes, letters, financial records, newsletters, bulletins and clippings, 1955-75. 3 reels of microfilm.
News of the Society of Ukrainian Engineers and Technicians in Canada, 1952 (4 issues). Microfilm.
News of the Society of Ukrainian Engineers in America. 1950-55 (25 issues). Microfilm.
Society of Ukrainian Engineers and Technicians of Canada. 1951-55 (13 issues). Microfilm.
Ukrainian Engineering News. 1956-77 (62 issues). Microfilm.

UKRAINIAN TORONTO CREDIT UNION
TORONTO, ONT.
Koordynator. 1970, 1973, 1974. Bulletin of the Ukrainian Credit Unions in Toronto (21 issues, quarterly). 3 cm, in English/Ukrainian.
Silver Jubilee Publication of Ukrainian Credit Union in Toronto. Toronto, 1969. 112 pp.

UKRAINIAN WORKINGMEN'S ASSOCIATION, LABOUR UNITY BRANCH
THOROLD, ONT.
The collection contains minutes book (with names and addresses of members), 1931-46; correspondence, 1935-43; financial statements, 1969; membership records (medical reports, statements of pensions), 1966-69; and miscellaneous items: donation form, flyer, almanac, and articles. 1 reel of microfilm.

UKRAINIAN WORKMEN'S CO-OPERATIVE (ROY LITWIN)
THOROLD, ONT.
Constitution, 1934, Co-op's financial

ledgers, 1936-43; and minutes of
Women's Association, 1942; also,
cash book of Ivan Franko Society in
Thorold. 3 cm. Photographs. Taped
interview.
10 photographs: mostly of members
of the "Ivan Franko" organization,
1920s, 1930s.

UKRAINIAN YOUTH ASSOCIATION
TORONTO, ONT.
The collection documents the policies
and activities of the Ukrainian Youth
Association and its related organizations in the period 1948-76. It
includes minutes of various committees, 1945-71, correspondence
between local branches and national
executives in other countries,
1948-76; as well as reports, bulletins,
membership lists, and scrapbooks,
1948-75. 2 meters. Complimenting
the collection are more than 2,000
photographs.
Over 2,000 photographs: showing
recreational (camping excursions,
sports), social and political activities
of the Youth Association, mostly in
Ont., 1952-81.

UNION OF UKRAINIAN BROTHER-
HOODS
KITCHENER, ONT.
Correspondence, 1933-35. .5 cm.
See records of the Ukrainian Catholic
Church of Transfiguration.

UNION OF UKRAINIAN STUDENTS OF
CANADA, QUEEN'S UNIVERSITY
KINGSTON, ONT.
The collection, consisting of minutes,
correspondence, conference reports
and resolutions, and documents the
cultural and political ambitions of the
Ukrainian Students' Union from
1969-75. 3 cm.

VERKHOVYNA WOMEN'S VOCAL
QUARTET
TORONTO, ONT.
7 photographs: the Quartet, Toronto,
1952-80.

YAROSLAV PASTERNAK'S ARCHAEOL-
OGY OF UKRAINE
TORONTO, ONT.
Minutes, 1959-64; correspondence,
1959-63; addresses, promotion
pamphlet, reviews and clippings, and
a distribution card catalogue. 2 reels
of microfilm.

VIETNAMESE COLLECTION

BUI, VAN BAO
TORONTO, ONT.
1 Vietnamese driving licence, 1958;
1 family tree, n.d.; an issue of a
magazine published by Vietnamese
refugees in the Dodwell's Ridge
Refugee Camp in Hong Kong, 1975;
and a collection of educational books
for children, published in Vietnam
and Canada in the 1970s. 8 cm.
Taped interview.
Interviewed on 20 July 1979; 1 hr.;
1 tape; Vietnamese; by H. T. Ngo.
Arrived in Canada in the late 1970s.

BUI, VAN LONG
TORONTO, ONT.
1 Vietnamese identification card,
1969; 1 diplomatic identification card,
1972; and a publication entitled
"Realites Vietnamiennes," 1966. 2
cm. Photograph. Taped interview.
1 photograph: Van Long Bui and his
brother, 1945-50.
Interviewed on 19 July 1979; 1.5
hrs.; 2 tapes; Vietnamese; by H. T.
Ngo. Emigrated from Vietnam in the
1970s.

DUONG, NHU HOA
TORONTO, ONT.
1 resume. .25 cm. Taped interview.
Interviewed on 10 July 1979; 1 hr.;
1 tape; Vietnamese; by H. T. Ngo.
Immigrated to Canada in 1967, recollections of Toronto's Vietnamese
community of the 1960s.

HOANG, TAT DAT
TORONTO, ONT.
Personal papers of Hoang family
1947-78. 3 cm. Taped interview.
Interviewed on 20 July 1979; .75
hr.; 1 tape; Vietnamese/English; by
H. T. Ngo. Fled Saigon a few days
prior to the Communist takeover on
30 April 1975.

HOANG-KIM, HAI
TORONTO, ONT.
Immigration papers and certificates
from Italy, 1959-68. 1 cm. Taped
interview.
Interviewed on 20 Sept. 1979; 1 hr.;
1 tape; Vietnamese/English; by H. T.
Ngo. Immigrated to Canada in the
early 1970s.

NGO, THE HOANH
TORONTO, ONT.
Personal papers, which include
immigration documents and a membership card of the Vietnamese Fraternal Association, 1940-78. 2 cm (29
items). Taped interview.
Self-interviewed on 10 March 1980;
1 hr.; 1 tape; English. Arrived in
Canada in 1969, active in organizing
Toronto's Vietnamese community.
Dac San Xuan: Dinhty. 1977. Almanac. 64 pp., in Vietnamese.

NGUYEN, DON PHU
TORONTO, ONT.
1 Canadian immigration record and
visa, 1979. .25 cm. Taped interview.

Interviewed on 7 Sept. 1979;
.75 hr.; 1 tape; Vietnamese; by H. T.
Ngo. Admitted to Canada in 1979.

NGUYEN, HUU HOI
TORONTO, ONT.
Personal documents, 1949-59 (14
items). Photographs.
3 photographs: donor in Vietnam, c.
1952.

NGUYEN, KHAC CAN
TORONTO, ONT.
Immigration papers and school certi-
ficates mainly from Vietnam, 1966-75
(48 items). Taped interview.
Interviewed on 10 Sept. 1979; .75
hr.; 1 tape; Vietnamese; by H. T.
Ngo. Moved to Canada in 1975.

NGUYEN, THI GOI
TORONTO, ONT.
Travel documents and school certifi-
cates, 1943-77 (30 items). Photo-
graphs. Taped interview.
2 photographs: the Nguyen family in
Vietnam, and Toronto, 1977.
Interviewed on 2 Dec. 1979; 1 hr.; 1
tape; Vietnamese; by H. T. Ngo.
Admitted to Canada with her family
in 1977 after 2 years in the
Philippines.

NGUYEN, VAN MY
MARKHAM, ONT.
Correspondence, including telegrams
from relatives, 1975, and 2 letters
from the Federation of Vietnamese
Employers, 1972 (24 items). Taped
interview.
Interviewed on 30 July 1979; 1 hr.;
1 tape; Vietnamese; by H. T. Ngo.
Fled Vietnam in 1975, helped found
the Evangelical Church of Vietnam in
Canada.

NGUYEN, VAN NGHIEN
TORONTO, ONT.
Personal papers and 1 Vietnamese
currency bill (200-piaster), 1942-52.
.5 cm. Taped interview.
Interviewed on 11 Sept. 1979; 1 hr.;
1 tape; Vietnamese; by H. T. Ngo.
Arrived in Canada in 1976, helped
found the Toronto Vietnamese Buddhist Association.

NGUYEN-DANG, DAT
TORONTO, ONT.
Personal documents, 1945-77, and a
music cassette (10 items). Photograph. Taped interview.
1 photograph: donor, c. 1970.
Interviewed on 12 Sept. 1979; .5
hr.; 1 tape; Vietnamese; by H. T.
Ngo. Immigrated to Canada in 1972.

NGUYEN-DANG, THINH PETER
TORONTO, ONT.
Personal papers from Vietnam, the
U.S., and Canada, 1961-72 (43
items).

TRAN, THI NGOC-BICH
TORONTO, ONT.
Immigration papers, 1970-77 (17
items). Photograph. Taped interview.
1 photograph: donor, c. 1972.
Interviewed on 23 July 1979; .5 hr.;
1 tape; Vietnamese; by H. T. Ngo.
Immigrated to Canada in 1972.

BOAT PEOPLE ORAL HISTORY PRO-
JECT
TORONTO AND OTTAWA, ONT.
The Boat People Oral History Project includes 264 interviews (673
cassettes) with South-East Asian refugees, most of whom are Vietnamese,

Cambodians, Chinese, or Laotians.
This project consists of three parts:
178 interviews conducted in Toronto
in 1981-82, and 86 interviews done in
Ottawa at the same time. Vietnamese
interviews represent a sizeable portion
of the collection. **RESTRICTED**

THE EVANGELICAL CHURCH OF VIET-
NAM IN CANADA
TORONTO, ONT.
 Constitution and patent letters of
Church, 1977; by-laws of the Church
Youth; by-laws of the Church Youth
Group, 1978; programmes, a
songbook, and bible study books
issued by the Church, 1973-75. 5 cm,
in Vietnamese. See Van My Nguyen.

VIETNAMESE COMMUNITY ASSOCI-
ATION OF OTTAWA-HULL (CAN, D.
LE)
OTTAWA, ONT.
 Ban Tin. 1978. Newsletter (3 issues).
In Vietnamese.
 Lua Viet. 1979. Almanac published
by the Vietnamese Community Asso-
ciation of Ottawa-Hull. 50 pp., in
Vietnamese.

VIETNAMESE FRATERNAL ASSOCI-
ATION (NGO, THE HOANH)
TORONTO, ONT.
 Records, 1972-79, which include a
constitution and letters patent, minutes
of general and executive meetings,
general correspondence, members'
lists, and a series of newsletters and
notices. 10 cm. 2 reels of microfilm.
 Tap-San Ban Viet. 1974-80. 9 cm.
 Vietnamese Association Newsletter.
Nos. 56-59, 1984-85. 1 cm.

WELSH COLLECTION

ANDREW, EVAN HUGH
OTTAWA, ONT.
 Interviewed on 7 Sept. 1977; .75
hr.; 1 tape; English; by Roger Jones.
Arrived in Canada in late 1920s.

BARKER, EIRLYS
SCARBOROUGH, ONT.
Newsclippings, 1957. Photographs.
Taped interview.
 7 photographs: William Thomas with
parents, 1886; his arrival in Canada,
1924; with Eirlys Barker at house on
Mutual Street, 1925; with priest on
Clinton Street; Welsh picnic; and
wedding group in Toronto, 1920s.
 Interviewed on 8 March 1977; 1 hr.;
1 tape; English; by Anne Dunets.
Father arrived at the turn of the cen-
tury.
 Edwards, J. M. *Drama: Rhys Lewis.*
Gwrecsam, 1910. 46 pp.
 Selected Welsh and English Hymns.
Toronto: Dewi Sant Welsh United
Church, n.d. Small booklet.
 Welsh Directory. Toronto, c. 1960s.
1 cm.

BENNETT, GWENDOLINE
TORONTO, ONT.
 Interviewed on 20 June 1977; .75
hr.; 1 tape; English; by Roger Jones.
Parents emigrated in 1907.

BOWEN, DAVID
HAMILTON, ONT.
 Hamilton Eisteddfod: syllabus,
1930-34, and financial statement,
1934. Hamilton Welsh Women's Club
minutes, Feb. 1962 - April 1963.

Hamilton Welsh Male Choir account
book, 1934-35. Hamilton Welsh
Society list and programme of meet-
ings, 1958. Miscellaneous items: St.
David's Day Annual Banquet pro-
gramme, 1931; Folk Festival of New
Canadians pamphlet, 1934; and
newsclippings on St. David's Welsh
Society and the Welsh community in
Hamilton, n.d. 9 cm. Taped inter-
view.
 Interviewed on 15 Aug. 1977; .5 hr.;
1 tape; English; by Roger Jones.
Emigrated in the 1920s.

CLEE, DAVID
TORONTO, ONT.
 Interviewed on 24 June 1977; .5 hr.;
1 tape; English; by Roger Jones.

DAVID, DAN
TORONTO, ONT.
 Interviewed in Jan./Feb. 1977; .5
hr.; 1 tape; English/Welsh; by Anne
Dunets.

DAVID, DAN
TORONTO, ONT.
 Interviewed on 10 Feb. 1977; .5 hr.;
1 tape; English; by Anne Dunets.

DAVIES, FRANK T.
OTTAWA, ONT.
 Personal papers, notes on donor. 5
cm. Taped interview.
 Interviewed on 7 Sept. 1977; .5 hr.;
1 tape; English; by Roger Jones.

DAVIES, MARY
OTTAWA, ONT.
Interviewed on 2, 3 Sept. 1977; .5
hr.; 1 tape; English; by Roger Jones.

ELLIS, WILLIAM
TORONTO, ONT.
Interviewed on 27 March 1978; .5
hr.; 1 tape; English; by Roger Jones.

EVANS, ANNIE
TORONTO, ONT.
Interviewed on 8 June 1977; 2 hrs.;
2 tapes; English; by Roger Jones.
Arrived in the 1920s.

EVANS, GLYNNE
TORONTO, ONT.
Interviewed on 6 June 1977; 2 hrs.;
2 tapes; English; by Roger Jones.

EVANS, MARGARET
HAMILTON, ONT.
Interviewed on 15 Aug. 1977; 1 hr.;
1 tape; English; by Roger Jones.

EVANS, NAN
TORONTO, ONT.
Interviewed on 8 June 1977; .75 hr.;
1 tape; English; by Roger Jones.
Arrived in Canada in the 1970s.

EVANS, NAN AND NELLIE GRIFFITHS
TORONTO, ONT.
Interviewed on 27 Feb. 1977; .75
hr.; 1 tape; English; by Roger Jones.
Parents arrived in 1905.

EVANS, OLWEN
TORONTO, ONT.
Diary of Megan Evan's voyage to
Canada, n.d. and biographical sketch
of Lewis Evans, n.d. .5 cm. Photographs.
11 photographs: Welsh community
banquet, c. 1914; Rev. J. R. Evans,

c. 1914; a group of people in
Toronto, 1917; interior and exterior
of the Rice Lewis and Son Ltd. store
on Victoria Street in Toronto, 1913;
art work done by E. L. Lewis.
Official Programme. Rhyl, 1904.
Royal National Eisteddfod of Wales.
68 pp.
_____. *Official Report of the Arts
and Crafts Committee.* Rhyl, 1904.
51 pp.

EVERY, GRETA AND SARA
TORONTO, ONT.
Toronto Welsh Players programme
for "Cobbler's Wax," 1954; pro-
gramme of Loyal Societies Dinner in
Honour of H. R. H. Princess
Alexandra, 1967; and newspaper
photograph "Red Dragon of Wales,"
1955. 1 cm. Taped interview with
Greta Evans.
Interviewed in Jan./Feb. 1977; 1 hr.;
1 tape; Welsh/English; by Anne
Dunets.

GARRESON, BILL
TORONTO, ONT.
Programme of dedication service of
New Dewi Sant, n.d.; Grand Trunk
Railway certificate, n.d.; and
newsclippings, including the Toronto
Welsh Male Choir, n.d. .5 cm.

GILMORE, JUDITH
OTTAWA, ONT.
Interviewed on 4 Sept. 1977; .5 hr;
1 tape; Welsh; by Roger Jones.
Taped recording.
Song, "Rachie," at Labour Day
Weekend Gymanfu Ganu.

GRIFFITHS, KATE O.
TORONTO, ONT.
Interviewed on 1 June 1977; .5 hr.;

1 tape; English; by Roger Jones. Discusses Welsh community in Kirkland Lake, Ont.

GRIFFITHS, NELLIE
TORONTO, ONT.
A selection of newsclippings on Welsh in Canada, 1961-77. Taped interview.
Interviewed in Jan./Feb. 1977; 1 hr.; 1 tape; English/Welsh; by Anne Dunets.

GRIFFITHS, TALFRYN AND SHIRLEY
OTTAWA, ONT.
Interviewed on 8 Oct. 1977; .75 hr.; 1 tape; English; by Roger Jones. Father immigrated to Canada in 1910.

HARRIES, MORFUDD
TORONTO, ONT.
Letter from C. T. Harries, to daughter Morfudd, c. 1920s; profile on Morfudd Harries, 1969; note on Royal National Eisteddfod, 1976; St. David's Day toast to Morfudd Harries, 1956; note on William Griffiths who immigrated to Canada in 1888; notes on George T. Harries, 1872-1945; notes on Gwerfyl Harries, 1909-73; copy of speech entitled "Welshmen in Canada" by Morfudd Harries. 2 cm. Photographs. Taped interview.
8 photographs: George Harries, 1936, and William Griffiths, Wales, 1930; Welsh choir, 1930, and St. David's Society banquet in Toronto, 1947.
Interviewed on 9 June 1977; 1 hr.; 1 tape; English; by Roger Jones.

HARRIES, TUDOR
TORONTO, ONT.
Welsh scrapbook, 1940s; miscellaneous clippings, n.d.; testimonials for Tudor Harries, 1910; and notes on 32nd Annual Kiwanis Music Festival. 1 reel of microfilm. 2 cm. Taped interview.
Interviewed on 9 June 1977; 1 hr.; 1 tape; English; by Roger Jones.

HEATHCOTE, ERIC T.
TORONTO, ONT.
Interviewed on 25 July 1977; .5 hr.; 1 tape; Eglish; by Roger Jones. Arrived in the 1910s.

HEATON, DAISY
TORONTO, ONT.
Interviewed on 1 Feb. 1977; .5 hr.; 1 tape; English; by Roger Jones. Discusses father's work in Dewi Sant Church.

HEATON, DAISY
TORONTO, ONT.
Clippings of Daisy Heaton and her father, Rev. D. Huhes, c. 1970s. 1 cm. Taped interview.
Interviewed in Jan./Feb. 1977; 1 hr.; 1 tape; English/Welsh; by Anne Dunets.
Thomas, Islyn. *Our Welsh Heritage.* New York: St. David's Society, 1972. 57 pp.

HODGE, FRED
TORONTO, ONT.
1 photograph: reception for Tommy Farr in Toronto, 1926. Taped interview.
Interviewed on 6 June 1977; 2 hrs.; 2 tapes; English; by Roger Jones. Recounts involvement in Dewi Sant Welsh Church and St. David's Society.

HODGE, GWEN AND BRENDA
KELSALL
TORONTO, ONT.
3 photographs: members of the
Davies and Hodge families in
Toronto, 1929-49. Taped interview.
Interviewed on 28 Feb. 1977; .75
hr.; 1 tape; English; by Roger Jones.
Recollections of the Depression, job
searches, evening prayer meetings,
and description of donated photo-
graphs.

HUDSON, JEANETTE
OTTAWA, ONT.
Interviewed in Oct. 1977; .5 hr.; 1
tape; English; by Roger Jones.
Dicusses church and choir activities in
Montreal, Quebec, and Ottawa.
*Favorite Welsh and English Hymns
and Melodies*. Welsh National
Gymanfa Ganu Association, Inc., n.d.
81 pp.

HUGHES, HUGH
TORONTO, ONT.
Interviewed on 27 June 1977; .75
hr.; 1 tape; English; by Roger Jones.
Immigrated to Canada in 1924,
worked in the construction trades.

JOHNSON, ANNETTE
OTTAWA, ONT.
Interviewed on 3 Sept. 1977; .5 hr.;
1 tape; English; by Roger Jones. Discusses sense of "Welshness."

JONES, CYNTHIA
OTTAWA, ONT.
Interviewed on 3 Sept. 1977; .5 hr.;
1 tape; English; by Roger Jones. Dis-
cusses involvement in Gymanfa Ganu
Association.

JONES, HOWELL E. WAYNE,
NEW JERSEY, U.S.
Complete file on Rev. Walter Jones
(Gwallter), the donor's father, d.
1937, which includes letters touching
on Rev. Jones's St. David's Day
speeches, and professional speech
writing; papers related to 1921 Eisteddfod; St. David's Day programme,
Montreal, n.d.; and newsclippings on
Jones and the Welsh United Church
in Montreal, n.d. 2 cm. Photograph.
1 photograph: W. H. Jones, 1936;
and newsclippings on Bardic Chair
awarded to Rev. Jones in 1921.

JONES, MYFANWY
TORONTO, ONT.
Interviewed on 8 July 1977; .5 hr.; 1
tape; English; by Roger Jones. Immigrated to Canada with mother in
1923, 2 years after father.

JONES, REV. J. H.
TORONTO, ONT.
Letter and translation of C.B.C.
broadcast to Wales, c. 1950s. .25 cm,
in Welsh/English. Taped interview.
Interviewed on 29 June 1977; .5 hr.;
1 tape; English; by Roger Jones.
Arrived in 1951, recounts history of
Welsh Church in Toronto.

JONES, ROGER
TORONTO, ONT.
Files on Welsh Ministers in Canada
(Rev. J. H. Micheal, 1878-1959;
Rev. T. H. Davies, 1871-1965;
Bishop D. T. Owen, 1876-1947; Rev.
R. Roberts, 1874-1945; and Bishop
D. Williams, 18?? - 1931); biographi-
cal material on Welsh personalities
(Ivor Rhys Lewis, Llewellyn Rees,
Caradoc Rhywen, Tudor and
Morfudd Harries, the Hughes Family,
the Jones Sisters, James H. Price, D.

E. Hughes, H. Pulman Evans, and Arthur Chambers); and printed matter (excerpts from books, journals and reports) on Welsh immigration, notes and miscellaneous clippings. 12 cm. Photographs.
 23 photographs: activities of the Welsh community in Toronto—celebrations such as Welsh Day, 1931, and St. David's Day, 1940; the Welsh Dramatic Society, 1939; and impressions of art work by I. R. Lewis; choirs and children's groups at the 46th Welsh National Gymanfa Ganu, 1977.
 Jones, Roger. *Gower: Fact and Fable*. Roger Jones, C. E. Watkins Ltd., c. 1970s. 33 pp., in English/Welsh.
 Selected Welsh and English Hymns. Toronto: Dewi Sant Welsh United Church, n.d. Booklet of hymns.
 W.A.Y. News. Winter 1977, Spring 1978. .25 cm.
 Yr Enfys. July/Aug. 1976. .25 cm.
 Y Gadwyn. Sept., Oct., Nov., Dec., 1977. .25 cm.
 Y Werin. Sept. 1977. .25 cm.

JONES, TOM
MALTON, ONT.
 Jones, W.J. *Adgofion Andronicus*. Caernarfon: Argraphwyd Gan y Welsh National Press Co., 1894. 220 pp., in Welsh.

LANGFORD, DAVID
TORONTO, ONT.
 Interviewed on 6 April 1977; 1.5 hrs.; 2 tapes; English; by Roger Jones. Father first immigrated to Canada in 1904.

MACMILLAN, ELUNED
TORONTO, ONT.
 Interviewed on 4 March 1977; 1 hr.; 1 tape; English; by Roger Jones.

MATTHEWS, CHARLES
TORONTO, ONT.
 4 photographs: art works done by Ivor Rhys Lewis, n.d. Taped interview.
 Interviewed on 7 June 1977; .5 hr.; 1 tape; English; by Roger Jones. Discusses the careers of Welsh artists in Toronto.

MORGAN, LILY
HAMILTON, ONT.
 Interviewed on 15 Aug. 1977; .5 hr.; 1 tape; English; by Roger Jones.

MORGAN, RICHARD
HAMILTON, ONT.
 Interviewed on 15 Aug. 1977; .5 hr.; 1 tape; English; by Roger Jones. Arrived in the 1930s, member of the Hamilton Welsh St. David's Society.

MORRIS, WILLIAM JOSEPH (JO)
TORONTO, ONT.
 Miscellaneous material on Welsh theatre and drama in Toronto such as notes by donor on first coast-to-coast broadcast, 1939; programme of Victory Review, 13 April 1943; the Welsh Players programme, "Quality Street," Lion's Club, Oct. 1947; C.B.C. script, "St. David's Eve," a pageant for St. David's Eve, 1939; and clippings on the Toronto Welsh Drama Society and Tommy Farr, n.d. Photographs. Taped interview.
 12 photographs: theatrical productions of the Welsh Dramatic Society of Toronto, 1936-49; Dewi Sant Welsh United Church in Toronto, 1960s.

Interviewed on 22 Feb. 1977; 2 hrs.; 2 tapes; English; by Roger Jones. Founder of the "Welsh Players," a drama group in Toronto.

PARKER, HORACE AND IRENE
ORANGEVILLE, ONT.
Interviewed on 14 March 1977; 1 hr.; 1 tape; English; by Gwen Hodge. Both arrived in Canada in 1929.

PEREGRINE, MURIEL AND GWILYM
TORONTO, ONT.
Letter of reference from D. J. Lewis, engineer at Nixon's Navigation Co. in Mountain Ash (Wales) for Mr. Gwylym Peregrine, Aug. 1927. .25 cm. Photographs. Taped interview.
4 photographs: 1928-35, at Fourth Annual Gymanfa Ganu, 1932.
Interviewed on March 1977; 1 hr.; 1 tape; English; by G. Hodge. Immigrated to Canada in 1926, immediately after the General Strike in Wales.

PHILLIPS, DAVID
TORONTO, ONT.
1 photograph: celebration of Welsh Day in Toronto, 1931; congregation at Dewi Sant Welsh United Church in Toronto, 1913. Taped interview.
Interviewed in March 1977; .75 hr.; 1 tape; English; by G. Hodge. He arrived in Canada in 1928, joined St. David's Society same year.

PRICE, WILLIAM
ARNPRIOR, ONT.
Price, William. *Celtic Odyssey; As Told to Eileen Sheila Hill.* Philadelphia: Dorrance and Co., 1970. 280 pp.

PRITCHETT, CERIDWEN
BOLTON, ONT.
Interviewed on 22 Aug. 1977; .5 hr.; 1 tape; English; by Roger Jones. Belonged to St. David's Society in the 1940s.

ROBERTS, DAVE
TORONTO, ONT.
Interviewed in Jan./Feb. 1977; .5 hr.; 1 tape; English/Welsh; by Anne Dunets.

ROBERTS, OWEN C.
MONTREAL, QUEBEC
A former president of the Montreal Welsh Society, donor's papers consist largely of records from the St. David's Society of Montreal: general correspondence, 1903-04, 1919-24, 1925-31, 1933-34, 1938-42; inter-society correspondence with lists of Welsh Societies across Canada, 1939-41; letters sent to Salem Welsh Church, 1926; minute books, 1918-43; financial records and subscription lists, 1903-34; membership lists, 1918-21; file on a 1926 Welsh church picnic in Montreal. In addition, a constitution and by-laws of the National Gymanfa Ganu Association of U.S. and Canada, n.d.; letters and programmes from St. David's Society of Winnipeg, 1952-53; and constitution and programmes from the Cambrian Society of Vancouver, 1927, 1952. .5 meters.
St. David's Day Banquet Golden Jubilee Programme. St. David's Society of Montreal, 1953. Pamphlet.
St. David's Society Montreal 58th Anniversary Programme. Montreal, 1958. Pamphlet.
Y Drych, March 1952, Oct.-Dec. 1972, Jan.-Dec. 1973, Jan. 1974. 2 cm.

THOMAS, DILYS
OTTAWA, ONT.
 Constitution, bulletins and announce-
ments from St. David's Society of
Ottawa, 1924, 1967-68; Eisteddfod
programmes, 1920-23, 1925, 1927;
Gymanfa Ganu programme, Ottawa,
1972; and clippings, 1940-1970s. 4
cm.
 Y Ddraig Goch: Xmas Greetings.
1939. Toronto: Dewi Sant Welsh
Young People's Society, 1939. 20 pp.

THOMAS, ELUNED
TORONTO, ONT.
 Biographical notes on Wilfred Powell
and Gaynor Jones for Gymanfa Ganu.
Taped interview.
 Interviewed on 23 Sept. 1977; .5
hr.; 1 tape; English; by Roger Jones.
Former president of Welsh National
Gymanfa Ganu Association.
 Thomas, Eluned. "The Welsh in
Canada." *Y Ddinas.* Vol. 2, no. 8,
May 1957.
 Williams, Galnmor. *A Prospect of
Paradise?.* B.B.C. Wales Annual
Radio Lecture, 1976. 30 pp.
 *Cymru ac America: Wales and
America.* Caerdydd, 1946. 90 pp., in
English.

THOMSON, CHARLES
TORONTO, ONT.
 Interviewed on 21 July 1977; .75
hr.; 1 tape; English; by Roger Jones.
Dicusses careers of Welsh artists in
Toronto since the 1910s.

WATSON, JOHN
TORONTO, ONT.
 Interviewed on April 1977; 1 hr.; 1
tape; English; by Roger Jones. Discusses his acting career in Toronto,
the Welsh Players, and Ivor Rhys
Lewis.

WILLIAMS, EILYS AND LEN
EDMONTON, ALBERTA
 Notes on "Memories of Welsh
Church in Demonton," by E.
Williams, 1978. .25 cm. Taped inter-
view donors.
 Interviewed on 31 March 1977; .5
hr.; 1 tape; English; by Roger Jones.
Discusses Welsh community activities
in Edmonton, Alberta since the
1920s.

WILLIAMS, REV. HEDD-WYN
TORONTO, ONT.
 Interviewed on 16 Aug. 1977; 1 hr.;
1 tape; English; by Roger Jones.
Post-WWII arrival, filled a post in
Toronto Welsh Church.

DEWI SANT WELSH UNITED CHURCH
TORONTO, ONT.
 Parish records, 1922-74; minutes of
congregational meetings, 1933-74;
board of trustees minutes, 1929-65;
financial records, 1934-35, 1945-72;
list of members, 1934, 1946, 1974;
and a scrapbook, n.d. Collection
papers from the Ladies' Aid Society
and the Young People's Society. 10
cm. and 5 reels of microfilm. Photographs. Taped interviews with Mr.
and Mrs. Barker.
 Over 150 photographs: 1925-75,
depicting religious life at Dewi Sant
Welsh United Church on Clinton
Street, Toronto; community activities
including choir and theatrical productions, picnics and St. David's Day
celebrations, rugby meets and
Gymfada Ganu sessions. (Finding aid
available).
 Davies, E. T. and S. Northcote. *The
National Songs of Wales.* Toronto:
Boosey and Hawkes, 1959. 148 pp.

A Short History of Dewi Sant Welsh United Church: Jubilee Celebration, 1907-57. Compiled by J. H. Jones. Toronto, 1957. Booklet. 19 pp.

Dewi Sant Newsletter. Vol. 1 , no. 2, Feb. 1958 - Dec. 1962. Incomplete. 4 cm.

Favorite Welsh and English Hymns and Melodies. Warren, Ohio: The National Gymanfa Ganu Association of the U.S. and Canada, n.d. 93 pp.

Y Gadwin (The Link). Vol. 1, no. 1, Jan. 1963 - vol. 13, no. 4, Dec. 1977. News of the Toronto Welsh community. 14 cm.

DEWI SANT YOUNG PEOPLE'S SOCIETY
TORONTO, ONT.
Minute book and newsletters, 1939. 2 cm.

Y Ddraig Goch. Vol. 1, no. 1, April 1939 - Dec. 1939. 1.5 cm.

EISTEDDFOD COMMITTEE (ST. DAVID'S SOCIETY)
TORONTO, ONT.
Minutes, 1961-64. 1 reel of microfilm.

GYMANFA GANU
OTTAWA, ONT.
Proceedings recorded on 4 Sep. 1977; .5 hr.; 1 tape; Welsh; by Roger Jones. C.B.C. recording of Noson Lawen at Ottawa Gymanfa Ganu, 1977.

LONDON WELSH SOCIETY
LONDON, ONT.
Letter from London, Ont. to London, England describing Canadian Welsh, published in *London Welshman.* Vol. 15, no. 11, Dec. 1960. .25 cm.

MULTICULTURAL HISTORY SOCIETY OF ONTARIO
TORONTO, ONT.
Chamberlain, M.E., ed. *The Welsh in Canada.* Swansea: Canadian Studies in Wales Group, 1986. Collection of essays.

Rosser, Frederick T. *The Welsh Settlement in Upper Canada.* London, Ont.: Lawson Memorial Library, 1954. 145 pp.

MONTREAL WELSH
MONTREAL, QUEBEC
Letter from member to *Western Mail* in Cardiff, Wales, 27 Nov. 1925; and notes on Montreal Welsh, n.d. .25 cm.

ONTARIO RUGGER UNION
TORONTO, ONT.
Letter regarding visiting Welsh team, 1973. .25 cm.

OTTAWA WELSH SOCIETY
OTTAWA, ONT.
Constitution of Ottawa Welsh Society, 1977; minutes and agendas of the society, 1973-76; general correspondence, 1973-76; correspondence concerning the Aberfan Disaster Fund, 1966; financial records, 1973; membership list, 1973-74; and bulletins. Miscellaneous items on Welsh conerts, rugby visits, St. David's Day banquets, and activities organized by the Gymanfa Ganu Association, 1970s. 13 cm. Taped interviews with J. Hudson, Tal and Shirley Griffiths (q.v.).

Ninnau. The North America Welsh Newsletter, 1976-78. 2 cm.

Y Bwletin. Ottawa Welsh Society, 1973-76. 3 cm.

Y Drych. Vol. 126, no. 3, March 1977. 1 issue.

ST. DAVID'S SOCIETY OF TORONTO
TORONTO, ONT.
This extensive collection documents
the histories of St. David's Society,
and its ancillary organizations. St.
David's Society, 1887-1974: charter,
minutes, correspondence financial
statements, reports, members' lists,
banquet brochures, programmes, and
clippings. Eisteddfod Committee: 7
entries in Eisteddfod writing competition, 1947, minutes, 1946-49, and
correspondence, 1971, and programmes, 1947-65. Incomplete.
Cymdeithas y Genhinen: constitution,
n.d., minutes, 1957-64, account
books, 1952-59, and correspondence,
1964. Yr Enfys: Annual reports,
1956-67, correspondence, 1956-66,
and miscellaneous material. .5 meter.
Photograph. Taped interviews with,
D. Clee, N. Griffiths (q.v.), D.
Heaton, and D. Roberts.
1 photograph: newsclipping on
Welsh picnic, 1907.
Guide for Newcomers. Toronto, c.
1950s. .5 cm.
Mawl a Chan, Praise and Song.
Detroit: Committee of the Welsh
Church of Detroit, 1952. Hymns. 320
pp.
Wales: Land of Opportunity. Text by
Brinley Thomas. Cardiff: Develop-
ment Corporation for Wales, 1960.
Illustrated. 112 pp. *Yr Enfys.* Journal
of the Welsh People in Dispersion.
Autumn, 1950, Oct.-Nov. 1960, Jan.-
Feb. 1961, Nov. 1962, Aug. 1967,
July-Aug. 1976, Jan.-Feb. 1977.

T. EATON MEMORIAL CHURCH
TORONTO, ONT.
Sermons, 1919-20, speech, 1918,
and notes on the history of the
Church, n.d. 1 cm.

TORONTO WELSH RUGBY FOOTBALL
CLUB
TORONTO, ONT.
List of Welsh R.F.C. team, and
newsclipping of one game, c.
1931-33. .25 cm.

WELSH NATIONAL EISTEDDFOD
WREXHAM, WALES
Recorded on 1-6 Aug. 1977; 1 hr.; 1
tape; English/Welsh; on the B.B.C.
Interviews with Welsh expatriates
from Vancouver and Australia.

WELSH NATIONAL GYMANFU GANU
OTTAWA, ONT.
Recorded on 4 Sept. 1977; 1 hr. ; 1
tape; Welsh; by Roger Jones. Selec-
tions from afternoon session of
Gymanfu Ganu Welsh songs.

WELSH NATIONAL GYMANFA GANU
TORONTO, ONT.
Gymanfa Ganu correspondence,
1956-64; financial records, 1958-59,
1967; constitution of Welsh National
Gymanfa Association, 1971; list of
committees and members at the 28th
N.G.G.A., 1959; brochures of
Annual Ontario Gymanfa Ganu Association, 1961, 1968-72, 1974-77 and
of the Annual National Gymanfa
Ganu, 1959, 1967, 1977; and
circulars and clippings. 8 cm. Taped
interview with H. Hughes, and audio
recordings of Gymanfu Ganu Welsh
songs. (See Roger Jones).
Hymns for Gymanfa Ganu. Toronto,
1913. Small booklet.
*T: Toronto-Welsh Canadian Centen-
nial Committee.* Jan. - July 1967. 1
cm.

TOMOVICH, VICTOR A.
ST. CATHARINES, ONT.
  Papers, 1945-56, which include min-
utes, reports, resolutions, and miscel-
laneous records from Canadian Yugo-
slav Youth Movement, Canadian
South Slavic Youth Federation,
League of Canadian Croats,
Communists-Decisions of the Work-
ing Committee, and the Council South
Slavs regarding Reconstruction of
Yugoslavia Fund. Collection also
includes correspondence from League
of Canadian Yugoslavs, *Jedinstvo*,
Yugoslav Red Cross, Council of
Canadian South Slavs, League of
Canadian Croats, and Federation of
Yugoslav-Canadians. 4 reels of
microfilm.

COUNCIL OF CANADIAN SOUTH
SLAVS
TORONTO, ONT.
  The collection contains minutes and
financial records of the Council of
Canadian South Slavs (Serbs, Croats,
Slovenians, and Macedonians),
1944-48; minutes and correspondence
from its executive, 1943-47; correspondence among associated organizations in Ont. and Canada, 1944-47;
and documents and correspondence
concerning Canadian aid to Yugoslavia, 1945-46. The collection also
includes minutes of Federation of
Yugoslav-Canadians, 1954-63; minutes of Yugoslav Club, "Advance,"
Toronto, 1951-55, 1957-58; constitu-

tion of the League of Canadian
Croats, 1945; reports and resolutions
from the Trieste convention, n.d.;
and miscellaneous records of League
of Yugoslav-Canadians, 1954-56. 12
reels of microfilm.

ISLAMIC FRATERNAL ASSOCIATION OF
MUSLIMS OF YUGOSLAVIA
TORONTO, ONT.
  Includes constitution, correspon-
dence, membership book, receipt
book, brochure and newsletters,
1974-78. 4 cm.
  Bosnia and Herzegovina. Sarajevo:
The Republican Secretariat for Infor-
mation, The Socialist Republic of
Bosnia and Herzegovina, 1974. Illus-
trated. 225 pp.

KANADSKOG JUGOSLAVENSKOG
KLUBA
WINDSOR, ONT.
  Minutes, 1929, 1933, 1935, 1949. 1
reel of microfilm.

LEAGUE OF YUGOSLAV CANADIANS
TORONTO, ONT.
  Papers, 1953-65, which include minutes of executive committee, correspondence, financial records of Council of Canadian South Slavs, biographies of Yugoslav immigrants, and 2
Yugoslavian dramas staged during
WWII. 1 reel of microfilm.

MULTICULTURAL HISTORY SOCIETY
OF ONTARIO
TORONTO, ONT.
  Adamic, Louis. *Laughing in the*

Jungle: The Autobiography of an Immigrant in America. New York: Harper and Brothers, 1932. 333 pp.

_____. *The Native's Return: An American Immigrant Visits Yugoslavia and Discovers His Old Country.* New York: Harper and Brothers, 1934. Illustrated. 370 pp.

_____. *Cradle of Life: The Story of One Man's Beginnings.* New York: Harper and Brothers, 1936. 468 pp.

_____. *From Many Lands.* New York: Harper and Brothers, 1939. 350 pp.

_____. *Two-Way Passage.* New York: Harper and Brothers, 1941. 350 pp.

_____. *What's Your Name?* New York: Harper and Brothers, 1942. 248 pp.

_____. *My Native Land.* New York: Harper and Brothers, 1943. 507 pp,

Bicanic, Rudolf. *How the People Live: Life in the Passive Regions (Peasant Life in Southwestern Croatia, Bosnia and Hercegovina; Yugoslavia in 1935).* Research Report No. 21, Dept. of Anthropology, University of Massachusetts, 1981.

Christian, Henry A. "Louis Adamic and Ethnic Autobiography." Translated into Japanese by Shozo Tahara. *Paulownia Review.* No. 4, 1986: 15-29.

_____. "Adamic's Struggle: The International History of a 'Radical' Pamphlet." In *Louis Adamic Symposium.* Ljubliana, 16-18 Sept. 1981. pp. 323-344.

_____. "Louis Adamic (1898-1951): His Life, Work, and Legacy." *Spectrum.* Vol. 4, no. 1, Fall 1982: 1-9. Immigration History Center, University of Minnesota.

Cizmic, Ivan. *Iz Dalmacije u Novi Zeland.* Zabreb: Globus, 1981. 185

pp. *Ostarivane Nacionalne Ravnopravnosti u Oblasti Vaspitanja i Obrazovanja.* Saopstenja, dokumenti i diskusija sa Medunarodnog simpozijuma, odrzanog u Novm Sadu od 14. do 16. septembra 1976. godine, Novi Sad, 1977. 430 pp.

Kosinski, Leszek A. *Yugoslavs in Canada.* Edmonton: Division of East European Studies, University of Alberta, 1980. 61 pp.

Magnusson, Kjell. *Jugoslaver i Sverige: Invandrare och identitet i ett kultursociologiskt perspektiv.* Uppsala Multiethnic Papers, no. 17, 1989. 307 pp., in Finnish.

Simic, Andrei. "Management of the Male Image in Yugoslavia." *Anthropological Quarterly.* Vol. 42, no. 2, April 1969: 89-101.

Velikonja, Josef. "Emigration." *Jugoslawien,* Sudosteuropa-Handbuch. Gottingen: Vandenhoeck and Ruprecht, 1975.

20 Godina: Kratki Pregled Historije Naprednog Pokreta Jugoslavenskih Iseljenika u Kanadi. Toronto: Izvrsnog Odbora Vijeca Kanadskih Juznih Slavena, 1950. 96 pp.

Iseljenistvo Naroda i Narodnosti Jugoslavije I Njegove Uzajamne Veze s Domovinom. Zagreb: Zbornik, 1978. 741 pp.

Jugoslav Survey: A Record of Facts and Information. Vol. 16, no. 2, May 1985 - vol. 30, no. 3, 1989. Quarterly Journal.

Jugoslavenski Kanadski Godisnjak: Kalendar 1970. Yugoslav Canadian Yearbook. Toronto: Yugoslav Canadian Publishers, 1970. 120 pp.

Louis Adamic Symposium. Ljubljana, 16-18 Sept. 1981, Univerza Edvarda Kardelja v Ljubljani. Articles commenting on the life and writings of Louis Adamic. 409 pp.

TESLA MEMORIAL SOCIETY OF
CANADA AND THE U.S.A.
LACKAWANNA, NEW YORK-ST.
CATHARINES, ONT.
 Records, 1979-1981, which include
minutes, correspondence and financial
statements. 1 reel of microfilm.

YUGOSLAV-CANADIAN PUBLISHERS
OF *NASE NOVINE*
TORONTO, ONT.
 Records from the first convention of
the Council of Canadian South Slavs,
1944; minutes of Executive of Council of South Slavs, 1947-48; correspondence of Council of South Slavs
with Yugoslavs of South Porcupine,
Vancouver, Montreal and telegrams
to Yugoslavia, 1945-46; and miscellaneous material pertaining to Aid to
Yugoslavia, 1946. Also, material
from the 3rd, 4th, 5th, and 6th Convention of the League of Yugoslav
Canadians, 1956; notes on M.
Kruzic, B. Mladenovic, B. Mihic,
and B. Stevanov, c. 1950s; list and
notes of Yugoslav immigrants returning from Canada, 1947-48; minutes
from the League of Canadian Croats,
1945, 1946; financial accounts and
minutes from the Federation of Yugoslav Canadians and Canadian Slav
Committee, 1952-55; and Serbian
"Kolo" correspondence, 1957-59. 3
reels of microfilm.

YUGOSLAVIAN-CANADIAN ORGANIZ-
ATIONS
TORONTO, ONT.
 Material concerning Yugoslavian
immigration in the immediate
post-WWII period, which was
obtained from Yugoslav Publishing
Co., *Nase Novine*. Formerly
Jedinstvo (Unity). Includes financial
records and convention material from
the Council of Canadian South Slavs,
1945-51; correspondence from the
Council of South Slavs; the Yugoslav
Embassy in Washington, D.C., the
Ministry of Trade of Yugoslavia, and
the Yugoslav People's Bank, 1947-48;
material regarding Soviet-Yugoslav
ideological split after 1948; items on
returning immigrants to Yugoslavia,
1947-49; and clippings from Serbian
newspapers published in Ont. and the
U.S., 1935-74. 2 reels of microfilm.

YUGOSLAV ORGANIZATIONS IN
CANADA
ST. CATHARINES, ONT.
 The collection contains correspondence, 1941-55, papers on returning
Yugoslav immigrants from Canada,
1946-47, material on Trieste convention, c. late 1940s, and records from
the Council of Yugoslav Canadians. 1
reel of microfilm.

YUGOSLAV PUBLISHERS
TORONTO, ONT.
 Receipts and disbursement books of
various Yugoslav publishers in
Toronto, 1940-44, 1951-56, 1956-68.
1 reel of microfilm.

INDEX

J

Printed in Canada